Adult Psychopathology
and Diagnosis

Adult Psychopathology and Diagnosis

Fourth Edition

Michel Hersen
and
Samuel M. Turner

WILEY

John Wiley & Sons, Inc.

Copyright © 1997, 2003 by John Wiley & Sons, Inc. All rights reserved.

Published by John Wiley & Sons, Inc., Hoboken, New Jersey.
Published simultaneously in Canada.

Library of Congress Cataloging-in-Publication Data:

Adult psychopathology and diagnosis / [edited by] Michel Hersen and Samuel M. Turner.—4th ed.
    p. cm.
  Includes bibliographical references and indexes.
  ISBN 0-471-41163-9 (cloth : alk. paper)
  1. Psychology, Pathological.   Mental illness—Diagnosis.   I. Hersen, Michel.   II. Turner, Samuel M., 1944–
  RC454.A324 2003
  616.89—dc21

                                        2002032384

Printed in the United States of America.

10 9 8 7 6 5 4

To Vicki and Brenda

Preface

This is the fourth edition of *Adult Psychopathology and Diagnosis*. Publication of this volume was necessitated by the continued rapid advancement in knowledge about psychopathology, its assessment, and remediation. Many new findings have emerged since publication of the third edition in 1997. The present revision includes a new chapter on "Dual Diagnosis" and some reordering of the material. Chapters on specific psychopathological states now have information on genetics within the section on etiological considerations rather than having one chapter solely devoted to genetics as in the third edition. And, as in the third edition, there is an emerging body of data describing similarities and differences in the manifestation of psychiatric disorders among ethnic and racial minority groups and differences associated with gender.

As in the previous editions of this text, the fourth edition is arranged to provide a discussion of the major adult psychiatric disorders using *DSM* nomenclature. Our intention in each of the four editions has been to present an integration of the empirical data and diagnostic criteria to permit the reader to become familiar with the bases for the diagnosis while concurrently examining ambiguities and inconsistencies. Treatment is discussed only insofar as it contributes to the understanding of the psychopathology for that specific condition. Many of the chapters include illustrative case material for heuristic purposes. Included in the chapters on specific psychopathology are sections on the description of the disorder, epidemiology, clinical picture, course and prognosis, diagnostic considerations, psychological and biological assessment, and etiological considerations (familial and genetic, learning and modeling, life events, gender and racial-ethnic, biological and physiological).

This volume contains 17 chapters, four of which constitute Part I: Overview, and the remaining 13 in Part II: Specific Disorders. Each of the authors selected to write chapters in both parts is an acknowledged expert in the field, and we are most grateful for every author's enthusiastic participation in this project.

In addition to the expertise of our contributors, many other individuals have been involved in bringing the fourth edition to fruition. We first thank Carole Londerée, Alex Duncan, and Angelina Marchand for their technical support. We are most appreciative of Jennifer Simon, our editor at John Wiley & Sons, who provided the right dosage of encouragement and prodding to bring this latest edition to completion. We also thank our students who, over the years, have sharpened our thinking about psychopathology as a result of their penetrating questions.

MICHEL HERSEN
SAMUEL M. TURNER

Forest Grove, Oregon
College Park, Maryland

Contributors

Candice Alfano
Department of Psychology
University of Maryland
College Park, Maryland

Jennifer R. Antick, PhD
School of Professional Psychology
Pacific University
Forest Grove, Oregon
PeaceHealth/St. John Medical Center
Longview, Washington

Patricia A. Areán, PhD
Department of Psychiatry
U. C. San Francisco
San Francisco, California

Belinda Barnett, PhD
 Mental Illness Research, Education,
    and Clinical Center (MIRECC)
VA Pittsburgh Healthcare System
Pittsburgh, Pennsylvania

Deborah C. Beidel, PhD, ABPP
Department of Psychology
University of Maryland
College Park, Maryland

Melanie E. Bennett, PhD
Department of Psychiatry
University of Maryland School of
    Medicine and VA Capital Network
    Mental Illness Research, Education,
    and Clinical Center (MIRECC)
Baltimore, Maryland

Etzel A. Cardeña, PhD
Department of Psychology and
    Anthropology
University of Texas-Pan American
Edinburg, Texas

Yael Chatav
Department of Psychiatry
U. C. San Francisco
San Francisco, California

Linda Anne Coker, MA
Department of Psychology
University of Kentucky
Lexington, Kentucky

Brian L. Cook, DO
Department of Psychiatry
University of Iowa
Iowa City, Iowa

Frederick L. Coolidge, PhD
Department of Psychology
University of Colorado at
    Colorado Springs
Colorado Springs, Colorado

Jack D. Edinger, PhD
Department of Psychiatry and
    Behavioral Sciences
Duke University Medical Center
Durham, North Carolina

David H. Gleaves
Department of Psychology
Texas A&M University
College Station, Texas

Gerald Goldstein, PhD
Research
VA Pittsburgh Healthcare System
Pittsburgh, Pennsylvania

Kimberly Goodale
School of Professional Psychology
Pacific University
Forest Grove, Oregon

Bill N. Kinder, PhD
Department of Psychology
University of South Florida
Tampa, Florida

Laurence J. Kirmayer, MD
Division of Social & Transcultural
    Psychiatry
McGill University
Montreal, Quebec, Canada

Ilan Lohr
Department of Psychiatry
University of Iowa
Iowa City, Iowa

Karl J. Looper, MD
Division of Social & Transcultural
    Psychiatry
McGill University
Montreal, Quebec, Canada

William L. Marshall, PhD
Department of Psychology
Queens University
Kingston, Canada

**Nathaniel McConaghy, DSc, MD,
FRANZCP**
Visiting Professor
School of Psychiatry
University of New South Wales
Sydney, Australia

Charles M. Morin, PhD
École de Psychologie
Université Laval
Sainte-Foy, Quebec, Canada

Kim T. Mueser, PhD
New Hampshire—Dartmouth
    Psychiatric Research Center
Department of Psychiatry
Dartmouth Medical School
Hanover, New Hampshire

Michelle P. Salyers, PhD
Department of Psychology
Indiana University—Purdue
    University at Indianapolis
Indianapolis, Indiana

Daniel L. Segal, PhD
Department of Psychology
University of Colorado at Colorado
    Springs
Colorado Springs, Colorado

Ralph C. Serin, PhD
Research Branch
Correctional Service Canada
Ottawa, Canada

Linda C. Sobell, PhD,ABPP
Center for Psychological Studies
Nova Southeastern University
Fort Lauderdale, Florida

Mark B. Sobell, PhD
Center for Psychological Studies
Nova Southeastern University
Fort Lauderdale, Florida

Suzanne Taillefer, MSc
Culture & Mental Health
    Research Unit
Sir Mortimer B. Davis-Jewish
    General Hospital
Montreal, Quebec, Canada

J. Kevin Thompson, PhD
Department of Psychology
University of South Florida
Tampa, Florida

Warren W. Tryon, PhD, ABPP
Department of Psychology
Fordham University
Bronx, New York

Samuel M. Turner, PhD, ABPP
Department of Psychology
University of Maryland
College Park, Maryland

Eric F. Wagner, PhD
Community-Based Intervention
    Research Group
Florida International University
Miami, Florida

Thomas A. Widiger, PhD
Department of Psychology
University of Kentucky
Lexington, Kentucky

Contents

PART I

OVERVIEW

Mental Disorders as Discrete Clinical Conditions: Dimensional versus Categorical Classification

THOMAS A. WIDIGER and LINDA ANNE COKER

"IN *DSM-IV*, THERE is no assumption that each category of mental disorder is a completely discrete entity with absolute boundaries dividing it from other mental disorders or from no mental disorder" (*Diagnostic and Statistical Manual of Mental Disorders, 4th Edition, Text Revision [DSM-IV-TR]*; American Psychiatric Association [APA], 2000, p. xxxi). This carefully worded disclaimer, is somewhat hollow because on the same page is the statement that "*DSM-IV* is a categorical classification that divides mental disorders into types based on criterion sets with defining features" (p. xxxi). Researchers and clinicians, following this lead, diagnose and interpret the conditions presented in *DSM-IV* as disorders that are qualitatively distinct from normal functioning and from one another.

The question of whether mental disorders are discrete clinical conditions or arbitrary distinctions along dimensions of functioning is a longstanding issue (Kendell, 1975), and its importance is escalating with the growing recognition of the limitations of the categorical model. For example, an issue that predominates much of the concern of clinicians and researchers is the excessive comorbidity among mental disorders (Caron & Rutter, 1991; Clark, Watson, & Reynolds, 1995; Sher & Trull, 1996; Widiger & Clark, 2000). A fundamental question is whether this apparent comorbidity is the co-occurring presence of multiple mental disorders or the presence of one disorder that is being given multiple diagnoses (Lilienfeld, Waldman, & Israel, 1994; Widiger & Clark, 2000).

Stoking the fire is the inadequacy of the diagnostic categories to fully cover many of the people in clinical treatment (Clark et al., 1995). The most common diagnosis in clinical practice is often the not-otherwise-specified diagnosis for disorders not covered by one of the discrete categories. Each of the recent editions of the *DSM* has added many new diagnoses, subtypes, and modifiers. These additions rarely concern newly discovered forms of psychopathology. Their purpose is instead to fill in holes and gaps along boundaries of existing diagnostic categories (Frances, First, Widiger, et al., 1991).

The purpose of this chapter is to review the *DSM-IV* categorical diagnosis of mental disorder. The chapter begins with a discussion of the fundamental categorical distinctions, including the boundaries with normality and among the mental disorders (the boundary with physical disorders was discussed briefly in the third edition). The discussion indicates the arbitrary nature of and problems created by these categorical distinctions. Reasons for maintaining a categorical model are then considered. The chapter concludes with a recommendation for an eventual conversion to a more quantitative, dimensional classification of mental disorders.

BOUNDARY WITH NORMALITY

In *DSM-IV*, each of the mental disorders is conceptualized as a clinically significant behavioral or psychological syndrome or pattern that occurs in an individual and that is associated with present distress (e.g., a painful symptom) or disability (i.e., impairment in one or more important areas of functioning) or with a significantly increased risk of suffering death, pain, disability, or an important loss of freedom. (APA, 2000, p. xxxi)

If we consider the fundamental, defining features of a mental disorder, there is no qualitative distinction from normal functioning. This is illustrated with respect to dyscontrol, impairment, and pathology—fundamental components of most concepts of mental disorder (Bergner, 1997; D. F. Klein, 1978, 1999; Spitzer & Williams, 1982; Wakefield, 1992; Widiger & Sankis, 2000; Widiger & Trull, 1991).

DYSCONTROL

Central to the concept of a mental disorder is dyscontrol (Bergner, 1997; D. F. Klein, 1999; Widiger & Trull, 1991). A mental disorder is an *"involuntary* [italics added] organismic impairment in psychological functioning" (Widiger & Trull, 1991, p. 112). "Involuntary impairment remains the key inference" (D. F. Klein, 1999, p. 424). Dyscontrol is not fundamental to the concept of a physical disorder, but it is fundamental to the concept of a mental disorder, since the latter concerns impairments to feelings, thoughts, and behaviors over which normal, healthy people attempt to exert volitional control. Normal psychological functioning presumably includes a degree of volitional control over thoughts, feelings, and behaviors (Bandura, 2001); fundamental to the concept of a mental disorder is a loss or at least diminution of this freedom (APA, 2000).

People who freely choose to engage in harmful or impairing behaviors are not said to have a mental disorder. Presumably, people can choose to consume alcohol, take anabolic steroids, shoot heroin, gamble, steal, assault, or engage in deviant sexual acts without being compelled to do so by the presence of a mental disorder. Not all instances of harmful drug usage are considered instances of psychopathology because it is believed that people can willfully and voluntarily decide to use drugs in a manner that is harmful to them. Gambling, drug usage, theft, assaults, and deviant sexual acts can be harmful and maladaptive, but the occurrence of a harmful (or deviant) act does not itself constitute a mental disorder (Gorenstein, 1984; Wakefield, 1992; Widiger & Trull, 1991). Similarly, to the extent that a person can control, modulate, manage, or regulate his or her painful or harmful feelings of sadness, anxiety, or anger, the person would not be considered to have a mood or anxiety disorder (Widiger & Sankis, 2000). "It is the ability to flexibly adjust the way one regulates one's emotions to environmental exigencies that is related to mental health" (Gross & Munoz, 1995, p. 151). It is only when a person lacks sufficient control of mood, anxiety, or a harmful behavior pattern that he or she could be diagnosed with a mental disorder (Frances, Widiger, & Sabshin, 1991).

There is, however, no qualitative distinction between the presence and absence of self-control. It is not even clear how much control a normal, healthy person has over adaptive, healthy behaviors (Bargh & Ferguson, 2000; Howard & Conway, 1986; Kirsch & Lynn, 2000; Wegner & Wheatley, 2000). Both normal and abnormal human functioning is, at best, the result of a complex interaction of apparent volitional choices with an array of biogenetic and environmental determinants. It does not appear that people have either full volitional control or absolutely no control of their behavior; at best, people vary in the extent to which they are in control of particular aspects of their behavior. Some people may have more control than others, and some may have more control over certain aspects of their behavior than other aspects; but even those who have recognized mental disorders appear to have some degree of control over important aspects of their maladaptive behavior patterns.

The continuum (or ambiguity) of self-control is particularly evident in disorders involving behaviors that provide immediate benefits or pleasures to the person, such as pedophilia, intermittent explosive disorder, transvestic fetishism, kleptomania, bulimia nervosa, anorexia nervosa, pathological gambling, and substance-related disorders, such as alcohol abuse, cocaine abuse, anabolic steroid abuse, and nicotine dependence. These disorders are difficult to diagnose and are often controversial because there is no distinct point at which dyscontrol occurs (Widiger & Smith, 1994). Each of the diagnostic criteria for pathological gambling can be seen as an indicator of harmful dyscontrol (Lesieur & Rosenthal, 1991). A person who displays "repeated unsuccessful efforts to control, cut back, or stop gambling" (APA, 2000, p. 674) is not in control of his or her behavior, but *DSM-IV* requires additional diagnostic criteria to be sufficiently confident that enough dyscontrol is present to warrant a diagnosis of mental disorder. At one time, people with alcohol dependence were thought to have a discrete pathology that rendered them entirely incapable of any control of their drinking. However, there is now sufficient research to indicate that individuals vary in the extent to which they are able to control their drinking behavior (Peele, 1984; Widiger & Smith, 1994). Treatment to control drinking is controversial because there is no absolute point of demarcation and people who lack sufficient control often deny the extent of their dyscontrol (Vaillant, 1995). In summary, the determination of adequate versus inadequate self-control is fundamental to many social and clinical decisions, but the boundary is at best grossly ill-defined and poorly understood (Alper, 1998; Golding, Skeem, Roesch, & Zapf, 1999).

IMPAIRMENT

An additional fundamental feature of mental disorders is impairment (APA, 1994, 2000; Wakefield, 1992; Widiger & Trull, 1991). "The definition of mental disorder in the introduction to *DSM-IV* requires that there be clinically significant impairment" (APA, 2000, p. 8). The purpose of this requirement is to distinguish between a mental disorder and simply a problem in living. "The ever-increasing number of new categories meant to describe the less impaired outpatient population raises the question of where psychopathology ends and the wear and tear of everyday life begins" (Frances, First, & Pincus, 1995, p. 15):

> To highlight the importance of considering this issue, the criteria sets for most disorders include a clinical significance criterion (usually worded ". . . causes clinically significant . . . impairment in social, occupational, or other important areas of functioning"). This criterion helps establish the threshold for the diagnosis of a disorder in those situations in which the symptomatic presentation by itself (particularly in its milder forms) is not inherently pathological and may be encountered in individuals for whom a diagnosis of "mental disorder" would be inappropriate. (APA, 2000, p. 8)

DSM-III-R (APA, 1987) failed to include this requirement in the criterion sets for many of the disorders, contributing to a confusion of harmless deviances, eccentricities, peculiarities, or annoyances with the presence of a mental disorder (Frances, First, Widiger, et al., 1991). For example, the attention-deficit hyperactivity and oppositional defiant disorders were diagnosed even if the behaviors resulted in "only minimal or no impairment in school and social functioning" (APA, 1987, pp. 53, 58). Similarly, transvestic fetishism could be diagnosed with *DSM-III-R* simply on the basis of intense sexual urges, fantasies, and behaviors involving cross-dressing that continued for more than six months (APA, 1987). A man who engaged in this behavior for longer than six months but experienced no impairment in functioning would still have been considered in *DSM-III-R* to have been mentally ill solely because he engaged in this deviant sexual behavior for longer than six months. It is possible that a six-month duration is a valid indicator for impairment (as well as dyscontrol), but deviant sexual preferences could also be ego-syntonic, controlled, and largely harmless. Therefore, *DSM-IV* required further that "the fantasies, sexual urges, or behaviors cause clinically significant distress or impairment in social, occupational, or other important areas of functioning" (APA, 1994, p. 531).

However, nowhere in *DSM-IV* is a "clinically significant" impairment defined, not even in the Criteria for Clinical Significance section of the manual (APA, 2000, p. 8). It is stated that this "is an inherently difficult clinical judgment" (p. 8), and it is advised that the clinician consider information obtained from family members and other third parties. Frances, First, and Pincus (1995) stated that "the evaluation of clinical significance is likely to vary in different cultures and to depend on the availability and interests of clinicians" (p. 15), an acknowledgment of no absolute or even explicit basis for the threshold. The absence of a clear basis for this distinction has helped fuel the considerable controversy of premenstrual dysphoric disorder, a mental disorder diagnosed when normal premenstrual experiences (that occur in a substantial proportion of normal adult women) reach an ill-defined level of clinically significant impairment (Gallant & Hamilton, 1990).

Spitzer and Williams (1982), the original authors of the *DSM-IV* definition of mental disorder, defined a *clinically significant impairment* as that point at which the attention of a clinician is indicated. "There are many behavioral or psychological conditions that can be considered 'pathological' but the clinical manifestations of which are so mild that clinical attention is not indicated" (p. 166). They provided three examples: caffeine withdrawal, jet lag syndrome, and insomnia resulting from environmental noise. Spitzer and Williams considered the impairments in each case too small to be "justified as syndromes that were clinically significant to mental health professionals" (p. 166). Nevertheless, jet lag syndrome was actually included in *DSM-III-R* as a variant of sleep-wake schedule disorder (APA, 1987, p. 306), caffeine withdrawal was subsequently included in the appendix to *DSM-IV* (APA, 1994), and a strong case has been made for the inclusion of caffeine dependence (Hughes, Oliveto, Helzer, Higgins, & Bickel, 1992).

The level of impairment that motivates people to seek treatment is likely to be highly subjective and idiosyncratic. What is considered a sufficient level of impairment to warrant treatment probably varies substantially across patients and across clinicians (Widiger & Corbitt, 1994). In addition, this threshold appears to be consistently below the threshold of many of the *DSM-IV* criterion sets. Clark et al. (1995) document well the reliance of clinicians on the category of "not otherwise specified" (NOS) to diagnose subthreshold cases. Whenever this catchall diagnosis is included in a study, it is often the most frequent diagnosis, as in the case of mood disorders (Angst, 1992), dissociative disorders (Spiegel & Cardena, 1991), and personality disorders (Widiger & Sanderson, 1995).

The purpose of many of the new diagnoses added to *DSM-IV* was to fill an apparent gap between an existing diagnosis and normal functioning. For example:

- Acute stress disorder is essentially posttraumatic stress disorder with a shorter duration (Liebowitz et al., 1998).
- Recurrent brief depressive disorder is major depression with shorter episodes (Merikangas, Hoyer, & Angst, 1996).
- Mixed anxiety-depressive disorder concerns subthreshold cases of mood and anxiety disorders (Zinbarg & Barlow, 1991).
- Binge eating disorder concerns subthreshold cases of bulimia nervosa (Devlin, Walsh, Spitzer, & Hasin, 1992).
- Mild neurocognitive disorder concerns subthreshold cases of dementia, delirium, or amnestic disorder (Gutierrez, Atkinson, & Grant, 1993).

A fundamental difficulty shared by all of these diagnoses is the lack of a clear distinction with normal functioning. Two cases that illustrate well the absence of a clear boundary between normal and abnormal functioning are minor depressive disorder (which is considered to be a mental disorder, although not yet officially recognized) and age-related cognitive decline (which is not considered to be a mental disorder).

Minor depressive disorder is a new addition to *DSM-IV* that attempts to plug the gap between *DSM-III-R* mood disorder diagnoses and normal sadness. It has been estimated that up to 50% of depressive symptomatology is currently being treated by primary care physicians without any consultation or involvement of a mental health clinician in part because the depression is below the threshold of a mood disorder diagnosis (Munoz, Hollon, McGrath, Rehm, & VandenBos, 1994). Many of these people would meet the *DSM-IV* criteria for minor depressive disorder. However, it is acknowledged in *DSM-IV* that "symptoms meeting . . . criteria for minor depressive disorder can be difficult to distinguish from periods of sadness that are an inherent part of everyday life" (APA, 2000, p. 776). Only two distinctions are provided. One is a two-week duration. If a person is sad for less than two weeks, it is normal sadness. If sadness lasts longer than two weeks, it is a mental disorder. This is comparable to indicating that normal cross-dressing becomes transvestic fetishism if it continues longer than six months (APA, 1987). The second distinction is that "the depressive symptoms must cause clinically significant distress or impairment" (APA, 2000, p. 776) but, again, *clinical significance* is left undefined.

Age-related cognitive decline is a new addition to the section of the manual for conditions that are not mental disorders but might be the focus of clinical attention. "Cognitive decline in the elderly can be considered dimensionally . . . , involving aging-associated cognitive decline, mild cognitive impairment, and dementia" (Caine, 1994, p. 335). "It may be very difficult to establish an arbitrary or numerical level where a disease state should be proclaimed" (p. 334). Age-related cognitive decline concerns "problems remembering names or appointments or . . . difficulty in solving complex problems" (APA, 2000, p. 740). People with this condition are often troubled by their cognitive deterioration, and they seek the help of clinicians who specialize in the treatment of dementia, thereby meeting the threshold for a clinically significant level of impairment proposed by Spitzer and Williams (1982). However, the *DSM-IV* Task Force decided that age-related cognitive decline should not be classified as a mental disorder because the decline in cognitive functioning is the result of "the aging process that is within normal limits given the person's age" (APA, 2000, p. 740). The level of impairment is sufficient to warrant professional intervention, but it is not considered a mental disorder because the level of impairment is normative for that time in life. We might question, however, whether being close to the norm is any more relevant to the issue of maladaptivity than being deviant from the norm (Frances, First, Widiger, et al., 1991; Gorenstein, 1984). The fact that age-related cognitive decline is the result of the normal process of aging does not indicate that it is adaptive, healthy, or without an underlying neuropathology. The aging process is simply the etiology for the deterioration in functioning. Fortunately, physicians do not apply the same reasoning by judging that deteriorations in the functioning of a person's vision, liver, or bladder are not disorders because they are simply the result of aging and are common to people in their age groups.

Pathology

Fundamental to many definitions of mental disorder is the presence of some form of pathology (D. F. Klein, 1978; Wakefield, 1992, 1997). "The necessary crucial inference is that something has gone wrong, not simply that something is undesirable or rare" (D. F. Klein, 1999, p. 421). Clinicians do not treat normal, healthy functioning; clinicians treat pathologies in cognitive, interpersonal, neurochemical, or psychodynamic functioning. Textbooks of psychopathology are largely efforts to identify and characterize pathologies that are the bases for each respective mental disorder. Presumably, there are people who lack these pathologies. Such people could be described as having normal, healthy psychological functioning. The boundary between normal and abnormal psychological functioning might then be identified by the presence versus absence of the respective pathology (D. F. Klein, 1978).

Missing from the diagnostic criterion sets in *DSM-IV*, however, are references to underlying pathologies (Wakefield, 1997). Explicit in the *DSM-IV* definition of mental disorder is that the condition "must currently be considered a manifestation of a behavioral, psychological, or biological dysfunction in the individual" (APA, 2000, p. xxxi), but few, if any, of the criterion sets refer explicitly to a behavioral, psychological, or biological dysfunction. The diagnostic criterion sets emphasize instead the distress or impairment that is presumably the manifestations of an underlying pathology. Perhaps inclusion of the underlying pathology in a diagnostic criterion set would provide a scientifically and clinically meaningful distinction between a respective mental disorder and normal (nonpathological) functioning (Spitzer & Wakefield, 1999; Wakefield, 1997).

A procedural limitation to this proposal, however, is absence of consensus as to fundamental pathologies that should be required. Pathologies are not currently included in diagnostic criterion sets in part because there is insufficient empirical support favoring one particular cognitive, interpersonal, neurochemical, or psychodynamic model of pathology over another. Wakefield (1997), for example, indicated that to provide a meaningful distinction between major depressive disorder and normal bereavement, it is "necessary to formulate some account . . . of the evolutionary programming of the mechanisms with respect to what kinds of triggering circumstances are supposed to cause which kinds of responses (e.g., loss-response mechanisms are designed so that perceptions of major losses trigger roughly proportional sadness responses)" (p. 647). Wakefield's (1992) conceptualization of mental disorder is tied to evolutionary theory. Evolutionary theory has enriched current understanding of the etiology and pathology of many mental disorders, but it is unclear whether the normal and pathologic behavioral response mechanisms from the perspective of evolutionary theory can be adequately specified for the purposes of a clinician's diagnosis. In addition, because it is a model of psychopathology that is derived from a particular theoretical perspective, it may not be capable of serving as a general definition of mental disorder that would be compatible with or suitable for alternative theoretical models (Bergner, 1997; Lilienfeld & Marino, 1995, 1999; Widiger & Sankis, 2000).

Even if clinicians and researchers agreed on a particular theoretical model of pathology, it is unclear whether qualitative distinctions between normal functioning and abnormal pathologies could be identified. D. F. Klein (1999) believes that there are qualitative distinctions between normal and abnormal neurochemical functioning that would provide a compelling basis for classification. As suggested by Klein, "currently, positive experience with psychopharmacological agents, which have little effect on normal people but have marked benefits on patients with chronic disorders, leads to the inference of something chronically but reversibly wrong" (p. 425). However, there has not been much research on the effects of current psychopharmacological agents on normal neurochemical functioning. Knutson et al. (1998) administered paroxetine, a selective serotonin reuptake inhibitor (SSRI), for four weeks in a double-blind study to 23 of 48 normal volunteers. None of the participants met currently, or throughout their lifetime, the *DSM-IV* diagnostic criteria for a mental disorder, as assessed with a semistructured interview. None of them had previously received a psychotropic medication, abused drugs, or been in treatment for a mental disorder; nor were any of them currently seeking or desiring treatment for a mental disorder. They were, in many respects, above normal in psychological functioning. The paroxetine and placebo treatments continued for four weeks. Knutson et al. reported that SSRI administration (relative to placebo) reduced negative affects and increased social facilitation. The magnitude of changes in functioning correlated with the plasma levels of SSRI in the treatment group. "This is the first empirical demonstration that chronic administration of a selective serotonin reuptake blockade can have significant personality and behavioral effects in normal humans in the absence of baseline depression or other psychopathology" (p. 378).

D. F. Klein's (1999) belief that current psychopharmacology would not have a meaningful effect on the neurochemical functioning of normal individuals is inferred "by the fact that they are not sold on the street as euphorants" (p. 425). However, many psychotropic agents are sold on the street for a variety of benefits, interests, and pleasures, and perhaps many are also being sold by primary care physicians for negative affects that would be conceptualized in psychiatry as within the realm of normal sadness or anxiety (Munoz et al., 1994). The effectiveness of anxiolytics and antidepressants for clinical treatment might be in their ability to impair, inhibit, or block normal neurochemical mechanisms of sadness and anxiousness rather than reversing or altering pathological neurochemical processes.

Mayberg et al. (1999) investigated with positron emission techniques two complementary alterations in mood: transient sadness provoked in healthy volunteers and treatment-induced resolution of dysphoria in clinically depressed patients. The results indicated "reciprocal changes involving nearly identical limbic-paralimbic and neocortical regions" (pp. 678–679). The neurophysiology of a mood disorder might be only quantitatively different from the neurophysiology of normal sadness. No neurophysiological laboratory technique is currently able to identify the presence of psychopathology independent of or blind to a clinician's diagnosis. The diagnosis of a mental disorder requires an assessment of the person's behavior in an environmental context as "functional impairment or disability, not the presence of a lesion, is the essential element in the medical concept of disease" (Bergner, 1997, p. 245).

BOUNDARIES AMONG MENTAL DISORDERS

DSM-IV provides diagnostic criterion sets to help guide the clinician in making the correct diagnosis and an additional section devoted to differential diagnosis that indicates "how to differentiate [the] disorder from other disorders that have similar presenting characteristics" (APA, 2000, p. 10). The intention of the diagnostic manual is to help the clinician determine which particular mental disorder is present, the selection of which indicates the presence of a specific pathology that explains the occurrence of the symptoms and suggests a specific treatment that will ameliorate the patient's suffering (Frances, First, & Pincus, 1995; Kendell, 1975).

However, it is evident that *DSM-IV* routinely fails in the goal of guiding the clinician to the presence of one specific disorder. Despite the best efforts of the leading clinicians and researchers who have been the primary authors of each revision of the diagnostic manual, diagnostic comorbidity rather than singularity is the norm (Clark et al., 1995; Sher & Trull, 1996). The high rate of multiple diagnoses at the time of clinical treatment is problematic to the conceptualization of mental disorders as distinct clinical conditions, and the extent of this comorbidity is even higher when lifetime as well as current comorbidity is included (Brown, Campbell, Lehman, Grisham, & Mancill, 2001; Kessler et al., 1994; Kessler, Crum, et al., 1997). "The greatest challenge that the extensive comorbidity data pose to the current nosological system concerns the validity of the diagnostic categories themselves—do these disorders constitute distinct clinical entities?" (Mineka, Watson, & Clark, 1998, p. 380). "It is clear that the classic Kraepelinian model in which all psychopathology is comprised of discrete and mutually exclusive diseases must be modified or rejected" (Maser & Cloninger, 1990, p. 12). Diagnostic comorbidity has become so prevalent that some researchers argue for an abandonment of the term *comorbidity* in favor of a term (e.g., *co-occurrence*) that is more simply descriptive and does not imply the presence of distinct clinical entities (Lilienfeld et al., 1994). There are instances in which the presence of multiple diagnoses do suggest the presence of distinct yet comorbid psychopathologies, but in most instances the presence of co-occurring diagnoses does appear to suggest the presence of a common, shared pathology (Widiger & Clark, 2000).

For example, in an extensive longitudinal epidemiological study, Krueger, Caspi, Moffitt, and Silva (1998) assessed a range of symptomatology in a large, unselected birth cohort in New Zealand at ages 18 and 21. Using structural equation modeling to examine cross-sectional and longitudinal co-occurrence patterns, they suggested that "stable, underlying 'core psychopathological processes'" (p. 216) underlie the many diagnoses given to the study participants. More specifically, a broad domain of internalization (neuroticism or negative affectivity) underlies mood and anxiety disorders, and a complementary factor of externalization (constraint, disinhibition) underlies disruptive behavior and substance use disorders. Krueger (1999) obtained similar results in a confirmatory factor analysis of the patterns of co-occurrence among the diagnoses included in the extensive National Comorbidity Survey (Kessler et al., 1994) that sampled more than 8,098 participants ranging in age from 15 to 54. Krueger (1999) concluded that "comorbidity results from common, underlying core psychopathological processes. The results thereby argue for focusing research on these core processes themselves, rather than on their varied manifestations as separate disorders" (p. 921).

Brown, Chorpita, and Barlow (1998) conducted a series of confirmatory factor analyses of the anxiety and mood disorder symptomatology evident among 350 anxiety and mood disorder patients. Their results confirmed the presence of latent dimensions of pathology (e.g., positive affectivity and arousal), some of which cut across the mood and anxiety disorders; more specifically, results confirmed a dimension of negative affectivity or neuroticism (Clark, Watson, & Mineka, 1994; Zinbarg & Barlow, 1996). Negative affectivity (neuroticism), positive affectivity (extraversion), and externalization (constraint, disinhibition) are also widely recognized in general personality research as fundamental domains of personality functioning that are evident universally in normal populations (John & Srivastava, 1999; McCrae & Costa, 1999) and that explain a substantial amount of the personality disorder diagnostic co-occurrence (Lynam & Widiger, 2001; Widiger & Costa, 1994).

DSM-IV appears to be replete with irresolvable boundary distinctions and, as suggested earlier, most of the new additions to *DSM-IV* were efforts to fill gaps between existing categories. Notable examples include bipolar II (filling a gap between *DSM-III-R* bipolar and cyclothymic mood disorders), mixed anxiety-depressive disorder (anxiety and mood disorders), depressive personality disorder (personality and mood disorders), and postpsychotic depressive disorder of schizophrenia (schizophrenia and major depression). These new diagnostic categories are helpful in decreasing clinicians' reliance on the NOS diagnostic category to plug the holes among the existing categories, but they also have the effect of creating additional boundary confusions.

Problematic boundaries in *DSM-IV* include the distinction between oppositional defiant, attention-deficit (with and without hyperactivity-impulsivity), and conduct disorder (Caron & Rutter, 1991; Loeber, Lahey, & Thomas, 1991; Milich, Balentine, & Lynam, in press); anorexia and bulimia (Wilson & Walsh, 1991); trichotillomania and obsessive-compulsive anxiety disorder (Liebowitz, 1992); depressive personality disorder and dysthymia (Huprich, 1998; Ryder & Bagby, 1999); conversion disorder and a dissociative disorder (Kihlstrom, 1992); bipolar and unipolar disorder (Blacker & Tsuang, 1992); and body dysmorphic disorder and anxiety disorder (Hollander, Neville, Frenkel, Josephson, & Liebowitz, 1992). To illustrate, we discuss briefly problematic boundaries for generalized social phobia, acute stress disorder, schizoaffective disorder, and hypochondriasis.

GENERALIZED SOCIAL PHOBIA

Social phobia was a new addition to *DSM-III* (Spitzer, Williams, & Skodol, 1980; Turner & Beidel, 1989). It was considered a distinct, circumscribed condition, consistent with the definition of a *phobia*, or a "persistent, irrational fear of a *specific* [italics added] object, activity, or situation" (APA, 1994, p. 770). However, it became apparent to anxiety disorder researchers and clinicians that the behavior of many of their patients was rarely so discrete and circumscribed (Spitzer & Williams, 1985). Therefore, the authors of *DSM-III-R* developed a generalized subtype when "the phobic situation includes most social situations" (APA, 1987, p. 243).

DSM-III-R generalized social phobia, however, merged into the *DSM-III* diagnosis of avoidant personality disorder. Both were concerned with a pervasive, generalized social insecurity, discomfort, and timidity. Efforts to distinguish them have indicated only that avoidant personality disorder tends to be, on average, relatively more dysfunctional than generalized social phobia (Turner, Beidel, & Townsley, 1992; Widiger, 1992b).

DSM-IV provided no solution. In fact, it was acknowledged that generalized social phobia emerges "out of a childhood history of social inhibition or shyness" (APA, 1994, p. 414), consistent with the concept of a personality disorder. An argument for classifying this condition as an anxiety rather than a personality disorder is that many people with the disorder benefit from pharmacologic interventions (Liebowitz, 1992). "One may have to rethink what the personality disorder concept means in an instance where 6 weeks of phenelzine therapy begins to reverse long-standing interpersonal hypersensitivity as well as discomfort in socializing" (p. 251). If so, we might have to rethink what the anxiety disorder concept means when an antidepressant is an effective form of treating an anxiety disorder. In addition, it is unclear why a maladaptive personality trait should not be responsive to a pharmacologic intervention (Silk, 1998), particularly if the response is confined simply to beginning to obtain a reversal in hypersensitivity and discomfort. In any case, *DSM-IV* fails to indicate how these two disorders could be distinguished, acknowledging that "they may be alternative conceptualizations of the same or similar conditions" (APA, 2000, p. 720).

ACUTE STRESS DISORDER

Spiegel and his colleagues proposed a new diagnosis for *DSM-IV* for inclusion in the dissociative disorders section that they titled *brief reactive dissociative disorder* (Cardena, Lewis-Fernandez, Bear, Pakianathan, & Spiegel, 1996; Task Force on *DSM-IV*, 1991). The predominant phenomenology consisted of symptoms of dissociation, including derealization, depersonalization, detachment, stupor, and amnesia. However, brief reactive dissociative disorder closely resembled post-traumatic stress disorder (PTSD), classified as an anxiety disorder (APA, 1987). The major distinction between them was simply that brief reactive dissociative disorder was of a shorter duration (two days to four weeks, whereas PTSD requires a duration of longer than four weeks).

Spiegel and Cardena (1991) made compelling arguments for moving PTSD to the dissociative disorders section. The etiology and treatment of people suffering from PTSD resemble more closely the etiology and treatment of dissociative disorders than most anxiety disorders (e.g., panic disorder, social phobia, obsessive-compulsive anxiety disorder, or specific phobia). Dissociative identity disorder and dissociative amnesia result almost invariably from having experienced, witnessed, or been confronted with a PTSD stressor. The cognitive pathology of PTSD and dissociative disorders concerns difficulties accepting, absorbing, or integrating a severe trauma (expressed through gross denial, avoidance, and/or recurrent recollections). The theories, treatment techniques, and concerns of people who specialize in crisis intervention, trauma, victimization, and abuse may overlap more with specialists in dissociative disorders than with specialists in anxiety disorders.

On the other hand, there are arguments to support the conceptualization of PTSD as an anxiety disorder (Davidson & Foa, 1991). Dissociative symptomatology is often seen in people with PTSD, but this dissociation could be understood as a cognitive avoidance of anxiety. In addition, dissociative symptoms are not as prevalent or predominant as anxious, avoidant symptoms in cases of PTSD. Finally, animal models can reproduce much of the PTSD symptomatology without invoking the notion that the animal is experiencing dissociation (March, 1990).

The final decision for *DSM-IV* was to classify brief reactive dissociative disorder within the anxiety disorders section and to rename it *acute stress disorder* (i.e., subthreshold PTSD). The best solution might have been to classify it as both an anxiety and as a dissociative disorder so that clinicians would recognize the importance of considering the presence of both a dysregulation of anxiety and dissociation in their understanding of the pathology and treatment of the condition. It is evident that the boundary between these conditions is uncertain, at best.

SCHIZOAFFECTIVE DISORDER

Schizoaffective disorder might be the prototypic boundary condition. It was included in *DSM-III* (APA, 1980) with no diagnostic criteria because it represented the gray area between schizophrenia and mood disorders (Spitzer et al., 1980). There are instances of mental disorder that are clearly mood or clearly schizophrenia, but these two major classes of disorder shade into each other, perhaps because of an overlap in their etiology and pathology (Blacker & Tsuang, 1992; Taylor, 1992). The *DSM-III* diagnosis of schizoaffective disorder represented those cases in which it was unclear whether it was more accurate to characterize the disorder as schizophrenic or mood (APA, 1980).

Researchers, though, had difficulty studying a condition with no diagnostic criteria. Therefore, specific and explicit diagnostic criteria were developed for *DSM-III-R* (APA, 1987). However, it may be paradoxical to create a distinct clinical entity to define a gray area between two other disorders. The diagnostic criteria for schizoaffective disorder have been notably complex and confusing (Frances, First, & Pincus, 1995). The solutions have been to develop increasingly more narrow definitions of the disorder, hoping to eventually identify a distinct clinical entity (Aubert & Rush, 1996; Blacker & Tsuang, 1992). These efforts may have the effect of simply creating even more problematic boundaries and gray areas.

HYPOCHONDRIASIS

Hypochondriasis is classified as a somatoform disorder, but it may also be considered an anxiety disorder (Liebowitz, 1992). Hypochondriasis involves the preoccupation with a person's fear of or belief that he or she has a serious physical disease based on the misinterpretation of one or more bodily signs or symptoms (APA, 2000). It shares with the other somatoform disorders "the presence of physical symptoms that suggest a general medical condition" (p. 485). People with this disorder initially seek treatment by a physician, and there is the need to exclude the presence of an actual physical disorder. As in the case of the somatization, pain, conversion, and body dysmorphic disorders, they may continually return to physicians in their belief that the disorder is physical rather than psychological.

However, people with hypochondriasis also share the rumination, doubt, and worry that is central to obsessive-compulsive anxiety disorder, the continuous and daily anxiety seen in people with generalized anxiety disorder, and the avoidant behavior seen in people with specific phobias. Many people with a phobia of getting a major disease ruminate over possibly having contracted a disease, and many people who are hypochondriacal are phobic of contracting a disease (Task Force, 1991). It is specified in *DSM-IV* that a *disease phobia* is the fear of contracting a disease (without the belief that it is already present), whereas *hypochondriasis* is the fear of having a disease (APA, 2000, p. 449). This distinction is seemingly discrete, but it is evident that hypochondriasis and specific phobia shade into each other.

RATIONALE AND JUSTIFICATION FOR CATEGORICAL MODEL

There are a number of reasons that diagnostic categories are used rather than clinical spectra or dimensions of functioning (Kendell, 1975), including simplicity, tradition, credibility, utility, and validity. Each of these reasons is considered in the following sections.

SIMPLICITY

It is human nature to categorize (Cantor & Genero, 1986). It is difficult to be cognizant of all shades of gray. Typologies are created in large part to render information into simpler, more succinct formats, and proponents of categorical systems argue that dimensional models are too complex and confusing for clinical use (Frances, First, & Pincus, 1995).

However, "there is a tendency, once having categorized, to exaggerate the similarity among nonidentical stimuli by overlooking within-group variability, discounting disconfirming evidence, and focusing on stereotypic examples" (Cantor & Genero, 1986, p. 235). Mental disorder categories are frustrating and troublesome to clinicians precisely because they suggest a uniformity of presentation and homogeneity of pathology that rarely seems to be present. To the extent that diagnostic categories are imposed on underlying dimensions, they are inaccurate and misleading when the information that is lost is relevant to an understanding of the etiology, pathology, and/or treatment of the condition. Describing the extent of a person's nearsightedness by the single diagnosis of myopia is succinct and informative, but ophthalmologists recognize that a more accurate and precise description of the extent of nearsightedness is necessary for clinical research and treatment decisions.

Widiger, Costa, and McCrae (2002) suggest that dimensional classifications that offer more precise and accurate descriptions may be less cumbersome and complex than the existing diagnostic categories that require the assessment of numerous diagnostic criteria in a frustratingly unsuccessful effort to make categorical distinctions. For example, semistructured interviews for the *DSM-IV* personality disorders must evaluate 80 diagnostic criteria, which does not even include the 14 additional criteria for the two personality disorders included in the appendix to *DSM-IV*, the NOS diagnosis, or the criteria for conduct disorder that are necessary for the diagnosis of antisocial personality disorder. In contrast, a semistructured interview for the five-factor model of personality that provides a comprehensive dimensional description of normal and maladaptive personality functioning requires the assessment of only 30 facets of personality functioning (Trull & Widiger, 1997).

TRADITION AND CREDIBILITY

The diagnosis of mental disorders has been largely in the domain of medicine, which has used since the days of Hippocrates a categorical model of classification (Kendell, 1975). It would be a major departure from this tradition to convert to a dimensional form of describing and diagnosing psychopathology. Many clinicians identify themselves as being in a branch of medicine, treating pathologies that are qualitatively distinct from normal functioning. A reformulation of mental disorders as shading imperceptibly into normal psychological functioning could complicate the identity of the profession (Guze & Helzer, 1987; Schacht & Nathan, 1977).

Advocates of categorical distinctions also suggest that dimensional models might trivialize the concept of mental disorder. If the distinction between mental disorders and normal psychological functioning is arbitrary, perhaps there is no meaningful justification for differentiating people as having versus not having a mental disorder. Perhaps there is a loss of credibility if mental disorders are not considered qualitatively distinct from normal psychological processes (Regier et al., 1998).

However, absence of a discrete, qualitative point of demarcation does not suggest absence of meaningful distinctions. Mental retardation is currently defined in large part as a level of intelligence below an intelligence quotient (IQ) of approximately 70 (APA, 1980, 2000). This point of demarcation does not carve nature at a discrete joint. It is an arbitrary point of demarcation along a continuous distribution, but the arbitrariness of this point of demarcation does not suggest that the disorder of mental retardation is illusory, invalid, or trivial. Mental retardation is well understood to be an involuntary organismic impairment to psychological functioning. People with IQs lower than 70 do suffer from a wide variety of significant and meaningful impairments secondary to their limited levels of intelligence, and it is very helpful and meaningful to identify a particular point of demarcation at which we would or should provide professional intervention to treat these impairments (Szymanski & Wilska, 1997).

A related concern is that a dimensional model of psychopathology might trivialize or hinder the study of psychopathology by suggesting that it can be meaningfully or adequately studied in nonclinical populations, such as college students enrolled in introductory psychology courses (Coyne, 1994; Flett, Vredenburg, & Krames, 1997; Tennen, Hall, & Affleck, 1995; Weary, Edwards, & Jacobson, 1995). Presence of a qualitative distinction between clinical depression and the level of depression commonly reported by college students would suggest that clinical depression is not meaningfully studied in college student samples (Coyne, 1994). However, absence of a qualitative point of demarcation between mild, moderate, and severe levels of depression does not necessarily mean that research on mild levels of depression generalizes meaningfully to high levels of depression. Being extremely tall, introverted, or depressed is not equivalent to being somewhat tall, introverted, or depressed. The experiences, social impairments, treatment implications, and other important correlates of depression vary with the severity of the disorder. Presence of a continuous distribution does not suggest that the psychopathology seen in clinical settings can be understood adequately by studies of the psychopathology seen in college students.

Regier et al. (1998) suggest that the thresholds for diagnosis in *DSM-IV* should be raised because epidemiologic research has obtained prevalence rates that are beyond expectations. They question whether the diagnostic criterion sets are identifying instances of "true psychopathologic disorder" (p. 114). However, Regier et al. are forthright in their acknowledgment that their concern is based in part on the implications of high prevalence rates for health care policy. "In the current U.S. climate of determining the medical necessity for care in managed health care plans, it is doubtful that 28% or 29% of the population would be judged to need mental health treatment" (p. 114). However, to protect availability of treatment for the most severe variants of psychopathology, many additional people in need of treatment are being neglected. At the same time that Regier et al. suggest raising the bar of diagnosis to limit health care coverage, other clinicians and researchers argue for lowering the bar to help gain access to health care coverage for people with subthreshold anxiety, mood, eating, and other forms of psychopathology (e.g., Magruder & Calderone, 2000; Shisslak, Crago, & Estes, 1995; Stein, Walker, Hazen, & Forde, 1997).

We suspect that a dimensional model might increase the credibility of mental disorder classification by avoiding the presence of misleading and illusory distinctions. The credibility of the profession is perhaps being undermined more by the problems and errors generated by a model that purports but fails to carve psychological or neurochemical functioning at discrete joints. A dimensional model of classification could be preferable to governmental, social, and professional agencies because it would provide more reliable, valid, and explicitly defined bases for making important social and clinical decisions.

UTILITY

Clinical decisions are categorical. Whether to provide medication, hospitalization, or insurance coverage are categorical decisions. Specific points of demarcation are needed along dimensions to guide clinical decisions. If these categorical distinctions inevitably occur, it might be more useful to have the initial diagnoses be categorical.

However, the cutoff points that will be optimal for one clinical decision (e.g., hospitalization) will not likely be optimal for another (e.g., medication). Kendler (1990), for example, indicates how the threshold for the diagnosis of schizophrenia that is associated with a family history is different from the threshold that is associated with an enduring course. Knowing that a person meets the *DSM-IV* diagnostic criteria for a particular mental disorder is insufficient for many social and clinical decisions. "Apologists for categorical diagnoses argue that the system has clinical utility being easy to use and valuable in formulating cases and planning treatment [but] there is little evidence for these assertions" (Livesley, 2001a, p. 278). Psychosocial and pharmacologic interventions, with few exceptions, target and have effects on broad domains of symptomatology rather than specifying individual diagnostic categories (Parker, 2000; Soloff, 1998).

Cutoff points can be placed along distribution of anxious, depressive, introverted, and other dimensions of functioning that will be more meaningful and specific to various social and clinical decisions. The optimal points along a distribution of aberrant cognition at which a particular medication, hospitalization, insurance coverage, or disability are optimally provided are unlikely to be equivalent. A classification system that provides different cutoff points specific to different clinical and social decisions would probably have greater utility than the existing diagnostic system.

VALIDITY

The major reason for retaining a categorical model should be its validity, and there is the concern that dimensional models mask underlying latent class taxons (Benjamin, 1993; Gunderson, Links, & Reich, 1991; Lenzenweger & Korfine, 1992; Meehl, 1995; Parker, 2000; Wittchen, Hofler, & Merikangas, 1999). A wide variety of statistical and methodological approaches for testing the validity of categorical and dimensional models of classification has been used, including (but not limited to) the search for evidence of incremental validity, bimodality, discrete breaks within distributions, and reproducibility of factor analytic solutions across groups, as well as taxometric, latent class, item response theory, and admixture analyses (D. N. Klein & Riso, 1993; Sher & Trull, 1996; Waller & Meehl, 1998). Researchers have at times obtained results that are more consistent with a categorical model than with a dimensional model of classification (e.g., Lenzenweger & Korfine, 1992; Santor & Coyne, 2001), but the body of research does appear to be more consistent with a dimensional model (Blacker & Tsuang, 1992; Flett et al., 1997; D. N. Klein & Riso, 1993; Sher & Trull, 1996; Widiger & Clark,

2000; Widiger & Trull, 1991). For the purpose of illustration, we summarize some of the more recent studies concerning posttraumatic stress, depressive, and personality disorders.

Posttraumatic Stress   "The boundary between normal and abnormal stress responses remains uncomfortably fuzzy" (McNally, 1999, p. 158). Difficulties specifying a distinct boundary have been problematic with respect to the severity of the disorder (Stein et al., 1997), the duration of its symptomatology (Bryant & Harvey, 1997), and the severity of the stressor that preceded the symptoms (Davidson & Foa, 1991).

A predominant conceptualization of PTSD is that it is a normal, natural, or expected response to an extraordinarily adverse stressor (Herman, 1992). *Stressor* was defined in *DSM-III* as a stimulus that "would evoke significant symptoms in almost everyone" (APA, 1980, p. 238). This conceptualization, however, was considered by some to be inconsistent with an understanding of PTSD as a disorder distinct from normal psychological functioning (Yehuda & McFarlane, 1995). It was noted further in *DSM-III-R* that the stressor was "outside the range of usual human experience" (APA, 1987, p. 250), but even if the event is rare, it might still be inconsistent to argue that it is pathological to respond normatively. Epidemiologic research has also indicated that the events considered in the realm of a PTSD stressor are not especially rare or unusual (Kessler, Sonnega, Bromet, Hughes, & Nelson, 1995; Kilpatrick et al., 1998).

PTSD, however, may not be a common, normal, or expected response to severe stressors. PTSD stressors might not be outside the range of usual human experience, but the occurrence of PTSD in response to this stress is the exception rather than the rule (Kessler et al., 1995; Kilpatrick et al., 1998). "PTSD is relatively rare compared to the prevalence of trauma" (Yehuda & McFarlane, 1995, p. 1707). PTSD does not occur in almost everyone who experiences these stressors; in fact, PTSD is an atypical, perhaps distinctly pathologic, reaction to being in combat, being raped, or being victimized by a natural disaster (Yehuda & McFarlane, 1995).

However, the low prevalence rate of PTSD in response to stress could result largely from an inordinately high threshold for its diagnosis. The diagnosis of PTSD requires that the symptoms be evident for at least four weeks, but the rationale for waiting until four weeks have passed to diagnose and treat the intrusive recollections, nightmares, feelings of detachment, and hypervigilance has been unclear (Frances, First, Widiger, et al., 1991). Failing to intervene early in the development of PTSD only makes the eventual treatment less likely to be effective (Frances, First, Pincus, 1995). Equally important, failing to respond to the significant distress and impairment experienced by people within the first month of a stressor is perhaps even callous or irresponsible. It is true that many of the symptoms might resolve without the intervention of a mental health clinician, but the existence of an involuntary organismic impairment to psychological functioning (or a harmful dysfunction) is not determined by the necessity of professional intervention (Frances, First, Widiger, et al., 1991; Widiger & Trull, 1991). Many acute physical disorders are treated adequately without the skills and knowledge of a physician. Acute stress disorder was, therefore, added to *DSM-IV* because a review of the empirical "literature provided evidence that the dissociative, intrusion, avoidance, and hyperarousal symptoms that make up the acute stress disorder diagnosis are prevalent in the immediate aftermath of trauma, are associated with the intensity of the trauma [and] co-occur with dysfunctional behavior during and after trauma" (Liebowitz et al., 1998, p. 1072).

The threshold for the diagnosis of PTSD might also be too high with respect to the number and severity of its diagnostic criteria. "Among the unresolved questions in the diagnosis and classification of PTSD is the taxonomic status and clinical importance of subsyndromal or subthreshold variants" (Stein et al., 1997, p. 1114). For example, extensive research of Vietnam veterans has indicated that subthreshold presentations (at times referred to as *partial PTSD*) are not uncommon and are associated with significant levels of distress and impairment (Weiss et al., 1992). Similar results have been reported in studies of survivors of sexual abuse, physical abuse, rape, natural disasters, and motor vehicle accidents (Stein et al., 1997). Stein et al. conducted a systematic epidemiologic study of the residents of Winnipeg, Manitoba, for the presence of *DSM-IV* PTSD and partial PTSD (i.e., four-week duration but lacking the necessary avoidance or arousal symptoms). They reported that partial PTSD did involve clinically significant levels of impairment, equaled the prevalence of *DSM-IV* PTSD, and resulted in as much treatment-seeking as *DSM-IV* PTSD. "Partial PTSD carries with it a burden of disability that approaches, if not entirely matches, that produced by full PTSD" (Stein et al., 1997, p. 1118).

Yehuda (1998) has conducted a number of studies that purportedly indicate that "the neuroendocrine alterations in PTSD are qualitatively, and sometimes directionally, different from those associated with the classic stress syndrome" (pp. 360–361). "Although most initial hypotheses about the biology of PTSD proposed very similar alterations in PTSD compared with those observed in major depression and other anxiety disorders, a review of the neuroendocrine findings in PTSD to date indicates very specific and qualitatively different abnormalities in this disorder" (p. 372). PTSD patients evidence an enhanced negative feedback inhibition characterized by an exaggerated cortisol response to dexamethasone, an increase in number of glucocorticoid receptors, and lower basal cortisol levels. These findings are in contrast to the blunted cortisol response to dexamethasone, decrease in number of glucocorticoid receptors, and increase in basal cortisol levels observed in people with major depressive disorder (Yehuda, 1998). However, these results do not indicate a neuroendocrine response to severe stress that is qualitatively distinct from a normal neuroendocrine response to equally severe stress. They simply indicate the neuroendocrine functioning that is associated with the sensitivity and hyperresponsivity that is observed in people with PTSD and not observed in people with major depressive disorder. More compelling support for a qualitatively distinct mental disorder would be provided by data indicating that the pathologic neuroendocrine functioning is qualitatively rather than quantitatively different from the neuroendocrine functioning observed in people with acute stress disorder, partial PTSD, and other people experiencing equal levels of stress.

A. Ruscio, Ruscio, and Keane (2002) conducted taxometric analyses of PTSD symptomatology (mean above minus below a cut [MAMBAC], maximum eigenvalue [MAXEIG], and latent mode factor analysis [L-MODE]; Waller & Meehl, 1998) to determine if a latent class taxon exists. The participants were 1,230 male combat veterans who received a psychological evaluation at the VA Boston Health Care System's National Center for Posttraumatic Stress Disorder from 1985 to 2000. The vast majority of the sample served in the Vietnam theater and reported a wide range of PTSD symptoms at the time of the assessment. Approximately 68% of the sample was estimated to have PTSD. Taxometric analyses were conducted on self-report and interview-based assessments and were based on alternative sets of items that were representative of PTSD symptomatology. None of the analyses indicated presence of a latent class taxon. A. Ruscio et al. concluded that "our empirical data were sufficiently valid to provide a meaningful test of latent structure, yielding compelling evidence for a dimensional latent structure of PTSD." Yehuda (1998) is correct that the experience of a traumatic stressor does not by itself determine who will develop the disorder, but the development of PTSD in response to combat is perhaps best understood to be the result of a series of graded factors (e.g., severity of the stressor, number of prior stressful life events, amount of postwar support, genetic vulnerability, and genetic resilience) that operate together to produce a particular level of symptom severity (King, King, Fairbank, Keane, & Adams, 1998).

Depression   "One of the most long-running controversies in the literature on depression concerns whether depression should be viewed as a distinct diagnostic category or as a single continuum occurring in normal and clinically diagnosed individuals" (Santor & Coyne, 2001, p. 216). Many studies have been conducted on the continuity or discontinuity of depression (Flett et al., 1997).

Kendler and Gardner (1998) used an extensive set of twin data to explore whether major depressive disorder is a discrete syndrome with points of rarity at its boundaries. They considered number of symptoms, level of severity or impairment, and duration of symptomatology. They examined how varying levels of these features predicted future episodes of depression and risk for major depression in co-twins. They failed to find evidence for discontinuity. Symptoms that were below diagnostic threshold, were of short duration, and even produced no impairment "had considerable predictive and familial validity" (p. 176). They concluded that "major depression—as articulated by *DSM-IV*—may be a diagnostic convention imposed on a continuum of depressive symptoms of varying severity and duration" (p. 172).

Kessler, Zhao, Blazer, and Swartz (1997) reported similar findings using data obtained through the National Comorbidity Survey ($N = 8,098$). They compared three levels of depression (minor, major, and severe) with respect to number of prior episodes, length of episode, level of impairment, comorbidity, and parental history of mental disorder. Cases of minor levels of depression had depressive symptomatology below the threshold for an officially recognized *DSM-IV* mood disorder. Kessler et al. could not find any indication of a discontinuous distribution and concluded that subclinical depression is on a continuum with major depressive disorder.

J. Ruscio and Ruscio (2000) conducted taxometric analyses of depressive symptomatology (maximum covariance [MAXCOV] and mean above minus below a cut [MAMBAC]; Waller & Meehl, 1998) to determine if a latent class taxon exists for major depression. The participants were 996 male veterans who received a psychological evaluation at the National Center for Posttraumatic Stress Disorder, approximately 60% of whom would receive a diagnosis of major depressive disorder. Subsets of items from two self-report measures of depression were used. The items selected were those with the highest correlations with total score and the least redundancy. The item sets were reasonably specific to the primary symptoms of a major depressive disorder, including significantly depressed mood, suicidality, anhedonia, and inappropriate guilt. The analyses consistently refuted the presence of an underlying latent class taxon. J. Ruscio and Ruscio (2000) concluded that the taxometric analyses "provided compelling evidence for the dimensionality of depression" (p. 482).

Lewinsohn, Solomon, Seeley, and Zeiss (2000) asked whether depressive symptomatology related in a continuous fashion or categorically to psychosocial impairment, mental health treatment utilization, and future episodes of major depression or substance-related disorders. The study participants were obtained from three large community samples of adolescents, adults, and older adults (total $N = 3,003$). Lewinsohn et al. concluded that "overall, the results suggest that what is consensually referred to as clinical depression is not categorically distinct from other degrees and patterns of depressive symptoms" (p. 349). Support for a continuous distribution of depression was observed across both self-reported and interview-based assessments, across gender, and across the life span from adolescence through older adulthood. "These findings suggest that (a) the clinical significance of depressive symptoms does not depend on crossing the major depressive diagnostic threshold and (b) depression may best be conceptualized as a continuum" (p. 345).

Cox, Enns, Borger, and Parker (1999) compared the correlations among major depressive disorder symptomatology obtained in a group of 101 adult patients diagnosed with major depressive disorder and in a group of 175 undergraduate college students with mildly elevated depression. The clinical sample reported significantly higher scores on almost all of the symptoms (the college students reported more alcohol use). However, there did not appear to be any qualitative differences in the structural nature of the depressive experience. The covariation among the depressive symptoms was quite similar across the two groups. Cox et al. concluded that "the differences observed between our analogue and clinical samples were of a quantitative rather than a qualitative nature" (p. 20).

Santor and Coyne (2001) reported results that they believe supported the existence of a qualitative distinction for depressive mood disorders. They conducted item response theory (IRT) analyses on items of the Hamilton Rating Scale for Depression (HRSD; Hamilton, 1960) in a sample of 67 clinically depressed primary care patients and 249 distressed, but not clinically depressed, primary care patients. They constructed a unidimensional scale of "global depression severity" (Santor & Coyne, 2001, p. 218) using a subset of seven HRSD items. Items from the HRSD that were explicitly diagnostic of anxiety or for which IRT analyses indicated differential item functioning between the depressed and nondepressed groups were not included. Santor and Coyne then obtained option characteristic curves for all 21 HRSD items for the depressed and nondepressed groups, with the groups equated for level of depression as assessed by the 7 HRSD items. They obtained a number of differences between the depressed and nondepressed groups. The clinically depressed patients evidenced higher levels of depressed mood, anhedonia, and suicidality than the nondepressed patients, even though they had been equated in terms of overall level of depression severity. In contrast, the nondepressed patients evidenced higher levels of middle insomnia and hypochondriasis. Santor and Coyne concluded that "a simple continuum of severity is inadequate to account for differences between depressed and nondepressed individuals" (p. 223).

The findings of Santor and Coyne, however, are not to the heart of the issue. The hypothesis that clinical depression and normal sadness exist along the same underlying continuum of functioning does not suggest that no differences between depressed and nondepressed people will be found. Higher levels of depression are associated with a wider array of impairments and dysfunction. These differences do not belie the existence of an underlying continuous distribution. More to the point is that the anhedonia, appetite disturbances, suicidal behavior, hopelessness, and worthlessness do not appear at a specific, discrete break. They instead accumulate progressively along continuously increasing quantitative degrees of depression. In addition, there is little reason to believe that "a simple continuum of severity" (Santor & Coyne, 2001, p. 223) would fully account for all of the differences that occur between arbitrarily distinguished groups. In fact, it is misleading to suggest that the depressed and nondepressed patients were equated with respect to "global depression severity" (p. 218). How could people who are not even depressed be said to have the same level of "depressive severity" (p. 219) as people who are significantly depressed? The groups were equated instead with respect to a particular subset of HRSD items; more specifically, seven items concerning guilt, weight loss, early insomnia, late insomnia, psychomotor agitation, psychomotor retardation, and loss of libido. Finally, it should not be particularly surprising that some symptoms are more evident in the distressed (but nondepressed people) than depressed patients, equated with the depressed people for level of guilt, loss of libido, early insomnia, late insomnia, and psychomotor disturbance. They must be distressed about something if it is not depression. It is hardly surprising that it could be middle insomnia or hypochondriasis.

Personality   It is stated in *DSM-IV* that "the diagnostic approach used in this manual represents the categorical perspective that Personality Disorders are qualitatively distinct clinical syndromes" (APA, 2000, p. 689). However, it is also now acknowledged that personality disorders may represent instead "maladaptive variants of personality traits that merge imperceptibly into normality and into one another" (p. 689). A personality disorder is diagnosed "when personality traits are inflexible and maladaptive and cause significant functional impairment or subjective distress" (p. 686), but no study has ever indicated that any one of the diagnostic thresholds for the personality disorders provided in any of the editions of the *DSM* identifies a point at which the respective personality traits are sufficiently or significantly maladaptive, impairing, or distressing to result in a valid, meaningful, or clinically useful distinction from normal personality functioning (Widiger & Corbitt, 1994).

Many studies, using a variety of methodologies, samples, and statistical approaches, have questioned the assumption that the *DSM-IV* personality disorders concern personality traits that are qualitatively distinct from general personality functioning (Clark, Livesley, & Morey, 1997; Livesley, 1998; Widiger, 1992a, 1993). For example, Livesley, Jang, and Vernon (1998) compared the phenotypic and genetic structure of a comprehensive set of personality disorder symptomatology in samples of 656 personality-disordered patients, 939 general community participants, and 686 twin pairs. Principal component analysis yielded four broad dimensions (emotional dysregulation, dissocial behavior, inhibitedness, and compulsivity) that were replicated across all three samples. Multivariate genetic analyses also yielded the same four factors. "The stable structure of traits across clinical and nonclinical samples is consistent with dimensional representations of personality disorders" (Livesley et al., 1998, p. 941). The structure and heritability of personality disorder symptomatology is just as evident in general community samples of people lacking the *DSM-IV* personality disorders as it is evident in people who have been diagnosed with these disorders. Livesley et al. and Widiger (1998) also noted the remarkable consistency of the four broad domains of personality disorder with four of the five broad domains consistently identified in studies of general personality functioning. Livesley et al. concluded that "the higher-order traits of personality disorder strongly resemble dimensions of normal personality" (p. 941).

A substantial amount of convergent and discriminant, temporal stability, developmental, cross-cultural, and heritability research has supported the validity of neuroticism, extraversion versus introversion, openness, agreeableness versus antagonism, and conscientiousness as constituting five broad domains of general personality functioning (John & Srivastava, 1999; McCrae & Costa, 1999). The personality traits that people in the general population consider most important in describing themselves and others are contained in these Big Five (Goldberg & Saucier, 1995), and they are remarkably congruent with the maladaptive personality functioning identified by the *DSM-IV* personality disorders, as follows (Widiger & Costa, 1994):

- Emotional dysregulation corresponds to five-factor model (FFM) neuroticism (identified by others as negative affectivity, as it includes traits such as fearfulness, depressiveness, anxiousness, anger, guilt, and vulnerability).
- The dissocial domain (defined by interpersonal hostility, judgmental attitudes, callousness, criminal behavior, and conduct problems) corresponds to FFM antagonism (which includes traits such as deceptiveness, exploitation, aggression, oppositionality, arrogance, and callousness).
- Inhibitedness (defined by intimacy problems and restricted affect) corresponds to FFM introversion (which includes traits such as placidity, withdrawal, reservation, aloofness, and passivity).
- *DSM-IV* compulsivity corresponds to FFM conscientiousness (which includes traits such as perfectionism, dutifulness, industriousness, discipline, deliberation, and organization).

It is "quite striking that an extensive history of research to develop a dimensional model of normal personality functioning that has been confined to community populations is so closely congruent with a model that was derived from an analysis confined to personality disorder symptoms" (Widiger, 1998, p. 865).

More than 50 studies have addressed the question of whether personality disorder symptomatology appears to be largely maladaptive variants of the personality traits included in the FFM of general personality functioning (Widiger & Costa, 2002). Almost all of the authors of these studies have concluded that their findings provided support for understanding personality disorder symptomatology from the perspective of the FFM. For example, joint factor analyses of measures of the FFM and personality disorder symptomatology have consistently confirmed a common underlying structure consistent with the FFM (e.g., Clark & Livesley, 1994; Schroeder, Wormworth, & Livesley, 1992). O'Connor and Dyce (1998) conducted independent principal-axes common factor analyses on the correlation matrices among the personality disorders using a variety of samples and assessment instruments provided by nine published studies. The personality disorder matrices were rotated to a least squares fit to the target matrices generated by alternative models. Their analyses were not exploratory searches of data sets, obtaining whatever factor analytic solution might capitalize on the particular measures and samples that were used. The confirmatory analyses "were powerful, support-seeking attempts to find the view on a correlational structure that was most consistent with a given model. Failures to find support are thus more likely due to shortcomings with a model than to shortcomings with the method" (p. 14). They found consistent support for the ability of the FFM to account for the personality disorder symptomatology: "The highest and most consistent level of fit were obtained for the five-factor model" (p. 14), along with a seven-factor model of Cloninger and Svrakic (1994).

Trull and his colleagues conducted a number of studies that document the correspondence of *DSM-IV* personality disorder symptomatology with maladaptive variants of common personality traits. Trull (1992) administered the NEO Personality Inventory (NEO-PI; Costa & McCrae, 1992), a self-report measure of the FFM, and three independent measures of the *DSM-III-R* personality disorders (APA, 1987) to a clinical outpatient sample. He concluded that "in general, the FFM appears to be useful in conceptualizing and differentiating among the *DSM-III-R* personality disorders" (Trull, 1992, p. 557). Trull et al. (1998) administered the self-report NEO PI-R (Costa & McCrae, 1992) and a semistructured interview for the assessment of the FFM (Structured Interview for the Five-Factor Model [SIFFM]; Trull & Widiger, 1997), along with measures of the *DSM-III-R* personality disorders to both outpatients and college students. The results confirmed again the ability of the FFM to account for the personality disorder symptomatology, particularly when the SIFFM and the NEO PI-R were used conjointly.

More specific findings were provided in a subsequent report by Trull, Widiger, and Burr (2001). The FFM is a hierarchical model of personality classification, consisting of five broad domains and 30 more specific facets (Costa & McCrae, 1992). For example, the general domain of agreeableness versus antagonism includes the more specific facets of trust (gullibility) versus skepticism (suspiciousness), straightforwardness (naive) versus cunning (deceptive), altruism (sacrificial) versus selfish (exploitative), compliance (docile) versus oppositional (aggressive), modesty (self-effacing) versus confident (arrogant), and tender-mindedness (soft) versus tough (callous). The *DSM-IV* personality disorders are more precisely described and differentiated at the level of the FFM facets, as demonstrated in studies by Axelrod, Widiger, Trull, and Corbitt (1997), Reynolds and Clark (2001), and Trull et al. (2001).

A few studies have questioned whether the *DSM-IV* personality disorders can be understood as variants of common personality traits. For example, Morey, Gunderson, Quigley, and Lyons (2000) concluded that the FFM was unsuccessful in providing much differentiation among any of the personality disorders because they obtained essentially equivalent FFM profiles for each of the *DSM-III-R* personality disorders. However, the primary reason for the failure of Morey et al. to obtain adequate differentiation could have been the inadequate differentiation among the disorders themselves (along with a reliance on an abbreviated measure of the FFM that was confined to an assessment of only the five broad domains). In their study, each of the 11 *DSM-III-R* personality disorders met, on average, the diagnostic criteria for 3 other personality disorders. Similar FFM profiles should be obtained in the presence of substantial diagnostic co-occurrence. The findings of Morey et al. could be more problematic for the validity of the *DSM-IV* diagnostic distinctions than for the validity of the FFM. Lynam and Widiger (2001) obtained expert consensus descriptions of each of the *DSM-IV* personality disorders in terms of the 30 facets of the FFM, and they indicated that the correlations among these FFM profiles largely accounted for the apparent comorbidity among the personality disorders previously reported in 15 published and unpublished studies. The *DSM-IV* personality disorders are not adequately differentiated from one another because they overlap substantially in the FFM personality traits included in their respective diagnostic criteria.

SUMMARY

The modern effort to demarcate a taxonomy of distinct clinical conditions is often traced to Kraepelin (1917). Kraepelin, however, had acknowledged that "wherever we try to mark out the frontier between mental health and disease, we find a neutral territory, in which the imperceptible change from the realm of normal life to that of obvious derangement takes place" (p. 295). The *DSM-IV* diagnostic categories do provide valid and useful information (as indicated in the chapters included in this text). There is good evidence that the personality disorder diagnoses, for example, are identifying clinically meaningful maladaptive personality traits (Livesley, 2001b; Millon et al., 1996). The *DSM-IV* antisocial (Stoff, Breiling, & Maser, 1997), borderline (Gunderson, 2001), narcissistic (Ronningstam, 1998), and dependent (Bornstein, 1992) personality disorder diagnoses do identify the presence of maladaptive personality traits of considerable social and clinical significance. However, undermining their validity is the false assumption that they are qualitatively distinct from one other and from general personality functioning. An adequate understanding of the diagnosis, etiology, pathology, comorbidity, and treatment of all mental disorders may require an acknowledgment that they are not conditions qualitatively distinct from the anxiety, depression, sexual functioning, sleep, and personality evident in all people.

A model for the future diagnosis of all mental disorders might be provided by one of the oldest and best validated diagnoses, mental retardation, a disorder for which much is known of its etiology, pathology, and classification. The point of demarcation for its diagnosis is an arbitrary, quantitative distinction along the normally distributed levels of intelligence. Alternative points of demarcation could have been selected. People with a level of intelligence of approximately 79 (i.e., borderline intellectual functioning; APA, 2000) experience significant impairments to success in school, career, and relationships. These impairments are not as severe as those with levels of intelligence of 69 but the distinction between an IQ of 69 and 79 is a quantitative, not a qualitative, distinction.

There are people below an IQ of 70 for whom a qualitatively distinct disorder is evident. However, the disorder in these cases is not mental retardation; it is a physical disorder (e.g., Down syndrome) that can be traced to a specific biological event (i.e., trisomy 21). "In approximately 30% to 40% of individuals seen in clinical settings, no clear etiology for the mental retardation can be determined despite extensive evaluation efforts" (APA, 2000, p. 45). Intelligence is distributed as a continuous variable because most individuals' level of intelligence is the result of a complex array of multiple genetic, fetal and infant development, and environmental influences (Neisser et al., 1996). "Etiological factors may be primarily biological or primarily psychosocial, or some combination of both" (APA, 2000, p. 45).

There are no discrete breaks in the distribution of intelligence that would provide an absolute distinction between normal intelligence and abnormal intelligence.

The diagnosis of anxiety, sleep, sexual, substance, mood, psychotic, personality, and other mental disorders should perhaps follow the model provided by mental retardation. Widiger et al. (2002), for example, provide a four-step procedure for the diagnosis of personality disorders that is similar in nature to the diagnosis of mental retardation:

1. Obtain a comprehensive description of the individual's general personality functioning with respect to the 5 domains and 30 facets of the FFM (thereby providing a description of adaptive as well as maladaptive personality traits).
2. Identify social and occupational impairments and distress associated with the individual's characteristic personality traits (commonly associated impairments are provided for each of the 60 poles of the 30 facets of the FFM by Widiger et al.)
3. Determine whether the dysfunction and distress reach a clinically significant level of impairment (using a scale modeled after Axis V of *DSM-IV*).
4. Match quantitatively the individual's FFM profile to prototypic profiles of diagnostic constructs.

The last step is provided for clinicians and researchers who wish to continue to provide single diagnostic labels to characterize a person's personality profile. However, we expect that prototypic profiles will be quite rare in clinical practice and the matching will serve largely to indicate how any particular diagnostic category will fail to be adequately descriptive and can be misleading (McCrae et al., 2001; Miller, Lynam, Widiger, & Leukefeld, 2001). The most precise and accurate description of an individual's personality will be provided by the FFM 30-facet profile.

We expect that researchers and clinicians in other domains of psychopathology will also develop comparable dimensional models of classification and diagnosis as the inadequacies of the categorical distinctions become increasingly problematic and unwieldy (Widiger & Clark, 2000; Widiger & Sankis, 2000). "Categorical disease models are being challenged . . . by the recent data indicating that individuals may carry a genetic risk factor to develop a disorder that can be measured premorbidly . . . and that may or may not ultimately be expressed as the full form of the disorder, depending on the occurrence of a variety of factors" (Andreasen 1997, p. 1587). The success of the categorical model in general medicine is in large part because medical conditions often have a quite specific etiology, pathology, and even phenomenology that allow for relatively homogeneous, uniform groups to be defined and diagnosed. Physical disorders and diseases often have a specific, discrete event, pathogen, or lesion that provides the condition with validity as a discrete clinical condition. This is not the case for most mental disorders. Mental disorders are typically the result of a complex interaction of an array of biological factors and environmental, psychosocial events, as indicated in each of the chapters in this text (Rutter, 1997). No mental disorder has been or will likely be reduced to a specific biological or psychological event. It is unrealistic to expect the maladaptive cognitions, affects, and behaviors present in any particular mental disorder to have a single, specific etiology. It is not that there are not physiological and environmental determinants worth identifying (e.g., sex abuse in the etiology of dissociative identity disorder). However, for a meaningful categorical diagnosis, not only would this etiology have to have provided a uniquely strong contribution to the development of the specific symptomatology, but also this symptomatology would have to have been largely resilient to the influence of other genetic and environmental influences (Widiger & Sankis, 2000). The symptomatology of mental disorders appears to be, in contrast, responsive to a variety of neurochemical, interpersonal, cognitive, and other mediating variables. Even schizophrenia may not be adequately characterized by a categorical diagnosis (Appelbaum, Robbins, & Roth, 1999). Molecular genetic studies have indicated that it is "most probable that genetic susceptibility to schizophrenic psychoses is polygenetic, and that their effects are dependent on interaction with physical and psychosocial environmental factors" (Portin & Alanen 1997, p. 73). As in the case of mental retardation, some specific etiologies and pathologies may eventually be discovered, but the bulk of psychopathology will be more complex and better understood multifactorially rather than categorically.

REFERENCES

Alper, J. S. (1998). Genes, free will, and criminal responsibility. *Social Science and Medicine, 46,* 1599–1611.

American Psychiatric Association. (1980). *Diagnostic and statistical manual of mental disorders* (3rd ed.). Washington, DC: Author.

American Psychiatric Association. (1987). *Diagnostic and statistical manual of mental disorders* (3rd ed., rev. ed.). Washington, DC: Author.

American Psychiatric Association. (1994). *Diagnostic and statistical manual of mental disorders* (4th ed.). Washington, DC: Author.

American Psychiatric Association. (2000). *Diagnostic and statistical manual of mental disorders* (4th ed., text rev.). Washington, DC: Author.

Andreasen, N. C. (1997). Linking mind and brain in the study of mental illnesses: A project for a scientific psychopathology. *Science, 275,* 1586–1593.

Angst, J. (1992). Recurrent brief psychiatric syndromes of depression, hypomania, neurasthenia, and anxiety from an epidemiological point of view. *Neurological, Psychiatric, and Brain Research, 1,* 5–12.

Appelbaum, P. S., Robbins, P. C., & Roth, L. H. (1999). Dimensional approach to delusions: Comparison across types and diagnoses. *American Journal of Psychiatry, 156,* 1938–1943.

Aubert, J. L., & Rush, A. J. (1996). Schizoaffective disorder. In T. A. Widiger, A. J. Frances, H. A. Pincus, R. Ross, M. B. First, & W. W. Davis (Eds.), *DSM-IV sourcebook* (Vol. 2, pp. 65–96). Washington, DC: American Psychiatric Association.

Axelrod, S. R., Widiger, T. A., Trull, T. J., & Corbitt, E. M. (1997). Relationships of five-factor model antagonism facets with personality disorder symptomatology. *Journal of Personality Assessment, 67,* 297–313.

Bandura, A. (2001). Social cognitive theory: An agentic perspective. *Annual Review of Psychology, 52,* 1–26.

Bargh, J. A., & Ferguson, M. J. (2000). Beyond behaviorism: On the automaticity of higher mental processes. *Psychological Bulletin, 126,* 925–945.

Benjamin, L. S. (1993). Dimensional, categorical, or hybrid analyses of personality: A response to Widiger's proposal. *Psychological Inquiry, 4,* 91–95.

Bergner, R. M. (1997). What is psychopathology? And so what? *Clinical Psychology: Science and Practice, 4,* 235–248.

Blacker, D., & Tsuang, M. T. (1992). Contested boundaries of bipolar disorder and the limits of categorical diagnosis in psychiatry. *American Journal of Psychiatry, 149,* 1473–1483.

Bornstein, R. F. (1992). The dependent personality: Developmental, social, and clinical perspectives. *Psychological Bulletin, 112,* 3–23.

Brown, T. A., Campbell, L. A., Lehman, C. L., Grisham, J. R., & Mancill, R. B. (2001). Current and lifetime comorbidity of the *DSM-IV* anxiety and mood disorders in a large clinical sample. *Journal of Abnormal Psychology, 110,* 585–599.

Brown, T. A., Chorpita, B. F., & Barow, D. H. (1998). Structural relationships among dimensions of the *DSM-IV* anxiety and mood disorders and dimensions of negative affect, positive affect, and autonomic arousal. *Journal of Abnormal Psychology, 107,* 179–192.

Bryant, R. A., & Harvey, A. G. (1997). Acute stress disorder: A critical review of diagnostic issues. *Clinical Psychology Review, 17,* 757–773.

Caine, E. D. (1994). Should aging-associated memory decline be included in *DSM-IV?* In T. A. Widiger, A. J. Frances, H. A. Pincus, M. B. First, R. Ross, & W. W. Davis (Eds.), *DSM-IV sourcebook* (Vol. 1, pp. 329–337). Washington, DC: American Psychiatric Association.

Cantor, N., & Genero, N. (1986). Psychiatric diagnosis and natural categorization: A close analogy. In T. Millon & G. Klerman (Eds.), *Contemporary directions in psychopathology* (pp. 233–256). New York: Guilford Press.

Cardena, E., Lewis-Fernandez, R., Bear, D., Pakianathan, I., & Spiegel, D. (1996). Dissociative disorders. In T. A. Widiger, A. J. Frances, H. A. Pincus, R. Ross, M. B. First, & W. W. Davis (Eds.), *DSM-IV sourcebook* (Vol. 2, pp. 973–1005). Washington, DC: American Psychiatric Association.

Caron, C., & Rutter, M. (1991). Comorbidity in child psychopathology: Concepts, issues and research strategies. *Journal of Child Psychology and Psychiatry, 32,* 1063–1080.

Clark, L. A., & Livesley, W. J. (1994). Two approaches to identifying the dimensions of personality disorder: Convergence on the five-factor model. In P. T. Costa & T. A. Widiger (Eds.), *Personality disorders and the Five-Factor Model of Personality* (pp. 261–278). Washington, DC: American Psychological Association.

Clark, L. A., Livesley, W. J., & Morey, L. C. (1997). Personality disorder assessment: The challenge of construct validity. *Journal of Personality Disorders, 11,* 205–231.

Clark, L. A., Watson, D., & Mineka, S. (1994). Temperament, personality, and the mood and anxiety disorders. *Journal of Abnormal Psychology, 103,* 103–116.

Clark, L. A., Watson, D., & Reynolds, S. (1995). Diagnosis and classification of psychopathology: Challenges to the current system and future directions. *Annual Review of Psychology, 46,* 121–153.

Cloninger, C. R., & Svrakic, D. M. (1994). Differentiating normal and deviant personality by the seven-factor personality model. In S. Strack & M. Lorr (Eds.), *Differentiating normal and abnormal personality* (pp. 40–64). New York: Springer.

Costa, P. T., & McCrae, R. R. (1992). *Revised NEO Personality Inventory (NEO-PI-R) and NEO Five-Factor Inventory (NEO-FFI) professional manual.* Odessa, FL: Psychological Assessment Resources.

Cox, B. J., Enns, M. W., Borger, S. C., & Parker, J. D. A. (1999). The nature of the depressive experience in analogue and clinically depressed samples. *Behavior Research and Therapy, 37,* 15–24.

Coyne, J. C. (1994). Self-reported distress: Analog or ersatz depression? *Psychological Bulletin, 116,* 29–45.

Davidson, J. R. T., & Foa, E. B. (1991). Diagnostic issues in posttraumatic stress disorder. *Journal of Abnormal Psychology, 100,* 346–355.

Devlin, M. G., Walsh, B. T., Spitzer, R. L., & Hasin, D. (1992). Is there another binge eating disorder? A review of the literature on overeating in the absence of bulimia nervosa. *International Journal of Eating Disorders, 11,* 333–340.

Flett, G. L., Vredenburg, K., & Krames, L. (1997). The continuity of depression in clinical and nonclinical samples. *Psychological Bulletin, 121,* 395–416.

Frances, A. J., First, M. B., & Pincus, H. A. (1995). *DSM-IV guidebook.* Washington, DC: American Psychiatric Press.

Frances, A. J., First, M. B., Widiger, T. A., Miele, G., Tilly, S., Davis, W. W., et al. (1991). An A to Z guide to *DSM-IV* conundrums. *Journal of Abnormal Psychology, 100,* 407–412.

Frances, A. J., Widiger, T. A., & Sabshin, M. (1991). Psychiatric diagnosis and normality. In D. Offer & M. Sabshin (Eds.), *The diversity of normal behavior* (pp. 3–38). New York: Basic Books.

Gallant, S. J., & Hamilton, J. A. (1990). Problematic aspects of diagnosing premenstrual phase dysphoria. *Professional Psychology, 20,* 60–68.

Goldberg, L. R., & Saucier, G. (1995). So what do you propose we use instead? A reply to Block. *Psychological Bulletin, 117,* 221–225.

Golding, S. L., Skeem, J. L., Roesch, R., & Zapf, P. A. (1999). The assessment of criminal responsibility: Current controversies. In A. K. Hess & I. B. Weiner (Eds.), *The handbook of forensic psychology* (2nd ed., pp. 379–408). New York: Wiley.

Gorenstein, E. (1984). Debating mental illness. *American Psychologist, 39,* 50–56.

Gross, J. J., & Munoz, R. F. (1995). Emotion regulation and mental health. *Clinical Psychology: Science and Practice, 2,* 151–164.

Gunderson, J. G. (2001). *Borderline personality disorder: A clinical guide.* Washington, DC: American Psychiatric Press.

Gunderson, J. G., Links, P. S., & Reich, J. H. (1991). Competing models of personality disorders. *Journal of Personality Disorders, 5,* 60–68.

Gutierrez, R., Atkinson, J. H., & Grant, I. (1993). Mild neurocognitive disorder. A needed addition to the nosology of cognitive impairment (organic mental) disorders. *Journal of Neuropsychiatry and Clinical Neurosciences, 5,* 161–177.

Guze, S. B., & Helzer, J. E. (1987). The medical model and psychiatric disorders. In R. Michels & J. Cavenar (Eds.), *Psychiatry* (Vol. 1, pp. 1–8). Philadelphia: Lippincott.

Hamilton, M. (1960). A rating scale for depression. *Journal of Neurology, Neurosurgery, and Mental Science, 105,* 985–987.

Herman, J. L. (1992). *Trauma and recovery.* New York: Basic Books.

Hollander, E., Neville, D., Frenkel, M., Josephson, S., & Liebowitz, M. R. (1992). Body dysmorphic disorder: Diagnostic issues and related disorders. *Psychosomatics, 33,* 156–165.

Howard, G. S., & Conway, C. G. (1986). Can there be an empirical science of volitional action? *American Psychologist, 41,* 1241–1251.

Hughes, J. R., Oliveto, A. H., Helzer, J. E., Higgins, S. T., & Bickel, W. K. (1992). Should caffeine abuse, dependence, or withdrawal be added to *DSM-IV* or ICD-10? *American Journal of Psychiatry, 149,* 33–40.

Huprich, S. K. (1998). Depressive personality disorder: Theoretical issues, clinical findings, and future research questions. *Clinical Psychology Review, 18,* 477–500.

John, O. P., & Srivastava, S. (1999). The Big Five trait taxonomy: History, measurement, and theoretical perspectives. In L. A. Pervin & O. P. John (Eds.), *Handbook of personality: Theory and research* (2nd ed., pp. 102–138). New York: Guilford Press.

Kendell, R. C. (1975). *The role of diagnosis in psychiatry.* Oxford, England: Blackwell.

Kendler, K. S. (1990). Toward a scientific psychiatric nosology: Strengths and limitations. *Archives of General Psychiatry, 47,* 969–973.

Kendler, K. S., & Gardner, C. O. (1998). Boundaries of major depression: An evaluation of *DSM-IV* criteria. *American Journal of Psychiatry, 155,* 172–177.

Kessler, R. C., Crum, R. M., Warner, L. A., Nelson, C. B., Schulenberg, J., & Anthony, J. C. (1997). Lifetime co-occurrence of *DSM-III-R* alcohol abuse and dependence with other psychiatric disorders in the National Comorbidity Survey. *Archives of General Psychiatry, 54,* 313–321.

Kessler, R. C., McGonagle, K. A., Zhao, S., Nelson, C. B., Hughes, M., Eshleman, S., et al. (1994). Lifetime and 12-month prevalence of *DSM-III-R* psychiatric disorders in the United States: Results from the National Comorbidity Survey. *Archives of General Psychiatry, 51,* 8–19.

Kessler, R. C., Sonnega, A., Bromet, E., Hughes, M., & Nelson, C. B. (1995). Posttraumatic stress disorder in the National Comorbidity Survey. *Archives of General Psychiatry, 52,* 1048–1060.

Kessler, R. C., Zhao, S., Blazer, D. G., & Swartz, M. (1997). Prevalence, correlates, and course of minor depression and major depression in the National Comorbidity Survey. *Journal of Affective Disorders, 45,* 19–30.

Kihlstrom, J. F. (1992). Dissociative and conversion disorders. In D. J. Stein & J. Young (Eds.), *Cognitive science and clinical disorders* (pp. 247–270). San Diego, CA: Academic Press.

Kilpatrick, D. G., Resnick, H. S., Freedy, J. R., Pelcovitz, D., Resick, P. A., Roth, S., et al. (1998). Posttraumatic stress disorder field trial: Evaluation of the PTSD construct–criteria A through E. In T. A. Widiger, A. J. Frances, H. A. Pincus, R. Ross, M. B. First, W. Davis, et al. (Eds.), *DSM-IV sourcebook* (Vol. 4, pp. 803–844). Washington, DC: American Psychiatric Association.

King, L. A., King, D. W., Fairbank, J. A., Keane, T. M., & Adams, G. A. (1998). Resilience-recovery factors in posttraumatic stress disorders among female and male Vietnam veterans: Hardiness, postwar social support, and additional stressful life vents. *Journal of Personality and Social Psychology, 74,* 420–434.

Kirsch, I., & Lynn, S. J. (2000). Automaticity in clinical psychology. *American Psychologist, 54,* 504–515.

Klein, D. F. (1978). A proposed definition of mental illness. In R. L. Spitzer & D. F. Klein (Eds.), *Critical issues in psychiatric diagnosis* (pp. 41–71). New York: Raven Press.

Klein, D. F. (1999). Harmful dysfunction, disorder, disease, illness, and evolution. *Journal of Abnormal Psychology, 108,* 421–429.

Klein, D. N., & Riso, L. P. (1993). Psychiatric disorders: Problems of boundaries and co-morbidity. In C. G. Costello (Ed.), *Basic issues in psychopathology* (pp. 19–66). New York: Guilford Press.

Knutson, B., Wolkowitz, O. M., Cole, S. W., Chan, T., Moore, E. A., Johnson, R. C., et al. (1998). Selective alteration of personality and social behavior by serotonergic intervention. *American Journal of Psychiatry, 155,* 373–379.

Kraepelin, E. (1917). *Lectures on clinical psychiatry* (3rd ed.). New York: William Wood.

Krueger, R. F. (1999). The structure of common mental disorders. *Archives of General Psychiatry, 56,* 921–926.

Krueger, R. F., Caspi, A., Moffitt, T. E., & Silva, P. A. (1998). The structure and stability of common mental disorders (*DSM-III-R*): A longitudinal-epidemiological study. *Journal of Abnormal Psychology, 107,* 216–227.

Lenzenweger, M. F., & Korfine, L. (1992). Confirming the latent structure and base rate of schizotypy: A taxometric analysis. *Journal of Abnormal Psychology, 101,* 567–571.

Lesieur, H. R., & Rosenthal, R. J. (1991). Pathological gambling: A review of the literature. *Journal of Gambling Studies, 7,* 5–40.

Lewinsohn, P. M., Solomon, A., Seeley, J. R., & Zeiss, A. (2000). Clinical implications of "subthreshold" depressive symptoms. *Journal of Abnormal Psychology, 109,* 345–351.

Liebowitz, M. R. (1992). Diagnostic issues in anxiety disorders. In A. Tasman & M. B. Riba (Eds.), *Review of psychiatry* (Vol. 11, pp. 247–259). Washington, DC: American Psychiatric Press.

Liebowitz, M. R., Barlow, D. H., Ballenger, J. C., Davidson, J., Foa, E. B., Fyer, A. J., et al. (1998). *DSM-IV* anxiety disorders: Final overview. In T. A. Widiger, A. J. Frances, H. A. Pincus, R. Ross, M. B. First, W. Davis, et al. (Eds.), *DSM-IV sourcebook* (Vol. 4, pp. 1047–1076). Washington, DC: American Psychiatric Association.

Lilienfeld, S. O., & Marino, L. (1995). Mental disorder as a Roschian concept: A critique of Wakefield's "harmful dysfunction" analysis. *Journal of Abnormal Psychology, 104,* 411–420.

Lilienfeld, S. O., & Marino, L. (1999). Essentialism revisited: Evolutionary theory and the concept of mental disorder. *Journal of Abnormal Psychology, 108,* 400–411.

Lilienfeld, S. O., Waldman, I. D., & Israel, A. C. (1994). A critical examination of the use of the term "comorbidity" in psychopathology research. *Clinical Psychology: Science and Practice, 1,* 71–83.

Livesley, W. J. (1998). Suggestions for a framework for an empirically based classification of personality disorder. *Canadian Journal of Psychiatry, 43,* 137–147.

Livesley, W. J. (2001a). Commentary on reconceptualizing personality disorder categories using trait dimensions. *Journal of Personality, 69,* 277–286.

Livesley, W. J. (Ed.). (2001b). *Handbook of personality disorders: Theory, research, and treatment.* New York: Guilford Press.

Livesley, W. J., Jang, K. L., & Vernon, P. A. (1998). Phenotypic and genetic structure of traits delineating personality disorder. *Archives of General Psychiatry, 55,* 941–948.

Loeber, R., Lahey, B. B., & Thomas, C. (1991). Diagnostic conundrum of oppositional defiant disorder and conduct disorder. *Journal of Abnormal Psychology, 100,* 379–390.

Lynam, D. R., & Widiger, T. A. (in press). Using the five factor model to represent the *DSM-IV* personality disorders: An expert consensus approach. *Journal of Abnormal Psychology.*

Magruder, K. M., & Calderone, G. E. (2000). Public health consequences of different thresholds for the diagnosis of mental disorders. *Comprehensive Psychiatry, 41,* 14–18.

March, J. S. (1990). The nosology of posttraumatic stress disorder. *Journal of Anxiety Disorders, 4,* 61–82.

Maser, J. D., & Cloninger, C. R. (1990). Comorbidity of anxiety and mood disorders: Introduction and overview. In J. D. Maser & C. R. Cloninger (Eds.), *Comorbidity of mood and anxiety disorders* (pp. 3–12). Washington, DC: American Psychiatric Press.

Mayberg, H. S., Liotti, M., Brannan, S. K., McGinnis, S., Mahurin, R. K., Jerabek, P. A., et al. (1999). Reciprocal limbic-cortical function and negative mood: Converging PET findings in depression and normal sadness. *American Journal of Psychiatry, 156,* 675–682.

McCrae, R. R., & Costa, P. T. (1999). A five-factor theory of personality. In L. A. Pervin & O. P. John (Eds.), *Handbook of personality: Theory and research* (2nd ed., pp. 139–153). New York: Guilford Press.

McCrae, R. R., Yang, J., Costa, P. T., Dai, X., Yao, S., Cai, T., et al. (2001). Personality profiles and the prediction of categorical personality disorders. *Journal of Personality, 69,* 155–174.

McNally, R. J. (1999). Posttraumatic stress disorder. In T. Millon, P. H. Blaney, & R. D. Davis (Eds.), *Oxford textbook of psychopathology* (pp. 144–165). New York: Oxford University Press.

Meehl, P. E. (1995). Bootstraps taxometrics: Solving the classification problem in psychopathology. *American Psychologist, 50,* 266–275.

Merikangas, K. R., Hoyer, E. B., & Angst, J. (1996). Recurrent brief depressive disorder. In T. A. Widiger, A. J. Frances, H. A. Pincus, R. Ross, M. B. First, & W. W. Davis (Eds.), *DSM-IV sourcebook* (Vol. 2, pp. 111–126). Washington, DC: American Psychiatric Association.

Milich, R., Balentine, A. C., & Lynam, D. R. (in press). ADHD combined type and ADHD predominantly inattentive type are distinct and unrelated disorders. *Clinical Psychology: Science and Practice.*

Miller, J. D., Lynam, D. R., Widiger, T. A., & Leukefeld, C. (2001). Personality disorders as extreme variants of common personality dimensions: Can the five-factor model adequately represent psychopathy? *Journal of Personality, 69,* 253–276.

Millon, T., Davis, R. D., Millon, C. M., Wenger, A. W., Van Zuilen, M. H., Fuchs, M., et al. (1996). *Disorders of personality: DSM-IV and beyond.* New York: Wiley.

Mineka, S., Watson, D., & Clark, L. A. (1998). Comorbidity of anxiety and unipolar mood disorders. *Annual Review of Psychology, 49,* 377–412.

Morey, L. C., Gunderson, J., Quigley, B. D., & Lyons, M. (2000). Dimensions and categories: The "Big Five" factors and the *DSM* personality disorders. *Assessment, 7,* 203–216.

Munoz, R. F., Hollon, S. D., McGrath, E., Rehm, L. P., & VandenBos, G. P. (1994). On the AHCPR Depression in Primary Care guidelines. *American Psychologist, 49,* 42–61.

Neisser, U., Boodoo, G., Bouchard, T. J., Boykin, A. W., Brody, N., Ceci, S. J., et al. (1996). Intelligence: Knowns and unknowns. *American Psychologist, 51,* 77–101.

O'Connor, B. P., & Dyce, J. A. (1998). A test of models of personality disorder configuration. *Journal of Abnormal Psychology, 107,* 3–16.

Parker, G. (2000). Classifying depression: Should paradigms lost be regained? *Archives of General Psychiatry, 157,* 1195–1203.

Peele, S. (1984). The cultural context of psychological approaches to alcoholism. *American Psychologist, 39,* 1337–1351.

Portin, P., & Alanen, Y. O. (1997). A critical review of genetic studies of schizophrenia. II: Molecular genetic studies. *Acta Psychiatrica Scandinavica, 95,* 73–80.

Regier, D. A., Kaelber, C. T., Rae, D. S., Farmer, M. E., Knauper, B., Kessler, R. C., et al. (1998). Limitations of diagnostic criteria and assessment instruments for mental disorders: Implications for research and policy. *Archives of General Psychiatry, 55,* 109–115.

Reynolds, S. K., & Clark, L. A. (2001). Predicting dimensions of personality disorder from domains and facets of the five-factor model. *Journal of Personality, 69,* 199–222.

Ronningstam, E. (Ed.). (1998). *Disorders of narcissism: Diagnostic, clinical, and empirical implications.* Washington, DC: American Psychiatric Press.

Ruscio, A. M., Ruscio, J., & Keane, T. M. (2002). The latent structure of posttraumatic stress disorder: A taxometric investigation of reactions to extreme stress. *Journal of Abnormal Psychology, 111,* 290–301.

Ruscio, J., & Ruscio, A. M. (2000). Informing the continuity controversy: A taxometric analysis of depression. *Journal of Abnormal Psychology, 109,* 473–487.

Rutter, M. L. (1997). Implications of genetic research for child psychiatry. *Canadian Journal of Psychiatry, 42,* 569–576.

Ryder, A. G., & Bagby, R. M. (1999). Diagnostic viability of depressive personality disorder: Theoretical and conceptual issues. *Journal of Personality Disorders, 13,* 99–117.

Santor, D. A., & Coyne, J. C. (2001). Evaluating the continuity of symptomatology between depressed and nondepressed individuals. *Journal of Abnormal Psychology, 110,* 216–225.

Schacht, T. E., & Nathan, P. E. (1977). But is it good for the psychologists? Appraisal and status of *DSM-III. American Psychologist, 32,* 1017–1025.

Schroeder, M. L., Wormworth, J. A., & Livesley, W. J. (1992). Dimensions of personality disorder and their relationship to the Big Five dimensions of personality. *Psychological Assessment, 4,* 47–53.

Sher, K. J., & Trull, T. J. (1996). Methodological issues in psychopathology research. *Annual Review of Psychology, 47,* 371–400.

Shisslak, C. M., Crago, M., & Estes, L. S. (1995). The spectrum of eating disturbances. *International Journal of Eating Disorders, 18,* 209–219.

Silk, K. (Ed.). (1998). *Biology of personality disorders.* Washington, DC: American Psychiatric Press.

Soloff, P. H. (1998). Algorithms for pharmacological treatment of personality dimensions: Symptom specific treatments for cognitive-perceptual, affective, and impulsive-behavioral dysregulation. *Bulletin of the Menninger Clinic, 62,* 195–214.

Spiegel, D., & Cardena, E. (1991). Disintegrated experience: The dissociative disorders revisited. *Journal of Abnormal Psychology, 100,* 366–378.

Spitzer, R. L., & Wakefield, J. C. (1999). The *DSM-IV* diagnostic criterion for clinical significance: Does it help solve the false positives problem? *American Journal of Psychiatry, 156,* 1856–1864.

Spitzer, R. L., & Williams, J. B. W. (1982). The definition and diagnosis of mental disorder. In W. Gove (Ed.), *Deviance and mental illness* (pp. 15–31). Beverly Hills, CA: Sage.

Spitzer, R. L., & Williams, J. B. W. (1985). Proposed revisions in the *DSM-III* classification of anxiety disorders based on research and clinical experience. In A. H. Tuma & J. Maser (Eds.), *Anxiety and the anxiety disorders* (pp. 759–773). Hillsdale, NJ: Erlbaum.

Spitzer, R. L., Williams, J. B. W., & Skodol, A. E. (1980). *DSM-III:* The major achievements and an overview. *American Journal of Psychiatry, 137,* 151–164.

Stein, M. B., Walker, J. R., Hazen, A. L., & Forde, D. R. (1997). Full and partial posttraumatic stress disorder: Findings from a community survey. *American Journal of Psychiatry, 154,* 1114–1119.

Stoff, D. M., Breiling, J., & Maser, J. D. (Eds.). (1997). *Handbook of antisocial behavior.* New York: Wiley.

Szymanski, L. S., & Wilska, M. (1997). Mental retardation. In A. Tasman, J. Kay, & J. A. Lieberman (Eds.), *Psychiatry* (Vol. 1, pp. 635). Philadelphia: Saunders.

Task Force on *DSM-IV.* (1991, September). *DSM-IV options book: Work in progress.* Washington, DC: American Psychiatric Association.

Taylor, M. A. (1992). Are schizophrenia and affective disorder related? A selective literature review. *American Journal of Psychiatry, 149,* 22–32.

Tennen, H., Hall, J. A., & Affleck, G. (1995). Depression research methodologies in the *Journal of Personality and Social Psychology:* A review and critique. *Journal of Personality and Social Psychology, 68,* 870–884.

Trull, T. J. (1992). *DSM-III-R* personality disorders and the Five-Factor Model of Personality: An empirical comparison. *Journal of Abnormal Psychology, 101,* 553–560.

Trull, T. J., & Widiger, T. A. (1997). *Structured Interview for the Five-Factor Model of Personality.* Odessa, FL: Psychological Assessment Resources.

Trull, T. J., Widiger, T. A., & Burr, R. (2001). A structured interview for the assessment of the Five-Factor Model of Personality. II: Facet-level relations to the Axis II personality disorders. *Journal of Personality, 69,* 175–198.

Trull, T. J., Widiger, T. A., Useda, J. D., Holcomb, J., Doan, D.-T., Axelrod, S. R., et al. (1998). A structured interview for the assessment of the Five-Factor Model of Personality. *Psychological Assessment, 10,* 229–240.

Turner, S. M., & Beidel, D. C. (1989). Social phobia: Clinical syndrome, diagnosis, and co-morbidity. *Clinical Psychology Review, 9,* 3–18.

Turner, S. M., Beidel, D. C., & Townsley, R. M. (1992). Social phobia: A comparison of specific and generalized subtypes and avoidant personality disorder. *Journal of Abnormal Psychology, 101,* 326–331.

Vaillant, G. E. (1995). *The natural history of alcoholism revisited.* Cambridge, MA: Harvard University Press.

Wakefield, J. C. (1992). Disorder as harmful dysfunction: A conceptual critique of *DSM-III-R's* definition of mental disorder. *Psychological Review, 99,* 232–247.

Wakefield, J. C. (1997). Diagnosing *DSM-IV* Part I: *DSM-IV* and the concept of disorder. *Behavioral Research and Therapy, 35,* 633–649.

Waller, N. G., & Meehl, P. E. (1998). *Multivariate taxometric procedures: Distinguishing types from continua.* Thousands Oaks, CA: Sage.

Weary, G., Edwards, J. A., & Jacobson, J. A. (1995). Depression research methodologies in the *Journal of Personality and Social Psychology:* A reply. *Journal of Personality and Social Psychology, 68,* 885–891.

Wegner, D. M., & Wheatley, T. (2000). Apparent mental causation: Sources of the experience of will. *American Psychologist, 54,* 480–492.

Weiss, D. S., Marmer, C. R., Schlenger, W. E., Fairbank, J. A., Jordan, B. K., Hough, R. L., et al. (1992). The prevalence of lifetime and partial posttraumatic stress disorder in Vietnam theater veterans. *Journal of Traumatic Stress, 5,* 365–376.

Widiger, T. A. (1992a). Categorical versus dimensional classification: Implications from and for research. *Journal of Personality Disorders, 6,* 287–300.

Widiger, T. A. (1992b). Generalized social phobia versus avoidant personality disorder: A commentary on three studies. *Journal of Abnormal Psychology, 101,* 340–343.

Widiger, T. A. (1993). The *DSM-III-R* categorical personality disorder diagnoses: A critique and an alternative. *Psychological Inquiry, 4,* 75–90.

Widiger, T. A. (1998). Four out of five ain't bad. *Archives of General Psychiatry, 55,* 865–866.

Widiger, T. A., & Clark, L. A. (2000). Toward *DSM-V* and the classification of psychopathology. *Psychological Bulletin, 126,* 946–963.

Widiger, T. A., & Corbitt, E. M. (1994). Normal versus abnormal personality from the perspective of the *DSM.* In S. Strack & M. Lorr (Eds.), *Differentiating normal and abnormal personality* (pp. 158–175). New York: Springer.

Widiger, T. A., & Costa, P. T. (1994). Personality and personality disorders. *Journal of Abnormal Psychology, 103,* 78–91.

Widiger, T. A., & Costa, P. T. (2002). FFM personality disorder research. In P. T. Costa & T. A. Widiger (Eds.), *Personality disorders and the Five-Factor Model of Personality* (2nd ed., pp. 59–87). Washington, DC: American Psychological Association.

Widiger, T. A., Costa, P. T., & McCrae, R. R. (2002). Proposal for Axis II: Diagnosing personality disorders using the five factor model. In P. T. Costa & T. A. Widiger (Eds.), *Personality disorders and the Five Factor Model of Personality* (2nd ed., pp. 431–456). Washington, DC: American Psychological Association.

Widiger, T. A., & Sanderson, C. J. (1995). Toward a dimensional model of personality disorders. In W. J. Livesley (Ed.), *The DSM-IV personality disorders* (pp. 433–458). New York: Guilford Press.

Widiger, T. A., & Sankis, L. (2000). Adult psychopathology: Issues and controversies. *Annual Review of Psychology, 51,* 377–404.

Widiger, T. A., & Smith, G. T. (1994). Substance use disorder: Abuse, dependence, and dyscontrol. *Addiction, 89,* 267–282.

Widiger, T. A., & Trull, T. J. (1991). Diagnosis and clinical assessment. *Annual Review of Psychology, 42,* 109–133.

Wilson, G. T., & Walsh, B. T. (1991). Eating disorders in the *DSM-IV. Journal of Abnormal Psychology, 100,* 362–365.

Wittchen, H., Hofler, M., & Merikangas, K. (1999). Toward the identification of core psychopathological processes? *Archives of General Psychiatry, 56,* 929–931.

Yehuda, R. (1998). Psychoneuroendocrinology of posttraumatic stress disorder. *Psychiatric Clinics of North America, 21,* 359–379.

Yehuda, R., & McFarlane, A. C. (1995). Conflict between current knowledge about posttraumatic stress disorder and its original conceptual basis. *American Journal of Psychiatry, 152,* 1705–1713.

Zinbarg, R. E., & Barlow, D. H. (1991). Mixed anxiety-depression: A new diagnostic category. In R. M. Rapee & D. H. Barlow (Eds.), *Chronic anxiety: Generalized anxiety disorder and mixed anxiety depression* (pp. 136–152). New York: Guilford Press.

Zinbarg, R. E., & Barlow, D. H. (1996). Structure of anxiety and anxiety disorders: A hierarchical model. *Journal of Abnormal Psychology, 105,* 181–193.

CHAPTER 2

Dual Diagnosis

MELANIE E. BENNETT and BELINDA BARNETT

IN RECENT YEARS, the issue of comorbidity of psychiatric disorders has gained increased attention. Research indicates that a substantial percentage of people in the general population with a lifetime psychiatric disorder have a history of some other disorder (Kessler, 1997; Kessler et al., 1994), and more than half of patients in psychiatric treatment meet criteria for more than one diagnosis (Wolf, Schubert, Patterson, Marion, & Grande, 1988). The issue of *comorbidity* broadly refers to combinations of any types of psychiatric disorders that co-occur in the same individual. A diagnostic pair that has received significant attention over the past two decades is that of mental illness and substance abuse. The term *dual diagnosis* has been used to describe individuals who meet diagnostic criteria for some Axis I or Axis II mental disorder (or disorders) along with one or more substance use disorders. Since the 1980s, rates of co-occurring mental illness and substance use disorders have increased sharply. This increase likely results from a range of factors including more specific diagnostic criteria for substance use disorders, as well as development of standardized diagnostic interviews that allow for reliable and valid assessments of Axis I disorders in a range of patient populations (Wittchen, Perkonigg, & Reed, 1996). It is likely that these increases in rates of dual diagnosis reflect what was truly there all along—a frequent association between mental and substance use disorders that we have only now begun to measure accurately.

It is now clear that dual diagnosis impacts all aspects of psychopathology research and clinical practice, from service utilization, treatment entry, and treatment retention, to assessment and diagnosis of psychological problems, to research on psychopathology and treatment outcome. In this chapter, we review current data on rates of dual diagnosis, both generally and for specific domains of disorders, as well as discuss some ways that dual diagnosis impacts the course, prognosis, assessment, and treatment of adult psychopathology. Finally, we review current research on the etiology of dual diagnosis, and highlight clinical and research directions.

EPIDEMIOLOGY OF DUAL DIAGNOSIS

METHODOLOGICAL ISSUES

There are several methodological issues to consider when evaluating the literature on the epidemiology of dual diagnosis. First, data come from both epidemiological and clinical studies. Several large-scale epidemiological studies examining rates of dual diagnosis in general population samples have been conducted since the mid-1980s. These studies provide representative information on rates of mental illness and substance use disorders, use structured diagnostic interviews, and generate results that are reliable and relevant to the population as a whole. Most information on rates of dual diagnosis comes from studies of clinical populations. Although such studies are not representative of the general population, they provide valuable information on the types of problems that are faced by individuals in treatment, as well as on the links between dual diagnosis, service utilization, impact on illness, and treatment outcome. Importantly, individuals with multiple disorders are more likely to seek treatment, a condition known as *Berkson's fallacy* (Berkson, 1949); therefore, estimates of prevalence of comorbid disorders are higher in clinical samples. In addition, factors such as inpatient or outpatient status and chronicity of illness may affect rates of dual diagnosis. For example, research on patients with schizophrenia has found that more severely impaired inpatients are less likely to abuse substances than patients who are less ill (Mueser et al., 1990). Dual-diagnosis rates have also been found to differ by setting, with hospital emergency rooms reflecting higher estimates than other settings (Barbee, Clark, Crapanzano, Heintz, & Kehoe, 1989; Galanter, Castaneda, & Ferman, 1988).

Second, definitions of what constitutes dual diagnosis are far from uniform. Studies of dual diagnosis often employ differing definitions of substance use disorders, making prevalence rates diverse and difficult to compare. For example, definitions of substance abuse vary, ranging from problem use of a substance, to abuse or dependence based on *Diagnostic and Statistical Manual of Mental Disorders (DSM)* criteria. Others do not specify the exact nature of the substance use they are assessing. Among studies that define the type of substance use they are assessing, different diagnostic criteria are often used, making interpretation and comparison difficult. In addition, methods used to determine psychiatric and substance use diagnoses can influence findings. Types of diagnostic measures used include structured research interviews, nonstructured clinical interviews, self-report ratings, and reviews of medical records. Although structured interviews are the most reliable method of diagnosis (Mueser, Bellack, & Blanchard, 1992), research with clinical samples often employs less well-standardized assessments. Studies measure different substances in their assessments of dual diagnosis, typically including alcohol, cocaine, heroin, hallucinogens, stimulants, and marijuana. Importantly, some substances are not typically considered in assessments of dual diagnosis. For example, nicotine is usually not considered a substance of abuse in dual-diagnosis research, despite high rates of use among individuals with both mental illness (Lasser et al., 2000) and substance abuse (Bien & Burge, 1990), as well as a growing literature that suggests nicotine dependence has links, perhaps biological in nature, to both major depression (Quattrocki, Baird, & Yurgelun-Todd, 2000) and schizophrenia (Dalack & Meador-Woodruff, 1996; Ziedonis & George, 1997). Others have found elevated rates of psychiatric and substance use disorders in smokers (Keuthen et al., 2000). Taken together, factors such as type of problematic substance use assessed, measures used, and specific substances included in an assessment contribute to varying meanings of the term dual diagnosis.

A final methodological issue involves the split between the mental health treatment system and the substance abuse treatment system, and the impact that this separation has on dual-diagnosis research. The literature on dual diagnosis really includes two largely separate areas of investigation:

1. Research on substance abuse in individuals with mental illness.
2. Research on mental illness in primary substance abusers.

To get an accurate picture of dual diagnosis and its full impact on clinical functioning and research in psychopathology, both aspects of this literature must be examined.

FINDINGS FROM MAJOR EPIDEMIOLOGICAL STUDIES

There are two major epidemiological studies that have examined rates of dual diagnosis for a range of psychiatric disorders. The Epidemiologic Catchment Area Study (ECA; Regier et al., 1990) surveyed more than 20,000 adults in five cities across the United States both in the community and in institutions. Data collection took place from 1980 to 1984, and trained interviewers used the Diagnostic Interview Schedule to determine *DSM-III-R* diagnoses for a range of psychopathological conditions. As the first large-scale study of comorbidity of psychiatric and substance use disorders in the general population, findings of the ECA study were significant in that they documented surprisingly high rates of dual diagnosis among individuals with primary mental disorders and those with primary substance use disorders. For example, 11% of respondents without mental illness were diagnosed with an alcohol use disorder, and 4% were diagnosed with a drug use disorder. The impact of mental illness on risk for substance use disorders was striking: 22% of respondents with mental illness met criteria for an alcohol use disorder, and 15% were diagnosed with a drug use disorder. Overall, individuals with a lifetime history of a mental illness had an odds ratio of 2:3 for a lifetime history of alcohol use disorder and 4:5 for drug use disorder, a clear illustration of how those with mental illness are at substantially increased risk of having a comorbid substance use diagnosis. When comorbidity was examined by type of psychopathology, antisocial personality disorder (ASP) showed the highest comorbidity rate (83.6%). High rates of dual diagnosis were also found for severe mental illnesses including bipolar disorder (60.7%), schizophrenia (47%), and major depression (27.2%), as well as for panic disorder (35.8%) and obsessive-compulsive disorder (32.8%). Further analysis of ECA data (Helzer, Robbins, & McEvoy, 1987) found that men and women with posttraumatic stress disorder (PTSD) were 5 times and 1.4 times more likely, respectively, to have a drug use disorder as men and women without PTSD.

Substantial rates of dual diagnosis were also found in primary substance abusers (Regier et al., 1990). Overall, 37% of individuals with an alcohol disorder and 53% of those with a drug use disorder had comorbid mental illness. Thus, having an alcohol use disorder was found to put an individual at an almost three times greater risk of mental illness, while having a drug use disorder was found to confer almost five times the risk of mental illness. Further analyses (Helzer & Pryzbeck, 1988) found that among those with alcohol use disorders, the strongest association was with ASP (odds ratio [OR] = 21:0), followed by mania (OR = 6:2) and schizophrenia (OR = 4:0). The ECA findings illustrate that rates of dual diagnosis are significant among individuals with mental illness and primary substance abusers and that many types of psychiatric disorders confer an increased risk of substance use disorder.

The second major epidemiological study of comorbidity is the National Comorbidity Survey (NCS; Kessler et al., 1994). The NCS-assessed 12-month and lifetime prevalence rates for a range of psychiatric disorders in more than 8,000 noninstitutionalized individuals ages 15 to 54 across 48 states from 1990 to 1992. Like the ECA study, the NCS found markedly high rates of dual diagnosis. In contrast to the 26.7% of the general population that met diagnostic criteria for a substance use disorder, 50.9% of those with mental illness had a lifetime substance use disorder. Respondents with mental illness had at least twice the risk of lifetime alcohol or drug use disorder, with even greater risk for individuals with certain types of mental illnesses. Like the ECA study, these findings suggest that a psychiatric diagnosis yields at least double the risk of a lifetime alcohol or drug use disorder. Findings were similar for primary substance abusers: The majority of respondents with an alcohol or drug use disorder had a history of some nonsubstance use psychiatric disorder (Kendler, Davis, & Kessler, 1997; Kessler, 1997). Overall, 56.8% of men and 72.4% of women with alcohol abuse met diagnostic criteria for at least one psychiatric disorder, as did 78.3% of men and 86% of women with alcohol dependence (Kendler et al., 1997). Moreover, 59% of those with a lifetime drug use disorder also met criteria for a lifetime psychiatric disorder (Kessler, 1997).

A final large-scale survey, the National Longitudinal Alcohol Epidemiology Study (NLAES; Grant et al., 1994), examined rates of co-occurrence of substance use disorders and affective disorders in a general population sample. Begun in 1992, the NLAES is a household survey of more than 42,000 adults in the United States who used structured diagnostic interviews to assess *DSM-IV* diagnostic criteria for alcohol use disorders. Grant and Harford (1995) found that among respondents with major depression, 32.5% met criteria for alcohol dependence during their lifetime, as compared to 11.2% of those without major depression. Those with primary alcohol use disorders were almost four times more likely to be diagnosed with lifetime depression, and associations were even stronger for drug use disorders: Individuals with drug dependence were nearly seven times more likely to report lifetime major depression than those without drug dependence (see Bucholz, 1999, for a review). In summary, epidemiological surveys show that dual diagnosis is highly prevalent in the general population, whether examined in individuals with primary mental illness or in those with primary substance abuse.

FINDINGS FROM STUDIES OF CLINICAL SAMPLES

The fact that dual diagnosis is fairly common in the general population serves to highlight even higher rates found in treatment settings. Clinical studies of dual diagnosis have assessed general psychiatric patients, patients with specific psychiatric disorders, and primary substance-abusing patients.

Dual Diagnosis in General Psychiatric Patients   Clinical studies of dual diagnosis over the past 20 years indicate that one-third to three-fourths of general psychiatric patients may meet criteria for comorbid psychiatric and substance use disorders, depending on diagnostic makeup of the sample and level of chronicity represented (Ananth et al., 1989; Galanter et al., 1988; McLellan, Druley, & Carson, 1978; Mezzich, Ahn, Fabrega, & Pilkonis, 1990; Safer, 1987). Rates seem to fall in the higher end of this range for samples composed of more impaired patient populations. For example, Ananth and colleagues (1989) found that 72% of a sample of patients with schizophrenia, bipolar disorder, and atypical psychosis received a comorbid substance use diagnosis. Mezzich et al. (1990) conducted a large-scale assessment of dual diagnosis in more than 4,000 patients presenting for evaluation and referral for mental health problems over an 18-month period and found substantial rates of dual diagnosis among a number of diagnostic subsamples. The highest rates were seen among patients with severe mental illnesses such as bipolar disorder (45% diagnosed with an alcohol use disorder and 39% diagnosed with a drug use disorder) and schizophrenia or paranoid disorders (42% and 38% were diagnosed with alcohol and other substance use disorders, respectively). However, dual diagnosis was also pronounced in other patient groups. Specifically, 33% of patients with major depression were diagnosed with an alcohol use disorder, and 18% were diagnosed with a drug use disorder. Among patients with anxiety disorders, 19% and 11% were diagnosed with alcohol and other substance use disorders, respectively.

Dual Diagnosis in Samples of Patients with Specific Disorders   Rates of dual diagnosis have been extensively studied among patients with severe mental illness, including schizophrenia (Dixon, Haas, Weiden, Sweeney, & Frances, 1991; Mueser et al., 1990), bipolar disorder (McElroy et al., 2001; Salloum & Thase, 2000; Vieta et al., 2000), and major depression (Goodwin & Jamison, 1990; Lynskey, 1998; Merikangas, Leckman, Prusoff, Pauls, & Weissman, 1985; Swendsen & Merikangas, 2000). Findings show that dual diagnosis is common in such samples. Mueser et al. (1990) evaluated 149 patients with schizophrenia spectrum disorders and found that 47% had a lifetime history of alcohol abuse, while many had abused stimulants (25%), cannabis (42%), and hallucinogens (18%). Dixon and colleagues found that 48% of a sample of schizophrenia patients met criteria for an alcohol or drug use disorder. Chengappa, Levine, Gershon, and Kupfer (2000) evaluated prevalence of substance abuse and dependence in patients with bipolar disorder. Among patients with bipolar I, 58% met abuse or dependence criteria for at least one substance, and 11% abused or were dependent on three or more substances. In the bipolar II group, rate of dual diagnosis was approximately 39%. Hasin, Endicott, and Lewis (1985) examined rates of comorbidity in a sample of patients with affective disorder presenting for treatment as part of the National Institute of Mental Health Collaborative Study of Depression and found that 24% of these patients reported serious problems with alcohol, and 18% met diagnostic criteria for an alcohol use disorder. In an examination of patients with major depression, bipolar disorder, and controls participating in National Institute of Mental Health Collaborative Program on the Psychobiology of Depression, Winokur and colleagues (1998) found that affective disorder patients had substantially higher rates of dual substance use disorders than did controls.

Dual diagnosis is also common among patients with anxiety disorders. In their review of studies of dual anxiety and substance use disorders, Kushner, Sher, and Beitman (1990) found that rates differed by type of anxiety disorder, with social phobia (ranging from 20% to 36% rate of dual diagnosis) and agoraphobia (ranging from 7% to 27% rate of dual diagnosis) showing the highest rates of substance abuse comorbidity. Others have found a 22% rate of lifetime alcohol use disorder among patients with social phobia (Himle & Hill, 1991), a 10% to 20% rate for patients with agoraphobia (Bibb & Chambless, 1986), and up to 12% rate of lifetime alcohol dependence among patients with obsessive-compulsive disorder (Eisen & Rasmussen, 1989). In addition, more attention is being given to dual substance abuse and PTSD in clinical samples. A growing literature examining this diagnostic combination finds high rates of dual diagnosis among patients with PTSD, with some findings as high as 80% (Keane, Gerardi, Lyons, & Wolfe, 1988). Research both with samples of veterans with PTSD and samples of women with assault- or trauma-related PTSD shows strikingly high rates of comorbid substance abuse and dependence (see Stewart, Pihl, Conrod, & Dongier, 1998 for a review). Moreover, Breslau, Davis, Peterson, and Schultz (1997) interviewed a sample of 801 women and found that PTSD significantly increased the likelihood for later alcohol use disorder.

Importantly, the highest rates of comorbidity are found for patients with personality disorders, especially ASP. Studies show that comorbid ASP accelerates development of alcoholism (V. M. Hesselbrock, Hesselbrock, & Workman-Daniels, 1986) and that 80% of patients with ASP have a history of problem use of alcohol (Schuckit, 1983). In a review of studies on dual substance use disorders and borderline personality disorder (BPD), Trull, Sher, Minks-Brown, Durbin, and Burr (2000) found that, across studies, more than 48% of patients with BPD met criteria for alcohol use disorders, and 38% of those with BPD met criteria for a drug use disorder.

Dual Diagnosis in Patients with Primary Substance Use Disorders Substance-abusing patients in treatment are a heterogeneous group, encompassing a range of substances and levels of severity. Nonetheless, researchers have found high rates of dual disorders across diverse samples of patients seeking substance abuse treatment (Herz, Volicer, D'Angelo, & Gadish, 1990; Mirin, Weiss, Griffin, & Michael, 1991; Mirin, Weiss, & Michael, 1988; Penick et al., 1984; Powell, Penick, Othmer, Bingham, & Rice, 1982; Ross, Glaser, & Stiasny, 1988; Rounsaville, Weissman, Kleber, & Wilber, 1982; Weissman & Meyers, 1980). Findings of lifetime rates of psychiatric disorder range from 73.5% of a sample of cocaine abusers (Rounsaville et al., 1991) to 77% of a sample of hospitalized alcoholics (M. N. Hesselbrock, Meyer, & Keener, 1985) to 78% of a sample of patients in an alcohol and drug treatment facility (Ross, Glaser, & Germanson, 1988). Findings of current psychiatric disorder are similarly high, ranging from 55.7% of a group of cocaine abusers (Rounsaville et al., 1991) to 65% in a general substance-abusing sample (Ross, Glaser, & Germanson, 1988).

Further reflecting their diagnostic heterogeneity, substance abusers in treatment experience a range of comorbid psychiatric disorders. Among the most widely studied have been affective disorders, and treatment-seeking substance abusers show high rates of both major depression (Hasin, Grant, & Endicott, 1988; M. N. Hesselbrock et al., 1985; Merikangas & Gelernter, 1990; Mezzich et al., 1990; Miller, Klamen, Hoffmann, & Flaherty, 1996; Rounsaville, Weissman, Wilber, Crits-Christoph, & Kleber, 1982; Weissman & Meyers, 1980) and bipolar disorder (Strakowski & DelBello, 2000). Miller and colleagues (1996) surveyed a sample of more than 6,000 substance abuse treatment patients from 41 sites and found that 44% had a lifetime history of major depression. In a review of comorbidity of affective and substance use disorders, Lynskey (1998) found that prevalence of unipolar depression among patients receiving treatment for substance use disorders ranged from a low of 25.8% for lifetime depression in a sample of 93 alcohol-dependent men (Sellman & Joyce, 1996) to a high of 67% meeting a lifetime diagnosis of major depression among a sample of 120 inpatients (Grant, Hasin, & Hartford, 1989). Busto, Romach, and Sellers (1996) evaluated rates of dual diagnosis in a sample of 30 patients admitted to a medical facility for benzodiazepine detoxification and found that 33% met *DSM-III-R* criteria for lifetime major depression. Results from large studies of treatment-seeking substance abusers find that these patients show five to eight times the risk of having a comorbid bipolar diagnosis (see Strakowski & DelBello, 2000, for a review).

An extensive literature documents high rates of comorbid personality disorders in primary substance abusers (Khantzian & Treece, 1985; Nace, 1990; Nace, Davis, & Gaspari, 1991), especially ASP (Herz et al., 1990; M. N. Hesselbrock et al., 1985; Liskow, Powell, Nickel, & Penick, 1991; Morgenstern, Langenbucher, Labouvie, & Miller, 1997; Penick et al., 1984; Powell et al., 1982). In their evaluation of a large sample of treatment-seeking substance abusers, Mezzich and colleagues (1990) found that 18% of those with alcohol use disorders and almost 25% of those with drug use disorders met criteria for an Axis II disorder. Busto and colleagues (1996) found that 42% of their sample of patients undergoing benzodiazepine detoxification met *DSM-III-R* criteria for ASP. Morgenstern et al. (1997) assessed prevalence rates of personality disorders in a multisite sample of 366 substance abusers in treatment. Results showed that more than 57% of the sample met criteria for at least one personality disorder. ASP was the most prevalent (22.7% of the sample), followed by borderline (22.4%), paranoid (20.7%), and avoidant (18%) personality disorders. Moreover, presence of a personality disorder doubled the likelihood of meeting criteria for a comorbid Axis I disorder. Brooner, King, Kidorf, Schmidt, and Bigelow (1997) assessed psychiatric disorders in 716 opioid abusers on methadone maintenance therapy and found that 47% of the sample met criteria for at least one disorder, with ASP and major depression diagnoses co-occurring most commonly. In addition, psychiatric comorbidity was associated with more severe substance use disorder. Kokkevi, Stephanis, Anastasopoulou, and Kostogianni (1998) surveyed 226 treatment-seeking individuals with drug dependence in Greece and found a 59.5% prevalence rate of personality disorder, with more than 60% of these patients meeting criteria for more than one personality disorder. Moreover, those with personality disorders were at twice the risk for meeting an additional Axis I diagnosis.

Findings are similar with anxiety disorders, with high rates of comorbid phobias (Bowen, Cipywnyk, D'Arcy, & Keegan, 1984; Hasin et al., 1988; Ross, Glaser, & Germanson, 1988), panic disorder (Hasin et al., 1988; Penick et al., 1984), and obsessive-compulsive disorder (Eisen & Rasmussen, 1989) documented in substance-abusing populations. S. E. Thomas, Thevos, and Randall (1999) reported a 23% prevalence rate of social phobia in a large study of both inpatients and outpatients with alcohol dependence. Substance abusers also appear to be especially affected by PTSD (Cottler, Compton, Mager, Spitznagel, & Janca, 1992; Davis & Wood, 1999; Triffleman, Marmar, Delucchi, & Ronfeldt, 1995). In an analysis of cocaine-dependent patients in the National Institute on Drug Abuse Collaborative Cocaine Treatment Study, Najavitis and colleagues (1998) found that 30.2% of women and 15.2% of men met *DSM-III-R* criteria for

PTSD. Back and colleagues (2000) found that 42.9% of a sample of cocaine-dependent individuals met criteria for PTSD; and Bonin, Norton, Asmundson, Dicurzio, and Pidlubney (2000) found a 37.4% rate of PTSD in a sample of patients attending a community substance abuse treatment program.

In summary, the literature documents high rates of dual substance abuse and psychiatric disorders for a variety of psychopathological conditions and in a range of patient populations. Findings from epidemiological studies show that dual diagnosis is relatively common in the general population, and results of clinical studies illustrate frequency of dual diagnosis among individuals in treatment. That rates of dual diagnosis are similarly high in both mentally ill and primary substance-abusing populations serves to highlight the serious difficulties in having two separate and independent systems of care for mental illness and substance abuse (Grella, 1996; Ridgely, Lambert, Goodman, Chichester, & Ralph, 1998) despite the fact that both populations of patients are quite likely to be suffering from both disorders.

CLINICAL IMPACT OF DUAL DISORDERS

The importance of dual diagnosis lies in its negative impact on the course and prognosis of both psychiatric and substance use disorders, as well as its influence on assessment, diagnosis, and treatment outcome. Individuals with dual disorders show more adverse social, health, economic, and psychiatric consequences than those with only one disorder; and they show more severe difficulties, often a more chronic course of psychiatric disorder, and a poorer response to both mental health and substance abuse treatment. In the next section, we review ways that dual diagnosis impacts three general areas: patient functioning, clinical care, and research.

IMPACT OF DUAL DIAGNOSIS ON PATIENT FUNCTIONING

Symptoms, Course of Illness, and Life Functioning   Dual diagnosis severely impacts the severity and course of many disorders, especially among patients with serious mental illnesses such as schizophrenia, bipolar disorder, and recurrent major depression. Often, these dually diagnosed individuals show a poorer and more chaotic course of disorder, with more severe symptoms (Alterman, Erdlen, Laporte, & Erdlen, 1982; Barbee et al., 1989; Hays & Aidroos, 1986; Negrete & Knapp, 1986), more frequent hospitalizations (Carpenter, Heinrichs, & Alphs, 1985; Drake & Wallach, 1989; Sonne, Brady, & Morton, 1994), and more frequent relapses than patients without co-occurring substance abuse (Linszen, Dingemans, & Lenior, 1994; O'Connell, Mayo, Flatow, Cuthbertson, & O'Brien, 1991; Sokolski et al., 1994). Haywood et al. (1995) found that substance abuse, along with medication noncompliance, was the most important predictor of more frequent rehospitalization among schizophrenia patients. Winokur and colleagues (1998) found that patients with drug abuse and bipolar disorder had an earlier onset age of bipolar disorder than those with bipolar disorder alone, as well as a stronger family history of mania. Lehman, Myers, Thompson, and Corty (1993) compared individuals with dual mental illness and substance use diagnoses to those with just a primary mental illness and found that the dual-diagnosis group had a higher rate of personality disorder and more legal problems. Hasin, Endicott, and Keller (1991) followed 135 individuals with dual mood and alcohol use disorders who were originally studied as part of the National Institute of Mental Health Collaborative Study on the Psychobiology of Depression. Although most had experienced at least one 6-month period of remission of the alcohol disorder at some point during the follow-up period, most had relapsed after five years. Mueller and colleagues (1994) examined the impact of alcohol dependence on the course of major depression over 10 years among individuals with depression who participated in the National Institute of Mental Health Collaborative Depression study. Those who were alcohol dependent at baseline had a much lower rate of recovery from major depression than those with major depression alone, illustrating the negative impact of alcohol use disorders on the course of major depressive disorder.

Dual diagnosis is also a serious issue for patients with anxiety disorders such as PTSD (Najavitis, Weiss, & Shaw, 1997; Ouimette, Brown, & Najavitis, 1998). Overall, the combination of substance abuse and PTSD appears to be linked to higher rates of victimization, more severe PTSD symptoms in general, more severe subgroups of PTSD symptoms, and higher rates of Axis II comorbidity (Ouimette, Wolfe, & Chrestman, 1996). Saladin, Brady, Dansky, and Kilpatrick (1995) compared 28 women with both substance abuse and PTSD to 28 women with PTSD only and found that the dual-diagnosis group reported more symptoms of avoidance and arousal, more sleep disturbance, and greater traumatic event exposure than the PTSD-only group. Back and colleagues (2000) similarly found higher rates of exposure to traumatic events, more severe symptomatology, and higher rates of Axis I and Axis II disorders among cocaine-dependent individuals with PTSD as compared to those without lifetime PTSD. Moreover, evidence suggests that the combination of PTSD and cocaine dependence remains harmful over several years, with patients showing a greater likelihood of continued PTSD, as well as revictimization several years after an initial substance abuse treatment episode (Dansky, Brady, & Saladin, 1998).

Dual diagnosis also exerts a profound impact on overall life functioning. Patients with severe mental illnesses such as schizophrenia who abuse substances appear to be particularly hard hit in this regard (see Bradizza & Stasiewicz, 1997 for a review; Kozaric-Kovacic, Folnegovic-Smalc, Folnegovic, & Marusic, 1995). Drake and colleagues consistently have found that individuals with schizophrenia and comorbid substance abuse show substantially poorer life adjustment than do their nonsubstance-abusing counterparts, including poorer self care, less stable living environments, and fewer regular meals (Drake, Osher, & Wallach, 1989; Drake & Wallach, 1989). Havassy and Arns (1998) surveyed 160 frequently hospitalized adult psychiatric patients and found not only high rates of dual disorders (48% of patients had at least one current substance use disorder; of these, 55.1% met criteria for polysubstance dependence), but also that dual diagnosis was related to increased depressive symptoms, poor life functioning, lower life satisfaction, and a greater likelihood of being arrested or in jail. Research similarly shows that patients with dual affective and alcohol use disorders show greater difficulties in overall functioning and social functioning than patients with depression alone (Hirschfeld, Hasin, Keller, Endicott, & Wunder, 1990). Newman, Moffitt, Caspi, and Silva (1998) examined the impact of different types of comorbidity (including, but not limited to, substance abuse-psychiatric disorder combinations) on life functioning in a large sample of young adults. Multiple disorder cases showed poorer functioning than single-disorder cases in almost every area measured, including health status, suicide attempts, disruption in performance of daily activities, number of months disabled because of psychiatric illness, greater life dissatisfaction, less social stability (more residence changes, greater use of welfare for support, greater rates of adult criminal conviction records), greater employment problems, lower levels of educational attainment, and greater reports of physical health problems. Moreover, toxic effects of psychoactive substances in individuals with schizophrenia and bipolar disorder may be present even at use levels that may not be problematic in the general population (Lehman, Myers, Dixon, & Johnson, 1994; Mueser et al., 1990).

Treatment Compliance and Violence   Substance abuse often interferes with compliance with both behavioral and psychopharmacological treatments. Lambert, Griffith, and Hendrickse (1996) surveyed patients on a general psychiatry unit in a Veterans Administration medical center and found that discharges against medical advice (AMA) were more likely to occur among patients with alcohol and/or substance use disorders. Pages and colleagues (1998) similarly assessed predictors of AMA discharge in psychiatric patients and found having a substance use diagnosis and a greater quantity and frequency of substance use to be among the most important predictors. Owen, Fischer, Booth, and Cuffel (1996) followed a sample of 135 inpatients after discharge and found that medication noncompliance was related to substance abuse and that this combination was significantly associated with lack of outpatient contact in the follow-up period. Specifically, those with dual diagnoses were more than eight times more likely to be noncompliant with their medication.

For many disorders, substance abuse and its associated noncompliance with treatment is linked not only to poorer outcomes but also to greater risk for violence (Marzuk, 1996; Poldrugo, 1998; Sandberg, McNiel, & Binder, 1998; Scott et al., 1998; Soyka, 2000; Steadman et al., 1998; Swanson, Borum, Swartz, & Hiday, 1999; Swartz et al., 1998). Fulwiler, Grossman, Forbes, and Ruthazer (1997) compared differences between two groups of outpatients with chronic mental illness: those with and without a history of violence. The only significant differences between the two groups involved alcohol or drug use. McFall, Fontana, Raskind, and Rosenheck (1999) examined 228 male Vietnam veterans seeking inpatient treatment for PTSD and found levels of substance abuse were positively correlated with violence and aggression. Substance abuse is also associated with greater suicidal ideation and risk of suicide among patients with mental illness, including those with schizophrenia (L. J. Cohen, Test, & Brown, 1990; Karmali et al., 2000; Landmark, Cernovsky, & Merskey, 1987), depression (Pages, Russo, Roy-Byrne, Ries, & Cowley, 1997), and bipolar disorder (reviewed in Goodwin & Jamison, 1990). Pages and colleagues (1997) surveyed 891 psychiatric inpatients with major depressive disorder and found that both substance use and substance dependence were associated with higher levels of suicidal ideation. Potash and colleagues (2000) examined the relationship between alcohol use disorders and suicidality in bipolar patients and found that 38% of subjects with dual bipolar and alcohol use disorders had attempted suicide as compared to 22% of those with bipolar disorder only.

IMPACT OF DUAL DIAGNOSIS ON CLINICAL CARE AND RELATED FACTORS

Service Utilization and Health Care Costs   The fact that clinical settings routinely demonstrate higher rates of dual-diagnosis patients points to the fact that having both psychiatric and substance use disorders increases rates of treatment seeking.

Increased service utilization among the dually diagnosed has been borne out in both large-scale household surveys and clinical studies. For example, Helzer and Pryzbeck (1988) examined data from the ECA study and found that, for respondents of both sexes with alcohol use disorders, number of additional nonsubstance use disorder diagnoses had a significant impact on treatment seeking: Those with more diagnoses reported greater utilization of treatment services. Grant (1997) examined the influence of comorbid major depression and substance abuse on rates of individuals seeking alcohol and drug treatment in data collected from the National Longitudinal Alcohol Epidemiological Survey (Grant et al., 1994). The percentage of individuals with alcohol use disorders seeking treatment practically doubled, from 7.8% to 16.9%, when a comorbid major depressive disorder was also present. Interestingly, the greatest rate of treatment seeking (35.3%) was found among respondents who met criteria for all three disorders—alcohol, drug, and depression—illustrating how the term dual diagnosis is somewhat misleading in that an individual can have two or more substance use and psychiatric disorders and each might have an additive effect on negative outcomes. Similarly, Wu, Kouzis, and Leaf (1999), analyzing data from the NCS, found that while 14.5% of patients with a pure alcohol disorder reported using mental health and substance abuse intervention services, more than 32% of patients with comorbid alcohol and mental disorders used such services. Menezes and colleagues (1996) studied the impact of substance use problems on service utilization over one year in a sample of 171 individuals with serious mental illness. Although the number of inpatient admissions was equivalent for those with dual disorders and those with mental illness only, the dual-diagnosis group used psychiatric emergency services 1.3 times more frequently and spent 1.8 times as many days in the hospital than the single-disorder group.

Given their increased rates of service utilization, it is not surprising that dual-diagnosis patients generally accrue greater health care costs than do patients with a single diagnosis (Maynard & Cox, 1998; McCrone et al., 2000). Dickey and Azeni (1996) examined costs of psychiatric treatment for more than 16,000 seriously mentally ill individuals with and without comorbid substance use disorders. Patients with dual diagnoses had psychiatric treatment costs that were nearly 60% higher than costs of psychiatrically impaired individuals without substance abuse. Most of the increased cost resulted from greater rates of inpatient psychiatric treatment, suggesting that the impact of substance abuse on psychiatric symptom and illness relapse is realized when patients require costly psychiatric hospitalization. Garnick, Hendricks, Comstock, and Horgan (1997) examined health insurance data files over three years from almost 40,000 employees and found that those with dual diagnoses routinely accrued substantially higher health care costs than those with substance abuse only. Such findings suggest that individuals with dual-disorder access the most expensive treatment options (inpatient hospitalization, visits to emergency rooms) that are short term to manage acute distress and fail to get the comprehensive and ongoing care that they require.

Other Societal Impacts

HIV AND AIDS   Individuals with dual diagnosis show greatly increased risk for HIV and AIDS. People with schizophrenia and other severe mental illness are now one of the highest risk groups for HIV (Gottesman & Groome, 1997; Krakow, Galanter, Dermatis, & Westreich, 1998), and data indicate that substance use substantially increases the likelihood of unsafe sex practices (M. P. Carey, Carey, & Kalichman, 1997) and other high-risk behaviors in those with mental illness. For example, McKinnon, Cournos, Sugden, Guido, and Herman (1996) found that 17.5% of a sample of psychiatric patients had a history of injection drug use, 35% reported using drugs during sex, and 30% traded sex for drugs—all substance use behaviors that are highly risky in terms of transmission of HIV and AIDS. In their sample of 145 psychiatric inpatients and outpatients in Australia, Thompson and colleagues (1997) found that 15.9% of dual-diagnosis patients reported injection drug use, a figure that is 10 times higher than that found in the general population. Hoff, Beam-Goulet, and Rosenheck (1997) examined data from the 1992 National Survey of Veterans and found that the combination of PTSD and substance abuse increased risk of HIV infection by almost 12 times over individuals with either disorder alone.

LEGAL PROBLEMS   There is also evidence that individuals with dual diagnoses have more frequent contacts with the legal system. Clark, Ricketts, and McHugo (1999) followed a sample of individuals with mental illness and substance use disorders over three years to longitudinally examine legal involvement and its correlates in this population. The sample consisted of 203 patients receiving treatment in a dual-diagnosis treatment program. Cost and use data were collected from a range of sources, including police, defenders, prosecutors, and jails. Interestingly, while rates of arrest were certainly high, patients were four times more likely to have encounters with the legal system that did not result in arrest. This suggests that frequency of arrest, while significant, is an underrepresentation of frequency of contact that dual-diagnosis patients have with the legal system. In addition, continued substance abuse over the follow-up period was significantly associated with a greater likelihood of arrest.

HOMELESSNESS   The combination of mental illness and substance abuse also increases risk for homelessness. In a study of patients with schizophrenia, Dixon (1999) found that those who used substances experienced not only greater psychotic symptoms and relapses, a higher incidence of violent behavior and suicide, elevated rates of HIV infection, increased mortality, and higher rates of treatment and medication noncompliance, but also were more likely to live in an unstable housing situation or to be homeless. Caton and colleagues (1994) compared a sample of mentally ill homeless men to a sample of mentally ill men who were not homeless and found higher rates of drug use disorders among the homeless group. Leal, Galanter, Dermatis, and Westreich (1999) assessed homelessness in a sample of 147 patients with dual diagnosis and found that the group with so-called *protracted* homelessness (no residence for one year or more) were significantly more likely to report a history of injection drug use than those patients without protracted homelessness.

ISSUES FOR WOMEN WITH SEVERE MENTAL ILLNESS AND SUBSTANCE ABUSE   Importantly, dual diagnosis is often particularly problematic for individuals who are underserved to begin with. As mentioned earlier, individuals with schizophrenia and substance use disorders appear to be particularly hard hit by the additional difficulties that substance abuse brings. Another such population is women with severe mental illness and substance abuse. Research on women with dual diagnoses has shown that those with comorbid severe mental illness and substance abuse show poorer retention in treatment (Brown, Melchior, & Huba, 1999) and elevated levels of anxiety, depression, and medical illness (Brunette & Drake,

1998), as well as being more difficult to engage in treatment and more underrepresented in treatment overall (Comtois & Ries, 1995). In addition, women with dual diagnoses appear to have alarmingly high rates of sexual and physical victimization that are substantially higher than those observed among women in the general population (Gearon & Bellack, 1999; Goodman, Rosenburg, Mueser, & Drake, 1997). Prevalence rates for physical victimization for women with serious mental illness have been found to be between 42% and 64% (Jacobson, 1989), and other research finds that 21% to 38% of women with serious mental illness report adult sexual abuse (Goodman, Dutton, & Harris, 1995). Palacios, Urmann, Newel, and Hamilton (1999) surveyed a cohort of women receiving treatment in a residential therapeutic community and found that 49% reported physical abuse and 40% reported sexual abuse. Similarly Gearon, Bellack, Nidecker, and Bennett (in press) examined data from 28 women and 24 men with serious mental illness and substance use disorders and found that, when compared with men, women were more likely to report being physically (60% of women vs. 29% of men) and sexually (47% of women vs. 17% of men) victimized. Finally, women with dual diagnosis are often affected by issues related to pregnancy and parenting. Grella (1997) summarized some of the many difficulties in terms of services for pregnant women with dual disorders, including receiving adequate prenatal care, use of substances and psychiatric medications while pregnant, and lack of coordinated treatment planning and provision among medical, psychiatric, and addictions professionals. Kelly and colleagues (1999) examined medical records of all women delivering babies in California hospitals in 1994 and 1995 and found that women with both psychiatric and substance use diagnoses were at greatly elevated risk of receiving inadequate prenatal care. There are also substantial barriers to treatment and medical care for these women, including fears of losing custody of the unborn child or other children the woman might have, lack of medical insurance, and the often-disjointed nature of services that are available for medical and psychiatric care of these patients (Grella, 1997).

Assessment and Diagnosis

SYMPTOM OVERLAP   Symptom overlap is a significant complication in terms of assessment and diagnosis. The symptoms of many psychiatric disorders overlap with those of substance use disorders, making diagnosis of either class of disorders difficult. For example, *DSM* lists problems in social functioning as symptoms of both schizophrenia and substance use disorders. That some criteria can count toward multiple diagnoses can potentially increase comorbidity rates and can make diagnosis of substance abuse difficult. This overlap can work against identification of the psychiatric disorder in some cases. For example, Evans (2000) suggests that the high rates of dual substance use and bipolar disorders lead to an underdiagnosing of bipolar disorder because of the often-incorrect assumption that behavioral manifestations of bipolar disorder are secondary to substance use. Others (Brady, Killeen, Brewerton, & Lucerini, 2000; Brunello et al., 2001) suggest that underdiagnosis can also be an issue with dual PTSD and substance use disorders.

MULTIPLE IMPAIRMENTS RESULTING FROM DIFFERENT DISORDERS   Substance use disorders are often overlooked in mental health settings in which patients present with a range of acute impairments that exert a negative impact on overall functioning. There is often diagnostic confusion in terms of whether a given impairment is caused by substance abuse, psychiatric disorder, both, or neither. For example, it is exceedingly difficult to determine the impact of substance abuse when serious mental illness profoundly affects all areas of functioning. Patients with severe mental illness in particular have a range of impairments in social, cognitive, occupational, and psychological functioning; and evaluating the negative impact of substance abuse is difficult when the functioning of individuals in this patient population is so poor to begin with. Moreover, *DSM-IV* diagnoses of substance abuse and dependence are based for the most part on diagnostic criteria that reflect substance use as becoming more pervasive in a person's life and interfering with normal functioning. For example, criteria involve substance use that impairs an individual's ability to work, engage in relationships, complete responsibilities, and participate in activities. However, such factors often do not apply to many with mental illness—their already-substantial level of impairment associated with the psychiatric disorder often precludes their having a job, being in relationships, or engaging in other activities. It becomes unclear how to measure the negative impact of substance use when there are few competing demands, activities, or responsibilities to be disrupted.

SUBSTANCE-INDUCED DISORDERS RESEMBLE PSYCHIATRIC DISORDERS   Diagnosis of psychopathology in the presence of substance abuse and dependence is especially difficult because symptoms of substance use and withdrawal can resemble psychiatric disorders (Schuckit, 1983; Schuckit & Monteiro, 1988). Schuckit and Monteiro review several instances in which symptoms of substance abuse resemble or mimic psychiatric symptoms. For example, long-term alcohol use and withdrawal can lead to psychotic symptoms, and abuse of amphetamines often results in psychotic symptoms that are identical to schizophrenia. Alcohol abuse and withdrawal also resemble symptoms of anxiety disorders (Kushner et al., 1990). Panic and obsessive behavior are often found with stimulant use and withdrawal from depressant drugs (Schuckit, 1983). Because symptoms of substance use and withdrawal can resemble psychiatric symptoms, differential diagnosis may be confounded. Lack of clear rules for differential diagnosis has important implications. Rates of dual diagnosis might be inflated, with individuals experiencing psychiatric disorders concurrently with alcohol or drug dependence being counted among those with dual disorder, despite the fact that many of these symptoms will likely fade following a period of abstinence. Or, incorrect treatment decisions may be made if interventions are aimed at what appear to be acute symptoms of psychiatric disorder but are actually substance-induced symptoms. For example, Rosenthal and Miner (1997) review the issue of differential diagnosis of substance-induced psychosis and schizophrenia and stress that medicating what appears to be acute psychosis resulting from schizophrenia but is actually substance-induced psychosis is not only incorrect but also ineffective treatment. Schuckit and colleagues (1997) suggest that too little attention has been paid to the "independent versus concurrent distinction" as it applies to dual diagnosis. Some alcoholics suffer from long-term psychiatric disorders that are present before, during, and after alcohol dependence and require treatment independent of that for alcohol abuse or dependence. However, many individuals present with substance-induced disorders, including depression, anxiety, and psychosis, that remit after several weeks of abstinence. Schuckit and colleagues suggest that much dual diagnosis, while distressing and clinically relevant in the short term, is temporary, likely to improve after several weeks, and thus holds different clinical and treatment implications from a true, independent psychiatric disorder. Their data, taken from the Collaborative Study on the Genetics of

Alcoholism, show that the majority of alcohol-dependent men and women did not meet diagnostic criteria for an "independent" mood or anxiety disorder that occurred outside the context of alcohol dependence. Specifically, there was no increased risk of a range of disorders in the alcohol-dependent sample, including major depression, obsessive-compulsive disorder, or agoraphobia. In contrast, there was an increased risk of independent bipolar, panic disorder, and social phobia.

Other studies have also found that a majority of dual-diagnosis patients have concurrent psychiatric diagnoses that likely result from the effects of heavy substance use. Rosenblum and colleagues (1999) used an algorithm to determine whether individuals with co-occurring mood and cocaine use disorders have either an *autonomous* mood disorder, that is, one that existed either before the cocaine use disorder or persists during times of abstinence (similar to Schuckit's independent distinction), or a *nonautonomous* mood disorder that followed from the cocaine use disorder and would remit during cocaine abstinence. Results showed that 27% of subjects were rated as having an autonomous mood disorder, while 73% were rated as having a nonautonomous mood disorder. At this point, differentiating independent from concurrent dual disorders requires significant investment in training interviewers and in interviewing patients. Such requirements often cannot be met in the day-to-day operations of mental health treatment programs.

IMPLICATIONS FOR NOSOLOGY   The fact that two disorders co-occur with great regularity raises the question of whether both categories actually represent two distinct disorders at all (Sher & Trull, 1996). For example, the literature regarding substance use disorders and ASP finds a high rate of comorbidity between the two disorders, one that is likely enhanced by the symptom overlap inherent in the ASP diagnosis. However, some (Widiger & Shea, 1991) suggest that such a high degree of co-occurrence between these two disorders may mean that these are not, in fact, unique diagnoses, but rather that such a pattern of comorbidity indicates presence of a single disorder.

Provision of Treatment and Treatment Outcome   Co-occurring substance use disorders raise problems for interventions that have been designed to impact specific psychiatric symptoms, or ones that have been validated on samples that have excluded dual-diagnosis patients. In addition, clinicians often experience difficulties in making referrals for dual-diagnosis patients in the current system of single-disorder treatment that effectively separates the treatment systems for mental illness and substance abuse. The fact that patients must often be forced into single diagnostic categories no doubt results in substance use disorders being overlooked or ignored by treatment professionals who have expertise in treating only single conditions or in dual-diagnosis patients not receiving both psychiatric and substance abuse treatment that they require (Blanchard, 2000).

Patients with dual diagnosis are more difficult to treat and show poorer retention in treatment as well as poorer treatment outcomes as compared to single-disorder patients. Such findings tend to be true for patients with both primary mental illness and co-occurring substance abuse (see Drake et al., 1989 and Polcin, 1992 for reviews; Goldberg, Garno, Leon, Kocsis, & Portera, 1999), as well as for patients identified through substance abuse treatment programs with comorbid mental illness (Glenn & Parsons, 1991; Ouimette, Ahrens, Moos, & Finney, 1998; Rounsaville, Kosten, Weissman, & Kleber, 1986). An early study by McLellan, Luborsky, Woody, O'Brien, and Cruley (1983) found that higher psychiatric severity was associated with poorer treatment outcome among alcohol and drug abuse treatment patients. T'omasson and Vaglum (1997) examined the impact of psychiatric comorbidity on 351 treatment-seeking substance abusers over a 28-month period and found that patients with comorbid psychiatric disorders at admission showed worse outcome in terms of mental health functioning at follow-up. More recently, Ouimette, Gima, Moos, and Finney (1999) reported findings of one-year follow-up of three groups of patients with dual substance use and psychiatric disorders (psychotic disorders, affective/anxiety disorders, and personality disorders) as compared to a group of substance abuse-only patients. Although all groups showed comparable decreases in substance use at follow-up, patients with dual diagnoses showed greater levels of psychological distress and psychiatric symptoms, and lower rates of employment than did patients with only substance use disorders. In a three-year follow-up of a sample of patients with alcohol use disorders, Kranzler, Del Boca, and Rounsaville (1996) found that presence of comorbid psychiatric disorders, including depression and ASP, is generally associated with worse three-year outcomes. V. H. Thomas, Melchert, and Banken (1999) examined treatment outcome in 252 patients in substance abuse treatment and found that likelihood of relapse within the year following treatment was significantly increased in patients with dual personality disorders. Specifically, 6% of patients with personality disorders were abstinent one-year posttreatment as compared with 44% of those with no diagnosed personality disorders. A study by Havassy, Shopshire, and Quigley (2000) examined the effects of substance dependence on treatment outcome in 268 psychiatric patients following two different case management programs. Regardless of program, dual-diagnosis patients showed more negative outcomes than patients with only a psychiatric disorder. Such results illustrate that the dually diagnosed fare worse than patients with either substance use disorders or psychiatric disorders alone following treatment. Importantly, the fact that dual-diagnosis patients are often found to still be adversely affected by psychiatric symptomatology following substance abuse treatment is a stark reminder that treatment strategies have yet to evolve that effectively address symptoms of both types of disorders.

IMPACT OF DUAL DIAGNOSIS ON PSYCHOPATHOLOGY RESEARCH

Dual diagnosis affects several areas that are critical to psychopathology research, including diagnosis, sample selection, and interpretation of research findings.

Diagnostic and Sample Selection Issues in Psychopathology Research An accurate diagnosis is a necessary starting point for any psychopathology study, and dual diagnosis presents an abundance of diagnostic challenges. Individuals with dual diagnoses may provide unreliable diagnostic information, or their data may be inaccurate because of greater severity of impairments. Alternatively, they may minimize their substance use and associated consequences, especially if they have much to lose by admitting to or honestly discussing their substance use, such as services, benefits (Ridgely, Goldman, & Willenbring, 1990), or child custody. Timing of a research diagnostic interview can also impact results, as answers and resulting diagnostic decisions may vary depending on type of use and stage of treatment. Method of assessment also can impact diagnostic findings (Regier et al., 1998), and diagnoses given in a clinical setting may vary with those obtained through more structured methods (Fennig, Craig, Tanenberg-Karant, &

Bromet, 1994). As discussed previously, establishing an accurate diagnosis in individuals with active substance use or withdrawal can be problematic, as the effects of substance use can imitate symptoms of various psychiatric disorders. Most diagnostic systems used in psychopathology research contend with this difficulty by asking if psychiatric symptoms have been experienced solely during the course of substance use and may recommend assessment only after a sustained period of abstinence. However, patient reports may be inaccurate, and histories may be too extensive and complicated to allow for this level of precise understanding. Finally, the issue of overlapping diagnostic criteria can pose a significant difficulty for psychopathology research, as common diagnostic criteria may contribute to the diagnosis of multiple disorders when actually the psychopathology is better understood as a single pathological process rather than two distinct disorders (Blashfield, 1990; Sher & Trull, 1996). As discussed previously, overlap of substance use disorders with ASP is notably problematic, and frequent comorbidity of substance abuse and ASP has long been recognized (Widiger & Shea, 1999). Krueger (1999) examined 10 common mental disorders using structural equation modeling and found that ASP loads onto a common "externalizing" factor along with alcohol and drug dependence, suggesting that substance dependence and ASP may share certain underlying features. Whether this overlap indeed results from common conceptual characteristics or is an artifact of similar diagnostic criteria is not known. All of these diagnostic issues impact research findings, in that poor diagnoses necessarily lead to poor quality data. Researchers can improve diagnostic reliability by using structured interviews, using collateral information and behavioral observation to inform diagnostic decisions, and assessing the patient at multiple time points (K. B. Carey & Correia, 1998).

In terms of sample selection, psychopathology and treatment outcome research tends to focus on single or pure disorders and routinely excludes dual-diagnosis cases, a practice that has several implications for research. First, screening out dual-diagnosis patients from psychopathology and treatment outcome research yields atypical samples. Most patients with one psychiatric disorder meet criteria for some other disorder. Eliminating patients with dual disorders means that the sample is less impaired and less representative of patients who actually seek treatment, resulting in limited generalizability of research findings (Krueger, 1999). In addition, dual-diagnosis patients often have other characteristics that are not adequately represented in a study in which such patients are excluded. For example, Partonen, Sihvo, and Lonnqvist (1996) report descriptive data on patients excluded from an antidepressant efficacy trial. The trial screened out individuals with "chronic alcohol or drug misuse." Results showed that younger male patients were likely to be excluded from the trial because of substance abuse, and that current substance abuse had the strongest excluding influence on selection of patients. Second, dual diagnosis impacts required sample sizes. In their examination of the impact of comorbid disorders on sample selection, Newman and colleagues (1998) discuss findings related to effect sizes of examining only single-disorder cases versus including dual-disorder cases when analyzing group differences. Results showed that if dual-disorder cases are screened out of psychopathology research, larger sample sizes are required to detect small effect sizes. The impact of retaining dual-disorder cases in the sample was seen in greater variance on study measures, resulting in larger effect sizes requiring smaller sample sizes. Third, psychopathology and treatment outcome research most often combines those with dual diagnoses without separating participants by the specific type of drug use disorder. While some might limit the scope of the study to alcohol only, most cast a wide net and include patients with alcohol, drug, and polysubstance use disorders. For example, research on substance abuse among patients with severe mental illness typically includes disorders of any number or combination of substances including alcohol, marijuana, cocaine, and heroin. Impact of grouping all substance use disorders together is unclear, but it certainly raises the possibility that research may miss important issues in dual diagnosis that are specific to substance. For example, it would not be surprising if patients with a greater number of drug use disorders or with both alcohol and drug use disorders required some unique adaptations of interventions that might not be necessary for patients with single drug or alcohol use disorders only. Similarly, there are likely to be meaningful differences between patients who inject drugs and those who do not, patients who have long histories of substance dependence and those who do not, or patients who are dependent on cocaine or heroin versus those who are abusing marijuana.

Interpretation of Psychopathology and Treatment Outcome Research   The overall result of screening out those with substance use disorders from psychopathology and treatment outcome research is that we are left with very little data to help us understand or treat dual disorders. For example, following completion of an antidepressant efficacy trial, Partonen and colleagues (1996) indicate that they were left without information as to efficacy of antidepressants among patients with dual disorders. Given significant rates of dual disorders found in clinical samples, such an omission is problematic. In their discussion of the many complex issues surrounding comorbidity and psychopathology research, Sher and Trull (1996) question the advantage of studying pure cases when certain disorders occur together with such great frequency that there really may be no ultimate benefit of studying either one alone. It also is unclear how well findings from psychopathology and treatment outcome research generalize to the larger population of individuals with a particular disorder if patients with dual diagnoses are not included. Epidemiological studies reviewed earlier illustrate that a significant number of those with mental illness or substance abuse experience dual disorders. Relevance of single-disorder research to this substantial population of dually impaired individuals is highly suspect. Thus, excluding dual-diagnosis cases yield samples that are not representative of patients who are likely to present for the treatments under study.

However, routinely including dual-diagnosis cases in psychopathology and treatment outcome research has its drawbacks. Sher and Trull (1996) and Krueger (1999) discuss the fact that if dual-diagnosis cases are included in psychopathology research, understanding of both mental and substance use disorders is compromised, in that samples would be less well defined. As a result, it would be unclear whether results could be attributed to the disorder under study or to comorbid disorders represented in the sample. In addition, comorbidity complicates longitudinal data because different patterns of comorbidity may emerge over time in individuals (Sher & Trull, 1996). Some have suggested strategies for dealing with dual disorders in psychopathology and treatment outcome research; for example, the idea that samples should include comorbid cases in percentages found in the general population to increase the generalizability of findings (Newman et al., 1998; Sher & Trull, 1996). Widiger and Shea (1991) offer several options, including having one diagnosis take precedence over another, adding criteria to make a differential diagnosis, or removing criteria shared by disorders. Sher and Trull additionally suggest statistically controlling for comorbidity via regression techniques but acknowledge that this practice can serve to mask important common features of disorders.

THEORIES OF DUAL DIAGNOSIS

This review makes two points clear: Dual diagnosis is highly prevalent and has a pervasive impact on both clinical and research domains in the field of psychopathology. At this point, there is general agreement that the time has come to define more precisely the mechanisms underlying dual diagnosis. This has been a complex task for several reasons. Most important, there is a great degree of heterogeneity found in dual-diagnosis populations. The numerous types of psychopathological disorders and substances of abuse ensure a great number of dual-diagnosis combinations. In addition, although the term *dual* is meant to describe cases with both mental illness and substance use problems, it can in actuality reflect more than two disorders (e.g., an individual might meet criteria for an affective disorder, an anxiety disorder, and a substance use disorder). Thus, it is unlikely that one explanation or causal model for dual diagnosis can explain the diversity of cases and experiences that are found.

Models to explain dual diagnoses tend to fall into one of four general categories (see Mueser, Drake, & Wallach, 1998 for a review). Third variable or common factors models suggest that some shared influence is responsible for development of both psychiatric and substance use disorders. The two types of causal models—secondary substance use disorder models and secondary psychiatric disorder models—posit that either type of disorder causes the other. Bidirectional models suggest that either psychiatric or substance use disorders can increase risk for and exacerbate the impact of the other. These models have been more or less described depending on the particular area of psychopathology. An overall look at this literature finds that models of dual diagnosis are typically organized by disorder, with research focused on specific combinations of dual disorders rather than at the issue of dual diagnosis across disorders. Extensive reviews of models in each of these categories can be found (Blanchard, 2000; Mueser et al., 1998). The following section provides a review of some models of dual diagnosis in their respective domains of psychopathology.

COMMON FACTORS MODELS

Common factors models suggest a shared etiological basis for psychiatric and substance use disorders. Most research has focused on genetics as the likely common factor linking psychiatric and substance use disorders. Results of numerous twin, adoption, and family studies show that both mental illness and substance abuse run in families and that familial aggregation of single disorders is substantial (Kendler et al., 1997; Kushner et al., 1990; Merikangas & Gelernter, 1990; Merikangas et al., 1985). Such findings have led to the hypothesis that commonly co-occurring disorders might be linked via common genetic factors. However, for genetics to serve as a viable common factor, family studies must show high rates of transmission of pure forms of both substance use and psychiatric disorders. For example, a proband with depression only should have an increased rate of alcoholism only in his or her relatives to provide evidence of shared genetic etiology. Studies of familial transmission of a range of comorbid psychiatric and substance use disorders find that evidence for a common genetic factor is lacking. Merikangas and Gelernter reviewed family, twin, and adoption studies of alcoholism and depression and concluded that familial transmission of pure forms of the disorders was not supported: *Depressed only* probands did not have increased rates of *alcoholism only* in their relatives, and *alcoholism only* probands did not have increased rates of *depression only* in their relatives. These authors stress that while familial aggregation of disorders is evident, the notion of a common genetic factor underlying the two is not supported and the disorders appear to be transmitted separately. In subsequent analyses of familial transmission of comorbid depression and substance use disorders using data from the Yale Family Study of Comorbidity of Substance Disorders, Swendsen and Merikangas (2000) similarly found that there was no support for a common factors model: Mood disorders in the proband were not associated with an increased risk of alcohol dependence in relatives. Similar results have been reported with schizophrenia (Kendler, 1985), ASP (V. M. Hesselbrock, 1986) and patients with schizoaffective and bipolar disorders (Gershon et al., 1982).

Importantly, common factors other than genetics may exist. For example, Mueser et al. (1998) discuss several possible common factors that might link substance use disorders and severe mental illness, including comorbid ASP, low socioeconomic status, and poor cognitive functioning. For example, ASP is associated with both substance use disorders and severe mental illness. Mueser and colleagues (1999) examined links between conduct disorder, ASP, and substance use disorders in patients with severe mental illness and found that both childhood conduct disorder and adult ASP were significant risk factors for substance use disorders. However, the status of ASP as a risk factor is unclear, given that problem substance use is part of the diagnosis of ASP, raising the possibility that ASP may be a by-product of substance use disorder. In addition, ASP is based in large part on criminality and socioeconomic status, both of which are difficulties that often accompany substance use disorder and severe mental illness (Mueser et al., 1998).

Other researchers are proposing multivariate approaches to identifying common factors of dual disorders. One such model is described by Trull and colleagues (2000) to explain the high prevalence of dual substance use disorders and BPD. These authors suggest that a family history of psychopathology inspires both dysfunctional family interactions and inheritance of deviant personality traits that are associated with development of both BPD and substance use disorders. Specifically, the personality traits of affective instability and impulsivity are central to both disorders and are conceptualized as stemming from a combination of "constitutional and environmental factors" (Trull et al., 2000) that include inherited deficiencies in serotonergic functioning, in combination with a deviant family environment that may include associated childhood trauma. These factors in turn impact development of BPD and substance use disorder, both alone and in combination. These authors stress that while this model is currently speculative, more prospective, longitudinal studies with a developmental and multivariate focus will enable the pieces of the models to be evaluated simultaneously. This model provides an example of combining strategies from family studies and psychopathology research into a multivariate framework that provides rich details as to how two disorders could be developmentally related.

SECONDARY SUBSTANCE ABUSE MODELS

Secondary substance abuse models contend that mental illness increases vulnerability to substance use disorders. Probably the most widely discussed model of this type is the self-medication model, which asserts that individuals with psychiatric disorders use substances as a way to self-medicate psychopathological symptoms and relieve discomfort associated with the primary psychiatric disorder. There are several types of studies used to examine applicability of a self-medication model to different forms of psychopathology. Some determine the ages of onset of dual disorders, with the idea that substance use disorders that develop following the start of other Axis I psychopathology are evidence in support of self-medication. Some examine subjective reasons for use among patients with different disorders, while others correlate levels of symptoms with levels of substance abuse (from a self-medication perspective, greater symptoms should correlate with greater substance abuse). Another line of self-medication research involves investigating types of substances used by different patient groups. According to a self-medication hypothesis, patients with certain psychopathological conditions should preferentially seek and use substances that directly impact symptoms associated with their specific psychopathology.

Varying levels of support for a self-medication model are seen depending on type of mental illness under investigation. For example, while the model is popular among treatment providers working with patients with severe mental illness, empirical support for a self-medication model has not been compelling (see Mueser et al., 1998 for a review). Although it has been suggested that schizophrenia patients preferentially abuse stimulants to self-medicate negative symptoms (Schneier & Siris, 1987), this finding has not been replicated in other studies (Mueser, Yarnold, & Bellack, 1992). Most important, studies fail to find evidence that specific substances are used in response to specific symptoms of severe mental illness. Rather, patterns of drug use appear to be strongly associated with demographic factors and drug availability (Mueser, Yarnold, et al., 1992). In addition, a self-medication model of substance use disorders in severe mental illness would predict that the more symptomatic patients would be at higher risk for substance use disorders (Mueser, Bellack, et al., 1992). Several studies, however, have found the opposite to be true: More severely ill patients are less likely to abuse substances (Chen et al., 1992; M. Cohen & Klein, 1970; Mueser, Yarnold, et al., 1992), and patients with substance use disorders have better premorbid social functioning (Dixon et al., 1991). Although individuals with schizophrenia and other severe mental illnesses report a range of reasons for substance use—to alleviate social problems, insomnia, or depression; to get high; to relieve boredom; and to increase energy—it is uncommon for them to report use of specific substances to combat particular psychiatric symptoms (see Brunette, Mueser, Xie, & Drake, 1997 for a review). Moreover, many studies have found that patients with schizophrenia report worsening of symptoms with substance abuse, including increased hallucinations, delusions, and paranoia (Barbee et al., 1989; Cleghorn et al., 1991; Dixon et al., 1991; Drake et al., 1989); and others have found that more severe symptoms of schizophrenia are not linked to more severe substance abuse

(Brunette et al., 1997). Similarly, findings of increased rates of cocaine use among patients with bipolar disorder, interpreted by some to indicate use of cocaine to self-medicate symptoms of depression, have been found on review to more likely reflect attempts to prolong euphoric feelings associated with mania (Goodwin & Jamison, 1990).

Other secondary substance abuse models may be more relevant to patients with severe mental illness. A social facilitation model suggests that patients with severe mental illness may have fewer available opportunities for social interaction and that substance abuse helps to smooth the progress of social interaction in patients who lack appropriate social and interpersonal skills. Dixon, Haas, Weiden, Sweeney, and Frances (1990) found that a large portion of drug use by individuals with schizophrenia occurs in a public setting, and they suggest that drug use may provide "isolated, socially handicapped individuals with an identity and a social group" (p. 74). Mueser, Bellack, et al. (1992) suggest that much substance abuse by individuals with schizophrenia occurs in a social context, and use may enable these individuals to fulfill needs for contact and acceptance. Others offer an alleviation of dysphoria model, which suggests that individuals with psychiatric disorders are more likely to experience negative affect and may have fewer occasions to experience feelings of pleasure, and that substance abuse represents an attempt to alleviate these negative mood states.

Evidence for self-medication may be more relevant to dual diagnosis in other psychopathological disorders. For example, several reviews have found that self-medication may apply to dual posttraumatic stress and substance use disorders, especially among women with trauma-related PTSD. Chilcoat and Breslau (1998) outline the three main theories that have been used to explain this high degree of comorbidity:

1. Self-medication hypothesis, which suggests that drugs are used to medicate PTSD symptoms.
2. High-risk hypothesis, which suggests that drug use puts individuals at heightened risk for trauma that can lead to PTSD.
3. Susceptibility hypothesis, which suggests that drug users are more likely to develop PTSD following exposure to a traumatic event.

They used data from a sample of more than 1,000 young adults who were randomly selected from enrollees in a large health maintenance organization and were followed longitudinally over five years to examine the timing of the development of both PTSD and substance use disorders. Those with a history of PTSD at baseline were four times more likely to develop drug abuse or dependence at some point during the five years of the study than did those without PTSD. In contrast, baseline drug abuse/dependence did not confer any increased risk of subsequent exposure to trauma or to developing PTSD in those who did experience some traumatic event during the follow-up period. Stewart and colleagues (1998) extensively reviewed data on dual substance use disorder and PTSD. They found that several lines of research lend support to a self-medication model, including:

- Development of substance abuse most often follows development of PTSD.
- Patients often report that they perceive substance use to be effective in controlling PTSD symptoms.

- Patients with both PTSD and substance use disorder report more severe trauma and a greater severity of PTSD symptoms, suggesting that substances are used in an effort to control greater psychiatric symptomatology.
- Drugs of abuse may be related to different clusters of PTSD symptoms, suggesting that substance abuse may be linked to attempts to control intrusion or arousal symptoms of PTSD.

These authors stress that although a self-medication model is likely too simplistic to explain all forms of PTSD-substance use disorder comorbidity, it provides a good fit with many aspects of the research to date.

SECONDARY PSYCHIATRIC DISORDER MODELS

These models suggest that substance abuse causes psychopathology. Different mechanisms for this connection have been suggested. Schuckit and Monteiro (1988; Schuckit, 1983) stress that use of or withdrawal from many psychoactive substances causes reactions that appear indistinguishable from psychiatric disorder. As reviewed earlier, these authors contend that often substance use disorders are diagnosed mistakenly as psychiatric disorders because the symptoms of the two are identical; and that while serious psychopathology can be expected in the course of substance use disorder, substance-induced disorders are likely to remit following several weeks of abstinence.

The case for substance-induced psychiatric disorder appears to be particularly relevant to dual substance use disorders and major depression. Raimo and Schuckit (1998) review the evidence in support of the idea that most cases of comorbid depression and alcohol dependence are substance induced, including findings that:

- Drinking can cause severe depressive symptoms.
- Treatment-seeking substance abusers show increased rates of depression that often remit following abstinence and in the absence of specific treatments for depression.
- Individuals with substance-induced depression do not show elevated rates of depression in family members.
- Children of alcoholics show higher rates of alcohol use disorders but do not show elevated rates of major depression.

These authors stress that, while having independent depression in addition to alcohol abuse or dependence is certainly possible, most of the depression that is comorbid with alcohol use disorders is substance-induced and not independent in nature. Following this example, Swendsen and Merikangas (2000) reviewed findings that are relevant to an etiological model of dual substance abuse and depression:

- Onset of alcohol dependence typically precedes onset of unipolar depression.
- Symptoms of depression often remit following several weeks of abstinence from alcohol.
- Studies do not support a shared genetic basis for comorbidity of depression and alcohol dependence.

They suggest that the association between unipolar depression and alcohol dependence may best be described via a secondary psychiatric disorder model, in which chronic alcohol use causes unipolar depression, through either considerable life stress that alcohol dependence promotes for the drinker in many important domains of functioning or through the pharmacological properties of alcohol as a depressant substance.

BIDIRECTIONAL MODELS

Bidirectional models propose there are ongoing, interactional effects between psychopathology and substance use disorders that account for increased rates of comorbidity. Kushner, Abrams, and Borchardt (2000) provide an example of a bidirectional model for anxiety and alcohol dependence. They first review the literature and find that:

- Self-report studies find that most patients with anxiety and alcohol use disorders report drinking to control fears and reduce tension.
- Drinking can cause anxiety (i.e., anxiety can result from long-term alcohol use; patients report increased anxiety after drinking; withdrawal from alcohol can cause physiological symptoms of anxiety).
- Alcohol dependence can lead to anxiety disorders (i.e., alcohol dependence increases risk for later development of an anxiety disorder; chronic drinking can cause neurochemical changes that cause anxiety and panic).
- Anxiety disorders can lead to alcohol dependence (i.e., having an anxiety disorder increases risk for later development of alcohol dependence; alcohol provides stress-response dampening and reduces the clinical symptoms of anxiety; many people use alcohol to self-medicate anxiety symptoms).

The authors conclude that alcohol and anxiety interact to produce an exacerbation of both anxiety symptoms and drinking. They suggest that initial use of alcohol provides short-term relief of anxiety symptoms, and this temporary relief encourages individuals to drink more, leading to increased physiological symptoms of anxiety. They then suggest that a so-called feed-forward cycle may develop wherein drinking is promoted by the short-term anxiety-reducing effects of alcohol, while at the same time anxiety symptoms are worsened by heavy drinking, leading to continued drinking in response to these worsened anxiety symptoms. While several caveats and issues remain to be clarified (i.e., the model seems to fit best with comorbid alcohol dependence, and its relevance to drug use disorders is unknown; those for whom the anxiety disorder begins first would not necessarily experience the anxiety-reducing properties of alcohol in a way that would initiate the feed-forward cycle), the authors suggest that a bidirectional model can best explain existing findings and can focus future research on comorbidity of anxiety and substance use disorders. Moreover, this sort of bidirectional model highlights the possibility that unidirectional causal models are likely too simplistic an approach in explaining comorbidity. Rather, the relationship between psychiatric and substance use disorders is more likely characterized by complex interactions between two disorders.

SUMMARY

We have learned much about the prevalence and impact of dual disorders from general population and clinical studies over the past several decades. Dual diagnosis is common, both in the general population and among clients in mental health and substance abuse treatment. While there remains much we need to understand about these rates of dual diagnosis, including how much of this problem represents independent mental illness versus the amount attributable to acute substance intoxication, the numbers illustrate the fact that comorbid psychiatric and substance use disorders impact a large percentage of people. Second, it is clear that dual diagnosis affects patient functioning, clinical service, and psychopathology research; and services designed to assist patients with either mental illness or substance abuse are ill equipped to address comorbidity of these problems. Moreover, research on psychopathology and its treatments is complicated by questions of dual diagnosis, including how it impacts findings and how it can be handled in data collection and analysis. Third, we are at the beginning of trying to develop models to explain dual diagnosis, a challenging task that must take into account the different types of psychopathology and substances of abuse, as well as differences in severity of both types of disorders.

The next step for research is to further examine causal mechanisms underlying dual diagnosis and to determine how these models work given the significant heterogeneity seen in the dual-diagnosis population. While a range of theories has been proposed, more specific work is required to fully examine the links between mental illness and substance use disorders. Moreover, many studies are finding that as the number of psychiatric disorders increases, the likelihood of co-occurring substance abuse increases as well. This means that research examining dual disorders must reflect current reality—individuals with dual disorders often have multiple diagnoses, each of which might have different impacts on functioning and treatment needs. It is unclear how prevailing models of dual disorders that are organized around a pair of problems are going to be relevant to individuals with three or more diagnoses. In addition, we need a better understanding of how to treat individuals with dual diagnosis. We are only at the very start of efforts to treat those with dual disorders comprehensively. Efforts aimed at treatment development must be linked to research on underlying causes of dual disorders. Improving our understanding of the causes of dual disorders will provide insight into interventions for treating these complex and recurring problems.

REFERENCES

Alterman, A. I., Erdlen, D. L., Laporte, D. L., & Erdlen, F. R. (1982). Effects of illicit drug use in an inpatient psychiatric setting. *Addictive Behaviors, 7*(3), 231–242.

Ananth, J., Vandewater, S., Kamal, M., Brodsky, A., Gamal, R., & Miller, M. (1989). Missed diagnosis of substance abuse in psychiatric patients. *Hospital and Community Psychiatry, 40,* 297–299.

Back, S., Dansky, B. S., Coffey, S. F., Saladin, M. E., Sonne, S., & Brady, K. T. (2000). Cocaine dependence with and without posttraumatic stress disorder: A comparison of substance use, trauma history, and psychiatric comorbidity. *American Journal on Addictions, 9*(1), 51–62.

Barbee, J. G., Clark, P. D., Crapanzano, M. S., Heintz, G. C., & Kehoe, C. E. (1989). Alcohol and substance abuse among schizophrenic patients presenting to an emergency psychiatric service. *Journal of Nervous and Mental Diseases, 177,* 400–407.

Berkson, J. (1949). Limitations of the application of four-fold tables to hospital data. *Biometric Bulletin, 2,* 47–53.

Bibb, J. L., & Chambless, D. L. (1986). Alcohol use and abuse among diagnosed agoraphobics. *Behavior Research and Therapy, 24*(1), 49–58.

Bien, T. H., & Burge, J. (1990). Smoking and drinking: A review of the literature. *International Journal of the Addictions, 25,* 1429–1454.

Blanchard, J. J. (2000). The co-occurrence of substance use in other mental disorders: Editor's introduction. *Clinical Psychology Review, 20*(2), 145–148.

Blashfield, R. K. (1990). Comorbidity and classification. In J. D. Master & C. R. Cloninger (Eds.), *Comorbidity of mood and anxiety disorders* (pp. 61–82). Washington, DC: American Psychiatric Press.

Bonin, M. F., Norton, G. R., Asmundson, G. J., Dicurzio, S., & Pidlubney, S. (2000). Drinking away the hurt: The nature and prevalence of posttraumatic stress disorder in substance abuse patients attending a community-based treatment program. *Journal of Behavior Therapy and Experimental Psychiatry, 31*(1), 55–66.

Bowen, R. C., Cipywnyk, D., D'Arcy, C., & Keegan, D. (1984). Alcoholism, anxiety disorders, and agoraphobia. *Alcoholism Clinical and Experimental Research, 8*(1), 48–50.

Bradizza, C. M., & Stasiewicz, P. R. (1997). Integrating substance abuse treatment for the seriously mentally ill into inpatient psychiatric treatment. *Journal of Substance Abuse Treatment, 14*(2), 103–111.

Brady, K. T., Killeen, T. K., Brewerton, T., & Lucerini, S. (2000). Comorbidity of psychiatric disorders and posttraumatic stress disorder. *Journal of Clinical Psychiatry, 61*(Suppl. 7), 22–32.

Breslau, N., Davis, G. C., Peterson, E. L., & Schultz, L. (1997). Psychiatric sequelae of posttraumatic stress disorder in women. *Archives of General Psychiatry, 54*(1), 81–87.

Brooner, R. K., King, V. L., Kidorf, M., Schmidt, C. W., & Bigelow, G. E. (1997). Psychiatric and substance use comorbidity among treatment-seeking opioid abusers. *Archives of General Psychiatry, 54*(1), 71–80.

Brown, V. B., Melchior, L. A., & Huba, G. J. (1999). Level of burden among women diagnosed with severe mental illness and substance abuse. *Journal of Psychoactive Drugs, 31*(1), 31–40.

Brunello, N., Davidson, J. R., Deahl, M., Kessler, R. C., Mendlewicz, J., Racagni, G., et al. (2001). Posttraumatic stress disorder: Diagnosis and epidemiology, comorbidity and social consequences, biology and treatment. *Neuropsychobiology, 43*(3), 150–162.

Brunette, M. F., & Drake, R. E. (1998). Gender differences in homeless persons with schizophrenia and substance abuse. *Community Mental Health Journal, 34,* 627–642.

Brunette, M. F., Mueser, K. T., Xie, H., & Drake, R. E. (1997). Relationships between symptoms of schizophrenia and substance abuse. *Journal of Nervous and Mental Diseases, 185,* 13–20.

Bucholz, K. K. (1999). Nosology and epidemiology of addictive disorders and their comorbidity. *Psychiatric Clinics of North America, 22*(2), 221–239.

Busto, U. E., Romach, M. K., & Sellers, E. M. (1996). Multiple drug use and psychiatric comorbidity in patients admitted to the hospital with severe benzodiazepine dependence. *Journal of Clinical Psychopharmacology, 16*(1), 51–57.

Carey, K. B., & Correia, C. J. (1998). Severe mental illness and addictions: Assessment considerations. *Addictive Behaviors, 23*(6), 735–748.

Carey, M. P., Carey, K. B., & Kalichman, S. C. (1997). Risk for human immunodeficiency virus (HIV) infection among persons with severe mental illnesses. *Clinical Psychology Review, 17,* 271–291.

Carpenter, W. T. J., Heinrichs, D. W., & Alphs, L. D. (1985). Treatment of negative symptoms. *Schizophrenia Bulletin, 11,* 440–452.

Caton, C. L., Shrout, P. E., Eagle, P. F., Opler, L. A., Felix, A., & Dominguez, B. (1994). Risk factors for homelessness among schizophrenic men: A case-control study. *American Journal of Public Health, 84,* 265–270.

Chen, C., Balogh, R., Bathija, J., Howanitz, E., Plutchik, R., & Conte, H. R. (1992). Substance abuse among psychiatric inpatients. *Comprehensive Psychiatry, 33,* 60–64.

Chengappa, K. N., Levine, J., Gershon, S., & Kupfer, D. J. (2000). Lifetime prevalence of substance or alcohol abuse and dependence among subjects with bipolar I and II disorders in a voluntary registry. *Bipolar Disorder, 2*(3, Pt. 1), 191–195.

Chilcoat, H. D., & Breslau, N. (1998). Investigations of causal pathways between posttraumatic stress disorder and drug use disorders. *Addictive Behaviors, 23*(6), 827–840.

Clark, R. E., Ricketts, S. K., & McHugo, G. J. (1999). Legal system involvement and costs for persons in treatment for severe mental illness and substance use disorders. *Psychiatric Services, 50*(5), 641–647.

Cleghorn, J. M., Kaplan, R. D., Szechtman, B., Szechtman, H., Brown, G. M., & Franco, S. (1991). Substance abuse and schizophrenia: Effect on symptoms but not on neurocognitive function. *Journal of Clinical Psychiatry, 52,* 26–30.

Cohen, L. J., Test, M. A., & Brown, R. J. (1990). Suicide and schizophrenia: Data from a prospective community treatment study. *American Journal of Psychiatry, 147,* 602–607.

Cohen, M., & Klein, D. F. (1970). Drug abuse in a young psychiatric population. *American Journal of Orthopsychiatry, 40,* 448–455.

Comtois, K. A., & Ries, R. (1995). Sex differences in dually diagnosed severely mentally ill clients in dual diagnosis outpatient treatment. *American Journal on Addictions, 4,* 245–253.

Cottler, L. B., Compton, W. M., Mager, D., Spitznagel, E. L., & Janca, A. (1992). Posttraumatic stress disorder among substance users from the general population. *American Journal of Psychiatry, 149*(5), 664–670.

Dalack, G. W., & Meador-Woodruff, J. H. (1996). Smoking, smoking withdrawal and schizophrenia: Case reports and a review of the literature. *Schizophrenia Research, 22,* 133–141.

Dansky, B. S., Brady, K. T., & Saladin, M. E. (1998). Untreated symptoms of posttraumatic stress disorder among cocaine-dependent individuals: Changes over time. *Journal of Substance Abuse Treatment, 15*(6), 499–504.

Davis, T. M., & Wood, P. S. (1999). Substance abuse and sexual trauma in a female veteran population. *Journal of Substance Abuse Treatment, 16*(2), 123–127.

Dickey, B., & Azeni, H. (1996). Persons with dual diagnoses of substance abuse and major mental illness: Their excess costs of psychiatric care. *American Journal of Public Health, 86*(7), 973–977.

Dixon, L. (1999). Dual diagnosis of substance abuse in schizophrenia: Prevalence and impact on outcomes. *Schizophrenia Research, 35,* S93–S100.

Dixon, L., Haas, G., Weiden, P., Sweeney, J., & Frances, A. J. (1990). Acute effects of drug abuse in schizophrenic patients: Clinical observations and patients' self-reports. *Schizophrenia Bulletin, 16*(1), 69–79.

Dixon, L., Haas, G., Weiden, P., Sweeney, J., & Frances, A. J. (1991). Drug abuse in schizophrenic patients: Clinical correlates and reasons for use. *American Journal of Psychiatry, 149,* 231–234.

Drake, R. E., Osher, F. C., & Wallach, M. A. (1989). Alcohol use and abuse in schizophrenia: A prospective community study. *Journal of Nervous and Mental Diseases, 177,* 408–414.

Drake, R. E., & Wallach, M. A. (1989). Substance abuse among the chronically mentally ill. *Hospital and Community Psychiatry, 40,* 1041–1046.

Eisen, J. L., & Rasmussen, S. A. (1989). Coexisting obsessive compulsive disorder and alcoholism. *Journal of Clinical Psychiatry, 50*(3), 96–98.

Evans, D. L. (2000). Bipolar disorder: Diagnostic challenges and treatment consideration. *Journal of Clinical Psychiatry, 61*(Suppl. 13), 26–31.

Fennig, S., Craig, T. J., Tanenberg-Karant, M., & Bromet, E. J. (1994). Comparison of facility and research diagnoses in first-admission psychotic patients. *American Journal of Psychiatry, 151*(10), 1423–1429.

Fulwiler, C., Grossman, H., Forbes, C., & Ruthazer, R. (1997). Early-onset substance abuse and community violence by outpatient with chronic mental illness. *Psychiatric Services, 48*(9), 1181–1185.

Galanter, M., Castaneda, R., & Ferman, J. (1988). Substance abuse among general psychiatric patients: Place of presentation, diagnosis, and treatment. *American Journal of Drug and Alcohol Abuse, 14*(2), 211–235.

Garnick, D. W., Hendricks, A. M., Comstock, C., & Horgan, C. (1997). Do individuals with substance abuse diagnoses incur higher charges than individuals with other chronic conditions? *Journal of Substance Abuse Treatment, 14*(5), 457–465.

Gearon, J. S., & Bellack, A. S. (1999). Women with schizophrenia and co-occurring substance use disorders: An increased risk for violent victimization and HIV. *Journal of Community Mental Health, 35,* 401–419.

Gearon, J. S., Bellack, A. S., Nidecker, M., & Bennett, M. E. (in press). Gender differences in drug use behavior in people with serious mental illness. *American Journal on Addictions.*

Gershon, E. S., Hamovit, J., Guroff, J. J., Dibble, E., Leckman, J. F., Sceery, W., et al. (1982). A family study of schizoaffective, bipolar I, bipolar II, and normal probands. *Archives of General Psychiatry, 39*(10), 1157–1167.

Glenn, S. W., & Parsons, O. A. (1991). Prediction of resumption of drinking in posttreatment alcoholics. *International Journal of the Addictions, 26*(2), 237–254.

Goldberg, J. F., Garno, J. L., Leon, A. C., Kocsis, J. H., & Portera, L. (1999). A history of substance abuse complicates remission from acute mania in bipolar disorder. *Journal of Clinical Psychiatry, 60*(11), 733–740.

Goodman, L. A., Dutton, M. A., & Harris, M. (1995). The relationship between violence dimensions and symptom severity among homeless, mentally ill women. *Journal of Traumatic Stress, 10*(1), 51–70.

Goodman, L. A., Rosenburg, S., Mueser, K. T., & Drake, R. (1997). Physical and sexual assault history in women with SMI: Prevalence, correlates, treatment, and future research directions. *Schizophrenia Bulletin, 23,* 685–696.

Goodwin, F. K., & Jamison, K. R. (1990). *Manic-depressive illness.* New York: Oxford University Press.

Gottesman, I. I., & Groome, C. S. (1997). HIV/AIDS risks as a consequence of schizophrenia. *Schizophrenia Bulletin, 23,* 675–684.

Grant, B. F. (1997). The influence of comorbid major depression and substance use disorders on alcohol and drug treatment: Results of a national survey. *NIDA Research Monograph, 172,* 4–15.

Grant, B. F., & Harford, T. C. (1995). Comorbidity between *DSM-IV* alcohol use disorders and major depression: Results of a national survey. *Drug and Alcohol Dependence, 39,* 197–206.

Grant, B. F., Harford, T. C., Dawson, D. A., Chou, P., Dufour, M., & Pickering, R. (1994). Prevalence of *DSM-IV* alcohol abuse and dependence: United States, 1992. *Alcohol Health and Research World, 18*(3), 243–248.

Grant, B. F., Hasin, D. S., & Hartford, T. C. (1989). Screening for major depression among alcoholics: An application of receiver operating characteristic analysis. *Drug and Alcohol Dependence, 23,* 123–131.

Grella, C. E. (1996). Background and overview of mental health and substance abuse treatment systems: Meeting the needs of women who are pregnant or parenting. *Journal of Psychoactive Drugs, 28*(4), 319–343.

Grella, C. E. (1997). Services for perinatal women with substance abuse and mental health disorders: The unmet need. *Journal of Psychoactive Drugs, 29*(1), 67–78.

Hasin, D. S., Endicott, J., & Keller, M. B. (1991). Alcohol problems in psychiatric patients: 5-year course. *Comprehensive Psychiatry, 32*(4), 303–316.

Hasin, D. S., Endicott, J., & Lewis, C. (1985). Alcohol and drug abuse in patients with affective syndromes. *Comprehensive Psychiatry, 26*(3), 283–295.

Hasin, D. S., Grant, B. F., & Endicott, J. (1988). Lifetime psychiatric comorbidity in hospitalized alcoholics: Subject and familial correlates. *International Journal of the Addictions, 23*(8), 827–850.

Havassy, B. E., & Arns, P. G. (1998). Relationship of cocaine and other substance dependence to well-being of high-risk psychiatric patients. *Psychiatric Services, 49*(7), 935–940.

Havassy, B. E., Shopshire, M. S., & Quigley, L. A. (2000). Effects of substance dependence on outcomes of patients in a randomized trial of two case management models. *Psychiatric Services, 51*(5), 639–644.

Hays, P., & Aidroos, N. (1986). Alcoholism followed by schizophrenia. *Acta Psychiatrica Scandinavica, 74*(2), 187–189.

Haywood, T. W., Kravitz, H. M., Grossman, L. S., Cavanaugh, J. L., Jr., Davis, J. M., & Lewis, D. A. (1995). Predicting the "revolving door" phenomenon among patients with schizophrenic, schizoaffective, and affective disorders. *American Journal of Psychiatry, 152,* 856–861.

Helzer, J. E., & Pryzbeck, T. R. (1988). The co-occurrence of alcoholism with other psychiatric disorders in the general population and its impact on treatment. *Journal of Studies on Alcohol, 49*(3), 219–224.

Helzer, J. E., Robbins, L. H., & McEvoy, L. (1987). Posttraumatic stress disorder in the general population. *New England Journal of Medicine, 317,* 1630–1634.

Herz, L. R., Volicer, L., D'Angelo, N., & Gadish, D. (1990). Additional psychiatric illness by Diagnostic Interview Schedule in male alcoholics. *Comprehensive Psychiatry, 30*(1), 72–79.

Hesselbrock, M. N., Meyer, R. E., & Keener, J. J. (1985). Psychopathology in hospitalized alcoholics. *Archives of General Psychiatry, 42,* 1050–1055.

Hesselbrock, V. M. (1986). Family history of psychopathology in alcoholics: A review and issues. In R. E. Meyer (Ed.), *Psychopathology and addictive disorders* (pp. 41–56). New York: Guilford Press.

Hesselbrock, V. M., Hesselbrock, M. N., & Workman-Daniels, K. L. (1986). Effect of major depression and antisocial personality on alcoholism: Course and motivational patterns. *Journal of Studies on Alcohol, 47*(3), 207–212.

Himle, J. A., & Hill, E. M. (1991). Alcohol abuse and anxiety disorders: Evidence from the Epidemiologic Catchment Area Survey. *Journal of Anxiety Disorders, 5,* 237–245.

Hirschfeld, R. M. A., Hasin, D., Keller, M. D., Endicott, J., & Wunder, J. (1990). Depression and alcoholism: Comorbidity in a longitudinal study. In J. D. Maser & C. R. Cloninger (Eds), *Comorbidity of mood and anxiety disorders* (pp. 293–303). Washington, DC: American Psychiatric Press.

Hoff, R. A., Beam-Goulet, J., & Rosenheck, R. A. (1997). Mental disorder as a risk factor for human immunodeficiency virus infection in a sample of veterans. *Journal of Nervous and Mental Diseases, 185*(9), 556–560.

Jacobson, A. (1989). Physical and sexual assault histories among psychiatric outpatients. *American Journal of Psychiatry, 146*(6), 755–758.

Karmali, M., Kelly, L., Gervin, M., Browne, S., Larkin, C., & O'Calleghan, E. (2000). The prevalence of comorbid substance misuse and its influence on suicidal ideation among in-patients with schizophrenia. *Acta Psychiatrica Scandinavica, 101*(6), 452–456.

Keane, T. M., Gerardi, R. J., Lyons, J. A., & Wolfe, J. (1988). The interrelationship of substance abuse and posttraumatic stress disorder: Epidemiological and clinical considerations. In M. Galanter (Ed.), *Recent developments in alcoholism* (pp. 27–48). New York: Plenum Press.

Kelly, R. H., Danielsen, B. H., Golding, J. M., Anders, T. F., Gilbert, W. M., & Zatzick, D. F. (1999). Adequacy of prenatal care among women with psychiatric diagnoses giving birth in California in 1994 and 1995. *Psychiatric Services, 50*(12), 1584–1590.

Kendler, K. S. (1985). A twin study of individuals with both schizophrenia and alcoholism. *British Journal of Psychiatry, 147,* 48–53.

Kendler, K. S., Davis, C. G., & Kessler, R. C. (1997). The familial aggregation of common psychiatric and substance use disorders in the National Comorbidity Survey: A family history study. *British Journal of Psychiatry, 170,* 541–548.

Kessler, R. C. (1997). The prevalence of psychiatric comorbidity. In S. Wetzler & W. C. Sanderson (Eds.), *Treatment strategies for patients with psychiatric comorbidity* (pp. 23–48). New York: Wiley.

Kessler, R. C., McGonagle, K. A., Zhao, S., Nelson, C. B., Hughes, M., Eshleman, S., et al. (1994). Lifetime and 12-month prevalence of *DSM-III-R* psychiatric disorders in the United States. *Archives of General Psychiatry, 51,* 8–19.

Keuthen, N. J., Niaura, R. S., Borrelli, B., Goldstein, M., DePue, J., Murphy, C., et al. (2000). Comorbidity, smoking behavior, and treatment outcome. *Psychotherapy and Psychosomatics, 69,* 244–250.

Khantzian, E. J., & Treece, C. (1985). *DSM-III* psychiatric diagnoses of narcotic addicts. *Archives of General Psychiatry, 42,* 1067–1071.

Kokkevi, A., Stephanis, N., Anastasopoulou, E., & Kostogianni, C. (1998). Personality disorders in drug abusers: Prevalence and their association with Axis I disorders as predictors of treatment retention. *Addictive Behaviors, 23*(6), 841–853.

Kozaric-Kovacic, D., Folnegovic-Smalc, V., Folnegovic, Z., & Marusic, A. (1995). Influence of alcoholism on the prognosis of schizophrenia patients. *Journal of Studies on Alcohol, 56,* 622–627.

Krakow, D. S., Galanter, M., Dermatis, H., & Westreich, L. M. (1998). HIV risk factors in dually diagnosed patients. *American Journal on Addictions, 7*(1), 74–80.

Kranzler, H. R., Del Boca, F. K., & Rounsaville, B. J. (1996). Comorbid psychiatric diagnosis predicts three-year outcomes in alcoholics: A posttreatment natural history study. *Journal of Studies on Alcohol, 57,* 619–626.

Krueger, R. F. (1999). The structure of common mental disorders. *Archives of General Psychiatry, 56,* 921–926.

Kushner, M. G., Abrams, K., & Borchardt, C. (2000). The relationship between anxiety disorders and alcohol use disorders: A review of major perspectives and findings. *Clinical Psychology Review, 20*(2), 149–171.

Kushner, M. G., Sher, K. J., & Beitman, B. D. (1990). The relation between alcohol problems and the anxiety disorders. *American Journal of Psychiatry, 147*(6), 685–695.

Lambert, M. T., Griffith, J. M., & Hendrickse, W. (1996). Characteristics of patients with substance abuse diagnoses on a general psychiatry unit in a VA medical center. *Psychiatric Services, 47*(10), 1104–1107.

Landmark, J., Cernovsky, Z. Z., & Merskey, H. (1987). Correlates of suicide attempts and ideation in schizophrenia. *British Journal of Psychiatry, 151,* 8–20.

Lasser, K., Boyd, J. W., Woolhandler, S., Himmelstein, D. U., McCormick, D., & Bor, D. H. (2000). Smoking and mental illness: A population-based study. *Journal of the American Medical Association, 284*(2), 2606–2610.

Leal, D., Galanter, M., Dermatis, H., & Westreich, L. (1999). Correlates of protracted homelessness in a sample of dually diagnosed psychiatric inpatients. *Journal of Substance Abuse Treatment, 16*(2), 143–147.

Lehman, A. F., Myers, C. P., Dixon, L. B., & Johnson, J. L. (1994). Defining subgroups of dual diagnosis patients for service planning. *Hospital and Community Psychiatry, 45*(6), 556–561.

Lehman, A. F., Myers, C. P., Thompson, J. W., & Corty, E. (1993). Implications of mental and substance use disorders: A comparison of single and dual diagnosis patients. *Journal of Nervous and Mental Diseases, 181*(6), 365–370.

Linszen, D. H., Dingemans, P. M., & Lenior, M. E. (1994). Cannabis abuse and the course of recent-onset schizophrenic disorders. *Archives of General Psychiatry, 51,* 273–279.

Liskow, B., Powell, B. J., Nickel, E. J., & Penick, E. (1991). Antisocial alcoholics: Are there clinically significant diagnostic subtypes? *Journal of Studies on Alcohol, 52*(1), 62–69.

Lynskey, M. T. (1998). The comorbidity of alcohol dependence and affective disorders: Treatment implications. *Drug and Alcohol Dependence, 52,* 201–209.

Marzuk, P. M. (1996). Violence, crime, and mental illness: How strong a link? *Archives of General Psychiatry, 53,* 481–486.

Maynard, C., & Cox, G. B. (1988). Psychiatric hospitalization of persons with dual diagnoses: Estimates from two national surveys. *Psychiatric Services, 49*(12), 1615–1617.

McCrone, P., Menezes, P. R., Johnson, S., Scott, H., Thornicroft, G., Marshall, J., et al. (2000). Service use and costs of people with dual diagnosis in South London. *Acta Psychiatrica Scandinavica, 101*(6), 464–472.

McElroy, S. L., Altshuler, L. L., Suppes, T., Keck, P. E., Frye, M. A., Denicoff, K. D., et al. (2001). Axis I psychiatric comorbidity and its relationship to historical illness variables in 288 patients with bipolar disorder. *American Journal of Psychiatry, 158*(3), 420–426.

McFall, M., Fontana, A., Raskind, M., & Rosenheck, R. (1999). Analysis of violent behavior in Vietnam combat veteran psychiatric inpatients with posttraumatic stress disorder. *Journal of Traumatic Stress, 12*(3), 501–517.

McKinnon, K., Cournos, F., Sugden, R., Guido, J. R., & Herman, R. (1996). The relative contributions of psychiatric symptoms and AIDS knowledge to HIV risk behaviors among people with severe mental illness. *Journal of Clinical Psychiatry, 57*(11), 506–513.

McLellan, A. T., Druley, K. A., & Carson, J. E. (1978). Evaluation of substance abuse in a psychiatric hospital. *Journal of Clinical Psychiatry, 39*(5), 425–430.

McLellan, A. T., Luborsky, L., Woody, G. E., O'Brien, C. P., & Cruley, K. A. (1983). Predicting response to alcohol and drug abuse treatments: Role of psychiatric severity. *Archives of General Psychiatry, 40,* 620–625.

Menezes, P. R., Johnson, S., Thornicroft, G., Marshall, J., Prosser, D., Bebbington, P., et al. (1996). Drug and alcohol problems among individuals with severe mental illnesses in South London. *British Journal of Psychiatry, 168,* 612–619.

Merikangas, K. R., & Gelernter, C. S. (1990). Comorbidity for alcoholism and depression. *Psychiatric Clinics of North America, 13*(4), 613–633.

Merikangas, K. R., Leckman, J. F., Prusoff, B. A., Pauls, D. L., & Weissman, M. M. (1985). Familial transmission of depression and alcoholism. *Archives of General Psychiatry, 42,* 367–372.

Mezzich, J. E., Ahn, C. W., Fabrega, H., & Pilkonis, P. (1990). Patterns of psychiatric comorbidity in a large population presenting for care. In J. D. Maser & C. R. Cloninger (Eds.), *Comorbidity of mood and anxiety disorders* (pp. 189–204). Washington, DC: American Psychiatric Press.

Miller, N. S., Klamen, D., Hoffmann, N. G., & Flaherty, J. A. (1996). Prevalence of depression and alcohol and other drug dependence in addictions treatment populations. *Journal of Psychoactive Drugs, 28,* 111–124.

Mirin, S. M., Weiss, R. D., Griffin, M. L., & Michael, J. L. (1991). Psychopathology in drug abusers and their families. *Comprehensive Psychiatry, 32*(1), 36–51.

Mirin, S. M., Weiss, R. D., & Michael, J. L. (1988). Psychopathology in substance abusers: Diagnosis and treatment. *American Journal of Drug and Alcohol Abuse, 14,* 139–157.

Morgenstern, J., Langenbucher, J., Labouvie, E., & Miller, K. J. (1997). The comorbidity of alcoholism and personality disorders in a clinical population: Prevalence rates and relation to alcohol topology variables. *Journal of Abnormal Psychology, 106*(1), 74–84.

Mueller, T. I., Lavori, P. W., Keller, M. B., Swartz, A., Warshaw, M., Hasin, D., et al. (1994). Prognostic effect of the variable course of alcoholism on the 10-year course of depression. *American Journal of Psychiatry, 151*(5), 701–706.

Mueser, K. T., Bellack, A. S., & Blanchard, J. J. (1992). Comorbidity of schizophrenia and substance abuse: Implications for treatment. *Journal of Consulting and Clinical Psychology, 60*(6), 845–856.

Mueser, K. T., Drake, R. E., & Wallach, M. A. (1998). Dual diagnosis: A review of etiological theories. *Addictive Behaviors, 23*(6), 717–734.

Mueser, K. T., Rosenberg, S. D., Drake, R. E., Miles, K. M., Wolford, G., Vidaver, R., et al. (1999). Conduct disorder, antisocial personality disorder, and substance use disorders in schizophrenia and major affective disorders. *Journal of Studies on Alcohol, 60*(2), 278–284.

Mueser, K. T., Yarnold, P. R., & Bellack, A. S. (1992). Diagnostic and demographic correlates of substance abuse in schizophrenia and major affective disorder. *Acta Psychiatrica Scandinavica, 85,* 8–55.

Mueser, K. T., Yarnold, P. R., Levinson, D. F., Singh, H., Bellack, A. S., Kee, K., et al. (1990). Prevalence of substance abuse in schizophrenia: Demographic and clinical correlates. *Schizophrenia Bulletin, 16*(1), 31–56.

Nace, E. P. (1990). Personality disorder in the alcoholic patient. *Psychiatric Annals, 19,* 256–260.

Nace, E. P., Davis, C. W., & Gaspari, J. P. (1991). Axis II comorbidity in substance abusers. *American Journal of Psychiatry, 148*(1), 118–120.

Najavitis, L. M., Gastfriend, D. R., Barber, J. P., Reif, S., Muenz, L. R., Blaine, J., et al. (1998). Cocaine dependence with and without posttraumatic stress disorder among subjects in the National Institute on Drug Abuse Collaborative Cocaine Treatment Study. *American Journal of Psychiatry, 155*(2), 214–219.

Najavitis, L. M., Weiss, R. D., & Shaw, S. R. (1997). The link between substance abuse and posttraumatic stress disorder in women: A review. *American Journal of Addiction, 6*(4), 273–283.

Negrete, J. C., & Knapp, W. P. (1986). The effects of cannabis use on the clinical condition of schizophrenics. *NIDA Research Monograph, 67,* 321–327.

Newman, D. L., Moffitt, T. E., Caspi, A., & Silva, P. (1998). Comorbid mental disorders: Implications for treatment and sample selection. *Journal of Abnormal Psychology, 107*(2), 305–311.

O'Connell, R. A., Mayo, J. A., Flatow, L., Cuthbertson, B., & O'Brien, B. E. (1991). Outcome of bipolar disorder on long-term treatment with lithium. *British Journal of Psychiatry, 159,* 23–129.

Ouimette, P. C., Ahrens, C., Moos, R. H., & Finney, J. W. (1998). During treatment changes in substance abuse patients with posttraumatic stress disorder: The influence of specific interventions and program environments. *Journal of Substance Abuse Treatment, 15*(6), 555–564.

Ouimette, P. C., Brown, P. J., & Najavitis, L. M. (1998). Course and treatment of patients with both substance use and posttraumatic stress disorders. *Addictive Behaviors, 23*(6), 785–795.

Ouimette, P. C., Gima, K., Moos, R. H., & Finney, J. W. (1999). A comparative evaluation of substance abuse treatment IV: The effect of comorbid psychiatric diagnoses on amount of treatment, continuing care, and 1-year outcomes. *Alcoholism: Clinical and Experimental Research, 23*(3), 552–557.

Ouimette, P. C., Wolfe, J., & Chrestman, K. R. (1996). Characteristics of posttraumatic stress disorder-alcohol abuse comorbidity in women. *Journal of Substance Abuse, 8*(3), 355–346.

Owen, R. R., Fischer, E. P., Booth, B. M., & Cuffel, B. J. (1996). Medication noncompliance and substance abuse among persons with schizophrenia. *Psychiatric Services, 47*(8), 853–858.

Pages, K. P., Russo, J. E., Roy-Byrne, P. P., Ries, R. K., & Cowley, D. S. (1997). Determinants of suicidal ideation: The role of substance use disorders. *Journal of Clinical Psychiatry, 58*(11), 510–515.

Pages, K. P., Russo, J. E., Wingerson, D. K., Ries, R. K., Roy-Byrne, P. P., & Cowley, D. S. (1998). Predictors and outcome of discharge against medical advice from the psychiatric units of a general hospital. *Psychiatric Services, 49*(9), 1187–1192.

Palacios, S., Urmann, C. F., Newel, R., & Hamilton, N. (1999). Developing a sociological framework for dually diagnosed women. *Journal of Substance Abuse Treatment, 17*(1/2), 91–102.

Partonen, T., Sihvo, S., & Lonnqvist, J. K. (1996). Patients excluded from an antidepressant efficacy trial. *Journal of Clinical Psychiatry, 57*(12), 572–575.

Penick, E. C., Powell, B. J., Othmer, E., Bingham, S. F., Rice, A. S., & Liese, B. S. (1984). Subtyping alcoholics by coexisting psychiatric syndromes: Course, family history, outcome. In D. W. Goodwin, K. T. Van Dusen, & S. A. Mednick (Eds.), *Longitudinal research in alcoholism* (pp. 167–196). Boston: Kluwer-Nijhoff.

Polcin, D. L. (1992). Issues in the treatment of dual diagnosis clients who have chronic mental illness. *Professional Psychology: Research and Practice, 23*(1), 30–37.

Poldrugo, F. (1998). Alcohol and criminal behavior. *Alcohol Alcohol, 33*(1), 12–15.

Potash, J. B., Kane, H. S., Chiu, Y. F., Simpson, S. G., MacKinnon, D. F., McInnis, M. G., et al. (2000). Attempted suicide and alcoholism in bipolar disorder: Clinical and familial relationships. *American Journal of Psychiatry, 157*(12), 2048–2050.

Powell, B. J., Penick, E. C., Othmer, E., Bingham, S. F., & Rice, A. S. (1982). Prevalence of additional psychiatric syndromes among male alcoholics. *Journal of Clinical Psychiatry, 43*(10), 404–407.

Quattrocki, E., Baird, A., & Yurgelun-Todd, D. (2000). Biological aspects of the link between smoking and depression. *Harvard Review of Psychiatry, 8*(3), 99–110.

Raimo, E. B., & Schuckit, M. A. (1998). Alcohol dependence and mood disorders. *Addictive Behaviors, 23*(6), 933–946.

Regier, D. A., Farmer, M. E., Rae, D. S., Locke, B. Z., Keither, S. J., Judd, L. L., et al. (1990). Comorbidity of mental disorders with alcohol and other drug abuse. *Journal of the American Medical Association, 264,* 2511–2518.

Regier, D. A., Kaelber, C. T., Rae, D. S., Farmer, M. E., Knauper, B., Kessler, R. C., et al. (1998). Limitations of diagnostic criteria and assessment instruments for mental disorders: Implications for research and policy. *Archives of General Psychiatry, 55,* 109–115.

Ridgely, M. S., Goldman, H. H., & Willenbring, M. (1990). Barriers to the case of persons with dual diagnoses: Organizational and financing issues. *Schizophrenia Bulletin, 16*(1), 123–132.

Ridgely, M. S., Lambert, D., Goodman, A., Chichester, C. S., & Ralph, R. (1998). Interagency collaboration in services for people with co-occurring mental illness and substance use disorder. *Psychiatric Services, 49,* 236–238.

Rosenblum, A., Fallon, B., Magura, S., Handelsman, L., Foote, J., & Bernstein, D. (1999). The autonomy of mood disorders among cocaine-using methadone patients. *American Journal of Drug and Alcohol Abuse, 25*(1), 67–80.

Rosenthal, R. N., & Miner, C. H. (1997). Differential diagnosis of substance-induced psychosis and schizophrenia in patients with substance use disorders. *Schizophrenia Bulletin, 23*(2), 187–193.

Ross, H. E., Glaser, F. B., & Germanson, T. (1988). The prevalence of psychiatric disorders in patients with alcohol and other drug problems. *Archives of General Psychiatry, 45,* 1023–1031.

Ross, H. E., Glaser, F. B., & Stiasny, S. (1988). Differences in the prevalence of psychiatric disorders in patients with alcohol and drug problems. *British Journal of Addiction, 83,* 1179–1192.

Rounsaville, B. J., Anton, S. F., Carroll, K., Budde, D., Prusoff, B. A., & Gawin, F. (1991). Psychiatric diagnoses of treatment seeking cocaine abusers. *Archives of General Psychiatry, 48,* 43–51.

Rounsaville, B. J., Kosten, T. R., Weissman, M. M., & Kleber, H. D. (1986). Prognostic significance of psychopathology in treated opiate addicts. *Archives of General Psychiatry, 43,* 739–745.

Rounsaville, B. J., Weissman, M. M., Kleber, H., & Wilber, C. (1982). Heterogeneity of psychiatric diagnosis in treated opiate addicts. *Archives of General Psychiatry, 39,* 161–166.

Rounsaville, B. J., Weissman, M. M., Wilber, C. H., Crits-Christoph, K., & Kleber, H. D. (1982). Diagnosis and symptoms of depression in opiate addicts: Course and relationship to treatment outcome. *Archives of General Psychiatry, 39,* 151–156.

Safer, D. J. (1987). Substance abuse by young adult chronic patients. *Hospital and Community Psychiatry, 38*(5), 511–514.

Saladin, M. E., Brady, K. T., Dansky, B. S., & Kilpatrick, D. G. (1995). Understanding co-morbidity between posttraumatic stress disorder and substance use disorders: Two preliminary investigations. *Addictive Behaviors, 20*(5), 643–655.

Salloum, I. M., & Thase, M. E. (2000). Impact of substance abuse on the course and treatment of bipolar disorder. *Bipolar Disorder, 2*(3, Pt. 2), 269–280.

Sandberg, D. A., McNiel, D. E., & Binder, R. L. (1998). Characteristics of psychiatric inpatients who stalk, threaten, or harass hospital staff after discharge. *American Journal of Psychiatry, 155*(8), 1102–1105.

Schneier, F. R., & Siris, S. G. (1987). A review of psychoactive substance use and abuse in schizophrenia: Patterns of drug choice. *Journal of Nervous and Mental Diseases, 175,* 641–650.

Schuckit, M. A. (1983). Alcoholism and other psychiatric disorders. *Hospital and Community Psychiatry, 34*(11), 1022–1027.

Schuckit, M. A., & Monteiro, M. G. (1988). Alcoholism, anxiety, and depression. *British Journal of Addiction, 83,* 1373–1380.

Schuckit, M. A., Tipp, J. E., Bucholz, K. K., Nurnberger, J. I., Hesselbrock, V. M., Crowe, R. R., et al. (1997). The life-time rates of three major mood disorder and four major anxiety disorders in alcoholics and controls. *Addiction, 92*(10), 1289–1304.

Scott, H., Johnson, S., Menezes, P., Thornicroft, G., Marshall, J., Bindman, J., et al. (1998). Substance misuse and risk of aggression and offending among the severely mentally ill. *British Journal of Psychiatry, 172,* 345–350.

Sellman, J. D., & Joyce, P. R. (1996). Does depression predict relapse in the 6 months following treatment for men with alcohol dependence? *Australian New Zealand Journal of Psychiatry, 30,* 573–578.

Sher, K. J., & Trull, T. J. (1996). Methodological issues in psychopathology research. *Annual Review of Psychology, 47,* 471–400.

Sokolski, K. N., Cummings, J. L., Abrams, B. I., DeMet, E. M., Katz, L. S., & Costa, J. F. (1994). Effects of substance abuse on hallucination rates and treatment responses in chronic psychiatric patients. *Journal of Clinical Psychiatry, 55,* 380–387.

Sonne, S. C., Brady, K. T., & Morton, W. A. (1994). Substance abuse and bipolar affective disorder. *Journal of Nervous and Mental Diseases, 182*(6), 349–352.

Soyka, M. (2000). Substance misuse, psychiatric disorder and violent and disturbed behavior. *British Journal of Psychiatry, 176,* 345–350.

Steadman, H. J., Mulvey, E. P., Monoahan, J., Robbins, P. C., Appelbaum, P. S., Grisson, T., et al. (1998). Violence by people discharged from acute psychiatric inpatient facilities and by others in the same neighborhoods. *Archives of General Psychiatry, 55*(5), 393–401.

Stewart, S. H., Pihl, R. O., Conrod, P. J., & Dongier, M. (1998). Functional associations among trauma, posttraumatic stress disorder and substance-related disorders. *Addictive Behaviors, 23*(6), 797–812.

Strakowski, S. M., & DelBello, M. P. (2000). The co-occurrence of bipolar and substance use disorders. *Clinical Psychology Review, 20*(2), 191–206.

Swanson, J., Borum, R., Swartz, M., & Hiday, V. (1999). Violent behavior preceding hospitalization among persons with severe mental illness. *Law and Human Behavior, 23*(2), 185–204.

Swartz, M. S., Swanson, J. W., Hiday, V. A., Borum, R., Wagner, H. R., & Burns, B. J. (1998). Violence and severe mental illness: The effects of substance abuse and nonadherence to medication. *American Journal of Psychiatry, 155*(2), 226–231.

Swendsen, J. D., & Merikangas, K. R. (2000). The comorbidity of depression and substance use disorders. *Clinical Psychology Review, 20*(2), 173–189.

Thomas, S. E., Thevos, A. K., & Randall, C. L. (1999). Alcoholics with and without social phobia: A comparison of substance use and psychiatric variables. *Journal of Studies on Alcohol, 60,* 472–479.

Thomas, V. H., Melchert, T. P., & Banken, J. A. (1999). Substance dependence and personality disorders: Comorbidity and treatment outcome in an inpatient treatment population. *Journal of Studies on Alcohol, 60*(2), 271–277.

Thompson, S. C., Checkley, G. E., Hocking, J. S., Crofts, N., Mijch, A. M., & Judd, F. K. (1997). HIV risk behavior and HIV testing of psychiatric patients in Melbourne. *Australia and New Zealand Journal of Psychiatry, 31*(4), 566–576.

T'omasson, K., & Vaglum, P. (1997). The 2-year course following detoxification treatment of substance abuse: The possible influence of psychiatric comorbidity. *European Archives of Psychiatry and Clinical Neuroscience, 247*(6), 320–327.

Triffleman, E. G., Marmar, C. R., Delucchi, K. L., & Ronfeldt, H. (1995). Childhood trauma and posttraumatic stress disorder in substance abuse inpatients. *Journal of Nervous and Mental Diseases, 183*(3), 172–176.

Trull, T. J., Sher, K. J., Minks-Brown, C., Durbin, J., & Burr, R. (2000). Borderline personality disorder and substance use disorders: A review and integration. *Clinical Psychology Review, 20*(2), 235–253.

Vieta, E., Colom, F., Martinez-Aran, A., Benabarre, A., Reinares, M., & Gasto, C. (2000). Bipolar II disorder and comorbidity. *Comprehensive Psychiatry, 41*(5), 339–343.

Weissman, M. M., & Meyers, J. K. (1980). Clinical depression in alcoholism. *American Journal of Psychiatry, 137,* 372–373.

Widiger, T. A., & Shea, T. (1991). Differentiation of Axis I and Axis II disorders. *Journal of Abnormal Psychology, 100*(3), 399–406.

Winokur, G., Turvey, C., Akiskal, H., Coryell, W., Solomon, D., Leon, A., et al. (1998). Alcoholism and drug abuse in three groups: Bipolar I, unipolars, and their acquaintances. *Journal of Affective Disorders, 50*(2/3), 81–89.

Wittchen, H., Perkonigg, A., & Reed, V. (1996). Comorbidity of mental disorders and substance use disorders. *European Addiction Research, 2,* 6–47.

Wolf, A. W., Schubert, D. S. P., Patterson, M. B., Marion, B., & Grande, T. P. (1988). Associations among major psychiatric disorders. *Journal of Consulting and Clinical Psychology, 56,* 292–294.

Wu, L., Kouzis, A. C., & Leaf, P. J. (1999). Influence of comorbid alcohol and psychiatric disorders on utilization of mental health services in the National Comorbidity Survey. *American Journal of Psychiatry, 156,* 230–1236.

Ziedonis, D. M., & George, T. P. (1997). Schizophrenia and nicotine use: Report of a pilot smoking cessation program and review of neurobiological and clinical issues. *Schizophrenia Bulletin, 23,* 247–254.

CHAPTER 3

Structured Interviewing and *DSM* Classification

DANIEL L. SEGAL and FREDERICK L. COOLIDGE

ASSESSMENT OF PSYCHIATRIC signs and symptoms has undergone significant change and maturation over the past three decades. More specifically, ability of clinicians and researchers to *accurately* diagnose psychiatric disorders and classify mental illness has improved with quantum leaps. Numerous structured diagnostic interviews have been developed for clinical, research, and training applications; and these instruments have contributed significantly to the advancement in diagnostic clarity and precision. Structured interviews have been devised to assist in diagnosis of all major Axis I (clinical) and all standard Axis II (personality) disorders. Most structured interviews are linked to *Diagnostic and Statistical Manual of Mental Disorders (DSM)* criteria and subsequently have been revamped to match refinements in the *DSM* classification system as it has evolved. Overall, structured interviews have improved clinical and research endeavors by providing a more standardized, scientific, and quantitative approach to the evaluation of psychiatric symptoms. This chapter reviews the prominent structured and semistructured interviews designed to enhance psychiatric diagnosis. For each instrument, the purpose, construction, psychometric properties, and clinical applications are discussed. First, however, some general issues about the nature and development of structured interviews are examined.

THE NATURE OF STRUCTURED INTERVIEWS

The heart and soul of clinical psychology may rest on twin pillars—diagnosis and psychotherapy. This chapter focuses on assessment and the diagnostic process, and, specifically, on the application of structured interviews. Traditional assessment methods have relied on a clinical interview (typically unstructured), behavioral and observational assessment, and psychometric testing. All of these methods are typically modified by the referral question, the philosophical nature of the clinical training program (e.g., psychoanalytic, behavioral), and the nature of the clinical setting (e.g., private vs. public, inpatient vs. outpatient). Although all of the traditional methods still have great value, the structured diagnostic interview adds much in developing clinical psychology into a true science (i.e., subject to evaluation, statistical analysis, modification, and improvement).

What are the differences between unstructured and structured interviews? Briefly, unstructured interviews are most often molded by the individual client's needs, the client's responses, and the clinician's intuitions. Any type of relevant question can be asked in any way that fits the mood, preferences, training, and philosophy of the clinician. Structured interviews, on the other hand, conform to a standardized list of questions, including follow-up questions, a standardized sequence of questioning, and, finally, systematized ratings of the client's responses. As Rogers (2001) has noted, it would be unwise to view the interviewing process as an either/or proposition (i.e., unstructured vs. structured interview). In certain situations, unstructured interviews can meet the objectives of a particular clinical inquiry more efficiently than a structured interview. However, structured interviewing allows for the assessment of the reliability of the interviewing process itself, as well as the assessment and validity of the diagnoses themselves.

As to reliability, unstructured interviews, because of their very nature, do not allow for any meaningful comparison among different clinicians or raters. A structured interview does allow for the determination of interrater reliability because all raters are asking the same questions. Furthermore, if the raters are using the same set of questions at a subsequent time, the test-retest reliability of the interview and of the symptoms themselves may be determined.

A structured interview also provides information about diagnostic validity. Perhaps, at the simplest level, a structured interview has face validity (i.e., the structured interview should cover fully the diagnostic criteria for a particular disorder). At a more complex level, a structured interview also provides an aspect of construct validity (i.e., the structured interview provides empirical, analyzable evidence that can be correlated to similar psychopathological diagnoses and uncorrelated to dissimilar ones). A simple convergence between a structured diagnostic interview and officially accepted diagnostic criteria does not validate the existence of the psychopathological condition, and the issue of the validity of mental disorders is beyond the scope of this chapter. However, it can be easily seen that the data supplied from a structured interview provides a solid framework for the study of the validity of mental disorders. It does this to some degree because it ensures greater reliability.

Some unstructured interviews may provide information about only the presence or absence of a particular disorder. Unstructured interviews may not often provide information about whether comorbid psychopathology exists, nor may they typically provide consistent information about the severity of the psychopathology. Structured interviews, because they incorporate systematic ratings, can provide information that allows for the determination of the level of severity and the level of impairment of a particular diagnosis and provide the same information about any comorbid conditions.

To be fair, however, there are some limitations of structured interviews. First, if clinicians become too bound by the interview protocol, they may fail to establish good rapport with their clients or fail to observe other important behavioral features. Thus, it behooves those who use structured interviews to engage their respondents in a meaningful way during the interview and to avoid a rote-like interviewing style that may serve to alienate. Second, as seen later in this chapter, no structured interview is entirely comprehensive (i.e., covering all psychiatric disorders). Thus, clinicians should be aware that some diagnoses may not be covered in structured interviews, or some diagnoses may receive limited attention when compared to others.

It is also important to emphasize that the term *structured interview* is a broad one and that the actual amount of *structure* provided by an interview varies considerably. Basically, structured interviews can be divided into one of two types: fully structured or semistructured. In a fully structured interview, the questions are asked verbatim to the respondent, the wording of probes used to follow up on initial questions is specified, and interviewers are trained to not deviate from this very specific format. In a semistructured interview, although the initial questions for each symptom are specified and are typically asked verbatim to the respondent, the interviewer has substantial latitude to follow up on responses. For example, existing questions and probes may be modified in any way, and completely new innovative questions may be asked for the explicit purpose of rating the presence or absence of the symptom more accurately. The amount of structure provided in a structured interview impacts the extent of clinical experience and judgment needed to administer the interview appropriately. Semistructured interviews require clinically experienced examiners to administer the interview and to make diagnoses, whereas fully structured interviews can be administered by nonclinicians who receive training on the specific instrument, thus making fully structured interviews economical to use, especially in very large studies.

One general issue concerning structured interviews is the problem of broadness versus depth. It has also been described as the *bandwidth-fidelity* issue (Widiger & Frances, 1987). If a structured interview has been designed to cover an entire diagnostic system, the inquiries about each disorder must be limited to a few inclusion criteria. Thus, the fidelity of the official diagnostic criteria has been compromised for the sake of a comprehensive interview. If the fidelity of the criteria is not compromised, the structured interview becomes unwieldy in terms of time and effort, on the part of both the interviewer and interviewee. Most structured interviews attempt some kind of compromise between these two approaches. Furthermore, most structured interviews allow for two types of questions—the standard ones and optional probes. The optional questions are typically used to clarify any ambiguities that may reside in the client's responses. As noted earlier, in some types of semistructured interviews, the interviewer may also ask atypical or unstructured questions to help the interviewer clarify a rating of the client's responses, but clinical experience and judgment are required.

Another advantage of the structured interview addresses the concern of clinicians about their clients' self-reports. As Rogers (1988) has noted, one overriding concern of clinicians during interviews is that the clients may consciously or unconsciously distort their responses by exaggerating, minimizing, or denying them. A client may intentionally prevaricate to gain money, notoriety, or escape punishment, as in the case of malingering. He or she may create symptoms to gain sympathy and attention, as in some factitious disorders. A client may also deny that he or she has any psychological problem or attempt to cover them up by confabulating responses. Clients may also minimize their problems, as in the case of some stoic individuals, or they may minimize because of their unique sociocultural environments where admission to psychological problems may be seen as socially undesirable or as a weakness. The referral question may also have a profound effect on the client's responses, as in the case of psychological evaluations during child custody determinations. These general issues have generated a great deal of research interest, not only in clinical psychology, but also in social psychology. There is a substantial body of literature on the issues of social desirability and acquiescence. Interestingly, the culmination of this research has provided the general consensus that while social desirability, acquiescence, and denial all may play a role in a patient's response, a majority of the variance in a response is accounted for by the content of the question. In other words, most answers to most questions are more affected by the nature of the question than by any other mitigating factors (Stone et al., 2000). Certainly, however, even in structured interviews, the client's self-reports may be discrepant with other corroborating evidence, such as history, observation, or family reports. In these cases, the clinician must use his or her own judgment. He or she may dismiss discrepant sources because of a lack of plausibility (Rogers, 2001). A clinician may also decide to seek additional information from other family members or informants. Finally, the clinician may decide to interpolate between two discrepant reports and assume some intermediate position (Rogers, 2001).

Quality structured interviews have been used in many different venues and for many different purposes. Application of structured interviews falls into three broad areas: research, clinical, and training use. The research domain is probably the most common for structured interviews, in which the interview is used to diagnose participants accurately so that etiology, comorbidity, and interventions (among other topics) can be investigated for a particular diagnosis or group of diagnoses. Indeed, good research requires that individuals assigned a diagnosis under study truly meet full criteria for the diagnosis. In the clinical setting, structured interviews may be used as a way to ensure standardized assessments. They may be used as part of a comprehensive intake evaluation, or parts of a structured interview may be used to clarify and confirm diagnoses based on an unstructured interview. Use of structured interviews for training in the mental health field is an ideal application because interviewers have the opportunity to learn (through repeated administrations) specific questions and follow-up probes used to elicit information and evaluate specific diagnostic criteria of the *DSM-IV.* Modeling his or her own questions and flow of the interview from a well-developed structured interview can be an invaluable source of training for the mental health clinician.

METHODOLOGICAL ISSUES IN INTERVIEW DEVELOPMENT

HISTORICAL PROBLEMS IN ACHIEVING ADEQUATE DIAGNOSTIC RELIABILITY

In general, psychiatric research has historically been hampered by the lack of agreement between two raters concerning presence or absence of a psychiatric diagnosis. Early landmark reports in the 1950s and 1960s documented consistently poor and unacceptable interclinician agreement (reliability) results (see Grove, 1987; Spitzer, Endicott, & Robins 1975). Indeed, credible findings from most early investigations were lacking for even the best-known and most prevalent diagnostic categories, such as major depression and schizophrenia (Grove, 1987). This notorious and disheartening unreliability of the first *DSM* (American Psychiatric Association [APA], 1952) and *DSM-II* (APA, 1968) classification systems was a grave cause of concern for psychiatric clinicians and researchers alike. Pervasive lack of agreement between clinicians and researchers when diagnosing clients is particularly troublesome because reliability is a necessary but insufficient prerequisite for validity.

Two primary reasons have been identified to account for this historically lamentable state of affairs. The first involves the actual diagnostic criteria in that inadequate nosology and poorly defined criteria play a substantial role in poor reliability (Ward, Beck, Mendelson, Mock, & Erbaugh, 1962). In the classic report by Ward et al., 80% of all diagnostic disagreements were attributed to inadequate diagnostic criteria. Spitzer et al. (1975) labeled this source of disagreement *criterion variance.* Disagreement about a diagnosis could result when two interviewers use different criteria for the same disorder. Indeed, early classification systems, such as the original *DSM* and *DSM-II,* lacked explicit diagnostic criteria for many disorders, provided a theoretical (often psychoanalytic) focus with respect to etiology, contained many inconsistencies, and confounded etiology with symptoms. Interviewers faced the formidable task of rating general or vague symptoms that often represented a theoretical construct that was difficult to operationalize. Consequently, these two early systems had poor reliability and validity.

The particular problem of nebulous and unclear criteria was partially addressed with publication of the *DSM-III* (APA, 1980), which greatly operationalized criteria and took a more descriptive, objective, and a theoretical approach concerning signs and symptoms of mental disorders. Empirical findings from clinical researchers were also included and the psychoanalytic influence was lessened. Additionally, the current multiaxial diagnostic system was introduced in *DSM-III,* which provided five separate axes on which more comprehensive diagnostic data could be recorded. Most notably here, clinical syndromes, such as bipolar disorder and generalized anxiety disorder, were recorded on Axis I, whereas personality disorders reflecting chronic interpersonal and self-image deficits were denoted separately on Axis II. Inclusion and exclusion criteria for many disorders were also more objectively defined in clear behavioral terms. These innovations have continued to be refined in subsequent versions of *DSM* including *DSM-III-R* (APA, 1987), *DSM-IV* (APA, 1994), and, most recently, the *DSM-IV-TR* (APA, 2000). Overall, these improvements in diagnostic criteria have greatly reduced criterion variance.

A second factor accounting for historically poor agreement rates between clinicians concerns the lack of standardization of questions that are asked to clients to evaluate psychiatric symptoms and ultimately to arrive at a formal diagnosis. Before standardized structured interviews, the unstructured interview format prevailed. As noted earlier, with unstructured interviews, clinicians are entirely responsible for asking whatever questions they decide are necessary for them to reach a diagnostic conclusion. The amount and kind of information gathered, as well as the way clinicians probe and assess psychiatric symptoms during an interview, are largely determined by their theoretical model, view of psychopathology, training, and interpersonal style, all of which can vary widely from clinician to clinician. The source of error involved when different clinicians obtain different information from the same client is referred to as *information variance* (Spitzer et al., 1975). The impetus for development of structured interviews was generated by the need to standardize questions asked of clients and provide guidelines for categorizing or coding responses. Adoption of such procedures serves to:

- Increase coverage of many disorders that previously might have been ignored.

- Enhance the diagnostician's ability to accurately determine if a particular symptom is present or absent.
- Reduce variability among interviewers (i.e., reduce information variance).

Introduction of operationalized, specified, empirically derived, and standardized criteria for mental disorders in conjunction with construction of standardized structured diagnostic interviews has served to revolutionize the diagnostic process and improve reliability and validity.

RELIABILITY AND VALIDITY OF STRUCTURED INTERVIEWS

Reliability and validity are important psychometric qualities to consider when critically evaluating diagnoses generated by structured interviews or any assessment device. *Reliability* refers to *replicability* and *stability.* If a structured interview does not provide reproducible data when readministered under identical conditions (i.e., poor reliability), what the instrument purports to measure is inconsequential. Indeed, it is a fact that acceptable levels of reliability must be confirmed *before* conclusions about validity can be drawn. Reliability constrains validity, but does not guarantee it. For example, with structured interviews, even if high reliability is attained, validity is not guaranteed because two clinicians may have perfect agreement but still be incorrect about all cases.

Two strategies have generally been implemented to ascertain reliability of a structured interview. The most commonly employed method is referred to as the *joint interview* or *simultaneous rating* design. In this type of study, the same interview is scored by at least two different raters who make independent diagnoses. This may be done in vivo when multiple raters simultaneously observe the same interview, or one rater may conduct the interview while additional raters are present and making judgments. A common variation involves audiotaped or videotaped interviews with post hoc analyses. Whether ratings are made live or post hoc, second or additional raters are always "blind" to diagnoses obtained based on the original evaluation, thus yielding an independent diagnostic appraisal. In many cases, the initial interviewer's diagnosis is included as a data point, which then is compared to judgments from at least one rater who made simultaneous live ratings or used taped interviews for post hoc ratings.

The type of variance encountered in simultaneous or joint interviewer designs is referred to as *rater variance* because raters are presented with the same responses from subjects but may *score* responses in different ways. For example, one rater may judge a symptom criterion for generalized anxiety disorder to be present (e.g., excessive unrealistic worrying), but another may judge the same response to indicate a clinically insignificant level of the symptom.

The second, and more stringent, reliability strategy has been referred to as the *test-retest* method. In such a study, two (or more) clinicians interview the same client on separate occasions, with clinicians formulating independent diagnoses. Reliability in test-retest investigations refers to the extent of agreement between multiple raters as to presence or absence of a disorder. A major source of variance in this type of study is *information variance,* in which separate interviewers elicit conflicting information from the same respondent. For example, a subject may deny experiencing suicidal thoughts to one interviewer, but admit such concerns to another. Obviously, there is a great potential for information variance when unstructured formats are used. However, information variance can also occur when structured interviews are used. For example, there can be differences in the manner in which clinicians phrase questions, probe about symptoms, or form a therapeutic alliance with the client. Clients themselves can also contribute to information variance by responding inconsistently from one interview to the next. Indeed, much anecdotal evidence supports the notion that some clients report inconsistent information from day to day and interview to interview.

In test-retest reliability investigations, there typically is a specified time period by which the second interview must be completed to decrease the probability that the respondent will change his or her symptom picture between interviews. For most conditions, second reliability interviews are conducted between one day and several weeks after the initial interview. For personality disorders, however, where there is an assumption of longstanding, inflexible, and enduring character traits, reliability intervals can be much longer.

An advantage of the test-retest method is that it approximates true clinical practice, in that clients in some settings can be examined by several clinicians with distinct orientations and interviewing styles. However, this may be burdensome for the client, especially if completion of a lengthy assessment battery is desirable. Conversely, an advantage of the simultaneous rating design is that it fits well with a normal flow of clients and does not cause any sort of clinical disruption. A drawback is that reliability estimates derived from this method are generally somewhat inflated compared to other reliability procedures (because the same interview is rated and thus there is no information variance). Given that both reliability strategies have particular advantages and shortcomings, it has been pointed out that the ideal procedure would be to combine both methods in one study (Grove, 1987). This would involve test-retest of subjects with different interviewers, while other raters make independent simultaneous or post hoc ratings of each interview. Such an approach requires considerable resources and effort, but it may be justified by the potential quality of data obtained.

Results of reliability studies are typically reported by the statistics of percentage agreement and/or the kappa index. Kappa is a better choice, however, because, unlike percentage agreement, kappa corrects for chance levels of agreement. Kappa coefficients range from −1.00 (perfect disagreement) to +1.00 (perfect agreement), with 0 indicating agreement no better or worse than chance. For structured interviews, kappas of .40 or .50 denote the lower limits of acceptability. Values below this cutoff suggest serious limitations of the interviewers, instrument, or diagnostic criteria.

Whereas *reliability* refers to reproducibility and stability, *validity* of a structured diagnostic interview refers to how well it measures the psychiatric conditions it purports to measure. The issue here is one of *accuracy*. Unfortunately, validity is much harder to accurately gauge and document, and thus represents a formidable challenge for psychiatric researchers. A common strategy used is to compare diagnoses generated by a structured interview with diagnoses from another source, such as a clinical interview, chart review, or other testing. However, such an endeavor is fraught with difficulties because these other diagnostic measures often suffer from questionable reliability and validity in the first place. Indeed, a major problem encountered by clinical researchers interested in validity is the lack of a solid criterion diagnosis with which to compare an interview-generated diagnosis. Lack of the so-called *gold standard* severely restricts conclusions drawn from many validity investigations.

Although reliability of a structured interview can be enhanced by improved training of raters and refinement of items, it appears that no quick fix for the validity problem is on the horizon in the field. In fact, lack of diagnostic validity is considered to be among the most serious issues facing the mental health community. This problem is especially noteworthy concerning Axis II personality disorders, which have always been plagued with poorer reliability and validity coefficients than most Axis I conditions (Coolidge & Segal, 1998). Indeed, there has been a long-standing debate among clinical researchers as to the validity of categorical diagnosis of personality disorders (Widiger, 1997) and usefulness of the three clusters (odd-eccentric, dramatic-erratic, anxious-fearful) proposed by the *DSM* system.

In his seminal and well-quoted paper, Spitzer (1983) proposed a method to establish procedural validity of a diagnostic instrument in the absence of clear-cut or flawed external validators. This type of validity refers to agreements between diagnoses made by structured interviews and expert clinicians. As such, Spitzer has postulated a standard diagnosis based on a thorough *clinical* assessment with three components: Longitudinal information, Expert clinicians, and use of All Data (LEAD). Use of the LEAD standard methodology no doubt results in a better criterion measure against which to ascertain validity. Despite many potential gains, this method has been infrequently applied in empirical work to date. Indeed, the time-consuming and thorough nature of such a methodology may be both a strength and limitation.

Another issue to consider is that reliability and validity are not tied to an interview in any direct way and are not constants. Therefore, it is a mistake to talk about the reliability or validity of a structured interview as a permanent attribute. Indeed, reliability and validity of interviewer-administered instruments are affected by many factors, such as the characteristics of the interviewers and the subject sample, type of reliability assessed (e.g., interrater or test-retest), true reliability of the diagnostic criteria, and the criterion measure. In addition, for validity, structured interviews are tied to specific diagnostic criteria. Unfortunately, these interviews do not provide an estimate of how good the criteria actually are, and no diagnostic assessment device can compensate for poor criteria. Each new version of a particular instrument requires its own full evaluation in studies with diverse interviewers, client populations, reliability designs, and comparison groups. Moreover, each particular study requires that some form of reliability and validity be established with the particular interviewers and patient population.

STRUCTURED AND SEMISTRUCTURED INTERVIEWS FOR AXIS I

Diagnostic interviews discussed in this section are the Schedule for Affective Disorders and Schizophrenia, the Diagnostic Interview Schedule for *DSM-IV,* and the Structured Clinical Interview for *DSM-IV* Axis I Disorders.

THE SCHEDULE FOR AFFECTIVE DISORDERS AND SCHIZOPHRENIA

The Schedule for Affective Disorders and Schizophrenia (SADS; Endicott & Spitzer, 1978) is a semistructured diagnostic interview designed to evaluate a range of clinical disorders, with a focus on mood and psychotic disorders. The original

SADS focused on psychiatric symptoms as specified by the Research Diagnostic Criteria (RDC; Spitzer, Endicott, & Robins, 1978). The SADS was developed in conjunction with the RDC, which provided specific inclusion and exclusion criteria for many psychiatric disorders. The RDC predated publication of the *DSM-III* and was a significant predecessor of that system. Many of the specified criteria outlined in the RDC were adopted for inclusion in *DSM-III*. As such, much information derived from SADS interviews can be applied to make *DSM*-based diagnoses. It should be noted, however, that while some sections of the SADS can be easily modified to accommodate *DSM* diagnoses, this is not easy for some disorders because the systems differ in coverage and conceptualizations of some disorders.

The SADS is intended to be used with adult psychiatric respondents and to be administered by trained mental health professionals. It focuses heavily on the differential diagnosis of mood and psychotic disorders but ancillary coverage is provided for anxiety symptoms, alcohol and drug use, treatment history, and antisocial traits. The full SADS is divided into two parts, each focusing on a different period of the respondent's life. Before administering those sections, a brief overview of the respondent's background and psychiatric problems is elicited in an open-ended inquiry. Then, Part I provides for a thorough evaluation of *current* psychiatric problems and concomitant functional impairment. Psychosocial functioning during the week *preceding* the interview is also assessed. A unique feature of the SADS is that for the current episode, symptoms are rated when they were at their worst levels to increase diagnostic sensitivity and validity. In contrast, Part II evaluates *past* episodes of psychopathology and treatment. Overall, the SADS covers more than 20 diagnoses in a systematic and comprehensive fashion and provides for diagnosis of both current and lifetime psychiatric disorders. Examples include schizophrenia (with six subtypes), schizoaffective disorder, manic disorder, hypomanic disorder, major depressive disorder (with eleven subtypes), minor depressive disorder, panic disorder, obsessive-compulsive disorder, phobic disorder, alcoholism, and antisocial personality disorder. In addition to collecting information to diagnose specific disorders, the SADS also yields scores for eight clinically relevant dimensional summary scales that were identified through factor analysis: Depressive Mood and Ideation, Endogenous Features, Depressive-Associated Features, Suicidal Ideation and Behavior, Anxiety, Manic Syndrome, Delusions-Hallucinations, and Formal Thought Disorder (Endicott & Spitzer, 1978).

In the SADS, questions are clustered according to specific diagnoses, which enables administration to simulate the natural flow characteristic of skilled unstructured interviews. For each disorder, standard probes are specified to evaluate specific symptoms of that disorder. Questions are either dichotomous or rated on a Likert scale, which allows for uniform documentation of levels of severity, persistence, and functional impairment associated with each symptom. For example, the mania syndrome criteria of *grandiosity* is rated from "(1) not at all or decreased self-esteem" to "(6) extremely preoccupied with grandiose delusions." Items are rated 0 if no information is available or the item is not applicable. To supplement patient self-report and obtain the most accurate symptom picture, the SADS allows for consideration of all available sources of information (i.e., chart records, input from relatives). Additionally, SADS interviewers are instructed to ask as many general and specific probes and gently challenge as necessary to accurately rate each symptom. To reduce length of administration and evaluation of symptoms that are not diagnostically significant, many diagnostic sections begin with screening questions, which provide for ("skip-outs" to the next section if the respondent shows no evidence of having the disorder. Administration of the SADS typically takes between 1.5 and 2.5 hours but can be extended if the respondent is currently severely impaired or has an extensive psychiatric history. After all symptoms are rated and the interview is completed, interviewers consult the RDC and make diagnostic appraisals according to specified criteria. At present, no reliable computer scoring applications have been designed because of the complex nature of the diagnostic process and the SADS' strong reliance on clinical judgment.

As noted, the SADS was designed for use by trained clinicians. Indeed, considerable clinical judgment, interviewing skills, and familiarity with diagnostic criteria and psychiatric symptoms are requisite for competent administration of the SADS. As such, it is recommended that the SADS be given only by professionals with graduate degrees and clinical experience, such as clinical psychologists, psychiatrists, and psychiatric social workers (Endicott & Spitzer, 1978). Training in the SADS is intensive and can encompass several weeks. The process includes reading articles about the SADS and the RDC and reviewing the most recent SADS manual. Practice is then provided in rating written case vignettes and videotaped SADS interviews. Additionally, trainees typically watch and score live interviews as if participating in a reliability study with a simultaneous-rating design. Throughout, discussion and clarification with expert interviewers concerning diagnostic disagreements or difficulties add to the experience. Finally, trainees conduct their own SADS interviews, which are observed and critiqued by the expert trainers.

Numerous additional versions of the SADS have been devised, each with a distinct focus and purpose. Perhaps the most common is the SADS-L (Lifetime version), which can be used to make both current and lifetime diagnoses but has significantly less details about current psychopathology than the full SADS. The SADS-L generally is used with nonpsychiatric samples, where there is no assumption of a significant current disturbance. Reduced emphasis on current symptoms of the SADS-L results in a quicker administration time. Also popular is the SADS-C (Change version), which provides for measurement of change in symptom levels over time that can be used in treatment planning and outcome studies. For family studies, the Family History-RDC (FH-RDC) version elicits diagnostic data from family members about other relatives who are not present.

Early psychometric data on the SADS came from its developers, who evaluated interrater reliability of SADS summary scales in two samples (Endicott & Spitzer, 1978). In the first study, 150 inpatients were jointly evaluated by two raters who made independent diagnostic appraisals. Reliability was excellent, with intraclass correlation coefficients (ICC) ranging from .82 (formal thought disorder) to .99 (manic syndrome). Similarly, internal consistency was high for all composite scales except formal thought disorder and anxiety. In the second study, which employed a test-retest design with 60 hospitalized subjects, agreement rates were slightly lower than in the joint evaluations, but still substantial for all summary scales except formal thought disorder (ICC = .49). With the same sample, Spitzer et al. (1978) reported test-retest concordance rates for many major diagnostic categories of the RDC. Agreement rates (kappa coefficients) were high for all eight current disorders, ranging from .65 for schizophrenia to 1.00 for alcoholism, whereas kappas for lifetime diagnoses tended to be lower, ranging from .40 for bipolar I to .95 for alcoholism. In a similar test-retest project with a nonpatient sample, reliability generally was good for the SADS-L (lifetime) version (Andreason et al., 1981). Later, Andreason et al. (1982) used a videotape design with eight clients selected from five centers. Overall, 36 raters viewed and rated the tapes. Results indicated excellent agreement rates for schizophrenia (ICC = 1.00) and major depressive disorder (.84), whereas a moderate value was found for manic disorder (.64). Subtypes of major depression (such as psychotic, endogenous, agitated) were also generally rated with acceptable reliability. Taken together, these studies suggest that sufficiently high diagnostic reliability can be achieved for summary scales and most major diagnoses of the SADS.

The SADS has been translated into several languages, it has been widely used in clinical research over the past three decades, and there is a large body of empirical data associated with it. As such, it is often the instrument of choice for clinical researchers interested in depression, schizophrenia, and anxiety. The extensive subtyping of disorders provided by the SADS is also highly valued by clinical researchers. However, because of its length and complexity, the SADS is less often chosen for use in pure clinical settings.

THE DIAGNOSTIC INTERVIEW SCHEDULE FOR *DSM-IV*

The Diagnostic Interview Schedule for *DSM-IV* (DIS-IV) is a *fully structured* diagnostic interview specifically designed for use by lay, nonprofessional interviewers. In 1978, development of the original DIS was begun by researchers at the Washington University Department of Psychiatry in St. Louis at the request of the National Institute of Mental Health (NIMH). At that time, the NIMH Division of Biometry and Epidemiology was planning a set of large-scale, multicenter epidemiological investigations of mental illness in the general adult population in America as part of its Epidemiological Catchment Area Program. Variables to be assessed included incidence and prevalence of many specific psychiatric disorders and utilization profiles of health and mental health services. With this grand purpose in mind, development of a structured interview that could be administered by nonclinicians was imperative because of the prohibitive cost of using professional clinicians for these expansive community studies. As a result, the DIS was designed as a fully structured diagnostic interview that specifies all questions and probes and minimizes the amount of clinical judgment and experience required to administer it. In fact, the DIS was explicitly crafted so that it can be administered and scored by lay, nonprofessional interviewers.

Since its inception as a draft version in 1978, there have been several major revisions of the original DIS. For example, the original DIS covered criteria for only 31 *DSM-III* diagnoses, with later versions adding more disorders. Another refinement was the addition of a comprehensive set of training materials, including mock interviews, professional training videotapes, and extensive training courses. Perhaps most importantly, DIS questions and diagnostic algorithms were revamped to match updated criteria and establish compatibility with *DSM-III-R* (Version DIS-III-R; Robins, Helzer, Cottler, & Goldring, 1989) and *DSM-IV* (Version DIS-IV; Robins, Cottler, Bucholz, & Compton, 1996). The DIS has been translated into many languages and applied in many countries, and enjoys widespread use in diverse clinical research, especially in large-scale studies.

As noted previously, the DIS is a fully structured interview, which can be administered by nonclinician or lay interviewers. The paper and pencil version of the DIS is no longer recommended because of its complicated format. Instead, a computerized version of the DIS-IV (C-DIS) is recommended. Notably, computerized administration may be interviewer-administered or self-administered. In both formats, the exact wording of all symptom questions and follow-up probes is delineated in an interview book, items are read (or presented) verbatim to the respondent in a standardized order, and clarification or rephrasing of questions is discouraged, although DIS interviewers can repeat any question as necessary to ensure that it is understood by the respondent. All DIS questions are written to be closed-ended, and replies are coded with a forced choice yes/no format, which eliminates the need for clinical judgment to rate responses. Given the yes/no format, clarification of responses is not required. The DIS gathers all necessary information about the subject from the subject, and collateral sources of information are not used, which again obviates the need for advanced clinical skills. The DIS is self-contained and covers all necessary symptoms to make many *DSM-IV* diagnoses. Responses are directly entered into a database during the interview, and diagnosis is made according to the explicit rules of the *DSM-IV* diagnostic system.

Because the DIS was designed for epidemiological research with normative samples, DIS interviewers do not elicit a presenting problem or chief complaint from the subject, as would be typical in unstructured clinical interviews. Rather, DIS interviews begin by asking questions about symptoms in a standardized order. Like other structured interviews, the DIS has sections that cover different disorders. Each diagnostic section is independent, except where one diagnosis preempts another. Once a symptom is reported to be present, further closed-ended questions are pursued to assess additional diagnostically relevant information such as severity, frequency, time frame, and possibility of organic etiology of the symptom. The DIS includes a set of core questions that are asked of each respondent; the core questions are followed by contingent questions administered only if the preceding core question is endorsed. DIS interviewers use a probe flowchart that indicates which probes to use in which circumstances.

For each symptom, the respondent is asked to state whether it has ever been present and how recently. All data about presence/absence of symptoms and time frames of occurrence are coded and then entered into a computer for scoring. Consistent with its use of lay interviewers who may not be familiar with the *DSM-IV* or psychiatric diagnosis, diagnostic output of the DIS is generated by a computer that analyzes the coded data from the completed interview. Output of the computer program provides estimates of prevalence for two periods: current and lifetime.

Because of its highly structured format, full administration of the DIS-IV interview typically requires between 90 and 120 minutes. Administration can be even longer with severely ill or loquacious subjects. To shorten administration time, it is possible to drop evaluation of disorders that are not of interest in a particular study. Another option is to drop further questioning for a particular disorder after it is clear that the threshold number of symptoms needed for diagnosis will not be met. Thus, modules can be dropped, shortened, or asked in full depending on the specific needs of the researchers.

Although designed for use by lay administrators, training for competent administration of the DIS is intensive and includes several components. Trainees typically attend a one-week training program at Washington University during which they review the DIS manual; listen to didactic presentations about the format, structure, and conventions of the DIS; view videotaped vignettes; and complete workbook exercises. Role-play practice interviews are also conducted with extensive feedback and review to ensure that trainees master the material. Finally, additional supervised practice is recommended.

The psychometric properties of the original DIS and its revisions have been evaluated in numerous investigations. Initial reliability results from St. Louis were encouraging (Robins, Helzer, Croughan, & Ratcliff, 1981), as concordance between lay administration and psychiatrist administration was assessed in a test-retest design with 216 clients. Psychiatrist interviews were used as the criterion measure. For *DSM-III* diagnoses, the mean kappa was .69, mean sensitivity was 75%, and mean specificity was 94%. In another study (Blouin, Perez, & Blouin, 1988), 80 psychiatric clients and 20 normal controls completed a self-administered computerized version of the DIS (C-DIS) on two occasions. Results showed generally acceptable test-retest reliability for the computerized DIS. With a similar test-retest design, Semler et al. (1987) examined 60 psychiatric inpatients on two occasions with a mean interval of 1.7 days. Results indicated respectable agreement values (kappa over .5) for 11 *DSM-III* lifetime diagnoses, with lower values found for dysthymic disorder (.47) and generalized anxiety disorder (.41). Further, Semler et al. noted that their results were improved over earlier versions of the DIS, especially for anxiety disorders. Vandiver and Sher (1991) investigated the temporal stability of the DIS by administering it to 486 college students at baseline and again approximately nine months later. Findings suggested that the DIS is a moderately reliable instrument for evaluating lifetime psychopathology, although reliability estimates tended to be lower for 12-month and 6-month diagnoses than for lifetime diagnoses. Unreliability was attributed to "borderline" cases, which historically have complicated reliability in categorical diagnostic systems.

Validity of the DIS has been evaluated in several studies that typically compare DIS diagnoses to clinician-generated diagnoses. Taken together, results have generally been quite variable depending on the sample, diagnosis, and criterion measure. An early study by Robins, Helzer, Ratcliff, and Seyfried (1982) compared DIS diagnoses to medical chart diagnoses, with generally poor concordance. With lay administration, mean agreement was 55%, whereas psychiatrist-administered DIS resulted in a 63% success rate. Anthony et al. (1985) compared lay-administered DIS diagnoses to standardized *DSM-III* diagnoses made by psychiatrists in a sample of 810 community residents. Their results also were discouraging, with agreement rates (kappa) ranging between −.02 (panic disorder) and .35 (alcohol-use disorder), with a mean of .15. In another study, psychiatrist-administered DIS diagnoses were examined in relation to clinical diagnoses from a *DSM-III* checklist (Helzer et al., 1985). Results were generally higher in this report, as kappas ranged from .12 to .63, with an average unweighted kappa of .40.

Erdman et al. (1987) used clinical diagnosis based on chart review and case staffing as the criterion measure to compare against DIS-generated diagnosis. Agreement (kappas) between clinical diagnoses and current DIS diagnoses for 220 psychiatric clients ranged from −.03 (social phobia) to .39 (obsessive-compulsive disorder), with 9 of 14 diagnoses achieving kappas below .20. Rates for lifetime DIS diagnoses were similarly poor, ranging from −.03 (schizophreniform) to .39 (bipolar disorder). Application of the DIS in pure clinical settings (as opposed to epidemiological research) has been a cause for some concern because of the rather poor relationship between DIS diagnoses and clinical diagnosis (Erdman et al., 1987). It is reiterated here, however, that chart or psychiatrist diagnoses are not the ideal gold standard with which to compare DIS diagnoses to assess validity, as problems with diagnoses from unstructured interviews precipitated development of structured interviews initially.

Overall, the DIS has proven to be a popular diagnostic assessment tool, especially for large-scale epidemiological research. The DIS has been translated into more than a dozen languages. It is used in many countries for epidemiological research, and it served as the basis for the Composite International Diagnostic Interview (CIDI/DIS) used by the World Health Organization. Presently, the DIS-IV is the only well-validated case-finding strategy that can make *DSM-IV* diagnoses in large-scale epidemiological research. Like earlier versions, the DIS-IV can be expected to enjoy widespread application in psychiatric research for many years to come. For information on DIS materials, training, and related procedures, consult the DIS Web site at http://epi.wustl.edu.

For MT

THE STRUCTURED CLINICAL INTERVIEW FOR *DSM-IV* AXIS I DISORDERS

The Structured Clinical Interview for *DSM-IV* Axis I Disorders (SCID-I) is a flexible, semistructured diagnostic interview designed for use by trained clinicians to diagnose most adult *DSM-IV* Axis I mental disorders. The current version is the product of many prior editions that were updated and modified over time. With each revision, the SCID has been reworked to enhance accuracy and ease of use. It is used primarily with adult respondents because of the language, format, coverage, and type of responses needed for administration. Since its inception, the SCID has enjoyed widespread popularity as an instrument to obtain reliable and valid psychiatric diagnoses for clinical, research, and training purposes. It has been translated into 12 languages and has been applied successfully in research studies in many countries.

The original SCID was designed for application in both research and clinical settings. Recently, the SCID was split into two distinct versions: the Research Version and the Clinician Version. The Research Version covers more disorders, subtypes, and course specifiers than the Clinician Version and, therefore, takes longer to complete. The benefit, however, is that it provides for a wealth of diagnostic data that is particularly valued by clinical researchers.

The Clinician Version of the SCID (SCID-CV; First, Spitzer, Gibbon, & Williams, 1997a) is designed for use in clinical settings. It has been trimmed down to encompass only those *DSM-IV* disorders that are most typically seen in clinical practice and can further be abbreviated on a module-by-module basis. The SCID-CV contains six self-contained modules of major diagnostic categories (mood episodes, psychotic symptoms, psychotic disorders, mood disorders, substance use disorders, and anxiety and other disorders). Specific *DSM-IV* diagnoses covered by the SCID-CV are shown in Table 3.1. The modular design of the SCID-CV is a major strength of the instrument because administration can be customized easily to meet the unique needs of the user. For example, the SCID can be shortened or lengthened to include only those categories of interest, and the order of modules can be altered.

The format and sequence of the SCID are designed to approximate the flowchart and decision trees followed by experienced diagnostic interviewers. The SCID begins with an open-ended overview portion, during which the development and

Table 3.1

Diagnoses Covered by the Structured Clinical Interview for
DSM-IV Axis I Disorders—Clinician Version

Mood Disorders
    Bipolar I disorder
    Bipolar II disorder
    Cyclothymic disorder
    Bipolar disorder NOS
    Major depressive disorder
    Dysthymic disorder
    Depressive disorder NOS
    Mood disorder due to a GMC
    Alcohol-induced mood disorder
    Other substance-induced mood disorder

Schizophrenia and Other Psychotic Disorders
    Schizophrenia
    Schizophreniform disorder
    Schizoaffective disorder
    Delusional disorder
    Brief psychotic disorder
    Psychotic disorder due to a GMC with delusions
    Psychotic disorder due to a GMC with hallucinations
    Alcohol-induced psychotic disorder with delusions
    Alcohol-induced psychotic disorder with hallucinations
    Other substance-induced psychotic disorder with delusions
    Other substance-induced psychotic disorder with hallucinations
    Psychotic disorder NOS

Substance Use Disorders
    Alcohol abuse/alcohol dependence
    Amphetamine abuse/amphetamine dependence
    Cannabis abuse/cannabis dependence
    Cocaine abuse/cocaine dependence
    Hallucinogen abuse/hallucinogen dependence
    Inhalant abuse/inhalant dependence
    Opioid abuse/opioid dependence
    Phencyclidine abuse/phencyclidine dependence
    Sedative, hypnotic, or anxiolytic abuse/sedative, hypnotic, or anxiolytic dependence
    Other (or unknown) substance abuse/other (or unknown) substance

Anxiety Disorders
    Panic disorder with agoraphobia
    Panic disorder without agoraphobia
    Obsessive-compulsive disorder
    Posttraumatic stress disorder
    Anxiety disorder NOS
    Anxiety disorder due to a GMC
    Alcohol-induced anxiety disorder
    Other substance-induced anxiety disorder
    Agoraphobia without history of panic disorder
    Social phobia
    Specific phobia
    Generalized anxiety disorder

Table 3.1 *(Continued)*

Somatoform Disorders
   Somatization disorder
   Undifferentiated somatoform disorder
   Hypochondriasis
   Body dysmorphic disorder

Eating Disorders
   Anorexia nervosa
   Bulimia nervosa

Adjustment Disorders
   Adjustment disorder with depressed mood
   Adjustment disorder with anxiety
   Adjustment disorder with mixed anxiety and depressed mood
   Adjustment disorder with disturbance of conduct
   Adjustment disorder with mixed disturbance of emotions and conduct
   Unspecified adjustment disorder

Note: NOS = Not otherwise specified; GMC = General medical condition.

history of the present psychological disturbance are elicited and tentative diagnostic hypotheses are generated. Then the SCID systematically presents modules that allow for assessment of specific disorders and symptoms. Most disorders are evaluated for two periods: current (meets criteria for previous month) and lifetime (ever-met criteria).

Consistent with its ties to *DSM-IV*, formal diagnostic criteria are included in the SCID booklet, thus permitting interviewers to see the exact criteria to which the SCID questions pertain. This unique feature makes the SCID an excellent training device for clinicians because it facilitates the learning of diagnostic criteria and appropriate probes. The SCID has many open-ended prompts that encourage respondents to elaborate freely about their symptoms. At times, open-ended prompts are followed by closed-ended questions to fully clarify a particular symptom. Although the SCID provides structure to cover criteria for each disorder, its flexible semistructured format provides significant latitude for interviewers to restate questions, ask for further clarification, probe, and challenge if the initial prompt was misunderstood by the interviewee or clarification is needed to fully rate a symptom. SCID interviewers are encouraged to use all sources of information about a respondent, and gentle challenging of the respondent is encouraged if discrepant information is suspected.

Each symptom criterion is rated as −, +, or ?. The minus (−) indicates that the symptom was absent or below threshold, whereas the plus sign (+) means that the symptom was present and clinically significant. The question mark (?) denotes that inadequate information was obtained to code the symptom. The SCID flowchart instructs interviewers to "skip-out" of a particular diagnostic section when essential symptoms are judged to be below threshold or absent. These skip-outs result in decreased time of administration, as well as the passing over of items with no diagnostic significance. Administration of the SCID is typically completed in one session and involves between 45 and 90 minutes, although application with a respondent manifesting extensive current and past psychopathology ı add considerable length. After administration is completed, all current and ıst disorders for criteria met are listed on a diagnostic summary sheet.

The SCID is optimally administered by trained clinicians who have knowledge about psychopathology, *DSM-IV* criteria, and diagnostic interviewing. With its semistructured format, proper administration often requires that interviewers restate or clarify questions in ways that are sometimes not clearly outlined in the manual to judge accurately if a particular symptom criterion has been met. The task requires that SCID assessors have a working knowledge of psychopathology and *DSM-IV* as well as basic interviewing skills. Standard procedures for training to use the SCID include carefully reading the SCID Users Guide (First, Spitzer, Gibbon, & Williams, 1997b), reviewing the SCID administration booklet and score sheet, viewing SCID videotape training materials that are available from the SCID authors, and conducting many role-playing practice administrations with extensive feedback discussions. Next, trainees may administer the SCID to representative participants who are jointly rated so that a discussion about sources of disagreements can ensue. In research settings with rich resources, a formal test-retest reliability study may also be done.

The reliability of the SCID in adult populations with diverse disorders has been evaluated in a number of investigations. A review of this literature indicated generally high reliability values for most major disorders, despite widely varied subject samples and experimental designs (see Segal, Hersen, & Van Hasselt, 1994), and these data are summarized here. Most impressive is an extensive multisite project, which involved test-retest reliability interviews of 592 subjects in four patient and two nonpatient sites in the United States and one patient site in Germany (Williams et al., 1992). Randomly matched pairs of two professionals independently evaluated and rated the same subject within a two-week period. The sample was divided into patient ($n = 390$) and nonpatient ($n = 202$) subjects for whom levels of agreement for current and lifetime disorders were reported. Results for the patient sample indicated that kappas for current and lifetime disorders ranged from a low of .40 (dysthymia) to a high of .86 (bulimia nervosa). Kappas were above .60 for most of the major disorders (e.g., bipolar disorder = .84; alcohol abuse/dependence = .75; schizophrenia = .65; major depression = .64). Combining all disorders yielded mean kappas of .61 for current and .68 for lifetime disorders. Results for the nonpatient sample suggested poorer concordance, with an overall weighted kappa of .37 for current and .51 for lifetime disorders. Overall, obtained kappas were judged to be comparable to data from other structured interviews (Williams et al., 1992), namely the SADS and DIS.

Riskind, Beck, Berchick, Brown, and Steer (1987) videotaped 75 psychiatric outpatients to assess interrater reliability of major depression and generalized anxiety disorder. Results showed that the SCID can reliably differentiate between the two disorders (major depression, kappa = .72; generalized anxiety disorder, kappa = .79). Skre, Onstad, Torgerson, and Kringlen (1991) investigated reliability using audiotaped SCID interviews of 54 Norwegian adults. Excellent interrater agreement (kappa above .80) was obtained for many disorders (e.g., schizophrenia, major depression, dysthymia, generalized anxiety disorder, panic disorder, alcohol abuse, and other nonalcohol abuse disorder), whereas moderate levels (kappa between .70 and .80) were found for most other major conditions (e.g., cyclothymia, PTSD, social phobia, simple phobia, bipolar disorder, and adjustment disorder). Poor reliability was indicated for obsessive-compulsive disorder (kappa = .40), agoraphobia without history of panic disorder (.32), and somato-form disorder (–.03). Interestingly, Skre et al. also tested reliability for combina-tions of diagnoses (e.g., mood and anxiety disorders). Reliability was generally favorable for combinations of two disorders (range = .53 to 1.00) and poorer but still decent for most combinations of three disorders (range = .38 to .87).

In our earlier review (Segal et al., 1994), we called for increased evaluation of the reliability of the SCID in minority populations, including older adults, and our research group has conducted two such studies. In the first study (Segal, Hersen, Van Hasselt, Kabacoff, & Roth, 1993), participants consisted of older psy-chiatric inpatients and outpatients (*N* = 33; *M* age = 67.3 years). SCID interviews were administered by master's-level clinicians, and audiotaped for retrospective review by an independent rater. Reliability estimates (kappa) were calculated for current major depression (47% base rate, kappa = .70), the broad diagnostic cate-gory of anxiety disorder (15% base rate, kappa = .77), and the broad category of somatoform disorder (12% base rate, kappa = 1.0). The second investigation (Segal, Kabacoff, Hersen, Van Hasselt, & Ryan, 1995) targeted older outpatients exclusively (*N* = 40; *M* age = 67.1 years) and evaluated a larger number of diag-noses. Diagnostic concordance was determined for the general groupings of mood disorder (60% base rate), anxiety disorder (25% base rate), somatoform disorder (9% base rate), and psychoactive substance use disorder (9% base rate). Three spe-cific disorders were evaluated: major depressive disorder (58% base rate), dys-thymia (9% base rate), and panic disorder (15% base rate). Agreement for the broad diagnostic group of somatoform disorder (kappa = .84) was almost perfect, and concordance was substantial for mood disorder (kappa = .79) and anxiety disorder (kappa = .73). Psychoactive substance use disorder (kappa = .23) had the lowest rate, reflecting poor agreement. For specific disorders, kappas were high for major depressive disorder (kappa = .90) and panic disorder (.80), but agree-ment for dysthymia (.53) was moderate. Taken together, these two studies suggest that reliability of the SCID administered by graduate-level clinicians to older adults appears very promising, although additional research with larger samples obviously is warranted.

Overall, the SCID is a widely used and respected assessment tool. Computer-assisted clinician-administered versions of the SCID-CV and SCID Research Ver-sion are available. A self-administered computerized screening version of the SCID, called the SCID-Screen-PQ, is also available, but it does not produce final diagnoses. Rather, likely diagnoses are further evaluated by a full SCID interview or a clinical evaluation. Finally, a childhood version of the SCID designed for clin-ical research has been developed—the Structured Clinical Interview for *DSM-IV*, Childhood Diagnoses (KID-SCID). For more information on the SCID, see the SCID Web site at www.scid4.org.

SEMISTRUCTURED INTERVIEWS FOR AXIS II

This section focuses on instruments that are consistent with *DSM-IV* conceptual-izations and yield as part of their output a wide range of personality disorder diagnoses. Interestingly, the diagnostic category of *personality disorders* has a long history, but research attention was limited until the creation of the multiaxial di-agnostic system in *DSM-III* (APA, 1980). Instruments reviewed include the Struc-tured Interview for *DSM-IV* Personality, the International Personality Disorder

Examination, and the Structured Clinical Interview for *DSM-IV* Axis II Personality Disorders. Personality disorders covered by the *DSM-IV* version of each instrument are shown in Table 3.2.

THE STRUCTURED INTERVIEW FOR *DSM-IV* PERSONALITY

The Structured Interview for *DSM-IV* Personality (SIDP-IV; Pfohl, Blum, & Zimmerman, 1995) is a comprehensive semistructured diagnostic interview for personality disorders as conceptualized by the *DSM-IV* system. The SIDP-IV covers 14 *DSM-IV* Axis II diagnoses, including the 10 standard personality disorders, mixed personality disorder, as well as self-defeating, depressive, and negativistic personality disorders. Before the SIDP-IV structured interview, a full evaluation of current mental state or Axis I conditions is required (Pfohl et al., 1995). This is not surprising given that self-report of enduring personality characteristics can be seriously compromised in a respondent who is experiencing acute psychopathology. Indeed, the aim of all personality assessment measures is to rate the respondent's typical, habitual, and lifelong personal functioning rather than acute or temporary states.

Interestingly, the SIDP-IV does not cover *DSM* personality categories on a disorder-by-disorder basis. Rather, *DSM-IV* personality disorder criteria are reflected in items that are grouped according to 10 topical sections that reflect a different dimension of personality functioning, including: interests and activities,

Table 3.2
Personality Disorders Covered by the SCID-II, IPDE, and SIDP-IV

Personality Disorders	Instrument		
	SCID-II	IPDE	SIDP-IV
Cluster A			
Paranoid	X	X	X
Schizoid	X	X	X
Schizotypal	X	X	X
Cluster B			
Antisocial	X	X	X
Borderline	X	X	X
Histrionic	X	X	X
Narcissistic	X	X	X
Cluster C			
Avoidant	X	X	X
Dependent	X	X	X
Obsessive-compulsive	X	X	X
Other Personality Disorders			
Mixed or personality disorder NOS	X	X	X
Sadistic (DSM-III-R)	No	No	No
Self-defeating (DSM-III-R)	No	No	X
Depressive (DSM-IV Appendix B)	X	No	X
Negativistic (passive-aggressive; DSM-IV Appendix B)	X	No	X

work style, close relationships, social relationships, emotions, observational criteria, self-perception, perception of others, stress and anger, and social conformity (Pfohl et al., 1995). It should be noted that these categories are not scored or rated in any way. Rather, they reflect broad areas of personal functioning under which personality disorder items can logically be subsumed.

Each SIDP-IV question corresponds to a unique *DSM-IV* Axis II criterion, except that one item addresses two criteria. An attractive feature is that the specific *DSM-IV* criterion associated with each question is provided for interviewers to easily see and reference. All questions are always administered to the client, and there are no skip-out options. Most questions are conversational in tone and open-ended to encourage respondents to talk about their *usual* behaviors and long-term functioning. In fact, respondents are specifically instructed to focus on their typical or habitual behavior when addressing each item and are prompted to "remember what you are like when you are your usual self." It is possible, however, that this distinction may be difficult for some psychiatrically impaired clients to make. Based on patient responses, each criterion is rated on a scale with four anchor points. A rating of 0 indicates that the criterion was not present, a 1 corresponds to a subthreshold level where there is some evidence of the trait but it is not sufficiently prominent, a 2 refers to the criterion being present for most of the last five years, and a 3 signifies a strongly present and debilitating level. The SIDP-IV requires that a trait be prominent for most of the last five years to be considered a part of the respondent's personality. This five-year rule helps ensure that the particular personality characteristic is stable and of long duration as required by the General Diagnostic Criteria for a Personality Disorder described in *DSM-IV*.

A strong point of the organizational format by personality dimensions (rather than by disorders) is that data for *specific* diagnoses are minimized until final ratings have been collated on the summary sheet. This feature can potentially reduce interviewer biases, such as the halo effect or changing thresholds, if it is obvious that a subject needs to meet one additional criterion to make the diagnosis. Like the SADS and SCID, significant clinical judgment is required to properly administer the SIDP-IV because interviewers are expected to ask additional questions to clarify patient responses when necessary. Also, data are not limited to self-report; rather, chart records and significant others such as relatives and friends who know the patient well should be consulted when available, and a standard informed consent is included for informant interviews. Such collateral information is particularly prized when evaluating personality-disordered individuals who may lack insight into their own maladaptive personality traits and distort facts about their strengths and limitations. Moreover, informants can provide diagnostic data that can help resolve the state/trait distinction about specific criterion behaviors.

If discrepancies between sources of information are noted, interviewers must consider all data and use their own judgment to determine veracity of each source. Making this distinction can be one of the challenges faced by SIDP-IV administrators. Given the multiple sources of diagnostic data, final ratings are made *after* all sources of information are considered. Such ratings are then transcribed onto a summary sheet that lists each criterion organized by personality disorder, and formal diagnoses are assigned. As required by the *DSM*, diagnoses are made only if the minimum number of criteria (or threshold) has been met for that particular disorder.

Minimum qualifications for competent administration consist of an interviewer with an undergraduate degree in the social sciences and six months' experience with diagnostic interviewing. Moreover, SIDP-IV developers note that such an interviewer requires an additional one month of specialized training and practice with the SIDP to become a competent interviewer (Pfohl et al., 1995). Administrators are required to possess an understanding of manifest psychopathology and the typical presentation and course of Axis I and II disorders. Training tapes and workshop information are available from the instrument authors. Overall, the SIDP typically requires 60 to 90 minutes for the patient interview, 20 minutes for interview of significant informants, and approximately 20 minutes to complete the summary score sheet.

Early interrater reliability values for the original SIDP were reported by its developers (Stangl, Pfohl, Zimmerman, Bowers, & Corentahl, 1985). In their study, psychiatric inpatients were independently rated by two interviewers ($N = 43$ with simultaneous ratings, $N = 20$ with test-retest ratings). Kappas for specific disorders diagnosed at least five times varied widely: avoidant (.45), schizotypal (.62), histrionic (.75), borderline (.85), and dependent (.90). Such values indicate excellent agreement, with the exception of avoidant personality disorder. Evidence for convergent validity between SIDP diagnoses and appropriate MMPI subscales was also adequately documented (Stangl et al., 1985).

Using a joint interview design, Nazikian, Rudd, Edwards, and Jackson (1990) investigated reliability of the SIDP in a sample of 10 inpatients and reported an overall kappa of .50. In contrast, high agreement was found when SIDP ratings were converted into trait percentage scores. Hogg, Jackson, Rudd, and Edwards (1990) studied personality disorders in recent onset schizophrenics and reported an overall kappa of .59 and a similarly adequate figure for the only specific disorder evaluated, schizotypal (.54). Their analysis of trait ratings (rather than categorical diagnoses) revealed widely discrepant results. Also employing a joint-reliability design, Brent, Zelenak, Bukstein, and Brown (1990) examined reliability of the SIDP in a sample of 23 depressed adolescents. Weighted kappas ranged from .24 for borderline to 1.0 for schizoid, with a mean kappa of .49. Jackson, Gazis, Rudd, and Edwards (1991) assessed interclinician agreement of the SIDP in psychiatric inpatients, reporting excellent kappas for histrionic (.70) and borderline (.77), moderate kappas for paranoid (.61) and schizotypal (.67), and a tolerable result for dependent (.42).

Validity of the SIDP has been assessed in several studies in which SIDP diagnoses typically were compared to diagnoses from self-report Axis II instruments. Generally poor diagnostic concordance has been documented between the SIDP and the self-report Millon Clinical Multiaxial Inventory (MCMI) with varied settings and methodologies (Hogg et al., 1990; Jackson et al., 1991; Miller, Streiner, & Parkinson, 1992; Nazikian et al., 1990; Turley, Bates, Edwards, & Jackson, 1992). It should be noted, however, that these studies may not be a fair test of the validity of the SIDP because of the differing nature of the instruments (interview vs. self-report) and the questionable validity of self-report personality disorder measures. Unfortunately, few studies exist in which SIDP diagnoses are compared to findings from other validated structured interviews or diagnoses made according to Spitzer's (1983) LEAD standard. Such studies are needed to fully document the validity of the SIDP for Axis II diagnoses and will undoubtedly enhance our understanding of the instrument. Moreover, most of the literature concerning the instrument pertains to the earlier versions, not the current SIDP-IV. Consequently, new studies investigating reliability and validity must be conducted.

Several additional versions of the SIDP are available and deserve mention. The SIDP-IV Modular Version uses the same items as the standard SIDP-IV but organizes them by personality disorders that are covered one at a time rather than by thematic area. This format lends itself to easy tailoring and shortening of the instrument as users can assess only those specific disorders of interest. The Self-Report Supplement for the SIDP-IV, a paper and pencil test, can provide research data that are not influenced by interviewers and can allow comparisons between different raters. Finally, the Super SIDP is a comprehensive version that allows clinicians and researchers to make diagnoses according to three diagnostic systems: *DSM-III-R, DSM-IV,* and the International Classification of Disease, 10th edition (ICD-10). This Super SIDP allows for useful comparisons between older and current *DSM* criteria to empirically evaluate the results of changes in disorder conceptualization and criterion operationalization. Further, its ties to the ICD system will enhance its application in international research on personality disorders. Although studies are required to formally test the psychometric properties of each of these new devices, it is likely that such instruments will prove valuable and psychometrically sound and be applied to enhance research on personality disorders for many years to come.

THE INTERNATIONAL PERSONALITY DISORDER EXAMINATION

The International Personality Disorder Examination (IPDE; Loranger, 1999) is an extensive, semistructured diagnostic interview administered by experienced clinicians to evaluate personality disorders. It is compatible with the *DSM-IV* and ICD-10 diagnostic schemes and was developed for the worldwide study of personality disorders. Notably, the IPDE seeks to secure reliable and uniform diagnosis of personality disorders that is both internationally and cross-culturally acceptable. The IPDE is an outgrowth of the Personality Disorder Examination (PDE), which was developed and refined over a five-year period from 1983 to 1988 (Loranger, Hirschfeld, Sartorius, & Regier, 1991). The first pilot version was tied to *DSM-III* classification system and was successfully field-tested by Loranger, Susman, Oldham, and Russakoff (1987). A revision of that early instrument was soon updated for draft criteria of the *DSM-III-R* and also favorably evaluated in a larger clinical trial. While some pilot items remain intact in the current version, others were replaced, refined, or dropped (Loranger et al., 1991), and the IPDE is substantially different from its predecessors. Impetus for the development of the IPDE came from the WHO and the U.S. Alcohol, Drug Abuse, and Mental Health Administration (ADAMHA) in their joint effort aimed at producing standardized assessment instruments to measure mental disorders on a worldwide basis. The PDE was chosen as the basis for an international instrument capable of diagnosing personality disorders. The IPDE was subsequently produced to tap *DSM-IV* and ICD-10 personality disorder criteria.

Items reflecting personality disorder criteria according to the *DSM* and ICD systems are grouped into six thematic headings: Work, Self, Interpersonal Relationships, Affects, Reality Testing, and Impulse Control (Loranger et al., 1991). Like the SIDP-IV, disorders are not covered on a one-by-one basis. Also similar to the SIDP-IV, respondents are encouraged to report their typical or usual functioning, rather than their often-altered personality functioning during times of acute psychiatric illness. Before the structured interview, a screening of Axis I conditions and the respondent's personal history is recommended.

IPDE sections typically begin with open-ended prompts to encourage respondents to elaborate about themselves in a less-structured fashion. Then, specific questions are asked to evaluate each *DSM* and ICD criterion. In the *DSM-III-R* version, the disorder name, criterion, and criterion number are printed above the question or questions designed to tap that criterion (Loranger et al., 1991, 1994). Some items tap a similar *DSM* and ICD criterion, while others relate to only one particular system. The *DSM-IV* version maintains the same format in terms of principles of administration and organization as the *DSM-III-R* IPDE, with the exception that there are separate modules for the *DSM-IV* and ICD-10 classification systems. This change was implemented because clinical researchers typically followed one system or the other, but rarely required diagnoses according to both. This modification also serves to reduce length and administration time of the interview.

The IPDE requires that a trait be prominent during the past five years to be considered a part of the respondent's personality. Information about age of onset of particular behaviors is also explored to determine if a late-onset diagnosis is appropriate. When a respondent acknowledges a particular trait, interviewers follow up by asking for examples and anecdotes to clarify the trait or behavior, gauge impact of the trait on the person's functioning, and fully substantiate the rating. Such probing requires significant clinical judgment and knowledge about each criterion on the part of interviewers. Moreover, some items are rated based on observation of the respondent's behavior during the session, and this, too, requires a certain level of clinical expertise. To supplement self-report, interview of informants is encouraged, and clinical judgment is needed to ascertain which source is more reliable if inconsistencies arise. Data from informants are recorded on a separate column, and final ratings on the score sheet are marked to indicate that they were obtained by informants.

Overall, all items are rated on a three-point scale with the following definitions: 0 indicates that the behavior or trait is denied or within normal limits, a 1 indicates that it is present to an accentuated degree, and a 2 signifies pathological/meets criterion (Loranger et al., 1994). A comprehensive item-by-item scoring manual is available, which clarifies the intent of each criterion and provides guidelines for scoring. At the end of the interview, final impressions are recorded on a summary score sheet. Ratings are then collated by either hand or computer. The ultimate output is quite extensive, including: presence or absence of each criterion, number of criteria met for each disorder, a dimensional score (sum of individual scores for each criteria for each disorder), and a categorical diagnosis (definite, probable, or negative; Loranger et al., 1994). Such comprehensive output is quite valued by clinical researchers who may analyze such data in multiple and creative ways.

Given that the IPDE evaluates many different diagnostic criteria according to two different diagnostic systems, administration time is typically longer than other interviews. The IPDE is intended to be administered by experienced clinicians, such as clinical psychologists and psychiatrists, who have also received specific training in the use of the IPDE. Such training typically involves a two-day workshop with demonstration videotapes, discussions, and practice. The WHO has established several training centers around the world. As noted earlier, this instrument was selected by the WHO for international application, and has been translated into numerous languages to facilitate transcultural research.

Reliability of the original PDE was first assessed by the instrument developers (Loranger et al., 1987) in a sample of 60 inpatients. This report focused on *DSM-III* personality disorders that were diagnosed at least five times. Kappas were quite impressive: antisocial (.70), histrionic (.77), schizotypal (.80), compulsive (.88), and borderline (.96). Later, Standage and Ladha (1988) examined the PDE in a clinical sample, reporting generally lower, but still acceptable, interclinician concordance rates that ranged from .38 to .78, and averaged .63. Also, Loranger et al. (1991) reported data from the field trial of the 1985 pilot version of the PDE, which was tied to *DSM-III-R* criteria. In a sample of 136 clients, diagnostic concordance between the PDE examiner and a silent independent observer ranged from .55 to .93, with a median of .83. Stability of diagnosis based on second interviews one to six months later in a subsample of the original population ($N = 86$) ranged from .52 to .57.

As noted earlier, the IPDE was selected by the WHO/ADAMHA for use in an international pilot study to assess personality disorders in different languages, cultures, and countries. In this large scale, multinational, reliability project (Loranger et al., 1994), the IPDE was administered by 58 experienced clinicians to 716 clients being treated at 14 field trial centers in 11 countries in North America, Europe, Africa, and Asia. A second clinician simultaneously rated 141 interviews to evaluate interrater reliability. Agreement rates were calculated for five definite (met full criteria) and nine definite/probable (met one criteria less than required number) *DSM-III-R* diagnoses. This strategy was used to increase base rates of some disorders so that more kappas could be computed. Results for the definite/probable diagnoses were higher than the definite cases (as can be expected) and generally were quite strong. Kappa values ranged from a low of .51 for paranoid to a high of .87 for schizoid. Moreover, kappas were above .70 (indicating excellent agreement) for six out of nine diagnoses. The weighted kappas for definite and probable/definite diagnoses were .57 and .69, respectively. Most impressively, these values are similar to those reported for many Axis I disorders, which previously were found to be substantially easier to accurately classify.

Temporal stability of the IPDE was also assessed in 243 cases that were reexamined with a mean interval of six months between administrations. Results for stability were somewhat more variable than those for interrater reliability, ranging from .28 for paranoid to .68 for both schizoid and schizotypal. For temporal stability, overall weighted kappas for definite and probable/definite diagnoses were .50 and .53, respectively. Interestingly, interrater reliability and temporal stability concordance rates were also reported for *dimensional* scores and the number of criteria met for each disorder. In fact, these rates were consistently higher than those obtained with categorical diagnoses, suggesting that the dimensional approach to personality disorder diagnosis and taxonomy may have some advantage over the existing scheme. A clear strong point of the IPDE is that the output always includes both dimensional and categorical scores for each disorder.

Two studies evaluated validity of the PDE by using the LEAD technique. Skodol, Oldham, Rosnick, Kellman, and Hyler (1991) compared the PDE with the Structured Clinical Interview for *DSM-IV* Axis II Personality Disorders (SCID-II), as well as with consensus diagnosis according to the LEAD technique in a sample of 100 inpatients. Agreement between the PDE and SCID-II was modest, ranging from .14 (schizoid) to .66 (dependent), with a mean of .45. When compared to LEAD diagnosis, positive predictive, negative predictive, and overall diagnostic power were calculated for each PDE diagnosis with modest results. Overall diagnostic power ranged from .47 (passive-aggressive) to .97 (schizoid), with 6 of 11 disorders having values of .70 or greater. However, kappas were consistently lower and moderate to poor. Pilkonis, Heape, Ruddy, and Serrao (1991) reported on the validity of PDE diagnosis in 40 depressed clients who were also diagnosed according to the LEAD standard. Use of the LEAD standard as the validity diagnosis resulted in high sensitivity (.71) but only fair specificity (.58) for the PDE. Relative to the LEAD method, the PDE diagnosed considerably fewer clients with personality dysfunction, and resulted in eight false negatives and five false positives out of 40 cases. Overall agreement (kappa) between the two sets of diagnoses about presence or absence of any personality disorder was poor at intake (.28) and follow-up (.29), with false negatives again prominent.

In other validity studies, Hunt and Andrews (1992) reported poor diagnostic concordance between the PDE and the self-report Personality Diagnostic Questionnaire-Revised (PDQ-R), while similarly disappointing results were found when the PDE and MCMI-II were administered to 34 wife assaulters (Hart, Dutton, & Newlove, 1993) and 97 psychiatric outpatients (Soldz, Budman, Demby, & Merry, 1993). However, these studies most likely suggest limitations of the self-report inventories rather than the structured interviews, with a tendency of the former to result in substantial false positives. The PDE has been also contrasted with another popular semistructured interview, the SCID-II, with better but still only fair concordance rates (see elaboration in following section on SCID-II). Because of the instrument's ties to the *DSM-IV* and ICD-10 classification systems and adoption by the WHO, the IPDE is a valuable instrument for international and transcultural investigations of personality pathology.

THE STRUCTURED CLINICAL INTERVIEW FOR *DSM-IV* AXIS II PERSONALITY DISORDERS

To complement the Axis I version of the SCID, a version focusing on Axis II personality disorders according to *DSM-IV* has been developed: the Structured Clinical Interview for *DSM-IV* Axis II Personality Disorders (SCID-II; First, Gibbon, Spitzer, Williams, & Benjamin, 1997). The SCID-II has a semistructured format similar to the Axis I version but it covers the 10 standard *DSM-IV* personality disorders, as well as personality disorders not otherwise specified (NOS), and depressive personality disorder and passive-aggressive personality disorder from *DSM-IV*, Appendix B (see Table 3.2).

The SCID-II is usually used in conjunction with the Axis I SCID, which typically is administered before personality assessment. This is encouraged so that the respondent's present mental state can be considered when judging accuracy of self-reported personality traits. The basic structure and conventions of the SCID-II closely resemble those of the Axis I SCID. One unique feature of the SCID-II is that it includes a personality questionnaire—a 119-item, self-report, forced choice yes/ no screening component that can be administered before the interview portion and takes about 20 minutes. The purpose of the questionnaire is to reduce overall administration time because only those items that are scored in the pathological direction are further evaluated in the structured interview portion.

During the structured interview component, the pathologically endorsed screening responses are further pursued to ascertain whether the symptoms are actually experienced at clinically significant levels. Here, the respondent is asked to elaborate about each suspected personality disorder criteria and specified prompts are provided. Like the Axis I SCID, the *DSM-IV* diagnostic criteria are printed on the interview page for easy review and responses are coded as follows: ? = Inadequate information, 1 = Absent or false, 2 = Subthreshold, and 3 = Threshold or true. Each personality disorder is assessed completely, and diagnoses are made before proceeding to the next disorder. The modular format permits researchers and clinicians to tailor the SCID-II to their specific needs and reduce administration time. Clinicians who administer the SCID-II are expected to use their clinical judgment to clarify responses, gently challenge inconsistencies, and ask for additional information as required to rate accurately each criterion and disorder. Collection of diagnostic information from ancillary sources is permitted. Complete administration of the SCID-II typically takes less than one hour. Training requirements and interviewer qualifications are similar to that of the Axis I SCID. There is no clinician version of the SCID-II.

Numerous studies have reported reliability data for the SCID-II. The largest and most recent study to date was a multisite, test-retest reliability project that included 284 subjects in four psychiatric and two nonclinical sites (First et al., 1995). At all sites, two raters independently evaluated the same subject at separate times, with intervals ranging from one day to two weeks. Agreement rates (kappa) for the patient sample ($N = 103$) ranged from a low of .24 for obsessive-compulsive to a high of .74 for histrionic. Kappas were above .50 for five of ten disorders, with an overall weighted kappa of .53. Similar to the Axis I project, agreement rates for nonpatient subjects were poorer, with an overall weighted kappa of .38. When compared to test-retest data from other structured interviews (SIDP and PDE), findings for the SCID-II were roughly comparable but achieved in a shorter administration time.

Two additional studies added to our current knowledge about test-retest reliability of the SCID-II. O'Boyle and Self (1990) examined reliability of personality disorders in a subsample of five inpatients participating in a larger validity study. The mean interval between administrations was 1.7 days. Agreement (kappa) for presence of any personality disorder was .74, but rates for specific disorders were not reported because of the small sample size. Malow, West, Williams, and Sutker (1989) also used a test-retest design (second interview within 48 hours); they reported excellent reliability of borderline (kappa = .87) and antisocial (.84) personality disorders in a sample of inpatients diagnosed with either cocaine or opioid dependence.

Several other studies have deployed the less stringent joint interview design. Fogelson, Nuechterlein, Asarnow, Subotnik, and Talovic (1991) evaluated interrater reliability of the SCID-II in a sample of 45 first-degree relatives of probands with schizophrenia, schizoaffective, or bipolar disorder. Intraclass correlation coefficients (ICC) for five disorders found in the sample were moderate to excellent: avoidant (ICC = .84), borderline (.82), schizotypal (.73), paranoid (.70), and schizoid (.60). Two similar investigations used a joint interviewer design to evaluate personality disorders in anxious outpatients. Renneberg, Chambless, and Gracely (1992) administered the SCID-II to 32 anxious outpatients. Audiotaped interviews were scored by a second rater, and reliability estimates (kappa) were calculated for four disorders: avoidant (.81), obsessive-compulsive (.71), borderline

(.63), and paranoid (.61). Interrater reliability for diagnosis of any personality disorder was .75. Similarly, personality disorders were rated in a sample of 30 outpatients with panic disorder with agoraphobia (Brooks, Baltazar, McDowell, Munjack, & Bruns, 1991). Audiotaped and videotaped SCID-II interviews were assessed retrospectively by two additional independent raters. Their findings indicated respectable agreement for 10 personality disorders, with kappas ranging from .43 for histrionic to .89 for schizotypal personality disorder. Kappas were not computed for schizoid and antisocial personality disorder, as neither disorder was diagnosed by any rater. A unique feature of this study is that interrater agreement was also evaluated for every criterion item for each personality disorder, and results revealed acceptable agreement (alpha less than .05) for 110 of 112 criteria. Similarly, Wonderlich, Swift, Slotnick, and Goodman (1990) retrospectively rated 14 audiotaped interviews of clients suffering from eating disorders. Kappas were obtained for five personality disorders: obsessive-compulsive (.77), histrionic (.75), borderline (.74), dependent (.66), and avoidant (.56), suggesting acceptable reliability.

In a larger-scale project carried out in Holland by Arntz, van Beijsterveldt, Hoekstra, Eussen, and Sallaerts (1992), two raters observed the same interview to compare diagnoses of 70 outpatients suffering from anxiety disorders. Interrater reliability (kappa) was moderate to excellent, ranging from .65 for schizotypal to 1.00 for dependent, self-defeating, and narcissistic personality disorders, with an impressive overall kappa of .80. Arntz et al. (1992) also calculated reliability levels for each *DSM-III-R* criteria for all personality disorders. Out of 116 criteria, results (using intraclass correlation coefficient) suggested "excellent" reliability for 84 ($r > .75$) and "good" reliability for 14 ($r > .65$); only six criteria showed disappointing levels ($r < .60$).

Considerably less empirical attention has been devoted to validity of SCID-II diagnoses, although several reports have been published. In an early study, SCID diagnoses were compared to those generated by Spitzer's (1983) LEAD standard in a sample of 20 psychiatric inpatients (Skodol, Rosnick, Kellman, Oldham, & Hyler, 1988). Positive predictive, negative predictive, and overall diagnostic power were calculated for each diagnosis. Overall diagnostic power ranged from .45 (narcissistic) to .95 (antisocial), with 8 of 12 disorders having values of .70 or greater. It was noted that the SCID appeared to more accurately diagnose disorders with clear-cut behavioral descriptors (i.e., antisocial, schizotypal) compared to less behaviorally defined disorders (i.e., narcissistic, self-defeating).

The SCID-II has been compared to the PDE in two studies (O'Boyle & Self, 1990; Skodol et al., 1991). In the O'Boyle and Self study, both measures were administered to 20 depressed inpatients. Diagnostic agreement between the two devices for any disorder was fair (kappa = .38). Rates for specific disorders diagnosed at least five times were poor for paranoid (.18) and dependent (.23) but moderate for borderline (.62). In the investigation by Skodol et al., 100 applicants for long-term inpatient treatment of personality pathology were independently assessed with both measures. Their results indicated better but still modest agreement, as kappa was over .50 (indicating acceptable levels) for 6 of 11 disorders, with a mean of .45. When compared to LEAD diagnoses, the SCID-II had slightly higher validity coefficients than the PDE for 8 of the 11 disorders studied, although values for both measures were moderate at best. In an interesting concurrent validity study (Hueston, Mainous, & Schilling, 1996), patients in a primary care clinic who received a personality disorder diagnosis according to the SCID-II had a lower functional status, lower satisfaction with health care, and were at increased risk for depression and alcohol abuse. Continued studies are needed to carefully evaluate and document the psychometric properties of the *DSM-IV* version of the SCID-II because most published studies used the *DSM-III-R* version of the SCID-II. Overall, the SCID-II will likely remain a popular and effective tool for *DSM-IV* personality disorder assessment. The SCID-II Web site is the same as for the SCID Axis I version: www.scid4.org.

SUMMARY

This chapter suggests that application of structured interviews in clinical and research endeavors has greatly facilitated the task of psychiatric diagnosis and *DSM-IV* classification. Current reliability estimates derived from the various Axis I interviews (SADS, DIS, SCID) are highly promising for a broad range of clinical disorders. For personality disorders, reliability values for the SIDP, IPDE, and SCID-II interviews generally indicate modest agreement with diverse patient populations and experimental designs. Most importantly, values from these structured interviews greatly surpass results from early investigations with unstructured interviews. In fact, prior efforts to classify personality disorders without structured interviews resulted in the lowest reliability rates in the entire *DSM* system. Improved criteria (in the classification system itself) in combination with structured assessment instruments have created this significant advancement.

For both Axis I and Axis II categories, however, it should be underscored that reliability in the absence of validity is meaningless. Grove (1987) cogently examined this issue and articulated that "reliability studies can never be more than a necessary first step in diagnostic research. Given the amorphous and overlapping nature of many psychiatric syndromes, one must be suspicious of highly reliable diagnoses until they are proven to be highly valid, too" (p. 116). Regrettably, although reliability rates are now more acceptable, relatively less investigative attention has been directed toward validity of diagnoses, especially for personality disorders. Most studies in this area have focused on basic reliability, differentiation of separate personality disorders from each other, and description of the conditions. Establishment of construct validity for these disorders is still lacking, and investigation in this area should be the major focus of future research attention. Structured interviews will be of great assistance in this endeavor. It is hoped that once these diagnostic constructs are well validated, comparisons between structured interviews can be carried out to assess the strengths and limitations of each instrument relative to each other for each personality disorder. Unfortunately, validity studies are more complex and difficult to conduct than pure reliability investigations, and questions about validity are paramount issues facing psychiatric researchers at present. Indeed, in the extant literature for Axis I and Axis II categories, there are too few studies in which diagnoses from one structured interview are compared to other structured interviews or Spitzer's LEAD standard for assessing validity. Now that reliability of diagnosis has been firmly established, enhancement of diagnostic validity appears the logical next area for active research attention.

The information in this chapter provides a broad overview of the many structured interviews that are available to the clinician and researcher. The nature of structured interviews was discussed, and descriptions, guidelines for use, and evidence for reliability and validity were summarized for each instrument. It is hoped that this review will enable clinicians and researchers to choose an instrument that will most appropriately suit their needs. It is also hoped that awareness of the thorny and troubling issue of diagnostic validity of structured interviews will stimulate state-of-the-art research in the future to move the field ahead.

REFERENCES

American Psychiatric Association. (1952). *Diagnostic and statistical manual of mental disorders.* Washington, DC: Author.

American Psychiatric Association. (1968). *Diagnostic and statistical manual of mental disorders* (2nd ed.). Washington, DC: Author.

American Psychiatric Association. (1980). *Diagnostic and statistical manual of mental disorders* (3rd ed.). Washington, DC: Author.

American Psychiatric Association. (1987). *Diagnostic and statistical manual of mental disorders* (3rd ed., rev.). Washington, DC: Author.

American Psychiatric Association. (1994). *Diagnostic and statistical manual of mental disorders* (4th ed.). Washington, DC: Author.

American Psychiatric Association. (2000). *Diagnostic and statistical manual of mental disorders* (4th ed., text rev.). Washington, DC: Author.

Andreason, N. C., Grove, W. M., Shapiro, R. W., Keller, M. B., Hirschfeld, R. M. A., & McDonald-Scott, P. (1981). Reliability of lifetime diagnosis. *Archives of General Psychiatry, 38,* 400–405.

Andreason, N. C., McDonald-Scott, P., Grove, W. M., Keller, M. B., Shapiro, R. W., & Hirschfeld, R. M. A. (1982). Assessment of reliability in multicenter collaborative research with a videotape approach. *American Journal of Psychiatry, 139,* 876–882.

Anthony, J. C., Folstein, M., Romanoski, A. J., Von Korf, M. R., Nestadt, G. R., Chahal, R., et al. (1985). Comparison of the lay Diagnostic Interview Schedule and a standardized psychiatric diagnosis. *Archives of General Psychiatry, 42,* 667–675.

Arntz, A., van Beijsterveldt, B., Hoekstra, R., Eussen, M., & Sallaerts, S. (1992). The interrater reliability of a Dutch version of the Structured Clinical Interview for *DSM-III-R* personality disorders. *Acta Psychiatrica Scandinavica, 85,* 394–400.

Blouin, A. G., Perez, E. L., & Blouin, J. H. (1988). Computerized administration of the Diagnostic Interview Schedule. *Psychiatry Research, 23,* 335–344.

Brent, D. A., Zelenak, J. P., Bukstein, O., & Brown, R. V. (1990). Reliability and validity of the Structured Interview for Personality Disorders in adolescents. *Journal of the American Academy of Child and Adolescent Psychiatry, 29,* 349–354.

Brooks, R. B., Baltazar, P. L., McDowell, D. E., Munjack, D. J., & Bruns, J. R. (1991). Personality disorders co-occurring with panic disorder with agoraphobia. *Journal of Personality Disorders, 5,* 328–336.

Coolidge, F. L., & Segal, D. L. (1998). Evolution of the personality disorder diagnosis in the *Diagnostic and Statistical Manual of Mental Disorders. Clinical Psychology Review, 18,* 585–599.

Endicott, J., & Spitzer, R. L. (1978). A diagnostic interview: The Schedule for Affective Disorders and Schizophrenia. *Archives of General Psychiatry, 35,* 837–844.

Erdman, H. P., Klein, M. H., Greist, J. H., Bass, S. M., Bires, J. K., & Machtinger, P. E. (1987). A comparison of the Diagnostic Interview Schedule and clinical diagnosis. *American Journal of Psychiatry, 144,* 1477–1480.

First, M. B., Gibbon, M., Spitzer, R. L., Williams, J. B. W., & Benjamin, L. (1997). *Structured Clinical Interview for DSM-IV Axis II Personality Disorders* (SCID-II). Washington, DC: American Psychiatric Press.

First, M. B., Spitzer, R. L., Gibbon, M., & Williams, J. B. W. (1997a). *Structured Clinical Interview for DSM-IV Axis I Disorders: Clinician version* (SCID-CV). Washington, DC: American Psychiatric Press.

First, M. B., Spitzer, R. L., Gibbon, M., & Williams, J. B. W. (1997b). *User's guide to the Structured Clinical Interview for DSM-IV Axis I Disorders: Clinician version* (SCID-CV). Washington, DC: American Psychiatric Press.

First, M. B., Spitzer, R. L., Gibbon, M., Williams, J. B. W., Davies, M., Borus, J., et al. (1995). The Structured Clinical Interview for *DSM-III-R* Personality Disorders (SCID-II). Part II: Multisite test-retest reliability study. *Journal of Personality Disorders, 9,* 92–104.

Fogelson, D. L., Nuechterlein, K. H., Asarnow, R. F., Subotnik, K. L., & Talovic, S. A. (1991). Interrater reliability of the Structured Clinical Interview for *DSM-III-R*. Axis II: Schizophrenia spectrum and affective spectrum disorders. *Psychiatry Research, 39,* 55–63.

Grove, W. M. (1987). The reliability of psychiatric diagnosis. In C. G. Last & M. Hersen (Eds.), *Issues in diagnostic research* (pp. 99–119). New York: Plenum Press.

Hart, S. D., Dutton, D. G., & Newlove, T. (1993). The prevalence of personality disorder among wife assaulters. *Journal of Personality Disorders, 7,* 329–341.

Helzer, J. E., Robins, L. N., McEvoy, M. A., Spitznagle, E. L., Stoltzman, R. K., Farmer, A., et al. (1985). A comparison of clinical and diagnostic interview schedule diagnoses: Physician reexamination of lay-interviewed cases in the general population. *Archives of General Psychiatry, 42,* 657–666.

Hogg, B., Jackson, H. J., Rudd, R. P., & Edwards, J. (1990). Diagnosing personality disorders in recent onset schizophrenia. *Journal of Nervous and Mental Diseases, 178,* 194–199.

Hueston, W. J., Mainous, A. G., & Schilling, R. (1996). Patients with personality disorders: Functional status, health care utilization, and satisfaction with care. *Journal of Family Practice, 42,* 54–60.

Hunt, C., & Andrews, G. (1992). Measuring personality disorder: The use of self-report questionnaires. *Journal of Personality Disorders, 6,* 125–133.

Jackson, H. J., Gazis, J., Rudd, R. P., & Edwards, J. (1991). Concordance between two personality disorder instruments with psychiatric inpatients. *Comprehensive Psychiatry, 32,* 252–260.

Loranger, A. W. (1999). *International Personality Disorder Examination. DSM-IV and ICD-10 Interviews.* Odessa, FL: Psychological Assessment Resources.

Loranger, A. W., Hirschfeld, R. M., Sartorius, N., & Regier, D. A. (1991). The WHO/ADAMHA International Pilot Study of Personality Disorders: Background and purpose. *Journal of Personality Disorders, 5,* 296–306.

Loranger, A. W., Sartorius, N., Andreoli, A., Berger, P., Buchheim, P., Channabasavanna, S. M., et al. (1994). The International Personality Disorder Examination: The World Health Organization/Alcohol, Drug Abuse, and Mental Health Administration International Pilot Study of Personality Disorders. *Archives of General Psychiatry, 51,* 215–224.

Loranger, A. W., Susman, V. L., Oldham, J. M., & Russakoff, L. M. (1987). The Personality Disorder Examination: A preliminary report. *Journal of Personality Disorders, 1,* 1–13.

Malow, R. M., West, J. A., Williams, J. L., & Sutker, P. B. (1989). Personality disorders classification and symptoms in cocaine and opioid addicts. *Journal of Consulting and Clinical Psychology, 57,* 765–767.

Miller, H. R., Streiner, D. L., & Parkinson, A. (1992). Maximum likelihood estimates of the ability of the MMPI and MCMI personality disorder scales and the SIDP to identify personality disorder. *Journal of Personality Assessment, 59,* 1–13.

Nazikian, H., Rudd, R. P., Edwards, J., & Jackson, H. J. (1990). Personality disorder assessment for psychiatric inpatients. *Australian and New Zealand Journal of Psychiatry, 24,* 37–46.

O'Boyle, M., & Self, D. (1990). A comparison of two interviews for *DSM-III-R* personality disorders. *Psychiatry Research, 32,* 85–92.

Pfohl, B., Blum, N., & Zimmerman, M. (1995). *Structured Interview for DSM-IV Personality SIDP-IV.* Iowa City: University of Iowa.

Pilkonis, P. A., Heape, C. L., Ruddy, J., & Serrao, P. (1991). Validity in the diagnosis of personality disorders: The use of the LEAD standard. *Psychological Assessment, 3,* 46–54.

Renneberg, B., Chambless, D. L., & Gracely, E. J. (1992). Prevalence of SCID-diagnosed personality disorders in agoraphobic outpatients. *Journal of Anxiety Disorders, 6,* 111–118.

Riskind, J. H., Beck, A. T., Berchick, R. J., Brown, G., & Steer, R. A. (1987). Reliability of *DSM-III-R* diagnoses for major depression and generalized anxiety disorder using the Structured Clinical Interview for *DSM-III-R. Archives of General Psychiatry, 44,* 817–820.

Robins, L. N., Cottler, L. B., Bucholz, K., & Compton, W. (1996). *The Diagnostic Interview Schedule, version IV.* St. Louis, MO: Washington University School of Medicine.

Robins, L. N., Helzer, J. E., Cottler, L. B., & Goldring, E. (1989). *The Diagnostic Interview Schedule, version III-R.* St. Louis, MO: Washington University School of Medicine.

Robins, L. N., Helzer, J. E., Croughan, J., & Ratcliff, K. S. (1981). National Institute of Mental Health Diagnostic Interview Schedule: Its history, characteristics, and validity. *Archives of General Psychiatry, 38,* 381–389.

Robins, L. N., Helzer, J. E., Ratcliff, K. S., & Seyfried, W. (1982). Validity of the Diagnostic Interview Schedule, version II: *DSM-III* diagnoses. *Psychological Medicine, 12,* 855–870.

Rogers, R. (1988). Structured interviews and dissimulation. In R. Rogers (Ed.), *Clinical assessment of malingering and deception* (pp. 250–268). New York: Guilford Press.

Rogers, R. (2001). *Handbook of diagnostic and structured interviewing.* New York: Guilford Press.

Segal, D. L., Hersen, M., & Van Hasselt, V. B. (1994). Reliability of the Structured Clinical Interview for *DSM-III-R:* An evaluative review. *Comprehensive Psychiatry, 35,* 316–327.

Segal, D. L., Hersen, M., Van Hasselt, V. B., Kabacoff, R. I., & Roth, L. (1993). Reliability of diagnosis in older psychiatric patients using the Structured Clinical Interview for *DSM-III-R. Journal of Psychopathology and Behavioral Assessment, 15,* 347–356.

Segal, D. L., Kabacoff, R. I., Hersen, M., Van Hasselt, V. B., & Ryan, C. F. (1995). Update on the reliability of diagnosis in older psychiatric outpatients using the Structured Clinical Interview for *DSM-III-R. Journal of Clinical Geropsychology, 1,* 313–321.

Semler, G., Wittchen, H. U., Joschke, K., Zaudig, M., von Gieso, T., Kaiser, S., et al. (1987). Test-retest reliability of a standardized psychiatric interview (DIS/CIDI). *European Archives of Psychiatry and Neurological Sciences, 236,* 214–222.

Skodol, A. E., Oldham, J. M., Rosnick, L., Kellman, H. D., & Hyler, S. E. (1991). Diagnosis of *DSM-III-R* personality disorders: A comparison of two structured interviews. *International Journal of Methods in Psychiatric Research, 1,* 13–26.

Skodol, A. E., Rosnick, L., Kellman, H. D., Oldham, J. M., & Hyler, S. E. (1988). Validating structured *DSM-III-R* personality disorders assessments with longitudinal data. *American Journal of Psychiatry, 145,* 1297–1299.

Skre, I., Onstad, S., Torgerson, S., & Kringlen, E. (1991). High interrater reliability for the Structured Clinical Interview for *DSM-III-R* Axis I (SCID-I). *Acta Psychiatrica Scandinavica, 84,* 167–173.

Soldz, S., Budman, S., Demby, A., & Merry, J. (1993). Diagnostic agreement between the Personality Disorder Examination and the MCMI-II. *Journal of Personality Assessment, 60,* 486–499.

Spitzer, R. L. (1983). Psychiatric diagnosis: Are clinicians still necessary? *Comprehensive Psychiatry, 24,* 399–411.

Spitzer, R. L., Endicott, J., & Robins, E. (1975). Clinical criteria for psychiatric diagnosis and *DSM-III. American Journal of Psychiatry, 132,* 1187–1192.

Spitzer, R. L., Endicott, J., & Robins, E. (1978). Research diagnostic criteria. *Archives of General Psychiatry, 35,* 773–782.

Standage, K., & Ladha, N. (1988). An examination of the reliability of the Personality Disorder Examination and a comparison with other methods of identifying personality disorders in a clinical sample. *Journal of Personality Disorders, 2,* 267–271.

Stangl, D., Pfohl, B., Zimmerman, M., Bowers, W., & Corentahl, C. (1985). A structured interview for the *DSM-III* personality disorders. *Archives of General Psychiatry, 42,* 591–596.

Stone, A. A., Turkkan, J. S., Bachrach, C. A., Jobe, J. B., Kurtzman, H. S., & Cain, V. S. (Eds.). (2000). *The science of self-report: Implications for research and practice.* Mahwah, NJ: Erlbaum.

Turley, B., Bates, G. W., Edwards, J., & Jackson, H. J. (1992). MCMI-II personality disorders in recent-onset bipolar disorders. *Journal of Clinical Psychology, 48,* 320–329.

Vandiver, T., & Sher, K. J. (1991). Temporal stability of the Diagnostic Interview Schedule. *Psychological Assessment, 3,* 277–281.

Ward, C. H., Beck, A. T., Mendelson, M., Mock, J. E., & Erbaugh, J. K. (1962). The psychiatric nomenclature: Reasons for diagnostic disagreement. *Archives of General Psychiatry, 7,* 198–205.

Widiger, T. A. (1997). Mental disorders as discrete clinical conditions: Dimensional versus categorical classification. In S. Turner & M. Hersen (Eds.), *Adult psychopathology and diagnosis* (3rd ed., pp. 3–23). New York: Wiley.

Widiger, T. A., & Frances, A. J. (1987). Interviews and inventories of the measurement of personality disorders. *Clinical Psychology Review, 7,* 49–75.

Williams, J. B. W., Gibbon, M., First, M. B., Spitzer, R. L., Davies, M., Borus, J., et al. (1992). The Structured Clinical Interview for *DSM-III-R* (SCID): Multisite test-retest reliability. *Archives of General Psychiatry, 49,* 630–636.

Wonderlich, S. A., Swift, W. J., Slotnick, H. B., & Goodman, S. (1990). *DSM-III-R* personality disorders in eating-disorder subtypes. *International Journal of Eating Disorders, 9,* 607–616.

CHAPTER 4

Activity Level and *DSM-IV*

WARREN W. TRYON

HERE ARE THEORETICAL and clinical reasons for psychologists' interest in activity level and for including a chapter on activity level in a text on adult psychopathology and diagnosis. The first section of this chapter considers the theoretical reasons that psychologists are interested in activity level. Activity level is the first personality variable to develop, and it continues across the life span. Several health-related applications create further theoretical interest in activity level.

The second section of this chapter provides practical clinical reasons explaining why psychologists wish to extend their assessment practices to include naturalistic activity measurement by discussing the role activity measurement plays in clinical diagnosis. The *Diagnostic and Statistical Manual of Mental Disorders* (*DSM-IV*; American Psychiatric Association [APA], 1994) refers to abnormal activity levels (agitation, psychomotor retardation) in its inclusion and exclusion criteria for 48 disorders. No other facet of behavior applies to this many psychiatric disorders. Special attention is paid to how nocturnal wrist activity informs the diagnosis of several sleep disorders, thereby extending behavioral assessment into a new domain.

Important measurement issues are addressed. The history of science is a history of measurement and measurement-driven theoretical advances (Tryon, 1996a, 1996b). Clinicians deserve high-quality assessment for the same reasons that research investigators do; both want as much good information as they can get to render accurate diagnoses and assess the effects of therapeutic interventions. Psychologists typically ask teachers, parents, and children to rate activity level because it is convenient and inexpensive to do so. Several reasons can be advanced against continuing this practice. For example, instruments, such as the Conners' Rating Scales (Conners, 1989), include items on their hyperactivity scales that do not pertain to motor excess (Kamphaus & Frick, 1996, pp. 348–352). This means that aspects of behavior other than motor excess are being rated and erroneously labeled *hyperactivity*. Instruments that quantify activity level—actigraphs—measure only movement. Tryon and Pinto (1994) discovered that some children rated by teachers as exhibiting motor excess were measurably less active than control children rated by teachers not to have a problem with activity level. Discrepancies such as these between rated and measured activity level can have important clinical implications, including whether to medicate a child. Instruments can be used to obtain activity measurements every minute of the day and night—1,440 measurements per 24-hour period. Parents see their children only when they are together at home or elsewhere. Teachers see children only at school. No one observes children while asleep. Only instruments can constantly measure activity level 24 hours a day. Porrino, Rapoport, Behar, Sceery, et al. (1983) reported that attention-deficit/hyperactivity disorder (ADHD) children are consistently more active than normal children at nearly all times, including night times when they are asleep. Gruber, Sadeh, and Raviv (2000) reported significant differences between ADHD and control children in measured but not self-reported sleep measures. Porrino, Rapoport, Behar, Ismond, and Bunney (1983) were able to measure the 6 P.M. behavioral rebound effect associated with 8 A.M. stat doses of methylphenidate in ADHD children, thereby demonstrating the ecological validity of actigraphy. The reliability and validity of actigraphs can be evaluated under laboratory conditions independent of the behavior of the people who wear these instruments (cf. Tryon & Williams, 1996). Rating and behavior observation systems necessarily confound the measurement properties with the behaviors being observed. Actigraphs quantify behavior on a ratio scale with an absolute zero and equal measurement intervals that can extend to 255 levels or more and do so over precisely controlled time intervals. Rating scales purport to measure on an interval scale extending five, seven, or nine levels at most with no supporting data that the intervals are equal. Raters rely on their memory for past events, which can be substantially in error (Rogler, Malgady, & Tryon, 1992). Ratings are single aggregates that do not reveal the temporal distribution of behavior.

Naturalists once sketched drawings of their specimens but now take high-resolution color photographs or digital images. Psychologists once depended on ratings and behavioral observations of activity level but can now obtain high-quality objective measurements at programmed intervals, typically every minute, over as many hours, days, weeks, or months as desired to reach firm clinical or research conclusions about activity level. The wide commercial availability of actigraphs and the fact that owning a personal computer and printer means that a person has half the equipment necessary for actigraphy makes it unacceptable to rate or observe rather than measure activity level. Step counters provide a very inexpensive alternative to actigraphy (cf. Tryon, 1991a). For these reasons and more, fundamental issues of actigraphy are integrated into this chapter on psychopathology.

DEVELOPMENTAL EVIDENCE

PERSONALITY

Activity level is a remarkable life span developmental variable because consistent individual differences arise *during gestation* that appear to persist through infancy, childhood, adolescence, and adulthood, into late life. Because activity level is relevant to normal development, it follows that activity level is distorted by psychopathology into recognizable symptoms.

Prenatal and Heritability Studies Eaton and Saudino (1992) reviewed 14 studies showing that mothers can reliably and validly detect fetal activity beginning with the 28th week of gestation. Fetal activity appears to increase to a peak at around week 34 and then decrease through week 39. They report the emergence of consistent individual differences in prenatal activity. These prenatal activity differences constitute the first stable individual difference in behavior and, therefore, the first personality trait.

Robertson (1985) reported that cyclic motility is relatively stable after midgestation. Robertson (1987) measured movements in 41 fetuses from one to seven times ($M = 3.5$, $SD = 1.7$) at postmenstrual ages ranging from 23 to 41 weeks. Motility measurements were taken again from 18 to 124 hours after birth ($M = 54$, $SD = 27$). Various between- and within-subject analyses were conducted. The most pertinent result for present purposes was the within-subject finding that cyclic movements during active sleep in the newborn are similar to fetal movements one month before birth. This direct connection between prenatal and postnatal activity supports the developmental continuity of activity level across the birth event.

Walters (1965) studied the relationship between fetal activity counts taken during the seventh, eighth, and ninth months of gestation with 12-week, 24-week, and 36-week postnatal Gesell development scores. Partial correlations controlling for birth weight were very similar—within .003 of the values reported in Table 4.1. Several findings deserve emphasis. Notice that many of the correlation coefficients between prenatal activity and postnatal development are statistically significant and have comparable size to other personality coefficients. Developmental trends can also be discerned. The first panel in the table shows that 12-week (three-month) postnatal behavior is more related to eighth- and ninth-month prenatal activity than it is to seventh-month prenatal activity. With a few exceptions, the correlations reported in the second panel for 24-week postnatal development are numerically larger than are the corresponding entries in the first panel for 12-week postnatal development. These larger correlations are mostly maintained in the third panel regarding 36-week postnatal development. Another way to view this development is to note that total activity across all three prenatal months is significantly correlated not only with 12-week postnatal Gesell Motor and Adaptive scores but also with all 36-week postnatal Gesell Motor, Adaptive, Language, and Personal-Social Gesell scores.

Other evidence indicates that activity level is heritable. Zuckerman (1991, pp. 7–8) reported that by age 9, activity level is among the temperament facets with the highest heritability ratios. Buss and Plomin (1984, pp. 114–118, Table 9.2) reported an identical twin activity correlation of .62 and a fraternal twin correlation of −.13 based on 228 identical and 172 fraternal twins whose average age was 61 months. Their Table 9.4 presents mean identical/fraternal twin concordance rates for activity of 45/26, 88/59, 78/54, and 75/57. Their Table 9.6 reports MA/DZ twin correlations of .24/.11 at 6 months, .33/.28 at 12 months, .43/.14 at 18 months, and .58/.14 at 24 months in the same longitudinally studied subjects. Plomin (1990, p. 94) details findings from a Swedish study reporting a heritability coefficient for 59-year-old adults of .27 for activity level.

All of the previous studies can be criticized because of their correlational methodology. It is always possible that a third uncontrolled variable is a common cause of both variables and, therefore, responsible for their correlation. Experimental studies avoid this pitfall by manipulating the variable in question in one

Table 4.1
Correlations between Prenatal Activity and Gesell Postnatal
Development Scores Reported by Walters (1965)

12-Week Postnatal Development				
Prenatal Activity Month	Motor	Adaptive	Language	Personal-Social	Total Gesell
7th ($N = 21$)	.28[a]	.33[a]	.24	.18	.29[a]
8th ($N = 25$)	.31[b]	.18	.28[a]	.38[c]	.37[c]
9th ($N = 26$)	.24[a]	.37[c]	.29[a]	.29[a]	.40[c]
Total ($N = 21$)	.54[d]	.54[d]	.24	.22	.42[c]

24-Week Postnatal Development				
Prenatal Activity Month	Motor	Adaptive	Language	Personal-Social	Total Gesell
7th ($N = 21$)	.52[d]	.26	.33[a]	.23	.44[c]
8th ($N = 25$)	.34[b]	.16	.33[a]	.29[a]	.31[a]
9th ($N = 26$)	.45[d]	.35[b]	.42[c]	.40[c]	.44[d]
Total ($N = 21$)	.48[c]	.23	.37[b]	.24	.34[b]

36-Week Postnatal Development				
Prenatal Activity Month	Motor	Adaptive	Language	Personal-Social	Total Gesell
7th ($N = 21$)	.53[d]	.34[a]	.35[a]	.47[d]	.51[d]
8th ($N = 25$)	.38[c]	.27	.11	.06	.23
9th ($N = 26$)	.47[d]	.35[b]	.37[c]	.14	.41[c]
Total ($N = 21$)	.53[d]	.36[a]	.44[c]	.34[a]	.51[d]

[a] $p < .05$.
[b] $p < .02$.
[c] $p < .009$.
[d] $p < .0008$.
Source: From "Prediction of Postnatal Development from Fetal Activity," by C. E. Walters, 1965, *Child Development, 36*, 801–807. Adapted with permission of the author.

group and comparing results to another group in which the putative cause is held constant. The following research definitively establishes that activity level is heritable. DeFries, Wilson, and McClearn (1970) published an initial description of this work. DeFries, Gervais, and Thomas (1978) published the results after 30 generations of selective breeding. They used an open-field test to measure activity level in 40 litters of mice. The most active male and female mice from each of 10 randomly chosen litters were selected and mated at random. Their offspring comprised the first selected generation (S1) of a high-active line (H1). The least active male and female from the same 10 litters were selected and mated at random to produce the first selected generation of a low-active line (L1). Two control groups were created from the remaining two sets of 10 litters. A male and a female were randomly chosen and randomly mated from 10 of the remaining 20 litters, and their offspring produced the first generation of a control-1 line (C1). Likewise, a male and a female were randomly chosen and randomly mated from the remaining set of 10 litters and their offspring produced the first generation of a control-2 line (C2). This process was repeated for 30 generations. The results were that the activity level distributions of the H and L strains gradually and consistently diverged from each other and from both control groups until the activity distributions of these two genetic lines became distinct. The distributions for H30 and L30 did not overlap at all. The high- and low-active lines also diverged from both control groups, whose activity level remained essentially the same and intermediate between the H and L strains over all 30 generations. These results conclusively demonstrate that activity level is heritable.

The studies cited previously indicate that activity level is established prenatally, is highly heritable, and is maintained across the birth event. Activity level is, therefore, the first stable individual difference, personality trait, to emerge. These findings support the expectation that activity level will continue to be a stable individual difference across the life span.

Infancy   Activity level was the first factor to emerge from the empirical longitudinal study by Thomas and Chess (1977, pp. 20–21). Every subsequent theoretical description and account of infant temperament has confirmed that activity level is a fundamental dimension of individual differences among infants (Goldsmith et al., 1987). It is extremely unusual for psychologists to completely agree on anything, but complete agreement has been reached with regard to the prominent role activity level plays in connection with infant temperament.

Middle Childhood   Shiner (1998) reviewed the temperament and personality literature regarding middle childhood and concluded that activity level was one of the personality dimensions for which the evidence is so robust that its status is well established.

Adulthood   Activity level has been found to be an important dimension of adult personality. Guilford, Zimmerman, and Guilford (1976) developed the Guilford-Zimmerman Temperament Survey to measure adult personality. They found clear evidence of an activity level factor in adults. Comrey (1994) developed the Comrey Personality Scales to measure adult personality, and he also found compelling evidence for an activity level factor. Buss and Plomin (1975, 1984) and Buss (1989) examined adult temperament and found a prominent activity level factor. Lerner, Palermo, Sprio, and Nessleroade (1982) and Lerner et al. (1986) developed the Dimensions of Temperament Scale—Revised for the study of adult temperament and also found a prominent activity level factor. Windle and Lerner (1986) and Waddington (1998) have convincingly replicated an activity level factor in adult temperament. These data demonstrate that an activity level factor characterizes adult personality.

Considerable evidence supports what is called the *five-factor model (FFM) of personality.* Personality can be described by the following five factors: Neuroticism, Extraversion, Openness, Agreeableness, and Conscientiousness (Costa & McCrae, 1980, 1992, 1994, 1995; Digman, 1990, 1994; Goldberg, 1990; Goldberg & Rosolack, 1994). *Neuroticism* entails self-piety, anxiety, insecurity, timidity, passivity, and immaturity. Its opposite pole is emotional stability. *Extraversion* entails being lively, talkativeness, sociability, spontaneity, adventure, energy, conceit, vanity, nosey, and sensual. Its opposite pole is introversion. *Openness* refers to new experiences: toleration and appreciation of the unfamiliar. Curious, creative, imaginative, and untraditional describe this pole. Conventional and narrow-minded describe the other pole. *Agreeableness* entails trust, amiability, generosity, tolerance, courtesy, altruism, warmth, and honesty. The opposite pole on this dimension involves vindictiveness, criticism, disdain, antagonism, aggressiveness, dogmatism, temper, distrust, greed, and dishonesty. *Conscientiousness* entails industry, order, self-discipline, consistency, grace, reliability, formality, foresight, maturity, and thrift. Its opposite pole entails negligence, inconsistency, rebelliousness, irreverence, and intemperance.

Digman (1994) refactored two data sets collected on first- and second-grade children more than 30 years ago and found striking support for the current five-factor model. The differences from the results first obtained were attributed to changes in factor analytic procedures. Van Lieshout and Haselager (1994) had 937 parents and 899 teachers administer a Dutch translation of the California Child Q-set (Block & Block, 1969/1980) to 1,836 children ages 3 to 14 years over six studies. They also reported that the first five principle components corresponded to the Big Five personality factors.

Block (1995) criticized the FFM by noting that it rests on what is called the *lexical hypothesis*—the assumption that the vocabulary used by the general population to describe individual differences provides a solid basis on which to erect a comprehensive scientific taxonomy of personality. The lexical hypothesis equates vocabulary used by the general population to describe a phenomenon, in this case, stable individual differences, with the phenomena itself. Would a common vocabulary list used by the general population to describe insects provide a solid basis for a comprehensive entomological taxonomy? Would a vocabulary list used by the general population to describe objects in the night sky provide a solid basis for a comprehensive astronomical taxonomy? Would a vocabulary list used by the general population to describe any field of science constitute a solid basis for a comprehensive taxonomy in that field? The answer to all of these questions is "probably not." The FFM is properly understood as an analysis of the way the general population describes stable individual differences. These practices seem consistent across cultures. The FFM has the potential problem of mistaking cultural practices for differentially describing the behavior of children and adults as a developmental progression.

Disagreement remains as to the exact number of factors needed to properly characterize the lexicon of adult personality (Block, 1995), but agreement exists across investigators that Extraversion and Neuroticism must be included because they are so well documented (Eysenck, 1991, 1994). Costa and McCrae (1992) describe activity level as the (E4) facet of Extraversion as follows: "A high Activity score is seen in rapid tempo and vigorous movement, in a sense of energy, and in a need to keep busy. Active people lead fast-paced lives. Low scorers are more leisurely and relaxed in tempo, although they are not necessarily sluggish or lazy" (p. 17). Rapid and vigorous movements, keeping busy, and living a fast-paced life are the kinds of behaviors that activity monitors respond to and, therefore, can be validated by actigraphy. The factor analytic studies that support the FFM have also shown that activity level develops into a facet of Extraversion. For example, Section II of Halverson, Kohnstamm, and Martin's (1994) edited book is titled "Emerging Conceptions of the Childhood Precursors of Personality Structure." In it, Martin, Wisenbaker, and Huttunen (1994) review factor analytic studies of temperament measures based on the work of Thomas and Chess (1977) and Thomas, Chess, and Birch (1968). The authors present the results of 12 large factor analytic studies. Their Table 8.2 consistently reveals an Activity factor. The authors conclude that the Activity factor develops into a facet of adolescent and adult extraversion. Hagekull's (1994) Figure 12.2 diagrams infant activity as making two contributions to childhood. First, infant activity contributes to childhood activity and to any external behavior problems that may develop during childhood. Second, Activity and Approach-Withdrawal infant temperaments are thought to combine to form adolescent shyness, which is also related to internal behavior disorders that develop during adolescence. Both childhood activity and adolescent shyness are thought to develop into adult Extraversion/Introversion. Hagekull also theorizes that infant activity influences childhood sociability that he believes helps determine adult Agreeableness (friendliness/hostility).

Another approach to the transformation of activity level into extraversion is to determine the earliest age at which the five-factor solution consistently emerges. Section III of Halverson, Kohnstamm, and Martin (1994) focuses on "Deriving the Five-Factor Model from Parental Ratings of Children and Adolescents." Robins, John, and Caspi (1994) provide evidence that five factors can be recovered from Block and Block's (1969/1980) California Child Q-set as adapted for use by laypersons (Caspi et al., 1992). However, evidence of two additional factors—Activity and Irritability—is found. These data suggest that activity level persists as an independent factor, separate from and additional to extraversion.

Because factor analysis is an atheoretical methodology, no theoretical explanation is available for why these five factors emerged or why activity level presumably metamorphosizes into extraversion. Moreover, the results of factor analysis are highly dependent on the variables used to form the underlying correlation matrix. Of specific interest is the fact that a general factor almost never emerges when few items (variables) are used to measure it. The term *items* is used here because FFM factor analyses typically involve personality test items. The reason a general factor is unlikely to emerge when relatively few test items are used to measure it is that these few items probably do not explain sufficient common variance to warrant being named as a primary factor. It is more likely that these items will be designated as a facet of a larger factor. This parsimonious approach is in keeping with the objectives of factor analysis: to represent many variables with a few factors. That few words are typically used to describe the activity level of adults almost guarantees that activity level will emerge as a facet of another factor in lexicon factor analytic studies. This fact formed the basis of a pilot study (Tryon & Forlenza, 2001) conducted to see if augmentation of the FFM item pool with additional activity level items and an instrumented activity level measure would cause an independent activity level factor to emerge. The instrumented activity measurement serves as an interpretive anchor or marker variable in that actigraphs can measure only activity and, consequently, only one interpretation can be made of their data. Twenty-six students from the psychology department subject pool participated in this study. Forty percent were male and 60% were female. The racial composition of the sample was as follows: 57.9% White, 15.8% Black, 21.1% Hispanic, and 5.3% Asian. Participants were administered the NEO-PI-R (Costa & McCrae, 1992) to measure the five personality factors mentioned previously. Participants were administered the Dimensions

Table 4.2

Principal Component Analysis of Six Extraversion Facet Scores

Extraversion Facet	Factor	
	1	2
NEO E1 (Warmth)	.601	−.718
NEO E2 (Gregariousness)	.776	−.014
NEO E3 (Assertiveness)	.821	−.120
NEO E4 (Activity)	.570	.710
NEO E5 (Excitement-Seeking)	.701	.226
NEO E6 (Positive Emotions)	.834	−.027

of Temperament-Revised (DOTS-R) (Lerner et al., 1982), and the Comrey Personality Inventory (Comrey, 1994) to obtain additional responses to activity level items. Activity level was objectively measured at the waist for all waking hours for one week, seven consecutive days, using a Computer Sciences and Applications (CSA) actigraph (Tryon & Williams, 1996). This device quantifies activity level into 128 intensity levels 10 times each second, averages the results over each minute, and does this 24 hours each day (1,440 minutes/day) for up to 88 days in the latest model. It is a small ($2.0 \times 1.5 \times 0.6$ in; 5.1 cm $\times 3.8$ cm $\times 1.5$ cm), lightweight (1.5 oz; 42.6 g) device that is attached to a thin belt and worn at the waist.

The first analysis was to replicate the NEO-PI five-factor solution. Too few subjects were available to factor-analyze item responses; therefore, we factor-analyzed facet scores instead using principal components analysis. All factors with an Eigen value greater than unity were extracted. Table 4.2 shows that two factors emerged. The first factor explained 52.5% of the variance, and the second factor explained 18.1% of the variance. A single factor solution explaining 57.6% of the variance was obtained by refactoring the data after removing facet E1 (Warmth). Table 4.3 shows that facets E2 through E6 all load positively and substantially on this factor.

A third factor analysis was conducted using the DOTS General Activity score, the Comrey Activity score, and the maximum activity level score recorded during one week of actigraphy. The results of a principal components analysis presented in Table 4.4 reveal the emergence of a second factor. The five NEO facets continued to load on Factor 1, thereby defining it as an Extraversion factor. The Comrey Activity Level Scale also loaded heavily on this factor. The DOTS—General

Table 4.3

Principal Component Analysis of Five
Extraversion Facet Scores

Extraversion Facet	Factor 1
NEO E2 (Gregariousness)	.778
NEO E3 (Assertiveness)	.785
NEO E4 (Activity)	.665
NEO E5 (Excitement-Seeking)	.724
NEO E6 (Positive Emotions)	.831

Table 4.4

Principal Component Analysis of Five Extraversion Facet Scores, the
DOTS-General Activity Score, Comrey Activity Level Score, and
Maximum Measured Activity Score

	Factor	
Extraversion Facet	1 (Extraversion)	2 (Activity Level)
NEO E2 (Gregariousness)	.730	−.269
NEO E3 (Assertiveness)	.824	−.078
NEO E4 (Activity)	.691	**.581**
NEO E5 (Excitement-Seeking)	.689	.071
NEO E6 (Positive Emotions)	.801	−.268
DOTS—General Activity	.075	**.767**
Comrey Activity Level	.857	−.055
Maximum Activity Score	.022	**.745**

Activity Score and Maximum Measured Activity Level loaded heavily on Factor 2 but negligibly on Factor 1, making this an Activity Level factor. This finding supports the hypothesis that adding additional self-reported activity items and/or measured activity data would allow a separate activity level factor to emerge. Notice also that the activity facet of the NEO-PI loads almost as heavily on the Activity Level factor as it does on the Extraversion factor.

Eaton, McKeen, and Campbell (2001) provide developmental evidence that may explain why the FFM differs from the measured activity level approach. They compiled data from 12 different studies that objectively measured activity levels of 840 subjects ranging in age from 1 to 24.6 years of age. These data revealed an inverted U-shaped function where activity level peaked between 2 and 6 years of age and then declined. This activity peak may be found across cultures and, therefore, may be what causes the associated lexicons to characterize child but not adult behavior in terms of activity level. The substantial developmental decrease in activity level around age 24.6 may explain why adult behavior is less characterized by the activity terms used to describe children. On this view, activity level remains a stable individual difference despite a decrease in the mean intensity. All people are expected to decrease their activity level proportionally as they develop. This reduction in absolute magnitude does not entail a metamorphic transform; it is just a magnitude decrement. It is easily understood that such a decrement could be mistakenly viewed as a possible transformation.

A related point is that instruments are better suited to quantify activity magnitude than are human observers. For example, one brand of actigraph quantifies activity into 127 equal intervals whereas human observers are mainly limited to five or nine categories. Actigraphs systematically measure activity level multiple times per second, hour after hour; raters take a more informal approach. These are some of the reasons that actigraphy is the method of choice when investigating activity level. The commercial availability of several brands of actigraphs means that there is no reason for serious investigators to rely on observers to quantify activity level. Observers should be restricted to making qualitative observations such as whether activity is socially appropriate or not.

PHYSICAL HEALTH

Good biological reason exists for activity beginning prenatally. Cyclic activation of motor circuits is required for the proper prenatal development of many vertebrates (Robertson & Dierker, 1986). Various structures including muscles, joints, spinal motor neurons, and neuromuscular synapses do not develop properly in the absence of such activity (Moessinger, 1988; Robertson & Dierker, 1986). Drachman and Sokoloff (1966) report that as little as 24 to 48 hours of curare-induced immobilization produces permanent joint malformation and muscle atrophy in chick embryos. It is, therefore, likely that all normal fetuses are active from time to time. Robertson (1985) has documented that normal fetuses are active and that cyclic activity emerges by the middle of gestation. Maternal diabetes has been shown to disrupt cyclic motility but appears to normalize by the end of gestation (Robertson, 1988).

Inactivity is a health risk later in life for:

- Cardiovascular disease (Fox, Naughton, & Haskell, 1971; Leon, Connett, Jacobs, & Rauramaa, 1987; Morris, Everitt, Pollard, Chave, & Semmence, 1980; Oberman, 1985; Paffenbarger & Hale, 1975; Paffenbarger, Hyde, Wing, & Steinmetz, 1984; Powell, Thompson, Caspersen, & Kendrick, 1987).
- Colon cancer (Gerhardsson, Norell, Kiviranta, Pedersen, & Ahlbom, 1986; Slattery, Schumacher, Smith, West, & Abd-Elghany, 1988; Vena et al., 1985).
- Diabetes mellitus, hypertension, and osteoporosis (Siscovick, LaPorte, & Newman, 1985).

Being more active reduces the risk of all-cause mortality (Blair et al., 1989; Paffenbarger, Hyde, Wing, & Hsieh, 1986). Consequently, the inclination or conscious decision to adopt an active lifestyle partly determines who survives to late life. This selective factor tends to remove inactive people from the population over time. Unfortunately, several chronic diseases (chronic obstructive pulmonary disease, coronary heart disease) diminish activity level and thereby restore the lower tail of the activity dimension in latter life (cf. Tryon, 1991a, pp. 209–220).

Palmore (1970) suggested that exercise is the single health practice most strongly associated with longevity in the elderly. Elderly people evaluate their own health, and the health of others, largely in terms of activity (Burnside, 1978; Gueldner & Spradley, 1988), with more active people perceived as healthier. McAuley, Courneya, and Lettunich (1991) reported self-efficacy increases following exercise in older people. Stewart, King, and Haskell (1993) report increased quality of life resulting from endurance exercise training in 50- to 65-year-old adults. Taylor (1991) reviews other psychological benefits of regular exercise. Some evidence supports the view that aerobic exercise improves neuropsychological function in older individuals by increasing cerebral metabolism (Dustman et al., 1984).

Many diseases reduce activity level. Coronary artery disease, chronic obstructive pulmonary disease, and arthritis are examples of diseases that decrease activity level. Actigraphy can be used to quantify the degree of activity reduction associated with these diseases. Activity increases are one of the expected benefits of coronary artery bypass surgery, and actigraphy can be used to document the extent to which these increases are realized. Patients who are not able to ambulate adequately may not be discharged from the hospital until they can do so. Redeker and Wykpisz (1999) used actigraphy to monitor recovery from coronary artery by-pass surgery in 8 middle-aged (*M* = 57 years) and 14 older (*M* = 72 years) patients. They found activity increases and improved circadian rhythms over postoperative days two through five. Redeker, Mason, Wykpisz, and Glica (1996) noted that these operations can disturb sleep for as long as one year postsurgery. They used wrist actigraphy to examine sleep patterns of 22 women over a six-month period and found that sleep became less fragmented over time. Hospitalization alters sleep patterns. Redeker, Tamburri, and Howland (1998) used wrist actigraphy to study the sleep of 33 hospitalized patients (23 men, 10 women) diagnosed with myocardial infarction and unstable angina from 1 to 10 days. Results showed that patients had more nighttime awakenings but similar duration of nighttime awakenings and somewhat poorer sleep efficiency than healthy community-residing people.

DSM-IV

Tryon (1986) reviewed activity-related inclusion and exclusion criteria for *DSM-I, DSM-II,* and *DSM-III.* Tryon (1991b) analyzed activity-related inclusion and exclusion criteria for *DSM-III-R.* Table 4.5 reveals that activity level is stated or strongly implied in either the inclusion or exclusion criteria of 48 *DSM-IV* diagnoses. No other assessment method pertains to so many diagnostic entities. This portion of the chapter reviews activity level-related *DSM-IV* disorders. Also discussed are:

- Instrument reliability and validity;
- Site of attachment chosen;
- Content validity of the behavioral sample taken; that is, its representativeness of natural situations and circumstances;
- Duration or extent of the behavioral sample obtained; and the
- Interpretation of the inclusion and exclusion criteria.

Tryon (1985, 1991a, pp. 23–63) reviewed the operating characteristics of activity-measuring instruments, including their reliability and validity. A comprehensive analysis of a fully proportional instrument capable of accurately measuring and storing the intensity of physical activity every minute of the day and night (1,440 minute/24 hours) for 22 days is presented by Tryon and Williams (1996). A newer version of this device collects data for 88 consecutive days using one-minute epochs.

Tryon (1991a, pp. 8, 42–43) and van Hilten, Middelkoop, Kuiper, Kramer, and Roos (1994) have previously discussed site of attachment issues. The waist (trunk) and wrist are the two most common sites of attachment. They are not equally active at all times. The dominant and nondominant wrists may be differentially active. Waist movements expend more energy because they entail displacement of the body's center of gravity. Wrist movements are greater than waist movements during sleep and, therefore, have been the preferred site of attachment for sleep-wake discriminations and circadian rhythm assessments for this reason. The ability to discriminate sleep from wake using wrist activity has been documented (Sadeh, Hauri, Kripke, & Lavie, 1995; Tryon, 1991a, pp. 149–184; Tryon, 1996c) and is discussed in more detail later in this chapter.

Behavioral samples are content valid to the extent that they are representative of the behavior being assessed, just as psychometric tests are content valid if they

Table 4.5

Summary of *DSM-IV* for Which Activity Level Is Part of Inclusion or Exclusion Criteria

Number	*DSM-IV* Code	*DSM-IV* Diagnosis	Inclusion Criterion (pages)	Exclusion Criterion Differential Diagnosis (pages)
1	314.01	Attention-Deficit/Hyperactivity Disorder, Combined Type	80, 83–85	
2	314.00	Attention-Deficit/Hyperactivity Disorder, Predominantly Inattentive Type	80, 83–85	
3	314.01	Attention-Deficit/Hyperactivity Disorder, Predominantly Hyperactive-Impulsive Type	80, 83–85	
4	312.8	Conduct Disorder		ADHD (89), Manic Episode (89)
5	313.81	Oppositional Defiant Disorder		ADHD (93), Conduct Disorder (93)
6	293.89	Catatonic Disorder	170–171	
7	291.8	Alcohol Withdrawal	198	
8	292.89	Amphetamine Intoxication	207–208	
9	292.0	Amphetamine Withdrawal	209	
10	305.90	Caffeine Intoxication	213	
11	292.89	Cocaine Intoxication	224	
12	292.0	Cocaine Withdrawal	225–226	
13	292.89	Inhalant Intoxication	239	
14	292.0	Nicotine Withdrawal	244–245	
15	292.0	Opioid Withdrawal	251	
16	292.0	Sedative, Hypnotic, or Anxiolytic Withdrawal	266	
17	295.20	Schizophrenia, Catatonic Type	289	
18	295.70	Schizoaffective Disorder	295–296	
19	298.8	Brief Psychotic Disorder	304	
20	296.2 or 3	Major Depressive Disorder	320–325	
21	296.0 or 4	Manic Episode	328–331	
22	300.4	Dysthymic Disorder	345	
23	311	Depressive Disorder Not Otherwise Specified	350	
24	296.xx	Bipolar I Disorder	350–358	
25	296.89	Bipolar II Disorder	359–363	
26	301.13	Cyclothymic Disorder	363–366	

(continued)

Table 4.5 *(Continued)*

Number	DSM-IV Code	DSM-IV Diagnosis	Inclusion Criterion (pages)	Exclusion Criterion Differential Diagnosis (pages)
27	296.80	Bipolar Disorder Not Otherwise Specified	366	
28	293.83	Mood Disorder Due to a General Medical Condition	366–370	
29	296.90	Mood Disorder Not Otherwise Specified	375	
30	309.81	Posttraumatic Stress Disorder	427–429	
31	308.3	Acute Stress Disorder	431–432	PTSD (435), Mood Disorders (435)
32	300.02	Generalized Anxiety Disorder	435–436	
33	307.1	Anorexia Nervosa*	540	Major Depressive Disorder (544)
34	307.51	Bulimia Nervosa	549	Major Depressive Disorder (549)
35	307.42	Primary Insomnia	557	
36	307.44	Primary Hypersomnia	557, 562	
37	347	Narcolepsy	562, 567	
38	780.59	Breathing Related Sleep Disorder	567, 573	
39	307.45	Circadian Rhythm Sleep Disorder	573, 578	
40	307.47	Dyssomnia Not Otherwise Specified	579	
41	307.47	Nightmare Disorder	583	
42	307.46	Sleep Terror Disorder	583, 587	
43	307.46	Sleepwalking Disorder	587, 591	
44	307.42	Insomnia Related to Another Mental Disorder	592, 596	
45	307.44	Hypersomnia Related to Another Mental Disorder	592, 597	
46	780.xx	Sleep Disorder Due to a General Medical Condition	597–601	
47	309.0	Adjustment Disorder with Depressed Mood		PTSD (626)
48	333.99	Neuroleptic-Induced Acute Akathesia	679	

*Excessive exercise is listed as a diagnostic feature of Anorexia Nervosa on p. 540 but is not listed as a diagnostic criterion in the box on pp. 544–545.

Source: From *Diagnostic and Statistical Manual of Mental Disorders, 4th Edition (DSM-IV);* American Psychiatric Association, 1994.

adequately survey the domain being measured (Anastasi, 1988, p. 140; Linehan, 1980; Tryon, 1993). Behavioral observations made under office or laboratory conditions may or may not validly represent behavior displayed at home or school. Test developers and behavioral assessors bear the burden of proof regarding content validity. Generalization must be demonstrated rather than assumed. Content validity depends on the duration of assessment as well as the conditions under which assessment occurs. *DSM-IV* frequently refers to a minimum of two weeks as the relevant duration. As to activity measurement, the two-week duration has the advantage of replicating each day of the week once. We do not all engage in the same activities each day of the week. Our behavior often differs on the weekend from that during the week.

The focus of this chapter is the activity-related diagnostic inclusion and exclusion criteria. Complete diagnostic criteria are tabled so that the reader can better evaluate their description in the text. We begin our coverage with sleep disorders for two main reasons. First, many psychologists are surprised to learn that several important aspects of sleep can be evaluated in the home using unobtrusive wrist activity monitors. Second, publication of "Practice Parameters for the use of Actigraphy in the Clinical Assessment of Sleep Disorders" by the Standards of Practice Committee (1995) of the American Sleep Disorders Association marks the clinical maturity of an important technology of which most psychologists are still unaware.

BEHAVIORAL SLEEP MEASUREMENT

Sleep was studied behaviorally before the polygraph was invented. Dropping a spool held between the thumb and forefinger was the gold standard for defining sleep onset before the advent of polysomnography (PSG) and was used to validate the newly discovered EEG changes associated with sleep onset (Blake, Gerard, & Kleitman, 1939). That the spool was dropped between 0.5 and 25 seconds after the disappearance of Alpha EEG patterns partially validated PSG sleep-onset criteria that include EEG (brain), EMG (muscle) and other parameters. This more complex neuroelectrical definition of sleep onset is now the gold standard. Sleep is typically studied in the laboratory for three nights, discarding the first night because sleep during the initial night in the laboratory is frequently unrepresentative. Sleep studies are expensive. Home PSG is also expensive and cumbersome given that the person must sleep with many electrodes attached to his or her head and elsewhere. Behavioral treatments for insomnia require nightly sleep measures over multiple weeks (Hauri, 1994, 1999; Lichstein & Riedel, 1994). Collecting PSG data over multiple weeks is too expensive to obtain. Hauri (1999) noted the behavior therapist's need for objective sleep measures. Stepanski (1994) noted that the absence of objective sleep measures has been a barrier to the use of behavioral treatments.

PSG sleep-scoring criteria distinguish between wake and several stages of sleep. This implies that sleep onset is a discrete event. Behavioral sleep measures such as actigraphy differ systematically from PSG measures; these differences are frequently characterized as actigraphy error. The presumption here is that sleep onset is a binary event that PSG measures without error despite the fact that sleep scoring is typically done by human judgment. The validity standard against which actigraphy is evaluated is much greater than that used to evaluate all psychological and medical tests. Research by Pollak, Tryon, Nagaraja, and Dzwonczyk (2001) makes all of these mistakes. These issues are addressed later.

On the other hand, sleep logs are routinely used with little question despite the fact that it has long been known that sleep logs can overestimate sleep latency and severely underestimate total sleep time (Baekeland & Hoy, 1971; Carskadon et al., 1976; Frankel, Coursey, Buchbinder, & Snyder, 1976; Freedman & Papsdorf, 1976; Hauri & Fisher, 1986). Some patients insist that they have not slept at all even after obtaining a full night's sleep as verified by PSG (McCall & Edinger, 1992). *Sleep State Misperception* is diagnosed when a complaint of excessive sleepiness or insomnia is accompanied by a normal polysomnogram (Hauri, 1994). That Sleep State Misperception occurs suggests that some objective sleep measure should always be used because, otherwise, Sleep State Misperception cannot be diagnosed.

Sleep logs are retained because they reflect how the person experiences his or her sleep, they are a psychological sleep measure, and they are simple to request and inexpensive. Instruments determine objective sleep. Research requires objective measures. Empirical validation of clinical practice should also require some objective measure to rule out the possibility that patients are acquiescing and telling therapists what they want to hear.

We now turn to several issues that explain why actigraphy sleep measures differ from PSG sleep measures.

SLEEP-ONSET SPECTRUM

Sleep onset is a gradual, not discrete, process that entails an orderly progression of behavioral, physiological, and psychological events. Ogilvie and Wilkinson (1988) and Harsh and Ogilvie (1994) refer to the *sleep-onset period* (SOP). Tryon (1991a) prefers the term *sleep-onset spectrum* (SOS) to emphasize the orderly sequence of events associated with sleep onset.

Phase 1: Immobility   Inactivity is necessarily the first sleep-onset phase. Six studies have reported that actigraph sleep-onset criteria are met before EEG Stage 1 sleep criteria (Cole & Kripke, 1989; Cole, Kripke, Gruen, Mullaney, & Gillin, 1992; Hauri & Wisbey, 1992; Mullaney, Kripke, & Messin, 1980; Stampi & Broughton, 1989; Webster, Kripke, Messin, Mullaney, & Wyborney, 1982). This difference is augmented in patients with insomnia. Hauri (1999) reported average actigraph sleep-onset time of 5.5 minutes (*SD* = 6.2 min) versus mean PSG sleep-onset time of 34.2 minutes (*SD* = 33.3 min) to the first 10 minutes of solid sleep. The corresponding mean sleep switch device time was 32.4 min (*SD* = 30.7 min).

Phase 2: Decreased Muscle Tone   Normal muscle tone decreases to a point where hand-held objects are dropped (Blake et al., 1939; Carskadon & Dement, 1994; Chase & Morales, 1994; Loomis, Harvey, & Hobart, 1937; Perry & Goldwater, 1987; Snyder & Scott, 1972). Before the EEG machine was invented, sleep was studied behaviorally. Rechtschaffen (1994) and Tryon (1996c) reviewed these sleep studies. Dropping hand-held objects is the gold standard against which EEG Sleep Stage 1 criteria were validated. Hence, contemporary behavioral measurements of dropping hand-held objects must continue to be acknowledged as valid measures of sleep onset if EEG validity is still to be claimed. Ogilvie, Wilkinson, and Allison (1989) used a hand-held "deadman" switch requiring 90 grams of pressure to maintain closure to measure the "drop-point." Franklin (1981) and Viens, De Koninck, Van den Bergen, Audet, and Christ (1988) describe variations of the Ogilvie et al.

apparatus suitable for home use. Perry and Goldwater (1987) instructed subjects to maintain constant pressure on a telegraph key. The drop point was identified at the point the switch opened. Hauri (1999) evaluated an inexpensive commercially available (www.sleepplace.com, RMP, Inc., 716 Sunset Road, Boynton Beach, FL 33435), sleep switch device that was found to correlate $r(23) = .98, p < .001$ in a sample of 19 insomnia patients and 6 normal sleepers with PSG-measured sleep onset. Discrepancies from PSG as to sleep-onset times are typically greatest with insomniacs. The arithmetic mean difference between sleep onset as defined by the sleep switch device and the first 10 minutes of solid sleep was −1.8 minutes. The mean of the absolute differences, without regard to sign, was 5.1 minutes. The largest single deviation for any sleeper was 13.5 minutes.

Phase 3: EEG Sleep Stage 1   The EEG changes defined by the widely used Rechtschaffen and Kales (1968) criteria mark the onset of the third SOS phase. Ogilvie and Wilkinson (1984) instructed subjects to squeeze a hand-held microswitch when they heard a tone while obtaining PSG data. Their results indicated that 99.3% of the tones were responded to during EEG Stage W (wake), 72.2% during Stage 1 sleep, 24% during Stage 2 sleep, and 5.3% during Stage 3 sleep. Hence, subjects are behaviorally awake to the degree that they systematically respond to environmental stimuli when PSG claims that they are asleep. PSG proponents may proclaim that people are not fully asleep during Stage 1, but they do not make the claim regarding Stages 2 and 3 when people remain behaviorally awake to a degree.

Phase 4: Auditory Threshold Increase   Bonnet and Moore (1982) report that auditory threshold rises rapidly within one minute of the first EEG sleep spindle. Auditory threshold increases take place mainly during EEG Stage 2 sleep (Bonato & Ogilvie, 1989). Subjects no longer respond to their names when spoken softly, to a light touch, or to normal external stimuli (Lindsley, 1957; Ogilvie & Wilkinson, 1984; Rechtschaffen, Hauri, & Zeitlin, 1966).

Phase 5: Perceived Sleep Onset   Birrell (1983), Bonato and Ogilvie (1989), and Lichstein, Nickel, Hoelscher, and Kelley (1982) found that self-reported sleep onset occurred after auditory threshold increases happened. Espie, Lindsay, and Espie (1989) found that self-reported sleep onset occurred concurrent with auditory threshold increase. Lichstein, Hoelscher, Eakin, and Nickel's study (1983) is the only study that found self-reported sleep onset to occur before auditory threshold increases occurred.

DISCRETE VERSUS GRADUAL SLEEP ONSET

Four sections of Rechtschaffen's (1994) chapter support the gradual sleep-onset view. In a section titled "No Specific Point of Sleep-Onset" he wrote, "Despite these and other significant relationships between behavioral sleep measures and physiological indicators, there appears to be no hope of defining a precise behavioral or physiological point of sleep-onset, except by *arbitrary criteria*" (p. 7, emphasis added). This view has been voiced since at least 1937 (Davis, Davis, Loomis, Harvey, & Hobart, 1937). Kleitman (1963) concurred in the opening sentence of his chapter on sleep onset. Ogilvie and Wilkinson (1988) have more recently expressed the same opinion. On this view, it is arbitrary to promote any one measure of sleep onset to the position of a gold standard and disparage all other measures of sleep onset as error.

Two other sections of Rechtschaffen's (1994) chapter titled "Wake-Sleep Transitions Are Gradual" and "Sleep-Onset Behaviors Not Synchronized" directly support the SOS as a gradual phase transition process. A fourth section of Rechtschaffen's (1994) chapter, "Individual Differences in Sleep-Onset," points to substantial variation across people in the sleep-onset process.

Nevertheless, once the EEG criteria associated with dropping hand-held objects were incorporated into EEG sleep-scoring criteria (e.g., Rechtschaffen & Kales, 1968), the behavioral basis on which they were validated was discarded both theoretically and procedurally. Kryger, Roth, and Dement's (1994) 95-chapter second edition of their comprehensive sleep medicine text excludes all but EEG and PSG approaches to sleep. Sleep onset remains largely defined as a binary event based on Rechtschaffen and Kales' EEG coding rules. All deviations from this gold standard that key on other portions of the SOS are defined as error. Rechtschaffen (1994) cautioned investigators against this view. He stated, "Physiological measures derive their value as indicators of sleep from their correlations with the behavioral criteria, not from any intrinsic ontological or explanatory superiority" (p. 5). He further concluded, "Any scientific definition of sleep that ignores the behaviors by which sleep is generally known unnecessarily violates common understanding and invites confusion" (p. 4). Kleitman (1963) cited a dozen studies showing discrepancies between behavioral and EEG sleep criteria and questioned using EEG as the sole basis for defining sleep.

WRIST ACTIGRAPHIC SLEEP ASSESSMENT

The fact that sleep onset is a process has at least two important implications. First, it means that there is no absolute point that discriminates sleep from wake. Unfortunately, all attempts to validate actigraphy against PSG are flawed by assuming that there is. Dichotomizing a continuous sleep-onset process creates categorization errors. All of these categorization errors are attributed to actigraphy, resulting in *lower bound* estimates of validity coefficients. Tryon (1996c) critically reviewed the literature validating actigraphy against PSG concerning sleep continuity and found exceptionally high validity coefficients despite this bias regarding computer-scored actigraphy total sleep time of .72, .77, .81, .82, .89, .91, .94, .97, and .98. Validity coefficients for percent sleep are .82, .89, and .96. Validity coefficients for sleep efficiency (time asleep/time in bed) are .56, .63, .71, .79, .81, .85, and .91. Validity coefficients for wake after sleep onset (WASO) are .49, .56, .63, .70, and .85. Percent agreement for sleep ranged from an unrepresentative low of 78.8% to a high of 99.7% but was mostly above 90%. W. J. Mason et al. (1992) reported that wrist actigraphy estimated total sleep time correlated $r(8) = .823$, $p < .005$ with PSG. Sadeh, Sharkey, and Carskadon (1994) reported agreement rates with PSG determined sleep from 93% to 99% across 36 subjects regardless of which wrist was used. Jean-Louis, Kripke, Cole, Assmus, and Langer (2001) reported validity coefficients against PSG on postmenopausal women sleeping at home ranging from .83 to .98, depending on sleep parameter. Jean-Louis et al. (2000) reported validity coefficients against PSG on patients meeting *DSM-IV* criteria for a Major Depressive Episode ranging from .58 to .87, depending on sleep parameter. Finally, Sadeh et al. (1995)

reviewed the actigraphy literature and concluded, "Actigraphy provides a cost-effective method for longitudinal, natural assessment of sleep-wake patterns (p. 300).

These validity coefficients presented are criticized by polysomnographers for being too *low* to justify clinical or research applications. However, Meyer et al. (2001) reviewed validity coefficients for medical and psychological tests. The validity coefficients reported previously are exceptionally *high* in this context. They substantially exceed those associated with all major psychological tests and most medical tests. Hence, actigraphy has at least the same empirical support for use in clinical and research settings as do all psychological and most medical tests. Sadeh, Alster, Urbach, and Lavie (1989), Webster et al. (1982), and Webster, Messin, Mullaney, and Kripke (1982) have conducted other relevant validational studies. Near-perfect agreement has never been a minimal validational criterion in psychology or medicine. Only actigraphy is held to this excessive empirical standard.

A second and corollary SOS implication is that deviations between actigraphic- and PSG-estimated sleep onset are systematic rather than random with actigraphic-estimated sleep onset occurring earlier than PSG-estimated sleep onset. Five of six studies in Tryon's (1996c) Table 4.1 reported that actigraph-estimated sleep onset precedes PSG-estimated sleep onset as theoretically predicted. These deviations are not random error but reflect the fact that actigraphy and PSG key on different SOS phases. Criticisms based on point-by-point sleep-wake comparisons between PSG and actigraphy are inadequate because they do not take the SOS into account. Interpreting all differences between actigraphy and PSG as actigraphy error is inappropriate and seriously underestimates validity coefficients. Insomnia appears to extend the SOS. This SOS magnification increases the differences between SOS elements, thereby clarifying the sleep-onset sequences. Hauri (1999) reported an average actigraphy-measured sleep-onset time of 5.5 minutes ($SD = 6.2$ min) for insomniacs compared to a 34.2-minute ($SD = 33.3$ min) PSG-measured sleep-onset time, showing that these sleepers became inactive long before they completed the sleep-onset process. Hauri also reported that the average sleep switch device-measured sleep-onset time was 32.4 minutes ($SD = 30.7$ min). That the sleep switch device and PSG sleep-onset measurements are so close (1.8 minutes) is a contemporary revalidation of PSG sleep-onset measurements. Hauri's data confirm that actigraphy measures the beginning of the SOS, whereas PSG and the sleep switch device measure more toward the end of the SOS. Auditory threshold increases mark the end of the SOS and come after PSG sleep-onset measures (Tryon, 1996c).

Unreliability of PSG measurement is an important source of actigraph-PSG difference. Actigraphy sleep scoring is done by computer and is perfectly repeatable on the same data set. Automatic sleep stagers are available but are not yet as good as hand scoring (Carskadon & Rechtschaffen, 1994). PSG-based sleep-wake discriminations entail manualized human judgments (Rechtschaffen & Kales, 1968) that are not 100% reliable. Ogilvie and Wilkinson (1988) reported that interrater EEG sleep scoring agreement values range from 80% to 98%. Spiegel (1981, p. 62) reported that the reliability of scoring Stage 1 sleep can be as low as 60%, whereas the reliability of scoring Stage 2 sleep is approximately 90%. Hence, up to 40% of EEG Stage 1 scoring and, therefore, sleep-wake scoring and PSG versus actigraphy differences can be questioned on measurement unreliability grounds. Studies that validate actigraphy against PSG frequently omit PSG reliability data and attribute all measurement error to actigraphy.

Another important source of actigraphy-PSG difference is that PSG is a multi-channel measurement procedure, and actigraphy is a single channel measurement procedure. It is unreasonable to expect unidimensional data to fully duplicate multidimensional data.

Even if the onset of EEG Sleep Stage 1 is *arbitrarily* selected as a reference point for defining sleep onset, this event can be behaviorally predicted using a "dead-man" device such as the one described by Ogilvie et al. (1989) because the onset of EEG Stage 1 sleep criteria was validated using the gold standard that people drop hand-held objects at the point of sleep onset (cf. Blake et al., 1939; Perry & Gold-water, 1987; Snyder & Scott, 1972). Behavioral measurements of dropping hand-held objects must continue to be acknowledged as valid measures of sleep onset if EEG and, therefore, PSG validity are still to be claimed. Ogilvie et al. (1989) instructed subjects to maintain closure of a 90-gram hand-held microswitch while in bed attempting to sleep. Hence, a battery-powered electric clock connected to a 90-gram hand-held deadman switch can be used to identify the point of sleep onset at home or elsewhere. This inexpensively provides sleep-onset latencies while people sleep at home with gold standard accuracy. Hauri (1999) has evaluated an inexpensive, commercially available sleep switch device that was found to correlate $r(23) = .98$, $p < .001$ in a sample of 19 insomnia patients and 6 normal sleepers with PSG-measured sleep onset. The mean sleep switch device sleep-onset time of 32.4 minutes agreed very closely to the mean PSG sleep-onset time of 34.2 minutes—a difference of but 1.8 minutes over more than a half-hour sleep latency for patients with insomnia.

SLEEP DISORDERS

DSM-IV distinguishes four major sleep disorders: Primary Sleep Disorders (Dys-somnias and Parasomnias), Sleep Disorder Related to Another Mental Disorder, Sleep Disorder Due to a General Medical Condition, and Substance-Induced Sleep Disorder. Each is discussed in the following sections.

PRIMARY SLEEP DISORDERS

Primary Sleep Disorders are "presumed to arise from endogenous abnormalities in sleep-wake generating or timing mechanisms, often complicated by condition-ing factors" (APA, 1994, p. 551).

Dyssomnias   Dyssomnias are "characterized by abnormalities in the amount, quality, or timing of sleep" (APA, 1994, p. 551).

PRIMARY INSOMNIA (307.42)   The five primary *DSM-IV* criteria that define this disorder are listed in Table 4.6. The patient has substantial difficulty *initiating or maintaining sleep for at least one month* that cannot be explained by Narcolepsy, Breathing-Related Sleep Disorder, Circadian Rhythm Sleep Disorder, a Parasom-nia, Major Depressive Disorder, Generalized Anxiety Disorder, delirium, pre-scription drugs, drug abuse, or a general medical condition. The clinical impact (criterion B) must necessarily rely on clinical judgment, patient self-report, and spouse/family report. Excluding other possible diagnoses entails evaluating the extent to which their diagnostic inclusion and exclusion criteria are met as dis-cussed elsewhere in this chapter. Difficulty initiating and maintaining sleep for

Table 4.6
DSM-IV Diagnostic Criteria for Sleep Disorders

Dyssomnias

Primary Insomnia (307.42) (p. 557)

A. **"The predominant complaint is difficulty initiating or maintaining sleep, or non-restorative sleep, for at least 1 month."**
B. "The sleep disturbance (or associated daytime fatigue) causes clinically significant distress or impairment in social, occupational, or other important areas of functioning."
C. "The sleep disturbance does not occur exclusively during the course of Narcolepsy, Breathing-Related Sleep Disorder, Circadian Rhythm Sleep Disorder, or a Parasomnia."
D. "The disturbance does not occur exclusively during the course of another mental disorder (e.g., Major Depressive Disorder, Generalized Anxiety Disorder, a delirium)."
E. "The disturbance is not due to the direct physiological effects of a substance (e.g., a drug of abuse, a medication) or a general medical condition."

Primary Hypersomnia (307.44) (p. 562)

A. **"The predominant complaint is excessive sleepiness for at least 1 month (or less if recurrent) as evidenced by either prolonged sleep episodes or daytime sleep episodes that occur almost daily."**
B. "The excessive sleepiness causes clinically significant distress or impairment in social, occupational, or other important areas of functioning."
C. "The excessive sleepiness is not better accounted for by insomnia and does not occur exclusively during the course of another Sleep Disorder (e.g., Narcolepsy, Breathing-Related Sleep Disorder, Circadian Rhythm Sleep Disorder, or a Parasomnia) and cannot be accounted for by an inadequate amount of sleep."
D. "The disturbance does not occur exclusively during the course of another mental disorder."
E. "The disturbance is not due to the direct physiological effects of a substance (e.g., a drug of abuse, a medication) or a general medical condition."

Narcolepsy (347) (p. 567)

A. **"Irrestible attacks of refreshing sleep that occur daily over at least 3 months."**
B. "The presence of one or both of the following:
   (1) cataplexy (i.e., brief episodes of sudden bilateral loss of muscle tone, most often in association with intense emotion),
   (2) recurrent intrusions of elements of rapid eye movement (REM) sleep into the transition between sleep and wakefulness, as manifested by either hypnopompic or hypnagogic hallucinations or sleep paralysis at the beginning or end of sleep episodes."
C. "The disturbance is not due to the direct physiological effects of a substance (e.g., a drug of abuse, a medication) or another general medical condition."

Breathing-Related Sleep Disorder (780.59) (p. 573)

A. **"Sleep disruption, leading to excessive sleepiness or insomnia, that is judged to be due to a sleep-related breathing condition** (e.g., obstructive or central sleep apnea syndrome or central alveolar hypoventilation syndrome)."
B. "The disturbance is not better accounted for by another mental disorder and is not due to the direct physiological effects of a substance (e.g., a drug of abuse, a medication) or another general medical condition (other than a breathing-related disorder)."

(continued)

Table 4.6 *(Continued)*

Circadian Rhythm Sleep Disorder (307.45) (p. 578)

A. **"A persistent or recurrent pattern of sleep disruption leading to excessive sleepiness or insomnia** that is due to a mismatch between the sleep-wake schedule required by a person's environment and his or her circadian sleep-wake pattern."
B. "The sleep disturbance causes clinically significant distress or impairment in social, occupational, or other important areas of functioning."
C. "The disturbance does not occur exclusively during the course of another Sleep Disorder or other mental disorder."
D. "The disturbance is not due to the direct physiological effects of a substance (e.g., a drug of abuse, a medication) or a general medical condition."

Parasomnias

Nightmare Disorder (307.47) (p. 583)

A. **"Repeated awakenings from the major sleep period or naps** with detailed recall of extended and extremely frightening dreams, usually involving threats to survival, security, or self-esteem. The awakenings generally occur during the **second half of the sleep period."**
B. "On awakening from the frightening dreams, the person rapidly becomes oriented and alert (in contrast to the confusion and disorientation seen in Sleep Terror Disorder and some forms of epilepsy)."
C. "The dream experience, or sleep disturbance resulting from the awakening, causes clinically significant distress or impairment in social, occupational, or other important areas of functioning."
D. "The nightmares do not occur exclusively during the course of another mental disorder (e.g., a delirium, Posttraumatic Stress Disorder) and are not due to the direct physiological effects of a substance (e.g., a drug of abuse, a medication) or a general medical condition."

Sleep Terror Disorder (307.46) (p. 587)

A. **"Recurrent episodes of abrupt awakening from sleep, usually occurring during the first third of the major sleep episode** and beginning with a panicky scream."
B. "Intense fear and signs of autonomic arousal such as tachycardia, rapid breathing, and sweating during each episode."
C. "Relative unresponsiveness to efforts of others to comfort the person during the episode."
D. "No detailed dream is recalled and there is **amnesia for the episode.** "
E. "The episodes cause clinically significant distress or impairment in social, occupational, or other important areas of functioning."
F. "The disturbance is not due to the direct physiological effects of a substance (e.g., a drug of abuse, a medication) or a general medical condition."

Sleepwalking Disorder (307.46) (p. 591)

A. **"Repeated episodes of rising from bed during sleep and walking about, usually occurring during the first third of the major sleep episode."**
B. "While sleepwalking, the person has a blank, staring fact, is relatively unresponsive to the efforts of others to communicate with him or her, and can be awakened only with great difficulty."
C. "On awakening (either from the sleepwalking episode or the next morning), the person has **amnesia for the episode.**"

Table 4.6   *(Continued)*

D. "Within several minutes after awakening from the sleepwalking episode, there is no impairment of mental activity or behavior (although there may initially be a short period of confusion or disorientation)."

E. "The sleepwalking causes clinically significant distress or impairment in social, occupational, or other important areas of functioning."

F. "The disturbance is not due to the direct physiological effects of a substance (e.g., a drug of abuse, a medication) or a general medical condition."

Note: Bold entries concern activity.

Source: From *Diagnostic and Statistical Manual of Mental Disorders, 4th Edition (DSM-IV);* American Psychiatric Association, 1994.

at least one month has traditionally been evaluated exclusively by self-report in that 30 consecutive nights of sleep laboratory assessment or home monitoring has not been done and is not likely to be done for several reasons. It is prohibitively expensive and most patients would probably not agree to sleep in a lab for an entire month. Home wrist actigraphy, supplemented with sleep switch device (Hauri, 1999) measures of initial sleep-onset latency, is a cost-effective practical method of monitoring sleep onset and maintaining sleep after initial onset in the patient's natural sleep environment for a month (cf. Middelkoop, 1994).

The one-month criterion is meant to distinguish temporary from chronic complaints. Continuous difficulty initiating or maintaining sleep is implied but greater specificity is lacking because there has not been a practical method of quantifying sleep onset and wake after sleep onset before actigraphy that can be used at home. The consistency with which primary insomniacs have difficulty initiating and maintaining sleep over 30 consecutive nights remains unknown because the relevant research has not yet been conducted. This is an instance in which the theoretical definition of a disorder exceeds quantitative evaluation by standard methods.

Perhaps a one-week behavioral sample will be found to accurately predict a one-month behavioral sample, thereby allowing a positive diagnosis to be based on seven consecutive nights of data collection plus self-report that the measured week is representative of at least the previous three weeks. The one-week behavioral sample might provide an adequate baseline evaluation against which the effectiveness of whatever therapeutic intervention is implemented can be evaluated.

PRIMARY HYPERSOMNIA (307.44)   The five primary *DSM-IV* criteria that define this disorder are listed in Table 4.6. The patient *sleeps too long or sleeps during the day* over a period of *at least one month* to the point that it compromises social and/or occupational functioning and cannot be explained by insomnia, another sleep disorder, another mental disorder, licit or illicit drugs, a general medical condition, or *insufficient sleep*. While impact on social and occupational functioning remains a clinical judgment, the clinician must have data showing the times the patient slept during each 24-hour period for 30 consecutive days. Standard methods are too expensive and invasive to provide these data and, consequently, this diagnosis is probably never reached on empirical grounds. Wrist actigraphy could be sleep-scored over each 24-hour period for one month to provide the necessary empirical support. These data could be inspected for the time the patient went to sleep at night, the time he or she awoke, whether he or she slept during the day, and, if so, for how long. It might be determined if daytime sleeping was responsive to inadequate nighttime sleep and if daytime napping occurred when the patient was at work or home.

NARCOLEPSY (347)   The *DSM-IV* criteria for Narcolepsy are presented in Table 4.6. The patient has uncontrollable periods of *diurnal sleep over a period of at least three months* that may be associated with cataplexy or intrusions of REM sleep during sleep-wake transitions that cannot be explained by a drug or general medical condition. Sleep laboratory or home PSG analysis is capable of detecting REM sleep during sleep-wake transitions. The problem is the degree to which this phenomenon occurs nightly and the maximum number of nights the patient can spend in the sleep laboratory. Standard methods do not provide information on diurnal sleep over at least three months' time.

Wrist actigraphy records could be continuously scored for sleep to detect instances of daytime sleeping over a three-month period. It may well be that a one- or two-week behavioral sample would accurately predict a three-month behavioral sample. In this case, a reduced behavioral sample, in combination with self-report that the measured period is representative of at least the prior three months, would provide an empirical basis for reaching this diagnosis.

BREATHING-RELATED SLEEP DISORDER (780.59)   The two primary criteria for this disorder are given in Table 4.6. *Abnormal breathing disrupts the patient's sleep* and leads to excessive daytime sleepiness or *insomnia* that cannot be explained by another mental disorder and is not due to a drug or other general medical condition. Abnormal breathing is generally evaluated in the sleep laboratory or with home PSG. However, Tryon (1991a, p. 189) described the use of abdominal actigraphy to detect spasmodic breathing, which results as patients come out of an Obstructive Sleep Apnea (OSA) episode. Normal breathing causes the abdominal actigraph to rise and fall so slightly and smoothly that little activity is recorded by the internal accelerometer. However, sudden movements of the diaphragm entail high degrees of acceleration despite relatively short movements. This activity causes clear spikes to occur in the actigraph record at the time this event occurs. Such information allows counting of the frequency with which OSA events occur and specifying the time of their occurrence with an accuracy of one minute or better if a shorter recording epoch is chosen. A one-second epoch is the shortest epoch that users can select with current software.

Wrist actigraphy can be used to determine if OSA events disturbed sleep by synchronizing the internal clocks of both the wrist and abdominal actigraphs. Wrist actigraphy can also be supplemented with the sleep switch device (Hauri, 1999) to evaluate whether OSA events lead to insomnia. All of these analyses can be conducted in the patient's home over as many nights as desired.

CIRCADIAN RHYTHM SLEEP DISORDER (307.45)   The four inclusion criteria for this *DSM-IV* disorder are provided in Table 4.6. The patient experiences clinically significant *persistent or recurrent sleep disruption* leading to excessive sleepiness or *insomnia* because of a mismatch between his or her internal sleep-wake schedule and environmental demands that cannot be explained by another sleep disorder, a drug, or a general medical condition. Data documenting sleep disruption over an unspecified number of consecutive nights and the concurrent possibility of delayed sleep onset, insomnia, are not presently available by standard methods. Wrist actigraphy supplemented with the sleep switch device sleep-onset timing (Hauri, 1999) can supply the desired information (cf. Brown, Smolensky, D'Alonzo, & Redman, 1990; Glod, Teicher, Polcari, McGreenery, & Ito, 1997; W. J. Mason & Tapp, 1992; Pollak, Perlick, & Linsner, 1992; Raoux et al., 1994).

Four subtypes are acknowledged. *Delayed Sleep Phase Type* is defined by "a persistent pattern of late sleep onset and late awakening times, with an inability to fall asleep and awaken at a desired earlier time" (APA, 1994, p. 578). Behavioral methods can determine sleep onset. Wrist actigraphy can document the time of awakening, which can be compared to the patient's target awakening time to verify the extent to which he or she cannot wake up at a chosen earlier time.

Jet Lag Type is defined by "*sleepiness* and alertness that occur at an inappropriate time of day relative to local time, occurring after repeated travel across more than one time zone" (APA, 1994, p. 578). Sleepiness is usually evaluated by a Multiple Sleep Latency Test (MLST; Carskadon, 1994). Because sleep latency is calculated from lights out until the first epoch-scored sleep, the behavioral methods described previously can accurately estimate sleep-onset latency. Carskadon indicates that MSLTs are generally conducted at least four times at two-hour intervals beginning 1.5 to 3 hours after the end of nocturnal sleep, generally beginning about 9 A.M. or 10 A.M. The test is discontinued after 20 minutes if the subject does not fall asleep. The standard MSLT continues for 15 minutes after sleep onset. The simplicity of behavioral methods means that patients can self-administer this test in their own homes. Awakening at home can be achieved by a preset alarm clock. Normal sleep onset occurs within 10 to 20 minutes. Sleep onset in 5 minutes or less indicates sleepiness.

Shift Work Type is defined as "*insomnia during the major sleep period* or *excessive sleepiness during the major wake period* associated with night shift work or frequently changing shift work" (APA, 1994, p. 578). Insomnia and daytime sleepiness can be evaluated by previously described behavioral and wrist actigraphic methods.

Parasomnias Parasomnias are "characterized by *abnormal behavioral* or physiological events occurring in association with sleep, specific sleep stages, or sleep-wake transitions" (APA, 1994, p. 551). Sleep is associated with very little activity. Abnormal behaviors entail substantial movement, which wrist actigraphy can detect.

NIGHTMARE DISORDER (370.47)   The four criteria constituting this sleep disorder are presented in Table 4.6. Patients experience distress or dysfunction because they *repeatedly awaken* and become alert during their *major sleep period* because of frightening dreams that cannot be explained by another mental disorder, a drug, or a general medical condition. Wrist actigraphy can clearly discriminate a highly vigilant, alert state from sleep. The emotional distress from the very frightening dream produces activity level far in excess of that associated with quiet sleep. Actigraphy documents the time of onset to an accuracy of one minute or better if a nonstandard epoch length is chosen.

DSM-IV requires a repeated pattern of such events without specifying their frequency. Wrist actigraphy could provide normative data by studying patients thought to have this disorder while they sleep at home over a month or two. Perhaps a one-week behavioral sample would accurately predict a one-month sample and, therefore, would be sufficient to empirically establish this diagnosis.

SLEEP TERROR DISORDER (307.46)   The six criteria used to diagnose this disorder are presented in Table 4.6. The patient experiences clinically significant stress or occupational dysfunction because of *abrupt awakening* from sleep due to intense fear that cannot be explained by a drug or general medication. The patient may *not remember* these events. Actigraphy can document the time of abrupt awakening with an accuracy of one minute or better if a nonstandard epoch is chosen. An objective record of nocturnal awakening is especially important given that the patient can have amnesia for these episodes. This factor is especially critical if the patient lives alone and no one is available to document the frequency of these events or if the person lives with an uncooperative or often-absent spouse.

SLEEPWALKING DISORDER (307.46)   The six *DSM-IV* criteria for this disorder are found in Table 4.6. The patient *repeatedly rises from bed during sleep and walks about* but may have *no recollection* of doing so the next morning. Wrist actigraphy detects awakening and is sufficient to detect ambulation. An additional waist actigraph decisively detects ambulation. That the patient may have no recollection of these events makes it important to have an objective record of their occurrence. Actigraphy can document the time these events occurred to an accuracy of one minute or better if a nonstandard epoch is chosen.

SLEEP DISORDERS RELATED TO ANOTHER MENTAL DISORDER

The essential feature of this disorder "is the presence of either insomnia or hypersomnia that is judged to be related temporally and causally to another mental disorder" (APA, 1994, p. 592).

Insomnia Related to Another Mental Disorder (307.42)   The ability of wrist actigraphy, supplemented with the sleep switch device (Hauri, 1999) to quantify sleep-onset latency makes it relevant to evaluating insomnia due to another mental disorder.

Hypersomnia Related to Another Mental Disorder (307.44)   The ability of wrist actigraphy, supplemented with the sleep switch device (Hauri, 1999) to quantify sleep-onset latency makes it relevant to evaluating hypersomnia due to another mental disorder.

SLEEP DISORDER DUE TO A GENERAL MEDICAL CONDITION (780.xx)

Some medical disorders can produce insomnia, hypersomnia, or a parasomnia. Wrist actigraphy supplemented with the sleep switch device (Hauri, 1999) to quantify sleep-onset latency is capable of quantifying all of these conditions as described previously. The subtypes of this disorder are Insomnia Type, Hypersomnia Type, Parasomnia Type, and Mixed Type. The latter is diagnosed when multiple sleep problems exist but no single type predominates.

SUBSTANCE-INDUCED SLEEP DISORDER

The subtypes of this disorder are also Insomnia Type, Hypersomnia Type, Parasomnia Type, and Mixed Type. Actigraphy and sleep switch device measurements are relevant to all three conditions as previously stated.

Two specifiers exist. The first is "With Onset during Intoxication," indicating that symptoms developed as a result of intoxication. The "With Onset during Withdrawal" specifier is used if the sleep disorder begins after discontinuing a substance.

MOOD DISORDERS

Tryon (1985, 1986, 1991a, 1991b) and Teicher (1995) have reviewed the use of actigraphy to quantify mood disorders. Aronen et al. (1996) reported that activity correlated significantly with clinical ratings of depressive severity across several mood disorders and concluded that actigraphy provides an objective measure of depressive severity. Teicher et al. (1995) used actigraphy to identify abnormal rest-activity circadian rhythms in patients with seasonal affective disorder (SAD).

The *DSM-IV* distinguishes *unipolar* Depressive Disorder from Bipolar Disorder. Both of these disorders are distinguished from Mood Disorder Due to a General Medical Condition and from Substance-Induced Mood Disorder. These disorders presume a definition of Major Depressive Episode, Manic Episode, Mixed Episode, and Hypomanic Episode, to which we now turn.

EPISODE DEFINITIONS

Major Depressive Episode   Table 4.7 presents the *DSM-IV* definition of a Major Depressive Episode (MDE). A patient must have five or more of the nine listed characteristics to qualify as having a MDE. Three of these criteria concern activity. Item 4 specifies "insomnia or hypersomnia nearly every day" (APA, 1994, p. 327). Wrist actigraphy supplemented by the sleep switch device (Hauri, 1999) can document the presence of insomnia and hypersomnia. Item 5 specifies "psychomotor agitation or retardation nearly every day (observable by others, not merely subjective feelings of restlessness or being slowed down)" (APA, 1994, p. 327). The parenthetical admonition insists on noticeable change, and activity monitors clearly measure such changes. Because the emphasis is on change rather than absolute level, the most relevant point of comparison is a one- or two-week activity measurement taken as part of a comprehensive physical examination before the onset of the MDE. The rationale is the same as having a healthy electrocardiogram on file when diagnosing heart disease. Unfortunately, behavioral specimens are not presently obtained as part of routine physical examinations but perhaps may be included in the future given the connection between exercise and health. The next best comparison is with a friend, coworker, or family member who most closely matches the patient's premorbid lifestyle. A one- or two-week behavioral sample could be obtained from this person as proxy for the patient's probable premorbid activity level. Futterman and Tryon (1994) found evidence of psychomotor retardation when comparing depressed and control subjects, and Barkley and Tryon (1995) found psychomotor retardation in a sample that varied widely in depression.

Item 6 specifies "fatigue or loss of energy nearly every day." Unless occupational or other necessity forces the person to remain active, fatigue should be reflected in a less active lifestyle, which can be tracked by activity measurement. People who elect to watch television rather than take a walk or who elect to stay home rather than shop are less active. It is especially important to use fully proportional actigraphy when attempting to measure fatigue to separate small or weak movements from normally energetic ones.

Manic Episode   Table 4.7 indicates that three of seven criteria must be met if mood is expansive, but four of seven criteria must be met if mood is only irritable. Two

Table 4.7
Episode Definitions

Major Depressive Episode (p. 327)

A. "Five (or more) of the following symptoms have been present during the same 2-week period and represent a change from previous functioning; at least one of the symptoms is either (1) depressed mood or (2) loss of interest or pleasure."

    (1) "Depressed mood most of the day, nearly every day, as indicated by either subjective report (e.g., feels sad or empty) or observation made by others (e.g., appears tearful)."

    (2) "Markedly diminished interest or pleasure in all or almost all, activities most of the day, nearly every day (as indicated by either subjective account or observation made by others)."

    (3) "Significant weight loss when not dieting or weight gain (e.g., a change of more than 5% of body weight in a month), or decrease or increase in appetite nearly every day."

    (4) **"Insomnia or hypersomnia nearly every day."**

    (5) **"Psychomotor agitation or retardation nearly every day (observable by others, not merely subjective feelings of restlessness or being slowed down)."**

    (6) **"Fatigue or loss of energy nearly every day."**

    (7) "Feelings of worthlessness or excessive or inappropriate guilt (which may be delusional) nearly every day (not merely self-reproach or guilt about being sick)."

    (8) "Diminished ability to think or concentrate, or indecisiveness, nearly every day (either by subjective account or as observed by others)."

    (9) "Recurrent thoughts of death (not just fear of dying), recurrent suicidal ideation without a specific plan, or a suicide attempt or a specific plan for committing suicide."

B. "The symptoms do not meet criteria for a Mixed Episode."

C. "The symptoms cause clinically significant distress or impairment in social, occupational, or other important areas of functioning."

D. "The symptoms are not due to the direct physiological effects of a substance (e.g., a drug of abuse, a medication) or a general medical condition (e.g., hypothyroidism)."

E. "The symptoms are not better accounted for by Bereavement, i.e., after the loss of a loved one, the symptoms persist for longer than 2 months or are characterized by marked functional impairment, morbid preoccupation with worthlessness, suicidal ideation, psychotic symptoms, or psychomotor retardation."

Manic Episode (p. 332)

A. "A distinct period of abnormally and persistently elevated, expansive, or irritable mood, lasting at least 1 week (or any duration if hospitalization is necessary)."

B. "During the period of mood disturbance, three (or more) of the following symptoms have persisted (four if the mood is only irritable) and have been present to a significant degree."

    (1) "Inflated self-esteem or grandiosity."

    (2) **"Decreased need for sleep (e.g., feels rested after only 3 hours of sleep)."**

    (3) "More talkative than usual or pressure to keep talking."

    (4) "Flight of ideas or subjective experience that thoughts are racing."

    (5) "Distractibility (i.e., attention too easily drawn to unimportant or irrelevant external stimuli)."

    (6) **"Increase in goal-directed activity (either socially, at work or school, or sexually) or psychomotor agitation."**

    (7) "Excessive involvement in pleasurable activities that have a high potential for painful consequences (e.g., engaging in unrestrained buying sprees, sexual indiscretions, or foolish business investments)."

Table 4.7   *(Continued)*

C. "The symptoms do not meet criteria for a Mixed Episode."
D. "The mood disturbance is sufficiently severe to cause marked impairment in occupational functioning or in usual social activities or relationships with others, or to necessitate hospitalization to prevent harm to self or others, or there are psychotic features."
E. "The symptoms are not due to the direct physiological effects of a substance (e.g., a drug of abuse, a medication, or other treatment) or a general medical condition (e.g., hyperthyroidism)."

Mixed Episode (p. 335)

A. **"The criteria are met both for a Manic Episode and for a Major Depressive Episode (except for duration) nearly every day during at least a 1-week period."**
B. "The mood disturbance is sufficiently severe to cause marked impairment in occupational functioning or in usual social activities or relationships with others, or to necessitate hospitalization to prevent harm to self or others, or there are psychotic features."
C. "The symptoms are not due to the direct physiological effects of a substance (e.g., a drug of abuse, a medication, or other treatment) or a general medical condition (e.g., hyperthyroidism)."

Hypomanic Episode (p. 338)

A. "A distinct period of persistently elevated, expansive, or irritable mood, lasting throughout at least 4 days, that is clearly different from the usual nondepressed mood."
B. During the period of mood disturbance, three (or more) of the following symptoms have persisted (four if the mood is only irritable) and have been present to a significant degree:
   (1) "Inflated self-esteem or grandiosity."
   (2) **"Decreased need for sleep (e.g., feels rested after only 3 hours of sleep)."**
   (3) "More talkative than usual or pressure to keep talking."
   (4) "Flight of ideas or subjective experience that thoughts are racing."
   (5) "Distractibility (i.e., attention too easily drawn to unimportant or irrelevant external stimuli)."
   (6) **"Increase in goal-directed activity (either socially, at work or school, or sexually) or psychomotor agitation."**
   (7) "Excessive involvement in pleasurable activities that have a high potential for painful consequences (e.g., the person engages in unrestrained buying sprees, sexual indiscretions, or foolish business investments)."
C. **"The episode is associated with an unequivocal change in functioning that is uncharacteristic of the person when not symptomatic."**
D. **"The disturbance in mood and the change in functioning are observable by others."**
E. "The episode is not severe enough to cause marked impairment in social or occupational functioning, or to necessitate hospitalization, and there are no psychotic features."
F. "The symptoms are not due to the direct physiological effects of a substance (e.g., a drug of abuse, a medication, or other treatment) or a general medical condition (e.g., hyperthyroidism)."

Note: Bold entries concern activity.
Source: From *Diagnostic and Statistical Manual of Mental Disorders, 4th Edition (DSM-IV);* American Psychiatric Association, 1994.

of these seven criteria entail activity. Item 2 specifies "decreased need for sleep (e.g., feels rested after only three hours of sleep)" (APA, 1994, p. 332). Wrist actigraphy supplemented by sleep switch device (Hauri, 1999) measurements can document total sleep time and thereby determine if the patient is sleeping as little as three hours.

Item 6 specifies "increase in goal-directed activity (either socially, at work or school, or sexually) or psychomotor agitation" (APA, 1994, p. 332). Combining psychomotor agitation with goal-directed activity means that both inappropriate and appropriate activity increases qualify. Actigraphy cannot distinguish between goal-directed activity and psychomotor agitation but, fortunately, item 6 does not require this discrimination to be made. Hence, actigraphy is very suitable for evaluating item 6. Site of attachment remains an issue. Waist activity consumes more calories than wrist or ankle activity because it is associated with the body's center of gravity. The waist is usually active only during ambulation. Hence, increased waist activity is probably a more conservative indicator of item 6 than is wrist or ankle activity.

Mixed Episode   Criteria for both a MDE and a Manic Episode must be met for at least one week as described previously. The requirement of a one-week behavioral sample can easily be met with actigraphy in between the intake and the first treatment session.

Hypomanic Episode   The criteria are the same for Hypomania as for Mania but duration need only extend to four rather than seven days. The "decreased need for sleep (e.g., feels rested after only three hours of sleep)" and "increase in goal-directed activity (either socially, at work or school, or sexually) or psychomotor agitation" (APA, 1994, p. 338) can be evaluated by actigraphy supplemented with the sleep switch device (Hauri, 1999) to quantify sleep-onset latency. These alterations must be unequivocal and observable by others, not merely self-reported.

DEPRESSIVE DISORDERS

All depressive disorders entail meeting the criteria for a MDE, as defined previously, for which actigraphy and sleep switch device measurements can be informative, as previously described.

Major Depressive Disorder, Single Episode (292.2x)   DSM-IV requires the presence of a single MDE, as previously defined, that cannot be "better accounted for by Schizoaffective Disorder and is not superimposed on Schizophrenia, Schizophreniform Disorder, Delusional Disorder, or Psychotic Disorder Not Otherwise Specified" (APA, 1994, p. 344). No history of a Manic, Hypomanic, or Mixed Episode is allowed. This exclusion does not apply if all the manic-like symptoms are caused by drugs or a general medical condition.

Major Depressive Disorder, Recurrent (296.3x)   Two or more MDEs are required. At least two months must transpire in which the MDE inclusion criteria are not met for two incidents to be considered separate. The same exclusions apply as for diagnosing a Single Episode.

Dysthymic Disorder (300.4)   The inclusion criteria (cf., *DSM-IV*, p. 349) require depressed mood, self-report or observable by others, for at least two years except in adolescents where duration must be at least one year. Presence of at least two of six criteria is required including "insomnia or hypersomnia" and "low energy or fatigue" for which actigraphy can be informative. Symptoms cannot be absent for longer than two months. Exclusion criteria entail not qualifying for a MDE; never having had a Manic Episode, a Hypomanic Episode, or a Mixed Episode; not meeting criteria for a Psychotic or Delusional Disorder; not due to a drug or medical condition; and that the symptoms produce "clinically significant distress or impairment . . ." (APA, 1994, p. 349).

BIPOLAR DISORDERS

Bipolar I Disorder   Having one or more Manic or Mixed Episodes is the essential defining feature of Bipolar I Disorder. Patients may have had previous MDEs or Substance-Induced Mood Disorders. Exclusion criteria include not being better accounted for by Schizoaffective Disorder or Delusional Disorder.

Bipolar I Disorder, Single Manic Episode (296.0x)   Patients qualify for a Manic Episode without ever having had a MDE. Symptoms cannot be better explained " by Schizoaffective Disorder and is not superimposed on Schizophrenia, Schizophreniform Disorder, Delusional Disorder, or Psychotic Disorder Not Otherwise Specified" (APA, 1994, p. 355).

Bipolar I Disorder, Most Recent Episode Hypomanic (296.40)   The patient is currently in or most recently had a Hypomanic Episode and has a history with at least one prior Manic or Mixed Episode. The same exclusion criteria apply.

Bipolar I Disorder, Most Recent Episode Manic (296.4x)   The patient is currently in or most recently had a Manic Episode and has a history with at least one prior MDE, Manic, or Mixed Episode. The same exclusion criteria apply.

Bipolar I Disorder, Most Recent Episode Mixed (296.6x)   The patient is currently in or most recently had a Mixed Episode and has a history with at least one prior Manic or Mixed Episode. The same exclusion criteria apply.

Bipolar I Disorder, Most Recent Episode Depressed (296.5x)   The patient is currently in or most recently had a MDE and has a history with at least one prior MDE. The same exclusion criteria apply.

Bipolar I Disorder, Most Recent Episode Unspecified (296.7)   The patient has symptoms of a Manic, Hypomanic, or Mixed Episode or for a MDE but does not meet the duration criteria. The patient has had at least one prior Manic or Mixed Episode.

Bipolar II Disorder   "The essential feature of Bipolar II disorder is a clinical course that is characterized by the occurrence of one or more Major Depressive Episodes accompanied by at least one Hypomanic Episode" (APA, 1994, p. 359).

Bipolar II Disorder (296.89)   The essential feature is "presence (or history) of one or more Major Depressive Episodes," and "presence (or history) of at least one

Hypomanic Episode. There has never been a Manic Episode or a Mixed Episode" (APA, 1994, p. 362). The same exclusion criteria apply as for Bipolar I disorder. Two specifiers are—Hypomanic and Depressed—depending on the current clinical condition.

Cyclothymic Disorder (301.13) Hypomanic symptoms are experienced over the past two years—one year for children and adolescents—and not asymptomatic for more than two consecutive months. Patients have not had a MDE or a Manic or Mixed Episode during the first two years of their illness.

MELANCHOLIC FEATURES SPECIFIER

DSM-IV provides for the specifier "With Melancholic Features" under the following conditions. First, either of the following criteria are met during a current or most recent episode:

1. "Loss of pleasure in all, or almost all activities."
2. "Lack of reactivity to usually pleasurable stimuli (does not feel much better, even temporarily, when something good happens)" (APA, 1994, p. 384).

Second, three or more of the following six features must apply:

1. "Distinct quality of depressed mood (i.e., the depressed mood is experienced as distinctly different from the kind of feeling experienced after the death of a loved one)."
2. "Depression regularly worse in the morning."
3. "Early morning awakening (at least two hours before usual time of awakening)."
4. "Marked psychomotor retardation or agitation."
5. "Significant anorexia or weight loss."
6. "Excessive or inappropriate guilt" (APA, 1994, p. 384).

Actigraphy can clearly document the time of awakening with an accuracy of one minute and, therefore, empirically determine if awakening is occurring at least two hours before usual. Psychomotor changes are said to be "nearly always present and are observable by others" (APA, 1994, p. 383). Actigraphy can quantify this frequently occurring symptom far more precisely and definitely more objectively than it can be self-reported or rated.

MOOD DISORDER DUE TO A GENERAL MEDICAL CONDITION (293.83)

This condition is diagnosed when patients meet criteria for a MDE, Manic, Hypomanic, or Mixed Episode because of a general medical condition. Actigraphy is as relevant to evaluating the psychological correlates of medical disorders as to primary psychological disorders.

SUBSTANCE-INDUCED MOOD DISORDER

This disorder is diagnosed if symptoms of a MDE, Manic, Hypomanic, or Mixed Episode occur within one month of intoxication or withdrawal from a substance.

ATTENTION-DEFICIT/HYPERACTIVITY DISORDER

DSM-IV provides the following six facets of hyperactivity:

1. "Often fidgets with hands or feet or squirms in seat."
2. "Often leaves seat in classroom or in other situations in which remaining seated is expected."
3. "Often runs about or climbs excessively in situations in which it is inappropriate (in adolescents or adults, may be limited to subjective feelings of restlessness)."
4. "Often has difficulty playing or engaging in leisure activities quietly.
5. "Is often 'on the go' or often acts as if 'driven by a motor.' "
6. "Often talks excessively" (APA, 1994, p. 84).

Three impulsivity facets are also defined.

Attention-Deficit/Hyperactivity Disorder, Predominantly Hyperactive-Impulsive Type (314.01) This disorder is diagnosed when six of the nine combined hyperactivity-impulsivity facets are documented but fewer than six of the inattention facets are found. Actigraphy can evaluate the degree and distribution of activity level because movement intensity can be quantified at precisely timed intervals 24 hours a day over days, weeks, or months while the person behaves in his or her natural environment, including home and school. These data, in conjunction with an activity diary and/or teacher and parent reports, can enable empirically informed estimates of the extent to which motor excess is pervasive or situational. Control data provided by another child in the same class with similar after-school activities currently constitutes the best method for determining if a target child's motor activity is excessive. Tryon and Pinto (1994) discovered that some children rated by teachers as exhibiting motor excess were measurably less active than control children rated by teachers not to have a problem with activity level. Actigraphy can provide an empirical "second opinion" in cases where medication may be prescribed to control presumed motor excesses.

Another approach to the question of motor excess is to determine the extent to which the child can be inactive. Waist movements should be small and infrequent when the child is seated and attending to the teacher or task at hand. Actigraphic records can be used to determine how long a child can remain relatively inactive, where activity level is below a threshold value. Failure to find quiescent periods may be as or more important than finding excessively high levels of activity.

Fidgeting with feet can probably be detected with ankle-worn actigraphs because relatively little foot movement is prompted by teachers of seated children. Fidgeting with hands may not be distinguishable from the constructively active child. Teicher, Ito, Glod, and Barber (1996) used an infrared motion analysis system to track the position of four markers placed on a cap, shoulder, back, and right elbow 50 times a second with a resolution of .04 mm (measurement error = 0.001%). ADHD boys were 2.3 to 3.8 times as active during a continuous performance test than control boys.

Sleep Problems Parents of children with ADHD consistently report that their children have disturbed sleep (e.g., Kaplan, McNicol, Conte, & Moghadam, 1987; Ross & Ross, 1982), yet a review of 16 PSG studies by Corkum, Tannock, and Moldofsky

(1998) failed to reveal any problems. Corkum, Tannock, Moldofsky, Hogg-Johnson, and Humphries (2001) found that children with ADHD sleep longer than normal children. Gruber et al. (2000) hypothesized that the failure to find sleep abnormalities in ADHD children was because sleep is studied for only a couple of nights in sleep laboratories. They studied sleep actigraphically in the child's home for five consecutive nights in 38 boys with ADHD and 64 control subjects and found significantly greater variability in sleep parameters of the ADHD boys. No significant differences were found between ADHD and control boys on any sleep parameter using multivariate analysis of covariance controlling for age. However, a similar analysis on the standard deviation of sleep parameters revealed significant differences regarding duration of sleep and sleep-onset time. Analysis of variability in corresponding subjective sleep self-ratings did not distinguish the two groups of boys, thereby showing the value of objective sleep measurement.

Attention-Deficit/Hyperactive Disorder, Predominantly Inattentive Type (314.00) This disorder is diagnosed when the inattention criteria are satisfied and the hyperactivity-impulsivity criteria are not. Not satisfying criteria always raises questions as to the thoroughness of the examination because the easiest way to not satisfy a criterion is to not assess it carefully or comprehensively.

Two behavioral sampling issues are pertinent. The first issue is whether observational data derive from the natural environment or were obtained during testing in an office setting or other evaluation environment. Behaviors must be assessed either in natural context or evidence provided that observations made under clinic or laboratory conditions generalize to these settings. The second issue concerns the size of the behavioral sample taken. Brief samples are more likely to overlook or minimize hyperactivity that becomes irritable to teachers and parents over weeks and months. These psychometric sampling issues pertain equally well to behavioral assessment (cf. Cone, 1988; Tryon, 1993, 1998).

Attention-Deficit/Hyperactive Disorder, Combined Type (314.01) This disorder is diagnosed when both inattentive and hyperactive-impulsive criteria are met.

Attention-Deficit/Hyperactive Disorder, Not Otherwise Specified (314.9) This disorder is diagnosed when prominent symptoms of inattention or hyperactivity exist but the full criteria for either subtype are not met.

ANXIETY DISORDERS

Actigraphy can be used to quantify certain correlates of anxiety because anxiety sets the occasion for increased activity.

Generalized Anxiety Disorder (300.02) Among other symptoms, patients must exhibit three or more of the following six:

1. "Restlessness or feeling keyed up or on edge."
2. "Being easily fatigued."
3. "Difficulty concentrating or mind going blank."
4. "Irritability."
5. "Muscle tension."
6. "Sleep disturbance (difficulty falling or staying asleep, or restless unsatisfying sleep)" (APA, 1994, p. 436).

Only one symptom is needed for children. Restlessness may result in pacing or other agitated behavior that actigraphy would easily detect. Fatigue can result in lifestyle changes favoring inactivity. Patients who curtail or avoid activities that they previously engaged in regularly reduce their 24-hour activity output. Difficulty initiating and/or maintaining sleep can be documented using wrist actigraphy supplemented by hand-pressure monitoring.

Posttraumatic Stress Disorder (309.81)   In addition to other criteria, patients must have two of the following five persistent symptoms:

1. "Difficulty falling or staying asleep."
2. "Irritability or outbursts of anger."
3. "Difficulty concentrating."
4. "Hypervigilance."
5. "Exaggerated startle response" (APA, 1994, p. 428).

Actigraphy, supplemented with the sleep switch device (Hauri, 1999) to quantify sleep-onset latency, can provide objective data regarding problems with sleep onset and sleep maintenance. Sadeh, Lavie, Scher, Tirosh, and Epstein (1991) demonstrated that 4.5 nights of wrist actigraphy can discriminate between sleep-disturbed and control children. Glod, Teicher, Hartman, and Harakal (1997) used 72 hours of continuous wrist actigraphy to show that 19 prepubertal children with documented abuse were twice as active at night as normal and depressed children. Abused children have more difficulty falling asleep and staying asleep.

SCHIZOPHRENIA AND OTHER PSYCHOTIC DISORDERS

Schizophrenia: Catatonic Type (295.20)   A schizophrenic receives this diagnosis if his or her clinical presentation is dominated by at least two of the following five features:

1. "Motoric immobility as evidenced by catalepsy (including waxy flexibility) or stupor."
2. "Excessive activity level (that is apparently purposeless and not influenced by external stimuli)."
3. "Extreme negativism (an apparently motiveless resistance to all instructions or maintenance of a rigid posture against attempts to be moved) or mutism."
4. "Peculiarities of voluntary movement as evidenced by posturing (voluntary assumption of inappropriate or bizarre postures), stereotyped movements, prominent mannerisms, or prominent grimacing."
5. "Echolalia or echopraxia" (APA, 1994, p. 289).

Actigraphy can quantify the first two features. Immobility and stupor results in hypoactivity. Actigraphy can also document excessive activity level, but observational data are needed to determine whether elevated activity levels are purposeless and/or not influenced by external stimuli.

Schizoaffective Disorder (295.70)   This diagnosis is given when criteria for a Major Depressive, Manic, or Mixed Episode are met concurrently with criterion A for Schizophrenia (cf. *DSM-IV*, pp. 285–286). Subtypes include Bipolar Type if a Manic or Mixed Episode occurs along with a MDE and Depressive Type if only a MDE is involved.

Catatonic Disorder Due to a General Medical Condition (293.89)   Actigraphy is as informative when catatonia is induced by a general medical condition as when it is the primary illness.

Substance-Related Disorders

The following disorders entail psychomotor agitation or retardation as one of their inclusion criteria: Amphetamine Intoxication (292.89), Amphetamine Withdrawal (292.0), Cocaine Intoxication (292.89), Cocaine Withdrawal (292.0). Psychomotor agitation, but not retardation, is associated with Alcohol Withdrawal (291.8), Caffeine Intoxication (305.90), and Sedative, Hypnotic, or Anxiolytic Withdrawal (292.0).

Insomnia is associated with Alcohol Withdrawal (291.8), Amphetamine Withdrawal (292.0), Caffeine Intoxication (305.90), Nicotine Withdrawal (292.0), Opioid Withdrawal (292.0), and Sedative, Hypnotic, or Anxiolytic Withdrawal (292.0). Hypersomnia is characteristic of Amphetamine Withdrawal (292.0) or Cocaine Withdrawal (292.0).

Medication-Induced Movement Disorders

Neuroleptic-Induced Parkinsonism (332.1)   This disorder can result within a few weeks of initiating or increasing the dose of neuroleptic medication. Van Hilten, Middelkoop, Kerkhof, and Roos (1991) demonstrated that it is possible to detect the 4 to 6 Hz tremor characteristic of Parkinson's Disease (PD) using a Geweiler wrist-worn actigraph (Sing Medical, Homberectikon, Switzerland) with a 0.1 g threshold and a bandpass filter of 0.25 to 3.0 Hz. Apparently, the band-pass window is not sharply defined, thereby enabling partial tremor detection. The authors recommend the construction of a 4 to 6 Hz sensitive device.

Van Someren et al. (1993) constructed an accelerometer-based, wrist-worn tremor-sensitive actigraph sensitive to the 3 to 12 Hz range. They were aware that normal arm movements produce transient 3 to 12 Hz vibrations that could be mistaken for 4 to 6 Hz Parkinsonian tremor. To distinguish valid tremor from these transients, the computer scored tremor only when at least six full waves of 2.94 to 12.5 Hz signal were detected. All signals not scored tremor were scored activity. They obtained wrist data on 8 patients with PD before and after a tremor-relieving thalamotomy and 10 age-matched and 10 young control subjects. Their data clearly discriminated between preoperative patients and control subjects and between pre- and postoperative patients. This type of device can be used to monitor patients as they first receive neuroleptic medication and when the dosage of such medication is increased to detect tremor onset early.

Medication-Induced Postural Tremor (331.1)   This disorder can occur in response to the administration of lithium, antidepressants, and valproate (*DSM-IV*, p. 680). Wrist tremography, described previously, could also be used to evaluate the onset of postural tremor.

Neuroleptic-Induced Tardive Dyskinesia (333.82)   This disorder may also be detected using a modified wrist actigraph, given the work of Tryon and Pologe (1987) on the accelerometric assessment of tardive dyskinesia.

Neuroleptic-Induced Acute Akathesia (333.99) This disorder causes restless movements of the leg, fidgeting, pacing, and the inability to sit or stand still. It is a form of drug-induced movement. The patient feels that he or she must move to obtain relief but movement does not bring relief. Yet, he or she continues to feel the necessity to move. Wrist, waist, and/or ankle actigraphy clearly reveals the presence of akathesia. Tryon (1991a, pp. 202–205) describes a protocol for evaluating akathesia. Essentially, the patient is asked to sit quietly in a chair for a chosen duration, perhaps while watching television. Actigraphs on all four limbs monitor the ability to remain motionless.

CRITERIA SETS AND AXES PROVIDED FOR FURTHER STUDY

Postconcussional Disorder entails disordered sleep for which actigraphy supplemented by hand-pressure monitoring could be informative (APA, 1994, p. 705). Longitudinal evaluation enables estimation of variability in sleep parameters.

Caffeine withdrawal entails "marked fatigue or drowsiness" (APA, 1994, p. 709). Fatigue may well be reflected in low energy lifestyle choices. Drowsiness may be evaluated by conducting the modified Multiple Sleep Latency Test using the sleep switch device (Hauri, 1999) described previously.

Postpsychotic Depressive Disorder of Schizophrenia requires that criteria for a Major Depressive Episode be superimposed on the residual phase of Schizophrenia (APA, 1994, p. 712).

Premenstrual Dysphoric Disorder includes insomnia or hypersomnia among its 11 inclusion criteria (APA, 1994, p. 717). Actigraphy supplemented by the sleep switch device (Hauri, 1999) may be informative here.

Minor Depressive Disorder entails "insomnia or hypersomnia nearly every day, psychomotor agitation or retardation nearly every day (observable by others, not merely subjective feelings of restlessness or being slowed down)," and "fatigue or loss of energy nearly every day" (APA, 1994, p. 720). The primary difference between this disorder and MDE is that it requires fewer (at least two but fewer than five) criteria to be met. However, all of the activity-related criteria are included.

Recurrent Brief Depressive Disorder requires that all MDE criteria be met over a period of at least two days but less than two weeks (APA, 1994, p. 723). Depressive periods must occur at least once per month for the last year and not be associated with the menstrual cycle. Actigraphy makes the same contributions here as when diagnosing MDE.

Mixed Anxiety-Depressive Disorder entails "sleep disturbance (difficulty falling or staying asleep, or restless unsatisfying sleep)" and "fatigue or low energy" (APA, 1994, p. 724). Wrist actigraphy supplemented with sleep switch device (Hauri, 1999) can quantify sleep-onset latency. Actigraphy can determine if sleep is maintained once initiated. Fatigue may result in selecting a less energetic lifestyle, which lowers 24-hour activity levels.

ANOREXIA NERVOSA

Epling and Pierce (1991) and Pierce and Epling (1994) describe an animal model of anorexia nervosa with close human parallels in which activity plays a central role. The primary observation is that when food availability is restricted to one meal per day, and access is given to an activity wheel, adolescent male as well as female rats decrease their food intake and run until they die! Running typically increases to 15 km per day, which is high for humans and enormous for the much smaller rat. The authors hypothesize that restricting food intake to one meal per day simulates famine conditions. Evolution has apparently favored continuous migration, with very little time spent feeding, until a more plentiful food supply is located. Hence, food restriction can set the occasion for sustained activity and heightened anorexia to facilitate migration. Because the rat cannot get anywhere in its activity wheel and because the experimenter does not increase the frequency of food presentation, the animals never *arrive* at a more plentiful food supply and so continue running, migrating, until death. Self-imposed food restriction and exercise opportunity appear to result in equally futile conditions for humans. Food restriction both increases activity, which burns more calories, and strengthens anorexia, thereby further reducing caloric intake. This artificial famine-escape migration state is maintained until exhaustion and/or death results. Activity increases are integral to this disorder but are not yet reflected in the inclusion criteria for Anorexia Nervosa (307.1) (APA, 1994, pp. 544–545). Perhaps *DSM*-V will address this omission. Two forms of Attention-Deficit Hyperactivity Disorder are diagnosed—one with hyperactivity and one without hyperactivity. If motor excess is causal to the development and maintenance of Anorexia Nervosa as the work of Epling and Pierce, and Pierce and Epling suggest, it may be prudent to include 24-hour actigraphy measurements as formal diagnostic criteria for this disorder. More generally, evidence of prior and current hyperactivity should become inclusion criteria for Anorexia Nervosa. Activity level reduces some percent of reduction in body weight. Healthy children are normally active, but starving children are inactive. Falk, Halmi, and Tryon (1985) found emaciated women to be hypoactive when hospitalized and that their activity levels increased as their body weight increased.

MINORITIES AND WOMEN

SEX

Women have routinely been included in activity research, but sex has not been used often as an independent variable. Eaton and Enns (1986) performed a meta-analysis of 90 studies involving 127 independent estimates of sex difference of people ages 2 months to 30 years (Median = 55.5 months = 4.6 yrs.) based on sample sizes ranging from 7 to 25,000 (Median = 68) using a variety of methodologies. They reported boys to be more active than girls by $d = .49$ standard deviations on average. Tryon (1991a, pp. 93–101) restricted his review of the developmental evidence to studies that actually measured activity level. Boys were found to be more active than girls by 6 to 8 months of age and to remain more active until about 10 years of age. By 12 years of age, boys' activity declined to the point where within-sex variability was as large as between-sex differences, precluding a significant difference.

Eaton et al. (2001) compiled data from 12 different studies that objectively measured activity levels of 840 subjects ranging in age from .1 to 24.6 years of age. They reported an inverted U-shaped function where activity level peaked between 2 and 6 years of age and then declined. This finding is consistent with Eaton and Yu's (1989) report of an age-related activity decrease in which older normal children were rated as less active than younger ones. Sex differences in measured activity have not been reported in teenagers or adults but could be easily studied. Two experimental designs could be used. The simplest approach is to use actigraphs (Tryon, 1991a; Tryon & Williams, 1996) to obtain minute-by-minute activity measurements 24 hours per day for two, three, or four weeks. In addition to analyzing these data for mean level, circadian rhythm analyses can be performed to determine if men and women distribute their activity similarly. A second approach is to use actigraphs to measure activity in one or more specific test situations. Clinicians should be careful to obtain an adequate behavioral sample and to limit conclusions to situations similar to those tested.

Sex effects regarding activity may largely reflect cultural preferences in how a person spends leisure time. If boys prefer active outdoor sports and girls prefer passive indoor activities, a sex difference emerges for this reason. Another possibility is that activity differences may reflect social roles. Caring for young children or delivering mail on foot probably occasions more activity than working as a secretary or accountant.

RACE

Racial composition of subjects participating in activity studies is not consistently reported and no known study has examined racial activity differences. No hypotheses have been suggested that a racial activity difference exists and, consequently, no tests of such hypotheses have been located.

SUMMARY

All observable behaviors entail motion and, therefore, have a measurable activity level ranging from a minimum of zero to some upper maximum value. Individual differences in activity level begin prenatally to stimulate proper neuromuscular and joint development. These activity level differences persist and are evident during infancy and childhood. They are described as a facet of extraversion regarding adult personality. Individual differences in activity level are related to all-cause mortality and strongly determine functional status during late life.

Many behavior and medical disorders alter normal activity patterns. Modern wrist- and waist-worn actigraphs objectively quantify the physical forces associated with behavior, average, and record these measurements every minute of the day and night for up to 88 consecutive days before filling memory. The history of medicine is a history of measurement in that modern medicine defines and diagnoses disease in terms of physical and chemical laboratory analyses of biological specimens. Actigraphy provides psychology and psychiatry with the opportunity to objectively collect and analyze behavioral specimens (samples) from the natural environment and under controlled laboratory conditions. This chapter articulates the relevance of activity measurements to 48 *DSM-IV* disorders of sleep and waking behaviors. Actigraphy can be used to evaluate change over time and, therefore, provide objective evidence of therapeutic efficacy for both behavioral and pharmacological interventions. Actigraphy is a cost-effective extension of behavioral assessment with broad applicability and relevance for clinicians as well as investigators.

The objectives of good clinical practice are those of good research. Clinicians' need for high-quality information on which to base diagnostic and treatment decisions is just as great as the researchers' need for high-quality information on which to evaluate theoretical hypotheses. Both clinicians and investigators are concerned with therapeutic efficacy; both are entitled to the same high-quality data. Clinicians often supplement client self-report with psychological testing regarding questions of anxiety, depression, and personality disorder but are reluctant to obtain instrumented behavioral samples of activity, preferring to rely exclusively on self-report, teacher report, and parent report for this information. No evidence exists that clients can more accurately self-report activity than they can self-report other aspects of their behavior and personality for which psychological testing is routinely ordered. The ability of teachers and parents to accurately report activity level has been assumed rather than demonstrated. One study by Tryon and Pinto (1994) reported serious discrepancies between teacher-rated and measured activity level.

Activity is ideally suited for instrumented measurement, and a broad range of devices are available—from simple pedometers and step counters to sophisticated, but easy-to-use, computerized actigraphs. Activity monitoring is especially suitable for continuous measurement over time and, therefore, is able to objectively quantify change throughout treatment and follow up. The state of the art regarding activity level measurement has moved well beyond self-report, parent report, and teacher report. The commercial availability of several different actigraphs makes these devices readily available to clinicians and investigators. Reliance on activity level estimates, given our ability to measure activity level, can no longer be justified.

REFERENCES

American Psychiatric Association. (1994). *Diagnostic and statistical manual of mental disorders* (4th ed.). Washington, DC: Author.

Anastasi, A. (1988). *Psychological testing* (6th ed.). New York: Macmillan.

Aronen, E. T., Teicher, M. H., Geenens, D., Curtin, S., Glod, C. A., & Pahlavan, K. (1996). Motor activity and severity of depression in hospitalized prepubertal children. *Journal of the American Academy of Child and Adolescent Psychiatry, 35,* 752–763.

Baekeland, F., & Hoy, P. (1971). Reported vs. recorded sleep characteristics. *Archives of General Psychiatry, 24,* 548–551.

Barkley, T. J., & Tryon, W. W. (1995). Psychomotor retardation found in college students seeking counseling. *Behavior Research and Therapy, 33,* 977–984.

Birrell, P. C. (1983). Behavioral, subjective, and electroencephalographic indices of sleep-onset latency and sleep duration. *Journal of Behavioral Assessment, 5,* 179–190.

Blair, S. N., Kohl, H. W., Paffenbarger, R. S., Clark, D. G., Cooper, K. H., & Gibbons, L. W. (1989). Physical fitness and all-cause mortality: A prospective study of healthy men and women. *Journal of the American Medical Association, 262,* 2395–2401.

Blake, H., Gerard, R. W., & Kleitman, N. (1939). Factors influencing brain potentials during sleep. *Journal of Neurophysiology, 2,* 48–60.

Block, J. (1995). A contrarian view of the five-factor approach to personality description. *Psychological Bulletin, 117,* 187–215.

Block, J., & Block, J. H. (1980). *The California Child Q-Set.* Palo Alto, CA: Consulting Psychologists Press. (Original work published 1969)

Bonato, R. A., & Ogilvie, R. D. (1989). A home evaluation of a behavioral response measure of sleep/wakefulness. *Perceptual and Motor Skills, 68,* 87–96.

Bonnet, M. H., & Moore, S. E. (1982). The threshold of sleep: Perception of sleep as a function of time asleep and auditory threshold. *Sleep, 5,* 267–276.

Brown, A. C., Smolensky, M. H., D'Alonzo, G. E., & Redman, D. P. (1990). Actigraphy: A means of assessing circadian patterns in human activity. *Chronobiology International, 7,* 125–133.

Burnside, I. M. (1978). *Working with the elderly.* North Scituate, MA: Duxbury Press.

Buss, A. H. (1989). Temperaments as personality traits. In G. A. Kohnstamm, J. E. Bates, & M. K. Rothbart (Eds.), *Temperament in childhood* (pp. 49–58). New York: Wiley.

Buss, A. H., & Plomin, R. (1975). *A temperament theory of personality development.* New York: Wiley.

Buss, A. H., & Plomin, R. (1984). *Temperament: Early developing personality traits.* Hillsdale, NJ: Erlbaum.

Carskadon, M. A. (1994). Measuring daytime sleepiness. In M. H. Kryger, T. Roth, & W. C. Dement (Eds.), *Principles and practice of sleep medicine* (2nd ed., pp. 961–966). London: Saunders.

Carskadon, M. A., & Dement, W. C. (1994). Normal human sleep: An overview. In M. H. Kryger, T. Roth, & W. C. Dement (Eds.), *Principles and practice of sleep medicine* (2nd ed., pp. 16–25). London: Saunders.

Carskadon, M. A., Dement, W. C., Mitler, M. M., Guilleminault, C., Zarcone, V. P., & Spiegel, R. (1976). Self-reports versus sleep laboratory findings in 122 drug-free subjects with complaints of chronic insomnia. *American Journal of Psychiatry, 133,* 1382–1388.

Carskadon, M. A., & Rechtschaffen, A. (1994). Monitoring and staging human sleep. In M. H. Kryger, T. Roth, & W. C. Dement (Eds.), *Principles and practice of sleep medicine* (2nd ed., pp. 943–960). London: Saunders.

Caspi, A., Block, J., Block, J. H., Klopp, B., Lynam, D., Moffitt, T. E., et al. (1992). A "common language" version of the California Child Q-Set for personality assessment. *Psychological Assessment, 4,* 512–523.

Chase, M. H., & Morales, F. R. (1994). The control of motoneurons during sleep. In M. H. Kryger, T. Roth, & W. C. Dement (Eds.), *Principles and practice of sleep medicine* (2nd ed., pp. 163–175). London: Saunders.

Cole, R. J., & Kripke, D. F. (1989). Progress in automatic sleep/wake scoring by wrist actigraph. *Sleep Research, 18,* 331.

Cole, R. J., Kripke, D. F., Gruen, W., Mullaney, D. J., & Gillin, J. C. (1992). Automatic sleep/wake identification from wrist activity. *Sleep, 15,* 461–469.

Comrey, A. L. (1994). *Manual and Handbook of Interpretations for the Comrey Personality Scales.* San Diego, CA: Edits Publishers.

Cone, J. D. (1988). Psychometric considerations and the multiple models of behavioral assessment. In A. S. Bellack & M. Hersen (Eds.), *Behavioral assessment: A practical handbook* (3rd ed., pp. 42–66). New York: Pergamon Press.

Conners, C. K. (1989). *Conners' Rating Scale.* Toronto, Ontario, Canada: Multi-Health Systems.

Corkum, P., Tannock, R., & Moldofsky, H. (1998). Sleep disturbances in children with attention-deficit/hyperactivity disorder. *Journal of the American Academy of Child and Adolescent Psychiatry, 37,* 637–646.

Corkum, P., Tannock, R., & Moldofsky, H., Hogg-Johnson, S., & Humphries, T. (2001). Actigraphy and parental ratings of sleep in children with Attention-Deficit/Hyperactivity Disorder (ADHD). *Sleep, 24,* 303–312.

Costa, P. T., Jr., & McCrae, R. R. (1980). Still stable after all these years: Personality as a key to some issues in adulthood and old age. In P. B. Baltes & O. G. Brim (Eds.), *Lifespan development and behavior* (Vol. 3, pp. 65–102). New York: Academic Press.

Costa, P. T., Jr., & McCrae, R. R. (1992). *Revised NEO Personality Inventory (NEO PI-R) and NEO Five-Factor Inventory (NEO-FFI): Professional manual.* Odessa, FL: Psychological Assessment Resources.

Costa, P. T., Jr., & McCrae, R. R. (1994). Stability and change in personality from adolescence through adulthood. In C. F. Halverson Jr., G. A. Kohnstamm, & R. P. Martin (Eds.), *The developing structure of temperament and personality from infancy to adulthood* (pp. 139–150). Hillsdale, NJ: Erlbaum.

Costa, P. T., Jr., & McCrae, R. R. (1995). Solid ground in the wetlands of personality: A reply to Block. *Psychological Bulletin, 117,* 216–220.

Davis, H., Davis, P. A., Loomis, A. L., Harvey, E. N., & Hobart, G. (1937). Changes in human brain potentials during the onset of sleep. *Science, 86,* 448–450.

DeFries, J. C., Gervais, M. C., & Thomas, E. A. (1978). Response to 30 generations of selection for open-field activity in laboratory mice. *Behavior Genetics, 8,* 3–13.

DeFries, J. C., Wilson, J. R., & McClearn, G. E. (1970). Open-field behavior in mice: Selection response and situational generality. *Behavior Genetics, 1,* 195–211.

Digman, J. M. (1990). Personality structure: Emergence of the five-factor model. *Annual Review of Psychology, 41,* 417–440.

Digman, J. M. (1994). Child personality and temperament: Does the five-factor model embrace both domains? In C. F. Halverson Jr., G. A. Kohnstamm, & R. P. Martin (Eds.), *The developing structure of temperament and personality from infancy to adulthood* (pp. 323–338). Hillsdale, NJ: Erlbaum.

Drachman, D. B., & Sokoloff, L. (1966). The role of movement in embryonic joint development. *Developmental Biology, 14,* 401–420.

Dustman, R. E., Ruhling, R. O., Russell, E. M., Shearer, D. E., Bonekat, W., Shigeoka, J. W., et al. (1984). Aerobic exercise training and improved neuropsychological function of older individuals. *Neurobiology of Aging, 5,* 35–42.

Eaton, W. O., & Enns, L. R. (1986). Sex differences in human motor activity level. *Psychological Bulletin, 100,* 19–28.

Eaton, W. O., McKeen, N. A., & Campbell, D. W. (2001). The waxing and waning of movement: Implications for psychological development. *Developmental Review, 21,* 205–223.

Eaton, W. O., & Saudino, K. J. (1992). Prenatal activity level as a temperament dimension? Individual differences and developmental functions in fetal movement. *Infant Behavior and Development, 15,* 57–70.

Eaton, W. O., & Yu, A. P. (1989). Are sex differences in child motor activity level a function of sex differences in maturational status? *Child Development, 60,* 1005–1011.

Epling, W. F., & Pierce, W. D. (1991). *Solving the anorexia puzzle: A scientific approach.* Toronto, Ontario, Canada: Hogrefe & Huber.

Espie, C. A., Lindsay, W. R., & Espie, L. C. (1989). Use of the sleep assessment device (Kelley and Lichstein, 1980) to validate insomniacs' self-report of sleep pattern. *Journal of Psychopathology and Behavioral Assessment, 11,* 71–79.

Eysenck, H. J. (1991). Dimensions of personality: Sixteen, 5, or 3?—Criteria for a taxonomic paradigm. *Personality and Individual Differences, 12,* 773–790.

Eysenck, H. J. (1994). The big five or giant three: Criteria for a paradigm. In C. F. Halverson Jr., G. A. Kohnstamm, & R. P. Martin (Eds.), *The developing structure of temperament and personality from infancy to adulthood* (pp. 37–51). Hillsdale, NJ: Erlbaum.

Falk, J. R., Halmi, K. A., & Tryon, W. W. (1985). Activity measures in anorexia nervosa. *Archives of General Psychiatry, 42,* 811–814.

Fox, S. M., Naughton, J. P., & Haskell, W. L. (1971). Physical activity and the prevention of coronary heart disease. *Annals of Clinical Research, 3,* 404–432.

Frankel, B. L., Coursey, R. D., Buchbinder, R., & Snyder, F. (1976). Recorded and reported sleep in chronic primary insomnia. *Archives of General Psychiatry, 33,* 615–623.

Franklin, J. (1981). The measurement of sleep-onset latency in insomnia. *Behavior Research and Therapy, 19,* 547–549.

Freedman, R., & Papsdorf, J. (1976). Biofeedback and progressive relaxation. Treatment of sleep-onset insomnia: A controlled, all-night investigation. *Biofeedback and Self Regulation, 1,* 253–271.

Futterman, C. S., & Tryon, W. W. (1994). Psychomotor retardation found in depressed outpatient women. *Journal of Behavior Therapy and Experimental Psychiatry, 25,* 41–48.

Gerhardsson, M., Norell, S. E., Kiviranta, H., Pedersen, N. L., & Ahlbom, A. (1986). Sedentary jobs and colon cancer. *American Journal of Epidemiology, 123,* 775–780.

Glod, C. A., Teicher, M. H., Hartman, C. R., & Harakal, T. (1997). Increased nocturnal activity and impaired sleep maintenance in abused children. *Journal of the American Academy of Child and Adolescent Psychiatry, 36,* 1236–1243.

Glod, C. A., Teicher, M. H., Polcari, A., McGreenery, C. E., & Ito, Y. (1997). Circadian rest-activity disturbances in children with seasonal affective disorder. *Journal of the American Academy of Child and Adolescent Psychiatry, 36,* 188–195.

Goldberg, L. R. (1990). An alternative "description of personality": The big five factor structure. *Journal of Personality and Social Psychology, 59,* 1216–1229.

Goldberg, L. R., & Rosolack, T. K. (1994). The big five factor structure as an integrative framework: An empirical comparison with Eysenck's P-E-N model. In C. F. Halverson Jr., G. A. Kohnstamm, & R. P. Martin (Eds.), *The developing structure of temperament and personality from infancy to adulthood* (pp. 7–35). Hillsdale, NJ: Erlbaum.

Goldsmith, H. H., Buss, A. H., Plomin, R., Rothbart, M. K., Thomas, A., Chess, S., et al. (1987). Roundtable: What is temperament? Four approaches. *Child Development, 58,* 505–529.

Gruber, R., Sadeh, A., & Raviv, A. (2000). Instability of sleep patterns in children with attention-deficit/hyperactivity disorder. *Journal of the American Academy of Child and Adolescent Psychiatry, 39,* 495–501.

Gueldner, S. H., & Spradley, J. (1988). Outdoor walking lowers fatigue. *Journal of Gerontological Nursing, 14,* 6–12.

Guilford, J. S., Zimmerman, W. S., & Guilford, J. P. (1976). *Guilford-Zimmerman Temperament Survey handbook: Twenty-five years of research and application.* San Diego, CA: Educational and Industrial Testing Service.

Hagekull, B. (1994). Infant temperament and early childhood functioning: Possible relations to the Five-Factor Model. In C. F. Halverson Jr., G. A. Kohnstamm, & R. P. Martin (Eds.), *The developing structure of temperament and personality from infancy to adulthood* (pp. 227–240). Hillsdale, NJ: Erlbaum.

Halverson, C. F., Jr., Kohnstamm, G. A., & Martin, R. P. (1994). *The developing structure of temperament and personality from infancy to adulthood.* Hillsdale, NJ: Erlbaum.

Harsh, J. R., & Ogilvie, R. D. (1994). Introduction: A first sketch. In R. D. Ogilvie & J. R. Harsh (Eds.), *Sleep-onset: Normal and abnormal processes* (pp. xvii–xxviii). Washington, DC: American Psychological Association.

Hauri, P. J. (1994). Primary insomnia. In M. H. Kryger, T. Roth, & W. C. Dement (Eds.), *Principles and practice of sleep medicine* (2nd ed., pp. 494–499). London: Saunders.

Hauri, P. J. (1999). Evaluation of a sleep switch device. *Sleep, 22,* 1110–1117.

Hauri, P., & Fisher, J. (1986). Persistent psychophysiologic (learned) insomnia. *Sleep, 9,* 38–53.

Hauri, P. J., & Wisbey, J. (1992). Wrist actigraphy in insomnia. *Sleep, 15,* 293–301.

Jean-Louis, G., Kripke, D. F., Cole, R. J., Assmus, J. D., & Langer. (2001). Sleep detection with an accelerometer actigraph: Comparisons with polysomnography. *Physiology and Behavior, 72,* 21–28.

Jean-Louis, G., Mendlowicz, M. V., Gillin, J. C., Rapaport, M. H., Kelsoe, J. R., Zizi, F., et al. (2000). Sleep estimation from wrist activity in patients with major depression. *Physiology and Behavior, 70,* 49–53.

Kamphaus, R. W., & Frick, P. J. (1996). *Clinical assessment of child and adolescent personality and behavior.* Boston: Allyn & Bacon.

Kaplan, B. J., McNicol, J., Conte, R. A., & Moghadam, H. K. (1987). Sleep disturbances in preschool aged hyperactive and nonhyperactive children. *Pediatrics, 80,* 839–844.

Kleitman, N. (1963). *Sleep and wakefulness.* Chicago: University of Chicago Press.

Kryger, M. H., Roth, T., & Dement, W. C. (1994). *Principles and practice of sleep medicine* (2nd ed.). Philadelphia: Saunders.

Leon, A. S., Connett, J., Jacobs, D. R., Jr., & Rauramaa, R. (1987). Leisure-time physical activity levels and risk of coronary heart disease and death: The Multiple Risk Factor International Trial. *Journal of the American Medical Association, 258,* 2388–2395.

Lerner, R. M., Lerner, J. V., Windle, M., Hooker, K., Lenerz, K., & East, P. L. (1986). In R. Plomin & J. Dunn (Eds.), *The structure of temperament: Changes, continuities and challenges* (pp. 99–114). Hillsdale, NJ: Erlbaum.

Lerner, R. M., Palermo, M., Sprio, A., & Nessleroade, J. (1982). Assessing the dimensions of temperamental individuality across the life-span: The Dimensions of Temperament Survey (DOTS). *Child Development, 53,* 149–160.

Lichstein, K. L., Hoelscher, T. J., Eakin, T. L., & Nickel, R. (1983). Empirical sleep assessment in the home: A convenient, inexpensive approach. *Journal of Behavioral Assessment, 5,* 111–118.

Lichstein, K. L., Nickel, R., Hoelscher, T. J., & Kelley, J. E. (1982). Clinical validation of a sleep assessment device. *Behavior Research and Therapy, 20,* 292–298.

Lichstein, K. L., & Riedel, B. W. (1994). Behavioral assessment and treatment of insomnia: A review with an emphasis on clinical application. *Behavior Therapy, 25,* 659–688.

Lindsley, O. R. (1957). Operant behavior during sleep: A measure of depth of sleep. *Science, 126,* 1290–1291.

Linehan, M. M. (1980). Content validity: Its relevance to behavioral assessment. *Behavioral Assessment, 2,* 147–159.

Loomis, A. L., Harvey, E. N., & Hobart, G. A. (1937). Cerebral states during sleep as studied by human brain potentials. *Journal of Experimental Psychology, 21,* 127–144.

Martin, R. P., Wisenbaker, J., & Huttunen, M. (1994). Review of factor analytic studies of temperament measures based on the Thomas-Chess structural model: Implications for the Big Five. In C. F. Halverson Jr., G. A. Kohnstamm, & R. P. Martin (Eds.), *The developing structure of temperament and personality from infancy to adulthood* (pp. 157–172). Hillsdale, NJ: Erlbaum.

Mason, D. J., & Tapp, W. (1992). Measuring circadian rhythms: Actigraph versus activation checklist. *Western Journal of Nursing Research, 14,* 358–379.

Mason, W. J., Ancoli-Israel, S., Kripke, D. F., Jones, D. W., Parker, L., Fell, R. L., et al. (1992). Reliability of actillume recordings in nursing home patients. *Sleep Research, 21,* 349.

McAuley, E., Courneya, K. S., & Lettunich, J. (1991). Effects of acute and long-term exercise on self-efficacy responses in sedentary, middle-aged males and females. *Gerontologist, 31,* 534–542.

McCall, W. V., & Edinger, J. D. (1992). Subjective total insomnia: An example of sleep state misperception. *Sleep, 15,* 71–73.

Meyer, G. J., Finn, S. E., Eyde, L. D., Kay, G. G., Moreland, K. L., Dies, R. R., et al. (2001). Psychological testing and psychological assessment: A review of evidence and issues. *American Psychologist, 56,* 128–165.

Middelkoop, H. A. M. (Ed.). (1994). *Actigraphic assessment of sleep and sleep disorders.* Delft, Holland: Eburon.

Moessinger, A. C. (1988). Morphological consequences of depressed or impaired fetal activity. In W. P. Smotherman & S. R. Robinson (Eds.), *Behavior of the fetus* (pp. 163–173). Caldwell, NJ: Telford Press.

Morris, J. N., Everitt, M. G., Pollard, R., Chave, S. P. W., & Semmence, A. M. (1980). Vigorous exercise in leisure time: Protection against coronary heart disease. *Lancet, 2,* 1207–1210.

Mullaney, D. J., Kripke, D. F., & Messin, S. (1980). Wrist-actigraphic estimation of sleep time. *Sleep, 3,* 83–92.

Oberman, A. (1985). Exercise and the primary prevention of cardiovascular disease. *American Journal of Cardiology, 55,* 10D-20D.

Ogilvie, R. D., & Wilkinson, R. T. (1984). The detection of sleep-onset: Behavioral and physiological convergence. *Psychophysiology, 21,* 510–520.

Ogilvie, R. D., & Wilkinson, R. T. (1988). Behavioral versus EEG-based monitoring of all-night sleep/wake patterns. *Sleep, 11,* 139–155.

Ogilvie, R. D., Wilkinson, R. T., & Allison, S. (1989). The detection of sleep-onset: Behavioral, physiological, and subjective convergence. *Sleep, 12,* 458–474.

Paffenbarger, R. S., Jr., & Hale, W. E. (1975). Work activity and coronary heart mortality. *New England Journal of Medicine, 292,* 545–550.

Paffenbarger, R. S., Jr., Hyde, R. T., Wing, A. L., & Hsieh, C. C. (1986). Physical activity, all-cause mortality, and longevity of college alumni. *New England Journal of Medicine, 314,* 605–613.

Paffenbarger, R. S., Jr., Hyde, R. T., Wing, A. L., & Steinmetz, C. H. (1984). A natural history of athleticism and cardiovascular health. *Journal of the American Medical Association, 252,* 491–495.

Palmore, E. (1970). Health practices and illness among the aged. *Gerontologist, 10,* 313–316.

Perry, T. J., & Goldwater, B. C. (1987). A passive behavioral measure of sleep-onset in high-alpha and low-alpha subjects. *Psychophysiology, 24,* 657–665.

Pierce, W. D., & Epling, W. F. (1994). Activity anorexia: An interplay between basic and applied behavior analysis. *The Behavior Analyst, 17,* 7–23.

Plomin, R. (1990). *Nature and nurture: An introduction to human behavioral genetics.* Pacific Grove, CA: Brooks/Cole.

Pollak, C. P., Perlick, D., & Linsner, J. P. (1992). Daily sleep reports and circadian rest-activity cycles of elderly community residents with insomnia. *Biological Psychiatry, 32,* 1019–1027.

Pollak, C. P., Tryon, W. W., Nagaraja, H., & Dzwonczyk, R. (2001). How accurately does wrist actigraphy identify the states of sleep and wakefulness? *Sleep, 24,* 957–965.

Porrino, L. J., Rapoport, J. L., Behar, D., Ismond, D. R., & Bunney, Jr., W. E. (1983). A naturalistic assessment of the motor activity of hyperactive boys. II: Stimulant drug effects. *Archives of General Psychiatry, 40,* 688–693.

Porrino, L. J., Rapoport, J. L., Behar, D., Sceery, W., Ismond, D. R., & Bunney, W. E., Jr. (1983). A naturalistic assessment of the motor activity of hyperactive boys. I: Comparison with normal controls. *Archives of General Psychiatry, 40,* 681–687.

Powell, K. E., Thompson, P. D., Caspersen, C. J., & Kendrick, J. S. (1987). Physical activity and the incidence of coronary heart disease. *Annual Review of Public Health, 8,* 253–287.

Raoux, N., Benoit, O., Dantchev, N., Denise, P., Franc, B., Allilaire, J. F., et al. (1994). Circadian pattern of motor activity in major depressed patients undergoing antidepressant therapy: Relationship between actigraphic measures and clinical course. *Psychiatric Research, 52,* 85–98.

Rechtschaffen, A. (1994). Sleep-onset: Conceptual issues. In R. D. Ogilvie & J. R. Harsh (Eds.), *Sleep-onset: Normal and abnormal processes* (pp. 3–17). Washington, DC: American Psychological Association.

Rechtschaffen, A., Hauri, P., & Zeitlin, M. (1966). Auditory awakening thresholds in REM and NREM sleep stages. *Perceptual and Motor Skills, 22,* 927–942.

Rechtschaffen, A., & Kales, A. (1968). *A manual of standard terminology, techniques and scoring system for sleep states of human subjects.* NIH Publication No. 204, Washington, Superintendent of Documents, Book 1–62 or Los Angeles: UCLA, Brain Information Service/Brain Research Institute.

Redeker, N. S., Mason, D. J., Wykpisz, E., & Glica, B. (1996). Sleep patterns in women after coronary artery bypass surgery. *Applied Nursing Research, 9,* 115–122.

Redeker, N. S., Tamburri, L., & Howland, C. L. (1998). Prehospital correlates of sleep in patients hospitalized with cardiac disease. *Research in Nursing and Health, 21,* 27–37.

Redeker, N. S., & Wykpisz, E. (1999). Effects of age on activity patterns after coronary artery bypass surgery. *Heart and Lung, 28,* 5–14.

Robertson, S. S. (1985). Cyclic motor activity in the human fetus after midgestation. *Developmental Psychobiology, 18,* 411–419.

Robertson, S. S. (1987). Human cyclic motility: Fetal-newborn continuities and newborn state differences. *Developmental Psychobiology, 20,* 425–442.

Robertson, S. S. (1988). Infants of diabetic mothers: Late normalization of fetal cyclic motility persists after birth. *Developmental Psychobiology, 21,* 477–490.

Robertson, S. S., & Dierker, L. J. (1986). The development of cyclic motility in fetuses of diabetic mothers. *Developmental Psychobiology, 19,* 223–234.

Robins, R. W., John, O. P., & Caspi, A. (1994). Major dimensions of personality in early adolescence: The big five and beyond. In C. F. Halverson Jr., G. A. Kohnstamm, & R. P. Martin (Eds.), *The developing structure of temperament and personality from infancy to adulthood* (pp. 267–291). Hillsdale, NJ: Erlbaum.

Rogler, L. H., Malgady, R., & Tryon, W. W. (1992). Evaluation of mental health issues of memory in the Diagnostic Interview Schedule. *Journal of Nervous and Mental Diseases, 180,* 215–222.

Ross, D. M., & Ross, S. A. (1982). *Hyperactivity: Current issues, research, and theory.* New York: Wiley.

Sadeh, A., Alster, J., Urbach, D., & Lavie, P. (1989). Actigraphically based automatic bedtime sleep-wake scoring: Validity and clinical applications. *Journal of Ambulatory Monitoring, 2,* 209–216.

Sadeh, A., Hauri, P. J., Kripke, D. F., & Lavie, P. (1995). The role of actigraphy in the evaluation of sleep disorders. *Sleep, 18,* 288–302.

Sadeh, A., Lavie, P., Scher, A., Tirosh, E., & Epstein, R. (1991). Actigraphic home-monitoring sleep-disturbed and control infants and young children: A new method for pediatric assessment of sleep-wake patterns. *Pediatrics, 87,* 494–499.

Sadeh, A., Sharkey, M., & Carskadon, M. A. (1994). Activity-based sleep-wake identification: An empirical test of methodological issues. *Sleep, 17,* 201–207.

Shiner, R. L. (1998). How shall we speak of children's personalities in middle childhood? A preliminary taxonomy. *Psychological Bulletin, 124,* 308–332.

Siscovick, D. S., LaPorte, R. E., & Newman, J. M. (1985). The disease-specific benefits and risks of physical activity and exercise. *Public Health Reports, 100,* 180–188.

Slattery, M. L., Schumacher, M. C., Smith, K. R., West, D. W., & Abd-Elghany, N. (1988). Physical activity, diet, and risk of colon cancer in Utah. *American Journal of Epidemiology, 128,* 989–999.

Snyder, F., & Scott, J. (1972). The psychology of sleep. In N. S. Greenfield & R. A. Sternback (Eds.), *Handbook of psychophysiology* (pp. 645–708). Toronto, Ontario, Canada: Holt, Rinehart and Winston.

Spiegel, R. (1981). *Sleep and sleeplessness in advanced age.* New York: SP Medical and Scientific Books.

Stampi, C., & Broughton, R. (1989). Ultrashort sleep-wake schedule: Detection of sleep state through wrist actigraph measures. *Sleep Research, 18,* 100.

Standards of Practice Committee. (1995). Practice parameters for the use of actigraphy in the clinical assessment of sleep disorders. *Sleep, 18,* 285–287.

Stepanski, E. J. (1994). Behavioral therapy for insomnia. In M. H. Kryger, T. Roth, & W. C. Dement (Eds.), *Principles and practice of sleep medicine* (2nd ed., pp. 535–541). London: Saunders.

Stewart, A. L., King, A. C., & Haskell, W. L. (1993). Endurance exercise and health-related quality of life in 50–65 year-old adults. *The Gerontologist, 33,* 782–789.

Taylor, S. E. (1991). *Health psychology* (pp. 119–123). New York: McGraw-Hill.

Teicher, M. H. (1995). Actigraphy and motion analysis: New tools for psychiatry. *Harvard Review of Psychiatry, 3,* 18–35.

Teicher, M. H., Glod, C. A., Magnus, E., Harper, D., Benson, G., Krueger, K., et al. (1995). *Circadian rest-activity disturbances in seasonal affective disorder.* Manuscript submitted for publication.

Teicher, M. H., Ito, Y., Glod, C. A., & Barber, N. I. (1996). Objective measurement of hyperactivity and attentional problems in ADHD. *Journal of the American Academy of Child and Adolescent Psychiatry. 35,* 334–342.

Thomas, A., & Chess, S. (1977). *Temperament and development.* New York: Brunner/Mazel.

Thomas, A., Chess, S., & Birch, H. (1968). *Temperament and behavior: Disorders in children.* New York: New York University Press.

Tryon, W. W. (1985). The measurement of human activity. In W. W. Tryon (Ed.), *Behavioral assessment in behavioral medicine* (pp. 200–256). New York: Springer.

Tryon, W. W. (1986). Motor activity measurements and *DSM-III.* In M. Hersen, R. M. Eisler, & P. Miller (Eds.), *Progress in behavior modification* (Vol. 20, pp. 35–66). New York: Academic Press.

Tryon, W. W. (1991a). *Activity measurement in psychology and medicine.* New York: Plenum Press.

Tryon, W. W. (1991b). Motoric assessment and *DSM-III-R* In M. Hersen & S. M. Turner (Eds.), *Adult psychopathology and diagnosis* (pp. 413–440). New York: Wiley.

Tryon, W. W. (1993). The role of motor excess and instrumented activity measurement in attention-deficit hyperactivity disorder. *Behavior Modification, 17,* 371–406.

Tryon, W. W. (1996a). Instrument driven theory. *Journal of Mind and Behavior, 17,* 21–30.

Tryon, W. W. (1996b). Measurement units and theory construction. *Journal of Mind and Behavior, 17,* 213–227.

Tryon, W. W. (1996c). Nocturnal activity and sleep assessment. *Clinical Psychology Review, 16,* 197–213.

Tryon, W. W. (1998). Behavioral observation. In M. Hersen & A. S. Bellack (Eds.), *Behavioral assessment: A practical handbook* (4th ed., pp. 79–103). Boston: Allyn & Bacon.

Tryon, W. W., & Forlenza, N. (2001, August). *Activity level as a personality factor.* Paper presented at the meeting of the American Psychological Association, San Francisco.

Tryon, W. W., & Pinto, L. P. (1994). Comparing activity measurements and ratings. *Behavior Modification, 18,* 251–261.

Tryon, W. W., & Pologe, B. (1987). Accelerometric assessment of tardive dyskinesia. *American Journal of Psychiatry, 144,* 1548–1587.

Tryon, W. W., & Williams, R. (1996). Fully proportional actigraphy: A new instrument. *Behavior Research Methods Instruments and Computers, 28,* 392–403.

van Hilten, J. J., Middelkoop, H. A. M., Kerkhof, G. A., & Roos, R. A. C. (1991). A new approach in the assessment of motor activity in Parkinson's disease. *Journal of Neurology, Neurosurgery, and Psychiatry, 54,* 976–979.

van Hilten, J. J., Middelkoop, H. A. M., Kuiper, S. I. R., Kramer, C. G. S., & Roos, R. A. C. (1994). Where to record motor activity: An evaluation of commonly used sites of placement for activity monitors. In H. A. M. Middelkoop (Ed.), *Actigraphic assessment of sleep and sleep disorders* (pp. 39–48). Delft, Holland: Eburon.

van Lieshout, C. F. M., & Haselager, G. J. T. (1994). The big five personality factors in Q-sort descriptions of children and adolescents. In C. F. Halverson Jr., G. A. Kohnstamm, & R. P. Martin (Eds.), *The developing structure of temperament and personality from infancy to adulthood* (pp. 293–318). Hillsdale, NJ: Erlbaum.

van Someren, E. J. W., van Gool, W. A., Vonk, B. F. M., Mirmiran, M., Speelman, J. D., Bosch, D. A., et al. (1993). Ambulatory monitoring of tremor and other movements before and after thalamotomy: A new quantitative technique. *Journal of the Neurological Sciences, 117,* 16–23.

Vena, J. E., Graham, S., Zielezny, M., Swanson, M. K., Barnes, R. E., & Nolan, J. (1985). Lifetime occupational exercise and colon cancer. *American Journal of Epidemiology, 122,* 357–365.

Viens, M., De Koninck, J., Van den Bergen, R., Audet, R., & Christ, G. (1988). A refined switch-activated time monitor for the measurement of sleep-onset latency. *Behavior Research and Therapy, 26,* 271–273.

Waddington, S. (1998). *Factor structure of the Revised Dimensions of Temperament Survey: College-aged and middle-aged adults.* Unpublished doctoral dissertation, Fordham University, New York.

Walters, C. E. (1965). Prediction of postnatal development from fetal activity. *Child Development, 36,* 801–808.

Webster, J. B., Kripke, D. F., Messin, S., Mullaney, D. J., & Wyborney, G. (1982). An activity-based sleep monitor system for ambulatory use. *Sleep, 5,* 389–399.

Webster, J. B., Messin, S., Mullaney, D. J., & Kripke, D. F. (1982). Transducer design and placement for activity recording. *Medical and Biological Engineering and Computing, 20,* 741–744.

Windle, M., & Lerner, R. M. (1986). Reassessing the dimensions of temperamental individuality across the life span: The Revised Dimensions of Temperament Survey (DOTS-R). *Journal of Adolescent Research, 1,* 213–229.

Zuckerman, M. (1991). *Psychobiology of personality.* Cambridge, England: Cambridge University Press.

PART II

SPECIFIC DISORDERS

CHAPTER 5

Delirium, Dementia, and Amnestic and Other Cognitive Disorders

GERALD GOLDSTEIN

MOST OF THE neurological disorders of mankind are ancient diseases, and developments in treatment and cure have been painfully slow. However, we continue to learn more about these disorders, and in the previous version of this chapter (G. Goldstein, 1997), we commented on two major events that took place during recent years that represented highly substantive developments. A new disorder, AIDS dementia, had appeared, and the marker for the Huntington's disease gene had been discovered. Since the time of that writing, there are, fortunately, no new diseases, with the possible exception of a still mysterious and controversial disorder sustained by military personnel during the war with Iraq in the Persian Gulf area, popularly known as the *Gulf War Syndrome*. An aspect of this syndrome has been said to involve impaired brain function (G. Goldstein, Beers, Morrow, Shemansky, & Steinhauer, 1996). We also commented on the substantial change in how the organic mental disorders are classified by psychiatry, reflected in the most recent *Diagnostic and Statistical Manual of Mental Disorders*, 4th Edition (*DSM-IV*; American Psychiatric Association [APA], 1994). The major developments over the past ten years have been technological in nature. Increasingly sophisticated techniques have been developed to image the brain, not only structurally as in an X-ray, but also functionally. We now have very advanced capacities to image brain activity while the individual is engaging in some form of behavior. At present, functional magnetic resonance imaging (fMRI) is the most widely used of these procedures. It involves performing magnetic resonance imaging while the individual is given tasks to perform and recording changes in brain activity. Thus, for example, it is possible to observe increased activity in the language area of the brain while the person is performing a language task.

Indebtedness is expressed to Medical Research Service, Department of Veterans Affairs, for support of this work.

153

Changes in *DSM-IV* have essentially codified the abandonment of the traditional distinction made in psychopathology between organic and functional disorders. The latter type of disorder was generally viewed as a reaction to some environmental or psychosocial stress, or as a condition in which the presence of a specific organic etiological factor is strongly suspected, but not proven. The anxiety disorders are examples of the first alternative, while schizophrenia is an example of the second. The organic mental disorders are those conditions that can be more or less definitively associated with temporary or permanent dysfunction of the brain. Thus, individuals with these illnesses are frequently described as "brain-damaged" patients or patients with "organic brain syndromes." Recent developments in psychopathological research and theory have gone a long way toward breaking down this distinction, and it is becoming increasingly clear that many of the schizophrenic, mood, and attentional disorders have their bases in some alteration of brain function. Psychiatric classification has, therefore, dropped use of the word *organic* to describe what was formerly called the *organic mental disorders*. The word has been replaced by several terms: *delirium, dementia, amnesia, cognitive disorders,* and *mental disorders due to a general medical condition*. Nevertheless, the clinical phenomenology, assessment methods, and treatment management procedures associated with patients generally described as brain damaged are sufficiently unique that the traditional functional versus organic distinction is probably worth retaining for certain purposes. Brain-damaged patients have clinical phenomenologies, symptoms, courses, and outcomes that are quite different from those of patients with other psychopathological disorders. However, to delineate the subject matter of this chapter as precisely as possible, we prefer to say that we are concerned with individuals having *structural brain damage* rather than with *organic* patients.

The theoretical approach taken here is neuropsychological in orientation, in that it is based on the assumption that clinical problems associated with brain damage can be understood best in the context of what is known about the relationships between brain function and behavior. Thus, attempts are made to expand our presentation beyond the descriptive psychopathology of *DSM-IV* (APA, 1994) in the direction of attempting to provide some material related to basic brain-behavior mechanisms. There are many sources of brain dysfunction, and the nature of the source has a great deal to do with determining behavioral consequences: morbidity and mortality. Thus, a basic grasp of key neuropathological processes is crucial to understanding the differential consequences of brain damage. Furthermore, it is important to have some conceptualization of how the brain functions. Despite great advances in neuroscience, we still do not know a great deal about this matter; therefore, it remains necessary to think in terms of brain models or conceptual schema concerning brain function. For example, we still do not know how memories are preserved in brain tissue. However, there are several neuropsychological models and hypotheses concerning memory, portions of which have been supported by neurochemical and neurophysiological research.

In recognition of the complexities involved in relating structural brain damage to behavioral consequences, a new field, clinical neuropsychology, has emerged as a specialty area in psychology. Clinical neuropsychological research has provided a number of specialized instruments for assessment of brain-damaged patients and a variety of rehabilitation methods aimed at remediation of neuropsychological deficits. This research has also pointed out that *brain damage,* far from being a single clinical entity, actually represents a wide variety of disorders. Initially, neuropsychologists were strongly interested in the relationship between localization of the brain damage and behavioral outcome. In recent years, however, localization has come to be seen as only one determinant of outcome, albeit often a very important one. Other considerations include age of the individual, individual's age when the brain damage was acquired, premorbid personality and level of achievement, and type of pathological process producing the brain dysfunction. Furthermore, neuropsychologists are now cognizant of the possible influence of various *nonorganic* factors on their assessment methods, such as educational level, socioeconomic status, and mood states. Thus, this chapter concerns concepts of brain dysfunction in historical and contemporary perspectives, the various causes of brain dysfunction, and the clinical phenomenology of a number of syndromes associated with brain damage in relation to factors such as localization, age of the individual, age of the lesion, and pathological process.

CHANGING VIEWS OF BRAIN FUNCTION AND DYSFUNCTION

Concepts of how mental events are mediated have evolved from vague philosophical speculations concerning the "mind-body problem" to rigorous scientific theories supported by objective experimental evidence. We may recall from our studies of the history of science that it was not always understood that the "mind" was in the brain and mental events were thought to be mediated by other organs of the body. Boring (1950) indicates that Aristotle thought that the mind was in the heart. After it was determined to be in the brain, scientists turned their interest to how the brain mediates behavior, thus ushering in a line of investigation that to this day is far from complete. Two major methodologies were used in this research: direct investigations of brain function through lesion generation or brain stimulation in animal subjects and studies of patients who had sustained brain damage, particularly localized brain damage. The latter method, with which we are mainly concerned here, can be reasonably dated to 1861 when Paul Broca produced his report on the case of a patient who had suddenly developed speech loss. An autopsy on this patient revealed that he had sustained an extensive infarct in the area of the third frontal convolution of the left cerebral hemisphere. Thus, an important center in the brain for speech had been discovered, but perhaps more significantly, this case produced what many would view as the first reported example of a neuropsychological or brain-behavior relationship in a human. Indeed, to this day, the third frontal convolution of the left hemisphere is known as *Broca's area*, and the type of speech impairment demonstrated by the patient is known as *Broca's aphasia*. Following Broca's discovery, much effort was devoted to relating specific behaviors to discrete areas of the brain. Wernicke made the very important discovery that the area that mediates the comprehension, as opposed to the expression of speech, is not the Broca area but in a more posterior region in the left temporal lobe: the superior temporal gyrus. Other investigators sought to localize other language, cognitive, sensory, and motor abilities in the tradition of Broca and Wernicke, some using animal lesion and stimulation methods, and others using clinical autopsy investigations of human brain-damaged patients. Various syndromes were described, and centers or pathways whose damage or disconnection produced these syndromes were suggested. These early neuropsychological investigations not only provided data concerning specific brain-behavior relationships, but also explicitly or implicitly evolved a theory of brain function, now commonly known as *classical localization theory*. In essence, the brain was viewed as consisting of centers for various functions connected by neural pathways. In human subjects, presence of these centers and pathways was documented through studies of individuals who had sustained damage to either a center or the connecting links between one center and another such that they became disconnected. To this day, behavioral consequences of this latter kind of tissue destruction is referred to as a *disconnection syndrome* (Geschwind, 1965). For example, there are patients who can speak and understand, but who cannot repeat what was just said to them. In such cases, it is postulated that there is a disconnection between the speech and auditory comprehension centers.

From beginnings of the scientific investigation of brain function, not all investigators advocated localization theory. The alternative view is that rather than functioning through centers and pathways, the brain functions as a whole in an integrated manner. Views of this type are currently known as *mass action, holistic*, or *organismic* theories of brain function. While we generally think of holistic theory as a reaction to localization theory, it actually can be seen as preceding localization theory, in that the very early concepts of brain function proposed by Galen and Descartes can be understood as holistic in nature. However, what is viewed as the first scientific presentation of holistic theory was made in 1824 by Flourens (1824), who proposed that the brain might have centers for special functions (*action propre*). But there is a unity to the system as a whole (*action commune*), and this unity dominates the entire system. Boring (1950) quotes Flourens' statement, "Unity is the great principle that reigns; it is everywhere, it dominates everything." The legacy of holistic theory has come down to us from Flourens through the neurologist Hughlings Jackson. Jackson proposed a distinction between primary and secondary symptoms of brain damage. The primary symptoms are the direct consequences of the insult to the brain itself, while the secondary symptoms are the changes that take place in the unimpaired stratum. Thus, a lesion produces changes not only at its site, but also throughout the brain. In contemporary neuropsychology, the strongest advocates of holistic theory were Kurt Goldstein, Martin Scheerer, and Heinz Werner. Goldstein and Scheerer (1941) are best known for their distinction between abstract and concrete behavior, their description of the *abstract attitude*, and the tests they devised to study abstract and concrete functioning in brain-damaged patients. Their major proposition was that many of the symptoms of brain damage could be viewed not as specific manifestations of damage to centers or connecting pathways but as some form of impairment of the abstract attitude. The abstract attitude is not localized in any region of the brain but depends on the functional integrity of the brain as a whole. K. Goldstein (1959) describes the abstract attitude as the capacity to transcend immediate sensory impressions and consider situations from a conceptual standpoint. Generally, it is viewed as underlying functions such as planning, forming intentions, developing concepts, and separating ourselves from immediate sensory experience. The abstract attitude is evaluated objectively primarily through the use of concept formation tests that involve sorting or related categorical abilities. In language, it is evaluated by testing the patient's ability to use speech symbolically. Often, this testing is accomplished by asking the patient to produce a narrative about some object that is not present in the immediate situation.

Heinz Werner and various collaborators applied many of Goldstein's concepts to studies of brain-injured and mentally retarded children (e.g., Werner & Strauss,

1942). His analyses and conceptualizations reflected an orientation toward Gestalt psychology and holistic concepts, dealing with matters such as figure-ground relationships and rigidity. Halstead (1947) made use of the concept of the abstract attitude in his conceptualizations of brain function, but in a modified form. Like most contemporary neuropsychologists, Halstead viewed abstraction as one component or factor in cognitive function among many and did not give it the central role attributed to it by K. Goldstein and his followers. Correspondingly, rather than adhering to an extreme position concerning the absence of localization, Halstead provided evidence to suggest that the frontal lobes were of greater importance concerning mediation of abstract behavior than were other regions of the brain. K. Goldstein (1936) also came to accept the view that the frontal lobes were particularly important concerning mediation of the abstract attitude.

The notion of a nonlocalized, generalized deficit underlying many of the specific behavioral phenomena associated with brain damage has survived to some extent in contemporary neuropsychology, but in a greatly modified form. Similarly, some aspects of classical localization theory are still with us, but also with major changes (Mesulam, 1985). None of the current theories accept the view that there is no localization of function in the brain, and, correspondingly, none would deny that there are some behaviors that cannot be localized to some structure or group of structures. This synthesis is reflected in a number of modern concepts of brain function, the most explicit one probably being that of Luria (1973). Luria has developed the concept of functional systems as an alternative to both strict localization and mass action theories. Basically, a functional system consists of a number of elements involved in the mediation of some complex behavior. For example, there may be a functional system for auditory comprehension of language. The concept of pluripotentiality is substituted for Lashley's (1960) older concept of equipotentiality. Equipotentiality theory suggests that any tissue in a functional area can carry out the functions previously mediated by destroyed tissue. Pluripotentiality is a more limited concept suggesting that one particular structure or element may be involved in many functional systems. Thus, no structure in the brain is involved in only a single function. Depending on varying conditions, the same structure may play a role in several functional systems.

Current neuropsychological thought reflects some elements of all of the general theories of brain function just outlined. In essence, it is thought that the brain is capable of highly localized activity directed toward control of certain behaviors, but also of mediating other behaviors through means other than geographically localized centers. Indeed, since discovery of the neurotransmitters (chemical substances that appear to play an important role in brain function), there appears to have been a marked change in how localization of function is viewed. To some authorities, at least, localization is important only because the receptor sites for specific neurotransmitters appear to be selectively distributed in the brain. Neuroscientists now tend to think in terms of not only geographical localization but also neurochemical localization. As to clinical neuropsychology, however, the main point seems to be that there are both specific and nonspecific effects of brain damage. Evidence for this point of view has been presented most clearly by Teuber and his associates (Teuber, 1959) and by Satz (1966). The Teuber group was able to show that patients with penetrating brain wounds that produced very focal damage had symptoms that could be directly attributed to the lesion site, but they also had other symptoms that were shared by all patients studied, regardless of their specific lesion sites. For example, a patient with a posterior lesion might have an area of cortical blindness associated with the specific lesion site in the visual projection areas, but he or she might also have difficulties in performing complex nonvisual tasks such as placing blocks into a formboard while blindfolded. Most of Teuber's patients had difficulty with formboard type and other complex tasks regardless of specific lesion site. In clinical settings, we may see brain-damaged patients with this combination of specific and nonspecific symptoms as well as patients with only nonspecific symptoms. One of the difficulties with early localization theory is that investigators tended to be unaware of the problem of nonspecific symptoms and so reported only the often more dramatic specific symptoms.

An old principle of brain function in higher organisms that has held up well and that is commonly employed in clinical neuropsychology involves contralateral control—the right half of the brain controls the left side of the body and vice versa. Motor, auditory, and somatosensory fibers cross over at the base of the brain and thus control the contralateral side of the body. In the case of vision, the crossover is atypical. The optic nerve enters a structure called the *optic chiasm,* at which point fibers coming from the outer or temporal halves of the retinas go to the ipsilateral side of the brain, while fibers from the inner or nasal halves cross over and go to the contralateral cerebral hemispheres. However, the pattern is thought to be complete and all fibers coming from a particular hemiretina take the same course. In the case of somesthesis, hearing, and motor function, the crossover is not complete, but the majority of fibers do cross over. Thus, for example, most of the fibers from the right auditory nerve find their way to the left cerebral hemisphere. The contralateral control principle is important for clinical neuropsychology because it explains why patients with damage to one side of the brain may become paralyzed on only the opposite side of the body or may develop sensory disturbances on that side. We see this condition most commonly in individuals who have had strokes, but it is also seen in some patients who have head injuries or brain tumors.

While aphasia, or impaired communicative abilities as a result of brain damage, was recognized before Broca (Benton & Joynt, 1960), it was not recognized as associated with destruction of a particular area of one side of the brain. Thus, the basic significance of Broca's discovery was not the discovery of aphasia, but of cerebral dominance. The term *cerebral dominance* is commonly employed to denote the fact that the human brain has a hemisphere that is dominant for language and a nondominant hemisphere. In most people, the left hemisphere is dominant, and left hemisphere brain damage may lead to aphasia. However, some individuals have dominant right hemispheres, while others do not appear to have a dominant hemisphere. What was once viewed as a strong relationship between handedness and choice of dominant hemisphere has not held up in recent studies. But the answers to questions as to why the left hemisphere is dominant in most people and why some people are right dominant or have no apparent dominance remain unknown. In any event, it seems clear that for individuals who sustain left hemisphere brain damage, aphasia is a common symptom, while aphasia is a rare consequence of damage to the right hemisphere. Following Broca's discovery, other neuroscientists discovered that just as the left hemisphere has specialized functions in the area of language, the right hemisphere has its own specialized functions. These functions all seem to relate to nonverbal abilities such as visual-spatial skills, perception of complex visual configurations, and, to some extent, appreciation of nonverbal auditory stimuli such as music. Some investigators have conceptualized the problem in terms of *sequential* as opposed to *simultaneous* abilities. The left hemisphere is said to deal with material in a sequential, analytic manner, while the right hemisphere functions more as a detector of patterns or configurations (Dean, 1986). Thus, while patients with left hemisphere brain damage tend to have difficulty with language and other activities that involve sequencing, patients with right hemisphere brain damage have difficulties with tasks such as copying figures and producing constructions, because such tasks involve either perception or synthesis of patterns. In view of these findings concerning specialized functions of the right hemisphere, many neuropsychologists now prefer to use the expression *functional asymmetries of the cerebral hemispheres* rather than *cerebral dominance.* The former terminology suggests that one hemisphere does not really dominate or lead the other. Rather, each hemisphere has its own specialized functions.

As indicated previously, localization alone is not the sole determinant of the behavioral outcomes of brain damage. While age, sociocultural, and personality factors make their contributions, perhaps the most important consideration is the type of brain damage. Some would argue that neuropsychological assessment is rarely the best method of determining type of brain damage because other techniques such as CT scan, cerebral blood flow studies, and magnetic resonance imaging (MRI) are more adequate for that purpose. While the point may be well taken, the problem remains that different types of lesions produce different behavioral outcomes even when they involve precisely the same areas of the brain. Thus, the clinician should be aware that the assessment methodology he or she uses may not be the best one to meet some specific diagnostic goal, and it is often necessary to use a variety of methods coming from different disciplines to arrive at an adequate description of the patient's condition. In the present context, an adequate description generally involves identification of the kind of brain damage the patient has as well as its location. A brief outline of the types of pathology that involve the brain and their physical and behavioral consequences is provided to point out the implications of this principle.

DESCRIPTION OF THE DISORDER

Neuropathological Considerations

The brain may incur many of the illnesses that afflict other organs and organ systems. It may be damaged by trauma or it may become infected. The brain can become cancerous or can lose adequate oxygen through occlusion of the blood vessels that supply it. The brain can be affected through acute or chronic exposure to toxins, such as carbon monoxide or other poisonous substances. Nutritional deficiencies can alter brain function just as they alter the function of other organs and organ systems. Aside from these general systemic and exogenous factors, there are diseases that more or less specifically target the central nervous system. These conditions, generally known as degenerative and demyelinating diseases, include Huntington's disease, multiple sclerosis, Parkinson's disease, and a number of disorders associated with aging. From the point of view of neuropsychological considerations, it is useful to categorize the various disorders according to temporal and topographical parameters. Thus, certain neuropathological conditions are static and do not change substantially; others are slowly progressive, and some are rapidly progressive. As to topography, certain conditions tend to involve focal, localized disease; others, multifocal lesions; and still others, diffuse brain damage without specific localization. Another very important consideration has to do with morbidity and mortality. Some brain disorders are more or less reversible, some are static and do not produce marked change in the patient over lengthy periods of time, while some are rapidly or slowly progressive, producing increasing morbidity and eventually leading to death. Thus, some types of brain damage produce a stable condition with minimal changes, some types permit substantial recovery, while other types are, in actuality, terminal illnesses. It is, therefore, apparent that the kind of brain disorder the patient suffers from is a crucial clinical consideration in that it has major implications for treatment, management, and planning.

HEAD TRAUMA

While the skull affords the brain a great deal of protection, severe blows to the head can produce temporary brain dysfunction or permanent brain injury. The temporary conditions, popularly known as *concussions,* are generally self-limiting and involve a period of confusion, dizziness, and, perhaps, double vision. However, there seems to be complete recovery. In these cases, the brain is not thought to be permanently damaged. More serious trauma is generally classified as *closed-* or *open-head* injury. In closed-head injury, which is more common, the vault of the skull is not penetrated, but the impact of the blow crashes the brain against the skull and thus may create permanent structural damage. A commonly occurring type of closed-head injury is the subdural hematoma in which a clot of blood forms under the dura—one of the protective layers on the external surface of the brain. These clots produce pressure on the brain that may be associated with clear-cut neurological symptoms. They may be removed surgically, but even when removed, there may be persistent residual symptoms of a localized nature, such as weakness of one side of the body. In the case of open-head injury, the skull is penetrated by a missile of some kind. Open-head injuries occur most commonly during wartime because of bullet wounds. They sometimes occur as a result of vehicular or industrial accidents, if some rapidly moving object penetrates the skull. Open-head injuries are characterized by the destruction of brain tissue in a localized area. There are generally thought to be more remote effects as well, but usually, the most severe symptoms are likely to be associated with the track of the missile through the brain. Thus, an open-head injury involving the left temporal lobe could produce an aphasia, while similar injury to the back of the head could produce a visual disturbance. A major neuropsychological difference between open- and closed-head injury is that while the open injury typically produces specific, localized symptoms, the closed-head injury, with the possible exception of subdural hematoma, produces diffuse dysfunction without specific focal symptoms. In both cases, some of these symptoms may disappear with time, while others may persist. There is generally a sequence of phases that applies to the course of both closed- and open-head injury. Often, the patient is initially unconscious and may remain that way for an extremely varying amount of time, ranging from minutes to weeks or months. After consciousness is regained, the patient generally goes through a so-called acute phase during which there may be confusion and disorientation.

Very often a condition called *posttraumatic amnesia* is present, in which the patient cannot recall events that immediately preceded the trauma up to the present time. Research has shown that the length of time spent unconscious and the length of posttraumatic amnesia are reasonably accurate prognostic signs; the longer either persists, the worse the prognosis. During this stage, seizures are common, and treatment with anticonvulsant drugs is often necessary. When the patient emerges from this acute phase, the confusion diminishes, amnesia may persist but may not be as severe as previously, the seizures may abate, and a better picture of long-term outcome emerges. The range of variability is extremely wide, extending from patients remaining in persistent vegetative states to essentially complete recovery of function. In general, the residual difficulties of the head trauma patient, when they are significant, represent a combination of cognitive and physical symptoms. As to the latter, these patients are often more or less permanently confined to wheelchairs because of partial paralysis. Frequently, there are sensory handicaps such as partial loss of vision or hearing.

Trauma to the head can do damage not only to the brain but also to other parts of the head, such as the eyes and ears. Additionally, there is sometimes substantial disfigurement in the form of scars, some of which can be treated with cosmetic surgery. The cognitive residual symptoms of head trauma are extremely varied as they are associated with whether the injury was open-head or closed-head and if there was clear tissue destruction. Most often, patients with closed-head injury have generalized intellectual deficits involving abstract reasoning ability, memory, and judgment. Sometimes, marked personality changes are noted, often having the characteristic of increased impulsiveness and exaggerated affective responsivity. Patients suffering from the residual of open-head injury may have classic neuropsychological syndromes such as aphasia, visual-spatial disorders, and specific types of memory or perceptual disorders. In these cases, the symptoms tend to be strongly associated with the lesion site. For example, a patient with left hemisphere brain damage may have an impaired memory for verbal material such as names of objects, while the right hemisphere patient may have an impaired memory for nonverbal material such as pictures or musical compositions. In these cases, there is said to be both modality (e.g., memory) and material (e.g., verbal stimuli) specificity. Head trauma is generally thought to be the most frequently seen type of brain damage in adolescents and young adults. It, therefore, generally occurs in a reasonably healthy brain. When the combination of a young person with a healthy brain exists, the prognosis for recovery is generally good if the wound itself is not devastating in terms of its extent or the area of the brain involved. For practical purposes, residual brain damage is a static condition that does not generate progressive changes for the worse. While there is some research evidence (Walker, Caveness, & Critchley, 1969) that following a long quiescent phase, head-injured individuals may begin to deteriorate more rapidly than normal when they become elderly, and there is some evidence that brain injury may be a risk factor for Alzheimer's disease (Lye & Shores, 2000), head-injured individuals may, nevertheless, have many years of productive functioning.

Since the first edition of this chapter appeared, there has been an increased interest in outcome following mild head injury (Levin, Eisenberg, & Benton, 1989), as well as in the specific problems associated with head injury in children (Goethe & Levin, 1986). It has been frequently pointed out in recent years that trauma is the major cause of death in children, and head trauma among children is not uncommon.

BRAIN TUMORS

Cancer of the brain is a complex area, particularly because cancer in general is not as yet completely understood. However, the conventional distinction between malignant and nonmalignant tumors is a useful one for the brain as it is for other organs and organ systems. Thus, some brain tumors are destructive, rapidly progressive, and essentially untreatable. Generally, these tissue structures are known as *intrinsic* tumors because they directly infiltrate the parenchyma of the brain. The most common type is a class of tumor known as *glioma*. Other types of tumors grow on the external surface of the brain and produce symptoms through the exertion of pressure on brain tissue. This type of tumor is described as *extrinsic,* and the most common type is a *meningioma.* Aside from these two types, there are metastases in which tumors have spread to the brain from some other organ of the body, often the lung. The extrinsic tumors are often treatable surgically, but metastases are essentially untreatable. The clinical symptoms of tumor include headache that frequently occurs at night or on awakening, seizures, and vomiting. There are often progressive cognitive changes, perhaps beginning with some degree of confusion and poor comprehension and progressing to severe dementia during the terminal stages. Because tumors often begin in quite localized areas of the brain, the symptoms associated with them tend to be dependent on the particular location affected. For example, there is a large literature on frontal lobe tumors in which impairment of judgment, apathy, and general loss of the ability to regulate and modulate behavior are the major symptoms (Berg, 1998). As in head injury, patients with left hemisphere tumors may develop aphasia, while patients with right hemisphere tumors may have visual-spatial disorders as their most prominent symptoms. The difference between head injury and brain tumors is that short of surgical intervention, the severity of symptoms increases with time, sometimes at a very slow and sometimes at a very rapid rate, depending on the type of tumor. On rare occasions, the clinical psychologist or psychiatrist may see patients with tumors that affect particular structures in the brain, thereby generating characteristic syndromes. Among the most common of these are the cranial pharyngiomas, the pituitary adenomas, and the acoustic neuromas.

The cranial pharyngiomas are cystic growths that lie near the pituitary gland and often depress the optic chiasm so that the primary symptoms may involve delayed development in children and waning libido and amenorrhea in adults, in combination with weakening of vision. The pituitary adenomas are similar in location but the visual loss is often more prominent, frequently taking the form of what is called a *bitemporal hemianopia*—a loss of vision in both peripheral fields. The acoustic neuromas are tumors of the auditory nerve and thereby produce hearing loss as the earliest symptom. However, because the auditory nerve also has a vestibular component, there may be progressive unsteadiness of gait and dizziness. Clinicians may also see patients who have had surgically treated tumors. When these patients demonstrate residual neuropsychological symptoms, they look like patients with histories of open-head injury. Perhaps that is because the brain lesion has, in a manner of speaking, been converted from a mass of abnormal tissue to a stable, nonmalignant wound. When neurosurgery has been successful, the changes are often rapid and very substantial. Recurrence is a normal concern, and these patients should remain under continued medical care. However, successful surgical treatment may leave the patient with many years of productive life.

BRAIN MALFORMATIONS AND EARLY LIFE BRAIN DAMAGE

Perhaps nowhere in the organic mental disorders is the type of lesion issue as significant as it is in the case of the developmental disorders of brain function. There is a great deal of difference between destruction of a function already acquired and destruction of the brain mechanisms needed to acquire that function before it has been developed. Thus, the consequences of being born with an abnormal brain or acquiring brain damage during the early years of life may be quite different from the consequences of acquiring brain damage as an adult. On the positive side, the young brain generally has greater plasticity than the older brain, and it is somewhat easier for preserved structures to take over functions of impaired structures. On the negative side, however, when the brain mechanisms usually involved in the acquisition of some function are absent or impaired, that function is often not learned or not learned at a normal level. While the relationship between age and consequences of brain damage remains an intensively researched area (Baron & Gioia, 1998), for practical purposes, it can be said that there is a population of individuals born with abnormal brain function, or who have sustained structural brain damage at or shortly after birth, who go on to have developmental histories of either generalized or specific cognitive subnormality. Those with generalized deficit, when it is sufficiently severe, are frequently described with a variety of terms such as minimal brain damage, learning disability, and attention deficit disorder.

One common subclass of this specific group consists of children who fail to learn to read normally despite adequate educational opportunity and average intelligence. These children are described as having dyslexia or developmental dyslexia. As to neuropathological considerations, several types of brain disorder may occur during the prenatal period. Some of them are developmental in nature in the sense that either the brain itself or the skull does not grow normally during gestation. When the skull is involved, the brain is damaged through the effects of pressure on it. Sometimes a genetic factor is present as in Down syndrome. Sometimes poor prenatal care is the responsible agent, the fetal alcohol syndrome perhaps being an extreme case of this condition. Sometimes an infection acquired during pregnancy, notably rubella (German measles), can produce severe mental retardation in the embryo. Probably most often, however, the causes of the developmental abnormality are unknown.

Damage to the brain can also occur as the result of a traumatic birth. Conditions such as cerebral anoxia, infection, and brain dysfunction associated with ongoing conditions such as malnutrition or exposure to toxic substances are the major agents. Children have strokes and brain tumors, but they are quite rare. In essence, brain damage can occur in the very young before, during, and after birth. While the neuropathological distinction among the various disorders is quite important, the life span development of individuals from all three categories shares some common characteristics. Retrospectively, it is often difficult to identify the responsible agent in the school-age child or adult. Thus, it is sometimes useful to think in terms of some general concept, such as perinatal or early life brain damage, rather than to attempt to specifically relate a particular developmental course or pattern of functioning to a single entity.

While early life brain damage is usually a static condition in the sense that the lesion itself does not change, it may have varying consequences throughout life. During the preschool years, the child may not achieve the generally accepted landmarks, such as walking and talking, at the average times. In school, these children often do not do well academically and may be either poor learners in general or have specific disabilities in areas such as reading, arithmetic, or visual-spatial skills. These academic difficulties may be accompanied by some form of behavior disorder, often manifested in the form of hyperactivity or diminished attentional capacity. During adulthood, it is often found that these individuals do not make satisfactory vocational adjustments, and many researchers now feel that they are particularly vulnerable to certain psychiatric disorders, notably alcoholism (Tarter, 1976) or schizophrenia (Green, 1998).

Note that, while this volume does not address itself to child psychopathology, there are several disorders that are now classed as organic mental, or neurobehavioral, disorders that begin during childhood, but persist into adulthood. There is growing evidence (Katz, Goldstein, & Beers, 2001; Spreen, 1987) that learning disability frequently persists into adulthood. Autism, which is now generally viewed as a neurobehavioral disorder (Minshew & Payton, 1988a, 1988b), generally persists into adulthood. A study (Rumsey & Hamburger, 1988) that followed up some of Kanner's (1943) original cases demonstrated persistence of neuropsychological deficit in these autistic adults.

DISEASES OF THE CIRCULATORY SYSTEM

Thinking about the significance of vascular disease has changed in recent years from the time when it was felt that cerebral arteriosclerosis or "hardening of the arteries" was the major cause of generalized brain dysfunction in the middle-aged and elderly. While this condition is much less common than was once thought, the status of the heart and blood vessels is significantly related to the intactness of brain function. The brain requires oxygen to function, and oxygen is distributed to the brain through the cerebral blood vessels. When these vessels become occluded, circulation is compromised and brain function is correspondingly impaired. This impairment occurs in a number of ways, perhaps the most serious and abrupt way being stroke. A stroke is a sudden total blockage of a cerebral artery caused by blood clot or a hemorrhage. The clot may be a thrombosis formed out of atherosclerotic plaque at branches and curves in the cerebral arteries or an embolism, which is a fragment that has broken away from a thrombus in the heart and has migrated to the brain. Cerebral hemorrhages are generally fatal, but survival from thrombosis or embolism is not at all uncommon. Following a period of stupor or unconsciousness, the most common and apparent postacute symptom is hemiplegia—paralysis of one side of the body. There is also a milder form of stroke known as a transient ischemic attack (TIA)—which is basically a temporary, self-reversing stroke that does not produce severe symptoms, or may be essentially asymptomatic.

A somewhat different picture emerges in another cerebral vascular disorder formerly known as *multiinfarct dementia*, but renamed *vascular dementia* in *DSM-IV* (APA, 1994). As opposed to the abruptly rapid onset seen in stroke, vascular dementia is a progressive condition based on a history of small strokes associated with hypertension. Patients with vascular dementia experience a stepwise deterioration of function, with each small stroke making the dementia worse in some way. There are parallels between vascular dementia and the older concept of cerebral arteriosclerosis in that they both relate to the role of generalized cerebral vascular disease in producing progressive brain dysfunction. However, vascular dementia is actually a much more precisely defined syndrome that, while not rare, is not extremely common either. Many of the patients who formerly would have been diagnosed as having cerebral arteriosclerosis would now be diagnosed as having one of the degenerative diseases associated with the presenile or senile period of life. Other relatively common cerebrovascular disorders are associated with aneurysms and other vascular malformations in the brain. An *aneurysm* is an area of weak structure in a blood vessel that may not produce symptoms until it balloons out to the extent that it creates pressure effects or it ruptures. A ruptured aneurysm is an extremely serious medical condition in that it may lead to sudden death. However, surgical intervention in which the aneurysm is ligated is often effective.

Arteriovenous malformations are congenitally acquired tangles of blood vessels. They may be asymptomatic for many years, but can eventually rupture and hemorrhage. They may appear anywhere in the brain, but commonly they occur in the posterior half. The symptoms produced, when they occur, may include headache and neurological signs associated with the particular site.

There are major neuropsychological differences between the individual with a focal vascular lesion, most commonly associated with stroke, and the patient with generalized vascular disease such as vascular dementia. The stroke patient is characterized not only by the hemiplegia or hemiparesis, but sometimes by an area of blindness in the right or left visual fields and commonly by a pattern of behavioral deficits associated with the hemisphere of the brain affected and the locus in that hemisphere. If the stroke involves a blood vessel in the left hemisphere, the patient will be paralyzed or weak on the right side of the body; the area of blindness, if present, involves the right field of vision and there is frequently an aphasia. Right hemisphere strokes may produce left-sided weakness or paralysis and left visual fields defects but no aphasia. Instead, a variety of phenomena may occur. The patient may acquire a severe difficulty with spatial relations, a condition known as *constructional apraxia.* The ability to recognize faces or to appreciate music may be affected. A phenomenon known as *unilateral neglect* may develop in which the patient does not attend to stimuli in the left visual field, although it may be demonstrated that basic vision is intact. Sometimes affective changes occur in which the patient denies that he or she is ill and may even develop euphoria. In contrast with this specific, localized symptom picture seen in the stroke patient, the individual with vascular dementia or other generalized cerebral vascular disease has quite a different set of symptoms. Generally, there is no unilateral paralysis, no visual field deficit, no gross aphasia, and none of the symptoms characteristic of patients with right hemisphere strokes. Rather, there is a picture of generalized intellectual, and to some extent physical, deterioration. If weakness is present, it is likely to affect both sides of the body, and, typically, there is general diminution of intellectual functions including memory, abstraction ability, problem-solving ability, and speed of thought and action. In the case of the patient with vascular dementia, there may be localizing signs, but there would tend to be several of them, and they would not point to a single lesion in one specific site.

The more common forms of cerebral vascular disease are generally not seen until at least middle age and, for the most part, are diseases of the elderly. Clinically significant cerebral vascular disease is often associated with a history of generalized cardiovascular or other systemic diseases, notably hypertension and diabetes. There are some genetic or metabolic conditions that promote greater production of atheromatous material than is normal, and some people are born with arteriovenous malformations or aneurysms, placing them at higher than usual risk for serious cerebral vascular disease. When a stroke is seen in a young adult, it is usually because of an aneurysm or other vascular malformation. Most authorities agree that stroke is caused basically by atherosclerosis; therefore, genetic and acquired conditions that promote atherosclerotic changes in blood vessels generate risk of stroke. With modern medical treatment, there is a good deal of recovery from stroke with substantial restoration of function. However, in the case of the diffuse disorders, there is really no concept of recovery because they tend to be slowly progressive. The major hope is to minimize the risk of future strokes, through means such as controlling blood pressure and weight.

An area of recently developed interest concerns the long-term effects of hypertension on cerebral function, as well as the long-term effects of antihypertensive medication. Reviews (Elias & Streeten, 1980; King & Miller, 1990) have demonstrated that hypertension in itself, as well as antihypertensive medication, can impair cognitive function, but there are no definite conclusions in this area as yet, with studies reporting mixed as well as benign outcomes associated with prudent use of the newer antihypertensive medications (G. Goldstein, 1986).

Degenerative and Demyelinating Diseases

The degenerative and demyelinating diseases constitute a variety of disorders that have a number of characteristics in common, but that are also widely different from each other in many ways. What they have in common is that they specifically attack the central nervous system; they are slowly progressive and incurable; and while they are not all hereditary diseases, they appear to stem from some often unknown but endogenous defect in physiology. Certain diseases, once thought to be degenerative, have been found not to be so, or are thought not to be so at present. For example, certain dementias have been shown to be caused by a *slow virus*, while multiple sclerosis, the major demyelinating disease, is strongly suspected of having a viral etiology. Thus, in these two examples, the classification would change from degenerative to infectious disease.

The term *degenerative disease* simply means that for some unknown reason, the brain or the entire central nervous system gradually wastes away. In some cases, this wasting, or atrophy, resembles what happens to the nervous system in very old people, but substantially earlier than the senile period—perhaps as early as the late forties. These diseases are known as presenile dementia, the commonest type being Alzheimer's disease. Alzheimer's disease also occurs in a senile form, but there is some controversy as to whether the senile and the presenile forms are in actuality the same disease. Senile dementia is generally diagnosed in elderly individuals when the degree of cognitive deficit is substantially greater than expected with normal aging. In other words, not all old people become significantly demented before death. Most of those who do, but do not have another identifiable disease of the central nervous system, are generally thought to have Alzheimer's disease. Indeed, Alzheimer's disease is now thought to account for more senile dementia than does vascular disease.

There is another disorder related to Alzheimer's disease called *Pick's disease*, but it is difficult to distinguish from Alzheimer's disease in living individuals.

The distinction becomes apparent only on autopsy, because the neuropathological changes in the brain are different. In psychiatry, there is no longer an attempt to differentiate clinically among Alzheimer's, Pick's, and some rarer degenerative diseases. *DSM-IV* (APA, 1994) describes them with the single term *dementia of the Alzheimer's type.*

Another frequently occurring degenerative disease found in younger adults is called *Huntington's chorea* or *Huntington's disease.* The disease is characterized by progressive intellectual deterioration and a motor disorder involving gait disturbance and involuntary jerky, spasmodic movements. It has definitely been established as a hereditary disorder, and there is a 50% chance of acquiring the disease if born to a carrier of the gene. Symptoms may begin to appear during the second or third decade, and survival from the time of appearance of symptoms is generally about eight years. The intellectual deterioration is characterized by progressively profound impairment of memory, with most cognitive functions eventually becoming involved. There is often a speech articulation difficulty because of the loss of control of the musculature involved in speech.

While much is still not known about the degenerative disorders, much has been discovered in recent years. The major discovery is that Alzheimer's and Huntington's diseases are apparently based on neurochemical deficiencies. In Alzheimer's disease, the deficiency is thought to be primarily the group of substances related to choline, one of the neurotransmitters. The disease process itself is characterized by progressive death of the choline neurons, the cells that serve as receptor sites for cholinergic agents. Huntington's disease is more neurochemically complex because three neurotransmitters are involved: choline, GABA, and substance P. The reasons for these neurochemical deficiency states remain unknown, but the states themselves have been described and treatment efforts have been initiated based on this information. For example, some Alzheimer's patients have been given choline or lecithin, a substance related to choline, and other newer drugs such as Aricept, in the hope of slowing down the progression of the illness. As indicated previously, the genetic marker for Huntington's disease has been discovered.

Multiple sclerosis is the most common of the demyelinating diseases, described as such because its pathology involves progressive erosion of the myelin sheaths that surround fibers in the central nervous system. Both the brain and the spinal cord are involved in this illness. Nerve conduction takes place along the myelin sheaths and, therefore, cannot occur normally when these sheaths erode. This abnormality leads to motor symptoms such as paralysis, tremor, and loss of coordination, but there are characteristic changes in vision if the optic nerve is involved, and in cognitive function. Obviously, cognitive skills that involve motor function tend to be more impaired than those that do not. Until its final stages, multiple sclerosis does not have nearly as devastating an effect on cognitive function as do the degenerative diseases. The crippling motor disorder may be the only apparent and significantly disabling symptom for many years. Less often, but not infrequently, progressive loss of vision also occurs. Multiple sclerosis acts much like an infectious disease, and some authorities feel that it is, in fact, caused by some unknown viral agent. Symptoms generally appear during young adulthood and may be rapidly or slowly progressive, leading some authorities to differentiate between acute and chronic multiple sclerosis. Individuals with this disorder may live long lives; there are sometimes lengthy periods during which no deterioration takes place. Sometimes temporary remission of particular symptoms is seen in the so-called *relapsing-remitting* form of multiple sclerosis. There have been extensive neuropsychological studies of multiple sclerosis (reviewed in Allen et al., 1998), and a particular interest in differences between relapsing-remitting and chronic-progressive forms of the disease (Heaton, Nelson, Thompson, Burks, & Franklin, 1985).

Alcoholism

The term *alcoholism* in the context of central nervous system function involves not only the matter of excessive consumption of alcoholic beverages, but also a complex set of considerations involving nutritional status, related disorders such as head trauma, physiological alterations associated with the combination of excessive alcohol consumption and malnutrition, and possible genetic factors. All of these elements, and perhaps others as well, may influence the status of the central nervous system in alcoholic patients. What is frequently observed in long-term chronic alcoholics is a pattern of deterioration of intellectual function not unlike what is seen in patients with degenerative dementia of the Alzheimer's type. However, it is not clear that the deteriorative process is specifically associated with alcohol consumption per se. Thus, while some clinicians use the term *alcoholic dementia,* this characterization lacks sufficient specificity, as it is rarely at all clear that the observed dementia is in fact solely a product of excessive use of alcohol. Looking at the matter in temporal perspective, there first may be a genetic propensity for acquisition of alcoholism that might ultimately have implications for central nervous system function (Goodwin, 1979). Second, Tarter (1976) has suggested that there may be an association between having minimal brain damage or a hyperactivity syndrome as a child and acquisition of alcoholism as an adult. These two considerations suggest the possibility that at least some individuals who eventually become alcoholics may not have completely normal brain function anteceding the development of alcoholism. Third, during the course of becoming chronically alcoholic, dietary habits tend to become poor and multiple head injuries may be sustained as a result of fights or accidents. As the combination of excessive alcohol abuse and poor nutrition progresses, major physiological changes may occur, particularly in the liver, and, to some extent, in the pancreas and gastrointestinal system. Thus, the dementia seen in long-term alcoholic patients may well involve a combination of all of these factors in addition to the always-present possibility of other neurological complications.

While the majority of alcoholics who develop central nervous system complications manifest it in the form of general deterioration of intellectual abilities, some develop specific syndromes. The most common of these is the Wernicke-Korsakoff syndrome. The Wernicke-Korsakoff disorder begins with the patient's going into a confusional state, accompanied by difficulty in walking and controlling eye movements, and by polyneuritis, a condition marked by pain or loss of sensation in the arms and legs. The latter symptoms may gradually disappear, but the confusional state may evolve into a permanent, severe amnesia. When this transition has taken place, the patient is generally described as having Korsakoff's syndrome or alcohol amnestic disorder, and is treated with large dosages of thiamine, as the etiology of the disorder appears to be a thiamine deficiency rather than a direct consequence of alcohol ingestion. There is now evidence (Blass & Gibson, 1977) that the thiamine deficiency must be accompanied by an inborn metabolic defect related to an enzyme that metabolizes thiamine. It should be noted that the amnesic and intellectual disorders found in chronic alcoholics are permanent and present even when the patient is not intoxicated. The acute effects of intoxication or withdrawal (e.g., delirium tremens [DTs]) are superimposed on these permanent conditions. These disorders are also progressive as long as the abuse of alcohol and malnutrition persists. Other than abstinence and improved nutrition, there is no specific treatment. Even thiamine treatment for the Korsakoff patient does not restore memory; it is used primarily to prevent additional brain damage.

It is probably fair to say that a major interest in recent years has been the genetics of alcoholism. Findings have been impressive thus far, and there is a growing, probably well justified, belief that the presence in an individual of a positive family history of alcoholism puts that individual at increased risk for becoming alcoholic if exposed to beverage alcohol. The research done has been broad ranging, including extensive family adoption studies (Goodwin, Schulsinger, Hermansen, Guze, & Winokur, 1973), neuropsychological studies of relatives (Schaeffer, Parsons, & Yohman, 1984) and children of alcoholics (Tarter, Hegedus, Goldstein, Shelly, & Alterman, 1984), psychophysiological studies emphasizing brain event-related potentials in siblings (Steinhauer, Hill, & Zubin, 1987) and children (Begleiter, Porjesz, Bihari, & Kissin, 1984) of alcoholics, and laboratory genetic studies. In summary, there is an extensive effort being made to find biological markers of alcoholism (Hill, Steinhauer, & Zubin, 1987) and to determine the transmission of alcoholism in families. One reasonable assumption is that alcoholism is a heterogeneous disorder, and there may be both hereditary and nonhereditary forms of it (Cloninger, Bohman, & Sigvardsson, 1981).

Toxic, Infectious, and Metabolic Illnesses

The brain may be poisoned by exogenous or endogenous agents or it may become infected. Sometimes, these events occur with such severity that the person dies, but more often, the individual survives with a greater or lesser degree of neurological dysfunction. Beginning with the exogenous toxins, we have already discussed the major one: alcohol. However, excessive use of drugs such as bromides and barbiturates may produce at least temporary brain dysfunction. This temporary condition, called *delirium* in *DSM-IV* (APA, 1994), is a loss of capacity to maintain attention with corresponding reduced awareness of the environment. Tremors and lethargy may be accompanying symptoms. Delirium is reversible in most cases, but may evolve into a permanent dementia or other neurological disorder.

In psychiatric settings, a frequently seen type of toxic disorder is carbon monoxide poisoning. This disorder and its treatment are quite complex because it usually occurs in an individual with a major mood or psychotic disorder who attempted to commit suicide by inhaling car fumes in a closed garage. The brain damage sustained during the episode may often be permanent, resulting in significant intellectual and physical dysfunction in addition to the previously existing psychiatric disorder. Other toxic substances that may affect central nervous system function include certain sedative and hypnotic drugs, plant poisons, heavy metals, and toxins produced by certain bacteria leading to conditions such as tetanus and botulism. The specific effects of these substances, as well as whether exposure is acute (as in the case of tetanus or arsenic poisoning) or chronic (as in the case of addiction to opiates and related drugs), influence outcome.

A very large number of brain disorders are associated with inborn errors of metabolism. In some way, a fault in metabolism produces a detrimental effect on the nervous system, generally beginning in early life. There are so many of these disorders that we mention only two of the more well-known ones as illustrations. First, *phenylketonuria* (PKU) is an amino acid uria, a disorder that involves excessive excretion of some amino acid into the urine. It is genetic and, if untreated, can produce mental retardation accompanied by poor psychomotor development and hyperactivity. The treatment involves a diet low in the substance *phenylalanine*. A second disorder is Tay-Sach's disease. The enzyme abnormality here is a deficiency in a substance called *hexasaminidase A,* which is important for the metabolism of protein and polysaccharides. It is hereditary, occurs mainly in Jewish children, and is present from birth. The symptoms are initially poor motor development and progressive loss of vision, followed by dementia, with death usually occurring before age 5. These two examples illustrate similarity in process, which is basically an inherited enzyme deficiency, but variability in outcome. PKU is treatable, with a relatively favorable prognosis, while Tay-Sachs is a rapidly progressive, incurable terminal illness.

Bacterial infections of the brain are generally associated with epidemics, but sometimes are seen when there are no epidemics at large. They are generally referred to as *encephalitis,* when the brain itself is infected, or *meningitis,* when the infection is in the membranous tissue that lines the brain—the meninges. Infections are produced by microorganisms that invade tissue and produce inflammation. During the acute phase of the bacterial infections, the patient may be quite ill and survival is an important issue. Headaches, fever, and a stiff neck are major symptoms. There may be delirium, confusion, and alterations in state of consciousness ranging from drowsiness, to excessive sleeping, to coma. Some forms of encephalitis formerly were popularly known as *sleeping sickness.* Following the acute phase of bacterial infection, the patient may be left with residual neurological and neuropsychological disabilities and personality changes. Sometimes, infections are local, and the patient is left with neurological deficits that correspond with the lesion site. The irritability, restlessness, and aggressiveness of postencephalitic children are mentioned in the literature. Jervis (1959) described them as overactive, restless, impulsive, assaultive, and wantonly destructive.

Neurosyphylis is another type of infection that has a relatively unique course. Most interesting, aside from the progressive dementia that characterizes this disorder, there are major personality changes involving the acquisition of delusions and a tendency toward uncritical self-aggrandizement. While neurosyphilis or general paresis played a major role in the development of psychiatry, it is now a relatively rare disease and is seldom seen in clinical practice. Similarly, the related neurosyphilitic symptoms, such as tabes dorsalis and syphilitic deafness, are also rarely seen. While incidence and, perhaps, interest in the bacterial infections and neurosyphilis have diminished, interest in viral infections has increased substantially during recent years. There are perhaps four reasons for this phenomenon:

1. Jonas Salk's discovery that poliomyelitis was caused by virus and could be prevented by vaccination.
2. Recent increase in the incidence of herpes simplex, a viral disorder.
3. Appearance of AIDS.
4. Discovery of the *slow viruses.*

The latter two reasons are probably of greatest interest in the present context. As to the slow viruses, it has recently been discovered that certain viruses have a long incubation period and may cause chronic degenerative disease, resembling Alzheimer's disease in many ways. Thus, some forms of dementia may be produced by a transmittable agent. Two of these appear to be diseases known as *kuru* and *Creutzfeldt-Jakab* disease. Recently, there has been an outbreak of a related disorder called *mad cow disease* or *bovine spongiform encephalopathy* (Balter, 2001). The importance of the finding is that the discovery of infection as the cause of disease opens the possibility of development of preventive treatment in the form of a vaccine. AIDS dementia, another form of viral encephalopathy, is a consequence of human immunovirus infection and apparently represents an illness that has not appeared on the planet previously. It has been characterized as a progressive *subcortical dementia* of the type seen in patients with Huntington's disease and other neurological disorders in which the major neuropathology is in the subcortex. The syndrome itself has not been completely described, but there is substantial evidence of neuropsychological abnormalities. The first papers in this area appeared circa 1987, with the most well-known study being that of Grant et al. (1987). A review is contained in the study of Bornstein, Nasrallah, Para, and Whitacre (1993).

EPILEPSY

Despite the usual manner in which this condition is described, epilepsy is really a symptom of many diseases and not really a disease in itself. Patients are generally diagnosed as *epileptic* when seizures are the major or only presenting symptoms and the cause cannot be determined. However, seizures are commonly associated with diagnosable disorders such as brain tumors, alcoholism, or head trauma. Furthermore, the view that epilepsy means that the patient has "fits" or episodes of falling and engaging in uncontrolled, spasmodic movements is also not completely accurate. These fits or convulsions do represent one form of epilepsy, but there are other forms as well. Several attempts have been made to classify epilepsy into subtypes, and we mention only the most recent one generally accepted by neurologists (Gastaut, 1970).

The major distinction made is between generalized and partial seizures. In the case of the generalized seizures, there is a bilaterally symmetrical abnormality of brain function, with one of two things generally happening. One is a massive convulsion with a sequence of spasmodic movements and jerking, while the other is a brief, abrupt loss of consciousness with little in the way of abnormal motor activity. There may be some lip smacking or involuntary movements of the eyelids. The former type was previously called a *grand mal seizure,* while the latter type was called a *petit mal seizure* or *absence.* The partial seizures may have what is described as a simple or complex symptomatology. In the simple case, the seizure may be confined to a single limb and may involve either motor or sensory function. When motor function is involved, there is often a turning movement of the head, accompanied by contractions of the trunk and limbs. There is a relatively rare form of this disorder called *Jacksonian motor seizure,* in which there is a spread of the spasmodic movements from the original site to the entire side of the body. The phenomenon is referred to as a *march.* In the case of sensory seizures, the epileptic activity may consist of a variety of sensory disorders such as sudden numbness, "pins and needles" feeling, seeing spits of light, or even a buzzing or roaring in the ears.

The complex partial seizures involve confused but purposeful-appearing behavior, followed by amnesia for the episode. In this condition, sometimes known as *temporal lobe* or *psychomotor epilepsy,* the patient may walk around in a daze, engage in inappropriate behavior, or have visual or auditory hallucinations. From this description, it is clear that not all seizures involve massive motor convulsions. What all of these phenomena have in common is that they are based on a sudden, abrupt alteration of brain function. The alteration is produced by an excessive, disorganized discharge of neurons. Thus, if looking at an epileptic individual's brain waves on an electroencephalograph (EEG), if a seizure occurred, there would be a sudden and dramatic alteration in the characteristics of the EEG. Presence and particular pattern of these alterations are often used to identify and diagnose various forms of epilepsy.

The question of whether there is an association between epilepsy and intellectual impairment is a complex one. According to Klove and Matthews (1974), individuals having complex partial (temporal lobe) seizures demonstrate little in the way of intellectual impairment. However, individuals with generalized seizures of unknown etiology that appear early in life are likely to have significant intellectual deficit. The matter is also complicated by the cause of the seizure. If an individual has seizures related to a brain tumor, it is likely that the neuropsychological deficits generally associated with the lesion sites involved can be expected to appear as well as the seizures. The question of intellectual deficit seems to arise primarily in the case of individuals who are epileptic but have no other apparent neurological signs of symptoms. This condition is known as *recurrent seizures of unknown cause* or as *idiopathic epilepsy.* Our tentative answer to the question is that there is a higher probability of significant intellectual deficit when the disorder involves generalized seizures and appears early in life.

The mental health practitioner should be aware that while epilepsy is an eminently treatable disorder through the use of a variety of anticonvulsant medications, the epileptic patient might have many difficulties of various types. There still appears to be some degree of social stigma attached to the disorder, either in the form of superstitious beliefs or the inaccurate stereotype that epileptics tend to be violent or impulsive people. More realistically, epileptics do have difficulties with matters such as obtaining drivers' licenses or insurance coverage that allows them to work around potentially hazardous equipment. It is possible that during a complex partial seizure, an individual can perform an antisocial act over which he or she honestly has no control and cannot remember. Epileptic seizures may be symptoms of some life-threatening illness. Children with petit mal epilepsy may have school difficulties because of their momentary lapses of consciousness. Individuals with motor seizures may injure their heads during the seizure and produce additional brain dysfunction through trauma. Thus, the epileptic may have many problems in living that are not experienced by the nonepileptic; they may frequently be assisted through an understanding of the nature of the condition and through counseling and support.

Myslobodsky and Mirsky (1988) have edited an extensive work on petit mal epilepsy that covers its genetic, neurophysiological, neuropsychological, metabolic, and electrophysiological aspects. There is a growing interest in psychosocial aspects of epilepsy. Having seizures clearly produces an impact on an individual's environment, and people in the environment may maintain the older superstitions and false beliefs about epilepsy. Furthermore, modifications of behavior in epileptics may be largely biologically determined because of the cerebral dysfunction associated with the disorder. Dodrill (1986) has reviewed the extensive literature on psychosocial consequences of epilepsy, providing a useful outline of the types of psychosocial difficulties epileptics commonly experience, the relationship between psychosocial and neuropsychological function, and treatment-related issues.

SOME COMMON SYNDROMES

In this section, we provide descriptions of the more commonly occurring disorders associated with structural brain damage. What is common in one setting may be rare in another. Thus, we focus on what is common in an adult neuropychiatric setting. The neuropsychological syndromes found in childhood are often quite different from what is seen in adults and deserve separate treatment. Furthermore, the emphasis is placed on chronic rather than acute syndromes because, with relatively rare exceptions, the psychologist and psychiatrist encounter the former type far more frequently that the latter. However, initially acute conditions such as stroke that evolve into chronic conditions are discussed in some detail.

Thus far, we have viewed matters from the standpoints of general concepts of brain function and of neuropathological processes. Now, we look at the behavioral manifestations of the interaction between various brain mechanisms and different types of pathology. It is useful to view these manifestations in the form of identified patterns of behavioral characteristics that might be described as neuropsychological syndromes. While there are admittedly other ways of describing and classifying neuropsychological deficit, the syndrome approach has the advantage of providing rather graphic phenomenological descriptions of different kinds of brain-damaged patients. However, it runs the risk of suggesting that every brain-damaged patient can be classified as having some specific, identifiable syndrome—something that is not at all true. It is, therefore, important to keep in mind that we are discussing classic types of various disorders seen in some actual patients. However, there are many brain-damaged patients who do not have classic-type syndromes, their symptomatology reflecting an often-complex combination of portions of several syndromes.

In their clinical neuropsychology text, Heilman and Valenstein (1993) have suggested a useful and workable classification of syndromes:

- Communicative disorders, which may be subdivided into aphasia and the specialized language or language-related disorders including reading impairment (alexia), writing disorders (agraphia), and calculation disorders (acalculia).
- Syndromes associated with some aspect of perception or motility. These include the perception of the individual's body (the body schema disturbances), the various visual-spatial disorders (which may involve perception, constructional abilities, or both), the gnostic disorders (impairment of visual, auditory, and tactile recognition), the neglect syndromes, and the disorders of skilled and purposeful movement, called apraxias.
- Syndromes that primarily involve general intelligence and memory-dementia and the amnesic disorders, including relatively unique syndromes associated with damage to the frontal lobes.

These three general categories account for most of the syndromes seen in adults, and our discussion here is limited to them.

The Communicative Disorders

In general, aphasia and related language disorders are associated with unilateral brain damage to the dominant hemisphere, which in most individuals is the left hemisphere. Most aphasias result from stroke, but some result from left hemisphere head trauma or brain tumor. While the definition has changed over the years, the most current one requires the presence of impairment of communicative ability associated with focal, structural brain damage. Thus, the term is not coextensive with all disorders of communicative ability and does not include, for example, the language disorders commonly seen in demented individuals with diffuse brain damage. The study of aphasia has in essence become a separate area of scientific inquiry, having its own literature and several theoretical frameworks. The term *aphasia* itself does not convey a great deal of clinically significant information as the various subtypes are quite different from each other. Numerous attempts have been made to classify the aphasias, and there is no universally accepted system. Contemporary theory indicates that perhaps the most useful major distinction is between fluent and nonfluent aphasias. To many authorities, this distinction is more accurate than the previously more common one between expressive and receptive aphasias. The problem is that aphasics with primarily expressive problems do not generally have normal language comprehension, and it is almost always true that aphasics with major speech comprehension disturbances do not express themselves normally. However, there are aphasics who talk fluently and aphasics whose speech is labored, very limited, and halting, if present at all in a meaningful sense. In the case of the former group, while speech is fluent, it is generally more or less incomprehensible because of a tendency to substitute incorrect words for correct ones—a condition known as *verbal paraphasia*. However, the primary disturbance in these patients involves profoundly impaired auditory comprehension. This combination of impaired comprehension and paraphasia is generally known as *Wernicke's aphasia*. The responsible lesion is generally in the superior gyrus of the left temporal lobe. In nonfluent aphasia, comprehension is generally somewhat better, but speech is accomplished with great difficulty and is quite limited. This condition is generally known as *Broca's aphasia*, the responsible lesion being in the lower, posterior portion of the left frontal lobe (i.e., Broca's area).

Several other types of aphasia that are relatively rare are not described here. However, it is important to point out that most aphasias are mixed, having components of the various pure types. Furthermore, the type of aphasia may change in the same patient, particularly during the course of recovery. Disorders of reading, writing, and calculation may also be divided into subtypes. In the case of reading, our interest is in the *acquired* alexias, in which an individual formerly able to read has lost that ability because of focal, structural brain damage. The ability to read letters, words, or sentences may be lost. Handwriting disturbances or agraphia might involve a disability in writing words from dictation or a basic disability in forming letters. Thus, some agraphic patients can write, but with omissions and distortions relative to what was dictated. However, some can no longer engage in the purposive movements needed to form letters. Calculation disturbances or *acalculias* are also of several types. The patient may lose the ability to read numbers, to calculate even if the numbers can be read, or to arrange numbers in a proper spatial sequence for calculation. The various syndromes associated with communicative disorders, while sometimes existing in pure forms, often merge. For example, alexia is frequently associated with Broca's aphasia, and difficulty with handwriting is commonly seen in patients with Wernicke's aphasia. However, there is generally a pattern of a clear primary disorder (e.g., impaired auditory comprehension), with other disorders (e.g., difficulty with reading or writing) occurring as associated defects. Sometimes, rather unusual combinations occur, as in the case of the syndrome of alexia without agraphia. In this case, the patient can write but cannot read, often to the extent that he or she cannot read what he or she has just written. Based on research done since the first version of this chapter was written, we add that academic deficits are frequently seen in adults that are not the product of brain damage acquired during adulthood, nor of inadequate educational opportunity. Rather, people with these deficits have developmentally based learning disabilities that they never outgrew. The view that learning disability is commonly outgrown has been rejected by most students of this area (Katz et al., 2001).

DISORDERS OF PERCEPTION AND MOTILITY

The disorders of perception can involve an individual's perception of his or her body as well as perception of the external world. In the case of the external world, the disorder can involve some class of objects or some geographical location. The disorders of motility discussed here are not primary losses of motor function as in the cases of paralysis or paresis, but losses in the area of the capacity to perform skilled, purposive acts. The set of impairments found in this area is called *apraxia*. There is also the borderline area in which the neuropsychological defect has to do with the coordination of a sense modality, usually vision, and purposive movement. These disorders are sometimes described as impairment of constructional or visual-spatial relations ability. In some patients, the primary difficulty is perceptual, while in others it is mainly motoric. The body schema disturbances most commonly seen are of three types. The first concerns the patient's inability to point to his or her own body parts on command. This syndrome is called *autotopognosia,* meaning lack of awareness of the surface of an individual's body. A more localized disorder of this type is *finger agnosia,* in which, while identification of body parts is otherwise intact, the patient cannot identify the fingers of his or her own hands, or the hands of another person. Finger agnosia has been conceptualized as a partial dissolution of the body schema. The third type of body schema disturbance is right-left disorientation, in which the patient cannot identify body parts as to whether they are on the right or left side. For example, when the patient is asked to show his or her right hand, he or she may become confused or show his or her left hand. More commonly, however, a more complex command is required to elicit this deficit, such as asking the patient to place his or her left hand on his or her right shoulder. The traditional thinking about this disorder is that both finger agnosia and right-left disorientation are part of a syndrome, the responsible brain damage being in the region of the left angular gyrus. However, Benton (1985) has pointed out that the matter is more complicated than that, and the issue of localization involves the specific nature of these defects in terms of the underlying cognitive and perceptual processes affected.

The perceptual disorders in which the difficulty is in recognition of some class of external objects are called *gnostic disorders* or *agnosias.* These disorders may be classified as to modality and verbal or nonverbal content. Thus, one form of the disorder might involve visual perception of nonverbal stimuli and is called *visual agnosia.* By definition, an agnosia is present when primary function of the affected modality is intact, but the patient cannot recognize or identify the stimulus. For example, in visual agnosia, the patient can see but cannot recognize what he or she has seen. To assure that visual agnosia is present, it should be determined that the patient can recognize and name the object in question when it is placed in his or her hand, so that it can be recognized by touch, or when it produces some characteristic sound, so that it can be recognized by audition. Brain lesions involved in the agnosias are generally in the association areas for the various perceptual modalities. Thus, visual agnosia is generally produced by damage to association areas in the occipital lobes. When language is involved, there is obviously a great deal of overlap between the agnosias and the aphasias. For example, visual-verbal agnosia can really be viewed as a form of alexia. In these cases, it is often important to determine through detailed testing whether the deficit is primarily a disturbance of perceptual recognition or a higher level conceptual disturbance involving language comprehension. A wide variety of gnostic disorders is reported in the literature involving phenomena such as the inability to recognize faces, colors, or spoken words. However, they are relatively rare conditions, and, when present, may persist during only the acute phase of the illness. In general, agnosia has been described as "perception without meaning," and it is important to remember that it is quite a different phenomenon from what we usually think of as blindness or deafness.

Sometimes, a perceptual disorder does not involve a class of objects but a portion of geographical space. The phenomenon itself is described by many terms; the most frequently used ones are *neglect* and *inattention.* It is seen most dramatically in vision, where the patient may neglect the entire right or left side of the visual world. It also occurs in the somatosensory modality, in which case the patient may neglect one side or the other of his or her body. While neglect can occur on either side, it is more common on the left side, because it is generally associated with right hemisphere brain damage. In testing for neglect, it is often useful to employ the method of double stimulation, for example, in the form of simultaneous finger wiggles in the areas of the right and left visual fields. Typically, the patient may report seeing the wiggle in the right field but not in the left. Similarly, when the patient with neglect is touched lightly on the right and left hands at the same time, he or she may report feeling the touch in only one hand or the other. As in the case of gnostic disorders, neglect is defined in terms of the assumption of intactness of the primary sensory modalities. Thus, the patient with visual neglect should have otherwise normal vision in the neglected half field, while the patient with tactile neglect should have normal somatosensory function. Clinically, neglect may be a symptom of some acute process and should diminish in severity or disappear as the neuropathological condition stabilizes. For example, visual neglect of the left field is often seen in individuals who have recently sustained right hemisphere strokes, but can be expected to disappear as the patient recovers.

The apraxias constitute a group of syndromes in which the basic deficit involves impairment of purposive movement occurring in the absence of paralysis, weakness, or unsteadiness. For some time, the distinction has been made among three major types of apraxia: ideomotor, limb-kinetic, and ideational. In ideomotor apraxia, the patient has difficulty in performing a movement to verbal command. In the case of limb-kinetic apraxia, movement is clumsy when performed on command or when the patient is asked to imitate a movement. In ideational apraxia, the difficulty is with organizing the correct motor sequences in response to language. In other words, it may be viewed as a disability in carrying out a series of acts. In addition, there are facial apraxias in which the patient cannot carry out facial movements to command. These four types are thought to involve different brain regions and different pathways. However, they are all generally conceptualized as a destruction or disconnection of motor engrams or traces that control skilled, purposive movement. Certain of the visual-spatial disorders are referred to as apraxias, such as constructional or dressing apraxia, but they are different in nature from the purer motor apraxias described previously.

The basic difficulty the patient with a visual-spatial disorder has relates to comprehension of spatial relationships and, in most cases, coordination between visual perception and movement. In extreme cases, the patient may readily become disoriented and lose his or her way when going from one location to another. However, in most cases, the difficulty appears to be at the cognitive level and may be examined by asking the patient to copy figures or solve jigsaw or block design-type puzzles. Patients with primarily perceptual difficulties have problems in localizing points in space, judging direction, and maintaining geographical orientation, as tested by asking the patient to describe a route or use a map. Patients with constructional difficulties have problems with copying and block building. *Dressing apraxia* may be seen as a form of constructional disability in which the patient cannot deal effectively with the visual-spatial demands involved in tasks such as buttoning clothing. While visual-spatial disorders can arise from lesions found in most parts of the brain, they are most frequently seen, and seen with the greatest severity, in patients with right hemisphere brain damage. Generally, the area that most consistently produces the severest deficit is the posterior portion of the right hemisphere. In general, while some patients show a dissociation between visual-spatial and visual-motor or constructional aspects of the syndrome of constructional apraxia, most patients have difficulties on both purely perceptual and constructional tasks.

DEMENTIA

Dementia is probably the most common form of organic mental disorder. There are several types of dementia, but usually they all involve slowly progressive deterioration of intellectual function. The deterioration is frequently patterned, with loss of memory generally the first function to decline, and other abilities deteriorating at later stages of the illness. One major class of dementia consists of disorders that arise during late life, either during late middle age or old age. In the former case, they are known as *presenile dementias,* while those that occur during old age are known as *senile dementia.* As the term is used now, dementia may occur at any age. In children, it is differentiated from mental retardation based on presence of deterioration from a formerly higher level. Dementia may result from head trauma or essentially any of the neuropathological conditions discussed previously. One common cause of dementia appears to be alcoholism and the nutritional disorders that typically accompany it. A specific type of dementia that generally appears before the presenile period is Huntington's disease. The term *dementia,* when defined in the broad way suggested here, is not particularly useful and does not really provide more information than do terms such as *organic brain syndrome* or *chronic brain syndrome*. However, when the term is used in a more specific way, it becomes possible to point out specific characteristics that may be described as syndromes. This specificity may be achieved by defining the dementias as disorders in which, for no exogenous reason, the brain begins to deteriorate and continues to do so until death. *DSM-IV* (APA, 1994) describes these conditions as dementia of the Alzheimer's type because the most common type of progressive degenerative dementia is Alzheimer's disease. Sufficient diagnostic methods are not yet available to specifically diagnose Alzheimer's disease in the living patient. However, its presence becomes apparent on examination of the brain at autopsy. Clinically, the course of the illness generally begins with signs of impairment of memory for recent events, followed by deficits in judgment, visual-spatial skills, and language. In recent years, the language deficit has become a matter of particular interest, perhaps because the communicative difficulties of dementia patients are becoming increasingly recognized. Generally, the language difficulty does not resemble aphasia, but can perhaps be best characterized as an impoverishment of speech, with word-finding difficulties and progressive inability to produce extended and comprehensible narrative speech. The same finding was noted in the descriptive writing of Alzheimer's disease patients (Neils, Boller, Gerdeman, & Cole, 1989). The patients wrote shorter descriptive paragraphs than age-matched controls and also made more handwriting errors of various types.

The end state of dementia is generalized, severe intellectual impairment involving all areas, with the patient sometimes surviving for various lengths of time in a persistent vegetative state. The progressive dementia seen in Huntington's disease also involves significant impairment of memory, with other abilities becoming gradually affected through the course of the illness. However, it differs from Alzheimer's disease in that it is accompanied by the choreic movements described earlier and by the fact that the age of onset is substantially earlier than is the case for Alzheimer's disease. Because of the chorea, there is also a difficulty in speech articulation frequently seen, which is not the case for Alzheimer's patients. A form of dementia that does not have an unknown etiology but that is slowly progressive is vascular dementia. This disorder is known to be associated with hypertension and a series of strokes, with the result being substantial deterioration. However, the course of the deterioration is not thought to be as uniform as in Alzheimer's disease, but rather, is generally described as stepwise and patchy. The patient may remain relatively stable between strokes, and the symptomatology produced may be associated with the site of the strokes. While these distinctions between vascular and Alzheimer's-type dementia are clearly described, in individual patients, it is not always possible to make a definitive differential diagnosis. Even sophisticated radiological methods such as the CT scan and MRI do not always contribute to the diagnosis. During the bulk of the course of the illness, the dementia patient typically appears confused, possibly disoriented, and lacks the ability to recall recent events. Speech may be very limited, and if fluent, is likely to be incomprehensible. Thus, these patients do not have the specific syndromes of the type described previously, surrounded by otherwise intact function. Instead, the deficit pattern tends to be global in nature with all functions more or less involved. Some investigators have attempted to identify syndromal subtypes, with some having more deficit in the area of abstraction and judgment, some in the area of memory, and some concerning affect and personality changes. However, this proposed typology has not been well established, with most patients having difficulties in all three areas. While there are some treatable dementias, particularly dementias associated with endocrine disorders or normal pressure hydrocephalus, there is no curative treatment for Alzheimer's-type dementia. Current research offers the hope that pharmacological treatment may eventually be able to ameliorate the course of Alzheimer's disease, but thus far, no such effective treatment is available.

In recent years, frontal lobe dementia has been proposed as a separate disorder. It is diagnosed only when Alzheimer's disease has been ruled out, and the patient must have symptoms that can be characterized as forming a "frontal lobe syndrome" (Rosenstein, 1998). The generic term commonly used to characterize the behaviors associated with this syndrome is *executive dysfunction,* a concept originally introduced by Luria (1966). Executive function is progressively impaired, and personality changes involving either apathy and indifference or childishness and euphoria occur. Compared with patients with Alzheimer's disease, frontal dementia patients have greater impairment of executive function but relatively better memory and visuoconstructional abilities. The outstanding features all may be viewed as relating to impaired ability to control, regulate, and program behavior. This impairment is manifested in numerous ways, including poor abstraction ability, impaired judgment, apathy, and loss of impulse control. Language is sometimes impaired, but in a rather unique way. Rather than having a formal language disorder, the patient loses the ability to control behavior through language. There is also often difficulty with narrative speech, which has been interpreted as a problem in forming the intention to speak or in formulating a plan for a narrative. Lack of insight or of the ability to produce goal-oriented behavior describes the frontal lobe patient. In many cases, these activating, regulatory, and programming functions are so impaired that the outcome looks like a generalized dementia with implications for many forms of cognitive, perceptual, and motor activities. Frontal dementia may result from a number of processes such as head trauma, tumor, or stroke, but the syndrome produced is more or less the same.

AMNESIA

While some degree of impairment of memory is a part of many brain disorders, there are some conditions in which loss of memory is clearly the most outstanding deficit. When loss of memory is particularly severe and persistent, and other cognitive and perceptual functions are relatively intact, the patient can be described as having an *amnesic syndrome.* Dementia patients are often amnesic, but their memory disturbance is embedded in significant generalized impairment of intellectual and communicative abilities. The amnesic patient generally has normal language and may be of average intelligence. As in the case of aphasia and several other disorders, there is more than one amnesic syndrome. The differences among them revolve around what the patient can and cannot remember. The structures in the brain that are particularly important for memory are the limbic system, especially the hippocampus, and certain brain stem structures including the mammilary bodies and the dorsomedial nucleus of the thalamus. There are many systems described in the literature for distinguishing among types of amnesia and types of memory. As to the amnesias, perhaps the most basic distinction is between anterograde and retrograde amnesia. *Anterograde amnesia* involves inability to form new memories from the time of the onset of the illness producing the amnesia, while *retrograde amnesia* refers to the inability to recall events that took place before the onset of the illness. This distinction dovetails with the distinction between recent and remote memory. It is also in some correspondence with the distinction made between short-term and long-term memory in the experimental literature. However, various theories define these terms somewhat differently, and perhaps it is best to use the more purely descriptive terms, *recent* and *remote* memory, in describing the amnesic disorders. It then can be stated that the most commonly appearing amnesic disorders involve dramatic impairment of recent memory with relative sparing of remote memory. Such sparing becomes greater as the events to be remembered become more remote. Thus, most amnesic patients can recall their early lives, but may totally forget what occurred during that last several hours. This distinction between recent and remote memory possibly aids in explaining why most amnesic patients maintain normal language function and average intelligence. In this respect, an amnesic disorder is not so much an obliteration of the past as it is an inability to learn new material.

Probably the most common type of relatively pure amnesic disorder is alcoholic Korsakoff's syndrome. These patients, while often maintaining average levels in a number of areas of cognitive function, demonstrate a dense amnesia for recent events with relatively well-preserved remote memory. Alcoholic Korsakoff's syndrome has been conceptualized by Butters and Cermak (1980) as an information processing defect in which new material is encoded in a highly degraded manner, leading to high susceptibility to interference. Butters and Cermak, as well as numerous other investigators, have accomplished detailed experimental studies of alcoholic Korsakoff's patients in which the nature of their perceptual, memory, and learning difficulties has been described in detail. Results of this research aid in explaining numerous clinical phenomena noted in Korsakoff's patients, such as their capacity to perform learned behaviors without recall of when or if those behaviors were previously executed, or their tendency to confabulate or "fill in" for the events of the past day that they do not recall. It may be noted that while confabulation was once thought to be a cardinal symptom of Korsakoff's syndrome, it is seen in only some patients. Another type of amnesic disorder is seen when there is direct, focal damage to the temporal lobes and, most importantly, to the hippocampus. These temporal lobe or limbic system amnesias are less common than Korsakoff's syndrome, but have been well studied because of the light they shed on the neuropathology of memory. These patients share many of the characteristics of Korsakoff's patients but have a much more profound deficit concerning basic consolidation and storage of new material. When Korsakoff's patients are sufficiently cued and given enough time, they can learn. Indeed, sometimes they can demonstrate normal recognition memory. However, patients with temporal lobe amnesias may find it almost impossible to learn new material under any circumstances.

In some cases, amnesic disorders are modality specific. In distinguishing between verbal and nonverbal memory, the translation can be made from the distinction between language and nonverbal abilities associated with the specialized functions of each cerebral hemisphere. It has, in fact, been reported that patients with unilateral lesions involving the left temporal lobe may have memory deficits for verbal material only, while right temporal patients have corresponding deficits for nonverbal material. Thus, the left temporal patient may have difficulty with learning word lists, while the right temporal patient may have difficulty with geometric forms. In summary, while there are several amnesic syndromes, they all have in common the symptom of lack of ability to learn new material following the onset of the illness. Sometimes, the symptom is modality specific, involving only verbal or nonverbal material, but more frequently, it involves both modalities. There are several relatively pure types of amnesia, notably Korsakoff's syndrome, but memory difficulties are cardinal symptoms of many other brain disorders, notably, the progressive dementias and certain disorders associated with infection. For example, people with herpes encephalitis frequently have severely impaired memories, but they have other cognitive deficits as well.

ALTERNATIVE DESCRIPTIVE SYSTEMS

As indicated, not all clinicians or researchers associated with brain-damaged patients have adopted the neuropsychologically oriented syndrome approach briefly described. There are many reasons for existence of these differing views, some of them methodological and some substantive in nature. Methodological issues largely revolve around the operations used by investigators to establish the existence of a syndrome. Critics suggest that syndromes may be established based on overly subjective inferences as well as on incomplete examinations. The alternative method proposed is generally described as a dimensional approach in which, rather than attempting to assign patients to categories, they are measured on a variety of neuropsychologically relevant dimensions such as intellectual function, language ability, and memory. Advocates of this approach are less concerned with determining whether the patient has a recognizable syndrome, and more involved with profiling the patient along a number of continuous dimensions and relating that profile to underlying brain mechanisms. Rourke and Brown (1986) have clarified this issue in a full discussion of similarities and differences between behavioral neurology and clinical neuropsychology.

Using a dimensional philosophy, there is no need to develop a classification system except perhaps in terms of certain characteristic profiles. For purposes of providing an overview of the descriptive phenomenology of structural brain damage, however, the substantive matters probably are of more relevance. In essence, the disciplines of neurology, neuropsychology, and psychiatry have all developed descriptive classificatory systems that differ in many respects. We have already discussed ways in which brain damage is described and classified by neurologists and neuropsychologists. However, psychiatric descriptions are also quite important, because they point to problems not uncommonly seen in brain-damaged patients that are not always clearly identifiable in the neurological and neuropsychological systems. There is an area of overlap concerning dementia and the amnesias, but *DSM-III* (APA, 1980), *DSM-III-R* (APA, 1987), and *DSM-IV* (APA, 1994) contain a number of categories that are not clearly defined neurologically or neuropsychologically. However, there has been a major reorganization of the categorization of these disorders in *DSM-IV*, largely revolving around an abandonment of the term *organic*. In general, what was previously characterized as an organic disorder, such as organic delusional syndrome, is now characterized as a mental disorder due to a general medical condition. Thus, the closest diagnosis to organic delusional syndrome is psychotic disorder due to a general medical condition, and the diagnostic criteria are listed under the heading of Schizophrenia and Other Psychotic Disorders. Patients with this disorder have delusional beliefs or hallucinations while in a normal state of consciousness as the primary symptom. It must be established that the delusions have an organic basis and the patient is not actually delusional because of a paranoid or schizophrenic disorder. The neurological basis for this syndrome is varied and may involve drug abuse, right hemisphere brain damage, or, in some cases, Huntington's disease or other dementias. This diagnosis incorporates what was previously described as *organic hallucinosis.* Delusions or hallucinations are specified as the predominant symptom. Other mental disorders due to a general medical condition include disorders of mood, anxiety, sexual dysfunction, sleep, and catatonic disorder. *DSM-IV* (APA, 1994) also contains a category of *personality change due to a general medical condition.* Such changes may be classified as disinhibited, aggressive, paranoid, other, or combined. The personality changes noted often involve increased impulsiveness, emotional lability, or apathy. Perhaps these are really mainly frontal lobes syndromes, but the syndrome may also be seen in conjunction with temporal lobe epilepsy. In *DSM-IV,* the specific medical condition, if known, becomes a part of the diagnosis.

DSM-IV also classifies under the organic mental disorders substance-induced delirium and persisting dementia. Delirium may be associated with intoxication or withdrawal. If cognitive symptoms persist beyond the period of delirium, intoxication, or withdrawal, the diagnosis of substance-induced persisting dementia is made. The specific substance or substance combination is indicated if known. Thus, for example, the diagnosis of alcohol-induced persisting dementia can be made. Typically, delirium is an acute phenomenon and does not persist beyond a matter of days. However, delirium, notably when it is associated with alcohol abuse, may eventually evolve into permanent disorders in the form of persistent dementia. The behavioral correlates of delirium generally involve personality changes such as euphoria, agitation, anxiety, hallucinations, and depersonalization. The more permanent cognitive changes might include impairment of memory and inability to concentrate. In the context of psychopathology, the commonality between these conditions and those related to more permanent, structural brain damage is that they all have an identified or presumed organic basis and are, therefore, distinct from the functional psychiatric disorders. The phraseology used throughout the organic mental disorders section of *DSM-IV* is: "There is evidence, from the history, physical examination, or laboratory findings of . . ." the presence of the disorder under consideration; for example, "that the deficits are etiologically related to the persisting effects of substance abuse" (APA, 1994).

Psychiatrically based categorization can perhaps be most productively viewed as supplemental to the type of neuropsychological system used by Heilman and Valenstein (1993), rather than as an alternative to it. It plays a major role in describing the noncognitive kinds of symptomatology that are often associated with structural brain damage, particularly for those cases in which these personality, mood, and affective changes are the predominant symptoms. These considerations are of the utmost clinical importance because the failure to recognize the organic basis for some apparently functional symptom such as a personality change may lead to the initiation of totally inappropriate treatment or the failure to recognize a life-threatening physical illness.

While alterations in brain function can give rise to symptoms that look like functional personality changes, the reverse can also occur. That is, a nonorganic personality change, notably acquisition of a depression, can produce symptoms that look as though they have been produced by alterations in brain function. This situation, generally called *pseudodementia,* is most frequently seen in elderly people who become depressed. The concept of pseudodementia or depressive pseudodementia is not universally accepted, but it is not uncommon to find elderly patients diagnosed as demented when the symptoms of dementia are actually produced by depression. The point is proven when the symptoms disappear or diminish substantially after the depression has run its course, or the patient is treated with antidepressant medication. Wells (1979, 1980) has pointed out that this differential diagnosis is a difficult one to make and cannot be accomplished satisfactorily with the usual examinational, laboratory, and psychometric methods. He suggests that perhaps the most useful diagnostic criteria are clinical features. For example, patients with pseudodementia tend to complain about their cognitive losses, while patients with dementia tend not to complain. Caine (1986) pointed to the many complexities of differential diagnosis in the elderly, referring in particular to the abundant evidence for neuropsychological deficits in younger depressed patients, and to the not-uncommon coexistence of neurological and psychiatric impairments in the elderly.

In recent years, there has been substantial rethinking about the concept of pseudodementia in the direction of characterizing it as a neurobiological disorder associated with demonstrable changes in brain structure. Clinicians have observed that depression may sometimes be the first indicator of Alzheimer's disease, and Nussbaum (1994), after an extensive review of the literature, concluded that pseudodementia or late-life depression has a neurological substrate involving subcortical structures and the frontal lobes. He indicated that the probable pathology is leukoaraiosis, diminution in the density of white matter, that particularly involves the subcortex in this disorder. Leukoaraiosis is frequently seen in the MRIs of elderly depressed individuals.

EPIDEMIOLOGY

The epidemiology of the organic mental disorders varies with the underlying disorder, and, therefore, is unlike most of the other diagnostic categories in *DSM-IV* (APA, 1994). Here, we sample from only those disorders in which epidemiological considerations are of particular interest. There are some exceptionally interesting and well-documented findings for multiple sclerosis, in which prevalence is directly related to latitude where the person resides; the farther from the equator, the higher the prevalence. Further study of this phenomenon has tended to implicate an environmental rather than an ethnic factor.

Epidemiology of head trauma has been extensively studied, with gender, age, and social class turning out to be important considerations. Head trauma has a higher incidence in males than in females (274 per 100,000 in males and 116 per 100,000 in females in one study; Levin, Benton, & Grossman, 1982). It is related to age, with risk peaking between ages 15 and 24, and occurs more frequently in individuals from lower social classes. Alcohol is a major risk factor, but marital status, preexisting psychiatric disorder, and previous history of head injury have also been implicated. The major causes of head injury are motor vehicle accidents, falls, assaults, and recreational or work activities, with motor vehicle accidents the major cause (50% to 60%; Smith, Barth, Diamond, & Giuliano, 1998).

Epidemiology of Huntington's disease has also been extensively studied. The disease is transmitted as an autosomal dominant trait, and the marker for the gene has been located on the short arm of chromosome 4 (Gusella et al., 1983). Prevalence estimates vary between 5 and 7 per 100,000. There are no known risk factors for acquiring the disorder; the only consideration is having a parent with the disease. If that is the case, the risk of acquiring the disorder is 50%. A test is now available to detect carriers of the defective gene, and its availability and usage may eventually reduce prevalence of Huntington's disease.

There is a great interest in the epidemiology of Alzheimer's disease because the specific cause of the disease is not fully understood and prevention of exposure to risk factors for Alzheimer's disease and related disorders remains a possibility. General health status considerations do not appear to constitute risk factors, but some time ago, there were beliefs that a transmissible infective agent existed and that exposure to aluminum might be a risk factor. The aluminum hypothesis has largely been discarded. It now seems well established that an infective agent is responsible in the case of a rare form of dementia called *Creutzfeldt-Jakob disease,* but Alzheimer's disease is apparently not associated with infection. It has been reported that Creutzfeldt-Jakob disease resembles mad cow disease, and it is thought that a risk factor may be eating beef from cattle possibly exposed to mad cow disease. Episodes of head trauma have been implicated as a possible risk factor for Alzheimer's disease (Lye & Shores, 2000). A reasonably solid genetic association involving chromosome 21 trisomy has been formed between what appears to be an inherited form of Alzheimer's disease and Down syndrome.

Much of the epidemiology of the organic mental disorders merges with general considerations concerning health status. Cardiovascular risk factors such as obesity and hypertension put a person at greater than usual risk for stroke. Smoking is apparently a direct or indirect risk factor for several disorders that eventuate in brain dysfunction. The diagnosis of dementia associated with alcoholism is now relatively widely accepted, although it was controversial at one time. Alcohol, most clearly, and perhaps several other abused substances make for significant risk factors. In some cases, the crucial risk factor is provided not by the individual, but by the mother of the individual during pregnancy. Existence of fetal alcohol syndrome is well established, and the evidence for association between birth defects and other forms of substance abuse during pregnancy is increasing. Until recently, risk of acquiring brain disease by infection had diminished substantially, but that situation has changed markedly with the appearance of human immunodeficiency virus, or HIV-1 infection, or acquired immunodeficiency syndrome (AIDS) dementia (Bornstein et al., 1993; Grant et al., 1987; Van Gorp, Miller, Satz, & Visscher, 1989). It has become increasingly clear that AIDS is frequently transmitted to children during pregnancy or in association with breast feeding. New anti-infection medication is going through extensive clinical trials, and there is great promise of effectiveness.

In summary, prevalence and incidence of the organic mental disorders vary substantially, ranging from very rare to common diseases. Number of risk factors also varies, ranging from complete absence to a substantial number. The genetic and degenerative diseases, notably Huntington's and Alzheimer's diseases, possess little in the way of risk factors, and there is not much that can be done to prevent their occurrence. Development of a test for risk of transmitting Huntington's disease has opened the admittedly controversial and complex matter of genetic counseling. On the other hand, disorders such as dementia associated with alcoholism and, perhaps, stroke are preventable by good health maintenance. Indeed, the incidence of major stroke has declined in recent years.

COURSE AND PROGNOSIS

Course and prognosis for the organic mental disorders also vary with the underlying disorder. We review the basic considerations here by first introducing some stages of acceleration and development. Then we provide examples of disorders that have courses and prognoses consistent with various acceleration and developmental combinations. Acceleration stages are steady state, slow, moderate, and rapid. Developmental stages are the perinatal period, early childhood, late childhood and adolescence, early adulthood, middle age, and old age. Acceleration stages concern the rate of progression of the disorder, while the developmental stages characterize the age of onset of symptoms.

Mental retardation is a disorder with a course involving onset during the perinatal period and steady-state acceleration. Mental retardation is one of those disorders in which there is little, if any, progression of neuropathology, but there may be a slowly progressive disability because of increasing environmental demands for cognitive abilities that the individual does not possess. Other developmental disorders, such as specific learning disability, do not have their onsets during the perinatal period but rather during early childhood when academic skills are first expected to be acquired.

In contrast to these disorders, stroke is typically characterized by onset during middle age. The acceleration of the disorder is first extremely rapid and then slows down, gradually reaching steady state. Thus, the stroke patient, at the time of the stroke, becomes seriously ill very rapidly, and this is followed by additional destructive processes in the brain. Assuming a good outcome, a gradual recovery period follows, and there is restoration of the brain to a relatively normal steady state. On the other hand, malignant brain tumors, which also tend to appear during middle age, progress rapidly and do not decelerate unless they are successfully surgically removed.

Progressive dementias generally appear during middle or old age and accelerate slowly or moderately. Huntington's disease generally progresses less rapidly than Alzheimer's disease; therefore, the Huntington's patient may live a long life with his or her symptoms. Head trauma is a disorder that may occur at any age, but once the acute phase of the disorder is over, the brain typically returns to a steady state. Thus, the head trauma patient, if recovery from the acute condition is satisfactory, may have a normal life expectancy with an often-dramatic picture of deterioration immediately following the trauma until completion of resolution of the acute phase, followed by substantial recovery. However, the degree of residual disability may vary widely.

Briefly summarizing these considerations from a developmental standpoint, the most common organic mental disorder associated with the perinatal period is mental retardation and its variants. During early childhood, the specific and pervasive developmental disorders begin to appear. Head trauma typically begins to appear during late childhood and adolescence, and incidence peaks during young adulthood. Systemic illnesses, notably cardiovascular, cardiopulmonary, and neoplastic disease, most commonly impact negatively on brain functions during middle age. Dementia associated with alcoholism also begins to appear during early middle age. The progressive degenerative dementias are largely associated with old age. As to acceleration, following the time period surrounding the acquisition of the disorder, developmental, vascular, and traumatic disorders tend to be relatively stable. Malignant tumors and certain infectious disorders may be rapidly progressive, and the degenerative disorders progress at a slow to moderate pace.

While connotation of the term *progressive* is progressively worse, not all of the organic mental disorders remain stable or get worse. There is recovery of certain disorders as a natural process or with the aid of treatment. In the case of head trauma, there is a rather typical history of initial unconsciousness, lapsing into coma for a varying length of time, awakening, a period of memory loss and incomplete orientation called *posttraumatic amnesia,* and resolution of the amnesia. Rehabilitation is often initiated at some point in this progression, sometimes beginning while the patient is still in a coma. Outcome of this combination of spontaneous recovery and rehabilitation is rarely, if ever, complete return to preinjury status, but often allows for a return to productive living in the community. Recovery from stroke is also common, and many poststroke patients can return to community living. Among the most important prognostic indicators for head trauma are length of time in coma and length of posttraumatic amnesia. General health status is a good predictor for stroke outcome and potential for recurrence. Patients who maintain poor cardiac status, hypertension, inappropriate dietary habits, or substance abuse are poorer candidates for recovery than are poststroke patients who do not have these difficulties. Some patients, particularly those with chronic, severe hypertension, may have multiple strokes, resolving into a vascular dementia.

Efficacy of rehabilitation in and of itself for head trauma and stroke patients remains a controversial area, but there is increasing evidence that rehabilitation may often have beneficial effects over and above spontaneous recovery. As to developmental disorders, enormous efforts have been made in institutional and school settings to provide appropriate educational remediation for developmentally disabled children—often with some success. Effective treatment at the time of onset of acute disorder also has obvious implications for prognosis. Use of appropriate medications and management following trauma or stroke and the feasibility and availability of neurosurgery are major considerations. Tumors can be removed, aneurysms can be repaired, and increased pressure can be relieved by neurosurgeons. These interventions during the acute phase of a disorder are often mainly directed toward preservation of life, but also have important implications for the outcomes of surviving patients.

FAMILIAL AND GENETIC PATTERNS

The organic mental disorders are based on some diseases of known genetic origin, some diseases in which a genetic or familial component is suspected, and some that are clearly acquired disorders. It is well established that Huntington's disease and certain forms of mental retardation, notably Down syndrome, are genetic disorders. There appears to be evidence of a hereditary form of Alzheimer's disease, although the genetic contribution to Alzheimer's disease in general is not fully understood. A relatively rare genetic subtype has been identified. The great majority of individuals with this subtype have a gene on chromosome 14 called *Apolipoprotein E* that promotes development of the amyloid plaques that constitute the major brain pathology associated with the disease. Whether multiple sclerosis has a genetic component remains under investigation, although it is clearly not a hereditary disorder such as Huntington's disease.

Of great recent interest is the role of genetics in the acquisition of alcoholism, and, subsequently, dementia associated with alcoholism or alcohol amnestic disorder. Evidence suggests that having an alcoholic parent places a person at higher than average risk for developing alcoholism. The specific genetic factors are far from understood, but the association in families appears to be present. Whether having a family history of alcoholism increases risk of acquiring dementia associated with alcoholism is not clear, but it has been shown that nonalcoholic sons of alcoholic fathers do more poorly on some cognitive tests than do matched controls. The matter is substantially clearer in the case of alcohol amnestic disorder of Korsakoff's syndrome. A widely cited study by Blass and Gibson (1977) showed acquisition of Korsakoff's syndrome is dependent on the existence of a genetic defect in transketolase, a liver enzyme, in combination with a thiamine deficiency.

Other genetic and familial factors associated with the organic mental disorders relate largely to the genetics of underlying systemic disorders. Thus, the genetics of cancer might have some bearing on the likelihood of acquiring a brain tumor, while the genetics of the cardiovascular system might have some bearing on the risk for stroke. Disorders such as hypertension and diabetes appear to run in families and have varying incidences in different ethnic groups. Ethnic specificity is sometimes quite precise (but this is rare), as in the case of Tay-Sachs disease, a degenerative disorder of early childhood found almost exclusively in Jewish people in Eastern Europe.

SUMMARY

The organic mental disorders are conditions in which behavioral changes may be directly associated with some basis in altered brain function. While the general diagnostic term *organic brain syndrome* has commonly been used to describe these conditions, wide variability in the manifestations of brain dysfunction makes this term insufficiently precise in reference to clinical relevance, and it has been abandoned. Variability is attributable to a number of factors, including the following considerations:

- Location of the damage in the brain.
- Neuropathological process producing the damage.
- Length of time the brain damage has been present.
- Age and health status of the individual at the time the damage is sustained.
- Individual's premorbid personality and level of function.

The neuropsychological approach to the conceptualization of the organic mental disorders has identified a number of behavioral parameters along which the manifestations of brain dysfunction can be described and classified. The most frequently considered dimensions are intellectual function, language, memory, visual-spatial skills, perceptual skills, and motor function. Some important concepts related to brain function and brain disorders include the principle of contralateral control of perceptual and motor functions and functional hemisphere asymmetries. In addition, studies of brain-damaged patients have shown that particular structures in the brain mediate relatively discrete behaviors. Neurologists and neuropsychologists have identified a number of syndromes in areas such as language dysfunction, memory disorder, and general intellectual impairment. There are major variations in the courses of the organic mental disorders. Some are transient, leaving little or no residual; some are permanent but not progressive; others are either slowly or rapidly progressive. While these disorders most profoundly and commonly involve impairment of cognitive, perceptual, and motor skills, sometimes personality changes of various types are the most prominent symptoms. More often than not, personality and affective changes appear in brain-damaged patients along with their cognitive, perceptual, and motor disorders. Thus, a mood disorder or symptoms such as delusions and hallucinations may be sequelae of brain damage for various reasons.

During the years spanning the writing of the various editions of this chapter, there have been several major developments in the area of what was originally called the organic mental disorders. These developments include at least one new disorder, AIDS dementia; major discoveries in the genetics of Huntington's disease and alcoholism; enormous developments in the technology of neuroimaging; and a reconceptualization by psychiatry of the previously held distinction between functional and organic disorders. The work in neuroimaging is particularly exciting because it goes beyond obtaining more refined pictures of the brain and now allows us to observe working of the brain during ongoing behavior through fMRI and to examine the molecular biology of brain function through another MRI-related procedure, magnetic resonance spectroscopy.

REFERENCES

Allen, D. N., Sprenkel, D. G., Heyman, R. A., Schramke, C. J., & Heffron, N. E. (1998). Evaluation of demyelinating and degenerative disorders. In G. Goldstein, P. D. Nussbaum, & S. R. Beers (Eds.), *Neuropsychology* (pp. 187–208). New York: Plenum Press.

American Psychiatric Association. (1980). *Diagnostic and statistical manual of mental disorders* (3rd ed.). Washington, DC: Author.

American Psychiatric Association. (1987). *Diagnostic and statistical manual of mental disorders* (3rd ed., rev.). Washington, DC: Author.

American Psychiatric Association. (1994). *Diagnostic and statistical manual of mental disorders* (4th ed.). Washington, DC: Author.

Balter, M. (2001). Genes and disease: Immune gene linked to vCJD susceptibility. *Science, 294*, 1438–1439.

Baron, I. S., & Gioia, G. A. (1998). Neuropsychology of infants and young children. In G. Goldstein, P. D. Nussbaum, & S. R. Beers (Eds.), *Neuropsychology* (pp. 9–34). New York: Plenum Press.

Begleiter, H., Porjesz, B., Bihari, B., & Kissin, B. (1984). Event-related potentials in boys at high risk for alcoholism. *Science, 225*, 1493–1496.

Benton, A. L. (1985). Body schema disturbances: Finger agnosia and right left disorientation. In K. M. Heilman & E. Valenstein (Eds.), *Clinical neuropsychology* (2nd ed., pp. 115–129). New York: Oxford University Press.

Benton, A. L., & Joynt, R. J. (1960). Early descriptions of aphasia. *Archives of Neurology, 3,* 205–222.

Berg, R. A. (1998). Evaluation of neoplastic processes. In G. Goldstein, P. D. Nussbaum, & S. R. Beers (Eds.), *Neuropsychology* (pp. 248–269). New York: Plenum Press.

Blass, J. P., & Gibson, G. E. (1977). Abnormality of a thiamine-requiring enzyme in patients with Wernicke-Korsakoff syndrome. *New England Journal of Medicine, 297,* 1367–1370.

Boring, E. G. (1950). *A history of experimental psychology* (2nd ed.). New York: Appleton-Century-Crofts.

Bornstein, R. A., Nasrallah, H. A., Para, M. F., & Whitacre, C. C. (1993). Neuropsychological performance in symptomatic and asymptomatic HIV infection. *AIDS, 7,* 519–524.

Broca, P. (1861). Perte de la parole. Ramollissement chronique et destruction partielle du lobe anterieur gauche du cerveau. *Bulletin de la Societe de' Anthropologie, 2,* 235–238.

Butters, N., & Cermak, L. S. (1980). *Alcoholic Korsakoff's syndrome.* New York: Academic Press.

Caine, E. D. (1986). The neuropsychology of depression: The pseudodementia syndrome. In I. Grant & K. M. Adams (Eds.), *Neuropsychological assessment of neuropsychiatric disorders* (pp. 221–243). New York: Oxford University Press.

Cloninger, C. R., Bohman, M., & Sigvardsson, S. (1981). Inheritance of alcohol abuse: Cross-fostering analysis of adopted men. *Archives of General Psychiatry, 38,* 861–868.

Dean, R. S. (1986). Lateralization of cerebral functions. In D. Wedding, A. M. Horton, Jr., & J. Webster (Eds.), *The neuropsychology handbook: Behavioral and clinical perspectives* (pp. 80–102). New York: Springer.

Dodrill, C. B. (1986). Psychosocial consequences of epilepsy. In S. B. Filskov & T. J. Boll (Eds.), *Handbook of clinical neuropsychology* (Vol. 2, pp. 338–363). New York: Wiley.

Elias, M. F., & Streeten, D. H. P. (1980). *Hypertension and cognitive processes.* Mount Desert, ME: Beech Hill.

Flourens, M. J. P. (1824). *Recherches experimentales sur les proprietes et les fonctons du systeme nerveux dans les animaux vertebres.* Paris: Crevot.

Gastaut, H. (1970). Clinical and electroencephalographical classification of epileptic seizures. *Epilepsia, 11,* 102–103.

Geschwind, N. (1965). Disconnection syndromes in animals and man. *Brain, 88,* 237–294.

Goethe, K. E., & Levin, H. S. (1986). Neuropsychological consequences of head injury in children. In G. Goldstein & R. E. Tarter (Eds.), *Advances in clinical neuropsychology* (Vol. 3, pp. 213–242). New York: Plenum Press.

Goldstein, G. (1986, February). *Neuropsychological effects of five antihypertensive agents.* Poster presented at annual meeting of International Neuropsychological Society, Denver, CO.

Goldstein, G. (1997). Delirium, dementia, and amnestic and other cognitive disorders. In S. M. Turner & M. Hersen (Eds.), *Adult psychopathology and diagnosis* (3rd ed., pp. 89–127). New York: Wiley.

Goldstein, G., Beers, S. R., Morrow, L. A., Shemansky, W. J., & Steinhauer, S. R. (1996, July). A preliminary neuropsychological study of Persian Gulf veterans. *Journal of the International Neuropsychological Society, 2,* 368–371.

Goldstein, K. (1936). The significance of the frontal lobes for mental performance. *Journal of Neurology and Psychopathology, 17,* 27–40.

Goldstein, K. (1959). Functional disturbances in brain damage. In S. Arieti (Ed.), *American handbook of psychiatry* (pp. 770–794). New York: Basic Books.

Goldstein, K., & Scheerer, M. (1941). Abstract and concrete behavior: An experimental study with special tests. *Psychological Monographs, 53*(2, Whole No. 239).

Goodwin, D. W. (1979). Alcoholism and heredity: A review and hypothesis. *Archives of General Psychiatry, 36,* 57–61.

Goodwin, D. W., Schulsinger, F., Hermansen, L., Guze, S. B., & Winokur, G. (1973). Alcohol problems in adoptees raised apart from alcoholic biological parents. *Archives of General Psychiatry, 28,* 238–243.

Grant, I., Atkinson, J. H., Hesselink, J. R., Kennedy, C. J., Richman, D. D., Spector, S. A., et al. (1987). Evidence for early central nervous system involvement in the acquired immunodeficiency syndrome (AIDS) and other human immunodeficiency virus (HIV) infections. *Annals of internal Medicine, 107,* 828–836.

Green, M. F. (1998). *Schizophrenia from a neurocognitive perspective.* Boston: Allyn & Bacon.

Gusella, J. F., Wexler, N. S., Conneallly, P. M., Naylor, S. L., Anderson, M. A., Tanzi, R. E., et al. (1983). A polymorphic DNA marker genetically linked to Huntington's disease. *Nature, 306,* 234–238.

Halstead, W. C. (1947). *Brain and intelligence.* Chicago: University of Chicago Press.

Heaton, R. K., Nelson, L. M., Thompson, D. S., Burks, J. S., & Franklin, G. M. (1985). Neuropsychological findings in relapsing-remitting and chronic-progressive multiple sclerosis. *Journal of Consulting and Clinical Psychology, 53,* 103–110.

Heilman, K. M., & Valenstein, E. (Eds.). (1993). *Clinical neuropsychology* (3rd ed.) New York: Oxford University Press.

Hill, S. Y., Steinhauer, S. R., & Zubin, J. (1987). Biological markers for alcoholism: A vulnerability model conceptualization. In P. C. Rivers (Ed.), *Nebraska Symposium on Motivation: Vol. 34. Alcohol and addictive behavior* (pp. 207–256). Lincoln: University of Nebraska Press.

Jervis, G. A. (1959). The mental deficiencies. In S. Arieti (Ed.), *American handbook of psychiatry* (Vol. 4, pp. 1289–1314). New York: Basic Books.

Kanner, L. (1943). Autistic disturbances of affective contact. *Nervous Child, 2,* 217–250.

Katz, L. J., Goldstein, G., & Beers, S. R. (2001). *Learning disabilities in older adolescents and adults.* New York: Kluwer Academic/Plenum Press.

King, H. E., & Miller, R. E. (1990). Hypertension: Cognitive and behavioral considerations. *Neuropsychology Review, 1,* 31–73.

Klove, H., & Matthews, C. G. (1974). Neuropsychological studies of patients with epilepsy. In R. M. Reitan & L. A. Davison (Eds.), *Clinical neuropsychology: Current status and applications* (pp. 237–265). New York: Winston-Wiley.

Lashley, K. S. (1960). In search of the engram. In F. A. Beach, D. O. Hebb, C. T. Morgan, & H. W. Nissen (Eds.), *The neuropsychology of Lashley* (pp. 478–505). New York: McGraw-Hill. (Original work published 1950)

Levin, H. S., Benton, A. L., & Grossman, R. G. (1982). *Neurobehavioral consequences of closed head injury.* New York: Oxford University Press.

Levin, H. S., Eisenberg, H. M., & Benton, A. L. (1989). *Mild head injury.* New York: Oxford University Press.

Luria, A. R. (1966). *Higher cortical functions in man* (B. Haigh, Trans.) New York: Basic Books.

Luria, A. R. (1973). *The working brain.* New York: Basic Books.

Lye, T. C., & Shores, E. A. (2000). Traumatic brain injury as a risk factor for Alzheimer's disease: A review. *Neuropsychology Review, 10,* 115–129.

Mesulam, M. M. (1985). *Principles of behavioral neurology.* Philadelphia: Davis.

Minshew, N. J., & Payton, J. B. (1988a). New perspectives in autism, Part 1: The clinical spectrum of infantile autism. *Current Problems in Pediatrics, 18,* 561–610.

Minshew, N. J., & Payton, J. B. (1988b). New perspectives in autism, Part 2: The differential diagnosis and neurobiology of autism. *Current Problems in Pediatrics, 19,* 615–694.

Myslobodsky, M. S., & Mirsky, A. F. (1988). *Elements of petit mal epilepsy*. New York: Peter Lang.

Neils, J., Boller, F., Gerdeman, B., & Cole, M. (1989). Descriptive writing abilities in Alzheimer's disease. *Journal of Clinical and Experimental Neuropsychology, 11,* 692–698.

Nussbaum, P. D. (1994). Pseudodementia: A slow death. *Neuropsychology Review, 4,* 71–90.

Rosenstein, L. D. (1998). Differential diagnosis of the major progressive dementias and depression in middle and late adulthood: A summary of the literature of the early 1990s. *Neuropsychology Review, 8,* 109–167.

Rourke, B. P., & Brown, G. G. (1986). Clinical neuropsychology and behavioral neurology: Similarities and differences. In S. B. Filskov & T. J. Boll (Eds.), *Handbook of clinical neuropsychology* (Vol. 2, pp. 3–18). New York: Wiley.

Rumsey, J. M., & Hamburger, S. D. (1988). Neuropsychological findings in high-functioning men with infantile autism, residual state. *Journal of Clinical and Experimental Neuropsychology, 10,* 201–221.

Satz, P. (1966). Specific and nonspecific effects of brain lesions in man. *Journal of Abnormal Psychology, 71,* 65–70.

Schaeffer, K. W., Parsons, O. A., & Yohman, J. R. (1984). Neuropsychological differences between male familial and nonfamilial alcoholics and nonalcoholics. *Alcoholism: Clinical and Experimental Research, 8,* 347–351.

Smith, R. J., Barth, J. T., Diamond, R., & Giuliano, A. J. (1998). Evaluation of head trauma. In G. Goldstein, P. D. Nussbaum, & S. R. Beers (Eds.), *Neuropsychology* (pp. 135–170). New York: Plenum Press.

Spreen, O. (1987). *Learning disabled children growing up: A follow-up into adulthood*. Lisse, The Netherlands: Swets & Zeitlinger.

Steinhauer, S. R., Hill, S. Y., & Zubin, J. (1987). Event related potentials in alcoholics and their first-degree relatives. *Alcoholism, 4,* 307–314.

Tarter, R. E. (1976). Neuropsychological investigations of alcoholism. In G. Goldstein & C. Neuringer (Eds.), *Empirical studies of alcoholism* (pp. 231–256). Cambridge, MA: Ballinger.

Tarter, R. E., Hegedus, A., Goldstein, G., Shelly, C., & Alterman, A. I. (1984). Adolescent sons of alcoholics: Neuropsychological and personality characteristics. *Alcoholism: Clinical and Experimental Research, 8,* 216–222.

Teuber, H.-L. (1959). Some alterations in behavior after cerebral lesions in man. In A. D. Bass (Eds.), *Evolution of nervous control from primitive organisms to man* (pp. 157–194). Washington, DC: American Association for the Advancement of Science.

Van Gorp, W. G., Miller, E. N., Satz, P., & Visscher, B. (1989). Neuropsychological performance in HIV-1 immunocompromised patients: A preliminary report. *Journal of Clinical and Experimental Neuropsychology, 11,* 763–773.

Walker, A. E., Caveness, W. F., & Critchley, M. (Eds.). (1969). *Late effects of head injury*. Springfield, IL: Charles C Thomas.

Wells, C. E. (1979). Pseudodementia. *American Journal of Psychiatry, 136,* 895–900.

Wells, C. E. (1980). The differential diagnosis of psychiatric disorders in the elderly. In J. O. Cole & J. E. Barrett (Eds.), *Psychopathology in the aged* (pp. 19–35). New York: Raven Press.

Werner, H., & Strauss, A. (1942). Experimental analysis of the clinical symptom "perseveration" in mentally retarded children. *American Journal of Mental Deficiency, 47,* 185–188.

CHAPTER 6

Substance-Related
Use Disorders: Alcohol

MARK B. SOBELL, ERIC F. WAGNER, and LINDA C. SOBELL

DESCRIPTION OF THE DISORDER

HISTORICALLY, THE SCIENTIFIC study of alcohol abuse has focused primarily on individuals who have been severely dependent on alcohol even though such people constitute a minority of the alcohol-abusing population. This chapter addresses diagnostic and assessment issues related to alcohol abusers all along the dependence continuum, ranging from those who are mildly dependent to those who are severely dependent.

Views about alcohol use disorders are a mix of concepts derived from research and from clinical anecdote. To understand present views about alcohol problems, you must understand how approaches have changed. Over the years, public opinion has ranged from viewing alcohol abusers as morally wrong to being victims of a disease. No matter how alcohol problems were conceptualized, however, the focus was on individuals who were severely dependent. Such individuals are highly visible and typically have experienced multiple serious consequences. In the United States, the view that alcohol problems are a disorder became dominant in the mid-1900s with the rise of Alcoholics Anonymous (AA) and the proclamation that alcoholism is a disease by the American Medical Association (Pattison, Sobell, & Sobell, 1977). The embracing of a disease concept, however, was not based on biological evidence. Rather, it was intended to shift responsibility for dealing with alcohol problems from the criminal justice system to the health care system. These views, referred to as *traditional* conceptualizations of alcohol problems (Pattison et al., 1977), stemmed primarily from AA (Bacon, 1973), and Jellinek (1960).

Alcoholics Anonymous viewed alcoholics as suffering from a biological aberration, an "allergy" to alcohol (i.e., with repeated exposure to alcohol, alcoholics would change to quickly become physically dependent on alcohol if they started to drink); and once dependent, they would continue to drink to avoid withdrawal symptoms. This, however, does not explain why people who have stopped drinking for some time would return to drinking. To explain relapse, AA stated that alcoholics had an "obsession" to drink like normal drinkers. In addition, alcoholism was thought to be a progressive disorder (i.e., if alcoholics continued to drink, their problem would inevitably worsen, even following a long abstinence period).

Jellinek, a scientist, attempted to bridge the gap between lay views and the little scientific knowledge available by postulating a disease concept of alcoholism. He and others felt that the medical profession should be responsible for treating alcohol abusers (Bacon, 1973). Although he alluded to genetic components, he did not speculate about why some drinkers develop alcohol problems and others do not. Jellinek postulated that alcoholics (a) use alcohol to cope with emotional problems, (b) over time develop tolerance to alcohol, thereby leading to increased consumption to achieve desired effects, and (c) eventually develop "loss of control." By loss of control, he hypothesized that consumption of even small amounts of alcohol would initiate physical dependence that would trigger continued drinking (Jellinek, 1960). Jellinek hypothesized that there were many types of alcohol problems. He called the type just described *gamma* alcoholism, which he felt was most common in the United States and was a progressive disorder.

Since these early views, considerable research has been conducted that is inconsistent with the traditional conceptualization. Although the research literature suggests that some individuals may be genetically predisposed to develop alcohol problems, a large proportion of individuals who have alcohol problems do not have a positive family history (Fingarette, 1988). Research also shows that social and cultural factors play a large role in the development of alcohol problems (Sigvardsson, Cloninger, & Bohman, 1985) and, in most cases, the natural history of the disorder is not progressive (Dawson, 1996; Institute of Medicine, 1990). Rather, it includes periods of alcohol problems of varying severity separated by periods of either nondrinking or of drinking limited quantities without problems (Cahalan, 1970).

Epidemiological studies have demonstrated that individuals with less serious alcohol problems outnumber those with severe problems (Institute of Medicine, 1990). As discussed later in this chapter, because alcohol use patterns lie along a continuum ranging from no problems to severe problems, conceptualizations must explain the entire continuum of cases. Treatment implications of the epidemiological findings are profound. Traditional conceptualizations view alcohol problems as a progressive disorder and people who are mildly dependent on alcohol as in the "early stages" of the development of alcoholism. Consequently, even those with mild problems are viewed as needing the same treatment as those who are severely dependent. That is, everyone who experiences problems with alcohol is labeled an *alcoholic* and told he or she can never drink again. Considerable research, however, shows that mildly dependent alcohol abusers not only respond well to brief interventions, but often recover by moderating rather than ceasing their drinking (Bien, Miller, & Tonigan, 1993; M. B. Sobell & Sobell, 1993a, 1995).

As to loss of control, research has demonstrated that even in very severe cases, physical dependence is not initiated by a small amount of drinking (Marlatt, 1978; Pattison et al., 1977). This suggests that other factors, such as conditioned cues (Niaura et al., 1988) and positive consequences of drinking (Orford, 2001), are necessary to explain why some people continue drinking despite having repeatedly suffered adverse consequences.

Case Study

The client described in this case study is a 27-year-old White, single male who voluntarily entered treatment at the Guided Self-Change (GSC) Clinic at the Addiction Research Foundation in Toronto, Canada. Guided Self-Change treatment, a motivationally based cognitive-behavioral intervention, emphasizes helping clients help themselves (M. B. Sobell & Sobell, 1993a). The intervention includes an assessment, four semistructured sessions, and an aftercare component. In addition, clients are given an opportunity to request additional sessions. The GSC treatment intervention has been evaluated in several clinical trials (M. B. Sobell & Sobell, 1998).

The client was in his last year of graduate school and was planning to pursue a postdoctoral fellowship in the coming year. He reported seeking treatment because of "hitting a personal rock bottom," and an "ultimatum from my girlfriend." The client reported that two years before treatment, the frequency and quantity of his drinking had increased and that he had tried to cut down and stop without success. He also reported that his university friends and colleagues drank heavily after seminars, and that he perceived there was a "stigma" attached to people who left after a few drinks. He also said he felt pressured to drink when others around him drank.

At treatment entry, he reported he was "extremely ready" to take action to change his drinking, and at the assessment, he stated, "I've started working on my problem, but I need some help." When the client was asked why he decided to seek treatment, he stated:

> A series of events, which started with increased drinking, behavioral change, fights when I was intoxicated, or drunk for a better word, breakups with friends, stupid arguments with friends, arguments with girlfriends. Just a lot of bad times and a lot of problems. I usually go for maybe two or three weeks and say, "I'm positively not going to have anything to drink," but when I would say "Okay, well I can handle this now," it seemed to get worse, so I thought it's time to talk to somebody about it.

Although the client reported drinking heavily for eight years, he felt that his drinking had been a problem for only the last four years. He scored 11 on the Alcohol Dependence Scale (ADS; Skinner & Allen, 1982) and 1 on the Drug Abuse Screening Test (DAST-20; Skinner, 1982). An ADS score of 11 is in the first quartile for ADS norms and is reflective of someone who has a mild alcohol problem. A DAST-20 score of 1 suggests no current drug problem. The client also reported no current use of prescription medications or other psychoactive substances, including nicotine. He reported no current health problems or past treatment for mental health or substance use problems. He also reported never having attended self-help group meetings (e.g., AA) and had no prior alcohol-related hospitalizations or arrests. He reported no morning drinking in the past year, and in terms of family history, reported that his father had had a problem with alcohol.

He reported experiencing several alcohol-related consequences in the six months before the assessment (e.g., fights in bars, personal problems, verbally abusive, spending too much money on alcohol). He reported that his highest risk situations for problem drinking were when home alone, bored and stressed, and when he was with friends after work at seminars. He also reported that about half the days when he drank alcohol, he was alone. Although this was his first treatment experience, he reported several prior attempts to quit or reduce his alcohol use. At the assessment, his subjective evaluation of the severity of his alcohol problem was "major," and he rated the overall quality of his life as "very unsatisfactory."

The client's self-report of his drinking in the past year using the Timeline Followback assessment (L. C. Sobell & Sobell, 1992b) was:

1. *Abstinence:* 59% of the days.
2. *Drinks per drinking day:* 4.5 standard drinks (*SDs*; 1 *SD* = 13.6 grams of absolute ethanol).
3. *Average weekly consumption:* 13 *SDs*.
4. *Highest single drinking day in the past year:* 14 *SDs*.
5. *Low consumption days* (1 to 3 *SDs*): 42% of all days.
6. *Heavy consumption:* 22% of all days (20% = 4 to 9 *SDs*, 2% were ≥ 10 *SDs*).

When the client was shown the personalized feedback based on his self-reports of drinking (L. C. Sobell & Sobell, 1996b; M. B. Sobell & Sobell, 1998; Substance Abuse and Mental Health Administration, 1999), he said: "I'm a little alarmed. More than a little alarmed, but I'm alarmed that I'm at the high end, but I know that's why I'm here. The other part that alarms me is that most of the people I know, I would put them in that."

Based on the assessment interview, this client met the criteria for a *Diagnostic and Statistical Manual of Mental Disorders, 4th Edition, Text Revision (DSM-IV-TR)* diagnosis of alcohol dependence (American Psychiatric Association [APA], 2000a). However, on a continuum of alcohol problems (M. B. Sobell & Sobell, 1993b), like most GSC clients (M. B. Sobell & Sobell, 1993a), the severity of his problem would be evaluated as mild. With such clients, a brief cognitive-behavioral motivational intervention is a good first treatment in a stepped-care model (M. B. Sobell & Sobell, 2000).

At the assessment, the client was given an explanation about the treatment (i.e., helping clients help themselves). Shortly into treatment when he was asked what he thought of the intervention, he replied: "I like it so far. It's making me think and I guess before, I always thought I was too busy to sit down and think about some of these things, and that's why I never had any success in curbing the problem. This is good because it puts the onus on me."

Another area of research that has relevance to treatment is natural recoveries. Several studies indicate that recovery from alcohol problems in the absence of treatment is more prevalent than once thought (Klingemann et al., 2001; L. C. Sobell, Cunningham, & Sobell, 1996; L. C. Sobell, Ellingstad, & Sobell, 2000). From a public health standpoint, this body of research suggests that community interventions might facilitate the self-change process by motivating people to identify their problems sooner than would otherwise have occurred and to attempt to recover on their own (L. C. Sobell, Cunningham, Sobell, Agrawal, et al., 1996).

EPIDEMIOLOGY

General population surveys provide information on rates of alcohol consumption as well as the prevalence of problem drinking. Next to caffeine, alcohol is the second most used psychoactive substance (APA, 1994). In North America, per capita consumption generally has been declining since the early 1980s (Schneider Institute for Health Policy, 2001). This decline is consistent with patterns observed in other developed countries (Smart, 1989) and is thought to be due either to an aging population (i.e., older people decrease use) or increased adoption of healthy lifestyles (National Institute on Alcohol Abuse and Alcoholism, 1993).

Drinking problems typically have been defined as either diagnosis-based or symptom-based. Reporting the prevalence of abuse and dependence using current *DSM* definitions has the advantage that those definitions generally are accepted by researchers and clinicians. However, a symptom-based approach in which rates of specific types of problems (e.g., physiological vs. psychosocial) are reported would be more congruent with a conceptualization of alcohol problems as lying along a severity continuum (Institute of Medicine, 1990).

The National Institute on Alcohol Abuse and Alcoholism surveyed a representative sample of 42,862 American individuals ages 18 and older in the National Longitudinal Alcohol Epidemiologic Survey (Grant, 1997). It was found that the lifetime prevalence of alcohol dependence was 13.3%, and the past year prevalence was 4.4%. Men were more likely than women to use alcohol and to have alcohol use disorders. In terms of the stability of diagnoses, Hasin, Grant, and Endicott (1990) found that of those individuals originally diagnosed as alcohol dependent, 46% were still classified as dependent four years later, 15% were classified as having alcohol abuse, and 39% could not be diagnosed with an alcohol problem. Similarly, in a national survey, Dawson (1996) found that of 4,585 adults who previously had met criteria for a *DSM-IV* diagnosis of alcohol dependence, 28% still met the criteria for alcohol abuse or dependence, 22% were abstinent, and 50% could not be diagnosed as having an alcohol problem. As compared to those who had not been in treatment, treated individuals were more likely to be abstinent (39% vs. 16%), while those who had not been treated were more likely to be drinking asymptomatically (58% vs. 28%). These findings indicate that alcohol problems are not necessarily progressive. In another national survey, Dawson (2000) reported that frequency of intoxication had the strongest association with the probability of having a diagnosable alcohol use disorder, followed by frequency of five or more drinks per day.

From the standpoint of symptom-based prevalence, the ratio of problem drinkers to severely dependent drinkers is a function of the definitions used and the populations sampled. Regardless of the definitions, on a problem severity continuum, the population of people with identifiable problems but no severe signs of dependence is much larger than the population with severe dependence (M. B. Sobell & Sobell, 1993a). Problem drinkers comprise 15% to 35% of individuals in the adult population, whereas severely dependent drinkers account for 3% to 7% (Hilton, 1991; Institute of Medicine, 1990).

Drinking problems are not distributed equally across sociodemographic groups. While males greatly outnumber females (Fillmore, 1988; Hilton, 1987), the gap has been narrowing since the Vietnam War (Grant, 1997). Besides gender differences in prevalence, problem drinking tends to occur later in life for women (Fillmore, 1987). In addition, women appear to be more vulnerable to the adverse physical consequences of heavy alcohol use (Dawson & Grant, 1993). For example, alcohol-dependent women may be at higher risk of dying of alcohol-related problems such as hypertension and liver disease (Ashley & Rankin, 1979; Hill, 1984). Compared to women without alcohol problems, women with alcohol problems have a higher incidence of menstrual irregularities, more difficulty becoming pregnant, more prenatal complications, and more gynecological and obstetric problems (Beckman, 1979; Collins, 1993b; S. C. Wilsnack & Wilsnack, 1995). This increased vulnerability may be because differences in body composition between men and women result in women having higher blood alcohol levels after consuming an equivalent amount of alcohol. Alcohol-related problems also appear to be inversely related to age, with the highest problem rates occurring for those 18 to 29 years of age (Fillmore, 1988; National Institute on Alcohol Abuse and Alcoholism, 2000; Robins & Regier, 1991). Marital status is similarly related to problem drinking, with single individuals experiencing more physiological symptoms of dependence and more psychosocial problems than those who are married (Hilton, 1991).

Even though epidemiological studies provide information on ethnic and racial differences in relation to alcohol use and abuse, the methods for categorizing respondents' cultural/ethnic backgrounds have been rudimentary. Consequently, data on ethnic differences must be considered preliminary. Across ethnic/racial groups, heavy drinking patterns occur at different points in the life span (Caetano & Kaskutas, 1995; National Institute on Alcohol Abuse and Alcoholism, 1993; Robins, 1991). Among White males, frequency of heavy drinking typically peaks in a man's 20s and decreases in his late 30s to 40s, while heavy drinking among young African American males is low at first (Caetano, 1984; Herd, 1989; Russell, 1989) but then increases during middle age. For example, African Americans before the age of 40 demonstrate a lower incidence of heavy drinking (i.e., four or more drinks a day) than Whites and Hispanics/Latinos (National Institute on Alcohol Abuse and Alcoholism, 2000). This late heavy drinking onset may explain why, despite similar heavy drinking rates among African American and White males, alcohol-related health problems (e.g., liver cirrhosis) were more common among African American males. Such age-related differences have not been observed between African American and White females.

The Hispanic/Latino population in the United States is very heterogeneous (e.g., Mexicans, Puerto Ricans, Cubans). Some studies show Hispanics/Latinos with lower rates of heavy drinking than other Americans (National Institute on Drug Abuse, 1991; Welte & Barnes, 1995), while other studies show Hispanics/Latinos with higher rates (Caetano, 1989; Caetano & Kaskutas, 1995). These latter studies have found increased prevalence of alcohol-related problems among Hispanic/Latino males, especially those who are young to middle age. This is consistent with research showing that acculturation appears to be associated with increased rates of heavy drinking among Hispanics/Latinos (Caetano, 1985; Cahalan & Room, 1974).

Among Asian Americans, alcohol problem rates are generally lower than the U.S. norms (National Institute on Alcohol Abuse and Alcoholism, 1993). As with other ethnic groups, there is marked variation in drinking patterns and problems among different Asian groups. Surveys of Hawaiians found that Whites report drinking significantly more alcohol than Japanese, Chinese, or Filipinos, and reports of alcohol problems paralleled use patterns (Ahern, 1985; Murakami, 1985). Across several studies, Chinese men and women report the lowest levels of alcohol use and abuse, with a large proportion reporting no drinking (Ahern, 1985; Yu, Liu, Xia, & Zhang, 1985). Low use has been attributed both to cultural norms and to physiological sensitivity to alcohol (W. B. Clark & Hesselbrock, 1988).

CLINICAL PICTURE

When someone is considering abandoning a valued behavior, unless the reasons for stopping are overwhelmingly adverse, ambivalence would be expected. For individuals whose alcohol problems are not severe, ambivalence can be very pronounced as the decision to stop or reduce drinking may be largely based on risks rather than actual consequences. Failure to recognize this ambivalence can have serious consequences during the assessment process and can affect how clients are perceived by clinicians.

Traditional conceptualizations assert that individuals with alcohol problems present in denial; that is, they fail to recognize that their drinking is a problem (Nowinski, Baker, & Carroll, 1992; Substance Abuse and Mental Health Administration, 1999). In this regard, traditional assessments attempt to confront and break through the denial. The rationale is that this procedure is consistent with the first step of AA (i.e., the individual's recognizing that he or she is powerless over alcohol; Nowinski et al., 1992). However, when individuals feel attacked, such as being labeled as alcoholic, they typically resist the label and its implications. In other words, a confrontational interviewing style can result in a client's denying or not adopting the label. An alternative approach considers the individual ambivalent and avoids the use of confrontation, labeling, or other tactics that provoke defensiveness and resistance. This alternative nonthreatening, nonconfrontational style of interviewing is called *motivational interviewing* (Miller & Rollnick, 1991; Substance Abuse and Mental Health Administration, 1999). Because individuals who present with alcohol problems in clinical settings can show impairment ranging from very mild symptoms (e.g., repeated hangovers) to severe symptoms (e.g., major withdrawal symptoms), use of a motivational interviewing style is recommended.

Because traditional views are based on a model that emphasizes severe dependence, many individuals who have less severe alcohol problems may not be identified. It is important, therefore, for clinicians to learn to recognize individuals with mild alcohol problems. Such individuals respond well to brief interventions that allow reduced drinking as a goal (Bien et al., 1993; Heather, 1990; M. B. Sobell & Sobell, 1993a).

COURSE AND PROGNOSIS

Traditional concepts of alcohol problems, based on Jellinek's work on progressivity (Jellinek, 1952), postulated that such problems develop in early adulthood (i.e., 20 to 30 years of age) and increase in severity for several years. As noted earlier, the notion of progressivity has not been supported by research, although some alcohol problems worsen over time. Research also shows that alcohol problems can occur at any age (Atkinson, 1994; Schonfeld & Dupree, 1991; S. C. Wilsnack, Klassen, Schur, & Wilsnack, 1991). The temporal pattern of problems can be variable, with problems sometimes remitting, worsening, or improving (Cahalan & Room, 1974; Dawson, 1996; Hasin et al., 1990; Mandell, 1983). If an individual is experiencing alcohol problems at one point, it is not possible to predict that, in the absence of treatment, the problem will worsen. It has been found, however, that men whose alcohol problems are severe are likely to continue to worsen over time if they continue to drink (Fillmore & Midanik, 1984).

Alcohol problems have been characterized as a recurrent disorder (Polich, Armor, & Braiker, 1981). This characteristic has given the disorder a reputation as difficult to treat and seldom cured. More recent research, however, has found that the probability of relapse in people who have been in remission for several years is low (De Soto, O'Donnell, & De Soto, 1989; Sobell & Sobell, 1992a; M. B. Sobell, Sobell, & Kozlowksi, 1995). Clinically, the high likelihood of recurrence has led to relapse prevention procedures (Marlatt & Gordon, 1985). Such procedures include advising clients that setbacks may occur during recovery from the disorder and that they should use these setbacks as learning experiences to prevent future relapses rather than as evidence that recovery is impossible. Finally, the presence of psychiatric comorbidity is associated with a more guarded prognosis for recovery (Modesto-Lowe & Kranzler, 1999).

DIAGNOSTIC CONSIDERATIONS

The classification of alcohol problems has evolved considerably. The two major sources of diagnostic classifications of mental disorders are the *Diagnostic and Statistical Manual of Mental Disorders* (*DSM*) and the Mental Disorder Section of the International Classification of Diseases (ICD). The first *DSM* (*DSM-I*) was published in 1952 by the American Psychiatric Association and was a variant of the ICD-6. Today, the terms in the *DSM-IV* are compatible with both the ICD-9 and ICD-10 (APA, 1994). Although the *DSM* and ICD diagnostic schema are highly similar, "agreement between *DSM-IV* and ICD-10 on whether subjects were dependent or not is less than optimal" (Caetano & Tam, 1995). According to Caetano and Tam, the ICD-10 finds a higher prevalence of dependence among young males. This is thought to be related to identifying consequences of episodic heavy drinking as signs of dependence. Because the primary diagnostic classification schema used in the United States is the *DSM*, this section focuses on *DSM* classifications.

Over the years, changes in the *DSM* classification criteria have reflected both the state of knowledge and contemporary attitudes. The most recent *DSM* is the *DSM-IV* (APA, 1994). Although a text revision of the *DSM-IV* (i.e., *DSM-IV-TR*) was more recently published (APA, 2000a), the criteria for alcohol use disorders are unchanged. While the *DSM-III-R* viewed alcohol dependence as a graded phenomenon ranging from mild (enough consequences to meet criteria but no major withdrawal symptoms) to severe (several negative consequences and withdrawal symptoms), the *DSM-IV* separates psychological from physiological dependence by making physical dependence a specifier rather than a central criterion. In other words, using the *DSM-IV*, it is possible to diagnose an individual as severely alcohol dependent "without physiological dependence."

The major difference between an alcohol dependence and an alcohol abuse diagnosis is that abuse is for less serious alcohol problems. A diagnosis of alcohol abuse is preempted by the diagnosis of alcohol dependence if the person's drinking pattern has *ever* met the criteria for dependence. Such a criterion implies that the disorder is progressive and that the condition will worsen unless an individual stops drinking. As reviewed earlier, several studies have failed to support the progressivity concept. Other problems relating to the lack of a sufficient empirical basis for the *DSM-IV* have been noted by Grant (1995).

A high prevalence of comorbidity of psychiatric disorders among alcohol abusers has been well documented (Anthony, Warner, & Kessler, 1994; Berglund & Ojehagen, 1998; Cox, Norton, Swinson, & Endler, 1990; Drake et al., 1990; Kessler et al., 1996; Modesto-Lowe & Kranzler, 1999; Regier et al., 1990). Psychiatric disorders reported as having exceptionally high co-occurrence with alcohol problems include mood disorders such as depression (Swendsen & Merikangas, 2000) and bipolar disorders (Drake & Mueser, 1996; Strakowski & DelBello, 2000), anxiety disorders (Kushner, Abrams, & Borchardt, 2000; Oei & Loveday, 1997), schizophrenia (Blanchard, Brown, Horan, & Sherwood, 2000; Drake & Mueser, 1996), and personality disorders such as antisocial personality disorder (D. B. Clark & Bukstein, 1998; Morgenstern, Langenbucher, Labouvie, & Miller, 1997) and borderline personality disorder (Trull, Sher, Minks-Brown, Durbin, & Burr, 2000). Although it is common to advocate using an integrated treatment approach with clients who have co-occurring disorders (Drake & Mueser, 1996; Woody, 1996) and such an approach has intuitive appeal, there is a lack of studies demonstrating the development and evaluation of such treatments (Modesto-Lowe & Kranzler, 1999).

DIAGNOSTIC ISSUES AND PROBLEMS

Because of the high comorbidity rates among alcohol abusers, diagnostic formulations are a two-step process. First, the extent and nature of the problem must be assessed. This can be done with instruments reviewed in the assessment section of this chapter. The second step is to establish whether other psychiatric disorders (i.e., anxiety, depression) are present, and, if so, to determine whether the alcohol problem is the primary or secondary disorder.

Diagnostic formulations have clinical utility beyond insurance and clinical recording requirements (L. C. Sobell, Sobell, Toneatto, & Shillingford, 1994; M. B. Sobell, Wilkinson, & Sobell, 1990; Sokolow, Welte, Hynes, & Lyons, 1981; Toneatto, Sobell, Sobell, & Leo, 1991). An accurate diagnosis is important because it defines the problem in a way that can be communicated and understood by clinicians and researchers. A diagnostic formulation, coupled with an assessment, provides an initial understanding of the problem as well as a foundation for initial treatment planning. Diagnostic formulations play an important role in decisions about treatment goals and intensities.

Over the past decade, there have been several significant developments in the alcohol field that call for differential treatment planning. Among these developments is a growing recognition of the importance of assessing and treating alcohol abusers with dual diagnoses, whether the second disorder is a psychiatric disorder or another substance use disorder. The *DSM-IV* (APA, 1994) provides a general discussion of the differential diagnoses of alcohol-induced disorders that resemble primary mental disorders (e.g., major depressive disorder versus alcohol-induced mood disorder with depressive features, with onset during intoxication). There are significant prognostic implications for alcohol abusers with comorbid psychiatric problems. Several studies have shown that alcohol abusers who have serious psychiatric problems generally have poorer treatment outcomes than alcohol abusers without major psychiatric symptoms (Berglund & Ojehagen, 1998; Meyer & Kranzler, 1988; Modesto-Lowe & Kranzler, 1999; Rounsaville, Dolinsky, Babor, & Meyer, 1987). Although it has been suggested that patients with serious psychiatric problems and a primary alcohol disorder should receive additional counseling, there is a lack of empirical data suggesting whether treatment of the comorbid problem reliably improves treatment outcomes. Although evidence is also lacking as to whether treatment for alcohol and other psychiatric problems should be concurrent or sequential and in separate or similar settings, most dually diagnosed clients with alcohol problems are currently treated in the mental health system (Carey, 1996). An important issue is the extent to which substance use may interfere with assessing psychiatric comorbidity. Thus, it has been suggested that individuals be alcohol free for several weeks before comorbidity can be accurately assessed (Schuckit, 1995).

For alcohol abusers who use or abuse other drugs, including nicotine, it is important to gather a comprehensive profile of psychoactive substance use. Over the course of an intervention, drug use patterns may change (e.g., decreased alcohol use, increased smoking; decreased alcohol use, increased cannabis use). Further, alcohol abusers who use other drugs raise the possibility of pharmacological synergism (i.e., a multiplicative effect of similarly acting drugs taken concurrently). Cross-tolerance (i.e., lessened drug effect because of past heavy use of pharmacologically similar drugs) should also be considered when assessing alcohol abusers who use other drugs. Finally, the treatment of alcohol abusers who abuse other drugs may not parallel that for individuals who abuse only alcohol (Battjes, 1988; Burglass & Shaffer, 1983; Burling & Ziff, 1988; Kaufman, 1982).

For alcohol abusers, diagnostic formulations may also play an important role in decisions about treatment goals and treatment intensity (M. B. Sobell & Sobell, 1987). Some research suggests that severity of alcohol dependence may interact with response to treatment goals, that is, abstinence or nonproblem drinking (Institute of Medicine, 1990; Miller, Leckman, Delaney, & Tinkcom, 1992; M. B. Sobell & Sobell, 1993a), and different treatment intensities (Annis, 1986; Orford & Keddie, 1986). Considering the most appropriate treatment for alcohol abusers with different levels of dependence (e.g., mild versus severe) is consistent with client-treatment matching (DiClemente, Carroll, Connors, & Kadden, 1994; Donovan et al., 1994; Mattson et al., 1994).

Because alcohol withdrawal symptoms are defining features for an alcohol dependence diagnosis, a careful history of past withdrawals is necessary. Thus, it is important that clients understand what is meant by withdrawal symptoms. For example, a critical term that often causes alcohol abusers confusion is *delirium tremens* or *DTs* (L. C. Sobell, Toneatto, & Sobell, 1994). This term, which is frequently confused with minor withdrawal symptoms (e.g., psychomotor agitation), refers to actual delirium and implies severe dependence on alcohol. A history of past with-drawal symptoms, coupled with reports of recent heavy ethanol consumption, can alert clinicians that withdrawal symptoms are likely to occur on cessation of drink-ing and require medical interventions.

PSYCHOLOGICAL AND BIOLOGICAL ASSESSMENT

A thorough and careful assessment is an important part of the treatment process for individuals with all types of alcohol problems. The assessment is critical to the development of meaningful treatment plans. Accurate diagnosis of alcohol and other concurrent disorders is integral to the assessment process. The assess-ment can serve several critical functions:

- It provides clinicians with an in-depth picture of a person's alcohol use and related consequences, particularly the severity of the disorder; this picture can be used to develop treatment plans tailored to the needs of each client.
- If change is not evident during treatment, ongoing assessment information can be used to make systematic changes in the treatment plan.
- Progress during treatment can be compared with the initial assessment to evaluate the extent and types of changes that have occurred, and to suggest where further interventions are needed.

The depth and intensity of an assessment is related to problem severity and the complexity of the presenting case as well as the individual needs of the clinician and/or researcher. Ultimately, assessments should be determined based on clini-cal judgment and current clinical needs. The instruments and methods described in this chapter can be used clinically to gather information relevant to the assess-ment and treatment planning process. The implications of assessment data for treatment issues, such as drinking goals and treatment intensity, show how the clinical interview can significantly impact treatment. Critical issues in assess-ment (e.g., self-reports, convergent data sources) are discussed as well.

CRITICAL ISSUES IN ASSESSMENT

In alcohol use assessment, most research and clinical information is obtained through retrospective self-reports (Babor, Brown, & Del Boca, 1990; L. C. Sobell & Sobell, 1990). Despite widespread skepticism among practitioners, several major re-views of the scientific literature have concluded that alcohol abusers' self-reports are generally accurate if clients are interviewed in clinical or research settings, when they are alcohol free, and when they are given assurances of confidentiality (Babor et al., 1990; Babor, Steinberg, Anton, & Del Boca, 2000; Brown, Kranzler, & Del Boca, 1992; Del Boca & Noll, 2000; L. C. Sobell & Sobell, 1990). Alcohol abusers' self-reports have been found to be inaccurate only when they are interviewed with any alcohol in their system (Leigh & Skinner, 1988; M. B. Sobell, Sobell, & Van-derSpek, 1979). However, because all studies find some proportion, albeit small, of self-reports to be inaccurate, one way to identify inaccurate self-reports is to obtain information from multiple sources (e.g., chemical tests, self-reports, collateral re-ports, official records). Data from different sources are then compared and conclu-sions are based on a convergence of information (Maisto, McKay, & Connors, 1990; L. C. Sobell & Sobell, 1990). When the measures converge, one can have confidence in the accuracy of the reports.

Information gathered through the assessment process can be used to provide feedback to clients to enhance their commitment to change. The feedback should be delivered in a nonconfrontational manner using principles of motivational interviewing. A comprehensive description of how to do motivational interviewing and how to use advice/feedback from an assessment has been published by the Substance Abuse and Mental Health Administration (1999).

With respect to the length of an assessment, intense and in-depth assessments are no longer justified for all clients. Because people with less severe alcohol problems often respond well to brief interventions (Bien et al., 1993; M. B. Sobell & Sobell, 1993a), an assessment that is longer than the intervention makes little sense. In contrast, severely dependent alcohol abusers may require a more intensive assessment covering areas such as organic brain dysfunction, psychiatric comorbidity, and social needs. Ultimately, an assessment should be based on clinical judgment and the client's needs.

The next section describes different assessment areas and reviews relevant assessment instruments, scales, and questionnaires that can be used for assessing alcohol use and abuse. A comprehensive listing of assessment tools for alcohol use and abuse can be found in several published directories (Allen & Columbus, 1995; American Psychiatric Association, 2000b). In this chapter, only instruments that have sound psychometric properties and clinical utility are discussed. When selecting an appropriate instrument, it is helpful to ask, "What will I learn from using the instrument that I would not otherwise know from a routine clinical interview?" (Sobell, Toneatto, et al., 1994).

ASSESSING ALCOHOL USE

Assessing alcohol consumption involves measuring the quantity and frequency of past and present use. When choosing an instrument to assess drinking, a decision must be made about the type of information desired, that is, level of precision and time frame (L. C. Sobell & Sobell, 1995; L. C. Sobell, Toneatto, et al., 1994). Two major dimensions along which measures differ are whether they gather summarized (e.g., "How may days per week on average do you drink any alcohol?") versus specific (e.g., "How many drinks did you have on each day of the following interval?") information, and whether the information was recalled retrospectively or recorded when it occurred. Specific measures are preferred over summary measures for pretreatment and within-treatment assessments because they provide information about patterns of drinking and opportunities to inquire about events associated with problem drinking that are not possible using summary data (e.g., "What was happening on Friday when you had 12 drinks?").

In terms of key instruments, there are four established methods for assessing past alcohol consumption:

1. *Lifetime Drinking History* (LDH; Skinner & Sheu, 1982; L. C. Sobell & Sobell, 1995; L. C. Sobell, Toneatto, et al., 1994).
2. *Quantity-Frequency (QF) methods* (Room, 1990; Skinner & Sheu, 1982; L. C. Sobell & Sobell, 1995).
3. *Timeline Followback* (TLFB; American Psychiatric Association, 2000b; L. C. Sobell & Sobell, 1992b, 1995, 2000).
4. *Self-Monitoring* (SM; L. C. Sobell & Sobell, 1995; M. B. Sobell, Bogardis, Schuller, Leo, & Sobell, 1989).

The first three are retrospective estimation methods (i.e., they obtain information about alcohol use after it has occurred). The TLFB can also be used in treatment as an advice-feedback tool to help increase clients' motivation to change (L. C. Sobell & Sobell, 1995). The fourth method, Self-Monitoring, asks clients to record their drinking at or about the same time that it occurred, and it has several clinical advantages:

- Provides feedback about treatment effectiveness.
- Identifies situations that pose a high-risk of relapse.
- Gives outpatient clients an opportunity to discuss their drinking since the previous session (L. C. Sobell, Toneatto, et al., 1994).

Because several reviews have detailed the advantages and disadvantages of these drinking instruments, they are not reviewed here.

CONSEQUENCES OF ALCOHOL USE

One of the key defining characteristics of a *DSM-IV* diagnosis is alcohol-related consequences. Several short self-administered scales have been developed to assess alcohol-related psychosocial consequences and dependence symptoms:

- *Alcohol Use Disorders Identification Test* (AUDIT; Saunders, Aasland, Babor, de la Fuente, & Grant, 1993).
- *Severity of Alcohol Dependence Questionnaire* (SADQ; Stockwell, Murphy, & Hodgson, 1983; Stockwell, Sitharthan, McGrath, & Lang, 1994).
- *Alcohol Dependence Scale* (ADS; Skinner & Allen, 1982).
- *Short Alcohol Dependence Data Questionnaire* (SADD; Raistrick, Dunbar, & Davidson, 1983).

These scales take about five minutes to administer and range from 10 to 25 items in length.

Although several scales are used for brief screening and identification of harmful and hazardous alcohol use, the AUDIT stands out for its psychometric characteristics, convenience, and cross-cultural validation. The AUDIT, developed as a multinational World Health Organization project, is a brief screening test for the early detection of harmful and hazardous alcohol use in primary health care settings (Saunders et al., 1993). The 10 questions are scored based on the frequency of the experience (i.e., from 0 = Never, to 4 = Daily use; Maximum score = 40). The AUDIT has been shown to be as good as or better than other screening tests (e.g., CAGE, MAST, ADS) in identifying individuals with probable alcohol problems when a cutoff score of 8 or greater is used (Barry & Fleming, 1993; Fleming, Barry, & MacDonald, 1991). According to the authors, the differences between the AUDIT and most other screening tests are that the AUDIT:

- Detects drinkers along the entire severity continuum from mild to severe.
- Emphasizes hazardous consumption and frequency of intoxication compared with drinking behavior and adverse consequences.

- Uses a time frame that asks questions about current (i.e., past year) and lifetime use.
- Avoids using a "yes/no" format and instead uses Likert rating scales to reduce face validity.

ASSESSING RISK SITUATIONS AND SELF-EFFICACY

Because relapse rates among treated alcohol abusers are extremely high, assessment of high-risk situations for problem drinking is important at assessment and during treatment (Marlatt & Gordon, 1985; M. B. Sobell & Sobell, 1993a). The Situational Confidence Questionnaire (SCQ-39) assesses situational (i.e., present time) self-efficacy by measuring how confident clients are that they will be able to resist the urge to drink heavily in particular situations. Clients are asked to imagine themselves in each situation and to rate their confidence on a six-point scale (100% confident to 0% confident) as to how they would resist urges to drink heavily or use drugs in that situation. The SCQ-39 takes about 10 to 20 minutes to complete and contains eight subscales (e.g., unpleasant emotions, pleasant emotions, testing personal control) based on research by Marlatt and Gordon (Marlatt & Gordon, 1985). For clinical purposes, an easy to score and interpret variant of the SCQ, the Brief SCQ (BSCQ), consists of the original eight items that represent the eight subscales (Breslin, Sobell, Sobell, & Agrawal, 2000). Although the BSCQ can be used clinically to enhance treatment planning, it identifies only generic situations/problem areas. To examine clients' individual high-risk situations or areas where they lack self-confidence, clinicians should explore specific situations with clients. For example, clients can be asked to describe their two or three highest risk situations for alcohol use in the past year (M. B. Sobell & Sobell, 1993a).

Another instrument to measure situational self-efficacy is the Drug-Taking Confidence Questionnaire-8 (DTCQ-8; Sklar & Turner, 1999). The DTCQ-8 is an eight-item questionnaire similar to the BSCQ but developed for a variety of different substance use disorders.

ASSESSMENT OF PSYCHIATRIC COMORBIDITY WITH ALCOHOL ABUSERS

As reviewed earlier, a substantial number of alcohol abusers have psychiatric problems (Modesto-Lowe & Kranzler, 1999; Woody, 1996) that need to be evaluated. While several diagnostic interviews and scales exist for assessing comorbidity with alcohol abusers, the comprehensiveness of assessments of individuals with comorbid disorders depends on the resources available, specificity of the information required, the treatment setting, and, most importantly, the assessor's skill level (L. C. Sobell, Toneatto, et al., 1994). Several brief instruments, while not yielding formal diagnoses, can serve to evaluate comorbidity:

- *Beck Depression Inventory* (Beck, Steer, & Garbin, 1988).
- *Beck Anxiety Inventory* (Beck, Epstein, Brown, & Steer, 1988).
- *Hamilton Rating Scale for Depression* (Hamilton, 1960).
- *Symptom Checklist-90-R* (Derogatis, 1983).

For brief descriptions of the clinical utility of these instruments, see two reviews (Carey & Correia, 1998; L. C. Sobell, Toneatto, et al., 1994).

Neuropsychological Assessment

Screening for organic brain damage related to alcohol abuse is important for treatment planning. The *Trail Making Test* (Davies, 1968) and the *Digit Symbol subscale of the WAIS* are recommended as brief screening tests for assessing probable organic brain dysfunction resulting from alcohol consumption (Lezak, 1976; Miller & Saucedo, 1983; Wilkinson & Carlen, 1980). Both tests are relatively easy and quick to administer (five minutes or less) and are highly sensitive to alcohol-related brain dysfunction. For application and interpretation of assessing neuropsychological impairment and functioning related to alcohol problems, see reviews of this literature (Miller & Saucedo, 1983; Neiman, 1998; Parsons, 1987; Parsons & Farr, 1981).

Barriers or Potential Barriers to Change

In developing a treatment plan, it is helpful to anticipate possible barriers that clients might encounter with respect to changing their behavior. Barriers can be both motivational and practical. If an individual is not motivated to change, there is little reason to expect that change will occur. Because many alcohol abusers are coerced into treatment (e.g., courts, significant others), such individuals might not have a serious interest in changing (Cunningham, Sobell, Sobell, & Gaskin, 1994). Thus, it is important to evaluate a client's motivation for and commitment to change. According to Miller and Rollnick (1991), "Motivation is a *state* of readiness or eagerness to change, which may fluctuate from one time or situation to another. This state is one that can be influenced" (p. 14). Thus, rather than a trait, motivation is a state that can be influenced by several variables, one of which is the therapist. An easy way to assess readiness to change is to use a Readiness Ruler (see p. 139; Substance Abuse and Mental Health Administration, 1999). The Readiness Ruler asks clients to indicate their readiness to change using a five-point scale ranging from "not ready to change" to "unsure" to "very ready to change." The ruler has face validity, is user friendly, and takes only a few seconds to complete. For a detailed description of methods for increasing motivation for change, see two excellent resources (Miller & Rollnick, 1991; Substance Abuse and Mental Health Administration, 1999).

Environmental factors can also present formidable obstacles to change. For example, individuals in an environment where alcohol is readily available and where there are many cues to drink might find it difficult to abstain. For some individuals, social avoidance strategies (e.g., avoiding bars, no alcohol in the house) might be the only effective alternative. Finally, clinicians should attend to individual barriers that can also affect a person's ability to enter and complete treatment (e.g., child care, transportation, inability to take time off from work, unwillingness to adopt an abstinence goal; Schmidt & Weisner, 1995).

Biochemical Measures

Because no self-report measure is error free, the use of measures complementary to self-reports is recommended with the set of measures yielding a convergent validity approach to assessment (L. C. Sobell & Sobell, 1980). Although there has been a tendency to consider biochemical measures as "gold standards" and superior to self-report, several reviews have found that even biochemical measures suffer from validity problems (Bernadt, Mumford, Taylor, Smith, & Murray, 1982; Leigh & Skinner, 1988; Levine, 1990; Maisto & Connors, 1992; O'Farrell & Maisto, 1987). In fact, some reviews have found self-reports to be superior to certain biochemical measures (Petersson, Trell, & Kristensson, 1983; Salaspuro, 1986).

Issues of self-report accuracy take on different meanings for clinical versus research purposes, where different levels of reporting precision are required (Baker & Brandon, 1990; Rankin, 1990). For example, clinicians do not routinely have to obtain information to confirm their client's alcohol use unless the situation warrants it. However, in clinical trials, researchers typically need to verify their clients' self-reports using an alternative measure (e.g., collateral reports).

Use of alcohol, tobacco, and other drugs can be detected in different body substances (e.g., breath, blood, urine, hair, saliva) and by several detection methods. Biochemical measures can be classified into two categories: (a) recent/current (i.e., past 24 hours) use, and (b) use over an extended period. Several sources provide an in-depth review of the advantages and disadvantages of different testing methods (Phelps & Field, 1992; Shute, 1988; Verebey & Turner, 1991).

BREATH ALCOHOL TESTS

Because of the phenomenon of tolerance, clinical judgment is not adequate to determine when clients are under the influence of alcohol (L. C. Sobell, Toneatto, et al., 1994). Furthermore, there is evidence that when individuals have a detectable blood alcohol concentration (BAC), their self-reports of drinking may be invalid (L. C. Sobell, Toneatto, et al., 1994). Thus, at least in the case of alcohol abusers, breath alcohol testers should be used routinely in assessments. A breath analyzer yields accurate readings of a person's BAC. Several portable testers differing in cost and precision are commercially available. Breath alcohol testers are noninvasive, inexpensive (a few dollars per test), easy to use, portable, and provide an immediate determination of BAC. To avoid false positives, clients should not smoke or drink anything for about 15 minutes before the test.

URINE TESTS

Urinalyses can provide qualitative (i.e., different types of drugs including alcohol and prescription medications) as well as quantitative (i.e., amount of the substance or the substance's metabolite currently in the body) information on drug use. However, all urine tests have limitations. Urinalyses cannot specify when a drug was taken. Rather, they provide evidence of whether consumption occurred and the amount of drug or the drug's metabolite in the system at the time of testing. For some drugs that have long half-lives (e.g., marijuana), the individual being tested might not have used for several weeks or even months, but still test positive. It is not uncommon for urine tests to yield both false positive and false negative results (Dilts, Gendel, & Williams, 1996; Sellers, Kadlec, Kaplan, & Naranjo, 1988).

HAIR ANALYSIS

Although hair analysis can detect drug use over several years and is highly accurate (Cook, Bernstein, & Andrews, 1997; Gibson & Manley, 1991; Magura, Freeman,

Siddiqi, & Lipton, 1992; Strang, Black, Marsh, & Smith, 1993), it is very costly. Presently, the clinical utility of hair analysis is undetermined.

LIVER FUNCTION TESTS

Blood tests to assess acute hepatic dysfunction are routinely used by physicians. Liver function tests, if results are elevated, can be used as an advice feedback tool to help motivate clients to consider changing their drinking habits (Romelsjö et al., 1989). Such tests have limited utility with drinkers whose problems are not severe and who do not drink daily. In fact, a sizeable percentage of problem drinkers, those who are not severely dependent on alcohol, show no elevations on liver function tests at assessment (Sobell, Agrawal, & Sobell, 1999). Clinicians who are not physicians and want to use liver function tests need to arrange for physicians to order and evaluate such tests.

Cirrhosis, permanent and nonreversible cellular liver damage (Maher, 1997), occurs in a small percentage of alcohol abusers (Klatsky & Armstrong, 1992), usually those with heavier drinking patterns (Sørensen et al., 1984; Wodak, Saunders, Ewusi-Mensah, Davis, & Williams, 1983). Unlike assessment of acute hepatic dysfunction, cirrhosis must be diagnosed through a liver biopsy.

CARBON MONOXIDE

Many clients with alcohol problems also smoke cigarettes, and several biochemical measures can be used to verify tobacco use (e.g., cotinine, thiocyanate, carbon monoxide). Carbon monoxide (CO), a by-product present in tobacco smoke, is rapidly absorbed through the lungs into the bloodstream. It has a very short half-life (three to five hours) that can be affected by various factors (e.g., exercise, pollutants). Compared to other tests of nicotine use, CO tests have major advantages (e.g., easily administered, highly correlated with exposure to cigarette smoke, portable testers) and disadvantages (e.g., short half-life).

ETIOLOGICAL CONSIDERATIONS

FAMILIAL AND GENETIC

It is well documented that close relatives of individuals with alcohol problems have an increased risk of demonstrating drinking problems, and both environmental and genetic explanations exist for this phenomenon. As to environmental factors, family issues are prominent in both the theoretical and empirical literature on etiology of alcohol problems. Familial factors (e.g., children's perception of their parents' and siblings' drinking, instability of family rituals because of parental drinking, poor parenting, impaired family communication and problem solving) have been found to increase the risk for alcohol problems (O'Farrell & Fals-Stewart, 1999). Currently, three models of familial influence are predominant (Hesselbrock, Hesselbrock, & Epstein, 1999):

1. The *family disease* model assumes a biological etiology of alcohol problems, with family members assuming roles of either alcoholic or codependent and these roles perpetuating drinking problems in the family.

2. The *family systems* model assumes that alcohol stabilizes family equilibrium and that families organize themselves to maintain alcohol problems despite its inherent repercussions.
3. The *behavioral family* model examines families' behaviors as antecedents to and reinforcing consequences of alcohol use.

Recent studies indicate that genetics explains 40% to 60% of the variance in alcohol abuse and dependence; these findings support the importance of both genetic and environmental contributions to the etiology of alcohol problems (Schuckit, 2000). Close relatives of people with alcohol problems, adopted-away children of men and women with alcohol problems, and identical twins whose parents had alcohol problems all have been found to demonstrate a much higher likelihood of alcohol use problems than the general population. While genetic studies have documented genetic influences on the risk of alcohol problems in men, this has occurred less so with women (McGue, 1999).

While many specific genes have been and continue to be evaluated as possible contributors to the risk of alcohol problems, variations of genetic material across a variety of genes likely contribute to the risk of drinking problems. Several endophenotypes, or subconditions, that increase the risk for a disorder have been identified concerning alcohol problems, and these endophenotypes appear to have strong genetic influences (Schuckit, 2000). The absence or limited production of alcohol-metabolizing enzymes (most common among Asians), low response level to alcohol (i.e., needing a greater number of drinks to have an effect), low amplitude of the P300 wave component of event-related potentials, and low alpha activity and voltage on electroencephalograms all are associated with an increased risk of drinking problems, and all have strong genetic influences.

LEARNING AND MODELING

Learning theory, as applied to alcohol use and abuse, assumes that drinking is largely learned, and that basic learning principles guide the acquisition, maintenance, and modification of drinking behavior (Carroll, 1999). Classical conditioning models posit that the development of a drinking problem occurs largely through the pairing of conditioned stimuli, such as locations or people, with the unconditioned stimulus of alcohol (Hesselbrock et al., 1999). Through repeated pairings with alcohol, the conditioned stimuli come to elicit a conditioned response, which is manifested in craving for alcohol. Tolerance to alcohol also has been explained using a classical conditioning model, where the conditioned stimuli come to elicit a conditioned compensatory response (i.e., an opposite reaction to initial drug effects) that resembles the unconditioned compensatory response elicited by alcohol consumption (Sherman, Jorenby, & Baker, 1988; Wikler, 1973). Operant conditioning models assume that alcohol consumption is governed by its reinforcing effects, including physiological and phenomenological changes in response to drinking, the social consequences of drinking, and/or the avoidance or cessation of withdrawal symptoms (Hesselbrock et al., 1999). In summary, learning models have been used to explain how drinking problems may develop, and have provided guidance in the design of interventions to modify drinking.

An especially influential variable in alcohol use and abuse that appears to be governed by basic learning principles is alcohol expectancies—the effects (positive and negative) attributed to alcohol that an individual anticipates experiencing when drinking (Goldman, Del Boca, & Darkes, 1999). Expectancies appear to develop early in life, are consistent across gender, and are learned according to social learning principles including classical conditioning, operant conditioning, and modeling (Hesselbrock et al., 1999). In several different studies, alcohol expectancies have been shown to be highly related to adult and adolescent drinking practices, including drinking problems and relapse to drinking following a period of abstinence (Goldman et al., 1999; Quigley & Marlatt, 1999).

Research on the modeling of alcohol consumption emerged from Bandura's (1969) social learning theory, which posits that modeling influences the acquisition and performance of a variety of social behaviors. Caudill and Marlatt (1975) were among the first to experimentally study the influence of social modeling on drinking behavior, and they found that participants exposed to a heavy drinking model (a research confederate) consumed significantly more wine than participants exposed to light drinking or no model. Collins and Marlatt (1981) reviewed the research in 1981 and concluded that modeling was a powerful influence on drinking that occurred regardless of study setting or moderating variables (e.g., gender, age). More recently, Quigley and Collins (1999) performed a meta-analysis on published studies concerning the modeling of alcohol consumption and found "a definitive effect" of modeling on drinking behavior. Large effect sizes for both amount of alcohol consumed and BAC were documented.

LIFE EVENTS

For centuries, stressful situations have been thought to be related to alcohol consumption, and drinking has been seen as relieving stress (Sayette, 1999). The relationship between drinking and stress can be traced to the sociological literature of the 1940s and the emergence of the tension-reduction hypothesis in the 1950s (Pohorecky, 1991). The tension-reduction hypothesis proposes that (a) alcohol consumption reduces stress under most circumstances, and (b) people are motivated to drink in times of stress. This hypothesis forms the basis of current research about the relationship between drinking and stress (Sayette, 1999). Although studies indicate that drinking can reduce stress in certain people and under certain circumstances, the relationship between drinking and stress is far more complex than originally thought. Individual differences—including a family history of alcohol problems; certain personality traits; extent of self-consciousness; level of cognitive functioning, gender, and situational factors such as distraction and the timing of drinking and stress—have been shown to be important moderators of the degree to which alcohol reduces the subjective, behavioral, neurochemical, and immunological consequences of stress (Sayette, 1999).

In alcohol-abusing populations, the relationship between alcohol use and stress has been difficult to establish, and studies vary widely in the strength and directionality of documented pathways (Johnson & Pandina, 2000). Some researchers have noted that the stress-relieving effects of alcohol are "neither robust or reliable" (Cooper, Russell, Skinner, Frone, & Mudar, 1992, p. 139), while others have concluded that alcohol is "a two-edged sword" because it can be both a response to stress and a cause of stress (Johnstone, Garrity, & Straus, 1997, p. 258). In a longitudinal study, Johnson and Pandina found that levels of stress, and especially stress related to life events, did not differentiate nonproblem and problem users during adolescence. Moreover, stress at ages 12 or 15 years was unrelated to drinking outcomes at age 25. Nonetheless, adults with alcohol problems do appear to experience more frequent, more severe, and more prolonged stress than those without alcohol problems (Pohorecky, 1991). Johnson and Pandina's study, however, suggests this may be more a consequence than a cause of drinking problems. Moreover, de Wit (1996) found that stressful life events may increase desire to drink and relapse to drinking among abstinent alcohol abusers. In summary, it appears that drinking and drinking problems are related to stress, at least among certain groups of people and under certain circumstances (Johnstone et al., 1997; Sayette, 1999).

Gender and Racial/Ethnic

Whenever and wherever women's and men's alcohol use has been measured, women drink less than men, and women's drinking leads to fewer social problems than their male counterparts (R. W. Wilsnack et al., 2000). However, few studies have gone beyond demonstrating that men use and abuse alcohol more than women do, and currently both biological and social-structural theoretical explanations exist for these gender differences (R. W. Wilsnack et al., 2000). The biological explanations emphasize gender differences in the metabolism of alcohol, and the social-structural explanations emphasize gender differences in social roles and how these differences may influence drinking behavior.

As to biological explanations, a number of animal studies have documented gender differences in alcohol metabolism, and it appears that hormonal differences between the sexes may modulate these differences (Smith & Lin, 1996). Moreover, women are more susceptible to alcoholic liver injury than are men, and this appears to be the result of less metabolism of alcohol in the stomach, and thus greater exposure to high alcohol concentrations (Frezza et al., 1990; Moack & Anton, 1999; Morgan, 1994; Schenker, 1997). While research has suggested that women's reproductive functioning influences alcohol metabolism, evidence is mixed as to how menstrual cycle phase may affect alcohol consumption, metabolism, and self-estimates of blood alcohol levels (Jensvold, 1996). Although one study has suggested that the use of oral contraceptives results in decreased alcohol metabolism, and thus increased alcohol effects (Jones & Jones, 1976), another study found no effect of oral contraceptives on alcohol metabolism (Hobbes, Boutagy, & Shenfield, 1985).

As to social-structural explanations, a number of investigators have examined how women's social roles vis-à-vis alcohol may explain lower rates of alcohol use and abuse among women than men. Cross-culturally, women's drinking has been more socially restricted than their male counterparts, primarily because it may negatively affect women's social behavior and responsibilities (R. W. Wilsnack et al., 2000). Consistent with this perspective, there is evidence that social influences play a greater role in women's than in men's drinking. For example, partners' heavy drinking has a greater influence on female problem drinking than on male problem drinking (Gomberg, 1994), and there is more marital disruption (i.e., never married, divorced or separated, widowed) among females (Gomberg, 1995).

It appears that both biological and social-structural explanations may be needed to account for gender differences in alcohol use and abuse. R. W. Wilsnack et al. (2000) conducted an in-depth review of international studies concerning gender differences in drinking and concluded "that gender differences in drinking are too consistent in direction for explanations based solely on variable social or cultural influences, but are too variable in size for explanations based solely on biological influences" (p. 261). Thus, conceptualizations of gender differences in alcohol use and misuse should include biological and social-structural considerations.

Several studies have examined personality factors as they relate to gender differences in the clinical presentations of men and women with alcohol problems. While there is evidence that male alcohol abusers may be more psychopathic, aggressive, and impulsive than women, and women may be more affectively affected than men (e.g., Hesselbrock, 1991), unfortunately, this literature is plagued with methodological problems. More recent studies have suggested that factors such as differential base rates of psychopathology among men and women, and differences in the age of onset of alcohol problems may explain gender differences in personality factors associated with alcohol problems (Sher, Trull, Bartholow, & Vieth, 1999). It should be noted that suicide attempts are almost twice as common among females than male alcohol abusers, with 41% of women and 21% of men reporting at least one suicide attempt (Hesselbrock, Hesselbrock, Syzmanski, & Weidenman, 1988).

Epidemiological studies show that alcohol use, morbidity, and mortality vary by race/ethnicity in seemingly paradoxical ways. For example, African Americans and some Hispanic/Latino groups have lower overall rates of alcohol involvement than non-Latino Whites (Vega & Gil, 1998). However, these groups demonstrate higher rates of alcohol-related and other drug-related morbidity and mortality than non-Latino Whites (Gilliland, Becker, Samet, & Key, 1995; Lee, Markides, & Ray, 1997). This paradox may result from ethnic/racial variations in the processes by which alcohol use can lead to alcohol problems. For example, the accelerated progression from use to problem use seen among these minority populations could result from socioeconomic polarization, criminal justice problems, or the lack of appropriate treatment options. Moreover, both African American and Hispanic/Latino populations have been shown to chronically underuse substance abuse treatment services (Giachello, 1994; Longshore, Hsieh, Anglin, & Annon, 1992; Molina & Aguirre-Molina, 1994; Neal & Turner, 1991; Neighbors, 1985), which also may contribute to the accelerated development of alcohol and other drug problems among these groups. Additional factors that may affect the progression to alcohol problems, as well as response to alcohol abuse treatment, include perceived discrimination and cultural mistrust for African Americans, and acculturation stress, nativity, and immigration history for Hispanics/Latinos.

While it has long been recognized that race/ethnicity is likely to impact multiple aspects of the alcohol abuse treatment process (Collins, 1993a), and several face valid explanations exist as to how race/ethnicity may influence alcohol use trajectories and responses to alcohol abuse treatment, little empirical research has examined the effectiveness of alcohol abuse treatment for ethnic minorities. Despite the recognition of problems related to alcohol use in the African American community, ranging from shorter life expectancy (U.S. Department of Health and Human Services, 1985) to perinatal substance use problems (Ernest & Sokoll, 1987; Roman, 1986), there is a paucity of knowledge about how to effectively intervene (Biafora & Zimmerman, 1998; Dawkins, 1996; Herd, 1985). Similar issues exist with Hispanics/Latinos. While alcohol problems are common in Hispanic/Latino communities, very little is known about how to address alcohol and other drug use problems in a culturally sensitive manner among Hispanics/

Latinos (Gil, Wagner, & Vega, 2000; Vega & Gil, 1998). While it appears that cultural sensitivity may enhance the degree to which a specific intervention may address alcohol problems among clients from specific racial/ethnic groups (Longshore & Grills, 2000; Longshore, Grills, & Annon, 1999; Perez-Arce, Carr, & Sorensen, 1993), how race/ethnicity may moderate treatment processes and outcomes and how interventions may be modified to improve cultural congruency remain areas in need of considerable research.

BIOLOGICAL AND PHYSIOLOGICAL

Multiple biological and physiological systems are impacted by and appear to influence alcohol consumption. As reviewed earlier, biological factors found to be associated with the development of alcohol problems include the absence or limited production of alcohol-metabolizing enzymes, low level of response to alcohol (i.e., needing more drinks to have an effect), low amplitude of the P300 wave component of event-related potentials, and low alpha activity and voltage on electroencephalograms. These factors all substantially raise the likelihood that an individual will develop alcohol problems, but none, alone or in combination, is a sufficient or necessary determinant of alcohol abuse or dependence.

In addition, two other biological systems are currently receiving considerable research attention. The hypothalamic-pituitary-adrenal (HPA) axis is a hormone system that plays a central role in the body's response to stress. Alcohol consumption has been shown to stimulate the HPA axis system, and several studies suggest that individuals who demonstrate greater HPA activity in response to various stimuli may find alcohol consumption more reinforcing than individuals who demonstrate lower HPA activity (Gianoulakis, 1998). The endogenous opioid system plays a central role in various physiological processes including pain relief, euphoria, and the rewarding and reinforcing effect of psychoactive substances. Alcohol consumption also stimulates the endogenous opioid system, and it appears that endogenous opioids help mediate the reinforcing effects of alcohol (Gianoulakis, 1998). Moreover, individuals at high risk for developing alcohol problems have been found to exhibit greater endogenous opioid system activity in response to alcohol consumption than low-risk individuals (Gianoulakis, Krishnan, & Thavundayil, 1996).

SUMMARY

Conceptualizations of alcohol problems have changed markedly over the past three decades, affecting thought about alcohol problems and their treatment. In particular, it is now recognized that severely dependent alcohol abusers represent only a small percentage of those who have alcohol problems. A one-size-fits-all approach is no longer seen as appropriate for all individuals with alcohol problems, and inpatient treatment has fallen out of favor. The concept that alcohol problems can be scaled along a continuum of severity has major implications for assessment and treatment. For example, less severely dependent alcohol abusers can benefit from brief treatment, accompanied by a brief assessment. The idea of a continuum of severity suggests that treatment for alcohol problems should be provided using a stepped-care model where the first treatment is the least intensive, least costly, least invasive, and has demonstrated effectiveness and consumer appeal. If treatment is not successful, it can be stepped up to include longer, more intensive, or different components.

Assessment of alcohol problems is critical to good treatment planning and continues throughout treatment. Besides using sound psychometric assessment instruments, the instruments should be clinically useful. There are also a number of important issues that need to be addressed at assessment. Tantamount among these is the assessment of other comorbidity, including psychiatric disorders and other drug and nicotine use.

Although many alcohol abusers voluntarily seek treatment, many are coerced to seek treatment, and they often exhibit resistance and a lack of commitment to change. Motivational enhancement techniques and a motivational interviewing style can be used to decrease resistance and increase commitment to change. Last, although alcohol problems can be treated successfully, there is still a high rate of relapse that must be addressed in treatment, but recurrence of problems should not be taken as an indication that the disorder is worsening as there is now abundant data showing that alcohol problems are not necessarily progressive.

REFERENCES

Ahern, F. M. (1985). *Alcohol use and abuse among four ethnic groups in Hawaii: Native Hawaiians, Japanese, Filipinos, and Caucasians* (DHHS Publication No. ADM 89–1435). Rockville, MD: National Institute on Alcohol Abuse and Alcoholism.

Allen, J. P., & Columbus, M. (1995). *Assessing alcohol problems: A guide for clinicians and researchers.* Rockville, MD: National Institute on Alcohol Abuse and Alcoholism.

American Psychiatric Association. (1994). *Diagnostic and statistical manual of mental disorders* (4th ed.). Washington, DC: Author.

American Psychiatric Association. (2000a). *Diagnostic and statistical manual of mental disorders (4th ed., rev.).* Washington, DC: Author.

American Psychiatric Association. (2000b). *Handbook of psychiatric measures.* Washington, DC: Author.

Annis, H. A. (1986). Is inpatient rehabilitation of the alcoholic cost effective? Con position. *Advances in Alcohol and Substance Abuse, 5,* 175–190.

Anthony, J. C., Warner, L. A., & Kessler, R. C. (1994). Comparative epidemiology of dependence on tobacco, alcohol, controlled substances, and inhalants: Basic findings from the National Comorbidity Survey. *Experimental and Clinical Psychopharmacology, 2,* 244–268.

Ashley, M. J., & Rankin, J. G. (1979). Alcohol consumption and hypertension: The evidence from hazardous drinking and alcoholic populations. *Australian and New Zealand Journal of Medicine, 9,* 201–206.

Atkinson, R. M. (1994). Late onset problem drinking in older adults. *International Journal of Geriatric Psychiatry, 9,* 321–326.

Babor, T. F., Brown, J., & Del Boca, F. K. (1990). Validity of self-reports in applied research on addictive behaviors: Fact or fiction? *Addictive Behaviors, 12,* 5–32.

Babor, T. F., Steinberg, K., Anton, R., & Del Boca, F. K. (2000). Talk is cheap: Measuring drinking outcomes in clinical trials. *Journal of Studies on Alcohol, 61,* 55–63.

Bacon, S. D. (1973). The process of addiction to alcohol: Social aspects. *Quarterly Journal of Studies on Alcohol, 34,* 1–27.

Baker, T. B., & Brandon, T. H. (1990). Validity of self-reports in basic research. *Behavioral Assessment, 12,* 33–52.

Bandura, A. (1969). *Principles of behavior modification.* New York: Holt, Rinehart and Winston.

Barry, K. L., & Fleming, M. F. (1993). The Alcohol Use Disorders Identification Test (AUDIT) and the SMAST-13: Predictive validity in a rural primary care sample. *Alcohol and Alcoholism, 28,* 33–42.

Battjes, R. J. (1988). Smoking as an issue in alcohol and drug abuse treatment. *Addictive Behaviors, 13,* 225–230.

Beck, A. T., Epstein, N., Brown, G., & Steer, R. A. (1988). An inventory for measuring clinical anxiety: Psychometric properties. *Journal of Consulting and Clinical Psychology, 56,* 893–897.

Beck, A. T., Steer, R. A., & Garbin, M. G. (1988). Psychometric properties of the Beck Depression Inventory: Twenty–five years of evaluation. *Clinical Psychology Review, 8,* 77–100.

Beckman, L. J. (1979). Reported effects of alcohol on the sexual feelings and behavior of women alcoholics and nonalcoholics. *Journal of Studies on Alcohol, 40,* 272–282.

Berglund, M., & Ojehagen, A. (1998). The influence of alcohol drinking and alcohol use disorders on psychiatric disorders and suicidal behavior. *Alcoholism: Clinical and Experimental Research, 22,* 333S–345S.

Bernadt, M. R., Mumford, J., Taylor, C., Smith, B., & Murray, R. M. (1982). Comparison of questionnaire and laboratory tests in the detection of excessive drinking and alcoholism. *Lancet, 1,* 325–328.

Biafora, F., & Zimmerman, R. S. (1998). Developmental patterns of African American adolescent drug use. In W. Vega & A. G. Gil (Eds.), *Drug use and ethnicity in early adolescence* (pp. 149–175). New York: Plenum Press.

Bien, T. H., Miller, W. R., & Tonigan, J. S. (1993). Brief interventions for alcohol problems: A review. *Addiction, 88,* 315–336.

Blanchard, J. J., Brown, S. A., Horan, W. P., & Sherwood, A. R. (2000). Substance use disorders in schizophrenia: Review, integration, and a proposed model. *Clinical Psychology Review, 20,* 207–234.

Breslin, F. C., Sobell, L. C., Sobell, M. B., & Agrawal, S. (2000). A comparison of a brief and long version of the Situational Confidence Questionnaire. *Behavior Research and Therapy, 38,* 1211–1220.

Brown, J., Kranzler, H. R., & Del Boca, F. K. (1992). Self-reports by alcohol and drug abuse inpatients: Factors affecting reliability and validity. *British Journal of Addiction, 87,* 1013–1024.

Burglass, M. E., & Shaffer, H. (1983). Diagnosis in the addictions. I: Conceptual problems. *Advances in Alcohol and Substance Abuse, 3,* 19–34.

Burling, T. A., & Ziff, D. C. (1988). Tobacco smoking: A comparison between alcohol and drug inpatients. *Addictive Behaviors, 13,* 185–190.

Caetano, R. (1984). Ethnicity and drinking in northern California: A comparison among Whites, Blacks, and Hispanics. *Alcohol and Alcoholism, 19,* 31–44.

Caetano, R. (1985). Two versions of dependence: *DSM-III* and the alcohol dependence syndrome. *Drug and Alcohol Dependence, 15,* 81–103.

Caetano, R. (1989). *Drinking patterns and alcohol problems in a national sample of U.S. Hispanics* (NIAAA Research Monograph No. 18). Rockville, MD: National Institute on Alcohol Abuse and Alcoholism.

Caetano, R., & Kaskutas, L. A. (1995). Changes in drinking patterns among Whites, Blacks, and Hispanics, 1984–1992. *Journal of Studies on Alcohol, 56,* 558–565.

Caetano, R., & Tam, T. W. (1995). Prevalence and correlates of *DSM-IV* and ICD-10 alcohol dependence: 1990 U.S. national alcohol survey. *Alcohol and Alcoholism, 30,* 177–186.

Cahalan, D. (1970). *Problem drinkers: A national survey.* San Francisco: Jossey-Bass.

Cahalan, D., & Room, R. (1974). *Problem drinking among American men*. New Brunswick, NJ: Rutgers Center of Alcohol Studies.

Carey, K. B. (1996). Substance use reduction in the context of outpatient psychiatric treatment: A collaborative, motivational, harm reduction approach. *Community Mental Health Journal, 32*, 291–306.

Carey, K. B., & Correia, C. J. (1998). Severe mental illness and addictions: Assessment considerations. *Addictive Behaviors, 23*, 735–748.

Carroll, K. M. (1999). Behavioral an cognitive behavioral treatments. In B. S. McCrady & E. E. Epstein (Eds.), *Addictions: A comprehensive guidebook* (pp. 250–267). New York: Oxford University Press.

Caudill, B. D., & Marlatt, G. A. (1975). Modeling influences in social drinking: An experimental analogue. *Journal of Clinical and Consulting Psychology, 43*, 405–415.

Clark, D. B., & Bukstein, O. G. (1998). Psychopathology in adolescent alcohol abuse and dependence. *Alcohol Health and Research World, 22*, 117–121.

Clark, W. B., & Hesselbrock, M. A. (1988). *A comparative analysis of U.S. & Japanese drinking patterns*. Rockville, MD: National Institute on Alcohol Abuse and Alcoholism.

Collins, R. L. (1993a). Sociocultural aspects of alcohol use and abuse: Ethnicity and gender. *Drugs and Society, 8*, 89–116.

Collins, R. L. (Ed.). (1993b). *Women's issues in alcohol use and smoking*. New York: Sage.

Collins, R. L., & Marlatt, G. A. (1981). Social modeling as a determinant of drinking behavior: Implications for prevention and treatment. *Addictive Behaviors, 6*, 233–239.

Cook, R. F., Bernstein, A. D., & Andrews, C. M. (1997). Assessing drug use in the workplace: A comparison of self-report, urinalysis, and hair analysis. In L. Harrison & A. Hughes (Eds.), *The validity of self-reported drug use: Improving the accuracy of survey estimates* (NIDA Research Monograph 167, pp. 247–272). Rockville, MD: National Institute on Drug Abuse.

Cooper, M. L., Russell, M., Skinner, J. B., Frone, M. R., & Mudar, P. (1992). Stress and alcohol use: Moderating effects of gender, coping, and alcohol expectancies. *Journal of Abnormal Psychology, 101*, 139–152.

Cox, B. M., Norton, R. G., Swinson, R. P., & Endler, N. S. (1990). Substance abuse and panic-related anxiety: A critical review. *Behavior Research and Therapy, 28*, 385–393.

Cunningham, J. A., Sobell, L. C., Sobell, M. B., & Gaskin, J. (1994). Alcohol and drug abusers reasons for seeking treatment. *Addictive Behaviors, 19*, 691–696.

Davies, A. D. M. (1968). The influence of age on trail making test performance. *Journal of Clinical Psychology, 24*, 96–98.

Dawkins, M. P. (1996). The social context of substance use among African American youth: Rural, urban, and suburban comparisons. *Journal of Alcohol and Drug Education, 41*, 68–86.

Dawson, D. A. (1996). Correlates of past-year status among treated and untreated persons with former alcohol dependence: United States, 1992. *Alcoholism: Clinical and Experimental Research, 20*, 771–779.

Dawson, D. A. (2000). Drinking patterns among individuals with and without *DSM-IV* alcohol use disorders. *Journal of Studies on Alcohol, 61*, 111–120.

Dawson, D. A., & Grant, B. F. (1993). Gender effects in diagnosing alcohol abuse and dependence. *Journal of Clinical Psychology, 49*, 298–307.

Del Boca, F. K., & Noll, J. A. (2000). Truth or consequences: The validity of self-report data in health services research on addictions. *Addiction, 95*, S347–S360.

Derogatis, L. R. (1983). *SCL-90 Revised version manual-1*. Baltimore: Johns Hopkins University School of Medicine.

De Soto, C. B., O'Donnell, W. E., & De Soto, J. L. (1989). Long-term recovery in alcoholics. *Alcoholism: Clinical and Experimental Research, 13,* 693–697.

de Wit, H. (1996). Priming effects with drugs and other reinforcers. *Experimental and clinical psychopharmacology, 4,* 5–10.

DiClemente, C. C., Carroll, K. M., Connors, G. J., & Kadden, R. M. (1994). Process assessment in treatment matching research. *Journal of Studies on Alcohol Supplement No. 12,* 156–162.

Dilts, S. L., Gendel, M. H., & Williams, M. (1996). False positives in urine monitoring of substance abusers: The importance of clinical context. *American Journal on Addictions, 5,* 66–68.

Donovan, D. M., Kadden, R. M., DiClemente, C. C., Carroll, K. M., Longabaugh, R., Zweben, A., et al. (1994). Issues in the selection and development of therapies in alcoholism treatment matching research. *Journal of Studies on Alcohol Supplement No. 12,* 138–148.

Drake, R. E., & Mueser, K. T. (1996). Alcohol-use disorder and severe mental illness. *Alcohol Health and Research World, 20,* 87–93.

Drake, R. E., Osher, F. C., Noordsy, D. L., Hurlbut, S. C., Teague, G. B., & Beaudett, M. S. (1990). Diagnosis of alcohol use disorders in schizophrenia. *Schizophrenia Bulletin, 16,* 57–67.

Ernest, A., & Sokoll, R. (1987). Incidence of fetal alcohol syndrome and economic impact of FAS-related anomalies. *Drug and Alcohol Dependence, 19,* 53–55.

Fillmore, K. M. (1987). Prevalence, incidence and chronicity of drinking patterns and problems among men as a function of age: A longitudinal and cohort analysis. *British Journal of Addiction, 82,* 77–83.

Fillmore, K. M. (1988). *Alcohol use across the life course: A critical review of 70 years of international longitudinal research.* Toronto, Ontario, Canada: Addiction Research Foundation.

Fillmore, K. M., & Midanik, L. (1984). Chronicity of drinking problems among men: A longitudinal study. *Journal of Studies on Alcohol, 45,* 228–236.

Fingarette, H. (1988). *Heavy drinking: The myth of alcoholism as a disease.* Berkeley: University of California Press.

Fleming, M. F., Barry, K. L., & MacDonald, R. (1991). The Alcohol Use Disorders Identification Test (AUDIT) in a college sample. *International Journal of Addictions, 26,* 1173–1185.

Frezza, M., di Padova, C., Pozzato, G., Terpin, M., Baraona, E., & Lieber, C. S. (1990). High blood alcohol levels in women. The role of decreased gastric alcohol dehydrogenase activity and first-pass metabolism. *New England Journal of Medicine, 322,* 95–99.

Giachello, A. L. M. (1994). Issues of access and use. In C. W. Molina & M. Aguirre-Molina (Eds.), *Latino health in the U.S.: A growing challenge* (pp. 83–111). Washington, DC: American Public Health Association.

Gianoulakis, C. (1998). Alcohol seeking behavior: The roles of the hypothalamic-pituitary-adrenal axis and the endogenous opioid system. *Alcohol Health and Research World, 22,* 202–210.

Gianoulakis, C., Krishnan, B., & Thavundayil, J. (1996). Enhanced sensitivity of pituitary beta-endorphin to ethanol in subjects at high risk of alcoholism. *Archives of General Psychiatry, 53,* 250–257.

Gibson, G. S., & Manley, S. (1991). Alternative approaches to urinalysis in the detection of drugs. *Social Behavior and Personality, 19,* 195–204.

Gil, A. G., Wagner, E. F., & Vega, W. A. (2000). Acculturation, familism, and alcohol use among Latino adolescent males: Longitudinal relations. *Journal of Community Psychology, 28,* 443–458.

Gilliland, F. D., Becker, T. M., Samet, J. M., & Key, C. R. (1995). Trends in alcohol-related mortality among New Mexico's American Indians, Hispanics, and non-Hispanic Whites. *Alcoholism: Clinical and Experimental Research, 19,* 1572–1577.

Goldman, M. S., Del Boca, F. K., & Darkes, J. (1999). Alcohol expectancy theory: The application of cognitive neuroscience. In K. E. Leonard & H. T. Blane (Eds.), *Psychological theories of drinking and alcoholism* (2nd ed., pp. 203–246). New York: Guilford Press.

Gomberg, E. S. (1995). Older women and alcohol. In M. Galanter (Ed.), *Recent developments in alcoholism* (Vol. 12, pp. 61–70). New York: Plenum Press.

Gomberg, E. S. (1994). Risk factors for drinking over a woman's life span. *Alcohol Health and Research World, 18,* 220–227.

Grant, B. F. (1995). The *DSM-IV* field trial for substance use disorders: Major results. *Drug and Alcohol Dependence, 38,* 71–75.

Grant, B. F. (1997). Prevalence and correlates of alcohol use and *DSM-IV* alcohol dependence in the United States: Results of the National Longitudinal Alcohol Epidemiologic Survey. *Journal of Studies on Alcohol, 58,* 464–473.

Hamilton, M. (1960). A rating scale for depression. *Journal of Neurology, Neurosurgery and Psychiatry, 23,* 56–62.

Hasin, D. S., Grant, B. F., & Endicott, J. (1990). The natural history of alcohol abuse: Implications for definitions of alcohol use disorders. *American Journal of Psychiatry, 147,* 1537–1541.

Heather, N. (1990). *Brief intervention strategies.* New York: Pergamon Press.

Herd, D. (1985). Rethinking Black drinking. *British Journal of Addiction, 82,* 219–223.

Herd, D. (1989). *The epidemiology of drinking patterns and alcohol-related problems among U.S. Blacks* (Research Monograph No. 18). Rockville, MD: National Institute on Alcohol Abuse and Alcoholism.

Hesselbrock, M. N. (1991). Gender comparison of antisocial personality disorder and depression in alcoholism. *Journal of Substance Abuse, 3,* 205–219.

Hesselbrock, M. N., Hesselbrock, V. M., & Epstein, E. E. (1999). Theories of etiology of alcohol and other drug use disorders. In B. S. McCrady & E. E. Epstein (Eds.), *Addictions: A comprehensive guidebook* (pp. 50–72). New York: Oxford University Press.

Hesselbrock, M. N., Hesselbrock, V. M, Syzmanski, K., & Weidenman, M. (1988). Suicide attempts and alcoholism. *Journal of Studies on Alcohol, 49,* 436–442.

Hill, S. Y. (Ed.). (1984). *Vulnerability to the biomedical consequences of alcoholism and alcohol-related problems among women.* New York: Guilford Press.

Hilton, M. E. (1987). Drinking patterns and drinking problems in 1984: Results from a general population survey. *Alcoholism: Clinical and Experimental Research, 11,* 167–175.

Hilton, M. E. (1991). Trends in U.S. drinking patterns: Further evidence from the past twenty years. In W. B. Clark & M. E. Hilton (Eds.), *Alcohol in America* (pp. 121–138). Albany: State University of New York Press.

Hobbes, J., Boutagy, J., & Shenfield, G. M. (1985). Interactions between ethanol and oral contraceptive steroids. *Clinical Pharmacology and Therapeutics, 38,* 371–380.

Institute of Medicine. (1990). *Broadening the base of treatment for alcohol problems.* Washington, DC: National Academy Press.

Jellinek, E. M. (1952). Phases of alcohol addiction. *Quarterly Journal of Studies on Alcohol, 13,* 673–684.

Jellinek, E. M. (1960). *The disease concept of alcoholism.* New Brunswick, NJ: Hillhouse Press.

Jensvold, M. F. (1996). Nonpregnant reproductive age women, Part I: The menstrual cycle and psychopharmacology. In M. F. Jensvold, U. Halbreich, & J. A. Hamilton (Eds.),

Psychopharmacology and women: Sex, gender, and hormones (pp. 139–169). Washington, DC: American Psychiatric Press.

Johnson, V., & Pandina, R. J. (2000). Alcohol problems among a community sample: Longitudinal influences of stress, coping, and gender. *Substance Use and Misuse, 35,* 669–686.

Johnstone, B. M., Garrity, T. F., & Straus, R. (1997). The relationship between alcohol and life stress. In T. W. Miller (Ed.), *Clinical disorders and stressful life events* (pp. 247–279). Madison, CT: International Universities Press.

Jones, B. M., & Jones, M. K. (1976). Male and female intoxication levels for three alcohol doses or do women really get higher than men. *Alcohol Technical Reports, 5,* 11–14.

Kaufman, E. (1982). The relationship of alcoholism and alcohol abuse to the abuse of other drugs. *American Journal of Drug and Alcohol Abuse, 9,* 1–17.

Kessler, R. C., Nelson, C. B., McGonagle, K. A., Edlund, M. J., Frank, R. G., & Leaf, P. J. (1996). The epidemiology of co-occurring addictive and mental disorders in the National Comorbidity Survey: Implications for prevention and service utilization. *American Journal of Orthopsychiatry, 66,* 17–31.

Klatsky, A. L., & Armstrong, M. A. (1992). Alcohol, smoking, coffee, and cirrhosis. *American Journal of Epidemiology, 136,* 1248–1257.

Klingemann, H. K., Sobell, L. C., Barker, J., Bloomquist, J., Cloud, W., Ellingstad, T. P., et al. (2001). *Promoting self-change from problem substance use: Practical implications for policy, prevention and treatment.* Boston: Kluwer Academic.

Kushner, M. G., Abrams, K., & Borchardt, C. (2000). The relationship between anxiety disorders and alcohol use disorders: A review of major perspectives and findings. *Clinical Psychology Review, 20,* 149–171.

Lee, D. J., Markides, K. S., & Ray, L. A. (1997). Epidemiology of self-reported past heavy drinking in Hispanic adults. *Ethnicity and Health, 2,* 77–88.

Leigh, G. L., & Skinner, H. A. (Eds.). (1988). *Physiological assessment.* New York: Guilford Press.

Levine, J. (1990). The relative value of consultation, questionnaires, and laboratory investigation in the identification of excessive alcohol consumption. *Alcohol and Alcoholism, 25,* 539–553.

Lezak, M. D. (1976). *Neuropsychological assessment.* New York: Oxford University Press.

Longshore, D., & Grills, C. (2000). Motivating illegal drug use recovery: Evidence for a culturally congruent intervention. *Journal of Black Psychology, 26,* 288–301.

Longshore, D., Grills, C., & Annon, K. (1999). Effects of a culturally congruent intervention on cognitive factors related to drug-use recovery. *Substance Use and Misuse, 34,* 1223–1241.

Longshore, D., Hsieh, S. C., Anglin, M. D., & Annon, T. A. (1992). Ethnic patterns in drug abuse treatment utilization. *Journal of Mental Health Administration, 19,* 268–277.

Magura, S., Freeman, R. C., Siddiqi, Q., & Lipton, D. S. (1992). The validity of hair analysis for detecting cocaine and heroin use among addicts. *International Journal of the Addictions, 27,* 51–69.

Maher, J. J. (1997). Exploring alcohol's effects on liver function. *Alcohol Health and Research World, 21,* 5–12.

Maisto, S. A., & Connors, G. J. (1992). Using subject and collateral reports to measure alcohol consumption. In R. Z. Litten & J. Allen (Eds.), *Measuring alcohol consumption: Psychosocial and biological methods* (pp. 73–96). Totowa, NJ: Humana Press.

Maisto, S. A., McKay, J. R., & Connors, G. J. (1990). Self-report issues in substance abuse: State of the art and future directions. *Behavioral Assessment, 12,* 117–134.

Mandell, W. (1983). Types and phases of alcohol dependence. In M. Galanter (Ed.), *Recent developments in alcoholism* (Vol. 3, pp. 415–448). New York: Plenum Press.

Marlatt, G. A. (Ed.). (1978). *Craving for alcohol, loss of control, and relapse.* New York: Plenum Press.

Marlatt, G. A., & Gordon, J. R. (1985). *Relapse prevention.* New York: Guilford Press.

Mattson, M. E., Allen, J. P., Longabaugh, R., Nickless, C. J., Connors, G. J., & Kadden, R. M. (1994). A chronological review of empirical studies matching alcoholic clients to treatment. *Journal of Studies on Alcohol Supplement No. 12,* 16–29.

McGue, M. (1999). Behavioral genetic models of alcoholism and drinking. In K. E. Leonard & H. T. Blane (Eds.), *Psychological theories of drinking and alcoholism* (2nd ed., pp. 372–421). New York: Guilford Press.

Meyer, R. E., & Kranzler, H. R. (1988). Alcoholism: Clinical implications of recent research. *Journal of Clinical Psychiatry, 49,* 8–12.

Miller, W. R., Leckman, A. L., Delaney, H. D., & Tinkcom, M. (1992). Long-term follow-up of behavioral self-control training. *Journal of Studies on Alcohol, 53,* 249–261.

Miller, W. R., & Rollnick, S. (1991). *Motivational interviewing: Preparing people to change addictive behavior.* New York: Guilford Press.

Miller, W. R., & Saucedo, C. F. (Eds.). (1983). *Assessment of neuropsychological impairment and brain damage in problem drinkers.* New York: Grune & Stratton.

Moack, D. H., & Anton, R. F. (1999). Alcohol. In B. S. McCrady & E. E. Epstein (Eds.), *Addictions: A comprehensive guidebook* (pp. 75–94). New York: Oxford University Press.

Modesto-Lowe, V., & Kranzler, H. R. (1999). Diagnosis and treatment of alcohol-dependent patients with comorbid psychiatric disorders. *Alcohol Health and Research World, 23,* 144–149.

Molina, C. W., & Aguirre-Molina, M. (1994). *Latino health in the U.S.: A growing challenge.* Washington, DC: American Public Health Association.

Morgan, M. Y. (1994). The prognosis and outcome of alcoholic liver disease. *Alcohol and Alcoholism Supplement No. 2,* 335–343.

Morgenstern, J., Langenbucher, J., Labouvie, E., & Miller, K. J. (1997). The comorbidity of alcoholism and personality disorders in a clinical population: Prevalence rates and relation to alcohol topology variables. *Journal of Abnormal Psychology, 106,* 74–84.

Murakami, S. R. (1985). An epidemiological survey of alcohol, drug, and mental health problems in Hawaii: A comparison of four ethnic groups. In D. L. Spiegler, D. A. Tate, S. S. Aitken, & C. M. Christian (Eds.), *Epidemiology of alcohol use and abuse among ethnic minority groups* (pp. 343–353). Rockville, MD: National Institute on Alcohol Abuse and Alcoholism.

National Institute on Alcohol Abuse and Alcoholism. (1993). *Eighth special report to the U.S. Congress on alcohol and health.* Washington, DC: U.S. Government Printing Office.

National Institute on Alcohol Abuse and Alcoholism. (2000). *Tenth special report to the U.S. Congress on alcohol and health.* Washington, DC: U.S. Government Printing Office.

National Institute on Drug Abuse. (1991). *National Household Survey on Drug Abuse.* Rockville, MD: U.S. Department of Health and Human Services.

Neal, A. M., & Turner, S. M. (1991). Anxiety disorders research with African Americans: Current status. *Psychological Bulletin, 109,* 400–410.

Neighbors, H. W. (1985). Seeking professional help for personal problems: African Americans' use of health and mental health services. *Community Mental Health Journal, 21,* 156–166.

Neiman, J. (1998). Alcohol as a risk factor for brain damage: Neurological aspects. *Alcoholism: Clinical and Experimental Research, 22,* 346S–351S.

Niaura, R. S., Rohsenow, D. J., Binkoff, J. A., Monti, P. M., Pedraza, M., & Abrams, D. B. (1988). Relevance of cue reactivity to understanding alcohol and smoking relapse. *Journal of Abnormal Psychology, 97*, 133–152.

Nowinski, J., Baker, S. C., & Carroll, K. (1992). *Twelve Step Facilitation Therapy manual* (Project MATCH Monograph Vol. 1). Rockville, MD: National Institute on Alcohol Abuse and Alcoholism.

Oei, T. P. S., & Loveday, W. A. L. (1997). Management of co-morbid anxiety and alcohol disorders: Parallel treatment of disorders. *Drug and Alcohol Review, 16*, 261–274.

O'Farrell, T. J., & Fals-Stewart, W. (1999). Treatment models and methods: Family methods. In B. S. McCrady & E. E. Epstein (Eds.), *Addictions: A comprehensive guidebook* (pp. 287–305). New York: Oxford University Press.

O'Farrell, T. J., & Maisto, S. A. (1987). The utility of self-report and biological measures of alcohol consumption in alcoholism treatment outcome studies. *Advances in Behavior Research and Therapy, 9*, 91–125.

Orford, J. (2001). Addiction as excessive appetite. *Addiction, 96*, 15–31.

Orford, J., & Keddie, A. (1986). Abstinence or controlled drinking in clinical practice: Indications at initial assessment. *Addictive Behaviors, 11*, 71–86.

Parsons, O. A. (Ed.). (1987). *Neuropsychological consequences of alcohol problems: Many questions—some answers*. New York: Guilford Press.

Parsons, O. A., & Farr, S. P. (Eds.). (1981). *The neuropsychology of alcohol and drug use*. New York: Wiley–Interscience.

Pattison, E. M., Sobell, M. B., & Sobell, L. C. (1977). *Emerging concepts of alcohol dependence*. New York: Springer.

Perez-Arce, P., Carr, K. D., & Sorensen, J. L. (1993). Cultural issues in an Outpatient Program for stimulant abusers. *Journal of Psychoactive Drugs, 25*, 35–44.

Petersson, B., Trell, E., & Kristensson, H. (1983). Comparison of g-glutamyltransferase and questionnaire test as alcohol indicators in different risk groups. *Drug and Alcohol Dependence, 11*, 279–286.

Phelps, G., & Field, P. (1992). Drug testing: Clinical and workplace issues. In M. F. Fleming & K. L. Barry (Eds.), *Addictive disorders* (pp. 125–142). St. Louis, MO: Mosby.

Pohorecky, L. A. (1991). Stress and alcohol interaction: An update of human research. *Alcoholism: Clinical and Experimental Research, 15*, 438–459.

Polich, J. M., Armor, D. J., & Braiker, H. B. (1981). *The course of alcoholism: Four years after treatment*. New York: Wiley.

Quigley, B. M., & Collins, R. L. (1999). The modeling of alcohol consumption: A meta-analytic review. *Journal of Studies on Alcohol, 60*, 90–98.

Quigley, L. A., & Marlatt, G. A. (1999). Relapse prevention: Maintenance of change after initial treatment. In K. E. Leonard & H. T. Blane (Eds.), *Psychological theories of drinking and alcoholism* (2nd ed., pp. 370–384). New York: Guilford Press.

Raistrick, D., Dunbar, G., & Davidson, R. (1983). Development of a questionnaire to measure alcohol dependence. *British Journal of Addiction, 78*, 89–95.

Rankin, H. (1990). Validity of self-reports in clinical settings. *Behavioral Assessment, 12*, 107–116.

Regier, D. A., Farmer, M. D., Rae, D. S., Locke, B. Z., Keith, S. J., Judd, L. L., et al. (1990). Comorbidity of mental disorders with alcohol and other drug abuse. *Journal of the American Medical Association, 264*, 2511–2518.

Robins, L. (1991). Assessing substance abuse and psychiatric disorders: History of problems, state of affairs. In L. Harris (Ed.), *Problems of drug dependence 1990: Proceeding of the 52nd annual Scientific Meeting of the Committee on Problems of Drug Dependence*

(NIDA Research Monograph 105, pp. 203–212). Rockville, MD: National Institute of Drug Abuse.

Robins, L. N., & Regier, D. A. (1991). *Psychiatric disorders in America: The Epidemiologic Catchment Area study*. New York: Free Press.

Roman, L. (1986, Winter). Alcohol-related health risks among African Americans. *Alcohol Health and Research World*, 36–39.

Romelsjö, A., Andersson, L., Barrner, H., Borg, S., Granstrand, C., Hultman, O., et al. (1989). A randomized study of secondary prevention of early stage problem drinkers in primary health care. *British Journal of Addiction, 84,* 1319–1327.

Room, R. (Ed.). (1990). *Measuring alcohol consumption in the United States: Methods and rationales*. New York: Plenum Press.

Rounsaville, B. J., Dolinsky, Z. S., Babor, T. F., & Meyer, R. E. (1987). Psychopathology as a predictor of treatment outcome in alcoholics. *Archives of General Psychiatry, 44,* 505–513.

Russell, M. (1989). *The epidemiology of drinking patterns and alcohol-related problems among U.S. Blacks* (Research Monograph No. 18). Rockville, MD: National Institute on Alcohol Abuse and Alcoholism.

Salaspuro, M. (1986). Conventional and coming laboratory markers of alcoholism and heavy drinking. *Alcoholism: Clinical and Experimental Research, 10*(Suppl. 6), 5S–10S.

Saunders, J. B., Aasland, O. G., Babor, T. F., de la Fuente, J. R., & Grant, M. (1993). Development of the Alcohol Use Disorders Identification Test (AUDIT): Who collaborative project on early detection of persons with harmful alcohol consumption—II. *Addiction, 88,* 791–804.

Sayette, M. A. (1999). Does drinking reduce stress? *Alcohol Health and Research World, 23,* 250–255.

Schenker, S. (1997). Medical consequences of alcohol abuse: Is gender a factor? *Alcoholism: Clinical and Experimental Research, 21,* 179–181.

Schmidt, L., & Weisner, C. (Eds.). (1995). *The emergence of problem-drinking women as a special population in need of treatment*. New York: Plenum Press.

Schneider Institute for Health Policy, Brandeis University. (2001). *Substance abuse: The nation's number one health problem*. Princeton, NJ: Robert Woods Johnson Foundation.

Schonfeld, L., & Dupree, L. W. (1991). Antecedents of drinking for early-onset and late-onset elderly alcohol abusers. *Journal of Studies on Alcohol, 52,* 587–592.

Schuckit, M. A. (1995). *Drug and alcohol abuse: A clinical guide to diagnosis and treatment* (4th ed.). New York: Plenum Medical Book Company.

Schuckit, M. A. (2000). Genetics of the risk for alcoholism. *American Journal on Addictions, 9,* 103–112.

Sellers, E. M., Kadlec, K. E., Kaplan, H. L., & Naranjo, C. A. (1988). Limitations in the measurement of urine ethanol in clinical trials to monitor ethanol consumption. *Journal of Studies on Alcohol, 49,* 567–570.

Sher, K. J., Trull, T. J., Bartholow, B. D., & Vieth, A. (1999). Personality and alcoholism: Issues, methods, and etiological processes. In K. E. Leonard & H. T. Blane (Eds.), *Psychological theories of drinking and alcoholism* (2nd ed., pp. 54–105). New York: Guilford Press.

Sherman, J. E., Jorenby, D. E., & Baker, T. B. (1988). Classical conditioning with alcohol: Acquired preferences and aversions, tolerance, and urges/cravings. In C. D. Chaudron & D. A. Wilkinson (Eds.), *Theories on Alcoholism* (pp. 173-237). Toronto, Ontario, Canada: Addiction Research Foundation.

Shute, P. A. (1988). Patients' alcohol drinking habits in general practice: Prevention and education. *Journal of the Royal Society of Medicine, 81,* 450–451.

Sigvardsson, S., Cloninger, C. R., & Bohman, M. (1985). Prevention and treatment of alcohol abuse: Uses and limitations of the high risk paradigm. *Social Biology, 32,* 185–193.

Skinner, H. A. (1982). The Drug Abuse Screening Test. *Addictive Behaviors, 7,* 363–371.

Skinner, H. A., & Allen, B. A. (1982). Alcohol dependence syndrome: Measurement and validation. *Journal of Abnormal Psychology, 91,* 199–209.

Skinner, H. A., & Sheu, W. J. (1982). Reliability of alcohol use indices: The lifetime drinking history and the MAST. *Journal of Studies on Alcohol, 43,* 1157–1170.

Sklar, S. M., & Turner, N. E. (1999). A brief measure for the assessment of coping self-efficacy among alcohol and other drug users. *Addiction, 94,* 723–729.

Smart, R. G. (1989). Is the postwar drinking binge ending? Cross-national trends in per capita alcohol consumption. *British Journal of Addictions, 84*(7), 743–748.

Smith, M., & Lin, K.-M. (1996). Gender and ethics differences in the pharmacogenetics of psychotropics. In M. F. Jensvold, U. Halbreich, & J. A. Hamilton (Eds.), *Psychopharmacology and women: Sex, gender, and hormones* (pp. 121–136). Washington, DC: American Psychiatric Press.

Sobell, L. C., Agrawal, S., & Sobell, M. B. (1999). Utility of liver function tests for screening "alcohol abusers" who are not severely dependent on alcohol. *Substance Use and Misuse, 34,* 1723–1732.

Sobell, L. C., Cunningham, J. A., & Sobell, M. B. (1996). Recovery from alcohol problems with and without treatment: Prevalence in two population surveys. *American Journal of Public Health, 86,* 966–972.

Sobell, L. C., Cunningham, J. C., Sobell, M. B., Agrawal, S., Gavin, D. R., Leo, G. I., et al. (1996b). Fostering self-change among problem drinkers: A proactive community intervention. *Addictive Behaviors, 21,* 817–833.

Sobell, L. C., Ellingstad, T. P., & Sobell, M. B. (2000). Natural recovery from alcohol and drug problems: Methodological review of the research with suggestions for future directions. *Addiction, 95,* 749–764.

Sobell, L. C., & Sobell, M. B. (Eds.). (1980). *Convergent validity: An approach to increasing confidence in treatment outcome conclusions with alcohol and drug abusers.* New York: Pergamon Press.

Sobell, L. C., & Sobell, M. B. (1990). Self-report issues in alcohol abuse: State of the art and future directions. *Behavioral Assessment, 12,* 91–106.

Sobell, L. C., & Sobell, M. B. (1992a, July). *Stability of natural recoveries from alcohol problems.* Paper presented at the second International Conference on Behavioral Medicine, Hamburg, Germany.

Sobell, L. C., & Sobell, M. B. (1992b). Time line Follow-back: A technique for assessing self-reported alcohol consumption. In R. Z. Litten & J. Allen (Eds.), *Measuring alcohol consumption: Psychosocial and biological methods* (pp. 41–72). Totowa, NJ: Humana Press.

Sobell, L. C., & Sobell, M. B. (1995). Alcohol consumption measures. In J. P. Allen & M. Columbus (Eds.), *Assessing alcohol problems: A guide for clinicians and researchers* (pp. 55–73). Rockville, MD: National Institute on Alcohol Abuse and Alcoholism.

Sobell, L. C., & Sobell, M. B. (1996). *Alcohol Time Line Followback (TLFB) users' manual.* Toronto, Ontario, Canada: Addiction Research Foundation.

Sobell, L. C., & Sobell, M. B. (2000). Alcohol Time Line Followback (TLFB). In American Psychiatric Association (Ed.), *Handbook of psychiatric measures* (pp. 477–479). Washington, DC: American Psychiatric Association.

Sobell, L. C., Sobell, M. B., Toneatto, T., & Shillingford, J. A. (1994). Alcohol problems. In M. Hersen & S. M. Turner (Eds.), *Diagnostic interviewing* (2nd ed., pp. 155–188). New York: Plenum Press.

Sobell, L. C., Toneatto, T., & Sobell, M. B. (1994). Behavioral assessment and treatment planning for alcohol, tobacco, and other drug problems: Current status with an emphasis on clinical applications. *Behavior Therapy, 25,* 533–580.

Sobell, M. B., Bogardis, J., Schuller, R., Leo, G. I., & Sobell, L. C. (1989). Is self-monitoring of alcohol consumption reactive? *Behavioral Assessment, 11,* 447–458.

Sobell, M. B., & Sobell, L. C. (Eds.). (1987). *Conceptual issues regarding goals in the treatment of alcohol problems.* New York: Haworth Press.

Sobell, M. B., & Sobell, L. C. (1993a). *Problem drinkers: Guided self-change treatment.* New York: Guilford Press.

Sobell, M. B., & Sobell, L. C. (1993b). Treatment for problem drinkers: A public health priority. In J. S. Baer, G. A. Marlatt, & R. J. McMahon (Eds.), *Addictive behaviors across the lifespan: Prevention, treatment, and policy issues* (pp. 138–157). Beverly Hills, CA: Sage.

Sobell, M. B., & Sobell, L. C. (1995). Controlled drinking after 25 years: How important was the great debate? *Addiction, 90,* 1149–1153.

Sobell, M. B., & Sobell, L. C. (1998). Guiding self-change. In W. R. Miller & N. Heather (Eds.), *Treating addictive behaviors* (2nd ed., pp. 189–202). New York: Plenum Press.

Sobell, M. B., & Sobell, L. C. (2000). Stepped care as a heuristic approach to the treatment of alcohol problems. *Journal of Consulting and Clinical Psychology, 68,* 573–579.

Sobell, M. B., Sobell, L. C., & Kozlowksi, L. T. (1995). Dual recoveries from alcohol and smoking problems. In J. B. Fertig & J. A. Allen (Eds.), *Alcohol and tobacco: From basic science to clinical practice* (NIAAA Research Monograph No. 30, pp. 207–224). Rockville, MD: National Institute on Alcohol Abuse and Alcoholism.

Sobell, M. B., Sobell, L. C., & VanderSpek, R. (1979). Relationships between clinical judgment, self-report and breath analysis measures of intoxication in alcoholics. *Journal of Consulting and Clinical Psychology, 47,* 204–206.

Sobell, M. B., Wilkinson, D. A., & Sobell, L. C. (1990). Alcohol and drug problems. In A. S. Bellack, M. Hersen, & A. E. Kazdin (Eds.), *International handbook of behavior modification and therapy* (2nd ed., pp. 415–435). New York: Plenum Press.

Sokolow, L., Welte, J., Hynes, G., & Lyons, J. (1981). Multiple substance use by alcoholics. *British Journal of Addiction, 76,* 147–158.

Sørensen, T., Orhdm, M., Bentsen, K. D., Hoybye, G., Eghoje, K., & Christoffersen, P. (1984). Prospective evaluation of alcohol abuse and alcoholic liver injury in men as predictors of development of cirrhosis. *Lancet, 2,* 241–244.

Stockwell, T., Murphy, D., & Hodgson, R. (1983). The Severity of Alcohol Dependence Questionnaire: Its use, reliability and validity. *British Journal of Addiction, 78,* 145–155.

Stockwell, T., Sitharthan, T., McGrath, D., & Lang, E. (1994). The measurement of alcohol dependence and impaired control in community samples. *Addiction, 89,* 167–174.

Strakowski, S. M., & DelBello, M. P. (2000). The co-occurrence of bipolar and substance use disorders. *Clinical Psychology Review, 20,* 191–206.

Strang, J., Black, J., Marsh, A., & Smith, B. (1993). Hair analysis for drugs: Technological breakthrough or ethical quagmire? *Addictions, 88,* 163–166.

Substance Abuse and Mental Health Administration. (1999). *Enhancing motivation for change in substance abuse treatment* (Treatment Improvement Protocol Series). Rockville, MD: U.S. Department of Health and Human Services.

Swendsen, J. D., & Merikangas, K. R. (2000). The comorbidity of depression and substance use disorders. *Clinical Psychology Review, 20,* 173–189.

Toneatto, T., Sobell, L. C., Sobell, M. B., & Leo, G. I. (Eds.). (1991). *Psychoactive substance use disorder (Alcohol).* New York: Wiley.

Trull, T. J., Sher, K. J., Minks-Brown, C., Durbin, J., & Burr, R. (2000). Borderline personality disorder and substance use disorders: A review and integration. *Clinical Psychology Review, 20,* 235–253.

U.S. Department of Health and Human Services. (1985). *Report of the Secretary's Task Force on Black and Minority volume VII, chemical dependency and diabetes.* Washington, DC: Author.

Vega, W. A., & Gil, A. G. (1998). *Drug use and ethnicity in early adolescence.* New York: Plenum Press.

Verebey, K., & Turner, C. E. (1991). Laboratory testing. In R. J. Frances & S. I. Miller (Eds.), *Clinical textbook of addictive disorders* (pp. 221–236). New York: Guilford Press.

Welte, J. W., & Barnes, G. M. (1995). Alcohol and other drug use among Hispanics in New York state. *Alcoholism: Clinical and Experimental Research, 19,* 1061–1066.

Wikler, A. (1973). Dynamics of drug dependence. *Archives of General Psychiatry, 28,* 611–616.

Wilkinson, D. A., & Carlen, P. L. (1980). Neuropsychological and neurological assessment of alcoholism: Discrimination between groups of alcoholics. *Journal of Studies on Alcohol, 41,* 129–139.

Wilsnack, R. W., Vogeltanz, N. D., Wilsnack, S. C., Harris, T. R., Ahlstrom, S., Bondy, S., et al. (2000). Gender differences in alcohol consumption and adverse drinking consequences: Cross-cultural patterns. *Addiction, 95*(2), 251–265.

Wilsnack, S. C., Klassen, A. D., Schur, B. E., & Wilsnack, R. W. (1991). Predicting onset and chronicity of women's problem drinking: A five-year longitudinal analysis. *American Journal of Public Health, 81,* 305–318.

Wilsnack, S. C., & Wilsnack, R. W. (Eds.). (1995). *Drinking and problem drinking in U.S. women: Patterns and recent trends.* New York: Plenum Press.

Wodak, A. D., Saunders, J. B., Ewusi-Mensah, I., Davis, M., & Williams, R. (1983). Severity of alcohol dependence in patients with alcoholic liver disease. *British Medical Journal, 287,* 1420–1422.

Woody, G. (1996). The challenge of dual diagnosis. *Alcohol Health and Research World, 20,* 76–80.

Yu, E. S. H., Liu, W. T., Xia, Z., & Zhang, M. (1985). Alcohol use, abuse, and alcoholism among Chinese Americans: A review of the epidemiologic data. In D. L. Spiegler, D. A. Tate, S. S. Aitken, & C. M. Christian (Eds.), *Epidemiology of alcohol use and abuse among minority groups* (pp. 329–341). Rockville, MD: National Institute on Alcohol Abuse and Alcoholism.

CHAPTER 7

Psychoactive Substance Use Disorders: Drugs

JENNIFER R. ANTICK and KIMBERLY GOODALE

T HE WORD *DRUGS,* in our society, generally implies illicit drugs. Although active addiction may involve illegal behavior, many substances of abuse are legal and sanctioned by our society. Those who question the presence of drugs in daily life should take note of the various over-the-counter (OTC) and prescription medications, caffeine, alcohol, and/or tobacco products around their own homes. In casual parlance, drugs are somehow distinguished from alcohol, tobacco, caffeine, and prescription medications. In the reality of substance use disorders, however, those cultural distinctions merely provide barriers to societal change and effective treatment development (Goldstein, 2001).

This chapter concerns substance use disorders that include intoxication, withdrawal states, abuse, and dependence on nicotine, opiates, cocaine and amphetamines, cannabis, caffeine, hallucinogens, inhalants, steroids, "club drugs," and the sedative hypnotics (with the exception of alcohol, which is covered in Chapter 6). Each of these groups of drugs differs from one another in neurochemical and molecular structure, routes of administration, physiological effects, rate of metabolism, general effects on behavior, and likelihood of instigating a harmful use pattern. The degree and type of danger for the user and those around the user vary as well.

HISTORICAL PERSPECTIVE

Every civilization has used chemicals to produce alterations in affect, thought, or behavior. Civilizations have also established expectations and norms for their use. The expected uses have historically included religious or ceremonial aspects but also accommodated recreational ones. Although alcohol is the drug most commonly used throughout history for recreational purposes, it is not the only one. Other naturally occurring substances have been used to relieve negative emotional states, to produce states of calm and relaxation, to provide relief from boredom, to manage pain, to increase strength or work tolerance, or to distort reality (Austin, 1979).

In addition, history suggests the presence of individuals who deviated from community custom with respect to when, how much, and in which situations drugs were used. These individuals produced problems for themselves, for those in their immediate communities, and for those in their extended social groups and societies. These individuals would likely be diagnosed with what is now termed a *psychoactive substance use disorder.* A key consideration is that in most communities, only a few substances were available at any time. A second consideration is that their use was closely monitored. Because of this, a relatively small percentage of individuals abused or became dependent on drugs.

Today, our patterns of abuse differ considerably from the traditional or historical pattern. We have available, at one time, almost all of the naturally occurring psychoactive substances. In most cases, the pharmacologically active ingredient in each natural product has been identified and, in many cases, enhanced through selective growing and processing. These "natural" substances are then made available to those who desire the drug. Of even more concern are the synthetic derivatives of naturally occurring drugs. Synthetic derivatives often contain pharmacologically active ingredients that are magnified 100 times or more than the psychoactive potency of the natural substance. In addition, contemporary users have available numerous methods of drug delivery. Contributions to this include invention of the hypodermic syringe in the 1860s, as well as the newest drugs, such as crack cocaine, and "designer" and "club" derivatives of fentanyl and mescaline. These developments have markedly increased options for delivery and dose, decreased time of onset to drug action, and increased both potency and toxicity of these agents compared with their naturally occurring counterparts.

Substantial heterogeneity exists among substance abusers in the nature and severity of their addiction-related problems. However, there are consistencies across users, such as comorbidity, that should inform diagnoses. Estimates suggest that between 50% and 80% of individuals with substance use disorders have a comorbid psychiatric disorder that requires additional services, such as specialized psychotherapy or psychotropic medications. An example of such comorbidity is that of eating disorders and substance-related disorders. Between 12% and 18% of people with anorexia nervosa abuse drugs, and 30% of bulimia patients struggle with substance abuse, according to the National Center on Addiction and Substance Abuse (CASA) at Columbia University, New York (Vastag, 2001).

COSTS TO SOCIETY

A second area of consistency is the cost of drug use disorders to individuals and to society. Drugs, alcohol, and tobacco use are reported to cause more deaths, illnesses, and disabilities than any other preventable health condition (Robert Wood Johnson, 2001). The most recent estimates (Office of Drug Control Policy [ONDCP], 2001) suggest the cost of illicit drugs and alcohol abuse in 1992 in the United States was $102.2 billion, and by 1998, this figure increased to $143.4 billion. The rate of increase in costs from 1992 to 1998 represented an excess of the combined increase of 3.5% for the adult population and the consumer price index for all services for this period. Projected overall costs of drug abuse for the year 2000 were $160.7 billion with $110.5 billion as projected lost productivity. This last figure was based on data suggesting that the fastest increases between 1992 and 1998 were for productivity losses associated with drug abuse-related illness and to incarceration, which increased 8.5% and 9.1%, respectively, annually. When examined in detail, the costs of drug abuse include premature death, institutionalization, short- and long-term hospitalization, productivity loss for victims of crime, and productivity loss for those who, because of crime careers, might have otherwise contributed to legal productivity. It is important to note that there are many other costs of drug abuse. These costs include, but are not limited to, running the criminal justice system (which is increasingly occupied with drug-related crimes), ensuring police protection, adjudicating defendants, maintaining the state and federal corrections facilities, and federal spending to reduce supply and social welfare costs (ONDCP, 2001). Additional factors to consider are costs to employers and private citizens. Employed drug abusers reportedly cost their employers about twice as much in medical and worker compensation claims as their drug-free coworkers. Additional costs to society include private sector costs such as private legal defense and property damage for victims of crime (National Institutes on Drug Abuse [NIDA], 1999).

Drug abuse also increases general health care costs. One set of consequences includes conditions directly caused by drug use such as polyneuropathy or the affects of narcotics on the fetus or newborn. Another set of general health care costs may be derived from calculating the contribution of drug use to the development, exacerbation, or complication of other illnesses or injuries that then require their own specific treatments or significantly longer lengths of hospitalization. In addition, individuals who use drugs are at higher risk for contracting and communicating tuberculosis, HIV/AIDS, and hepatitis B and C (ONDCP, 2001; Spittal & Schechter, 2001). Prevalence of medical disorders is high among substance abuse patients and includes hypertension, coronary artery disease, chronic liver disease, and hepatitis C (Weisner, Mertens, Parthasarathy, Moore, & Lu, 2001). Drug abuse is also likely to represent the most common cause of stroke in young adults, largely from the abuse of amphetamine, cocaine, or MDMA (Ecstasy; McEvoy, Kitchen, & Thomas, 1998).

There are other costs as well, since drug abuse precipitates violent crimes such as assault, rape, robbery, and homicide. These episodes of violence often result in injuries requiring medical care or additional hospital days resulting from comorbid drug abuse and other mental health disorders. Rivara et al. (1997) investigated the risk of violent death in the home associated with alcohol use or chronic abuse and use of illicit drugs. The authors found that subjects who reportedly drank alcohol were at increased risk of violent death by homicide. Similarly, reported use of illicit drugs or being arrested were also associated with an increased risk of homicide. Subjects who reportedly used both alcohol and drugs were at a markedly increased risk of homicide, relative to those who used neither substance. Reported use of drugs was associated with a seven-fold increased risk of suicide. The highest elevation in suicide risk was observed for those who reportedly used both alcohol and drugs. The authors also found an increased risk of homicide and suicide for nonsubstance-abusing individuals living in households in which other members abused alcohol or drugs.

IMPLICATIONS FOR TRAINING

Given the previous discussion, it is evident that individuals with substance use disorders may present for services at any number of places other than treatment centers. They may be identified in primary care clinics, emergency departments, correctional facilities, detoxification centers, or mental health clinics (privately or publicly funded). Because of this, research suggests that it is increasingly important to have adequately cross-trained professionals in primary care, emergency medicine, psychology, psychiatry, and social work so that issues of substance use can be identified wherever patients present for services and appropriate referrals can be made. Importantly, a very small percentage of primary care, emergency medicine, psychiatry, psychology, or social work practitioners have had sufficient didactics and/or practical training in the identification, assessment, or treatment of substance use disorders. Current reports suggest that many medical programs do not offer any training or didactics in the assessment of substance use disorders. In those practitioner programs that do commonly offer training (i.e., psychiatry residencies, psychology internships, and social work internships), training is elective (McCarty, Caspi, Panas, Krakow, & Mulligan, 2000; Soderstrom et al., 1997).

Case Study 1

Jane is a 39-year-old mother of two children, ages 6 and 9. She is a European-descent American, middle class, and addicted to OxyContin. She is not prescribed the drug but was given one by a friend on an evening when she had a headache two years ago. Since that time, she has been taking the drug illegally once or twice per day. She states that her friend gives them to her from his own prescription. She openly admits that "it is wrong" but she is "afraid of being sick" (experiencing the withdrawal symptoms). She has tried several times to stop using, and these attempts have resulted in the onset of unremitting severe headaches, nausea, irritability, and "like the flu." In two years, she has not managed to stay clean for more than two days before the withdrawal symptoms become "unbearable" and she takes another pill to feel better. She reports that the headaches "are almost instantly gone" and that she feels like "all of the stresses of life are manageable" when she is taking the medication/drug.

Case Study 2

Madge is a 56-year-old married woman with three grown children. She has been smoking cigarettes since she was 15 years old. She reports that she would like to quit, that smoking interferes with her ability to take part in pleasurable activities (she says she is the only smoker in the social group), and that she is ashamed to "still be smoking after all these years," primarily because she reportedly understands it to be "self-destructive behavior." She is beginning to notice physical limitations that she attributes to smoking cigarettes, and she is very afraid of lung cancer. Despite all of this, she continues to smoke every day.

Case Study 3

John is a 37-year-old single, highly educated man. He is career driven and very motivated to succeed in his work. He is also addicted to crack cocaine. He indulges on Fridays to accommodate the aftereffects of use before returning to work on Mondays. He reports establishing lengthy requirements to make use more difficult, but this instead results in binge use between three and six days after enduring cravings for up to four weeks.

Case Study 4

David is a 29-year-old married man working in health care. He uses marijuana on a daily basis. He was recently tested for drugs as part of his hospital's drug-free policy. A result of a positive test now means that his job is in jeopardy, and he has been referred for an evaluation of his drug use. Although he has seniority in his job class and his department, and he is the sole support of his family, he is considering leaving his job rather than quitting marijuana use.

Case Study 5

Janice is a 40-year-old married woman with two school-age children. She is bright and verbal, has a good social life, and has all that she needs financially. She is being treated for generalized anxiety disorder and is prescribed Xanax by her psychiatrist. She has been instructed to take the drug only as prescribed, but she admits that she has needed more than the prescribed dose recently. She is experiencing breakthrough symptoms and anticipatory anxiety about running out of medication. When her psychiatrist insisted on maintaining the current dose and began to discuss "tapering down" and "changing meds," she became even more anxious in anticipation of being without the medication that she perceived as "saving her life" for the past few years. Two weeks later, a local pharmacy called the psychiatrist to say that it had what looked like forged prescriptions for a doubled dose.

Case Study 6

Leslie is a 19-year-old premed student in her sophomore year of college. She had never "done drugs" before and has good grades and a good part-time work history. She is expected to accomplish a great deal in her chosen field of medicine. Twelve weeks ago, she tried heroin for the first time. Her friends told her that getting "hooked" only happens with needles and smoking it is "no big deal." She reports that she has never felt anything so good as her first high. Since that time, she has not been attending classes and is spending most of her time obtaining, using, or recovering from heroin use.

Case Study 7

Stan is a 42-year-old veteran who has presented to a Veterans Administration homeless program for entry. He apparently "served his country well" and received an honorable discharge after two tours of duty. Since he left the armed service, he has been making his living as a photographer and appears to have great skill. He is verbal and bright. He has also been living in a tent for the past year, moving from place to place. It is now beginning to snow, requiring the "winter plan." Each year in the past 10 years, he has been homeless most of the year until the cold threatens, at which point he presents to a Veterans Administration or other treatment program in hopes of finding shelter and a place to "dry out." He has taken multiple psychoactive substances over the years but his "drug of choice" is cocaine. He has had as much as two years clean in the past 10 years; most of that time, however, was in an extended-stay treatment environment. Today, he has four days clean.

These cases demonstrate both the chronicity and relapsing nature of the disorders that we collectively call *substance use disorders*. Each of these individuals began using with a "choice," and each found they were seemingly controlled by the chemical(s) they had been using.

EPIDEMIOLOGY

Substance use, like many human behaviors, occurs on a continuum of frequency and intensity. As we prepare to discuss the frequency and intensity of use, it is important to first discuss common drugs of abuse and general terminology.

Commonly abused drugs, according to Julien (1997) and National Institute on Drug Abuse (NIDA, 1998a, 1998b, 1999, 2000a, 2000b, 2000c), include:

- Cannabinoids: hashish and marijuana.
- Central nervous system depressants (the traditional sedative-hypnotic drugs and antiepileptic drugs): barbiturates, benzodiazepines (other than flunitrazepam), flunitrazepam, gamma hydroxybutyrate (GHB), methaqualone.
- Dissociative anesthetics: ketamine, phencyclidine (PCP), and analogs.
- Hallucinogens/psychedelics: lysergic acid diethylamide (LSD), mescaline, psilocybin.
- Opioids, morphine derivatives, and synthetic opiates: codeine, fentanyl, heroin, morphine, opium, Demerol, oxycodone, OxyContin.
- Stimulants: amphetamine, cocaine, methamphetamine, methylenedioxymethamphetamine (MDMA), methylphenidate, nicotine.
- Anabolic-andronergic steroids: synthetic substances related to the male sex hormones (androgens) that may be taken orally (such as oxymetholone [Anadrol]), injectable (such as nandrolone phenpropionate [Duabolin]), or rubbed on the skin (various compounds).
- Inhalants: volatile solvents (e.g., paint thinners, gasoline, glues), aerosols (e.g., spray paints, hair sprays, vegetable oil sprays for cooking), gases (e.g., medical anesthetics such as ether, chloroform, or nitrous oxide), and nitrites (e.g., amyl nitrite or butyl nitrite).

- "Club drugs": drugs from other categories that are grouped by use patterns, such as MDMA, LSD, GHB, ketamine, rohypnol, methamphetamine.

Glossary—General Definitions (American Psychiatric Association [APA], 2000; Julien, 1997; Substance Abuse and Mental Health Services Administration [SAMHSA], 2000)

Addiction A chronic, relapsing disease characterized by compulsive drug-seeking and drug use and by neurochemical and molecular changes in the brain.

Comorbid disorders Psychiatric disorders that coexist with a second psychiatric disorder.

Cross tolerance A condition in which one drug can prevent the withdrawal symptoms associated with physical dependence on a different drug.

Current use Use of alcohol or a drug at least once in the past 30 days.

Drugs Chemical substances used for their effects on bodily processes.

Drug interactions Modifications of the action of one drug by the concurrent or prior administration of another drug.

Drug misuse Use of any drug (legal or illegal) for a medical or recreational purpose when other alternatives are available, practical, or warranted, or when drug use endangers either the user or others with whom he or she may interact.

Drug tolerance A state of progressively decreasing responsiveness to a drug.

Heavy use The use of any drug or alcohol on five or more occasions in the past 30 days.

Intoxication Development of a reversible condition after recent ingestion of a psychoactive substance.

Physical dependence A state in which the use of a substance is required for a person to function normally. (Note that a person may be physically dependent on a substance without meeting criteria for addiction or substance dependence.)

Psychoactive drugs Chemical substances that alter mood or behavior as a result of alterations in the functioning of the brain.

Psychological dependence Compulsion to use a drug for its pleasurable effects. Such dependence may lead to a compulsion to misuse a drug.

Routes of administration The ways drugs can be taken into the body. These are by oral dose, intravenous dose, intramuscular dose, topical dose, subcutaneous dose, intranasal dose, inhalation, and smoking. The method of ingestion affects how the drug is broken down in the body and how long the chemical has a psychoactive effect.

Substance abuse A maladaptive pattern of substance use leading to clinically significant impairment or distress.

Substance use Ingestion of alcohol or drugs without the experience of any negative consequences.

Withdrawal A substance-specific state that is reached on cessation or reduction of substance use that has been heavy and/or prolonged.

GENERAL STATISTICS

The most recent National Household Survey on Drug Abuse (NHSDA; SAMHSA, 1999, 2000) included approximately 70,000 people. Based on this survey, an estimated 14 million Americans were current illicit drug users, representing 6.3% of the population 12 years and older in 2000. Although surveys consistently suggest that more men than women use illicit drugs, rates of nonmedical use of psychotherapeutic drugs (pain relievers, tranquilizers, stimulants, and sedatives) were similar for men and women. Of women who use illicit drugs, about half are of childbearing age. Among adolescents ages 12 to 17, 9.7% had used an illicit drug within 30 days before the interview. Another important estimate was that 7 million people reported driving under the influence of an illicit drug in the past year. Adults between the ages of 18 and 25 use more cigarettes, marijuana, and alcohol by their own report than any other age group.

The National Institute on Drug Abuse (NIDA) reports that 4 million people age 12 years and older misused pain relievers, sedatives, tranquilizers, and stimulants in 1999. Data from the National Household Survey on Drug Abuse place the total number of people misusing prescription drugs at 9.3 million. NIDA most recently suggested that the "true number" is between these two figures (Vastag, 2001).

"First use" statistics are also an important source of information. An estimated 2.1 million U.S. residents first used marijuana in 1997, approximately 5,800 people per day. An estimated 81,000 people used heroin for the first time in 1997. There were 730,000 new cocaine users in 1997 and 1.1 million new hallucinogen users in 1997. About 2.1 million people began smoking cigarettes daily in 1997, more than half of whom were younger than 18, which translates into 3,000 new youth smokers per day (SAMHSA, 1999).

Illicit drug use rates have been, and remain, highly correlated with educational status. Among young adults ages 26 to 34 in 1998, those who had not completed high school had the highest rate of current use while college graduates had the lowest rate of use. The authors of the SAMHSA report indicate that this is in spite of the fact that young adults at different educational levels are equally likely to have tried illicit drugs in their lifetimes. About 15.4% of unemployed adults (age 18+) were current illicit drug users versus 6.3% of full-time employed adults and 7.8% of part-time employed adults. Of the 11.8 million adult illicit drug users in 2000, 9.1 million (77%) were employed either full time or part time. About 3.5 million Americans age 12 and older are estimated to meet criteria for dependence on illicit drugs (SAMHSA, 1999, 2000).

CLINICAL PICTURE

Leshner (1999) gives two general categories of individuals who use drugs and states that these two groups of people present different clinical pictures. One category is that of individuals who might appear to be "sensation seekers." These people begin use for the pleasant sensations the drugs can produce and/or to feel accepted by peers. Many of these individuals begin to have problems with their use because the drugs interfere with daily functioning. Leshner notes that this behavior is most consistent with adolescence and young adulthood. The second category is that of the individual who appears to use drugs as a way to cope with life stressors and negative emotional states. These individuals are more likely to have other mental health problems and may subscribe later in life to the "self-medication" hypothesis to explain their prolonged drug use and the exacerbations of the psychological symptoms that come from extended use. Regardless of the reasons for first use or prolonged use, the most salient feature of addiction is an "uncontrollable compulsion to seek and use drugs" (Leshner, 1999). Most of the life problems that develop in substance use disorders stem from the "uncontrollable compulsion" and accompanying inappropriate or illegal behaviors to satisfy the compulsion. Although use usually begins with a voluntary act, once addiction has developed, it is almost impossible for people to stop the spiral without treatment. The severity of the clinical picture varies by the number of risk factors, the point of onset, the consequences of use, the physical response to the substance(s), the psychological needs for use, and the psychosocial structure's support for use versus limited tolerance for abuse. For most people, addiction is a chronic, relapsing disorder in which multiple treatment episodes are likely to be required over the life span (Minkoff, 2000).

DIAGNOSTIC CONSIDERATIONS

The *DSM-IV-TR* (APA, 2000) is a prominent method of classifying the behaviors and consequences of substance use. The *DSM-IV-TR* divides the Substance-Related Disorders into the Substance Use Disorders and Substance-Induced Disorders. The focus of this chapter is the Substance Use Disorders, Abuse and Dependence. For more information about Substance-Induced Disorders, see APA (2000).

The diagnostic criteria for Substance Abuse are:

A. A maladaptive pattern of substance use leading to clinically significant impairment or distress, as manifested by one (or more) of the following, occurring within a 12-month period:
   (1) Recurrent substance use resulting in a failure to fulfill major role obligations at work, school, or home (e.g., repeated absences or poor work performance related to substance use; substance-related absences, suspensions, or expulsions from school; neglect of children or household).
   (2) Recurrent substance use in situations in which it is physically hazardous (e.g., driving an automobile and operating a machine when impaired by substance use).
   (3) Recurrent substance-related legal problems (e.g., arrests for substance-related disorderly conduct).
   (4) Continued substance use despite having persistent or recurrent social or interpersonal problems caused or exacerbated by the effects of the substance (e.g., arguments with spouse about consequences of intoxication, physical fights).
B. The symptoms have never met the criteria for Substance Dependence for the class of substance.

The diagnosis of Substance Abuse may be applied to alcohol, amphetamines, cannabis, cocaine, hallucinogens, inhalants, opioids, phencyclidine, sedatives, hypnotics, or anxiolytics, and other or unknown substances.

The diagnostic criteria for substance dependence are:

A. A maladaptive pattern of substance use, leading to clinically significant impairment or distress, as manifested by three (or more) of the following, occurring at any time in the same 12-month period:

(1) Tolerance, as defined by either of the following:
  (a) A need for markedly increased amounts of the substance to achieve intoxication or desired effect.
  (b) Markedly diminished effect with continued use of the same amount of the substance.
(2) Withdrawal, as manifested by either of the following:
  (a) The characteristic withdrawal syndrome for the substance (refer to criteria A and B of the criteria sets for Withdrawal from the specific substances).
  (b) The same (or a closely related) substance is taken to relieve or avoid withdrawal symptoms.
(3) The substance is often taken in larger amounts or over a longer period than was intended.
(4) There is a persistent desire or unsuccessful efforts to cut down or control substance use.
(5) A great deal of time is spent in activities necessary to obtain the substance (e.g., visiting multiple doctors or driving long distances), use the substance (e.g., chain-smoking), or recover from its effects.
(6) Important social, occupational, or recreational activities are given up or reduced because of substance use.
(7) The substance use is continued despite knowledge of having a persistent or recurrent physical or psychological problem that is likely to have been caused or exacerbated by the substance (e.g., current cocaine use despite recognition of cocaine-induced depression, or continued drinking despite recognition that an ulcer was made worse by alcohol consumption).

Specify if:

With Physiological Dependence: Evidence of tolerance or withdrawal (i.e., either item 1 or 2 is present).

Without Physiological Dependence: No evidence of tolerance or withdrawal (i.e., neither item 1 nor 2 is present).

Course Specifiers

Early Full Remission

Early Partial Remission

Sustained Full Remission

Sustained Partial Remission

On Agonist Therapy

In a Controlled Environment

The Substance Dependence diagnosis may be applied to all of the drugs specified for inclusion in Substance Abuse, with the additions of Nicotine and Polysubstance Dependence. The Polysubstance Dependence diagnosis is used when a person repeatedly uses at least three groups of substances (not including caffeine and nicotine), but no single substance predominated and when Dependence criteria were met for substances as a group but not for the specific substances (APA, 2000).

Dual diagnosis considerations include what Kenneth Minkoff (1998, 2000) calls a "welcoming expectation" or an assumption that any client is likely to have a co-morbid condition. Each of the *DSM* diagnoses for each class of substances requires the ruling out of the symptoms as occurring due to a general medical condition or better accounted for by another mental health disorder. The primary difficulty in accurately diagnosing a psychoactive substance use disorder versus another mental health disorder versus two co-occurring disorders is that, by definition, psychoactive substances mimic mental health disorders. A practical approach allows for a careful, structured assessment, preferably over time, that facilitates disclosure by clients. If co-occurring disorders are the norm and not the exception, assessment and reassessment during treatment and aftercare phases of treatment are indicated. An integrated approach addressing both mental health and substance use disorders as primary is considered more effective than either sequential or concurrent approaches.

SCREENING AND ASSESSMENT

Friedmann, McCullough, and Saitz (2001) sent a survey to a national sample of 2,000 practicing general internists, physicians, obstetricians and gynecologists, and psychiatrists to assess their screening and intervention practices for illicit drug abuse. Greater confidence in obtaining a history of drug abuse, fewer perceived time constraints, and fewer patients with a history of substance abuse were associated with a greater likelihood to screen and intervene. However, the authors concluded that a substantial minority of physicians adequately intervene with patients presenting with substance use disorders. This finding is particularly noteworthy because, as stated previously, physicians may be in a prime position to identify and refer individuals with substance use disorders. Physicians specializing in addiction medicine, however, are increasingly prominent in determining the guidelines by which treatment options are generated. The American Society of Addiction Medicine (ASAM) has established a rigorous set of criteria for patient placement decisions. The ASAM Patient Placement Criteria—Revised (PPC-2R; ASAM, 2001; Center for Substance Abuse Treatment [CSAT], 2001) requires assessment in six areas of an individual's life:

1. Dimension 1: Acute intoxication and withdrawal potential.
2. Dimension 2: Biomedical conditions and complications.
3. Dimension 3: Emotional, behavioral, or cognitive conditions and complications.
4. Dimension 4: Readiness to change.
5. Dimension 5: Relapse, continued use, or continued problem potential.
6. Dimension 6: Recovery/living environment.

The purpose of assessing each area mirrors the research reflecting the multidimensional nature of the problems known as *substance use disorders*. The specific methods for assessment vary considerably across practitioners, as do the reliability and validity information for specific tools. The ASAM criteria lend consistency to the weight placed on specific aspects of an individual's impairment and the best placement or intensity of treatment for his or her individual clinical picture.

According to the Northwest Frontier Addiction Technology Transfer Center (NFATTC; 2001), assessment of substance use disorders should be approached as an ongoing, collaborative process to gather sufficient information for treatment planning. They provide specific criteria for the determination of what makes a competent "developing counselor," "proficient counselor," and the "exemplary counselor." The NFATTC guidelines may provide a roadmap for training in substance use assessment for professionals from different disciplines.

Many clinical researchers also suggest that assessment and goal-setting are not separate; they are related processes. Assessment begins with the first interview and screening, may proceed through an intensive assessment, and continues throughout the treatment process. Individuals in treatment often report that they were able to establish brief periods of pretreatment or between-treatment abstinence. These episodes of abstinence may reveal clients' skills, resources, and coping strategies that are useful in designing treatment. To this end, clinicians must be prepared to assess for past successes in addition to their failures, in a manner consistent with each client's age, developmental level, and gender. Culture, race, language, ethnicity, spirituality, and disabilities are all major considerations and may indicate the need for specialized assessment procedures as well as diagnostic consideration (APA, 2000; ASAM, 2001; S. D. Miller & Berg, 1992; Riehman, Hser, & Zeller, 2000; Rosengren, Downey, & Donovan, 2000).

Motivational interviewing was first developed by William Miller and associates (CSAT, 1999; Miller & Rollnick, 1991) as an assessment methodology and later developed into a treatment strategy. One of the major premises of motivational interviewing is that ambivalence about change is normal. This assumption allows for an alliance between the therapist and client that may be more difficult to establish when using a confrontational approach to break through resistance. In fact, motivational interviewing assumes that ambivalence is an important aspect of the process of recovery. Reflective listening in an empathic, supportive, yet directive, counseling style is said to provide conditions in which change can occur. In addition, this type of interviewing assumes that the alliance between client and clinician is a collaborative partnership to which each brings important expertise. Ambivalence can then be resolved by working with the client's intrinsic motivations and values. A successful motivational interview is characterized by the expression of empathy through reflective listening, communication of respect for and acceptance of the clients, a collaborative relationship, and an understanding that change is always ultimately up to the client. It is also characterized by the development of discrepancy between the client's goals, values, and current behavior; adjustment to resistance (rather than opposition); and support for self-efficacy and optimism by focusing on the client's strengths instead of his or her pathology. This provides the foundation for the hope and optimism the client needs to make the difficult changes he or she needs to make. Because of the flexibility of this model and the successes reported in the clinical research literature, motivational interviewing is now being used with other clinical populations whose treatment requires significant behavioral changes, such as cardiac rehabilitation and diabetes treatment.

A different but complementary model is that of J. O. Prochaska and C. C. DiClemente's *Stages of Change* (Prochaska & DiClemente, 1991; Prochaska, DiClemente, & Norcross, 1992). This model, like motivational interviewing, applies to any desired changes in human behavior, including those involved in substance use changes. Brady et al. (1996) suggest that the use of this model is both pragmatic and appropriate to conceptualize a client's change in substance abuse as well as mental health problems. This model provides a method of assessing client readiness to accept different types of treatment, measure progress in treatment, and provide a foundation for both client and treatment provider in understanding the client's strengths as well as the illness.

The five Stages of Change, sequentially, are:

1. *Precontemplation:* The person is not yet considering treatment and may be "in denial" of a substance use problem.
2. *Contemplation:* In this stage, the individual acknowledges having a problem but is not yet ready to make specific behavioral changes.
3. *Preparation:* Planning for change takes place in this stage.
4. *Action:* The person begins to modify his or her behavior, environment, or experiences to overcome his or her problems.
5. *Maintenance:* The person works to maintain the gains and prevent relapse in this stage.

One key benefit of this approach is that it can be used across different theoretical paradigms including behavioral, dynamic, or 12-step approaches, hence the name *transtheoretical.* A second benefit is that it allows for a common language across different levels of staff training, ultimately unifying what is otherwise confusing rhetoric to clientele. The most compelling finding is that even one session using motivational interviewing informed by the Stages of Change approach was found to improve treatment outcomes, even when motivational interviewing methods did not continue during treatment (W. R. Miller & Rollnick, 1991; Prochaska & DiClemente, 1991; Prochaska et al., 1992; SAMHSA, 1999).

Although the assessment interview lays the groundwork for treatment as described previously, getting information is still one of the main outcomes. Because most clients have had experience making changes in their lives, it can be very informative to explore what they already understand about their current challenges and problems as well as what they have done in the past that has worked for them. It may also be very important to determine what healthy efforts are already being implemented by a client at the time of the interview. Some basic questions that may be helpful in highlighting healthy efforts already being implemented by a client include:

- Has your substance use ever changed?
- Is this a slip from a previous sobriety? (Follow-up: How did you manage to stay clean for that length of time?)
- Is this new behavior?
- Is this situation-specific?
- Is this in response to a new stressor at home, school, or with family? (Follow-up: What other things are you doing to cope that are even slightly effective?)
- When are you able to refuse use even when substances are available? (Follow-up: How do you accomplish that?)
- Who else might notice that you have been making an effort?

Brief screening tools may also be a very useful way for busy clinicians to begin the assessment process. They include a sampling of items that are consistent with problematic substance use. For children and adolescents, begin with general assessment questions concerning school, extracurricular activities, friends, nighttime activities, neighborhood, and family life. At this point, the clinician can move into alcohol and drug questions:

- Does anyone you know smoke, drink, or use drugs?
- Does anyone in your family smoke, drink, or use drugs?
- Do any of your friends smoke, drink, or use drugs?
- Have you ever used tobacco, alcohol, or other drugs in the past?
- How about now?

It is then appropriate to ask about any consequences of drug or alcohol use. The authors recommend that the clinician include questions about physical health, including suicidal ideation; family and social relations, including sexual activity; physical and sexual abuse; school work; and financial or legal problems, including driving while intoxicated or arrests. An excellent brief screening for adolescents is the RAFFT (Relax, Alone, Friends, Family, Trouble; Bastiens, Francis, & Lewis, 2000):

- Do you use to *Relax*?
- Do you use when *Alone*?
- How many of your *Friends* use?
- Is there a history of substance use/abuse in the *Family*?
- Have you experienced any problems/*Trouble* because of your use?

In the screening of adults, it is appropriate to include questions about tobacco use separately from alcohol and drugs. If the client uses tobacco, there are several questions that may be helpful to ask:

- How much do you smoke? (amount and frequency)
- Is that the same or different from use patterns in the past?
- How long have you smoked?
- Have you ever tried to quit? (Follow-up: When?)
- What helped or hindered quitting in the past?

At this point, it is useful to ask if the person has used any alcohol or drugs in the past year. If he or she has not used either in the past year, it is important to know if the person is in recovery and to assess past use and family history. If the person answers that he or she has used in the past year, there are two common screening tools that are useful—one more useful for men and the second more useful for women. The CAGE (Cutting, Annoyed, Guilty, Eye opener; Cooney, Zweben, & Fleming, 1995), more useful for men, should be considered a "positive" screen with two of four yes answers. The CAGE consists of the following questions:

- Have you ever thought about *Cutting* down on your drinking?
- Have you ever been *Annoyed* by people's criticism of your drinking/drug use?
- Have you ever felt *Guilty* about your drinking/drug use?
- Have you ever used alcohol/drugs to get you going in the morning? (*Eye opener*).

The CAGE is anecdotally reported to produce false positives for women, reportedly because of the item regarding guilt. If that is a consideration, consider the TACE (Take, Annoyed, Cutting, Eye opener). Instead of asking about guilt, the TACE asks about indicators for tolerance. Like the CAGE, two of four yes answers indicate a positive screen. The TACE consists of the following questions:

- How many drinks does it *Take* for you to feel high? (>3 is a positive response).
- Have you ever been *Annoyed* by people's criticism of your drinking/drug use?
- Have you ever thought about *Cutting* down on your drinking/drug use?
- Have you ever used alcohol/drugs to get you going in the morning? (*Eye opener*).

There are also special considerations for older adults. It is important to begin with questions regarding stresses in the client's life and his or her methods of coping with those stresses. It is then useful to ask whether the individual has used any alcohol or drugs in the past year. It is particularly important with elders to ask about the use of alcohol and about prescribed medications. The clinician should investigate past difficulties with alcohol or drugs. If the person answers positively to use of alcohol or drugs in the past year, the CHARMM (Cutting, How, Anyone, Role, More, Medications) screen may be very useful. It consists of the following questions:

- Have you ever thought about *Cutting* down?
- *How*? Do you have rules about drinking or drug use? Has your pattern of drinking or drug use changed recently?
- Has *Anyone* expressed concern about your alcohol or drug use?
- What *Role* does alcohol/drugs play in your life?
- Have you ever used alcohol/drugs *More* than you intended?
- Have you ever had problems with your *Medications* or taken more than prescribed?

In all cases, follow-up questions for adults should include drug(s) used, method of use, amount and frequency of use, duration of use, periods of abstinence, role of alcohol/drugs in the person's life, consequences of use, additional coping strategies, and support systems that are consistent with changes in use.

There are a number of standardized tools available for assessments of substance use disorders. The following are instruments either designed for use with adolescents or developed primarily for adults and later adapted for adolescents:

1. *Drug and Alcohol Problem (DAP) Quick Screen* (Schwartz & Wirtz, 1990): A 30-item questionnaire that measures overall alcohol and drug problem severity. The reliability and validity have not yet been evaluated.

2. *Drug Use Screening Inventory—Revised* (DUSI-R; Tarter, Laird, Bukstein, & Kaminer, 1992): The adolescent version of the DUSI-R assesses alcohol and drug use patterns as well as psychosocial functioning using 159 true/false questions. This tool yields scores on 10 different functional adolescent problem areas: alcohol and drug use, physical health, mental health, family relations, peer relations, educational status, vocational status, social skills, leisure and recreation, and

aggressive behavior/delinquency. The adolescent version of the DUSI-R has shown good reliability and validity.

3. *Perceived Benefit of Drinking and Drug Use* (Petchers & Singer, 1990): A 10-item questionnaire, which asks about the perceived benefits of alcohol and drug use. It is a nonthreatening problem-severity screen based on the approach that beliefs about drug use tend to be associated with actual alcohol and drug use. The perceived benefits may give useful information in motivational interviewing.

4. *Personal Experiences Screening Questionnaire* (PESQ; Winters, 1992): A 40-item questionnaire that provides measures of overall problem severity, alcohol and other drug use history, psychosocial problems, and response-distortion tendencies. Cutoff scores indicate the need for further assessment. The use of this instrument has been validated for normal adolescents, juvenile offenders, and adolescents in addiction treatment.

5. *Problem Oriented Screening Instrument for Teenagers* (POSIT; Rahdert, 1991): A 139-item yes/no questionnaire, which addresses 10 areas of adolescent functioning.

6. *Substance Abuse Subtle Screening Inventory* (SASSI; G. A. Miller, 1997): The adolescent version of the SASSI consists of 81 questions pertaining to the severity of alcohol and other drug problems. The SASSI yields scores for alcohol problems, drug problems, and defensiveness (i.e., the tendency to minimize or deny problems; Martin & Winters, 1998).

For adult assessment, there are many tools. A few are:

1. The *Addiction Severity Index* is a structured interview designed to assess problem severity in seven commonly affected areas of alcohol and/or drug abusers' lives: medical condition, employment, drug use, alcohol use, illegal activity (other than purchase and possession of illicit drugs), family relationships, and psychiatric condition (McLellan et al., 1992; McLellan, Luborsky, Woody, & O'Brien, 1980).

2. Tarter and Hegedus (1991) developed the *Drug Use Screening Inventory* (DUSI), a screening instrument that assesses multiple problems of individuals who abuse alcohol and other drugs, as described previously. The DUSI-R (Tarter, 1990) is a multidimensional screening tool, which detects disturbances in the following 10 domains: substance use, behavior patterns, health status, psychiatric disorders, social competency, family system, school performance/adjustment, work adjustment, peer relationships, and leisure/recreation. The relative severity of each of these problem domains is rank ordered, which helps in prioritizing treatment for each client. It is reported to be relatively brief to administer and is useful for monitoring treatment progress.

3. One of the few brief screenings designed specifically for drug use is the *Drug Abuse Screening Test* (DAST-10; Skinner, 1982). It is a 10-item questionnaire that yields a "suggested action" based on the score including a "monitor, reassess at a later date," "further investigation" warranted, and "intensive assessment" warranted, assisting the clinician in identifying the next step in the assessment or treatment process.

4. The *Substance Abuse Subtle Screening Inventory* (SASSI-3; G. A. Miller, 1997) is intended to be a relatively brief, inexpensive assessment tool that can accurately differentiate between use, abuse, and dependence in clients. It addresses issues

of validity encountered by other instruments and earlier versions of the SASSI and is easy to score and use with clients.

5. The *Structured Clinical Interview for DSM* (First, Spitzer, Gibbon, & Williams, 1997) is important to consider as well. Although it is time consuming, it is also quite thorough, completely compatible with the diagnostic nomenclature, and very useful in ensuring consistency in diagnoses and problem identification.

6. For several instruments consistent with the Motivational Interviewing and Stages of Change models, see *SAMHSA Treatment Improvement Protocol Series No. 35* (CSAT, 1999).

None of the tools mentioned previously are recommended for use outside the context of a complete biopsychosocial evaluation. Additional considerations for assessment include assessing for the chemical evidence of drug use as well as assessing for criminal justice issues, risk for contraction and spread of HIV/AIDS, hepatitis, and tuberculosis, and co-occurring mental health disorders that require integrated treatment. Any of these considerations require a concomitant adjustment in assessment and then treatment strategy.

ETIOLOGICAL CONSIDERATIONS

Most people who use drugs do not become dependent on them. There are many factors, including drug availability, route of administration, genetics, family environment and history of drug use, stress, and life events, that contribute to the transition from drug use to drug addiction. A few of the notable recent findings are elucidated in the following discussion. For a more complete evaluation of etiological considerations, see Ott, Tarter, and Ammerman (1999).

According to Kendler, Karkowski, Neale, and Prescott (2000), to develop appropriate prevention and treatment approaches to substance abuse, we need to understand the sources of individual differences in risk. Evidence suggests that psychoactive substance use disorder aggregates in families and may be due to genetic factors. The authors found that twin resemblance for substance use, heavy use, abuse, and dependence was substantial and consistently greater in monozygotic twins than dizygotic twins. Two factors must be considered: type of drug and level of use/abuse. For cannabis and hallucinogen use, model fitting suggested that twin resemblance was due to both genetic and environmental/familial factors. For sedative, stimulant, cocaine, and opiate use, however, twin resemblance was caused solely by genetic factors. However, twin resemblance for heavy use, abuse, and dependence resulted from only genetic factors (with the exception of cocaine abuse and stimulant dependence), with heritability of liability ranging from 60% to 80%. The authors concluded that the family environment plays a role in twin resemblance for some forms of substance use; however, heavy use, abuse, and dependence in men is caused mostly by genetic factors, and heritability estimates are high.

Additional familial factors often cited anecdotally include early exposure to use in the environment, significant negative events in the home of a child such as parental-marital distress, and a history of sexual abuse or physical abuse.

According to Koob and LeMoal (1997), the current challenge is to discover what neurobiological elements convey the individual differences in vulnerability to addiction. The authors use the concept of spiraling distress to describe the progressive dysregulation of the brain reward system in the context of repeated addiction cycles. The focus for the neurobiological mechanism for the positive-reinforcing effects of drugs has been the mesocorticolimbic dopamine system and its connections in the basal forebrain. In addition, the drug abstinence syndrome, which leads to negative affective states, may be playing a role reinforcing drug abuse. There is increasing evidence in both animals and humans that the presence of a negative affective state may not only signal the beginning of the development of dependence, but also contribute to vulnerability to relapse and have motivational significance. At the neurobiological level, two models have been conceptualized to explain the changes in motivation for drug-seeking behavior: counteradaptation and sensitization. Both of these models focus on neurobiological changes at the molecular, cellular, and systems levels leading to reinforcing effects of drugs. In terms of relapse, studies suggest that stressful stimuli and neuropharmacological agents that activate the mesocorticolimbic dopamine system can rapidly lead to increases in drug use that has been previously extinguished. Vulnerability to relapse, however, has both genetic and environmental components.

Volkow and colleagues (as cited in Moore, 1999) reported that people with few dopamine D2 receptors may be at greater risk of abusing psychostimulants than those with more receptors. The authors suggest that there is an "optimal range for dopamine D2 stimulation," and for people with few receptors, psychostimulants boost stimulation into that optimal range. For those with many receptors, however, a similar drug dose causes overstimulation and unpleasant drug responses. According to Volkow, individuals who are addicted to a substance, whether they are using cocaine, alcohol, or heroin, have low numbers of dopamine D2 receptors. The authors suggest that assessing the number of receptors may indicate whether a person is likely to abuse drugs.

Numerous risk and several protective factors have been identified for special populations in the United States. A few of the sociocultural risk issues identified include the stresses of living between cultures, economic deprivation, racism, language barriers, difficulties with the educational system, and early exposure to use (Bettes, Dusenbury, Kerner, James-Ortiz, & Botvin, 1990; Gordon, 1994). For an excellent review of considerations for culturally and ethnically diverse groups in the United States, see Fisher and Harrison (2000).

SUMMARY

Psychoactive drugs have been available to specific cultures at specific times throughout history for ritualized, ceremonial, or celebratory use. Currently, almost all psychoactive substances are available to anyone seeking them, and each substance may be as much as 100 times more potent than its historical counterpart. The costs to individuals, their natural supports, and their extended community are taxing our collective personal and economic resources. The most current epidemiological studies suggest that individuals who use, abuse, and become dependent on substances are a heterogeneous group requiring multiple and flexible methods of study and application. They also require that practitioners of different stripes become competent and skilled in the identification, screening, assessment, referral, and participation in the treatment of people with psychoactive substance use disorders. There are numerous screening and assessment tools available, as well as a growing appreciation for consistency in clinical decision making. However, the most useful assessment methodologies are those that enhance treatment outcomes as well as assist practitioners in gathering information necessary for treatment planning. Last, if comorbidity and client complexity are the expectation and not the exception, diagnostic methods and assessments that are designed to elicit cooperation and focus on clients' strengths and resources are essential in building a well-rounded clinical picture. This chapter serves as one brief foray into a burgeoning literature concerning psychoactive substance use disorders involving drugs. The reader is encouraged to explore many of the citations as extensive chapters, texts, and peer-reviewed articles precede the writing of this chapter.

REFERENCES

American Psychiatric Association. (2000). *Diagnostic and statistical manual of mental disorders* (4th ed., text rev.). Washington, DC: Author.

American Society of Addiction Medicine. (2001). *Patient placement criteria for the treatment of substance-related disorders* (2nd ed., rev.). Washington, DC: Author.

Austin, G. A. (1979). *Perspectives on the history of psychoactive substance use* (DHEW Publication No. ADM-79-810, out of print). Retrieved June 6, 2002, from http://itsa.ucsf.edu /~ddrc/histdrg_frset.html.

Bastiens, L., Francis, G., & Lewis, K. (2000). The RAFFT as a screening tool for adolescent substance use disorders. *American Journal on Addictions, 9,* 10–16.

Bettes, B. L., Dusenbury, L., Kerner, J., James-Ortiz, S., & Botvin, G. L. (1990). Ethnicity and psychosocial factors in alcohol and tobacco use in adolescence. *Child Development, 61,* 557–565.

Brady, S., Hiam, C. M., Saemann, R., Humbert, L., Fleming, M. Z., & Dawkins-Brickhouse, K. (1996). Dual-diagnosis: A treatment model for substance abuse and major mental illness. *Community Mental Health Journal, 32,* 573–578.

Center for Substance Abuse Treatment. (1999). *Enhancing motivation for change in substance abuse treatment* (Treatment Improvement Protocol [TIP] Series). Washington, DC: U.S. Government Printing Office.

Center for Substance Abuse Treatment. (2001). *The role and current status of patient placement criteria in the treatment of substance use disorders* (Treatment Improvement Protocol [TIP] Series). Washington, DC: U.S. Government Printing Office.

Cooney, N. L., Zweben, A., & Fleming, M. F. (1995). Screening for alcohol problems and at-risk drinking in health-care settings. In R. K. Hester & W. R. Miller (Eds.), *Handbook of alcoholism treatment approaches: Effective approaches* (2nd ed., pp. 45–60). Boston: Allyn & Bacon.

First, M. B., Spitzer, R. L., Gibbon, M., & Williams, J. B. W. (1997). *User's guide to the Structured Clinical Interview for DSM-IV Axis I Disorders: Clinician version* (SCID-CV). Washington, DC: American Psychiatric Press.

Fisher, G. L., & Harrison, T. C. (2000). *Substance abuse: Information for school counselors, social workers, therapists, and counselors* (2nd ed.). Boston: Allyn & Bacon.

Friedmann, P. D., McCullough, D., & Saitz, R. (2001). Screening and intervention for illicit drug abuse: A national survey of primary care physicians and psychiatrists. *Archives of Internal Medicine, 161,* 248–251.

Goldstein, A. (2001). *Addiction: From biology to drug policy* (2nd ed.). New York: Oxford University Press.

Gordon, J. U. (Ed.). (1994). *Managing multiculturalism in substance abuse services.* Thousand Oaks, CA: Sage.

Julien, R. M. (1997). *A primer of drug action: A concise, nontechnical guide to the actions, uses, and side effects of psychoactive drugs* (8th ed.). New York: Freeman.

Kendler, K. S., Karkowski, L. M., Neale, M. C., & Prescott, C. A. (2000). Illicit psychoactive substance use, heavy use, abuse, and dependence in a U.S. population-based sample of male twins. *Archives of General Psychiatry, 57,* 261–269.

Koob, G., & LeMoal, M. (1997). Drug abuse: Hedonic homeostatic dysregulation. *Science, 279,* 52–58.

Leshner, A. I. (1999). Science-based views of drug addiction treatment. *Journal of the American Medical Association, 282,* 1314–1316.

Martin, C. S., & Winters, K. C. (1998). Screening instruments for adolescent alcohol use disorders. *Alcohol Health and Research World, 22,* 102–104.

McCarty, D., Caspi, Y., Panas, L., Krakow, M., & Mulligan, D. H. (2000). Detoxification centers: Who's in the revolving door? *Journal of Behavioral Health Services and Research, 27,* 245–257.

McEvoy, A. W., Kitchen, N. D., & Thomas, D. G. T. (1998). Intracerebral hemorrhage caused by drug abuse. *Lancet, 351,* 1029–1030.

McLellan, A. T., Kushner, H., Metzger, D., Peters, R., Smith, I., Grissom, G., et al. (1992). The Addiction Severity Index (5th ed.). *Journal of Substance Abuse Treatment, 9,* 199–213.

McLellan, A. T., Luborsky, L., Woody, G. E., & O'Brien, C. P. (1980). An improved diagnostic evaluation instrument for substance abuse patients: The Addiction Severity Index. *Journal of Nervous and Mental Diseases, 168,* 26–33.

Miller, G. A. (1997). *The Substance Abuse Subtle Screening Inventory-3 manual.* Spencer, IN: Spencer Evening World.

Miller, S. D., & Berg, I. K. (1992). *Working with the problem drinker.* New York: Norton.

Miller, W. R., & Rollnick, S. (1991). *Motivational interviewing: Preparing people to change addictive behavior.* New York: Guilford Press.

Minkoff, K. (1998). *Individuals with co-occurring psychiatric and substance disorders in managed care systems: Standards of care, practice guidelines, workforce competencies and training curricula.* University of Pennsylvania Center for Mental Health Policy and Services Research. Available from www.upenn.edu/cmhpsr.

Minkoff, K. (2000). *State of Arizona service planning guidelines: Co-occurring psychiatric and substance disorders* (edited version). Acton, MA: Author.

Moore, P. (1999). Brain chemistry behind drug abuse investigated. *Lancet, 354,* 924.

National Institute on Drug Abuse. (1998a). *Methamphetamine abuse and addiction.* National Institute on Drug Abuse Research Report Series (NIH Publication No. 98-4210). Washington, DC: U.S. Department of Health and Human Services.

National Institute on Drug Abuse. (1998b). *Nicotine addiction.* National Institute on Drug Abuse Research Report Series (NIH Publication No. 98-4342). Washington, DC: U.S. Department of Health and Human Services.

National Institute on Drug Abuse. (1999). *Cocaine abuse and addiction.* National Institute on Drug Abuse Research Report Series (NIH Publication No. 99-4342). Washington, DC: U.S. Department of Health and Human Services.

National Institute on Drug Abuse. (2000a). *Anabolic steroid abuse.* National Institute on Drug Abuse Research Report Series (NIH Publication No. 00-3721). Washington, DC: U.S. Department of Health and Human Services.

National Institute on Drug Abuse. (2000b). *Heroin abuse and addiction.* National Institute on Drug Abuse Research Report Series (NIH Publication No. 00-4165). Washington, DC: U.S. Department of Health and Human Services.

National Institute on Drug Abuse. (2000c). *Inhalant abuse.* National Institute on Drug Abuse Research Report Series (NIH Publication No. 00-3818). Washington, DC: U.S. Department of Health and Human Services.

Northwest Frontier Addiction Technology Transfer Center. (2001). *Performance assessment rubrics for the addiction counseling competencies* (Oregon Office of Alcohol and Drug Abuse Programs). Salem: Author.

Office of National Drug Control Policy. (2001). *The economic costs of drug abuse in the United States, 1992–1998* (Publication No. NCJ-190636). Washington, DC: Executive Office of the President.

Ott, P. J., Tarter, R. E., & Ammerman, R. T. (1999). *Sourcebook on substance abuse: Etiology, epidemiology, assessment, and treatment.* Boston: Allyn & Bacon.

Petchers, M., & Singer, M. (1990). Clinical applicability of a substance abuse screening instrument. *Journal of Adolescent Chemical Dependency, 1,* 47–56.

Prochaska, J. O., & DiClemente, C. C. (1991). Stages of change in the modification of problem behaviors. In M. Hersen, R. M. Eisler, & P. M. Miller (Eds.), *Progress in behavior modification* (pp. 184–214). Newbury Park, CA: Sage.

Prochaska, J. O., DiClemente, C. C., & Norcross, J. C. (1992). In search of how people change: Applications to addictive behaviors. *American Psychologist, 47,* 1102–1114.

Rahdert, E. (1991). *The adolescent assessment and referral manual* (DHHS Publication No. ADM-91-1735). Rockville, MD: National Institute on Drug Abuse.

Riehman, K. S., Hser, Y.-I., & Zeller, M. (2000). Gender differences in how intimate partners influence drug treatment motivation. *Journal of Drug Issues, 30,* 823–839.

Rivara, F. P., Muelle, B. A., Somes, G., Mendoza, C. T., Rushforth, N. B., & Kellerman, A. L. (1997). Alcohol and illicit drug abuse and the risk of violent death in the home. *Journal of the American Medical Association, 278,* 569–575.

Robert Wood Johnson Foundation. (2001). *Substance abuse: The nation's number one health problem: Key indicators for policy.* Princeton, NJ: Author.

Rosengren, D. B., Downey, L., & Donovan, D. M. (2000). I already stopped: Abstinence prior to treatment. *Addiction, 95,* 65–77.

Schwartz, R. H., & Wirtz, P. W. (1990). Potential substance abuse: Detection among adolescent patients using the Drug and Alcohol Problem (DAP) Quick Screen, a 30-item questionnaire. *Clinical Pediatrics, 29,* 322–326.

Skinner, H. (1982). The Drug Abuse Screening Test. *Addictive Behaviors, 7,* 363–371.

Soderstrom, C. A., Smith, G. S., Dischinger, P. C., McDuff, D. R., Hebel, J. R., Gorelick, D. A., et al. (1997). Psychoactive substance use disorders among seriously injured trauma center patients. *Journal of the American Medical Association, 277,* 1769–1774.

Spittal, P. M., & Schechter, M. T. (2001). Injection drug use and despair through the lens of gender. *Canadian Medical Association Journal, 164,* 802–804.

Substance Abuse and Mental Health Services Administration. (1999). *National Household Survey on Drug Abuse: Population estimates, 1999.* Retrieved May 13, 2002, from www .samhsa.gov/OAS/NHSDA/tobacco/highlights.htm.

Substance Abuse and Mental Health Services Administration. (2000). *National Household Survey on Drug Abuse: Population estimates, 2000.* Retrieved May 13, 2002, from www .samhsa.gov/oas/NHSDA/2kNHSDA/highlights.htm.

Tarter, R. E. (1990). Evaluation and treatment of adolescent substance abuse: A decision tree method. *American Journal of Drug and Alcohol Abuse, 16,* 1–46.

Tarter, R. E., & Hegedus, A. M. (1991). The Drug Use Screening Inventory. *Alcohol Health and Research World, 15,* 65–76.

Tarter, R. E., Laird, S. B., Bukstein, O., & Kaminer, Y. (1992). Validation of the adolescent Drug Use Screening Inventory: Preliminary findings. *Psychology of Addictive Behaviors, 6,* 322–326.

Vastag, B. (2001). Mixed message on prescription drug abuse. *Journal of the American Medical Association, 285,* 2183–2184.

Weisner, C., Mertens, J., Parthasarathy, S., Moore, C., & Lu, Y. (2001). Integrating primary care with addiction treatment: A randomized controlled trial. *Journal of the American Medical Association, 286,* 1715–1723.

Winters, K. (1992). Development of an adolescent alcohol and other drug abuse screening scale: Personal Experiences Screening Questionnaire. *Addictive Behavior, 17,* 479–490.

CHAPTER 8

Schizophrenia

KIM T. MUESER and MICHELLE P. SALYERS

DESCRIPTION OF THE DISORDER

SCHIZOPHRENIA IS THE most severely debilitating of all adult psychiatric illnesses. Despite the recent trend toward community-oriented treatment, more psychiatric hospital beds are occupied by patients with schizophrenia than any other disorder. Even when patients receive optimal treatments, many continue to experience substantial impairments throughout most of their lives.

Since schizophrenia was first described more than 100 years ago, the nature of the disorder has been hotly debated, and public misconceptions about it have been commonplace. In recent years, there has been a growing consensus among clinicians and researchers to more rigorously define the psychopathology and diagnostic features of this disorder. Once referred to as a "wastebasket diagnosis," the term *schizophrenia* is now used to describe a specific clinical syndrome. An understanding of the core clinical features of schizophrenia is necessary for differential diagnosis and treatment planning. After many years of struggling to improve the long-term course of schizophrenia, there is now abundant evidence that combined pharmacological and psychosocial interventions can have a major impact on improving functioning. This chapter provides an up-to-date review of schizophrenia, with a particular focus on the psychopathology of the illness and its impact on other domains of functioning.

Schizophrenia is characterized by impairments in social functioning, including difficulty establishing and maintaining interpersonal relationships, problems working or fulfilling other instrumental roles (e.g., student, homemaker), and difficulties caring for oneself (e.g., poor grooming and hygiene). These problems in daily living, in the absence of significant impairment in intellectual functioning, are the most distinguishing characteristics of schizophrenia, and are a necessary criterion for its diagnosis according to most diagnostic systems (e.g., *Diagnostic and Statistical Manual of Mental Disorders,* fourth edition [*DSM-IV*], American Psychiatric Association [APA], 1994). Consequently, many patients with the illness depend on others to meet their daily living needs. For example, estimates suggest that between 40% and 60% of patients with schizophrenia live with relatives, and an even higher percentage rely on relatives for caregiving (Goldman, 1982; Torrey, 1995). Patients without family contact typically rely on mental health, residential, and case management services to get their basic needs met. In the worst-case scenario, patients who have insufficient contact with relatives and who fall between the cracks of the social service delivery system end up in jail (Torrey et al., 1992) or become homeless, with between 10% and 20% of homeless people having schizophrenia (Susser, Struening, & Conover, 1989).

In addition to the problems in daily living that characterize schizophrenia, patients with the illness experience a range of different symptoms. The most common symptoms include positive symptoms (e.g., hallucinations and delusions), negative symptoms (e.g., social withdrawal, apathy, anhedonia), cognitive impairments (e.g., memory difficulties, planning ability, abstract thinking), and problems with mood (e.g., depression, anxiety, anger). The specific nature of these symptoms is described in greater detail in the Clinical Picture section. The symptoms of schizophrenia appear to account for some, but not all, of the problems in social functioning (Glynn, 1998).

The various impairments associated with schizophrenia tend to be long term, punctuated by fluctuations in severity over time. For this reason, schizophrenia has a broad impact on the family, and patients are often impeded from pursuing personal life goals. Despite the severity of the disorder, advances in the treatment of schizophrenia provide solid hope for improving the outcome.

Case Study

Jamie is a 25-year-old man who was diagnosed with schizophrenia five years ago. During the summer before his junior year in college, he was working in a busy office. He became increasingly concerned that his office mates were "out to get him" and that there was an intricate plot to discredit him. He also believed that his coworkers were secretly communicating with each other about him through certain facial expressions, choice of clothing, and configuration of items on their desks. As his paranoia escalated, he became more disorganized in his thinking and behavior, he was less able to take care of his daily activities, and he could no longer come to work. He began to believe he was dying and attributed a variety of factors that were playing a role in his demise, including being poisoned by indoor air pollution. These symptoms led to a psychiatric hospitalization where he was first diagnosed with provisional schizophreniform disorder and treated with antipsychotic medication. At that time, he had to leave his job, quit school, and move back home with his parents. After six months of impairment, his diagnosis was changed to schizophrenia.

Jamie benefited from his treatment, and his most flagrant symptoms improved substantially, including his belief that others were plotting against him. Nevertheless, he continues to struggle with schizophrenia today, five years later. Even in the absence of psychotic symptoms, he maintains poor eye contact and shows little facial expression. For example, he rarely smiles

(Continued)

spontaneously. His hygiene is generally good, but when his psychotic symptoms increase, he becomes more disheveled, smokes more cigarettes, and becomes agitated. He is prescribed medications, which he says help him feel better, less paranoid, and decrease his ideas of reference (i.e., beliefs that things around him have special meaning for him). However, Jamie lacks basic insight into his psychiatric disorder, and he does not believe he has a mental illness. Jamie also does not like having to take medications, partly because of the weight gain he has experienced from his antipsychotic medication. He periodically stops taking his medications when he feels better. These breaks from taking medication often lead to relapses in his symptoms, a deterioration in functioning, and sometimes rehospitalization.

Although Jamie continues to have symptoms and impairments of schizophrenia, he has also made some positive steps toward improving the quality of his life, with the help of his treatment team and his family. When Jamie first moved back home, there was a significant amount of tension in the household, as Jamie's parent and younger sisters did not understand the nature of his illness and were upset by his occasionally disruptive living habits, such as staying up much of the night. With the help of a clinician who worked with Jamie and his family for 15 months after Jamie returned home, his family was able to learn more about schizophrenia, the principles of its treatment, and strategies for solving problems together. After several years of living at home, Jamie moved out two years ago to his own apartment. Jamie has been able to live on his own with the support of his family members and his case manager, who coordinates his care with the treatment team. After attending a local day treatment program, Jamie became interested in working. The mental health center where he receives his treatment had a supported employment program in which an employment specialist was assigned to Jamie to help him find a job in his area of interest, and to stay on the job through support and help with his employer. Jamie said he liked working with animals, and he was able to get a job working part-time at a local pet store, where he cares for the animals, feeds them, and cleans their cages. Jamie has kept this job for almost two years; on two occasions, he has had to take some time off when he had a relapse of his symptoms and had to return to the hospital. His employment specialist arranged with his employer for him to return to his job when he had recovered from his relapse.

Many of the symptoms described in this vignette are highlighted in *DSM-IV* criteria (see Diagnostic Considerations section and Table 8.1). Jamie experienced at least two *characteristic symptoms*, including delusions (e.g., his beliefs about his coworkers) and negative symptoms (e.g., flat facial expression). He experienced clear impairments in social/occupational functioning—at the time of diagnosis, he was no longer able to care for himself or to come to work. Duration criteria of *DSM-IV* were met because these difficulties lasted longer than six months. In addition, other diagnoses were ruled out (e.g., mood disorders, substance abuse, developmental disorders). In addition to describing some of the symptoms of schizophrenia, this vignette illustrates that people with this illness are often able to lead rewarding and productive lives, usually with the help of pharmacological and psychological treatment, as well as social supports, despite continued symptoms and impairment from the illness.

Table 8.1
DSM-IV Criteria for the Diagnosis of Schizophrenia

A. Presence of at least two or more of the following characteristic symptoms in the active phase for at least 1 month (unless the symptoms are successfully treated):

1. Delusions
2. Hallucinations
3. Disorganized speech (e.g., frequent derailment or incoherence)
4. Grossly disorganized or catatonic behavior
5. Negative symptoms (i.e., affect flattening, alogia, or avolition)

Note: Only one of these symptoms is required if delusions are bizarre or hallucinations consist of a voice keeping up a running commentary on the person's behavior or thoughts, or two or more voices conversing with each other.

B. Social/occupational dysfunction: For a significant proportion of the time from the onset of the disturbance, one or more areas of functioning, such as work, interpersonal relations, or self-care, is markedly below the level achieved prior to the onset (or, when the onset is in childhood or adolescence, failure to achieve expected level of interpersonal, academic, or occupational achievement).

C. Duration: Continuous signs of the disturbance persist for at least 6 months. This 6-month period must include at least 1 month of symptoms that meet criterion A (i.e., active-phase symptoms) and may include periods of prodromal or residual symptoms. During these prodromal or residual periods, the signs of the disturbance may be manifested by only negative symptoms or by two or more symptoms listed in criterion A present in an attenuated form (e.g., odd beliefs, unusual perceptual experiences).

D. Schizoaffective and mood disorders exclusion: Schizoaffective disorder and mood disorder with psychotic features have been ruled out because either (1) no major depressive or manic episodes have occurred concurrently with the active-phase symptoms or (2) if mood episodes have occurred during active-phase symptoms, their total duration has been brief relative to the duration of the active and residual periods.

E. Substance/general medical condition exclusion: The disturbance is not due to the direct effects of a substance (e.g., drugs of abuse, medication) or a general medical condition.

Source: From *Diagnostic and Statistical Manual of Mental Disorders*, 4th Edition (*DSM-IV*), 1994, American Psychiatric Association.

EPIDEMIOLOGY

The lifetime prevalence of schizophrenia (including the closely related disorders of schizoaffective disorder and schizophreniform disorder) is approximately 1% (Keith, Regier, & Rae, 1991). In general, prevalence of schizophrenia is remarkably stable across a wide range of different populations, such as gender, race, religion, or level of industrialization (Jablensky, 1999). However, schizophrenia is more common in urban areas of industrialized countries (Peen & Dekker, 1997; Takei, Sham, O'Callaghan, Glover, & Murray, 1995; Torrey, Bowler, & Clark, 1997). This increased risk appears to be related not only to the likelihood that people with schizophrenia drift to urban areas, but also to being born in urban areas (Torrey et al., 1997).

As schizophrenia frequently has an onset during early adulthood, people with the illness are less likely to marry or remain married, particularly males (Eaton, 1975; Munk-Jørgensen, 1987), and are less likely to complete higher levels of education (Kessler, Foster, Saunders, & Stang, 1995). It has long been known that there is an association between poverty and schizophrenia, with people belonging to lower socioeconomic classes more likely to develop the disorder (Hollingshead & Redlich, 1958; Salokangas, 1978). Historically, two theories have been advanced to account for this association. The *social drift* hypothesis postulates that the debilitating effects of schizophrenia on capacity to work result in a lowering of socioeconomic means—hence poverty (Aro, Aro, & Keskimäki, 1995). The *environmental stress* hypothesis proposes that the high levels of stress associated with poverty precipitate schizophrenia in some individuals who would not otherwise develop the illness (Bruce, Takeuchi, & Leaf, 1991). Both of these explanations may be partly true, and longitudinal research on changes in socioeconomic class status and schizophrenia provide conflicting results. For example, Fox (1990) reanalyzed data from several longitudinal studies and found that after controlling for initial levels of socioeconomic class, downward drift was not evident. However, Dohrenwend et al. (1992) did find evidence for social drift, even after controlling for socioeconomic class. Thus, more work is needed to sort out the relationships between socioeconomic status and schizophrenia.

CLINICAL PICTURE

Most studies on the dimensions of schizophrenia agree on at least three major groups of symptoms (Liddle, 1987; Mueser, Curran, & McHugo, 1997; Van Der Does, Dingemans, Linszen, Nugter, & Scholte, 1993), including positive symptoms, negative symptoms, and cognitive impairments. *Positive symptoms* refer to thoughts, sensory experiences, and behaviors that are present in patients, but are ordinarily absent in people without the illness. Common examples of positive symptoms include hallucinations (e.g., hearing voices), delusions (e.g., believing that people are persecuting you), and bizarre behavior (e.g., maintaining a peculiar posture for no apparent reason). *Negative symptoms,* on the other hand, refer to the absence or diminution of cognitions, feelings, or behaviors, which are ordinarily present in people without the illness. Common negative symptoms include blunted or flattened affect (e.g., diminished facial expressiveness), poverty of speech (i.e., diminished verbal communication), anhedonia (i.e., inability to experience pleasure), apathy, psychomotor retardation (e.g., slow rate of speech), and physical inertia. *Cognitive impairments* refer to difficulties in memory, attention, abstract reasoning (i.e., understanding a concept), and executive functions (e.g., ability to anticipate or plan). These impairments may interfere with patients' abilities to focus for sustained periods on work or recreational pursuits, interact effectively with others, perform basic activities of daily living, or participate in conventional psychotherapeutic interventions (Bellack, Gold, & Buchanan, 1999; Brekke, Raine, Ansel, Lencz, & Bird, 1997; Sevy & Davidson, 1995; Velligan et al., 1997). Cognitive impairments also result in difficulties generalizing training or knowledge to other areas (i.e., transfer of training problems). Thus, many rehabilitative efforts focus on teaching patients directly in the environment in which skills will be used.

The positive symptoms of schizophrenia tend to fluctuate over the course of the disorder and are often in remission between episodes of the illness. In addition, positive symptoms tend to be responsive to the effects of antipsychotic medication (Kane & Marder, 1993). In contrast, negative symptoms and cognitive impairments tend to be stable over time and are less responsive to antipsychotic medications (Greden & Tandon, 1991). However, there is some evidence that atypical antipsychotic medications, such as clozapine, risperidone, and olanzapine, have a beneficial impact on negative symptoms and cognitive functioning (Green et al., 1997; Tollefson & Sanger, 1997; Wahlbeck, Cheine, Essali, & Adams, 1999).

Aside from the core symptoms of schizophrenia, many patients with schizophrenia experience negative emotions (e.g., depression, anxiety, and anger) because of their illness. Depression is very common among people with schizophrenia and has been associated with poor outcomes (e.g., increased hospital use, lower employment rates) and suicidal tendencies (Sands & Harrow, 1999). In addition, it is generally estimated that approximately 10% of the people with this illness die from suicide (Drake, Gates, Whitaker, & Cotton, 1985; Roy, 1986). However, recent data and modeling techniques show lifetime rates of suicide for schizophrenia at 4%, compared to 6% for affective disorders and 7% for alcohol dependence (Inskip, Harris, & Barraclough, 1998). Difficulties with anxiety are common, and are often due to positive symptoms, such as hallucinations or paranoid delusions (Argyle, 1990; Penn, Hope, Spaulding, & Kucera, 1994). Finally, anger and hostility may also be present, especially when the patient is paranoid (Bartels, Drake, Wallach, & Freeman, 1991).

In addition to the symptoms and negative emotions commonly present in schizophrenia, individuals with this diagnosis often have comorbid substance use disorders. Epidemiological surveys have repeatedly found that people with psychiatric disorders are at increased risk for alcohol and drug abuse (Mueser, Yarnold, & Bellack, 1992; Mueser, Yarnold, et al., 1990). This risk is highest for people with the most severe psychiatric disorders, including schizophrenia and bipolar disorder. For example, individuals with schizophrenia are more than four times as likely to have a substance abuse disorder than individuals in the general population (Regier et al., 1990). In general, approximately 50% of all patients with schizophrenia have a lifetime history of substance use disorder, and 25% to 35% have a recent history of such a disorder (Mueser, Bennett, & Kushner, 1995).

Presence of comorbid substance use disorders in schizophrenia has consistently been found to be associated with a worse course of the illness, including increased vulnerability to relapses and hospitalizations, housing instability and homelessness, violence, economic family burden, and treatment noncompliance (Drake & Brunette, 1998). For these reasons, recognition and treatment of substance use disorders in patients with schizophrenia are crucial to the overall management of the illness.

Another important clinical feature of schizophrenia is lack of insight and compliance with treatment (Amador & Gorman, 1998; Amador, Strauss, Yale, & Gorman, 1991). Many patients with schizophrenia have little or no insight into the fact that they have a psychiatric illness, or even that they have any problems at all. This denial of illness can lead to noncompliance with recommended treatments, such as psychotropic medications and psychosocial therapies (McEvoy et al., 1989). Furthermore, fostering insight into the illness is a difficult and often impossible task with these patients.

Noncompliance with treatment is a related problem, but can also occur because of the severe negativity often present in the illness, independent of poor insight. Problems with paranoia and distrust may contribute to noncompliance, in that some patients may believe medications or treatment providers are dangerous to them. Further, side effects of some medications, particularly the conventional antipsychotics, are unpleasant and can also lead to noncompliance. Medication noncompliance increases the risk of patients to relapse, and is, therefore, a major concern to clinical treatment providers (A. Buchanan, 1992). Strategies for enhancing compliance include helping the patient become a more active participant in his or her treatment, identifying personal goals of treatment that have high relevance for that individual, and helping patients develop strategies for incorporating the taking of medication into their daily routines (Azrin & Teichner, 1998; Corrigan, Liberman, & Engle, 1990; Kemp, Hayward, Applewhaite, Everitt, & David, 1996; Kemp, Kirov, Everitt, Hayward, & David, 1998).

People with schizophrenia are sometimes assumed to be violent or otherwise dangerous. Indeed, rates of violence have been found to be higher in people with schizophrenia and other severe mental illnesses as compared to the general population (Hodgins, Mednick, Brennan, Schulsinger, & Engberg, 1996; Swanson, Holzer, Ganju, & Jono, 1990). Actual rates of violence are difficult to ascertain. Rates vary widely depending on source of information (e.g., self-report vs. collateral reports), definition of violence, population studied (e.g., inpatients vs. outpatients), and where the research takes place (e.g., country). However, the majority of people with schizophrenia and other mental illnesses are not violent (Swanson, 1994). When violence does occur, it is often associated with substance abuse (Steadman et al., 1998) or the combination of substance abuse and medication noncompliance (Swartz, Swanson, Hiday, Borum, Wagner, & Burns, 1998). Other factors such as psychopathy (Nolan, Volavka, Mohr, & Czobor, 1999) or antisocial personality disorder (Hodgins & Côté, 1993, 1996) also have been implicated. Finally, targets of violence tend to be family members or friends rather than strangers (Steadman et al., 1998).

While there is an increased rate of violence in schizophrenia, people with schizophrenia are much more likely to be the victims of violence. For example, in a recent survey of a large number of people with severe mental illness, one third of the men and women with schizophrenia reported severe physical or sexual assault in the past year (Goodman et al., 2001). These numbers are striking compared to estimates of the general population, in which 0.3% of women and 3.5% of men reported assault in the past year (Tjaden & Thoennes, 1998). Similarly, people with severe mental illness have been found to be more likely than a community sample to be victims of violent crime (Hiday, Swartz, Swanson, Borum, & Wagner, 1999). In addition, between 34% and 53% of patients with severe mental illness report childhood sexual or physical abuse (Greenfield, Strakowski, Tohen, Batson, & Kolbrener, 1994; Jacobson & Herald, 1990; Rose, Peabody, & Stratigeas, 1991; Ross, Anderson, & Clark, 1994), and 43% to 81% report some type of victimization over their lives (Carmen, Rieker, & Mills, 1984; Hutchings & Dutton, 1993; Jacobson, 1989; Jacobson & Richardson, 1987; Lipschitz et al., 1996). Studies of the prevalence of interpersonal trauma in women with severe mental illness indicate especially high vulnerability to victimization, with rates ranging as high as 77% to 97% for episodically homeless women (Davies-Netzley, Hurlburt, & Hough, 1996; Goodman, Dutton, & Harris, 1995). Thus, interpersonal violence is so common in people with severe mental illness that it can be considered a normative experience (Goodman, Dutton, & Harris, 1997).

COURSE AND PROGNOSIS

Schizophrenia usually has an onset in late adolescence or early adulthood, most often between the ages of 16 and 25. Because schizophrenia usually occurs during early adulthood, many developmental tasks are disrupted, including forming close interpersonal or dating relationships, pursuing higher education, career development, separating from parents, and identity formation. Increased attention to first break or early onset psychosis may potentially avoid some of the long-term problems in these areas (C. V. Lincoln & McGorry, 1995). It is extremely rare for the first onset of schizophrenia to occur before adolescence (e.g., before the age of twelve), with most diagnostic systems considering childhood-onset schizophrenia to be a disorder different from adolescent or adult-onset schizophrenia (APA, 1994). More common than childhood schizophrenia, but, nevertheless, rare in the total population of people with schizophrenia, are individuals who develop the illness later in life, such as after the age of 45 (C. I. Cohen, 1990). Late-onset schizophrenia is characterized by positive symptoms, but is less likely to involve formal thought disorder and negative symptoms (Bartels, Mueser, & Miles, 1998). Late-onset schizophrenia is further complicated by the lack of clear-cut distinguishing characteristics that discriminate this disorder from a variety of disorders that develop later in old age (Howard, Almeida, & Levy, 1994).

Before onset of schizophrenia, some, but not all, people have impairments in their premorbid social functioning (Zigler & Glick, 1986). For example, some people who later develop schizophrenia were more socially isolated, passed fewer social-sexual developmental milestones, and had fewer friends in childhood and adolescence. Aside from problems in social functioning, before developing schizophrenia, some individuals in childhood display a maladaptive pattern of behaviors, including disruptive behavior, problems in school, and impulsivity (Baum & Walker, 1995; Hans, Marcus, Henson, Auerbach, & Mirsky, 1992). Similarly, symptoms of conduct disorder in childhood, such as repeated fighting, truancy, and lying, have been found to be predictive of the later development of schizophrenia (Asarnow, 1988; Cannon et al., 1993; Neumann, Grimes, Walker, & Baum 1995; Robins, 1966; Robins & Price, 1991; Rutter, 1984; Watt, 1978). However, other patients display no unusual characteristics in their premorbid functioning.

A second moderating factor related to the prognosis of schizophrenia is patient gender (Haas & Garratt, 1998). Women tend to have later onset of the illness, spend less time in hospitals, and demonstrate better social competence and social functioning than men with the illness (Goldstein, 1988; Häfner et al., 1993; Mueser, Bellack, Morrison, & Wade, 1990). The benefits experienced by women do not appear to be explained by societal differences in tolerance for deviant behavior. Several hypotheses have been advanced to account for the superior outcome of women with schizophrenia (e.g., biological differences, interactions with socioenvironmental stressors; Castle & Murray, 1991; Flor-Henry, 1985), but no single theory has received strong support.

In general, onset of schizophrenia can be described as either gradual or acute. The gradual onset of schizophrenia can take place over many months, and it may be difficult for family members and others to clearly distinguish onset of the illness. In cases of acute onset, symptoms develop rapidly over a period of a few weeks, with dramatic and easily observed changes occurring over this time. People with acute onset of schizophrenia have a somewhat better prognosis than those with a more insidious illness (Fenton & McGlashan, 1991; Kay & Lindenmayer, 1987).

Although schizophrenia is a long-term and severe psychiatric illness, there is considerable interindividual variability in the course of illness (Marengo, 1994). Generally, though, once schizophrenia has developed, the illness usually continues to be present at varying degrees of severity throughout most of the person's life. Schizophrenia is usually an episodic illness with periods of acute symptom severity requiring more intensive, often inpatient, treatment interspersed by periods of higher functioning between episodes. Despite the fact that most patients with schizophrenia live in the community, it is comparatively rare, at least in the short term, for patients to return to their premorbid levels of functioning between episodes.

Some general predictors of the course and outcome of schizophrenia have been identified, such as premorbid functioning, but overall, the ability to predict outcome is rather poor (Avison & Speechley, 1987; Tsuang, 1986). The primary reason is that symptom severity and functioning are determined by the dynamic interplay between biological vulnerability, environmental factors, and coping skills (Nuechterlein & Dawson, 1994; Liberman et al., 1986). Factors such as compliance with medication (A. Buchanan, 1992), substance abuse (Drake, Osher, & Wallach, 1989), exposure to a hostile or critical environment (Butzlaff & Hooley, 1998), availability of psychosocial programming (Bellack & Mueser, 1993), and assertive case management and outreach (Mueser, Bond, Drake, & Resnick, 1998; Mueser, Drake, & Bond, 1997; Phillips et al., 2001; Quinlivan et al., 1995) are environmental factors that in combination play a large role in determining outcome.

The importance of environmental factors and rehabilitation programs in determining the outcome of schizophrenia is illustrated by two long-term outcome studies conducted by Harding and her associates (DeSisto, Harding, McCormick, Ashikaga, & Brooks, 1995; Harding, Brooks, Ashikaga, Strauss, & Breier, 1987a, 1987b). The first study was conducted in Vermont, which had a highly developed system of community-based rehabilitation programs for people with severe mental illness. Patients in this study demonstrated surprisingly positive outcomes over the 20- to 40-year follow-up period. In contrast, similar patients in Maine, where more traditional hospital-based treatment programs existed, fared substantially worse over the long-term course of their illnesses. Thus, the outcome of most cases of schizophrenia is not predetermined by specific biological factors but, rather, is influenced by the interaction between biological and environmental factors.

In summary, prognosis of schizophrenia is usually considered fair, and there is general agreement that it is worse than for other major psychiatric disorders, such as bipolar disorder or major depression. Despite widespread acceptance that schizophrenia is usually a lifelong disability, recent research on the long-term outcome of schizophrenia has challenged this assumption. Several long-term studies that have followed up patients 20 to 40 years after developing schizophrenia suggest that previous estimates of recovery from schizophrenia are overly conservative (Harding & Keller, 1998). Although definitions of *recovery* vary from one study to the next, some studies suggest as many as 20% to 50% of patients fully recover from schizophrenia later in life (Ciompi, 1980; Harding et al., 1987a, 1987b).

DIAGNOSTIC CONSIDERATIONS

The diagnostic criteria for schizophrenia are fairly similar across a variety of different diagnostic systems. In general, the diagnostic criteria specify some degree of social impairment, combined with positive and negative symptoms lasting a significant duration (e.g., six months or more). The diagnostic criteria for schizophrenia according to *DSM-IV* (APA, 1994) are summarized in Table 8.1.

The diagnosis of schizophrenia requires a clinical interview with the patient, a thorough review of all available records, and standard medical evaluations to rule out the possible role of organic factors (e.g., CAT scan to rule out a brain tumor). In addition, because many patients are poor historians or may not provide accurate accounts of their behavior, information from significant others, such as family members, is often critical to establish a diagnosis of schizophrenia. Because of the wide variety of symptoms characteristic of schizophrenia and variations in interviewing style and format across different clinical interviewers, the use of structured clinical interviews, such as the Structured Clinical Interview for *DSM-IV* (First, Spitzer, Gibbon, & Williams, 1996) can greatly enhance the reliability and validity of psychiatric diagnosis.

Structured clinical interviews have two main advantages over more open clinical interviews. First, structured interviews provide definitions of the key symptoms agreed on by experts, thus making explicit the specific symptoms required for diagnosis. Second, by conducting the interview in a standardized format, including a specific sequence of asking questions, variations in interviewing style are minimized, thus enhancing the comparability of diagnostic assessments across different clinicians. The second point is especially crucial considering that most research studies of schizophrenia employ structured interviews to establish diagnoses. If the findings of clinical research studies are to be generalized into clinical practice, efforts must be taken to ensure the comparability of the patient populations and the assessment techniques employed.

The symptoms of schizophrenia overlap with many other psychiatric disorders. Establishing a diagnosis of schizophrenia requires particularly close consideration of three other overlapping disorders: substance use disorders, affective disorders, and schizoaffective disorder. We discuss issues related to each of these disorders and the diagnosis of schizophrenia in the following sections.

Substance Use Disorders

Substance use disorder, such as alcohol dependence or drug abuse, can be either a differential diagnosis to schizophrenia or a comorbid disorder (i.e., the patient can have both schizophrenia *and* a substance use disorder). With respect to differential diagnosis, substance use disorders can interfere with a clinician's ability to diagnose schizophrenia and can lead to misdiagnosis if the substance abuse is covert (Corty, Lehman, & Myers, 1993; Kranzler et al., 1995). Psychoactive substances, such as alcohol, marijuana, cocaine, and amphetamine, can produce symptoms that mimic those found in schizophrenia, such as hallucinations, delusions, and social withdrawal (Schuckit, 1995). Because diagnosis of schizophrenia requires presence of specific symptoms in the absence of identifiable organic factors, schizophrenia can be diagnosed in people with a history of substance use disorder only by examining the individual's functioning during sustained periods of abstinence from drugs or alcohol. When such periods of abstinence can be identified, a reliable diagnosis of schizophrenia can be made. However, patients who have a long history of substance abuse, with few or no periods of abstinence, are more difficult to assess. For example, in a sample of 461 patients admitted to a psychiatric hospital, a psychiatric diagnosis could not be confirmed or ruled out because of history of substance abuse in 71 patients (15%) (Lehman, Myers, Dixon, & Johnson, 1994).

Substance use disorder is the most common comorbid diagnosis for people with schizophrenia. As substance abuse can worsen the course and outcome of schizophrenia, recognition and treatment of substance abuse in schizophrenia is a critical goal of treatment. The diagnosis of substance abuse in schizophrenia is complicated by several factors. Substance abuse, as in the general population, is often denied because of social and legal sanctions (Galletly, Field, & Prior, 1993; Stone, Greenstein, Gamble, & McLellan, 1993), a problem that may be worsened in this population because of a fear of losing benefits. Denial of problems associated with substance abuse, a core feature of primary substance use disorders, may be further heightened by psychotic distortions and cognitive impairments present in schizophrenia. Furthermore, the criteria used to establish a substance use disorder in the general population are less useful for diagnosis in schizophrenia (Corse, Hirschinger, & Zanis, 1995). For example, the common consequences of substance abuse in the general population—loss of employment, driving under the influence of alcohol, and relationship problems—are less often experienced by people with schizophrenia, who are often unemployed, do not own cars, and have limited interpersonal relationships. Rather, patients with schizophrenia more often experience increased symptoms and rehospitalizations, legal problems, and housing instability because of substance abuse (Drake & Brunette, 1998).

Patients with schizophrenia tend to use smaller quantities of drugs and alcohol (M. Cohen & Klein, 1970; Crowley, Chesluk, Dilts, & Hart, 1974; Lehman et al., 1994) and rarely develop the full physical dependence syndrome that is often present in people with a primary substance use disorder (Corse et al., 1995; Drake et al., 1990; Test, Wallisch, Allness, & Ripp, 1989) or show other physical consequences of alcohol such as stigmata (Mueser et al., 1999). Even very low scores on instruments developed for the primary substance use disorder population, such as the Addiction Severity Inventory, are indicative of substance use disorder in patients with schizophrenia (Appleby, Dyson, Altman, & Luchins, 1997; Corse et al., 1995; Lehman, Myers, Dixon, & Johnson, 1996). Because of the difficulties in using existing measures of substance abuse for people with schizophrenia and other severe mental illnesses, a screening tool was developed specifically for these populations—the Dartmouth Assessment of Lifestyle Instrument (DALI; Rosenberg et al., 1998). The DALI is an 18-item questionnaire that has high classification accuracy for current substance use disorders of alcohol, cannabis, and cocaine for people with severe mental illness.

Despite difficulties involved in assessing comorbid substance abuse in patients with schizophrenia, recent developments in this area indicate that if appropriate steps are taken, reliable diagnoses can be made (Drake, Rosenberg, & Mueser, 1996; Maisto, Carey, Carey, Gordon, & Gleason, 2000). The most critical recommendations for diagnosing substance abuse in schizophrenia include:

- Maintain a high index of suspicion of substance abuse, especially if a patient has a history of substance abuse.
- Use multiple assessment techniques, including self-report instruments, interviews with patients, clinician reports, reports of significant others, and biological assays.
- Be alert to signs that may be subtle indicators of the presence of a substance use disorder, such as unexplained symptom relapses, familial conflict, money management problems, and depression or suicidality.

When a substance use disorder has been diagnosed, integrated treatment that addresses both the schizophrenia and the substance use disorder is necessary to achieve a favorable clinical outcome (Drake, Mercer-McFadden, Mueser, McHugo, & Bond, 1998).

AFFECTIVE DISORDERS

Schizophrenia overlaps more prominently with the major affective disorders than any other psychiatric disorder. The differential diagnosis of schizophrenia from affective disorders is critical because the disorders respond to different treatments, particularly pharmacological interventions. Two different affective disorders can be especially difficult to distinguish from schizophrenia—bipolar disorder and major depression. The differential diagnosis of these disorders from schizophrenia is complicated by the fact that affective symptoms (e.g., depression, grandiose delusions) are frequently present in people with schizophrenia, and psychotic symptoms (e.g., hallucinations, delusions) may be present in people with a major affective disorder (APA, 1994; Pope & Lipinski, 1978).

The crux of making a differential diagnosis between schizophrenia and a major affective disorder is determining whether psychotic symptoms are present *in the absence of* affective symptoms. If there is strong evidence that psychotic symptoms persist even when the person is not experiencing symptoms of mania or depression, the diagnosis is either schizophrenia or the closely related disorder of schizoaffective disorder (discussed later). If, on the other hand, symptoms of psychosis are present during an affective syndrome, but disappear when the person's mood is stable, the appropriate diagnosis is either major depression or bipolar disorder. For example, it is common for people with bipolar disorder to have hallucinations and delusions during the height of a manic episode but for these psychotic symptoms to subside when the person's mood becomes stable again. Similarly, people with major depression often experience hallucinations or delusions during a depressive episode, which subside as their mood improves. If the patient experiences chronic mood problems, meeting criteria for manic, depressive, or mixed episodes, it may be difficult or impossible to establish a diagnosis of schizophrenia, as there are no sustained periods of stable mood.

SCHIZOAFFECTIVE DISORDER

Schizoaffective disorder is a diagnostic entity that overlaps with the affective disorders and schizophrenia (APA, 1994). Three conditions must be met for a person to be diagnosed with schizoaffective disorder:

1. The person must meet criteria for an affective syndrome (i.e., a two-week period in which manic, depressive, or mixed affective features are present to a significant degree).
2. The person must meet criteria for the symptoms of schizophrenia during a period when he or she is not experiencing an affective syndrome (e.g., hallucinations or delusions in the absence of manic or depressive symptoms).
3. The affective syndrome must be present for a substantial period of the person's psychiatric illness (i.e., a patient who experiences brief affective syndromes and who is chronically psychotic and has other long-standing impairments would be diagnosed with schizophrenia, rather than schizoaffective disorder).

Table 8.2 lists *DSM-IV* criteria for the diagnosis of schizoaffective disorder.

Schizoaffective disorder and major affective disorder are frequently mistaken for each other because it is incorrectly assumed that schizoaffective disorder

Table 8.2

DSM-IV Criteria for the Diagnosis of Schizoaffective Disorder

A. An uninterrupted period of illness during which at some time there is either a major depressive episode (which must include depressed mood) or manic episode concurrent with symptoms that meet criterion A of schizophrenia.

B. During the same period of illness, there have been delusions or hallucinations for at least 2 weeks in the absence of prominent mood symptoms.

C. Symptoms meeting the criteria for a mood disorder are present for a substantial portion of the total duration of the active and residual periods of the illness.

D. The disturbance is not due to the direct effects of a substance (e.g., drugs of abuse, medication) or a general medical condition.

Source: From *Diagnostic and Statistical Manual of Mental Disorders*, 4th Edition (*DSM-IV*), 1994, American Psychiatric Association.

requires simply the presence of both psychotic and affective symptoms. Rather, as described in the preceding section, if psychotic symptoms always coincide with affective symptoms, the person has an affective disorder, whereas if psychotic symptoms are present in the absence of an affective syndrome, the person meets criteria for either schizoaffective disorder or schizophrenia. The distinction between schizophrenia and schizoaffective disorder can be more difficult to make, because judgment must be made as to whether the affective symptoms have been present for a substantial part of the person's illness. Decision rules for determining the extent to which affective symptoms must be present to diagnose a schizoaffective disorder have not been established.

Although the differential diagnosis between schizophrenia and schizoaffective disorder is difficult to make, the clinical implications of this distinction are less important than between the affective disorders and either schizophrenia or schizoaffective disorder. Research on family history and treatment response suggests that schizophrenia and schizoaffective disorder are similar disorders and respond to the same interventions (Kramer et al., 1989; Levinson & Levitt, 1987; Levinson & Mowry, 1991; Mattes & Nayak, 1984). In fact, many studies of schizophrenia routinely include patients with schizoaffective disorder and find few differences. Therefore, the information provided in this chapter on schizophrenia also pertains to schizoaffective disorder, and the differential diagnosis between the two disorders is not of major importance from a clinical perspective.

PSYCHOLOGICAL AND BIOLOGICAL ASSESSMENT

Diagnostic assessment provides important information about the potential utility of interventions for schizophrenia (e.g., antipsychotic medications). However, assessment does not end with a diagnosis. It must be supplemented with additional psychological and biological assessments.

PSYCHOLOGICAL ASSESSMENT

A wide range of different psychological formulations has been proposed for understanding schizophrenia. For example, there are extensive writings about psychodynamic and psychoanalytic interpretations of schizophrenia. Although this work has contributed to the further development of these theories, these formulations do not appear to have improved the ability of clinicians to understand patients with this disorder or led to more effective interventions (Mueser & Berenbaum, 1990). Therefore, the use of projective assessment techniques based on psychodynamic concepts of personality, such as the Rorschach and Thematic Apperception Test, are not considered here.

As noted earlier, schizophrenia is often associated with impairments in memory, attention, abstract reasoning, and executive functioning. These impairments result in difficulties generalizing new knowledge to different situations (i.e., transfer of training problems). Thus, assessment needs to be conducted in the environments in which the skills are to be used. For example, successful employment interventions incorporate assessment on the job on an ongoing basis rather than extensive prevocational testing batteries that do not generalize to real-world settings (Bond, 1998; Drake & Becker, 1996). Similarly, when assessing independent living skills, these need to be measured directly in the living environment of the patient or in simulated tests (Wallace, Liberman, Tauber, & Wallace, 2000).

A great deal of research has been done on the functional assessment of social skills in people with schizophrenia. *Social skills* refer to the individual behavioral components, such as eye contact, voice loudness, and the specific choice of words, which in combination are necessary for effective communication with others (Mueser & Bellack, 1998). As previously described, poor social competence is a hallmark of schizophrenia. Although not all problems in social functioning are the consequence of poor social skill, many social impairments appear to be related to skill deficits (Bellack, Morrison, Wixted, & Mueser, 1990).

A number of different strategies can be used to assess social skill. Direct interviews with patients can be a good starting place for identifying broad areas of social dysfunction. These interviews can focus on answering questions such as: Is the patient lonely? Would the patient like more or closer friends? Is the patient able to stand up for his or her rights? Is the patient able to get others to respond positively to him or her? Patient interviews are most informative when combined with interviews with significant others, such as family members and clinicians who are familiar with the nature and quality of the patient's social interactions, as well as naturalistic observations of the patient's social interactions. The combination of these sources of information is useful for identifying specific areas in need of social skills training.

One strategy for assessing social skills that yields the most specific type of information is role-play assessments. Role plays involve brief simulated social interactions between the patient and a confederate taking the role of an interactive partner. During role plays, patients are instructed to act as though the situation were actually happening in real life. Role plays can be as brief as 15 to 30 seconds to assess skill areas such as initiating conversations, or as long as several minutes to assess skills such as problem-solving ability. Role plays can be audiotaped or videotaped and later rated on specific dimensions of social skill. Alternatively, role playing can be embedded into the procedures of social skills training, in which patients practice targeted social skills in role plays, followed by positive and corrective feedback and additional role-play rehearsal. In the latter instance, the assessment of social skills is integrated into the training of new skills, rather than preceding skills training.

Research on the reliability and validity of social skill assessments, and the benefits of social skills training for patients with schizophrenia, has demonstrated the utility of the social skills construct. Patients with schizophrenia have consistently been found to have worse social skills than patients with other psychiatric disorders (Bellack, Morrison, Wixted, et al., 1990; Bellack, Mueser, Wade, Sayers, & Morrison, 1992; Mueser, Bellack, Douglas, & Wade, 1991), and approximately half of the patients with schizophrenia demonstrate stable deficits in basic social skills compared to the nonpsychiatric population (Mueser, Bellack, Douglas, & Morrison, 1991). In the absence of skills training, social skills tend to be stable over periods of time as long as six months to one year (Mueser, Bellack, Douglas, & Morrison, 1991). Social skill in patients with schizophrenia is moderately correlated with level of premorbid social functioning, current role functioning, and quality of life (Mueser, Bellack, Morrison, & Wixted, 1990). Social skills tend to be associated with negative symptoms (Appelo et al., 1992; Bellack, Morrison, Wixted, et al., 1990; Lysaker, Bell, Zito, & Bioty, 1995; Penn, Mueser, Spaulding, Hope, & Reed, 1995) but not with positive symptoms (Mueser, Douglas, Bellack, & Morrison, 1991; Penn et al., 1995). Furthermore, role-play assessments of social skill are also strongly related to social skill in more natural contexts, such as interactions with significant others (Bellack, Morrison, Mueser, Wade, & Sayers, 1990). Patients with schizophrenia show a wide range of impairments in social skill, including areas such as conversational skill, conflict resolution, assertiveness, and problem solving (Bellack, Sayers, Mueser, & Bennett, 1994; Douglas & Mueser, 1990). Thus, ample research demonstrates that social skills are impaired in patients with schizophrenia, tend to be stable over time in the absence of intervention, and are strongly related to other measures of social functioning. Furthermore, there is growing evidence supporting the efficacy of social skills training for schizophrenia (Heinssen, Liberman, & Kopelowicz, 2000; Liberman et al., 1998; Marder et al., 1996).

FAMILY ASSESSMENT

Assessment of family functioning has high relevance in schizophrenia for two reasons. First, *expressed emotion* (EE), which refers to presence of hostile, critical, or emotionally overinvolved attitudes and behaviors on the part of close relatives of patients, is an important stressor that can increase the chance of relapse and rehospitalization (Butzlaff & Hooley, 1998). Second, caring for a mentally ill loved one can lead to significant burden on relatives (Webb et al., 1998), which ultimately can threaten their ability to continue to provide emotional and material support to the patient. Family burden has its own negative consequences, and can be related to EE and the ability of the family to care for the person with schizophrenia. Thus, a thorough assessment of these family factors is important to identify targets for family intervention.

A number of specific methods can be used to assess a negative emotional climate in the family and burden of the illness. Interviews with individual family members, including the patient, as well as the entire family, coupled with observation of more naturalistic family interactions, can provide invaluable information about the quality of family functioning. The vast majority of research on family EE has employed a semistructured interview with individual family members—the Camberwell Family Interview (Leff & Vaughn, 1985). This instrument is primarily a research instrument, and it is too time consuming to be used in clinical practice. Alternatives to the Camberwell Family Interview have been proposed (e.g., Magaña et al., 1986), although none have gained widespread acceptance yet. Several studies have successfully employed the Family Environment Scale (Moos & Moos, 1981), a self-report instrument completed by family members, which has been found to be related to symptoms and outcome in patients with schizophrenia (Halford, Schweitzer, & Varghese, 1991).

Many instruments have been developed for the assessment of family burden. The most comprehensive instrument, with well-established psychometric properties, is the Family Experiences Interview Schedule (Tessler & Gamache, 1995). This measure provides information concerning dimensions of both subjective burden (e.g., emotional strain) and objective burden (e.g., economic impact), as well as specific areas in which burden is most severe (e.g., household tasks).

The importance of evaluating family functioning is supported by research demonstrating clinical benefits of family intervention for schizophrenia. Numerous controlled studies of family treatment for schizophrenia have shown that family intervention has a significant impact on reducing relapse rates and rehospitalizations (Dixon et al., 2001; Pitschel-Walz, Leucht, Bäuml, Kissling, & Engel, 2001). The critical elements shared across different models of family intervention are education about schizophrenia, the provision of ongoing support, improved communication skills, and a focus on helping all family members improve the quality of their lives (Dixon & Lehman, 1995; Glynn, 1992; Lam, 1991).

BIOLOGICAL ASSESSMENT

Biological assessments are becoming more common in the clinical management of schizophrenia. For diagnosis, biological assessments may be used to rule out possible organic factors such as tumor, stroke, or covert substance abuse. Urine and blood specimens are sometimes obtained to evaluate the presence of substance abuse. Similarly, blood samples may be obtained to determine whether the patient is compliant with the prescribed antipsychotic medication, although the specific level of medication in the blood has not been conclusively linked to clinical response. Blood levels may also be monitored to ensure appropriate levels of mood stabilizers (e.g., lithium). Some newer medications also require ongoing blood tests to detect very rare, but potentially lethal, blood disorders (Alvir, Lieberman, & Safferman, 1995; Young, Bowers, & Mazure, 1998).

Biological measures are sometimes used to characterize impairments in brain functioning associated with schizophrenia, although these assessments do not have clear implications for treatment of the illness at this time. For example, CAT scans of the brain indicate that between one half and two thirds of all patients with schizophrenia display enlarged cerebral ventricles, indicative of cortical atrophy (Liddle, 1995). Similarly, magnetic resonance imaging (MRI) studies show reduced brain volume in several brain structures for people with schizophrenia (Lawrie & Abukmeil, 1998). In addition, MRI studies, positron emission tomography (PET), and single photon emission computerized tomography (SPECT) have shown reduced metabolism and blood flow in several cortical and subcortical areas (Kindermann, Karimi, Symonds, Brown, & Jeste, 1997; Liddle, 1997; McClure, Keshavan, & Pettegrew, 1998). Gross structural impairments in brain functioning, such as enlarged ventricles, tend to be associated with a wide range of neuropsychological impairments and negative symptoms often present in schizophrenia (Andreasen, Flaum, Swayze, Tyrrell, & Arndt, 1990; R. W. Buchanan et al., 1993; Merriam, Kay, Opler, Kushner, & van Praag, 1990).

To date, most of the advances in the treatment of schizophrenia have been in psychopharmacology. Biological assessments are still not useful for diagnosing the illness or for guiding treatment. However, the clinical utility of biological assessment is likely to increase in the years to come as advances continue to be made in the understanding of the biological roots of schizophrenia.

ETIOLOGICAL CONSIDERATIONS

FAMILIAL AND GENETIC CONSIDERATIONS

The etiology of schizophrenia has been a topic of much debate over the past 100 years. Kraepelin (1919/1971) and Bleuler (1911/1950) viewed the illness as having a biological origin. However, from the 1920s to the 1960s, alternative theories gained prominence, speculating that the disease was the result of disturbed family interactions (Bateson, Jackson, Haley, & Weakland, 1956). Psychogenic theories of the etiology of schizophrenia, positing that the illness was psychological in nature, rather than biological, played a dominant role in shaping the attitudes and behavior of professionals toward patients with schizophrenia and their relatives (Fromm-Reichmann, 1950; Searles, 1965). These theories have not been supported empirically (Jacob, 1975; Waxler & Mishler, 1971). Moreover, in many cases, psychogenic theories fostered poor relationships between mental health professionals and relatives (Terkelsen, 1983), which have only begun to mend in recent years (Mueser & Glynn, 1999).

For more than a century, clinicians have often noted that schizophrenia tends to "run in families." However, the clustering of schizophrenia in family members could reflect learned behavior that is passed on from one generation to the next, rather than predisposing biological factors. In the 1950s and 1960s, two paradigms were developed for evaluating the genetic contributions to the illness. The first approach, the *high risk* paradigm, involves examining the rate of schizophrenia in adopted-away offspring of mothers with schizophrenia. If the rate of schizophrenia in children of biological parents with schizophrenia is higher than in the general population, even in the absence of contact with those parents, a role for genetic factors in developing the illness is supported. The second approach, the *monozygotic/dizygotic twin* paradigm involves comparing the concordance rate of schizophrenia in identical twins (monozygotic) with fraternal twins (dizygotic). Because monozygotic twins share the same gene pool, whereas dizygotic twins share only approximately half their genes, a higher concordance rate of schizophrenia among monozygotic twins than dizygotic twins, even reared in the same environment, would support a role for genetic factors in the etiology of schizophrenia.

Over the past 30 years, numerous studies employing either the high-risk or twin paradigm have been conducted examining the role of genetic factors in schizophrenia. There has been almost uniform agreement across studies indicating that the risk of developing schizophrenia in biological relatives of people with schizophrenia is greater than in the general population, even in the absence of any contact between the relatives (Kendler & Diehl, 1993). Thus, strong support exists for the role of genetic factors in the etiology of at least some cases of schizophrenia. For example, the risk of a woman with schizophrenia giving birth to a child who later develops schizophrenia is approximately 10%, compared to only 1% in the general population (Gottesman, 1991). Similarly, the risk of one identical twin developing schizophrenia if his or her co-twin also has schizophrenia is between 25% and 50%, compared to a risk of about 10% for fraternal twins (Walker, Downey, & Caspi, 1991).

The fact that identical twins do not have a 100% concordance rate of schizophrenia, as might be expected if the disorder were purely genetic, has raised intriguing questions about the etiology of schizophrenia. Some have proposed that the development of schizophrenia might be the consequence of an interaction between genetic and environmental factors. The results of one study suggest this might be the case. Tienari (1991; Tienari et al., 1987) compared the likelihood of developing schizophrenia in three groups of children raised by adoptive families. Two groups of children had biological mothers with schizophrenia; the third group had biological mothers with no psychiatric disorder. The researchers divided the adoptive families of the children into two broad groups based on the level of disturbance present in the family: healthy adoptive families and disturbed adoptive families. Follow-up assessments were conducted to determine the presence of schizophrenia and other severe psychiatric disorders in the adopted children raised in all three groups. The researchers found that biological children of mothers with schizophrenia who were raised by adoptive families with high levels of disturbance were significantly more likely to develop schizophrenia or another psychotic disorder (46%) than either similarly vulnerable children raised in families with low levels of disturbance (5%), or children with no biological vulnerability raised in either disturbed (24%) or healthy (3%) adoptive families. This study raises the intriguing possibility that some cases of schizophrenia develop because of the interaction between biological vulnerability and environmental stress.

Although families do not cause schizophrenia, there are important interactions between the family and patient that deserve consideration. First, as previously mentioned, it has repeatedly been found that critical attitudes and high levels of emotional overinvolvement (expressed emotion [EE]) on the part of the relatives toward the patient are strong predictors of the likelihood of patient relapse and rehospitalization (Butzlaff & Hooley, 1998). The importance of family factors is underscored by the fact that the severity of patients' psychiatric illness or their social skill impairments are not related to family EE (Mueser et al., 1993). Rather, family EE seems to act as a stressor, increasing the vulnerability of patients with schizophrenia to relapse.

A second important family consideration is the amount of burden on relatives caring for a mentally ill person. Family members of patients with schizophrenia typically experience a wide range of negative emotions related to coping with the illness, such as anxiety, depression, guilt, and anger (Hatfield & Lefley, 1987, 1993; Oldridge, & Hughes, 1992). Burden is even associated with negative health consequences for relatives (Dyck, Short, & Vitaliano, 1999). Family burden may be related to levels of EE, ability to cope with the illness, and, ultimately, the ability of the family to successfully monitor and manage the schizophrenia in a family member (Mueser & Glynn, 1999). Thus, EE and family burden are important areas for assessment and intervention.

Learning and Modeling

While schizophrenia is broadly accepted as a biologically based disorder and not a learned one, learning and modeling may play a role in the course and outcome of the disorder. As described in the following section, the stress-vulnerability model of schizophrenia posits that coping skills mediate the noxious effects of stress on psychobiological vulnerability on symptoms and relapses (Liberman et al., 1986). Coping skills, such as social skills for developing and maintaining close relationships with others and strategies for managing negative emotions and distorted thinking processes, can be acquired either naturalistically through access to good role models (e.g., family, friends) or through social learning-based programs, such as social skills training (Bellack, Mueser, Gingerich, & Agresta, 1997) or cognitive-behavior therapy (Chadwick, Birchwood, & Trower, 1996; Fowler, Garety, & Kuipers, 1995). Thus, improving coping skills, as well as other life skills, through the systematic application of social learning methods is a common treatment goal in schizophrenia.

Life Events

Although stressful life events alone are not the *cause* of schizophrenia, some theories hypothesize that life events may contribute to the development of the disorder and can play an important role in the course of schizophrenia. The stress-vulnerability model (Liberman et al., 1986; Zubin & Spring, 1977) assumes that symptom severity and related impairments of psychiatric disorders such as schizophrenia have a biological basis (*psychobiological vulnerability*) determined by a combination of genetic and early environmental factors. This vulnerability can be decreased by medications and worsened by substance use disorder. *Stress,* including discrete events such as traumas and exposure to ongoing conditions such as a hostile environment, can impinge on vulnerability, precipitating relapses, and worse outcomes. Finally, *coping* resources, such as coping skills or the ability to obtain social support, can minimize the effects of stress on relapse and the need for acute care.

As described previously, EE represents a stressful environment that may increase relapse and hospitalization in people with schizophrenia. In addition, in the Clinical Picture section, we discussed that people with schizophrenia are often the targets of violence and have frequently been exposed to physical and/or sexual assault. Exposure to traumatic events may lead to posttraumatic stress disorder (PTSD), a condition characterized by reliving the traumatic experience (e.g., nightmares, intrusive memories); avoidance of people, places, and things that remind the person of the event; and increased arousal symptoms (e.g., irritability, sleep problems). The prevalence of PTSD among people with schizophrenia and other severe mental illnesses ranges from 29% to 43% (Cascardi, Mueser, DeGirolomo, & Murrin, 1996; Craine, Henson, Colliver, & MacLean, 1988; Mueser, Goodman, et al., 1998; Switzer et al., 1999). These rates of *current* PTSD are far in excess of the *lifetime* prevalence of PTSD in the general population, with estimates ranging between 8% and 12% (Breslau, Davis, Andreski, & Peterson, 1991; Kessler, Sonnega, Bromet, Hughes, & Nelson, 1995; Resnick, Kilpatrick, Dansky, Saunders, & Best, 1993). Exposure to trauma and the presence of PTSD are likely to worsen the course of schizophrenia and complicate treatment (Mueser, Rosenberg, Goodman, & Trumbetta, 2002.) For example, research shows that both discrete stressors (e.g., life events) and exposure to a stressful environment can worsen psychotic disorders (Butzlaff & Hooley, 1998). PTSD is also associated with substance abuse (Chilcoat & Breslau, 1998), which, as described earlier, can have severe consequences for people with schizophrenia.

GENDER, ETHNIC, AND CULTURAL ISSUES

A number of issues related to gender are important for understanding the psychopathology in the course of schizophrenia. As described in the section on course and prognosis, women tend to have a milder overall course of schizophrenia than men. The net consequence is that, although similar numbers of men and women have schizophrenia, men are more likely to receive treatment for the disorder. In fact, most research on the treatment of schizophrenia is conducted on samples ranging from 60% to 100% male.

Because treatment studies usually sample patients who are currently receiving treatment, often inpatient treatment, the efficacy of widely studied psychosocial interventions, such as social skills training and family therapy, has been less adequately demonstrated in women. For example, some research suggests that social skills training may be more helpful to men than to women (Mueser, Levine, Bellack, Douglas, & Brady, 1990; Schaub, Behrendt, Brenner, Mueser, & Liberman, 1998; Smith et al., 1997). There is a need for more research on the effects of treatments for women with schizophrenia. At the same time, further consideration needs to be given to the different needs of women with this illness. For example, women with schizophrenia are much more likely to marry and have children than are men. It is crucial, therefore, that psychosocial interventions be developed to address the relationship, family planning, and parenting needs of women with schizophrenia (Apfel & Handel, 1993; Brunette & Dean, 2002; Coverdale & Grunebaum, 1998).

Another issue related to gender in need of further consideration is exposure to trauma. As described earlier, people with schizophrenia are at risk for being the victims of violence. Although both men and women with schizophrenia report histories of abuse and assault, women report more sexual assault (Goodman et al., 2001; Mueser, Goodman, et al., 1998). Further, in the general population, women are more likely to be abused than men, are more likely to sustain injuries, and are more likely to be economically dependent on perpetrators of domestic violence. Thus, there is particular need to recognize and address trauma in the lives of women with schizophrenia. Accurate detection of trauma is further complicated by the fact that most severely mentally ill people who have been physically or sexually assaulted deny that they have been *abused* (Cascardi et al., 1996). The development of programs that address both the cause of domestic violence and their sequelae, especially for women with schizophrenia, is a priority in this area (Harris, 1996; Rosenberg et al., 2001).

Research on the relationships between race, ethnicity, and severe psychiatric disorders demonstrates that cultural factors are critical to understanding how people with schizophrenia are perceived by others in their social milieu, as well as the course of the illness. Although the prevalence of schizophrenia is comparable across different cultures, several studies have shown that the course of the illness is more benign in developing countries compared to industrialized nations (Lo & Lo, 1977; Murphy & Raman, 1971; Sartorius et al., 1986). Westermeyer (1989) has raised questions about the comparability of patient samples in cross-cultural studies, but a consensus remains that the course of schizophrenia tends to be milder in non-industrialized countries (Jablensky, 1989).

Several different interpretations have been offered to account for the better prognosis of schizophrenia in some cultures (Lefley, 1990). It is possible that the strong stigma and social rejection that results from severe mental illness and poses an obstacle to the ability of patients to cope effectively with their disorder and assimilate into society (Fink & Tasman, 1992) are less prominent in some cultures (Parra, 1985). Greater cultural and societal acceptance of the social deviations present in schizophrenia may enable patients to live less stressful and more productive lives. Family ties, in particular, may be stronger in developing countries or in certain ethnic minorities, and less vulnerable to the disorganizing effects of mental illness (Lin & Kleinman, 1988). For example, Liberman (1994) has described how the strong functional ties of severely mentally ill people to their families and work foster the reintegration of patients back into Chinese society following psychiatric hospitalization. In contrast, until recently, families of patients with schizophrenia in many Western societies were viewed by mental health professionals as either irrelevant, or worse, as causal agents in the development of the illness (Lefley, 1990; Mueser & Glynn, 1999), thus precluding them from a role in psychiatric rehabilitation. Furthermore, the use of other social supports may vary across different ethnic groups or cultures, such as importance of the church to the African American community and its potential therapeutic benefits (Griffith, Young, & Smith, 1984; E. C. Lincoln & Mamiya, 1990).

Some have hypothesized that different cultural interpretations of the individual's role in society and of the causes of mental illness may interact to determine course and outcome. Estroff (1989) has suggested that the emphasis on the "self" in Western countries, compared to a more family-based or societally based identification, has an especially disabling effect on people with schizophrenia, whose sense of self is often fragile or fragmented. Another important consideration is the availability of adaptive concepts for understanding mental illness. For example, *espiritismo* in Puerto Rican culture is a system of beliefs involving the interactions between the invisible spirit world and the visible world in which spirits can attach themselves to people (Comas-Díaz, 1981; Morales-Dorta, 1976). Spirits are hierarchically ordered in terms of their moral perfection, and the practice of espiritismo is guided by helping individuals who are spiritually ill achieve higher levels of this perfection. Troubled people are not identified as "sick" nor are they blamed for their difficulties; in some cases, symptoms such as hallucinations may be interpreted favorably as signs that the person is advanced in his or her spiritual development, resulting in some prestige (Comas-Díaz, 1981). Thus, certain cultural interpretations of schizophrenia may promote more acceptance of people who display the symptoms of schizophrenia, as well as avoid the common assumption that these phenomenological experiences are the consequence of a chronic, unremitting condition.

Understanding different cultural beliefs, values, and social structures can have important implications for the diagnosis of schizophrenia. Religious practices and beliefs may complicate diagnosis. For example, high levels of religiosity have been found in people with schizophrenia (Brewerton, 1994). Without a clear understanding of the religious and cultural background, patients may be misdiagnosed (May, 1997). Ethnic groups may differ in their willingness to report symptoms, as illustrated by one study that reported that African American patients were less likely to report symptoms than Hispanics or non-Hispanic Whites (Skilbeck, Acosta, Yamamoto, & Evans, 1984). Other studies have found that African Americans are more likely to be diagnosed with schizophrenia than other ethnic groups (e.g., Adams, Dworkin, & Rosenberg, 1984). Knowledge of cultural norms appears critical to avoid the possible misinterpretation of culturally bound beliefs and practices when arriving at a diagnosis. Several studies have shown that ethnic differences in diagnosis vary as a function of both the patient's and the interviewer's ethnicity (Baskin, Bluestone, & Nelson, 1981; Loring & Powell, 1988). Misdiagnosis of affective disorders such as schizophrenia is the most common problem with the diagnosis of ethnic minorities in the United States (e.g., Jones, Gray, & Parsons, 1981, 1983).

Cultural differences are also critical in the treatment of schizophrenia, both with respect to service utilization and the nature of treatment provided. There is a growing body of information documenting that ethnic groups differ in their use of psychiatric services. A number of studies have indicated that Hispanics and Asian Americans use fewer psychiatric services than non-Hispanic Whites, whereas Blacks use more emergency and inpatient services (Cheung & Snowden, 1990; Hough et al., 1987; Hu, Snowden, Jerrell, & Nguyen, 1991; Padgett, Patrick, Burns, & Schlesinger, 1994; S. Sue, Fujino, Hu, Takeuchi, & Zane, 1991). Aside from cultural-based practices that may cause some individuals to seek assistance outside the mental health system (e.g., practitioners of *santeria*; González-Wippler, 1992), access to and retention in mental health services may be influenced by the proximity of mental health services (Dworkin & Adams, 1987) and by the ethnicity of treatment providers. S. Sue et al. (1991) reported that matching clinician and client ethnicity resulted in higher retention of ethnic minorities in mental health services. Increasing access to needed services for racial/ethnic minorities may require a range of strategies, including ensuring that services are available in the communities where clients live, working with the natural social supports in the community, awareness of relevant cultural norms, and adequate representation of ethnic minorities as treatment providers.

Cultural factors may have an important bearing on psychotherapeutic treatments provided for schizophrenia. D. W. Sue and Sue (1990) have described the importance of providing psychotherapy driven by goals that are compatible with clients' cultural norms. This requires both knowledge of subcultural norms and familiarity with the other social support mechanisms typically available to those clients. Interventions developed for one cultural group may need substantial modification to be effective in other groups. For example, Telles et al. (1995) reported that behavioral family therapy, which has been found to be effective at reducing relapse in schizophrenia for samples of non-Hispanic White and African American patients (Mueser & Glynn, 1999), was significantly less effective for Hispanic Americans (of Mexican, Guatemalan, and Salvadoran descent) with low levels of acculturation than more acculturated patients. However, adaptations of the same family model were effective for samples of Chinese patients (Xiong et al., 1994; Zhang, Wang, Li, & Phillips, 1994). These findings underscore the importance of tailoring psychosocial interventions to meet the unique needs of clients from different cultural backgrounds.

A final cultural factor is stigma; that is, negative attitudes that lead to prejudice and discrimination against people with schizophrenia. Although stigma can be present for a variety of disabilities, attitudes toward people with severe mental illness tend to be more negative (Corrigan & Penn, 1999). Stigma may stem from characteristics of the disorder itself, such as poor social skills, bizarre behavior, and unkempt appearance; and stigma may develop and be maintained through negative media portrayals and myths (e.g., dangerousness, unpredictability; Farina, 1998). Stigma and discrimination can greatly undermine the person's ability to recover from the effects of schizophrenia and integrate into society. For example, people with severe mental illness identify role functioning, such as employment, developing and maintaining friendships and intimate relationships, and regular activities as critical to their recovery (Uttaro & Mechanic, 1994). However, many studies have shown that these are the very areas most affected by stigma (Farina, 1998). Much is being done to try to reduce stigma associated with schizophrenia and other mental illness. In particular, strategies that involve active education and increased contact with people with mental illness may be most effective for eradicating this serious problem (Corrigan & Penn, 1999).

BIOLOGICAL AND PHYSIOLOGICAL ISSUES

Although there is strong evidence that genetic factors can play a role in the development of schizophrenia, there is also a growing body of evidence pointing to the influence of other biological, nongenetic factors playing a critical role. For example, obstetric complications, maternal exposure to the influenza virus, and other environmentally based insults to a developing fetus (e.g., maternal starvation) are associated with an increased risk of developing schizophrenia (Geddes & Lawrie, 1995; Kirch, 1993; Rodrigo, Lusiardo, Briggs, & Ulmer, 1991; Susser & Lin, 1992; Susser et al., 1996; Takei et al., 1996; Thomas et al., 2001; Torrey, Bowler, Rawlings, & Terrazas, 1993). Thus, there is a growing consensus that the etiology of schizophrenia may be heterogeneous, with genetic factors playing a role in the development of some cases, and early environmentally based factors playing a role in the development of other cases. This heterogeneity may account for the fact that the genetic contribution to schizophrenia has consistently been found to be lower than the genetic contribution to bipolar disorder (Goodwin & Jamison, 1990). Other biological and physiological factors include alterations in brain chemistry and structure.

Pharmacological research has identified many neurochemical changes associated with schizophrenia. By far, the neurotransmitter most commonly implicated in the onset of schizophrenia is dopamine. The dopamine hypothesis proposes that alterations in levels of dopamine are responsible for the symptoms of schizophrenia. Originally, this hypothesis was based on findings that substances that increase dopamine (e.g., levadopa used to treat Parkinson's Disease) increase psychotic symptoms, and substances that decrease dopamine reduce psychotic symptoms. Current versions of this hypothesis suggest that an overabundance of dopamine in certain limbic areas of the brain may be responsible for positive symptoms, while a lack of dopamine in cortical areas may be responsible for negative symptoms (Davis, Kahn, Ko, & Davidson, 1991; Moore, West, & Grace, 1999). Other neurochemicals appear to be implicated in schizophrenia. In particular, serotonin may directly or indirectly (e.g., by mediating dopamine) affect symptoms of schizophrenia as several of the newer antipsychotic medications impact serotonin levels (Lieberman et al., 1998). In addition, glutamate and GABA may be altered in schizophrenia (Pearlson, 2000).

As discussed in the Biological Assessment section, abnormalities in several brain structures also have been identified. In particular, enlarged ventricles and decreased brain volume and blood flow to cortical areas have been associated with a wide range of cognitive impairments and negative symptoms of schizophrenia (Andreasen, Flaum, Swayze, Tyrrell, & Arndt, 1990; R. W. Buchanan et al., 1993; Merriam et al., 1990).

SUMMARY

Schizophrenia is a severe, long-term psychiatric illness characterized by impairments in social functioning, the ability to work, self-care skills, positive symptoms (hallucinations, delusions), negative symptoms (social withdrawal, apathy), and cognitive impairments. Schizophrenia is a relatively common illness, afflicting approximately 1% of the population, and tends to have an episodic course over the lifetime, with symptoms gradually improving over the long term. Most evidence indicates that schizophrenia is a biological illness that may be caused by a variety of factors, such as genetic contributions and early environmental influences (e.g., insults to the developing fetus). Despite the biological nature of schizophrenia, environmental stress can precipitate either the onset of the illness or symptom relapses. Schizophrenia can be reliably diagnosed with structured clinical interviews, with particular attention paid to the differential diagnosis of affective disorders. There is a high comorbidity of substance use disorders in people with schizophrenia, which must be treated if positive outcomes are to accrue. Psychological assessment of schizophrenia is most useful when it focuses on behavioral, rather than dynamic, dimensions of the illness. Thus, assessments and interventions focused on social skill deficits and family functioning have yielded promising treatment results. Biological assessments are useful at this time primarily for descriptive, rather than clinical, purposes. Finally, there are a great many issues related to gender and racial or ethnic factors that remain unexplored. Although schizophrenia remains one of the most challenging psychiatric illnesses to treat, substantial advances have been made in recent years in developing reliable diagnostic systems, understanding the role of various etiological factors, development of effective pharmacological and psychosocial treatments, and the identification of factors that mediate the long-term outcome of the illness, such as stress and substance abuse. These developments bode well for the ability of researchers and clinicians to continue to make headway in treating this serious illness.

REFERENCES

Adams, G. L., Dworkin, R. J., & Rosenberg, S. D. (1984). Diagnosis and pharmacotherapy issues in the care of Hispanics in the public sector. *American Journal of Psychiatry, 141,* 970–974.

Alvir, J. M. J., Lieberman, J. A., & Safferman, A. Z. (1995). Do white-cell count spikes predict agranulocytosis in clozapine recipients? *Psychopharmacology Bulletin, 31,* 311–314.

Amador, X. F., & Gorman, J. M. (1998). Psychopathologic domains and insight in schizophrenia. *Psychiatric Clinics of North America, 21,* 27–42.

Amador, X. F., Strauss, D., Yale, S., & Gorman, J. M. (1991). Awareness of illness in schizophrenia. *Schizophrenia Bulletin, 17,* 113–132.

American Psychiatric Association. (1994). *Diagnostic and statistical manual of mental disorders* (4th ed.). Washington, DC: American Psychiatric Association.

Andreasen, N. C., Flaum, M., Swayze, V. W., II, Tyrrell, G., & Arndt, S. (1990). Positive and negative symptoms in schizophrenia: A critical reappraisal. *Archives of General Psychiatry, 47*, 615–621.

Apfel, R. J., & Handel, M. H. (1993). *Madness and loss of motherhood: Sexuality, reproduction, and long-term mental illness.* Washington, DC: American Psychiatric Press.

Appelo, M. T., Woonings, F. M. J., van Nieuwenhuizen, C. J., Emmelkamp, P. M. G., Sloof, C. J., & Louwerens, J. W. (1992). Specific skills and social competence in schizophrenia. *Acta Psychiatrica Scandinavica, 85*, 419–422.

Appleby, L., Dyson, V., Altman, E., & Luchins, D. (1997). Assessing substance use in multi-problem patients: Reliability and validity of the Addiction Severity Index in a mental hospital population. *Journal of Nervous and Mental Diseases, 185*, 159–165.

Argyle, N. (1990). Panic attacks in chronic schizophrenia. *British Journal of Psychiatry, 157*, 430–433.

Aro, S., Aro, H., & Keskimäki, I. (1995). Socioeconomic mobility among patients with schizophrenia or major affective disorder: A 17-year retrospective follow-up. *British Journal of Psychiatry, 166*, 759–767.

Asarnow, J. R. (1988). Children at risk for schizophrenia: Converging lines of evidence. *Schizophrenia Bulletin, 14*, 613–631.

Avison, W. R., & Speechley, K. N. (1987). The discharged psychiatric patient: A review of social, social-psychological, and psychiatric correlates of outcome. *American Journal of Psychiatry, 144*, 10–18.

Azrin, N. H., & Teichner, G. (1998). Evaluation of an instructional program for improving medication compliance for chronically mentally ill outpatients. *Behavior Research and Therapy, 36*, 849–861.

Bartels, S. J., Drake, R. E., Wallach, M. A., & Freeman, D. H. (1991). Characteristic hostility in schizophrenic outpatients. *Schizophrenia Bulletin, 17*, 163–171.

Bartels, S. J., Mueser, K. T., & Miles, K. M. (1998). Schizophrenia. In M. Hersen & V. B. Van Hasselt (Eds.), *Handbook of clinical geropsychology* (pp. 173–194). New York: Plenum Press.

Baskin, D., Bluestone, H., & Nelson, M. (1981). Ethnicity and psychiatric diagnosis. *Journal of Clinical Psychology, 37*, 529–537.

Bateson, G., Jackson, D. D., Haley, J., & Weakland, J. (1956). Toward a theory of schizophrenia. *Behavioral Science, 1*, 251–264.

Baum, K. M., & Walker, E. F. (1995). Childhood behavioral precursors of adult symptom dimensions in schizophrenia. *Schizophrenia Research, 16*, 111–120.

Bellack, A. S., Gold, J. M., & Buchanan, R. W. (1999). Cognitive rehabilitation for schizophrenia: Problems, prospects, and strategies. *Schizophrenia Bulletin, 25*, 257–274.

Bellack, A. S., Morrison, R. L., Mueser, K. T., Wade, J. H., & Sayers, S. L. (1990). Role play for assessing the social competence of psychiatric patients. *Psychological Assessment, 2*, 248–255.

Bellack, A. S., Morrison, R. L., Wixted, J. T., & Mueser, K. T. (1990). An analysis of social competence in schizophrenia. *British Journal of Psychiatry, 156*, 809–818.

Bellack, A. S., & Mueser, K. T. (1993). Psychosocial treatment for schizophrenia. *Schizophrenia Bulletin, 19*, 317–336.

Bellack, A. S., Mueser, K. T., Gingerich, S., & Agresta, J. (1997). *Social skills training for schizophrenia: A step-by-step guide.* New York: Guilford Press.

Bellack, A. S., Mueser, K. T., Wade, J. H., Sayers, S. L., & Morrison, R. L. (1992). The ability of schizophrenics to perceive and cope with negative affect. *British Journal of Psychiatry, 160*, 473–480.

Bellack, A. S., Sayers, M., Mueser, K. T., & Bennett, M. (1994). An evaluation of social problem solving in schizophrenia. *Journal of Abnormal Psychology, 103,* 371–378.

Bleuler E. (1950). *Dementia praecox or the group of schizophrenias* (J. Zinkin, Trans.). New York: International Universities Press. (Original work published 1911)

Bond, G. R. (1998). Principles of the individual placement and support model: Empirical support. *Psychiatric Rehabilitation Journal, 22,* 11–23.

Brekke, J. S., Raine, A., Ansel, M., Lencz, T., & Bird, L. (1997). Neuropsychological and psychophysiological correlates of psychosocial functioning in schizophrenia. *Schizophrenia Bulletin, 23,* 19–28.

Breslau, N., Davis, G. C., Andreski, P., & Peterson, E. (1991). Traumatic events and posttraumatic stress disorder in an urban population of young adults. *Archives of General Psychiatry, 48,* 216–222.

Brewerton, T. D. (1994). Hyperreligiosity in psychotic disorders. *Journal of Nervous and Mental Diseases, 182,* 302–304.

Bruce, M. L., Takeuchi, D. T., & Leaf, P. J. (1991). Poverty and psychiatric status: Longitudinal evidence from the New Haven Epidemiologic Catchment Area study. *Archives of General Psychiatry, 48,* 470–474.

Brunette, M. F., & Dean, W. (2002). Community mental health care of women with severe mental illness who are parents. *Community Mental Health Journal, 38*(2), 153–165.

Buchanan, A. (1992). A two-year prospective study of treatment compliance in patients with schizophrenia. *Psychological Medicine, 22,* 787–797.

Buchanan, R. W., Breier, A., Kirkpatrick, B., Elkashef, A., Munson, R. C., Gellad, F., et al. (1993). Structural abnormalities in deficit and nondeficit schizophrenia. *American Journal of Psychiatry, 150,* 59–65.

Butzlaff, R. L., & Hooley, J. M. (1998). Expressed emotion and psychiatric relapse: A meta-analysis. *Archives of General Psychiatry, 55,* 547–552.

Cannon, T. D., Mednick, S. A., Parnas, J., Schulsinger, F., Praestholm, J., & Vestergaard, A. (1993). Developmental brain abnormalities in the offspring of schizophrenic mothers. *Archives of General Psychiatry, 50,* 551–564.

Carmen, E., Rieker, P. P., & Mills, T. (1984). Victims of violence and psychiatric illness. *American Journal of Psychiatry, 141,* 378–383.

Cascardi, M., Mueser, K. T., DeGirolomo, J., & Murrin, M. (1996). Physical aggression against psychiatric inpatients by family members and partners: A descriptive study. *Psychiatric Services, 47,* 531–533.

Castle, D. J., & Murray, R. M. (1991). Editorial: The neurodevelopmental basis of sex differences in schizophrenia. *Psychological Medicine, 21,* 565–575.

Chadwick, P., Birchwood, M., & Trower, P. (1996). *Cognitive therapy for delusions, voices and paranoia.* Chichester, West Sussex, England: Wiley.

Cheung, F. K., & Snowden, L. R. (1990). Community mental health and ethnic minority populations. *Community Mental Health Journal, 26,* 277–289.

Chilcoat, H. D., & Breslau, N. (1998). Posttraumatic stress disorder and drug disorders: Testing causal pathways. *Archives of General Psychiatry, 55,* 913–917.

Ciompi, L. (1980). Catamnestic long-term study of life and aging in chronic schizophrenic patients. *Schizophrenia Bulletin, 6,* 606–618.

Cohen, C. I. (1990). Outcome of schizophrenia into later life: An overview. *Gerontologist, 30,* 790–797.

Cohen, M., & Klein, D. F. (1970). Drug abuse in a young psychiatric population. *American Journal of Orthopsychiatry, 40,* 448–455.

Comas-Díaz, L. (1981). Puerto Rican espiritismo and psychotherapy. *American Journal of Orthopsychiatry, 51,* 636–645.

Corrigan, P. W., Liberman, R. P., & Engle, J. D. (1990). From noncompliance to collaboration in the treatment of schizophrenia. *Hospital and Community Psychiatry, 41,* 1203–1211.

Corrigan, P. W., & Penn, D. L. (1999). Lessons from social psychology on discrediting psychiatric stigma. *American Psychologist, 54,* 765–776.

Corse, S. J., Hirschinger, N. B., & Zanis, D. (1995). The use of the Addiction Severity Index with people with severe mental illness. *Psychiatric Rehabilitation Journal, 19,* 9–18.

Corty, E., Lehman, A. F., & Myers, C. P. (1993). Influence of psychoactive substance use on the reliability of psychiatric diagnosis. *Journal of Consulting and Clinical Psychology, 61,* 165–170.

Coverdale, J. H., & Grunebaum, H. (1998). Sexuality and family planning. In K. T. Mueser & N. Tarrier (Eds.), *Social functioning in schizophrenia* (pp. 224–237). Boston: Allyn & Bacon.

Craine, L. S., Henson, C. E., Colliver, J. A., & MacLean, D. G. (1988). Prevalence of a history of sexual abuse among female psychiatric patients in a state hospital system. *Hospital and Community Psychiatry, 39,* 300–304.

Crowley, T. J., Chesluk, D., Dilts, S., & Hart, R. (1974). Drug and alcohol abuse among psychiatric admissions. *Archives of General Psychiatry, 30,* 13–20.

Davies-Netzley, S., Hurlburt, M. S., & Hough, R. (1996). Childhood abuse as a precursor to homelessness for homeless women with severe mental illness. *Violence and Victims, 11,* 129–142.

Davis, K. L., Kahn, R. S., Ko, G., & Davidson, M. (1991). Dopamine in schizophrenia: A review and reconceptualization. *American Journal of Psychiatry, 148,* 1474–1486.

DeSisto, M. J., Harding, C. M., McCormick, R. V., Ashikaga, T., & Brooks, G. W. (1995). The Maine and Vermont three-decade studies of serious mental illness. I: Matched comparison of cross-sectional outcome. *British Journal of Psychiatry, 167,* 331–342.

Dixon, L. B., & Lehman, A. F. (1995). Family interventions for schizophrenia. *Schizophrenia Bulletin, 21,* 631–643.

Dixon, L. B., McFarlane, W. R., Lefley, H. P., Lucksted, A., Cohen, M., Falloon, I., et al. (2001). Evidence-based practices for services to family members of people with psychiatric disabilities. *Psychiatric Services, 52,* 903–910.

Dohrenwend, B. R., Levav, I., Shrout, P. E., Schwartz, S., Naveh, G., Link, B. G., et al. (1992). Socioeconomic status and psychiatric disorders: The causation-selection issue. *Science, 255,* 946–952.

Douglas, M. S., & Mueser, K. T. (1990). Teaching conflict resolution skills to the chronically mentally ill: Social skills training groups for briefly hospitalized patients. *Behavior Modification, 14,* 519–547.

Drake, R. E., & Becker, D. R. (1996). The individual placement and support model of supported employment. *Psychiatric Services, 47,* 473–475.

Drake, R. E., & Brunette, M. F. (1998). Complications of severe mental illness related to alcohol and drug use disorders. In M. Galanter (Ed.), *Recent developments in alcoholism: The consequences of alcoholism* (Vol. 14, pp. 285–299). New York: Plenum Press.

Drake, R. E., Gates, C., Whitaker, A., & Cotton, P. G. (1985). Suicide among schizophrenics: A review. *Comprehensive Psychiatry, 26,* 90–100.

Drake, R. E., Mercer-McFadden, C., Mueser, K. T., McHugo, G. J., & Bond, G. R. (1998). Review of integrated mental health and substance abuse treatment for patients with dual disorders. *Schizophrenia Bulletin, 24,* 589–608.

Drake, R. E., Osher, F. C., Noordsy, D. L., Hurlbut, S. C., Teague, G. B., & Beaudett, M. S. (1990). Diagnosis of alcohol use disorders in schizophrenia. *Schizophrenia Bulletin, 16,* 57–67.

Drake, R. E., Osher, F. C., & Wallach, M. A. (1989). Alcohol use and abuse in schizophrenia: A prospective community study. *Journal of Nervous and Mental Diseases, 177,* 408–414.

Drake, R. E., Rosenberg, S. D., & Mueser, K. T. (1996). Assessment of substance use disorder in persons with severe mental illness. In R. E. Drake & K. T. Mueser (Eds.), *Dual diagnosis of major mental illness and substance abuse disorder. II: Recent research and clinical implications. New directions in mental health services* (Vol. 70, pp. 3–17). San Francisco: Jossey-Bass.

Dworkin, R. J., & Adams, G. L. (1987). Retention of Hispanics in public sector mental health services. *Community Mental Health Journal, 23,* 204–216.

Dyck, D. G., Short, R., & Vitaliano, P. P. (1999). Predictors of burden and infectious illness in schizophrenia caregivers. *Psychosomatic Medicine, 61,* 411–419.

Eaton, W. W. (1975). Marital status and schizophrenia. *Acta Psychiatrica Scandinavica, 52,* 320–329.

Estroff, S. E. (1989). Self, identity, and subjective experiences of schizophrenia. In search of the subject. *Schizophrenia Bulletin, 15,* 189–196.

Farina, A. (1998). Stigma. In K. T. Mueser & N. Tarrier (Eds.), *Handbook of social functioning in schizophrenia* (pp. 247–279). Boston: Allyn & Bacon.

Fenton, W. S., & McGlashan, T. H. (1991). Natural history of schizophrenia subtypes. II: Positive and negative symptoms and long term course. *Archives of General Psychiatry, 48,* 978–986.

Fink, P. J., & Tasman, A. (Eds.). (1992). *Stigma and mental illness.* Washington, DC: American Psychiatric Press.

First, M. B., Spitzer, R. L., Gibbon, M., & Williams, J. B. W. (1996). *Structured Clinical Interview for Axes I and II DSM-IV Disorders-Patient edition (SCID-I/P).* New York: New York State Psychiatric Institute, Biometrics Research Department.

Flor-Henry, P. (1985). Schizophrenia: Sex differences. *Canadian Journal of Psychiatry, 30,* 319–322.

Fowler, D., Garety, P., & Kuipers, E. (1995). *Cognitive behavior therapy for psychosis: Theory and practice.* Chichester, West Sussex, England: Wiley.

Fox, J. W. (1990). Social class, mental illness, and social mobility: The social selection-drift hypothesis for serious mental illness. *Journal of Health and Social Behavior, 31,* 344–353.

Fromm-Reichmann, F. (1950). *Principles of intensive psychotherapy.* Chicago: University of Chicago Press.

Galletly, C. A., Field, C. D., & Prior, M. (1993). Urine drug screening of patients admitted to a state psychiatric hospital. *Hospital and Community Psychiatry, 44,* 587–589.

Geddes, J. R., & Lawrie, S. M. (1995). Obstetric complications and schizophrenia: A meta-analysis. *British Journal of Psychiatry, 167,* 786–793.

Glynn, S. M. (1992). Family-based treatment for major mental illness: A new role for psychologists. *California Psychologist, 25,* 22–23.

Glynn, S. M. (1998). Psychopathology and social functioning in schizophrenia. In K. T. Mueser & N. Tarrier (Eds.), *Handbook of social functioning in schizophrenia* (pp. 66–78). Boston: Allyn & Bacon.

Goldman, H. H. (1982). Mental illness and family burden: A public health perspective. *Hospital and Community Psychiatry, 33,* 557–560.

Goldstein, J. M. (1988). Gender differences in the course of schizophrenia. *American Journal of Psychiatry, 146,* 684–689.

González-Wippler, M. (1992). *Powers of the Orishas: Santeria and the worship of saints.* New York: Original Publications.

Goodman, L. A., Dutton, M. A., & Harris, M. (1995). Physical and sexual assault prevalence among episodically homeless women with serious mental illness. *American Journal of Orthopsychiatry, 65,* 468–478.

Goodman, L. A., Dutton, M. A., & Harris, M. (1997). The relationship between violence dimensions and symptom severity among homeless, mentally ill women. *Journal of Traumatic Stress, 10,* 51–70.

Goodman, L. A., Salyers, M. P., Mueser, K. T., Rosenberg, S. D., Swartz, M., Essock, S. M., et al. (2001). Recent victimization in women and men with severe mental illness: Prevalence and correlates. *Journal of Traumatic Stress, 14,* 615–632.

Goodwin, F. K., & Jamison, K. R. (1990). *Manic-depressive illness.* New York: Oxford University Press.

Gottesman, I. I. (1991). *Schizophrenia genesis: The origins of madness.* New York: Freeman.

Greden, J. F., & Tandon, R. (Eds.). (1991). *Negative schizophrenic symptoms: Pathophysiology and clinical implications.* Washington, DC: American Psychiatric Press.

Green, M. F., Marshall, B. D., Jr., Wirshing, W. C., Ames, D., Marder, S. R., McGurk, S., et al. (1997). Does risperidone improve verbal working memory in treatment-resistant schizophrenia? *American Journal of Psychiatry, 154,* 799–804.

Greenfield, S. F., Strakowski, S. M., Tohen, M., Batson, S. C., & Kolbrener, M. L. (1994). Childhood abuse in first-episode psychosis. *British Journal of Psychiatry, 164,* 831–834.

Griffith, E. E. H., Young, J. L., & Smith, D. L. (1984). An analysis of the therapeutic elements in a Black church service. *Hospital and Community Psychiatry, 35,* 464–469.

Haas, G. L., & Garratt, L. S. (1998). Gender differences in social functioning. In K. T. Mueser & N. Tarrier (Eds.), *Handbook of social functioning in schizophrenia* (pp. 149–180). Boston: Allyn & Bacon.

Häfner, H., Riecher-Rössler, A., An Der Heiden, W., Maurer, K., Fätkenheuer, B., & Löffler, W. (1993). Generating and testing a causal explanation of the gender difference in age at first onset of schizophrenia. *Psychological Medicine, 23,* 925–940.

Halford, W. K., Schweitzer, R. D., & Varghese, F. N. (1991). Effects of family environment on negative symptoms and quality of life on psychotic patients. *Hospital and Community Psychiatry, 42,* 1241–1247.

Hans, S. L., Marcus, J., Henson, L., Auerbach, J. G., & Mirsky, A. F. (1992). Interpersonal behavior of children at risk for schizophrenia. *Psychiatry, 55,* 314–335.

Harding, C. M., Brooks, G. W., Ashikaga, T., Strauss, J. S., & Breier, A. (1987a). The Vermont longitudinal study of persons with severe mental illness. I: Methodology, study sample, and overall status 32 years later. *American Journal of Psychiatry, 144,* 718–726.

Harding, C. M., Brooks, G. W., Ashikaga, T., Strauss, J. S., & Breier, A. (1987b). The Vermont longitudinal study of persons with severe mental illness. II: Long-term outcome of subjects who retrospectively met *DSM-III* criteria for schizophrenia. *American Journal of Psychiatry, 144,* 727–735.

Harding, C. M., & Keller, A. B. (1998). Long-term outcome of social functioning. In K. T. Mueser & N. Tarrier (Eds.), *Social functioning in schizophrenia* (pp. 134–148). Boston: Allyn & Bacon.

Harris, M. (1996). Treating sexual abuse trauma with dually diagnosed women. *Community Mental Health Journal, 32,* 371–385.

Hatfield, A. B., & Lefley, H. P. (Eds.). (1987). *Families of the mentally ill: Coping and adaptation.* New York: Guilford Press.

Hatfield, A. B., & Lefley, H. P. (Eds.). (1993). *Surviving mental illness: Stress, coping, and adaptation.* New York: Guilford Press.

Heinssen, R. K., Liberman, R. P., & Kopelowicz, A. (2000). Psychosocial skills training for schizophrenia: Lessons from the laboratory. *Schizophrenia Bulletin, 26,* 21–46.

Hiday, V. A., Swartz, M. S., Swanson, J. W., Borum, R., & Wagner, H. R. (1999). Criminal victimization of persons with severe mental illness. *Psychiatric Services, 50,* 62–68.

Hodgins, S., & Côté, G. (1993). Major mental disorder and antisocial personality disorder: A criminal combination. *Bulletin of the American Academy of Psychiatry Law, 21,* 155–160.

Hodgins, S., & Côté, G. (1996). Schizophrenia and antisocial personality disorder: A criminal combination. In L. B. Schlesinger (Ed.), *Explorations in criminal psychopathology: Clinical syndromes with forensic implications* (pp. 217–237). Springfield, IL: Charles C Thomas.

Hodgins, S., Mednick, S. A., Brennan, P. A., Schulsinger, F., & Engberg, M. (1996). Mental disorder and crime: Evidence from a Danish birth cohort. *Archives of General Psychiatry, 53,* 489–496.

Hollingshead, A. B., & Redlich, F. C. (1958). *Social class and mental illness: A community study.* New York: Wiley.

Hough, R. L., Landsverk, J. A., Karno, M., Burnam, A., Timbers, D. M., Escobar, J. I., et al. (1987). Utilization of health and mental health services by Los Angeles Mexican Americans and non-Hispanic Whites. *Archives of General Psychiatry, 44,* 702–709.

Howard, R., Almeida, O., & Levy R. (1994). Phenomenology, demography and diagnosis in late paraphrenia. *Psychological Medicine, 24,* 397–410.

Hu, T., Snowden, L. R., Jerrell, J. M., & Nguyen, T. D. (1991). Ethnic populations in public mental health: Services choices and level of use. *American Journal of Public Health, 81,* 1429–1434.

Hutchings, P. S., & Dutton, M. A. (1993). Sexual assault history in a community mental health center clinical population. *Community Mental Health Journal, 29,* 59–63.

Inskip, H. M., Harris, E. C., & Barraclough, B. (1998). Lifetime risk of suicide for affective disorder, alcoholism, and schizophrenia. *British Journal of Psychiatry, 172,* 35–37.

Jablensky, A. (1989). Epidemiology and cross-cultural aspects of schizophrenia. *Psychiatric Annals, 19,* 516–524.

Jablensky, A. (1999). Schizophrenia: Epidemiology. *Current Opinion in Psychiatry, 12,* 19–28.

Jacob, T. (1975). Family interaction in disturbed and normal families: A methodological and substantive review. *Psychological Bulletin, 82,* 33–65.

Jacobson, A. (1989). Physical and sexual assault histories among psychiatric outpatients. *American Journal of Psychiatry, 146,* 755–758.

Jacobson, A., & Herald, C. (1990). The relevance of childhood sexual abuse to adult psychiatric inpatient care. *Hospital and Community Psychiatry, 41,* 154–158.

Jacobson, A., & Richardson, B. (1987). Assault experiences of 100 psychiatric inpatients: Evidence of the need for routine inquiry. *American Journal of Psychiatry, 144,* 508–513.

Jones, B. E., Gray, B. A., & Parsons, E. B. (1981). Manic-depressive illness among poor urban Blacks. *American Journal of Psychiatry, 138,* 654–657.

Jones, B. E., Gray, B. A., & Parsons, E. B. (1983). Manic-depressive illness among poor urban Hispanics. *American Journal of Psychiatry, 140,* 1208–1210.

Kane, J. M., & Marder, S. R. (1993). Psychopharmacologic treatment of schizophrenia. *Schizophrenia Bulletin, 19,* 287–302.

Kay, S. R., & Lindenmayer, J. (1987). Outcome predictors in acute schizophrenia: Prospective significance of background and clinical dimensions. *Journal of Nervous and Mental Diseases, 175,* 152–160.

Keith, S. J., Regier, D. A., & Rae, D. S. (1991). Schizophrenic disorders. In L. N. Robins & D. A. Regier (Eds.), *Psychiatric disorders in America: The Epidemiologic Catchment Area Study* (pp. 33–52). New York: Free Press.

Kemp, R., Hayward, P., Applewhaite, G., Everitt, B., & David, A. (1996). Compliance therapy in psychotic patients: Randomised controlled trial. *British Medical Journal, 312,* 345–349.

Kemp, R., Kirov, G., Everitt, B., Hayward, P., & David, A. (1998). Randomised controlled trial of compliance therapy: 18-month follow-up. *British Journal of Psychiatry, 173,* 271–272.

Kendler, K. S., & Diehl, S. R. (1993). The genetics of schizophrenia. *Schizophrenia Bulletin, 19,* 261–285.

Kessler, R. C., Foster, C. L., Saunders, W. B., & Stang, P. E. (1995). Social consequences of psychiatric disorders. I: Educational attainment. *American Journal of Psychiatry, 152,* 1026–1032.

Kessler, R. C., Sonnega, A., Bromet, E., Hughes, M., & Nelson, C. B. (1995). Posttraumatic stress disorder in the national comorbidity survey. *Archives of General Psychiatry, 52,* 1048–1060.

Kindermann, S. S., Karimi, A., Symonds, L., Brown, G. G., & Jeste, D. V. (1997). Review of functional magnetic resonance imaging in schizophrenia. *Schizophrenia Research, 27,* 143–156.

Kirch, D. G. (1993). Infection and autoimmunity as etiologic factors in schizophrenia: A review and reappraisal. *Schizophrenia Bulletin, 19,* 355–370.

Kraepelin E. (1971) *Dementia praecox and paraphrenia* (R. M. Barclay, Trans.). New York: Robert E. Krieger. (Original work published 1919)

Kramer, M. S., Vogel, W. H., DiJohnson, C., Dewey, D. A., Sheves, P., Cavicchia, S., et al. (1989). Antidepressants in depressed schizophrenic inpatients. *Archives of General Psychiatry, 46,* 922–928.

Kranzler, H. R., Kadden, R. M., Burleson, J. A., Babor, T. F., Apter, A., & Rounsaville, B. J. (1995). Validity of psychiatric diagnoses in patients with substance use disorders: Is the interview more important than the interviewer? *Comprehensive Psychiatry, 36,* 278–288.

Lam, D. H. (1991). Psychosocial family intervention in schizophrenia: A review of empirical studies. *Psychological Medicine, 21,* 423–441.

Lawrie, S. M., & Abukmeil S. S. (1998). Brain abnormality in schizophrenia: A systematic and quantitative review of volumetric magnetic resonance imaging studies. *British Journal of Psychiatry, 172,* 110–120.

Leff, J., & Vaughn, C. (1985). *Expressed emotion in families: Its significance for mental illness.* New York: Guilford Press.

Lefley, H. P. (1990). Culture and chronic mental illness. *Hospital and Community Psychiatry, 41,* 277–286.

Lehman, A. F., Myers, C. P., Dixon, L. B., & Johnson, J. L. (1994). Defining subgroups of dual diagnosis patients for service planning. *Hospital and Community Psychiatry, 45,* 556–561.

Lehman, A. F., Myers, C. P., Dixon, L. B., & Johnson, J. L. (1996). Detection of substance use disorders among psychiatric inpatients. *Journal of Nervous and Mental Diseases, 184,* 228–233.

Levinson, D. F., & Levitt, M. M. (1987). Schizoaffective mania reconsidered. *American Journal of Psychiatry, 144,* 415–425.

Levinson, D. F., & Mowry, B. J. (1991). Defining the schizophrenia spectrum: Issues for genetic linkage studies. *Schizophrenia Bulletin, 17,* 491–514.

Liberman, R. P. (1994). Treatment and rehabilitation of the seriously mentally ill in China: Impressions of a society in transition. *American Journal of Orthopsychiatry, 64,* 68–77.

Liberman, R. P., Mueser, K. T., Wallace, C. J., Jacobs, H. E., Eckman, T., & Massel, H. K. (1986). Training skills in the psychiatrically disabled: Learning coping and competence. *Schizophrenia Bulletin, 12,* 631–647.

Liberman, R. P., Wallace, C. J., Blackwell, G., Kopelowicz, A., Vaccaro, J. V., & Mintz, J. (1998). Skills training versus psychosocial occupational therapy for persons with persistent schizophrenia. *American Journal of Psychiatry, 155,* 1087–1091.

Liddle, P. F. (1987). Schizophrenic syndromes, cognitive performance and neurological dysfunction. *Psychological Medicine, 17,* 49–57.

Liddle, P. F. (1995). Brain imaging. In S. R. Hirsch & D. R. Weinberger (Eds.), *Schizophrenia* (pp. 425–439). Cambridge, MA: Blackwell Science.

Liddle, P. F. (1997). Dynamic neuroimaging with PET, SPET or fMRI. *International Review of Psychiatry, 9,* 331–337.

Lieberman, J. A., Mailman, R. B., Duncan, G., Sikich, L., Chakos, M., Nichols, D. E., et al. (1998). A decade of serotonin research: Role of serotonin in treatment of psychosis. *Biological Psychiatry, 44,* 1099–1117.

Lin, K.-M., & Kleinman, A. M. (1988). Psychopathology and clinical course of schizophrenia: A cross-cultural perspective. *Schizophrenia Bulletin, 14,* 555–567.

Lincoln, C. V., & McGorry, P. (1995). Who Cares? Pathways to psychiatric care for young people experiencing a first episode of psychosis. *Psychiatric Services, 46,* 1166–1171.

Lincoln, E. C., & Mamiya, L. H. (1990). *The Black church in the African American experience.* Durham, NC: Duke University Press.

Lipschitz, D. S., Kaplan, M. L., Sorkenn, J. B., Faedda, G. L., Chorney, P., & Asnis, G. M. (1996). Prevalence and characteristics of physical and sexual abuse among psychiatric outpatients. *Psychiatric Services, 47,* 189–191.

Lo, W. H., & Lo, T. (1977). A ten-year follow-up study of Chinese schizophrenics in Hong Kong. *British Journal of Psychiatry, 131,* 63–66.

Loring, M., & Powell, B. (1988). Gender, race, and *DSM-III:* A study of the objectivity of psychiatric diagnostic behavior. *Journal of Health and Social Behavior, 29,* 1–22.

Lysaker, P. H., Bell, M. D., Zito, W. S., & Bioty, S. M. (1995). Social skills at work: Deficits and predictors of improvement in schizophrenia. *Journal of Nervous and Mental Diseases, 183,* 688–692.

Magaña, A. B., Goldstein, M. J., Karno, M., Miklowitz, D. J., Jenkins, J., & Falloon, I. R. H. (1986). A brief method for assessing expressed emotion in relatives of psychiatric patients. *Psychiatry Research, 17,* 203–212.

Maisto, S. A., Carey, M. P., Carey, K. B., Gordon, C. M., & Gleason, J. R. (2000). Use of the AUDIT and the DAST-10 to identify alcohol and drug use disorders among adults with a severe and persistent mental illness. *Psychological Assessment, 12,* 186–192.

Marder, S. R., Wirshing, W. C., Mintz, J., McKenzie, J., Johnston, K., Eckman, T. A., et al. (1996). Two-year outcome for social skills training and group psychotherapy for outpatients with schizophrenia. *American Journal of Psychiatry, 153,* 1585–1592.

Marengo, J. (1994). Classifying the courses of schizophrenia. *Schizophrenia Bulletin, 20,* 519–536.

Mattes, J. A., & Nayak, D. (1984). Lithium versus fluphenazine for prophylaxis in mainly schizophrenic schizoaffectives. *Biological Psychiatry, 19,* 445–449.

May, A. (1997). Psychopathology and religion in the era of "enlightened science": A case report. *European Journal of Psychiatry, 11,* 14–20.

McClure, R. J., Keshavan, M. S., & Pettegrew, J. W. (1998). Chemical and physiologic brain imaging in schizophrenia. *Psychiatric Clinics of North America, 21,* 93–122.

McEvoy, J. P., Freter, S., Everett, G., Geller, J. L., Appelbaum, P., Apperson, L. J., et al. (1989). Insight and the clinical outcome of schizophrenic patients. *Journal of Nervous and Mental Diseases, 177,* 48–51.

Merriam, A. E., Kay, S. R., Opler, L. A., Kushner, S. F., & van Praag, H. M. (1990). Neurological signs and the positive-negative dimension in schizophrenia. *Biological Psychiatry, 28,* 181–192.

Moore, H., West, A. R., & Grace, A. A. (1999). The regulation of forebrain dopamine transmission: Relevance to the pathophysiology and psychopathology of schizophrenia. *Biological Psychiatry, 46,* 40–55.

Moos, R. H., & Moos, B. S. (1981). *Family Environment Scale manual.* Palo Alto, CA: Consulting Psychologists Press.

Morales-Dorta, J. (1976). *Puerto Rican espiritismo: Religion and psychotherapy.* New York: Vantage Press.

Mueser, K. T., & Bellack, A. S. (1998). Social skills and social functioning. In K. T. Mueser & N. Tarrier (Eds.), *Social functioning in schizophrenia* (pp. 79–96). Boston: Allyn & Bacon.

Mueser, K. T., Bellack, A. S., Douglas, M. S., & Morrison, R. L. (1991). Prevalence and stability of social skill deficits in schizophrenia. *Schizophrenia Research, 5,* 167–176.

Mueser, K. T., Bellack, A. S., Douglas, M. S., & Wade, J. H. (1991). Prediction of social skill acquisition in schizophrenic and major affective disorder patients from memory and symptomatology. *Psychiatry Research, 37,* 281–296.

Mueser, K. T., Bellack, A. S., Morrison, R. L., & Wade, J. H. (1990). Gender, social competence, and symptomatology in schizophrenia: A longitudinal analysis. *Journal of Abnormal Psychology, 99,* 138–147.

Mueser, K. T., Bellack, A. S., Morrison, R. L., & Wixted, J. T. (1990). Social competence in schizophrenia: Premorbid adjustment, social skill, and domains of functioning. *Journal of Psychiatric Research, 24,* 51–63.

Mueser, K. T., Bellack, A. S., Wade, J. H., Sayers, S. L., Tierney, A., & Haas, G. (1993). Expressed emotion, social skill, and response to negative affect in schizophrenia. *Journal of Abnormal Psychology, 102,* 339–351.

Mueser, K. T., Bennett, M., & Kushner, M. G. (1995). Epidemiology of substance use disorders among persons with chronic mental illnesses. In A. Lehman & L. Dixon (Eds.), *Double jeopardy: Chronic mental illness and substance abuse* (pp. 9–25). Chur, Switzerland: Harwood Academic.

Mueser, K. T., & Berenbaum, H. (1990). Psychodynamic treatment of schizophrenia: Is there a future? *Psychological Medicine, 20,* 253–262.

Mueser, K. T., Bond, G. R., Drake, R. E., & Resnick, S. G. (1998). Models of community care for severe mental illness: A review of research on case management. *Schizophrenia Bulletin, 24,* 37–74.

Mueser, K. T., Curran, P. J., & McHugo, G. J. (1997). Factor structure of the Brief Psychiatric Rating Scale in schizophrenia. *Psychological Assessment, 9,* 196–204.

Mueser, K. T., Douglas, M. S., Bellack, A. S., & Morrison, R. L. (1991). Assessment of enduring deficit and negative symptom subtypes in schizophrenia. *Schizophrenia Bulletin, 17,* 565–582.

Mueser, K. T., Drake, R. E., & Bond, G. R. (1997). Recent advances in psychiatric rehabilitation for patients with severe mental illness. *Harvard Review of Psychiatry, 5,* 123–137.

Mueser, K. T., & Glynn, S. M. (1999). *Behavioral family therapy for psychiatric disorders* (2nd ed.). Oakland, CA: New Harbinger.

Mueser, K. T., Goodman, L. B., Trumbetta, S. L., Rosenberg, S. D., Osher, F. C., Vidaver, R., et al. (1998). Trauma and posttraumatic stress disorder in severe mental illness. *Journal of Consulting and Clinical Psychology, 66,* 493–499.

Mueser, K. T., Levine, S., Bellack, A. S., Douglas, M. S., & Brady, E. U. (1990). Social skills training for acute psychiatric patients. *Hospital and Community Psychiatry, 41,* 1249–1251.

Mueser, K. T., Rosenberg, S. D., Drake, R. E., Miles, K. M., Wolford, G. L., Vidaver, R., et al. (1999). Conduct disorder, antisocial personality disorder, and substance use disorders in schizophrenia and major affective disorders. *Journal of Studies on Alcohol, 60,* 278–284.

Mueser, K. T., Rosenberg, S. D., Goodman, L. A., & Trumbetta, S. L. (2002). Trauma, PTSD, and the course of schizophrenia: An interactive model. *Schizophrenia Research, 53,* 123–143.

Mueser, K. T., Yarnold, P. R., & Bellack, A. S. (1992). Diagnostic and demographic correlates of substance abuse in schizophrenia and major affective disorder. *Acta Psychiatrica Scandinavica, 85,* 48–55.

Mueser, K. T., Yarnold, P. R., Levinson, D. F., Singh, H., Bellack, A. S., Kee, K., et al. (1990). Prevalence of substance abuse in schizophrenia: Demographic and clinical correlates. *Schizophrenia Bulletin, 16,* 31–56.

Munk-Jørgensen, P. (1987). First-admission rates and marital status of schizophrenics. *Acta Psychiatrica Scandinavica, 76,* 210–216.

Murphy, H. B. M., & Raman, A. C. (1971). The chronicity of schizophrenia in indigenous tropical peoples. *British Journal of Psychiatry, 118,* 489–497.

Neumann, C. S., Grimes, K., Walker, E., & Baum, K. (1995). Developmental pathways to schizophrenia: Behavioral subtypes. *Journal of Abnormal Psychology, 104,* 558–566.

Nolan, K. A., Volavka, J., Mohr, P., & Czobor, P. (1999). Psychopathy and violent behavior among patients with schizophrenia or schizoaffective disorder. *Psychiatric Services, 50,* 787–792.

Nuechterlein, K. H., & Dawson, M. E. (1984). A heuristic vulnerability/stress model of schizophrenic episodes. *Schizophrenia Bulletin, 10,* 300–312.

Oldridge, M. L., & Hughes, I. C. T. (1992). Psychological well-being in families with a member suffering from schizophrenia. *British Journal of Psychiatry, 161,* 249–251.

Padgett, D. K., Patrick, C., Burns, B. J., & Schlesinger, H. J. (1994). Women and outpatient mental health services: Use by Black, Hispanic, and White women in a national insured population. *Journal of Mental Health Administration, 21,* 347–360.

Parra, F. (1985). Social tolerance of the mentally ill in the Mexican American community. *International Journal of Social Psychiatry, 31,* 37–47.

Pearlson, G. D. (2000). Neurobiology of schizophrenia. *Annals of Neurology, 48,* 556–566.

Peen, J., & Dekker, J. (1997). Admission rates for schizophrenia in The Netherlands: An urban/rural comparison. *Acta Psychiatrica Scandinavica, 96,* 301–305.

Penn, D. L., Hope, D. A., Spaulding, W. D., & Kucera, J. (1994). Social anxiety in schizophrenia. *Schizophrenia Research, 11,* 277–284.

Penn, D. L., Mueser, K. T., Spaulding, W. D., Hope, D. A., & Reed, D. (1995). Information processing and social competence in chronic schizophrenia. *Schizophrenia Bulletin, 21,* 269–281.

Phillips, S. D., Burns, B. J., Edgar, E. R., Mueser, K. T., Linkins, K. W., Rosenheck, R. A., et al. (2001). Moving assertive community treatment into standard practice. *Psychiatric Services, 52,* 771–779.

Pitschel-Walz, G., Leucht, S., Bäuml, J., Kissling, W., & Engel, R. R. (2001). The effect of family interventions on relapse and rehospitalization in schizophrenia: A meta-analysis. *Schizophrenia Bulletin, 27,* 73–92.

Pope, H. G., & Lipinski, J. F. (1978). Diagnosis in schizophrenia and manic-depressive illness. *Archives of General Psychiatry, 35,* 811–828.

Quinlivan, R., Hough, R., Crowell, A., Beach, C., Hofstetter, R., & Kenworthy, K. (1995). Service utilization and costs of care for severely mentally ill clients in an intensive case management program. *Psychiatric Services, 46,* 365–371.

Regier, D. A., Farmer, M. E., Rae, D. S., Locke, B. Z., Keith, S. J., Judd, L. L., et al. (1990). Comorbidity of mental disorders with alcohol and other drug abuse. *Journal of the American Medical Association, 264,* 2511–2518.

Resnick, H. S., Kilpatrick, D. G., Dansky, B. S., Saunders, B. E., & Best, C. L. (1993). Prevalence of civilian trauma and posttraumatic stress disorder in a representative national sample of women. *Journal of Consulting and Clinical Psychology, 61,* 984–991.

Robins, L. N. (1966). *Deviant children grown up.* Huntington, NY: Krieger.

Robins, L. N., & Price, R. K. (1991). Adult disorders predicted by childhood conduct problems: Results from the NIMH Epidemiologic Catchment Area project. *Psychiatry, 54,* 116–132.

Rodrigo, G., Lusiardo, M., Briggs, G., & Ulmer, A. (1991). Differences between schizophrenics born in winter and summer. *Acta Psychiatrica Scandinavica, 84,* 320–322.

Rose, S. M., Peabody, C. G., & Stratigeas, B. (1991). Undetected abuse among intensive case management clients. *Hospital and Community Psychiatry, 42,* 499–503.

Rosenberg, S. D., Drake, R. E., Wolford, G. L., Mueser, K. T., Oxman, T. E., Vidaver, R. M., et al. (1998). Dartmouth Assessment of Lifestyle Instrument (DALI): A substance use disorder screen for people with severe mental illness. *American Journal of Psychiatry, 155,* 232–238.

Rosenberg, S. D., Mueser, K. T., Friedman, M. J., Gorman, P. G., Drake, R. E., Vidaver, R. M., et al. (2001). Developing effective treatments for posttraumatic disorders: A review and proposal. *Psychiatric Services, 52,* 1453–1461.

Ross, C. A., Anderson, G., & Clark, P. (1994). Childhood abuse and the positive symptoms of schizophrenia. *Hospital and Community Psychiatry, 45,* 489–491.

Roy, A. (Ed.). (1986). *Suicide.* Baltimore: Williams & Wilkins.

Rutter, M. (1984). Psychopathology and development. I: Childhood antecedents of adult psychiatric disorder. *Australian and New Zealand Journal of Psychiatry, 18,* 225–234.

Salokangas, R. K. R. (1978). Socioeconomic development and schizophrenia. *Psychiatria Fennica,* 103–112.

Sands, J. R., & Harrow, M. (1999). Depression during the longitudinal course of schizophrenia. *Schizophrenia Bulletin, 25,* 157–171.

Sartorius, N., Jablensky, A., Korten, A., Ernberg, G., Anker, M., Cooper, J. E., et al. (1986). Early manifestations and first-contact incidence of schizophrenia in different cultures. *Psychological Medicine, 16,* 909–928.

Schaub, A., Behrendt, B., Brenner, H. D., Mueser, K. T., & Liberman, R. P. (1998). Training schizophrenic patients to manage their symptoms: Predictors of treatment response to the German version of the Symptom Management Module. *Schizophrenia Research, 31,* 121–130.

Schuckit, M. A. (1995). *Drug and alcohol abuse: A clinical guide to diagnosis and treatment: Critical issues in psychiatry* (4th ed.). New York: Plenum Press.

Searles, H. (1965). *Collected papers on schizophrenia and related subjects.* New York: International Universities Press.

Sevy, S., & Davidson, M. (1995). The cost of cognitive impairment in schizophrenia. *Schizophrenia Research, 17,* 1–3.

Skilbeck, W. M., Acosta, F. X., Yamamoto, J., & Evans, L. A. (1984). Self-reported psychiatric symptoms among Black, Hispanic, and White outpatients. *Journal of Clinical Psychology, 40,* 1184–1189.

Smith, T. E., Hull, J. W., Anthony, D. T., Goodman, M., Hedayat-Harris, A., Felger, T., et al. (1997). Posthospitalization treatment adherence of schizophrenic patients: Gender differences in skill acquisition. *Psychiatry Research, 69,* 123–129.

Steadman, H. J., Mulvey, E. P., Monahan, J., Robbins, P. C., Appelbaum, P. S., Grisso, T., et al. (1998). Violence by people discharged from acute psychiatric inpatient facilities and by others in the same neighborhoods. *Archives of General Psychiatry, 55,* 393–401.

Stone, A., Greenstein, R., Gamble, G., & McLellan, A. T. (1993). Cocaine use in chronic schizophrenic outpatients receiving depot neuroleptic medications. *Hospital and Community Psychiatry, 44,* 176–177.

Sue, D. W., & Sue, D. (1990). *Counseling the culturally different: Theory and practice* (2nd ed.). New York: Wiley, Interscience.

Sue, S., Fujino, D. C., Hu, L.-T., Takeuchi, D. T., & Zane, N. W. S. (1991). Community mental health services for ethnic minority groups: A test of the cultural responsiveness hypothesis. *Journal of Consulting and Clinical Psychology, 59,* 533–540.

Susser, E., & Lin, S. (1992). Schizophrenia after prenatal exposure to the Dutch hunger winter of 1944–1945. *Archives of General Psychiatry, 49,* 983–988.

Susser, E., Neugebauer, R., Hoek, H. W., Brown, A. S., Lin, S., Labovitz, D., et al. (1996). Schizophrenia after prenatal famine: Further evidence. *Archives of General Psychiatry, 53,* 25–31.

Susser, E. Struening, E. L., & Conover, S. (1989). Psychiatric problems in homeless men: Lifetime psychosis, substance use, and current distress in new arrivals at New York City shelters. *Archives of General Psychiatry, 46,* 845–850.

Swanson, J. W. (1994). Mental disorder, substance abuse, and community violence: An epidemiological approach. In J. Monahan & H. Steadman (Eds.), *Violence and mental disorder: Developments in risk assessment* (pp. 101–136). Chicago: University of Chicago Press.

Swanson, J. W., Holzer, C. E., Ganju, V. K., & Jono, R. T. (1990). Violence and psychiatric disorder in the community: Evidence from the Epidemiologic Catchment Area Surveys. *Hospital and Community Psychiatry, 41,* 761–770.

Swartz, M. S., Swanson, J. W., Hiday, V. A., Borum, R., Wagner, H. R., & Burns, B. J. (1998). Violence and severe mental illness: The effects of substance abuse and nonadherence to medication. *American Journal of Psychiatry, 155,* 226–231.

Switzer, G. E., Dew, M. A., Thompson, K., Goycoolea, J. M., Derricott, T., & Mullins, S. D. (1999). Posttraumatic stress disorder and service utilization among urban mental health center clients. *Journal of Traumatic Stress, 12,* 25–39.

Takei, N., Mortensen, P. B., Klaening, U., Murray, R. M., Sham, P. C., O'Callaghan, E., et al. (1996). Relationship between in utero exposure to influenza epidemics and risk of schizophrenia in Denmark. *Biological Psychiatry, 40,* 817–824.

Takei, N., Sham, P. C., O'Callaghan, E., Glover, G., & Murray, R. M. (1995). Schizophrenia: Increased risk associated with winter and city birth—a case-control study in 12 regions within England and Wales. *Journal of Epidemiology and Community Health, 49,* 106–109.

Telles, C., Karno, M., Mintz, J., Paz, G., Arias, M., Tucker, D., et al. (1995). Immigrant families coping with schizophrenia: Behavioral family intervention v. case management with a low-income Spanish-speaking population. *British Journal of Psychiatry, 167,* 473–479.

Terkelsen, K. G. (1983). Schizophrenia and the family. II: Adverse effects of family therapy. *Family Process, 22,* 191–200.

Tessler, R., & Gamache, G. (1995). *Evaluating family experiences with severe mental illness: To be used in conjunction with The Family Experiences Interview Schedule (FEIS): The Evaluation Center @ HSRI toolkit.* Cambridge, MA: The Evaluation Center @ HSRI.

Test, M. A., Wallisch, L. S., Allness, D. J., & Ripp, K. (1989). Substance use in young adults with schizophrenic disorders. *Schizophrenia Bulletin, 15,* 465–476.

Thomas, H. V., Dalman, C., David, A. S., Gentz, J., Lewis, G., & Allebeck, P. (2001). Obstetric complications and risk of schizophrenia: Effect of gender, age at diagnosis, and maternal history of psychosis. *British Journal of Psychiatry, 179,* 409–414.

Tienari, P. (1991). Interaction between genetic vulnerability and family environment: The Finnish adoptive family study of schizophrenia. *Acta Psychiatrica Scandinavica, 84,* 460–465.

Tienari, P., Sorri, A., Lahti, I., Naarala, M., Wahlberg, K., Moring, J., et al. (1987). Genetic and psychosocial factors in schizophrenia: The Finnish Adoptive Family Study. *Schizophrenia Bulletin, 13,* 477–484.

Tjaden, P., & Thoennes, N. (1998, November). *Prevalence, incidence, and consequences of violence against women: Findings from the national violence against women survey.* Washington, DC: U.S. Department of Justice, National Institute of Justice, Research in Brief.

Tollefson, G. D., & Sanger, T. M. (1997). Negative symptoms: A path analytic approach to a double-blind, placebo- and haloperidol-controlled clinical trial with olanzapine. *American Journal of Psychiatry, 154,* 466–474.

Torrey, E. F. (1995). *Surviving schizophrenia: A manual for families, consumers, and providers* (3rd ed.). New York: HarperCollins.

Torrey, E. F., Bowler, A. E., & Clark, K. (1997). Urban birth and residence as risk factors for psychoses: An analysis of 1880 data. *Schizophrenia Research, 25,* 169–176.

Torrey, E. F., Bowler, A. E., Rawlings, R., & Terrazas, A. (1993). Seasonality of schizophrenia and stillbirths. *Schizophrenia Bulletin, 19,* 557–562.

Torrey, E. F., Stieber, J., Ezekiel, J., Wolfe, S. M., Sharfstein, J., Noble, J. H., et al. (1992). *Criminalizing the seriously mentally ill: The abuse of jails as mental hospitals.* Joint report of the National Alliance of the Mentally Ill, Arlington, VA and Public Citizen's Health Research Group, Washington, DC.

Tsuang, M. T. (1986). Predictors of poor and good outcome in schizophrenia. In: L. Erlenmeyer-Kimling & N. E. Miller (Eds.), *Life-span research on the prediction of psychopathology,* Hillsdale NJ: Erlbaum.

Uttaro, T., & Mechanic, D. (1994). The NAMI consumer survey analysis of unmet needs. *Hospital and Community Psychiatry, 45,* 372–374.

Van Der Does, A. J. W., Dingemans, P. M. A. J., Linszen, D. H., Nugter, M. A., & Scholte, W. F. (1993). Symptom dimensions and cognitive and social functioning in recent-onset schizophrenia. *Psychological Medicine, 23,* 745–753.

Velligan, D. I., Mahurin, R. K., Diamond, P. L., Hazleton, B. C., Eckert, S. L., & Miller, A. L. (1997). The functional significance of symptomatology and cognitive function in schizophrenia. *Schizophrenia Research, 25,* 21–31.

Wahlbeck, K., Cheine, M., Essali, A., & Adams, C. (1999). Evidence of clozapine's effectiveness in schizophrenia: A systematic review and meta-analysis of randomized trials. *American Journal of Psychiatry, 156,* 990–999.

Walker, E., Downey, G., & Caspi, A. (1991). Twin studies of psychopathology: Why do the concordance rates vary? *Schizophrenia Research, 5,* 211–221.

Wallace, C. J., Liberman, R. P., Tauber, R., & Wallace, J. (2000). The Independent Living Skills Survey: A comprehensive measure of the community functioning of severely and persistently mentally ill individuals. *Schizophrenia Bulletin, 26,* 631–658.

Watt, N. F. (1978). Patterns of childhood social development in adult schizophrenics. *Archives of General Psychiatry, 35,* 160–165.

Waxler, N. E., & Mishler, E. G. (1971). Parental interaction with schizophrenic children and well siblings. *Archives of General Psychiatry, 25,* 223–231.

Webb, C., Pfeiffer, M., Mueser, K. T., Mensch, E., DeGirolamo, J., & Levenson, D. F. (1998). Burden and well-being of caregivers for the severely mentally ill: The role of coping style and social support. *Schizophrenia Research, 34,* 169–180.

Westermeyer, J. (1989). Psychiatric epidemiology across cultures: Current issues and trends. *Transcultural Psychiatric Research Review, 26,* 5–25.

Xiong, W., Phillips, M. R., Hu, X., Ruiwen, W., Dai, Q., Kleinman, J., et al. (1994). Family-based intervention for schizophrenic patients in China: A randomised controlled trial. *British Journal of Psychiatry, 165,* 239–247.

Young, C. R., Bowers, M. B., & Mazure, C. M. (1998). Management of the adverse effects of clozapine. *Schizophrenia Bulletin, 24,* 381–390.

Zhang, M., Wang, M., Li, J., & Phillips, M. R. (1994). Randomised-control trial of family intervention for 78 first-episode male schizophrenic patients: An 18-month study in Suzhou, Jiangsu. *British Journal of Psychiatry, 165,* 96–102.

Zigler, E., & Glick, M. (1986). *A developmental approach to adult psychopathology.* New York: Wiley.

Zubin, J., & Spring, B. (1977). Vulnerability: A new view of schizophrenia. *Journal of Abnormal Psychology, 86,* 103–123.

CHAPTER 9

Mood Disorders: Depressive Disorders

PATRICIA A. AREÁN and YAEL CHATAV

DESCRIPTION OF THE DISORDERS

DEPRESSIVE DISORDERS ARE among the most common psychiatric disorders, characterized by feelings of sadness, lack of interest in formerly enjoyable pursuits, sleep and appetite disturbance, feelings of worthlessness, and thoughts of death and dying. All depressive disorders are extremely disabling, second only to heart disease as the illness most responsible for poor quality of life and disability (Pincus & Pettit, 2001). Depression is also associated with increased suicide risk. Statistics show that 15% of people with major depression kill themselves (Satcher, 2000). Fortunately, depressive disorders can be treated successfully with antidepressant medication and psychotherapy (Moore & Bona, 2001). The research on these disorders grows daily, and we know quite a bit about how depressive disorders are presented, their etiology, and their course and prognosis. This chapter describes the depressive disorders, discusses their prevalence and effects on people afflicted by these disorders, examines best methods for assessing depressive disorders, and presents the latest research on their etiology.

According to the fourth edition of the *Diagnostic and Statistical Manual of Mental Disorders* (*DSM-IV*; American Psychiatric Association [APA], 1994), *depressive disorders* include three categories of illnesses: *major depression (MDD)*, *dysthymia*, and *depressive disorder not otherwise specified (depression NOS)*. As shown in Table 9.1, all three categories share common symptoms and clinical features. First, all three disorders consist of *mood symptoms*, which include feeling sad, empty, worried, and irritable. Second, these disorders are characterized by *vegetative symptoms*, which include fatigue, social withdrawal, and agitation. Changes in sleep and appetite are also common, with lack of sleep and appetite being more typical in depression, although patients with an atypical presentation complain of hypersomnia or weight gain due to frequent eating. Finally, all three disorders consist of *cognitive*

Table 9.1
DSM-IV Symptoms Required for Major Depressive Disorder and Dysthymia

Major Depressive Disorder	Dysthymia
Five of nine symptoms must be present most of the day, nearly every day, for at least two weeks:	Depressed mood most days, for most of the week, for two years, plus two or more of six symptoms:
1. Depressed mood.	1. Poor appetite or overeating.
2. Diminished interest or pleasure in all, or almost all, activities. (One of the above is required.)	2. Insomnia or hypersomnia.
3. Significant weight loss or weight gain or a decrease or increase in appetite.	3. Low energy or fatigue.
4. Insomnia or hypersomnia.	4. Low self-esteem.
5. Psychomotor agitation or retardation.	5. Poor concentration or difficulty making decisions.
6. Fatigue or loss of energy.	6. Feelings of hopelessness.
7. Feelings of worthlessness or excessive or inappropriate guilt.	
8. Diminished ability to think or concentrate, or to make decisions.	
9. Recurrent thoughts of death, suicidal ideation, plans, or attempts.	

Source: From *Diagnostic and Statistical Manual of Mental Disorders,* 4th Edition (*DSM-IV*), 1994, Washington, DC: American Psychiatric Association.

symptoms. These include trouble concentrating; difficulty making decisions; low self-esteem; negative thoughts about self, the world, and others; guilt; suicidal ideation; and, in its most severe forms, hallucinations and delusions. The degree to which these features are present and the number of symptoms present determine which depressive disorder a person may be suffering from. We discuss each disorder to clarify how the disorders can be distinguished from one another.

Major Depressive Disorder

Major depressive disorder (MDD) is the most serious and widely studied depressive disorder. It is characterized by at least one *major depressive episode,* with no history of mania. A major depressive episode consists of at least five of nine possible symptoms (listed in Table 9.1) present during the same period, and the episode must last at least two weeks. The symptoms must be severe enough to interfere with the individual's social or occupational functioning. Either depressed mood or lack of interest in usual activities must be present, most of the day, nearly every day, during the episode. MDD is further qualified by its severity, chronicity, and remission status. Severity is generally determined by the degree of disability experienced by the afflicted person. If individuals can continue to pursue their obligations (work, family, and social activities), the depression is ranked as *mild.* If the person has trouble getting out of bed and can no longer engage in any obligated activities, the depression is ranked as *moderate*. If a person is thinking of death or dying, or is so vegetative that he or she has not left his or her bed, eaten or engaged in any self-management activities, or is exhibiting psychotic behavior, the depression is ranked as *severe*. A person is diagnosed as having *MDD, recurrent type* if there has been more than one episode of MDD. *Chronic MDD* is characterized by having symptoms of MDD for as long as two years. Because research has found MDD to be a typically recurrent disorder (single episodes are rare), if a person has had an episode of MDD but is no longer experiencing any depressive symptoms, that person is considered to be *in remission*. Although rare, a depressed person can also exhibit symptoms of catatonia, which is characterized by immobility, excessive motor activity, and extreme negativism or mutism.

MDD can be further delineated by type. The *DSM-IV* describes the concept of *endogenous depression* and is subsumed under the category of *melancholic depression*. This category is characterized by lack of reactivity to pleasurable stimuli, experiencing more severe depression in the morning, and excessive guilt. Some researchers have suggested that this subtype is more typically associated with biological etiology and that it may be more responsive to psychopharmacological intervention (Simons & Thase, 1992). *Atypical features* of depression include brightening of mood in response to actual or potential positive events, weight gain, hypersomnia, heavy feelings in arms or legs, and interpersonal rejection sensitivity. These symptoms tend to be interpreted as suggesting a depressive disorder that is more likely to respond to psychosocial interventions and may be more stress related (Beck, 1979; Klerman, 1986).

Dysthymia

Dysthymic disorder is typically thought to be a chronic depression (lasting two years or more), but one that is not as severe as MDD. Unlike MDD, dysthymia has only one typical presentation. Because of its chronicity and lack of responsiveness to existing treatments, some feel that dysthymia may be best considered a personality disorder, rather than an acute illness such as MDD. This opinion, however, is hotly contested.

The symptoms of dysthymia (listed in Table 9.1) must be present for more than two months at a time during the two-year period that defines the episode. Additionally, no major depressive episode during the first two years of dysthymia should have been present, although one could occur after the initial two-year period. The symptoms must not be due exclusively to other disorders (including medical conditions) or to the direct physiological effects of a substance (including medication). As in MDD, the person must not have ever met criteria for manic episode, hypomanic episode, or cyclothymic disorder. If dysthymia occurs before age 21, it is described as having *early onset;* otherwise, it is described as having *late onset*.

Depressive Disorder Not Otherwise Specified

This category is a catchall for depressive conditions that are provisionary and have yet to be studied in depth. This category includes:

- *Premenstrual dysphoric disorder:* A mood disorder thought to be due to hormonal fluctuations in the female menstrual cycle.
- *Minor depressive disorder:* Depressive episodes lasting for at least two weeks, but with fewer than the five items needed to meet criteria for major depressive episode.
- *Recurrent brief depressive disorder:* Characterized by repeated episodes of depression that last for a period of less than two weeks.
- *Postpsychotic depressive disorder of schizophrenia:* Depression that follows a psychotic episode.
- *Major depressive episode superimposed on psychotic or delusional disorders:* Depression that co-occurs with a psychotic disorder.
- *Depression due to general medical conditions:* Depression that is thought to be present but cannot be determined to be primary, due to medical conditions, or substance induced.

DISCRETE VERSUS CONTINUOUS CONCEPTUALIZATIONS OF DEPRESSION

There has been considerable debate about whether depression types are best thought of as discrete illnesses or if depression is one illness along a severity continuum. As knowledge on depression advances, there is a strong movement toward considering both arguments in diagnosis and treating patients. As an example, most clinicians consider MDD to be a different disorder from dysthymia, requiring different treatment choices. However, clinicians also believe that in each disorder, there is considerable variation in the degree to which the illness affects each patient. Moreover, it is very likely that minor depression is a precursor to a major depressive episode, and thus may be important to treat to prevent clinical episodes of depression (Munoz, 1993).

WHEN DEPRESSION IS NOT A DEPRESSIVE DISORDER

Sometimes symptoms of depression may be present but not diagnosed as one of the depressive disorders. It is important to note that depressive disorders are different from sadness brought on by grief or the loss of a loved one. If *bereavement* accounts for symptoms of depression, and if these symptoms have not persisted longer than two months after such loss, the episode is not MDD. People who become depressed after a significant life stressor for a short period of time are more likely to be suffering from an *adjustment disorder,* rather than a mood disorder. Furthermore, a previous *manic episode* also excludes a diagnosis of MDD. Finally, if the depressed person has a medical disorder known to cause symptoms of depression (e.g., hyperthyroidism), the symptoms are classified as *depression due to a general medical condition.*

It is important to note that everyone experiences feelings of sadness from time to time. This is a normal experience that should not be pathologized. Depressive symptoms are considered problematic when the symptoms persist for two weeks or more and are accompanied by considerable difficulty coping with day-to-day activities. In the next section, we provide examples of these disorders.

Case Studies

To illustrate the disorders just discussed, we present three cases—one that describes the presentation of MDD; one, dysthymia; and the third, depression NOS.

Major Depression

K. G. was a 45-year-old White, single woman seeking mental health services for what she called "depression." K. G. was the middle child of three female children from the northeastern part of the United States. She was always a good student, had many friends, and remembers her childhood as a happy one. Her father died when she was three years old, and K. G. does not remember him. She had a large extended family and did not feel that she missed having a father figure. K. G. was successful in school and in her work. She has never lost a job. K. G. said that she had suffered from depression twice before in her adult life, but had always been able to overcome depression on her own. In both instances, she had ended a relationship and felt quite depressed for a number of weeks. She never sought help for her depression before because she thought her symptoms were a normal reaction to these events and because she could always come out of the depression on her own. Further, she indicated that it was not like her to talk with someone about her feelings. She indicated that her family were "stoic New Englanders" and rarely shared their feelings. She suspected that an uncle had committed suicide and that her father was an alcoholic, but was unsure of these facts, as these issues were never discussed.

Six months before seeking services, K. G. had ended a one-year relationship; and one month before her visit, she had begun working for a new company. She was managing several large projects for the company and felt that she was the only one of her staff who was doing any work. K. G. had noticed over the last four months that she had been gaining weight and that this weight gain was the result of her continued snacking. This weight gain was also quite distressing to her. K. G. sought services now because she was unable to "snap out of it" and was concerned that she may need therapy or medication. Her symptoms included feeling depressed nearly all day, every day for the last seven months, feeling a lack of interest in her usual activities (skiing and ballet) for three months, hypersomnia, increased appetite, feeling worthless and hopeless, trouble making decisions about her life (but not at work), and increased irritability. She also reported feeling physically slowed down. Although she had occasionally felt that she would be better off dead, she was not suicidal. She did not feel that suicide was an option and had no plan to harm herself. She was not perimenopausal and had no medical illnesses.

Dysthymia

B. G. is a 55-year-old retired man who sought services for "depression" after a doctor recommended he talk to a mental health professional. B. G. is the oldest of five in his family and was currently married with three grown children who all live in other parts of the country. He completed high school and, shortly after, trade school. He had been employed with one construction company his entire adult life. He was living with his wife at the time of his intake. He had no serious health problems, other than chronic pain due to a back injury. B. G. retired because of a back injury that prevented him from performing his job. Three years ago, his wife took on a part-time job to earn extra money, and B. G. began looking after the house. Before this visit, he had never sought mental health services, nor had he ever felt depressed. B. G. stated that for the last three years, he occasionally felt worthless, depressed, and irritable. He reported that some days, he often had to get himself going to complete his chores for the day but would somehow manage to do so. He indicated that he was unsure of treatment, because he had "my good days"; but on further probing, he reported that these days were infrequent (no more than one or two days a week). Although he said he and his wife did not have marital problems, he felt guilty that she worked and he did not. The primary symptoms he complained about were feeling sad on occasion, lack of energy, irritability, and feelings of worthlessness and guilt.

Depression NOS

T. J. was a 40-year-old woman who was referred by her physician for treatment of depression. She was an only child and was living with her mother at the time of referral. She had a college education and had been employed as an administrative assistant for 10 years. She was divorced with no children. According to the physician, T. J. was struggling with placing her elderly mother in a nursing home and this struggle made her quite depressed. The provider indicated that T. J. had a recent diagnosis of hyperthyroidism and was being treated with medication. T. J. stated that she had been feeling quite depressed for a number of months, since her mother became more seriously ill and she needed to find a home for her mother. T. J. had indicated that she had been her mother's caregiver for most of her life, and that they had a "love-hate" relationship. Her mother was being verbally abusive to T. J. as to the placement, making T. J. feel guilty. T. J. indicated that she would normally be able to let her mother's abuse roll off her back, having long ago accepted that her mother was a difficult person. However, the last four months were hard to cope with, even though she had a good caseworker helping her, and her mother would be placed in a pleasant assisted-living facility within the next month. Her primary complaints were depression and sadness nearly all day, every day, feeling slowed down, and trouble with concentration. She also indicated that having had a recent diagnosis of hyperthyroidism complicated matters for her and that she had been unable to take her medication regularly. T. J. was encouraged to start taking her medication for hyperthyroidism and was educated about the link between the illness and depressive symptoms. T. J. and her therapist agreed to meet again

(Continued)

in two weeks. At that meeting, T. J. reported that her mother had been placed in the assisted-living facility and that while T. J. felt guilty for a few days, she found that her mother was actually quite happy at the facility. She also reported taking the medication regularly and stated she already felt much better, "like my old self," although she was still somewhat symptomatic of depression (occasional sadness and poor energy). Now that her mother had been successfully placed, T. J. indicated that she would like to work on rebuilding her social life.

EPIDEMIOLOGY

These cases are representative of a growing number of people in the United States suffering from depressive disorders. There have been two large-scale epidemiological studies on mental illness in the United States. The Epidemiological Catchment Area Study, conducted in the 1980s (Regier et al., 1988), was the first to definitively determine the prevalence of psychiatric problems in the United States. The National Comorbidity Study (NCS; Kessler, McGonagle, Zhao, et al., 1994) focused specifically on adults between the ages of 18 and 65 and was mostly concerned with prevalence of co-occurring psychiatric disorders in the United States. Data from these two studies demonstrate that prevalence of depressive disorders varies from population to population. The following discussion presents prevalence of depressive disorders by the different populations.

COMMUNITY SAMPLES

Lifetime prevalence rates, or number of persons who have *ever* experienced an episode of major depression, range from 5.8% (Regier et al., 1988) to 12% (Kessler, McGonagle, Zhao, et al., 1994) in community-dwelling individuals. These studies also indicate that in a given six-month period, approximately 3% to 9% of the general population experience an episode of major depression (Kessler, McGonagle, Zhao, et al., 1994; Regier et al., 1988). Lifetime prevalence rates for dysthymia are lower than the rates of major depression. According to the NCS, 6% of the general population have had a period of dysthymia in their lifetime. Rates of other depressive disorders were not available.

PREVALENCE BY GENDER

The ECA and the NCS show differential prevalence rates by gender. In the ECA studies, lifetime prevalence rates of affective disorders for adult women average 6.6%, whereas in the NCS, rates are significantly higher, at 21.3% (Kessler, McGonagle, Nelson, et al., 1994; Regier et al., 1988). Lifetime rates for men, on the other hand, were 8.2% in the ECA and 12.7% in the NCS. While the rates for depression varied between these two studies, a consistent theme emerges: More women report having depressive episodes than men. Differences in rates between men and women have been found repeatedly throughout the world, and thus appear to be accurate reflections of true differences in the prevalence of the disorder between men and women (Angold, Weissman, John, Wickramaratne, & Prusoff, 1991;

Kessler, McGonagle, Nelson, et al., 1994). Although reasons for these differences are relatively unknown, some speculate that biological differences, differences in cognitive and behavioral patterns of mood control, and social influences, including differential expectations for the two genders, account for the difference in prevalence (Nolen-Hoeksema, 2000).

PREVALENCE BY AGE COHORT

It has been nearly 30 years since there has been a national survey of the prevalence of psychiatric disorders in older adults. The NCS purposely excluded people ages 65 and older because the ECA data indicated that psychiatric comorbidity was an uncommon problem in this population. Thus, information on the differential prevalence rates of depression between younger and older people is dated and likely to be inaccurate because of the shifting life experiences and attitudes about mental health in more recent cohorts of older people. As Burke, Burke, Rae, and Regier (1991) point out, rates for all psychiatric disorders are increasing with each decade, indicating that disorders such as depression may be influenced by cohort effects. Thus, the rates of depressive disorders in older people in the ECA studies are thought to be underestimates.

With this caveat in mind, it is important to highlight what is known about the prevalence of depression in older adults. Prevalence of depression among elderly populations exceeds that of any other mental disorder (Baldwin, 2000). According to the ECA, the rate for major depression in people over the age of 65 is 0.7% (Regier et al., 1988), while rates for subsyndromal depressions, such as minor depression and dysthymia, are greater, approximately 10% to 20% (Koenig & Blazer, 1992). The prevalence rate of depression in the United States appears to have been increasing steadily since World War II: Each 10-year cohort reports earlier onset of depression and a higher rate throughout the life span (Klerman, 1986). These apparent increases have been examined carefully and are found in several epidemiological databases.

PREVALENCE IN MINORITIES

Rates of depression also vary by ethnic group. According to the NCS data, African Americans have rates of depression similar to the Caucasian population. Approximately 3.1% of African Americans have had a MDD episode, and 3.2% have had dysthymia (Jackson-Triche et al., 2000). However, Asian Americans have the lowest rates, with only 0.8% saying they had experienced a major depression and 0.8% experiencing dysthymia (Jackson-Triche et al., 2000). Hispanics were found to have an interesting presentation of prevalence that depended on immigration status. According to Alderete, Vega, Kolody, and Aguilar-Gaxiola (1999), Hispanics who have recently emigrated from Latin America were less likely to be depressed than Hispanics who were born and raised in the United States. U.S.-born Hispanics had prevalence rates of depression much like the rates of Caucasians (3.5% for MDD and 5% for dysthymia), while immigrants reported only half the prevalence rates of U.S.-born Hispanics. Although unconfirmed empirically, Vega, Kolody, Valle, and Hough (1986) believe that lower rates in immigrants result from a heartiness factor; those able to withstand the stress related to immigration are more likely to cope with stress related to depression.

Prevalence of depression in certain settings is greater than that found in the general community. For instance, people who are depressed are more likely to seek help in primary care settings (Wagner et al., 2000). Estimates as to prevalence of depressive disorders vary, but most studies indicate that minor depression is the most common depressive disorder, with as many as 25% of patients meeting criteria for that disorder (Judd et al., 1998; Wagner et al., 2000). While prevalence of depressive disorders may be high, the recurrence rate is lower in these settings than in the community. According to van Weel-Baumgarten and colleagues (van Weel-Baumgarten, Schers, van den Bosch, van den Hoogen, & Zitman, 2000), patients treated in primary care medicine are less likely to suffer a relapse or remission than those treated in psychiatric settings, likely because more severely depressed people are being managed in psychiatry than in primary care medicine.

Another setting with high rates for depression is the skilled nursing facility. According to Masand (1995), as many as 15% to 25% of people residing in these settings suffer from MDD. Given the impact depressive disorders have on rehabilitation, the high rate of these disorders in these settings is cause for concern and argues for more vigilant and proactive treatment of depression in skilled nursing facilities.

CLINICAL PICTURE

Major depression, dysthymia, and depression NOS all vary to a degree in their presentations but share several features that distinguish these disorders from other mental illnesses. People with depressive disorders can be identified by their pessimism and negativistic thinking, difficulty solving even everyday problems, and lack of initiative. People with depressive disorders are also quite disabled by the illness and often report having multiple somatic symptoms.

Most people with depressive disorders exhibit what is called *negativistic thinking*. This term was coined by Aaron Beck (1979) and has since been used extensively to describe the cognitive style of people suffering from depressive disorders. Negativistic thinking is best described as a style of thinking that is overly pessimistic and critical. People with depression tend to expect failure and disappointment at every turn and focus only on their past failures as a way to confirm these beliefs (Alloy et al., 2000). As an example, in the first case study, K. G.'s faith in herself and others was impaired by her pessimism. Her problems with work-related stress resulted in part from her belief that no one at her new place of employment was working hard enough, and no one was inclined to help her. She would take on extra work rather than delegate to her staff because she was afraid they did not like her and that they would refuse to do the extra work or that they would do it poorly.

People with negativistic thinking also have poor self-esteem and are passive when difficulty arises (Lewinsohn, Hoberman, & Rosenbaum, 1988). In the second case study presented, B. G. often felt that because he was no longer working, he was a failure; he feared that his wife saw him in the same way. When faced with a problem to solve at home, B. G. often doubted his decisions and would then avoid the problem, feeling that he was incapable of dealing with even small, mundane tasks. Even in the face of success, someone who is depressed downplays a successful experience as an unusual event or an event that occurred despite the odds against it. In the last case example, while T. J. was glad to have found a residential facility for her mother, she was also cautious about this success, believing that her mother's good mood was likely to be short lived and that she would probably be ejected from the new home.

Presence of negativistic thinking in depression is a bit of a "chicken or the egg" problem: Does depression cause negativistic thinking, or does negativistic thinking cause depression? Recent research suggests that the cause of depression is more likely an imbalanced thinking style and that negativistic thinking may have a clearer association with repeated exposure to failure and disappointment. In a study by Isaacowitz and Seligman (2001), people both with pessimistic thinking and optimistic thinking were at risk for developing depressive symptoms after exposure to stressful life events. In fact, optimists were at higher risk for depression than pessimists were, although pessimists tended to have more persistent depression. Therefore, objective perceptions of a person's abilities, of his or her environment, and of other people are likely to be more protective than overly optimistic or pessimistic styles of thinking.

Negativistic thinking is primarily responsible for depressed people finding it difficult to engage in and enjoy activities that once gave them pleasure; thus *social isolation* is a common feature of depressive disorders (Brugha et al., 1987). Many people suffering from a depressive disorder report that they have stopped socializing or engaging in pleasant activities, largely because they anticipate no enjoyment from the activity (Vinokur, Schul, & Caplan, 1987). K. G., for example, often reported that she did not feel "up to" her dance classes, particularly on days when she felt most depressed. It is important, however, that people who are depressed try to reengage in social activities. Increased social isolation puts the depressed person at greater risk of severe depression. Several studies show that social support can offset occurrence or worsening of depression, and thus, increasing exposure to socialization is an important process in recovering from depression (Brugha et al., 1987).

People suffering from a depressive disorder also tend to use passive coping skills or to avoid solving problems (Nolen-Hoeksema, Larson, & Grayson, 1999). This sometimes results from a preexisting skills deficit or from *learned helplessness*, a condition caused by repeated attempts and failures to cope with problems (Folkman & Lazarus, 1986). Most often, after people become depressed, they avoid proactive attempts to solve problems because they anticipate that they are not capable of implementing a successful solution (Nezu, 1986). Such avoidance often results in more problems; for instance, avoiding marital problems potentially results in divorce. In the case study, B. G.'s marriage, while not in trouble yet, was certainly strained. He felt guilty about his wife's having to work, yet never spoke to her about this problem. Instead, he withdrew from her completely, which resulted in her feeling unsupported by him. Similarly, T. J.'s nonadherence to her new medication was a result of her avoiding "yet another problem." Unfortunately, for T. J., not treating her illness most likely exacerbated her depressive symptoms.

Many people are surprised to discover how disabling depression is. People who are depressed complain of somatic problems, such as fatigue, stomach upset, headaches, and joint pain (Davidson, Krishnan, France, & Pelton, 1985; Viinamaeki et al., 2000). These symptoms, coupled with the pessimism and avoidant style associated with depression, are related to the increased number of disability days reported by people with depressive disorders (Pincus & Pettit, 2001). In the NCS (Kessler & Frank, 1997), people with depression reported a five-fold increase in time lost from work compared to nondepressed people. In fact, patients treated for depression incurred greater disability costs to employers than did people needing treatment for hypertension and had costs comparable to more severe chronic illnesses such as diabetes (Conti & Burton, 1995; Druss, Rosenheck, & Sledge, 2000). Interestingly, costs related to treating depression are almost as great as costs due to disability days from depression (Kessler et al., 1999), and some studies show that treatment of depression yields decreased disability days (Simon et al., 2000).

COURSE AND PROGNOSIS

Research has begun to identify variables that can predict toward better or worse course and outcome, but there is still a great deal of uncertainty. Here we present the descriptive data concerning length, severity, and prognosis of depressive disorders.

Course

Beyond the basic diagnostic criteria, MDD has several delineating features. Early-onset depression tends to appear before age 20 and has a more malignant course than the late-onset group. It is also associated with a family history of depression and other mood disorders. Late-onset depression, on the other hand, tends to emerge in the mid-30s and is associated with fewer recurrent episodes, comorbid personality disorders, and substance abuse disorders relative to early-onset depression (Klein et al., 1999). However, there is a much greater variation in the age of onset than in disorders such as schizophrenia. Second, the course of MDD tends to be time limited. The average episode lasts six months, although this varies greatly from person to person. Third, MDD tends to be a recurrent disorder. Patients who have one major depressive episode have a 36.7% chance of experiencing a second; those who have two previous episodes have a 11% increased chance of developing a third episode. With each additional episode, chances for an additional episode increase by approximately 15% (Kessing & Andersen, 1999).

Dysthymia, on the other hand, is a more chronic, long-lasting illness. The mean duration of dysthymia is 30 years, and almost half of patients who have dysthymia will develop a major depressive episode in their lifetimes (Shelton et al., 1997; Wells, Burnam, Rogers, Hays, & Camp, 1992). Dysthymics have been found to have worse clinical prognosis than people with either MDD or depression NOS, and are as disabled as those with MDD (Griffiths, Ravindran, Merali, & Anisman, 2000). Thankfully, dysthymia is responsive to both psychotherapy and medication treatment, at least in the short term (Kocsis et al., 1997), with some studies suggesting that the most robust intervention is a combination of psychotherapy and medication (Barrett et al., 2001). Unfortunately, few people with dysthymia ever receive treatment. Less than half will ever receive any kind of mental health treatment, and those who do receive treatment do so only after having experienced a major depressive episode (Shelton et al., 1997).

PROGNOSIS

Early diagnosis and treatment with therapy and/or medication result in a better chance of recovery from MDD, dysthymia, and depression NOS (Wells et al., 1992). The ease of recovery from depression, however, is related to several factors. Prognosis is best when the patient is faced with few stressful life events (Keitner, Ryan, Miller, & Zlotnick, 1997; Sherrington, Hawton, Fagg, Andrew, & Smith, 2001) and has a solid support network on which to rely (Keitner et al., 1997). Furthermore, individuals with an initial early recovery are less likely to develop recurring symptoms. Early improvements indicate that the patient has access to coping mechanisms that allow for a quick recovery, and this often suggests an overall positive long-term prognosis. The prognosis for dysthymia is less certain. As of this writing, there have been few treatment studies demonstrating any long-lasting positive effect for any intervention.

Another factor involved in the prognosis for both MDD and dysthymia are levels of self-esteem. A higher self-esteem predicts an increasingly positive prognosis (Sherrington et al., 2001). Poor self-esteem, on the other hand, predicts a longer and more delayed recovery.

Prognosis of depressive disorders is also poor when the person has an early onset and a premorbid personality disorder, and when there has been a previous episode (Brodaty et al., 1993). More intensive and extended treatment can improve the remission and maintenance of remission from MDD episodes, even with a high severity of the depression, although the evidence on dysthymia is limited. Longevity in the use of treatment is predictive of an improved long-term course of the appearance of symptoms. In a study by Dawson, Lavori, Coryell, Endicott, and Keller (1998), evidence showed that extended use of psychopharmacology in a past recovery resulted in fewer recurrent depressive episodes. Thus, though symptoms may have abated, prognosis can be significantly improved when treatment continues for a more extended period. This evidence shows that despite seemingly greater costs for continued treatment, the benefits from prolonged treatment are a worthwhile long-term investment.

DIAGNOSTIC CONSIDERATIONS

Although the *DSM-IV* provides a guideline for the diagnosis of depressive disorders, the comorbidity of other medical and psychiatric disorders can complicate a diagnostic decision. To make an accurate diagnosis of depression, physical health, medications, family and personal history, and medical history need to be considered.

MEDICAL ILLNESS

The first important step in diagnosing depressive disorders is to have the patient get a complete physical. Many medical illnesses are related to onset of a depressive episode, and at times, treating both the illness and depression is a more efficient way to affect symptom change (Areán & Miranda, 1996; Zubenko et al., 1997). Endocrinological disorders such as hyperthyroidism and hypothyroidism have as one of the diagnostic signs a change in affect and mood. Moreover, people with chronic illnesses, such as diabetes mellitus, have high rates of depressive disorder (de Groot, Jacobson, Samson, & Welch, 1999; Wilkinson et al., 1988).

Acute medical illnesses, such as stroke (Starkstein et al., 1991), Parkinson's disease (Caap-Ahlgren & Dehlin, 2001; Starkstein, Berthier, Bolduc, Preziosi, & Robinson, 1989), pancreatic cancer (Holland et al., 1986), coronary heart disease (Kubzansky & Kawachi, 2000), and myocardial infarction (Fielding, 1991), are associated with depressive symptoms. Although it is unclear whether these illnesses directly cause depression or the depression is the result of the life changes brought on by the illness, recovery from these diseases (when possible) will help alleviate depressive symptoms.

Drug and Alcohol Abuse

The next step in establishing a diagnosis is to determine to what extent the person drinks or uses drugs. Often, substance abuse/dependence disorders are strongly associated with depressive symptoms (Gunnarsdottir et al., 2000; Kessler, McGonagle, Zhao, et al., 1994; Merikangas & Avenevoli, 2000). Currently, scientists are debating whether depressive symptoms are a consequence of substance abuse and the problems related to this disorder, or if the substance use is a means of "self-medicating" depressive symptoms. Whatever the true relationship is, it is important for patients to abstain from using substances to obtain a clearer picture of the person's affective state.

Grief and Bereavement

Grief over the loss of a special person or presence of a major life stress or change can also complicate attempts to diagnose depressive disorders. Both uncomplicated bereavement and adjustment disorder have many symptoms of depression, but neither is considered a mood disorder. People with these problems are best helped by understanding that their symptoms are common reactions to their recent stress. Although it is possible that those with uncomplicated bereavement or adjustment disorder can develop a depressive disorder, little is known about the extent to which grief can develop into depression.

Depression Due to Other Psychiatric Disorders

People with other psychiatric disorders can have co-occurring depressive symptoms, and thus, a differential rule-out for these other disorders is often important. For instance, people with anxiety disorders, particularly generalized anxiety disorder, report feelings of sadness and hopelessness (Hopko et al., 2000). When under stress, people with personality disorders also report significant symptoms of depression. In fact, they can become quite acutely depressed. Specifically, depressive episodes are most prevalent with avoidant, borderline, and obsessive-compulsive personality disorders (Rossi et al., 2001). Furthermore, personality disorders have an association with a longer remission onset from a depressive episode (O'Leary & Costello, 2001). In addition, depression is common in prodromal phases of schizophrenia and is a recurrent feature in bipolar disorder.

PSYCHOLOGICAL AND BIOLOGICAL ASSESSMENT

Assessment of depression has evolved over the decades, but many issues and controversies about the most adequate means of detecting this disorder still remain.

Controversies over cultural differences, age differences, and the setting in which a client is being evaluated are still under investigation. This section focuses on the strengths and weaknesses of different methods for assessing depression, ranging from screening instruments to structured clinical interviews.

ASSESSING THE DEPRESSED PERSON

The most common way to assess for depressive disorders is to conduct an in-person interview with the patient. The interviewer, usually a mental health professional or trained clinic worker, asks the patient a number of questions concerning the current episode of depression, including the symptoms the patient is experiencing, how long he or she has been depressed, what he or she thinks caused the depression, and what the patient would like to do about the depressive episode. In addition, intake clinicians also ask for family and personal history, past and current medical history, previous psychiatric history, and impact the depression has had on day-to-day functioning. All this information is compiled to determine whether the patient has a depressive disorder, the type of disorder, and the degree of suffering. This information is then used to determine the appropriate treatment.

Most mental health professionals use their own methods of assessment. Some conduct an open-ended interview that is guided not by any instrumentation, but only by the patient's responses to questions. Although this method is most commonly practiced, it also carries the greatest risk of misdiagnosis, particularly if the interviewer is not an expert in depressive disorders. Because of this risk, many mental health organizations prefer to use a combination of an open-ended interview with a screening instrument or a guide, such as a semistructured interview form, to help remind the clinician to ask for all relevant information. In using a screening instrument or semistructured interview, it is imperative that the instruments chosen be highly reliable and valid. Other than a medical examination to rule out physical causes for depressive symptoms, there is no biological test to diagnose depression; therefore, accurate diagnosis rests with the clinician and the instrumentation used to confirm a diagnosis.

SCREENING INSTRUMENTS

Many health settings are concerned with identifying as many people as possible that have the disorder so that quick and effective interventions can take place. This tradition comes from medical practice, where physicians routinely conduct medical tests when they suspect a particular illness. These screening tests help the doctor rule out need for further tests to make a specific diagnosis. Standardized screening instruments are used for similar purposes in psychiatry. Screening instruments should be highly *sensitive*. That is, they should detect depression in *everyone* with the disorder. Otherwise, their utility is limited. When someone screens positive for depression, further assessment is required to confirm a diagnosis and refine the specifics.

The most common mechanism for diagnosing depression is a *self-report measure,* such as the Beck Depression Inventory (BDI; Beck, 1961), the Center for Epidemiological Studies-Depression Scale (CES-D; Radloff, 1977), the Geriatric Depression Scale (GDS; Yesavage et al., 1982), the Zung Depression Scale (Zung, 1972), the Montgomery Asberg Depression Rating Scale (MADRS-S; Montgomery & Asberg,

1979), and the Profile of Mood States (POMS; Plutchik, Platman, & Fieve, 1968). These instruments are completed by the patient and hand scored by the person administering the scale. A patient's score on the instrument reflects the severity of depression. These instruments are considered cost-effective and efficient. They are useful in primary care settings in making quick diagnoses, especially when followed with a second-stage interview (Schmitz, Kruse, Heckrath, Alberti, & Tress, 1999). However, they are often too inclusive in that they tend to identify some people as depressed who are not. They also differ in their assessments of depression and specifications in the diagnosis. For example, the BDI and the MADRS-S are equivalent in their assessment of depression, but the MADRS-S has a greater focus on core depressive symptoms than does the BDI (Svanborg & Asberg, 2001). An issue that arises is that these instruments are designed to be screening devises and not diagnostic tools. Furthering the problem, research indicates that such scales may be efficient in identifying psychological distress that might then be identified as major depression (Areán & Miranda, 1997; Schein & Koenig, 1997).

Because of the prevalence of depression in primary care medicine, a number of instruments have been created specifically for that environment. These instruments are meant to be used as red flags to the provider so that a more thorough assessment can be done if a patient appears to be depressed. The Primary Care Evaluation of Mental Disorders (PRIME-MD; Spitzer et al., 1994) is a good example of such an instrument. The patient completes a brief questionnaire, of which two questions are red flags for depression. If the patient endorses one of the two red-flag questions, the provider then asks more specific questions to finalize the diagnosis. The PRIME-MD has satisfactory reliability and validity (Spitzer, Kroenke, & Williams, 1999). Another brief self-report questionnaire for medical patients is the Beck Depression Inventory—Primary Care. This questionnaire is one page and consists of some of the same items from the full BDI. No data exist supporting its psychometric properties.

Structured and Semistructured Clinical Interviews

When a person screens positive for a depressive disorder, the next step is to confirm the diagnosis. This is best done by using a structured or semistructured interview. As stated earlier, most people who are expert in the diagnosis of depression disorders do not need assistance of a structured instrument. However, because these experts are not always available and can be quite costly, structured and semistructured interviews have been developed for use by less experienced personnel. The best-known instruments are the Structured Clinical Interview for *DSM-IV* (SCID) and the Composite International Diagnostic Interview (CIDI). The Diagnostic Interview for *DSM* (DIS) has also been used widely but has been largely replaced by the CIDI and, therefore, is not discussed in this chapter.

The Structured Clinical Interview for *DSM-IV*

The SCID was developed for clinical research to determine presence of *DSM-IV* disorders. It is a semistructured interview to be used by formally trained staff. Although interviewers use the instrument as a guide to structure the interview, the interview can also rely on interviewers' judgment in interpreting patients' answers to questions. Because there is a reliance on clinical judgment, the SCID functions best when administered by a mental health professional.

The SCID interview is divided into a number of sections: a historical overview of the presenting complaint; a screening list to determine beforehand whether the patient has symptoms of MDD, alcohol or substance abuse, obsessive-compulsive disorder and anxiety disorders; and the different diagnostic modules to reflect all the Axis I diagnoses of *DSM-IV*. While the SCID has been used extensively in research studies, it has only fair reliability and validity. According to the SCID's creators, this instrument has a kappa coefficient of agreement equal to only .31 in nonpatient samples, indicating a poor validity.

The main advantage to using the SCID is in its structured nature, thus decreasing the amount of variation of diagnosis from clinician to clinician. However, it is still a costly instrument in that staff administering the SCID must be trained in its use and must be of a professional level. However, costs can be lowered while maintaining effectiveness of the assessment by using trained research assistants rather than senior investigators to administer the test (Miller et al., 1999).

COMPOSITE INTERNATIONAL DIAGNOSTIC INTERVIEW

The CIDI was developed by the World Health Organization for the purpose of providing a variety of diagnoses that are in accord with definitions from the *DSM-IV*. This structured clinical interview is a fully computerized interview and, therefore, is able to attain a complexity and depth of diagnosis with carefully programmed skip patterns and flow charts. Its great advantage is that is does not require a mental health professional to administer the instrument—in fact, the CIDI can be used as a patient-only administered instrument although it is also common for it to be administered by a researcher. Because the program makes the diagnosis, the researcher giving the interview does not need to make any independent clinical judgments (Cooper, Peters, & Andrews, 1998).

The obvious benefits of the CIDI are that it is computerized and thus cuts down on costs of training interviewers and costs of using health practitioners to make diagnoses. There are, however, simultaneous negative aspects to the CIDI. One important negative aspect is that because it is computerized, certain disorders may be more difficult to diagnose due to individuals' desire to maintain secrecy or denial of mental disorders (Thornton, Russell, & Hudson, 1998). Additionally, because it is computerized, differences between individuals that are not accounted for by the program cannot be adjusted in the interview. However, the CIDI can be a useful tool, provided that it is used with a follow-up interview with a clinician.

COMMENT

Determining the presence of depressive disorder requires skill and effort to gather information about depression and their potential causes. The most efficient method to determine the presence of a depressive disorder is to first screen patients, and if screened positive, to perform an in-depth interview.

ETIOLOGICAL CONSIDERATIONS

The most debated topic in depression research is the area of causality. To date, the majority of research in this area has focused on the etiology of MDD, with very little research studying the etiology of dysthymia. Depression NOS appears to be related to whatever is thought to be the comorbid cause. Most scientists now believe that depressive disorders are multifaceted, with causes resulting from the inter-actions of psychological, social, and biological factors (Kendler, Thornton, & Gard-ner, 2001; O'Keane, 2000). For example, stressful life events have been found to in-crease risk for developing depression. However, the person's coping style, social support, and genetic makeup all mediate the impact that stress has on depression. If someone loses his or her job, but has good social support and coping skills, that person will be less likely to develop depression than another unemployed person who has weak coping skills and no social support. Though depression is related to many variables, it is their intermingling that can most clearly predict development of depression, rather than the ability of any single factor to determine the onset. Genetics, learning, and life experiences work together to cause depression.

FAMILIAL AND GENETIC CONSIDERATIONS

The most fascinating research on the etiology of depression has been the recent work on the role of genetics in mental health. With the mapping of the human genome, the prospect of clearly identifying the influence of genetics on mental health is in our reach. However, with depressive disorders, the contribution of ge-netics may take longer to uncover than for other disorders that have already demonstrated a clear genetic and biological cause (i.e., schizophrenia). While past evidence from twin studies has demonstrated some genetic involvement in de-pressive disorders, those links thus far have been weak.

Historically, the principal method for studying the influence of genetics on psychopathology was to compare concordance of depression in identical twins (monozygotic twins [MZ]) to that of fraternal twins (dizgotic [DZ]). Because fre-quency of twin births is low, genetic researchers also observe rates of depressive disorder in first-degree relatives (often parents and children). According to the twin studies, MZ twins have greater concordance rates for depressive disorders than do DZ twins (Englund & Klein, 1990). The correlation between MZ twins is .46, compared to DZ twins, whose concordance rates are .20, although much con-cordance is lower than what is found in schizophrenia studies (McGuffin, Katz, Watkins, & Rutherford, 1996). Family studies also find that onset of depression is more likely in people with depressed relatives than in those who do not have de-pressed family members (Marazita et al., 1997). Again, rates are not that com-pelling, with relatives having only a 21% risk for developing depression (Kupfer, Frank, Carpenter, & Neiswanger, 1989).

Direct genetic comparisons are becoming a more popular method for determin-ing genetic links to mood. These methods are considered to be superior to the methods discussed previously, because DNA is a specific measure that is unlikely to be modified by environmental influences. Results from twin and family studies cannot account for the impact of learning on development of depression, whereas DNA is less likely to be influenced by personal experience. DNA studies are able to compare depressed with nondepressed controls on characteristics of certain genes that are associated with neurotransmitters related to depressive disorder (see Biological and Physiological section). Although still in its infancy, this re-search has been very helpful in confirming the role of genetics in the development of depressive disorders. For instance, Dikeos et al. (1999) studied whether the ge-netic location of the D3 dopamine receptor differed in patients with MDD and those with no history or current MDD. The investigators observed that genotypes carrying the allele (DNA structure) associated with D3 polymorphisms were found in 75% of the MDD patients and in 50% of the controls, suggesting genetic influences in MDD. Other studies, however, have not found such robust effects (Frisch et al., 1999; Neiswanger et al., 1998; Qian et al., 1999). At best, the literature on the genetics of depressive disorders suggests a propensity to develop these disorders, but this propensity can be offset by learning and environment.

LEARNING AND MODELING

Depressive disorders also appear to be related to three psychological variables:

1. People's cognitive appraisals of themselves, their lives, and others (Alloy et al., 2000).
2. Whether people proactively solve problems or avoid them (D'Zurilla & Nezu, 1999).
3. Degree to which proactive attempts to cope with stress have been successful (Folkman & Lazarus, 1988).

In this paradigm, people who have negative expectations about their ability to cope with problems generally acquire these expectations through past learning experience. Repeated failed attempts to solve problems, for instance, leaves a person feeling hopeless and helpless, abandoning his or her usual methods for solving problems, and becoming depressed (Seligman, Weiss, Weinraub, & Schulman, 1980). These factors—cognitive attributions, coping skills, and learned helplessness—have all been found to be predictive of depression.

People with negative expectations, or cognitive vulnerabilities, are more likely to become depressed when faced with a stressor than people who do not possess cognitive vulnerability. Grazioli and Terry (2000) found that in women with postpartum depression, both general and maternal-specific dysfunctional attitudes were associated with self-reported depression, particularly in women who had children found to be temperamentally difficult (Grazioli & Terry, 2000). Another study found that individuals with negative cognitive styles had higher lifetime prevalence of depression than people who were not cognitively vulnerable (Alloy et al., 2000). Therefore, people with negative perceptions of themselves and their environment are at risk for becoming depressed.

Coping skills have also been found to be related to depression. Most research has found that people who use active forms of coping, such as problem solving, are less likely to become depressed than people who use passive forms of coping, such as avoidance. In fact, one study found that the prevalence of major depression was 59.4% in people with avoidant coping styles (Garcia, Valdes, Jodar, Riesco, & de Flores, 1994; Welch & Austin, 2001). Studies show that when faced with a problem to solve, depressed people are more likely to produce less effective solutions than nondepressed people, such as using distraction to cope with a stressor, rather than trying to solve it (Marx, Williams, & Claridge, 1992).

Although coping skill deficits and cognitive style contribute to depression, it is really the interaction of these two factors that seems to have the biggest impact on the development of depression. This interaction in learned helplessness has been supported by several studies. Originally, these theories were tested in animal models, where insolvable problems were presented to animals and all attempts to solve the problem were met with unpleasant consequences, such as a shock. After repeated attempts to solve the problem failed, these animals would exhibit depressogenic behavior—withdrawal, acting as if they were in pain—and, even after a solution was presented to them, the animals would refuse to try the solution (Altenor, Volpicelli, & Seligman, 1979). Scientists have been able to draw a relationship between learned helplessness and depression in research. For instance, Swendsen (1997) found that people with high-risk attributional styles were more likely to experience depressed mood after exposure to negative stressful events. Kapci and Cramer (2000) also found that people were more likely to become depressed when they were exposed to numerous negative life events, but only if their faith in their ability to solve problems was impaired. Thus, it is the interaction of negative life events, coping skills, and attributions about coping skill that influences depression.

Life Events

The literature is replete with data indicating that stressful life events contribute to the development of a depressive episode. Although not everyone who is faced with difficult problems becomes depressed, it is evident that prolonged exposure to psychosocial stress can precipitate a depressive episode (Brown, Bifulco, Harris, & Bridge, 1986). A number of studies have found that most depressive episodes are preceded by a severe life event or difficulty in the six months before onset (Brown, Bifulco, & Harris, 1987). In addition, patients with more long-term or chronic depression were more likely to report past abuse, though the causal relationship is unclear (Keitner et al., 1997).

Because depression is a multifaceted disorder, it is difficult to pinpoint the specific role life events have on the development of a depressive disorder. Most people face severe life stress at some time, yet not everyone becomes depressed. How severe life events are viewed and the individual's perceived control over the situation play an important role in determining the vulnerability to depression. For instance, several studies find that the relationship of life events to depression is mediated by other factors such as social support, cognitive style, and coping abilities (Alloy et al., 2000; Brugha et al., 1987). Severe life events are significantly more likely to provoke a major depressive episode in individuals without social support (Bifulco, Brown, & Harris, 1987; Keitner et al., 1997). Support systems give an individual external support when internal coping skills are put to the test. Without the external support, however, an individual must rely exclusively on his or her own internal resources, which under severe duress might not be entirely effective. Therefore, while negative life events do influence occurrence of depressive disorders, social and psychological resources available to the person facing the stressful life event generally mediate the impact on mood.

Gender and Racial-Ethnic

We have already reported that prevalence of depression is higher among women and some minority populations. Many researchers have been trying to discern the reasons for the discrepant rates of depressive disorders in these populations. Is the reason genetic or biological? Is it that these populations are exposed to more stress and have fewer resources to cope with stress and, therefore, are more vulnerable than men and nonminority groups? Or, is the reason that depression is presented differently across these groups and, therefore, the estimates in prevalence for depressive disorders in these populations are inaccurate? Mental health researchers are still struggling with these questions and have only partially been able to explain the discrepancy.

Some theorists believe that the reason minorities have differing rates of depressive disorder is that they present their symptoms of depression differently than do Caucasians. Many researchers have spent years trying to discern the most appropriate way to assess depression in different cultures. While research from the World Health Organization indicates that depression is similar across cultures, how people report the symptoms and their cultural attitudes about mental health can cloud diagnoses. Screening instruments and scales that were developed for Anglo populations can be problematic if they are simply translated without regard for translation bias. Additionally, many studies have found that the factor structures and reliabilities of these instruments tend to differ across ethnic groups, indicating that groups vary in their reports of depressive symptoms (Areán & Miranda, 1997; Azocar, Areán, Miranda, & Munoz, 2001). For instance, lower rates of depression in Asians may result from their tendency to underreport affective symptoms of depression and rely more on somatic presentation (Iwamasa, 1993).

Others have hypothesized that different rates of depression in certain ethnic groups result from the fact that in this country, minorities such as African Americans and Hispanics are more likely to be impoverished and having to cope with financial and urban stress. Studies have demonstrated that socioeconomic status and exposure to trauma related to racism, urban living, and financial strain are correlated with depression and other mental illnesses such as anxiety and substance abuse (Ostler et al., 2001). Other studies have found that rates for depression in middle-class and affluent minorities are more similar to the national rates of depression for Caucasians (Badger, McNiece, & Gagan, 2000). These studies seem to argue that in the case of minority populations, increased exposure to stress is the reason for the differing rates of depressive disorder (Olfson et al., 2000).

The differing rate of depressive disorders between men and women is an interesting, yet complicated, finding. Researchers initially thought that the different prevalence rates were due to reluctance on the part of men to admit feelings of depression and a tendency to cope with stress through substance use. Others suggest that the increased prevalence of depression in women is due to the fact that women tend to be victims of sexual abuse and, therefore, suffer a significant psychosocial stressor that is not as common in men. However, because discrepancy between men and women seems to be universal, others claim that it is the hormonal and biological differences that account for the differential prevalence rates. Whatever the differential effect, the fact remains that depression is more commonly reported in women than in men.

BIOLOGICAL AND PHYSIOLOGICAL

Much research effort has gone into determining biological determinants of depression. The literature shows evidence not only of the effects from both neurotransmitters and hormones, but also physiological changes arising from stress that can increase susceptibility to depression (Maes, Maes, & Suy, 1990).

The role of neurotransmitters in affecting mood regulation is an area of ongoing research. Clinicians initially believed that depression was caused, in part, by lack of the two neurotransmitters, norepinephrine and serotonin. Now, however, it is known that the dysregulation rather than the deficiency of these neurotransmitters causes depression (Moore & Bona, 2001). Antidepressants to regulate the production and distribution of norepinephrine and serotonin are effective in their ability to increase the availability of receptor sites rather than increase the production of the neurotransmitters (Veenstra-VanderWeele, Anderson, & Cook, 2000). Neurotransmitters provide an important, but still only partial, picture of the biological origin of depression because abnormalities in neurotransmitter regulation do not necessarily lead to a depressed mood.

Neuroendocrinology also adds to the more complete understanding of the biological causes of depression. Evidence points to an overabundance of cortisol in the systems of depressed patients. Additionally, abnormalities in the thyroid functions are often related to symptoms of depression, further indicating an important role for the neuroendocrine system in depression. In a study by Ghaziuddin et al. (2000), neuroendocrine imbalances in adolescents with MDD, compared to their nondepressed counterparts, demonstrated that depression is associated with abnormal baseline levels of prolactin as well as sharper prolactin and cortisol responses to serotonergic challenges. Evidence for such abnormalities not only yields a more complete understanding of causation, but also aids in the development of more effective drug treatments.

Finally, physiological changes in the brain structure of depressed individuals lend further support for structural changes in the brains of people with MDD. In a study by Sheline (2000), brain changes in early-onset depression were localized in the hippocampus, amygdala, caudate nucleus, putamen, and frontal cortex, whereas late-onset depression was noted to frequently occur with comorbid physical illnesses that often affect brain structures involved in emotion regulation. These physical changes that can occur during stress and that are associated so closely to depression give a more comprehensive picture and explanation of the causes of depression.

SUMMARY

Depressive disorders are common and widely studied. Given the extent of our knowledge of MDD and dysthymia, however, research continues to address issues around the best means of recognizing depression, how to treat depression in different settings and in different cultures, and in further clarifying the etiology of these disorders. The causes and symptoms of depressive disorders are extremely variable and intermingled. The causes range from physiological to environmental, and the expressions of depression vary from short, severe episodes to chronic symptomology. Because of the immense complexity of the depressive disorders, further research will aid in the ability to tailor diagnosis and therapy for each particular manifestation.

REFERENCES

Alderete, E., Vega, W. A., Kolody, B., & Aguilar-Gaxiola, S. (1999). Depressive symptomatology: Prevalence and psychosocial risk factors among Mexican migrant farmworkers in California. *Journal of Community Psychology, 27*(4), 457–471.

Alloy, L. B., Abramson, L. Y., Hogan, M. E., Whitehouse, W. G., Rose, D. T., Robinson, M. S., et al. (2000). The Temple-Wisconsin Cognitive Vulnerability to Depression Project:

Lifetime history of Axis I psychopathology in individuals at high and low cognitive risk for depression. *Journal of Abnormal Psychology, 109*(3), 403–418.

Altenor, A., Volpicelli, J. R., & Seligman, M. E. (1979). Debilitated shock escape is produced by both short- and long-duration inescapable shock: Learned helplessness versus learned inactivity. *Bulletin of the Psychonomic Society, 14*(5), 337–339.

American Psychiatric Association. (1994). *Diagnostic and statistical manual of mental disorders* (4th ed.). Washington, DC: Author.

Angold, A., Weissman, M. M., John, K., Wickramaratne, P., & Prusoff, B. A. (1991). The effects of age and sex on depression ratings in children and adolescents. *Journal of the American Academy of Child and Adolescent Psychiatry, 30*(1), 67–74.

Areán, P. A., & Miranda, J. (1996). Do primary care patients accept psychological treatments? *General Hospital Psychiatry, 18*(1), 22–27.

Areán, P. A., & Miranda, J. (1997). The utility of the Center of Epidemiological Studies-Depression Scale in older primary care patients. *Aging and Mental Health, 1*(1), 47–56.

Azocar, F., Areán, P. A., Miranda, J., & Munoz, R. F. (2001). Differential item functioning in a Spanish translation of the Beck Depression Inventory. *Journal of Clinical Psychology, 57*(3), 355–365.

Badger, T. A., McNiece, C., & Gagan, M. J. (2000). Depression, service need, and use in vulnerable populations. *Archives of Psychiatric Nursing, 14*(4), 173–182.

Baldwin, R. C. (2000). Poor prognosis of depression in elderly people: Causes and actions. *Annals of Medicine, 32*(4), 252–256.

Barrett, J. E., Williams, J. W., Jr., Oxman, T. E., Frank, E., Katon, W., Sullivan, M., et al. (2001). Treatment of dysthymia and minor depression in primary care: A randomized trial in patients aged 18 to 59 years. *Journal of Family Practice, 50*(5), 405–412.

Beck, A. T. (1961). A systematic investigation of depression. *Comprehensive Psychiatry, 2*(3), 163–170.

Beck, A. T. (1979). *Cognitive therapy of depression.* New York: Guilford Press.

Bifulco, A. T., Brown, G. W., & Harris, T. O. (1987). Childhood loss of parent, lack of adequate parental care and adult depression: A replication. *Journal of Affective Disorders, 12*(2), 115–128.

Brodaty, H., Harris, L., Peters, K., Wilhelm, K., Hickie, I., Boyce, P., et al. (1993). Prognosis of depression in the elderly: A comparison with younger patients. *British Journal of Psychiatry, 163,* 589–596.

Brown, G. W., Bifulco, A., & Harris, T. O. (1987). Life events, vulnerability and onset of depression: Some refinements. *British Journal of Psychiatry, 150,* 30–42.

Brown, G. W., Bifulco, A., Harris, T. O., & Bridge, L. (1986). Life stress, chronic subclinical symptoms and vulnerability to clinical depression. *Journal of Affective Disorders, 11*(1), 1–19.

Brugha, T., Bebbington, P. E., MacCarthy, B., Potter, J., Sturt, E., & Wykes, T. (1987). Social networks, social support and the type of depressive illness. *Acta Psychiatrica Scandinavica, 76*(6), 664–673.

Burke, K. C., Burke, J. D., Rae, D. S., & Regier, D. A. (1991, September). Comparing age at onset of major depression and other psychiatric disorders by birth cohorts in five U.S. community populations. *Archives of General Psychiatry, 48,* 789–795.

Caap-Ahlgren, M., & Dehlin, O. (2001). Insomnia and depressive symptoms in patients with Parkinson's disease: Relationship to health-related quality of life. An interview study of patients living at home. *Archives of Gerontology and Geriatrics, 32*(1), 23–33.

Conti, D. J., & Burton, W. N. (1995). The cost of depression in the workplace. *Behavioral Health Care Tomorrow, 4*(4), 25–27.

Cooper, L., Peters, L., & Andrews, G. (1998). Validity of the Composite International Diagnostic Interview (CIDI) psychosis module in a psychiatric setting. *Journal of Psychiatric Research, 32*(6), 361–368.

Davidson, J., Krishnan, R., France, R., & Pelton, S. (1985). Neurovegetative symptoms in chronic pain and depression. *Journal of Affective Disorders, 9*(3), 213–218.

Dawson, R., Lavori, P. W., Coryell, W. H., Endicott, J., & Keller, M. B. (1998). Maintenance strategies for unipolar depression: An observational study of levels of treatment and recurrence. *Journal of Affective Disorders, 49*(1), 31–44.

de Groot, M., Jacobson, A. M., Samson, J. A., & Welch, G. (1999). Glycemic control and major depression in patients with type 1 and type 2 diabetes mellitus. *Journal of Psychosomatic Research, 46*(5), 425–435.

Dikeos, D. G., Papadimitriou, G. N., Avramopoulos, D., Karadima, G., Daskalopoulou, E. G., Souery, D., et al. (1999). Association between the dopamine D3 receptor gene locus (DRD3) and unipolar affective disorder. *Psychiatric Genetics, 9*(4), 189–195.

Druss, B. G., Rosenheck, R. A., & Sledge, W. H. (2000). Health and disability costs of depressive illness in a major U.S. corporation. *American Journal of Psychiatry, 157*(8), 1274–1278.

D'Zurilla, T. J., & Nezu, A. M. (1999). *Problem-solving therapy: A social competence approach to clinical intervention.* New York: Springer.

Englund, S. A., & Klein, D. N. (1990). The genetics of neurotic-reactive depression: A reanalysis of Shapiro's (1970) twin study using diagnostic criteria. *Journal of Affective Disorders, 18*(4), 247–252.

Fielding, R. (1991). Depression and acute myocardial infarction: A review and reinterpretation. *Social Science and Medicine, 32*(9), 1017–1027.

Folkman, S., & Lazarus, R. S. (1986). Stress-processes and depressive symptomatology. *Journal of Abnormal Psychology, 95*(2), 107–113.

Folkman, S., & Lazarus, R. S. (1988). The relationship between coping and emotion: Implications for theory and research. *Social Science and Medicine, 26*(3), 309–317.

Frisch, A., Postilnick, D., Rockah, R., Michaelovsky, E., Postilnick, S., Birman, E., et al. (1999). Association of unipolar major depressive disorder with genes of the serotonergic and dopaminergic pathways. *Molecular Psychiatry, 4*(4), 389–392.

Garcia, L., Valdes, M., Jodar, I., Riesco, N., & de Flores, T. (1994). Psychological factors and vulnerability to psychiatric morbidity after myocardial infarction. *Psychotherapy and Psychosomatics, 61*(3/4), 187–194.

Ghaziuddin, N., King, C. A., Welch, K. B., Zaccagnini, J., Weidmer-Mikhail, E., Mellow, A. M., et al. (2000). Serotonin dysregulation in adolescents with major depression: Hormone response to meta-chlorophenylpiperazine (mCPP) infusion. *Psychiatry Research, 95*(3), 183–194.

Grazioli, R., & Terry, D. J. (2000). The role of cognitive vulnerability and stress in the prediction of postpartum depressive symptomatology. *British Journal of Clinical Psychology, 39*(Pt. 4), 329–347.

Griffiths, J., Ravindran, A. V., Merali, Z., & Anisman, H. (2000). Dysthymia: A review of pharmacological and behavioral factors. *Molecular Psychiatry, 5*(3), 242–261.

Gunnarsdottir, E. D., Pingitore, R. A., Spring, B. J., Konopka, L. M., Crayton, J. W., Milo, T., et al. (2000). Individual differences among cocaine users. *Addictive Behaviors, 25*(5), 641–652.

Holland, J. C., Korzun, A. H., Tross, S., Silberfarb, P., Perry, M., Comis, R., et al. (1986). Comparative psychological disturbance in patients with pancreatic and gastric cancer. *American Journal of Psychiatry, 143*(8), 982–986.

Hopko, D. R., Bourland, S. L., Stanley, M. A., Beck, J. G., Novy, D. M., Averill, P. M., et al. (2000). Generalized anxiety disorder in older adults: Examining the relation between clinician severity ratings and patient self-report measures. *Depression and Anxiety, 12*(4), 217–225.

Isaacowitz, D. M., & Seligman, M. E. (2001). Is pessimism a risk factor for depressive mood among community-dwelling older adults? *Behavior Research and Therapy, 39*(3), 255–272.

Iwamasa, G. Y. (1993). Asian Americans and cognitive behavioral therapy. *Behavior Therapist, 16*(9), 233–235.

Jackson-Triche, M. E., Sullivan, J. G., Wells, K. B., Rogers, W., Camp, P., & Mazel, R. (2000). Depression and health-related quality of life in ethnic minorities seeking care in general medical settings. *Journal of Affective Disorders, 58*(2), 89–97.

Judd, L. L., Akiskal, H. S., Maser, J. D., Zeller, P. J., Endicott, J., Coryell, W., et al. (1998). A prospective 12-year study of subsyndromal and syndromal depressive symptoms in unipolar major depressive disorders. *Archives of General Psychiatry, 55*(8), 694–700.

Kapci, E. G., & Cramer, D. (2000). The mediation component of the hopelessness depression in relation to negative life events. *Counseling Psychology Quarterly, 13*(4), 413–423.

Keitner, G. I., Ryan, C. E., Miller, I. W., & Zlotnick, C. (1997). Psychosocial factors and the long-term course of major depression. *Journal of Affective Disorders, 44*(1), 57–67.

Kendler, K. S., Thornton, L. M., & Gardner, C. O. (2001). Genetic risk, number of previous depressive episodes, and stressful life events in predicting onset of major depression. *American Journal of Psychiatry, 158*(4), 582–586.

Kessing, L. V., & Andersen, P. K. (1999). The effect of episodes on recurrence in affective disorder: A case register study. *Journal of Affective Disorders, 53*(3), 225–231.

Kessler, R. C., Barber, C., Birnbaum, H. G., Frank, R. G., Greenberg, P. E., Rose, R. M., et al. (1999). Depression in the workplace: Effects on short-term disability. *Health Affairs, 18*(5), 163–171.

Kessler, R. C., & Frank, R. G. (1997). The impact of psychiatric disorders on work loss days. *Psychological Medicine, 27*(4), 861–873.

Kessler, R. C., McGonagle, K. A., Nelson, C. B., Hughes, M., Swartz, M., & Blazer, D. G. (1994). Sex and depression in the National Comorbidity Survey. II: Cohort effects. *Journal of Affective Disorders, 30*, 15–26.

Kessler, R. C., McGonagle, K. A., Zhao, S., Nelson, C. B., Hughes, M., Eshleman, S., et al. (1994). Lifetime and 12-month prevalence of *DSM-III-R* psychiatric disorders in the United States: Results from the National Comorbidity Survey. *Archives of General Psychiatry, 51*(1), 8–19.

Klein, D. N., Schatzberg, A. F., McCullough, J. P., Keller, M. B., Dowling, F., Goodman, D., et al. (1999). Early- versus late-onset dysthymic disorder: Comparison in outpatients with superimposed major depressive episodes. *Journal of Affective Disorders, 52*(1/3), 187–196.

Klerman, G. L. (1986). The National Institute of Mental Health—Epidemiologic Catchment Area (NIMH-ECA) program: Background, preliminary findings and implications. *Journal of Social Psychiatry, 21*(4), 159–166.

Kocsis, J. H., Zisook, S., Davidson, J., Shelton, R., Yonkers, K., Hellerstein, D. J., et al. (1997). Double-blind comparison of sertraline, imipramine, and placebo in the treatment of dysthymia: Psychosocial outcomes. *American Journal of Psychiatry, 154*(3), 390–395.

Koenig, H. G., & Blazer, D. G. (1992). Epidemiology of geriatric affective disorders. *Clinics in Geriatric Medicine, 8*(2), 235–251.

Kubzansky, L. D., & Kawachi, I. (2000). Going to the heart of the matter: Do negative emotions cause coronary heart disease? *Journal of Psychosomatic Research, 48*(4/5), 323–337.

Kupfer, D. J., Frank, E., Carpenter, L. L., & Neiswanger, K. (1989). Family history in recurrent depression. *Journal of Affective Disorders, 17*(2), 113–119.

Lewinsohn, P. M., Hoberman, H. M., & Rosenbaum, M. (1988). A prospective study of risk factors for unipolar depression. *Journal of Abnormal Psychology, 97*(3), 251–264.

Maes, M., Maes, L., & Suy, E. (1990). Symptom profiles of biological markers in depression: A multivariate study. *Psychoneuroendocrinology, 15*(1), 29–37.

Marazita, M. L., Neiswanger, K., Cooper, M., Zubenko, G. S., Giles, D. E., Frank, E., et al. (1997). Genetic segregation analysis of early onset recurrent unipolar depression. *American Journal of Human Genetics, 61*(6), 1370–1378.

Marx, E. M., Williams, J. M., & Claridge, G. C. (1992). Depression and social problem solving. *Journal of Abnormal Psychology, 101*(1), 78–86.

Masand, P. S. (1995). Depression in long-term care facilities. *Geriatrics, 50*(Suppl. 1), S16–S24.

McGuffin, P., Katz, R., Watkins, S., & Rutherford, J. (1996). A hospital-based twin register of the heritability of *DSM-IV* unipolar depression. *Archives of General Psychiatry, 53*(2), 129–136.

Merikangas, K. R., & Avenevoli, S. (2000). Implications of genetic epidemiology for the prevention of substance use disorders. *Addictive Behaviors, 25*(6), 807–820.

Miller, N. L., Markowitz, J. C., Kocsis, J. H., Leon, A. C., Brisco, S. T., & Garno, J. L. (1999). Cost effectiveness of screening for clinical trials by research assistants versus senior investigators. *Journal of Psychiatric Research, 33*(2), 81–85.

Montgomery, S. A., & Asberg, M. (1979). A new depression scale designed to be sensitive to change. *British Journal of Psychiatry, 134,* 382–389.

Moore, J. D., & Bona, J. R. (2001). Depression and dysthymia. *Medical Clinics of North America, 85*(3), 631–644.

Munoz, R. F. (1993). The prevention of depression: Current research and practice. *Applied and Preventive Psychology, 2*(1), 21–33.

Neiswanger, K., Zubenko, G. S., Giles, D. E., Frank, E., Kupfer, D. J., & Kaplan, B. B. (1998). Linkage and association analysis of chromosomal regions containing genes related to neuroendocrine or serotonin function in families with early onset, recurrent major depression. *American Journal of Medical Genetics, 81*(5), 443–449.

Nezu, A. M. (1986). Cognitive appraisal of problem solving effectiveness: Relation to depression and depressive symptoms. *Journal of Clinical Psychology, 42*(1), 42–48.

Nolen-Hoeksema, S. (2000). Further evidence for the role of psychosocial factors in depression chronicity. *Clinical Psychology: Science and Practice, 7*(2), 224–227.

Nolen-Hoeksema, S., Larson, J., & Grayson, C. (1999). Explaining the gender difference in depressive symptoms. *Journal of Personality and Social Psychology, 77*(5), 1061–1072.

O'Keane, V. (2000). Evolving models of depression as an expression of multiple interacting risk factors. *British Journal of Psychiatry, 177,* 482–483.

O'Leary, D., & Costello, F. (2001). Personality and outcome in depression: An 18-month prospective follow-up study. *Journal of Affective Disorders, 63*(1/3), 67–78.

Olfson, M., Shea, S., Feder, A., Fuentes, M., Nomura, Y., Gameroff, M., et al. (2000). Prevalence of anxiety, depression, and substance use disorders in an urban general medicine practice. *Archives of Family Medicine, 9*(9), 876–883.

Ostler, K., Thompson, C., Kinmonth, A. L. K., Peveler, R. C., Stevens, L., & Stevens, A. (2001). Influence of socioeconomic deprivation on the prevalence and outcome of depression in primary care: The Hampshire Depression Project. *British Journal of Psychiatry, 178,* 12–17.

Pincus, H. A., & Pettit, A. R. (2001). The societal costs of chronic major depression. *Journal of Clinical Psychiatry, 62*(Suppl. 6), 5–9.

Plutchik, R., Platman, S. R., & Fieve, R. R. (1968). Repeated measurements in the manic-depressive illness: Some methodological problems. *Journal of Psychology, 70*(1), 131–137.

Qian, Y., Lin, S., Jiang, S., Jiang, K., Wu, X., Tang, G., et al. (1999). Studies of the DXS7 polymorphism at the MAO loci in unipolar depression. *American Journal of Medical Genetics, 88*(6), 598–600.

Radloff, L. S. (1977). The CES-D Scale: A self-report depression scale for research in the general population. *Applied Psychological Measurement, 1*(3), 385–401.

Regier, D. A., Hirschfeld, R. M. A., Goodwin, F. K., Burke, J., Jack D., Lazar, J. B., et al. (1988). The NIMH Depression Awareness, Recognition, and Treatment Program: Structure, aims, and scientific basis. *American Journal of Psychiatry, 145*(11), 1351–1357.

Rossi, A., Marinangeli, M. G., Butti, G., Scinto, A., Di Cicco, L., Kalyvoka, A., et al. (2001). Personality disorders in bipolar and depressive disorders. *Journal of Affective Disorders, 65*(1), 3–8.

Satcher, D. (2000). Mental health: A report of the Surgeon General—Executive summary. *Professional Psychology: Research and Practice, 31*(1), 5–13.

Schein, R. L., & Koenig, H. G. (1997). The Center for Epidemiological Studies-Depression (CES-D) Scale: Assessment of depression in the medically ill elderly. *International Journal of Geriatric Psychiatry, 12*(4), 436–446.

Schmitz, N., Kruse, J., Heckrath, C., Alberti, L., & Tress, W. (1999). Diagnosing mental disorders in primary care: The General Health Questionnaire (GHQ) and the Symptom Check List (SCL-90-R) as screening instruments. *Social Psychiatry and Psychiatric Epidemiology, 34*(7), 360–366.

Seligman, M. E., Weiss, J., Weinraub, M., & Schulman, A. (1980). Coping behavior: Learned helplessness, physiological change and learned inactivity. *Behavior Research and Therapy, 18*(5), 459–512.

Sheline, Y. I. (2000). 3D MRI studies of neuroanatomic changes in unipolar major depression: The role of stress and medical comorbidity. *Biological Psychiatry, 48*(8), 791–800.

Shelton, R. C., Davidson, J., Yonkers, K. A., Koran, L., Thase, M. E., Pearlstein, T., et al. (1997). The undertreatment of dysthymia. *Journal of Clinical Psychiatry, 58*(2), 59–65.

Sherrington, J. M., Hawton, K. E., Fagg, J., Andrew, B., & Smith, D. (2001). Outcome of women admitted to hospital for depressive illness: Factors in the prognosis of severe depression. *Psychological Medicine, 31*(1), 115–125.

Simon, G. E., Revicki, D., Heiligenstein, J., Grothaus, L., VonKorff, M., Katon, W. J., et al. (2000). Recovery from depression, work productivity, and health care costs among primary care patients. *General Hospital Psychiatry, 22*(3), 153–162.

Simons, A. D., & Thase, M. E. (1992). Biological markers, treatment outcome, and 1-year follow-up in endogenous depression: Electroencephalographic sleep studies and response to cognitive therapy. *Journal of Consulting and Clinical Psychology, 60*(3), 392–401.

Spitzer, R. L., Kroenke, K., & Williams, J. B. W. (1999). Validation and utility of a self-report version of PRIME-MD: The PHQ Primary Care Study. *Journal of the American Medical Association, 282*(18), 1737–1744.

Spitzer, R. L., Williams, J. B. W., Kroenke, K., Linzer, M., Mulsant, B. H., Pasternak, R. E., et al. (1994). Utility of a new procedure for diagnosing mental disorders in primary care: The PRIME-MD 1000 study. *Journal of the American Medical Association, 272*(22), 1749–1756.

Starkstein, S. E., Berthier, M. L., Bolduc, P. L., Preziosi, T. J., & Robinson, R. G. (1989). Depression in patients with early versus late onset of Parkinson's disease. *Neurology, 39*(11), 1441–1445.

Starkstein, S. E., Bryer, J. B., Berthier, M. L., Cohen, B., Price, T. R., & Robinson, R. G. (1991). Depression after stroke: The importance of cerebral hemisphere asymmetries. *Journal of Neuropsychiatry and Clinical Neurosciences, 3*(3), 276–285.

Svanborg, P., & Asberg, M. (2001). A comparison between the Beck Depression Inventory (BDI) and the self-rating version of the Montgomery Asberg Depression Rating Scale (MADRS). *Journal of Affective Disorders, 64*(2/3), 203–216.

Swendsen, J. D. (1997). Anxiety, depression, and their comorbidity: An experience sampling test of the Helplessness-Hopelessness Theory. *Cognitive Therapy and Research, 21*(1), 97–114.

Thornton, C., Russell, J., & Hudson, J. (1998). Does the Composite International Diagnostic Interview underdiagnose the eating disorders? *International Journal of Eating Disorders, 23*(3), 341–345.

van Weel-Baumgarten, E. M., Schers, H. J., van den Bosch, W. J., van den Hoogen, H. J., & Zitman, F. G. (2000). Long-term follow-up of depression among patients in the community and in family practice settings. *Journal of Family Practice, 49*(12), 1113–1120.

Veenstra-VanderWeele, J., Anderson, G. M., & Cook, E. H., Jr. (2000). Pharmacogenetics and the serotonin system: Initial studies and future directions. *European Journal of Pharmacology, 410*(2/3), 165–181.

Vega, W. A., Kolody, B., Valle, R., & Hough, R. (1986). Depressive symptoms and their correlates among immigrant Mexican women in the United States. *Social Science and Medicine, 22*(6), 645–652.

Viinamaeki, H., Tanskanen, A., Hintikka, J., Haatainen, J., Antikainen, R., Honkalampi, K., et al. (2000). Effect of somatic comorbidity on alleviation of depressive symptoms. *Australian and New Zealand Journal of Psychiatry, 34*(5), 755–761.

Vinokur, A., Schul, Y., & Caplan, R. D. (1987). Determinants of perceived social support: Interpersonal transactions, personal outlook, and transient affective states. *Journal of Personality and Social Psychology, 53*(6), 1137–1145.

Wagner, H. R., Burns, B. J., Broadhead, W. E., Yarnall, K. S., Sigmon, A., & Gaynes, B. N. (2000). Minor depression in family practice: Functional morbidity, comorbidity, service utilization and outcomes. *Psychological Medicine, 30*(6), 1377–1390.

Welch, J. L., & Austin, J. K. (2001). Stressors, coping and depression in haemodialysis patients. *Journal of Advanced Nursing, 33*(2), 200–207.

Wells, K. B., Burnam, M. A., Rogers, W., Hays, R., & Camp, P. (1992). The course of depression in adult outpatients: Results from the Medical Outcomes Study. *Archives of General Psychiatry, 49*(10), 788–794.

Wilkinson, G., Borsey, D. Q., Leslie, P., Newton, R. W., Lind, C., & Ballinger, C. B. (1988). Psychiatric morbidity and social problems in patients with insulin-dependent diabetes mellitus. *British Journal of Psychiatry, 153,* 38–43.

Yesavage, J. A., Brink, T. L., Rose, T. L., Lum, O., Huang, V., Adey, M., et al. (1982). Development and validation of a geriatric depression screening scale: A preliminary report. *Journal of Psychiatric Research, 17*(1), 37–49.

Zubenko, G. S., Marino, L. J., Sweet, R. A., Rifai, A. H., Mulsant, B. H., & Pasternak, R. E. (1997). Medical comorbidity in elderly psychiatric inpatients. *Biological Psychiatry, 41*(6), 724–736.

Zung, W. W. (1972). The Depression Status Inventory: An Adjunct to the Self-Rating Depression Scale. *Journal of Clinical Psychology, 28*(4), 539–543.

CHAPTER 10

Mood Disorders: Bipolar Disorders

ILAN LOHR and BRIAN L. COOK

DESCRIPTION OF THE DISORDER

BIPOLAR DISORDER IS a disorder of mood, characterized by recurrent episodes of mania and depression. People with bipolar disorder manifest a variety of mood, cognitive, and physiological symptoms, coupled with social and occupational dysfunction, frequent substance abuse, and even suicide. While a person may experience elation, increased speech production, hyperactivity, decreased need for sleep, and feelings of grandiosity during the manic phase of the illness, he or she may feel down, hopeless, worthless, fatigued, withdrawn, and unable to experience pleasure during the depressed phase. Combined, these mood states constitute what we refer to as *bipolar disorder* or *manic-depressive illness*.

More than 2 million Americans carry the diagnosis of bipolar disorder at any given time, although recent studies show that lifetime prevalence rates for bipolar spectrum disorder may be as high as 5%, depending on how exhaustive and inclusive the diagnosis may be. Although bipolar disorder has distinct features, symptomatic variability, episodic course, and comorbidity still present obstacles to timely and/or proper diagnosis. For example, a person experiencing recurrent major depressive episodes cannot be diagnosed with bipolar disorder until after having exhibited a manic or hypomanic episode. Similarly, childhood/ adolescent bipolar disorder has been misdiagnosed or underdiagnosed for many years, resulting in inadequate treatment and poor prognosis. Modern pharmacological treatments have made bipolar disorder more manageable, and treatment options are far greater today than ever before.

Recent advances in neurobiological research and methods (e.g., neuroimaging techniques) have helped elucidate some of the abnormal underlying mechanisms in bipolar disorder. Bipolar disorder is believed to be a genetically heterogeneous illness, evolving from a single (defective) gene or an interaction of multiple genes through complex genetic processes. The results are wide ranging, including neuroanatomical abnormalities, neurophysiological changes, and neuropsychological deficits. Coupled with psychological and behavioral dysfunction, bipolar disorder constitutes a serious psychiatric disorder, with debilitating effects on the individual and significant societal costs.

HISTORY

Occurrence of bipolar disorder was noted as far back as the ancient Greek times. The earliest record in Indo-Germanic cultures is that of the melancholia of Bellerophontes in the Homeric sagas (White, Davis, & Frantz, 1931). In second century A.D., Aretaeus of Cappadocia, a student of Hippocrates, described mania and melancholia specifically. He noted that overactive, irritable, or excitable individuals were more likely to develop mania, whereas depressive individuals were more likely to develop melancholia—a state of depressed, restless, agitated mood, accompanied by a feeling of futility and a desire to die. Although Aretaeus identified correctly the symptomatology and phases of manic-depressive illness, he did not realize that they constitute a single disorder (Campbell, 1953). Hippocratic psychiatry also classified mania and melancholia, among other psychoses (e.g., amnesia, hysteria, epilepsy, etc.), as distinct chronic disorders within the general framework of medicine. They were all separated from phrenitis—any type of psychotic picture accompanied by (or resulting from) fever (White et al., 1931). Likewise, Greek tragedy writers often used the terms *mania, melancholia,* and *paranoia* interchangeably to describe craziness, acknowledging exaggerated mood, thinking, and behavioral patterns.

Conversely, the Middle Ages contributed little to our understanding of mental illness, focusing on religious and superstitious explanations and treatments. In the thirteenth century, for example, Arnold of Villanova related melancholia to a phase of the moon. Mania was often viewed as synonymous with alcoholic intoxication. The fifteenth-century Paduan professor Savanarola treated melancholia with warm baths and irritants. Other contemporaries believed salt, sulphur, or mercury to be precursors of these disorders. Mostly all mental disorders were reduced to *mania* and *melancholia* by the sixteenth century (White et al., 1931).

It was not until 1686 that Bonet used the term *maniacomelancholicus* in describing a group of his patients. In 1854, Falret adopted the term *circular insanity (folie circulaire)* for the same kinds of patients, while his colleague Baillarger used the term *double-form insanity (folie à double forme)*, stirring a controversy on the origins of bipolar disorder (Pichot, 1995). But it was Emil Kraepelin (1893) who combined melancholia and circular insanity into a single category, describing it as *manic-depressive insanity (Manisch-depressives Irresein)*. Further, Kraepelin separated manic-depressive illness from dementia praecox (schizophrenia), based on the clinical descriptions and the natural history of the illnesses, arguing that manic-depression was characterized by recurrent episodes, while schizophrenia was associated with chronic deterioration (Kraepelin, 1921). Although the original descriptions of the illness required presence of both manias and depressions in the same patient, it was generally accepted that patients with only depressions also belonged to the group of manic-depressive illnesses.

EPIDEMIOLOGY

Results from epidemiological studies may be used to estimate the prevalence of bipolar illness in the general population. The lifetime prevalence of bipolar I disorder (see Classification section) in community samples has varied from 0.4% to

1.6%. Approximately 10% to 15% of adolescents with recurrent major depression will eventually develop this disorder. Bipolar II disorder affects approximately 0.5% of the population, with a 5% to 15% chance of bipolar II patients' experiencing four or more mood episodes in a given year (rapid cycling). Males and females are affected equally in bipolar I disorder, but females may be more common in bipolar II disorder (Leibenluft, 1996). Further, males' first episode is likely to be manic as compared with depressive in females, and females report more mixed or depressive symptoms overall. Lifetime prevalence of cyclothymia ranges from 0.4% to 1%, with a 15% to 50% risk of developing into bipolar I or bipolar II disorder (American Psychiatric Association [APA], 2000).

To interpret the significance of these studies, it is important to recognize that many of the epidemiological studies conducted before use of criteria-based psychiatric diagnoses ascertained the prevalence of psychiatric symptomatology and not of psychiatric disorder. Prevalence rates for bipolar illness may be either point prevalence (i.e., the number of individuals ill at some time in a given year) or lifetime prevalence, a potentially more meaningful piece of information.

It is becoming increasingly apparent that all forms of affective illness (unipolar plus bipolar) are more prevalent than once thought. Before the 1970s, meaningful data were available only from studies done outside the United States. European investigators at that time were reporting on specific psychiatric disorders, not simply symptomatology; however, their definitions for given illnesses must be carefully noted because they differ from present-day nosology. These conservative estimates of prevalence represented the state-of-the-art of epidemiology at that time.

One European study that is often cited was conducted by Helgason (1964) in Iceland. Using the biographic method (long-term follow-up of a randomly obtained sample), Helgason reported the lifetime prevalence for manic-depressive psychosis. Again, the problem of a nosology that combines bipolar illness with some forms of unipolar illness must be considered in interpreting these data. Helgason defined manic-depressive psychosis as an illness characterized by attacks of affective disturbance, either elated or depressed, without apparent external cause and associated with psychomotor dysfunction and periods of disability. He also included involutional depression, a form of unipolar illness. Results were reported for both certain and uncertain diagnoses as a single diagnostic group.

Helgason drew his sample by identifying all Icelanders born in Iceland from 1895 to 1897 and living there on December 1, 1910. His period of observation began on that date and extended to July 1, 1957. Information was obtained on 99.4% of his probands, including those who had emigrated. Probands were followed from 13 to 15 years of age through 59 to 62 years of age. Thus, all had essentially passed through the age of risk for bipolar illness. A lifetime prevalence (certain plus uncertain diagnoses) was found to be 1.50 and 2.07 for men and women, respectively. The combined prevalence figure was 1.80%. It is impossible to determine what portion of these probands had bipolar illness and what portion had a form of unipolar illness; therefore, we can only conclude that these figures are high estimates for the true bipolar lifetime prevalence. No data exist that permit generalization of this information to other populations of European descent. Helgason (1979) reanalyzed his data, using criteria that differentiated bipolar disorder from other affective illnesses, and reported the expectancy (morbidity risk) for bipolar illness in his probands. The resultant finding, 0.79%, is not the lifetime prevalence, but approximates this figure closely because of the protracted period of follow-up. Tsuang, Winokur, and Crowe (1980) also reported morbidity risk for bipolar illness in the relatives of their surgical controls. Their value of 0.30% is generally considered a conservative figure that underestimates the true lifetime risk.

A study conducted by Weissman and Myers (1978) determined illness rates in an urban population in the United States. These investigators interviewed 515 randomly selected adults 25 years of age or older using a structured interview. Diagnoses were made using research diagnostic criteria (RDC; Spitzer, Endicott, & Robins, 1977). Weissman and Myers found lifetime prevalence of 1.2% for bipolar illness (depressions associated with mania or hypomania).

The National Institute of Mental Health (NIMH) Epidemiological Catchment Area (ECA) study provides prevalence rates for criteria-based affective disorders (Weissman et al., 1988). Five urban sites in the United States were used to assess more than 18,000 people. Bipolar illness was defined as depression occurring with at least one manic or hypomanic episode. The two-week prevalence rate of bipolar disorder was 0.7%. Lifetime prevalence rate was 1.2%. Bipolar illness was found to be significantly less prevalent than unipolar depression. The study reported the prevalence rate for major depression for the two weeks before the interview to be 4.4%. In contrast to unipolar illness, bipolar disorders were found to have an earlier age of onset and no significant sex differences for prevalence rates. Further analysis of the ECA data by Akiskal et al. (2000) demonstrated a mean onset of bipolar illness to be 21 years for bipolar disorder. The peak age of onset of bipolar disorder appears to be between ages 15 and 19 years, followed by ages 20 to 24. Age of onset in bipolar disorder is complicated by the difficulty of making the diagnosis in younger individuals, as symptoms may be atypical and overlap with symptoms of attention-deficit disorder. Late-onset (after age 60 years) is uncommon and is associated with organic (i.e., medical) conditions. Because bipolar disorder often begins with depression, rates of bipolar disorder are always underestimates until these individuals have their first manic or hypomanic episode.

A cross-national study of approximately 38,000 subjects conducted by Weissman et al. (1996) provides rates and patterns of depression and bipolar disorder in 10 countries—the United States, Canada, Puerto Rico, France, West Germany, Italy, Lebanon, Taiwan, Korea, and New Zealand. *Diagnostic and Statistical Manual of Mental Disorders, 3rd Edition (DSM-III)* criteria were used to determine major affective disorder in all communities sampled. The lifetime rate per 100 for bipolar disorder ranged from 0.3 in Taiwan, 0.4 in Korea, 0.5 in West Germany, 0.6 in Canada and Puerto Rico, 0.9 in the United States, to 1.5 in New Zealand. Men showed higher rates than women in Canada, Puerto Rico, Korea, and New Zealand. Mean age of onset of bipolar disorder was an average six years younger than for major depression, ranging from 17 years in Canada, 18 years in the United States and New Zealand, 22 and 23 years in Taiwan and Korea, respectively, to 27 years in Puerto Rico. Calculations for age-specific rates for bipolar disorder by age at onset showed an onset age of between 15 and 19 years in all sites.

More recent epidemiological studies support the notion of a wider bipolar spectrum. When bipolar disorder was surveyed using traditional assessment tools, the prevalence rate in the general population was typically under 1%. However, when milder expressions of bipolarity were taken into account, prevalence rates increased significantly to 5% (Szádóczky, Papp, Vitrai, Rihmer, & Furedi, 1998), 5.7% (Lewinsohn, Klein, & Seeley, 1995), and 8.3% (Angst, 1998). Thus, it seems that the 1% figure is highly conservative, excluding many softer symptoms and conditions, and ignoring a continuum of bipolar illness expression.

UNIPOLAR-BIPOLAR DISTINCTION

Bipolar disorder is characterized by recurrent episodes of mania and depression. To best understand the concept of bipolar disorder, it is necessary to separate it from unipolar affective disorder, in which an individual shows only depressions and no manic episodes. Most people with bipolar disorder have one or more episodes of both depression and mania; however, patients occasionally report only manias and no depressions.

The distinction between unipolar (monopolar) and bipolar disorder, first proposed by Leonhard in 1959, was eventually incorporated into the RDC in 1978 and into *DSM-III* in 1980. Specifically, Leonhard studied 238 bipolar and 288 unipolar patients, examining the prevalence of endogenous psychosis among their family members. He found that 39.9% of first-degree relatives of the bipolar patients were ill, as compared to 25.7% in the unipolar patients' sample. The fact that bipolar patients had more frequent endogenous psychosis in their families as compared to unipolar patients supported his idea that unipolar and bipolar depressions represent separate illnesses. Additional findings from Switzerland, Sweden, and the United States further strengthened the unipolar-bipolar distinction. For example, Angst (1966) in Switzerland reported that the morbidity risk for affective disorders in the first-degree relatives of bipolar probands was higher than for those of unipolar probands, and that bipolar patients had more bipolar illness in their families than unipolar patients did. Likewise, Perris (1966) in Sweden showed that bipolar patients were more likely than unipolar patients to have bipolar illness in their families. Winokur and Clayton (1967) further showed that one third of the first-degree relatives of bipolar patients who had an affective illness had bipolar illness. Table 10.1 summarizes these and similar studies. Winokur (1984), however, presented data showing that psychotic and nonpsychotic, bipolar and unipolar patients (four groups) all manifested the same amount of familial affective illness. In families with mania present, 36% to 75% of ill relatives exhibit depression only; other affectively ill family members have manic or both manic and depressive episodes over the course of their illnesses (Winokur, 1979).

Accumulating neurobiological evidence over the past several decades continues to strengthen the unipolar-bipolar dichotomy (Yatham, Srisurapanont, Zis, & Kusumakar, 1997). For example, in several studies urinary amines (norepinephrine and epinephrine) and norepinephrine metabolite 3-methoxy-4-hydroxyphenylethylene glycol (MHPG) consistently appear lower in bipolar versus unipolar patients (Bowden et al., 1987; Koslow et al., 1983; Schatzberg et al., 1989; and Deleon-Jones, Maas, Dekirmenjian, & Sanchez, 1975; Beckmann & Goodwin, 1980; Schatzberg et al., 1982; and Muscettola, Potter, Pickar, & Goodwin, 1984, respectively). Similarly, activity of monoamine oxidase and catechol-o-methyltransferase, two of the major enzymes responsible for degrading catecholamines, showed decreased activity in bipolar versus unipolar patients (Eckert et al., 1980; Mann, 1979; D. L. Murphy & Weiss, 1972). One study found gamma-aminobatyric acid (GABA) plasma levels to be higher in bipolar manic and euthymic patients versus depressed unipolars (Petty & Sherman, 1984). Several studies investigating ion and intracellular signal transduction,

Table 10.1
Morbidity Risk (%) of Affective Disorders in
First-Degree Relatives of Bipolar Probands

Study	Morbidity Risk in Relatives	
	Bipolar Disorder	Unipolar Disorder
Stenstedt (1952)	5.0	8.0
Angst (1966)	4.0	4.0
Perris (1966)	11.0	0.6
Winokur & Clayton (1967)	10.2	20.4
Goetzl, Green, Whybrow, & Jackson (1974)	4.0	21.0
Helzer & Winokur (1974)	5.0	12.0
Gershon, Mark, Cohen, Belizon, Baron et al. (1975)	4.0	7.0
Videbech (1975)	8.0	6.0
James & Chapman (1975)	6.0	13.0
Tsuang, Woolson, & Fleming. (1980)	1.9	11.3
Taylor & Abrams (1980)	4.8	4.2
Gershon et al. (1982)	8.0	14.9
Rice, Reich, Andreasen, Endicott, Van Eerdewegh et al. (1987)	10.4	23.1

such as Na-K ATPase activity and calcium concentration, showed greater activity or concentration levels in bipolar patients as compared to unipolar patients (Hesketh, Glen, & Reading, 1977; and Bowden et al., 1988; Dubovsky et al., 1989; and Dubovsky, Lee, Christiano, & Murphy, 1991, respectively). Further, a number of neuroendocrinological studies showed higher growth hormone (GH) response to levodopa stimulation in bipolar patients (P. W. Gold, Goodwin, Wehr, Rebar, & Sack, 1976; Sachar, Frantz, Altman, & Sassin, 1973), higher cortisol response to 5-hydroxytryptophan challenge test in bipolar patients (Meltzer, Perline, Tricou, Lowy, & Robertson, 1984), greater growth hormone responses to insulin-induced hypoglycemia in bipolar patients (Amsterdam & Maislin, 1991), and better thyroid stimulating hormone (TSH) response to thyroid releasing hormone (TRH) in bipolar patients as compared to unipolar patients (P. W. Gold, Goodwin, Wehr, & Rebar, 1977; M. S. Gold et al., 1979). A few neuroanatomical studies showed that bipolar depressed patients seemed to have higher density values in left and right occipital regions, and that male bipolar depressed patients had higher ventricle-brain ratio than unipolar patients (Andreasen, Swayze, Flaum, Alliger, & Cohen, 1990; Schlegel & Kretzschmar, 1987). A neuroimaging study showed that bipolar patients had lower whole brain glucose metabolic rates and lower regional rates in the frontal, temporal, occipital, and parietal lobes as well as in the cingulated, caudate, and thalamic regions in both hemispheres as compared to unipolar patients (Baxter et al., 1985). Yet, other neurophysiological studies showed better sleep patterns and more delta wave sleep in bipolar patients, albeit less rapid eye movement (REM) efficiency as compared with unipolar patients (Duncan, Pettigrew, & Gillin, 1979; Mendels & Chernik, 1973).

Still, some investigators suggest an alternative hypothesis to the idea of bipolar and unipolar disorders as distinct illnesses. Gershon, Bunney, Leckman, Eerdewegh, and DeBauche (1976) and Gershon et al. (1982) proposed that a common genetic diathesis might account for both illnesses, which are represented along an illness severity continuum, with nonpsychotic unipolars having the mildest type of affective disorder and bipolars with psychotic symptoms having the most severe form of the illness. Thus, if unipolar and bipolar illness represent opposite poles of the continuum, both illness frequency and illness severity would be expected to be greater in the families of patients with illnesses of greater severity (i.e., with bipolar and bipolar with psychosis as compared to unipolar). Gershon and colleagues' ideas are interesting, but genetic evidence has provided inconclusive evidence concerning such an explanation thus far.

Additional differences between unipolar and bipolar patients, summarized in Table 10.2, are reflected in the results of a collaborative study of 189 bipolar

Table 10.2
Differences in Characteristics of Probands with Bipolar versus Unipolar Disorder

Characteristic	Bipolar Disorder	Unipolar Disorder
Clinical Picture:		
Presence of mania in proband.	Yes	No
Biphasic or triphasic immediate course with episodes of depression and mania.	Yes	No
Age of onset in proband mean, years (SD).	24.7 (9.4)	32.1 (15.4)
Percent alcoholism in proband.	46.2	16.5
Duration of illness before hospitalization mean, weeks (SD).	48.3 (112.9)	75.9 (121.7)
Course of Illness:		
Mean total number of episodes (5-year follow-up).	8.7	4.0
Predictors of multiple episodes.	Family history of mania and/or schizoaffective mania.	Early onset age.
Chronicity of illness:		
Males	15% at 2 years; 3% at 5 years	17% at 2 years; 8% at 5 years
Females	13% at 2 years; 4% at 5 years	21% at 2 years; 13% at 5 years
Family Background:		
Family history of bipolar illness in proband.	21.7%	8.3%
Mania in relatives.	4%–10%	
Affective illness in parent.	51%	26%
Families having two generations of affective illness (proband parent, proband child).	54%	32%
Affective illness in parents or extended family.	63%	36%
Bipolar psychosis in first-degree relatives.	3.7%–10.8%	0.29%–0.35%
Childhood hyperactive syndrome in relatives.	18.9%	7.2%

Source: Data from "A Prospective Follow-Up of Patients with Bipolar and Primary Unipolar Affective Disorder," by G. Winokur, W. Coryell, M. Keller, J. Endicott, and H. S. Akiskal, 1993, *Archives of General Psychiatry, 50,* pp. 457–465; and "Further Distinctions between Manic-Depressive Illness (Bipolar Disorder) and Primary Depressive Disorder (Unipolar Depression)," by G. Winokur, W. Coryell, J. Endicott, and H. S. Akiskal, 1993, *American Journal of Psychiatry, 150*(8), pp. 1176–1181.

patients and 218 unipolar patients at a five-year follow-up (Winokur, Coryell, Endicott, & Akiskal, 1993; Winokur, Coryell, Keller, Endicott, & Akiskal, 1993). Bipolar patients had an earlier age of onset, more acute onset of illness, and more total episodes than people with unipolar illness. Also, bipolar patients had higher rates of overall family affective illness and were more likely to have shown traits of hyperactivity as children.

CLASSIFICATION

The mood disorders are divided into depressive disorders, bipolar disorders, and those resulting from a medical condition or are substance induced. The bipolar disorders group consists of bipolar I disorder, bipolar II, cyclothymia, and bipolar disorder not otherwise specified. Descriptions of major depressive episode, manic episode, hypomanic episode, dysthymia, and mixed episodes are included in the Clinical Picture section.

DSM-IV-TR (APA, 2000) describes *bipolar I disorder* as occurrence of one or more manic episodes or mixed episodes, and possibly one or more major depressive episodes. Recurrence requires shifting in episodic polarity (e.g., manic to mixed or to depressive) or an episodic interval of at least two months without manic symptoms. Bipolar I may or may not include psychotic and catatonic features. On the other hand, bipolar II disorder is characterized by recurrent major depressive episodes coupled with at least one hypomanic episode. Psychotic symptoms are not seen in the hypomanic episodes and are less frequent during the bipolar II depressive episodes. If a manic or mixed episode develops, the diagnosis changes to bipolar I.

Cyclothymic disorder is "a chronic, fluctuating mood disturbance involving numerous periods of hypomanic symptoms and numerous episodes of depressive symptoms" (APA, 2000). Neither the hypomanic nor the depressive symptoms are sufficiently severe, frequent, or pervasive to qualify as a manic or depressive episode, respectively, but they recur within a two-year period with no more than a two-month symptom-free interval (one year in children/adolescents). If a manic or depressive episode appears after the initial two-year period, a respective bipolar I or bipolar II disorder may be concurrently diagnosed.

Finally, *bipolar disorder not otherwise specified* may result from manic, depressive, hypomanic, or mixed state symptoms, which are too infrequent or too short in duration for a formal diagnosis; concurrent with other symptoms; or superimposed on other psychotic or delusional disorders.

Alternative classification schemes have been proposed. For example, Akiskal (1992) described three types of bipolar illness. According to these formulations, type I is generally psychotic, consisting of a basic depressive temperament coupled with mood-congruent or mood-incongruent psychotic symptoms (which makes it difficult to differentiate these patients from ones with schizoaffective illness). Type II is generally not psychotic but is characterized by cyclothymic bursts during a depressive episode, causing symptoms such as mood lability, irritability, flight of ideas, sexual impulsivity, or even substance abuse. These types of patients are sometimes wrongly diagnosed with *borderline personality disorder.* Finally, type III originates from a hyperthymic temperament coupled with major depression, with typical symptoms of agitation, sexual arousal, and pressure of speech (Marneros, 2001).

Young and Klerman (1992) suggested six bipolar subtypes:

1. Bipolar I: depression with full-blown mania.
2. Bipolar II: hypomania and depression.
3. Bipolar III: hypomania and depressive symptoms.
4. Bipolar IV: bipolar disorder secondary to disease or drugs.
5. Bipolar V: major depression with a family history of bipolar disorder.
6. Bipolar VI: unipolar mania.

More recently, Akiskal and Pinto (1999) suggested a wider bipolar spectrum of seven subtypes, which is more inclusive in nature, incorporating not only mania and depression, but also hypomanic, cyclothymic, and hyperthymic states, as well as conditions associated with pharmacotherapy and family background. These include:

- Bipolar I: depression with full-blown mania.
- Bipolar I½: depression with protracted hypomania.
- Bipolar II: depression with hypomania.
- Bipolar II½: cyclothymic depression.
- Bipolar III: antidepressant-associated hypomania.
- Bipolar III½: stimulant-associated bipolarity.
- Bipolar IV: hyperthymic depression.

These researchers believe that because most patients seek treatment for depression, failure to consider mood swings and mania often leads to misdiagnosis. Refining the bipolar spectrum disorder increases diagnostic accuracy as well as consideration of softer symptomatology coupled with familial and drug-related factors. As mentioned earlier, recent epidemiological data supports the broader definition of bipolar spectrum disorder.

CLINICAL PICTURE

An individual experiencing an episode of bipolar illness may present clinically in a manic phase, a depressed phase, or occasionally, a mixed state, combining both manic and depressive symptoms. Thus, a description of the symptomatic behavior of bipolar disorder encompasses the uniqueness of manic and hypomanic behavior, the ubiquity of depressive symptomatology, and the clinically confusing state, in which symptoms of both phases of the illness are mixed. Clinical researchers investigating mania and hypomania often describe the signs and symptoms of a relatively homogeneous patient population. All manic episodes are attributed to bipolar disorder when neurological or medical etiologies are ruled out. The situation with depressive episodes is more complex, however. Depressed patients are diagnosed or suspected of having bipolar illness only if they report a history of a manic episode, a familial history of mania or hypomania, or both. These individuals are the source of our clinical picture of bipolar depression. Unfortunately, this clinical picture of bipolar depression is not easily differentiated from that seen in the unipolar depressive disorders. Subtle differences exist, but none are pathognomonic.

MANIA AND HYPOMANIA

The manic phase of bipolar illness is divided by severity into hypomania and mania, with hypomania being less severe than mania. Mania is defined in *DSM-IV-TR* (APA, 2000) as a "distinct period of abnormally and persistently elevated, expansive, or irritable mood, lasting at least 1 week." A manic episode is characterized by a clustering of three or more of the following symptoms that present significant behavioral changes. The mood changes need to be sufficiently severe to cause a major impairment in occupational, social, and interpersonal functioning, and may warrant hospitalization to prevent harm to self or others, especially if accompanied by psychotic symptoms. Symptoms include:

- Inflated self-esteem or grandiosity.
- Decreased need for sleep.
- More talkative than usual or pressure to keep talking.
- Flight of ideas or subjective experience that thoughts are racing.
- Distractibility.
- Increase in goal-directed activities (either socially, at work or school, or sexually) or psychomotor agitation.
- Excessive involvement in pleasurable activities that have a high potential for painful consequences (e.g., spending sprees, sexual indiscretions, foolish business decisions).

In hypomania, a clustering of three or more of the same symptoms needs to be present, lasting at least four days. The episode is not severe enough to cause a marked impairment in social or occupational functioning or to require hospitalization, but it does represent a clear change from the usual, nondepressed mood. No psychotic features are seen in a hypomanic state.

Acute mania may be heralded by a period of hypomanic signs and symptoms or begin acutely in its full form. All of the characteristics of hypomania are increased in severity in mania; thoughts and speech become disconnected, fleeting grandiose delusions may be present, and the individual's mood becomes expansive and exalted. Extreme irritability may appear and be associated with destructive actions. If changes in consciousness or psychotic features are present, they often dominate the clinical picture; delusions are frequently religious in nature, and visual and auditory hallucinations may occur. Regardless of the severity of accompanying manic symptoms, patients with psychotic symptoms (delusions or hallucinations) are always classified as experiencing a manic episode. The clinical picture of a manic episode can vary considerably, but most often contains the three cardinal symptoms of mania: elevated mood, flight of ideas, and psychomotor overactivity.

People in a hypomanic state may exhibit similar symptomatology, though to a lesser degree of severity. Their moods are cheerful and expansive, but irritability may appear at the slightest provocation. Self-confidence is high, and actions may be impulsive. Psychomotor activity is increased with a lively quality. Speech rate may be minimally increased, but they are often verbose and bombastic. Rate of thought production is accelerated, coupled with an incapacity to complete a definite series of thoughts. There is increased involvement in goal-directed activities, with a marked increase in efficiency, productivity, or creativity. These individuals may recognize the abnormality of their mood, but they do not identify themselves as ill. Notably, they are neither in a state requiring hospitalization nor do they exhibit psychotic features.

DEPRESSION AND DYSTHYMIA

Kraepelin's (1921) original conceptions of melancholia still provide a vivid accounting of the many ways bipolar depression may present clinically. In his classical description of depressive states, Kraepelin defined six groups according to severity—melancholia simplex, stupor, melancholia gravis, paranoid melancholia, fantastic melancholia, and delirious melancholia.

In melancholia simplex, a sense of profound inward dejection dominates the mood. The patient's view of life is markedly pessimistic and flavored with hopelessness and despair. Feelings of worthlessness are prominent, and torment from guilt is frequent. Endogenous features of decreased libido, anorexia, weight loss, and sleep disturbance with early morning awakening are often present. Energy is markedly decreased, and psychomotor retardation is demonstrated. Phobias may also be part of the clinical picture. Various combinations of these signs and symptoms characterize simple melancholia.

In depressive stupor, the prominent feature is the patient's difficulty in perceiving surroundings and assimilating these external stimuli. Apathy is readily observed, and the patient makes detached statements with confused ideas. However, the patient is most commonly observed to be mute and shows minimal physical activity. The other features of depression are present, but the stuporous quality is most striking clinically.

Melancholia gravis is characterized by the presence of ideas of sin and persecution. The patient is preoccupied with his or her present and past sins, both real and imaginary. His or her life has been without any saving grace, and damnation is viewed as the final reward. Somatic delusions concerning the rotting away of various organs may be experienced, as well as hallucinations of figures or spirits of relatives. Persecutory ideation, when present, is closely related to sinful delusions.

Paranoid melancholia is characterized by persecutory ideation centered on beliefs that the patient is being watched or spied on. He or she often imagines being the target of others, and auditory hallucinations reflect the paranoid theme. The patient's mood is gloomy and despondent, and the risk for suicide is significant.

Fantastic melancholia is characterized by multiple delusions and hallucinations. An individual patient may demonstrate delusions of guilt and persecution, bizarre somatic dysfunction, and hypochondriasis. Abundant hallucinations of spirits, the devil, monsters, and angels are present. Cognitive function appears impaired, and psychomotor activity may range from one extreme to the other.

Finally, in delirious melancholia, the total clinical picture described in fantastic melancholia is present, but, in addition, cognitive function and consciousness are significantly impaired.

DSM-IV-TR (APA, 2000), like previous editions, does not differentiate between the clinical picture of bipolar and unipolar depression. The central feature of depression in either affective illness category is a pervasive depressed mood or loss of interest or pleasure. To meet the criteria of a depressive episode, a patient must exhibit five or more of the following symptoms for a consecutive two-week period, representing a change from previous functioning. At least one of the symptoms must be either depressed mood or loss of interest or pleasure:

- Depressed mood most of the day, nearly every day.
- Markedly diminished interest or pleasure in all, or almost all activities, most of the day, nearly every day.
- Significant weight loss when not dieting or weight gain (e.g., a change of more than 5% of body weight in a month), or decrease or increase in appetite nearly every day.
- Insomnia (classically presenting as early morning awakening) or hypersomnia.
- Psychomotor agitation or retardation (e.g., of speech and movement).
- Fatigue or loss of energy.
- Decreased self-esteem, manifested by feelings of worthlessness, or excessive or inappropriate guilt.
- Diminished ability to think or concentrate, or indecisiveness.
- Recurrent thoughts of death, recurrent suicidal ideation without a specific plan, or a suicide attempt or specific plan for committing suicide.

When a person has been chronically depressed, sad, or "down" most of the day more days than not for at least two years, he or she is diagnosed with dysthymic disorder (in children, only one year). At least two of the following symptoms should be present as well: poor appetite or overeating, insomnia or hypersomnia, low energy or fatigue, low self-esteem, poor concentration or difficulty making decisions, and feelings of hopelessness. This diagnosis is made only in the absence of a major depressive episode during the two-year period.

MIXED EPISODES

A mixed form of bipolar illness, with both manic and depressive features, may be seen. Once given little attention and thought to be rare, the patient experiencing a mixed episode is now recognized frequently in the clinical setting. The identification of this phase of the bipolar illness is critical, as it may be the first time mood stabilizers are considered in the therapeutic management of the patient's recurring "depression."

The clinical picture presents both manic and depressive symptoms, as outlined previously, lasting for at least a one-week period. The mood disturbance is sufficiently severe to cause a significant impairment in occupational and/or interpersonal functioning that sometimes necessitates hospitalization, particularly when psychotic features are present. Individuals in a mixed episode experience more dysphoria than do those in a *pure* manic state and are more likely to seek help. Mixed states are more common in younger individuals or in people over age 60 years with bipolar disorder, and are believed to be more common among males (APA, 2000).

DIAGNOSIS, COURSE, AND PROGNOSIS

Bipolar disorder is a lifelong, usually episodic condition with an unpredictable course. The first episode of illness may be either depressed, manic, or even hypomanic in character. Females tend to present more often with depression in their first episode than males, but both are much more likely to have depressive episodes that precede manic episodes. Because episodes of hypomania may be subtle and patients may fail to report manic episodes, correct diagnosis is often delayed. Substance abuse may also delay proper diagnosis.

The clinical pictures of unipolar and bipolar depressive episodes generally share a broad range of affective symptomatology. While characteristics that differentiate the unipolar depressive from the bipolar depressive may have some validity in distinguishing groups of patients, application to an individual patient is of little clinical value. The wise clinician attempts to differentiate one from the other by using information on the course of the patient's illness and the family history of affective illness and not by eliciting subtle behavioral differences in depressive symptomatology. Many researchers have reported subtle differences; however, other investigators report no differences between bipolar and unipolar depressive episodes when cross-sectional symptoms are compared (Abrams & Taylor, 1980).

While the differential diagnosis between bipolar depression and unipolar depression represents the most frequent diagnostic challenge, other diagnostic considerations may present clinical confusion. The distinction between schizoaffective disorder and bipolar disorder in a patient with both affective symptoms and psychosis can be particularly problematic. Studies using the RDC definition of schizoaffective disorder have shown that in people with bipolar disorder, the manic states are similar to those in schizoaffective manics, although the schizoaffective manic probably has an earlier age of onset and a more malignant course (Clayton, 1987). Previous episodes of mania or depression without psychosis and family history of bipolar illness make bipolar illness more likely than schizoaffective disorder in patients who present with both affective and psychotic symptoms. Distinguishing bipolar illness from schizophrenia can be difficult if the patient's history and family history are unknown. It may not be possible to distinguish psychotic illness from affective illness in the initial presentation of patients who do not have a family history of either schizophrenia or bipolar illness. Finally, patients with certain personality disorders (e.g., antisocial or borderline personality disorders) and patients with alcohol and drug abuse can present with symptoms of hypomania or, in extreme cases, mania; these conditions must be considered in the differential diagnosis of bipolar illness.

Bipolar illness starts generally before age 30. Table 10.3 presents the cumulative risk for age of onset for both males and females (Winokur, 1970). Over half the patients become ill before age 30, and, in fact, a quarter of the patients become ill before age 20. Although bipolar illness frequently begins in adolescence, historically, the occurrence of early onset was interpreted by clinicians as suggesting the presence of schizophrenia.

Bipolar disorder may first manifest itself by a depression. In one study, 225 unipolar depressive patients were identified and then followed for as long as 40 years. In the first few years after follow-up, about 4% of the patients went from unipolarity to bipolarity (Winokur & Morrison, 1973); however, in the long-term follow-up, 9.7% became bipolar (Winokur, Tsuang, & Crowe, 1982).

Episodes of bipolar illness are often biplasic or triplasic. Often, there is a short depression (few weeks), followed by a mania (two to three months), followed in turn by a longer depression (six to nine months). Short-term follow-ups in bipolar

Table 10.3

Age of Onset and Age at Index Admission in Manic Patients (*N* 89)

Age Range	Number with Index Admission (both sexes)	Number within Age Range at Onset of Illness		Both sexes	Cumulative Risk (% both sexes)
		Males	Females		
10–19	6	8	14	22	25
20–29	16	12	13	25	53
30–39	18	3	12	15	70
40–49	18	5	8	13	84
50–59	18	5	6	11	97
60–69	11	2	1	3	100
70–79	2	0	0	0	
Total	89	35	54	89	

Source: From "Genetic Findings and Methodological Considerations in Manic-Depressive Disease," by G. Winokur, 1970, *British Journal of Psychiatry, 117,* pp. 267–274. Copyright 1970 by The Royal College of Psychiatrists. Adapted with permission of the author.

patients are in reasonable agreement. Commonly, the patient has subsequent episodes, either superimposed on partial remission or wellness. Bratfos and Haug (1968) followed 42 patients for six years. They found that 7% recovered without relapse, 48% had one or more episodes, and 45% had chronic courses.

Winokur, Clayton, and Reich (1969) followed 28 bipolar patients for 18 to 36 months after index admission. Notably, about 39% were chronically ill or only partially remitted, and 14% were well in every way. In a 10-year follow-up study of 131 bipolar patients (Winokur et al., 1994), chronicity from index episode to the end of the 10-year follow-up was uncommon (4%).

In a study conducted by Angst et al. (1973), only two of 393 bipolar patients from five different countries suffered single episodes of the illness. Sixty-four percent of people with bipolar psychoses were followed for at least 10 years and 49% for 15 years. Median number of episodes for the observation period was seven to nine, and the mean number of episodes in patients who had been observed for 40 years was not higher than in patients who had been observed for only 15 years. The authors concluded that there was a certain self-limitation in the mean number of episodes. It is important to note that these data refer to bipolars who had been treated. Between 70% and 80% of the patients had been treated in the hospital, and very few patients had received no treatment at all. The length of the episodes remains rather constant, varying only between 2.7 months in the first episode to 2.4 months in the tenth. Cycle length, or the time from the beginning of one episode to the beginning of the next, was shortened from episode to episode, but approached a certain threshold value.

Winokur et al. (1994) published a prospective and systematic evaluation of the course of bipolar illness in 131 patients over a 10-year period of follow-up based on data available from the NIMH Collaborative Study of the Psychobiology of Depression (Coryell, Lavori, Endicott, Keller, & Van Eerdewegh, 1984; Katz, Secunda, Hirschfeld, & Koslow, 1979; Keller et al., 1984). In contrast to the Angst study, cycle lengths showed no systematic decrease in duration over a 10-year follow-up period. Cycle lengths in the first five years of follow-up were similar in length to the last five years of follow-up. Furthermore, the number of episodes in the first five years of follow-up was not correlated with the number of episodes in the last five years of follow-up. This was a naturalistic study, and treatment intensity was not related to decreasing episodes or to changes in cycle length. Data from this study are presented in Table 10.4.

Reasons for the differences in the findings between the Winokur and the Angst studies are not readily apparent. With a longer period of follow-up, the Angst findings may turn out to be accurate. Marked differences in the methods of the Winokur and the Angst study exist and may explain some of the differences. Assessment of episodes in the Angst study was dependent on hospitalization, whereas in the Winokur study, assessment of an episode depended on the development of a set of symptoms with or without hospitalization or any other medical care. Therefore, the episodes in the Angst study probably were more severe. It also is possible that the cycle length is not decreased or that the number of episodes is increased in bipolar illness, but that there is a decrease in cycle length for episodes that meet the criteria of severity leading to hospitalization. Finally, the Angst study was largely historical (hospitalizations and records) and the period of observation concerns the beginning of the illness to the end of the time of follow-up. In contrast, the surveillance of the Winokur study was more intense in that it provided systematic follow-up of every patient on an individual basis, for the same period of time, and with the same methods.

Data presented by Angst and Winokur as to the proportion of people who have only one episode of illness are not consistent with data presented by Pollock in the early part of the century (1909 to 1920). Pollock (1931) reported that about 55% of manic patients had only one recorded episode as opposed to Angst, who reported single episodes in 3 of 393 patients, and Winokur, who reported single episodes in 14 of 126 bipolar patients. Like the Angst study, Pollock's study depended on hospital admissions. More recently, Fukuda, Etoh, and Iwandate (1983) followed 100 bipolars in Japan for 12 years and reported a much higher percentage (39%) of patients who had only one or two episodes. Reasons for the differences between the modern Japanese study and Angst's study, as well as the reasons for the differences in the material from today and Pollock's material, are not apparent.

While these studies demonstrate that chronic hospitalization and chronic symptom progression are not common, they do not suggest that the person with

Table 10.4
Course of Illness in Bipolar Patients at 10-Year Period Follow-Up

Characteristics	Male ($n = 48$)	Female ($n = 83$)
Percentage chronically ill (never had an 8-week period of wellness)	2.1	4.8
Number of manic, schizoaffective manic episodes (mean)	2.2	3.0
Number of depressive episodes (mean)	2.0	2.5
Total number of affective episodes	2.8	3.1
Percentage with only one episode (i.e., no further episodes of illness)	12.8	10.1
Percentage with no further hospitalizations	25.5	21.5

Source: Data from "Manic-Depressive (Bipolar) Disorder: The Course in Light of a Prospective Ten-Year Follow-Up of 131 Patients," by G. Winokur et al., 1994, *Acta Psychiatrica Scandinavica, 89,* p. 104.

bipolar illness is immune to psychosocial morbidity. This illness takes a toll on interpersonal relationships and may lead to disrupted family and occupational pursuits and many other aspects of a person's life. Treatments geared toward improved stabilization of these areas, as opposed to symptom control only, are still in their infancy and may improve the lives of those with this disorder as they become better understood and more widely available.

BIPOLAR DISORDER AND SUICIDE

Several studies report a higher risk of suicide in bipolar patients as compared to patients with other psychiatric or medical disorders. According to *DSM-IV-TR* (APA, 2000), completed suicide occurs in 10% to 15% of patients with bipolar I disorder and within a similar range among bipolar II patients. Typically, suicide attempts and suicidal ideation are greatest during the depressed phase or mixed state of the illness. The suicide attempt rate is much higher than that of successful suicides.

Goodwin and Jamison's (1990) review reported a mean suicide rate of 18.9% in bipolar patients based on several existing studies. Isometsae, Henriksson, Aro, and Loennqvist (1994) found that 79% of bipolar I patients in a given year in Finland committed suicide during a major depressive episode, versus 11% during a mixed state, and another 11% during a psychotic manic state. The ECA study (Eaton & Kessler, 1985) found an even higher rate of suicide attempts in bipolar or unipolar patients than in individuals over their lifetime history of psychiatric illness: About 25% to 50% of bipolar patients attempted suicide at least once in their lives, and they were mostly female, with an attempt rate two to three times that of males. Rihmer and Pestality's (1999) meta-analysis revealed that the lifetime risk of suicide attempts is highest in bipolar II patients, intermediate in bipolar I patients, and lowest in unipolar patients. It is believed that rapid mood changes in the beginning or end of a mood episode (mainly depressive, but also hypomanic) or changes in bipolar mood states (e.g., when depression escalates into mania or when mania turns into depression) are associated with increased suicide risk, which may be further exacerbated by patients' substance abuse, disorganized lives, and noncompliance with medication. Comorbid personality disorders and a family history of suicide are additional risk factors. Although lithium proved effective in treating suicide, still little is known about the effects of other mood-altering drugs on bipolar patients' mortality rates (Jamison, 2000).

Increased mortality in bipolar patients from natural causes has also been reported. For example, Tsuang, Winokur, and Crowe (1980) reported data from the "Iowa 500" on follow-up of patients admitted to the hospital in the 1930s. The researchers found excessive death from unnatural causes (e.g., suicide) in both primary unipolar depressives and manics. The unnatural deaths were higher in the unipolar depressives, but manic patients experienced excessive natural death. Likewise, in a large study of hospitalized patients with affective disorders, excessive death from natural causes was found in female bipolar depression and in male and female manics who had concurrent organic mental disorders or serious medical illness (Black, Winokur, & Nasrallah, 1987). In the absence of these conditions, however, natural death was not excessive. Alternately, unnatural deaths, mainly suicides, were significantly increased. Taken together (bipolars of both sexes admitted for either depression or mania), no increased natural death rate was found after the patients with organic medical disorders were omitted; however, unnatural deaths (mainly suicides) were significantly increased, mainly in males. Increase in the unnatural death rate of bipolars was not as large as that in unipolars. Consequently, it is assumed that bipolar illness is associated with increased suicide rate, but the increased natural death rate is the result of patients with two diseases, bipolar illness and serious medical disease.

BIPOLAR DISORDER AND SUBSTANCE USE DISORDERS

The association between bipolar disorder and substance use disorders has become a subject of recent interest. Such increased interest stems from the recognition of how often these disorders co-occur in the same individual. In the NIMH ECA study, 60.7% of people with bipolar I disorder had a lifetime diagnosis of drug or alcohol abuse (Regier et al., 1990). Rate of alcohol abuse or dependence in this study was 46% in individuals with bipolar illness, as opposed to the general population rate of 13%. Other substance abuse rates were 41% versus 6% in the bipolars versus general population, respectively.

Mechanisms responsible for co-occurrence of these disorders were reviewed by Swann (1997). In this review, the following mechanisms were considered: Are they independent conditions? Do they share an underlying pathophysiology? Is the substance use a form of self-treatment? Does bipolar illness provide an environmental risk factor for development of substance abuse? This review demonstrated a variety of methodological difficulties in teasing apart these mechanisms, and concluded that there are probably distinct subgroups of patients with bipolar disorder who differ in their predisposition to substance use disorders. Similar conclusions about alcoholism and bipolar illness were demonstrated in a 10-year follow-up study of 131 bipolar patients by Winokur et al. (1994). This study found that co-occurrence of alcoholism was associated with recurrent episodes of bipolar illness in patients whose affective illness predated the onset of the alcoholism, but not in patients whose alcoholism predated the onset of their affective illness. This suggests that alcoholism seen in bipolar illness is related to the bipolar illness itself rather than being independent. It is also possible that alcoholism will precipitate a bipolar illness in a person less predisposed to develop episodes than in patients in whom the bipolar illness came first. In either case, the alcoholism may be of a different quality in bipolar patients than the alcoholism that is ordinarily seen as a separate primary illness. In a study of 445 male veterans, bipolar patients with alcoholism were compared to nonalcoholic bipolar patients on clinical and family history variables. There was no increase in the family history of alcoholism in the alcoholic/bipolar patients, which argues against separate transmission of alcoholism and bipolar illness. This does not exclude the possibility that alcoholism is secondary to the bipolar illness in some cases or that preexisting alcoholism could produce an induced "organic" bipolar picture (Winokur, Cook, Liskow, & Fowler, 1993).

Regardless of how these conditions co-occur, it is important to recognize each to maximize treatment outcome. Treatment outcome in general is negatively influenced by substance use. In addition to precipitating episodes, substance abuse may mask detection of episodes that require pharmacological management. Suicide attempts and completed suicide have been linked to substance use in bipolar patients. Pharmacological management of bipolar disorder is negatively influenced by substance use because of drug-drug interactions, as well as renal and hepatic effects. These negative effects point to the need for aggressive treatment of bipolar patients with substance use disorders. This treatment should be approached in an integrated fashion. Integrated treatment of co-occurring disorders does not necessarily require stabilization of one disorder before treatment of the other one. Treatment of both conditions concurrently, preferably by the same treatment team, is recommended (Drake et al., 2001).

GENETICS OF BIPOLAR DISORDER

Major improvements in genetic research and methodologies have contributed significantly to our understanding of the genetics of bipolar disorder. Family, twin, adoption, and linkage studies point to a major contribution of genetic factors in bipolar disorder, which is assumed to be a genetically heterogeneous illness. Craddock and Jones (1999) believe that although a single gene may play a major role in determining illness susceptibility, the majority of bipolar disorders involve an interaction of multiple genes or more complex genetic mechanisms such as genetic mutations, imprinting, and anticipation (i.e., increased symptom severity and/or earlier illness onset in offspring). Although no specific gene has been identified yet, specific regions on chromosomes 4p, 4q, 5q, 10p, 11p, 12q, 16p, 18q, 21q, 22q, and Xq have been implicated in the etiology of the illness (Craddock & Jones, 1999, 2001; Kato, 2001; Nurnberger & Foroud, 2000; Souery, Rivelli, & Mendlewicz, 2001).

Genetic research of bipolar disorder has many potentials. As Potash and DePaulo (2000) note, identifying the "bipolar" genes may facilitate diagnosis, as in the case of Huntington's disease. Given our understanding of the underlying genetic mechanisms, treatments may be designed to repair genetically linked pathophysiology (e.g., in intracellular transmission, receptor blockade), or gene therapy might be specially developed to modify specific gene action. Further, precision in diagnosis may improve illness management and increase prognostic accuracy. Genetic counseling may help determine familial risk or susceptibility to bipolar disorder. Regardless, the Human Genome Project—aimed at identifying the estimated 70,000 human genes—will certainly facilitate researchers' efforts in identifying the causative genes in bipolar disorder.

Bipolar disorder genetic research still faces many limitations. It is quite clear that the mode of inheritance of bipolar disorder is complex and does not follow traditional Mendelian principles. In families with high mood disorder incidence, a spectrum of illness phenotype is seen, including unipolar depression, alcoholism, suicide, schizophrenia, and other psychoses, thereby making it difficult to isolate the appropriate defective loci on suspect genes (Craddock & Jones, 2001). As Blackwood, Visscher, and Muir (2001) suggest, "mutations in one of several independent genes may produce a similar clinical phenotype, and different mutations in the same gene may cause a variety of related symptoms" (p. S134). Further, bipolar symptoms may develop because of the cumulative effects of mutations in several genes, coupled by other internal and external risk factors. Thus, complex interactions among genes, their transmutations, translocations, and environmental factors should all be considered as building blocks for a genetic model of bipolar disorder.

Family Studies

Family studies have shown that a lifetime prevalence of bipolar and unipolar disorders in families of bipolar patients is higher than in healthy controls (see

Table 10.1). Such aggregation of bipolar disorder in families implies a genetic effect. For example, in a study of 57 bipolar patients, Winokur et al. (1969) found that the morbidity risk for parents was 35% and for siblings, 35%. As no male subject had an ill father, it was speculated that the "bipolar" gene is linked to the sex chromosome X. Female subjects, on the other hand, had both ill fathers and ill mothers. Further, among first-degree relatives, females were much more likely to be affected than males; of 99 male first-degree relatives at risk, 19 had an affective illness, whereas of 100 female relatives at risk, 50 had an affective illness.

TWIN STUDIES

Craddock and Jones (1999) report results of six twin studies, which—using the modern concept of bipolar I disorder—consistently found greater concordance rates in monozygotic (MZ) twins as compared to dizygotic (DZ) twins. Two Norwegian studies found a lifetime rate of affective illness in the MZ co-twin of a bipolar proband (probandwise concordance rate) to be 67% (Kringlen, 1967) and 75% (Torgersen, 1986), respectively. Likewise, a Danish study of 34 MZ and 37 DZ twins found a concordance rate of 62% for bipolar disorder or a 79% concordance rate for either bipolar or unipolar disorder in the MZ co-twin as compared with 8% concordance rate for bipolar disorder or 19% concordance rate for either bipolar or unipolar in the DZ co-twin (Bertelsen, Harvald, & Hauge, 1977). A small-sample American study (Allen, Cohen, Pollin, & Greenspan, 1974) of 5 MZ and 15 DZ twins found bipolar illness concordance rates of 20% in MZ co-twins versus 0% in DZ co-twins, respectively. Further, a Swedish twin study of 13 MZ and 22 DZ twin pairs found the concordance rates for bipolar disorder to be 39% for MZ twins and 5% for DZ twins or 62% concordance rate for either bipolar or unipolar disorder in the MZ co-twin versus 14% in the DZ co-twin (Kendler, Pedersen, Johnson, Neale, & Mathe, 1993). And finally, a British study (Cardno et al., 1999) found a concordance rate of 36% for bipolar disorder in a group of 22 MZ twins as compared with a 7% concordance rate among 27 DZ twin pairs. Combined, these studies reveal a lifetime risk of bipolar disorder in the MZ co-twin to range between 40% and 70%, with an additional risk of 15% to 25% for unipolar depression as well. In comparison, the lifetime risk for bipolar disorder in the general population is 0.5% to 1.5% with an additional 5% to 10% risk of lifetime unipolar depression (Craddock & Jones, 1999). These findings strongly support a genetic model of bipolar disorder, as increase in genetic coinheritance is highly correlated with increased risk for bipolar disorder.

ADOPTION STUDIES

Mendlewicz and Rainer (1977) studied the lifetime risk of affective disorder (bipolar, unipolar, and schizoaffective illness) in the biological versus adoptive parents of 29 adopted bipolar patients, 22 adopted normal controls, and 31 non-adopted bipolar subjects, finding significant differences between these groups. They found an 18% risk for affective illness in the biological parents of bipolar adoptees and a similar risk rate in the biological parents of nonadoptees, as compared to 7% risk in the adoptive parents. Likewise, in a study of 10 bipolar probands, Wender et al. (1986) found a similar, though nonsignificant, trend for increased risk of affective illness in the biological relatives of bipolar patients as compared with their adoptive parents. Both of these studies further support a genetic basis for bipolar illness.

Gene Linkage Studies

Genetic linkage studies aim at identifying a chromosomal region that contains a susceptibility gene. This is done by identifying well-known DNA markers on a chromosome and determining whether they are physically close (cosegregate) to the suspected gene, so that they are passed together from parents to children. If they cosegregate, diseased children carry the marker on the same location where the defective gene is located. Using sophisticated statistical techniques to determine cosegregation of DNA markers and suspected bipolar genes, researchers have been able to identify several chromosomal regions, which may be implicated in bipolar disorder, as follows:

- *Chromosome 18.* The most widely studied regions have been on chromosome 18. Berrettini et al. (1994) evaluated 22 manic-depressive families for linkage to 11 loci on chromosome 18. Although overall linkage analysis score (LOD) was not significant, several families yielded LOD scores consistent with linkage under dominant or recessive modes. These results are consistent with the hypothesis that a susceptibility gene in the pericentromeric region of chromosome 18 (specifically, 18p11.2) with a complex mode of inheritance may exist. Furthermore, two plausible candidate genes, a corticotropin receptor and the alpha subunit of a GTP binding protein, have been localized to this region. More recently, a sample of 57 German families who were tested for linkage to 23 loci on chromosome 18 also revealed linkage to 18p11.2 (Nothen et al., 1999), and Freimer et al. (1996) showed linkage to region 18q22–23. A study of a large Belgian family with affective disorder provided support for linkage to 18q21 (Verheyen et al., 1999).
- *Chromosome 12.* Linkage to chromosome 12 has also been established, especially in connection with a rare autosomal dominant skin disorder called *Darier's disease*. Craddock, McGuffin, and Owen (1994) studied a family, in which the mother and five of eight offspring had both Darier's disease and severe affective illness, suggesting a cosegregation of a susceptibility gene for bipolar disorder and the Darier's disease gene, which was mapped to chromosome 12q23–q24.1. Similarly, Morissette et al. (1999) studied 130 members of a large family of French origin, many of whom had bipolar disorder coupled with Darier's disease, producing a high LOD score on the Darier region on chromosome 12q.
- *Chromosome 11.* Chromosome 11 has been repeatedly investigated, because of the location of important genes involved in catecholamine neurotransmission, such as tyrosine hydroxylase and tryptophan hydroxylase (both on 11p15), tyrosinase (11q14–21), and dopamine receptors D2 and D4 (11q22–23 and 11p15.5, respectively). Overall, however, none of these sites have shown linkage to bipolar disorder, except dopamine receptor 4, which has not been ruled out (Souery et al., 2001). Egeland et al. (1987) reported a finding of an autosomal linkage to the Harvey-ras locus and the insulin gene locus, both on chromosome 11 in a large Amish pedigree. However, reanalysis of a large lateral extension of the original pedigree excluded this linkage (Kelsoe et al.,

1989). More recently, De Bruyn et al. (1994) examined linkage in 14 bipolar families with several candidate genes on chromosome 11, including the c-Harvey-ras-oncogene and the insulin gene, resulting again in the exclusion of close linkage between bipolar illness and each gene.

- *Chromosome 21.* Straub et al. (1994) reported linkage to chromosome 21q22.3 with the marker for liver-type phosphofructokinase enzyme (PFKL) in a large multigenerational pedigree, predisposing at least one family to bipolar disorder. Linkage between bipolar disorder and the PFLK region has also been confirmed in other studies (Ewald, Eiberg, Mors, Flint, & Kruse, 1996; Smyth et al., 1997), as well as the adjacent region to the gene for PFKL, area 21q21–22 (Kwok et al., 1999; LaBuda, Maldonado, Marshall, Otten, & Gerhard, 1996).
- *Chromosome 4.* Genes for dopamine receptor D5 and the alpha-adrenergic 2C receptor are located on this chromosome (4p16), a region that showed positive linkage with bipolar disorder in one study (Byerley, Hoff, Holik, & Coon, 1994). A study by Asherson et al. (1998) of 24 pedigrees with significant number of schizophrenic family members also supported linkage to this region, causing the researchers to conclude that a candidate gene on this chromosome produces susceptibility to a broad spectrum of illness phenotype, including unipolar and bipolar disorders, schizophrenia, and schizoaffective disorder.
- *Chromosome 5.* Preliminary data suggested linkage to three DNA markers on chromosome 5, including a dopamine transporter gene DAT1 on 5p15.3, and candidate genes for serotonergic receptor 5HT1A and a protein subunit of GABA A receptor, on region 5q35 (Coon et al., 1993). However, only a locus near the dopamine transporter gene produced positive LOD score, implying a possible linkage with bipolar disorder.
- *Chromosome X.* Conflicting results have been reported on linkage to the X chromosome. Reich, Clayton, and Winokur (1969) provided support for transmission of bipolar illness via a dominant gene on chromosome X in two families. Mendlewicz, Linkowski, and Wilmotte (1980) studied a large family with bipolar illness in Israel, reporting that the illness was specifically linked to the G6PD region of the X chromosome. Yet, results of several other studies are somewhat contradictory. Gershon, Targum, Mattysse, and Bunney (1979) published results for linkage with red-green color blindness and concluded that bipolar illness is not transmitted by a single gene close to the region on the X chromosome that transmits color blindness. Del Zompo, Bocchetta, Goldin, and Corsini (1984) also found linkage between bipolar illness and color blindness on region G6PD of the X chromosome in two Sardinian pedigrees. Likewise, Baron et al. (1987) reported a positive finding of linkage between bipolar disorders and X chromosome markers, however, reevaluation of the pedigree data greatly diminished support for linkage to Xq28 (Baron et al., 1993). Bocchetta, Piccardi, and Del Zompo (1994) suggested that an X-linked gene, perhaps G6PD itself, may contribute to the susceptibility of bipolar illness in some ethnic groups.

Since many cases of male-to-male transmission have been reported, the role of X-linked inheritance in the transmission of bipolar illness remains unclear. Clearly, X-linked inheritance can account for neither the transmission of bipolar illness per se nor all cases of bipolar illness.

NEUROPSYCHOLOGY AND NEUROIMAGING
STUDIES OF BIPOLAR DISORDER

Patients with affective disorders manifest a variety of cognitive impairments, particularly with respect to attention, learning, memory, and psychomotor functioning. Behavioral observations of hospitalized depressed patients reveal psychomotor retardation or agitation, energy loss, difficulties in learning new information, increased negative thinking, short attention span, and loss of motivation. In contrast, relatively little is known about cognitive deficits in bipolar patients and how they might relate to the clinical symptoms and neurobiological substrates of bipolar disorder (F. C. Murphy & Sahakian, 2001).

Neuropsychological abnormalities in depression include a decrease in auditory sensitivity (Bruder, Spring, Yozawitz, & Sutton, 1980; Bruder et al., 1975); prolonged recognition time for common objects (Friedman, 1964); reduced pain sensitivity (Hemphill, Hall, & Crookes, 1952); slowed motor performance (Cornell, Suarez, & Brent,1984; Donnelly, Murphy, Goodwin, & Waldman, 1982; Friedman, 1964; Raskin, Friedman, & DiMascio, 1982); reduced spontaneous activity (Wolff, Putnam, & Post, 1985); deficits in time estimation and in visuomotor coordination, integration, and accuracy (Raskin et al., 1982); deficits in sensory registration, short-term memory, long-term memory, and semantic storage and retrieval failures; as well as disturbances in the efficiency of information processing strategies (Kaszniak, 1986; Mayes, 1986; Weingartner, Cohen, Murphy, Martello, & Gerdt, 1981). Depressed patients scored lower on IQ tests (Payne, 1973), showed decreased motivation (R. M. Cohen, Weingartner, Smallberg, Pickar, & Murphy, 1982), and exhibited severe problems in attention, vigilance, and concentration (Byrne, 1977; Frith et al., 1983; Malone & Helmsley, 1977; Raskin et al., 1982). Silberman, Weingartner, and Post (1983) argued that while depressed patients can successfully attend to information, remember, and perform logical operations under conditions of low information load, they cannot effectively coordinate these cognitive functions under more demanding processing conditions. Accordingly, Lohr (1999) and Cohen, Lohr, Paul, and Boland (2001) demonstrated that depressed patients performed incrementally worse on tasks requiring sustained and focused attention, under high effortful processing conditions. The question arises as to what cognitive disturbances are manifested during the manic or hypomanic phases of the illness.

Murphy and Sahakian (2001) summarize findings of the several existing neuropsychological studies of manic patients. According to Bunney and Hartmann (1965), a patient with 48-hour manic-depressive cycle exhibited memory loss during the manic phase of the cycle. Similarly, Henry, Weingartner, and Murphy (1971) found that manic patients had difficulty learning serial word lists, with greater impairments seen in more severe cases. Andreasen and Powers (1974) claimed that the memory structures of manic patients were loose, over-inclusive, and idiosyncratic, leading to difficulties in filtering information and a tendency to overgeneralize. On a battery of attention, visuospatial, and memory tests, half of the manic subjects demonstrated moderate-to-severe global cognitive impairment (Taylor & Abrams, 1986). Likewise, manic patients showed memory impairments on tests of pattern and spatial recognition as well as on delayed visual recognition tests (F. C. Murphy et al., 1999). Given the disinhibited nature of a manic state, it was suggested that manic patients experience *dysexecutive syndrome,* that is, disrupted executive functioning in the frontal cortex (Bechara, Damasio, Damasio, & Anderson, 1994). Accordingly, on tasks of attentional set-shifting (Morice, 1990), planning ability (F. C. Murphy et al., 1999), and decision making (Clark, Iversen, & Goodwin, 2001; F. C. Murphy & Sahakian, 2001), manic patients have shown significant executive dysfunction.

Cognitive deficits have been demonstrated to be more common in bipolar patients with poor prognosis. Atre-Vaidya et al. (1998) examined the relationship between poor functioning, cognition, and psychopathology in 36 bipolar patients, using tests of general intelligence and language, verbal and visual memory, and visuospatial functioning along with ratings of psychosocial dysfunction and maladjustment. Patients who exhibited substantial cognitive and memory deficits were associated with poorer psychosocial functioning. Likewise, Van Gorp, Altshuler, Theberge, Wilkins, and Dixon (1998) showed that euthymic bipolar patients who were tested on a neuropsychological battery assessing a range of cognitive functions showed poorer verbal memory and executive functioning as compared to normal controls. As in other psychotic disorders, cognitive deficits in bipolar patients may predict outcome (Zarate, Tohen, Land, & Cavanagh, 2000).

Neuroimaging studies of bipolar disorder have also contributed to our improved understanding of its underpinnings, despite producing conflicting results. Most structural neuroimaging studies (including computed tomography [CT] and magnetic resonance imaging [MRI]) that examined whole brain volume or cortical atrophy in bipolar patients found no differences when compared to healthy controls. Likewise, most studies examining prefrontal cortical, anterior cingulate, or temporal cortical volumes showed no significant differences. When differences were found, they were either minimal or nonreplicable (Strakowski, DelBello, Adler, Cecil, & Sax, 2000). Yet, several studies found cerebellar atrophy (e.g., in the vermal V3 area), particularly in patients with multiple prior episodes (DelBello, Strakowski, Zimmerman, Hawkins, & Sax, 1999). Of 20 studies of lateral ventricular sizes, about half found lateral ventriculomegaly in bipolar patients' samples, but no decreased periventricular brain areas volumes. Measurements of the basal ganglia provided mixed results, with some showing enlarged caudate and globus pallidus (Aylward et al., 1994; Strakowski et al., 1999). Similarly, some studies of thalamic volumes reported enlargements in bipolar patients (Dupont et al., 1995; Strakowski et al., 1999). Strakowski et al. (1999) and Altshuler, Bartzokis, Grieder, Curran, and Mintz (1998) observed bilateral amygdala enlargement in bipolar disorder, but not in the hippocampus. Swayze, Andreasen, Alliger, Yuh, and Ehrhardt (1992) conversely reported right hippocampal enlargement in 48 bipolar patients, but no differences in amygdala volumes. Given the fact that bipolar subjects take a variety of medications for prolonged periods, as well as often suffer from comorbid disorders, it is difficult to reach unequivocal conclusions based on these findings.

Functional neuroimaging studies have also provided valuable data (e.g., positron emission tomography [PET] and single-photon emission computed tomography [SPECT]), because they enable researchers to observe cognitive function in vivo, while radioactive glucose is metabolized cellularly in specific brain regions. Alternatively, functional magnetic resonance imaging (fMRI) allows researchers to identify increased blood flow (and oxygen consumption) in active brain regions. Early PET studies of bipolar disorder found reduced metabolic rates in the prefrontal cortex as compared with the occipital lobe, which is reversed from what was seen in normal controls (Buchsbaum, Cappelletti, et al., 1984; Buchsbaum, DeLisi, et al., 1984). Also, increased metabolic rate was seen in the superior temporal gyrus with decreases in the temporal pole (Buchsbaum et al., 1986). Baxter et al. (1985), however, found that manic patients showed lower glucose metabolism globally, without regional decreases in the prefrontal cortex, caudate, cingulate, or thalamus. Additional studies supported the finding of decreased frontal lobe function, especially in depressed bipolar patients, but examination of smaller subcortical structures, including the thalamus, caudate, and putamen, provided no consistent results (Buchsbaum, Someya, Wu, Tang, & Bunney, 1997). O'Connell et al. (1995) found increased temporal and basal ganglia blood flow in manic bipolar patients compared with healthy controls, whereas Rubin et al. (1995) found lower blood flow in certain frontal and temporal brain regions of manic patients, thereby providing no definite conclusions on cerebral blood flow changes in mania.

ASSESSMENT

Assessment of bipolar disorder patients relies heavily on the clinical picture and symptomatology as reported by affected individuals, coupled with close scrutiny of their clinical response to medications. Because patients may present in either depressed or manic phases of the illness, it is especially important to evaluate depressed patients for history suggestive of mania or hypomania as this may directly influence treatment. At the time of initial assessment, and in ongoing fashion, the patient's safety, level of functioning, and reaction to prescribed treatment are crucial. The initial and ongoing assessment of these patients also requires careful attention to their general medical status, particularly concerning their thyroid, renal, and hepatic status as these may all be influenced by the treatment required for management of the illness.

Abnormalities and variability in biochemical, neuroendocrine, and neuropsychological function in people with bipolar disorder have been described, but the cause of illness has not been determined. The "biogenic amine hypothesis" has been the most popular theory used to explain depression; according to this hypothesis, a functional deficit in the noradrenergic or serotonergic neurotransmitter systems occurs in the central nervous system. It may be implied from this theory that an excess or overactivation of these systems results in mania. Other biogenic amines, such as dopamine, have also been implicated. Other neurotransmitters or neuromodulators, including the cholinergic system, the GABAergic system, and the endorphin system, may also play a role in bipolar disorder. For example, Janowski et al. (1983) suggested that an affective state may be related to the balance between central cholinergic and adrenergic neurotransmitters, with depression a disorder of cholinergic predominance whereas mania is a disorder of adrenergic predominance. However, no unchallenged body of evidence supports any of these theories. Furthermore, there is no evidence that mania and depression are opposites of each other in terms of their neurobiological bases.

Laboratory findings in manic episodes include, among others, polysomnographic abnormalities, increased cortisol secretion, and absence of dexamethasone nonsuppression, which may imply a hypothalamic-pituitary-adrenal dysfunction in bipolar disorder (Schlesser, Winokur, & Sherman, 1980). Also, bipolar depressed patients demonstrated a variety of sleep disturbances, including shortened REM latency, higher REM density, and problems with sleep continuity (Kupfer, 1983).

While some of these findings have been used to theorize about the etiology of bipolar disorder, it is difficult to distinguish course from effect, and the central defect in bipolar illness has not been determined.

As Clayton (1994) suggested, causes of *induced mania* include neurological conditions such as neoplasm, epilepsy, head injury, and cerebrovascular lesions. Drugs that have been associated with acute symptoms of mania include corticosteroids, methamphetamine, cocaine, and L-dopa. Finally, metabolic or endocrine disturbances, infections, or other systemic conditions can also precipitate manic symptoms. Such reports have an important heuristic value as they may provide insight into the key pathophysiology of bipolar disorder. The same idea applies to findings from neuropsychological and neuroimaging studies of bipolar disorder. While a variety of cognitive deficits and neuroanatomical changes have been implicated in depression, fewer and more controversial findings have been reported in bipolar illness, making it difficult to draw definite conclusions about the primary etiology of bipolar disorder.

Finally, traditional psychological testing has not proved very useful in the diagnosis or treatment of bipolar disorder (Hirschfeld, Klerman, Keller, Andreason, & Clayton, 1986), although neuropsychological testing has been more effective in assessing hemispheric deficiencies among bipolar patients (Powell & Miklowitz, 1994). Hence, good clinical skills, as opposed to evolving technology, are still the key to assessment of bipolar disorders.

TREATMENT

Treatment of bipolar disorder must incorporate strategies that address management of acute episodes of depression, mania and mixed episodes, as well as maintenance treatment to prevent recurrent episodes of illness. Current approaches to treatment of bipolar disorder emphasize somatic therapies (i.e., pharmacotherapy and electroconvulsive therapy [ECT]). Family and psychosocial factors also appear to be important in the outcome of lithium-maintained bipolar patients (O'Connell, Mayo, & Flatow, 1991), and comprehensive treatment of bipolar patients should also address these issues. Recently, the American Psychiatric Association (APA) comprehensively reviewed the management of bipolar illness, and revised treatment guidelines have been published (APA, 2002). These new guidelines update the previous 1994 APA bipolar disorder practice guidelines, and were approved for publication at their board meeting in December 2001. The new treatment guidelines are divided into sections that describe approaches to all phases of bipolar disorder and take into consideration various clinical considerations that may alter treatment strategies. These guidelines also provide a wealth of references and a section on background information that helps understand the treatment recommendations. Recommendations in the guidelines are rated as to whether they are made with "substantial clinical confidence," "moderate clinical confidence," or recommended "on the basis of individual circumstances." The following sections review general recommendations found in these guidelines. Specific medication doses are not addressed in this review, but can be found in the APA treatment guidelines or in the Physician Desk Reference (PDR). Comparison of cost is also not considered in the discussion of treatment choices; but for atypical antipsychotic agents, the issue of cost may influence treatment choice, as these are some of the most expensive medications used in psychiatry.

Treatment of Acute Mania

In the acute treatment of severe manic episodes, lithium or divalproex (valproate), in combination with an antipsychotic medication, have been demonstrated to be effective. Atypical antipsychotics are recommended over typical antipsychotics because of their relative lack of extrapyramidal symptoms and better efficacy. Atypical antipsychotics with the most evidence for efficacy include olanzapine or risperidone, but research with others is ongoing. Milder episodes may be approached with monotherapy with any of these agents individually. Refractory patients may be best treated with clozapine, but alternative options may include carbamazepine or oxcarbazine. ECT should also be considered in circumstances of patient preference, pregnancy, severe refractory cases, or in life-threatening medical situations where rapid relief is sought. Psychotherapy alone has not been demonstrated to be effective during acute manic episodes.

If refractory patients present with mania while already on appropriate first-line medications, efforts to optimize medication dosage should first be considered, along with resumption of antipsychotic treatment if it has been discontinued. Mixed episodes generally require antipsychotic treatment, and valproate may be preferred over lithium. ECT may also be of benefit for mixed episodes. Benzodiazepines, specifically lorazepam and clonazepam, possess possible specific antimanic effects and can provide sedation. Thus, they are often used along with lithium or valproate in the acute treatment. As control of the episode is obtained, the antipsychotic or other adjunctive medication is tapered and ultimately discontinued while the lithium or valproate is continued for maintenance and prophylactic therapy.

Electroconvulsive therapy is a very effective treatment for acute mania and may be the treatment of choice if the illness is life threatening and rapid resolution of manic symptoms is imperative. ECT has been demonstrated to be particularly effective in rapid resolution of the catatonic syndrome, a life-threatening condition that can occur in either the manic or depressive phases of bipolar illness (Rohland, Carroll, & Jacoby, 1993). With increasing availability of effective pharmacological management, ECT is infrequently used for the acute management of mania. ECT is also effective in the treatment of depressive symptoms in bipolar illness (see next section).

Side effects differ significantly across these medications. Lithium may cause tremor, polyuria, polydypsia, gastrointestinal (GI) upset, weight gain, and a sense of mental slowing even at therapeutic doses. Less common lithium side effects include rash, acne, psoriasis, and hair loss. Lithium-induced hypothyroidism occurs in a small number of patients (primarily women) and requires monitoring of thyroid functioning for detection. This form of hypothyroidism is most common in the first one to two years of lithium therapy and is treated with thyroid hormone supplementation, or a switch to another medication such as valproate. Long-term lithium treatment has not been shown unequivocally to cause renal failure, but morphologic kidney changes have been detected with its use and case reports suggest that renal failure may occur in very rare instances.

Valproate is most often associated with GI upset, sedation, tremor, and mild liver enzyme elevations. Weight gain, leukopenia, and hair loss are also potential side effects. Very rare, but extremely important, side effects to warn patients of include hemorrhagic pancreatitis, liver failure, thrombocytopenia, and agranulocytosis. Polycystic ovarian syndrome remains a controversial issue, but females on valproate should be advised of this potential risk.

Olanzapine has as its most common side effects weight gain and sedation. Some orthostatic hypotension is possible early in treatment. Long-term risks of type-II diabetes and cardiovascular risk associated with weight gain and lipid alternations should also be considered, along with the very small chance of tardive dyskinesia (TD) when this agent is used. For these reasons, olanzapine and other atypical antipsychotic agents are generally discontinued following initial stabilization on lithium or valproate.

Side effects of carbamazepine are similar to, but generally more severe than, those seen with valproate. Typical antipsychotics carry much higher rates of extrapyramidal side effects including TD. Benzodiazepines may cause excessive sedation, motor and memory impairment, and risk for abuse.

Toxicity of lithium and valproate is quite different, and this difference has led many clinicians to use valproate preferentially as a first-line agent in the treatment of mania. Lithium toxicity is associated with 12-hour serum blood levels above 1.5 mEq/liter, and levels above 2.0 mEq/liter can be life threatening. Patients need to be careful to maintain good hydration when they experience diarrhea or vomiting, or when they exercise in extremely hot conditions. Drug interactions may also raise lithium levels to a toxic point. Lithium levels should be monitored closely on initiation of diuretics, ACE inhibitors, nonsteroidal anti-inflammatory drugs (including Cox-2 inhibitors). Valproate has a very wide therapeutic window and generally does not lead to overdoses when taken as prescribed. Intentional overdose can result in obtundation, coma, and death.

TREATMENT OF BIPOLAR DEPRESSION

Treatment of depressive episodes in bipolar disorder is complicated by the potential risk of precipitating a manic episode or a rapid-cycling course by use of antidepressant agents. The APA bipolar disorder guidelines recommend initiation of either lithium or lamotrigine for the depressed phase of bipolar disorder if the patient is not already being treated with a maintenance medication. If a depression occurs when the patient is already on maintenance medication, optimization of that agent's dosage is also suggested. Whether treatment of depression in bipolar I versus bipolar II disorder requires different approaches is unknown.

Following these steps for initial management, those who fail to respond are generally treated with an antidepressant agent. The 1950s saw the development of the first drugs with truly effective antidepressant properties. Two classes of antidepressants, monoamine oxidase inhibitors (MAOIs) and tricyclic antidepressants, were serendipitously discovered during this period. The MAOIs came from research in drug therapy for tuberculosis, whereas the tricyclics were derived from work with the antipsychotics. Since that time, other antidepressants have been developed with additions such as bupropion, mirtazepine, venlafaxine, nefazadone, and the serotonin-specific reuptake inhibitors (fluoxetine, fluvoxamine, paroxetine, sertraline, and citalopram). These newer drugs may possess unique therapeutic benefits, but their roles in the specific treatment of bipolar depression remain unclear. Because of side-effect considerations and the aforementioned risk of rapid-cycling or mania inducement, the newer antidepressant medications are used preferentially in bipolar depression.

ECT as an organic treatment in psychiatry dates back to 1938 when Cerletti first reported its use. Its introduction was a refinement in artificially induced convulsive therapy in use at that time. Although schizophrenia was the illness that was thought to benefit by convulsive therapy, it soon became apparent that ECT's most dramatic effects were in affective disorder, most commonly depression. Early reports were anecdotal in nature, but, as scientific methodology improved in psychiatry, well-designed, controlled studies demonstrated the efficacy of this treatment modality for depression. The therapeutic response of depressive signs and symptoms to ECT appears not to be a function of diagnosis (unipolar vs. bipolar illness). ECT is clinically indicated for the treatment of depressive episodes if the patient has proven unresponsive to antidepressant medication, if psychotic features are present, if there is serious suicidal risk, or if the depression is especially severe and has led to medical complications such as weight loss or severe inanition.

The safety of ECT was increased dramatically by the introduction of two methodological advances in the 1950s. A short-acting hypnotic and a muscle relaxant are administered before the production of the seizure; thus, a modified convulsion is produced. The most recent advance is the use of brief pulse wave stimulation to produce seizures. This technique minimizes transient memory impairment and confusion that was previously observed in ECT treatment. Pharmacotherapy remains the mainstay for the treatment of severe depression, but ECT retains indications under certain clinical situations.

Rapid Cycling

Patients with a rapid-cycling course should be evaluated for potential causes such as hypothyroidism or antidepressant medication usage. The dosage of lithium or valproate should be optimized, and combination therapy may be used. Lamotrigine or atypical antipsychotics may also play a role in management of these patients.

Maintenance Therapy

Because bipolar disorder is an episodic illness characterized by recurrence, prevention of future manic and depressive episodes is central to therapy. The Consensus Development Panel (1985) concluded that studies addressing prevention of recurrence of bipolar episodes support lithium carbonate's prophylactic properties. It is estimated, however, that 50% or more of bipolar patients receive incomplete or no preventive benefit from lithium. More recent studies have supported the use of lithium and valproate (either alone or in combination with lithium) as maintenance therapy. Maintenance ECT has been used to prevent manic and depressive episodes in some bipolar patients, but the evidence for its usefulness is mainly anecdotal.

Psychotherapy

Psychosocial support, illness management groups, peer-support groups, and efforts to help patients adhere to their treatment plan all help to improve treatment outcome. Acute mania does not response to psychotherapy, but it may help in situations where patients refuse medications and involuntary treatment is not feasible. Depression in bipolar illness can be approached with cognitive behavioral therapy (CBT) or interpersonal therapy (IPT), but definitive studies as to their efficacy in bipolar (as opposed to unipolar) depression have not yet been published.

CHILDHOOD AND ADOLESCENT BIPOLAR DISORDER

Although Kraepelin reported that 4% of people with bipolar disorder show symptoms of mania before puberty, bipolar disorder in children and youth has been underdiagnosed for many years. Kupfer et al. (2002) report that half of the patients in their sample had a first bipolar episode before age 17, with about 20% between ages 10 and 14, and 10% with a first episode between ages 5 and 9. Lewinsohn et al. (1995), conducting a large community study of psychiatric disorders in adolescents ages 14 and 18 in Oregon, reported that 0.1% of their subjects met diagnostic criteria for bipolar I, 0.6% for bipolar II, and 0.3% for cyclothymia (a total of 1% overall), in addition to 5.7% who met subthreshold criteria for a manic episode. Lish, Dime-Meenan, Whybrow, Price, and Hirschfeld (1994) noted that adults with childhood onset of bipolar disorder typically report an initial depressive episode.

Comorbidity with attention-deficit hyperactivity disorder (ADHD), conduct disorder, anxiety disorder, substance abuse, bulimia, Tourette's disorder, head trauma, and pervasive developmental disorder is one complicating factor in diagnosis or misdiagnosis. According to Geller and Luby (1997), approximately 90% of bipolar children and 30% of bipolar adolescents have ADHD. Because many more young children report ADHD symptoms as compared to bipolar adolescents, it is suggested that hyperactivity is a developmentally based predictive factor in the onset of bipolar disorder. Further, approximately 22% of children and 18% of adolescents with bipolar disorder have conduct disorder. As to anxiety disorders, approximately 33% of bipolar children and 12% of bipolar adolescents report multiple symptoms. Bipolar adolescents also exhibit more personality disorders and are at higher risk for suicide as compared to adolescents with other psychiatric diagnoses (44% of bipolar adolescents in Lewinsohn's study had attempted suicide). Räsänen, Tiihonen, and Hakko (1998) reported that substance use disorders occurred in 65.2% of youths under age 21 at the onset of bipolar disorder (vs. 17.2% in older subjects) in a Finnish sample.

The clinical presentation of prepubertal bipolar disorder is variable but includes a waxing and waning course, marked disruptive behavior, extreme moodiness, difficulty falling asleep, impulsivity, and hyperactivity. Hypomanic or manic children often exhibit excessive cheerfulness, inappropriate silliness, giddiness, and elation. Because of short attention span, decreased concentration, low frustration tolerance, and explosive anger, their academic performance deteriorates. Adolescents also show psychotic features, including mood-incongruent hallucinations, grandiose and paranoid delusions, hypersexuality, and labile mood, with rapid shifting and mixed features. Pressured speech, racing thoughts, and flight of ideas are as common as in adults. Irritable mood is more common than elated mood during a manic episode, and episodes are often mixed, short, and acute (Bowden & Rhodes, 1996; Geller & Luby, 1997; Mohr, 2001; Weller, Weller, & Fristad, 1995).

Treatment of childhood and adolescent bipolar disorder is similar to that of adults, although few studies examined the pharmacokinetics of lithium and other drugs in this population group. In addition to lithium, which appears beneficial in 40% to 60% of youth-onset mania, anticonvulsant mood stabilizers such as valproate and carbamazepine have proved useful in treating acute, mixed, and rapid-cycling episodes, as well as lithium-resistant adolescents. Given high comorbidity rates, rapid cycling and mixed features, and chronic course, the usefulness of pharmacotherapy in childhood and adolescent bipolar disorder is complex with yet unstudied prognosis.

GENDER AND RACIAL-ETHNIC ISSUES

GENDER

Unlike major depressive disorder, which is more common in women, bipolar I disorder is equally common in women and men. Yet, the course of bipolar disorder is somewhat different in women: Males' first episode is more likely to be manic, whereas in females, it is more likely to be depressive. Females more often exhibit a rapid-cycling course, more episodes of depression or dysphoric mania, later age of onset, more depressive than manic episodes overall, and longer duration of depressive episodes (Robb, Young, Cooke, & Joffe, 1998). Further, women have been reported to demonstrate more switching with antidepressants, more mixed states, less substance abuse, a tendency toward a seasonal pattern, and greater severity than bipolar I males (Benazzi, 1999). The female reproductive transitions also have a significant effect on the course of the illness (Leibenluft, 2000). Some women have their first episode during the postpartum period, and women with bipolar I disorder have an increased risk of relapse, often with psychotic features, immediately following delivery. The premenstrual period may be associated with worsening of an ongoing major depressive, manic, mixed, or hypomanic episode (Winokur et al., 1994).

The NIMH Genetics Initiative study (Blehar et al., 1998) attempted to examine risk factors associated with liability to bipolar I disorder. The sample consisted of 186 bipolar I women and 141 bipolar I males. Seventy-five percent of the women reported having been pregnant and 31% had experienced menopause. As to childbearing, 45.3% experienced severe emotional problems during their pregnancy or for one month thereafter; 37% reported mood episodes during pregnancy; and 13.7% reported episodes from pregnancy onward. Mood changes included manic episodes, rapid cycling, but primarily depressive episodes (86%). Moreover, almost half of the women reported postpartum mood disturbances. Concerning the menstrual cycle, 75% of the bipolar women described abnormal mood changes, including increased irritability, anger bursts, and mood lability, whereas 25% reported depression. As to menopause, almost 20% of the postmenopausal women reported severe emotional problems, including manic episodes, anxiety and agitation, and depressions. The authors conclude that childbearing is a period of increased risk for the onset of a bipolar I disorder in women, whereas the menstrual cycle is associated with exacerbation of symptoms. Menopause changes pose a lesser risk for mood episodes, though still a period of higher risk than in the general female population. Combined, reproductive risks play an important role in the clinical course of bipolar disorder in women.

An MRI study (Lewine, Hudgins, Brown, Caudle, & Risch, 1995) comparing 5 male and 15 female bipolar disorder patients (along with other psychiatric disorders) found significantly higher rates of brain anomalies in bipolar females. These included deep white matter lesions (6.7% in females vs. 0% in males) and volume loss (33.3% of females vs. 0% in bipolar males). No ventricular differences (e.g., enlargement or asymmetry) were found or differentiated between bipolar females and males, although women were found to have greater rates of hyperintensity signals, suggesting physiological pathology as well. Additional studies on gender differences in brain function in bipolar males and females are needed to elucidate these issues.

Finally, treatment considerations should include factors in the clinical course and drug response of females with bipolar disorder, particularly concerning increased rapid-cycling, depressive, and dysphoric symptoms. As Wehr and Goodwin (1987) suggested, women have a higher risk of drug-induced mania and drug-induced rapid cycling than men. It is possible that females develop rapid cycling more often than men because they are treated more frequently with antidepressants, which may cause switching into hypomania, mania, or rapid cycling. Further, thyroid impairment, which is more prevalent among women, may also be associated with rapid cycling, as well as lithium-induced hypothyroidism. Reproductive status (e.g., pregnancy, menstrual cycle, menopause) and reproductive changes in thyroid function and hormonal levels should also be considered in treating bipolar females (Leibenluft, 1996, 1997). Finally, medication effects on the developing fetus during pregnancy and on breast-fed babies must be carefully considered when choosing the course of treatment.

RACIAL-ETHNIC ISSUES

Cultural differences may affect the experience and communication of manic and depressive symptomatology. For example, in Latin and Mediterranean cultures, patients complain about "nerves"; in Chinese/Asian cultures, there are complaints of weakness, tiredness, and "imbalance"; in Middle Eastern cultures, there are problems of the "heart"; or among the Hopi, being "heartbroken" is a complaint. In some cultures, depression may be experienced largely in somatic terms, rather than subjective cognitive symptoms of sadness or guilt. Further, cultures differ in their perception of the seriousness of certain emotions.

A growing body of evidence suggests that ethnicity affects kinetic and dynamic response to medications. Lin, Poland, and Lesser's (1986) review of several studies suggests that Asian bipolar patients respond clinically to lower lithium blood levels as compared to Caucasians. Because neuroleptics and benzodiazepines are used in the management of acute manic episodes and antidepressants in the treatment of acute depressive episodes, possible interethnic variations in response to these drugs may exist. Generally, Asians report significantly higher extrapyramidal side effects than Caucasians or African Americans, while African Americans experience a greater number than Caucasians. Similar findings in clozapine-treated Korean Americans were reported by Matsuda et al. (1996). As to tricyclic antidepressants and benzodiazepines, African Americans, Asians, and Hispanics have been reported to respond to lower doses than Caucasians (Lin et al., 1986; Macros & Cancro, 1982; Yamamoto, Fung, Lo, & Reece, 1979; Ziegler & Biggs, 1977). Thus, it is assumed that ethnic variation in dosage requirements reflects a complex interaction of cultural, environmental, and genetic factors. These may include differences in body weight and fat distribution, genetically based differences in enzyme systems that metabolize drugs, and variations in receptor-mediated responses. Differences in diet related to ethnicity may also affect drug plasma levels. Further, culturally related habits such as smoking, alcohol, and drug ingestion may affect the metabolism of psychotropic agents. Finally, responses to medication may be affected by cultural variation in symptom expression.

SUMMARY

Bipolar illness is a mood disorder characterized by recurrent episodes of mania and depression. Although it was described as early as ancient Greek times, it was not until the mid-nineteenth century when French and German psychiatrists conceived it as a singular, dual polar disorder (*mania [with] melancholy, circular insanity, double form insanity, manic-depressive insanity,* and, more recently, *bipolar disorder*). Bipolar I disorder includes one or more manic (or mixed) episodes with possibly one or more major depressive episodes. Bipolar II disorder is characterized by recurrent major depressive episodes coupled with at least one hypomanic episode. Hypomania occurs when symptoms do not amount to full-blown mania, whereas cyclothymia has a chronic, fluctuating course with numerous hypomanic and depressive episodes. Recent classification systems have proposed including softer bipolar signs in the diagnosis of the disorder, using the term *bipolar spectrum disorder.*

Lifetime prevalence of bipolar I disorder in community samples has varied from 0.4% to 1.6%, with bipolar II disorder affecting approximately 0.5% of the population, and cyclothymia affecting from 0.4% to 1%. About 90% of individuals with a single episode experience recurrent episodes. Males and females are affected equally in bipolar I, but females may be more common in bipolar II. While males' first episode is more likely to be manic, first episode is more likely to be depressive in females. Further, females report more rapid cycling, more depressive or mixed episodes, and more prolonged and severe depressions. In a large community sample of adolescents, prevalence rates were reported to be 0.1% for bipolar I, 0.6% for bipolar II, and 0.3% for cyclothymia (Lewinsohn et al., 1995), although the diagnosis of bipolar disorder in children and adolescents is often confounded by comorbid symptoms of ADHD, conduct, anxiety, substance abuse, and pervasive developmental disorders. Bipolar adolescents are also at higher risk for suicide, as is the general bipolar individual: About 10% to 15% of people with bipolar I and bipolar II commit successful suicides, with an even greater number of suicide attempts and suicidal ideation. Additionally, individuals with bipolar illness are at higher risk for alcohol dependence and/or drug abuse, with more than half of the patients having had a lifetime diagnosis of substance abuse.

The clinical picture, course of illness, psychosocial backgrounds, and neurobiological and genetic factors differentiate bipolar from unipolar disorder. However, some evidence suggests that bipolar and unipolar affective disorders represent a continuum of severity rather than two distinct illnesses. Further research is needed to resolve this controversial issue. Meanwhile, family, twin, adoption, and molecular studies all suggest that genetic factors play an important role in bipolar disorder, although the mode of inheritance remains uncertain. Since a variety of chromosomal regions have been implicated in its etiology, bipolar disorder is believed to involve an interaction of multiple genes or complex genetic mechanisms, such as mutations, imprinting, and anticipation. Recent neuropsychological and (functional) neuroimaging findings further support a neurobiological basis in the etiology of bipolar disorder.

Treatment of bipolar disorder has continued to evolve over the past several decades. Pharmacological treatment of mania has evolved from lithium as the preferred agent, to anticonvulsants, particularly valproate, being chosen as first-line therapy. The atypical (second generation) antipsychotics are also gaining momentum for use as their efficacy becomes better appreciated. Treatment of the depressed phase of bipolar disorder remains more controversial and the path to treatment is less clear. Psychotherapy, particularly cognitive therapy and interpersonal therapies, play a role. Antidepressant agents have carried concern as to whether they may induce mania or rapid cycling, but this debate remains. The newer antidepressants, psychotherapy, and lamotrigine are treatments that are often added to other mood-stabilizing agents such as lithium, valproate, carbamazepine, or atypical antipsychotics for management of bipolar depression. Long-term follow-up studies provide the best information about the natural history of bipolar patients, and thus will continue to be important in providing insight into the etiology, pathophysiology, and treatment effectiveness in bipolar patients.

REFERENCES

Abrams, R., & Taylor, M. A. (1980). A comparison of unipolar and bipolar depressive illness. *American Journal of Psychiatry, 137*, 1084–1087.

Akiskal, H. S. (1992). The distinctive mixed states of bipolar I, II, and II. *Clinical Neuropharmacology, 15*(1), 632–633.

Akiskal, H. S., Bourgeois, M. L., Angst, J., Post, R., Möller, H. J., & Hirschfeld, R. (2000). Re-evaluating the prevalence of and diagnostic composition within the broad clinical spectrum of bipolar disorders. *Journal of Affective Disorders, 59*, S5–S30.

Akiskal, H. S., & Pinto, O. (1999). The evolving bipolar spectrum: Prototypes I, II, III, and IV. *Psychiatric Clinics of North America, 22*, 517–534.

Allen, M. G., Cohen, S., Pollin, W., & Greenspan, S. I. (1974). Affective illness in veteran twins: A diagnostic review. *American Journal of Psychiatry, 131*, 1234–1239.

Altshuler, L. L., Bartzokis, G., Grieder, T., Curran, J., & Mintz, J. (1998). Amygdala enlargement in bipolar disorder and hippocampal reduction in schizophrenia: An MRI study demonstrating neuroanatomic specificity. *Archives of General Psychiatry, 55*(7), 663–664.

American Psychiatric Association. (2000). *Diagnostic and statistical manual of mental disorders* (4th ed., text rev.). Washington, DC: Author.

American Psychiatric Association. (2002). Practice guideline for the treatment of patients with bipolar disorder (revision). *American Journal of Psychiatry, S159*(4), 1–50.

Amsterdam, J. D., & Maislin, G. (1991). Hormonal responses during insulin-induced hypoglycemia in manic-depressed, unipolar depressed, and healthy control subjects. *Journal of Clinical Endocrinology and Metabolism, 73*(3), 541–548.

Andreasen, N. C., & Powers, P. S. (1974). Overinclusive thinking in mania and schizophrenia. *British Journal of Psychiatry, 125*, 452–456.

Andreasen, N. C., Swayze, V., II, Flaum, M., Alliger, R., & Cohen, G. (1990). Ventricular abnormalities in affective disorder: Clinical and demographic correlates. *American Journal of Psychiatry, 147*(7), 893–900.

Angst, J. (1966). On the etiology and nosology of endogenous depressive psychoses: A genetic, sociologic and clinical study. *Monographien aus dem Gesamtgebiete der Neurologie und Psychiatrie, 112*, 1–118.

Angst, J. (1998). The emerging epidemiology of hypomania and bipolar II disorder. *Journal of Affective Disorders, 50,* 143–151.

Angst, J., Baastrup, H., Grof, P., Hippius, H., Poldinger, W., & Weis, P. (1973). The course of monopolar depression and bipolar psychoses. *Psychiatrica Neurologia, Neurochirurgia, 76,* 489–500.

Asherson, P., Mant, R., Williams, N., Cardno, A., Jones, L., Murphy, K., et al. (1998). A study of chromosome 4p markers and dopamine D5 receptor gene in schizophrenia and bipolar disorder. *Molecular Psychiatry, 3*(4), 310–320.

Atre-Vaidya, N., Taylor, M. A., Seidenberg, M., Reed, R., Perrine, A., & Glick-Oberwise, F. (1998). Cognitive deficits, psychopathology, and psychosocial functioning in bipolar mood disorder. *Neuropsychiatry, Neuropsychology, and Behavioral Neurology, 11*(3), 120–126.

Aylward, E. H., Roberts-Twillie, J. V., Barta, P. E., Kumar, A. J., Harris, G. J., Geer, M., et al. (1994). Basal ganglia volumes and white matter hyperintensities in patients with bipolar disorder. *American Journal of Psychiatry, 151*(5), 687–693.

Baron, M., Freimer, N. F., Risch, N., Lerer, B., Alexander, J. R., Straub, R. E., et al. (1993). Diminished support for linkage between manic depressive illness and X-chromosome markers in three Israeli pedigrees. *Nature Genetics, 3,* 49–55.

Baron, M., Risch, N., Hamburger, R., Mandel, B., Kushner, S., Newman, M., et al. (1987). Genetic linkage between X-chromosome markers and affective illness. *Nature, 326,* 289–292.

Baxter, L. R., Jr., Phelps, M. E., Mazziotta, J. C., Schwartz, J. M., Gerner, R. H., Selin, C. E., et al. (1985). Cerebral metabolic rates for glucose in mood disorders; studies with positron emission tomography and fluorodeoxyglucose F 18. *Archives of General Psychiatry, 42*(5), 441–447.

Bechara, A., Damasio, A. R., Damasio, H., & Anderson, S. W. (1994). Insensitivity to future consequences following damage to human prefrontal cortex. *Cognition, 50,* 7–15.

Beckmann, H., & Goodwin, F. K. (1980). Urinary MHPG in subgroups of depressed patients and normal controls. *Neuropsychobiology, 6*(2), 91–100.

Benazzi, F. (1999). Gender differences in bipolar II and unipolar depressed outpatients: A 557-case study. *Annals of Clinical Psychiatry, 11*(2), 55–59.

Berrettini, W. H., Ferraro, T. N., Goldin, L. R., Weeks, D. E., Detera-Wadleigh, S., Burnberger, J. I., et al. (1994). Chromosome 18 DNA markers and manic-depressive illness: Evidence for a susceptibility gene. *Proceedings of the National Academy of Sciences, USA, 91,* 5918–5921.

Bertelsen, A., Harvald, B., & Hauge, M. (1977). A Danish twin study of manic-depressive disorders. *British Journal of Psychiatry, 130,* 330–351.

Black, D. W., Winokur, G., & Nasrallah, A. (1987). Is death from natural causes still excessive in psychiatric patients? A follow-up of 1,593 patients with major affective disorder. *Journal of Nervous and Mental Diseases, 175*(11), 674–680.

Blackwood, D. H. R., Visscher, P. M., & Muir, W. J. (2001). Genetic studies of bipolar affective disorder in large families. *British Journal of Psychiatry, 178*(S41), 134–136.

Blehar, M. C., DePaul, J. R., Gershon, E. S., Reich, T., Simpson, S. G., & Nurnberger, J. I. (1998). Women with bipolar disorder: Findings from the NIMH Genetics Initiative Sample. *Psychopharmacology Bulletin, 34*(3), 239–243.

Bocchetta, A., Piccardi, M. L., & Del Zompo, M. (1994). Is bipolar disorder linked to Xq28? (Correspondence), *Nature Genetics, 6,* 224.

Bowden, C. L., Huang, L. G., Javors, M. A., Johnson, J. M., Seleshi, E., McIntyre, K., et al. (1988). Calcium function in affective disorders and healthy controls. *Biological Psychiatry, 23*(4), 367–376.

Bowden, C. L., Koslow, S., Maas, J. W., Davis, J., Garver, D. L., & Hanin, I. (1987). Changes in urinary catecholamines and their metabolites in depressed patients treated with amitriptyline or imipramine. *Journal of Psychiatric Research, 21*(2), 111–128.

Bowden, C. L., & Rhodes, L. J. (1996). Mania in children and adolescents: Recognition and treatment. *Psychiatric Annals, 26*(7), S430–S434.

Bratfos, O., & Haug, J. (1968). The course of manic-depressive psychosis. *Acta Psychiatrica Scandinavica, 44,* 89–112.

Bruder, G., Spring, B., Yozawitz, A., & Sutton, S. (1980). Auditory sensitivity in psychiatric patients and nonpatients: Monotic click detection. *Psychological Medicine, 10,* 133–138.

Bruder, G., Sutton, S., Babkoff, H., Gurland, B., Yozawitz, A., & Fleiss, J. (1975). Auditory signal detectibility and facilitation of simple reaction time in psychiatric patients and nonpatients. *Psychological Medicine, 5,* 260–272.

Buchsbaum, M. S., Cappelletti, J., Ball, R., Hazlett, E., King, A. C., Johnson, J., et al. (1984). Positron emission tomographic image measurement in schizophrenia and affective disorders. *Annals of Neurology, 15*(Suppl.), S157–S165.

Buchsbaum, M. S., DeLisi, L. E., Holcomb, H. H., Cappelletti, J., King, A. C., Johnson, J., et al. (1984). Anteroposterior gradients in cerebral glucose use in schizophrenia and affective disorders. *Archives of General Psychiatry, 41*(12), 1159–1166.

Buchsbaum, M. S., Someya, T., Wu, J. C., Tang, C. T., & Bunney, W. E. (1997). Neuroimaging bipolar illness with positron emission tomography and magnetic resonance imaging. *Psychiatric Annals, 27*(7), 489–495.

Buchsbaum, M. S., Wu, J., DeLisi, L. E., Holcomb, H., Kessler, R., Johnson, J., et al. (1986). Frontal cortex and basal ganglia metabolic rates assessed by positron emission tomography with [18F]2-deoxyglucose in affective illness. *Journal of Affective Disorders, 10*(2), 137–152.

Bunney, W. E. J., & Hartmann, E. L. (1965). A study of a patient with 48-hour manic-depressive cycles, I. An analysis of behavioral factors. *Archives of General Psychiatry, 12,* 611–618.

Byerley, W., Hoff, M., Holik, J., & Coon, H. (1994). A linkage study with D5 dopamine and alpha 2C-adrenergic receptor genes in six multiplex bipolar pedigrees. *Psychiatric Genetics, 4*(3), 121–124.

Byrne, D. (1977). Affect and vigilance performance in depressive illness. *Journal of Psychiatric Research, 13,* 185–191.

Campbell, J. D. (1953). *Manic-depressive disease: Clinical and psychiatric significance.* Philadelphia: Lippincott.

Cardno, A. G., Marshall, E. J., Coid, B., Macdonald, A. M., Ribchester, T. R., Davies, N. J., et al. (1999). Heritability estimates for psychotic disorders: The Maudsley twin psychosis series. *Archives of General Psychiatry, 56*(2), 162–168.

Clark, L., Iversen, S. D., & Goodwin, G. M. (2001). A neuropsychological investigation of prefrontal cortex involvement in acute mania. *American Journal of Psychiatry, 158*(10), 1605–1611.

Clayton, P. J. (1987). Bipolar and schizoaffective disorder. In G. Tischler (Ed.), *Diagnosis and classification in psychiatry.* Cambridge, MA: Cambridge University Press.

Clayton, P. J. (1994). Bipolar illness. In G. Winokur & P. J. Clayton (Eds.), *The medical basis of psychiatry* (2nd ed.). Philadelphia: Saunders.

Cohen, R. A., Lohr, I., Paul, R., & Boland, B. (2001). Impairments of attention and effort in patients with affective disorders. *Journal of Neuropsychiatry and Clinical Neurosciences, 13*(3), 385–395.

Cohen, R. M., Weingartner, H., Smallberg, D. P., Pickar, D., & Murphy, D. L. (1982). Effort and cognition in depression. *Archives of General Psychiatry, 39,* 593–597.

Consensus Development Panel. (1985). Mood disorders: Pharmacologic prevention of recurrence. *American Journal of Psychiatry, 142,* 469–476.

Coon, H., Jensen, S., Hoff, M., Holik, J., Plaetke, R., Reimherr, F., et al. (1993). Genome-wide search for genes predisposing to manic-depression, assuming autosomal dominant inheritance. *American Journal of Human Genetics, 52*(6), 1234–1249.

Cornell, D., Suarez, R., & Brent, S. (1984). Psychomotor retardation in melancholic and nonmelancholic depression: Cognitive and motor components. *Journal of Abnormal Psychology, 93,* 150–157.

Coryell, W., Lavori, P., Endicott, J., Keller, M., & Van Eerdewegh, M. (1984). Outcome in schizoaffective psychotic and nonpsychotic depression. *Archives of General Psychiatry, 120,* 787–791.

Craddock, N., & Jones, I. (1999). Genetics of bipolar disorder. *Journal of Medical Genetics, 36,* 585–594.

Craddock, N., & Jones, I. (2001). Molecular genetics of bipolar disorder. *British Journal of Psychiatry, 178*(S41), 128–133.

Craddock, N., McGuffin, P., & Owen, M. (1994). Darier's disease cosegregating with affective disorder. *British Journal of Psychiatry, 165*(2), 272.

De Bruyn, A., Mendelbaum, K., Sandkuijl, L. A., Delvenne, V., Hirsch, D., Staner, L., et al. (1994). Nonlinkage of bipolar illness to tyrosine hydroxylase, tyrosinase, and D2 and D4 dopamine receptor genes on chromosome 11. *American Journal of Psychiatry, 151,* 102–106.

DelBello, M. P., Strakowski, S. M., Zimmerman, M. E., Hawkins, J. M., & Sax, K. W. (1999). MRI analysis of the cerebellum in bipolar disorder: A pilot study. *Neuropsychopharmacology, 21*(1), 63–68.

Deleon-Jones, F., Maas, J. W., Dekirmenjian, H., & Sanchez, J. (1975). Diagnostic subgroups of affective disorders and their urinary excretion of catecholamine metabolities. *American Journal of Psychiatry, 132*(11), 1141–1148.

Del Zompo, M., Bocchetta, A., Goldin, L., & Corsini, G. (1984). Linkage between X chromosome markers and manic depressive illness. *Acta Psychiatrica Scandinavica, 70,* 282–287.

Donnelly, E., Murphy, D., Goodwin, F., & Waldman, I. (1982). Intellectual function in primary affective disorder. *British Journal of Psychiatry, 140,* 633–636.

Drake, R. E., Essock, S. M., Shaner, A., Carey, K. B., Minkoff, K., Kola, L., et al. (2001). Implementing dual diagnosis services for clients with severe mental illness. *Psychiatric Services, 52*(4), 469–476.

Dubovsky, S. L., Christiano, J., Daniell, L. C., Franks, R. D., Murphy, J., Adler, L., et al. (1989). Increased platelet intracellular calcium concentration in patients with bipolar affective disorders. *Archives of General Psychiatry, 46*(7), 632–638.

Dubovsky, S. L., Lee, C., Christiano, J., & Murphy, J. (1991). Elevated platelet intracellular calcium concentration in bipolar depression. *Biological Psychiatry, 29*(5), 441–450.

Duncan, W. C., Pettigrew, K. D., & Gillin, J. C. (1979). REM architecture changes in bipolar and unipolar depression. *American Journal of Psychiatry, 136*(11), 1424–1427.

Dupont, R. M., Butters, N., Schafer, K., Wilson, T., Hesselink, J., & Gillin, J. C. (1995). Diagnostic specificity of focal white matter abnormalities in bipolar and unipolar mood disorder. *Biological Psychiatry, 38*(7), 482–486.

Eaton, W. W., & Kessler, R. G. (1985). *Epidemiological field methods in psychiatry: The NIMH Epidemiologic Catchment Area Program.* Orlando, FL: Academic Press.

Eckert, B., Gottfries, C. G., Von Knorring, L., Oreland, L., Wiberg, A., & Winblad, B. (1980). Brain and platelet monoamine oxidase in mental disorders; schizophrenics and cycloid psychotics. *Progress in Neuro-Psychopharmacology, 4*(1), 57–68.

Egeland, D., Gerhard, D., Pauls, D., Sussex, J., Kidd, K., Allen, C., et al. (1987). Bipolar affective disorders linked to DNA markers on chromosome 11. *Nature, 325,* 783–787.

Ewald, H., Eiberg, H., Mors, O., Flint, T., & Kruse, T. A. (1996). Linkage study between manic-depressive illness and chromosome 21. *American Journal of Medical Genetics, 67*(2), 218–224.

Freimer, N. B., Reus, V. I., Escamilla, M. A., McInnes, L. A., Spesny, M., Leon, P., et al. (1996). Genetic mapping using haplotype, association and linkage methods suggests a locus for severe bipolar disorder (BPI) at 18q22–q23. *Nature Genetics, 12*(4), 436–441.

Friedman, A. (1964). Minimal effects of severe depression on cognitive functioning. *Journal of Abnormal Psychology, 69,* 237–243.

Frith, C., Stevens, M., Johnstone, E., Deakin, J., Lawler, P., & Crow, T. (1983). Effects on ECT and depression various aspects of memory. *British Journal of Psychiatry, 142,* 610–617.

Fukuda, L., Etoh, T., & Iwandate, T. (1983). The course and prognosis of manic-depressive psychosis: A quantitative analysis of episodes and intervals. *Journal of Experimental Medicine, 139,* 299–307.

Geller, B., & Luby, J. (1997). Child and adolescent bipolar disorder: A review of the past 10 years. *Journal of the American Academy of Child and Adolescent Psychiatry, 36*(9), 1168–1176.

Gershon, E. S., Bunney, W. E., Leckman, J. F., Eerdewegh, M., & DeBauche, B. A. (1976). The inheritance of affective disorders: A review of data and of hypotheses. *Behavior Genetics, 6*(3), 227–261.

Gershon, E. S., Hamovit, J., Guroff, J., Dibble, E., Leckman, J. F., Sceery, W., et al. (1982). A family study of schizoaffective bipolar I, bipolar II, unipolar, and normal control probands. *Archives of General Psychiatry, 39,* 1157–1167.

Gershon, E. S., Mark, A., Cohen, N., Belizon, N., Baron, M., & Knobe, K. E. (1975). Transmitted factors in the morbid risk of affective disorders: A controlled study. *Journal of Psychiatric Research, 12,* 283–299.

Gershon, E. S., Targum, S., Mattysse, S., & Bunney, W. E. (1979). Color blindness not closely linked to bipolar illness. *Archives of General Psychiatry, 36,* 1423–1430.

Goetzl, U., Green, R., Whybrow, P., & Jackson, R. (1974). X linkage revisited: A further family study of manic-depressive illness. *Archives of General Psychiatry, 31*(5), 665–672.

Gold, M. S., Pottash, A. L., Davies, R. K., Ryan, N., Sweeney, D. R., & Martin, D. M. (1979). Distinguishing unipolar and bipolar depression by thyrotropin release test. *Lancet, 2*(8139), 411–412.

Gold, P. W., Goodwin, F. K., Wehr, T., & Rebar, R. (1977). Pituitary thyrotropin response to thyrotropin-releasing hormone in affective illness: Relationship to spinal fluid amine metabolites. *American Journal of Psychiatry, 134*(9), 1028–1031.

Gold, P. W., Goodwin, F. K., Wehr, T., Rebar, R., & Sack, R. (1976). Growth-hormone and prolactin response to levodopa in affective illness. *Lancet, 2*(7998), 1308–1309.

Goodwin, F. K., & Jamison, K. R. (1990). *Manic-depressive illness.* New York: Oxford University Press.

Helgason, T. (1964). Epidemiology of mental disorders in Iceland. *Acta Psychiatrica Scandinavica, 40*(S173), 11–251.

Helgason, T. (1979). Epidemiological investigations concerning affective disorders. In M. Schou & E. Stromgren (Eds.), *Origin, prevention, and treatment of affective disorders* (pp. 214–255). New York: Academic Press.

Helzer, J. E., & Winokur, G. (1974). A family interview study of male manic depressives. *Archives of General Psychiatry, 31*(1), 73–77.

Hemphill, R., Hall, K., & Crookes, T. (1952). A preliminary report on fatigue and pain tolerance in depressive and psychoneurotic patients. *Journal of Mental Science, 98,* 433–440.

Henry, G. M., Weingartner, H., & Murphy, D. L. (1971). Idiosyncratic patterns of learning and word association during mania. *American Journal of Psychiatry, 128*(5), 564–574.

Hesketh, J. E., Glen, A. I., & Reading, H. W. (1977). Membrane ATPase activities in depressive illness. *Journal of Neurochemistry, 28*(6), 1401–1402.

Hirschfeld, R., Klerman, G., Keller, M., Andreason, N., & Clayton, P. J. (1986). Personality of recovered patients with bipolar affective disorder. *Journal of Affective Disorders, 11,* 81–89.

Isometsae, E. T., Henriksson, M. M., Aro, H. M., & Loennqvist, J. K. (1994). Suicide in bipolar disorder in Finland. *American Journal of Psychiatry, 151*(7), 1020–1024.

James, N. M., & Chapman, C. J. (1975). A genetic study of bipolar affective disorder. *British Journal of Psychiatry, 126,* 449–456.

Jamison, K. R. (2000). Suicide and bipolar disorder. *Journal of Clinical Psychiatry, 61*(S9), 47–51.

Janowski, D., Risch, S., Judd, L., Parker, D., Kalin, N., & Huey, L. (1983). Behavioral and neuroendocrine effects of physostigmine in affective disorder patients. In P. J. Clayton & J. Barrett (Eds.), *Treatment of depression: Old controversies and new approaches.* New York: Raven.

Kaszniak, A. (1986). The neuropsychology of dementia. In I. Grant & K. M. Adams (Eds.), *Neuropsychological assessment of neuropsychiatric disorders* (pp. 172–220). New York: Oxford University Press.

Kato, T. (2001). Molecular genetics of bipolar disorder. *Neuroscience Research, 40,* 105–113.

Katz, M., Secunda, S., Hirschfeld, R., & Koslow, S. H. (1979). NIMH Clinical Research Branch collaborative program on the psychobiology of depression. *Archives of General Psychiatry, 36,* 765–771.

Keller, M., Klerman, G., Lavori, P., Coryell, W., Endicott, J., & Taylor, J. (1984). Long-term outcome of episodes of major depression. *Journal of the American Medical Association, 252,* 788–792.

Kelsoe, J. R., Ginns, E. I., Egeland, J. A., Gerhard, D. S., Goldstein, A. M., Bale, S. J., et al. (1989). Reevaluation of the linkage relationship between chromosome 11p loci and the gene for bipolar affective disorder in the Old Order Amish. *Nature, 342,* 238–242.

Kendler, K. S., Pedersen, N., Johnson, L., Neale, M. C., & Mathe, A. A. (1993). A pilot Swedish twin study of affective illness, including hospital- and population-ascertained subsamples. *Archives of General Psychiatry, 50*(9), 699–706.

Koslow, S. H., Maas, J. W., Bowden, C. L., Davis, J. M., Hanin, I., & Javaid J. (1983). CSF and urinary biogenic amines and metabolites in depression and mania: A controlled, univariate analysis. *Archives of General Psychiatry, 40*(9), 999–1010.

Kraepelin, E. (1893). *Psychiatrie, ein kurzes Lehrbuch für Studirende und Aerzte.* Leipzig, Germany: Verlag von Ambr. Abel (Arthur Meiner).

Kraepelin, E. (1921). *Manic-depressive insanity and paranoia* (R. M. Barclay & G. M. Livingston, Eds. & Trans.). Edinburgh, Scotland: E & S Livingstone.

Kringlen, E. (1967). *Heredity and environment in the functional psychoses.* London: Heinemann.

Kupfer, D. J. (1983). Application of sleep EEG in affective disorders. In J. Davis & J. Haas (Eds.), *The affective disorders.* Washington, DC: American Psychiatric Press.

Kupfer, D. J., Frank, E., Grochocinski, V. J., Cluss, P. A., Houck, P. R., & Stapf, D. A. (2002). Demographic and clinical characteristics of individuals in a bipolar disorder case registry. *Journal of Clinical Psychiatry, 63*(2), 120–125.

Kwok, J. B., Adams, L. J., Salmon, J. A., Donald, J. A., Mitchell, P. B., & Schofield, P. R. (1999). Nonparametric simulation-based statistical analyzes for bipolar affective disorder locus on chromosome 21q22.3. *American Journal of Medical Genetics, 88*(1), 99–102.

LaBuda, M. C., Maldonado, M., Marshall, D., Otten, K., & Gerhard, D. S. (1996). A follow-up report of a genome search for affective disorder predisposition loci in the Old Order Amish. *American Journal of Human Genetics, 59*(6), 1343–1362.

Leibenluft, E. (1996). Women with bipolar illness: Clinical and research issues. *American Journal of Psychiatry, 153*(2), 163–173.

Leibenluft, E. (1997). Issues in the treatment of women with bipolar illness. *Journal of Clinical Psychiatry, 58*(S15), 5–11.

Leibenluft, E. (2000). Women and bipolar disorder: An update. *Bulletin of the Meninger Clinic, 64*(1), 5–17.

Leonhard, K. (1959). *Aufteilung der Endogenen Psychosen* (2nd ed.). Berlin, Germany: Academie Verlag.

Lewine, R. R. J., Hudgins, P., Brown, F., Caudle, J., & Risch, S. C. (1995). Differences in qualitative brain morphology findings in schizophrenia, major depression, bipolar disorder, and normal volunteers. *Schizophrenia Research, 15*, 253–259.

Lewinsohn, P. M., Klein, D. L., & Seeley, J. R. (1995). Bipolar disorders in a community sample of older adolescents: Prevalence, phenomenology, comorbidity, and course. *Journal of the American Academy of Child and Adolescent Psychiatry, 34*, 454–463.

Lin, K. M., Poland, R. E., & Lesser, I. M. (1986). Ethnicity and psychopharmacology. *Culture, Medicine and Psychiatry, 10*(2), 151–165.

Lish, J. D., Dime-Meenan, S., Whybrow, P. C., Price, R. A., & Hirschfeld, R. M. (1994). The National Depressive and Manic-Depressive Association (DMDA) survey of bipolar members. *Journal of Affective Disorders, 31*, 281–294.

Lohr, I. (1999). *The influence of effort on impairments of attention associated with major affective disorders*. Parkland, FL: UPublish.com.

Malone, J., & Helmsley, D. (1977). Lowered responsiveness and auditory signal detectability during depression. *Psychological Medicine, 7*, 717–722.

Mann, J. (1979). Altered platelet monoamine oxidase activity in affective disorders. *Psychological Medicine, 9*(4), 729–736.

Marcos, L. R., & Cancro, R. (1982). Pharmacotherapy of Hispanic depressed patients: Clinical observations. *American Journal of Psychotherapy, 36*, 505–512.

Marneros, A. (2001). Expanding the group of bipolar disorders. *Journal of Affective Disorders, 62*, 39–44.

Matsuda, K. T., Cho, M. C., Lin, K. M., Smith, M. W., Yong, A. S., & Adams, J. A. (1996). Clozapine dosage, serum levels, efficacy and side-effect profiles: A comparison of Korean American and Caucasian patients. *Psychopharmacology Bulletin, 32*, 253–257.

Mayes, A. (1986). Learning and memory disorders and their assessment. *Neuropsychologia, 24*, 25–39.

Meltzer, H. Y., Perline, R., Tricou, B. J., Lowy, M., & Robertson, A. (1984). Effect of 5-hydroxytryptophan on serum cortisol levels in major affective disorders. II: Relation to suicide, psychosis, and depressive symptoms. *Archives of General Psychiatry, 41*(4), 379–387.

Mendels, J., & Chernik, D. A. (1973). The effect of lithium carbonate on the sleep of depressed patients. *International Pharmacopsychiatry, 8*(3), 184–192.

Mendlewicz, J., Linkowski, P., & Wilmotte, J. (1980). Linkage between glucose-6-phosphate dehydrogenase deficiency and manic-depressive psychosis. *British Journal of Psychiatry, 137,* 337–342.

Mendlewicz, J., & Rainer, J. (1977). Adoption studies supporting genetic transmission in manic-depressive illness. *Nature, 268,* 327–329.

Mohr, W. K. (2001). Bipolar disorder in children. *Journal of Psychosocial Nursing and Mental Health Services. 39*(3), 12–23.

Morice, R. (1990). Cognitive inflexibility and prefrontal dysfunction in schizophrenia and mania. *British Journal of Psychiatry, 157,* 50–54.

Morissette, J., Villeneuve, A., Bordeleau, L., Rochette, D., Laberge, C., Gagne, B., et al. (1999). Genome-wide search for linkage of bipolar affective disorders in a very large pedigree derived from a homogeneous population in Quebec points to a locus of major effect on chromosome 12q23–q24. *American Journal of Medical Genetics, 88*(5), 567–587.

Murphy, D. L., & Weiss, R. (1972). Reduced monoamine oxidase activity in blood platelets from bipolar depressed patients. *American Journal of Psychiatry, 128*(11), 1351–1357.

Murphy, F. C., & Sahakian, B. J. (2001). Neuropsychology of bipolar disorder. *British Journal of Psychiatry, 178*(S41), 120–127.

Murphy, F. C., Sahakian, B. J., Rubinsztein, J. S., Michael, A., Rogers, R. D., Robbins, T. W., et al. (1999). Emotional bias and inhibitory control processes in mania and depression. *Psychological Medicine, 29*(6), 1307–1321.

Muscettola, G., Potter, W. Z., Pickar, D., & Goodwin, F. K. (1984). Urinary 3-methoxy-4-hydroxyphenylglycol and major affective disorders: A replication and new findings. *Archives of General Psychiatry, 41*(4), 337–342.

Nothen, M. M., Cichon, S., Rohleder, H., Hemmer, S., Franzek, E., Fritze, J., et al. (1999). Evaluation of linkage of bipolar affective disorder to chromosome 18 in a sample of 57 German families. *Molecular Psychiatry, 4*(1), 76–84.

Nurnberger, J. I., & Foroud, T. (2000). Genetics of bipolar affective disorders. *Current Psychiatry Reports, 2*(2), 147–157.

O'Connell, R. A., Mayo, J. A., & Flatow, L. (1991). Outcome of bipolar disorder on long-term treatment with lithium. *British Journal of Psychiatry, 159,* 123–129.

O'Connell, R. A., Van Heertum, R. L., Luck, D., Yudd, A. P., Cueva, J. E., Billick, S. B., et al. (1995). Single-photon emission computed tomography of the brain in acute mania and schizophrenia. *Journal of Neuroimaging, 5*(2), 101–104.

Payne, R. (1973). Cognitive abnormalities. In H. J. Eysenck (Ed.), *Handbook of abnormal psychology* (3rd ed., pp. 420–483). San Diego, CA: Knapp.

Perris, C. (1966). A study of bipolar (manic-depressive) and unipolar recurrent depressive psychoses. *Acta Psychiatrica Scandinavica, 42*(S194), 7–184.

Petty, F., & Sherman, A. D. (1984). Plasma GABA levels in psychiatric illness. *Journal of Affective Disorders, 6*(2), 131–138.

Pichot, P. (1995). The birth of the bipolar disorder. *European Psychiatry, 10*(1), 1–10.

Pollock, H. (1931). Recurrence of attacks in manic-depressive psychoses. *American Journal of Psychiatry, 22,* 567–574.

Potash, J. B., & DePaulo, J. R. (2000). Searching high and low: A review of the genetics of bipolar disorder. *Bipolar Disorders, 2*(1), 8–26.

Powell, K. B., & Miklowitz, D. J. (1994). Frontal lobe dysfunction in the affective disorders. *Clinical Psychology Review, 14,* 525–546.

Räsänen, P., Tiihonen, J., & Hakko, H. (1998). The incidence and onset-age of hospitalized bipolar affective disorder in Finland. *Journal of Affective Disorders, 48,* 63–68.

Raskin, A., Friedman, A., & DiMascio, A. (1982). Cognitive and performance deficits in depression. *Psychopharmacology Bulletin, 18,* 196–202.

Regier, D. A., Farmer, M. E., Rae, D. S., Locke, B. Z., Keith, S. J., Judd, L. L., et al. (1990). Comorbidity of mental disorders with alcohol and other drug abuse. *Journal of the American Medical Association, 264,* 2511–2518.

Reich, T., Clayton, P. J., & Winokur, G. (1969). Family history studies: The genetics of mania. *American Journal of Psychiatry, 125,* 358–360.

Rice, J., Reich, T., Andreasen, N. C., Endicott, J., Van Eerdewegh, M., Fishman, R., et al. (1987). The familial transmission of bipolar illness. *Archives of General Psychiatry, 44*(5), 441–447.

Rihmer, Z., & Pestality, P. (1999). Bipolar II disorder and suicidal behavior. *Psychiatric Clinics of North America, 22*(3), 667–673.

Robb, J. C., Young, L. T., Cooke, R. G., & Joffe, R. T. (1998). Gender differences in patients with bipolar disorder influence outcome in the medical outcomes survey (SF-20) subscale scores. *Journal of Affective Disorder, 49,* 189–193.

Rohland, B. M., Carroll, B. T., & Jacoby, R. G. (1993). ECT in the treatment of the catatonic syndrome. *Journal of Affective Disorder, 29,* 255–261.

Rubin, E., Sackeim, H. A., Prohovnik, I., Moeller, J. R., Schnur, D. B., & Mukherjee, S. (1995). Regional cerebral blood flow in mood disorders. IV: Comparison of mania and depression. *Psychiatry Research, 61*(1), 1–10.

Sachar, E. J., Frantz, A. G., Altman, N., & Sassin, J. (1973). Growth hormone and prolactin in unipolar and bipolar depressed patients: Responses to hypoglycemia and L-dopa. *American Journal of Psychiatry, 130*(12), 1362–1367.

Schatzberg, A. F., Orsulak, P. J., Rosenbaum, A. H., Maruta, T., Kruger, E. R., Cole, J. O., et al. (1982). Toward a biochemical classification of depressive disorders, V: Heterogeneity of unipolar depressions. *American Journal of Psychiatry, 139*(4), 471–475.

Schatzberg, A. F., Samson, J. A., Bloomingdale, K. L., Orsulak, P. J., Gerson, B., Kizuka, P. P., et al. (1989). Toward a biochemical classification of depressive disorders, X. Urinary catecholamines, their metabolites, and D-type scores in subgroups of depressive disorders. *Archives of General Psychiatry, 46*(3), 260–268.

Schlegel, S., & Kretzschmar, K. (1987). Computed tomography in affective disorders. Part II: Brain density. *Biological Psychiatry, 22*(1), 15–23.

Schlesser, M., Winokur, G., & Sherman, B. (1980). Hypothalamic-pituitary-adrenal axis activity in depressive illness. *Archives of General Psychiatry, 37,* 737–743.

Silberman, E. K., Weingartner, H., & Post, R. M. (1983). Thinking disorder in depression. *Archives of General Psychiatry, 40,* 775–780.

Smyth, C., Kalsi, G., Curtis, D., Brynjolfsson, J., O'Neill, J., Rifkin, L., et al. (1997). Two-locus admixture linkage analysis of bipolar and unipolar affective disorder supports the presence of susceptibility loci on chromosomes 11p15 and 21q22. *Genomics, 39*(3), 271–298.

Souery, D., Rivelli, S. K., & Mendlewicz, J. (2001). Molecular genetic and family studies in affective disorders: State of the art. *Journal of Affective Disorders, 62,* 45–55.

Spitzer, R., Endicott, J., & Robins, E. (1977). *Research diagnostic criteria: Rationale and reliability.* Paper presented at the annual meeting of the American Psychiatric Association, Toronto, Ontario, Canada.

Stenstedt, A. (1952). A study in manic depressive psychosis: Clinical, social, and genetic investigations. *Acta Psychiatrica Scandinavica, S79,* 1–112.

Strakowski, S. M., DelBello, M. P., Adler, C., Cecil, D. M., & Sax, K. W. (2000). Neuroimaging in bipolar disorder. *Bipolar Disorders, 2*(3, Pt. 1), 148–164.

Strakowski, S. M., DelBello, M. P., Sax, K. W., Zimmerman, M. E., Shear, P. K., Hawkins, J. M., et al. (1999). Brain magnetic resonance imaging of structural abnormalities in bipolar disorder. *Archives of General Psychiatry, 56*(3), 254–260.

Straub, R. E., Lehner, T., Luo, Y., Loth, J. E., Shao, W., Sharpe, L., et al. (1994). A possible vulnerability locus for bipolar affective disorder on chromosome 21q22.3. *Nature Genetics, 8,* 291–296.

Swann, A. C. (1997). Manic-depressive illness and substance abuse. *Psychiatric Annals, 27*(7), 507–511.

Swayze, V. W., II, Andreasen, N. C., Alliger, R. J., Yuh, W. T., & Ehrhardt, J. C. (1992). Subcortical and temporal structures in affective disorder and schizophrenia: A magnetic resonance imaging study. *Biological Psychiatry, 31*(3), 221–240.

Szádóczky, E., Papp, Z., Vitrai, I., Rihmer, Z., & Furedi, J. (1998). The prevalence of major depressive and bipolar disorder in Hungary. *Journal of Affective Disorders, 50,* 155–162.

Taylor, M. A., & Abrams, R. (1986). Cognitive dysfunction in mania. *Comprehensive Psychiatry, 27*(3), 186–191.

Torgersen, S. (1986). Genetic factors in moderately severe and mild affective disorders. *Archives of General Psychiatry, 43*(3), 222–226.

Tsuang, M., Winokur, G., & Crowe, R. (1980). Morbidity risk of schizophrenia and affective disorders among first-degree relatives of patients with schizophrenia, mania, depression, and surgical conditions. *British Journal of Psychiatry, 137,* 497–504.

Tsuang, M., Woolson, R., & Fleming, J. (1980). Cause of death in schizophrenia and manic depression. *British Journal of Psychiatry, 136,* 239–242.

Van Gorp, W. G., Altshuler, L., Theberge, D. C., Wilkins, J., & Dixon, W. (1998). Cognitive impairment in euthymic bipolar patients with and without prior alcohol dependence: A preliminary study. *Archives of General Psychiatry, 55,* 41–46.

Verheyen, G. R., Villafuerte, S. M., Del-Favero, J., Souery, D., Mendlewicz, J., Van Broeckhoven, C., et al. (1999). Genetic refinement and physical mapping of a chromosome 18q candidate region for bipolar disorder. *European Journal of Human Genetics, 7*(4), 427–434.

Videbech, T. (1975). A study of genetic factors, childhood bereavement, and premorbid personality traits in patients with anancastic endogenous depression. *Acta Psychiatrica Scandinavica, 52*(3), 178–222.

Wehr, T. A., & Goodwin, F. K. (1987). Can antidepressants cause mania and worsen the cause of affective illness? *American Journal of Psychiatry, 144,* 1403–1411.

Weingartner, H., Cohen, R., Murphy, D., Martello, J., & Gerdt, C. (1981). Cognitive processes in depression. *Archives of General Psychiatry, 38,* 42–47.

Weissman, M., Bland, R. C., Canino, G. J., Faravelli, C., Greenwald, S., Hwu, H. G., et al. (1996). Cross-national epidemiology of major depression and bipolar disorder. *Journal of the American Medical Association, 276*(4), 293–299.

Weissman, M., Leaf, P., Tischler, G., Blazer, D., Karno, M., Bruce, M., et al. (1988). Affective disorder in five United States communities. *Psychological Medicine, 18,* 141–153.

Weissman, M., & Myers, J. (1978). Affective disorders in a U.S. urban community. *Archives of General Psychiatry, 35,* 1304–1311.

Weller, E. B., Weller, R. A., & Fristad, M. A. (1995). Bipolar diagnosis in children: Misdiagnosis, underdiagnosis, and future directions. *Journal of the American Academy of Child and Adolescent Psychiatry, 34*(6), 709–714.

Wender, P. H., Kety, S. S., Rosenthal, D., Schulsinger, F., Ortmann, J., & Lunde, I. (1986). Psychiatric disorders in the biological and adoptive families of adopted individuals with affective disorders. *Archives of General Psychiatry, 43*(10), 923–929.

White, W. A., Davis, T. A., & Frantz, A. M. (1931). *Manic-depressive psychosis: An investigation of the most recent advances.* Baltimore: Williams & Wilkins.

Winokur, G. (1970). Genetic findings and methodological considerations in manic-depressive disease. *British Journal of Psychiatry, 117,* 267–274.

Winokur, G. (1979). Unipolar depression, is it divisible into autonomous subtypes? *Archives of General Psychiatry, 36,* 47–52.

Winokur, G. (1984). Psychosis in bipolar and unipolar affective illness with special reference to schizoaffective disorder. *British Journal of Psychiatry, 145,* 236–242.

Winokur, G., & Clayton, P. J. (1967). Family history studies: Two types of affective disorder separated according to genetic and clinical factors. In J. Wortis (Ed.), *Recent advances in biological psychiatry.* New York: Plenum Press.

Winokur, G., Clayton, P. J., & Reich, T. (1969). *Manic-depressive illness.* St. Louis: Mosby.

Winokur, G., Cook, B., Liskow, B., & Fowler, R. (1993). Alcoholism in manic depressive (bipolar) patients. *Journal on Studies on Alcohol, 54,* 574–576.

Winokur, G., Coryell, W., Akiskal, H. S., Endicott, J., Keller, M., & Mueller, T. (1994). Manic-depressive (bipolar) disorder: The course in light of a prospective ten-year follow-up of 131 patients. *Acta Psychiatrica Scandinavica, 89,* 102–110.

Winokur, G., Coryell, W., Endicott, J., & Akiskal, H. S. (1993). Further distinctions between manic-depressive illness (bipolar disorder) and primary depressive disorder (unipolar depression). *American Journal of Psychiatry, 150,* 1176–1181.

Winokur, G., Coryell, W., Keller, M., Endicott, J., & Akiskal, H. S. (1993). A prospective follow-up of patients with bipolar and primary unipolar affective disorder. *Archives of General Psychiatry, 50,* 457–465.

Winokur, G., & Morrison, J. (1973). The Iowa 500: Follow-up of 225 depressives. *British Journal of Psychiatry, 123,* 543–548.

Winokur, G., Tsuang, M., & Crowe, R. R. (1982). The Iowa 500: Affective disorder in relatives of manic and depressed patients. *American Journal of Psychiatry, 139,* 209–212.

Wolff, E., Putnam, F., & Post, R. (1985). Motor activity and affective illness. The relationship of amplitude and temporal distribution to changes in affective state. *Archives of General Psychiatry, 42,* 288–294.

Yamamoto, J., Fung, D., Lo, S., & Reece, S. (1979). Psychopharmacology for Asian Americans and Pacific Islanders. *Psychopharmacology Bulletin, 15*(4), 29–31.

Yatham, L. N., Srisurapanont, M., Zis, A. P., & Kusumakar, V. (1997). Comparative studies of the biological distinction between unipolar and bipolar depressions. *Life Sciences, 61*(15), 1445–1455.

Young, R. C., & Klerman, G. L. (1992). Mania in late life: Focus on age at onset. *American Journal of Psychiatry, 149,* 867–876.

Zarate, C. A., Tohen, M., Land, M., & Cavanagh, S. (2000). Functional impairment and cognition in bipolar disorder. *Psychiatric Quarterly, 71*(4), 309–329.

Ziegler, V. E., & Biggs, J. T. (1977). Tricyclic plasma levels—effects of age, race, sex, and smoking. *Journal of the American Medical Association, 238,* 2167–2169.

CHAPTER 11

Anxiety Disorders

DEBORAH C. BEIDEL, SAMUEL M. TURNER, and CANDICE ALFANO

T HE PAST 20 YEARS have witnessed a remarkable period of scientific development in the study of anxiety disorders. Initially, the third edition of the *Diagnostic and Statistical Manual of Mental Disorders* (*DSM-III*; American Psychiatric Association [APA], 1980) radically altered conceptualization of these disorders. Rather than three broad categories (phobic neurosis, obsessive-compulsive neurosis, or anxiety neurosis), nine different diagnoses were introduced. In 1987, further classificatory changes were made, including subsuming agoraphobia under panic disorder (*DSM-III-R*; APA, 1987). The most recent revision (*DSM-IV*; APA, 1994) expanded the number of distinct diagnostic categories. The substantial attention directed at anxiety disorders is well justified as data indicate they constitute the most common psychiatric problem in the United States, with the exception of substance abuse disorders (Aalto-Setaelae, Marttunen, Tuulio-Henriksson, & Loennqvist, 2001; Beekman et al., 1998; Kessler, McGonagle, Zhao, & Nelson, 1994).

DESCRIPTION OF THE DISORDERS

PANIC ATTACKS

A panic attack consists of a discrete period of intense fear or discomfort in which four (or more) somatic and cognitive symptoms develop abruptly and reach a peak within 10 minutes (*DSM-IV*; APA, 1994, p. 395). Symptoms include palpitations; pounding heart or accelerated heart rate; sweating; trembling or shaking; sensations of shortness of breath or smothering; feelings of choking; chest pain or discomfort; nausea or abdominal distress; feeling dizzy, unsteady, lightheaded, or faint; derealization or depersonalization; fear of losing control or going crazy; fear of dying; paresthesias; and chills or hot flushes. As noted in *DSM-IV*, panic attacks occur in the context of many different anxiety states as well as nonanxiety disorders.

There are three types of panic attacks:

1. *Unexpected (uncued):* Onset is not associated with a situational trigger.
2. *Situationally bound (cued):* The attack occurs immediately on exposure to or in anticipation of exposure to the anxiety-producing stimulus.
3. *Situationally predisposed:* The attack is more likely to occur on exposure although not immediately on exposure and not necessarily every time the individual is exposed to the event.

Uncued attacks are more characteristic of panic disorder and frequently occur in generalized anxiety disorder (GAD), whereas situationally bound attacks are more characteristic of specific and social phobia. However, there is not a one-to-one relationship between type of attack and particular disorder. Furthermore, although not specifically mentioned in the *DSM-IV,* patients with obsessive-compulsive disorder often report panic attacks. Finally, panic attacks are not unique to people with anxiety disorders. In the general population, about 15% of individuals reported occurrence of panic symptoms at some time in their lives, and 3% reported a panic attack in the previous month (Eaton, Kessler, Wittchen, & Magee, 1994; Reed & Wittchen, 1998).

PANIC DISORDER WITHOUT AGORAPHOBIA

When panic attacks are recurrent and unexpected, and at least one attack is followed by a one-month period of concern about (a) additional attacks, (b) worry about the implications of the attack, or (c) changes in behavior, a diagnosis of panic disorder might be appropriate. The work of Klein and his associates is usually credited with differentiating panic from other forms of anxiety. Klein and Fink (1962) reported that antidepressants were effective in decreasing phobic inpatients' episodic anxiety or panic attacks but were ineffective for anticipatory anxiety or avoidance. On the other hand, benzodiazepines were effective for anticipatory anxiety. Through an apparent semantic drift, *anticipatory anxiety* became synonymous with *generalized anxiety* (Turner, Beidel, & Jacob, 1988). This pharmacological dissection strategy was thought to have delineated two distinct types of anxiety. However, imipramine (an antidepressant) is effective for GAD (e.g., R. J. Kahn et al., 1981; Rickels et al., 2000), and the high-potency benzodiazepines are effective for treating panic disorder, thus calling into question this early model of psychopathology (Lydiard, Roy-Byrne, & Ballenger, 1988).

PANIC DISORDER WITH AGORAPHOBIA

Agoraphobia, considered to be a complication of panic disorder, is a fear of being in public places or situations where escape might be difficult or where help may be unavailable in case a panic attack occurs. However, one study (Jacob, Furman, Durrant, & Turner, 1996) reported that this conceptualization may not describe all individuals who suffer from this disorder (see Psychological and Biological Assessment section). Despite the specific reason for the fear, patients with agoraphobia avoid (or endure with marked distress) certain situations. In the most severe form, patients may refuse to travel long distances from home or even leave the house. Thus, this disorder encompasses panic attacks plus behavioral avoidance of situations that are associated with their potential onset. Agoraphobics commonly fear crowded places, such as supermarkets, shopping malls, restaurants, churches, and theaters; riding in buses, cars, or planes; and traveling over bridges or through tunnels. Some individuals with agoraphobia will enter these situations but only with a trusted companion or by carrying certain items that serve as a safety signal.

AGORAPHOBIA WITHOUT HISTORY OF PANIC

Some patients with agoraphobia report fear and avoidance of public places but deny panic attacks. Thus, although their behavior is similar to those suffering from panic disorder with agoraphobia, it does not appear to have been triggered by the sudden, unexpected onset of panic. According to *DSM-IV*, these patients usually fear the occurrence of incapacitating or extremely embarrassing physical symptoms or report limited symptom attacks (anxiety that consists of no more than three panic symptoms). Patients with this disorder also may fear dizziness or falling, loss of bowel or bladder control, or vomiting (APA, 1994). Interestingly, for some patients, the event they fear has never occurred, at least not in public places that elicit distress. The fact that patients have not necessarily experienced the feared physical symptoms appears to differentiate agoraphobia without panic from panic disorder with agoraphobia. In the latter disorder, the actual sudden onset of panic constitutes the first stage of the disorder. Agoraphobia without history of panic is seen only rarely in clinic settings and, thus, has not been the subject of much empirical study. Some agoraphobics without history of panic (e.g., those who fear losing control of their bodily functions) possess other clinical characteristics reminiscent of obsessive-compulsive disorder and may actually fall within the obsessional realm (Beidel & Bulick, 1990; Jenike, Vitagliano, Rabinowitz, Goff, & Baer, 1987). Initial studies suggested that the prevalence rate for agoraphobia without history of panic disorder ranged from 1% to 2.9% (Jacob & Turner, 1988; Weissman, Leckman, Merikangas, Gammon, & Prusoff, 1984). However, when those originally diagnosed with agoraphobia without panic were reassessed by clinicians using standard interview schedules, most were discovered to have specific phobias rather than agoraphobia without panic attacks (APA, 1994). Therefore, the nature and proper classification of this condition must await further study.

SOCIAL PHOBIA

Although fears when in the presence of others have been documented as far back as the days of the Hippocratic Corpus (Marks, 1985) and have been addressed in the literature since 1966 (Marks & Gelder, 1966), *social phobia* refers to a marked and persistent fear of social or performance situations in which embarrassment may occur (APA, 1994). Exposure almost invariably provokes an anxiety response, which can result in a situationally-bound or situationally-predisposed panic attack. Social or performance situations are avoided or endured with significant distress. Individuals with social phobia may feel uncomfortable performing certain activities in the presence of others (e.g., speaking, eating, drinking, or writing), fearing that he or she may do something that will cause humiliation or embarrassment (e.g., forgetting a speech, mispronouncing a word, or shaking uncontrollably). Some social phobics also fear that others will detect their nervousness by observing signs of somatic distress, such as blushing or trembling. For some, the fear is not limited to circumscribed social situations but is present in most social interactions, including one-on-one conversations. Those who fear a broad range of social situations are considered to have the *generalized* subtype, which is associated with more severe anxiety, depression, social inhibition, fear of negative evaluation, avoidance, fearfulness, and self-consciousness (Herbert, Hope, & Bellack, 1992; Holt, Heimberg, & Hope, 1992; Turner, Beidel, & Townsley, 1992; Wittchen, Stein, & Kessler, 1999). Those with generalized social phobia appear to have an earlier age of onset (Herbert et al., 1992; Holt et al., 1992; Wittchen et al., 1999) and are more neurotic, more frequently shy as children, and more introverted than the specific (nongeneralized) subtype (Stemberger, Turner, Beidel, & Calhoun, 1995).

Many social phobics (86%) avoid at least some social situations (Turner, Beidel, Dancu, & Keys, 1986), although strict avoidance is not necessary for the diagnosis. With respect to social functioning, several investigations (Liebowitz, Gorman, Fyer, & Klein, 1985; Turner et al., 1986; Wittchen & Beloch, 1996) document that an inability to work, incomplete educational attainment, lack of career advancement, and severe social restrictions are common features of this disorder. Lost productivity is also common (Van Ameringen, Mancini, & Streiner, 1993). Social phobics in a community sample were more dependent on others and relied more heavily on public assistance (Schneier, Johnson, Hornig, Liebowitz, & Weissman, 1992), further documenting the severe and impairing nature of this disorder.

SPECIFIC PHOBIA

Because phobias are rarely simple, a significant change in *DSM-IV* was the renaming of *simple phobia* to *specific phobia*, referring to a marked and persistent fear of clearly discernible, circumscribed objects or situations (APA, 1994). When confronted with the feared situation, specific phobics experience internal emotional reactions and may have panic attacks that are situationally bound or situationally predisposed. The situations are either avoided or endured with significant distress. In the general population, common specific phobias include fears of animals, such as dogs, snakes, insects, and mice, as well as fears of blood/injury, heights, and enclosed spaces (Agras, Sylvester, & Oliveau, 1969; APA, 1994; Curtis, Magee, Eaton, Wittchen, & Kessler, 1998). In clinical settings, claustrophobia (fear of closed spaces) and acrophobia (fear of heights) are those most commonly encountered (Emmelkamp, 1988).

As noted, the renaming of these phobic conditions from simple to specific phobia is a clear recognition that these disorders are not necessarily minor abreactions. Although a significant percentage of the general population appears to suffer a specific phobia, this disorder accounts for a very small percentage of those treated in anxiety disorders clinics (Barlow, DiNardo, Vermilyea, Vermilyea, & Blanchard, 1986). Those who do seek treatment often present with additional Axis I or II conditions, or both (Barlow, 1988). Furthermore, the greater the number of specific phobias, the greater the predisposition toward other types of psychopathology (Curtis et al., 1998).

There are four subtypes of specific phobias:

1. *Animal* type, in which the fear is cued by animals or insects.
2. *Natural environment* type, cued by objects or events in the environment such as storms, heights, or water.

3. *Blood/injection/injury* type, cued by blood, injuries, or needles.
4. *Situational* type, cued by specific situations such as public transportation, tunnels, bridges, elevators, flying, driving, or enclosed places (APA, 1994).

In addition, an *other* type is for fears related to any other stimuli. In clinical settings, the situational subtype is most frequent, followed by natural environment, blood/injection/injury, and animal.

OBSESSIVE-COMPULSIVE DISORDER

Obsessive-compulsive disorder (OCD) is characterized by intrusive thoughts, often coupled with repetitive behaviors that are elaborate, time consuming, and distressful for the individual or significant others (APA, 1994). *Obsessions* are recurrent and persistent thoughts, impulses, or images that are intrusive and inappropriate and cause marked anxiety or distress. In most cases, the irrationality of obsessions is recognized by the individual, and there is an attempt to ignore or suppress the thoughts by neutralizing them with other thoughts or actions. Furthermore, individuals recognize that the obsessions are a product of their own minds and that they are not imposed externally—an important distinction that separates obsessions from delusions. Delusional individuals do not recognize the irrationality of their thoughts and frequently view them as having been imposed externally. The most common forms of obsessions are doubts, thoughts, impulses, fears, images, and urges. The most common obsessional content areas include dirt and contamination, aggression, inanimate-interpersonal objects or behaviors (e.g., locks, bolts, other safety devices, and orderliness), sex, religion, and a miscellaneous category (Antony, Downie, & Swinson, 1998; Khanna & Channabasavanna, 1988; Kolada, Bland, & Newman, 1994).

Compulsions are repetitive behaviors or mental acts that an individual feels driven to perform in response to obsessions or according to rules that must be applied rigidly (APA, 1994). Compulsions are designed to prevent occurrence of a future event or to neutralize the aftereffects of an event, such as coming into contact with germs. Completion may be negatively reinforcing because it temporarily decreases anxiety for most patients, although a few individuals do report increased anxiety (e.g., Walker & Beech, 1969). Common forms of compulsions are hand washing and bathing, cleaning, checking, counting, and ordering. Repetitive cleaning behaviors often coexist with contamination fears, while checking behaviors are common in those who experience self-doubt or dread the onset of some future event (Turner & Beidel, 1988). However, it also is common for more than one type of obsession or compulsion, or both, to be present. In addition, patients often develop elaborate avoidance strategies to avoid feared objects or situations, thereby lessening daily distress and limiting the necessity to engage in ritualistic behaviors. OCD is considered to have the most chronic course among the anxiety disorders.

POSTTRAUMATIC STRESS DISORDER

When individuals are exposed to a traumatic event in which (a) the individual experienced, witnessed, or was confronted with actual or threatened death or serious injury, or a threat to the physical integrity of self or others, and (b) the response involved intense fear, helplessness, or horror, they may develop *DSM-IV* posttraumatic stress disorder (PTSD). Examples of traumatic events include combat experiences, assault, rape, or observing the serious injury or violent death of another individual. Patients with PTSD report that they "reexperience" the event in one of the following ways: recurrent and intrusive recollections, recurrent and intrusive dreams, suddenly acting or feeling as if the event were recurring, intense psychological or physical reactivity, and distress when exposed to events that symbolize or resemble some aspect of the trauma. As a result, there is an attempt to avoid associated stimuli, including thoughts, feelings, activities, or situations, and there may be difficulty recalling important aspects of the event. Furthermore, patients usually describe numbing of general emotions, including diminished interest in activities, feeling of detachment or estrangement, restricted range of affect, and a sense of a foreshortened future. Occurrence of general and persistent autonomic arousal also is a component of PTSD and may include difficulty sleeping, irritability or anger, difficulty concentrating, hypervigilance, exaggerated startle responses, and physiologic reactivity on exposure to stimuli associated with the event (APA, 1994).

The symptoms must persist for at least one month, and there are two subtypes: acute, if symptom duration is less than three months, and chronic, if symptom duration is three months or more. There is also a delayed onset specifier, if onset occurs at least six months after the event. Historically, PTSD was applied to people who had participated in combat, but now also is used for those who experience natural disasters, assault or rape (Kilpatrick et al., 1989), or a host of other noncombat-related events. In the community, rates for PTSD range from 1% to 14%, depending on the method of assessment and the type of population (APA, 1994). For example, Davidson, Hughes, Blazer, and George (1991) reported a 1.3% lifetime prevalence rate and a 0.44% six-month prevalence rate for PTSD in a community sample. Although most people experience some traumatic event in their lifetimes, Hidalgo and Davidson (2000) estimated that up to 25% will develop PTSD. Similar to rates for civilian PTSD, epidemiological estimates of combat-related PTSD vary, but most studies report a lifetime prevalence of between 15% and 30% of combat veterans (Center for Disease Control, 1988; Kulka et al., 1988). There is some indication that many of the civilian forms of PTSD do not meet the classic criteria associated with combat-related PTSD, thus raising the question of whether some of these "disorders" are not the same reactions as "classic" PTSD (Blanchard et al., 1996; Norris & Kaniasty, 1994).

Acute Stress Disorder

The criteria for *acute stress disorder* (ASD) are similar to those of PTSD. In fact, the description of the stress-inducing event and the individual's possible reaction are very similar to those for PTSD; only the duration requirement distinguishes the two disorders. Individuals with this disorder report a subjective sense of numbing, detachment, or absence of emotion; a reduction in awareness of surroundings; derealization; depersonalization; or dissociative amnesia. Symptoms of reexperiencing, avoidance of the stimuli, and symptoms of anxiety or arousal are identical to those for PTSD. The one difference is that the criteria for ASD emphasize dissociative symptoms (Bryant, Harvey, Dang, & Sackville, 1998). In addition, there must be clinically significant distress or functional impairment. The disturbance lasts for a minimum of two days and a maximum of four weeks. The short symptom duration (maximum of four weeks) for this condition makes it unclear if someone with this disorder would require treatment. If the symptoms persist for longer than four weeks, a diagnosis of PTSD would be warranted. Clearly, this is a condition that is in need of better definition and differentiating from other syndromes.

Introduction of this diagnostic category was in response to the criticism that the one-month minimum duration criteria required for a diagnosis of PTSD did not address the substantial distress experienced by many patients in the immediate weeks following their exposure to a traumatic event (Bryant & Harvey, 1999) and to identify those who might be a risk for developing PTSD (Bryant et al., 1998). For example, among eight adults injured and traumatized as a result of a plane crash, four developed ASD and three developed PTSD (Birmes, Arrieu, Payen, Warner, & Schmitt, 1999). However, there was no relationship between presence of ASD and development of PTSD one month later. In contrast, among motor vehicle accident victims, 13% met criteria for ASD (with a further 21% manifesting subclinical ASD symptoms). Six months later, 78% of those with ASD and 60% of those with subclinical ASD met criteria for PTSD (Harvey & Bryant, 1999). Symptoms predicting those who would develop PTSD included acute numbing, depersonalization, sense of reliving the trauma, and motor restlessness. This is important inasmuch as dissociative symptoms (considered to be the differentiating feature of ASD) did not predict the onset of PTSD. Conducting a two-year follow-up study, Harvey and Bryant reported that 13% of the original sample who were never diagnosed with ASD nevertheless met PTSD criteria two years later. As noted, one of the disorder's proposed distinctions is its brief and highly reactive nature (Bryant et al., 1998), but even this is controversial. In a comprehensive review of the ASD diagnosis, Marshall, Spitzer, and Liebowitz (1999) concluded that currently, there is insufficient evidence of the need for the separate diagnostic categories of PTSD and ASD. Specifically, there appears to be limited validity and utility for the requirement of peritraumatic dissociative symptoms as a core and distinctive feature of this disorder. Furthermore, there appears to be limited utility for having essentially continuous symptomatology differentiated into two theoretically different disorders based solely on whether the symptoms persist for 30 days. This category remains quite controversial and further studies as to its diagnostic validity are necessary.

GENERALIZED ANXIETY DISORDER

Generalized anxiety disorder (GAD) was at one time reserved for those who did not meet criteria for any other anxiety disorder (Barlow, 1988). Basically, GAD was a residual diagnostic category and was quite controversial. Currently in *DSM-IV,* the essential feature is excessive anxiety and worry occurring more days than not, for a period of at least six months, about a number of events or activities (APA, 1994). Worry is difficult to control and is associated with a number of somatic and cognitive symptoms: muscle tension, restlessness or feeling keyed up or on edge, being easily fatigued, difficulty concentrating or mind going blank, sleep disturbance, and irritability. Six out of 18 cognitive and somatic complaints are necessary to meet diagnostic criteria. Focus of the anxiety is not confined to the features of any other Axis I disorder, and anxiety, worry, or physical symptoms must cause clinically significant distress or functional impairment. Individuals with the disorder tend to believe that worrying may be an effective means of avoidance and/or preventing the occurrence of negative consequences. Both one-month and lifetime prevalence rates have been estimated at 5% to 10% in community and clinic samples (Maier et al., 2000; Weiller, Bisserbe, Maier, & Lecrubier, 1998; Wittchen & Hoyer, 2001), making it one of the most prevalent anxiety disorders in the primary care setting. However, it should be noted that studies examining GAD generally report unacceptable levels of interrater reliability, raising questions as to whether GAD deserves to be an independent syndrome or at least whether the current diagnostic criteria are valid.

OTHER ANXIETY DISORDERS

Panic attacks, worry, obsessions, compulsions, or phobias can result from a variety of medical conditions (anxiety disorder due to a general medical condition). Thus, before assigning an anxiety disorder diagnosis, it is necessary to rule out general medical disorders, including endocrine, cardiovascular, respiratory, metabolic, and neurological conditions. Jacob and Turner (1988) noted a number of medical conditions that may be related to the presence of panic disorder. These include mitral valve prolapse, other cardiovascular conditions, vestibular abnormalities, hyperthyroidism, hypothyroidism, hypoglycemia, partial complex seizures, phenochromocytoma, hypoparathyroidism, hyperparathyroidism, and Cushing's syndrome. The challenge to clinicians is to determine if the anxiety symptoms result from one of these general medical conditions. Temporal order of the disease and the specific anxiety symptoms may assist in differential diagnosis. Similarly, presence of anxiety symptoms only during an episode of the physical illness or an atypical age of onset may suggest an etiological role for a medical condition (APA, 1994). Before beginning any intervention for anxiety, the patient's medical condition should be evaluated and treated by a physician, if necessary.

Anxiety symptoms also can be induced by ingestion of or withdrawal from various substances, including alcohol, drugs, or caffeine (substance-induced anxiety disorder). Substances specifically listed by the *DSM-IV* include alcohol, amphetamine, caffeine, cannabis, cocaine, hallucinogen, inhalants, phencyclidine, sedatives, hypnotics, or anxiolytics. Also included are medications such as anesthetics, analgesics, sympathomimetics, anticholinergics, insulin, thyroid preparations, oral contraceptives, antihistamines, anti-Parkinsonian medications, corticosteroids, antihypertensive and cardiovascular medications, anticonvulsants, lithium carbonate, antipsychotic medications, and antidepressant medications. Another class of anxiety precipitants includes heavy metals and toxins (e.g., gasoline, organophosphate insecticides, and carbon monoxide). If anxiety is caused by any one of these conditions, treatment for the medical disorder should result in a remediation of the anxiety symptoms.

EPIDEMIOLOGY

During the early 1980s, data from the National Institute of Mental Health (NIMH) Epidemiological Catchment Area (ECA) survey provided some initial estimates of prevalence rates for anxiety disorders. Six-month rates (adjusted to control for slight variations in age and gender distributions across the five ECA sites) for the combined anxiety/somatoform categories ranged from 6.6%, 7.2%, and 7.4% (St. Louis, Los Angeles, and New Haven sites) to 14.8% (Baltimore and

Piedmont sites) in adult populations (Burnam et al., 1987). Somatoform disorders contributed only minimally to these prevalence rates (less than 0.4%). About 10 years later, findings from a new study suggested that the previous ECA data were an underestimate (Kessler et al., 1994). According to results from the National Comorbidity Survey (NCS), 24.9% of the general population reported the lifetime occurrence of an anxiety disorder, and 17.2% of the sample reported the presence of an anxiety disorder in the past 12 months. This 12-month prevalence rate was higher than for any other diagnostic category, and the lifetime prevalence rate was second only to substance use/abuse disorders. Although there are reasons to suggest that these figures may be overestimates, they do suggest that anxiety disorders affect a substantial portion of the general population. Data for lifetime and 12-month prevalence rates are presented in Table 11.1.

Different rates of disorders between the two epidemiological surveys are likely due, at least in part, to methodological differences. The NCS study used a national sample, concentrated on a younger age range than previous surveys (ages 15 to 54), used a correction weight to adjust for nonresponse bias, and based diagnoses on *DSM-III-R* rather than *DSM-III* (Kessler et al., 1994).

CLINICAL PICTURE

Differentiation of "normal" anxiety from the clinical syndromes discussed previously is based not only on symptom severity but also on degree of functional interference. Consideration of impairment is most important in determining whether symptoms actually are disorders. For example, in the case of social anxiety/social phobia, 61% of a telephone survey sample reported that they were much or somewhat more anxious than others in social situations, but only 18.7% reported at least moderate interference or distress. This percentage dropped to 7.1% when strict diagnostic criteria were applied and further dropped to 1.9% when only "at least moderate impairment" was considered (Stein, Walker, & Forde, 1994).

Anxiety is a multidimensional construct, commonly conceptualized as a tripartite system (Lang, 1977). Anxiety responses usually are divided into three dimensions: subjective distress (self-report), physiological response, and avoidance or escape behavior (overt behavioral response). Consistent with the transient "fight or flight" response, the somatic complaints of anxiety patients are characterized primarily by sympathetic nervous system activation. Thus, complaints of tachycardia,

Table 11.1

Lifetime and 12-Month Prevalence Rates for Anxiety Disorders

Disorder	Lifetime	12-Month
Panic disorder	3.5	2.3
Agoraphobia without panic	5.3	2.8
Social phobia	13.3	7.9
Specific phobia	11.3	8.8
Generalized anxiety disorder	5.1	3.1
Any anxiety disorder	24.9	17.2

Source: From "Lifetime and 12-Month Prevalence of *DSM-III-R* Psychiatric Disorders in the United States: Results from the National Comorbidity Survey," by R. C. Kessler et al., 1994, *Archives of General Psychiatry, 51*, pp. 8–19.

tremulousness, dizziness, lightheadedness, parasthesias, and dyspnea are common. Certain types of anxiety disorder patients differentially experience somatic symptomatology. Dizziness, difficulty breathing, weakness in limbs, fainting episodes, and buzzing or ringing in the ears were endorsed significantly more often by agoraphobics than social phobics, whereas patients with social phobia were significantly more likely to endorse blushing and muscle twitching than agoraphobics (Amies, Gelder, & Shaw, 1983). In a more recent study, patients with panic disorder were more likely than social phobics to endorse parasthesias, choking or smothering, feeling dizzy or lightheaded, and feeling faint, as well as worrying that they might die, collapse, or go crazy (Page, 1994), and the symptoms are likely to be worse in patients who have panic disorder with agoraphobia (De Jong & Majella-Bouman, 1995). Individuals with GAD sometimes report gastrointestinal distress, including indigestion, nausea, constipation, diarrhea, and urinary urgency and frequency. Brown, Marten, and Barlow (1995) reported a predominance of muscle tension, irritability, and fatigue in patients with GAD. Others have noted a predominant central nervous system hyperarousal (Noyes et al., 1992). In *DSM-IV*, muscle tension is considered the primary somatic complaint. Finally, the reaction of needle/blood/injury phobics is defined by parasympathetic (rather than sympathetic) activation manifested by bradycardia and hypotension (Ost, 1996), which is clearly different from the somatic responses found in other phobic states.

Cognitive symptoms of anxiety usually entail worry about specific events involving the possibility of danger or harm to self or others. Although most often in the form of specific thoughts, cognitive symptoms also may occur as ideas, images, or impulses. Occurrence of the fearful event, although a possibility, is usually of very low probability, thus fear is out of proportion to situational demand. Anxiety patients are usually aware that the fear is excessive or unreasonable, yet such knowledge does little to assuage the overly aroused emotional state.

In specific or social phobias, thoughts usually have a specific theme and are most often triggered by actual or anticipated contact with the feared stimulus. On the other hand, those with more pervasive anxiety states, such as GAD present with a broader constellation of anxious cognitions, termed worry that encompasses several thematic areas, has the characteristics of mental problem solving, and the possibility of at least one negative outcome (Borkovec, Robinson, Pruzinsky, & DePress, 1983, p. 10). It has been suggested that intolerance of uncertainty about any particular situation or thing may trigger the worry process (Dugas, Gagnon, Ladoucer, & Freeston, 1998).

A final category of cognitive phenomena is obsessions that consist of intrusive unwanted thoughts, images, or impulses that are often horrific and perceived by the patient as uncontrollable, yet always as a product of his or her own mind and not outside forces. Differentiation among the types of anxious cognitions can be quite subtle and may be tied to the severity of the specific disorder. An attempt to differentiate worry from obsessionality (Turner, Beidel, & Stanley, 1992) highlighted several distinguishing characteristics, including thematic content (GAD patients do not often report excessive concern with dirt, contamination, aggressive impulses, or horrific images), form of the cognition (GAD patients do not report images or impulses but primarily conceptual, verbal linguistic activity as described by Borkovec & Shadick, 1989, p. 22), and intrusive quality (worry is perceived as less intrusive and less egodystonic than obsessions). More recent evidence confirms that the intrusive quality (i.e., the egodystonic/egosyntonic distinction) appears to be a key dimension in distinguishing obsessive thought from worry (Langlois, Freeston, & Ladoucer, 2000). Thus, although there are some similarities, there are important differences as well.

The characteristic behavior of anxiety patients is escape from, or avoidance of, the feared stimulus. Many patients devise elaborate strategies, often eliciting the cooperation of others to avoid the feared object or situation. In severe cases of panic disorder with agoraphobia, avoidance may become so restrictive that the affected individual becomes housebound. In the case of OCD, avoidance is usually accompanied by ritualistic behaviors, such as washing or checking, which serve to "undo" or "prevent" occurrence of the feared event. Although almost always present, escape or avoidance is not required for a diagnosis as individuals sometimes are able to engage in feared situations but suffer great distress as a consequence. In addition, behavioral avoidance is sometimes manifested in subtle ways that may not be readily apparent to the patient but can be detected by a trained clinician.

Other aspects of the clinical presentation often include appetite or sleep disturbances and concentration and memory difficulties. Suicidal ideation and suicide attempts have been reported in patients with panic disorder or social phobia. In an early study (Cox, Direnfeld, Swinson, & Norton, 1994), 31% of patients with panic disorder and 34% of patients with social phobia reported suicidal ideation in the past year. Only one panic patient and two social phobic patients actually had made suicide attempts in the past year, and 18% of panic patients and 12% of social phobia patients reported lifetime occurrence of suicide attempts. Those who made suicide attempts were more likely to report past psychiatric hospitalizations and treatment for depression, and those with current ideation had higher scores on a depression inventory. A more recent study (Warshaw, Dolan, & Keller, 2000) assessed suicidal behavior in a large sample of panic disorder (PD) patients over a period of five years. Patients with PD had a .06 probability of suicidal behavior. However, in this study, comorbid affective, eating, and personality disorders posed specific risk factors for such behavior, leading the authors to conclude that PD is not associated with suicidal behavior in the absence of these other disorders. In fact, both studies highlight the role of depression as a mediating factor in the relationship of suicidality and anxiety disorders.

Even if not significantly depressed, anxiety patients often present with a dysphoric mood, usually attributed to the impairment that results from their disorder (i.e., depression mostly is secondary). Many of these dysphoric symptoms are similar to those experienced by primarily depressed patients, making it sometimes difficult to differentiate these two affective states. For example, in France, depression was the most frequent comorbid diagnosis, affecting approximately 70% of patients with social phobia (Lecrubier & Weiller, 1997). That study also reported that although highly associated with suicidal ideation, only 11% of social phobics (with comorbid depression) who presented to general practitioners were identified as having an anxiety disorder. Thus, anxiety disorders are sometimes overlooked by nonmental health professionals.

COURSE AND PROGNOSIS

In this section, behavioral and cognitive theories of etiology, age of onset, course, and prognosis (treated or untreated) are discussed. Biological theories of etiology are discussed in the Familial and Genetic Considerations section.

Behavioral Theories of Etiology

Studies investigating the etiology of anxiety disorders indicate that conditioning experiences are instrumental in the onset of agoraphobia (76.7% to 84%), claustrophobia (66.7%), and dental phobias (68.4%; Ost, 1987; Ost & Hugdahl, 1983). Although still evident, conditioning experiences appear less frequent in the onset of social phobia (58%), animal phobias (48%), and blood phobias (45%; Ost, 1987). In the case of the latter two specific phobias, vicarious conditioning accounts for fear onset in approximately 25% of the cases. Behavioral theories enjoy a prominent role in explaining the acquisition of anxiety and phobic states. However, no single theory can adequately account for the onset of these disorders. In the ensuing paragraphs, behavioral theories addressing the acquisition and maintenance of anxiety disorders are discussed. In light of the voluminous literature on the subject, this review touches briefly on important perspectives and highlights some of the more recent formulations.

One of the earliest accounts of fear acquisition, the case of Little Albert (Watson & Rayner, 1920), was based on a strict Pavlovian model. Delprato and McGlynn (1984) provided a summary of 25 studies that support Pavlovian conditioning as a mechanism for fear acquisition. Also, a combination of classical and operant conditioning is inherent in the two-factor theory (e.g., Mowrer, 1947), a model frequently used to explain anxiety. However, traditional conditioning models have been subject to a variety of criticisms. First, despite instances where conditioning is evident in the case histories of anxiety patients, there are almost an equivalent number of instances in which there appears to be no direct conditioning experience. Second, there are certain individuals who, under even the most ideal traumatic conditioning situations, fail to acquire fear (Rachman, 1990). Third, types of learning other than classical conditioning can effectively explain the acquisition of fear (Bandura, 1969). Rachman (1977) proposed a "three-pathway" hypothesis in which classical conditioning is considered as one method through which fear may be acquired. According to the theory, other mechanisms include vicarious learning and transmission via information, instruction, or both.

Another problem for traditional conditioning models is that they do not adequately explain the unequal distribution of fears in the general population (Agras et al., 1969). For example, a significant proportion of the population fears heights and snakes, yet few actually have had traumatic conditioning experiences. To account for this, Seligman (1971) proposed the notion of preparedness. Essentially, preparedness theory postulates that the unequal distribution of fears in the general population stems from a biological bias, such that certain fears are more easily acquired because they enhance the species' survival. Nonhuman primate studies provided some support for the preparedness theory. Fearful reactions were more easily acquired when laboratory-reared monkeys observed other monkeys behaving fearfully in the presence of fear-relevant stimuli such as snakes or lizards than when they behaved fearfully in the presence of rabbits or flowers (Cook & Mineka, 1989).

Seligman (1971) argued that biological preparedness accounts for phobia characteristics such as rapid acquisition, irrationality, belongingness, and high resistance to extinction. Initial laboratory studies (e.g., Ohman, 1986; Ohman, Eriksson, & Olafsson, 1975; Ohman, Fredrikson, Hugdahl, & Rimmo, 1976) appeared to provide some support, but McNally's (1987) comprehensive and thoughtful review argued persuasively that the entire body of experimental evidence for preparedness is equivocal. Only enhanced resistance to extinction of laboratory-conditioned electrodermal responses has been demonstrated consistently, whereas data supporting ease of acquisition, belongingness, and irrationality have received only minimal support (McNally, 1987).

Conditioning theories also must address the issue of previously acquired information. The observer monkeys in the Cook and Mineka (1989) study had no prior information about any of the stimuli as dangerous or safe, yet conditioning was more evident for those objects feared "naturally" by wild-bred monkeys. Other studies provide further evidence that prior information and experience may be significant factors. Also, Mineka and Cook (1986) demonstrated that monkeys could be immunized against snake fear by prior observational learning. Laboratory-bred monkeys first observed other monkeys behaving nonfearfully in the presence of a toy snake, then monkeys who behaved fearfully when confronted with the same snake. When the observer monkeys were exposed to the toy snake, they did not react fearfully, suggesting that prior exposure to nonfearful models "immunized" the observer monkeys against the later acquisition of fear. These data suggest that prior positive environmental experiences may explain why only some individuals acquire fear after a traumatic event. Also, conditioning experiences can be cumulative (Mineka, Davidson, Cook, & Heir, 1985), and there are factors before, within, and following the conditioning experience that are relevant for the onset of fear (Mineka & Zinbarg, 1991).

In summary, behavioral theories have evolved from simple, straightforward classical conditioning theories toward more complex conceptualizations. First, as noted by Rachman (1977), fear may be acquired because of vicarious conditioning, information transmission, or classical conditioning. Vicarious conditioning may be a particularly powerful mechanism for fear acquisition. In Cook and Mineka's studies, learning occurred within a very brief period of time (eight minutes) and produced strong emotional responses that were easily observable and approximately equivalent in intensity to those of the models. Although extant family studies often have attributed strong familial prevalence rates of anxiety to a biological etiology, the vicarious conditioning literature indicates that other pathways may be equally important, or that some combination of biological and psychological-environmental parameters might provide a more robust explanation. However, behavioral theories may never fully account for the acquisition or maintenance of fear. Even under the strictest environmental controls, not all rhesus monkeys acquired a fear of snakes. Thus, it is likely that multiple mechanisms are involved, and we turn now to an examination of other possible contributors.

COGNITIVE THEORIES OF ETIOLOGY

One of the first cognitive theories (Beck & Emery, 1985) used an information-processing model to explain maladaptive anxiety. Specifically, the basic elements of cognitive organization are cognitive schemas. Schemas are organized into cognitive constellations (cognitive sets). When a set is activated, the content directly influences the individual's perceptions, interpretations, associations, and memories, which in turn assign meaning to the stimuli. Cognitive sets contain rules. For the anxiety disorders, rules relate to the estimation of danger, vulnerability, and capacity for coping. If there is a perception of high vulnerability, the rules result in conclusions that the individual is incapable of dealing with the situation. Unlike the rules for depression, which are absolute, rules for anxiety disorders have a conditional form: If A happens, it *may* (rather than *will*) have a negative result. Thus, the crux of an anxiety disorder is "a cognitive process that takes the form of an automatic thought or image that appears rapidly, as if by reflex, after the initial stimulus that seems plausible (e.g., shortness of breath), and that is followed by a wave of anxiety" (pp. 5–6; Beck & Emery, 1985). If a specific thought or image cannot be identified, it still is possible to infer that a cognitive set with a meaning relevant to danger has been activated. However, the schemata themselves appear to develop because of behavioral or environmental experiences. Because the cognitive schemata result from other experiences, this would appear to remove maladaptive cognition from a primary etiological function to one that might function to maintain the disorder. Thus, cognitive theory does not appear to have a unique explanatory role in illuminating etiology or in treatment outcome (Beidel & Turner, 1986; Brewin, 1985).

Other cognitive theories are the "fear of fear" model (A. J. Goldstein & Chambless, 1978) and the expectancy model and its associated construct of anxiety sensitivity (Reiss, 1991; Reiss & McNally, 1985). Fear of fear posits that an individual who has experienced panic attacks may, through the process of interoceptive conditioning, learn to fear any change in physiological state that could signal the onset of panic. In effect, low-level bodily sensations become a conditioned stimulus that triggers worry concerning the onset of panic. Of course, this is not a purely cognitive model because interoceptive conditioning has a central role. Fear of fear seems to be a particularly important characteristic of individuals with panic disorder, and interventions built on this model typically involve treatment in which the individual is exposed not only to places where panic might occur but also to the physical sensations of panic itself. Building on the fear of fear hypothesis, Reiss and his colleagues introduced the construct of *anxiety sensitivity*, defined as a belief that the experience of anxiety causes illness, embarrassment, or additional anxiety (Reiss & McNally, 1985; Reiss, Peterson, Gursky, & McNally, 1986). However, whereas the emergence of fear of fear was considered a consequence of panic attacks (A. J. Goldstein & Chambless, 1978), Reiss and McNally consider fear of fear to result from several factors: panic attacks, biological predisposition, and personality needs to avoid embarrassment or illness or to maintain control (see Reiss, 1991). Anxiety sensitivity is the quantification of belief that anxiety causes illness or embarrassment and, like fear of fear, is considered more prevalent in patients with agoraphobia.

Salkovskis (1996) proposed a cognitive model for OCD, which begins with the concept that intrusive thoughts occur often and are experienced by everyone. However, in individuals where intrusive thoughts activate preexisting cognitive schemata, and the thought is evaluated in a negative light (i.e., "it is bad to have a thought about killing my child"), emotional distress may result. These individuals also believe that they have the "pivotal power" to bring about or prevent negative consequences (i.e., actually killing the child). Such beliefs and cognitive schemata create distress that leads to attempts to control and undo the thoughts, which, in turn, increases the thoughts' saliency and frequency and creates emotional distress. There also is a feedback loop; beliefs about pivotal power (responsibility) are reinforced because rituals that eliminate the thoughts prevent disconfirmation of the belief. In a recent review of OCD, Turner and colleagues (Turner, Beidel, Stanley, & Heiser, 2001) used existing empirical data to evaluate the veracity of this model (see the review for a full discussion). For example, a review of the current literature does not support the notion of a unitary overresponsibility construct among patients with OCD. In fact, inflated responsibility associated with OCD appears to be situation-specific, connected primarily to checking (and not washing or hoarding), and does not prevent an individual with OCD from accepting other forms of responsibility (Rachman, Thordarson, Shafran, & Woody, 1995).

In the past 15 years, cognitive theories have dominated explanations of the etiology of anxiety disorders. McNally (1995) noted that a core assumption of this approach is that those with disorders process threat information differently than do those without a disorder. Furthermore, the assumption is that the cognitive biases figure in the maintenance, and perhaps the etiology, of anxiety disorders. To fit this theory, thoughts must fit the definition of *automatic*; that is, they must be capacity free, unconscious, and involuntary. *Capacity free* means that the information processing does not consume resources (i.e., the thoughts are produced effortlessly). In reviewing this literature, McNally concluded that cognitive biases are involuntary, may sometimes be unconscious, but are not capacity free. Therefore, the most parsimonious explanation is that cognitions must be driven by some other function. In summary, cognitive theories allow a direct examination of the role of beliefs and cognitions in the etiology and maintenance of anxiety disorders. Although important syndromal phenomena and, perhaps, important in maintaining fear and avoidance, their role as primary etiological catalysts remains uncertain. High-risk studies may well be necessary to resolve the issue of primacy or secondary status for cognitive features of anxiety.

AGE OF ONSET

Among the anxiety disorders, specific phobias have the earliest age of onset, usually appearing during early childhood. Interestingly, ages of onset for certain specific phobias mirror developmental stages established for "normal" childhood fears. Developmentally, animal fears are common in preschool children, and two studies reported that specific animal phobias first appear between the ages of 4.4 and 6.9 years (Marks & Gelder, 1966; Ost, 1987); in a third study, 100% of a sample of animal and insect phobics had an age of onset before age 10 (McNally & Steketee, 1985). Similarly, younger elementary school children commonly fear natural events such as lightning and thunder and health-related concerns, while fear of injury is seen in older elementary school children (Silverman, La Greca, & Wasserstein, 1995). With respect to phobias, Liddell and Lyons (1978) reported that age of onset was 11.9 years for thunderstorm phobics, 8.8 years for blood phobics, and 10.8 years for dental phobics, although more recent research documents a younger median age of onset for blood phobia (5.5 years; Bienvenu & Eaton, 1998). Studies of normal fears in children often are fraught with methodological limitations including data based almost solely on parental report rather than child self-report or behavioral observation. Thus, it is unclear how many of these normal fears may have been the initial expression of a specific phobia. Furthermore, it is tempting to speculate that certain constitutional or environmental characteristics may differentiate normal fear from specific phobia. Certainly, the relationship between normal childhood fears and age of onset for specific phobias is deserving of further investigation.

Certain specific phobias (especially claustrophobia) appear to have a later average age of onset, ranging from 16.1 to 22.7 years (Marks & Gelder, 1966; Sheehan,

Sheehan, & Minichiello, 1981; Thyer, Parrish, Curtis, Nesse, & Cameron, 1985). Age of onset for claustrophobia in the Ost (1987) study also was later than for other specific phobias (20.2 years). Interestingly, these ages are more similar to the age of onset for panic disorder (see next paragraph), supporting the hypothesis proposed by Klein (1981), and discussed by Ost, that claustrophobia may be a restricted but functional and descriptive equivalent of panic disorder with agoraphobia.

The generally accepted age of onset for panic disorder usually is early adulthood (McNally, 2001). Ost (1987) compiled data from 13 samples of panic and agoraphobic patients, reporting an age of onset ranging from 19.7 to 32 years of age, with a mean of 26.5 years across all studies. Although some researchers have described a bimodal age distribution with the first period occurring during late adolescence and the second around age 30 (Marks & Gelder, 1966), others found a unimodal distribution (Ost, 1987; Thorpe & Burns, 1983). Based on the analysis of the NCS (Magee, 1999), three unpredictable and uncontrollable events (that threaten or result in physical harm) appear to be uniquely related to agoraphobia onset. These include life-threatening accidents, combat in war (for men), and fire/flood or other natural disaster. However, although these events might be uniquely related to agoraphobia, they are not necessarily in the life history of every individual who develops agoraphobia, and every individual who experiences these events does not necessarily develop agoraphobia. Therefore, although these events may be related, they are neither necessary or sufficient for the onset of agoraphobia.

Age of onset for social phobia falls somewhere between those for specific phobias and panic disorder with agoraphobia, usually occurring during adolescence. Age of onset reported by adult samples ranges from 15.7 to 20.0 years (Amies et al., 1983; Liebowitz, Gorman, et al., 1985; Marks & Gelder, 1966; Ost, 1987; Thyer et al., 1985; Turner et al., 1986). However, Regier, Rae, Narrow, Kaelber, and Schatzberg(1998) found age of onset to be somewhat younger than mid-adolescence (i.e., 11.6 years) in socially phobic patients with comorbid depression, and social phobia often occurs in children as young as age 8 (Beidel & Turner, 1988; Beidel, Turner, & Morris, 1999).

For OCD, typical age of onset ranges from late adolescence to early adulthood (e.g., Nestadt, Bienvenu, Cai, Samuels, & Eaton, 1998; Rasmussen & Tsuang, 1986; Turner & Beidel, 1988), and the frank onset of this disorder has been witnessed in those as young as age 4 (Turner & Beidel, 1988). Furthermore, even for those who report an actual onset in early adulthood, retrospective reports from OCD patients indicate that vestiges of the disorder often are present at a much earlier age (Turner & Beidel, 1988). Early-onset OCD (before age 18) is characterized by a greater number of obsessions and compulsions and greater levels of clinical impairment than cases of adult onset (Sobin, Blundell, & Karayiorgou, 2000).

A review of the literature did not reveal any figures for a typical age of onset for GAD or PTSD. Overall, prevalence rates of GAD are low in adolescents and young adults but increase significantly with age (Wittchen & Hoyer, 2001). In the case of PTSD, given that the disorder is triggered by a traumatic event, the onset of the disorder can be expected to occur at any age (see McNally, 2001).

COURSE AND COMPLICATIONS

Anxiety disorders tend to have a chronic course. In an early study, Breier, Charney, and Heninger (1986) reported that agoraphobia was chronic and unremitting.

Similarly, once severe animal phobias are established, fear intensity remained constant or gradually increased over subsequent years (McNally & Steketee, 1985). The same pattern has been noted for OCD (Rasmussen & Tsuang, 1986), although a subset of OCD cases with a later age of onset may be best described as episodic (Perugi et al., 1998). Along these lines, Eaton et al. (1998) reported that panic with agoraphobia is associated with a less intense onset but slower recovery than panic disorder without agoraphobia.

In a multicenter study of panic disorder, panic disorder with agoraphobia, and agoraphobia without panic disorder (Goisman et al., 1994), there was a .42 probability that a panic disorder patient would be symptom free for eight weeks. Probabilities for the two groups with agoraphobia were both .15, indicating they were very unlikely to have symptom-free periods. Similar figures were reported by Keller et al. (1994), who found a .39 probability of full remission (eight weeks symptom free) at one-year follow-up for uncomplicated panic disorder and a .17 probability of full remission for panic disorder with agoraphobia. At 18 months, the probabilities increased to .49 and .20, respectively. However, there was a high rate of relapse (within one year) after remission. Probability of relapse rates were .31 for panic disorder patients and .35 for panic disorder with agoraphobia. Eaton et al. (1998) also reported that panic disorder with agoraphobia is associated with a less intense onset but slower recovery than panic disorder without agoraphobia. Comorbidity of Axis II disorders may play a role in chronicity as 59% of those without a personality disorder had a two-month period of remission compared to 29% of those with a comorbid personality disorder (Pollack, Otto, Rosenbaum, & Sachs, 1992). Although more than 80% of these patients received pharmacological treatment and 75% received psychological treatment as well, interpretation of the study results is difficult because of:

- The mixed method of treatment.
- Psychological treatment that primarily consisted of nonspecific dynamic intervention rather than highly efficacious behavioral and cognitive-behavioral treatments.

In a follow-up investigation of pharmacological treatment, Andersch, Hanson, and Haellstroem (1997) assessed 52 panic patients who had been part of a double-blind placebo-controlled multicenter study. At five-year follow-up, 85% no longer met criteria for panic disorder, although 62% still reported occasional panic attacks.

Davidson (1993) reported that onset of social phobia before age 11 was predictive of nonrecovery in adulthood. A prospective follow-along study of social phobia (Reich, Goldenberg, Goisman, Vasile, & Keller, 1994) reported that no demographic (gender or age) or clinical variables (age of onset, duration of illness, comorbidity, or level of functioning) accurately predicted outcome 65 weeks after intake. G. A. Fava, Grandi, Rafanelli, Conti, and Belluardo (2001) reported social phobia remission rates of 85% 10 years after psychological treatment. Noyes et al. (1992) reported that, compared to panic patients, those with GAD were significantly more likely to describe a gradual onset for their disorder but, like panic patients, they had an unremitting course of illness. In fact, in a five-year follow-up study, significantly fewer GAD patients achieved full remission (18%) as compared to panic patients (45%; Woodman, Noyes, Black, Schlosser, & Yagla, 1999). In another follow-up study, patients with GAD were interviewed an average of 15.7 months after completing a clinical drug trial (Mancuso, Townsend, & Mercante, 1993); 50% continued to meet criteria for GAD, whereas 50% did not. Interestingly, there were an equal number of "treatment responders" (designated at the end of the clinical trial) in each group. However, those who continued to have GAD symptoms were also more likely to have concurrent diagnoses of dysthymia, social phobia, or both, as well as a higher prevalence of Axis II cluster B and C personality disorders.

The few empirical data that do exist, along with our clinical experience, lead us to draw the following tentative conclusions:

- Symptom exacerbation often is correlated with onset of significant life stressors (Klein & Fink, 1962; Kukleta & Franc, 2000; Magee, 1999; Turner & Beidel, 1988).
- Once the disorder is established, behavioral avoidance often functions to reduce general emotional distress, but this is associated with social impairment, and symptoms tend to reemerge or worsen when there is contact with the phobic environment.
- It is likely that a subset of anxiety disorder patients do overcome their disorder without professional intervention, but the personality or environmental characteristics associated with these successful outcomes are currently unknown.

Anxiety disorders can result in significant life complications. Schneier et al. (1992) reported that social phobics were significantly more likely to receive disability and welfare payments than normal controls (22% vs. 11%). Furthermore, because of a consistent inability to hold a job, 22% of their sample was on welfare (Schneier et al., 1994). Similarly, Goisman et al. (1994) noted that 50% of those with panic disorder, agoraphobia, or both were receiving some form of financial assistance (unemployment, disability, welfare, or social security payments). With respect to educational attainment, failure to complete high school was positively and significantly associated with anxiety disorders or conduct disorders in females, whereas only anxiety disorders were positively related to women's failure to enter college and failure to complete college (Kessler, Foster, Saunders, & Stang, 1995). Among men, all of these transitions were significantly related only to conduct disorders. Furthermore, the economic burden of anxiety disorders is quite severe, with an annual cost of approximately $42.3 billion or $1,542 per sufferer (Greenberg et al., 1999). This includes $23 billion in nonpsychiatric medical treatment costs, $13.3 billion in psychiatric medical costs, $4.1 billion in indirect workplace costs, $1.2 billion in mortality costs, and $0.8 billion in prescription pharmaceutical costs. Thus, anxiety disorders result in substantial cost to American society.

TREATMENT OUTCOME

Pharmacological Treatments Pharmacological treatments for anxiety disorders primarily consist of antidepressants, high-potency benzodiazepines, or beta-blocking agents. It is beyond the scope of this chapter to provide a thorough review for each pharmacological agent with each disorder. Thus, we comment on the efficacy of the various classes of agents and note factors that may predict treatment outcome. It is important to note that what constitutes improvement in pharmacological treatment studies in many cases differs from outcome measures used in behavioral and cognitive-behavioral studies. Thus, comparisons of outcome across behavioral and pharmacological treatment are fraught with limitations.

There is no evidence for efficacy of any drug in the treatment of a specific phobia (Lydiard et al., 1988). Initially, panic disorder and panic disorder with agoraphobia were treated successfully with tricyclic antidepressants such as imipramine (Ballenger, 1986; Barlow, Gorman, Shear, & Woods, 2000; Liebowitz, 1997), and the benzodiazepine, alprazolam (Ballenger, 1990; Ballenger et al., 1988; Cross National Collaborative Panic Study Second Phase Investigation, 1992; Sheikh & Swales, 1999). Curtis et al. (1993) noted that benzodiazepines may have a more rapid effect at the initiation of treatment, but that within a month, the antidepressants "catch up," such that differences were no longer apparent, and eight months later, outcome for the two drugs appeared equal. Currently, selective serotonin reuptake inhibitors (SSRIs) are the treatment of choice for panic disorder with or without agoraphobia. For example, fluvoxamine appears effective when compared to placebo (Hoehn-Saric, McLeod, & Hipsley, 1993). Recently, fluvoxamine was compared to inositol for the treatment of panic disorder (Palatnik, Frolov, Fux, & Benjamin, 2001). Inositol is a natural isomer of glucose that also affects serotonin receptor sites within the cell membrane whereas fluvoxamine also affects serotonin but at receptor sites outside the cell membrane. Both groups showed significant decreases on clinician ratings of anxiety and agoraphobia. However, after one month, only inositol was superior in reducing panic attacks when compared to placebo. Sertraline (another SSRI) also appears to be effective for the treatment of panic disorder (Pohl, Wolkow, & Clary, 1998), even for those who had been previously treated with benzodiazepines (Rapaport, Pollack, Clary, Mardekian, & Wolkow, 2001). Finally, with respect to beta blockers, the bulk of the evidence at this time does not indicate any effectiveness in the treatment of panic disorder (Fyer & Sandberg, 1988; Gorman et al., 1983), although there is some evidence that they may be effective for more general anxiety symptoms (Bailly, 1996).

The pharmacological treatment of social phobia has a shorter history than that of panic disorder and agoraphobia; however, a number of studies have appeared over the past 20 years. Initially, phenelzine, a monoamine oxidase inhibitor (MAOI), was reported effective in treating social phobia (Liebowitz et al., 1992), particularly the generalized subtype (Liebowitz et al., 1988), but its side-effect profile and dietary restrictions limit its use as a first-line treatment. Currently, SSRIs are the treatment of choice, particularly for the generalized subtype. For example, Stein et al. (1998) reported paroxetine to be significantly more effective than placebo in a large controlled trial for generalized social phobia. Similar positive outcome was reported for sertraline (Katzelnick et al., 1995) and fluvoxamine (Stein, Fyer, Davidson, Pollack, & Wiita, 1999; Van Vliet, den Boer, & Westenberg, 1994), although only 43% to 47% of those treated with fluvoxamine were judged as treatment responders in both trials. Other pharmacological interventions have had only mixed results. For example, outcome for buspirone is equivocal; open trials indicated some efficacy (Munjack et al., 1991; Schneier et al., 1993), but controlled trials (Clark & Agras, 1991; VanVliet, den Boer, Westenberg, & Pian, 1997) do not report a difference between buspirone and placebo. Clark and Agras found that the combination of buspirone and cognitive-behavioral treatment did more poorly than cognitive-behavioral treatment alone. Imipramine, a tricyclic antidepressant, has been found to be ineffective (Simpson et al., 1998). The beta blocker atenolol also does not appear to be more effective than placebo (Liebowitz et al., 1988; Turner,

Beidel, & Jacob, 1994). Finally, with respect to benzodiazepines, Davidson et al. (1993) reported that clonazepam was superior to placebo, and a more recent study indicated that when clonazepam is tapered slowly, relapse rate is 21%, and 28% of those who were tapered off the medication experienced withdrawal symptoms (Connor et al., 1998). Meta-analyses of pharmacological and psychosocial treatments for social phobia suggest that effect sizes were larger for benzodiazepines and SSRIs in comparison to psychological treatments (Fedoroff & Taylor, 2001; Gould, Buckminster, Pollack, Otto, & Yap, 1997). However, benzodiazepines have side effects including psychological and physical dependency, and discontinuation of all pharmacological agents results in high rates of relapse (e.g., Gelernter, Uhde, Cimbolic, & Arnkoff, 1991). In contrast, those treated with behavioral or cognitive-behavioral treatments maintain their treatment gains at follow-up and a subset demonstrate continued improvement (see Beidel & Turner, 1998).

Antidepressants (older and newer compounds) have a history of use to treat OCD, and the results of recent studies support their use, particularly for the SSRIs (Rivas-Vazquez, 2001; Stanley & Turner, 1995). In a comprehensive review of the OCD pharmacological treatment literature, Pigott and Seay (1999) noted that fluoxetine, sertraline, fluvoxamine, and paroxetine (all SSRIs) all have been the subjects of multicenter trials, and all have shown demonstrated efficacy and tolerability in comparison to placebo. Furthermore, meta-analyses or direct comparisons of clomipramine (an SRI) to fluoxetine, paroxetine, or fluvoxamine result in equal outcome, but the SSRIs have a lower incidence of side effects. For a review, see Pigott and Seay (1999). The equal effectiveness of the SSRIs and clomipramine are disputed by others, however, particularly with respect to refractory OCD in which clomipramine still might be considered the treatment of choice (Todorov, Freeston, & Borgeat, 2000). Overall, pharmacological treatment results are reported in terms of improvement in symptomatology. The improvement rate ranges from 22% to 62% for SSRIs (Ellingrod, 1998), although decreases of 25% to 30% in symptomatology are usually considered as indicative of "positive treatment response" (e.g., Koran, Ringold, & Elliott, 2000). More recently, citalopram, one of the most selective SSRIs, also has been reported to be more efficacious than placebo (Marazziti et al., 2001; Montgomery, Kasper, Stein, Bang, & Lemming, 2001). Currently, research on pharmacological interventions for OCD has focused on SSRI augmentation trials. Specifically, a number of agents such as citalopram (Pallanti, Quercioli, Paiva, & Koran, 1999), risperidone (McDougle, Epperson, Pelton, Wasylink, & Price, 2000), and olanzapine (Koran et al., 2000), in combination with an SSRI or SRI, have been reported to have increased efficacy over the SSRI or SRI alone. However, sample sizes for these studies are small and firm conclusions cannot be drawn at this time.

Benzodiazepines have been widely used for treating GAD (Ballenger, 1984). Beta-blockers also have been used by primary care physicians (Lydiard et al., 1988), but they are rarely more effective than placebo (Noyes, 1985). Rickels and colleagues (Rickels, Downing, Schweizer, & Hassman, 1993) reported that 73% of patients treated with imipramine, 69% of patients treated with trazedone, 66% of patients treated with diazepam, and 47% of patients treated with placebo were judged as moderately to markedly improved. This high placebo response rate has been noted in many recent drug trials. Although the reason is unclear, one likely explanation is that assessment of treatment outcome in drug trials relies heavily on clinician judgment, ratings that are known to be more susceptible to placebo effects than behavioral assessment or self-report inventories (Turner, Beidel, & Jacob,

1994). Most recently, Rickels et al. (2000) found imipramine to be highly effective in treating GAD patients who were previous long-term benzodiazepines users and who reported several prior unsuccessful taper attempts from these drugs. In fact, there appears to be a shift in the pharmacotherapy of GAD (Salzman, Goldenberg, Bruce, & Keller, 2001). Based on the findings of a longitudinal study, Salzman and colleagues reported that between 1989 and 1991, 67% of patients diagnosed with GAD alone were being treated with medication. Of those patients on medication, 61% were receiving benzodiazepines alone and none was receiving both antidepressants and benzodiazepines. By 1996, the percentage receiving medication increased to 73%; but only 36% were receiving benzodiazepines alone, and 36% were receiving both antidepressants and benzodiazepines. Thus, even within this short period of time, there has been a dramatic shift in the pharmacotherapy for this disorder, with a growing use of antidepressants.

There are only a few controlled trials of pharmacological treatment for PTSD. These studies have been reviewed by Davidson (1992, 2000), who reported positive treatment outcome for the tricyclic antidepressants amitriptyline or imipramine, but not for desipramine. Outcome for MAOIs was equivocal, with only one of two studies reporting a positive outcome. Fluoxetine (an SSRI) also has been reported to be effective in decreasing the specific symptoms of arousal and numbing (van der Kolk et al., 1994), and there also is some preliminary evidence for the efficacy of nefazodone (a neuroleptic) in treating PTSD symptoms (Zisook et al., 2000).

In summary, although the overall outcome for pharmacological treatments is positive, not all patients respond to these treatments, and there has been little attention to patient factors that might predict positive outcome. Only two studies have addressed this issue. As noted earlier, a naturalistic study of panic disorder patients indicated that panic-free periods were more likely to occur in patients without comorbid Axis I or II disorders (Pollack et al., 1992). Although a host of possible predictor variables for OCD has been the subject of discussion (e.g., schizotypal personality, fixidity of beliefs), no clear findings have been reported to date (Stanley & Turner, 1995). Furthermore, many of these studies, and particularly the earlier ones, suffer from methodological confounds, such as the almost-total reliance on clinician and patient rating scales to judge outcome. Finally, the positive outcome from these studies must be tempered by acknowledgment that withdrawal of these medications has produced relapse rates ranging from 23% to 86% (Fontaine & Chouinard, 1986; Pato, Zohar-Kadouch, Zohar, & Murphy, 1988; Versiani, Amrein, & Montgomery, 1997). Particularly for the most refractory patients, a combination of medication and psychosocial interventions may be the treatment of choice (see following discussion).

Behavioral and Cognitive-Behavioral Treatments   Although numerous psychosocial treatments exist, more than 25 years of empirical data are so compelling that there can be no doubt that behavioral and cognitive-behavioral interventions are the psychosocial treatments of choice for anxiety disorders (Beidel, Turner, & Ballenger, 1997). Although engineered differently, these interventions share a common element: exposure to the anxiety-producing stimuli (e.g., Hoffart, 1993; Turner, Cooley-Quille, & Beidel, 1996). Interestingly, numerous demographic and clinical factors have been examined in an attempt to predict positive treatment outcome from behavioral and cognitive-behavioral treatments. In short, across all disorders (with the exception of specific phobia), poorer treatment outcome is predicted by greater severity of either the primary anxiety disorder (Basoglu et al., 1994; Castle et al., 1994; Keijsers, Hoogduin, & Schapp, 1994a; Steketee & Shapiro, 1995; Turner, Beidel, Wolff, Spaulding, & Jacob, 1996), comorbid affective and anxiety states (Albus & Scheibe, 1993; Brown, Antony, & Barlow, 1995; Keijsers, Hoogduin, & Schaap, 1994b; Steketee & Shapiro, 1995; Turner, Beidel, Wolff, Spaulding, et al., 1996), or comorbid Axis II disorders (AuBuchon & Malatesta, 1994; Stanley & Turner, 1995; Turner, Beidel, Wolff, Spaulding, et al., 1996). The literature on behavioral and cognitive-behavioral interventions is reviewed in the following section.

PANIC DISORDER

For panic disorder with agoraphobia, in vivo exposure (with or without the concomitant use of medication or cognitive interventions) appears to be the treatment of choice (Barlow & Lehman, 1996; Clum, 1989; Craske, Rapee, & Barlow, 1992). Ballenger, Lydiard, and Turner (1995) concluded that exposure-based interventions produce improvement in the 60% to 70% range. Treatment effects last at least nine years, and many patients show further improvement (without additional treatment) during the follow-up period. In a long-term follow-up study of panic patients treated with exposure therapy, G. A. Fava, Rafanelli, et al. (2001) reported remission rates of 93% after 2 years and 62% after 10 years. Positive results are usually achieved in 10 to 20 sessions. Furthermore, gradual or intensive approaches appear equally effective (Craske et al., 1992). The empirical evidence for adding coping or cognitive strategies to standard exposure procedures is equivocal. Although one review suggested some effect (Clum, 1989), this conclusion was based on the fact that cognitive strategies appeared to reduce the number of treatment dropouts. There was no superiority for cognitive strategies based on treatment outcome measures. Others also have reported that addition of cognitive components do not generate improvement rates that are higher than exposure alone (Jansson, Jerremalm, & Ost, 1986; Michelson, Mavissakalian, & Marchione, 1985).

As noted by Barlow and Lehman (1996), changing conceptualizations of panic disorder with agoraphobia began to focus treatment efforts more specifically on the presence of panic attacks. Results of several trials suggest that cognitive-behavioral treatment (e.g., cognitive restructuring, respiratory training) may be effective for those with uncomplicated panic disorder (Beck, 1988; Clark, Salkovskis, & Chalkley, 1985). Panic control therapy (PCT; Barlow, Craske, Cerney, & Klosko, 1989; Craske, Maidenberg, & Bystritsky, 1995) incorporates exposure to somatic symptoms as well as cognitive restructuring. Clark and his colleagues (e.g., Beck, Sokol, Clark, Berchick, & Wright, 1992) developed a more cognitive view of panic treatment that also addresses physiological, cognitive, and behavioral components. Focused cognitive therapy was effective when compared to supportive therapy or applied relaxation (e.g., Beck et al., 1992). Reviewing all of the available literature, Barlow and Lehman (1996) concluded that when comparisons are made, PCT or cognitive therapy results in approximately 80% of treated patients reporting themselves to be panic-free at posttreatment when compared to no treatment controls or other psychological interventions. Although the findings are not surprising given the central role of exposure in these interventions, it also must be noted that these studies have narrowed their treatment outcome criteria to focus quite specifically on frequency of panic attacks. Other aspects of the clinical syndrome, such as state anxiety or functional impairment, are not often considered as "primary" outcome measures, and often do not show the same degree of improvement.

SPECIFIC PHOBIA

Although few individuals with specific phobias seek treatment (Myers et al., 1984), available outcome data indicate that behavioral interventions, such as systematic desensitization, imaginal and in vivo flooding, graduated in vivo exposure, participant modeling, and applied tension, are effective. In a review of the literature, Ost (1996) noted that positive treatment rates are quite high (averaging about 80% improvement) with very minimal treatment lengths (1.9 to 9.0 hours, depending on the particular phobia). For animal phobias, therapist-directed exposure and participant modeling are the treatments of choice. Flying phobias appear to respond to self-instructional training, applied relaxation, and various methods of exposure. Participant modeling and guided mastery are effective for acrophobia. The biphasic physiological response of blood/illness/injury phobias (an initial increase in blood pressure and heart rate, then a rapid drop so sharp that readings often fall below resting baseline levels) requires special consideration. Fainting on the part of the patient needs to be prevented to eliminate the possibility of injury and also to allow the exposure to take place. Applied tension (tensing during the exposure sessions; see Ost, 1996, for details) has been markedly successful in the treatment of these phobias.

SOCIAL PHOBIA

Social phobia has been successfully treated by traditional behavioral and cognitive-behavioral interventions (see Turner, Cooley-Quille, et al., 1996, for a review). As noted earlier, the key ingredient is exposure (imaginal or in vivo) to the fear-producing stimuli. Social skills training also has been demonstrated to be effective (Newman, Hofmann, Trabert, Roth, & Taylor, 1994; Van Dam-Baggen & Kraaimaat, 2000; Wlazlo, Schroeder-Hartwig, Hand, Kaiser, & Munchau, 1990), and Social Effectiveness Therapy (which combines exposure and social skills training; Turner, Beidel, & Cooley, 1994) appears to be particularly promising, especially for the generalized subtype. Cognitive-behavioral group therapy combines exposure with cognitive restructuring and has shown some degree of efficacy (Heimberg et al., 1990), as have other cognitive-behavioral interventions (Mattick & Peters, 1988; Mattick, Peters, & Clarke, 1989). Recently, the preponderance of evidence from substantive reviews (Turner, Cooley-Quille, et al., 1996), dismantling studies (Hope, Heimberg, & Bruch, 1995; Salaberria & Echeburua, 1998), and meta-analyses (Feske & Chambless, 1995; Taylor, 1996; Wenzel, Statler-Cowen, Patton, & Holt, 1998) indicates that, for this disorder, the addition of cognitive procedures does not produce superior outcome to that of exposure alone. In the most recent review, Wenzel et al. reported that for all forms of cognitive-behavioral treatments (with the exception of relaxation therapy alone), pre- and posteffect sizes were .80 or above. When differences across behavioral and cognitive-behavioral interventions were reported, they were (a) only on a relatively small subset of variables; and (b) never on the same variables across different studies, even when several studies were conducted by the same research team. Also, treatments appear about equally efficacious when delivered in individual or group formats (Scholing & Emmelkamp, 1993). Follow-up data indicate that effects of behavioral or cognitive-behavioral treatment are maintained for at least two years (Turner, Beidel, & Cooley-Quille, 1995; Wlazlo et al., 1990) and up to five years posttreatment (G. A. Fava, Grandi, et al., 2001; Heimberg, Salzman, Holt, & Blendell, 1993).

GENERALIZED ANXIETY DISORDER

Few controlled trials document efficacy of behavioral treatments for GAD, although systematic desensitization, in vivo desensitization, stress inoculation, social skills training, problem-solving strategies, cognitive therapy, and cognitive restructuring are considered to be useful (Craske et al., 1992). Butler, Fennell, Robson, and Gelder (1991) reported that cognitive-behavioral therapy (Beck's cognitive therapy) was consistently superior to a wait-list control, whereas there were fewer differences between behavior therapy (relaxation, graduated exposure, and pleasant events scheduling) and a wait-list group. In an early review of the literature, outcome data were collapsed across five controlled studies that included three behavioral and five cognitive interventions (Durham & Allan, 1993). Using the averaged score across all treated groups, average improvement rates were 14% for treated patients and 11% for wait-list control patients based on the Hamilton Rating Scale for Anxiety, and 11% for the treated group and 4% for the wait-list control group for a trait anxiety self-report measure. Better improvement rates were reported by Borkovec and Costello (1993), and at 12-month follow-up, 57.9% of those treated with cognitive-behavioral treatment were judged as treatment responders, compared with 33% in the applied relaxation condition and 22.2% of those who received nondirective treatment. Finally, Ladoucer and colleagues (2000; Dugas & Ladoucer, 2000) reported positive treatment effects in GAD patients in comparison to a wait-list control group, following the use of a cognitive-behavioral therapy strategy that used:

- Correction of erroneous beliefs about amenable worries and effective problem-solving strategies for these worries.
- Cognitive exposure for worries not amenable to problem solving.

Results from one investigation (Ladoucer et al., 2000) revealed that 77% of patients no longer met diagnostic criteria for GAD at posttreatment, with results maintained at 6- and 12-month follow-up. It must be noted that, in this trial, approximately 33% of the patients also were receiving medication concurrently with the cognitive-behavioral treatment, and results were not analyzed separately for these two subgroups. Furthermore, the intervention included both cognitive and traditional behavioral components, and it is unclear whether either intervention alone might have produced the same results. Finally, the intervention has been compared only to a wait-list control group; further studies addressing its efficacy, in comparison to either an attention-placebo control or another active intervention, are necessary. In summary, empirical data addressing the treatment of GAD lags far behind that of the other anxiety disorders. Some of the difficulty may relate to high rates of comorbidity for this disorder, making it extremely difficult to find samples of patients with GAD alone and thereby determine the efficacy of interventions specifically for this disorder.

OBSESSIVE-COMPULSIVE DISORDER

For OCD, the psychosocial treatment of choice is exposure combined with response prevention (see Stanley & Turner, 1995, for an extended review of the literature). Graduated exposure strategies appear less effective than a more intensive procedure (Turner & Beidel, 1988) but more effective than cognitive-behavior therapy (McLean et al., 2001) or general anxiety management (Lindsay, Crino, & Andrews, 1997). Substantive reviews (Stanley & Turner, 1995) and meta-analyses (Abramowitz, 1997) confirm early estimates of Foa, Steketee, and Ozarow (1985) that approximately 51% of patients achieve at least a 70% reduction in symptoms. The most conservative estimates (adjusting for dropout and refusal rates that account for about 20% of the patients seeking behavioral treatment) are that 72% of patients benefit from exposure and response prevention. Positive treatment outcome is maintained over time (79% remain improved or much improved one to six years later; Stanley & Turner, 1995). Hiss, Foa, and Kozak (1994) added relapse prevention procedures commonly used with substance abuse patients to enhance exposure and response-prevention procedures for the treatment of OCD. In comparison to an attention placebo control, relapse and reoccurrence rates were lower at six-month follow-up when these prevention strategies were implemented. Most recently, group treatment of cognitive (based on Salkovski's 1996 model) versus behavior (exposure and response prevention) therapy was examined (McLean et al., 2001). Both treatments were superior to a wait-list control group, but behavior therapy was judged as marginally more effective than cognitive therapy at posttreatment and follow-up. At three-month follow-up, significantly more behaviorally treated patients were recovered in comparison to the cognitive group. Finally, the extent of cognitive change was equivalent across the two interventions. Although the utility of exposure and response prevention treatment for OCD has been firmly established, the results of randomized, controlled trials often have been criticized as not being generalizable to "nonresearch" patients. However, two studies (Franklin, Abramowitz, Kozak, Levitt, & Foa, 2000; Warren & Thomas, 2001) indicate that exposure and response prevention also are effective when delivered in clinical or private practice settings. For example, Franklin et al. treated 110 patients without regard to treatment history, concomitant pharmacotherapy, psychiatric comorbidity, age, or OCD severity. These patients demonstrated substantial reductions in OCD symptomatology, and outcome was comparable to that reported in randomized, controlled trials. Thus, exposure and response prevention appear to be the psychosocial treatment of choice for OCD.

POSTTRAUMATIC STRESS DISORDER

Treatment outcome data for PTSD encompass both civilian and combat populations and are based on behavioral or cognitive-behavioral interventions. Extant data indicate that prolonged or massed exposure to relevant cues led to anxiety and fear reduction. Among civilian populations, exposure has been demonstrated to be effective in randomized, controlled trials (Echeburua, de Corral, Zubizarreta, & Sarasua, 1997; Foa, Rothbaum, Riggs, & Murdock, 1991; Foa et al.,1999; Marks, Lovell, Noshirvani, Livanou, & Thrasher, 1998; Tarrier et al., 1999). Among combat veterans, exposure treatments are considered partially efficacious, but the data are weaker than for the civilian populations. In general, intensive exposure (imaginal or in vivo) for combat veterans results in significant decreases on some clinical measures, including anxiety, depression, startle responses, memory disturbance, sleep, nightmares, and intrusive thoughts (Boudewyns & Hyer, 1990; Cooper & Clum, 1989; Frueh, Turner, Beidel, Mirabella, & Jones, 1996; Keane, Fairbank, Caddell, & Zimering, 1989), but not on measures of "negative" symptoms (behavioral avoidance, social withdrawal, interpersonal difficulties, occupational maladjustment, and emotional numbing) or on measures of emotion management (anger control; see

Frueh, Turner, & Beidel, 1995, for a review of this treatment literature). In response to this limited outcome, several researchers have suggested that adding other interventions to exposure treatment may be necessary to address the myriad of symptoms associated with combat-related PTSD. Behavioral family therapy (Glynn et al., 1999) and trauma management therapy (Turner, Beidel, & Frueh, 2000) have been the subjects of investigations and both have shown positive treatment outcome. However, more controlled trials are necessary to determine the effects of augmenting exposure with these additional interventions.

Eye Movement Desensitization and Reprocessing (EMDR; Shapiro, 1989, 1994) is a controversial treatment strategy that combines multisaccadic eye movements with a cognitive exposure element (Acierno, Hersen, Van Hasselt, Tremont, & Meuser, 1994). Several randomized clinical trials indicated that patients treated with EMDR reported decreased immediate subjective distress but did not differ from controls on standardized measures (Boudewyns, Stwertka, Hyer, Albrecht, & Sperr, 1993; Jensen, 1994). In a comparison of EMDR and cognitive-behavioral treatment (Devilly & Spence, 1999), cognitive-behavioral treatment was more effective, and dismantling efforts indicated that the eye movement component is not necessary (Boudewyns et al., 1993; Steketee & Goldstein, 1994). Furthermore, individuals participating in EMDR trials frequently have experienced a traumatic event but often the subjects are not diagnosed with PTSD, thus questioning the severity of their disorder. Finally, treatment gains from EMDR may not be maintained at follow-up (Macklin et al., 2000).

COMBINED OR COMPARATIVE PHARMACOLOGICAL AND PSYCHOSOCIAL TREATMENTS

Several studies have compared behavioral and cognitive-behavioral procedures with pharmacological treatment for panic disorder. A comparison of alprazolam and PCT revealed that only PCT was more effective than placebo and wait-list controls (Klosko, Barlow, Tassinari, & Cerny, 1990). Percentages of patients who were free from panic disorder at posttreatment were 87% for the PCT group, 50% for alprazolam, 36% for placebo, and 33% for wait-list control. Although current data do not consistently show a synergistic effect for the combination of pharmacological and behavioral treatments for panic disorder, one study (Hegel, Ravaris, & Ahles, 1994) reported that one year after the cessation of cognitive-behavioral treatment and alprazolam withdrawal, 76% of the sample was medication free, and 85% remained panic free. Furthermore, the positive outcome suggests that use of alprazolam in combination with cognitive-behavioral treatment was not contraindicated, as concerns about the impact of state-dependent learning would suggest. Finally, ability to enhance the effects of exposure treatment by first treating the patients with either fluvoxamine or psychological panic management was examined in a group of panic patients (DeBeurs, van Balkom, Lange, Koele, & van Dyck, 1995). The combination of fluvoxamine and exposure in vivo was significantly superior (and had twice as large an effect size) when compared to psychological panic management plus exposure in vivo, placebo plus exposure in vivo, or exposure in vivo alone on self-reported agoraphobic avoidance. There were no other differences among groups, indicating that psychological panic management, combined with exposure in vivo, was not superior to exposure in vivo alone. Finally, behavioral and cognitive-behavioral treatments have been used successfully to aid in the withdrawal of patients from benzodiazepines (Otto et al., 1993).

Flooding (an intensive exposure procedure) is more effective than atenolol (a beta blocker) in the treatment of social phobia (Turner, Beidel, & Jacob, 1994). In one of the largest comparative trials (Heimberg et al., 1998), patients were treated with cognitive-behavioral group treatment (CBGT), phenelzine, pill placebo, or an educational support group (psychological placebo). After 12 weeks, patients treated with phenelzine or CBGT were more likely to be treatment responders than those in the placebo groups. Both groups were equally improved, although effect sizes were higher for the phenelzine group in comparison to CBGT and phenelzine had a more rapid treatment effect. At six-month follow-up, all patients who responded to CBGT maintained their treatment gains, whereas 50% of the phenelzine responders had relapsed (Heimberg et al., 1994). Thus, although the initial treatment response may be positive, as previously noted, substantial relapse rates remain an issue for patients treated with medication. Only one study (Falloon, Lloyd, & Harpin, 1981) addressed the combination of pharmacological and behavioral treatment for social phobia. Results indicated that propranolol did not result in superior outcome over exposure treatment alone.

A meta-analysis examining behavioral and pharmacological treatment for OCD indicated that on self- and assessor ratings of obsessive-compulsive symptoms, both serotonin blocking antidepressants (clomipramine, fluoxetine, and fluvoxamine) and behavior therapy were significantly superior to placebo (Christensen, Hadzi-Pavlovic, Andrews, & Mattick, 1987). On assessor ratings, there was no difference in effect sizes between the two classes of active treatments. However, on self-report ratings, behavior therapy was significantly more effective than the pharmacological agents. A review (Westra & Stewart, 1998) addressing the combination of cognitive-behavior therapy and pharmacotherapy for treatment of anxiety disorders (other than OCD) indicated that high potency benzodiazepines exert a detrimental effect on outcome of cognitive-behavioral treatment. According to this review, low potency benzodiazepines and antidepressants neither enhance nor attenuate cognitive-behavioral treatment response. However, because of the few outcome studies that exist, these conclusions may require reexamination when a database sufficient to examine each specific anxiety disorder is available.

FAMILIAL AND GENETIC CONSIDERATIONS

As with other areas of psychopathology, there has been increased interest in biological factors in anxiety disorders, and the possibility of a biological etiology has been pursued through twin studies and family or family history studies. Family and family history studies reveal increased morbidity rate among first-degree relatives of patients with an anxiety disorder. Data consistently demonstrate higher lifetime prevalence rates of panic disorder in relatives of patient probands (7.7 to 20.5 of 100) compared to relatives of normal controls (0.8 to 7.7 of 100; Weissman, 1993). Fyer (1993) reported that rates of social phobia in first-degree relatives of social phobia probands were higher than in first-degree relatives of normal controls (16% vs. 5%), whereas rates for other disorders were not different between these two groups. Similarly, Fyer et al. (1990) reported higher rates of specific (simple) phobia among first-degree relatives of specific (simple) phobic probands compared to rates among relatives of normal control probands (31% vs. 11%). Again, rates for other disorders did not differ. Two family studies of OCD have produced inconsistent findings. Black, Noyes, Goldstein, and Blum (1992) did not find a higher prevalence of OCD among relatives of OCD probands when compared to normal controls. They did find, however, a higher prevalence of anxiety disorders in general among relatives of OCD probands, primarily because of the presence of GAD. When OCD was more broadly defined to include subclinical levels, there was a higher prevalence of OCD among parents of OCD probands compared to normal controls (16% vs. 3%). Using a larger sample, rates of OCD and subthreshold OCD were significantly higher among OCD probands than normal controls (10.3% vs. 1.9% for OCD and 7.9% vs. 2.0% for subthreshold OCD; Pauls, Alsobrook, Goodman, Rasmussen, & Leckman, 1995). Nestadt et al. (2000) also reported a higher lifetime prevalence of OCD in OCD probands compared to control relatives. Age of onset of OCD symptoms was strongly associated with familiality. Adults with early onset OCD (before age 18) were much more likely to have a relative with OCD than adults with late onset OCD (after age 18). For an overview of family and genetic studies of OCD, see Hanna (2000).

In some cases, these conflictual outcomes may be explained by different assessment methodologies (family studies vs. family history studies) or perhaps different patient characteristics. In other cases, age of onset also may impact familial rates of anxiety disorders. For example, R. B. Goldstein, Wickramaratne, Horwath, and Weissman (1997) examined age of onset in adult probands as a predictor of panic disorder in first-degree relatives. Results indicated that first-degree relatives of early-onset panic patients had significantly higher rates of panic disorder than first-degree relatives of later onset panic. If earlier age of onset is considered an indicator of more severe psychopathology (as appears to be the case for social phobia), these results might be interpreted as indicating that the more severe form of the disorder is more likely to be the type that "runs in families."

In addition to their ability to document familial relationships, family studies have provided data to support the validity of GAD as a distinctive diagnosis. Weissman (1990) reported results of three family studies, which indicated:

- Rates of panic disorder were not different among relatives of GAD patients compared to normal controls.
- Rates of GAD were not different among relatives of panic patients versus controls.
- Rates of GAD were higher among relatives of GAD patients (19.5 of 100) compared to relatives of panic patients (5.4 of 100) or normal controls (5.3 of 100).

Similar results were presented by Noyes et al. (1992). There was a higher frequency of GAD in families of GAD patients when compared to families of panic disorder patients. In contrast, there was more panic disorder in families of panic disorder patients than in families of GAD patients.

The majority of these studies assessed all available first-degree relatives. Other investigations have examined increased familial prevalence by focusing more specifically on the parent-child relationship. These studies are one of two types:

1. Those in which a child with an anxiety disorder is the proband and the rates of anxiety disorders in the parents are assessed.
2. Those in which the proband is an adult with an anxiety disorder and the investigator seeks to establish the incidence and prevalence of anxiety disorders in the patients' children.

Studies of Children of Patients with Anxiety Disorders

In an early study examining prevalence of anxiety disorders in parents and their children, offspring of panic patients or depressed patients were more anxious and depressed than offspring of normal control parents, whereas there were few differences between children of the two patient groups (Sylvester, Hyde, & Reichler, 1988). However, offspring of panic patients reported higher trait anxiety than any other group, and children of depressed parents reported fewer pleasurable experiences and more depression than normal controls, suggesting some specificity between parent disorder and children's symptoms. In a more recent study, children of patients with panic disorder were found to have significantly more severe diagnoses and a greater number of diagnoses than offspring of parents with animal phobias or no disorder (Unnewehr, Schneider, Florin, & Margraf, 1998). In this study, children of patients with panic disorder had significantly higher rates of separation anxiety disorder (SAD) than the other two groups. However, the evidence for a specific relationship between parental panic disorder and childhood SAD is controversial. Although some studies have indicated a relationship (e.g., Martin, Cabrol, Bouvard, Lepine, & Mouren-Simeoni, 1999; Unnewehr et al., 1998), other studies have not (e.g., Biederman et al., 2001). To examine the issue of specific transmission of anxiety disorders versus a general anxiety "proneness," Biederman and colleagues evaluated familial predisposition of anxiety and depressive disorders in a sample of 380 children. There was mixed support for familial transmission of anxiety proneness and perhaps for the specific transmission of panic and agoraphobia. Overall, children of parents with both anxiety and depressive disorders were at greatest risk for multiple diagnoses.

The substantial impact of comorbid anxiety and depression also has been illustrated in the results of other investigations. For example, anxiety disorders were more common in children whose parents had early-onset major depression disorder (MDD) than in children of normal controls (Warner, Mufson, & Weissman, 1995), but there were no differences in rates of anxiety disorder among offspring of parents with panic disorder and depression, panic disorder without depression, and normal controls. An offspring's risk of anxiety disorder was increased by proband recurrent early-onset major depression and impaired functioning in the co-parent. Furthermore, the relationship between major depression in the parent and panic spectrum disorders in the offspring was largely due to the family's chaotic environment. The authors' definition of anxiety disorder was very broad, including subthreshold conditions such as limited symptom attacks, near panic attacks, and situational panic attacks. When rates for presence of *DSM-IV* anxiety disorders were compared, the only group difference was that offspring of probands with panic plus major depression had higher rates of separation anxiety disorder than offspring of normal controls.

Behavioral inhibition (Kagan, 1982, see later discussion) describes a child's degree of sociability as displayed by behaviors ranging along an approach-withdrawal dimension. Briefly, inhibited children consistently emit few spontaneous vocalizations when in the presence of a stranger and cry and cling to their mothers rather than approach other children in play settings. These behaviors resemble those of individuals who consider themselves "shy or socially phobic" although empirical studies relating these constructs have yet to be conducted. Rosenbaum et al. (1988) compared rates of behavioral inhibition in the offspring of four groups: panic disorder patients with or without comorbid major depression, major depression alone, and a psychiatric control group, and found that 86% of the panic disorder offspring were judged to be "behaviorally inhibited" compared to 70% of the anxious and depressed group, 50% in the major depression only group, and 15% in the psychiatric control group. More recent studies from this group of investigators started with "behaviorally inhibited children" and examined psychopathology in the parents. A discussion of results of those studies is presented later in this chapter.

In an early study, Turner, Beidel, and Costello (1987) reported that children of anxiety probands were:

- Almost three times as likely to have a psychiatric disorder as the children of dysthymic patients.
- Twice as likely as the children of dysthymic parents to have an anxiety disorder.
- More than nine times as likely to have a psychiatric disorder as the children of normal parents.

More recently, Beidel and Turner (1997) replicated these results with a much larger sample. Rates of anxiety disorders among offspring were 33% for children of anxious parents, 21% for children of depressed parents, 33% for children of anxious and depressed parents, and 8% for children of normal control parents. Furthermore, offspring of anxious parents were significantly more likely to have only anxiety disorders, whereas offspring of depressed or mixed anxious/depressed parents had a broader range of disorders and higher rates of comorbidity. Similarly, McClure, Brennan, Hammen, and LeBrocque (2001) examined the relationship between parental and child anxiety/depressive disorders in a sample of 816 children age 15. Findings revealed that after parental depression was covaried out, a maternal (but not paternal) anxiety disorder significantly predicted anxiety disorders in children. In summary, rates of anxiety disorders are higher in children with parents with emotional disorders but not specifically just parents with anxiety disorders. Finally, in one of the few studies to focus specifically on the offspring of parents with social phobia (Mancini, Van Ameringen, Szatmari, & Fugere, 1996), 49% of the offspring met criteria for an anxiety disorder including overanxious disorder (30%), social phobia (23%), and separation anxiety disorder (19%). In summary, all of these studies provide data indicating that anxiety disorders "run in families," but do not indicate the specific mode of transmission.

STUDIES OF RELATIVES OF CHILDREN WHO HAVE ANXIETY DISORDERS

Several studies have examined the incidence and prevalence of anxiety disorders in the relatives of children with anxiety disorders. Last and her colleagues (Last, Hersen, Kazdin, Francis, & Grubb, 1987; Last, Hersen, Kazdin, Orvaschel, & Ye, 1990) conducted an extensive family investigation of the first- and second-degree relatives of child probands diagnosed with anxiety disorders. In addition, relatives of children with attention-deficit hyperactivity disorder and normal controls were included in one study (Last et al., 1990). There was an increased risk for anxiety disorders in the first- and second-degree relatives of children with anxiety disorders when compared to relatives of normal control children. Similarly, there was a trend for increased risk for anxiety disorders in the first- and second-degree relatives of children with anxiety disorders when compared to relatives of children with attention-deficit disorder.

Behavioral Inhibition and Anxiety Disorders

Rosenbaum and Biederman and their colleagues (Biederman et al., 1990; Hirshfeld, Biederman, Brody, Faraone, & Rosenbaum, 1997; Rosenbaum et al., 1991, 1992) examined the existence of parental pathology in "behaviorally inhibited" children. Results indicated that there was higher rate of parental anxiety disorders among behaviorally inhibited children, but primarily among those children who also had anxiety disorders. Rates of parental pathology were not higher among children who had only behavioral inhibition (e.g., Rosenbaum et al., 1992). In one of the few long-term outcome studies of children initially identified as vulnerable (i.e., behaviorally inhibited), Hirshfeld et al. (1992) reported that children who maintained a stable pattern of behavioral inhibition (over a five- to six-year period) were significantly more likely to have anxiety disorders, and in particular, phobic disorders. When reassessed at ages 13 to 14, children from the original Harvard cohort who had been designated as behaviorally inhibited were diagnosed with social phobia "more frequently" than children who were initially judged as uninhibited (Kagan, 1997). In contrast, there were no differences in rates of specific phobias, separation anxiety, or compulsive symptoms. However, the report did not indicate if "more frequently" represented a statistically significant difference. As noted by Turner, Beidel, and Wolff (1996), there are methodological limitations to each of these investigations that require cautious interpretation of the findings. For an extended review and discussion of these studies, see Turner, Beidel, and Wolff.

Twin Studies

In addition to family studies, twin studies also address hypotheses about genetic contributions. Torgersen (1983) reported that the proband-wise concordance rate for any anxiety disorders category, with the exception of GAD, was higher for monozygotic (MZ) than for dizygotic (DZ) twins. The overall concordance rate for MZ twins was 34% compared to 17% for DZ twins, but no co-twin had the same anxiety disorder as the proband, and concordance rates for GAD were higher for DZ than MZ twins. Thus, the data did not support a one-to-one genetic transmission. Andrews, Stewart, Allen, and Henderson (1990) reached similar conclusions. Initially, Kendler, Neale, Kessler, Heath, and Eaves (1992a, 1992b), based on a study of 1,033 female-female twin pairs, reported that GAD is a moderately familial disorder with heritability estimates of about 30%, but more recently, Hettema, Prescott, and Kendler (2001) reported a more modest heritability of GAD ranging from 15% to 20%. Rasmussen (1993) noted that twin studies of OCD patients also support the heritability of a neurotic anxiety factor, but not a specific OCD factor. Using 4,042 twin pairs from the Vietnam era twin registry, True et al. (1993) demonstrated that heritability plays a substantial role in susceptibility to PTSD symptoms; and Kendler and his colleagues (Kendler et al., 1992a, 1992b) reported that the familial aggregation of agoraphobia, social phobia, situational phobics, and specific phobia was consistent with "phobia proneness," with heritability estimates indicating that "genetic factors play a significant but by no means overwhelming role in the etiology of phobias" (Kendler et al., 1992b, p. 279). Individual-specific environmental effects appeared to account for twice as much variance in liability as did the genetic factors. Perna, Caldirola, Arancio, and Bellodi (1997) investigated the role of genetic factors in panic disorder in a sample of MZ and DZ twins. There was a high concordance rate among MZ rather than DZ twins with panic disorder (73% vs. 0%), but rates for sporadic panic attacks did not show the same association (57% vs. 43%). Thus, all of these studies are consistent in noting evidence for the heritability of some general factor, but not necessarily for a specific anxiety disorder.

In summary, some general trends appear to be consistent across all studies that have used family or twin designs in the search for a genetic etiology. First, significantly higher rates of anxiety disorders appear in the families of anxiety probands when compared to normal controls. However, when other types of psychopathology are included (e.g., a psychiatric control group), the outcome becomes less clear. Significant differences among psychiatric groups for familial prevalence or morbidity risks are not always evident. At this time, twin studies do not support the direct transmission of a particular anxiety disorder. Therefore, at least two other factors warrant consideration in explaining the observed familial pattern:

1. The increased prevalence rates among the probands' families could reflect the stress of coping with a psychiatrically ill individual in the family structure.
2. Some underlying vulnerability is manifested in different fashions, dependent on environmental circumstances.

PSYCHOLOGICAL AND BIOLOGICAL ASSESSMENT

The issue of vulnerability is one that has been noted consistently throughout this chapter. Numerous investigators have attempted to shed light on this concept from several different perspectives. Non-human primate studies of individual differences in anxiety have significant implications for the study of vulnerability in humans. There are substantial individual differences both in the intensity and range of anxiety-like behaviors in infant and juvenile rhesus monkeys (Suomi, 1986). When in novel situations or when separated from familiar surroundings, some infant monkeys show evidence of behavioral, autonomic, and endocrinological signs of fearfulness, while others respond with exploratory or play behaviors (Suomi, Kraemer, Baysinger, & Delizio, 1981). Longitudinal studies indicate that these characteristics remain stable throughout adolescence and young adulthood. Furthermore, it appears that environmental conditions cannot alter completely constitutional vulnerability. When faced with challenging situations, biological monkey siblings "adopted away" at birth and raised in adoptive families continued to show greater similarity in both cortisol levels and behavioral fear scores than the similarity between adopted siblings (Suomi, 1986).

Kagan and his associates (Kagan, 1982; Kagan, Reznick, & Snidman, 1987; Kagan, Reznick, Snidman, Gibbons, & Johnson, 1988; Reznick et al., 1986) have conducted a series of studies on behavioral inhibition (BI). From an initial pool of 300 children, these investigators identified 60 children who consistently displayed inhibited or uninhibited behaviors in the presence of novel events (Kagan, 1982). Inhibited children were those who cried, clung to their mothers when approached by a stranger, were reluctant to interact with their peers in a play situation, and emitted few spontaneous vocalizations when in the presence of an unknown investigator. When placed in these situations, inhibited children had higher heart rates and less heart-rate variability than the noninhibited children, and the preponderance of evidence supports the usefulness of the BI construct.

However, although BI is a stable pattern of behavior for some children, others become less inhibited with increasing age. Thus, specific behaviors defining BI do not appear to be immutable even if they have a biological basis (Turner, Beidel, & Wolff, 1996). However, the *tendency* to react in an inhibited fashion, under particular environmental circumstances, might be biologically based (see Turner, Beidel, & Wolff, 1996, for an extended discussion of BI and its relationship to anxiety disorders).

An initial study that addressed another aspect of biological vulnerability was reported by Turner, Beidel, and Epstein (1991). Skin conductance responses of children with an anxiety disorder were compared to normal controls when presented with novel or fear-producing stimuli, including a 100 db tone and a picture of a snake that appears ready to strike (see Turner et al., 1991, for assessment details). With respect to skin conductance, exposure to the tone or the snake resulted in a significantly higher mean response amplitude for the anxious children, indicative of increased arousal. In addition, anxious children had five times the number of spontaneous fluctuations during baseline and tone condition, and twice the number of spontaneous fluctuations during the snake condition. Furthermore, habituation rates were significantly lower among the anxious children than normal controls. Interestingly, both groups of children reported only minimal levels of subjective distress during the assessment. A more recent investigation (Turner, Beidel, Roberson-Nay, & Tervo, 2001) replicated these results using a group of children who did not have an anxiety disorder but were the offspring of a patient with an anxiety disorder (i.e., a high-risk sample). Results indicated that children without an anxiety diagnosis, but who were the offspring of a parent with a diagnosis, had significantly more spontaneous fluctuations (skin conductance) than children of normal controls or children of depressed parents. In addition, these children were less likely to habituate (as measured by skin conductance response) to repeated presentations of the same stimulus, whereas the offspring of normal control parents habituated rapidly. Unlike the earlier Turner et al. (1991) study, where these differences may have been attributed to the child's psychopathology, results of this second study suggest that children of anxious parents who do not themselves have a disorder show similar psychophysiological characteristics as those who have a disorder when exposed to fearful or novel stimuli. This suggests that these children might have vulnerability features that could predispose them to develop maladaptive anxiety.

The studies reviewed to this point have focused on general vulnerability and indicate that certain individuals may be more prone or vulnerable to anxiety reactions. However, none of these studies provided any indication about the exact nature of the vulnerability. In the following sections, other research investigations that have sought to determine if specific structures or neurochemicals are related to the anxiety disorders are discussed.

STRUCTURAL, FUNCTIONAL, AND NEUROCHEMICAL ABNORMALITIES IN THE ANXIETY DISORDERS

Historically, most studies addressing biological parameters in anxiety disorders have directed their research endeavors at panic disorder. During the late 1970s and early 1980s, a high prevalence of mitral valve prolapse in patients with panic attacks was reported (e.g., Gorman, Fyer, Glicklich, King, & Klein, 1981), but subsequent studies found that the prevalence rate was no higher than in the general population (e.g., Kathol et al., 1980; Shear, Devereux, Kranier-Fox, Mann, & Frances, 1984). The vestibular system has also been the subject of investigation as a correlate of panic disorder. Jacob, Moller, Turner, and Wall (1985) reported that 67% of 21 panic disorder or agoraphobic patients had some type of vestibular abnormality. In 39% of those with an abnormality, results were consistent with a peripheral vestibular lesion. This study was replicated using a much larger sample of patients, including those with panic disorder and no agoraphobia to mild agoraphobia, panic disorder with moderate to severe agoraphobia, anxiety disorders but no panic attacks, depression, and normal controls (Jacob et al., 1996). Vestibular laboratory abnormalities were common in all groups, but most prevalent in patients with panic disorder with moderate to severe agoraphobia. The dysfunction was associated with presence of vestibular symptoms between panic attacks and with ratings of space and motion discomfort and could not be explained by higher patient subjective distress during the tasks. These findings suggest that many agoraphobics rely on visual or proprioceptive cues for spatial orientation to compensate for their disordered vestibular system, thus avoiding or fearing situations such as heights, open spaces, long corridors, tunnels, or shopping malls where visual spatial cues are misleading or absent (Jacob et al., 1996). The findings from this study hold significant implications for theories of the etiology of agoraphobia.

Other studies attempted to evaluate biochemical changes when panic is produced in the laboratory. Initial studies focused on inducing panic by infusing panic patients with lactate (e.g., Pitts & McClure, 1967). Subsequently, numerous challenge paradigms were developed and substances that appear to induce panic include lactate, bicarbonate, CO, caffeine, yohimbine, tricyclic antidepressants, isoprenaline, noradrenaline, chlorimipramine, MCPP, flumazenil, cholecystokinin, and hypoglycemia (Nutt & Lawson, 1992). In addition, panic can be induced by hyperventilation and through behavioral methods such as putting claustrophobics in confining places (Rachman, 1988). Only lactate and flumazenil appear to induce panic only in panic patients and not other anxiety patients. Reactivity to so many different substances suggests many different neurochemical and neurobiological systems, several of which contradict each other. There is also the problem of expectancy effects (see Turner et al., 1988). Furthermore, these studies have serious methodological limitations, including:

- Inadequate criteria for defining panic attacks.
- Strict reliance on patient report that a panic attack was occurring.
- Use of only single-blind criteria.
- Failure to account for group differences in baseline anxiety levels.

When baseline differences are considered, there appear to be no differences in the responses of panic patients compared to other diagnostic or control groups (see Margraf, Ehlers, & Roth, 1986, for a complete discussion). To summarize, it is likely that the laboratory findings are influenced by non-biological factors present in the individual or the environment. Of late, there appears to be little interest in further pursuing this line of research.

Other investigators have pursued the potential etiological roles of catecholamines, norepinephrine, and serotonin for many of the anxiety disorders. Although the relationship between increased catecholamine levels and stress is well documented, there is little conclusive evidence that levels of catecholamines are higher in chronically anxious patients when compared to normal controls. Findings of group differences (Liebowitz, Fyer, et al., 1985; Mathew, Ho, Francis, Taylor, & Weinman, 1982) have been reported as often as no group differences (Ballenger et al., 1984; Nesse, Cameron, Curtis, McCann, & Huber-Smith, 1984). More recently, there has been an acknowledgment that none of these systems function in isolation. For example, investigations have focused on both the noradrenergic system and the corticotropin-releasing factor (CRF) system, both of which appear to be the central systems responsible for stress responses and to cross-regulate their activities. An excellent review of the relationship of the noradrenergic system to pathological anxiety is provided by Sullivan, Coplan, Kent, and Gorman (1999; see review for specific details). With respect to the CRF system, Heim and Nemeroff (1999) examined the relationship of CRF to early life stress, anxiety, and depression. A high density of CRF neurons is found in the hypothalamus (which mediates behavioral stress responses and cognitive appraisal of stress situations) and the amygdala (which is involved in the processing of emotions). In animals, the central administration of CRF produces physiologic and behavioral responses characteristic of depression and anxiety. In addition, preclinical studies suggest that early life stress results in persistent CRF hyperactivity in these brain centers and increased stress reactivity in adulthood (Heim & Nemeroff, 1999; Sanchez, Ladd, & Plotsky, 2001). These adverse experiences include animal models of separation and loss, abuse or neglect, and social deprivation. Although further research is necessary, these findings suggest that early life experiences may produce vulnerability, which could put an individual at risk for the development of anxiety and/or depressive disorders.

A review by Tancer (1993) found few data to support a biological basis for social phobia. Infusions of lactate or epinephrine did not produce phobic symptoms in social phobic patients. Caffeine did induce anxiety, but the symptoms were not those experienced by social phobic patients in social settings. Furthermore, there does not appear to be any global dysfunction in either the hypothalamic-pituitary adrenal (HPA) or hypothalamic-pituitary-thyroid (HPT) endocrine axes (Tancer, 1993). Catecholamine responses when giving a speech did not differ between social phobics and normal volunteers (Levin et al., 1989). Finally, neuroendocrine challenges for the noradrenergic, serotonergic, and dopaminergic systems indicate that there may be some dysregulation in serotonergic transmission, but activity in the noradrenergic and dopaminergic systems remain normal (Tancer, 1993).

Among all of the neurotransmitters that have been studied, most research has examined the relationship between serotonin functioning and the anxiety disorders. An early review of this literature can be found in R. S. Kahn, van Praag, Wetzler, Asnis, and Barr (1988). In brief, much of the interest in serotonin is derived from the successful results of pharmacological trials of potent serotonergic drugs in patients with anxiety disorders, leading investigators (correctly or incorrectly) to hypothesize abnormal serotonin functioning as an etiological determinant (see section on treatment for a review of biological treatment studies). Early studies reported decreased number of serotonin uptake sites in blood platelets (Weizman, Carmi, & Hermesh, 1986), but the findings were not replicated (Bastani, Arora, & Meltzer, 1991; Insel, Mueller, Gillin, Siever, & Murphy, 1985). Similarly, a few studies have reported an increase in cerebrospinal fluid 5-HIAA (serotonin) in OCD patients (Insel et al., 1985); however, these findings also have not been replicated (see McDougle, Barr, Goodman, & Price, 1999; Turner, Beidel, Stanley, et al., 2001, for a review). Finally, laboratory studies using various challenge tasks have reported mixed results; some studies report increased 5-HT (serotonin) mediated responses, whereas others report normal or decreased responses (Fineberg, Cowen, Kirk, & Montgomery, 1994; Hewlett, Vinogradov, Martin, Berman, & Csernansky, 1992; Hollander et al., 1992; Lopez-Ibor, Saiz, & Vinas, 1994; Lucey, Butcher, O'Flynn, Clare, & Dinan, 1994). These conflicting results indicate that 5-HT mediated neuroendocrine responses probably do not play an important role in the pathophysiology of OCD (Fineberg et al., 1994).

Others have directed their attention to the role of basal ganglia dysfunction in OCD. Rapoport (1991) proposed that dysfunction of the basal ganglia-thalamic frontal cortical loops produces symptoms, such as excessive grooming, checking, and doubting behaviors. Data from clinical trials of trichotillomania, nail biting, and canine acral lick dermatitis demonstrated that clomipramine was superior to desipramine in remediating each of these behaviors. Furthermore, fluoxetine treatment for canine acral lick dermatitis also resulted in decreased grooming behaviors. Thus, Rapoport proposed that the basal ganglia is a repository for species-typical behavior and the frontal cortex-basal ganglia-thalamic circuit is the center for phylogenetic self-protective behaviors such as grooming or checking. In those with OCD, trichotillomania, nail biting, or dogs with acral lick dermatitis, this system has gone awry (see Rapoport, 1991, for an extensive discussion of this issue). Although intriguing, this hypothesis is not without its difficulties. First, no specific dysregulation or neuroanatomical abnormality has been identified (although neuroimaging studies described later suggest some possibilities). Second, as noted by Rapoport, this model cannot account for the efficacy of behavioral treatment. Third, anatomically, existence of these basal ganglia "loops" is still undetermined.

The past ten years also has witnessed a plethora of structural and functional neuroimaging studies designed to detect abnormalities primarily in OCD patients. A thorough review of this literature is beyond the scope of this chapter (see Turner, Beidel, Stanley, et al., 2001, for a review). In brief, structural imaging using computerized tomography (CT) or magnetic resonance imaging (MRI) has not resulted in any conclusive data that would document structural brain abnormalities. With respect to functional neuroimaging studies, PET and SPECT neuroimaging studies provide some limited support for a basal ganglia dysfunction. Initially, Baxter (1992) concluded that the preponderance of the data provides evidence of abnormalities in the orbital prefrontal cortex. The caudate nucleus also may be involved although the data are less consistent. Three studies have noted that effective treatment of OCD (either with medication or behavior therapy) reduced the abnormalities, although not all studies have noted decreases in the same regions. In a study of possible predictors of treatment response to both behavioral and pharmacotherapy in OCD patients, Brody et al. (1998) examined PET scan results of glucose metabolic rates in the orbitofrontal cortex and anterior cingulate gyrus. Results indicated that the left orbitofrontal cortex alone was predictive of treatment response in those treated with behavior therapy but not those treated with fluoxetine. Activation of the left orbitofrontal cortex also has been reported in non-treated OCD patients (Adler et al., 2000). Furthermore, although psychological challenge studies (i.e., exposing OCD patients to feared contaminants during PET or SPECT scans) appear to implicate the orbitofrontal cortex, anterior cingulate, striatum, and thalamus (Trivedi, 1996), pharmacological challenges do not implicate any one particular site (see Turner, Beidel, Stanley, et al., 2001, for a review). In fact, Insel and Winslow (1992) and Trivedi (1996) noted a number of limitations of all of these functional neuroimaging studies, including different technologies, different scanning environments, different methods for analyzing and comparing regions, small sample sizes coupled with multiple comparisons, anatomical ambiguity, and the issue of epiphenomenon versus causality. Finally, as noted by Turner, Beidel, Stanley, et al. (2001), although the data often document differences between OCD patients and normal controls, there are no differences when an anxious control group (such as those with PTSD) is included in the analysis. Thus, these findings may reflect the presence of an anxiety state rather than one particular disorder. In summary, the results of all of these studies still provide only equivocal support for the etiological role of biological factors in anxiety disorders.

DIAGNOSTIC CONSIDERATIONS

As noted, a clear advancement of the *DSM-IV* was acknowledgment (long known by experienced clinicians) that individuals with anxiety disorders *other* than panic disorder also have panic attacks. Thus, one diagnostic consideration when assessing a primary complaint of panic attacks pertains to the stimuli under which the attacks occur. Similarly, presenting complaints of specific phobias of knives (Barlow, 1988) or thunderstorms (Turner & Beidel, 1988) may indicate presence of a more pervasive anxiety disorder, such as OCD. Patients with extensive washing rituals often present at dermatology clinics with contact dermatitis. Similarly, the OCD-related condition of dysmorphophobia often is found in the plastic surgeon's office (Rasmussen & Eisen, 1992). Among a sample of 80 outpatients seeking treatment for anxiety disorders, 7% met criteria for body dysmorphic disorder (BDD; Wilhelm, Otto, Zucker, & Pollack, 1997). Among patients with BDD, rates were highest for social phobia (12%), with the onset of social phobia preceding the onset of BDD.

Differential diagnosis often is difficult because of the substantial comorbidity among the anxiety disorders. For example, Brown and Barlow (1992) reported that 50% of anxiety patients with a principal anxiety disorder had at least one other clinically significant anxiety or depressive disorder. Among panic-disordered patients, 20% had secondary GAD, whereas 36% of panic-disordered patients with mild agoraphobia also had secondary GAD. A high rate of comorbidity also has been reported for panic disorder and specific phobias, with 65% of panic patients in one study also meeting criteria for a specific phobia (Starcevic & Bogojevic, 1997). Nine percent of social phobics also had secondary panic disorder, and 29% of patients with primary GAD had secondary social phobia, as did 24% of OCD patients. Seventeen percent of OCD patients had a lifetime prevalence of eating disorders (Rasmussen & Eisen, 1992). As to GAD, those presenting at anxiety disorders clinics typically do not have a singular diagnosis of GAD. Only 26% of primary GAD patients had GAD as the sole diagnosis (Brawman-Mintzer et al., 1993). The most common comorbid diagnoses were social phobia (23%) and specific phobia (21%). Forty-two percent of GAD patients had a major depressive episode in their lifetimes. In fact, some research has found GAD to share some of the same genetic factors as major depression (Kendler, 1996; Kendler, Neale, Kessler, Heath, & Eaves, 1992c). Prevalence of GAD across all of the other diagnostic categories has led some investigators to suggest that it may not be a distinct disorder, but perhaps the basis from which other disorders arise and the residual state often remaining following treatment for other specific disorders (Turner & Beidel,

1989a, 1989b). Brown, Barlow, and Liebowitz (1994) provided some evidence for the validity of GAD, but diagnostic unreliability and high rates of comorbidity continue to plague this diagnostic category.

In addition to comorbidity among the anxiety disorders, anxiety and depressive states share many symptoms, leading some investigators to suggest that many anxiety disorders, most specifically OCD and PD, are merely variants of depressive disorder. However, the bulk of evidence based on actual symptoms, childhood characteristics and childhood events, differential predictors of outcome, personality characteristics, and analysis of genetic models based on large samples of twin data support the hypothesis that anxiety and depression are indeed different disorders (e.g., Kendler, Heath, Martin, & Eaves, 1987). Kendler et al. examined anxiety and depressive symptoms in an unselected sample of twins (3,798 pairs). Based on factor analytic scores, symptoms of anxiety and depression tend to form separate symptom clusters (depression-distress and general anxiety), and it is the environment rather than any specific genetic influence that is depressogenic or anxiogenic.

Although depression and anxiety may be separate disorders, the clinician is still confronted with distinguishing between affective states that often have a high rate of concordance. One method for drawing distinctions has been to examine the disorder's etiology and designate as "primary" the one with the earliest age of onset. Thus, secondary depression is defined as depression that occurs after the onset of the anxiety disorder. Along these lines, Parker and colleagues (Parker, Wilhelm, & Asghari, 1997; Parker, et al., 1999) reported that depression before age 25 was associated with family history of anxiety, early childhood expressions of anxiety, and lifetime episode of an anxiety disorder. Secondary depression is common among anxiety patients, with estimates ranging from 17.5% to 60% and averaging approximately 30% to 35% for panic disorder and agoraphobic patients (Barlow et al., 1986; Breier, Charney, & Heninger, 1984; Lesser et al., 1988; Uhde et al., 1985; Van Valkenburg, Akiskal, Puzantian, & Rosenthal, 1984). Using epidemiological data, Andrade, Eaton, and Chilcoat (1994) reported that 2.1% of their total sample was comorbid for panic attacks and major depression. However, 62% of those with panic attacks reported presence of a dysphoric mood.

Another method of determining primacy is to determine the longitudinal course of the disorders. Breier et al. (1984) examined the course of depression in 60 patients with agoraphobia or panic disorder. Seventy percent had an episode of depression, with 43% reporting that depression occurred before the first panic attack. The average time between remission of the depression and the subsequent onset of the panic attack was four years. In contrast, 57% of those patients who had both anxiety and depressive disorders reported that the depression occurred following the onset of the panic. For those patients, symptoms of panic, anticipatory anxiety, and generalized anxiety were chronic and unremitting, while symptoms of depression were episodic in nature, with 63% of those patients having remissions of depression that lasted for one year or more (Breier et al., 1986). In such cases, the depressive disorder would clearly be seen as secondary to the anxiety disorder. Similarly, M. Fava et al. (2000) examined comorbidity rates and clinical impact of anxiety disorders to major depression. Comorbid anxiety disorders were present in 50% of patients, with social phobia (27%), simple phobia (17%), panic disorder (14.5%), and generalized anxiety disorder (10%) as the most common diagnoses. Furthermore, the authors found that both social phobia and generalized anxiety disorder preceded the first major depressive episode in approximately 65% of cases, while panic disorder (21%) and agoraphobia (14%) were much less likely to precede the first major depressive episode than to emerge subsequently. These findings also indicate different temporal relationships between major depression and comorbid anxiety disorders.

Using data from the ECA study, Regier et al. (1998) also examined co-occurrence of anxiety disorders and mood disorders. Forty-seven percent of subjects meeting criteria for major depression also had at least one comorbid anxiety disorder. Moreover, among depressed subjects, social phobia showed the youngest age of onset (11.5 years) as compared to panic disorder with a much later age of onset (23 years). Thus, similar to the findings of M. Fava et al. (2000), it appears that certain anxiety disorders (e.g., social phobia) may pose specific risk factors for the onset of major depression, while depression may represent a specific predisposing factor for other anxiety disorders (e.g., panic disorder).

Depression also is common in OCD, where the majority of patients may experience at least some dysphoric mood (Barlow et al., 1986). Again, the most common distinction has been based on the chronological onset of the disorders. Depression that occurs after the onset of OCD is considered secondary. Even though considered secondary, presence of significant depression in a patient with OCD could have important treatment implications. Recent research has attempted to determine personality dimensions that may be able to differentiate the two disorders. For example, in a comparison of OCD and MDD patients, Kusunoki et al. (2000) reported that OCD patients were significantly lower on the trait of novelty-seeking than MDD patients or controls.

Often, it is necessary to differentiate between patients with anxiety that represents one symptom of a primary Axis II personality disorder and those who truly manifest comorbid Axis I and II disorders. For example, although individuals with paranoid personality disorder are often anxious when in the company of others, their anxiety stems from concern about the motives of others. This differs from social phobics, who fear doing something to humiliate or embarrass themselves when in the company of others. However, even with careful diagnosis and the use of hierarchical diagnostic rules, there will be a subset of individuals with anxiety disorders and personality disorders. Several investigators (Mavissakalian & Hamann, 1986, 1988; Pollack et al. 1992; Reich & Noyes, 1987; Rennenberg, Chambless, & Gracely, 1992) reported Axis II disorders in approximately 30% to 56% of panic patients—primarily histrionic, dependent, avoidant, and obsessive-compulsive subtypes. Turner et al. (1991) found that 41% of a socially phobic sample met criteria for a personality disorder, most commonly avoidant personality disorder or obsessive-compulsive personality disorder. In fact, introversion and depressive symptoms correctly predicted the presence (or absence) of avoidant personality disorder in 85% of a sample of social phobics (Van Velzen, Emmelkamp, & Scholing, 2000). Cluster C (anxious) personality disorders were identified in 17% of patients with GAD, whereas 2% of GAD patients had cluster B (unstable) personality disorder. The most common Axis II disorders in OCD patients are avoidant, histrionic, and paranoid personality disorders (Sciuto et al., 1991), and there is evidence that those with OCD and comorbid schizotypal symptoms, which may account for up to 20% of obsessive-compulsive patients, have a significantly poorer prognosis than those without such features (Jenike, Baer, Minichiello, Schwartz, & Carey, 1986; Stanley, Turner, & Borden, 1990). Furthermore, evidence indicates that OCD patients with schizotypal symptoms represent a specific subgroup of OCD and can be distinguished by earlier age of onset of OCD symptoms, a higher number of comorbid diagnoses, and higher rates of learning disabilities (Sobin, Blundell, Weiller, et al., 2000).

In summary, differential diagnosis is necessary to fully understand the psychopathology of anxiety disorders. Moreover, certain treatments that may be effective for one disorder may be relatively ineffective for another. Although differentiation is possible, it can be complicated because a substantial percentage of anxiety patients are comorbid for an additional anxiety disorder, a depressive disorder, or a personality disorder. In the majority of cases, patients with additional diagnoses appear to be more symptomatic (Curtis et al., 1998; Jenike et al., 1986; Mavissakalian & Hamann, 1988; Turner & Beidel, 1989a, 1989b) and may have a poorer treatment prognosis (Brown, Antony, et al., 1995; Mavissakalian & Hamann, 1988).

GENDER, RACIAL, AND ETHNIC ISSUES

The Epidemiological Catchment Area (ECA) Survey was the first modern comprehensive epidemiological survey of psychopathology in the United States. One of the findings was that African Americans had higher lifetime prevalence than Whites for simple phobia and agoraphobia (Blazer et al., 1985; Robins et al., 1984). The lifetime prevalence for panic disorder was 1.2% for African Americans and 1.4% for Whites. There were no differences in prevalence of anxiety disorders between Mexican Americans and non-Hispanic Whites. However, the data are difficult to interpret because the sampling strategy over-included severely disadvantaged African Americans (Baltimore and St. Louis sites) and elderly African Americans, under-included low-income African American males, and virtually excluded middle-class African Americans. There were no differences in symptom presentation, except that African Americans reported a higher mean number of symptoms during their worst episode. Similar sampling difficulties occurred with other minority participants. For example, Hispanics in the ECA study consisted solely of Mexican Americans in the Los Angeles area. The more recent National Comorbidity Study (NCS; Kessler et al., 1994) used a national sample and provides a clearer picture with respect to race and ethnicity. Based on the findings from this study, African Americans had anxiety disorder prevalence rates that were no different from those of Whites. Thus, the NCS findings are consistent with the ECA findings on panic disorder but not for specific phobia and agoraphobia. The NCS data also did not find any differences between Hispanics and Whites for any anxiety disorder.

Panic disorder without agoraphobia occurs twice as often in women as in men (Eaton et al., 1994, 1998; Reed & Wittchen, 1998), and panic disorder with agoraphobia occurs three times as often in women as in men (APA, 1994). Those with panic disorder and agoraphobia constitute more than 50% of patients seeking treatment at anxiety disorders clinics (Barlow et al., 1986; Chambless, 1982). Epidemiological data suggest that social phobia is more common in women, but the genders are equally represented in clinic samples. Among individuals with situational, animal, and natural environment phobia types, 75% to 90% are female (except for heights, where 55% to 70% are female). Similarly, Curtis et al. (1998) reported that animal fears were most prevalent among women, while fear of heights was the most common among men. Among blood/injection/injury subtypes, 55% to 70% are female (Bienvenu & Eaton, 1998). Obsessive-compulsive disorder affects men and women in equal proportions (Turner & Beidel, 1989a). In epidemiological samples, about 3% of the population meets criteria for GAD, two thirds of whom are women (Wittchen & Hoyer, 2001). In clinical samples, approximately 55% to 60% of patients are women.

The data indicate that there likely are no differences in the rates of anxiety disorders with respect to various ethnic groups. There may be some differences, however, in the symptomatic expression of these disorders or in other conditions that covary with them. For example, *ataque de nervios* (attack of nerves) is a description used by Hispanics to describe a group of symptoms that bears some similarities to panic disorder. In addition to many of the same features of panic, *ataque de nervios* includes becoming hysterical, screaming, hitting self or others, breaking things, nervousness, and feeling depressed before or after the episode. These episodes typically occur in stressful situations, such as funerals or family disputes (Kirmayer, Young, & Hayton, 1995). Liebowitz et al. (1994) examined the presence of *ataque de nervios* and panic symptoms in 156 Hispanic patients seeking treatment for anxiety disorders. Results indicated that 70% reported at least one episode of *ataque de nervios* in their lifetime; 80% of those were female and 41.3% had panic disorder as a primary diagnosis. In this subgroup, 80% referred to their panic attacks as *ataque de nervios*. However, like the current reconceptualization of panic attacks, *ataque de nervios* was present in individuals with a variety of anxiety disorders as well as major depression. Common symptoms included increased rates of sweating, depersonalization, fear of going crazy, and fear of losing control. These findings suggest that *ataque de nervios* constitutes a condition that is broader than panic disorder. It remains unclear whether it is a separate condition or whether it is a culturally specific manifestation of the same vulnerabilities associated with panic.

Another example of cultural differences in the expression of anxious symptoms can be found in Japanese culture and *Taijin Kyofusho,* a form of social phobia. *Taijin Kyofusho* differs from social phobia in terms of the underlying (or core) feature of the disorder (Kirmayer, 2001; Kirmayer et al., 1995). In social phobia, individuals fear public evaluation, scrutiny, or humiliation. *Taijin Kyofusho,* however, consists of a core fear of offending and/or making others feel uncomfortable due to inappropriate social behavior or having some form of a physical blemish/ deformity. Kirmayer et al. (1995) have described this fear in terms of the importance of presenting oneself positively in the Japanese culture, and the importance of harmonious relationships and successful negotiation.

In their seminal article, Neal and Turner (1991) reviewed the literature on anxiety disorders in African Americans and noted the paucity of empirical data. There has been some improvement since that review, and studies are beginning to emerge addressing the epidemiology, clinical presentation, and treatment outcome for African Americans with anxiety disorders. As noted previously, the best epidemiological data suggest that prevalence rates are about the same for African Americans and Whites. Likewise, the clinical presentation of the anxiety disorders in African Americans appears to be similar in White patients.

Although the core features of anxiety disorders appear to be essentially the same for all racial and ethnic groups, secondary features or other syndromes may covary with the primary disorder and complicate the diagnostic process. Bell and Jenkins (1994) conducted substantial research on the phenomenon of isolated sleep paralysis. As described by these investigators, sleep paralysis, lasting from several seconds to a few minutes, is a state of consciousness that occurs while falling asleep or on awakening, during which time the individual is unable to move. The individual is fully conscious of the experience, which can be accompanied by terrifying hallucinations (hypnopompic or hypnagogic) and a sense of acute danger. After the paralysis passes, the individual may experience panic symptoms and the realization that the distorted perceptions were false. Sleep paralysis that occurs in the absence of narcolepsy is referred to as *isolated sleep paralysis.* Isolated sleep paralysis (ISP) appears to be far more common and recurring among African Americans than among White Americans or Nigerian Blacks (Bell, Hildreth, Jenkins, & Carter, 1988; Neal-Barnett & Crowther, 2000). Among a group of African American patients receiving treatment at a local health center, 41% reported occurrence of at least one episode of ISP (Bell & Jenkins, 1994). This is higher than the 15% that had been reported for Whites (Hufford, 1982). Furthermore, among African American patients who experience episodes of ISP, 36% reported the occurrence of panic attacks and 16% met criteria for panic disorder (Bell, Dixie-Bell, & Thompson, 1986). Bell and his colleagues have hypothesized that panic disorder in African Americans may be manifested differently than in White Americans, with recurrent ISP and increased frequency of panic attacks as the core features. Alternatively, ISP could be a culturally specific manifestation of the same underlying vulnerability responsible for panic. In fact, Bell and Jenkins have proposed a stress-response hypothesis to explain the relationship of panic, ISP, and high rates of essential hypertension in African Americans.

With respect to treatment-seeking behavior, Neighbors (1985) found that 87% of a sample of African Americans experiencing psychological distress sought help from an informal network. Among the 48% who sought help from professionals, 22% went to emergency rooms, 22% went to general physicians, and 19% went to ministers. Only 9% went to mental health clinicians. Thus, it does not appear that most African Americans seek help from mental health professionals (Paradis, Hatch, & Friedman, 1994) and thus, treatment outcome data are few. Chambless and Williams (1995) reported that both African American and White patients with agoraphobia benefited from an in vivo exposure program. However, African Americans were more severely phobic at pretreatment. At posttreatment, although both groups improved, African American patients were still more symptomatic. At follow-up, differences were less evident. It is unclear from these data, however, if these differences reflect symptom severity rather than racial group differences. Culturally sensitive factors were reported as important in the treatment outcome of an African American social phobic treated with Social Effectiveness Therapy (Fink, Turner, & Beidel, 1996). The treatment package used in this study was effective, but only when racial factors, central to the development of the disorder, specifically were included in the exposure program. This suggests that in certain cases, specifically addressing ethnicity or racial factors might be critical to achieving a positive treatment outcome.

Although relatively few psychotropic drug treatment studies report efficacy data for ethnic and racial groups, and still fewer studies are conducted to directly address this issue (Turner & Cooley-Quille, 1996), a growing number of studies demonstrate that various racial/ethnic groups respond differently to these drugs (Lin, 2001; Lin, Poland, & Silver, 1993). Asians consistently require smaller doses of tricyclic antidepressants (TCAs) than Caucasians to achieve the same therapeutic effect (Lin, Poland, & Lesser, 1986; Yamamoto, Fungi, Loa, & Reecho, 1979). Similarly, lower dosages of lithium and benzodiazepines are required in Asians to achieve the same results required by higher dosages in Caucasians. In addition, African Americans and Hispanics appear to respond to lower doses of TCAs than do Caucasians (Marcos & Cancro, 1982; Ziegler & Biggs, 1977).

Emerging data indicate that Hispanics and African Americans experience greater side effects than Caucasians from various pharmacological compounds, which suggests a difference in pharmacokinetics among various racial and ethnic groups (Lin et al., 1986; Matsuda, Cho, Lin, & Smith, 1995; Sellwood & Tarrier, 1994). It appears, then, that ethnicity and racial factors should be considered when various psychotropic drugs are used in the treatment of anxiety, and the control of these factors in drug treatment studies is essential to allow unambiguous interpretation of outcome and to make recommendations for use in treatment. Additionally, because cultural differences may exist in terms of patients' expectation of pharmacological treatment and compliance with prescribed medication regimens, it also is important to consider patient attitudes toward psychotropic drugs (Kirmayer & Minas, 2000).

SUMMARY

Over the past two decades, conceptualization of the anxiety disorders has undergone a radical evolution. Increased attention to classification and diagnostic differentiation, along with the high prevalence of these conditions in the general population, has contributed to a burgeoning interest in the area. Questions of etiology are emerging as central to our further understanding of the nature of these disorders and will, no doubt, intensely occupy the attention of researchers over the next decade. Currently, it seems clear that the anxiety disorders are familial, but the exact nature of this familial factor is poorly understood. Human and non-human primate data suggest that the high likelihood of early temperamental factors is related to increased vulnerability to anxiety in some individuals. Longitudinal studies with those considered to be at high risk are necessary to fully address the issue of vulnerability. However, based on the extant literature, the nature of this vulnerability is likely to be complex, encompassing biological, psychological, and environmental parameters.

Although many questions remain, there are now a number of treatment interventions (behavioral and drug) with demonstrated efficacy. Questions of efficacy for ethnic minority groups, however, are just now beginning to be addressed. Although the treatment for some of the anxiety disorders is better understood than others, such treatment of these disorders has evolved to the point that few additional advances are likely possible without increased understanding of the basic psychopathology and the further elucidation of the mechanisms of change.

REFERENCES

Aalto-Setaelae, T., Marttunen, M., Tuulio-Henriksson, A., & Loennqvist, J. (2001). One month prevalence of depression and other *DSM-IV* disorders among young adults. *Psychological Medicine, 31,* 791–801.

Abramowitz, J. S. (1997). Effectiveness of psychological and pharmacological treatments for obsessive-compulsive disorder: A quantitative review. *Journal of Consulting and Clinical Psychology, 65,* 44–52.

Acierno, R., Hersen, M., Van Hasselt, V. B., Tremont, G., & Meuser, K. T. (1994). Review of the validation and dissemination of eye-movement desensitization and reprocessing: A scientific and ethical dilemma. *Clinical Psychology Review, 14,* 287–299.

Adler, C. M., McDonough-Ryan, P., Sax, K. W., Holland, S. K., Arndt, S., & Strakowski, S. M. (2000). fMRI of neuronal activation with symptom provocation in unmedicated patients with obsessive compulsive disorder. *Journal of Psychiatric Research, 34,* 317–324.

Agras, W. S., Sylvester, D., & Oliveau, D. (1969). The epidemiology of common fear and phobia. *Comprehensive Psychiatry, 10,* 151–156.

Albus, M., & Scheibe, G. (1993). Outcome of panic disorder with or without concomitant depression: A two-year prospective follow-up study. *American Journal of Psychiatry, 150,* 1878–1880.

American Psychiatric Association. (1980). *Diagnostic and statistical manual of mental disorders* (3rd ed.). Washington, DC: Author.

American Psychiatric Association. (1987). *Diagnostic and statistical manual of mental disorders* (3rd ed., rev.). Washington, DC: Author.

American Psychiatric Association. (1994). *Diagnostic and statistical manual of mental disorders* (4th ed.). Washington, DC: Author.

Amies, P. L., Gelder, M. G., & Shaw, P. M. (1983). Social phobia: A comparative clinical study. *British Journal of Psychiatry, 142,* 174–179.

Andersch, S., Hanson, L., & Haellstroem, T. (1997). Panic disorder: A five year follow-up study in 52 patients. *European Journal of Psychiatry, 11,* 145–155.

Andrade, L., Eaton, W. W., & Chilcoat, H. (1994). Lifetime comorbidity of panic attacks and major depression in a population-based study: Symptom profiles. *British Journal of Psychiatry, 165,* 363–369.

Andrews, G., Stewart, G., Allen, R., & Henderson, A. S. (1990). The genetics of six anxiety disorders: A twin study. *Journal of Affective Disorders, 19,* 23–29.

Antony, M. M., Downie, F., & Swinson, R. P. (1998). Diagnostic issues and epidemiology in obsessive-compulsive disorder. In R. P. Swinson et al. (Eds.), *Obsessive-compulsive disorder: Theory research and treatment* (pp. 3–32). New York: Guilford Press.

AuBuchon, P. G., & Malatesta, V. J. (1994). Obsessive-compulsive patients with comorbid personality disorder: Associated problems and response to a comprehensive behavior therapy. *Journal of Clinical Psychiatry, 55,* 448–453.

Bailly, D. (1996). The role of beta-adrenoceptor blockers in the treatment of psychiatric disorders. *CNS Drugs, 5,* 115–136.

Ballenger, J. C. (1984). Psychopharmacology of the anxiety disorders. *Psychiatric Clinics of North America, 7,* 757–771.

Ballenger, J. C. (1986). Pharmacotherapy of the panic disorders. *Journal of Clinical Psychiatry, 47*(Suppl. 6), 27–32.

Ballenger, J. C. (1990). Efficacy of benzodiazepines in panic disorder and agoraphobia. *Journal of Psychiatric Research, 24*(Suppl. 2), 15–25.

Ballenger, J. C., Burrows, G. D., DuPont, R. L., Lesser, I. M., Noyes, R., Jr., Pecknold, J. C., et al. (1988). Alprazolam in panic disorder and agoraphobia: Results from a multicenter trial. *Archives of General Psychiatry, 45,* 413–422.

Ballenger, J. C., Lydiard, R. B., & Turner, S. M. (1995). The treatment of panic disorder and agoraphobia. In G. O. Gabbard (Editor-in-Chief), *Treatment of psychiatric disorders* (2nd ed., pp. 1422–1452). Washington, DC: American Psychiatric Press.

Ballenger, J. C., Peterson, G. A., Laraia, M., Hucek, A., Lake, C. R., Jimerson, D., et al. (1984). A study of plasma catecholamines in agoraphobia and the relationship to serum. In J. C. Ballenger (Ed.), *Biology of agoraphobia* (pp. 27–63). Washington, DC: American Psychiatric Press.

Bandura, A. (1969). *Principles of behavior modification.* New York: Holt, Rinehart and Winston.

Barlow, D. H. (1988). *Anxiety and its disorders.* New York: Guilford Press.

Barlow, D. H., Craske, M. G., Cerny, J. A., & Klosko, J. S. (1989). Behavioral treatment of panic disorder. *Behavior Therapy, 20,* 261–282.

Barlow, D. H., DiNardo, P. A., Vermilyea, B. B., Vermilyea, J. A., & Blanchard, E. B. (1986). Comorbidity and depression among the anxiety disorders: Issues in diagnosis and classification. *Journal of Nervous and Mental Diseases, 174,* 63–72.

Barlow, D. H., Gorman, J. M., Shear, M. K., & Woods, S. W. (2000). Cognitive-behavioral therapy, imipramine, or their combination for panic disorder. *Journal of the American Medical Association, 283,* 2529–2536.

Barlow, D H., & Lehman, C. L. (1996). Advances in the psychosocial treatment of anxiety disorders: Implications for national health care. *Archives of General Psychiatry, 53,* 727–735.

Basoglu, M., Marks, I. M., Kilic, C., Swinson, R. P., Noshirvani, H., Kuch, K., et al. (1994). Relationship of panic, anticipatory anxiety, agoraphobia, and global improvement in panic disorder with agoraphobia treated with alprazolam and exposure. *British Journal of Psychiatry, 164,* 647–652.

Bastani, B., Arora, R., & Metzler, H. (1991). Serotonin uptake and imipramine binding in the blood platelets of obsessive-compulsive disorder patients. *Biological Psychiatry, 30,* 13–139.

Baxter, L. R. (1992). Neuroimaging studies of obsessive-compulsive disorder. *Psychiatric Clinics of North America, 15,* 871–884.

Beck, A. T. (1988). Cognitive approaches to panic disorder: Theory and therapy. In S. Rachman & J. D. Maser (Eds.), *Panic: Psychological perspectives* (pp. 91–109). Hillsdale, NJ: Erlbaum.

Beck, A. T., & Emery, G. (1985). *Anxiety disorders and phobias: A cognitive perspective.* New York: Basic Books.

Beck, A. T., Sokol, L., Clark, D. A., Berchick, R., & Wright, F. (1992). A crossover study of focused cognitive therapy for panic disorder. *American Journal of Psychiatry, 149,* 778–783.

Beekman, A. T. F., Bremmer, M. A., Deeg, D. J. H., van Balkom, A. J., Snut, J. H., DeBeurs, E., et al. (1998). Anxiety disorders in later life: A report from the longitudinal aging study Amsterdam. *International Journal of Geriatric Psychiatry, 13,* 717–726.

Beidel, D. C., & Bulick, C. M. (1990). Flooding and response prevention as a treatment for bowel obsessions. *Journal of Anxiety Disorders, 4,* 247–256.

Beidel, D. C., & Turner, S. M. (1986). A critique of the theoretical bases of cognitive behavior theories and therapies. *Clinical Psychology Review, 6,* 177–197.

Beidel, D. C., & Turner, S. M. (1988). Comorbidity of test anxiety and other anxiety disorders in children. *Journal of Abnormal Child Psychology, 16,* 275–287.

Beidel, D. C., & Turner, S. M. (1997). At risk for anxiety. I: Psychopathology in the offspring of anxious parents. *Journal of the American Academy of Child and Adolescent Psychiatry, 36,* 918–924.

Beidel, D. C., & Turner, S. M. (1998). *Shy children, phobic adults: Nature and treatment of social phobia.* Washington, DC: American Psychological Association.

Beidel, D. C., Turner, S. M., & Ballenger, J. C. (1997). A review of psychosocial treatments for anxiety disorders. In D. Dunner (Ed.), *Current psychiatric therapy II* (pp. 339–345). New York: Saunders.

Beidel, D. C., Turner, S. M., & Morris, T. L. (1999). Psychopathology of childhood social phobia. *Journal of the American Academy of Child and Adolescent Psychiatry, 38,* 643–650.

Bell, C. C., Dixie-Bell, D. D., & Thompson, B. (1986). Further studies on the prevalence of isolated sleep paralysis in Black subjects. *Journal of the National Medical Association, 78,* 649–659.

Bell, C. C., Hildreth, C. J., Jenkins, E. J., & Carter, C. (1988). The relationship of isolated sleep paralysis and panic disorder to hypertension. *Journal of the National Medical Association, 80,* 289–294.

Bell, C., & Jenkins, E. J. (1994). Isolated sleep paralysis and anxiety disorders. In S. Friedman (Ed.), *Anxiety disorders in African Americans* (pp. 117–127). New York: Springer.

Biederman, J., Faraone, S. V., Hirshfeld-Becker, D. R., Friedman, D., Robin, J. A., & Rosenbaum, J. F. (2001). Patterns of psychopathology and dysfunction in high-risk children of parents with panic disorder and major depression. *American Journal of Psychiatry, 158,* 49–57.

Biederman, J., Rosenbaum, J. F., Hirshfeld, D. R., Faraone, S. V., Bolduc, E. A., Gersten, M., et al. (1990). Psychiatric correlates of behavior inhibition in young children of parents with and without psychiatric disorders. *Archives of General Psychiatry, 47,* 21–26.

Bienvenu, O. J., & Eaton, W. W. (1998). The epidemiology of blood-injection-injury phobia. *Psychological Medicine, 28,* 1129–1136.

Birmes, P., Arrieu, A., Payen, A., Warner, B. A., & Schmitt, L. (1999). Traumatic stress and depression in a group of plane crash survivors. *Journal of Nervous and Mental Diseases, 187,* 754–755.

Black, D. B., Noyes, R., Goldstein, R. B., & Blum, N. (1992). A family study of obsessive-compulsive disorder. *Archives of General Psychiatry, 49,* 362–368.

Blanchard, E. B., Hickling, E. J., Taylor, A. E., & Loos, W. R. (1996). Who develops PTSD from motor vehicle accidents? *Behaviour Research and Therapy, 34,* 1–10.

Blazer, D., Goerge, L. K., Landerman, R., Pennybacker, M., Melville, M. L., Woodbury, M., et al. (1985). Psychiatric disorders: A rural-urban comparison. *Archives of General Psychiatry, 42,* 652–656.

Borkovec, T. D., & Costello, E. (1993). Efficacy of applied relaxation and cognitive-behavioral therapy in the treatment of generalized anxiety disorder. *Journal of Consulting and Clinical Psychology, 61,* 611–619.

Borkovec, T. D., Robinson, E., Pruzinsky, T., & DePress, J. A. (1993). Preliminary exploration of worry: Some characteristics and processes. *Behavior Research and Therapy, 21,* 9–16.

Borkovec, T. D., & Shadick, R. (1989). *The nature of normal versus pathological worry.* Paper prepared for the *DSM-IV* Task Force.

Boudewyns, P. A., & Hyer, L. (1990). Physiological response to combat memories and preliminary treatment outcome in Vietnam veteran PTSD patients treated with direct therapeutic exposure. *Behavior Therapy, 21,* 63–87.

Boudewyns, P. A., Stwertka, S. A., Hyer, L. A., Albrecht, J. W., & Sperr, E. V. (1993). Eye movement desensitization for PTSD of combat: A treatment outcome pilot study. *Behavior Therapist, 16,* 29–33.

Brawman-Mintzer, O., Lydiard, R. B., Emmamuel, N., Payeur, R., Johnson, M., Roberts, J., et al. (1993). Psychiatric comorbidity in patients with generalized anxiety disorder. *American Journal of Psychiatry, 150,* 1216–1218.

Breier, A., Charney, D. S., & Heninger, G. R. (1984). Major depression in patients with agoraphobia and panic disorder. *Archives of General Psychology, 41,* 1129–1135.

Breier, A., Charney, D. S., & Heninger, G. R. (1986). Agoraphobia with panic attacks. *Archives of General Psychology, 43,* 1029–1036.

Brewin, C. R. (1985). Depression and causal attributions: What is their relation? *Psychological Bulletin, 98,* 297–309.

Brody, A. L., Saxena, S., Schwartz, J. M., Stoessel, J. M., Maidment, K., Phelps, M. E., et al. (1998). FDG-PET predictors of response to behavior therapy and pharmacotherapy in obsessive compulsive disorder. *Psychiatry Research: Neuroimaging, 84,* 1–6.

Brown, T. A., Antony, M. M., & Barlow, D. H. (1995). Diagnostic comorbidity in panic disorder: Effect on treatment outcome and course of comorbid diagnoses following treatment. *Journal of Consulting and Clinical Psychology, 63,* 408–418.

Brown, T. A., & Barlow, D. H. (1992). Comorbidity among anxiety disorders: Implications for treatment and *DSM-IV. Journal of Consulting and Clinical Psychology, 60,* 835–844.

Brown, T. A., Barlow, D. H., & Liebowitz, M. R. (1994). The empirical basis of generalized anxiety disorder. *American Journal of Psychiatry, 151,* 1272–1280.

Brown, T. A., Marten, P. A., & Barlow, D. H. (1995). Discriminant validity of the symptoms constituting the *DSM-III-R* and *DSM-IV* associated symptom criterion of generalized anxiety disorder. *Journal of Anxiety Disorders, 9,* 317–328.

Bryant, R. A., & Harvey, A. G. (1999). Acute stress disorder following motor vehicle accidents. In E. J. Hickling & E. B. Blanchard (Eds.), *The international handbook of road traffic accidents and psychological trauma: Current understanding, treatment and law* (pp. 29–44). New York: Elsevier.

Bryant, R. A., Harvey, A. G., Dang, S. T., & Sackville, T. (1998). Assessing acute stress disorder: Psychometric properties of a structured clinical interview. *Psychological Assessment, 10,* 215–220.

Burnam, M. A., Hough, R. L., Escobar, J. I., Karno, M., Timbers, D. M., Telles, C. A., et al. (1987). Six-month prevalence of specific psychiatric disorders among Mexican Americans and Non-Hispanic Whites in Los Angeles. *Archives of General Psychiatry, 44,* 687–694.

Butler, G., Fennell, M., Robson, P., & Gelder, M. (1991). Comparison of behavior therapy and cognitive behavior therapy in the treatment of generalized anxiety disorder. *Journal of Consulting and Clinical Psychology, 59,* 167–175.

Castle, D. J., Deale, A., Marks, I. M., Cutts, E., Chadhoury, Y., & Stewart, A. (1994). Obsessive-compulsive disorder: Prediction of outcome from behavioral psychotherapy. *Acta Psychiatrica Scandinavica, 89,* 393–398.

Center for Disease Control. (1988). Health status of Vietnam veterans. *Journal of the American Medical Association, 259,* 2701–2724.

Chambless, D. L. (1982). Characteristics of agoraphobia. In D. L. Chambless & A. J. Goldstein (Eds.), *Agoraphobia* (pp. 1–18). New York: Wiley.

Chambless, D. L., & Williams, K. E. (1995). A preliminary study of African Americans with agoraphobia: Symptom severity and outcome of treatment with in vivo exposure. *Behavior Therapy, 26,* 501–515.

Christensen, H., Hadzi-Pavlovic, D., Andrews, G., & Mattick, R. (1987). Behavior therapy and tricyclic medication in the treatment of obsessive-compulsive disorder: A quantitative review. *Journal of Consulting and Clinical Psychology, 55,* 701–711.

Clark, D., & Agras, S. (1991). The assessment and treatment of performance anxiety in musicians. *American Journal of Psychiatry, 148,* 598–605.

Clark, D., Salkovskis, P., & Chalkley, A. (1985). Respiratory control as a treatment for panic attacks. *Journal of Behavior Therapy and Experimental Psychiatry, 16,* 23–30.

Clum, G. A. (1989). Psychological interventions versus drugs in the treatment of panic disorder. *Behavior Therapy, 20,* 429–457.

Connor, K. M., Davidson, J. R. T., Potts, N. L. S., Tupler, L. A., Miner, C. M., Malik, M. L., et al. (1998). Discontinuation of clonazepam in the treatment of social phobia. *Journal of Clinical Psychopharmacology, 18,* 373–378.

Cook, M., & Mineka, S. (1989). Observational conditioning of fear to fear-relevant versus fear-irrelevant stimuli in rhesus monkeys. *Journal of Abnormal Psychology, 98,* 448–459.

Cooper, N. A., & Clum, G. A. (1989). Imaginal flooding as a supplementary treatment for PTSD in combat veterans: A controlled study. *Behavior Therapy, 20,* 381–391.

Cox, B. J., Direnfeld, D. M., Swinson, R. P., & Norton, G. R. (1994). Suicidal ideation and suicide attempts in panic disorder and social phobia. *American Journal of Psychiatry, 151,* 882–887.

Craske, M. M., Maidenberg, E., & Bystritsky, A. (1995). Brief cognitive-behavioral versus nondirective therapy for panic disorder. *Journal of Behavior Therapy and Experimental Psychiatry, 26,* 113–120.

Craske, M. M., Rapee, R. M., & Barlow, D. H. (1992). Cognitive-behavior treatment of panic disorder, agoraphobia, and generalized panic disorder. In S. M. Turner, K. S. Calhoun, & H. E. Adams (Eds.), *Handbook of clinical behavior therapy* (2nd ed., pp. 39–66). New York: Wiley.

Cross National Collaborative Panic Study Second Phase Investigation. (1992). Drug treatment of panic disorder: Comparative efficacy of alprazolam, imipramine, and placebo. *British Journal of Psychiatry, 160,* 191–202.

Curtis, G. C., Magee, W. J., Eaton, W. W., Wittchen, H. U., & Kessler, R. C. (1998). Specific fears and phobias: Epidemiology and classification. *British Journal of Psychiatry, 173,* 212–217.

Curtis, G. C., Massana, J., Udina, C., Ayuso, J. L., Cassanos, G. B., & Perugi, G. (1993). Maintenance drug therapy of panic disorder. *Journal of Psychiatric Research, 27,* 127–142.

Davidson, J. R. T. (1992). Drug therapy of posttraumatic stress disorder. *British Journal of Psychiatry, 160,* 309–314.

Davidson, J. R. T. (1993, March). *Childhood histories of adult social phobics.* Paper presented at the Anxiety Disorders Association of America annual convention, Charleston, South Carolina.

Davidson, J. R. T. (2000). Pharmacotherapy of posttraumatic stress disorder: Treatment options, long-term follow-up, and predictors of outcome. *Journal of Clinical Psychiatry, 61,* 52–56.

Davidson, J. R. T., Hughes, D., Blazer, D. G., & George, L. K. (1991). Posttraumatic stress disorder in the community: An epidemiological study. *Psychological Medicine, 21,* 713–721.

Davidson, J. R. T., Potts, N., Ruchichi, E., Krishnan, R., Ford, S. M., Smith, R., et al. (1993). Treatment of social phobia with clonazepam and placebo. *Journal of Clinical Psychopharmacology, 13,* 423–428.

DeBeurs, E., van Balkom, A. J. L. M., Lange, A., Koele, P., & van Dyck, R. (1995). Treatment of panic disorder with agoraphobia: Comparison of fluvoxamine, placebo, and psychological panic management combined with exposure and of exposure in vivo alone. *American Journal of Psychiatry 152,* 683–691.

De Jong, G., & Majella-Bouman, T. K. (1995). Panic disorder: A baseline period. Predictability of agoraphobic avoidance behavior. *Journal of Anxiety Disorders, 9,* 185–199.

Delprato, D. J., & McGlynn, F. D. (1984). Behavioral theories of anxiety disorders. In S. M. Turner (Ed.), *Behavioral theories and treatment of anxiety* (pp. 1–49). New York: Plenum Press.

Devilly, G. J., & Spence, S. H. (1999). The relative efficacy and treatment distress of EMDR and a cognitive-behavior trauma treatment protocol in the amelioration of posttraumatic stress disorder. *Journal of Anxiety Disorders, 13,* 131–157.

Dugas, M. J., Gagnon, F., Ladoucer, R., & Freeston, M. H. (1998). Generalized anxiety disorder: A preliminary test of a conceptual model. *Behavior Therapy and Research, 36,* 215–226.

Dugas, M. J., & Ladoucer, R. (2000). Treatment of GAD: Targeting intolerance of uncertainty in two types of worry. *Behavior Modification, 24,* 635–657.

Durham, R., & Allan, T. (1993). Psychological treatments of generalized anxiety disorder: A review of the clinical significance of results in outcome studies since 1980. *British Journal of Psychiatry, 156,* 19–26.

Eaton, W. W., Anthony, J. C., Romanoski, A., Tien, A., Gallo, J., Cai, G., et al. (1998). Onset and recovery from panic disorder in the Baltimore epidemiologic catchment area follow-up. *British Journal of Psychiatry, 173,* 501–507.

Eaton, W. W., Kessler, R. C., Wittchen, H. U., & Magee, W. J. (1994). Panic and panic disorder in the United States. *American Journal of Psychiatry, 151,* 413–420.

Echeburua, E., de Corral, P., Zubizarreta, I., & Sarasua, B. (1997). Psychological treatment of chronic posttraumatic stress disorder in victims with sexual aggression. *Behavior Modification, 21,* 433–456.

Ellingrod, V. L. (1998). Pharmacotherapy of primary obsessive-compulsive disorder: Review of the literature. *Pharmacotherapy, 18,* 936–960.

Emmelkamp, P. M. G. (1988). Phobic disorders. In C. G. Last & M. Hersen (Eds.), *Handbook of anxiety disorders* (pp. 66–86). New York: Pergamon Press.

Falloon, I. R. H., Lloyd, G. G., & Harpin, R. E. (1981). The treatment of social phobia: Real life rehearsal with nonprofessional therapists. *Journal of Nervous and Mental Diseases, 169,* 180–184.

Fava, G. A., Grandi, S., Rafanelli, C., Conti, S., & Belluardo, P. (2001). Long-term outcome of social phobia treated by exposure. *Psychological Medicine, 31,* 899–905.

Fava, G. A., Rafanelli, C., Grandi, S., Conti, S., Ruini, C., Mangelli, L., et al. (2001). Long-term outcome of panic disorder with agoraphobia treated by exposure. *Psychological Medicine, 31,* 891–898.

Fava, M., Rankin, M. A., Wright, E. C., Alpert, J. E., Nierenberg, A. A., Pava, J., et al. (2000). Anxiety disorders in major depression. *Comprehensive Psychiatry, 41,* 97–102.

Fedoroff, I. C., & Taylor, S. T. (2001). Psychological and pharmacological treatments of social phobia: A meta-analysis. *Journal of Clinical Psychopharmacology, 21,* 311–324.

Feske, U., & Chambless, D. (1995). Cognitive-behavioral versus exposure treatment for social phobia: A meta-analysis. *Behavior Therapy, 26,* 695–720.

Fineberg, N. A., Cowen, P. J., Kirk, J. W., & Montgomery, S. A. (1994). Neuroendocrine responses to intravenous L-tryptophan in obsessive compulsive disorder. *Journal of Affective Disorders, 32,* 97–104.

Fink, C. M., Turner, S. M., & Beidel, D. C. (1996). Culturally relevant factors in the behavioral treatment of social phobia: A case study. *Journal of Anxiety Disorders, 10,* 201–209.

Foa, E. B., Dancu, C. V., Hembree, E. A., Jaycox, L. H., Meadows, E. A., & Street, G. P. (1999). A comparison of exposure therapy, stress inoculation training, and their combination for reducing posttraumatic stress disorder in female assault victims. *Journal of Consulting and Clinical Psychology, 67,* 194–200.

Foa, E. B., Rothbaum, B. O., Riggs, D. S., & Murdock, T. B. (1991). Treatment of posttraumatic stress disorder in rape victims: A comparison between cognitive-behavioral procedures and counseling. *Journal of Consulting and Clinical Psychology, 59,* 715–723.

Foa, E. B., Steketee, G. A., & Ozarow, B. J. (1985). Behavior therapy with obsessive-compulsives: From theory to treatment. In M. Mavissakalian, S. M. Turner, & L. Michelson (Eds.), *Obsessive-compulsive disorder: Psychological and pharmacological treatments* (pp. 49–120). New York: Plenum Press.

Fontaine, R., & Chouinard, G. (1986). An open clinical trial of fluoxetine in the treatment of obsessive-compulsive disorder. *Journal of Clinical Psychopharmacology, 6,* 98–101.

Franklin, M. E., Abramowitz, J. S., Kozak, M. J., Levitt, J. T., & Foa, E. B. (2000). Effectiveness of exposure and ritual prevention for obsessive-compulsive disorder: Randomized compared with nonrandomized samples. *Journal of Consulting and Clinical Psychology, 68,* 594–602.

Frueh, B. C., Turner, S. M., & Beidel, D. C. (1995). Exposure therapy for combat-related PTSD: A critical review. *Clinical Psychology Review, 15,* 799–817.

Frueh, B. C., Turner, S. M., Beidel, D. C., Mirabella, R. F., & Jones, W. J. (1996). Trauma management therapy: A preliminary evaluation of a multicomponent behavioral treatment for chronic combat-related PTSD. *Behavior Research and Therapy, 34,* 533–543.

Fyer, A. J. (1993). Heritability of social anxiety: A brief review. *Journal of Clinical Psychiatry, 54,* 10–12.

Fyer, A. J., Mannuzza, S., Gallops, M. S., Martin, L. Y., Aaronson, C., Gorman, J. M., et al. (1990). Familial transmission of simple phobias and fears: A preliminary report. *Archives of General Psychiatry, 47,* 252–256.

Fyer, A. J., & Sandberg, D. (1988). Pharmacologic treatment of panic disorder. In A. J. Francis & R. E. Hales (Eds.), *Review of psychiatry* (Vol. 7, pp. 88–137). Washington, DC: American Psychiatric Press.

Gelernter, C. S., Uhde, T. W., Cimbolic, P., & Arnkoff, D. (1991). Cognitive-behavioral and pharmacological treatments of social phobia. *Archives of General Psychiatry, 48,* 938–945.

Glynn, S. M., Eth, S., Randolph, E. T., Foy, D. W., Urbaitis, M., Boxer, L., et al. (1999). A test of behavioral family therapy to augment exposure for combat-related posttraumatic stress disorder. *Journal of Consulting and Clinical Psychology, 67,* 243–251.

Goisman, R. M., Warshaw, M. G., Peterson, L. G., Rogers, M. P., Cuneo, P., Hunt, M. E., et al. (1994). Panic, agoraphobia, and panic disorder with agoraphobia: Data from a multicenter anxiety disorders study. *Journal of Nervous and Mental Disease, 182,* 72–79.

Goldstein, A. J., & Chambless, D. L. (1978). A reanalysis of agoraphobia. *Behavior Therapy, 9,* 47–59.

Goldstein, R. B., Wickramaratne, P. J., Horwath, E., & Weissman, M. M. (1997). Familial aggregation and phenomenology of early onset (at or before age 20 years) panic disorder. *Archives of General Psychiatry, 54,* 271–278.

Gorman, J. M., Fyer, A. J., Glicklich, J., King, D. W., & Klein, D. E. (1981). Effect of imipramine on prolapsed mitral valves of patients with panic disorder. *American Journal of Psychiatry, 138,* 977–978.

Gorman, J. M., Levy, G. F., Liebowitz, M. R., McGrath, P., Appleby, I. L., Dillon, D. J., et al. (1983). Effect of acute b-adrenergic blockade of lactate-induced panic. *Archives of General Psychiatry, 40,* 1079–1082.

Gould, R. A., Buckminster, S., Pollack, M. H., Otto, M. W., & Yap, L. (1997). Cognitive-behavioral and pharmacological treatment for social phobia: A meta-analysis. *Clinical Psychology: Science and Practice, 4,* 291–306.

Greenberg, P. E., Sisitsky, T., Kessler, R. C., Finkelstein, S. N., Berndt, E. R., Davidson, J. R. T., et al. (1999). The economic burden of anxiety disorders in the 1990s. *Journal of Clinical Psychiatry, 60,* 427–435.

Hanna, G. L. (2000). Clinical and family-genetic studies of childhood obsessive-compulsive disorder. In W. K. Goodman et al. (Eds.), *Obsessive-compulsive disorder: Contemporary issues in treatment: Personality and clinical psychology series* (pp. 87–103). Mahwah, NJ: Erlbaum.

Harvey, A. G., & Bryant, R. A. (1999). The relationship between acute stress disorder and posttraumatic stress disorder: A 2-year prospective evaluation. *Journal of Consulting and Clinical Psychology, 67,* 985–988.

Hegel, M. T., Ravaris, C. L., & Ahles, T A. (1994). Combined cognitive-behavioral and time-limited alprazolam treatment of panic disorder. *Behavior Therapy, 25,* 183–195.

Heim, C., & Nemeroff, C. B. (1999). The impact of early adverse experiences on brain systems involved in the pathophysiology of anxiety and affective disorders. *Biological Psychiatry, 46,* 1509–1522.

Heimberg, R. G., Dodge, C. S., Hope, D. A., Kennedy, C. R., Zollo, L., & Becker, R. E. (1990). Cognitive behavioral treatment of social phobia: Comparison to a credible placebo control. *Cognitive Therapy and Research, 14,* 1–23.

Heimberg, R. G., Juster, H. R., Brown, E. J., Holle, C., Makris, G. S., Leung, A. W., et al. (1994, November). *Cognitive-behavioral versus pharmacological treatment of social phobia: Posttreatment and follow-up effects.* Poster presented at the annual meeting of the Association for the Advancement of Behavior Therapy, San Diego, CA.

Heimberg, R. G., Liebowitz, M. R., Hope, D. A., Schneier, F. R., Holt, C. S., Welkowitz, L. A., et al. (1998). Cognitive-behavioral group therapy vs. phenelzine therapy for social phobia. *Archives of General Psychiatry, 55,* 1133–1141.

Heimberg, R. G., Salzman, D. G., Holt, C. S., & Blendell, K. A. (1993). Cognitive-behavioral group treatment of social phobia: Effectiveness at five-year follow-up. *Cognitive Therapy and Research, 17,* 325–339.

Herbert, J. D., Hope, D. A., & Bellack, A. S. (1992). Validity of the distinction between generalized social phobia and avoidant personality disorder. *Journal of Abnormal Psychology, 104,* 332–339.

Hettema, J. M., Prescott, C. A., & Kendler, K. S. (2001). A population-based twin study of generalized anxiety disorder in men and women. *Journal of Nervous and Mental Disease, 189,* 413–420.

Hewlett, W. A., Vinogradov, S., Martin, K., Berman, S., & Csernansky, J. G. (1992). Fenfluramine stimulation of prolactin in obsessive-compulsive disorder. *Psychiatry Research, 42,* 81–92.

Hidalgo, R. B., & Davidson, J. R. T. (2000). Posttraumatic stress disorder: Epidemiology and health-related concerns. *Journal of Clinical Psychiatry, 61,* 5–13.

Hirshfeld, D. R., Biederman, J., Brody, L., Faraone, S. V., & Rosenbaum, J. F. (1997). Expressed emotion toward children with behavioral inhibition: Associations with maternal anxiety disorder. *Journal of the American Academy of Child and Adolescent Psychiatry, 36,* 910–917.

Hirshfeld, D. R., Rosenbaum, J. F., Biederman, J., Bolduc, E. A., Faraone, S. V., Snidman, N., et al. (1992). Stable behavioral inhibition and its association with anxiety disorder. *Journal of the American Academy of Child and Adolescent Psychiatry, 31,* 301–311.

Hiss, H., Foa, E. B., & Kozak, M. J. (1994). Relapse prevention program for treatment of obsessive-compulsive disorder. *Journal of Consulting and Clinical Psychology, 62,* 801–808.

Hoehn-Saric, R., McLeod, D. R., & Hipsley, P. A. (1993). Effect of fluvoxamine on panic disorder. *Journal of Clinical Psychopharmacology, 13,* 321–326.

Hoffart, A. (1993). Cognitive treatments of agoraphobia: A critical evaluation of theoretical bases and outcome evidence. *Journal of Anxiety Disorders, 7,* 75–91.

Hollander, E., DeCaria, C. M., Nitescu, A., Gully, R., Suckow, R. F., Cooper, T. B., et al. (1992). Serotonergic function in obsessive-compulsive disorder: Behavioral and neuroendocrine responses to oral m-chlorophenylpiperazine and fenfluramine in patients and healthy volunteers. *Archives of General Psychiatry, 49,* 21–28.

Holt, C. S., Heimberg, R. G., & Hope, D. A. (1992). Avoidant personality disorder and the generalized subtype of social phobia. *Journal of Abnormal Psychology, 101,* 318–325.

Hope, D. A., Heimberg, R. G., & Bruch, M. A. (1995). Dismantling cognitive-behavioral therapy for social phobia. *Behavior Research and Therapy, 33,* 637–650.

Hufford, D. (1982). *The terror that comes in the night.* Philadelphia: University of Pennsylvania Press.

Insel, T. R., Mueller, E. A., Gillin, C., Siever, L. J., & Murphy, D. L. (1985). Tricyclic response in obsessive-compulsive disorder. *Progress in Neurological-Psychopharmacology and Biological Psychiatry, 9,* 25–31.

Insel, T. R., & Winslow, J. T. (1992). Neurobiology of obsessive-compulsive disorder. *Psychiatric Clinics of North America, 15,* 813–824.

Jacob, R. G., Furman, J. M., Durrant, J. D., & Turner, S. M. (1996). Panic, agoraphobia, and vestibular dysfunction. *American Journal of Psychiatry, 153,* 503–512.

Jacob, R. G., Moller, M. B., Turner, S. M., & Wall, C. (1985). Otoneurological examination in panic disorders and agoraphobia with panic attacks: A pilot study. *American Journal of Psychiatry, 142,* 715–720.

Jacob, R. G., & Turner, S. M. (1988). Panic disorder: Diagnosis and assessment. In A. J. Francis & R. E. Hales (Eds.), *Review of psychiatry* (pp. 67–87). Washington, DC: American Psychiatric Press.

Jansson, L., Jerremalm, A., & Ost, L. G. (1986). Follow-up of agoraphobic patients treated with exposure in-vivo or applied relaxation. *British Journal of Psychiatry, 149,* 486–490.

Jenike, M. A., Baer, L., Minichiello, W. E., Schwartz, C. E., & Carey, R. J., Jr. (1986). Concomitant obsessive-compulsive disorders and schizotypal personality disorder. *American Journal of Psychiatry, 143,* 530–532.

Jenike, M. A., Vitagliano, H. L., Rabinowitz, J., Goff, D. C., & Baer, L. (1987). Bowel obsessions responsive to tricyclic antidepressants in four patients. *American Journal of Psychiatry, 144,* 1347–1348.

Jensen, J. A. (1994). An investigation of eye movement desensitization and reprocessing (EMD/R) as a treatment for posttraumatic stress disorder (PTSD) symptoms of Vietnam combat veterans. *Behavior Therapy, 25,* 311–325.

Kagan, J. (1982). Heart rate and heart rate variability as signs of a temperamental dimension in infants. In C. E. Izard (Ed.), *Measuring emotions in infants and children* (pp. 38–66). Cambridge, England: Cambridge University Press.

Kagan, J. (1997). Temperamental contributions to the development of social behavior. In D. Magnusson (Ed.), *The lifespan development of individuals: Behavioral, neurobiological, and psychosocial perspectives: A synthesis* (pp. 376–393). New York: Cambridge University Press.

Kagan, J., Reznick, J. S., & Snidman, N. (1987). The physiology and psychology of behavioral inhibition in children. *Child Development, 58,* 1459–1473.

Kagan, J., Reznick, J. S., Snidman, N., Gibbons, J., & Johnson, M. O. (1988). Childhood derivatives of inhibition and lack of inhibition to the unfamiliar. *Child Development, 59,* 1580–1589.

Kahn, R. J., McNair, D. M., Covi, L., Downing, R. W., Fisher, S., Lipman, R. S., et al. (1981). Effects of psychotropic agents on high anxiety subjects. *Psychopharmacology Bulletin, 17,* 97–100.

Kahn, R. S., van Praag, H. M., Wetzler, G. M., Asnis, G. M., & Barr, G. (1988). Serotonin and anxiety revisited. *Biological Psychiatry, 23,* 189–208.

Kathol, R. G., Noyes, R., Slyman, D. J., Crowe, R. R., Clancy, J., & Kerber, R. E. (1980). Propranolol in chronic anxiety disorders. *Archives of General Psychiatry, 37,* 1361–1365.

Katzelnick, D. J., Kobak, K. A., Greist, J. H., Jefferson, J. W., Mantle, J. M., & Serlin, R. C. (1995). Sertraline for social phobia: A double-blind, placebo-controlled crossover study. *American Journal of Psychiatry, 152,* 1368–1371.

Keane, T. M., Fairbank, J. A., Caddell, J. M., & Zimering, R. T. (1989). Implosive (flooding) therapy reduces symptoms of PTSD in Vietnam combat veterans. *Behavior Therapy, 20,* 245–260.

Keijsers, G. P. J., Hoogduin, C. A. L., & Schapp, C. P. D. (1994a). Predictors of treatment outcome in the behavioral treatment of obsessive-compulsive disorder. *British Journal of Psychiatry, 165,* 781–786.

Keijsers, G. P. J., Hoogduin, C. A. L., & Schapp, C. P. D. (1994b). Prognostic factors in the behavioral treatment of panic disorder with and without agoraphobia. *Behavior Therapy, 25,* 689–708.

Keller, M. B., Yonkers, K. A., Warshaw, M. G., Pratt, L. A., Gollan, J. K., Massion, A. O., et al. (1994). Remission and relapse in subjects with panic disorder and panic with agoraphobia. *Journal of Nervous and Mental Diseases, 182,* 290–296.

Kendler, K. S. (1996). Major depression and generalized anxiety disorder: Same genes, (partly) different environments-Revisited. *British Journal of Psychiatry, 168,* 68–75.

Kendler, K. S., Heath, A. C., Martin, N. G., & Eaves, L. J. (1987). Symptoms of anxiety and symptoms of depression: Same genes, different environments. *Archives of General Psychiatry, 44,* 451–457.

Kendler, K. S., Neale, M. C., Kessler, R. C., Heath, A. C., & Eaves, L. J. (1992a). Generalized anxiety disorder in women: A population-based twin study. *Archives of General Psychiatry, 49,* 267–272.

Kendler, K. S., Neale, M. C., Kessler, R. C., Heath, A. C., & Eaves, L. J. (1992b). The genetic epidemiology of phobias in women: The interrelationship of agoraphobia, social phobia, situational phobia, and simple phobia. *Archives of General Psychiatry, 49,* 273–281.

Kendler, K. S., Neale, M. C., Kessler, R. C., Heath, A. C., & Eaves, L. J. (1992c). Major depression and generalized anxiety disorder: Same genes, (partly) different environments? *Archives of General Psychiatry, 49,* 716–722.

Kessler, R. C., Foster, C. L., Saunders, W. B., & Stang, P. E. (1995). Social consequences of psychiatric disorders. I: Educational attainment. *American Journal of Psychiatry, 152,* 1026–1032.

Kessler, R. C., McGonagle, K. A., Zhao, S., & Nelson, C. B. (1994). Lifetime and 12-month prevalence of *DSM-Ill-R* psychiatric disorders in the United States: Results from the national comorbidity survey. *Archives of General Psychiatry, 51,* 8–19.

Khanna, S., & Channabasavanna, S. M. (1988). Phenomenology of obsessions in obsessive-compulsive neurosis. *Psychopathology, 21,* 12–18.

Kilpatrick, D. G., Saunders, B. E., Amick-McMullan, A., Best, C. L., Veronen, L. J., & Resnick, H. S. (1989). Victim and crime factors associated with the development of crime-related posttraumatic stress disorder. *Behavior Therapy, 20,* 199–214.

Kirmayer, L. J. (2001). Cultural variations in the clinical presentation of depression and anxiety: Implications for diagnosis and treatment. *Journal of Clinical Psychiatry, 62,* 22–28.

Kirmayer, L. J., & Minas, H. (2000). The future of cultural psychiatry: An international perspective. *Canadian Journal of Psychiatry, 45,* 438–446.

Kirmayer, L. J., Young, A., & Hayton, B. C. (1995). The cultural context of anxiety disorders. *Psychiatric Clinics of North America, 18,* 503–521.

Klein, D. F. (1981). Anxiety reconceptualized. In D. R. Klein & J. R. Rabkin (Eds.), *Anxiety: New research and changes concepts* (pp. 235–263). New York: Raven Press.

Klein, D. F., & Fink, M. (1962). Psychiatric reaction patterns to imipramine. *American Journal of Psychiatry, 119,* 432–438.

Klosko, J. S., Barlow, D. H., Tassinari, R., & Cerney, J. A. (1990). A comparison of alprazo-lam and behavior therapy in treatment of panic disorder. *Journal of Consulting and Clinical Psychology, 58,* 77–84.

Kolada, J. L., Bland, R. C., & Newman, S. C. (1994). Obsessive-compulsive disorder. *Acta Psychiatrica Scandinavica, 376,* 24–35.

Koran, L. M., Ringold, A. L., & Elliott, M. A. (2000). Olanzapine augmentation for treatment-resistant obsessive-compulsive disorder. *Journal of Clinical Psychiatry, 61,* 514–517.

Kukleta, M., & Franc, Z. (2000). Anxiety, depressive symptoms, and psychosocial stress in general population. *Homeostasis in Health and Disease, 40,* 14–19.

Kulka, R. A., Schlenger, W. E., Fairbank, J. A., Hough, R. L., Jordan, B. K., Marmar, C. R., et al. (1988). *National Vietnam Veterans Readjustment Study (NVVRS): Description, current status, and initial PTSD prevalence estimates, final report.* Washington, DC: Veterans Administration.

Kusunoki, K., Sato, T., Taga, C., Yoshida, T., Komori, K., Narita, T., et al. (2000). Low-novelty seeking differentiates obsessive-compulsive disorder from major depression. *Acta Psychiatrica Scandinavica, 101,* 403–405.

Ladoucer, R., Dugas, M. J., Freeston, M. H., Leger, E., Gagnon, F., & Thibodeau, N. (2000). Efficacy of a cognitive-behavioral treatment for generalized anxiety disorder: Evaluation in a controlled clinical trial. *Journal of Consulting and Clinical Psychology, 68,* 957–964.

Lang, P. J. (1977). Physiological assessment of anxiety and fear. In J. D. Cone & R. P. Hawkins (Eds.), *Behavioral assessment: New directions in clinical psychology* (pp. 178–195). New York: Brunner/Mazel.

Langlois, F., Freeston, M. H., & Ladoucer, R. (2000). Differences and similarities between obsessive intrusive thoughts and worry in a nonclinical population: Studies 1 & 2. *Behavior Research and Therapy, 38,* 157–189.

Last, C. G., Hersen, M., Kazdin, A. E., Francis, G., & Grubb, H. J. (1987). Psychiatric illness in the mothers of anxious children. *American Journal of Psychiatry, 144,* 1580–1583.

Last, C. G., Hersen, M., Kazdin, A. E., Orvaschel, H., & Ye, W. (1990). *Anxiety disorders in children and their families.* Unpublished manuscript, Nova Southeastern University, Fort Lauderdale, FL.

Lecrubier, Y., & Weiller, E. (1997). Comorbidities in social phobia. *International Clinical Psychopharmacology, 12,* S17–S21.

Lesser, I. M., Rubin, R. T., Pecknold, J. C., Rifkin, A., Swinson, R. P., Lydiard, R. B., et al. (1988). Secondary depression in panic disorder and agoraphobia. *Archives of General Psychiatry, 45,* 437–443.

Levin, A. R., Sandberg, D., Stein, J., Cohen, B., Strauman, T., Gorman, J. M., et al. (1989). *Responses of generalized and limited social phobics during public speaking.* Unpublished manuscript, Columbia University, New York.

Liddell, A., & Lyons, M. (1978). Thunderstorm phobias. *Behavior Research and Therapy, 16,* 306–308.

Liebowitz, M. R. (1997). Imipramine in the treatment of panic disorder and its complications. *Psychiatric Clinics of North America, 8,* 37–47.

Liebowitz, M. R., Fyer, A. J., Gorman, J. M., Dillon, D., Davies, S., Stein, J. M., et al. (1985). Specificity of lactate infusions in social phobia versus panic disorders. *American Journal of Psychiatry, 142,* 947–950.

Liebowitz, M. R., Gorman, J. M., Fyer, A. J., Campeas, R., Levin, A. P., Sandberg, D., et al. (1988). Pharmacotherapy of social phobia: A placebo-controlled comparison of phenelzine and atenolol. *Journal of Clinical Psychiatry, 49,* 252–257.

Liebowitz, M. R., Gorman, J. M., Fyer, A. J., & Klein, D. R (1985). Social phobia. *Archives of General Psychiatry, 42,* 729–736.

Liebowitz, M. R., Salman, E., Jusino, C. M., Garfinkel, R., Street, L., Cardenas, D. L., et al. (1994). Ataque de nervios and panic disorder. *American Journal of Psychiatry, 151,* 871–875.

Liebowitz, M. R., Schneier, F. R., Campeas, R., Hollander, J., Fyer, A. J., Gorman, J. M., et al. (1992). Phenelzine vs. Atenolol in social phobia. A placebo-controlled comparison. *Archives of General Psychiatry, 49,* 290–300.

Lin, K. M. (2001). Biological differences in depression and anxiety across races and ethnic groups. *Journal of Clinical Psychiatry, 62,* 13–19.

Lin, K. M., Poland, R. E., & Lesser, I. M. (1986). Ethnicity and psychopharmacology. *Culture, Medicine, and Psychiatry, 10,* 151–165.

Lin, K. M., Poland, R. E., & Silver, B. (1993). The interface between psychobiology and ethnicity. In K. M. Lin, R. E. Poland, & G. Nagasaki (Eds.), *Psychopharmacology and psychobiology of ethnicity* (pp. 11–35). Washington, DC: American Psychiatric Press.

Lindsay, M., Crino, R., & Andrews, G. (1997). Controlled trial of exposure and response prevention in obsessive-compulsive disorder. *British Journal of Psychiatry, 171,* 135–139.

Lopez-Ibor, J. J., Jr., Saiz, J., & Vinas, R. (1994). Obsessive-compulsive disorder and depression. In S. A. Montgomery & T. H. Corn (Eds.), *Psychopharmacology of depression* (pp. 185–217). New York: Oxford University Press.

Lucey, J. V., Butcher, G., O'Flynn, K., Clare, A. W., & Dinan, G. (1994). The growth hormone response to baclofen in obsessive compulsive disorder: Does the GABA-B receptor mediate obsessive anxiety? *Pharmacopsychiatry, 27,* 23–26.

Lydiard, R. B., Roy-Byrne, P. P., & Ballenger, J. C. (1988). Recent advances in psychopharmacological treatment of anxiety disorders. *Hospital and Community Psychiatry, 39,* 1157–1165.

Macklin, M. L., Metzger, L. J., Lasko, N. B., Berry, N. J., Orr, S. P., & Pitman, R. K. (2000). Five-year follow-up study of eye-movement desensitization and reprocessing therapy for combat-related posttraumatic stress disorder. *Comprehensive Psychiatry, 41,* 24–27.

Magee, W. J. (1999). Effects of negative life experiences on phobia onset. *Social Psychiatry and Psychiatric Epidemiology, 34,* 343–351.

Maier, W., Gansicke, M., Freyberger, H. J., Linz, M., Heun, R., & Lecrubier, Y. (2000). Generalized anxiety disorder (ICD-10) in primary care from a cross-cultural perspective: A valid diagnostic entity? *Acta Psychiatrica Scandinavica, 101,* 29–36.

Mancini, C., Van Ameringen, M., Szatmari, P., & Fugere, C. (1996). A high-risk pilot study of the children of adults with social phobia. *Journal of the American Academy of Child and Adolescent Psychiatry, 35,* 1511–1517.

Mancuso, D. M., Townsend, M. H., & Mercante, D. E. (1993). Long-term follow-up of generalized anxiety disorder. *Comprehensive Psychiatry, 34,* 441–446.

Marazziti, D., Dell'Osso, L., Gemignani, A., Ciapparelli, A., Presta, S., DiNasso, E., et al. (2001). Citalopram in refractory obsessive-compulsive disorder: An open study. *International Clinical Psychopharmacology, 16,* 215–219.

Marcos, L. R., & Cancro, R. (1982). Pharmacotherapy of Hispanic depressed patients: Clinical observations. *American Journal of Psychotherapy, 36,* 505–512.

Margraf, J., Ehlers, A., & Roth, W. T. (1986). Sodium lactate infusions and panic attacks: A review and critique. *Psychosomatic Medicine, 48,* 23–51.

Marks, I. M. (1985). Behavioral treatment of social phobia. *Psychopharmacology Bulletin, 21,* 615–618.

Marks, I. M., & Gelder, M. G. (1966). Different onset ages in varieties of phobias. *American Journal of Psychiatry, 123,* 218–221.

Marks, I. M., Lovell, K., Noshirvani, H., Livanou, M., & Thrasher, S. (1998). Treatment of posttraumatic stress disorder by exposure and/or cognitive restructuring: A controlled study. *Archives of General Psychiatry, 55,* 317–325.

Marshall, R. D., Spitzer, R. L., & Liebowitz, M. R. (1999). Review and critique of the new *DSM-IV* diagnosis of acute stress disorder. *American Journal of Psychiatry, 156,* 1677–1685.

Martin, C., Cabrol, S., Bouvard, M. P., Lepine, J. P., & Mouren-Simeoni, M. (1999). Anxiety and depressive disorders in fathers and mothers of anxious school-refusing children. *Journal of the American Academy of Child and Adolescent Psychiatry, 38,* 916–922.

Mathew, R. J., Ho, B. T., Francis, D. J., Taylor, D. L., & Weinman, M. L. (1982). Catacholamines and anxiety. *Acta Psychiatrica Scandinavica, 65,* 142–147.

Matsuda, K. T., Cho, M. C., Lin, K. M., & Smith, M. W. (1995, May). *Clozapine dosage, efficacy, side-effect profiles: A comparison of Asian and Caucasian patients.* Paper presented at the New Clinical Drug Evaluation Unit (NCDEU) annual meeting, Orlando, Florida.

Mattick, R. P., & Peters, L. (1988). Treatment of severe social phobia: Effects of guided exposure with and without cognitive restructuring. *Journal of Consulting and Clinical Psychology, 56,* 251–260.

Mattick, R. P., Peters, L., & Clarke, J. C. (1989). Exposure and cognitive restructuring for severe social phobia. *Behavior Therapy, 20,* 3–23.

Mavissakalian, M., & Hamann, M. S. (1986). *DSM-III* personality disorder in agoraphobia. *Comprehensive Psychiatry, 27,* 471–479.

Mavissakalian, M., & Hamann, M. S. (1988). Correlates of *DSM-III* personality disorder in panic disorder and agoraphobia. *Comprehensive Psychiatry, 29,* 535–544.

McClure, E. B., Brennan, P. A., Hammen, C., & LeBrocque, R. M. (2001). Parental anxiety disorders, child anxiety disorders, and the perceived parent-child relationship in an Australian high-risk sample. *Journal of Abnormal Child Psychology, 29,* 1–10.

McDougle, C. J., Barr, L. C., Goodman, W. K., & Price, L. H. (1999). Possible role of neuropeptides in obsessive-compulsive disorder. *Psychoneuroendocrinology, 24,* 1–24.

McDougle, C. J., Epperson, C. N., Pelton, G. H., Wasylink, S., & Price, L. H. (2000). A double-blind, placebo-controlled study of resperidone addition in serotonin reuptake inhibitor-refractory obsessive-compulsive disorder. *Archives of General Psychiatry, 57,* 794–801.

McLean, P. D., Whittal, M. L., Thordarson, D. S., Taylor, S., Soechting, I., Koch, W. J., et al. (2001). Cognitive versus behavior therapy in the group treatment of obsessive-compulsive disorder. *Journal of Consulting and Clinical Psychology, 69,* 205–214.

McNally, R. J. (1987). Preparedness and phobias: A review. *Psychological Bulletin, 101,* 283–303.

McNally, R. J. (1995). Automaticity and the anxiety disorders. *Behavior Research and Therapy, 33,* 747–754.

McNally, R. J. (2001). Vulnerability to anxiety disorders in adulthood. In R. E. Ingram & J. M. Price (Eds.), *Vulnerability to psychopathology: Risk across the lifespan* (pp. 304–321). New York: Guilford Press.

McNally, R. J., & Steketee, G. S. (1985). The etiology and maintenance of severe animal phobias. *Behavior Research and Therapy, 23,* 431–435.

Michelson, L., Mavissakalian, M., & Marchione, K. (1985). Cognitive and behavioral treatments of agoraphobia: Clinical, behavioral, and psychophysiological outcomes. *Journal of Consulting and Clinical Psychology, 53,* 913–925.

Mineka, S., & Cook, M. (1986). Immunization against the observational conditioning of snake fear in rhesus monkeys. *Journal of Abnormal Psychology, 95,* 307–318.

Mineka, S., Davidson, M., Cook, M., & Heir, R. (1985). Observational conditioning of snake fear in rhesus monkeys. *Journal of Abnormal Psychology, 93,* 355–372.

Mineka, S., & Zinbarg, R. (1991). Animal models of psychopathology. In C. E. Walker (Ed.), *Clinical psychology: Historical and research foundations* (pp. 51–86). New York: Plenum Press.

Montgomery, S. A., Kasper, S., Stein, D. J., Bang Hedegaard, K., & Lemming, O. M. (2001). Citalopram 20 mg, 40 mg, and 60 mg are all effective and well tolerated compared with placebo in obsessive-compulsive disorder. *International Journal of Clinical Psychopharmacology, 16,* 75–86.

Mowrer, O. H. (1947). On the dual nature of learning: A reinterpretation of "conditioning" and "problem-solving." *Harvard Education Review, 17,* 102–148.

Munjack, D. J., Bruns, J., Baltazar, P. L., Brown, R., Leonard, M., Nagy, R., et al. (1991). A pilot study of buspirone in the treatment of social phobia. *Journal of Anxiety Disorders, 5,* 87–98.

Myers, J. K., Weissman, M. M., Tischler, G. L., Holzer, C. E., Leaf, P. J., Orvaschel, H., et al. (1984). , Six month prevalence of psychiatric disorders in three communities. *Archives of General Psychiatry, 41,* 287–292.

Neal, A. M., & Turner, S. M. (1991). Anxiety disorders research with African Americans: Current status. *Psychological Bulletin, 109,* 400–410.

Neal-Barnett, A. M., & Crowther, J. H. (2000). To be female, middle class, anxious, and Black. *Psychology of Women Quarterly, 24,* 129–136.

Neighbors, H. W. (1985). Seeking help for personal problems: African Americans' use of health and mental health services. *Community Mental Health Journal, 21,* 156–166.

Nesse, R. M., Cameron, O. G., Curtis, G. C., McCann, D. S., & Huber-Smith, M. J. (1984). Adrenergic function in patients with panic anxiety. *Archives of General Psychiatry, 41,* 771–776.

Nestadt, G., Bienvenu, O. J., Cai, G., Samuels, J., & Eaton, W. W. (1998). Incidence of obsessive-compulsive disorder in adults. *Journal of Nervous and Mental Diseases, 186,* 401–406.

Nestadt, G., Samuels, J., Riddle, M., Bienvenu, O. J., Liang, K. Y., LaBuda, M., et al. (2000). A family study of obsessive compulsive disorder. *Archives of General Psychiatry, 57,* 358–363.

Newman, M. G., Hofmann, S. G., Trabert, W., Roth, W. T., & Taylor, C. B. (1994). Does behavioral treatment of social phobia lead to cognitive changes? *Behavior Therapy, 25,* 503–517.

Norris, F. H., & Kaniasty, K. (1994). Psychological distress following criminal victimization in the general population: Cross-sectional, longitudinal, and prospective analyzes. *Journal of Consulting and Clinical Psychology, 62,* 111–123.

Noyes, R., Jr. (1985). Beta-adrenergic blocking drugs in anxiety and stress. *Psychiatric Clinics of North America, 8,* 119–132.

Noyes, R., Woodman, C., Garvey, M. J., Cook, B. L., Suelzer, M., Clancy, J., et al. (1992). Generalized anxiety disorder versus panic disorder: Distinguishing characteristics and patterns of comorbidity. *Journal of Nervous and Mental Diseases, 180,* 369–378.

Nutt, D., & Lawson, C. (1992). Panic attacks: A neurochemical overview of models and mechanisms. *British Journal of Psychiatry, 160,* 165–178.

Ohman, A. (1986). Face the beast and fear the face: Animal and social fears as prototypes for evolutionary analyzes of emotion. *Psychophysiology, 23,* 123–145.

Ohman, A., Eriksson, A., & Olafsson, C. (1975). One-trial learning and superior resistance to extinction of autonomic responses conditioned to potentially phobic stimuli. *Journal of Comparative and Physiological Psychology, 88,* 619–627.

Ohman, A., Fredrikson, M., Hugdahl, K., & Rimmo, P. A. (1976). The premise of equipotentiality in human classical conditioning: Conditioned electrodermal responses to potentially phobic stimuli. *Journal of Experimental Psychology: General, 105,* 313–337.

Ost, L. G. (1987). Age of onset in different phobias. *Journal of Abnormal Psychology, 96,* 223–229.

Ost, L. G. (1996). Long-term effects of behavior therapy for specific phobia. In M. Mavissakalian & R. R Prien (Eds.), *Long-term treatments of anxiety disorders* (pp. 121–170). Washington, DC: American Psychiatric Press.

Ost, L. G., & Hugdahl, K. (1983). Acquisition of phobias and anxiety response patterns in clinical patients. *Behavior Research and Therapy, 21,* 623–631.

Otto, M. W., Pollack, M. H., Sachs, G. S., Reiter, S. R., Meltzer-Brody, S., & Rosenbaum, J. R. (1993). Discontinuation of benzodiazepine treatment: Efficacy of cognitive-behavioral therapy for patients with panic disorder. *American Journal of Psychiatry, 150,* 1485–1490.

Page, A. C. (1994). Distinguishing panic disorder and agoraphobia from social phobia. *Journal of Nervous and Mental Diseases, 182,* 611–617.

Palatnik, A., Frolov, K., Fux, M., & Benjamin, J. (2001). Double-blind, controlled, crossover trial of inositol versus fluvoxamine for the treatment of panic disorder. *Journal of Clinical Psychopharmacology, 21,* 335–339.

Pallanti, S., Quercioli, L., Paiva, R. S., & Koran, L. M. (1999). Citalopram for treatment-resistant obsessive-compulsive disorder. *European Psychiatry, 14,* 101–106.

Paradis, C. M., Hatch, M., & Friedman, S. (1994). Anxiety disorders in African Americans: An update. *Journal of the National Medical Association, 86,* 609–612.

Parker, G., Wilhelm, K., & Asghari, A. (1997). Early onset depression: The relevance of anxiety. *Social Psychiatry and Psychiatric Epidemiology, 32,* 30–37.

Parker, G., Wilhelm, K., Mitchell, P., Austin, M. P., Roussos, J., & Gladstone, G. (1999). The influence of anxiety as a risk to early onset depression. *Journal of Affective Disorders, 52,* 11–17.

Pato, M. T., Zohar-Kadouch, R., Zohar, J., & Murphy, D. L. (1988). Return of symptoms after discontinuation of clomipramine in patients with obsessive-compulsive disorder. *American Journal of Psychiatry, 145,* 1521–1525.

Pauls, D. L., Alsobrook, J. P., Goodman, W., Rasmussen, S., & Leckman, J. F. (1995). A family study of obsessive-compulsive disorder. *American Journal of Psychiatry, 152,* 76–84.

Perna, G., Caldirola, D., Arancio, C., & Bellodi, L. (1997). Panic attacks: A twin study. *Psychiatry Research, 66,* 69–71.

Perugi, G., Akiskal, H. S., Gemignani, A., Pfanner, C., Presta, S., Milanfranchi, A., et al. (1998). Episodic course in obsessive-compulsive disorder. *European Archives of Psychiatry and Clinical Neuroscience, 248,* 240–244.

Pigott, T. A., & Seay, S. M. (1999). A review of the efficacy of selective serotonin reuptake inhibitors in obsessive-compulsive disorder. *Journal of Clinical Psychiatry, 60,* 101–106.

Pitts, E. N., Jr., & McClure, J. N., Jr. (1967). Lactate metabolism in anxiety neuroses. *New England Journal of Medicine, 277,* 1328–1336.

Pohl, R. B., Wolkow, R. M., & Clary, C. M. (1998). Sertraline in the treatment of panic disorder: A double-blind multicenter trial. *American Journal of Psychiatry, 155,* 1189–1195.

Pollack, M. H., Otto, M. W., Rosenbaum, J. F., & Sachs, G. S. (1992). Personality disorders in patients with panic disorder: Association with childhood anxiety disorders, early trauma, comorbidity, and chronicity. *Comprehensive Psychiatry, 33,* 78–83.

Rachman, S. (1977). The conditioning theory of fear-acquisition. A critical examination. *Behavior Research and Therapy, 15,* 375–387.

Rachman, S. (1988). Panics and their consequences: A review and prospect. In S. Rachman & J. D. Maser (Eds.), *Panic: Psychological perspectives* (pp. 259–303). Hillsdale, NJ: Erlbaum.

Rachman, S. (1990). *Fear and courage* (2nd ed.). New York: Freeman.

Rachman, S., Thordarson, D. S., Shafran, R., & Woody, S. R. (1995). Perceived responsibility: Structure and significance. *Behavior Research and Therapy, 33*, 779–784.

Rapaport, M. H., Pollack, M. H., Clary, C. M., Mardekian, J., & Wolkow, R. (2001). Panic disorder and response to sertraline: The effect of previous treatment with benzodiazepines. *Journal of Clinical Psychopharmacology, 21*, 104–107.

Rapoport, J. L. (1991). Recent advances in obsessive-compulsive disorder. *Neuropsychopharmacology, 5*, 1–10.

Rasmussen, S. (1993). Genetic studies of obsessive-compulsive disorder. *Annals of Clinical Psychiatry, 5*, 241–248.

Rasmussen, S. A., & Eisen, J. L. (1992). The epidemiology and differential diagnosis of obsessive-compulsive disorder. *Journal of Clinical Psychiatry, 53*, 4–10.

Rasmussen, S. A., & Tsuang, M. T. (1986). Clinical characteristics and family history in *DSM-III* obsessive-compulsive disorder. *American Journal of Psychiatry, 143*, 317–322.

Reed, V., & Wittchen, H. U. (1998). *DSM-IV* panic attacks and panic disorder in a community sample of adolescents and young adults: How specific are panic attacks? *Journal of Psychiatric Research, 32*, 335–345.

Regier, D. A., Rae, D. S., Narrow, W. E., Kaelber, C. T., & Schatzberg, A. F. (1998). Prevalence of anxiety disorders and their comorbidity with mood and addictive disorders. *British Journal of Psychiatry, 173*, 24–28.

Reich, J., Goldenberg, I., Goisman, R., Vasile, R., & Keller, M. (1994). A prospective, follow-along study of the course of social phobia. II: Testing for basic predictors of course. *Journal of Nervous and Mental Diseases, 182*, 297–301.

Reich, J. H., & Noyes, R., Jr. (1987). A comparison of *DSM-III* personality disorders in acutely ill panic and depressed patients. *Journal of Anxiety Disorders, 1*, 123–131.

Reiss, S. (1991). Expectancy theory of fear, anxiety, and panic. *Clinical Psychology Review, 11*, 141–153.

Reiss, S., & McNally, R. J. (1985). The expectancy model of fear. In S. Reiss & R. R. Bootzin (Eds.), *Theoretical issues in behavior therapy* (pp. 107–121). New York: Academic Press.

Reiss, S., Peterson, R. A., Gursky, D. M., & McNally, R. J. (1986). Anxiety sensitivity, anxiety frequency, and the prediction of fearfulness. *Behavior Research and Therapy, 24*, 1–8.

Rennenberg, B., Chambless, D. L., & Gracely, E. J. (1992). Prevalence of SCID diagnosed personality disorders in agoraphobic outpatients. *Journal of Anxiety Disorders, 6*, 111–118.

Reznick, J. S., Kagan, J., Snidman, N., Gersten, M., Baak, K., & Rosenberg, A. (1986). Inhibited and uninhibited children: A follow-up study. *Child Development, 57*, 660–680.

Rickels, K., De Martinis, N., Garcia-Espana, F., Greenblatt, D. J., Mandos, L. A., & Rynn, M. (2000). Imipramine and buspirone in treatment of patients with generalized anxiety disorder who are discontinuing long-term benzodiazepine therapy. *American Journal of Psychiatry, 157*, 1973–1979.

Rickels, K., Downing, R., Schweizer, E., & Hassman, H. (1993). Antidepressants for the treatment of generalized anxiety disorder: A placebo-controlled comparison of imipramine, trazodone, and diazepam. *Archives of General Psychiatry, 50*, 884–895.

Rivas-Vazquez, R. A. (2001). Antidepressants as first-line agents in the current pharmacotherapy of anxiety disorders. *Professional Psychology, 32*, 101–104.

Robins, L. N., Helzer, J. E., Weissman, M. M., Orvaschel, H., Greenberg, E., Burke, J. D., Jr., et al. (1984). Lifetime prevalence of specific psychiatric disorders at three sites. *Archives of General Psychiatry, 41*, 949–958.

Rosenbaum, J., Biederman, J., Bolduc, E. A., Faraone, S. V, Hirshfeld, D. R., & Kagan, J. (1992). Comorbidity of parental anxiety disorders at risk for childhood-onset anxiety in inhibited children. *American Journal of Psychiatry, 149,* 475–481.

Rosenbaum, J., Biederman, J., Gersten, M., Hirshfeld, D. R., Meminger, S. R., Herman, J. B., et al. (1988). Behavioral inhibition in children of parents with panic disorder and agoraphobia. *Archives of General Psychiatry, 45,* 463–470.

Rosenbaum, J., Biederman, J., Hirshfeld, D. R., Bolduc, E. A., Kagan, J., Snidman, N., et al. (1991). Further evidence of an association between behavioral inhibition and anxiety disorders: Results from a family study of children from a nonclinical sample. *Journal of Psychiatric Research, 25,* 49–65.

Salaberria, K., & Echeburua, E. (1998). Long-term outcome of cognitive therapy's contribution to self-exposure in vivo to the treatment of social phobia. *Behavior Modification, 22,* 262–284.

Salkovskis, P. M. (1996). The cognitive approach to anxiety: Threat beliefs, safety-seeking behavior, and the special case of health anxiety and obsessions. In P. M. Salkovskis (Ed.), *Frontiers of cognitive therapy* (pp. 48–74). New York: Guilford Press.

Salzman, C., Goldenberg, I., Bruce, S. E., & Keller, M. B. (2001). Pharmacological treatment of anxiety disorders in 1989 versus 1996: Results from the Harvard/Brown anxiety disorders research program. *Journal of Clinical Psychiatry, 62,* 149–152.

Sanchez, M. M., Ladd, C. O., & Plotsky, P. M. (2001). Early adverse experiences as a developmental risk factor for later psychopathology: Evidence from rodent and primate models. *Development and Psychopathology, 13,* 419–449.

Schneier, F. R., Heckelman, L. R., Garfinkel, R., Campeas, R., Fallon, B. A., Gitow, A., et al. (1994). Functional impairment in social phobia. *Journal of Clinical Psychiatry, 55,* 322–331.

Schneier, F. R., Johnson, J., Hornig, C. D., Liebowitz, M. R., & Weissman, M. M. (1992). Social phobia: Comorbidity and morbidity in an epidemiological sample. *Archives of General Psychiatry, 49,* 282–288.

Schneier, F. R., Saoud, J. B., Campeas, R., Fallon, B. A., Hollander, E., Coplan, J., et al. (1993). Buspirone in social phobia. *Journal of Clinical Psychopharmacology, 13,* 251–256.

Scholing, A., & Emmelkamp, P. M. (1993). Exposure with and without cognitive therapy for generalized social phobia: Effects of individual and group treatment. *Behavior Research and Therapy, 31,* 667–681.

Sciuto, G., Diaferia, G., Battaglia, M., Perna, G., Gabriele, A., & Bellodi, L. (1991). *DSM-III-R* personality disorders in panic and obsessive-compulsive disorder: A comparison study. *Comprehensive Psychiatry, 32,* 450–457.

Seligman, M. (1971). Phobias and preparedness. *Behavior Therapy, 2,* 307–320.

Sellwood, W., & Tarrier, N. (1994). Demographic factors associated with extreme noncompliance in schizophrenia. *Social Psychiatry and Epidemiology, 29,* 172–177.

Shapiro, F. (1989). Eye movement desensitization: A new treatment for posttraumatic stress disorder. *Journal of Behavior Therapy and Experimental Psychiatry, 51,* 323–329.

Shapiro, F. (1994). EMDR: In the eye of a paradigm shift. *Behavior Therapist, 17,* 153–156.

Shear, M. K., Devereux, R. B., Kranier-Fox, R., Mann, J. J., & Frances, A. (1984). Low prevalence of mitral valve prolapse in patients with panic disorder. *American Journal of Psychiatry, 141,* 302–303.

Sheehan, D. V, Sheehan, K. E., & Minichiello, W. E. (1981). Age of onset of phobic disorders. *Comprehensive Psychiatry, 22,* 544–553.

Sheikh, J. I., & Swales, P. J. (1999). Treatment of panic disorder in older adults: A pilot study comparison of alprazolam, imipramine, and placebo. *International Journal of Psychiatry in Medicine, 29,* 107–117.

Silverman, W. K., La Greca, A. M., & Wasserstein, S. (1995). What do children worry about? Worries and their relation to anxiety. *Child development, 66,* 671–686.

Simpson, H. B., Schneier, F. R., Campeas, R. B., Marshall, R. D., Fallon, B. A., Davies, S., et al. (1998). Imipramine in the treatment of social phobia. *Journal of Clinical Psychopharmacology, 18,* 132–135.

Sobin, C., Blundell, M. L., & Karayiorgou, M. (2000). Phenotypic differences in early and late onset obsessive-compulsive disorder. *Comprehensive Psychology, 41,* 373–379.

Sobin, C., Blundell, M. L., Weiller, F., Gavigan, C., Haiman, C., & Karayiorgou, M. (2000). Evidence of a schizotypy subtype in OCD. *Journal of Psychiatric Research, 34,* 15–24.

Stanley, M. A., & Turner, S. M. (1995). Current status of pharmacological and behavioral treatment of obsessive-compulsive disorder. *Behavior Therapy, 26,* 163–186.

Stanley, M. A., Turner, S. M., & Borden, J. W. (1990). Schizotypal features in obsessive-compulsive disorder. *Comprehensive Psychiatry, 31,* 511–518.

Starcevic, V., & Bogojevic, G. (1997). Comorbidity of panic disorder with agoraphobia and specific phobia: Relationship with the subtypes of specific phobia. *Comprehensive Psychiatry, 38,* 315–320.

Stein, M. B., Fyer, A. J., Davidson, J. R. T., Pollack, M. H., & Wiita, B. (1999). Fluoxetine treatment of social phobia (social anxiety disorder): A double-blind, placebo-controlled study. *American Journal of Psychiatry, 156,* 756–760.

Stein, M. B., Liebowitz, M. R., Lydiard, R. B., Pitts, C. D., Bushnell, W., & Gergel, I. (1998). Paroxetine treatment of generalized social phobia (social anxiety disorders): A randomized controlled trial. *Journal of the American Medical Association, 280,* 708–713.

Stein, M. B., Walker, J. R., & Forde, D. R. (1994). Setting diagnostic thresholds for social phobia: Considerations from a community survey of social anxiety. *American Journal of Psychiatry, 151,* 408–412.

Steketee, G., & Goldstein, A. J. (1994). Reflections on Shapiro's reflections: Testing EMDR within a theoretical context. *Behavior Therapist, 17,* 156–157.

Steketee, G., & Shapiro, L. J. (1995). Predicting behavioral treatment outcome for agoraphobia and obsessive-compulsive disorder. *Clinical Psychology Review, 15,* 317–346.

Stemberger, R. I., Turner, S. M., Beidel, D. C., & Calhoun, K. (1995). Social phobia: An analysis of possible developmental factors. *Journal of Abnormal Psychology, 104,* 526–531.

Sullivan, G. M., Coplan, J. D., Kent, J. M., & Gorman, J. M. (1999). The noradrenergic system in pathological anxiety: A focus on panic with relevance to generalized anxiety and phobias. *Biological Psychiatry, 46,* 1192–1204.

Suomi, S. J. (1986). Anxiety in young nonhuman primates. In R. Gittelman (Ed.), *Anxiety disorders of childhood* (pp. 1–23). New York: Guilford Press.

Suomi, S. J., Kraemer, G. U., Baysinger, C. M., & Delizio, R. D. (1981). Inherited and experiential factors associated with individual differences in anxious behavior displayed by rhesus monkeys. In D. Klein & J. Rabkin (Eds.), *Anxiety: New research and changing concepts* (pp. 179–200). New York: Raven Press.

Sylvester, C. E., Hyde, T. S., & Reichler, R. J. (1988). Clinical psychopathology among children of adults with panic disorder. In D. L. Dunner, E. S. Gershon, & J. E. Barrett (Eds.), *Relatives at risk for mental disorder* (pp. 87–98). New York: Raven Press.

Tancer, M. E. (1993). Neurobiology of social phobia. *Journal of Clinical Psychiatry, 54,* 26–30.

Tarrier, N., Pilgrim, H., Sommerfield, C., Faragher, B., Reynolds, M., Graham, E., et al. (1999). A randomized trial of cognitive therapy and imaginal exposure in the treatment of chronic posttraumatic stress disorder. *Journal of Consulting and Clinical Psychology, 67,* 13–18.

Taylor, S. (1996). Meta-analysis of cognitive-behavioral treatments for social phobia. *Journal of Behavior Therapy and Experimental Psychiatry, 27,* 1–9.

Thorpe, G. L., & Burns, L. E. (1983). *The agoraphobic syndrome.* New York: Wiley.

Thyer, B. A., Parrish, R. T., Curtis, G. E., Nesse, R. M., & Cameron, O. G. (1985). Age of onset of *DSM-III* anxiety disorders. *Comprehensive Psychiatry, 26,* 113–121.

Todorov, C., Freeston, M. H., & Borgeat, F. (2000). On the pharmacotherapy of obsessive-compulsive disorder: Is a consensus possible? *Canadian Journal of Psychiatry, 45,* 257–262.

Torgersen, S. (1983). Genetic factors in anxiety disorders. *Archives of General Psychiatry, 40,* 1085–1089.

Trivedi, M. H. (1996). Functional neuroanatomy of obsessive-compulsive disorder. *Journal of Clinical Psychiatry, 57,* 26–36.

True, W. R., Rice, J., Eisen, S. A., Heath, A. C., Goldberg, J., Lyons, M. J., et al. (1993). A twin study of genetic and environmental contributions to liability for posttraumatic stress symptoms. *Archives of General Psychiatry, 50,* 257–264.

Turner, S. M., & Beidel, D. C. (1988). *Treating obsessive-compulsive disorder.* New York: Pergamon Press.

Turner, S. M., & Beidel, D. C. (1989a). *On the nature of obsessional thoughts and worry: Similarities and dissimilarities.* Paper prepared for the *DSM-IV* Task Force.

Turner, S. M., & Beidel, D. C. (1989b). Social phobia: Clinical syndrome, diagnosis, and co-morbidity. *Clinical Psychology Review, 9,* 3–18.

Turner, S. M., Beidel, D. C., & Cooley, M. R. (1994). *Social effectiveness therapy: A program for overcoming social anxiety and phobia.* Mount Pleasant, SC: Turndel.

Turner, S. M., Beidel, D. C., & Cooley-Quille, M. R. (1995). Two-year follow-up of social phobias treated with Social Effectiveness Therapy. *Behaviour Research and Therapy, 33,* 553–555.

Turner, S. M., Beidel, D. C., & Costello, A. (1987). Psychopathology in the offspring of anxiety disorders patients. *Journal of Consulting and Clinical Psychology, 55,* 229–235.

Turner, S. M., Beidel, D. C., Dancu, C. V., & Keys, D. J. (1986). Psychopathology of social phobia and comparison to avoidant personality disorder. *Journal of Abnormal Psychology, 95,* 389–394.

Turner, S. M., Beidel, D. C., & Epstein, L. H. (1991). Vulnerability and risk for anxiety disorders. *Journal of Anxiety Disorders, 5,* 151–166.

Turner, S. M., Beidel, D. C., & Frueh, B. C. (2000). *Trauma management therapy for chronic combat-related PTSD: A multicomponent behavioral treatment program.* Unpublished treatment manual, Medical University of South Carolina, Charleston.

Turner, S. M., Beidel, D. C., & Jacob, R. G. (1988). Assessment of panic. In S. Rachman & J. D. Maser (Eds.), *Panic: Psychological perspectives* (pp. 37–50). Hillsdale, NJ: Erlbaum.

Turner, S. M., Beidel, D. C., & Jacob, R. G. (1994). Behavioral and pharmacological treatment of social phobia. *Journal of Consulting and Clinical Psychology, 62,* 350–358.

Turner, S. M., Beidel, D. C., Roberson-Nay, R., & Tervo, K. (2001). *Parenting behaviors in parents with anxiety disorders.* Manuscript submitted for review.

Turner, S. M., Beidel, D. C., & Stanley, M. A. (1992). Are obsessional thoughts and worry different cognitive phenomena? *Clinical Psychology Review, 12,* 257–270.

Turner, S. M., Beidel, D. C., Stanley, M. A., & Heiser, N. (2001). Obsessive-compulsive disorder. In P. B. Sutker & H. E. Adams (Eds.), *Comprehensive handbook of psychopathology* (3rd ed., pp. 155–182). New York: Kluwer Academic/Plenum Press.

Turner, S. M., Beidel, D. C., & Townsley, R. M. (1992). Social phobia: A comparison of specific and generalized subtypes and avoidant personality disorder. *Journal of Abnormal Psychology, 101,* 326–331.

Turner, S. M., Beidel, D. C., & Wolff, P. (1996). Behavioral inhibition: Relationship to anxiety disorders. *Clinical Psychology Review, 16,* 157–172.

Turner, S. M., Beidel, D. C., Wolff, P., Spaulding, S., & Jacob, R. G. (1996). Clinical features affecting treatment outcome in social phobia. *Behavior Research and Therapy, 34,* 795–804.

Turner, S. M., & Cooley-Quille, M. R. (1996). Socioecological and sociocultural variables in psychopharmacological research: Methodological considerations. *Psychopharmacology Bulletin, 32,* 183–192.

Turner, S. M., Cooley-Quille, M. R., & Beidel, D. C. (1996). Behavioral and pharmacological treatment of social phobia: Long-term outcome. In M. Mavissakalian & R. Prien (Eds.), *Anxiety disorders: Psychological and pharmacological treatments* (pp. 291–300). Washington, DC: American Psychiatric Press.

Uhde, T. W., Boulenger, J. P., Roy-Byrne, P. P., Geraci, M. E., Vittone, B. I., & Post, R. M. (1985). Longitudinal course of panic disorder: Clinical and biological considerations. *Progress in Neuro-Psychopharmacology and Biological Psychiatry, 9,* 39–51.

Unnewehr, S., Schneider, S., Florin, I., & Margraf, J. (1998). Psychopathology in children of patients with panic disorder or animal phobia. *Psychopathology, 31,* 69–84.

Van Ameringen, M., Mancini, C., & Streiner, D. (1993). Fluoxetine efficacy in social phobia. *Journal of Clinical Psychiatry, 54,* 27–32.

Van Dam-Baggen, R., & Kraaimaat, F. (2000). Social skills training or cognitive group therapy as the clinical treatment of choice for generalized social phobia? *Journal of Anxiety Disorders, 14,* 437–451.

van der Kolk, B. A., Dreyfuss, D., Michaels, M., Shera, D., Berkowitz, R., Fisler, R., et al. (1994). Fluoxetine in posttraumatic stress disorder. *Journal of Clinical Psychiatry, 55,* 517–523.

Van Valkenburg, C., Akiskal, H. G., Puzantian, V., & Rosenthal, T. (1984). Anxious depressions: Clinical, family history, and naturalistic outcome-comparisons with panic and major depressive disorders. *Journal of Affective Disorders, 6,* 67–82.

Van Velzen, C. J. M., Emmelkamp, P. M. G., & Scholing, A. (2000). Generalized social phobia versus avoidant personality disorder: Differences in psychopathology, personality traits, and social and occupational functioning. *Journal of Anxiety Disorders, 14,* 395–411.

Van Vliet, I. M., den Boer, J. A., & Westenberg, H. G. M. (1994). Psychopharmacological treatment of social phobia; a double-blind placebo-controlled study with fluoxetine. *Psychopharmacology, 115,* 128–134.

VanVliet, I. M., den Boer, J. A., Westenberg, H. G. M., & Pian, K. L. (1997). Clinical effects of buspirone in social phobia: A double-blind placebo-controlled study. *Journal of Clinical Psychiatry, 58,* 164–168.

Versiani, M., Amrein, R., & Montgomery, S. A. (1997). Social phobia: Long-term treatment outcome and prediction of response—a moclobemide study. *International Clinical Psychopharmacology, 12,* 239–254.

Walker, V. J., & Beech, H. R. (1969). Mood states and the ritualistic behavior of obsessional patients. *British Journal of Psychiatry, 150,* 1261–1268.

Warner, V., Mufson, L., & Weissman, M. M. (1995). Offspring at high and low risk for depression and anxiety: Mechanisms of psychiatric disorder. *Journal of the American Academy of Child and Adolescent Psychiatry, 34,* 786–797.

Warren, R., & Thomas, J. C. (2001). Cognitive-behavioral therapy of obsessive-compulsive disorder in private practice: An effectiveness study. *Journal of Anxiety Disorders, 15,* 277–285.

Warshaw, M. G., Dolan, R. T., & Keller, M. B. (2000). Suicidal behavior in patients with current or past panic disorder: Five years of prospective data from the Harvard/Brown anxiety research program. *American Journal of Psychiatry, 157,* 1876–1878.

Watson, J. B., & Rayner, R. (1920). Conditional emotional reactions. *Journal of Experimental Psychology, 3,* 1–14.

Weiller, E., Bisserbe, J. C., Maier, W., & Lecrubier, Y. (1998). Prevalence and recognition of anxiety syndromes in five European primary care settings: A report from the WHO Study on Psychological Problems in General Health Care. *British Journal of Psychiatry, 173,* 18–23.

Weissman, M. M. (1990). Panic and generalized anxiety: Are they separate disorders? *Journal of Psychiatric Research, 24,* 157–162.

Weissman, M. M. (1993). Family genetic studies of panic disorder. *Journal of Psychiatric Research, 27,* 69–78.

Weissman, M. M., Leckman, J. F., Merikangas, K. R., Gammon, G. D., & Prusoff, B. A. (1984). Depression and anxiety disorders in parents and children. *Archives of General Psychiatry, 41,* 845–852.

Weizman, A., Carmi, M., & Hermesh, H. (1986). High affinity imipramine binding and serotonin uptake in platelets of eight adolescent and ten adult obsessive-compulsive patients. *American Journal of Psychiatry, 143,* 335–339.

Wenzel, A., Statler-Cowen, T., Patton, G. K., & Holt, C. S. (1998). *A comprehensive meta-analysis of psychosocial and pharmacological interventions for social phobia and social anxiety.* Poster presented at the 19th annual conference of the Anxiety Disorders Association of America, San Diego, CA.

Westra, H. A., & Stewart, S. H. (1998). Cognitive-behavioral therapy and pharmacotherapy: Complementary or contradictory approaches to the treatment of anxiety. *Clinical Psychology Review, 18,* 307–340.

Wilhelm, S., Otto, M. W., Zucker, B. G., & Pollack, M. H. (1997). Prevalence of body dysmorphic disorder in patients with anxiety disorders. *Journal of Anxiety Disorders, 11,* 499–502.

Wittchen, H. U., & Beloch, E. (1996). The impact of social phobia on quality of life. *International Clinical Psychopharmacology, 11,* 15–24.

Wittchen, H. U., & Hoyer, J. (2001). Generalized anxiety disorder: Nature and course. *Journal of Clinical Psychiatry, 62,* 15–19.

Wittchen, H. U., Stein, M. B., & Kessler, R. C. (1999). Social fears and social phobia in a community sample of adolescents and young adults: Prevalence, risk factors, and comorbidity. *Psychological Medicine, 29,* 309–323.

Wlazlo, A., Schroeder-Hartwig, K., Hand, I., Kaiser, G., & Munchau, N. (1990). Exposure in vivo versus social skills training for social phobia: Long-term outcome and differential effects. *Behavior Research and Therapy, 28,* 181–193.

Woodman, C. L., Noyes, R., Black, D. W., Schlosser, S., & Yagla, S. J. (1999). A 5-year follow-up study of generalized anxiety disorder and panic disorder. *Journal of Nervous and Mental Diseases, 187,* 3–9.

Yamamoto, J., Fungi, D., Loa, S., & Reecho, S. (1979). Psychopharmacology for Asian Americans and Pacific Islanders. *Psychopharmacology Bulletin, 15,* 29–31.

Ziegler, V. E., & Biggs, J. T. (1977). Tricyclic plasma levels-effects of age, race, sex, and smoking. *Journal of the American Medical Association, 238,* 2167–2169.

Zisook, S., Chentsova-Dutton, Y. E., Smith-Vaniz, A., Kline, N. A., Ellenor, G. L., Kodsi, A. B., et al. (2000). Nefazodone in patients with treatment-refractory posttraumatic stress disorder. *Journal of Clinical Psychiatry, 61,* 203–208.

CHAPTER 12

Somatoform Disorders

LAURENCE J. KIRMAYER, KARL J. LOOPER, and SUZANNE TAILLEFER

DESCRIPTION OF THE DISORDERS

THE SOMATOFORM DISORDERS are a group of problems in which people suffer from somatic symptoms or worry about bodily illness or deformity that cannot be accounted for by an organic medical condition or another psychiatric disorder, such as depression or anxiety. While *psychosomatic diseases* are no longer recognized as distinct disorders—as psychological and behavioral factors may affect any medical condition—the somatoform disorders retain the implication of being wholly or predominantly caused by psychological processes. In some cases, this presumption may be unwarranted.

The *Diagnostic and Statistical Manual of Mental Disorders, 4th Edition (DSM-IV;* American Psychiatric Association, 1994) category of *somatoform disorders* emerged from earlier notions of hysteria (Hyler & Spitzer, 1978) and includes seven related disorders: *somatization disorder* (formerly Briquet's syndrome or hysteria), *conversion disorder, pain disorder* (formerly psychogenic or somatoform pain disorder), *hypochondriasis, body dysmorphic disorder,* and two residual categories for patients who do not meet full criteria for any of the previously mentioned disorders—*undifferentiated somatoform disorder* and *somatoform disorder not otherwise specified.*

Despite many conceptual problems, the somatoform disorders survive as a useful set of diagnoses in the *DSM-IV* largely because of their relevance to Western health care systems where patients with medically unexplained somatic symptoms, or bodily distress in excess of what can be explained by organic pathophysiology, present a common clinical problem. Diagnosis of a somatoform disorder serves to label and situate patients who would otherwise fall through the cracks of a diagnostic system increasingly oriented around laboratory tests and biological treatments for specific pathophysiology.

Somatoform disorders are diagnoses that reproduce two fundamental dualisms that are deeply embedded in Western medicine, health psychology, and, indeed, in the everyday concept of the person (Kirmayer, 1988). First, mind and body are distinct realms, so there is something noteworthy or even exceptional about

420

people who express problems in somatic terms that a clinician would situate in the psychological or social realm. Second, what is bodily is somehow more real, substantial, and, ultimately, more legitimate as illness than what is purely psychological. The concept of somatoform disorders emerges from this dualistic conception, contributes to it, and, in consequence, is part of social processes that challenge the legitimacy and reality of people's suffering. The obverse of somatization might be psychologization: the tendency to attribute to psychological factors symptoms that others see as fundamentally somatic in nature. Many mental health practitioners tend to be psychologizers, confidently attributing somatic distress to psychological conflicts, personality traits, or social stressors even when physiological explanations are available (Kirmayer, 2000).

With this cultural construction of the category in mind, in this chapter we review what is known about the somatoform disorders. We argue that, just as the notion of *psychophysiological disorder* has been replaced by that of *psychological factors affecting physical condition*—a shift from a categorical, disorder-based scheme to one of diagnosing specific situations—so, too, should the somatoform disorders be reconceptualized as symptoms or patterns of illness behavior that interact with other medical and psychiatric conditions. As illness behavior, somatoform disorders can be best typified and understood in terms of dimensions rather than categories, processes rather than symptoms and signs, and social contexts rather than isolated behaviors. We think this social and dimensional approach to somatization not only fits the research data better than the individual psychopathology-oriented perspective, but also has important implications for clinical assessment and treatment. Rethinking the category of somatoform disorders from a social and cultural perspective allows us to avoid some of the negative attitudes and stigmatization that plague patients who receive these diagnoses (Kirmayer, 1999).

The *DSM-IV* somatoform disorders share two features:

1. They involve predominantly somatic symptoms or bodily preoccupation.
2. The focus on the body cannot be fully explained by any known medical disease or substance use.

In addition to these features, the diagnostic criteria generally stipulate that symptoms do not result from faking, malingering, or another psychiatric disorder. Although not a specific diagnostic criterion for each diagnosis, use of a somatoform diagnosis to describe a patient's condition reflects the clinician's assessment that psychological factors are a large contributor to the symptom's onset, severity, and duration. To warrant diagnosis, these symptoms must result in significant distress, medical help seeking, and/or impairment of functioning in work or other social roles.

Somatization disorder (SD) is characterized by a pattern of multiple somatic symptoms recurring over a period of several years. Criterion A stipulates that symptoms must begin before age 30 and result in medical help seeking or lead to significant social or occupational impairment. Based on clinical reports and a field trial, *DSM-IV* has simplified the B criteria found in *DSM-III-R* (APA, 1987) to require four different types of symptoms:

1. A history of pain related to at least four different anatomical sites or functions.

2. A history of at least two gastrointestinal symptoms other than pain (e.g., nausea, bloating, vomiting other than during pregnancy, diarrhea, or multiple food intolerance).
3. At least one sexual or reproductive symptom other than pain.
4. At least one pseudoneurological (conversion) symptom not related to pain (American Psychiatric Association [APA], 1994).

A third criterion (C) requires that either there be no medical condition that can fully explain the symptoms or that the distress and disability are in excess of what can be medically explained. The simplified *DSM-IV* criteria show high concordance with the *DSM-III* (APA, 1980) and *DSM-III-R* (APA, 1987) diagnostic criteria based on longer explicit symptom lists (Yutsy et al., 1995).

Undifferentiated somatoform disorder is a broad category that includes patients who do not reach criteria for SD because their symptoms are fewer in number or less severe. Undifferentiated SD simply requires one or more medically unexplained physical complaints lasting at least six months and resulting in "clinically significant" distress or impairment of functioning. This category includes specific constellations of somatic symptoms for which there is no medical explanation. These syndromes are collectively referred to as *functional somatic syndromes* and are found in most areas of medicine (see Table 12.1). Examples include neurasthenia or chronic fatigue syndrome, fibromyalgia, and irritable bowel syndrome.

The status of the common functional somatic syndromes remains ambiguous in *DSM-IV* because of continuing controversy over the validity of medical diagnoses (Barsky & Borus, 1999; Wessely, Nimnuan, & Sharpe, 1999). Thus, irritable bowel syndrome (abdominal symptoms such as pain, bloating, and distension associated with alteration of bowel habits) is presumed to reflect disturbed gut motility and widely viewed as a valid medical disorder. Fibromyalgia syndrome (widespread bodily pain with tenderness at specific anatomical sites called *tender points*) has steadily gained acceptance as a discrete rheumatological disease, while chronic fatigue syndrome (the persistence of debilitating fatigue for at least six months associated with symptoms of malaise) continues to be a hotly contested diagnosis. In spite of many years of medical research and the growing acceptance of some functional somatic syndromes as medical diagnoses, their underlying organic pathology has not been demonstrated. The pressure to label these syndromes as medical diseases and to identify underlying medical causes is as much driven by patient groups and the popular media as it is by the process of scientific development and the medical community (Barsky & Borus, 1999). This may reflect the greater acceptance of medical diagnoses over psychological or ambiguous diagnoses in our culture and the resulting desire to avoid stigmatizing labels (Raguram, Weiss, Channabasavanna, & Devins , 1996). For these and other functional somatic syndromes, the diagnosis remains a process of excluding other organic medical explanations and inferring the relevance of psychological mechanisms because this process of exclusion is never complete, uncertainty about diagnosis remains. Indeed, uncertainty about diagnosis and the self-doubt and social ambiguity that ensue are central to patients' experience of somatoform disorders.

Conversion disorder involves one or more symptoms that affect the voluntary motor or sensory systems and that mimic a neurological or other medical condition. Diagnostic criteria stipulate that psychological factors (i.e., conflicts or other stressors) are judged to be associated with the symptom because they antecede its

Table 12.1
Symptoms and Syndromes of Uncertain Etiology in Medical Specialties

Ear, Nose, and Throat
    Burning tongue or mouth   (Van Houdenhove & Joostens, 1995)
    Intractable sneezing   (Fochtmann, 1995)
    Stridor   (Lacy & McManis, 1994)
    Tinnitus   (Sullivan et al., 1988)

Cardiology
    Chest pain with normal angiogram   (Eifert, 1991)

Endocrinology
    Pseudocyesis   (Starkman et al., 1985)

Gastroenterology
    Dysphagia (difficulty swallowing)   (Kim et al., 1996)
    Irritable bowel   (Thompson & Pigeon-Reesor, 1990)
    Nonulcer dyspepsia   (Wilhelmsen, Haug, Ursin, & Berstad, 1995)

Gynecology
    Chronic pelvic pain   (Walker et al., 1988)
    Dysmenorrhea   (Whitehead et al., 1986)
    Dyspareunia   (Meana & Binik, 1994)
    Hyperemesis gravidarum   (Katon, Ries, Bokan, & Kleinman, 1980)
    Premenstrual tension   (Kuczmierczyk, Labrum, & Johnson, 1995)
    Vaginismus
    Vulvidynia   (McKay & Farrington, 1995)

Infectious Disease and Immunology
    Chronic fatigue   (Abbey & Garfinkel, 1991)
    Environmental sensitivity   (Göthe, Molin, & Nilsson, 1995)
    Multiple or *total* allergy   (Simon, Katon, & Sparks, 1990)

Neurology
    Conversion   (Toone, 1990)
      Pseudoseizures   (Savard, 1990)
      Paralysis   (Fishbain & Goldberg, 1991)
      Paresthesias
      Sensory loss   (Rada, Meyer, & Kellner, 1978)
    Dizziness   (O'Connor, Hallam, Beyts, & Hinclife, 1988)
    Headache   (Blanchard, 1992)
    Post-concussion syndrome   (Lishman, 1988)
    Syncope   (Kapoor, Fortunato, Hanusa, & Schulberg, 1995)

Pulmonology
    Dyspnea (shortness of breath)   (Bass, 1992)

Rheumatology
    Fibromyalgia   (Bennett, 1981)
    Myofascial pain syndromes   (Merskey, 1993)
    Repetitive strain injury   (Sinclair, 1988)

Urology
    Interstitial cystitis   (Ratliff, Klutke, & McDougall, 1994)

onset or exacerbation. Conversion disorder may be subtyped as *with motor symptom or deficit* (e.g., paralyses, ataxia, aphonia, difficulty swallowing, or *globus hystericus* [lump in throat]), *with sensory symptom or deficit* (e.g., paresthesias, diplopia, blindness, deafness, or hallucinations), *with seizures or convulsions* (pseudoepilepsy), or *with mixed presentation.*

Pain disorder involves any clinically significant pain that causes distress and/or impaired functioning for which "psychological factors are judged to have an important role in the onset, severity, exacerbation, or maintenance of the pain" (APA, 1994, p. 461). Pain due to mood, anxiety, or psychotic disorders and dyspareunia (painful intercourse in women) are specifically excluded from the category. Pain disorder is subtyped as associated exclusively with psychological factors or with both psychological factors and a medical condition. In each case, it may be acute or chronic. If no psychological factors are associated with the pain, it is not given a somatoform diagnosis.

Hypochondriasis is characterized by at least six months of preoccupation with fears of having, or the idea that the person has, a serious disease "based on the person's misinterpretation of bodily symptoms" (APA, 1994, p. 465). Preoccupation, fear, or idea must persist despite "appropriate medical evaluation and reassurance" (APA, 1994, p. 465). Hypochondriasis is distinguished from delusional disorder and other somatoform and anxiety disorders. If the person generally does not recognize the excessive or unreasonable nature of his or her illness worry, but the disease conviction does not reach delusional intensity, the diagnosis may be qualified as "with poor insight."

Body dysmorphic disorder involves a "preoccupation with an imagined defect in appearance" (APA, 1994, p. 468) or, if a mild physical anomaly is present, a preoccupation markedly in excess of what is reasonable or appropriate. Dissatisfaction with overall body shape and anorexia nervosa are explicitly excluded.

Somatoform disorder not otherwise specified is a residual category for people with clusters of symptoms that do not meet full criteria for any specific somatoform disorder. Examples given in *DSM-IV* are:

- Pseudocyesis (hysterical pregnancy).
- Nonpsychotic hypochondriacal symptoms of less than six-months' duration (i.e., acute or transient hypochondriacal worry).
- Unexplained physical symptoms of less than six months' duration.

The International Classification of Diseases (ICD-10; World Health Organization [WHO], 1992) uses a very similar nosology. One distinction is that it classifies conversion as a dissociative disorder in recognition of the mechanism through which the symptoms may arise. *Dissociation* refers to the disruption of the usual integration of motor and sensory function with awareness and conscious control. The ICD-10 has the additional category of *somatoform autonomic dysfunction,* which involves *psychogenic* bodily symptoms in organs regulated by the autonomic nervous system. These autonomic syndromes are subdivided by system into heart and cardiovascular (e.g., cardiac neurosis), upper gastrointestinal tract (functional dyspepsia, aerophagia), lower gastrointestinal tract (irritable bowel syndrome), respiratory system (psychogenic hyperventilation, hiccup, cough), genitourinary system (frequent micturation, dysuria), and other organ or system. ICD-10 also includes neurasthenia (chronic mental and/or physical fatigue) as a distinct diagnosis under the rubric of *other neurotic disorders;* many isolated functional somatic symptoms and culture-related somatic syndromes would also be classified under this rubric. To a greater degree than *DSM-IV*, the ICD criteria conflate symptoms and somatic preoccupation, thus making hypochondriacal anxiety more closely related to functional symptoms.

EPIDEMIOLOGY

Somatoform disorder is the single most frequent class of problem in primary care medicine. Medically unexplained symptoms—especially pain, fatigue, and generalized malaise—constitute from 25% to 60% of family medicine practice (Kirkwood et al., 1982; Barsky & Borus, 1999; Katon & Walker, 1998). Every medical specialty has its own collection of *idiopathic* (unexplained) or functional somatic syndromes that reflect the limitations of current medical knowledge more than any identified psychopathology (see Table 12.1). These syndromes occupy a large portion of clinicians' time and effort and account for substantial health care costs. Still, patients who present to the clinic with somatoform disorders represent a fraction of those in the general population with functional somatic syndromes. Many people cope with these problems without medical help. Patients who do come to the clinic often are prompted by coexisting problems such as depression, anxiety, or life stresses. Studies then find much higher rates of psychiatric comorbidity among patients with somatoform disorders in clinical settings compared to community samples. Such comorbidity may partially reflect the cumulative effect of multiple problems on help seeking rather than an intrinsic connection between the mood and anxiety disorders and common functional symptoms. This tendency for clinical studies to overestimate the strength of the association in the general population (a form of what is called *Berkson's bias* in epidemiology) points to the need for community studies to establish the causes of somatoform disorders. Unfortunately, community epidemiological studies are hampered by the necessity for medical evaluation to rule out organic explanations before the diagnosis of somatoform disorders can be made with confidence.

The Epidemiologic Catchment Area (ECA) studies in the United States assessed prevalence of SD in the general population (Robins & Regier, 1991). This was done using the Diagnostic Interview Schedule, a structured interview that lists 38 somatic symptoms and establishes the severity and lack of medical explanation for each symptom. The prevalence of SD varied across the five ECA sites from 0% (Los Angeles) to 0.44% (Durham, North Carolina) with a mean of 0.13% (Swartz, Landerman, George, Blazer, & Escobar, 1991). Other studies of community populations of SD based on different diagnostic criteria found somewhat higher rates, in the range of 0.3% to 0.7% (Faravelli et al., 1997; Rief, Hessel, & Braehler, 2001; Weissman, Myers, & Harding, 1978). SD was more common among women than men, with a ratio of approximately 10 : 1 in the ECA study and 5 : 1 in the study by Rief and colleagues (2001). Prevalence rates also varied across ethnic groups in the ECA study, ranging from 0.08% of Hispanics, to 0.1% of non-Hispanic Whites, and 0.45% of Blacks. All subjects with SD also met criteria for at least one other psychiatric disorder, including phobias (in 69% of SD subjects), major depression (55%), panic disorder (38%), alcohol abuse (23%), schizophrenia (21%), and dysthymia (19%). Only 5% of respondents with SD met criteria for antisocial personality disorder, contrary to previous research and theory linking the two disorders (Lilienfeld, 1992). In general, respondents were equally divided among those with onset of SD before or after a coexisting psychiatric disorder, implying that SD cannot be understood as simply due to an underlying affective or anxiety disorder. However, the development of major depression tended to follow SD, while the development of panic disorder was more closely associated with the onset of SD, suggesting that it may be implicated in the evolution of SD, possibly by increasing health anxiety.

Somatization disorder has also been investigated in primary care settings. The World Health Organization (WHO) Study of Mental Illness in Primary Care (Gureje, Simon, Ustun, & Goldberg, 1997) surveyed 5,438 patients drawn from primary care clinics in 14 countries. The study used a two-stage design with screening for distressed patients using the General Health Questionnaire, followed by diagnosis of SD using the Composite International Diagnostic Inventory (CIDI), a structured diagnostic interview for making both *DSM-IV* and ICD-10 diagnoses (WHO, 1992). The study found that SD was relatively uncommon, ranging from 0.1% to 3% in 13 of 15 sites. Prevalence rates were much higher in two South American sites, which may result from cultural differences in symptom reporting, but no other geographical differences were reported. The mean age of patients diagnosed with SD was 43.3 years. Female gender, older age, and lower education were associated with the diagnosis, but no patterns of cultural differences (other than in the two South American sites) were observed. Somatizing patients reported more disease burden, negative health perception, higher rates of comorbid depression, and generalized anxiety disorder, as well as greater occupational and social disability.

Most patients presenting to physicians with unexplained physical symptoms do not meet the full criteria for SD and fall into the category of *undifferentiated somatoform disorder*. Common medically unexplained symptoms involve pain in various parts of the body (head, back, chest, abdominal, joint), fatigue, dizziness, palpitations, shortness of breath, insomnia, numbness, bloating, and nausea (Kroenke & Price, 1993; Rief et al., 2001; Simon, Gater, Kisely, & Piccinelly, 1996). While no study has explicitly addressed the epidemiology of undifferentiated somatoform disorder, there have been surveys of a wide range of related functional somatic symptoms and conditions (Mayou, Bass, & Sharpe, 1995). Escobar and colleagues (Escobar, Rubio-Stipec, Canino, & Karno, 1989) used the Diagnostic Interview Schedule (DIS), which provides a count of medically unexplained somatic symptoms, to construct a measure of an abridged somatization syndrome (SS). This involves a lifetime occurrence of four medically unexplained symptoms for men and six for women. Somatization syndrome approximates the combined prevalence of undifferentiated somatoform disorder and somatoform disorder not otherwise specified (NOS). In two large community samples from Los Angeles and Puerto Rico, the lifetime rates of SS identified by these criteria were 11.6% (ranging from 4.4% to 20%); 4% of the sample met criteria for *active* SS based on symptoms within the past year. Other surveys have identified higher rates of clinically significant functional or unexplained somatic symptoms in primary care, in the range of 16% to 17% (Garcia-Campayo, Lobo, Perez-Echeverria, & Campos, 1998; Kirmayer & Robbins, 1991b). These studies have led to suggestions for modifications to the diagnostic criteria that currently result in a very restrictive diagnosis of SD and excessive heterogeneity within the diagnosis of undifferentiated somatoform disorder (Escobar et al., 1989; Hiller, Rief, & Fichter, 1995; Katon et al., 1991; Kroenke et al., 1997). Kroenke et al. proposed multisomatoform disorder (MSD) as an alternative to the diagnosis of undifferentiated somatoform disorder. MSD requires three or more currently bothersome unexplained physical complaints from a symptom checklist and a history of chronic somatization. They developed a symptom checklist of 15 physical symptoms to screen for MSD primary care (Kroenke, Spitzer, deGruy, & Swindle, 1998) and found a prevalence of 8.2% in a large primary care sample.

Most studies of the prevalence of conversion disorder have relied on clinical samples, particularly patients referred to psychiatry or neurology (Akagi & House, 2001; Folks, Ford, & Regan, 1984). Thus, prevalence of conversion disorder is reported to be in the range of 0.87% to 7% of psychiatric patients (Guze, Woodruff, & Clayton, 1971; Stefansson, Messina, & Meyerowitz, 1976) and 1% to 9% of neurology patients (Folks et al., 1984; C. Smith, Clarke, Handrinos, Dunsis, & McKenzie, 2000; Toone, 1990). Studies of community populations have reported the point prevalence to be 33 and 55 per 100,000 (Singh & Lee, 1997; Watts, Cawte, & Kuenssberg, 1964) and yearly prevalence of 0.3% and 0.7% (Faravelli et al., 1997; Nandi et al., 1980). Although the dramatic nature of many conversion symptoms ensures that they come to medical attention, referral samples may, nonetheless, underestimate both community and primary care prevalence. In general, conversion symptoms are thought to be more common in rural regions and in those of lower socioeconomic class and with less formal Western-style education (Folks et al., 1984; Lazare, 1981), although elevated rates have also been found in some urban populations (Swartz, Landerman, Blazer, & George, 1989). Cultural differences are important and may explain elevated rates and specific symptoms reported in various parts of the world (Kirmayer & Santhanam, 2001). Several authors have described a decline in the prevalence of conversion disorder in Britain and the United States over the last half-century (Leff, 1988). However, because most studies are based on referral populations, it remains unclear to what extent this apparent decrease simply represents changes in symptoms and patterns of help seeking (Akagi & House, 2001).

Prevalence of hypochondriasis in the community population is not well established. One study (Looper & Kirmayer, 2001) reports a relatively low rate of 0.2% for the full disorder and 1.3% for the less restrictive syndrome described in the WHO primary care study. Other community-based studies reported a higher rate of 4.5% (Faravelli et al., 1997) for the full diagnosis and 7% for hypochondriacal symptoms (Rief et al., 2001). These differences may result from recruitment of patients through primary care registries (Faravelli et al., 1997), less stringent diagnostic criteria (Rief et al., 2001), and other methodological issues. Illness phobia, reported in 5% of subjects in a community survey (Noyes et al., 2000), is distinguished from hypochondriacal fear in that the individual has a fear or discomfort when exposed to thoughts of illness without necessarily having the fear of being ill. Prevalence of hypochondriasis in primary care patients was assessed by a large multinational study conducted by the WHO (Gureje et al., 1997). The full disorder was found to be relatively uncommon, affecting 0.8% of the sample, and reported a less restrictively defined syndrome in 2.2%. Other studies have identified clinically relevant levels of hypochondriacal symptoms in 4% to 8% of primary care patients (Barsky, Wyshak, Klerman, & Latham, 1990; Kirmayer & Robbins, 1991b). Patients with hypochondriasis have high rates of other Axis I disorders, in particular, mood and anxiety disorders (Barsky, Wyshak, & Klerman, 1992; Gureje et al., 1997). Studies of both clinical and community samples demonstrate that hypochondriasis is associated with psychological distress, help seeking, and impaired functioning (Barsky et al., 1990; Gureje et al., 1997; Looper & Kirmayer, 2001).

Epidemiology of pain disorder has not been well studied. One community survey reported the prevalence of pain disorder as 0.6% in the general population. Other reports indicate that 15% to 33% of the community population between the ages of 25 and 74 report some form of sustained musculoskeletal pain (Magni, Caldieron, Rigatti-Luchini, & Merskey, 1990; Magni, Marchetti, Moreschi, Merskey, & Rigatti Luchini, 1993), and up to 10% to 15% of adults in the United States have some degree of work disability from back pain alone (Von Korff, Dworkin, Le Resche, & Kruger, 1990). Discrepancy between these findings and the relatively low rate reported for somatoform pain disorder may result from diagnostic criteria that requires psychological factors to be clearly associated with the onset, course, or outcome of the pain symptom for the diagnosis to be made.

The prevalence of body dysmorphic disorder (BDD) has been reported to be 0.7% in the community by two independent studies (Faravelli et al., 1997; Otto, Wilhelm, Cohen, & Harlow, 2001). This may be an underestimate because patients are reluctant to acknowledge their symptoms and seek psychological or psychiatric treatment (Cororve & Gleaves, 2001). Although rate of BDD in clinical samples has not been thoroughly assessed, it would be expected to be considerably higher in medical specialties, such as dermatology and plastic surgery, where patients with BDD tend to seek help to correct what they perceive to be physical abnormalities. The broader issue of body image dissatisfaction may apply to a large proportion of the population and, in one survey, was reported to be of concern to 28% of college students (Fitts, Gibson, Redding, & Deister, 1989). The focus of concern in BDD is usually an aspect of the face or head, but may involve any area of the body, multiple body parts, or the overall shape and size of the body (Phillips, McElroy, Keck, Pope, & Hudson, 1993). Mood, anxiety, and personality disorders are common comorbid diagnoses in patients with BDD (Veale et al., 1996). BDD has been associated with obsessive-compulsive disorder (Phillips et al., 1993; Simeon, Hollander, Stein, Cohen, & Aronowitz, 1995), but the two are distinguished by the restricted focus of concern about bodily appearance in BDD. The degree of insight into the excessive concern of patients with BDD is variable and includes an extreme at which the additional diagnosis of delusional disorder may be applied (Phillips & McElroy, 1993). Patients with BDD tend to not present spontaneously to mental health professionals, but are occasionally referred by primary care physicians, surgeons, and specialists who identify excessive distress and treatment for relatively minor physical problems.

Somatoform disorder NOS is an ill-defined residual category intended to identify clinically relevant cases that do not meet the criteria of the other somatoform diagnoses. No global prevalence can be given for this diagnosis, because the vague diagnostic criteria collect a vast array of disparate symptoms and syndromes. One example is a transient form of hypochondriasis that tends to resolve spontaneously or with a doctor's reassurance, which is found in approximately 4% of primary care patients (Barsky, Cleary, Sarnie, & Klerman, 1993; Robbins & Kirmayer, 1996). Other types of problems categorized as somatoform disorder NOS may be very rare, such as pseudocyesis, or very common, as in various functional somatic symptoms.

CLINICAL PICTURE

The clinical picture of the somatoform disorders varies with the social and cultural background of patients, their specific somatic symptoms, and the clinical context in which patients are seen. Most patients with somatoform disorders seek medical care and are referred to mental health practitioners when medical diagnosis and treatment prove ineffective. As a result of such failure of conventional treatment, patients may seek many alternative forms of care (Kirmayer, 1999). By the time the mental health practitioner sees these patients, they may be frustrated and angry about the care they have received. Patients are often made to feel "it's all in your head." Clinicians, in turn, feel frustrated that ordinary reassurances or symptomatic treatments have been ineffective. The mutual disappointment and blaming of patient and physician sometimes erupt into hostility. In this context, it is easy for the consultant to misattribute anxious, hostile, or paranoid thoughts and behavior in the patient to personality traits when such behavior is, at least in part, a response to circumstances.

SOMATIZATION DISORDER

While age of onset of SD is before age 30 by definition, in the ECA study, 55% of cases reported an onset before age 15 (Swartz et al., 1991, p. 231). This points to a development of SD in early adolescence or childhood. The most common symptoms in SD include chest pain, palpitations, abdominal bloating, depressed feelings, dizziness, weakness, quitting work because of poor health, shortness of breath without exertion, headache, and fatigue (G. Smith, Monson, & Ray, 1986a). This list, however, does not capture the richness of patients' language of suffering.

Case Study 1

A 31-year-old man was referred to a behavioral medicine clinic by an internist for treatment of abdominal pain. He arrived with a carefully written list of his current symptoms ranked by the degree of distress they caused him (from most to least):

- Constant ringing in the ears.
- Dizziness, lightheadedness.
- Headaches with numbness in the face.
- Squeezing at the temples with bands of pressure and fuzzy head.
- Pain in the lower right abdomen.
- Jerking sensations in the throat, chest, and stomach.
- Rapid, steady throbbing throughout the entire body.
- Pains in the middle back, left shoulder, and arm.
- Numbness in the left forearm and hand (right forearm and hand less often).
- Spots before eyes—occasionally.
- Hard-to-breathe feeling.
- Rapid irregular heartbeat and pounding slow heartbeat, both usually accompanied by nausea and lasting several hours.

(Continued)

He denied any personal or emotional problems and said that all was well with his work and home life except that his wife and daughter were upset that his many illnesses prevented them from ever having a family vacation. Treatment focused on developing coping strategies for the four most distressing symptoms with the goal of taking a family vacation. He was able to accomplish this after six sessions of cognitive behavioral therapy with hypnosis for relaxation and symptom management. Three months later, he went to another hospital's emergency room where his recurrent abdominal pain was diagnosed as irritable bowel syndrome. He felt relieved to have a "definite" diagnosis and embarked on a program to control his symptoms through dietary changes (Kirmayer, 1986).

In addition to their somatic complaints, patients with SD commonly suffer from the gamut of psychological symptoms and often meet criteria for mood and anxiety disorders (Wetzel, Guze, Cloninger, & Martin, 1994). It is misleading, therefore, to view SD patients as having predominately somatic problems. More than 70% of patients with SD also meet criteria for personality disorder (Stern, Murphy, & Bass, 1993). Although SD was classically related to histrionic personality (Slavney, 1990), the most commonly associated personality disorders are avoidant, paranoid, self-defeating, and obsessive-compulsive (G. Smith, Golding, Kashner, & Rost, 1991).

Undifferentiated Somatoform Disorder

The number and diversity of functional somatic symptoms may identify subgroups of patients with undifferentiated somatoform disorder:

- A *diversiform* group that reports many different symptoms in different systems, particularly pain complaints that approximates SD.
- An *asthenic* group that reports fewer and less diverse symptoms, mainly fatigue, weakness, and minor illnesses such as upper respiratory tract infections and resembles neurasthenia or chronic fatigue syndrome (Bohman, Cloninger, von Knorring, & Sigvardsson, 1984; Cloninger, Sigvardsson, von Knorring, & Bohman, 1984; Sigvardsson, Bohman, von Knorring, & Cloninger, 1986).

There is evidence both for discrete somatic syndromes, which are common and hence often co-occur, and a general tendency to report many somatic symptoms across diverse physiological systems because of generalized effects of somatic amplification (Barsky & Borus, 1999; Deary, 1999; Wessely et al., 1999). In general, patients with isolated functional symptoms or functional somatic syndromes resemble patients with other medical disorders in having elevated rates of depression, anxiety, and other psychological problems that may be both contributors to and consequences of their somatic illness (Kirmayer & Robbins, 1991a).

CONVERSION DISORDER

Conversion disorder occurs across the life span and tends to affect women more frequently than men (Akagi & House, 2001). By definition, patients with conversion disorder have symptoms resembling a neurological disorder. The most common symptoms include gait disturbances; pseudoseizures; episodes of fainting (syncope) or loss of consciousness; muscle tremors; spasms; weakness or paralysis; sensory changes, including paresthesias or anesthesia; speech disturbances (aphonia); and visual disturbances (blindness, diplopia) (Folks et al., 1984; Tomasson, Dent, & Coryell, 1991; Toone, 1990; Watson & Buranen, 1979a). Among the symptoms classically described as hysterical conversion, the main exception to these pseudoneurological symptoms is pseudocyesis (hysterical pregnancy), which is classified in *DSM-IV* as somatoform disorder NOS (Martin, 1996). Pseudocyesis may be associated with endocrine disturbances, which sets it apart from other conversion symptoms (Small, 1986; Starkman, Marshall, La Ferla, & Kelch, 1985).

Case Study 2

A 52-year-old woman presented to the general hospital emergency room with sudden onset paralysis of her left arm and the inability to straighten her torso, walking and sitting bent over at the waist (a symptom termed *camptocormia*). She described the symptoms as having started abruptly while she was working at her typewriter in the office where she was employed as a secretary. She feared that she had suffered a stroke. Initially, she could give no precipitating stressful event. On later questioning by her regular family physician, she revealed that she had discovered that morning that her employer had promoted a coworker with less seniority, with whom he was having an affair, to a more senior position. She recalled that she initially felt shocked, angry, and betrayed, but these feelings were forgotten when her alarming paralysis suddenly developed. She accepted an explanation from this trusted family physician that her symptoms were a "stress reaction," and she connected the intensity of her reaction to having witnessed the sexual abuse of a sibling when she was a child. Her symptoms gradually resolved over the next two weeks with two sessions of counseling in her doctor's office to validate her feelings, identify other stressors, and plan an appropriate response to her predicament at work.

Although patients with conversion symptoms were classically described as blandly indifferent to their symptoms, showing *la belle indifférence*, clinical experience suggests they are more often concerned and distressed. Such distress, however, may be mitigated by the intimation that there are other even more distressing recent events from which the conversion symptoms serve as a distraction. The form of conversion symptoms may have symbolic meaning in some situations but usually is more readily attributed to available models of illness (Slavney, 1994). For example, patients with epilepsy may develop pseudoseizures (Savard, 1990). About 70% of unilateral conversion symptoms affect the left side of the body (Axelrod, Noonan, & Atanacio, 1980).

HYPOCHONDRIASIS

Patients with hypochondriasis show varying degrees of concern, worry, fear, and preoccupation with the notion that they have an illness. They remain concerned or convinced that something is wrong despite medical reassurance. At times, this conviction may reach near delusional intensity. More typically, patients have anxieties that they view as irrational but find they cannot rid themselves of bodily preoccupation and catastrophizing thoughts.

Case Study 3

A 24-year-old man presented to the mental health clinic with depression and the persistent fear that he had cancer or another mortal illness. Since the age of 12, when he learned of the sudden death of a cousin, he had suffered from constant worries about his health. His parents had responded to his fears by taking him on frequent visits to a pediatrician, where his hyperventilation was misdiagnosed at first as asthma. He viewed himself as vulnerable to illness and was preoccupied with symptoms of weakness, malaise, and a chronically stuffy nose for which he had become dependent on decongestant spray. He described sporadic panic attacks, usually triggered by events that should have made him angry. During these attacks, he feared that he would lose his mind or die of a heart attack. Afterward, he was left feeling still more worried that he had a physical illness. Over many sessions of cognitive-behavioral therapy, it became apparent that he misidentified the bodily concomitants of strong emotions such as anger, fear, or even intense happiness as possible symptoms of illness. Learning to reattribute these somatic symptoms to specific emotions and to the effects of physiological arousal resolved his hypochondriacal worries but did not entirely eliminate his panic attacks.

Hypochondriacal fears commonly accompany depression and anxiety disorders but may arise and persist even when mood and other anxiety symptoms are not present (Noyes et al., 1994a). Hypochondriacal preoccupation often has an obsessional quality and may occur with other symptoms of obsessive-compulsive disorder (Starcevic, 1990). A sense of bodily vulnerability may be associated with more pervasive feelings of fragility of the self or with fears of loss of control.

BODY DYSMORPHIC DISORDER

Patients with BDD are preoccupied with the notion that some aspect of their bodies is misshapen and ugly. This bodily defect is imagined or grossly exaggerated. The most common complaints involve the face (e.g., wrinkles, complexion, facial hair, asymmetric or disproportionate features), hair, nose, and skin, but any body part can be the focus of preoccupation (Phillips, 1991). Patients engage in frequent checking in the mirror to monitor their "defect" and may attempt to camouflage it, usually without success. They are convinced that others are reacting negatively to them and commonly have ideas or delusions of reference. They fear embarrassment and avoid social situations, sometimes to the point of being housebound. As a result, the condition may result in severe social disability.

Case Study 4

A 34-year-old married mother of four was referred to the mental health clinic by a concerned friend. She complained of a five-year history of increasing social isolation caused by an intense fear of offending others with her physical appearance. She believed that her nose had been gradually growing and her eyes shrinking in size, leading to such profound ugliness that no one could stand to look at her. She had isolated herself from neighbors and family. She shopped only in stores on the other side of town where she would not encounter people who knew her. She parked her car outside her children's school but would not go inside to pick them up. She never left her home unless she had a specific errand to run.

She dated the onset of her "physical change" to the birth of her youngest child, at which time the family moved to a new city so that she could care for her elderly parents. Over the three months before consulting the clinic, she had become increasingly distressed and hopeless about her appearance. When others reassured her that her appearance was, in fact, attractive, she thanked them for their kindness but was left completely unconvinced. She asked that therapy be conducted by telephone so that the therapist would not be offended by her appearance and so that she would not have to travel in public to get to appointments.

In a series of 30 cases of BDD referred to psychiatry, all but two cases had mood disorders, mainly major depression (Phillips et al., 1993). Anxiety disorders were the next most common current and lifetime diagnoses, including 50% with social phobia and 37% with obsessive-compulsive disorder (OCD). Fully 77% had a history of psychotic symptoms either associated with a mood disorder (43%) or as a primary psychotic disorder (33%). Given the predominance of obsessive thinking and compulsive behaviors, BDD may be related to OCD and respond to similar pharmacological and behavioral treatments (Hollander, Neville, Frenkel, Josephson, & Liebowitz, 1992). As with OCD, BDD patients' symptoms range along a spectrum of severity from obsession to delusion (Phillips, Kim, & Hudson, 1995).

SOMATIC PRESENTATIONS OF OTHER PSYCHIATRIC DISORDERS

DSM-IV somatoform disorders leave out a group of patients, sometimes described as "somatizing," who have underlying psychiatric disorders (mainly depression, anxiety, or personality disorders but sometimes also psychotic disorders) but who make exclusively somatic clinical presentations. The majority of these patients are willing to acknowledge a psychosocial contribution to their distress provided it is not presented as an explanation that excludes somatic factors (Kirmayer, Robbins, Dworkind, & Yaffe, 1993). As a group, "presenting" somatizers tend to be less depressed than patients who "psychologize," show less social dissatisfaction, have a more negative attitude toward mental illness, and are more likely to have been a medical inpatient (Bridges, Goldberg, Evans, & Sharpe, 1991). They make more normalizing and fewer psychologizing attributions for common somatic symptoms, are less introspective, and are less likely to seek help if they are anxious or depressed (Kirmayer & Robbins, 1996).

COURSE AND PROGNOSIS

There is wide variation in course, disability, and outcome across the somatoform disorders. Patients who meet the relatively stringent diagnostic criteria of SD or hypochondriasis have a more severe and chronic course of illness. However, the majority of patients with a somatoform disorder and, in particular, those with fewer somatic symptoms of shorter duration, usually classified as undifferentiated or NOS, have a much better prognosis, improving either spontaneously or with relatively brief interventions. In general, psychiatric comorbidity is one of the most important factors contributing to chronicity for the range of somatoform disorders (Rief, Hiller, Geissner, & Fichter, 1995). Nevertheless, research demonstrates that cognitive behavioral interventions can significantly reduce symptomatology, distress, disability, and excessive or inappropriate health care utilization (Looper & Kirmayer, 2002; Sharpe et al., 1996; Speckens et al., 1995). Psychopharmacological management of somatoform disorders has not been rigorously studied, although antidepressants have been reported effective in treating functional somatic syndromes (O'Malley et al., 1999).

Somatization disorder is defined as a chronic condition, and patients generally accrue the requisite number of symptoms over a period of several years. The ECA study found that of patients with a lifetime diagnosis of SD, fully 90% had symptoms in the past year, yielding a remission rate of less than 8% (Swartz et al., 1991, p. 227). This high rate of diagnostic stability was also found in a study in which patients were reassessed after 4.5 years of the original diagnosis (Kent, Tomasson, & Coryell, 1995). Patients with SD are likely to continue to experience multiple somatic symptoms in shifting functional systems. They are at risk for iatrogenic illness because of complications of invasive diagnostic procedures and unnecessary medication or surgery. In contrast, patients with subthreshold SD have a much better outcome. In one study, 76% improved, including 30% recovered after a mean of 15.2 months (Speckens, Van Hemert, Bolk, Rooijmans, & Hengeveld, 1996).

For patients with SD, a simple intervention consisting of a consultation letter to the patient's primary care physician has been shown to significantly reduce expenditures for health care and improve health outcomes (Rost, Kashner, & Smith, 1994; G. Smith et al., 1986a). The letter includes information on the diagnosis of SD and suggestions for the frequency of scheduled visits, reduction of investigations of new symptoms, and avoidance of hospitalization and surgery unless clearly indicated. Similar benefits have been demonstrated in psychiatric consultations for primary care patients with undifferentiated somatoform disorder or subsyndromal somatization (G. Smith, Rost, & Kashner, 1995).

Bass and Benjamin (1993) outlined a general approach to the clinical management of the chronic somatizing patient geared to general practitioners. They include the following strategies:

- In the initial interview, identify psychosocial issues but avoid direct confrontation.
- Provide unambiguous information about medical findings.
- Plan time for gradual discussion of psychosocial issues.
- Work out a problem list and negotiate an agenda with the patient.
- Set limits for diagnostic investigations.

Additional efforts at psychological support and reattribution training may further improve outcome (Kashner, Rost, Cohen, Anderson, & Smith, 1995; Lidbeck, 1997; McLeod, Budd, & McClelland, 1997; Speckens et al., 1995; Sumathipala, Hewege, Hanwella, & Mann, 2000).

Conversion disorder tends to be an acute, self-limited condition, with approximately 50% to 90% improved or recovered in studies that reassessed patients after two to six years (Binzer & Kullgren, 1998; Crimlisk et al., 1998; Kent et al., 1995). Conversion symptoms usually have an abrupt onset in relation to some acute stressor, cause substantial impairment, and resolve spontaneously or respond to a wide variety of suggestive therapeutics (Ford & Folks, 1985). Patients who progress to chronicity have less recent onset of symptoms, greater psychiatric comorbidity, intractable social circumstances, and a broader propensity to experience and report multiple somatic symptoms through which they eventually reach criteria for SD (Couprie, Wijdicks, Rooijmans, & van Gijn, 1995; Kent et al., 1995). Longitudinal studies of patients with conversion disorders have found that 10% to 50% are eventually diagnosed with an organic disease, which may have accounted for their conversion symptoms (Cloninger, 1987; Slater, 1965; Watson & Buranen, 1979b); however, results of more recent studies are in the lower end of this range of outcomes (Binzer & Kullgren, 1998; Crimlisk et al., 1998; Kent et al., 1995). The development of SD was found in about 20% of patients with conversion disorder followed for two years in a general hospital (Kent et al., 1995; Tomasson et al., 1991). The link between conversion disorder and SD is overstated in *DSM-IV*, however, because in the general population, sporadic conversion symptoms are much more common than SD. The few recent studies of the treatment of conversion disorder have emphasized a cognitive-behavior therapy, the use of physical rehabilitation methods, and the use of hypnosis (Halligan, Bass, & Marshall, 2001).

Although hypochondriasis is defined as a chronic condition, about 50% of patients with high levels of hypochondriacal worry in primary care have their anxiety at least temporarily resolved with standard reassurance and so have *transient* hypochondriasis (Barsky, Wyshak, & Klerman, 1990b). Medical illness or other life events may give rise to transient hypochondriasis (Barsky et al., 1993). Previous or coexisting psychiatric disorder, including Axis I disorders and personality disorders, predisposes a person to the development of persistent hypochondriasis (Barsky, Cleary, Wyshak, et al., 1992; Robbins & Kirmayer, 1996). Psychoeducational and cognitive-behavioral approaches to reduce hypochondriacal anxiety can improve the prognosis in this group with persistent worry (Barsky, 1996; Warwick & Salkovskis, 1990). Similar results have been reported for patients with BDD (Rosen, Reiter, & Orosan, 1995b).

As noted previously, up to 33% of the adult population in the United States suffers from some form of chronic pain. An eight-year follow-up study suggests that about one third of people with chronic musculoskeletal pain will recover while two thirds continue to be symptomatic (Magni et al., 1993). Patients with multiple, anatomically unrelated pains differ from those with discrete, localized chronic pain in having greater psychiatric comorbidity. Data from the ECA study suggest that the total number of pain complaints is more predictive of associated psychopathology and use of health care services than the specific location, duration, severity, or medical explanation of the pain complaints (S. F. Dworkin, Von Korff, & Le Resche, 1990; Von Korff, Wagner, Dworkin, & Saunders, 1991). People with single pain complaints did not differ from those with no history of pain in rates of psychiatric disorders and health service utilization. Psychological factors contribute to the risk that acute pain will become a chronic condition. In a study of patients with acute herpes zoster (shingles), patients who went on to develop chronic pain had higher state and trait anxiety, more depressive symptoms, lower life satisfaction, and greater disease conviction at the time of their initial assessment (R. H. Dworkin et al., 1992).

ETIOLOGICAL CONSIDERATIONS

Studies of somatoform disorders have considered the role of personality, psychodynamic, cognitive, and social factors in shaping symptom experience. In this section, we consider putative etiological factors in terms of temperamental differences, personality and psychiatric comorbidity; sensory-perceptual mechanisms; cognitive-evaluative processes; emotion suppression or inhibition; and social-interactional factors. Finally, we discuss the role of specific development experiences, including trauma, and present an integrative model of somatization.

PERSONALITY AND PSYCHIATRIC COMORBIDITY

The tendency to experience high levels of both somatic symptoms and emotional distress may reflect underlying temperamental traits, particularly the trait that has been termed *neuroticism* or *negative affectivity* in factorial studies of the dimensions of personality (Pennebaker & Watson, 1991). Individuals high on negative affectivity are more prone to experience affective and anxiety disorders, which give rise to somatic symptoms. Health anxiety and hypochondriacal worry are strongly associated with neuroticism (Cox, Borger, Asmundson, & Taylor, 2000). Lower levels of dysphoria may also give rise to significant somatic symptoms through physiological mechanisms such as hyperventilation or sleep disturbance (Sharpe & Bass, 1992). Individuals with high levels of negative affectivity may also experience more frequent, intense, and distressing bodily sensations because of the dysregulation of autonomic or pain control systems even in the absence of dysphoric mood.

The majority of patients with SD meet criteria for personality disorders (Stern et al., 1993). Indeed, it has been suggested that SD itself is best conceptualized as a personality disorder based on an interaction between temperamental traits of negative affectivity and family experiences modeling and reinforcing the sick role (Kirmayer, Robbins, & Paris, 1994). First-degree relatives of patients with SD have elevated rates of SD, antisocial personality disorder, major depression, and alcoholism (Cloninger, Martin, Guze, & Clayton, 1986). Cross-fostering adoption studies of SD provide evidence for both heritable pathophysiological mechanisms and family environment in somatization (Bohman et al., 1984; Sigvardsson et al., 1986).

In a classic paper, Engel (1959) introduced the notion of the *pain-prone personality* characterized by perfectionistic striving, minimization, or denial of emotional distress. Blumer and Heilbronn (Blumer & Heilbronn, 1982) later expanded this notion to include *ergomania* or *workaholism* and a familial tendency toward depression. Personality factors may play a role in aggravating pain whatever its origins but do not reliably distinguish patients with clear-cut medical explanations for the pain from those whose problems are more complicated and obscure. Turk and Melzack (1992) concluded that "the search for a 'pain prone personality' . . . or psychogenic pain has proved futile" (p. 9).

Studies of clinical populations with pain show high levels of comorbid Axis I disorders. Depression is the most common diagnosis and is found in 25% to 50% of hospital patients with acute pain referred to psychiatric evaluation, and from 10% to 100% of patients with chronic pain (Blumer & Heilbronn, 1982; Romano & Turner, 1985). However, earlier claims that chronic pain was essentially a variant of major depressive disorder (Blumer & Heilbronn, 1982, 1984) have not been borne out by more recent studies showing that many chronic pain patients have little or no evidence of depressed mood (Ahles, Yunus, & Masi, 1987) and that major depression is somewhat more likely to be a consequence of chronic pain than an antecedent (Brown, 1990; Magni, Moreschi, Rigatti-Luchini, & Merskey, 1994). Specific types of pains may be associated with other specific psychiatric disorders; for example, up to one third of patients with noncardiac chest pain have concurrent panic disorder (Beitman, Mukerji, Flaker, & Basha, 1988).

Somatic Perception, Attention, and Amplification

Mechanic and others have studied the effect of "introspectiveness" on the increased reporting of both psychological and somatic symptoms (Hansell & Mechanic, 1986; Mechanic, 1979). Individual differences in the tendency to focus attention on the self and on bodily sensations are associated with elevated symptom reporting in the laboratory and in epidemiological studies (Pennebaker, 1982; Robbins & Kirmayer, 1986, 1991b). While self-focused patients tend to report both somatic and psychological symptoms, patients who preferentially attend to the body may be more likely to report somatic rather than cognitive or emotional symptoms.

Barsky and Klerman (1983) introduced the notion of *somatic amplification,* a hypothesized tendency for individuals to experience bodily sensations as intense, noxious, and disturbing. Related concepts include augmenting-reducing and perceptual sensitivity. Amplification may involve sensory, perceptual, and cognitive-evaluative processes. The background level of everyday bodily discomfort (a sort of bodily "white noise"), as well as the higher levels of distress that ordinarily accompany illness or injury, may be selectively focused on and amplified by some individuals, giving rise to more varied and intense symptom reports and hypochondriacal worry.

To test this hypothesis, Barsky and colleagues (Barsky, Wyshak, & Klerman, 1990a) developed the Somatosensory Amplification Scale (SSAS), an 11-item self-report questionnaire with adequate internal consistency and test-retest reliability. Higher levels on the SSAS were found in hypochondriacal patients as well as in patients making frequent use of medical care (Barsky, 1992; Barsky, Cleary, & Klerman, 1992). Unfortunately, despite its name, the SSAS does not really tap underlying perceptual processes of amplification. It includes many symptom experience items that represent the outcome of hypochondriacal cognitions. There is a need for longitudinal studies to determine the direction of causality between hypochondriasis and less symptom-based measures of amplification.

While selective attention and preoccupation with the body may lead to amplified somatic sensations, conversion symptoms seem to involve a different deployment of attention, in which the affected body part, function, or sensory system is selectively ignored. This form of selective inattention or alternate control is usually subsumed under the construct of dissociation (Kihlstrom, 1992). Evidence that conversion disorders are related to dissociative mechanisms comes from observations of their frequent occurrence in patients with dissociative identity disorder (Putnam, Guroff, Silberman, Barban, & Post, 1986), high levels of hypnotic susceptibility in patients with conversion symptoms (Bliss, 1984), the ability to create laboratory models of conversion symptoms with hypnosis (Sackeim, Nordlie, & Gur, 1979), and a dramatic therapeutic response to hypnosis (Williams, Spiegel, & Mostofsky, 1978).

Dissociative mechanisms may also contribute to other somatic symptoms to the extent that individuals high on hypnotizability or openness to absorbing experiences may be more likely to become intensely focused on and absorbed by bodily sensations. Wickramasekera (1995) has suggested that there are two groups of somatizing patients: one with high levels of hypnotizability and the tendency to be absorbed by their symptoms and the other with unusually low levels and the inability to block out noxious sensations.

COGNITIVE EVALUATION, ATTRIBUTION, AND COPING

Attention is guided by cognitive schemas that indicate potential sources of threat (Cioffi, 1991; Lazarus & Folkman, 1984). Somatizers may be primed by preexisting schemas or beliefs about their own vulnerability to disease to interpret the generalized malaise and symptoms that accompany affective or anxiety disorders as indicating serious physical illness. The literature on hypochondriasis and abnormal illness behavior has demonstrated the role of worry, fear, disease conviction, and self-rated bodily sensitivity or intolerance to noxious stimuli as important correlates of somatic symptom reporting (Barsky, Goodson, Lane, & Cleary, 1988; Barsky & Klerman, 1983; Pilowsky, 1967). Hypochondriacal worry often accompanies depression and anxiety disorders and, when sufficiently intense, may overshadow other symptoms (Barsky, Wyshak, & Klerman, 1992; Kenyon, 1976).

A lack of effective coping with common bodily symptoms or illnesses may result in greater anxiety about the body, increased body-focus, persistent symptoms, and hypochondriacal worry. Hypochondriacal college women (as indicated by high scores on the Minnesota Multiphasic Personality Inventory [MMPI] hypochondriasis scale) tend to spend more time on health-related pursuits than those who are less symptomatic (Karoly & Lecci, 1993). This preoccupation with efforts to assess and maintain health interacts with more specific thoughts linking bodily sensations to illness. Hypochondriacal patients are prone to catastrophizing thoughts in which they equate specific bodily sensations or events with the idea that they are sick (Salkovskis, 1989). For example, a patient may think, "This tightness in my chest is not normal. It's probably from my heart. Maybe I'm going to have a heart attack." These thoughts create more anxiety and focus attention on the chest area. Both the anxiety and the attentional focus may increase muscle tension in the chest wall, leading to more symptoms, which, in turn, increase the conviction that the person is ill. The more dire the symptom interpretation, the greater anxiety, tension, and distress.

Somatic amplification affects both somatic and emotional distress and, therefore, cannot account for the denial of coexisting emotional problems found in some somatizing patients. The selective emphasis on somatic symptoms and explanations for distress may have more to do with attributional style, defense style, or structural factors influencing help seeking and stigmatization. An unwillingness or inability to attribute the bodily concomitants of emotional arousal or affective disorder to psychosocial causes may lead patients to present clinically with somatic symptoms while minimizing underlying emotional distress (Kleinman, 1980; Robbins & Kirmayer, 1986, 1991a; Stoeckle & Barsky, 1980).

Robbins and Kirmayer (1991a) developed the Symptom Interpretation Questionnaire (SIQ), a self-report measure that asks respondents to rate the extent to which they would attribute common somatic symptoms to each of three types of hypothetical causes:

1. *Somatic* (physical disorder or disease).
2. *Psychological* (emotional distress or problem).
3. *Normalizing* (environmental or other ordinary external event; e.g., "If I felt fatigued, I would probably think that it is because I'm emotionally exhausted or discouraged, because I'm anemic or my blood is weak, or because I've been overexerting myself or not exercising enough").

Among family medicine patients, the SIQ has been found to predict somatizing or psychologizing clinical presentations of depression and anxiety (Kirmayer & Robbins, 1996; Robbins & Kirmayer, 1991a). Patients with psychiatric disorders are more likely to attribute common somatic symptoms to psychological causes on the SIQ (Wise & Mann, 1995). A subset of items of the SIQ predicted the tendency for primary care patients with fatigue associated with an acute viral illness to subsequently develop chronic fatigue (Cope, David, Pelosi, & Mann, 1994). Patients who are high-frequency users of medical care are less able to generate normalizing explanations for common somatic symptoms (Rigby, MacLeod, & Sensky, 1993).

Bridges and colleagues (1991) found that patients who make somatized presentations of depression or anxiety in primary care have more hostile attitudes toward mental illness than those who make psychosocial presentations. Somatizers may live in familial or cultural contexts where mental illness is stigmatized. These negative attitudes toward mental illness extend to a greater hesitancy among somatizers to talk to a doctor about any emotional problem and a greater reluctance to seek specialty mental health care (Kirmayer & Robbins, 1996).

Attributions of distress to physical illness may also act to limit the dysphoria and loss of self-esteem that would otherwise result when distress is attributed to personal character or emotional weakness. Bridges and colleagues (1991) suggest that insisting on a physical illness explanation for symptoms and holding the doctor responsible for missing the correct organic diagnosis remove personal blame from the somatizer. The blame-avoidance function of somatization may explain why patients who make somatic presentations of depression or anxiety in primary care tend to report lower levels of dysphoria than do psychosocial presenters (Bridges et al., 1991; Powell, Dolan, & Wessely, 1990; Verhaak & Tijhuis, 1994).

The interaction between anxiety, attention, and attributions is well demonstrated by the phenomenon of "medical students' disease" (Mechanic, 1972). A substantial proportion of medical students experience transient hypochondriasis. The pressures of study, sleep loss, and apprehension about examinations lead to anxiety. Inundated by information about pathophysiology, students scan their bodies and misinterpret benign sensations as signs and symptoms of disease. The hypochondriacal worry that results usually resolves when the stress of examinations passes and when students acquire additional information to clarify that their unusual sensations do not fit the pattern of any disease. To the extent that this is a useful model of transient hypochondriasis, what must be added to explain clinical hypochondriasis are the factors that lead to chronicity.

EMOTION SUPPRESSION, INHIBITION, AND DENIAL

There is limited empirical support for an earlier generation of psychodynamic hypotheses about the relationship of intrapsychic conflict, personality, and defense mechanisms to somatization. Much of this literature assumed an either/or relationship between somatization and psychological mindedness in which distress was either adequately cognized and expressed in symbolic terms through the language of psychology or suppressed, repressed, and converted into physiological distress. This either/or theory has not been borne out in large-scale epidemiological studies where somatic and emotional distress is found to be highly positively correlated rather than inversely correlated as psychodynamic theory might suggest (Simon & Von Korff, 1991). However, these epidemiological studies have not attempted to separate out a subgroup for whom emotional and somatic distress might be inversely correlated, nor can they deal with the possibility that self-reports are not accurate reflections of underlying distress or physiological disturbance. It is possible that epidemiological studies based on self-report questionnaires or lay interviewers incorrectly classify as healthy some people who deny both emotional distress and somatic symptoms (Shedler, Mayman, & Manis, 1993). Study of the consequences of this type of illusory mental health requires careful clinical assessments and measures of dysfunction that are independent of self-report.

A group of related concepts—including *repression-sensitization, alexithymia, levels of emotional awareness,* and *level of thinking*—involves the tendency to suppress emotional expression or the inability to cognitively elaborate emotional conflict. The relevance of these concepts for somatization derives from the theory that suppression or hypocognition of strong emotions leads to more prolonged emotional arousal, which in turn may result in higher levels of somatic symptoms and distress (Pennebaker, 1995).

Some support for the notion of somatization versus verbalization as either/or phenomena comes from studies of repressive coping style (Schwartz, 1990). There is evidence that while individuals who are repressors initially report less emotional distress in response to an acute stressor, they show more prolonged levels of physiological arousal and increased depressive and somatic symptomatology over the long run (Bonanno & Singer, 1990). Similarly, an individual's suppressing or not telling his or her story of stress or trauma may lead to persistent somatic symptoms. Conversely, telling his or her story can relieve symptoms (Pennebaker, 1990).

It often has been claimed that somatizing patients lack *psychological mindedness*—that is, the ability to label, symbolize, and describe their emotions, fantasies, conflicts, or other aspects of their inner lives. Efforts have been made to operationalize this deficit in the concept of *alexithymia*—a term coined by Sifneos (1973) from Greek roots to mean "no words for feeling." Alexithymic individuals are said to lack the ability to discriminate feelings and bodily sensations, tend not to express their psychological states, think in a concrete and action-oriented rather than a reflective way about the world, and lack a rich fantasy life. The Toronto Alexithymia Scale (TAS) is currently the most psychometrically sound self-report measure of alexithymia (Taylor, Bagby, Ryan, & Parker, 1990). The most recent version of the

TAS has three distinct dimensions, which correlate differently with symptom and personality measures (Hendryx, Haviland, Gibbons, & Clark, 1992; Hendryx, Haviland, & Shaw, 1991; Kirmayer & Robbins, 1993). Scores on the TAS are also significantly affected by level of education (Kauhanen, Kaplan, Julkunen, Wilson, & Salonen, 1993; Kirmayer & Robbins, 1993).

There is some preliminary evidence that high scores on the TAS may be predictive of chronicity among somatizing patients (Bach & Bach, 1995) and of somatic complaints among psychiatric patients (Wise & Mann, 1994). However, a community study found no relationship between alexithymia and somatic symptom reporting when anxiety and neuroticism were controlled (Lundh & Simonsson-Sarnecki, 2001). In fact, alexithymia is more closely related to measures of depressive symptoms than to somatization (Cohen, Auld, & Brooker, 1994; Honkalampi, Kintikka, Tanskanen, Lehtonen, & Viinamaki, 2000). Depression or dysphoria may be associated with a range of confusing sensations that cannot be clearly separated into emotions and bodily symptoms. At present, the TAS has little utility in clinical settings and should not be used to exclude patients from psychotherapy because they are deemed "not psychologically minded," because this is likely to be a state secondary to preoccupation with somatic symptoms that can change as these symptoms are directly addressed through techniques of behavioral medicine (Wise, Mann, Mitchell, Hryniak, & Hill, 1990). In some cases, the inability or reluctance of mental health practitioners to address patients' somatic symptoms and concerns may lead to a breakdown in communication that is attributed to psychological deficits in the patient (Kirmayer, 1987).

FAMILY, SOCIAL, AND DEVELOPMENTAL FACTORS

Developmental experiences of reinforcement and modeling of illness behavior play a role in shaping adult illness behavior (Whitehead, Busch, Heller, & Costa, 1986; Whitehead, Winget, Fedoravicius, Wooley, & Blackwell, 1982; Wilkinson, 1988). Somatization is common among children and adolescents (Campo & Fritsch, 1994). Exaggerated parental concerns with illness, pathologizing of normal sensations (or misattribution of bodily concomitants of emotional distress), and medical help seeking may predispose children to develop bodily preoccupation and anxiety as adults (Benjamin & Eminson, 1992; Watt, Stewart, & Cox, 1998). For example, childhood reinforcement of illness behavior in response to menstruation correlates with adult premenstrual symptoms and associated disability; similarly, reinforcement of illness behavior in response to colds predicts adult levels of symptomatology and disability with colds (Whitehead et al., 1994). These effects are specific to illness and independent of the effects of life stress and neuroticism. A lack of parental protection in childhood may also increase the likelihood of high rates of health care utilization for somatoform symptoms in adulthood (Craig, Drake, Mills, & Boardman, 1994).

There has been increasing recognition of the role of childhood trauma and sexual abuse in somatization (Walker, Gelfand, Gelfand, Koss, & Katon, 1995; Walker, Katon, Neraas, Jemelka, & Massoth, 1992). Traumatic experiences in adulthood, such as domestic violence or state violence experienced by refugees, may also lead to persistent somatic problems (McCauley et al., 1995; Westermeyer, Bouafuely, Neider, & Callies, 1989).

Along with dissociative disorders and SD, conversion symptoms may be associated with high rates of childhood sexual abuse (Alper, Devinsky, Perrine, Vazquez, & Luciano, 1993; Coryell & Norten, 1981; Morrison, 1989). However, the association is nonspecific as histories of trauma and abuse are found among patients with a wide range of psychological disorders. A more specific link may exist between suppression or inhibition of verbal response to trauma and subsequent somatic distress (Pennebaker, 1985, 1990).

AN INTEGRATIVE MODEL

The physiological, psychological, and social factors discussed previously may interact in a series of nested vicious cycles to give rise to persistent somatoform disorders. Figure 12.1 depicts some of these loops. Bodily sensations arise from everyday physiological disturbances or common illness, such as viral infections, or from emotional arousal or major mood or anxiety disorders. These sensations may be more or less insistent, capturing attention despite efforts to ignore them, but even mild sensations can become magnified once attention is focused on the affected region of the body. Selective attention to the body or to specific sensations is guided by cognitive-interpretive processes, which make use of symptom and illness schemas. These include attributional processes by which sensations may be interpreted as symptoms or signs of an illness. When an illness schema is accessed, it may guide subsequent attention to identify further symptoms confirmatory of the illness out of the background noise of bodily sensations (Arkes & Harkness, 1980). More or less neutral sensations may also be reevaluated as uncomfortable and threatening. To the extent that the ensuing thoughts and images represent the putative illness as serious, cognitive evaluation leads to illness worry, catastrophizing, and demoralization. Identification of a potentially worrisome symptom leads to the search for a remedy and, if it persists, to adoption of the sick role with restrictions in activity. The response of care providers may validate the sick role or question the reality of the person's symptoms and suffering.

Specific traits and external factors may act at many levels in this evolution of illness cognition and behavior. Constitutional or acquired differences in autonomic and emotional reactivity may make some individuals more prone to experience uncomfortable bodily sensations because of physiological dysregulation or dysphoric mood. Differences in attentional set, attributional style, and coping influence the tendency to minimize, ignore, or explain symptoms away on the one hand, or become absorbed in sensations and convince the person that they are symptoms of a serious illness.

All of these processes are normal aspects of the response to any illness. They may reach disabling levels for some individuals either because of the intensity of specific factors or because of runaway feedback loops. Only some of these potential loops have been drawn in the diagram. One loop involves feedback from illness worry and catastrophizing to emotional arousal, which in turn generates more symptoms. This loop is the focus of the cognitive assessment and treatment of hypochondriasis (Warwick & Salkovskis, 1990). A second loop runs from sick role behavior back to physiological disturbance; this occurs, for example, when restriction or avoidance of activity leads to physical deconditioning with consequent feelings of fatigue, weakness, and muscular discomfort. This loop has been postulated to play a key role in the genesis of chronic fatigue syndrome,

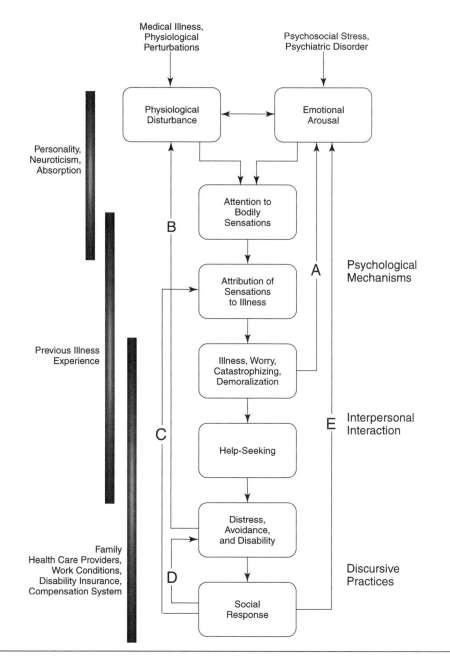

Figure 12.1 An Integrative Model of Somatization. Physiological, psychological, interpersonal, and sociocultural processes all contribute to vicious cycles of symptom amplification that can result in disabling, medically unexplained somatic symptoms. Only a few of these potential cycles are depicted: (A) Illness worry and catastrophizing thoughts result in increased emotional arousal and anxiety, which, in turn, give rise to somatic symptoms associated with autonomic arousal and hyperventilation; (B) avoidance of activity and sick role behavior lead to physical deconditioning, sleep disturbance, and other forms of physiological dysregulation; (C and D) cultural interpretations of symptoms and sick role behavior reinforce pathologizing attributions for new sensations, as well as distress and disablement; (E) sick role behavior may lead to interpersonal conflict, which, in turn, increases emotional arousal, leading to more somatic symptoms.

and cognitive-behavioral interventions aimed at modifying this cycle have proven therapeutically efficacious (Wessely & Sharpe, 1995).

Finally, two loops are drawn to suggest the importance of social processes in exacerbating and maintaining somatization. There is much evidence that the response of family members, employers, health care professionals, and the larger society to a person's illness behavior may either aggravate or resolve somatoform disorders (McDaniel, Hepworth, & Doherty, 1992). Many of these studies involve patients with chronic pain. Couple and family response is known to influence the intensity and disability associated with chronic pain (Block, Kremer, & Gaylor, 1980).

The course of somatoform disorders is strongly influenced by the response of care providers and the health care system. Excessive and invasive diagnostic investigations may increase patients' worry and conviction that they are ill, heighten body consciousness, and lead to the reporting of more somatic symptoms. Conversely, realistic reassurance and opportunities to receive support and clinical care without the need to present fresh somatic symptoms as a "ticket" to see the doctor can reduce the intensity of somatic distress, health care utilization and costs, and the risk of iatrogenic illness (G. Smith, Monson, & Ray, 1986b). The single best predictor of return to work after back injury is preinjury level of job satisfaction (Kleinman, Brodwin, Good, & Good, 1992).

Wider societal attitudes and cultural notions about specific illnesses and vulnerabilities may also contribute to the emergence of specific syndromes. This was observed in the sudden rise in repetitive strain injury syndrome in Australia in response to insurance and disability coverage (Hall & Morrow, 1988). Similar stories could be told about environmental sensitivity syndrome, hypoglycemia, chronic candidiasis, and other historically popular diagnoses that may be promoted by mass media (Shorter, 1994). Chronic fatigue syndrome may be an example of an enduring problem that is undergoing a renaissance due, in part, to media coverage (Abbey & Garfinkel, 1991). In the case of chronic fatigue, the influence from social responses also runs back to attributions. Patients who find their illness doubted or discounted by health care providers may become more insistent on a disease explanation for their distress in an effort to gain legitimacy and counteract the stigma associated with psychological and psychiatric problems (Wessely, 1994). Clinicians' power to ratify illness is a double-edged sword. There is evidence, for example, that primary care patients with an acute viral illness who are intensively investigated are more likely to go on to develop chronic fatigue (Cope et al., 1994). It is particularly important to reassess these social loops when problems do not respond to interventions focused exclusively at an individual level.

DIAGNOSTIC CONSIDERATIONS

The category of somatoform disorders arises from the assumption that medically unexplained somatic distress and worry can be attributed to psychopathology. In fact, this determination is often difficult to make (Kirmayer, 1994). Diagnostic criteria for somatoform disorders raise a number of thorny diagnostic problems including:

- When is a symptom medically unexplained?
- When is worry or distress excessive?

- When can a symptom be called *psychogenic,* that is, predominately caused by psychological factors?

The notion that a symptom is medically unexplained is based on efforts to rule out identifiable organic causes. The extent of the medical investigation depends on available technology and clinical practices. The offering of a plausible explanation for symptoms, even in the absence of definite laboratory confirmation, depends on current medical knowledge. New theories and technology allow further investigations and provide new explanations for previously obscure symptoms. To some extent, the decision that a symptom or syndrome is idiopathic or unexplained reflects diagnostic conventions in the medical community that are, in turn, influenced by larger social forces. For many patients and practitioners, calling a syndrome *unexplained* is tantamount to saying that symptoms are imaginary. However, there are many types of physiological perturbation that can give rise to significant somatic distress (Sharpe & Bass, 1992). For example, unnoticed hyperventilation can give rise to feelings of faintness, shortness of breath, paresthesias, and other unusual sensations. Our ability to measure abnormalities in the functioning of many physiological systems is still quite rudimentary. It is likely that many functional symptoms and syndromes result from disturbances of physiological process rather than gross structural abnormalities and, hence, will lie beyond the power of clinical and laboratory measures to resolve for some time to come.

In the case of hypochondriasis, there is an assumption that worry and emotional distress are greater than appropriate for the severity or likelihood of organic disease. However, there are no established norms for how much distress is appropriate to a given condition; therefore, clinical judgments that distress is exaggerated may be influenced by factors other than the relative level of patients' worry. The diagnostic criteria for hypochondriasis also include the notion that the patient's illness worry does not respond to appropriate medical reassurance. But how much reassurance is enough? Do most patients given the label *hypochondriacal* actually receive adequate reassurance? When assessed in primary care, each laboratory investigation the clinician conducts causes apprehension and uncertainty, so the clinician's ultimate declaration that "nothing is wrong" may be met with some doubt. When hypochondriacal patients are evaluated and treated by mental health practitioners, they may find that a sudden shift to focus on their anxiety and related psychological or social problems conflicts with the experiential primacy of their somatic distress. In either case, the assumption that they have been "adequately" reassured may not be justified as features of the clinical encounter may aggravate hypochondriacal concerns. The observation that many hypochondriacal patients respond well to systematic reassurance and reattribution training points to the limitations of their earlier encounters with physicians (Kellner, 1992; Warwick, 1992).

It is a short segue from the notion that symptoms are medically unexplained or amplified by patients' anxieties, to the assumption that symptoms are caused by psychological factors. Given the epistemological constraints of the clinical setting, however, this assumption often is difficult to support with concrete data. The difficulty of ascertaining psychological causation was openly acknowledged in the *DSM-III-R* criteria for somatoform pain disorder where there was a retreat from the causal imputations of psychogenic pain to the judgment that pain simply persists too long or is too intense. *DSM-IV* pain disorder reinstates a judgment of whether pain is entirely or partially caused by medical or psychological factors as a diagnostic qualifier but this faces the same epistemological difficulties. Melzack, Wall, and Ty (1982) have noted the low correlation between size of tissue injury and severity of pain. Indeed, such observations are basic to their theory of pain, which emphasizes the ability of central cognitive evaluative processes to regulate somatic pain no matter what its origin. This problem is compounded by the fact that observers are not able to reliably discriminate individual differences in style of expression or coping with pain from actual pain experience (Poole & Craig, 1992). In practice, any distinction between psychogenic and organic pain reflects patients' style of self-presentation, credibility, and the larger functioning of the hospital ward or health care team as a system in which the patient is made to carry the brunt of diagnostic uncertainty and treatment failure.

In *DSM-II*, conversion disorder was classified as "hysterical neurosis, conversion type" and characterized by "involuntary psychogenic loss or disorder of function" involving the special senses or voluntary motor system (APA, 1968, p. 39). This definition was broadened in *DSM-III* (APA, 1980) to include any symptom that involved "a loss of, or alteration in," attributed to "a psychological conflict or need" (p. 247). It has proved to be difficult to operationalize and of limited use in discriminating conversion symptoms from symptoms that ultimately prove to have organic causation (Cloninger, 1987; Watson & Buranen, 1979b).

Neither *medically explained, exaggerated distress,* nor *psychogenic causation* are easy criteria to apply, and these diagnostic judgments remain liable to clinician bias and other extraneous factors (Kirmayer, 1988). It may be more useful, therefore, to approach somatoform disorders in terms of psychosocial factors than shape the reporting of all distress—although whether these will prove sufficient to explain the extreme variants that form the prototypical definitions of the *DSM* remains to be seen.

DSM-IV stipulates that to receive a diagnosis of somatoform disorder, symptoms must not be caused by another psychiatric disorder. In many cases, however, symptoms of somatoform disorder are clearly secondary to another antecedent or underlying psychiatric disorder. Somatic symptoms commonly accompany mood and anxiety disorders. Pain, fatigue, and a wide range of other vegetative symptoms are among the most frequent symptoms of major depression. Palpitations, feelings of faintness or dizziness, and other symptoms of autonomic hyperarousal are cardinal signs of panic disorder and other anxiety disorders. Hypochondriacal worry and disease conviction also are common in depression and anxiety disorders. It has been claimed that many somatizing patients have "masked" depressions in which the emotional and cognitive symptoms are muted, hidden, or denied. More commonly, the emotional distress is quite evident but patients insist that it is secondary to their original somatic illness. A somatoform diagnosis serves to acknowledge the prominence of physical symptoms and patients' own somatic causal attributions.

All symptoms should be treated as having both physiological and psychosocial dimensions and should be investigated and treated at multiple levels. This integrative approach avoids the danger that, in labeling symptoms as *psychogenic,* clinicians will no longer search for or discount evidence of underlying organic disease that requires medical attention.

Case Study 5

A 22–year-old Laotian man, who had immigrated to Canada four years earlier, was brought to the hospital emergency room by his brothers and mother. Several hours earlier while comfortably watching television and experiencing no distress, he had the sudden onset of pain in his lower back, radiating forward through his buttocks. This was followed by a paralysis affecting all four limbs. His trunk was unaffected and he had no difficulty breathing. In the emergency room, he appeared to be in little distress, answering the doctor's questions in good humor and apparently only mildly worried about his dramatic symptoms. His physical examination was inconsistent. He had some power in his extremities though deep tendon reflexes could not be elicited. He stated that these symptoms had occurred several times in the last year and always subsided after a few hours. He had stopped work several months earlier and was living with his parents because of fear of recurrent symptoms. A psychiatric consultation was requested to "rule out conversion disorder."

The psychiatric consultant was unable to elicit any history of emotional trauma or stress that might account for the acute onset of symptoms. He considered the impact of migration and the possibility of a poor social adjustment but felt this was too remote to account for increasing symptoms over the last year. He attempted hypnosis to assess the availability of dissociative mechanisms for symptom production; but while the patient relaxed and appeared to enjoy the experience, his paralysis persisted.

On hearing the history of the symptoms, an astute neurologist made the diagnosis of familial periodic hypokalemic paralysis (Stedwell, Allen, & Binder, 1992). The diagnosis was confirmed by the finding of a low serum potassium level, which returned to normal as the patient's paralysis spontaneously resolved over the next few hours.

Determination that symptoms are medically unexplained can involve extensive investigation to rule out occult or obscure diseases. Many chronic illnesses, such as asthma or hypothyroidism, have systemic effects resulting in fatigue and other somatic symptoms. The manifestations and course of these diseases have a high degree of individual variability, and often it remains uncertain whether patients' somatic symptoms are due to a pathophysiological process. Table 12.2 lists some of the many uncommon diseases that give rise to symptoms that are readily mistaken for conversion symptoms. In some cases, laboratory tests or diagnostic maneuvers can elicit physical signs that distinguish between conversion and organic disease.

Psychological factors contributing to somatic distress should be assessed whatever the evidence for or against organic disease. From the illness behavior perspective, the same cognitive and social factors that affect functional illness also influence the symptoms and course of organic illness. The principal difference is the social response to illness based on whether it is viewed as medically validated or remains ambiguous. This underscores the fact that the making of a diagnosis is

Table 12.2
Diseases That May Be Mistaken for
Conversion Symptoms

Basilar artery migraine
Brain tumors
Creutzfeldt-Jakob disease
Diabetic neuropathy
Drug-induced dystonic reactions
Endocrine disorders (e.g., Addison's disease)
Hypokalemic periodic paralysis
Multiple sclerosis
Myasthenia gravis
Temporal lobe epilepsy
Torsion dystonia
Toxic neuropathy
Porphyria
Sensory seizures
Spinal cord tumors
Parkinson's disease
Wilson disease

Source: From *Neuropsychiatric Features of Medical Disorders* (p. 000), by J. W. Jefferson and J. R. Marshall, 1981, New York: Plenum Press. Adapted with permission.

itself an intervention. Diagnostic terms carry personal and social meanings that have immediate implications for patients' wellness, self-esteem, interpretation of subsequent sensations, and potential stigmatization. Diagnostic labels may also function as metaphors that influence subsequent illness experience, coping, and self-image (Kirmayer, 1994).

PSYCHOLOGICAL AND BIOLOGICAL ASSESSMENT

Assessment of patients with somatoform disorders occurs in the context of outpatient or hospital management, disability or compensation evaluation, and research (see Table 12.3). Depending on context, the goals of assessment include:

- To rule out coexisting medical disorders.
- To make a psychiatric diagnosis that can guide clinical treatment planning and intervention.
- To determine the level and types of symptoms, illness impact, and disability.
- To predict outcome or prognosis.
- To assess mediating processes relevant to research or clinical intervention (Barsky, 1996; Bass & Benjamin, 1993; Creed & Guthrie, 1993; Warwick, 1995).

The diagnosis of a somatoform disorder does not indicate the specific symptoms, their meaning and impact for the patient, or their interaction with other psychological, medical, and social problems. Assessment must go well beyond the mere

Table 12.3
An Outline for the Assessment of
Somatizing Patients

Medical comorbidity

Psychiatric comorbidity

Symptom characteristics
    Type
        Location
        Intensity
        Sensory qualities
    Temporal pattern
        Frequency
        Duration
        Contours of onset and resolution

Amplifying factors
    Attention
        Body focus
        Self-focus (introspectiveness)
        Hypnotizability
    Cognition
        Symptom attributions
        Perception of vulnerability and risk
        Catastrophizing thoughts

Coping strategies

Symptom context
    Recent life events
    Chronic stressors
    Marital and family adjustment
    Economic situation
    Work satisfaction
    Social supports

establishment of a diagnosis to include a clinically rich and useful picture of the person's pathology, resources, and life world.

Establishing a collaborative relationship with somatizing patients can pose special challenges (Bass & Benjamin, 1993; McDaniel, Campbell, & Seaburn, 1989). Patients who fear their own emotional vulnerability or who have experienced rejection and stigmatization by doctors, employers, and others may vigorously resist any implication that their problems are psychological in nature. This may reflect both psychological defensiveness and an effort to avoid further stigmatization and negation of the seriousness of their symptoms. The clinician can offer himself or herself as a consultant who is expert in assessing the psychosocial factors that can aggravate any physical illness and in teaching strategies to improve coping with illness. The clinician cannot arbitrate the ontological distinction between "real" organic disease and "imaginary" psychological disorder but must focus instead on factors that maintain symptoms and that are relevant to treatment. It is important to start from the assumption that all pain and other somatic symptoms are real regardless of the relative contribution of physiological and psychological, or peripheral and central, processes. Even pain from identifiable physical lesions is always the outcome of psychological processes (Merskey, 1991). What is at stake in the psychological assessment and diagnosis of somatic symptoms is the identification, for each individual in a specific life context, of factors that exacerbate and/or maintain symptoms and that may be modified to reduce suffering and disability.

Situating the evaluation process in a medical setting may help avoid some of the implicit message that the patients' problems are essentially psychological. In general, somatizing patients are not averse to considering a psychosocial dimension to their problems but rightly reject the implication that their problems are entirely psychological or "all in their head." Frequently, as patients see that the clinician is interested in the details of their somatic symptoms, they volunteer information about emotional distress, social problems, and psychological issues. Sometimes, this opening does not occur until the clinician has succeeded in helping the patient to reduce symptoms. Wickramasekera (1989) argues for a more frontal approach in which the links between emotional distress and conflict and somatic symptoms are directly demonstrated to patients with biofeedback monitoring during a stress-inducing interview in the clinician's office.

Assessment usually begins with the collection of detailed information on the presenting symptoms, their intensity, quality, temporal characteristics, and impact on the patient's life. Using the symptoms as a focus, it is possible to collect detailed information about other aspects of psychological and social functioning, which are introduced in terms of their possible impact on somatic distress, or as areas of functioning where somatic illness may be having disruptive effects. It is often useful to obtain a symptom diary in which the patient records each occurrence of major symptoms, their characteristics, the situations or context in which they occur, the associated cognitive, emotional, and behavioral responses, and the responses of others. This diary involves a form of self-monitoring, which may have immediate therapeutic effects and sets the stage for subsequent cognitive and family interventions.

Although for most clinical purposes simple visual analog scales suffice, there are a number of self-report or interview-based measures for assessing the intensity and quality of specific somatic symptoms including pain (Melzack, 1975), nausea (Melzack, Rosberger, Hollingsworth, & Thirlwell, 1985), and fatigue (Smets, Garssen, Bonke, & De Haes, 1995). These provide sensitive indicators of level of distress as well as various qualitative dimensions and can be used to monitor treatment progress.

PSYCHIATRIC DIAGNOSIS

Several screening interviews and self-report measures for SD have been devised based on the assumption that common *nonspecific* somatic symptoms are more likely to be an indication of underlying psychiatric disorder than of organic medical illness, particularly when symptoms involve many different functional physiological systems. Othmer and De Souza (1985) found seven symptoms that highly discriminated SD patients from a sample of other psychiatric outpatients: vomiting, pain in the extremities, shortness of breath without exertion, amnesia, difficulty swallowing, a burning sensation of the genitals or rectum, and painful menstruation. A similar 11-item index was developed by Swartz and colleagues

(1986) based on statistical analysis of data from the ECA study (Robins & Regier, 1991). The discriminating symptoms included a history of feeling sickly most of one's life, abdominal pain and gas, nausea, diarrhea, dizziness, chest pain, fainting spells, pain in the extremities, vomiting, and weakness. Both indices are useful for screening in epidemiological surveys or clinical settings (G. Smith & Brown, 1990). In *DSM-IV*, a simplified set of criteria for SD has been introduced and validated in a field trial (Yutsy et al., 1995). Clinical screening based on these criteria first ascertains whether patients have a lifetime history of at least four separate pain complaints; if not, the diagnosis of SD can be excluded. Otherwise, the clinician proceeds to inquire about gastrointestinal, sexual or reproductive symptoms, and conversion symptoms. If at least one of each is identified, the patient meets *DSM-IV* criteria for SD.

A variety of structured diagnostic interviews has been devised to assess psychiatric diagnoses in community and clinical populations by standardized criteria. The Diagnostic Interview Schedule (DIS) has been the most widely used instrument of this type (Robins, Helzer, & Orvaschel, 1985). Despite this wide use, the DIS has been criticized by many authors (Bass & Murphy, 1990). Robins and colleagues (Robins, Helzer, Ratcliff, & Seyfired, 1982) found low concordance between psychiatrist and lay interviewers for the diagnosis of SD using the DIS and a sensitivity of only 41%. The DIS asks about lifetime occurrence of symptoms, and the patient's memory may be poor for details of remote illnesses. As well, some patients suffering with somatoform disorders may conceal information in the fear that the physicians will not take their current symptoms seriously. Nonphysician interviewers may have difficulty recognizing SD because they are less able to reject implausible medical explanations offered by patients.

The Composite International Diagnostic Interview (CIDI) is a standardized diagnostic instrument based on the DIS that assesses mental disorders according to both *DSM-III-R* and ICD-10 criteria (Robins et al., 1989). The CIDI assesses more somatoform disorders than the DIS, including SD, conversion disorder, somatoform pain disorder, and hypochondriasis. It is available in 16 languages and incorporates some efforts to make distinctions relevant to cross-cultural diagnosis. The CIDI has been used in a cross-national study of somatoform disorders (Janca, Isaac, Bennett, & Tacchini, 1995).

Barsky and colleagues (Barsky, Cleary, Wyshak, et al., 1992) developed the Structured Diagnostic Interview for Hypochondriasis (SDIH), a clinician-administered diagnostic interview for hypochondriasis modeled on the Structured Clinical Interview for *DSM-III-R* (Spitzer, Williams, Gibbon, & First, 1990). In a sample of general medical clinic patients, the SDIH had an interrater agreement on the diagnosis of 96%, and there was high concordance between the interview and the Whiteley Index (WI) of hypochondriasis (Pilowsky, 1967) and physician's ratings of patients as hypochondriacal. Similar findings were reported by Noyes and colleagues (1993). A seven-item version of the Whiteley Index has also shown promise as a screening tool for both hypochondriasis and other somatoform disorders in primary care (Fink et al., 1999).

Pope and Hudson (1991) developed a structured interview modeled on the SCID to diagnose several common functional somatic syndromes, which the authors hypothesized were variant forms of *affective spectrum disorder*. Although these authors have not published psychometric characteristics of their interview, they have used it to examine the overlap between functional syndromes and their relationship to major depression (Hudson, Goldenberg, Pope, Keck, & Schlesinger, 1992). Robbins and colleagues (Kirmayer, Robbins, Taillefer, & Helzer, 1995) developed the Diagnostic Interview for Functional Syndromes (DIFS), modeled on the DIS for use by trained lay interviewers, to estimate the prevalence of the three most common functional syndromes by currently accepted criteria: fibromyalgia syndrome (FMS), irritable bowel syndrome (IBS), and chronic fatigue syndrome (CFS). However, there was substantial discrepancy between clinician and interview-based diagnoses. This may reflect inconsistencies in clinicians' diagnostic practices and the waxing and waning of symptoms in functional syndromes, as well as inherent limitations of the instrument.

Several instruments have been developed for the assessment of patients with BDD. Jorgensen, Castle, Roberts, and Groth-Marnat (2001) and Phillips, Atala, and Pope (1995) developed the Body Dysmorphic Disorder Questionnaire for use in psychiatric settings. Dufresne, Phillips, Vittorio, and Wilkel (2001) developed a brief self-report questionnaire for use in settings such as dermatology clinics. The Dysmorphic Concern Questionnaire (DCQ; Jorgensen et al., 2001) identifies body-related symptoms in patients who present with depression, OCD, social phobia, or BDD based on the Body Dysmorphic Disorder Questionnaire (Phillips et al., 1995) to screen for BDD in dermatology settings. The Overvalued Ideas Scale (OVIS) is an 11-item clinician-administered scale that measures the severity of overvalued ideation (Neziroglu, McKay, Yaryura-Tobias, Stevens, & Todaro, 1999), which may be predictive of treatment outcome in OCD and BDD patients.

The Irritable Bowel Syndrome Misconception Scale (IBS-MS; Dancey, Fox, & Devins, 1999) is a 17-item questionnaire that measures misconceptions held by people with IBS. It can be used to evaluate the changes in illness-related knowledge gained during intervention programs.

ASSOCIATED FACTORS: PERSONALITY, AMPLIFICATION, AND COPING

Determination of the intensity, duration, and quality of specific symptoms allows diagnosis of somatoform disorders and other possibly comorbid conditions by standardized criteria. However, *DSM-IV* diagnosis is only one aspect of the clinical evaluation. In addition to diagnosis, the clinical assessment of patients with SD requires attention to illness cognitions and coping skills, somatic amplification, attributional biases, related personality traits, as well as the family system, work, and larger social contexts of suffering. These domains can be explored with clinical interviews that start from the nature of somatic symptoms and inquire about the patients' cognitive response as well as their impact on others.

Psychological testing using standard instruments must be adapted to the experience of patients with predominately somatic symptomatology. Test results may be subject to *physiogenic invalidity*—misinterpreting symptoms that arise from the disturbed physiology of disease as evidence of psychopathology.

Neuropsychological testing has limited utility but should be considered where there is a history or signs suggestive of dementia or other organic mental disorder. On formal cognitive testing, CFS patients have mild cognitive impairments that usually are correlated with depressive symptomatology and cannot account for the magnitude of their subjective complaints (Cope, Pernet, Kendall, & David, 1995; DeLuca, Johnson, Beldowicz, & Natelson, 1995; Krupp, Sliwinski, Masur, Friedberg, & Coyle, 1994; McDonald, Cope, & David, 1993).

The Minnesota Multiphasic Personality Inventory (MMPI), in both its original and second-generation versions (MMPI-2), generates several scales relevant to the assessment of somatizing patients (Hathaway & McKinley, 1989). The hypochondriasis scale consists of 32 items, all of which deal with somatic preoccupation or general physical functioning. The standard interpretation of the MMPI suggests that patients with high scores on hypochondriasis have excessive bodily concern; may have conversion disorder or somatic delusions; are likely to be diagnosed as having somatoform, somatoform pain, or depressive or anxiety disorders; are not good candidates for psychotherapy; and tend to be critical of therapists and may terminate therapy prematurely when therapists suggest psychological reasons for symptoms. The MMPI does not provide an adequate assessment of hypochondriacal beliefs for which more specialized instruments are needed.

The 60-item MMPI Hysteria Scale identifies individuals who tend to react to stress by demonstrating physical symptoms such as headaches, stomach discomfort, chest pains, weakness, and somatic symptoms that do not fit the pattern of any known organic disorder. The typical high scorer is said to be someone who avoids responsibility through the development of physical symptoms and is self-centered, narcissistic, egocentric, psychologically immature, and resistant to psychological interpretations. The Hysteria Scale has been divided into two subscales: items that primarily address denial of psychological problems (DH) and items relating to admission of physical problems (AD; McGrath & O'Malley, 1986).

In addition to individual scale scores, the MMPI yields profiles based on multiple scales. A high score on both Hypochondriasis and Hysteria Scales may indicate the presence of a somatoform disorder, particularly if the score on the Depression Scale is low (the so-called *conversion V* pattern). With few exceptions, however, more recent studies with the MMPI have shown that it is not able to reliably distinguish patients with symptoms caused by organic disease and those with medically unexplained symptoms (Blakely et al., 1991; Kim, Hsu, Williams, Weaver, & Zinsmeister, 1996; Pincus, Callahan, Bradley, Vaughn, & Wolfe, 1986). MMPI profile patterns also have not been shown to consistently predict treatment outcome among chronic pain patients (Chapman & Pemberton, 1994). Patients' specific beliefs about pain are better predictors of satisfaction and response to treatment (Deyo & Diehl, 1988). This points to the need for more specific inventories that assess cognitions involved in coping with somatic distress (DeGood & Shutty, 1992).

The Whiteley Index is a self-report measure of hypochondriacal beliefs (Pilowsky, 1967). It contains 14 items tapping three factors:

1. *Bodily preoccupation* (e.g., "Are you bothered by many pains and aches?")
2. *Disease phobia* (e.g., "If a disease is brought to your attention—through radio, television, newspapers, or someone you know—do you worry about getting it yourself?")
3. *Conviction of the presence of disease with nonresponse to reassurance* (e.g., "If you feel ill and someone tells you that you are looking better, do you become annoyed?")

The WI has good test-retest reliability and internal consistency. It has been widely used in studies of hypochondriasis and provides a useful screening measure (Pilowsky, 1990). Although it might be thought to measure *illness worry* rather than hypochondriasis, in fact, it has a low correlation with estimates of the severity of disease and seems to reflect patient characteristics more than disease burden (Robbins & Kirmayer, 1996).

Subsequently, Pilowsky and colleagues (Pilowsky, Murrell, & Gordon, 1979; Pilowsky & Spence, 1983; Pilowsky, Spence, Cobb, & Katsikitis, 1984) developed the Illness Behavior Questionnaire (IBQ) to study the association to assess forms of *abnormal illness behavior* (Pilowsky, 1978). The IBQ is a 62-item self-report instrument measuring patients' attitudes, ideas, affects, and attributions in relation to illness. It generates scores on seven factors of illness behavior, including general hypochondriasis, disease conviction, and denial. While there is a lack of information concerning the IBQ's internal and test-retest reliability (Bradley, Prokop, Gentry, Van der Heide, & Prieto, 1981), an interview form of the questionnaire has been shown to have adequate interrater reliability, with a mean percentage of agreement of 88% (Pilowsky & Spence, 1983).

Several studies have shown that patients with diverse chronic pain syndromes or pain symptoms without organic cause have elevated scores on relevant IBQ scales (Bradley, McDonald Haule, & Jaworski, 1992). However, a study of outpatients visiting a gastroenterology clinic, whose primary complaint was upper abdominal pain, found that among the patients with no organic cause for their pain, only patients with a psychiatric diagnosis had indications of abnormal illness behavior on the IBQ (Colgan, Creed, & Klass, 1988). Other studies have found little difference between patients with CFS and multiple sclerosis (Trigwell, Hatcher, Johnson, Stanley, & House, 1995). Despite its questionable use to discriminate somatoform disorders from other medical conditions, the IBQ remains a useful clinical and research tool to systematically assess a range of important illness cognitions.

The IBQ measures beliefs and attitudes rather than actual behaviors. One of the few attempts to develop an instrument that taps illness behavior is the Illness Behavior Inventory (IBI), developed by Turkat and Pettegrew (1983). The IBI is a 20-item self-report questionnaire assessing two dimensions of illness-related behaviors: *Work-Related Illness Behavior* (9 items pertaining to work and activity when feeling ill; e.g., "I work fewer hours when I'm ill") and *Social Illness Behavior* (11 items concerning illness behaviors in social situations; e.g., "Most people who know me are aware that I take medication"). It has good internal consistency and concurrent validity with the McGill Pain Questionnaire (Melzack, 1980), but has been little used in subsequent research.

The Illness Attitude Scale (IAS) is a 21-item self-report questionnaire measuring seven components of hypochondriasis including generic worry about illness, concern about pain, health beliefs, and bodily preoccupation (Kellner, Abbott, Winslow, & Pathak, 1987). The IAS reflects the authors' hypothesis that the most distinctive characteristic of hypochondriasis is not the fact that patients worry about health but that their fears are not eliminated by a satisfactory medical examination and they are resistant to medical reassurance (Fava & Grandi, 1991). The IAS differentiates between patients with *DSM-III* hypochondriasis and various other clinical groups (Hitchcock & Mathews, 1992).

Instruments also have been devised for the assessment of body image. For example, the Body Dysmorphic Disorder Examination assesses self-consciousness, preoccupation with appearance, overvalued ideas about the importance of appearance to self-worth, and body image avoidance and checking behaviors (Rosen, Reiter, & Orosan, 1995a).

The assessment of symptom and illness meanings and attributions follows standard cognitive therapy strategies developed for work with anxiety and depressive disorders (Salkovskis, 1989; Sharpe, Peveler, & Mayou, 1992; Warwick, 1995). Assessment involves eliciting automatic thoughts and images, exploring cognitive and behavioral coping strategies, and testing alternative thoughts and behaviors. This type of assessment is typically woven into ongoing treatment.

The Social Context of Illness

Assessment of the social context of illness should be a routine part of the assessment of all individual psychopathology. In addition to recent life events, chronic stressors, and social supports, couple and family interviews may reveal crucial interactions that are aggravating or maintaining symptoms—or uncover important resources to aid the clinician in devising treatment strategies (Griffith & Griffith, 1994; McDaniel et al., 1989; Rolland, 1987). New research and clinical instruments are being developed to tap the perceptions and responses of family members to patients with chronic pain and somatic syndromes (Cordingley, Wearden, Appleby, & Fisher, 2001; Sharp & Nicholas, 2000). *DSM-IV* provides an outline for a cultural formulation in Appendix I that should be part of the assessment of all patients with somatoform disorders. When there is significant cultural distance between patient and clinician, other family and community members, culture brokers, and anthropologists can be consulted to explore the local meanings of the symptoms and appropriate treatment approaches.

GENDER AND CULTURAL ISSUES

As discussed earlier in this chapter, SD is about nine times more common among women than men in the general population of North America, and women are more likely to report the range of somatic symptoms (Kroenke & Spitzer, 1998). Similarly, the most common forms of undifferentiated somatoform disorder (e.g., the functional somatic syndromes of fibromyalgia, irritable bowel, and chronic fatigue) are diagnosed from two to nine times more frequently among women than men (Toner, 1995). In contrast, hypochondriasis is equally represented across the genders, and somatized presentations of depression and anxiety may actually be proportionately more common among men (Kirmayer & Robbins, 1991b).

Potential explanations for these gender differences in prevalence include a higher prevalence of related psychiatric disorders among women (i.e., mood and anxiety disorders), which secondarily gives rise to somatoform disorders; differences in illness behavior and help seeking; differential exposure to sexual and physical abuse; social stresses and psychological conflicts associated with gender roles; hormonal or other physiological differences; and gender bias in the diagnostic process (Toner, 1995; Wool & Barsky, 1994). These six hypotheses are discussed in the following paragraphs:

1. Prevalence of major depression (Nolen-Hoeksma, 1995) and several anxiety disorders (Yonkers & Gurguis, 1995) is higher among women than among men. As noted previously, patients with somatoform disorders often have underlying mood or anxiety disorders that may account, in part, for their symptoms. A higher prevalence of these disorders among women could give rise to part of the gender difference in prevalence of somatoform disorders. However, many patients with somatoform disorders do not have identifiable mood or anxiety disorders. Further, the gender difference in somatoform disorders is much greater than that for mood or anxiety, suggesting that other factors must be involved.

2. Women may have a greater tendency to focus on their bodies and, hence, notice and report more symptoms (Pennebaker & Watson, 1991). In addition, women may be more likely to seek help because they are more willing than are men to admit distress and acknowledge the need for assistance (Verbrugge, 1985). In some circumstances, women may be more able to seek help because they are less constrained than men are by full-time employment. More commonly, however, women face considerable barriers to help seeking because of heavy work and family responsibilities. Indeed, Ginsburg and Brown (1982) found that many women with postpartum depression presented their babies to the pediatrician for minor somatic complaints in a sort of "somatization-by-proxy" both because they could not justify taking time for themselves to seek help and because others around them normalized their seriously depressed mood as ordinary "baby-blues."

3. A number of studies have demonstrated high prevalence of sexual or physical abuse among women with somatoform disorders, including IBS and other functional gastrointestinal disorders as well as chronic pelvic pain (Walker et al., 1988; Walker, Gelfand, Gelfand, & Katon, 1995). Women are generally more likely than men to experience sexual and physical abuse; and although somatization is only one possible outcome (Walker, Katon, Hansom, et al., 1992), this could account for some of the differential prevalence. Childhood and domestic violence are common contributors to a wide range of somatic and psychological forms of distress.

4. Gender roles may subject women to increased social stressors, causing elevated levels of both emotional and somatic distress (Verbrugge, 1985). Women may face narrow standards and rigid expectations for physical attractiveness and reproductive fitness that make them preoccupied with their bodies and prone to somatoform disorders (Cash & Pruzinsky, 1990).

5. Physiological differences between men and women may result in differential rates and patterns of functional somatic symptoms. Female sex hormones have effects on smooth muscle throughout the gut and other organ systems and may contribute directly to a higher prevalence of IBS among women (Talley, 1991). The menstrual cycle itself may be associated with a wide range of somatic symptoms and with the intensification of preexisting functional somatic symptoms to a level that prompts help seeking and clinical attention, although perception of menstrual symptoms is itself influenced by other psychological factors (Whitehead et al., 1986).

6. Finally, there may be gender bias in the diagnostic process itself, where-by clinicians are more likely to attribute symptoms to psychosocial causes for women than for men (Kirmayer, 1988). Such a gender bias has been found for the diagnosis of histrionic personality (Chodoff, 1982; Fernbach, Winstead, & Derlega, 1989; Warner, 1978; Winstead, 1984), although the diagnostic criteria themselves are not obviously gender biased, at least when applied by a standardized diagnostic interview (Nestadt et al., 1990). To the extent that women are more forthcoming about psychosocial problems and emotions in the clinician-patient interaction, clinicians may be more likely to view women as emotionally distressed and/or histrionic. Women may be more likely to have their medically unexplained or functional symptoms explicitly labeled as a somatoform disorder (Slavney, Teitelbaum, & Chase, 1985).

Although somatoform disorders are common worldwide, they show great variation in form and prevalence across geographical regions and ethnocultural groups

(Hsu & Folstein, 1997; Kirmayer, 1984). Indeed, the gender ratio itself differs markedly across cultures, giving some evidence of the importance of sociocultural factors in shaping illness experience. A review of cultural aspects of the somatoform disorders for *DSM-IV* suggests three major issues for existing nosology:

1. The overlap between somatoform, affective, and anxiety disorders.
2. Cultural variations in symptomatology.
3. The use of somatic symptoms as idioms of distress (Kirmayer & Weiss, 1996).

Most basically, cross-cultural work challenges the separation of affective, anxiety, dissociative, and somatic categories in the *DSM*. The requirement that patients with somatoform disorders not have another disorder that explains their symptoms seems overly restrictive because somatic symptoms may be such a prominent part of depressive and anxiety disorders. Further, syndromes resembling depression or anxiety but without prominent mood symptoms are common. Neurasthenia may represent an example of this overlap that is not well captured by existing nosology (Ware & Weiss, 1994).

A wealth of clinical observations and anthropological fieldwork demonstrates that there are many culture-specific symptoms. For example, feelings of heat in the head or body are common in equatorial regions as are peppery feelings and the sensations of "worms crawling in the head." In South Asia, men may complain of losing semen in the urine. There have been several attempts to develop expanded symptom inventories with items tapping culture-specific somatic symptoms but these have not been widely used (Ebigbo, 1982; Mumford et al., 1991). Some of the symptoms that appear culture-specific may, in fact, occur in other places but lack salience in terms of local illness categories and so are rarely noticed or reported.

The preferential use of a bodily idiom to express suffering has been linked to cognitive factors in symptom expression, as well as to social, familial, and cultural responses to distress (Angel & Thoits, 1987; Kirmayer, 1986; Kleinman, 1986). In Appendix I, *DSM-IV* lists a variety of cultural idioms of distress with prominent somatic symptoms, including: *ataques de nervios, bilis* or *colera, brain fag, dhat, falling out* or *blacking out, hwa-byung, koro, nervios, shenjing shuairuo,* and *shenkui.* Many of these terms refer to illness causes or explanations rather than to discrete syndromes. They direct attention to the links between social circumstances and somatic distress. They are tied to ethnophysiological notions about how the body works and to local ways of talking about everyday problems. Worldwide, sociosomatics is a more common mode of illness experience and explanation than psychosomatics—that is, people see the connections between untoward social situations and bodily distress and put more emphasis on this than on an individual's psychological characteristics. In a somatic idiom of distress, bodily symptoms may serve to communicate a person's plight to others (Kirmayer & Young, 1998).

Anthropological research suggests several potential ways in which symptoms may have meaning (see Table 12.4). Symptoms may be direct indices of underlying disease or physiological disturbance, occurring as one manifestation of abnormalities in structure or process. To the extent that this meaning is available to the patient, it may play a role in exacerbating illness worry and somatic distress.

Symptoms may also be indices of underlying psychopathology, as when, for example, conversion symptoms are taken to indicate dissociative pathology. The classical psychoanalytic interpretation of somatic symptoms understood them as

Table 12.4
Levels of Potential Meaning of Somatic Symptoms

---

1. Index of disease or physiological disorder.
2. Index of psychopathology.
3. Symbolic representation of psychological conflict.
4. Representation of illness model.
5. Metaphor for experience.
6. Cultural idiom of distress.
7. Act of positioning in a local world.
8. Form of social commentary or protest.

Source: L. J. Kirmayer, T. H. Dao, and A. Smith, 1998, *Clinical Methods in Transcultural Psychiatry*, pp. 240–247.

symbolic expressions of underlying (unconscious) conflicts, which they either represented through analogy or displaced. More recent clinical experience suggests that symptoms more often are related to available illness models in the individual's local world (Slavney, 1990).

Somatic symptoms may also have meaning as metaphors for other domains of experience. These may be idiosyncratic to the individual or drawn from common cultural idioms. These communicative meanings of symptoms may be conscious and explicit or hidden and implicit to patients and their entourage.

Finally, symptoms may function as moves in a local system of power, serving to position the individual and providing more or less explicit social commentary, criticism, or protest. For example, in many families, women who suffer persistent physical complaints may be able to command more resources for help and gain more control over their time and activities than those who try to criticize their spouses directly.

These meanings are not intrinsic to the somatic symptoms but arise from how they are used by patients, their families, and others. In fact, the epistemological limitations of the clinical situation are such that the meaning of symptoms remains largely indeterminate (Kirmayer, 1994). The interpretation of a symptom as having symbolic meaning or as a rhetorical strategy on the part of a patient should always be made because it is helpful to the patient rather than simply because it gives the clinician a satisfying feeling of closure or the license to blame the patient for the limitations of current therapeutics.

SUMMARY

The *DSM-IV* category of somatoform disorder implies that persistent complaints of somatic distress in the absence of a medical explanation represent a distinctive form of psychopathology. Somatic symptoms, however, can arise from a wide range of physiological perturbations, as well as being a normal concomitant of emotional distress. Milder forms of somatoform disorders do not represent a distinctive type of psychopathology. More severe forms (e.g., SD) may reflect the generalized effects of intense emotional distress, as well as other psychological and social factors that contribute to chronicity and disability.

While the *DSM-IV* somatoform disorder diagnoses have utility for research purposes, they may be misleading in clinical contexts: They reify patterns of illness behavior that cut across other psychiatric disorders as discrete conditions; they situate interactional problems inside the person and so promote biological and psychological reductionism; they ignore the social context of suffering and so point away from exactly those social contingencies that explain the onset of symptoms and that hold clues to their alleviation.

An approach in terms of dimensions of illness cognition and behavior may be more fruitful in terms of assessing the psychological factors that may contribute to somatic distress and help seeking. In this view, there are three basic forms of somatization:

1. Functional somatic symptoms that arise from a wide range of different physiological and psychological mechanisms, including autonomic dysregulation, hyperventilation, cognitive-attentional amplification, and dissociation (this category includes undifferentiated somatoform disorder and conversion disorder).
2. Hypochondriacal illness worry, which has similar roots to other anxiety disorders, including panic and generalized anxiety disorder with pathologizing attributions and catastrophizing cognitions that specifically invoke the threat of disease or deformity (dysmorphophobia also fits this model).
3. Somatic presentations of depression, anxiety, and other psychiatric disorders or psychosocial distress, which reflect patients' efforts to avoid the stigma of psychiatric illness and present the doctor with an appropriate somatic complaint.

A broader social focus on family, work, disability, and health care systems may provide explanations for persistent distress and functional impairment that appear inexplicable at purely physiological or even psychological levels. From this perspective, symptoms have potential meanings that may be taken up by patients, their families, and others in ways that either reinforce illness or serve to further invalidate the afflicted person. To the extent that patients must struggle to prove the reality of their suffering to skeptical physicians and incredulous family and friends, they may be forced into a rigid position that exacerbates their illness. For this reason, we have emphasized the importance of understanding the physical and social roots of somatic distress as an entree into the life world of the patient.

REFERENCES

Abbey, S. E., & Garfinkel, P. E. (1991). Neurasthenia and chronic fatigue syndrome: The role of culture in the making of a diagnosis. *American Journal of Psychiatry, 148,* 1638–1646.

Ahles, T. A., Yunus, M. B., & Masi, A. T. (1987). Is chronic pain a variant of depressive disease? The case of primary fibromyalgia syndrome. *Pain, 29,* 105–111.

Akagi, H., & House, A. (2001). The epidemiology of hysterical conversion. In P. W. Halligan, C. M. Bass, & J. C. Marshall (Eds.), *Contemporary approaches to the study of hysteria: Clinical and theoretical perspectives* (pp. 73–87). Oxford, England: Oxford University Press.

Alper, K., Devinsky, O., Perrine, K., Vazquez, B., & Luciano, D. (1993). Nonepileptic seizures and childhood sexual and physical abuse. *Neurology, 43*(10), 1950–1953.

American Psychiatric Association. (1968). *Diagnostic and statistical manual of mental disorders* (2nd ed.). Washington, DC: Author.

American Psychiatric Association. (1980). *Diagnostic and statistical manual of mental disorders* (3rd ed.). Washington, DC: Author.

American Psychiatric Association. (1987). *Diagnostic and statistical manual of mental disorders* (3rd ed., rev.). Washington, DC: Author.

American Psychiatric Association. (1994). *Diagnostic and statistical manual of mental disorders* (4th ed.). Washington, DC: Author.

Angel, R., & Thoits, P. (1987). The impact of culture on the cognitive structure of illness. *Culture, Medicine, and Psychiatry, 11,* 465–494.

Arkes, H. R., & Harkness, A. R. (1980). Effect of making a diagnosis on subsequent recognition of symptoms. *Journal of Experimental Psychology, 6,* 568–575.

Axelrod, S., Noonan, M., & Atanacio, B. (1980). On the laterality of psychogenic somatic symptoms. *Journal of Nervous and Mental Diseases, 168*(9), 517–528.

Bach, M., & Bach, D. (1995). Predictive value of alexithymia: A prospective study in somatizing patients. *Psychotherapy and Psychosomatics, 64*(1), 43–48.

Barsky, A. J. (1992). Amplification, somatization, and the somatoform disorders. *Psychosomatics, 33*(1), 28–34.

Barsky, A. J. (1996). Hypochondriasis: Medical management and psychiatric treatment. *Psychosomatics, 37*(1), 48–56.

Barsky, A. J., & Borus, J. F. (1999). Functional somatic syndromes. *Annals of Internal Medicine, 130,* 910–921.

Barsky, A. J., Cleary, P. D., & Klerman, G. L. (1992). Determinants of perceived health status of medical outpatients. *Social Science and Medicine, 10,* 1147–1154.

Barsky, A. J., Cleary, P. D., Sarnie, M. K., & Klerman, G. L. (1993). The course of transient hypochondriasis. *American Journal of Psychiatry, 150*(3), 484–488.

Barsky, A. J., Cleary, P. D., Wyshak, G., Spitzer, R. L., Williams, J. B. W., & Klerman, G. L. (1992). A structured diagnostic interview for hypochondriasis: A proposed criterion standard. *Journal of Nervous and Mental Diseases, 180*(1), 20–27.

Barsky, A. J., Goodson, J. D., Lane, R. S., & Cleary, P. D. (1988). The amplification of somatic symptoms. *Psychosomatic Medicine, 50,* 510–519.

Barsky, A. J., & Klerman, G. L. (1983). Overview: Hypochondriasis, bodily complaints and somatic styles. *American Journal of Psychiatry, 140*(3), 273–283.

Barsky, A. J., Wyshak, G., & Klerman, G. L. (1990a). The Somatosensory Amplification Scale and its relationship to hypochondriasis. *Journal of Psychiatry Research, 24*(4), 323–334.

Barsky, A. J., Wyshak, G., & Klerman, G. L. (1990b). Transient hypochondriasis. *Archives of General Psychiatry, 47*(8), 746–753.

Barsky, A. J., Wyshak, G., & Klerman, G. L. (1992). Psychiatric comorbidity in *DSM-III-R* hypochondriasis. *Archives of General Psychiatry, 49,* 101–108.

Barsky, A. J., Wyshak, G., Klerman, G. L., & Latham, K. S. (1990). The prevalence of hypochondriasis in medical outpatients. *Social Psychiatry and Psychiatric Epidemiology, 25,* 89–94.

Bass, C. (1992). Chest pain and breathlessness: Relationship to psychiatric illness. *American Journal of Medicine, 92*(Suppl. 1A), 12–15.

Bass, C., & Benjamin, S. (1993). The management of chronic somatisation. *British Journal of Psychiatry, 162,* 472–480.

Bass, C. M., & Murphy, M. R. (1990). Somatization disorder: Critique of the concept and suggestions for further research. In C. M. Bass & R. H. Cawley (Eds.), *Somatization:*

Physical symptoms and psychological illness (pp. 301–332). Oxford, England: Blackwell Scientific Publications.

Beitman, B. D., Mukerji, V., Flaker, G., & Basha, I. M. (1988). Panic disorder, cardiology patients, and atypical chest pain. *Psychiatric Clinics of North America, 11*(2), 387–397.

Benjamin, S., & Eminson, D. M. (1992). Abnormal illness behavior: Childhood experiences and long-term consequences. *International Review of Psychiatry, 4,* 55–70.

Bennett, R. M. (1981). Fibrositis: Misnomer for a common rheumatic disorder. *Western Journal of Medicine, 134,* 405–413.

Binzer, M., & Kullgren, G. (1998). Motor conversion disorder: A prospective 2- to 5-year follow-up study. *Psychosomatics, 39,* 519–527.

Blakely, A. A., Howard, R. C., Sosich, R. M., Murdoch, J. C., Menkes, D. B., & Spears, G. F. (1991). Psychiatric symptoms, personality and ways of coping in chronic fatigue syndrome. *Psychological Medicine, 21*(2), 347–362.

Blanchard, E. B. (1992). Psychological treatment of benign headache disorders. *Journal of Consulting and Clinical Psychology, 60*(4), 537–551.

Bliss, E. L. (1984). Hysteria and hypnosis. *Journal of Nervous and Mental Diseases, 172*(4), 203–206.

Block, A. R., Kremer, E. F., & Gaylor, M. (1980). Behavioral treatment of chronic pain: The spouse as a discriminative cue for pain behavior. *Pain, 8*(3), 367–375.

Blumer, D., & Heilbronn, M. (1982). Chronic pain as a variant of depressive disease: The pain-prone disorder. *Journal of Nervous and Mental Diseases, 170*(7), 381–406.

Blumer, D., & Heilbronn, M. (1984). Chronic pain as a variant of depressive disease: A rejoinder. *Journal of Nervous and Mental Diseases, 172*(7), 405–407.

Bohman, M., Cloninger, C. R., von Knorring, A.-L., & Sigvardsson, S. (1984). An adoption study of somatoform disorders. III: Cross-fostering analysis and genetic relationship to alcoholism and criminality. *Archives of General Psychiatry, 41,* 863–871.

Bonanno, G. A., & Singer, J. L. (1990). Repressive personality style: Theoretical and methodological implications for health and pathology. In J. L. Singer (Ed.), *Repression and dissociation: Implications for personality theory, psychopathology, and health* (pp. 435–470). Chicago: University of Chicago Press.

Bradley, L. A., McDonald Haule, J., & Jaworski, T. M. (1992). Assessment of psychological status using interviews and self-report instruments. In D. C. Turk & R. Melzack (Eds.), *Handbook of pain assessment* (pp. 193–213). London: Guilford Press.

Bradley, L. A., Prokop, C. K., Gentry, W. D., Van der Heide, L. H., & Prieto, E. J. (1981). Assessment of chronic pain. In C. K. Prokop & L. A. Bradley (Eds.), *Medical psychology: Contributions to behavioral medicine* (pp. 91–117). New York: Academic Press.

Bridges, K., Goldberg, D., Evans, B., & Sharpe, T. (1991). Determinants of somatization in primary care. *Psychological Medicine, 21,* 473–483.Brown, G. K. (1990). A causal analysis of chronic pain and depression. *Journal of Abnormal Psychology, 99*(2), 127–137.

Brown, G. K. (1990). A causal analysis of chronic pain and depression. *Journal of Abnormal Psychology, 99*(2), 127–137.

Campo, J. V., & Fritsch, S. L. (1994). Somatization in children and adolescents. *Journal of the American Academy of Child and Adolescent Psychiatry, 33*(9), 1223–1235.

Cash, T. F., & Pruzinsky, T. (Eds.). (1990). *Body images: Development, deviance and change.* New York: Guilford Press.

Chapman, S. L., & Pemberton, J. S. (1994). Prediction of treatment outcome from clinically derived MMPI clusters in rehabilitation for chronic low back pain. *Clinical Journal of Pain, 10*(4), 267–276.

Chodoff, P. (1982). Hysteria and women. *American Journal of Psychiatry, 139,* 545–551.

Cioffi, D. (1991). Beyond attentional strategies: A cognitive-perceptual model of somatic interpretation. *Psychological Bulletin, 109*(1), 25–41.

Cloninger, C. R. (1987). Diagnosis of somatoform disorders: A critique of *DSM-III*. In G. L. Tischler (Ed.), *Diagnosis and classification in psychiatry: A critical appraisal of DSM-III* (pp. 243–259). New York: Cambridge University Press.

Cloninger, C. R., Martin, R. L., Guze, S. B., & Clayton, P. J. (1986). A prospective follow-up and family study of somatization in men and women. *American Journal of Psychiatry, 143*(7), 873–878.

Cloninger, C. R., Sigvardsson, S., von Knorring, A.-L., & Bohman, M. (1984). An adoption study of somatoform disorders. II. Identification of two discrete somatoform disorders. *Archives of General Psychiatry, 41*, 863–871.

Cohen, K., Auld, F., & Brooker, H. (1994). Is alexithymia related to psychosomatic disorder and somatizing? *Journal of Psychosomatic Research, 38*(2), 119–127.

Colgan, S., Creed, F., & Klass, H. (1988). Symptom complaints, psychiatric disorder and abnormal illness behavior in patients with upper abdominal pain. *Psychological Medicine, 18*, 887–892.

Cope, H., David, A., Pelosi, A., & Mann, A. (1994). Predictors of chronic "postviral" fatigue. *Lancet, 344*, 864–868.

Cope, H., Pernet, A., Kendall, B., & David, A. (1995). Cognitive functioning and magnetic resonance imaging in chronic fatigue. *British Journal of Psychiatry, 167*, 86–94.

Cordingley, L., Wearden, A. J., Appleby, L., & Fisher, L. (2001). The family Response Questionnaire: A new scale to assess the responses of family members to people with chronic fatigue syndrome. *Journal of Psychosomatic Research, 51*, 417–424.

Cororve, M. B., & Gleaves, D. H. (2001). Body dysmorphic disorder: A review of conceptualizations, assessment, and treatment strategies. *Clinical Psychology Review, 21*(6), 949–970.

Coryell, W., & Norten, S. (1981). Briquet's syndrome (somatization disorder) and primary depression: Comparison of background and outcome. *Comprehensive Psychiatry, 22*(3), 249–255.

Couprie, W., Wijdicks, E. F., Rooijmans, H. G., & van Gijn, J. (1995). Outcome in conversion disorder: A follow up study. *Journal of Neurology, Neurosurgery and Psychiatry, 58*(6), 750–752.

Cox, B. J., Borger, S. C., Asmundson, G. J. G., & Taylor, S. (2000). Dimensions of hypochondriasis and the five-factor model of personality. *Personality and Individual Differences, 29*(1), 99–108.

Craig, T. K. J., Drake, H., Mills, K., & Boardman, A. P. (1994). The South London Somatisation Study. II: Influence of stressful life events, and secondary gain. *British Journal of Psychiatry, 165*, 248–258.

Creed, F., & Guthrie, E. (1993). Techniques for interviewing the somatising patient. *British Journal of Psychiatry, 162*, 467–471.

Crimlisk, H. L., Bhatia, K., Cope, H., David, A., Marsden, C. D., & Ron, M. A. (1998). Slater revisited: 6 year follow up study of patients with medically unexplained motor symptoms. *British Medical Journal, 316*, 582–586.

Dancey, C. P., Fox, R., & Devins, G. M. (1999). The measurement of irritable bowel syndrome (IBS)-related misconceptions in people with IBS. *Journal of Psychosomatic Research, 47*(3), 269–276.

Deary, I. J. (1999, November). A taxonomy of medically unexplained symptoms. *Journal of Psychosomatic Research, 30*(5), 1080–1089.

DeGood, D. E., & Shutty, M. S. J. (1992). Assessment of pain beliefs, coping, and self-efficacy. In D. C. Turk & R. Melzack (Eds.), *Handbook of pain assessment* (pp. 214–234). New York: Guilford Press.

DeLuca, J., Johnson, S. K., Beldowicz, D., & Natelson, B. H. (1995). Neuropsychological impairments in chronic fatigue syndrome, multiple sclerosis, and depression. *Journal of Neurology, Neurosurgery and Psychiatry, 58*(1), 38–43.

Deyo, R. A., & Diehl, A. K. (1988). Psychosocial predictors of disability in patients with low back pain. *Journal of Rheumatology, 15,* 1557–1564.

Dufresne, R. G., Phillips, K. A., Vittorio, C. C., & Wilkel, C. S. (2001). A screening questionnaire for body dysmorphic disorder in a cosmetic dermatologic surgery practice. *Dermatologic Surgery, 27*(5), 457–462.

Dworkin, R. H., Hartstein, G., Rosner, H. L., Walther, R. R., Sweeney, E. W., & Brand, L. (1992). A high-risk method for studying psychosocial antecedents of chronic pain: The prospective investigation o herpes zoster. *Journal of Abnormal Psychology, 101*(1), 200–205.

Dworkin, S. F., Von Korff, M., & Le Resche, L. (1990). Multiple pains and psychiatric disturbance: An epidemiologic investigation. *Archives of General Psychiatry, 47,* 239–244.

Ebigbo, P. O. (1982). Development of a culture specific (Nigeria) screening scale of somatic complaints indicating psychiatric disturbance. *Culture, Medicine and Psychiatry, 6,* 29–43.

Eifert, G. (1991). Cardiophobia: A paradigmatic behavioral model of heart-focused anxiety and nonanginal chest pain. *Behavior Research and Therapy, 30*(4), 329–345.

Engel, G. E. (1959). "Psychogenic" pain and the pain-prone patient. *American Journal of Medicine, 26,* 899–918.

Escobar, J. L., Rubio-Stipec, M., Canino, G., & Karno, M. (1989). Somatic Symptom Index (SSI): A new and abridged somatization construct. *Journal of Nervous and Mental Diseases, 177*(3), 140–146.

Faravelli, C., Salvatori, S., Galassi, F., Aiazzi, L., Drei, C., & Cabras, P. (1997). Epidemiology of somatoform disorders: A community survey in Florence. *Social Psychiatry and Psychiatric Epidemiology, 32,* 24–29.

Fava, G. A., & Grandi, S. (1991). Differential diagnosis of hypochondriacal fears and beliefs. *Psychotherapy and Psychosomatics, 55*(2/4), 114–119.

Fernbach, B. E., Winstead, B. A., & Derlega, V. J. (1989). Sex differences in diagnosis and treatment recommendations for antisocial personality and somatization disorders. *Journal of Social and Clinical Psychology, 8*(3), 238–255.

Fink, P., Ewald, H., Jensen, J., Sorensen, L., Engberg, M., Holm, M., et al. (1999). Screening for somatization and hypochondriasis in primary care and neurological patients: A seven-item scale for hypochondraisis and somatization. *Journal of Psychosomatic Research, 46*(3), 261–273.

Fitts, S. N., Gibson, P., Redding, C. A., & Deister, P. J. (1989). Body dysmorphic disorder: Implications for its validity as a *DSM-III-R* disorder. *Psychological Reports, 64,* 655–658.

Fochtmann, L. J. (1995). Intractable sneezing as a conversion symptom. *Psychosomatics, 36*(2), 103–112.

Folks, D. G., Ford, C. V., & Regan, W. M. (1984). Conversion symptoms in a general hospital. *Psychosomatics, 25*(4), 285–289, 291, 294–295.

Ford, C. V., & Folks, D. G. (1985). Conversion disorders: An overview. *Psychosomatics, 26*(5), 371–383.

Garcia-Campayo, J., Lobo., A., Perez-Echeverria, J., & Campos, R. (1998). Three forms of somatization presenting in primary care settings in Spain. *Journal of Nervous and Mental Diseases, 186,* 554–560.

Ginsburg, S., & Brown, G. W. (1982). No time for depression: A study of help-seeking among mothers of preschool children. In D. Mechanic (Ed.), *Symptoms, illness behavior, and help-seeking* (pp. 87–114). New York: Neale Watson Academic.

Griffith, J. L., & Griffith, M. E. (1994). *The body speaks: Therapeutic dialogues for mind-body problems.* New York: Basic Books.

Gureje, O., Simon, G. E., Ustun, T. B., & Goldberg, D. P. (1997). Somatization in cross-cultural perspective: A world health organization study in primary care. *American Journal of Psychiatry, 154,* 989–995.

Guze, S. B., Woodruff, R. A., & Clayton, P. J. (1971). A study of conversion symptoms in psychiatric outpatients. *American Journal of Psychiatry, 128*(5), 643–646.

Hall, W., & Morrow, L. (1988). Repetition strain injury: An Australian epidemic of upper limb pain. *Social Science and Medicine, 27*(6), 645–649.

Halligan, P. W., Bass, C., & Marshall, J. C. (Eds.). (2001). *Contemporary approaches to the study of hysteria: Clinical and theoretical perspectives.* Oxford, England: Oxford University Press.

Hansell, S., & Mechanic, D. (1986). The socialization of introspection and illness behavior. In S. McHugh & T. M. Vallis (Eds.), *Illness behavior* (pp. 253–260). New York: Plenum Press.

Hathaway, S. R., & McKinley, J. C. (1989). *Minnesota Multiphasic Personality Inventory-2: Manual for administration.* Minneapolis: University of Minnesota Press.

Hendryx, M. S., Haviland, M. G., Gibbons, R. D., & Clark, D. C. (1992). An application of item response theory to alexithymia assessment among abstinent alcoholics. *Journal of Personality Assessment, 58*(3), 506–515.

Hendryx, M. S., Haviland, M. G., & Shaw, D. G. (1991). Dimensions of alexithymia and their relationships to anxiety and depression. *Journal of Personality Assessment, 56*(2), 227–237.

Hiller, W., Rief, W., & Fichter, M. M. (1995). Further evidence for a broader concept of somatization disorder using the somatic symptoms index. *Psychosomatics, 36,* 285–294.

Hitchcock, P. B., & Mathews, A. (1992). Interpretation of bodily symptoms in hypochondriasis. *Behavior Research and Therapy, 30*(3), 223–234.

Hollander, E., Neville, D., Frenkel, M., Josephson, S., & Liebowitz, M. R. (1992). Body dysmorphic disorder: Diagnostic issues and related disorders. *Psychosomatics, 33*(2), 156–165.

Honkalampi, K., Hintikka, J., Tanskanen, A., Lehtonen, J., & Viinamaki, H. (2000). Depression is strongly associated with alexithymia in the general population. *Journal of Psychosomatic Research, 48,* 99–104.

Hsu, L. K. G., & Folstein, M. F. (1997). Somatoform disorders in Caucasian and Chinese Americans. *Journal of Nervous and Mental Diseases, 185*(6), 382–387.

Hudson, J. I., Goldenberg, D. L., Pope, H. G., Jr., Keck, P. E., Jr., & Schlesinger, L. (1992). Comorbidity of fibromyalgia with medical and psychiatric disorders. *American Journal of Medicine, 92,* 363–367.

Hyler, S. E., & Spitzer, R. L. (1978). Hysteria split asunder. *American Journal of Psychiatry, 135*(12), 1500–1503.

Janca, A., Isaac, M., Bennett, L. A., & Tacchini, G. (1995). Somatoform disorders in different cultures: A mail questionnaire survey. *Social Psychiatry and Psychiatric Epidemiology, 30,* 44–48.

Jefferson, J. W., & Marshall, J. R. (1981). *Neuropsychiatric features of medical disorders.* New York: Plenum Press.

Jorgensen, L., Castle, D., Roberts, C., & Groth-Marnat, G. (2001). A clinical validation of the Dysmorphic Concern Questionnaire. *Australian and New Zealand Journal of Psychiatry, 35,* 124–128.

Kapoor, W. N., Fortunato, M., Hanusa, B. H., & Schulberg, H. C. (1995). Psychiatric illnesses in patients with syncope. *American Journal of Medicine, 99*(5), 505–512.

Karoly, P., & Lecci, L. (1993). Hypochondriasis and somatization in college women: A personal projects analysis. *Health Psychology, 12*(2), 103–109.

Kashner, T. M., Rost, K., Cohen, B., Anderson, M., & Smith, G. R. (1995). Enhancing the health of somatization disorder patients: Effectiveness of short-term group therapy. *Psychosomatics, 36,* 462–470.

Katon, W., Lin, E., Von Korff, M., Russo, J., Lipscomb, P., & Bush, T. (1991). Somatization: A spectrum of severity. *American Journal of Psychiatry, 148,* 34–40.

Katon, W. J., Ries, R. K., Bokan, J. A., & Kleinman, A. (1980). Hyperemesis gravidarum: A biopsychosocial perspective. *International Journal of Psychiatry in Medicine, 10*(2), 151–162.

Katon, W. J., & Walker, E. A. (1998). Medically explained symptoms in primary care. *Journal of Clinical Psychiatry 59*(Suppl. 20), 15–21.

Kauhanen, J., Kaplan, G. A., Julkunen, J., Wilson, T. W., & Salonen, J. T. (1993). Social factors in alexithymia. *Comprehensive Psychiatry, 34*(5), 330–335.

Kellner, R. (1992). The case for reassurance. *International Review of Psychiatry, 4,* 71–80.

Kellner, R., Abbott, P., Winslow, W. W., & Pathak, D. (1987). Fears, beliefs, and attitudes in *DSM-III* hypochondriasis. *Journal of Nervous and Mental Diseases, 175*(1), 20–25.

Kent, D. A., Tomasson, K., & Coryell, W. (1995). Course and outcome of conversion and somatization disorders. *Psychosomatics, 36,* 138–144.

Kenyon, F. E. (1976). Hypochondriacal states. *British Journal of Psychiatry, 129,* 1–14.

Kihlstrom, J. F. (1992). Dissociation and conversion disorders. In D. J. Stein, J. Young, & F. L. Orlando (Eds.), *Cognitive science and clinical disorders* (pp. 247–270). New York: Academic Press.

Kim, C. H., Hsu, J. J., Williams, D. E., Weaver, A. L., & Zinsmeister, A. R. (1996). A prospective psychological evaluation of patients with dysphagia of various etiologies. *Dysphagia, 11*(1), 34–40.

Kirkwood, C. R., Clure, H. R., Brodsky, R., Gould, G. H., Knaak, R., Metcalf, M., et al. (1982). The diagnostic content of family practice: 50 most common diagnoses recorded in the WAMI community practices. *Journal of Family Practice, 15*(3), 485–492.

Kirmayer, L. J. (1984). Culture, affect and somatization. *Transcultural Psychiatric Research Review, 21*(3, 4), 159–188, 237–262.

Kirmayer, L. J. (1986). Somatization and the social construction of illness experience. In S. McHugh & T. M. Vallis (Eds.), *Illness behavior: A multidisciplinary perspective* (pp. 111–133). New York: Plenum Press.

Kirmayer, L. J. (1987). Languages of suffering and healing: Alexithymia as a social and cultural process. *Transcultural Psychiatric Research Review, 24,* 119–136.

Kirmayer, L. J. (1988). Mind and body as metaphors: Hidden values in biomedicine. In M. Lock & D. Gordon (Eds.), *Biomedicine examined* (pp. 57–92). Dordrecht, The Netherlands: Kluwer Press.

Kirmayer, L. J. (1994). Improvisation and authority in illness meaning. *Culture, Medicine and Psychiatry, 18*(2), 183–214.

Kirmayer, L. J. (1999). Rhetorics of the body: Medically unexplained symptoms in sociocultural perspective. In Y. Ono, A. Janca, M. Asai, & N. Sartorius (Eds.), *Somatoform disorders: A worldwide perspective* (pp. 271–286). Tokyo: Springer-Verlag.

Kirmayer, L. J. (2000). Broken narratives: Clinical encounters and the poetics of illness experience. In C. Mattingly & L. Garro (Eds.), *Narrative and the cultural construction of illness and healing* (pp. 153–180). Berkeley: University of California Press.

Kirmayer, L. J., Dao, T. H. T., & Smith, A. (1998). Somatization and psychologization: Understanding cultural idioms of distress. In S. Okpaku (Ed.), *Clinical methods in transcultural psychiatry* (pp. 233–265). Washington, DC: American Psychiatric Press.

Kirmayer, L. J., & Robbins, J. M. (1991a). Functional somatic syndromes. In L. J. Kirmayer & J. M. Robbins (Eds.), *Current concepts of somatization: Research and clinical perspectives* (pp. 79–106). Washington, DC: American Psychiatric Press.

Kirmayer, L. J., & Robbins, J. M. (1991b). Three forms of somatization in primary care: Prevalence, co-occurrence and sociodemographic characteristics. *Journal of Nervous and Mental Diseases, 179*(11), 647–655.

Kirmayer, L. J., & Robbins, J. M. (1993). Cognitive and social correlates of the Toronto Alexithymia Scale. *Psychosomatics, 34*(1), 41–52.

Kirmayer, L. J., & Robbins, J. M. (1996). Patients who somatize in primary care: A longitudinal study. *Psychological Medicine, 26*(5), 937–951.

Kirmayer, L. J., Robbins, J. M., Dworkind, M., & Yaffe, M. (1993). Somatization and the recognition of depression and anxiety in primary care. *American Journal of Psychiatry, 150*(5), 734–741.

Kirmayer, L. J., Robbins, J. M., & Paris, J. (1994). Somatoform disorders: Personality and the social matrix of somatic distress. *Journal of Abnormal Psychology, 103*(1), 125–136.

Kirmayer, L. J., Robbins, J. M., Taillefer, S., & Helzer, J. (1995). *Development of a Structured Diagnostic Interview for Functional Somatic Syndromes* (Working Paper No. 5). Montréal, Canada: Sir Mortimer B. Davis—Jewish General Hospital, Department of Psychiatry, Culture and Mental Health Research Unit.

Kirmayer, L. J., & Santhanam, R. (2001). The anthropology of hysteria. In P. W. Halligan, C. Bass, & J. C. Marshall (Eds.), *Contemporary approaches to the study of hysteria: Clinical and theoretical perspectives* (pp. 251–270). Oxford, England: Oxford University Press.

Kirmayer, L. J., & Weiss, M. G. (1996). Cultural considerations on somatoform disorders. In T. A. Widiger, A. J. Frances, H. A. Pincus, R. Ross, M. B. First, & W. W. Davis (Eds.), *DSM-IV sourcebook* (pp. 933–941). Washington, DC: American Psychiatric Press.

Kirmayer, L. J., & Young, A. (1998). Culture and somatization: Clinical, epidemiological, and ethnographic perspectives. *Psychosomatic Medicine, 60*(4), 420–430.

Kleinman, A. (1980). *Patients and healers in the context of culture.* Berkeley: University of California Press.

Kleinman, A. (1986). *Social origins of distress and disease.* New Haven, CT: Yale University Press.

Kleinman, A., Brodwin, P. E., Good, B. J., & Good, M. J. D. (1992). Pain as a human experience: An introduction. In M. J. D. Good, P. E. Brodwin, B. J. Good, & A. Kleinman (Eds.), *Pain as human experience: Anthropological perspectives* (pp. 1–28). Berkeley: University of California Press.

Kroenke, K., & Price, R. K. (1993). Symptoms in the community: Prevalence, classification, and psychiatric comorbidity. *Archives of Internal Medicine, 153,* 2474–2480.

Kroenke, K., & Spitzer, R. L. (1998). Gender differences in the reporting of physical and somatoform symptoms. *Psychosomatic Medicine, 60,* 150–155.

Kroenke, K., Spitzer, R. L., deGruy, F. V., Hahn, S. R., Linzer, M., Williams, J. B., et al. (1997). Multisomatoform disorder: An alternative to undifferentiated somatoform disorder for the somatizing patient in primary care. *Archives of General Psychiatry, 54,* 352–358.

Kroenke, K., Spitzer, R. L., deGruy, F. V., & Swindle, R. (1998). A symptom checklist to screen for somatoform disorders in primary care. *Psychosomatics, 39*(30), 263–272.

Krupp, L. B., Sliwinski, M., Masur, D. M., Friedberg, F., & Coyle, P. K. (1994). Cognitive functioning and depression in patients with chronic fatigue syndrome and multiple sclerosis. *Archives of Neurology, 51*(7), 705–710.

Kuczmierczyk, A., Labrum, A. H., & Johnson, C. C. (1995). The relationship between mood, somatization, and alexithymia in premenstrual syndrome. *Psychosomatics, 36,* 26–32.

Lacy, T. J., & McManis, S. E. (1994). Psychogenic stridor. *General Hospital Psychiatry, 16,* 213–223.

Lazare, A. (1981). Conversion symptoms. *New England Journal of Medicine, 305,* 745–748.

Lazarus, R., & Folkman, S. (1984). *Stress, appraisal and coping.* New York: Springer.

Leff, J. (1988). *Psychiatry around the globe: A transcultural view.* London: Gaskell.

Lidbeck, J. (1997). Group therapy for somatization disorders in general practice: Effectiveness of a short cognitive-behavioral treatment model. *Acta Psychiatrica Scandinavica, 96,* 14–24.

Lilienfeld, S. O. (1992). The association between antisocial personality and somatization disorders: A review and integration of theoretical models. *Clinical Psychology Review, 12,* 641–662.

Lishman, W. A. (1988). Physiogenesis and psychogenesis in the postconcussional syndrome. *British Journal of Psychiatry, 153,* 460–469.

Looper, K., & Kirmayer, L. J. (2001). Hypochondriacal concerns in a community population. *Psychological Medicine, 31,* 577–584.

Looper, K. J., & Kirmayer, L. J. (2002). Behavioral medicine approaches to somatoform disorders. *Journal of Consulting and Clinical Psychology, 70*(3), 810–827.

Lundh, L. G., & Simonsson-Sarnecki, M. (2001). Alexithymia, emotion and somatic complaints. *Journal of Personality, 69,* 483–510.

Magni, G., Caldieron, C., Rigatti-Luchini, S., & Merskey, H. (1990). Chronic musculoskeletal pain and depressive symptoms in the general population: An analysis of the 1st National Health and Nutrition Examination Survey data. *Pain, 43,* 299–307.

Magni, G., Marchetti, M., Moreschi, C., Merskey, H., & Rigatti-Luchini, S. (1993). Chronic musculoskeletal pain and depressive symptoms in the National Health and Nutrition Examination. I: Epidemiologic follow-up study. *Pain, 53,* 163–168.

Magni, G., Moreschi, C., Rigatti-Luchini, S., & Merskey, H. (1994). Prospective study on the relationship between depressive symptoms and chronic musculoskeletal pain. *Pain, 56,* 289–297.

Martin, R. L. (1996). Conversion disorder, proposed autonomic arousal disorder, and pseudocyesis. In T. A. Widiger, A. J. Frances, H. A. Pincus, R. Ross, M. B. First, & W. W. Davis (Eds.), *DSM-IV sourcebook* (Vol. 2, pp. 893–914). Washington, DC: American Psychiatric Press.

Mayou, R., Bass, C., & Sharpe, M. (1995). Overview of epidemiology, classification and aetiology. In R. Mayou, C. Bass, & M. Sharpe (Eds.), *Treatment of functional somatic symptoms* (pp. 42–65). Oxford, England: Oxford University Press.

McCauley, J., Kern, D. E., Kolodner, K., Dill, L., Schroeder, A. F., Dechant, H. K., et al. (1995). The battering syndrome: Prevalence and clinical characteristics of domestic violence in primary care internal medicine practices. *Annals of Internal Medicine, 123*(10), 774–781.

McDaniel, S. H., Campbell, T., & Seaburn, D. (1989). Somatic fixation in patients and physicians: A biopsychosocial approach. *Family Systems Medicine, 7*(1), 5–16.

McDaniel, S. H., Hepworth, J., & Doherty, W. J. (1992). *Medical family therapy.* New York: Basic Books.

McDonald, E., Cope, H., & David, A. (1993). Cognitive impairment in patients with chronic fatigue: A preliminary study. *Journal of Neurology, Neurosurgery and Psychiatry, 56*(7), 812–815.

McGrath, R. E., & O'Malley, W. B. (1986). The assessment of denial and physical complaints: The validity of the Hy Scale and associated MMPI signs. *Journal of Clinical Psychology, 42*(5), 754–760.

McKay, M., & Farrington, J. (1995). Vulvodynia: Chronic vulvar pain syndromes. In A. Stoudemire & B. S. Fogel (Eds.), *Medical-psychiatric practice* (Vol. 3, pp. 381–414). Washington, DC: American Psychiatric Press.

McLeod, C. C., Budd, M. A., & McClelland, D. C. (1997). Treatment of somatization in primary care. *General Hospital Psychiatry, 19*, 251–258.

Meana, M., & Binik, Y. M. (1994). Painful coitus: A review of female dyspareunia. *Journal of Nervous and Mental Diseases, 182*(5), 264–272.

Mechanic, D. (1972). Social psychologic factors affecting the presentation of bodily complaints. *New England Journal of Medicine, 286*(21), 1133–1139.

Mechanic, D. (1979). Development of psychological distress among young adults. *Archives of General Psychiatry, 36*, 1233–1239.

Melzack, R. (1975). The McGill Pain Questionnaire: Major properties and scoring methods. *Pain, 1*, 277–299.

Melzack, R. (1980). Psychological aspects of pain. In J. J. Bonica (Ed.), *Pain*. New York: Raven Press.

Melzack, R., Rosberger, Z., Hollingsworth, M. L., & Thirlwell, M. (1985). New approaches to measuring nausea. *Canadian Medical Association Journal, 133*, 755–759.

Melzack, R., Wall, P. D., & Ty, T. C. (1982). Acute pain in an emergency clinic: Latency of onset and descriptor patterns related to different injuries. *Pain, 14*(1), 33–43.

Merskey, H. (1991). The definition of pain. *European Psychiatry, 6*, 153–159.

Merskey, H. (1993). The classification of fibromyalgia and myofascial pain. In H. Vaerøy & H. Merskey (Eds.), *Progress in fibromyalgia and myofascial pain* (pp. 191–194). New York: Elsevier.

Morrison, J. (1989). Childhood sexual histories of women with somatization disorder. *American Journal of Psychiatry, 146*, 239–241.

Mumford, D. B., Bavington, J. T., Bhatnagar, K. S., Hussain, Y., Mirza, S., & Naraghi, M. H. (1991). The Bradford Somatic Inventory: A multiethnic inventory of somatic symptoms reported by anxious and depressed patients in Britain and the Indo-Pakistan subcontinent. *British Journal of Psychiatry, 158*, 379–386.

Nandi, D. N., Mukherjee, S. P., Boral, G. C., Banerjee, G., Ghosh, A., Sarkar, S., et al. (1980). Socioeconomic status and mental morbidity in certain tribes and castes in India: A cross-cultural study. *British Journal of Psychiatry, 136*, 73–85.

Nestadt, G., Romanoski, A. J., Chahal, R., Merchant, A., Folstein, M. F., Gruenbeg, E. M., et al. (1990). An epidemiological study of histrionic personality disorder. *Psychological Medicine, 20*(2), 413–422.

Neziroglu, F., McKay, D., Yaryura-Tobias, J. A., Stevens, K. P., & Todaro, J. (1999). The Overvalued Ideas Scale: Development, reliability and validity in obsessive-compulsive disorder. *Behavior Research and Therapy, 37*, 881–902.

Nolen-Hoeksma, S. (1995). Epidemiology and theories of gender differences in unipolar depression. In M. V. Seeman (Ed.), *Gender and psychopathology* (pp. 63–87). Washington, DC: American Psychiatric Press.

Noyes, R., Jr., Hartz, A. J., Dobbeling, C. C., Malis, R. W., Happel, R. L., Werner, L. A., et al. (2000). Illness fears in the general population. *Psychosomatic Medicine, 62*, 318–325.

Noyes, R., Jr., Kathol, R. G., Fisher, M. M., Philips, B. M., Suelzer, M. T., & Holt, C. S. (1993). The validity of *DSM-III-R* hypochondriasis. *Archives of General Psychiatry, 50*, 961–970.

Noyes, R., Jr., Kathol, R. G., Fisher, M. M., Phillips, B. M., Suelzer, M. T., & Woodman, C. L. (1994a). One-year follow-up of medical outpatients with hypochondriasis. *Psychosomatics, 35,* 533–545.

Noyes, R., Jr., Kathol, R. G., Fisher, M. M., Phillips, B. M., Suelzer, M. T., & Woodman, C. L. (1994b). Psychiatric comorbidity among patients with hypochondriasis. *General Hospital Psychiatry, 16,* 78–87.

O'Connor, K. P., Hallam, R., Beyts, J., & Hinclife, R. (1988). Dizziness: Behavioral, subjective and organic aspects. *Journal of Psychosomatic Research, 32*(3), 291–302.

O'Malley, P. G., Jackson, J. L., Santoro, J., Tomkins, G., Balden, E., & Kroenke, K. (1999). Antidepressant therapy for unexplained symptoms and symptom syndromes. *Journal of Family Practice, 48,* 980–990.

Othmer, E., & De Souza, C. (1985). A screening test for somatization disorder (hysteria). *American Journal of Psychiatry, 142*(10), 1146–1149.

Otto, M. W., Wilhelm, S., Cohen, L. S., & Harlow, B. L. (2001). Prevalence of body dysmorphic disorder in a community sample of women. *American Journal of Psychiatry, 158,* 2061–2063.

Pennebaker, J. W. (1982). *The psychology of physical symptoms.* New York: Springer.

Pennebaker, J. W. (1985). Traumatic experience and psychosomatic disease: Exploring the roles of behavioral inhibition, obsession, and confiding. *Canadian Psychology, 26,* 82–95.

Pennebaker, J. W. (1990). *Opening up: The healing power of confiding in others.* New York: Morrow.

Pennebaker, J. W. (Ed.). (1995). *Emotion, disclosure, and health.* Washington, DC: American Psychological Association.

Pennebaker, J. W., & Watson, D. (1991). The psychology of somatic symptoms. In L. J. Kirmayer & J. M. Robbins (Eds.), *Current concepts of somatization* (pp. 21–35). Washington, DC: American Psychiatric Press.

Phillips, K. A. (1991). Body dysmorphic disorder: The distress of imagined ugliness. *American Journal of Psychiatry, 148,* 1138–1149.

Phillips, K. A., Atala, K. D., & Pope, H. G. (1995). *Diagnostic instruments for body dysmorphic disorder.* New Research program and abstracts, American Psychiatric Association 148th annual meeting, Miami, FL.

Phillips, K. A., Kim, J. M., & Hudson, J. I. (1995). Body image disturbance in body dysmorphic disorder and eating disorders: Obsessions or delusions? *Psychiatric Clinics of North America, 18*(2), 317–334.

Phillips, K. A., & McElroy, S. L. (1993). Insight, overvalued ideation, and delusional thinking in body dysmorphic disorder: Theoretical and treatment implications. *Journal of Nervous and Mental Diseases, 181,* 699–702.

Phillips, K. A., McElroy, S. L., Keck, P. E., Pope, H. G., & Hudson, J. L. (1993). Body dysmorphic disorder: 30 cases of imagined ugliness. *American Journal of Psychiatry, 150,* 302–309.

Pilowsky, I. (1967). Dimensions of hypochondriasis. *British Journal of Psychiatry, 113,* 89–93.

Pilowsky, I. (1978). A general classification of abnormal illness behaviors. *British Journal of Medical Psychology, 51,* 131–137.

Pilowsky, I. (1990). The concept of abnormal illness behavior. *Psychosomatics, 31*(2), 207–213.

Pilowsky, I., Murrell, G. C., & Gordon, A. (1979). The development of a screening method for abnormal illness behavior. *Journal of Psychosomatic Research, 23,* 203–207.

Pilowsky, I., & Spence, N. D. (1983). *Manual for the Illness Behavior Questionnaire (IBQ):* University of Adelaide, Adelaide, South Australia.

Pilowsky, I., Spence, N. D., Cobb, J., & Katsikitis, M. (1984). The illness behavior questionnaire as an aid to clinical assessment. *General Hospital Psychiatry, 6,* 123–130.

Pincus, T., Callahan, L. F., Bradley, L. A., Vaughn, W. K., & Wolfe, F. (1986). Elevated MMPI scores for hypochondriasis, depression, and hysteria in patients with rheumatoid arthritis reflect disease rather than psychological status. *Arthritis and Rheumatism, 29*(12), 1456–1466.

Poole, G. D., & Craig, K. D. (1992). Judgments of genuine, suppressed, and faked facial expressions of pain. *Journal of Personality and Social Psychology, 63*(5), 797–805.

Pope, H. G., Jr., & Hudson, J. I. (1991). A supplemental interview for forms of affective spectrum disorder. *International Journal of Psychiatry in Medicine, 21*(3), 205–232.

Powell, R., Dolan, R., & Wessely, S. (1990). Attributions and self-esteem in depression and chronic fatigue syndromes. *Journal of Psychosomatic Research, 34*(6), 665–673.

Putnam, F. W., Guroff, J. J., Silberman, E. K., Barban, L., & Post, R. M. (1986). The clinical phenomenology of multiple personality disorder. *Journal of Clinical Psychiatry, 47*(6), 285.

Raguram, R., Weiss, M. G., Channabasavanna, S. M., & Devins, G. M. (1996). Stigma, depression, and somatization in South India. *American Journal of Psychiatry, 153*(8), 1043–1049.

Ratliff, T. L., Klutke, C. G., & McDougall, E. M. (1994). The etiology of interstitial cystitis. *Urologic Clinics of North America, 21*(1), 21–30.

Rief, W., Hessel, A., & Braehler, E. (2001). Somatization symptoms and hypochondriacal features in the general population. *Psychosomatic Medicine, 63,* 595–602.

Rief, W., Hiller, W., Geissner, E., & Fichter, M. M. (1995). A two-year follow-up study of patients with somatoform disorders. *Psychosomatics, 36,* 376–386.

Rigby, M., MacLeod, A., & Sensky, T. (1993). *Causal attributions of somatic sensations by people who frequently seek medical help.* Paper presented at the 12th International Congress of Psychosomatic Medicine, Bern, Switzerland.

Robbins, J. M., & Kirmayer, L. J. (1986). Illness cognition, symptom reporting and somatization in primary care. In S. McHugh & T. M. Vallis (Eds.), *Illness behavior: A multidisciplinary model* (pp. 283–302). New York: Plenum Press.

Robbins, J. M., & Kirmayer, L. J. (1991a). Attributions of common somatic symptoms. *Psychological Medicine, 21,* 1029–1045.

Robbins, J. M., & Kirmayer, L. J. (1991b). Cognitive and social factors in somatization. In L. J. Kirmayer & J. M. Robbins (Eds.), *Current concepts of somatization: Research and clinical perspectives* (pp. 107–141). Washington, DC: American Psychiatric Press.

Robbins, J. M., & Kirmayer, L. J. (1996). Transient and persistent hypochondriacal worry in primary care. *Psychological Medicine, 26*(3), 575–589.

Robins, L. N., Helzer, J. E., & Orvaschel, H. (1985). The Diagnostic Interview Schedule. In W. W. Eaton & L. G. Kessler (Eds.), *Epidemiologic field methods in psychiatry* (pp. 143–170). Orlando, FL: Academic Press.

Robins, L. N., Helzer, J. E., Ratcliff, K. S., & Seyfired, W. (1982). Validity of the diagnostic interview schedule, version II: *DSM-III* diagnoses. *Psychological Medicine, 12*(4), 855–870.

Robins, L. N., & Regier, D. A. (1991). *Psychiatric disorders in America: The Epidemiologic Catchment Area Study.* New York: Free Press.

Robins, L. N., Wing, J., Wittchen, H. U., Helzer, J. E., Babor, T. F., Burke, J., et al. (1989). The Composite International Diagnostic Interview: An epidemiologic instrument suitable for use in conjunction with different diagnostic systems and in different cultures. *Archives of General Psychiatry, 45,* 1069–1077.

Rolland, J. S. (1987). Chronic illness and the life cycle: A conceptual framework. *Family Process, 26*(2), 203–222.

Romano, J. M., & Turner, J. A. (1985). Chronic pain and depression: Does the literature support a relationship? *Psychological Bulletin, 97,* 18–34.

Rosen, J. C., Reiter, J., & Orosan, P. (1995a). Assessment of body image in eating disorders with the body dysmorphic disorder examination. *Behavior Research and Therapy, 33*(1), 77–84.

Rosen, J. C., Reiter, J., & Orosan, P. (1995b). Cognitive-behavioral body image therapy for body dysmorphic disorder [published erratum appears in *Journal of Consulting and Clinical Psychology,* 1995, June, 63(3):437]. *Journal of Consulting and Clinical Psychology, 63*(2), 263–269.

Rost, K., Kashner, T. M., & Smith, G. R., Jr. (1994). Effectiveness of psychiatric intervention with somatization disorder patients: Improved outcomes at reduced cost. *General Hospital Psychiatry, 16,* 381–387.

Sackeim, H. A., Nordlie, J. W., & Gur, R. C. (1979). A model of hysterical and hypnotic blindness: Cognition, motivation, and awareness. *Journal of Abnormal Psychology, 88*(5), 474–489.

Salkovskis, P. M. (1989). Somatic problems. In K. Hawton, P. M. Salkovskis, J. Kirk, & D. M. Clark (Eds.), *Cognitive behavior therapy for psychiatric problems* (pp. 235–276). Oxford, England: Oxford University Press.

Savard, G. (1990). Convulsive pseudoseizures: A review of current concepts. *Behavioral Neurology, 3*(3), 133–141.

Schwartz, G. E. (1990). Psychobiology of repression and health: A systems approach. In J. L. Singer (Ed.), *Repression and dissociation: Implications for personality theory, psychopathology, and health* (pp. 405–434). Chicago: University of Chicago Press.

Sharp, T. J., & Nicholas, M. K. (2000). Assessing the significant others of chronic pain patients: The psychometric properties of significant other questionnaires. *Pain, 88,* 135–144.

Sharpe, M., & Bass, C. (1992). Pathophysiological mechanisms in somatization. *International Review of Psychiatry, 4,* 81–97.

Sharpe, M., Hawton, K., Simkin, S., Surawy, C., Hackmann, A., Klimes, I., et al. (1996). Cognitive behavior therapy for the chronic fatigue syndrome: A randomised controlled trial. *British Medical Journal, 312,* 22–26.

Sharpe, M. J., Peveler, R., & Mayou, R. (1992). The psychological treatment of patients with functional somatic symptoms: A practical guide. *Journal of Psychosomatic Research, 36*(6), 515–529.

Shedler, J., Mayman, M., & Manis, M. (1993). The illusion of mental health. *American Psychologist, 48*(11), 1117–1131.

Shorter, E. (1994). *From the mind into the body: The cultural origins of psychosomatic symptoms.* New York: Free Press.

Sifneos, P. E. (1973). The prevalence of alexithymic characteristics in psychosomatic patients. *Psychotherapy and Psychosomatics, 22,* 255–262.

Sigvardsson, S., Bohman, M., von Knorring, A.-L., & Cloninger, C. R. (1986). Symptom patterns and causes of somatization in men: I. Differentiation of two discrete disorders. *Genetic Epidemiology, 3*(3), 153–69.

Simeon, D., Hollander, E., Stein, D. J., Cohen, L., & Aronowitz, B. (1995). Body dysmorphic disorder in the *DSM-IV* field trial for obsessive-compulsive disorder. *American Journal of Psychiatry, 152*(8), 1207–1209.

Simon, G., Gater, R., Kisely, S., & Piccinelly, M. (1996). Somatic symptoms of distress: An international primary care study. *Psychosomatic Medicine, 58,* 481–488.

Simon, G. E., Katon, W. J., & Sparks, P. J. (1990). Allergic to life: Psychological factors in environmental illness. *American Journal of Psychiatry, 147*(7), 901–908.

Simon, G. E., & Von Korff, M. (1991). Somatization and psychiatric disorder in the NIMH Epidemiologic Catchment Area study. *American Journal of Psychiatry, 148*(11), 1494–1500.

Sinclair, D. S. (1988). Repetitive strain syndrome: An Australian experience. *Journal of Rheumatology, 15*(11), 1729–1730.

Singh, S. P., & Lee, A. S. (1997). Conversion disorders in Nottingham: Alive, but not kicking. *Journal of Psychosomatic Research, 43,* 425–430.

Slater, E. (1965, May 29). Diagnosis of "hysteria." *British Medical Journal,* 1395–1399.

Slavney, P. R. (1990). *Perspectives on hysteria.* Baltimore: Johns Hopkins University Press.

Slavney, P. R. (1994). Pseudoseizures, sexual abuse, and hermeneutic reasoning. *Comprehensive Psychiatry, 35*(6), 471–477.

Slavney, P. R., Teitelbaum, M. L., & Chase, G. A. (1985). Referral for medically unexplained somatic complaints: The role of histrionic traits. *Psychosomatics, 26*(2), 103–109.

Small, G. W. (1986). Pseudocyesis: An overview. *Canadian Journal of Psychiatry, 31,* 452–457.

Smets, E. M., Garssen, B., Bonke, B., & De Haes, J. C. (1995). The Multidimensional Fatigue Inventory (MFI) psychometric qualities of an instrument to assess fatigue. *Journal of Psychosomatic Research, 39*(3), 315–325.

Smith, C. G., Clarke, D. M., Handrinos, D., Dunsis, A., & McKenzie, D. P. (2000). Consultation-liaison psychiatrists' management of somatoform disorders. *Psychosomatics, 41,* 481–489.

Smith, G. R., & Brown, F. W. (1990). Screening indexes in *DSM-III-R* somatization disorder. *General Hospital Psychiatry, 12,* 148–152.

Smith, G. R., Golding, J. M., Kashner, T. M., & Rost, K. (1991). Antisocial personality disorder in primary care patients with somatization disorder. *Comprehensive Psychiatry, 32*(4), 367–372.

Smith, G. R., Monson, R. A., & Ray, D. C. (1986a). Patients with multiple unexplained symptoms: Their characteristics, functional health, and health care utilization. *Archives of Internal Medicine, 146,* 69–72.

Smith, G. R., Monson, R. A., & Ray, D. C. (1986b). Psychiatric consultation in somatization disorder: A randomized controlled study. *New England Journal of Medicine, 314,* 1407–1413.

Smith, G. R., Jr., Rost, K., & Kashner, M. (1995). A trial of the effect of a standardized psychiatric consultation on health outcomes and costs in somatizing patients. *Archives of General Psychiatry, 52,* 238–243.

Speckens, A. E., Van Hemert, A. M., Bolk, J. H., Rooijmans, H. G., & Hengeveld, M. W. (1996). Unexplained physical symptoms: Outcome, utilization of medical care and associated factors. *Psychological Medicine, 26,* 745–752.

Speckens, A. E., Van Hemert, A. M., Spinhoven, P., Hawton, K. E., Bolk, J. H., & Rooijmans, H. G. (1995). Cognitive behavioral therapy for medically unexplained physical symptoms: A randomised controlled trial. *British Medical Journal, 311*(7016), 1328–1332.

Spitzer, R. L., Williams, J. B. W., Gibbon, M., & First, M. B. (1990). *Structured clinical interview for* DSM-III-R-*nonpatient edition.* Washington, DC: American Psychiatric Press.

Starcevic, V. (1990). Relationship between hypochondriasis and obsessive compulsive disorder: Close relatives separated by nosological schemes? *American Journal Psychotherapy, 44*(3), 340.

Starkman, M. N., Marshall, J. C., La Ferla, J., & Kelch, R. P. (1985). Pseudocyesis: Psychologic and neuroendocrine interrelationships. *Psychosomatic Medicine, 47*(1), 46–57.

Stedwell, R. E., Allen, K. M., & Binder, L. S. (1992). Hypokalemic paralyses: A review of the etiologies, pathophysiology, presentation, and therapy. *American Journal of Emergency Medicine, 10*(2), 143–148.

Stefansson, J. D., Messina, J. A., & Meyerowitz, S. (1976). Hysterical neurosis, conversion type: Clinical and epidemiological considerations. *Acta Psychiatrica Scandinavica, 53,* 119–138.

Stern, J., Murphy, M., & Bass, C. (1993). Personality disorders in patients with somatisation disorder: A controlled study. *British Journal of Psychiatry, 363,* 785–789.

Stoeckle, J. D., & Barsky, A. J. (1980). Attributions: Uses of social science knowledge in the doctoring of primary care. In L. Eisenberg & A. Kleinman (Eds.), *The relevance of social science for medicine* (pp. 223–240). Dordrecht, The Netherlands: Reidel.

Sullivan, M. D., Katon, W., Dobie, R., Sakai, C., Russo, J., & Harrop-Griffiths, J. (1988). Disabling tinnitus: Association with affective disorder. *General Hospital Psychiatry, 10,* 285–291.

Sumathipala, A., Hewege, S., Hanwella, T., & Mann, A. H. (2000). Randomized controlled trial of cognitive behavior therapy for repeated consultations for medically unexplained complaints: A feasibility study in Sri Lanka. *Psychological Medicine, 30,* 747–757.

Swartz, M., Hughes, D., George, L., Blazer, D., Landerman, R., & Bucholz, K. (1986). Developing a screening index for community studies of somatization disorder. *Journal of Psychiatric Research, 20,* 335–343.

Swartz, M., Landerman, R., Blazer, D. G., & George, L. K. (1989). Somatization symptoms in the community: A rural/urban comparison. *Psychosomatics, 30*(1), 44–53.

Swartz, M., Landerman, R., George, L. K., Blazer, D. G., & Escobar, J. (1991). Somatization disorder. In L. N. Robins & D. A. Regier (Eds.), *Psychiatric disorders in America: The Epidemiologic Catchment Area Study* (pp. 220–257). New York: Free Press.

Talley, N. J. (1991). Diagnosing an irritable bowel: Does sex matter? *Gastroenterology, 110,* 834–837.

Taylor, G. J., Bagby, R. M., Ryan, D. P., & Parker, J. D. A. (1990). Validation of the alexithymia construct: A measurement-based approach. *Canadian Journal of Psychiatry, 35,* 290–297.

Thompson, W. G., & Pigeon-Reesor, H. (1990). The irritable bowel syndrome. *Seminars in Gastrointestinal Disease, 1*(1), 57–73.

Tomasson, K., Dent, D., & Coryell, W. (1991). Somatization and conversion disorders: Comorbidity and demographics at presentation. *Acta Psychiatrica Scandinavica, 84,* 288–293.

Toner, B. B. (1995). Gender differences in somatoform disorders. In M. V. Seeman (Ed.), *Gender and psychopathology* (pp. 287–310). Washington, DC: American Psychiatric Press.

Toone, B. K. (1990). Disorders of hysterical conversion. In C. M. Bass & R. H. Cawley (Eds.), *Somatization: Physical symptoms and psychological illness* (pp. 207–234). Oxford, England: Blackwell Scientific Publications.

Trigwell, P., Hatcher, S., Johnson, M., Stanley, P., & House, A. (1995). "Abnormal" illness behavior in chronic fatigue syndrome and multiple sclerosis. *British Medical Journal, 311*(6996), 15–18.

Turk, D. C., & Melzack, R. (Eds.). (1992). *Handbook of pain assessment.* New York: Guilford Press.

Turkat, I. D., & Pettegrew, L. S. (1983). Development and validation of the Illness Behavior Inventory. *Journal of Behavioral Assessment, 5*(1), 35–47.

Van Houdenhove, B., & Joostens, P. (1995). Burning mouth syndrome: Successful treatment with combined psychotherapy and pharmacotherapy. *General Hospital Psychiatry, 17,* 385–388.

Veale, D., Boocock, A., Gournay, K., Dryden, W., Shah, F., Willson, R., et al. (1996). Body dysmorphic disorder, a survey of fifty cases. *British Journal of Psychiatry, 169,* 196–201.

Verbrugge, L. M. (1985). Gender and health: An update on hypotheses and evidence. *Journal of Health and Social Behavior, 26,* 156–182.

Verhaak, P. F. M., & Tijhuis, M. A. R. (1994). The somatizing patient in general practice. *International Journal of Psychiatry in Medicine, 24*(2), 157–177.

Von Korff, M., Dworkin, S. F., Le Resche, L., & Kruger, A. (1990). An epidemiologic comparison of pain complaints. *Pain, 32,* 173–183.

Von Korff, M., Wagner, E. H., Dworkin, S. F., & Saunders, K. W. (1991). Chronic pain and use of ambulatory health care. *Psychosomatic Medicine, 53,* 61–79.

Walker, E., Katon, W., Harrop-Griffiths, J., Holm, L., Russo, J., & Hickok, L. R. (1988). Relationship of chronic pelvic pain to psychiatric diagnosis and childhood sexual abuse. *American Journal of Psychiatry, 145,* 75–80.

Walker, E. A., Gelfand, A. N., Gelfand, M. D., & Katon, W. J. (1995). Psychiatric diagnoses, sexual and physical victimization, and disability in patients with irritable bowel syndrome or inflammatory bowel disease. *Psychological Medicine, 25,* 1259–1267.

Walker, E. A., Gelfand, A. N., Gelfand, M. D., Koss, M. P., & Katon, W. J. (1995). Medical and psychiatric symptoms in female gastroenterology clinic patients with histories of sexual victimization. *General Hospital Psychiatry, 17,* 85–92.

Walker, E. A., Katon, W. J., Hansom, J., Harrop-Griffiths, J., Holm, L., Jones, M. L., et al. (1992). Medical and psychiatric symptoms in women with childhood sexual abuse. *Psychosomatic Medicine, 54,* 658–664.

Walker, E. A., Katon, W. J., Neraas, K., Jemelka, R. P., & Massoth, D. (1992). Dissociation in women with chronic pelvic pain. *American Journal of Psychiatry, 149*(4), 534–537.

Ware, N. C., & Weiss, M. G. (1994). Neurasthenia and the social construction of psychiatric knowledge. *Transcultural Psychiatric Research Review, 31*(2), 101–124.

Warner, R. (1978). The diagnosis of antisocial and hysterical personality disorders: An example of sex bias. *Journal of Nervous and Mental Diseases, 166,* 839–845.

Warwick, H. (1992). Provision of appropriate and effective reassurance. *International Review of Psychiatry, 4,* 76–80.

Warwick, H. (1995). Assessment of hypochondriasis. *Behavior Research and Therapy, 33*(7), 845–853.

Warwick, H., & Salkovskis, P. (1990). Hypochondriasis. *Behavior Research and Therapy, 28,* 105–117.

Watson, C. G., & Buranen, C. (1979a). The frequencies of conversion reaction symptoms. *Journal of Abnormal Psychology, 88*(2), 209–211.

Watson, C. G., & Buranen, C. (1979b). The frequency and identification of false positive conversion reactions. *Journal of Nervous and Mental Diseases, 167,* 243–247.

Watt, M. C., Stewart, S. H., & Cox, B. J. (1998). A retrospective study of the learning history origins of anxiety sensitivity. *Behavior Research and Therapy, 36*(5), 505–525.

Watts, C. A. H., Cawte, E. C., & Kuenssberg, E. V. (1964). Survey of mental illness in general practice. *British Medical Journal, 2,* 1351–1359.

Weissman, M. M., Myers, J. K., & Harding, P. S. (1978). Psychiatric disorders in a U.S. urban community: 1975–1976. *American Journal of Psychiatry, 135*(4), 459–462.

Wessely, S. (1994). Neurasthenia and chronic fatigue: Theory and practice in Britain and America. *Transcultural Psychiatric Research Review, 31*(2), 173–208.

Wessely, S., Nimnuan, C., & Sharpe, M. (1999). Functional somatic syndromes: One or many? *Lancet, 354,* 936–939.

Wessely, S., & Sharpe, M. (1995). Chronic fatigue, chronic fatigue syndrome, and fibromyalgia. In R. Mayou, C. Bass, & M. Sharpe (Eds.), *Treatment of functional somatic symptoms* (pp. 285–312). Oxford, England: Oxford University Press.

Westermeyer, J., Bouafuely, M., Neider, J., & Callies, A. (1989). Somatization among refugees: An epidemiologic study. *Psychosomatics, 30,* 34–43.

Wetzel, R. D., Guze, S. B., Cloninger, C. R., & Martin, R. L. (1994). Briquet's syndrome (hysteria) is both a somatoform and a "psychoform" illness: A Minnesota Multiphasic Personality Inventory study. *Psychosomatic Medicine, 56*(6), 564–569.

Whitehead, W. E., Busch, C. M., Heller, B. R., & Costa, P. T. (1986). Social learning influences on menstrual symptoms and illness behavior. *Health Psychology, 5,* 13–23.

Whitehead, W. E., Crowell, M. D., Heller, B. R., Robinson, J. C., Schuster, M. M., & Horn, S. (1994). Modeling and reinforcement of the sick role during childhood predicts adult illness behavior. *Psychosomatic Medicine, 56,* 541–550.

Whitehead, W. E., Winget, C., Fedoravicius, A. S., Wooley, S., & Blackwell, B. (1982). Learned illness behavior in patients with irritable bowel syndrome and peptic ulcer. *Digestive Diseases and Sciences, 27*(3), 202–208.

Wickramasekera, I. (1989). Enabling the somatizing patient to exit the somatic closet: A high risk model. *Psychotherapy, 26*(4), 530–544.

Wickramasekera, I. (1995). Somatization: Concepts, data. and predictions from the high risk model of threat perception. *Journal of Nervous and Mental Diseases, 183*(1), 15–23.

Wilhelmsen, I., Haug, T. T., Ursin, H., & Berstad, A. (1995). Discriminant analysis of factors distinguishing patients with functional symptoms from patients with duodenal ulcer Significance of somatization. *Digestive Diseases and Sciences, 40*(5), 1105–1111.

Wilkinson, S. R. (1988). *The child's world of illness: The development of health and illness behavior.* Cambridge, England: Cambridge University Press.

Williams, D. T., Spiegel, H., & Mostofsky, D. I. (1978). Neurogenic and hysterical seizures: Differential diagnostic and therapeutic considerations. *American Journal of Psychiatry, 135*(1), 82–86.

Winstead, B. A. (1984). Hysteria. In C. S. Widom (Ed.), *Sex roles and psychopathology* (pp. 73–100). New York: Plenum Press.

Wise, T. N., & Mann, L. S. (1994). The relationship between somatosensory amplification, alexithymia and neuroticism. *Journal of Psychosomatic Research, 38,* 515–521.

Wise, T. N., & Mann, L. S. (1995). The attribution of somatic symptoms in psychiatric outpatients. *Comprehensive Psychiatry, 36*(6), 407–410.

Wise, T. N., Mann, L. S., Mitchell, J. D., Hryniak, M., & Hill, B. (1990). Secondary alexithymia: An empirical validation. *Comprehensive Psychiatry, 31*(4), 284–285.

Wool, C. A., & Barsky, A. J. (1994). Do women somatize more than men? Gender differences in somatization. *Psychosomatics, 35*(5), 445–452.

World Health Organization. (1992). *The ICD-10 classification of mental and behavioral disorders: Clinical descriptions and diagnostic guidelines.* Geneva, Switzerland: Author.

Yonkers, K. A., & Gurguis, G. (1995). Gender differences in the prevalence and expression of anxiety disorders. In M. V. Seeman (Ed.), *Gender and psychopathology* (pp. 113–130). Washington, DC: American Psychiatric Press.

Yutsy, S. H., Cloninger, C. R., Guze, S. B., Pribor, E. F., Martin, R. L., Kathol, R. G., et al. (1995). DSM-IV field trial: Testing a new proposal for somatization disorder. *American Journal of Psychiatry, 152*(1), 97–101.

CHAPTER 13

Dissociative Disorders: Phantoms of the Self

ETZEL CARDEÑA and DAVID H. GLEAVES

I look at my reflection in the window, and find myself to be strange, novel. For a moment I was almost afraid of the image the windowpane returned to me—of this phantom of myself.

L. Dugas and F. Moutier (1911) in Nemiah (1995)

DESCRIPTION OF THE DISORDER

FEW CATEGORIES OF psychopathology are as controversial as the dissociative disorders (DD). Detractors find some of these disorders, particularly dissociative identity disorder, suspect, if not outright iatrogenic; supporters maintain that the disregard of dissociation diagnoses has condemned many patients to inadequate diagnosis and treatment. Leaving aside for a moment this debate, it is undeniable that the study of dissociation and DD has grown exponentially in the last couple of decades, after considerable neglect since the turn of the century (e.g., Hilgard, 1994; D. Spiegel & Cardeña, 1991). Besides a specialized journal, the *Journal of Trauma & Dissociation,* and a professional society, International Society for the Study of Dissociation (ISSD), there have been a number of volumes dedicated to clinical and theoretical issues, including several comprehensive anthologies (e.g., Cohen, Berzoff, & Elin, 1995; Lynn & Rhue, 1994; Michelson & Ray, 1996; D. Spiegel, 1994).

The rise of systematic research on dissociation has been fostered by recent cognitive (e.g., Freyd & DePrince, 2001) and neural-developmental models (Forrest, 2001) consistent with dissociative theories, and by the development of specific measures of dissociation, including paper-and-pencil questionnaires of trait (e.g., Dissociative Experiences Scale [DES], Carlson & Putnam, 1993; Questionnaire of

Experiences of Dissociation [QED], Riley, 1988) and state dissociation (e.g., Stanford Acute Stress Reaction Questionnaire [SASRQ], see Cardeña, Koopman, Classen, Waelde, & Spiegel, 2000; Peritraumatic Dissociative Experiences Questionnaire [PDEQ], Marmar et al., 1994). A mental status examination (Loewenstein, 1991a) and structured clinical interviews have also been developed (e.g., Structured Clinical Interview of Dissociative Disorders [SCID-D], Steinberg, 1993; Dissociative Disorders Interview Schedule [DDIS], Ross, 1991; see Gleaves, May, & Cardeña, 2001, for a review of the psychometric properties of many of these measures).

Despite these developments, there is no consensus on what *dissociation* actually means. Although in simple terms, it refers to a lack of integration of psychological processes that should normally be integrated, the term has been used for different phenomena, such as the activation of behavioral subroutines (e.g., driving while focusing on a conversation), a lack of mental contents (e.g., "blanking out"), the recollection of forgotten traumatic memories, experiences in which the phenomenal self seems to be located outside the physical body (i.e., out-of-body experiences), the partial independence of explicit and implicit forms of memory, the apparently painless piercing of flesh in some rituals, and intrusive and realistic memories (flashbacks), among others. Dissociation has been used as a descriptive term or as a hypothetical construct, sometimes synonymous with repression, sometimes as a distinct defense mechanism.

Erdelyi (1994) subsumed the notion of the *unconscious* under the idea of *dissociation,* which he defined as the discrepancy between two indicators of information (e.g., conscious experience of calmness, concurrent with physiological indicators of distress) or as memories that, while inaccessible at one point, may be later recovered. Besides this use (compartmentalization of experience), Cardeña (1994) also pointed out that other uses of the term include an alteration of consciousness characterized by detachment from the self or the environment, and a purposeful mechanism of defense to ward off the emotional impact of traumatic events and memories.

The concept of dissociation, according to the *Diagnostic and Statistical Manual of Mental Disorders* (*DSM-IV;* American Psychiatric Association [APA], 1994) is narrower and, arguably, descriptive rather than explanatory. In contrast, other authors use *dissociation* to denote a mental process that gives rise to the DD (e.g., Nemiah, 1985). The *DSM-IV* defines DD as being characterized by a "disruption in the usually integrated functions of consciousness, memory, identity, or perception of the environment" (APA, 1994, p. 477) that is distressing or impairs basic areas of functioning. To qualify as dissociative, such discrepancies cannot be the product of malingering or other forms of conscious deception, and cannot be directly caused by a medical condition.

The *DSM-IV* does not assume that DD develop as the result of a defense mechanism invoked to cope with ongoing trauma, but it nonetheless asserts that these disorders are typically linked to traumatic events. Some researchers have argued that the clinical conditions most similar to the DD are the posttraumatic diagnoses (acute stress disorder and posttraumatic stress disorder [PTSD]) and that all of these conditions might be classified under the same category (e.g., Barlow & Durand, 2001; Cardeña, Butler, & Spiegel, in press). Nonetheless, although traumatic events are related to DD, they are not a sufficient cause for these conditions. Other risk factors proposed include repeated exposure to trauma in an inescapable situation, at least among children (Terr, 1991), especially when brought about by a parental figure (Freyd, DePrince, & Zurbriggen, 2001), even when controlling for family background (Nelson et al., 2002). Important research is providing evidence that disturbed forms of early attachment (especially avoidant and disorganized) predict pathological dissociation (e.g., Ogawa, Sroufe, Weinfield, Carlson, & Egeland, 1997).

An inborn disposition to dissociate has been proposed as a diathesis (e.g., Braun, 1993; Butler, Duran, Jasiukaitis, Koopman, & Spiegel, 1996), but the evidence for heritability of pathological dissociation is mixed (Jang, Paris, Zweig-Frank, & Livesley, 1998; Waller & Ross, 1997). There is more consistent evidence for heritability of the related phenomena of hypnotizability (Morgan, 1973) and absorption (Tellegen et al., 1988).

Repression and *dissociation* have been frequently used to refer to the same manifestations, that is, the inability to remember a traumatic event. Some authors differentiate *repression* as a defense mechanism to ward off internal pressures from *dissociation* as an alteration in consciousness to deflect the overwhelming impact of ongoing trauma. This distinction, although problematic and not consensually accepted, does make some reference to the historical fact that Pierre Janet, the originator of the term *dissociation* saw it as a lack of integration produced by the impact of trauma on a psychologically deficient system, whereas Freud saw it more as the product of conflict among psychological structures. *Dissociation* can be used as a descriptive term to encompass disorders centered on the lack of integration among psychological processes such as the sense of self and/or the environment (e.g., depersonalization), emotions (e.g., emotional behaviors without the related feeling), physical sensations and agency (e.g., conversion disorders), memory (e.g., dissociative amnesia), and identity (e.g., dissociative identity disorder; Butler et al., 1996; Cardeña, 1997). Janet also had a useful distinction between *positive* symptoms (exaggerations or additions to normal processes such as flashbacks in PTSD) and *negative* symptoms (diminution of normal processes, such as lack of memory for personal information; Janet, 1907/1965).

The effort to conceptualize DD according to their observable characteristics follows the move of the *DSM* taxonomy from a psychoanalytic characterization in its first two editions to the more descriptive model adopted later. However, some changes in the nosology have been controversial. Foremost among them, conversion and related somatoform disorders were moved from the dissociative category to the somatoform category. Critics of this taxonomic change have invoked historical, conceptual, and empirical arguments. Many of the "hysterical" cases described at the turn of the century involved concurrent somatoform and dissociative phenomena such as conversion paralysis and dissociated identities (Kihlstrom, 1994). Conceptually, dissociation as a discrepancy or lack of integration between behaviors, experiences, and conscious experience would fit the nature of the somatoform disorders in which experiences of pain, motor, visceral, and sensory dysfunctions are present in the absence of pathophysiology. A substantial comorbidity of somatization disorders with traumatic history and dissociative symptomatology has been replicated in various studies (e.g., Cardeña & Nijenhuis, 2000; Nijenhuis, 2000; Pribor, Yutzi, Dean, & Wetzel, 1993; Saxe et al., 1994).

Another clarification about DD is that they refer to conditions with a sociocultural/psychological etiology rather than a neurological one. For instance, the *DSM-IV* distinguishes between the presumed psychological etiology of dissociative amnesia and the biological etiology of alcohol amnestic syndrome. This distinction may be somewhat lost now, after some of these disorders were renamed in the last edition; for instance, *psychogenic* amnesia became *dissociative* amnesia. The presumption of a psychological etiology does not, of course, imply absence of biological underpinnings to these conditions (APA, 1994; P. Brown, 1994).

It should be borne in mind that dissociative *experiences* are associated with various medical conditions and biological factors, including damage to the central nervous system, prescription and nonprescription drugs, and seizure disorders (Good, 1993). Some authors use the term *dissociation* to address neurologically based conditions such as *blindsight*, in which there is a discrepancy between conscious experience and behavior (Farthing, 1992).

Even in the strict province of psychological conditions, other clarifications must be made. Dissociative phenomena, though they may be present as part of a clinical condition, are also experienced by normal individuals and may be associated with hypnosis, rituals, artistic activities, or personal development practices such as meditation (Cardeña, 1997). Furthermore, dissociative experiences in general were once viewed as occurring on a continuum of severity (e.g., Braun, 1993), but Waller, Putnam, and Carlson (1996) found that, whereas some dissociative phenomena (i.e., absorption) overlap in clinical and nonclinical populations, others seem to distinguish nonpathological from pathological conditions (e.g., severe depersonalization, amnesia). Thus, types of dissociative experiences that occur in the general population may be qualitatively different from those experienced by people with DD. Besides the general issues of distress and dysfunction, other dimensions such as controllability, recurrence, and organization of the experience help distinguish pathological from nonpathological manifestations.

The previous considerations refer mostly to our culture and do not even address the fact that cultural beliefs and practices can pathologize or normalize diverse gaps in experience (Kirmayer, 1994), an issue discussed in a later section, which describes the proposed new diagnosis of *dissociative trance disorder*.

The diagnosis of acute stress disorder (ASD), initially proposed as *brief reactive dissociative disorder* (D. Spiegel & Cardeña, 1991), and PTSD also involve substantial dissociative symptomatology; but they are discussed in Chapter 11, Anxiety Disorders (see also Cardeña et al., in press). Dissociative symptoms may also occur in the context of other conditions, including somatoform and panic disorders, psychosis, and some severe types of depression. Whether to assign one of these diagnoses a dissociative disorder or a dual diagnosis depends on the constellation and presentation of symptoms.

The following sections address DD in adults, by far the most studied group. The DD are usually manifested in early to middle adulthood. Nonetheless, reports of childhood DD can be traced at least to the eighteenth century. Their assessment is particularly difficult because some manifestations (e.g., spontaneous staring spells, imaginary companions) are normal in some age groups. Putnam (1997) and Silberg (1998) provide authoritative introductions to the diagnosis and treatment of DD in children and adolescents.

EPIDEMIOLOGY

Epidemiological studies have rarely used instruments that evaluate DD directly (e.g., Kessler et al., 1994). Mezzich, Fabrega, Coffman, and Haley (1989), reported that these disorders, using *DSM-III* criteria, were rare in a psychiatric population. However, the assessment instrument that these authors used did not systematically inquire about dissociative experiences and only defined them as a "narrowing of consciousness" (Mezzich, Dow, Rich, Costello, & Himmelhoch, 1981, p. 471). In a more recent review of studies using systematic measures, Gleaves (1996) found that rate of DD among various clinical populations ranged from a low of 10% among obsessive-compulsive disorder patients to a high of 88% among women in treatment for severe sexual abuse.

Ross (1991) used careful methodology to evaluate the epidemiology of DD in clinical and nonclinical samples. Using *DSM-III-R* criteria (which are different in some important ways from the current *DSM-IV* criteria), he found that approximately 21% of psychiatric patients also fulfilled criteria for DD (5% to 14% fulfilled criteria for dissociative identity disorder). In a nonclinical Canadian sample ($N = 454$), Ross reported the following rates: 7% dissociative amnesia, 3.1% dissociative identity disorder (DID), 2.4% depersonalization disorder, 0.2% dissociative fugue, 0.2% of dissociative disorders not otherwise specified (11.2%, a dissociative disorder of some type). The 3.1% prevalence of DID in the general population seems very high, but Ross himself commented that it included individuals who were high functioning, and the *DSM-III-R* criteria he used did not include the requirements for amnesia or for the symptoms to be clinically distressing or to produce maladjustment. Ross's description of a pathological type of DID in about 1% of his sample is likely to be closer to the actual prevalence of this condition.

In a more recent and careful study in an inpatient setting, Ross, Duffy, and Ellason (2002) found a lifetime prevalence of some type of DD of 41%, 44.5%, and 27%, using structured, semistructured interviews, or a masked clinician, respectively. However, there was not a single instance of dissociative fugue, and the diagnostic reliability for dissociative amnesia and depersonalization disorder were not adequate.

Studies in Turkey and the Netherlands have also found substantial rates of DD in clinical samples (10% in Tutkun et al., 1998; 8% in Friedl & Draijer, 2000).

DEMOGRAPHIC VARIABLES

Studies in the United States and Europe (see Vanderlinden, van der Hart, & Varga, 1996) suggest that, at least among nonclinical populations, dissociativity reaches its peak somewhere in early adolescence and then gradually declines with age. It is of interest that hypnotizability has a similar age distribution (Hilgard, 1968).

There is scant information on the impact of socioeconomic status or ethnicity on the incidence of dissociative pathology. Some researchers reported that dissociative symptoms (not necessarily disorders) were more common among minorities, but when socioeconomic status was controlled, that difference disappeared (Zatzick, Marmar, Weiss, & Metzler, 1994). Nor have European studies found that ethnicity affects dissociativity (Vanderlinden et al., 1996), but an important caveat is that these studies have been conducted only in Western technological societies. Dissociative phenomena and disorders seem to have a different presentation in some societies (see later discussion). With respect to the so-called culture-bound syndromes with a dissociative component, both pathological spirit possession and *ataque de nervios* are predominantly found among women of lower socioeconomic status, while *amok, berserk,* and similar "assault" conditions are mostly found among men (Lewis-Fernández, 1994; Simons & Hughes, 1985).

It is fair to say that, other than for some culture-bound syndromes and DID, we do not have consistent findings as to the gender distribution of other DD (e.g.,

Vanderlinden et al., 1996). Some proponents of a strong skeptic position affirm that DID is mostly a condition of affluent U.S. Caucasian women, but research shows that this condition is found in other countries (e.g., Coons, Bowman, Kluft, & Milstein, 1991). It is also the case that, in the United States, DID does not affect only either Caucasian or affluent women (or men). For instance, Coons, Bowman, and Milstein (1988) described 50 cases, 40 of whom came from a state psychiatric hospital and could not afford private care. The largest occupational level (28%) of these clients was clerical/sales/technician (Coons, personal communication, 1996). Similarly, Ross, Joshi, and Currie (1991) found that, in a large representative sample of Canadians, socioeconomic status was unrelated to the distribution of reported dissociative experiences.

What remains true is that, at least in the United States, DID is found at much higher rates among women than among males. As Kluft (1996) maintains, however, the ratio of about 9:1 female to male found in many studies may be excessive because some males with DID end up being part of the legal system and are not assessed in epidemiological studies (see also Lewis, Yeager, Swica, Pincus, & Lewis, 1997).

DEPERSONALIZATION DISORDER

Case Study 1

Frank, a 20-year-old college student, visited his student counseling center with a presenting problem that he described as a "freaked-out feeling." He described that, often while studying in his room, he would begin to feel somewhat disconnected from his body, as if he could barely feel his arms, face, or body. If he got up to walk around, he would become more distressed because it felt as if his feet were not touching the floor. The problems were not something that occurred only while taking some sort of drug, but he did report that it started one night when he had stayed up late studying and drinking several cups of coffee. Frank found the experiences very distressful (although they never led to episodes of panic), and they began to interfere with his academic functioning. His initial suspicion was that there was something physically wrong with him (such as a neurological problem) and, before going to the student counseling service, he had gone to the medical clinic. He was referred to the counseling service after no physical cause could be determined.

The therapist recognized that Frank was experiencing both depersonalization and derealization. In assessing the problem, it became clear that the episodes were generally associated with stress, lack of sleep, and Frank's keeping his mind focused on one target (such as staring at a book) for a long period. It was as if he were putting himself into a hypnotic trance. However, because of hypersensitivity to unexpected bodily sensations, interpreted as a loss of control, he found the experience very frightening, and his heightened fear led to increased depersonalization. In treatment, Frank acquired stress management skills and learned to break up his study habits to avoid inducing depersonalization while studying. However, the therapist also incorporated exercises to directly induce depersonalization (as is sometimes done in treating panic disorder) to desensitize him to the experiences and the bodily sensations.

Feeling estranged from bodily or psychological processes is not that unusual, although it is not a common topic of conversation. Poets (e.g., Trakl, Villaurrutia) have written about these experiences. Perhaps the most extreme form is autoscopy, in which an individual encounters a self-image outside the body. The experience of a "double" of oneself was studied by the psychoanalyst Otto Rank and described by Poe ("William Wilson") and Dostoevsky, among others. Researchers have distinguished among various alterations of the self such as out-of-body experiences, autoscopy, and depersonalization proper (Gabbard, Twemlow, & Jones, 1982).

DSM-IV (APA, 1994) defines *depersonalization* as persistent or recurrent experiences of feeling detached from one's mental processes or body, without loss of reality testing. It involves a perception or experience in which the usual sense of one's reality is temporarily lost or altered. The individual may experience a sense of being unreal, of being dead or unfeeling. Five different types of depersonalization have been proposed: inauthenticity, self-negation, self-objectification, derealization, and body detachment (Jacobs & Bovasso, 1992). In the Jacobs and Bovasso study, self-objectification was more closely related to psychological disorganization than the other factors, but because only students participated in the study, it is unknown to what extent this finding would generalize to actual depersonalization disorder.

Depersonalization experiences are distinguished from psychotic ones in that the former describe *experiences* of alienation with intact reality testing, whereas psychotic episodes involve delusional beliefs. A depersonalized individual may feel like a robot or as if body movements are mechanical; a psychotic, on the other hand, would hold delusional beliefs that he or she may have actual mechanical implants, is turning into metal, and so on.

A literature review found that the four most common features of depersonalization are:

1. An altered sense of self (e.g., "My body doesn't belong to me").
2. A precipitating event (e.g., an accident, marijuana use).
3. A sense of unreality or a dream-like state (e.g., "Nothing seems real"; "I'm not real").
4. Sensory alterations (e.g., "Colors are less vibrant"; "Voices sound strange"; Kubin, Pakianathan, Cardeña, & Spiegel, 1989).

Depersonalization *syndrome* should be distinguished from isolated or transient symptoms. The syndrome involves depersonalization as the predominant disturbance with recurrent and chronic episodes that cause distress or maladjustment. Depression and anxiety are frequently present in depersonalization syndrome, and there is evidence that early emotional abuse is an important risk factor for this condition (Simeon, Guralnik, Schmeidler, Sirof, & Knutelska, 2000).

Isolated depersonalization symptoms may be the third most common psychiatric symptom, present in about 40% of psychiatric patients (cf. Steinberg, 1990). Depersonalization symptoms are frequent in other dissociative disorders and in panic attacks. When depersonalization occurs exclusively in the presence of another psychological disorder, the latter is the superordinate diagnosis. Because depersonalization *symptoms* occur often in conjunction with anxiety, the construct of depersonalization *disorder* has been questioned, but empirical work has upheld its validity (Simeon, Gross, Guralnik, Stein, Schmeidler, & Hollander, 1997).

Depersonalization episodes are also not that uncommon among nonclinical populations and frequently occur during or shortly after a traumatic event (Cardeña & Spiegel, 1993; Koopman, Classen, Cardeña, & Spiegel, 1995; Noyes & Kletti, 1977). They can also occur as a byproduct of meditation (Lazarus, 1976) or psychedelic ingestion, and some hypnotic suggestions are specifically geared to producing a sense of disconnection with the individual's movements or sensations (Cardeña & Spiegel, 1991). In a survey of more than 1,000 nonclinical adults, Aderibigbe, Bloch, and Walker (2001) reported prevalence rates of 19.1% for depersonalization, 14.4% for derealization, and 23.4% for either experience.

To remedy the lack of systematic research on the disorder, Simeon and collaborators initiated a program of research on depersonalization. Their findings about depersonalization include:

- Related attentional and memory problems (Guralnik, Schmeidler, & Simeon, 2000).
- Functional abnormalities in cortical areas associated with sensory integration and body schema (Simeon et al., 2000).
- Hypothalamic-pituitary-adrenal dysregulation (Simeon, Guralnik, Knutelska, Hollander, & Schmeidler, 2001).

The terms *depersonalization* and *derealization* are often used interchangeably. However, they describe different concepts. Whereas depersonalization involves detachment from or sense of unreality about self, in derealization, this sense of detachment or unreality refers to the external world. Experiencers may describe feeling as if they were seeing the world "through a fog . . . as if it were a dream," or as if they were watching a film. It is rare to find a case of chronic depersonalization without derealization, or vice versa.

Derealization as a dissociative symptom differs from a psychotic symptom. In derealization, the individual may experience that his or her relatives are not quite real but will know them to be real; in contrast, some neurological conditions and psychoses would be associated with the belief that the relatives had been exchanged by impostors (i.e., *l'illusion des sosies,* Reed, 1972).

Initial diagnosis may be difficult because patients may not report depersonalization initially, but complain of depression, general anxiety, or fear of becoming mad. They may lack the language to describe how they feel or may confuse their experiences with incipient psychosis. Because of this communication problem, the clinician should consider using direct queries as to whether the individual may have chronic episodes of disconnections with the body or emotions, out-of-body experiences, sensations of the world being unreal at times, besides inquiring about other dissociative phenomena such as episodes of amnesia, other alterations of consciousness, and so on.

Differential diagnoses include other conditions in which depersonalization is one but not the central symptom (e.g., DID, panic attacks), depression, obsessive-compulsive disorder, and hypochondriasis. Other conditions to rule out include schizophrenia, borderline personality disorder, substance abuse disorders, medical conditions, and medication side effects. The diagnostician should be particularly careful to rule out seizure disorders, particularly temporal lobe epilepsy, which often include depersonalization episodes (Litwin & Cardeña, 1993).

DISSOCIATIVE AMNESIA

Case Study 2

A soldier in his early 20s was found in the bathroom of an airport, with his pants down (and no evidence of sexual assault, but see Kaszniak, Nussbaum, Berren, & Santiago, 1988), and without his wallet or any recollection of his name, family, where he came from, where he was going, and so on. He also showed various signs of anxiety, including heavy stuttering. Initially, he did not recognize his family or his girlfriend, but after he was taken to a military hospital and started treatment with medications and hypnosis, his anxiety symptoms started to subside and he began to recognize his relatives and girl-friend. He was eventually "boarded out" of the military and went back to his family's home, where he seemed to respond and enjoy the care he was receiving. His memories continued coming back, although a follow-up six months after the incident still found him amnesic for the precipitating event. Analysis of his personality strongly suggested immaturity personality, although this is not necessarily generalizable to other individuals with dissociative amnesia.

This disorder is important for its own sake and because it serves as the basis for two other DD: dissociative fugue and dissociative identity disorder.

According to the *DSM-IV* (APA, 1994), *dissociative amnesia* (previously called *psychogenic*) is characterized by one or more instances of amnesia for important personal information that cannot be explained by ordinary forgetfulness, by the common developmental amnesia for the first years of life, or by an organic condition.

The distinction between psychogenic amnesia and that caused by a neurological condition is critical for diagnosis. However, the two conditions typically have very different presentations. In the case of dissociative amnesia after a traumatic event, loss of memory is typically retrograde in the sense that the patient does not remember all or part of the trauma or previous events, while he or she usually has no problem with learning new material or remembering what occurred after the trauma. Such presentation is in sharp contrast with a number of organic amnesias (e.g., various dementias, alcohol amnestic syndrome) in which the amnesia is anterograde; that is, the patient is unable to remember events occurring after the onset of amnesia, although he or she may preserve older memories and may show implicit, but not explicit, memory for new material. Generally, dissociative amnesia involves loss of explicit or declarative memory (i.e., awareness of personal information or previous experience), whereas implicit memory (i.e., general knowledge such as language, habits, conditioned responses, and such) may be preserved (Kihlstrom, 1987). A second distinction is that psychogenic amnesia is believed to be, at least potentially, a reversible memory impairment. In contrast, explicit memories for neurologically based amnesias are typically inaccessible, or whatever recovery occurs is very gradual and incomplete.

Dissociative amnesia is closely related to severe stress or exposure to trauma, including experiences of combat, natural disaster, being the victim of violence, or childhood abuse. Legal problems, financial disaster, severe marital problems, depression, and suicide attempts have also triggered this disorder (Coons & Milstein, 1992; Kopelman, 1987; Loewenstein, 1991b).

The precipitating event(s) for dissociative amnesia, although usually traumatic in nature (APA, 1994), can be complex and involve idiosyncratic elements. In the case study, the only obvious external event before the amnesia episode was the impending sale of the soldier's childhood home (which seemed to have a greater personal impact for him than for most individuals), but forgotten fantasies about that event or about something else might have played an equal or more important role. In a Gulf War veteran with PTSD, hearing a cannon shot made him slide under a parked car. Even weeks after the incident, he had no memory of the period from the moment of the shooting to the time when other soldiers eventually got him from under the car. Not uncharacteristically, he did not respond to his colleagues for a few minutes.

The presentation of amnesia can vary according to frequency of episodes, extent of amnesia, and temporal parameters. As to frequency, patients can have one or very few episodes of amnesia, or have a chronic condition. Coons and Milstein (1992) described a group of patients, typically with reported history of early abuse, with chronic forms of amnesia. These recurrent episodes usually involved one or more of the following: episodes of "missing time," unexplainable forgetfulness, chronic amnesia for periods that should be remembered (e.g., nor remembering any event that occurred when the individual was 13 years of age), and so on.

Episode(s) of amnesia can be generalized, selective, localized, or systematized. *Generalized* amnesia involves amnesia for all or most personal information, including name, personal history, and identity of relatives and friends. *Localized* amnesia refers to forgetting what transpired during a certain period although the individual remembers previous and subsequent events (e.g., an individual involved in an automobile accident, but who did not suffer neurological damage, may nonetheless not remember *anything* that occurred some minutes before and after the accident). With *selective* amnesia, the individual may recall some but not all features of a specified event or circumstance (e.g., a victim of a violent armed robbery may recall some of the events that transpired but not others that we would expect the individual to be able to recall). *Systematized* amnesia is perhaps the most bizarre experience and involves an inability to remember certain categories of experiences. For example, following the tragic death of a sibling, an individual may be unable to recall memories containing the lost sibling. The controversial type of amnesia in which an individual is unable to remember a series of sexually abusive experiences, but retains memories of other events, would technically fall into the *systematized amnesia* category, assuming the individual did not meet the diagnostic criteria for a more severe dissociative disorder. Sometimes the concepts of *systematized* and *selective* amnesia are used interchangeably, although they differ along the lines just described. In any case, typically, dissociative amnesia is organized according to emotional rather than temporal parameters (Schacter, Wang, Tulving, & Freedman, 1982). Along these lines, Coons and Milstein (1992) found that more than 76% of the amnesias for the 25 patients in their study were for selective (and systematized) information.

Depression, anxiety, episodes of depersonalization, and trance (i.e., apparent unawareness of the surroundings) frequently predate or are associated with dissociative amnesia. In cases with a history of early and chronic abuse, a more complex syndrome that may also include relationship problems, PTSD symptoms, self-injurious behavior, substance abuse, sexual problems, and various other symptoms may be present (see Cardeña et al., in press, for a review).

When dissociative amnesia is not chronic and follows a traumatic event, the prognosis is usually good. Once the client is in a safe environment, therapy can gradually bring a complete or substantial recovery of the memories in a matter of days or weeks; there can also be spontaneous recovery of material without therapeutic intervention. Chronic and recurrent episodes of amnesia, on the other hand, are much more complex, may require therapy, and have a less certain outcome.

Differential diagnoses of this condition includes other dissociative disorders that are superordinate to amnesia (dissociative fugue, DID), ASD, PTSD, and somatization disorder. Other diagnoses includes various medical conditions that can produce amnesia, among them transient global amnesia (TGA), a brief amnestic episode involving confusion and probably caused by transient vascular insufficiency (Rollinson, 1978); amnestic alcohol or Korsakoff's syndrome; head injury; epilepsy; dementia; stroke; postoperative amnesia; postinfectious amnesia; and anoxic amnesia (Benson, 1978; Keller & Shaywitz, 1986; Kopelman, 1987). Dissociative amnesia must be differentiated also from that produced by various drugs, foremost alcohol (e.g., "black-outs"). In a legal context, the clinician should also consider the possibility of malingering.

Usually, presentation of the amnesia (i.e., selective, retrograde, associated with depression or anxiety) and the surrounding circumstances (i.e., precipitating trauma or severe stress without head injury), give an indication of the likely diagnosis (Sivec & Lynn, 1995). A detailed clinical history and laboratory analyses can usually rule out other possibilities. The clinician has to be mindful that amnesia may not be a presenting problem. There are a number of reasons for this; among them, the individual may have amnesia for the amnestic episodes, that is, he or she may be aware of suddenly finding himself or herself in a place without knowing how he or she got there, but may later forget that this event occurred; or he or she may assume that these episodes of "forgetfulness" are shared by everybody else. Assessment for this and other DD may include one or more of the questionnaires and clinical interviews mentioned previously. At the very least, if the clinician suspects amnesia, a number of areas should be investigated, including "gaps" of memory in everyday life, failure to give an account of at least the salient episodes from late childhood onward, finding items that must have recently been bought but for which the client has no memory, and so on (cf. Loewenstein, 1991a).

Although the earlier reports of dissociative amnesia and fugue concentrated on male soldiers in time of war, more recent work (e.g., Coons & Milstein, 1992) has reported a preponderance of females, and as with the other DD, dissociative amnesia seems to affect young adults more than other groups.

As with the other DD, at present, there are no biological techniques to evaluate dissociative amnesia, although cognitive procedures are being developed to distinguish real from simulated amnesia (e.g., Kopelman, Christensen, Puffett, & Stanhope, 1994). Given the possibility of simulated, or otherwise nongenuine, amnesia, mention should be made of the skepticism (e.g., Loftus, 1993) concerning reports of apparently recovered memories, particularly concerning early abuse, which could be interpreted as denying the existence of dissociative amnesia. Although a full coverage of these issues is beyond the scope of this chapter, there is good reason to question the view that false memories are easily or commonly produced by psychotherapists (D. Brown, 1995); more importantly, evidence for the reality of dissociative amnesia has accumulated for decades and in contexts independent of therapy or early abuse, including combat-trauma, torture, traumatic loss, and crime (e.g., van der Hart & Nijenhuis, 1995). D. Brown, Scheflin, and Whitfield (1999) reviewed the clinical research in this area and concluded: "In just this past decade alone, 68 research studies have been conducted on naturally occurring dissociative or traumatic amnesia for childhood sexual abuse. Not a single one of the 68 data-based studies failed to find it" (p. 126).

At this stage, the debate should no longer be on whether most recovered memories are completely accurate or inaccurate, untenable positions, given the evidence, but on the individual and social characteristics that facilitate or hinder accurate retrieval. Even in less controversial examples than early abuse, an evaluation of the validity of the amnesia is likely to be more complex than has been usually considered. For instance, Kopelman and collaborators (1994) thoroughly studied a case of functional retrograde amnesia in which there was a probable mixture of actual amnesia and simulation. The authors proposed that dissociative amnesia involves different levels of awareness for different memories, in accord with current models of memory and cognition, rather than a simple conscious/nonconscious dichotomy. Amnesia may fluctuate in time and cognitive (Schooler, 1994) and neurophysiological (Bremner, Krystal, Southwick, & Charney, 1995) mechanisms may explain both dissociative amnesia and the recovery of the forgotten material. Finally, it bears mentioning that the external validity of some recovered memories does not in any way negate the reality of confabulation and suggestive influences on memory (Loftus, 1993). Both phenomena show the malleability of memory and the effect of suggestive influences (self- or other-generated) on forgetfulness of matters that did occur or remembrance of matters that did not occur (Butler & Spiegel, 1997).

DISSOCIATIVE FUGUE

Case Study 3

Marta, a middle-aged, single mother, arrived at a health clinic in the Mexican countryside. While trying to interview her, it became clear that she seemed to be unable to stand still or remain seated; and during the rare moments when she sat, she kept on fidgeting. She was lucid and could give a coherent account of her life. Some months before arriving at the clinic, a man had attempted to rape one of her nieces. He was caught by the child's relatives, who nearly hanged him from the house ceiling. A few days later, Marta left her home for a short while and when she came back, she noticed that the door was open. The thought that one of her daughters had been raped immediately came to her mind (nothing had actually happened), and the next thing she remembers is walking by Mexico City's cathedral, hundreds of miles from her hometown. She was referred to a medical center, and the physician prescribed neuroleptics. When seen by a psychiatrist and the first author, she was taking four different neuroleptics. Her restlessness was very likely neuroleptic-induced akathisia. When her medications were tapered down, the symptoms disappeared. The other symptoms are indicative of dissociative fugue.

Dissociative fugue is defined by the sudden wandering away from place of residence or employment, amnesia for the past, and confusion about personal identity or adoption of a new identity. It is not surprising that generalized amnesia and personal confusion would be associated with leaving one's customary surroundings. To what extent dissociative fugue should be considered more than an extreme case of generalized amnesia is debatable.

Before the current edition of the *DSM*, the diagnosis was circumscribed to individuals who actually changed their identity for another one. This form was probably immortalized by William James's description of the Reverend Ansel Bourne, who left his hometown and adopted a new name and profession, only to "wake up" at a later point to the knowledge of his previous identity (James, 1890/1923; see also Kenny, 1986). It is not very uncommon to read in newspapers of modern day "Bournes." Nonetheless, more recent studies show that it is by far more common to find a presentation in which the individual is, at least initially, confused about his or her identity (Loewenstein, 1991b; Riether & Stoudemire, 1988); an undetected and unresolved case of identity confusion may resolve into a new identity.

The nature of the confusion of identity is not clear at present, but some authors have described it as some type of alteration of consciousness. William James (1890/1923) saw fugue as a long-lasting "trance"; Stengel (1941, p. 255, in Loewenstein, 1991b) defined it as "states of altered or narrowed consciousness with the impulse to wander." These definitions are consistent with Pierre Janet's view of dissociation as involving a focusing and narrowing of consciousness (van der Kolk & van der Hart, 1989). Although there are no studies that directly evaluate this hypothesis, nonclinical groups exposed to the 1989 Bay Area earthquake reported that their attention was significantly narrower and more focused during the earthquake week than four months afterwards (Cardeña & Spiegel, 1993), a finding consistent with laboratory studies (e.g., Christianson & Loftus, 1987). Some authors propose other constructs such as strategic self-presentation and a culturally prescribed "idiom of distress" (Kenny, 1986; Spanos, 1994), but these concepts are not necessarily incompatible with an experienced alteration of consciousness.

As in the case of dissociative amnesia, traumatic events and severe stress are the common precipitants of this condition. Older references on dissociative amnesia and fugue centered on soldiers at time of war. Grinker and Spiegel (1945, p. 372) wrote that "the psychotic reactions seen mostly in ground troops were due to a negation of reality by the process of dissociation." While the aftereffects of war continue producing dissociative symptomatology, most fugue patients seen in hospitals are civilians fleeing the terrors of urban life.

Loewenstein (1991b) maintains that, in our nomadic modern societies, some patients have a "nonclassic" presentation in which they do not complain of fugue unless queried about it. He maintains that, in urban settings, isolated or abused individuals may have episodes of fugue without anyone noticing, much less bringing this fact to official agencies; some may become homeless people, others, particularly teenagers having a fugue episode after abuse, may be easily lured or forced into illegal activities. For these reasons, we may never have accurate estimates of the prevalence of fugue.

The symptoms associated with dissociative fugue are the same as those for dissociative amnesia. If the fugue is part of a DID, the *DSM* nosology makes the latter a superordinate diagnosis. Differential diagnoses of fugue include complex partial seizure involving postictal episodes of aimless wandering, amnesia, and disorientation, also known as *poriomania* (Mayeux, Alexander, Benson, Brandt, & Rosen, 1979). Episodes of poriomania tend to be short-lived, usually a matter of minutes, in contrast to the longer duration of a fugue; and, as compared with poriomanias, fugues are more likely to be responsive to hypnosis and similar techniques (Sivec & Lynn, 1995). Other diagnoses to consider are manic or schizophrenic episodes accompanied by traveling, organic, nonepileptic factors such as brain tumors, and alcohol- and drug-related loss of memory and wandering (cf. Akhtar & Brenner, 1979). Generally, the characteristic symptoms of other diagnoses (e.g., the grandiosity and impulsivity in mania) can easily differentiate the conditions. Nonetheless, clinicians unfamiliar with the dissociative disorders may easily conclude that they are dealing with a psychosis, as in the case study.

DISSOCIATIVE IDENTITY DISORDER

Case Study 4

Joan, a 30-year-old married mother of two, presented for treatment of a sexual dysfunction that was reportedly affecting her marriage. Although Joan reported also having problems with depression dating back to childhood, she denied other problems. Because of the presenting problem, Joan's therapist asked that the spouse come in for an information gathering session and to discuss possible sex therapy. During the first discussion with the spouse, it became clear that Joan had a variety of problems that she had not disclosed during the initial assessment. Most striking to her husband were her memory problems. He described how frequently she would do things and then not remember having done them. He also described sometimes finding her in a terrified state, hiding in her closet or under her bed, acting as if she did not recognize him during these times. Joan's husband also reported that she had grown up in a violent, abusive family and that several of Joan's siblings reported having also been severely abused, both physically and sexually.

Joan was very frightened about discussing many of these problems with the therapist because she felt they meant that she was "crazy." However, when reassured by the therapist and supported by her husband, she described striking episodes of amnesia lasting for hours, days, or even weeks. She described having no memory for a variety of significant events in her life, including the birth of her two children, her marriage, her sexual experiences, and several events from her childhood and adolescence. Joan also described frequent episodes of depersonalization and derealization, nightmares, and flashbacks; she also disclosed that she frequently heard voices coming from within her head. She described that some of the voices sounded angry and others comforting. She perceived the voices as coming from other people inside her head, and the voices expressed a belief that they were different people. It became clear that these voices were of the alter identities that sometimes took control of Joan's functioning. These

(Continued)

"alters" also seemed to remember the events (both recent and remote) that Joan could not otherwise remember.

The therapist arrived at primary diagnoses of DID and PTSD. The sexual problems and depression were seen as secondary features of the DID and co-morbid PTSD, and it was decided to not directly target these problems until progress had been made on the primary problems. In the early phases of treatment, Joan's therapist worked on improving Joan's overall level of functioning, first orienting her to the fact that she was one individual, working to reduce internal conflict, and restoring continuity of memory. In the middle and later phases of the treatment, Joan and her therapist directed their efforts toward processing memories of the physical and sexual abuse that she had experienced as a child. As this work progressed, the perceived separateness of the alter identities diminished, and she developed a cohesive memory for her life. Joan's sexual aversion, as well as her depression, also began to dissipate.

The possibility that two or more different streams of consciousness or identity states coexist in one body has intrigued scientists and writers for a number of centuries. At the turn of the century, William James, Morton Prince, Pierre Janet, and other eminent clinicians studied this phenomenon (Kenny, 1986). Although long regarded as an exotic and extremely rare curiosity, this condition has been systematically studied in recent years.

Dissociative identity disorder (DID) is the current label for what was formerly called *multiple personality disorder*. According to the *DSM-IV* (APA, 1994), its defining features are the presence in the person of two or more distinct identities or personality states with enduring patterns of perceiving, relating to, and thinking about the environment and the self, which recurrently take control of the individual. The other essential feature is psychogenic amnesia. In the case of DID, the issue of amnesia is more complex than in pure dissociative amnesia, because an alter may claim to have memory for events of which another alter is amnesic.

There is a core set of features of DID that may be as essential as the diagnostic criteria. They include the other dissociative symptoms such as chronic depersonalization and derealization, a variety of disturbances in memory, identity alteration and confusion, and experiences of auditory hallucinations perceived as coming from inside the individual's head (Boon & Draijer, 1993; Gleaves et al., 2001; Steinberg, Cicchetti, Buchanan, Rakfeldt, & Rounsaville, 1994). Some researchers have argued that the *DSM* criteria should be revised to focus on these features, and a recent issue of the *Journal of Trauma and Dissociation* was devoted to this topic (see Dell, 2001, and commentaries).

The *DSM-IV* made more changes to the diagnostic criteria of this condition than to those of any other DD. There were two main reasons to change the name from *multiple personality disorder* to *dissociative identity disorder*. First, the older term emphasized the concept of "many" personalities, whereas the current view is that the main problem of these individuals does not involve having a number of personalities, but failing to have the sort of complex, multifaceted, but unified, personality that most of us have. That is, the many aspects of our personality, acquiescent or aggressive, playful or serious, are not integrated in these patients, but remain as isolated and personalized nuclei. The International Society for the Study of Dissociation (1997) states it this way: "The DID patient is a single individual who experiences him/herself as having separate parts of the mind that function with some autonomy. The patient is not a collection of separate people sharing the same body."

Another reason for the name change is that the term *personality* refers to the characteristic pattern of thoughts, feelings, moods, and behaviors of the whole individual. From this perspective, the fact that DID patients consistently switch between different identities, behavior styles, and so on, constitutes their characteristic personality. This is also the main reason that the current phraseology of the *DSM* refers to "distinct identities or personality states," rather than to personalities. Other phrasing changes in diagnostic criteria clarified that while alters may be personalized by the individual, they are not to be considered as having an objective, independent existence.

The *DSM-IV* readopted the criterion of amnesia, which had been abandoned by the *DSM-III-R* (APA, 1987). The rationale then had been that, although amnesia may indeed be an essential characteristic of the condition, individuals might fail to report this symptom either because they might not remember their own amnesic episodes, or for other reasons (Kluft, Steinberg, & Spitzer, 1988). Analysis of various publications and datasets revealed, however, that an increase in false negative diagnoses with the readoption of the new criterion is very unlikely because amnesia was a symptom in all DID patients who had been systematically evaluated by different authors (Cardeña et al., 1996). These data confirmed that amnesia is a central component of the condition (see Dorahy, 2001, for a review of memory functioning in DID).

DID is generally considered the most severe of the DD, and it is the most thoroughly researched. Initially, only a few authors accounted for most of the research in this area, but there has been a steady growth in the number of contributors to the field. Although acceptance of the diagnosis among psychologists and psychiatrists is considerable (Dunn, Paolo, Ryan, & van Fleet, 1994), DID remains the most controversial of all DD. Two issues have been vigorously debated in the mental health field—first, the etiology/reality of the phenomenon, and second, its diagnostic validity. There are currently two primary positions on the etiology of DID: the posttraumatic and iatrogenic perspectives.

Proponents of the *posttraumatic,* or *traumatogenic,* model (e.g., Gleaves, 1996; Kluft, 1985) suggest that DID is a form of developmental psychopathology that occurs as a response to overwhelming childhood trauma. Some authors (e.g., Butler et al., 1996; Kluft, 1985) have proposed a diathesis-stress model, in which a disposition to use dissociative skills, including hypnotic ability, interacts with early trauma in the development of DD.

The *DSM-IV* (APA, 1994, p. 486) maintains that DID is more common among first-degree biological relatives, but there is no current information on whether this relationship is caused by genetic or environmental factors, or, more likely, an interaction of both (see earlier sections).

In contrast with the posttraumatic model, proponents of the *iatrogenesis* (sometimes referred to as *sociocognitive*) position (e.g., McHugh, 1993; Merskey, 1992; Spanos, 1994) maintain that DID is an artifact of psychotherapy and/or the popular media. There is some variability among this camp with positions ranging from those who believe that the condition is mostly or completely iatrogenic (e.g., Aldridge-Morris, 1989), produced by naive therapists and the media, to those who state that the condition is not necessarily iatrogenic but is molded by cultural expectations and social roles and strategies (e.g., Spanos, 1994). Proponents of the iatrogenic explanation point out that DID patients show significantly higher hypnotizability than other clinical groups and normal individuals (Frischholz, Lipman, Braun, & Sachs, 1992) and are thus prone to follow manifest or subtle suggestions provided by hypnotists probing for possible hidden personalities or alters. Two studies (Putnam, Guroff, Silberman, Barban, & Post, 1986; Ross, Norton, & Fraser, 1989) have answered this objection by showing that neither the use of hypnosis nor other proposed therapist characteristics can account for the majority of DID diagnoses. Also, if DID patients were just following clinicians' suggestions, they would present with other conditions because the vast majority have previously received other diagnoses (Coons et al., 1988; Putnam et al., 1986; Ross, Norton, & Wozney, 1989).

Although more research is needed, the available evidence generally supports the posttraumatic conceptualization for most cases. People with DID almost invariably report a history of childhood trauma, with some research demonstrating independent corroboration through medical and legal records, or other means (Coons, 1994; Coons & Milstein, 1986; Hornstein & Putnam, 1992). This does not mean, of course, that all reports, or all details of every report, are valid or accurate, but it shows that at least a significant proportion of DID patients have verifiable histories of abuse. A large percentage of people with DID also have comorbid PTSD, and many of the symptoms of PTSD are dissociative in nature (see Cardeña et al., in press). There is also now accumulating data on the psychobiology of chronic trauma that support the posttraumatic formulation (Forrest, 2001).

Inter-alter amnesia is both complex and not consistent with a simple malingering hypothesis (Eich, Macaulay, Loewenstein, & Patrice, 1997). Studies using brain imaging technology support the validity for the concept of *switching* between alters (Tsai, Condie, Wu, & Chang, 1999) and the diagnosis as a whole (Sar, Unal, Kiziltan, Kundakci, & Ozturk, 2001).

Gleaves (1996) proposed that most, if not all, of the assumptions of the iatrogenesis/sociocognitive model are inaccurate and based on an inaccurate understanding of the psychopathology, assessment, and treatment of DID. Perhaps the greatest misconception is equating DID with the concept of *multiple identity enactment* (e.g., Spanos, 1994). As noted previously, DID is characterized by a pattern of dissociative experiences including amnesia, depersonalization, and derealization. The identity disturbance is better understood as a perception of having separate selves, rather than as having different individuals coexisting in the same body. People with DID also appear to actively conceal what they perceive to be a set of separate selves.

DID is more frequently diagnosed in the United States than in most other places, but there is considerable evidence for its existence in other countries (e.g., Boon & Draijer, 1991; Coons et al., 1991; Martínez-Taboas, 1991; Tutkun, Yargic, & Sar, 1995). An alternative explanation to iatrogenesis is that the characteristics and method of evaluation of DID have just recently become part of the clinician's awareness in the United States, and other countries are lagging behind. For instance, when the first author taught a course in Spain on DD, three clinicians without previous knowledge of dissociation independently described clients from their practices who were almost textbook descriptions of DID, but had received other diagnoses. That DID, as well as our nonpathological sense of self, is mediated by cultural notions of self, identity, personal consistency, and so on (e.g., Kirmayer, 1994) is an issue different from whether DID is an iatrogenic condition.

The high hypnotic susceptibility of DID patients, coupled with the incompetent use of hypnosis or other suggestive techniques by some practitioners, increases the possibility of iatrogenesis. The empirical support for the traumatogenic theory does not deny the likelihood that a few cases have therapist suggestion or malingering causal factors (Ross, 1997), but this is the case for all disorders, not only DID. In a balanced overview of the DID controversy, Horevitz (1994, p. 447) stated that "Critics who claim MPD [multiple personality disorder] is nonexistent, rare, iatrogenic, or overdiagnosed may be right or they may be wrong. However, no data at present exists [sic] to directly support these contentions." There are problems with the iatrogenesis model, and even the model's proponents admit that there is "a paucity of data" to support it (Lilienfeld et al., 1999, p. 36).

Similarly, D. Brown, Frischolz, and Scheflin (1999) concluded that "these sparse data fail to meet a minimal standard of scientific evidence justifying the claim that a major psychiatric diagnosis like dissociative identity disorder per se can be produced through suggestive influences in therapy" (p. 549).

As to the second area of controversy, that of diagnostic validity, some researchers and/or clinicians regard the phenomenology as genuine (i.e., not iatrogenic), but symptomatic of other disorders, and not an independent diagnostic entity (North, Ryall, Ricci, & Wetzel, 1993). Fahy (1988), for example, described DID as "an intriguing symptom of a wide range of psychological disturbances" (p. 603). Ross (1997) reviewed much of the most recent data on this issue and concluded that "although the data are not definitive, the burden of proof lies on extreme disbelievers to establish through scientific studies that DID is not valid and reliable, since the existing data point to the opposite conclusion" (p. 79). More recently, after reviewing three different guidelines to establish diagnostic validity, Gleaves et al. (2001) concluded that considerable converging evidence supports the validity of the diagnosis and its inclusion in the *DSM.* They demonstrated that the reliability and validity data for DID were generally equal to or better than those for most well-accepted diagnosis, and that DID is one of the few disorders currently supported by taxometric research. Data suggest that DID can be quite reliably discriminated from other conditions with which it is sometimes allegedly confused (schizophrenia, borderline personality disorder, and seizure disorder). Consistent with the posttraumatic model of the disorder's etiology, the greatest degree of diagnostic overlap may be with PTSD.

The clinical presentation of people with DID can vary widely. Even among DID patients, there is a wide range of symptom severity and level of adaptation, with some individuals being able to perform adequately in various areas of functioning (Kluft, 1994). Symptom presentation can vary across time in the same patient, sometimes fulfilling all the criteria for DID, sometimes fulfilling criteria only for DDNOS (dissociative disorders not otherwise specified; see later discussion). Besides the "textbook" presentation, Kluft (1991) provides an extensive list of variants, including epochal or sequential (i.e., switches are rare), latent (alters are manifested only at times of stress), posttraumatic DID, and others.

At least until some years ago, DID individuals usually received, on average, about four previous diagnoses (e.g., depression and other affective disorders, personality disorders, and schizophrenia) before the final DID diagnosis (Coons et al., 1988; Putnam et al., 1986). Later studies have found substantial comorbidity between DID and depression and affective liability (including self-injury attempts); anxiety, conversion, and other somatoform disorders (headaches are almost always found among DIDs); personality disorders (especially borderline) and first-rank symptoms; substance abuse and eating disorders are not infrequent either (see Cardeña & Spiegel, 1996, for a review). Individuals with DID report some first-rank symptoms such as auditory hallucinations, but they typically have adequate reality testing outside of specific events such as fugues or flashbacks and do not present the negative symptoms of schizophrenia.

Because DID patients are multisymptomatic and often have previous diagnoses, a thorough evaluation is essential. A careful differential diagnosis of DID should rule out other DD (DID is the superordinate diagnosis), dissociative symptoms produced by epilepsy, psychotic states, some personality disorders, transient effects of medications and drugs, malingering and factitious disorder, somatoform disorders, depression, and sexual disorders such as gender identity disorder (Cardeña & Spiegel, 1996; Coons & Milstein, 1994; Ross, 1997).

In most cases, thorough assessment with a systematic interview and one or more of the instruments mentioned previously can provide enough information for a diagnosis. While a questionnaire such as the DES can provide valuable information, more thorough clinical interviews such as the SCID-D are recommended. The *Guidelines for Treating Dissociative Identity Disorder* of ISSD (1997) explicitly recommend that hypnosis and amytal interviews not be used during evaluation unless there is uncertainty, and even then, caution should be exercised not to provide leading or suggestive questions. Considering the high suggestibility of these patients, this caution seems warranted.

The course and prognosis depends on symptom severity and the psychological fragility of the patient. There is a wide variety of therapy trajectories even while maintaining a number of therapy variables constant (Kluft, 1994); nonetheless, it is widely accepted that therapy for these patients typically takes a number of years (Putnam & Loewenstein, 1993).

DISSOCIATIVE DISORDERS NOT OTHERWISE SPECIFIED

Case Study 5

A young Brazilian man described that he became possessed by spirits from the Afro-Brazilian pantheon, which would take over his body and voice, and make him act in a style that was uncharacteristic of him. Unless someone told him what he had done, he could not remember what had transpired during these episodes. He was very distressed about it, because he could not control the episodes and they sometimes happened while he was in his job. The local *Candomble* priest recommended that he be initiated into that religion. After a number of rituals and instruction, the young man had spirit possession experiences only in the midst of carefully arranged ritual settings.

The *dissociative disorders not otherwise specified* (DDNOS) include dissociative pathologies of consciousness, identity, or memory, that do not fulfill the criteria of the DD described so far. A substantial proportion of dissociative patients fall under this category. In a large general psychiatric sample ($N = 11,292$), Mezzich et al. (1989) found the majority (57%) of dissociative disorder diagnoses to be atypical (a previous designation for DDNOS). This figure is very similar (60%) to the one obtained by Saxe and collaborators (1993) in a subgroup of general psychiatric patients reporting clinical levels of dissociation. However, the epidemiological study by Ross (1991), who used a thorough evaluation of dissociation, found a smaller percentage. Diagnostic criteria have changed, and new epidemiological studies with detailed evaluation of dissociation are needed to clarify this issue.

Lynn and Rhue (1988), H. Spiegel (1974), and Hartmann (1984), respectively, have described subgroups of high fantasizers, hypnotic "virtuosos," and "thin boundaried" individuals who are vulnerable to distressing fantasies, excessive suggestibility, and uncontrolled loss of boundaries, which increase their risk for psychopathology. Uncontrolled and disorganized fluctuations of consciousness seem to increase the risk of pathology in this and other cultures (Cardeña, 1992), but the clinician should bear in mind that the mere presence of unusual experiences is not synonymous with psychological dysfunction (Cardeña, Lynn, & Krippner, 2000).

What little evidence we have suggests that the majority of dissociative patients in other cultures have presentations different from the ones described so far (Cardeña et al., 1996; Saxena & Prasad, 1989). Social, political, gender, and cultural variables must be considered to understand these syndromes (Littlewood, 1998).

The *DSM-IV* contains the following examples of DDNOS:

- Cases similar to DID that do not fulfill all its criteria; for instance, an individual presenting with two or more identities but without amnesia. The instances of identity alteration without amnesia, and typically with a greater integration of personality, have been called *ego states.* Coons (1992) has described different personality states associated with gender identity disorder.

- Derealization without depersonalization; for example, sensing self as "normal," but the world as not quite real or as diffuse. This example is specific to adults; children without any pathology might blur the distinction between their fantasy and consensual reality.

- Dissociative states in individuals who have been subjected to chronic forms of coercion, suggestion, "brainwashing," and so on. West and Martin (1994) have described the presentation of captivity and cult victims. Among the phenomena they describe are having an emotionally and intellectually restricted "pseudo-identity," which, at least temporarily, substitutes for the previous identity; episodes of unawareness and disorientation; emotional unresponsiveness and lack of motivation; and so on.

- Dissociative trance disorder (see next section).

- Loss of consciousness, being stuporous, or comatose without a medical reason. For instance, a medically unexplained epidemic of fainting among Bhutanese refugees was found to be significantly related to recent and early loss (Van Ommeren et al., 2001), and similar epidemics have been observed in Western countries.

- Ganser's syndrome or the giving of approximate answers (e.g., "a car has three wheels"), that cannot be explained by dementia, psychosis, or malingering. Ganser's syndrome is often accompanied by other alterations of consciousness such as time alteration. The *DSM-IV* considers dissociative amnesia and fugue as superordinate diagnoses to Ganser's syndrome.

The assessment of DDNOS is the same as that for the other dissociative disorders, and its prognosis depends on factors such as the severity of the disorder and its chronicity and history. Differential diagnosis should include dissociative-like phenomena occurring as the byproduct of medication (e.g., Finestone & Manly, 1994) and seizure or other medical conditions (cf. Cardeña et al., 1996; Good, 1993). As with the other dissociative disorders, DDNOS can be diagnosed only when there is evidence of clinical levels of distress or maladjustment.

DISSOCIATIVE TRANCE DISORDER

One of the examples of DDNOS is *dissociative trance disorder*, which includes trance or spirit possession phenomena. Cardeña, Lewis-Fernández and colleagues (Cardeña, Lewis-Fernández, Beahr, Pakianathan, & Spiegel, 1996) proposed that dissociative trance disorder be removed from the list of DDNOS and considered a dissociative disorder in its own right. This action would enhance the cross-cultural applicability of the *DSM* taxonomy because there is evidence that many, if not most, of the dissociative manifestations in other cultures might fall under this rubric. Although we do not yet have a cross-cultural comparative database for other cultures, there are indications that they often differ in important ways from the criteria used by the *DSM-IV*. For instance, Saxena and Prasad (1989) reported that 90% of clinic outpatients in India with a *DSM-III* dissociative diagnosis had *atypical dissociative disorder*, or DDNOS; many of those patients specifically complained of distressing or maladjusting forms of spirit possession. Alterations of consciousness that could be defined as spirit possession or trance are frequently a common aspect of cultural and religious practices in many parts of the world (Bourguignon, 1976), and the proposal for a dissociative trance disorder explicitly excludes culturally accepted practices and experiences from the disorder. The *DSM-IV* included the proposal of a *dissociative trance disorder* in an appendix for "further study."

The word *trance* has been used in many, often inconsistent, ways. In the *DSM-IV*, it is defined as a consciousness state characterized by a narrow focus of consciousness and/or stereotypical behaviors experienced as alien to the subject. The notion of trance entails a diminution of the temporal, spatial, and memory context for the self, or what Shor called "generalized reality orientation" (Shor, 1959), and a decrease in reflective awareness (Cardeña & Spiegel, 1991). Examples of *trance* include a patient who suddenly becomes unaware of and/or unresponsive to the therapist (either because he or she has no apparent mental contents, or because he or she is fully absorbed in a memory or a fantasy), and a patient who starts writing lines on a paper and becomes temporarily unable to stop the scribbling on the paper. Although amnesia has been mentioned as a central component of most DD, lack of reflective consciousness and control of behavior are often seen in the clinical context and are central to modern views of dissociation (Hilgard, 1994; Nijenhuis, 2000; Woody & Bowers, 1994).

Spirit possession is defined by the *DSM-IV* as an alteration of identity and consciousness characterized by the replacement of the individual's usual identity by a different one, commonly believed to be that of an ancestor or some form of noncorporeal being; it is typically accompanied by amnesia. Spirit possession in this sense is different from the mere *belief* that illnesses or other occurrences are caused by metaphysical forces. It might be tempting to conclude that spirit possession is nothing but a metaphysical explanation for what we call DID, but, at this point, such conclusion would require further research. In contrast with DID, dysfunctional spirit possession has not been unequivocally associated with a history of early abuse, the possessing entity is experienced as external to the individual and generally conforms to a specific religious pantheon, and the disorder seems to be more reactive to a current stressor and less chronic than DID.

Examples of culture-bound pathological manifestations with a central dissociative component include:

- Cases of long-lasting, dysfunctional, and uncontrolled spirit possession involving identity substitution, harming or self-harming acts, amnesia, and so on.
- *Ataque de nervios,* a condition characterized by dysphoric feelings after exposure to trauma, somatic complaints and paresthesias, unawareness of the surroundings, and partial or total amnesia for the event.
- *Latah* and other startle syndromes in which the victim, after a sudden fright, may start mimicking others without apparent control.
- *Amok, berserk,* and similar phenomena in which, after "losing face," the experiencer may brood for a while, have a narrow focus of consciousness, and then go on an apparently automatic killing rampage until he or she is stopped (cf. Cardeña et al., 1996; Simons & Hughes, 1985).

Assessment of general dissociative alterations in our culture may be done through the instruments mentioned, but an evaluation of dissociative manifestations in a member from another culture or subculture requires that clinicians be conversant with the semantic network of disease and health of that group, and be able to find a common language. As the APA states (1995, p. 76), diagnostic evaluation "must be sensitive to the patient's ethnicity and place of birth, gender, social class, sexual orientation, and religious/spiritual beliefs," a principle that is even more crucial in the evaluation of complex experiential and behavioral phenomena.

There is no systematic database on which to evaluate the prognosis of dissociative trance disorder, but we have considerable anthropological literature on the efficacy of indigenous treatment for some of these manifestations.

SUMMARY

This chapter gives an overview of DD. Considering the brief span in which systematic research on dissociation and the DD has been conducted, it is likely that our conception of, and diagnostic criteria for, these disorders will change in the future. This chapter has just skimmed the surface in some areas such as consideration of cultural variations. The dissociative disorders have been, and will probably remain, mired in controversy for a number of years, but actual empirical investigation has been gradually substituting uninformed speculation. It is now established, for example, that traumatic events and attachment dysfunctions are commonly associated with dissociative phenomena and symptomatology, that DD are much more common than was once thought, and that DD can be present at an early age. Many other areas remain open for debate; for example: What personal characteristics predispose individuals to react to trauma with dissociativity rather than with other symptoms? What is the nature of DID alters? What neurophysiological and perceptual processes underlie dissociative experiences?

Whatever the outcome of some of these debates, we now have psychometrically sound instruments to measure dissociative experiences and disorders, but many more theoretical and empirical developments need to occur before we can state that we have really gone beyond the conceptualization of brilliant observers and thinkers such as Sigmund Freud, Pierre Janet, and William James. It seems that the dissociative disorders, in some shape or another, are here to stay.

REFERENCES

Aderibigbe, Y. A., Bloch, R. M., & Walker, W. R. (2001). Prevalence of depersonalization and derealization experiences in a rural population. *Social Psychiatry and Psychiatric Epidemiology, 36,* 63–69.

Akhtar, S., & Brenner, I. (1979). Differential diagnosis of fugue-like states. *Journal of Clinical Psychiatry, 9,* 381–385.

Aldridge-Morris, R. (1989). *Multiple personality: An exercise in deception.* Hillside, NJ: Erlbaum.

American Psychiatric Association. (1987). *Diagnostic and statistical manual of mental disorders* (3rd ed., rev). Washington, DC: Author.

American Psychiatric Association. (1994). *Diagnostic and statistical manual of mental disorders* (4th ed.). Washington, DC: Author.

American Psychiatric Association. (1995). Practice guidelines for psychiatric evaluation of adults. *American Journal of Psychiatry, 152*(Suppl. 1), 67–80.

Barlow, D. H., & Durand, V. M. (2001). *Abnormal psychology: An integrative approach.* Stamford, CT: Wadsworth/Thomson Learning.

Benson, D. F. (1978). Amnesia. *Southern Medical Journal, 71,* 1221–1227.

Boon, S., & Draijer, N. (1991). Diagnosing dissociative disorders in the Netherlands: A pilot study with the Structured Clinical Interview for the *DSM-III-R* Dissociative Disorders. *American Journal of Psychiatry, 148,* 458–462.

Boon, S., & Draijer, N. (1993). *Multiple personality disorder in the Netherlands: A study on reliability and validity of the diagnosis.* Amsterdam: Swets & Zeitlinger.

Bourguignon, E. (1976). *Possession.* San Francisco: Chandler.

Braun, B. G. (1993). Multiple personality disorder and posttraumatic stress disorder. In J. P. Wilson & B. Raphael (Eds.), *International handbook of traumatic stress syndromes* (pp. 35–47). New York: Plenum Press.

Bremner, J. D., Krystal, J. H., Southwick, S. M., & Charney, D. S. (1995). Functional neuroanatomical correlates of the effects of stress on memory. *Journal of Traumatic Stress, 8,* 527–553.

Brown, D. (1995). Pseudo-memories, the standard of science and the standard of care in trauma treatment. *American Journal of Clinical Hypnosis, 37,* 1–24.

Brown, D., Frischolz, E. J., & Scheflin, A. W. (1999). Iatrogenic dissociative identity disorder: An evaluation of the scientific evidence. *Journal of Psychiatry and Law, 27,* 549–637.

Brown, D., Scheflin, A. W., & Whitfield, C. L. (1999). Recovered memories: The current weight of the evidence in science and in the courts. *Journal of Psychiatry and Law, 27,* 5–156.

Brown, P. (1994). Toward a psychobiological model of dissociation and posttraumatic stress disorder. In S. J. Lynn & J. Rhue (Eds.), *Dissociation: Clinical and theoretical perspectives* (pp. 94–122). New York: Guilford Press.

Butler, L. D., Duran, E. E., Jasiukaitis, P., Koopman, C., & Spiegel, D. (1996). Hypnotizability and traumatic experience: A diathesis-stress model of dissociative symptomatology. *American Journal of Psychiatry, 153,* 42–63.

Butler, L. D., & Spiegel, D. (1997). Trauma and memory. In L. J. Dickstein, M. B. Riba, & J. O. Oldham (Eds.), *Review of psychiatry* (Vol. 16, pp. 1113–1115). Washington, DC: American Psychiatric Press.

Cardeña, E. (1992). Trance and possession as dissociative disorders. *Transcultural Psychiatric Research Review, 29,* 287–300.

Cardeña, E. (1994). The domain of dissociation. In S. J. Lynn & J. Rhue (Eds.), *Dissociation: Clinical and theoretical perspectives* (pp. 15–31). New York: Guilford Press.

Cardeña, E. (1997). The etiologies of dissociation. In S. Powers & S. Krippner (Eds.), *Broken images, broken selves* (pp. 61–87). New York: Brunner/Mazel.

Cardeña, E., Butler, L., & Spiegel, D. (2003). Stress disorders. In G. Stricker & T. Widiger (Eds.), *Handbook of psychology* (pp. 229–249). New York: Wiley.

Cardeña, E., Butler, L., & Spiegel, D. (in press). Disorders of extreme stress. In T. Widiger (Ed.), *Comprehensive handbook of psychology.* New York: Wiley.

Cardeña, E., Koopman, C., Classen, C., Waelde, L., & Spiegel, D. (2000). Psychometric properties of the Stanford Acute Stress Reaction Questionnaire (SASRQ): A valid and reliable measure of acute stress reactions. *Journal of Traumatic Stress, 13,* 719–734.

Cardeña, E., Lewis-Fernández, R., Beahr, D., Pakianathan, I., & Spiegel, D. (1996). Dissociative disorders. In T. A. Widiger, A. J. Frances, H. J. Pincus, R. Ross, M. B. First, & W. W. Davis (Eds.), *Sourcebook for the DSM-IV* (Vol. 2, pp. 973–1005) Washington, DC: American Psychiatric Press.

Cardeña, E., Lynn, S. J., & Krippner, S. (2000). *Varieties of anomalous experience.* Washington, DC: American Psychological Association.

Cardeña, E., & Nijenhuis, E. (Eds.). (2000). Special issue on Somatoform dissociation. *Journal of Trauma and Dissociation, 1*(4).

Cardeña, E., & Spiegel, D. (1991). Suggestibility, absorption, and dissociation: An integrative model of hypnosis. In J. F. Schumaker (Ed.), *Human suggestibility: Advances in theory, research and application* (pp. 93–107). New York: Routledge.

Cardeña, E., & Spiegel D. (1993). Dissociative reactions to the Bay Area earthquake. *American Journal of Psychiatry, 150,* 474–478.

Cardeña, E., & Spiegel, D. (1996). Diagnostic issues, criteria and comorbidity of dissociative disorders. In L. Michelson & W. Ray (Eds.), *Handbook of dissociation: Theoretical, empirical, and clinical perspectives* (pp. 227–250). New York: Plenum Press.

Carlson, E. B., & Putnam, F. W. (1993). An update on the Dissociative Experiences Scale. *Dissociation, 6,* 16–27.

Christianson, S. A., & Loftus, E. F. (1987). Memory for traumatic events. *Applied Cognitive Psychology, 1,* 225–239.

Cohen, L., Berzoff, J., & Elin, M. (Eds.). (1995). *Dissociative identity disorder.* Northvale, NJ: Aronson.

Coons, P. M. (1992). Dissociative disorders not otherwise specified: A clinical investigation of 50 cases with suggestions for typology and treatment. *Dissociation, 5,* 187–195.

Coons, P. M. (1994). Confirmation of childhood abuse in child and adolescent cases of multiple personality and dissociative disorder not otherwise specified. *Journal of Nervous and Mental Diseases, 182,* 461–464.

Coons, P. M., Bowman, E. S., Kluft, R. P., & Milstein, V. (1991). The cross-cultural occurrence of MPD: Additional cases from a recent survey. *Dissociation, 4,* 124–128.

Coons, P. M., Bowman, E. S., & Milstein, V. (1988). Multiple personality disorder: A clinical investigation of 50 cases. *Journal of Nervous and Mental Disorders, 176,* 519–527.

Coons, P. M., & Milstein, V. (1986). Psychosexual disturbances in multiple personality: Characteristics, etiology and treatment. *Journal of Clinical Psychiatry, 47,* 106–110.

Coons, P. M., & Milstein, V. (1992). Psychogenic amnesia: A clinical investigation of 25 cases. *Dissociation, 5,* 73–79.

Coons, P. M., & Milstein, V. (1994). Factitious or malingered multiple personality disorder: Eleven cases. *Dissociation, 7,* 81–85.

Dell, P. F. (2001). Why the diagnostic criteria for dissociative identity disorder should be changed. *Journal of Trauma and Dissociation, 2,* 7–37.

Dorahy, M. J. (2001). Dissociative identity disorder and memory dysfunction: The current state of experimental research and its future directions. *Clinical Psychology Review, 21,* 771–795.

Dunn, G. E., Paolo, A. M., Ryan, J. J., & van Fleet, J. N. (1994). Belief in the existence of multiple personality disorder among psychologists and psychiatrists. *Journal of Clinical Psychology, 50,* 454–457.

Eich, E., Macaulay, D., Loewenstein, R., & Patrice, H. (1997). Memory, amnesia, and dissociative identity disorder. *Psychological Science, 8,* 417–422.

Erdelyi, M. E. (1994). Dissociation, defense, and the unconscious. In D. Spiegel (Ed.), *Dissociation: Culture, mind, and body* (pp. 3–20). Washington, DC: American Psychiatric Press.

Fahy, T. (1988). The diagnosis of multiple personality disorder: A critical review. *British Journal of Psychiatry, 153,* 597–606.

Farthing, G. W. (1992). *The psychology of consciousness.* Englewood Cliffs, NJ: Prentice-Hall.

Finestone, D. H., & Manly, D. T. (1994). Dissociation precipitated by propranolol. *Psychosomatics, 35,* 83–87.

Forrest, K. A. (2001). Toward an etiology of dissociative identity disorder: A neurodevelopmental approach. *Consciousness and Cognition, 10,* 259–293.

Freyd, J. J., & DePrince, A. P. (2001). *Trauma and cognitive science: A meeting of minds, science, and human experience.* New York: Haworth Press.

Freyd, J. J., DePrince, A. P., & Zurbriggen, E. L. (2001). Self-reported memory for abuse depends upon victim-perpetrator relationship. *Journal of Trauma and Dissociation, 2*(5), 5–16.

Friedl, M. C., & Draijer, N. (2000). Dissociative disorders in Dutch psychiatric inpatients. *American Journal of Psychiatry, 157*(6), 1012–1013.

Frischholz, E. J., Lipman, L. S., Braun, B. G., & Sachs, R. G. (1992). Psychopathology, hypnotizability, and dissociation. *American Journal of Psychiatry, 149,* 1521–1525.

Gabbard, G. O., Twemlow, S. W., & Jones, F. C. (1982). Differential diagnosis of altered mind/body perception. *Psychiatry, 45,* 361–369.

Gleaves, D. H. (1996). The sociocognitive model of dissociative identity disorder: A reexamination of the evidence. *Psychological Bulletin, 120,* 42–59.

Gleaves, D. H., May, M. C., & Cardeña, E. (2001). An examination of the diagnostic validity of dissociative identity disorder. *Clinical Psychology Review, 21,* 577–608.

Good, M. I. (1993). The concept of an organic dissociative disorder: What is the evidence? *Harvard Review of Psychiatry, 1,* 145–157.

Grinker, R. R., & Spiegel, J. P. (1945). *Men under stress.* Philadelphia: Blakiston.

Guralnik, O., Schmeidler, J., & Simeon, D. (2000). Feeling unreal: Cognitive processes in depersonalization. *American Journal of Psychiatry, 157,* 103–109.

Hartmann, E. (1984). *The nightmare.* New York: Basic Books.

Hilgard, E. R. (1968). *The experience of hypnosis.* New York: Harcourt, Brace & World.

Hilgard, E. R. (1994). Neodissociation theory. In S. J. Lynn & J. Rhue (Eds.), *Dissociation: Clinical and theoretical perspectives* (pp. 32–51). New York: Guilford Press.

Horevitz, R. (1994). Dissociation and multiple personality: Conflicts and controversies. In S. J. Lynn & J. Rhue (Eds.), *Dissociation: Clinical and theoretical perspectives* (pp. 434–461). New York: Guilford Press.

Hornstein, N. L., & Putnam, F. W. (1992). Clinical phenomenology of child and adolescent dissociative disorders. *Journal of the American Academy of Child and Adolescent Psychiatry, 31,* 1077–1085.

International Society for the Study of Dissociation. (1997). *Guidelines for treating dissociative identity disorder (multiple personality disorder) in adults.* Retrieved June 27, 2002, from http://issd.org/indexpage/isdguide.htm.

Jacobs, J. R., & Bovasso, G. B. (1992). Toward the clarification of the construct of depersonalization and its association with affective and cognitive dysfunctions. *Journal of Personality Assessment, 59,* 352–365.

James, W. (1923). *Principles of psychology.* New York: Holt. (Original work published 1890)

Janet, P. (1965). *The major symptoms of hysteria* (2nd ed.). New York: Hafner. (Original work published 1907)

Jang, K. L., Paris, J., Zweig-Frank, H., & Livesley, W. J. (1998). Twin study of dissociative experience. *Journal of Nervous and Mental Diseases, 186,* 345–351.

Kaszniak, A. W., Nussbaum, P. D., Berren, M. R., & Santiago, J. (1988). Amnesia as a consequence of male rape: A case report. *Journal of Abnormal Psychology, 97,* 100–104.

Keller, R., & Shaywitz, B. A. (1986). Amnesia or fugue state: A diagnostic dilemma. *Developmental and Behavioral Pediatrics, 7,* 131–132.

Kenny. (1986). *The passion of Ansel Bourne: Multiple personality in American culture.* Washington, DC: Smithsonian Press.

Kessler, R. C., McGonagle, K. A., Zhao, S., Nelson, C. B., Hughes, M., Eshleman, S., et al. (1994). Lifetime and 12-month prevalence of *DSM-III-R* psychiatric disorders in the United States. *Archives of General Psychiatry, 51,* 8–19.

Kihlstrom, J. F. (1987). The cognitive unconscious. *Science, 237,* 1445–1452.

Kihlstrom, J. F. (1994). One hundred years of hysteria. In S. J. Lynn & J. W. Rhue (Eds.), *Dissociation: Clinical and theoretical perspectives* (pp. 365–394). New York: Guilford Press.

Kirmayer, L. J. (1994). Pacing the void: Social and cultural dimensions of dissociation. In D. Spiegel (Ed.), *Dissociation: Culture, mind, and body* (pp. 91–122). Washington, DC: American Psychiatric Press.

Kluft, R. P. (1985). The natural history of multiple personality disorder. In R. P. Kluft (Ed.), *Childhood antecedents of multiple personality disorder* (pp. 197–238). Washington, DC: American Psychiatric Press.

Kluft, R. P. (1991). Clinical presentations of multiple personality disorder. *Psychiatric Clinics of North America, 14,* 605–629.

Kluft, R. P. (1994). Treatment trajectories in multiple personality disorder. *Dissociation, 7,* 63–76.

Kluft, R. P. (1996). Dissociative identity disorder. In L. K. Michelson & W. J. Ray (Eds.), *Handbook of dissociation: Theoretical, empirical and clinical perspectives* (pp. 337–366). New York: Plenum Press.

Kluft, R. P., Steinberg, M., & Spitzer, R. L. (1988). *DSM-III-R* revisions in the dissociative disorders: Exploration of their derivation and rationale. *Dissociation, 1,* 39–46.

Koopman, C., Classen, C., Cardeña, E., & Spiegel, D. (1995). When disaster strikes, acute stress disorder may follow. *Journal of Traumatic Stress, 8,* 29–46.

Kopelman, M. D. (1987). Amnesia: Organic and psychogenic. *British Journal of Psychiatry, 150,* 428–442.

Kopelman, M. D., Christensen, H., Puffett, A., & Stanhope, N. (1994). The great escape: A neuropsychological study of psychogenic amnesia. *Neuropsychologia, 32,* 675–691.

Kubin, M., Pakianathan, I., Cardeña, E., & Spiegel, D. (1989). *Depersonalization disorder.* Unpublished manuscript, Stanford University, Stanford, CA.

Lazarus, A. (1976). Psychiatric problems precipitated by transcendental meditation. *Psychological Reports, 10,* 39–74.

Lewis, D. O., Yeager, C. A., Swica, Y., Pincus, J. H., & Lewis, M. (1997). Objective documentation of child abuse and dissociation in 12 murderers with dissociative identity disorder. *American Journal of Psychiatry, 154,* 1703–1710.

Lewis-Fernández, R. (1994). Culture and dissociation: A comparison of *Ataque de Nervios* among Puerto Ricans and possession syndrome in India. In D. Spiegel (Ed.), *Dissociation: Culture, mind, and body* (pp. 123–167). Washington, DC: American Psychiatric Press.

Lilienfeld, S. O., Lynn, S. J., Kirsch, I., Chaves, J. F., Sarbin, T. R., Ganaway, G. K., et al. (1999). Dissociative identity disorder and the sociocognitive model: Recalling the lessons of the past. *Psychological Bulletin, 125,* 507–523.

Littlewood, R. (1998). Mental illness as ritual theatre. *Performance Research, 3,* 41–52.

Litwin, R. G., & Cardeña, E. (1993). *Dissociation and reported trauma in organic and psychogenic seizure patients.* Paper presented at the 101st annual convention of the American Psychological Association, Toronto, Canada.

Loewenstein, R. J. (1991a). An office mental status examination for chronic complex dissociative symptoms and dissociative identity disorder. *Psychiatric Clinics of North America, 14,* 567–604.

Loewenstein, R. J. (1991b). Psychogenic amnesia and psychogenic fugue: A comprehensive review. In A. Tasman & S. M. Goldfinger (Eds.), *Review of psychiatry* (Vol. 10, pp. 189–222). Washington, DC: American Psychiatric Press.

Loftus, E. F. (1993). The reality of repressed memories. *American Psychologist, 48,* 518–537.

Lynn, S. J., & Rhue, J. W. (1988). Fantasy proneness: Hypnosis, developmental antecedents, and psychopathology. *American Psychologist, 43,* 35–44.

Lynn, S. J., & Rhue, J. W. (1994). *Dissociation: Clinical and theoretical perspectives.* New York: Guilford Press.

Marmar, C. R., Weiss, D. S., Schlenger, W. E., Fairbank, J. A., Jordan, B. K., Kulka, R. A., et al. (1994). Peritraumatic dissociation and posttraumatic stress in male Vietnam theater veterans. *American Journal of Psychiatry, 151,* 902–907.

Martínez-Taboas, A. (1991). Multiple personality in Puerto Rico: Analysis of fifteen cases. *Dissociation, 4,* 189–192.

Mayeux, R., Alexander, M. P., Benson, F., Brandt, J., & Rosen, J. (1979). Poriomania. *Neurology, 29,* 1616–1619.

McHugh, P. (1993). Multiple personality disorder. *Harvard Medical School Mental Health Letter, 10*(3), 4–6.

Merskey, H. (1992). The manufacture of personalities: The production of multiple personality disorder. *British Journal of Psychiatry, 160,* 327–340.

Mezzich, J. E., Dow, J. T., Rich, C. L., Costello, A. J., & Himmelhoch, J. M. (1981). Developing an efficient clinical information system for a comprehensive psychiatric institute. II: Initial evaluation form. *Behavior Research Methods and Instrumentation, 13,* 464–478.

Mezzich, J. E., Fabrega, H., Coffman, G. A., & Haley, R. (1989). *DSM-III* disorders in a large sample of psychiatric patients: Frequency and specificity of diagnoses. *American Journal of Psychiatry, 146,* 212–219.

Michelson, L. K., & Ray, W. J. (Eds.). (1996). *Handbook of dissociation: Theoretical, empirical and clinical perspectives.* New York: Plenum Press.

Morgan, A. H. (1973). The heritability of hypnotic susceptibility in twins. *Journal of Abnormal Psychology, 82,* 55–61.

Nelson, E. C., Heath, A. C., Madden, P. A., Cooper, M. L., Dinwiddle, S. H., Bucholz, K., et al. (2002). Association between self-reported childhood sexual abuse and adverse psychosocial outcomes. *Archives of General Psychiatry, 59,* 139–145.

Nemiah, J. C. (1995). Dissociative disorders. In H. I. Kaplan & B. J. Sadock (Eds.), *Comprehensive textbook of psychiatry* (Vol. 6, pp. 1281–1293). Baltimore: Williams & Wilkins.

Nijenhuis, E. R. S. (2000). Somatoform dissociation: Major symptoms of dissociative disorders. *Journal of Trauma and Dissociation, 1*(4), 7–32.

North, C. S., Ryall, J. M., Ricci, D. A., & Wetzel, R. D. (1993). *Multiple personalities, multiple disorders: Psychiatric classification and media influence.* New York: Oxford University Press.

Noyes, R., & Kletti, R. (1977). Depersonalization in response to life-threatening danger. *Comprehensive Psychiatry, 18,* 375–384.

Ogawa, J. R., Sroufe, L. A., Weinfield, N. S., Carlson, E. A., & Egeland, B. (1997). Development and the fragmented self: Longitudinal study of dissociative symptomatology in a nonclinical sample. *Development and Psychopathology, 9,* 855–879.

Pribor, E. E., Yutzi, S. H., Dean, T. J., & Wetzel, R. D. (1993). Briquet's syndrome, dissociation, and abuse. *American Journal of Psychiatry, 150,* 1507–1511.

Putnam, F. W. (1994). Dissociative disorders in children and adolescents. In S. J. Lynn & J. Rhue (Eds.), *Dissociation: Clinical and theoretical perspectives* (pp. 175–189). New York: Guilford Press.

Putnam, F. W. (1997). *Dissociation in children and adolescents: A developmental approach.* New York: Guilford Press.

Putnam, F. W., Guroff, J. J., Silberman, E. K., Barban, L., & Post, R. M. (1986). The clinical phenomenology of multiple personality disorder: Review of 100 recent cases. *Journal of Clinical Psychiatry, 47,* 285–293.

Putnam, F. W., & Loewenstein, R. J. (1993). Treatment of multiple personality disorder: A survey of current practices. *American Journal of Psychiatry, 150,* 1048–1052.

Reed, G. (1972). *The psychology of anomalous experience.* London: Hutchinson University.

Riether, A. M., & Stoudemire, A. (1988). Psychogenic fugue states: A review. *Southern Medical Journal, 81,* 568–571.

Riley, K. C. (1988). Measurement of dissociation. *Journal of Nervous and Mental Diseases, 176,* 449–450.

Rollinson, R. D. (1978). Transient global amnesia: A review of 213 cases from the literature. *Australian and New Zealand Journal of Medicine, 8,* 547–549.

Ross, C. A. (1991). Epidemiology of multiple personality and dissociation. *Psychiatric Clinics of North America, 14,* 503–517.

Ross, C. A. (1997). The validity and reliability of dissociative identity disorder. In L. Cohen, J. Berzoff, & M. Elin (Eds.), *Dissociative identity disorder* (pp. 65–84. Northvale, NJ: Aronson.

Ross, C. A., Duffy, C. M., & Ellason, J. W. (2002). Prevalence, reliability, and validity of dissociative disorders in an inpatient setting. *Journal of Trauma and Dissociation, 3,* 7–17.

Ross, C. A., Joshi, S., & Currie, R. (1991). Dissociative experiences in the general population: A factor analysis. *Hospital and Community Psychiatry, 42,* 297–301.

Ross, C. A., Norton, G. R., & Fraser, G. A. (1989). Evidence against the iatrogenesis of multiple personality disorder. *Dissociation, 2,* 61–65.

Ross, C. A., Norton, G. R., & Wozney, K. (1989). Multiple personality disorder: An analysis of 236 cases. *Canadian Journal of Psychiatry, 34,* 413–418.

Sar, V., Unal, S. N., Kiziltan, E., Kundakci, T., & Ozturk, E. (2001). HMPAO SPECT study of regional cerebral blood flow in dissociative identity disorder. *Journal of Trauma and Dissociation, 2,* 5–25.

Saxe, G. N., Chinman, G., Berkowitz, R., Hall, K., Lieberg, G., Schwartz, J., et al. (1994). Somatization in patients with dissociative disorders. *American Journal of Psychiatry, 151,* 1329–1334.

Saxe, G. N., van der Kolk, B. A., Berkowitz, R., Chinman, G., Hall, K., Lieberg, G., et al. (1993). Dissociative disorders in psychiatric patients. *American Journal of Psychiatry, 150,* 1037–1042.

Saxena, S., & Prasad, K. V. (1989). *DSM-III* subclassification of dissociative disorders applied to psychiatric outpatients in India. *American Journal of Psychiatry, 146,* 261–262.

Schacter, D. L., Wang, P. L., Tulving, E., & Freedman, M. (1982). Functional retrograde amnesia: A quantitative case study. *Neuropsychologia, 20,* 523–532.

Schooler, J. W. (1994). Seeking the core: The issues and evidence surrounding recovered accounts of sexual trauma. *Consciousness and Cognition, 3,* 452–469.

Shor, R. E. (1959). Hypnosis and the concept of the generalized reality-orientation. *American Journal of Psychotherapy, 13,* 582–602.

Silberg, J. L. (Ed.). (1998). *The dissociative child.* Lutherville, MD: Sidran Press.

Simeon, D., Gross, S., Guralnik, O., Stein, D., Schmeidler, J., & Hollander, E. (1997). Feeling unreal: 30 cases of *DSM-III-R* depersonalization disorder. *American Journal of Psychiatry, 154,* 1107–1113.

Simeon, D., Guralnik, O., Knutelska, M., Hollander, E., & Schmeidler, J. (2001). Hypothalamic-pituitary-adrenal axis dysregulation in depersonalization disorder. *Neuropsychopharmacology, 5,* 793–795.

Simeon, D., Guralnik, O., Schmeidler, J., Sirof, B., & Knutelska, M. (2000). The role of childhood interpersonal trauma in depersonalization disorder. *American Journal of Psychiatry, 157,* 1027–1033.

Simons, R. C., & Hughes, C. C. (Eds.). (1985). *The culture bound syndromes.* Dordrecht, The Netherlands: Reidel.

Sivec, H. J., & Lynn, S. J. (1995). Dissociative and neuropsychological symptoms: The question of differential diagnosis. *Clinical Psychology Review, 15,* 297–316.

Spanos, N. P. (1994). Multiple identity enactments and multiple personality disorder: A sociocognitive perspective. *Psychological Bulletin, 116,* 143–165.

Spiegel, D. (Ed.). (1994). *Dissociation: Culture, mind, and body.* Washington, DC: American Psychiatric Press.

Spiegel, D., & Cardeña, E. (1991). Disintegrated experience: The dissociative disorders revisited. *Journal of Abnormal Psychology, 100,* 366–378.

Spiegel, H. (1974). The grade 5 syndrome: The highly hypnotizable person. *International Journal of Clinical and Experimental Hypnosis, 22,* 303–319.

Steinberg, M. (1990). The spectrum of depersonalization: Assessment and treatment. In A. Tasman & S. M. Goldfinger (Eds.), *Review of psychiatry* (Vol. 10, pp. 223–247). Washington, DC: American Psychiatric Press.

Steinberg, M. (1993). *The structured clinical interview for DSM-IV dissociative disorders.* Washington, DC: American Psychiatric Press.

Steinberg, M., Cicchetti, D., Buchanan, J., Rakfeldt, J., & Rounsaville, B. (1994). Distinguishing between multiple personality disorder (Dissociative Identity disorder) and schizophrenia using the Structured Clinical Interview for *DSM-IV* Dissociative disorders. *Journal of Nervous and Mental Diseases, 182,* 495–502.

Tellegen, A., Lykken, D. T., Bouchard, T. J., Wilcox, K. J., Segal, N. L., & Rich S. (1988). Personality similarity in twins reared apart and together. *Journal of Personality and Social Psychology, 54,* 1031–1039.

Terr, L. C. (1991). Childhood traumas: An outline and overview. *American Journal of Psychiatry, 148,* 10–20.

Tsai, G. E., Condie, D., Wu, M. T., & Chang, I. W. (1999). Functional magnetic resonance imaging of personality switches in a woman with dissociative identity disorder. *Harvard Review of Psychiatry, 7,* 119–122.

Tutkun, H., Sar, V., Yargic, L., Ozpulat, T., Yanik, M., & Kiziltan, E. (1998). Frequency of dissociative disorders among psychiatric inpatients in a Turkish university clinic. *American Journal of Psychiatry, 155,* 800–805.

Tutkun, H., Yargic, L. I., & Sar, V. (1995). Dissociative identity disorder: A clinical investigation of 20 cases in Turkey. *Dissociation, 8,* 3–9.

van der Hart, O., & Nijenhuis, E. (1995). Amnesia for traumatic experiences. *Hypnos, 22,* 73–86.

van der Kolk, B. A., & van der Hart, O. (1989). Pierre Janet and the breakdown of adaptation in psychological trauma. *American Journal of Psychiatry, 146,* 1530–1540.

Vanderlinden, J., van der Hart, O., & Varga, K. (1996). European studies of dissociation. In L. K. Michelson & W. J. Ray (Eds.), *Handbook of dissociation: Theoretical, empirical, and clinical perspectives* (pp. 25–49). New York: Plenum Press.

Van Ommeren, M. V., Sharma, B., Komproe, I., Sharma, G. K., Cardeña, E., de Jong, J. T., et al. (2001). Trauma and loss as determinants of medically unexplained epidemic illness in a Bhutanese refugee camp. *Psychological Medicine, 31,* 1259–1267.

Waller, N. G., Putnam, F. W., & Carlson, E. B. (1996). Types of dissociation and dissociative types: A taxometric analysis of dissociative experiences. *Psychological Methods, 1,* 300–321.

Waller, N. G., & Ross, C. A. (1997). The prevalence and biometric structure of pathological dissociation in the general population: Taxometric and behavior genetic findings. *Journal of Abnormal Psychology, 106,* 499–510.

West, L. J., & Martin, P. R. (1994). Pseudo-identity and the treatment of personality change in victims of captivity and cults. In S. J. Lynn & J. Rhue (Eds.), *Dissociation: Clinical and theoretical perspectives* (pp. 268–288). New York: Guilford Press.

Woody, E. Z., & Bowers, K. S. (1994). A frontal assault on dissociated control. In S. J. Lynn & J. Rhue (Eds.), *Dissociation: Clinical and theoretical perspectives* (pp. 52–79). New York: Guilford Press.

Zatzick, D. F., Marmar, C. R., Weiss, D. S., & Metzler, T. (1994). Does trauma-linked dissociation vary across ethnic groups? *Journal of Nervous and Mental Diseases, 182,* 576–582.

CHAPTER 14

Sexual and Gender Identity Disorders

NATHANIEL McCONAGHY

DESCRIPTION OF THE DISORDERS

SEXUAL AND GENDER identity disorders, as classified in the *Diagnostic and Statistical Manual of Mental Disorders, Fourth Edition* (*DSM-IV*; American Psychiatric Association [APA], 1994), include sexual dysfunctions, paraphilias, and gender identity disorders. Criteria for seven categories of dysfunction are presented.

Criteria A provide clinical features for four groups of disorders. *Sexual desire disorders* include hypoactive sexual desire, deficiency or absence of sexual fantasies and desire for sexual activity; and sexual aversion disorder, aversion to and active avoidance of genital sexual contact with a sexual partner. *Sexual arousal disorders* include female sexual arousal disorder, inability to attain, or to maintain until completion of the sexual activity, an adequate lubrication-swelling response of sexual excitement; and male erectile disorder, a similar inability in relation to adequate erection. *Orgasm disorders* include female and male orgasmic disorders, delay in, or absence of, orgasm following a normal sexual excitement phase; and premature ejaculation, onset of orgasm and ejaculation with minimal sexual stimulation before, on, or shortly after penetration and before the person wishes. To diagnose hypoactive sexual desire, arousal, and orgasmic disorders, *DSM-IV* states the clinician should take into account factors affecting sexual functioning. These may include adequacy of sexual stimulation, novelty of the sexual partner, frequency of sexual activity, and the subject's age and sexual experience. *Sexual pain disorders* include dyspareunia, genital pain in either males or females before, during, or after sexual intercourse; and vaginismus, involuntary spasm of the musculature of the outer third of the vagina that interferes with sexual intercourse. Vaginismus usually prevents penetration of any object above a certain size into the vagina, such as the subject's finger or a tampon. If intercourse is attempted, vaginismus is commonly accompanied by spasm of the adductor muscles of the thighs, preventing their separation. Vaginismus does not prevent women from experiencing sexual arousal and orgasm with activities other than coitus.

To receive the diagnosis of sexual disorder in these four categories, criteria A require that the condition described be recurrent or persistent, and criteria B require that it cause marked distress or interpersonal difficulty. This allows absence of orgasmic capacity to be considered not a dysfunction in women who report they enjoy intercourse although they do not reach orgasm. Indeed, it could include all sexual dysfunctions that meet criteria A in the large number of subjects who, as discussed subsequently, do not consider the condition a problem for themselves or their partners. Criteria C states that the dysfunctions are not better accounted for by another Axis I disorder (except another sexual dysfunction) and are not due exclusively to the direct physiological effect of a substance (e.g., a drug of abuse or a medication) or a general medical condition.

Sexual dysfunctions that meet criteria A and B but are *due to a general medical condition,* or are *substance-induced,* make up the fifth and sixth categories of dysfunctions. The final category of *sexual dysfunctions not otherwise specified* includes those that do not meet the criteria of specific dysfunctions, including situations in which the clinician cannot determine if a sexual dysfunction is primary or due to a medical condition or substance. The *DSM-IV* classification of sexual dysfunction provides no description of the sexual difficulties shown both in surveys of healthy couples and in those presenting with lack of sexual satisfaction to be more common and more strongly related to lack of such satisfaction than *DSM-IV*-defined dysfunctions (see Epidemiology section).

The terms *paraphilias* and *gender identity disorders* are employed in the *DSM-IV* for conditions previously referred to as sexual deviations, behaviors seen as deviating from those currently socially acceptable. With recent changes in social values, masturbation and homosexuality are no longer classified as deviations. The essential features of paraphilias are stated to be recurrent, intense, sexually arousing fantasies, sexual urges, or behaviors generally involving (a) nonhuman objects, (b) the suffering or humiliation of self or partner, or (c) children or other nonconsenting people, that occur over a period of at least six months (criterion A). It is important to note that the fantasies or urges do not have to be carried out. The behaviors, sexual urges, or fantasies cause significant distress or impairment in social, occupational, or other important areas of functioning (criterion B). *DSM-IV* provides a series of specific criteria A for some common paraphilias. These include exhibitionism—exposure of genitals to an unsuspecting stranger, fetishism—use of nonliving objects (e.g., female undergarments), and frotteurism—touching and rubbing against a nonconsenting person. Rape or sexual assault is not classified as a paraphilia. *Pedophilia,* defined as sexual activity with a prepubescent child or children (generally age 13 years or younger) by a person who is at least 16 years old and 5 years older than the child, is classified; *hebephilia,* defined as sexual activity of an adult with pubertal or immediately postpubertal subjects, is not. *Sexual masochism* involves the act (real, not simulated) of being humiliated, beaten, bound, or otherwise made to suffer. *Sexual sadism* involves acts (real, not simulated) in which the psychological or physical suffering (including humiliation) of the victim is sexually exciting. *Transvestic fetishism* involves cross-dressing; and *voyeurism* is the act of observing an unsuspecting person who is naked, in the process of disrobing, or engaged in sexual activity.

DSM-IV requires for the diagnosis of gender identity disorder a strong and persistent cross-gender identity as criterion A. It is manifested in children by four or more of these features:

1. Desire to be, or the insistence that one is, of the other sex.
2. Cross-dressing.
3. Preference for cross-sex roles in play or fantasy.
4. Intense desire to participate in opposite-sex games and pastimes.
5. Strong preference for opposite sex playmates.

In adolescents and adults, it is manifested by the stated desire to be, to live, or to be treated as of the opposite sex; frequent passing as the other sex; or the conviction that he or she has the typical feelings and reactions of the other sex. Criterion B is persistent discomfort or sense of inappropriateness with his or her sex; criterion C requires that the disturbance is not concurrent with a physical intersex condition; and criterion D requires that the disturbance cause clinically significant distress or impairment in social, occupational, or other important areas of functioning.

Case Study

Case Identification

N. S. was a 25-year-old married man studying to become a minister in an evangelical Christian religion. Two years before consulting the psychotherapist, he had traveled to a religious institution in another country, where he had severe panic attacks and suicidal thoughts. After consulting a psychiatrist there and receiving medication with some improvement, he returned home. He had received psychiatric treatment for anxiety and depression since then.

Presenting Complaints

He was referred for treatment of sexual difficulties, which followed his marriage six months earlier. From the day of his marriage, he became depressed and lost all sexual desire. He also experienced some loss of general enjoyment, which responded to the antidepressant venlafaxine. His sexual interest toward women apart from his wife returned, as did his desire to masturbate. His sleep was unimpaired, his appetite was good, he had no difficulty in concentrating on his studies, and his academic results were very good. Though he and his wife continued to kiss and cuddle, he felt a growing repulsion to intercourse. This was unrelated to any concern that his wife would become pregnant—he said he would love to have children. He then pointed out that this repulsion may always have been present to some extent and that he had never had sexual fantasies that involved intercourse. He felt he found female genitals off-putting, because of the "liquid mess," and he found breasts "the most beautiful part." He had never seen pictures of women's genitals. He had some aversion to touching his wife's genitals as she got "quite moist," and he had to shower after doing so. He related this to a negative response to what he termed "slime getting on his hands." He had a similar response to other forms of moisture. After eating fruit such as bananas and apples, he could not work until he washed his hands. In addition, he had negative feelings if his wife touched his penis when he was wet and sweaty. Both before and after having sexual relations, he liked to shower. As to saliva, he was put off by tongue contact in kissing.

When he saw the psychotherapist, he no longer wanted any sexual relations. Because his wife did, though, they compromised by having relations once a week. He found it very difficult and at times impossible to ejaculate with intercourse. His wife did not reach a climax with intercourse or manual stimulation, which he attributed to her knowing he wasn't sexually interested. He could ejaculate if his wife manually stimulated him, though aware of a degree of anxiety that if he did not, his wife might conclude he did not find her attractive. Without his wife's knowledge, he would masturbate to fantasies of attractive women, such as film stars. He found this arousing and pleasurable, but he also felt guilt. He had developed a fear that his pattern of sexual behavior had become entrenched and he would not be able to change it. He felt that the force of his ejaculation was reduced, which had occurred before he began taking venlafaxine. Asked about his wife's response to their sexual difficulties, he said that it moved from depression to anger to depression. She could be irritable and complained of tiredness but still wanted to have sex. When asked about their emotional relationship, he said it was excellent. They kissed and cuddled several times through the day for from five to thirty minutes, had afternoon naps together naked, and also slept together naked at night. I asked about their attitudes to possible alternatives to intercourse. He said his wife would consider fellatio immoral, and she would consider cunnilingus the ultimate contamination.

History

His parents were in their late 50s and in good health. He had a younger brother. He remembered his childhood as being very happy, saying the family had a lot of fun together. He added that they didn't talk deeply or about anything close. His parents encouraged him to attend sex education sessions for a period in his adolescence, but he added that he couldn't imagine his parents having a sexual life. While he lived at home, he saw no indication they were sexually active. He enjoyed school and was successful scholastically, but was not very good at sports. However, he mixed well with other students. He had always felt an interest in spiritual issues and left home to study philosophy at the university in a neighboring city. He did well scholastically and obtained an arts degree with honors. His family did not have a strong commitment to religion, but he became a born-again Christian in his first year at the university. His social life was with his peers, who were also Christians. He commenced dating girls at the same time he became a Christian, having fairly stable relationships, three lasting about a year in each of his first, second, and fourth years at the university. In the relationships, he touched his partners' naked breasts, and they touched his penis. He would obtain erections, but did not ejaculate. After he left the

(Continued)

university, before starting work, he decided to attend a religious institution in another country for three months, where his panic attacks and suicidal ideation commenced. He was started on paroxetine with some improvement. The psychiatrist who saw him on his return related his attacks to the stress of his recent final year examinations and his uncertainty about his career plans. The psychiatrist reported that the attacks had a marked obsessional flavor, with pronounced doubts about theological issues and philosophical questions, but were much milder than they had been initially. He continued N. S. on paroxetine. N. S. worked in a clerical position for 18 months, enjoying the work; he continued to work there during holidays. Initially, when he began work, he became highly anxious and couldn't eat in social situations. After six months, he said it settled to a medium level of anxiety without panic attacks. He was able to work effectively but felt that when his mind wasn't engaged, he would be aware of feeling anxious. He did not feel there were specific things about which he was anxious. He denied any checking behaviors or avoiding any situations other than those discussed. His symptoms gradually improved sufficiently that four months before his marriage, he stopped taking the paroxetine.

He began full-time religious studies, with the intention of becoming a minister in his church. He met his wife at the training institute, where she was studying religion and hoped to work in a religious capacity. In the year before their marriage, they agreed that, in view of their Christian beliefs, their sexual activity would be restricted to kissing, without breast or genital touching. He masturbated three or four times a week with fantasies of making love to women he did not know. His fantasies did not include intercourse. Since their marriage six months before, they have lived in an apartment, attending lectures every morning and studying in the afternoons. They napped together part of each afternoon. He said he adhered to the principle that he would work two-thirds of each day during the week, and they would take time off to walk before preparing dinner. They drank a small amount of beer with dinner about five days out of seven, but did not smoke or take any other substances. They had an active social life with friends in the church and visited his parents every few weeks. His wife's family were in another city, but she was emotionally close to them and kept in regular contact by phone. On Saturdays, they went to the movies or to a local park. He preached in a country church on Sundays as part of his training.

Assessment

The initial *DSM-IV* diagnosis in relation to N. S.'s presenting complaint is that of sexual aversion disorder. Criterion A for this disorder is persistent or recurrent extreme aversion to and avoidance of all or almost all genital sexual contact with a partner. N. S.'s complaint was of persistent aversion to genital contact with his wife, both by intercourse and touching. He continued both activities at least weekly, so it is arguable whether his aversion was sufficiently extreme to meet criterion A. If it is considered insufficient, it is equally arguable that his condition did not meet criterion A for hypoactive sexual disorder. Though he reported deficient desire for intercourse, he could not be considered to have deficient (or absent) sexual fantasies and desire for sexual activity. Criterion B is that the disturbance cause marked distress and interpersonal difficulty. N. S.'s disturbance caused sufficient distress for him to seek treatment, and it was likely that the interpersonal difficulty in relation to his wife's reactions of anger and depression contributed to this distress. Criterion C is that the sexual dysfunction is not better accounted for by another Axis I disorder (except another sexual dysfunction). Possible other Axis I diagnoses to consider were mood disorder and/or anxiety disorder, in particular, obsessive-compulsive disorder. At the time he was interviewed, he was not showing marked symptoms of depression or anxiety. The episodes of mild depression he experienced he related to his concern about his sexual difficulty, and in particular, his concern that it was entrenched and irreversible. He did not show any of the nine symptoms, five or more of which are required, for the *DSM-IV* diagnosis of major depressive episode. Nor did he show any of the six symptoms required for most of the preceding two years for the diagnosis of dysthymic disorder. He had no panic attacks in the preceding 18 months, and the level of anxiety of which he was aware when his mind was not engaged was not sufficiently severe to meet the *DSM-IV* criteria for generalized anxiety. His obsessive-compulsive symptoms were more marked. These were his feelings of aversion to what he termed slime, which included his wife's genital secretions and saliva, and to being sweaty, when he did not like being touched. He, therefore, had features of an obsessive-compulsive disorder, which contributed to his sexual dysfunction. However, he did not appear to regard the feelings or avoidance behaviors as excessive or unreasonable, and they had not caused him marked anxiety or distress. He had not attempted to ignore or suppress the feelings, nor did he feel he was driven in relation to the behaviors. He thus failed to meet these criteria for the *DSM-IV* diagnosis of obsessive-compulsive disorder. He demonstrated acceptance of rules and a degree of perfectionism in his adherence to the principle that he would work two-thirds of each day during the week, but not to the extent that the major point of the activity was lost or that he was prevented from completing tasks. In addition, he showed none of the other features required for the Axis II diagnosis of obsessive-compulsive personality disorder.

In summary, his principal complaint was of sexual aversion. He was aware he had a level of depression and generalized anxiety but felt that his response to medication for these feelings was adequate. He was less aware of the symptoms that indicated a degree of obsessive-compulsive disorder, which contributed to his sexual aversion. It is arguable whether the symptoms of any of these conditions were sufficient to justify a *DSM-IV* diagnosis. He also had features of an obsessive-compulsive personality, but it would seem these, at least in large measure, contributed to his success in relation to his life goals. They could also be employed positively in increasing the likelihood of his complying with treatment.

EPIDEMIOLOGY

There is limited epidemiological data concerning the prevalence of sexual dysfunctions in representative population samples despite indications it is high compared to other disorders. Spector and Carey (1990) pointed out that of the National Institute of Mental Health (NIMH) Epidemiologic Catchment Area (ECA) Program studies of the prevalence of psychiatric disorders in representative population samples, only the ECA study carried out in St. Louis investigated sexual dysfunctions. It did not report the prevalence of individual dysfunctions but found the total prevalence to be 24%. This was the highest prevalence after tobacco use disorder. Spector and Carey reviewed about 20 studies investigating the prevalence of dysfunctions in community samples, few of which were representative. High prevalence figures were reported by Frank, Anderson, and Rubinstein (1978) in a study of 100 predominantly White, well-educated, happily married couples. Dysfunctions were reported by 65% of the women and 40% of the men. However, 85% of both men and women stated their sexual relations were "very" or "moderately satisfying," so that most would not receive a *DSM-IV* diagnosis of dysfunction, because criterion B requires that the disturbance cause marked distress or interpersonal difficulty. The most common dysfunctions in women were difficulty getting excited (48%) and difficulty reaching orgasm (44%); in men, common dysfunctions were ejaculating too quickly (36%) and difficulty getting (7%) and maintaining (9%) erection.

The community studies, as summarized by Spector and Carey (1990), reported prevalence in women of inhibited female orgasm, 5% to 20%; of sexual arousal disorder, 11% to 48%; of hypoactive sexual desire disorder, 34%; and of dyspareunia, 8% to 23%. There were no data reported concerning the prevalence of vaginismus. Prevalence rates in men were for erectile difficulty, 3% to 9%; for premature ejaculation, 36% to 38%; for hypoactive sexual desire disorder, 16%; and for inhibited male orgasm, 1% to 10%. Nathan (1986) reviewed 22 general population sex surveys, only six of which were included in Spector and Carey's review. Prevalence rates were in the same range, indicating the findings of both were reliable. Spector and Carey concluded that inhibited orgasm was one of the least common dysfunctions in men, both in community and clinical samples. However, varying over the age range, from 19% to 30% of a 78% representative sample of 18- to 59-year-old men in the United States reported they did not always have an orgasm during sex with their primary partner (Laumann, Gagnon, Michael, & Michaels, 1994). It may not be experienced as a problem. Several studies reported that a significant number of women enjoy intercourse although they do not reach orgasm (McConaghy, 1993). The possibility that this is true of men has received less attention. In a 60% representative sample of British men and women ages 16 to 59, 50% of women and 34% of men disagreed with the statement that sex without orgasm or climax cannot be really satisfying for a person of their sex (Johnson, Wadsworth, Wellings, Field, & Bradshaw, 1994).

Spector and Carey (1990) pointed out the lack of data relating the prevalence of sexual dysfunctions to social and biological variables including age, possibly the most important determinant of the major dysfunctions of inhibited female orgasm and male erectile disorders. In his 1973 representative study of adolescents, Sorensen found that more than 50% of the girls rarely or never reached orgasm in sexual relationships. This was reported by 25% of women in their first year of marriage, but 11% or less in their 20th year (Hunt, 1974; Kinsey, Pomeroy, Martin, &

Gebhardt, 1953). A similar but weaker trend was found by Laumann et al. (1994) in their investigation of a 78% representative sample of 18- to 59-year-old men and women in the United States. The subjects were asked whether, in the previous 12 months, there had ever been a period of several months or more when they experienced particular sexual dysfunctions. In the total sample, lack of interest in having sex was reported by 16% of men and 33% of women; being unable to come to a climax (8% and 24%); coming to a climax too quickly (28% and 10%); experiencing physical pain during intercourse (3% and 14%); not finding sex pleasurable (8% and 21%); feeling anxious about their ability to perform sexually (17% and 11%); and (for men) having trouble achieving or maintaining erection (10%) and (for women) having trouble lubricating (19%). In women, all the dysfunctions defined in this way decreased with increasing age except lack of interest in sex, which reached 37% in those ages 55 to 59, and having trouble lubricating, which was experienced by 21% to 24% of women ages 45 to 59. Other studies have found decline in women's sexual interest to commence from the perimenstrual period (Hallstrom & Samuelsson, 1990). In men, only having trouble achieving or maintaining erection showed a clear relationship with age, as reported by more than 20% of men ages 50 to 59. Prevalence rates in community studies of men for complete inability to attain erection were 1% at 30, 2% at 40, 7% at 50, 18% at 60, 27% at 70, 55% at 75, and 76% at 80 years of age (Kinsey, Pomeroy, & Martin, 1948; Weizman & Hart, 1987). In the Massachusetts Male Aging Study, complete inability to attain erection was reported by 5% of 40-year-olds and 25% of 75-year-olds (Mulhall, 2000). Prevalence in men of the same age is markedly lower in healthy than unhealthy older subjects (McConaghy, 1993). The onset of difficulty in achieving erection without manual stimulation of the penis is commonly reported by men in middle age if they are questioned concerning this. Its prevalence and relationship with age does not appear to have been documented, although it often causes men to reduce frequency of attempts to have intercourse.

The number of men and women who seek treatment for sexual problems is only a small percentage of those identified, both among patients reporting other illnesses and in community studies, as having sexual dysfunctions (McConaghy, 1993). The majority of men and women, when identified, were not interested in having treatment. Spector and Carey (1990) pointed out that the prevalence of sexual dysfunctions in men and women who seek treatment could be influenced by the popular conception of what disorders are treatable. The introduction of known treatments for erectile dysfunction, initially penile prostheses and intracavernous injections, appeared to encourage men to seek treatment for this disorder compared to others where a specific cure was not widely known. Since its approval by the U.S. Food and Drug Administration in March 1998, sildenafil citrate (Viagra) has been used by millions of men for the treatment of erectile dysfunction (Boyce & Umland, 2001). There is concern about the effect of cost on national health systems for the increasing number of men seeking treatment for this dysfunction. Applying prevalence data from the Massachusetts Male Aging Study, Aytac, McKinley, and Krane (1999) estimated that in 1995, more than 152 million men worldwide had erectile disorder and, by 2025, there would be 322 million. The studies reviewed by Spector and Carey indicated erectile disorder could have become the most common complaint in men seeking treatment for sexual dysfunction even before the introduction of known treatments. It was reported by 40% to 60% of men, with figures in the same range being reported in the 1970s for premature ejaculation but lower figures in the 1980s. Inhibited male orgasm was infrequent, being reported by less than 8% of subjects. The percentage of women seeking treatment for inhibited orgasms ranged from 18% to 76% and for sexual arousal disorder, 50% to 80%. Vaginismus rates varied from 12% to 17%, and dyspareunia, 3%. In the small number of studies they reviewed, Spector and Carey found complaints of hypoactive sexual desire in men increased markedly in the 1980s, reaching more than 50% and outnumbering the percentage of women with this complaint in some studies. This increase was not found in three studies they did not examine, in which its prevalence remained below that of women, and, in one, was very low (McConaghy, 1993).

The absence of reports of sexual aversion in the studies of prevalence of sexual dysfunctions is noteworthy and presumably results from neglect to investigate it as a diagnostic category. Sexual aversion may be present as a contributory cause in a number of patients who report in answers to questions that they lack sexual interest or desire, but overlooked if specific questions are not asked. Patients experiencing sexual aversion would then be diagnosed as having hypoactive sexual desire. As discussed in relation to N. S.'s symptoms (see case study), the *DSM-IV* diagnosis of sexual aversion disorder is very restrictive, requiring extreme aversion to and avoidance of all or almost all genital sexual contact with a partner. Snyder and Berg (1983a) pointed out that studies of couples seeking therapy focused on a relatively narrow range of specific dysfunctions. Little attention was given to the impact of more general or interpersonal difficulties. Frank et al. (1978), in their study of happily married couples, found difficulties related to the emotional tone of sexual relations more common and significant than dysfunctions. In women, the most frequent difficulties were inability to relax (47%), too little foreplay before intercourse (38%), disinterest (35%), partner choosing an inconvenient time (31%), and being turned off (28%). In men, the most common were attraction to people other than the spouse and too little foreplay before intercourse (21%), too little tenderness after intercourse (17%), and disinterest and partner choosing an inconvenient time (16%). Snyder and Berg (1983a), in their study of 45 couples with sexual dissatisfaction, also found the incidence of specific dysfunctions to be lower than more general interpersonal difficulties.

DSM-IV diagnoses have not been used in studies of prevalence of paraphilias in representative community samples. In the representative U.S. population sample investigated by Laumann et al. (1994), 2.8% of men and 1.5% of women reported they had forced a person of the opposite sex to do something sexual they did not want to do; 0.1% of women and 0.2% of men reported they had forced a person of the same sex. Twenty-two percent of women and 1.3% of men reported having been forced by a person of the opposite sex; 0.3% of women and 1.9% of men reported having been forced by a person of the same sex; and 0.5% of women and 0.4% of men reported having been forced by both men and women. The total percentage of men and women who reported being forced by women was 1.6%. In contrast, women were reported to be the perpetrators in 25% of sexual assaults of adults in a supplementary study of the Los Angeles NIMH Epidemiologic Catchment Area survey (Sorenson, Stein, Siegel, Golding, & Burnam, 1987). Whereas, in the study by Laumann et al., 2.8% of men reported forcing a woman, Ageton (1983) found 10% of a national sample of male adolescents reported forcing females into genital contact over a three-year period. Presumably, these marked differences resulted from differences in the methods of obtaining the information. Ageton contrasted the high percentage of male adolescents forcing women into sexual activity with the low percentage of one in 200 who were arrested yearly over the three years of her study. Ageton did not report sexually assaultive behavior by women. Women rarely seek treatment for, or are charged with, sexual assault or pedophilia. Women were convicted of 1% of sexual offenses and 1.5% of acts of indecency against children in Britain (O'Connor, 1987). Factors contributing to the low rate of conviction are that male child partners of women do not usually regard the experience negatively, and few men would report being victims of sexual assault by women. Russell (1986), in her nonrepresentative study of the sexual experiences of female children with adults, classified them as abusive even if the girl considered her reactions neutral or positive. This procedure has been less commonly followed concerning the sexual experiences of boys with older women. When the procedure was followed, the number of women perpetrators, particularly with boy victims, was much higher than when it was not. Laumann et al. found that 17% of women and 12% of men reported they had been touched sexually before puberty or when they were 12 or 13 by someone over age 14. The perpetrators were men only, women only, and both, in 91%, 4%, and 4%, respectively, of the offenses against girls; and 38%, 54%, and 7%, respectively, of the offenses against boys. Finkelhor, Hotaling, Lewis, and Smith (1990) requested a national U.S. population sample, of whom 76% complied, to answer four questions concerning experiences when they were children (age 18 or younger) that they would now consider sexual abuse. Twenty-seven percent of women and 16% of men indicated they had at least one experience. Perpetrators were men in 98% of the offenses against girls and 83% of those against boys. The higher percentage of women and men who reported abusive experiences in the Finkelhor study was due in part to the addition of experiences that occurred when they were ages 14 to 18. Noncontact forms of potential sexual abuse were not assessed by Laumann et al. However, they made up only a small percentage of the abuse reported in the Finkelhor et al. study. Perpetrators in the Laumann et al. study were relatives of 52% and strangers to 7% of the women, and relatives of 19% and strangers to 4% of the men. Most of the remainder were family friends. In the Finkelhor et al. study, perpetrators were relatives of 29% and strangers to 21% of the women, and relatives of 11% and strangers to 40% of the men. Most of the remainder were family friends or acquaintances. If both studies validly reported the experiences of representative samples of the U.S. population, girls and boys were much more likely to be sexually touched by relatives than by strangers, but were much more likely to regard being touched by strangers as abusive. Boys were more likely than girls to be touched by family friends and acquaintances, but were less likely to regard the experience as abusive.

The sexual behaviors experienced by the subjects in the Laumann et al. (1994) study were vaginal intercourse in 14% of women and anal sex in 18% of men with male perpetrators, and vaginal intercourse in 42% of the men with female perpetrators. Oral sexual contact was reported by 30% of men and 10% of women with male perpetrators and 10% of men but no women with women perpetrators. The majority of men and women were ages 7 to 10 when sexually touched by men; the majority of men were ages 11 to 13 years when sexually touched by women. The prevalence of the different forms of pedophilic acts investigated by Finkelhor et al. (1990) was:

- Someone trying or succeeding in having any kind of sexual intercourse was reported by 14.6% of women and 9.5% of men.

- Someone touching, grabbing, kissing, or rubbing against their bodies was reported by 20% of women and 4.5% of men.
- Having nude photos taken, being exhibited to, or having a sex act performed in their presence was reported by 1.6% of men and 3.7% of women.
- Oral sex or sodomy was reported by 0.4% of men and 0.1% of women.

Force was used in 15% of the incidents with boys and 19% of those with girls. Median age at the time of abuse was 9.9 years for both men and women. Basing their conclusion on the age of the subjects when the sexual experiences occurred, both Laumann et al. and Finkelhor et al. agreed that there had not been an increased incidence in those growing up in the wake of the "sexual revolution" of the 1960s. As with sexual assault, the number of cases of child-adult sexual activity reported to authorities is only a fraction of that reported in community surveys. In Russell's study (1983), 2% of the intrafamilial and 6% of the extrafamilial experiences of child sexual abuse were reported to the police. Only 2.5 per 1,000 children or adolescents in 14 states in the United States were reported in 1988 to be sexually abused (Kilpatrick, 1992). Finkelhor (1998) found that there had been a decline in nationally reported cases of child sexual abuse since 1992, reversing the earlier pattern of increase dating back to the 1970s. Estimates for 1997 put the number at 84,000, down 40% from the early 1990s. In the absence of appropriate research, it was impossible to determine the cause for the decline, which had also occurred in relation to sexual assault and crime in general.

Laumann et al. (1994), in their representative study, did not question their subjects as to whether they had carried out pedophilic acts. Herman (1990) cited a nationwide random-sample survey finding that between 4% and 17% of men acknowledged having molested a child, the sex of whom was not specified. Clinical and forensic data indicate that many men who molest boys do so on one occasion with hundreds of victims, whereas those who molest girls typically do so repeatedly with at most a few victims (McConaghy, 1993). McConaghy estimated that, because an average of one to two females are victims of a pedophile, if it is accepted that 90% of pedophiles are male, 30% of women are their victims; and because there are about four times as many adults as children in the population, about 5% of men and 0.5% of women molest girls. These figures seem not unduly high in view of the percentage of men and women with sexual interest in children. About 15% of male and 2% of female university students in the United States and Australia reported some likelihood of having sexual activity with a prepubertal child if they could do so without risk (Malamuth, 1989; McConaghy, Zamir, & Manicavasagar, 1993). A similar percentage of men showed sexual arousal to children, as assessed by their penile responses (Fedora et al., 1992). Because about twice as many girls as boys report being sexually abused in childhood and because perpetrators against boys have many more victims than perpetrators against girls, perpetrators against girls must markedly outnumber those with boy victims. Freund and Watson (1992) calculated the ratio to be approximately 11:1.

The prevalence of paraphilias other than non-*DSM-IV* pedophilia has been investigated only in nonrepresentative samples. Person, Terestman, Myers, Goldberg, and Salvadori (1989) investigated the sexual activities of university students. Men reported that, over the previous three months, 4% had exhibited in public; 4% had watched others make love; 3% had been tied or bound during sexual activities; 2% had whipped or beaten a partner; 1% had degraded a partner; 1% had tortured a partner; 1% had been forced to submit; 1% had dressed in the clothes of the opposite sex; and 1% had been whipped, beaten, or degraded by a partner. Twenty-one percent reported a lifetime prevalence of having exhibited in public; the lifetime prevalence of the other practices was not stated. Women reported that 6% had been forced to submit to sexual acts, 4% had been tied or bound during sex activities, 4% had been sexually degraded, 1% had been tortured by a partner, 1% had been whipped or beaten by a partner, and 1% had tortured a sexual partner. The authors described the activities as sadomasochistic, which would suggest that the subjects being hurt or humiliated consented to them. This was consistent with the prevalence and nature of the students' reported fantasies. Comparable frequencies of sadomasochistic acts were found by Hunt (1974) in a national survey of 2,000 subjects. Sexual pleasure was obtained by 4.8% of men and 2.1% of women by inflicting pain and by 2.5% of men and 4.6% of women by receiving pain.

It is possible that as many as half the male population has carried out occasional paraphilic acts, mainly in adolescence. Templeman and Stinnett (1991) found that 65% of 57 male undergraduates had engaged in some form of sexual misconduct, though only two had been arrested for sexual offenses. Two others had been in trouble with parents, school, or employers for their sexual behavior. Voyeurism was the most common offense, reported by 42%; frottage was reported by 35%; and making obscene phone calls, by 8%. Only one subject reported exhibitionism. Because exhibitionism is one of the most common sex offenses, this inconsistent finding may have been because the undergraduates had been raised and educated in rural areas rather than cities where they would not be known to victims (McConaghy, 1993). Thirty percent of 500 women in Albuquerque reported being victims of exhibitionists, compared with 8% who reported being victims of obscene phone calls, and 4% victims of voyeurs (DiVasto et al., 1984). Three (5%) of the undergraduates reported coercive sexual behaviors, consistent with the percentage of male students reporting the use of some physical force to obtain sexual acts in the United States and Australia (McConaghy, 1993). Two reported sexual contacts with girls under 12 years of age and three reported sexual contact with girls ages 13 to 15 when the students were over 20 years old. This is consistent with the calculation that 5% of men molest girls, as previously discussed.

Abel, Becker, Cunningham-Rathner, Mittelman, and Rouleau (1988) interviewed 561 men seeking evaluation and/or treatment for possible paraphilia. These men were given protection from reporting by a certificate of confidentiality. More than 70% of the men who were not transsexuals had carried out more than one paraphilia, including female and male incestuous and nonincestuous pedophilia, rape, exhibitionism, voyeurism, and frottage. The authors pointed out that the findings were at variance with the traditional view of the paraphiliac—one who is fixated on one type of paraphilia to the exclusion of other kinds. They believed that the traditional view resulted from the use of inadequate interviewing and the lack of guarantee of confidentiality. However, if the traditional view is incorrect, it is difficult to understand why offenders who are repeatedly charged are usually charged with the same offense (Day, 1994). In addition, in clinical experience with offenders seeking treatment, the majority report having carried out mainly the same deviant behavior. If they were charged repeatedly, it was usually for the same form of deviation (McConaghy, Blaszczynski, Armstrong, & Kidson, 1989). Many of the paraphilias reported by the offenders in the study of Abel et al. may have been equivalent to those found by Templeman and

Stinnett (1991) in that they were carried out infrequently and mainly in adolescence. Knight, Prentky, and Cerce (1994) reported that 81% of 59 incarcerated rapists reported they had engaged in some paraphilic behavior at least more than twice. The clinical records of 74.6% of the same sample did not contain any evidence of paraphilias, suggesting the behaviors had been carried out infrequently. Marshall (1996) emphasized the need for comparisons of sex offenders with nonoffenders to evaluate the finding of Abel et al. In the population of sex offenders whom he studied, few had more than one paraphilia, and only one had three, though he took careful steps to ensure confidentiality and to instill confidence in the subjects.

Consistent with the prevalence of deviant behaviors, regular use of deviant sexual fantasies is also common. In Hunt's study (1974), masturbatory fantasies of forcing someone to have sex were reported by 13% of men and 3% of women, and masturbatory fantasies of being forced to have sex were reported by 10% of men and 19% of women. The coital fantasy of being overpowered or forced to surrender was the second most popular fantasy in 50% of married upper-class New York women (Hariton & Singer, 1974). More than 30% of normal men reported sexual fantasies of tying up and raping a woman, and 10% to 20% reported fantasies of torturing or beating up a woman (Crepault & Couture, 1980; Person et al., 1989). A significant percentage of normal men are aroused by descriptions of rape in which the woman experiences pain or is humiliated (Malamuth & Check, 1983; Pfaus, Myronuk, & Jacobs, 1986). Penile circumference assessment of paraphilias in 66 normal controls demonstrated clinically significant arousal to images of sadism, defined as nonsexual violence against fully clothed females, in 5%; pedophilia, in 18%; and at least one paraphilia, in 28% (Fedora et al., 1992).

Prevalence of gender identity disorders in children has not been investigated in community studies. Zuger and Taylor (1969) compared the incidence of feminine behaviors in 95 schoolboys and 26 boy patients who showed marked effeminacy likely to be diagnosed as gender identity disorder using *DSM-IV* criteria. The behaviors included dressing in female clothes, wearing lipstick, and so on, preferring girl playmates, desire to be female, feminine gesturing, doll-play, and aversion to boys' games. Overlap in the frequency of the behaviors occurred with six schoolboys and one patient. Zuger and Taylor decided that the patient may have been incorrectly diagnosed, enabling them to conclude the behavior of the patients was clearly differentiated from that of the schoolboys. Although their results indicated that a quarter of the schoolboys showed some feminine behaviors, Zuger and Taylor did not attribute any significance to this. They thus reinforced the belief that opposite sex-linked behaviors of interest to sex researchers were extreme and categorical, present in only one or two boys in a 1,000. Several studies additional to that of Zuger and Taylor have found that a percentage of normal children show some degree of opposite sex-linked behaviors (McConaghy, 1993).

Relationships between a degree of opposite gender identity, opposite sex-linked behaviors, and homosexual feelings have been found in the childhood and adulthood of both men and women. In four studies of medical students, 27% to 45% of men and 28% to 51% of women anonymously reported current awareness of a degree of homosexual, as compared with heterosexual, feelings, ranging from 10% in the majority to 100% in the minority (McConaghy, 1987; McConaghy & Silove, 1991). In a subsequent study of male twins educationally more representative of the total population, 12% anonymously reported a similar awareness (McConaghy, Buhrich, & Silove, 1994). In all groups, the degree of their homosexual to heterosexual feelings correlated in the men with an increased incidence of opposite-sex behaviors in childhood and adolescence, and in both sexes with desire to be of the opposite sex in childhood and with current feelings of having opposite sex traits and identity. The correlations remained present in the men who reported predominant heterosexual feelings in the two later studies, when the reports of the men who reported bisexual or predominant homosexual interest were excluded. Fifty-nine percent of lesbian, 32% of bisexual, and 22% of heterosexual women reported that, as children, they felt like boys or men (Phillips & Over, 1995). In an anonymous study of 2,905 female and 1,725 male twins, 21% percent of men, and 19% of women reported they had been sexually attracted to, or had sexual contact (which included sexual excitement) with, someone of the same sex, or both sexes (Dunne, Bailey, Kirk, & Martin, 2000). Compared with the men and women who denied either experience, they reported greater levels of gender nonconforming behavior before the age of 12 and current opposite sex identity. Nevertheless, as discussed later (see Psychological and Biological Assessment section), the view that gender identity is categorical remains accepted by some authoritative researchers.

The *DSM-IV* classification abandoned use of the term *transvestism* and instead classified the men previously receiving this diagnosis as having either *paraphilia, transvestic fetishism with or without gender dysphoria,* or *gender identity disorder* in adolescents or adults. The term is still employed by most clinicians and in studies of its prevalence. This disorder has not been investigated in representative community samples, though Schott (1995) cited an estimate of as many as 1 million for the population of transvestic males in the United States. Person et al. (1989) found that 4% of female and 1% of male university students reported dressing in the clothes of the opposite sex in the previous three months. The motivation for the behavior was not reported, but 3% of the men and 2% of the women reported recent sexual fantasies of dressing in clothes of the opposite sex. Fifteen of 138 male medical students, but none of 58 female medical students, reported they had obtained sexual arousal from dressing in the external or underclothes of the opposite sex (McConaghy, 1982). The term *transsexualism* also was abandoned in *DSM-IV*, replaced with that of *gender identity disorder* in adolescents and adults. Clinicians appear to be replacing it with the diagnosis of *gender dysphoria* or *transgender*. Available studies of prevalence use the term transsexualism and demonstrate a steady increase since the condition was first identified (McConaghy, 1993). Reported rates in Europe and the United States in the 1960s ranged from one in 40,000 to 100,000 for male-to-female transsexuals and a third of that number for female-to-male transsexuals. In 1991, rates were one in 12,000 and 30,000, respectively, for the two groups in the Netherlands, the highest figure in the Western world (Van Kesteren, Gooren, & Megens, 1996). In most countries, the ratio of male-to-female, as compared to female-to-male transsexuals, has remained consistent at about 3:1. More transsexuals now seek sex conversion because of the increasingly benevolent social climate concerning the procedure.

CLINICAL PICTURE

Earlier studies failed to find consistent associations between subjects' sexual dysfunctions and psychological adjustment (Stuart, Hammond, & Pett, 1987), presumably because of the use of less sensitive, though possibly not less valid, assessments than those employed in recent studies. These studies, discussed in relation to dual diagnosis (see Diagnostic Considerations section), found high levels of psychiatric and personality disorders in subjects with sexual dysfunctions, using assessments that also found high levels of these conditions in the normal population. Frank et al. (1978) found the sexual difficulties not diagnosed in *DSM-IV* not only more prevalent than dysfunctions but also more significant. They correlated more highly with subjects' and their spouses' lack of sexual satisfaction than did dysfunctions. In men, the correlations between presence of dysfunctions and lack of sexual satisfaction were not statistically significant. Reporting a similar finding in older men, Schiavi, Schreiner-Engel, Mandeli, Schanzer, and Cohen (1990) found that older healthy couples with appropriate attitudes and coping strategies were able to continue to engage in satisfying sexual intercourse in the face of significant decrements in erectile function. Other studies reviewed by McConaghy (1993) also found little or no relationship between the presence of sexual dysfunctions and sexual satisfaction in both community and clinical populations. Despite the consistent evidence of the importance of sexual difficulties rather than dysfunctions in couples' sexual satisfaction, most subjects seeking treatment for sexual problems tend to report dysfunctions rather than reduced satisfaction. Possibly, they feel dysfunctions are clinically more legitimate complaints for which to seek treatment. This could account for the focus on dysfunctions in the treatment literature. The importance of relationship factors, rather than sexual dysfunctions, in sexual satisfaction could explain the common finding of outcome studies discussed subsequently. That is, despite minimal improvement of the specific dysfunction with which the subjects presented, many reported increased sexual interest and enjoyment following psychological treatment. Hawton, Catalan, Martin, and Fagg (1986) found that the improvement in couples' general relationships frequently reported to follow therapy for sexual problems could result from the equally frequently reported improvement in their communication. Stuart et al. (1987) noted that, based on clinical impression, therapists commonly believed that a variety of interpersonal difficulties influence the development and maintenance of sexual dysfunctions, such as couples' power struggles, poor or destructive communication, and lack of respect and affection. In support of this belief, the authors cited a study that found that 91% of women with normal sexual functioning, but only 35% of women with a disorder of sexual desire, rated communication with their partners as good or very good. In their own study, they found a similar relationship.

The importance of their partners in relation to the sexual activity of men and women has been consistently demonstrated. Partners of men with psychogenic, compared to organic, erectile dysfunctions reported more relationship problems, but also higher levels of vaginismus and dyspareunia, which usually preceded the erectile dysfunctions (Speckens, Hengeveld, Lycklama a Nijeholt, van Hemert, & Hawton, 1995). Absence or inability of a male partner to perform sexually is the most common cause for the cessation of sexual activity in older women (McConaghy, 1993). Anorgasmia in women was reported to decline greatly over the first year of marriage in a series of studies (Nathan, 1986). All the studies Nathan cited were conducted before 1956, when more women would have married without having had intercourse. Nathan also cited studies reporting that only 1% to 3% of men and married women, but 15% to 20% of unmarried, heterosexual women, claimed never to have any desire for sex. In Hunt's (1974) U.S. survey of sexual behavior in the 1970s, women emphasized the role of men in helping them to learn to become aroused by encouraging them to express their feelings. Men emphasized the importance of encouraging their partners to become aroused. In a 1996 Swedish nationally representative sex survey, one-third of women experienced their first orgasm during sexual intercourse, and almost a quarter, when caressed by a partner's hand. One-third experienced their first orgasm during masturbation, whereas almost all men did (Helmius, 1998). Women who consistently experienced orgasm during coitus, compared to those who did not, were found to be more likely to report inability to control their thinking or movements as they approached orgasm. They also obtained higher scores on a hypnotic susceptibility scale (Bridges, Critelli, & Loos, 1985). This was considered to reflect a greater ability to suspend effortful, controlled cognitive processes. Heiman, Gladue, Roberts, and LoPiccolo (1986) found that sexually functional women were distinguished from sexually dysfunctional women by greater arousal, pleasure and sexual interest, a positive reaction to their current partner's body (touch, smell, genitals, and physical appearance), and less emotional involvement with the partner in first coitus. Sexually functional, as compared to dysfunctional, men were more likely to obtain pleasure from varied sexual activities; to attach less importance to emotional closeness, holding, and expression of care during sex; to have more frequent oral and coital sex; and to use fantasy in partner sex, including atypical and deviant fantasy. Dysfunctional subjects would appear to have a more romantic and less physical attitude to sexual activity. Studies have consistently found that 60% of women pretend to reach orgasm on occasion (McConaghy, 1993). Steiner (1981) commented that male pretense of orgasm had not been investigated and found that 36% of male junior college students reported it. Hunt (1974) reported that some men, after failing to reach orgasm, could shortly afterwards pretend they were successful. Reasons given for the pretence suggest that both men and women fake orgasm to satisfy male expectations.

Traditional measures of personality and psychopathology have yielded inconsistent results when administered to mainly incarcerated sex offenders (Knight et al., 1994). This is likely because of the lack of validity of the tests, as behavioral evidence has strongly indicated the presence of psychopathic features, both in incarcerated offenders (Herman, 1990) and in adolescent males and male college students who carried out mainly unreported sexual assaults (Ageton, 1983; Koss & Dinero, 1988). Knight, Rosenberg, and Schneider (1985) found marked behavioral similarities between convicted rapists, child molesters, and the general prison population. The similarities included low socioeconomic status, high rate of school failure or dropout, subsequent unstable employment record of an unskilled nature, and previous convictions for nonsexual offenses. It would seem likely that these features contributed to the detection and conviction, both of incarcerated sex offenders and the rest of the prison population. If so, they would be less frequently found in the majority of perpetrators whose offenses are not reported or who are charged but not convicted. This is consistent with the finding of Knight et al. that defendants referred for evaluation as possible child molesters had less extensive criminal histories than the convicted group. Deficiencies in social skills and accomplishments found in several studies in child molesters and rapists were not found when the offenders were compared with socioeconomically matched community controls (Stermac, Segal, & Gillis, 1990). Bard et al. (1987) commented concerning investigations of incarcerated offenders that the only distinction that received consistent empirical scrutiny was that between rapists and child molesters. Rapists were younger than child molesters, who were more evenly distributed by age. U.S. Department of Justice studies consistently found that about 25% of rapists were under 18 years of age (Herman, 1990). Knight et al. (1985) found that a number of studies reported a higher incidence of mental retardation and organic brain syndrome in child molesters. As could be expected, rapists were more likely to show behavioral excesses, to be overassertive or explosive, and to have greater heterosexual experience. Knight and Prentky (1990) found it difficult to substantiate the distinction made in the *DSM-III-R* (APA, 1987) between nonsadistic rapists who used no more aggression than necessary to ensure compliance, and sadistic rapists who used excessive aggression.

The differentiation by Burgess and Holmstrom (1980) of *blitz* and *confidence* rapes was replicated by Bowie, Silverman, Kalick, and Edbril (1990). They found the same two types predominated in their study of 1,000 consecutive rape victims seen at a Boston rape crisis intervention program over a 10-year period. Blitz rapes were sudden surprise attacks by an unknown assailant. Confidence rapes involved some nonviolent interaction between the rapist and the victim before the attacker's intention to commit rape emerged. Blitz rape occurred in settings where the victims felt secure, such as their homes. They were more likely to have their lives threatened than victims of confidence rapes. The latter were three times more likely than blitz victims to have consumed alcohol or other drugs, to have spent some time with the assailant in a public or private place, or to have been in transit with the assailant before the assault. Confidence victims waited significantly longer before seeking medical attention or help from the crisis program. Some, particularly victims of date rapes, were unclear that the assault or forced sexual encounter to which they were subjected constituted rape. Confidence rape assailants were more likely to be of the same race as their victim, to have known the victim's name or address, to have consumed alcohol or other drugs before committing the rape, and to have prolonged the incident beyond five hours. In Ageton's study (1983) of sexual assault in adolescents, most of the offenders were boyfriends or dates in the age range of the victims. Less than 20% were unknown to them. Only 5% of the assaults were reported to the police; these were mainly blitz rapes carried out by unknown or multiple assailants and involving threats or employment of violence.

Pedophilia, unlike sexual assault or hebephilia, is classified as a paraphilia in the *DSM-IV.* Most pedophiles are male and offend against only male or only female children. The homosexual offenders, like hebephiles, commonly begin their deviant activity in adolescence. In adulthood, when they seek treatment or are charged, a number report having had a large number of victims who were strangers or casual acquaintances. Many male homosexual pedophiles and hebephiles, though of average or above-average intelligence, report an inability to be socially or sexually interested in adults of either sex. The offenses of heterosexual pedophiles commonly commence in adulthood, and they have one or a few victims who are related or well-known to them. Male heterosexual pedophiles are more likely to be heavy drinkers, of lower socioeconomic class, to have had little schooling, and to have committed other criminal offenses (McConaghy, 1993). Some brain-damaged or developmentally delayed men are drawn to the company of children of both sexes who are at their intellectual or emotional level. Sexual activity may be initiated by these men, or they may be regularly approached for such activity by one or more young adolescent males for monetary or other gains. In Laumann et al.'s (1994) representative sample, men who touched girls or boys age 13 or less were typically over 18 with victims of ages 7 to 10. Women who touched boys were typically ages 14 to 17, and their partners were ages 11 to 13. These women would not be diagnosed as pedophiles according to *DSM-IV* criteria, which require them to be at least 16 and 5 years older than the child.

Exhibitionism, which appears to be the most common sex offense and paraphilia, rarely results in incarceration. It typically takes the form of the unsolicited exposure of the genitals by postpubertal males to one or a few females, usually strangers, around the age of puberty. The behavior commonly begins in adolescence when it is experienced as sexually exciting. When they become adults, subjects seek treatment, at times without having been charged, as they find themselves unable to cease the behavior in the situations where they have previously carried it out. At this stage, they usually report that the excitement is largely nonsexual but rather a state of heightened arousal approaching panic. Exhibitionism associated with sexual arousal is rare in women (McConaghy, 1993). *Voyeurism* appears related to exhibitionism in that it is also rare in woman, it commences in adolescent men when it is experienced as sexually exciting, and, when in their adulthood it has become compulsive, the excitement is largely nonsexual. Its best-known form has been termed *peeping*—males looking into a private area to observe a partially or completely nude woman without her consent. Forms of voyeurism less likely to come to attention are observation by heterosexual men of heterosexual couples having intercourse in parked automobiles and by homosexual men of homosexual activity in public lavatories or steam baths. When exhibitionists and voyeurs present for treatment in adulthood, most are in satisfactory sexual relationships, report a stable work history, and appear to show no obvious personality problems (Langevin & Lang, 1987; Smukler & Schiebel, 1975). *DSM-IV* criterion A for frotteurism is that it involves the touching and rubbing against a nonconsenting person. At times, the victim is male and the behavior may be used as a form of sexual invitation. Freund (1990) defined *frotteurism* as the pressing of the subject's penis against the body of an unknown woman and used *toucheurism* for the intimate touching of an unknown woman. Using this terminology, both are carried out in public, with frotteurism usually in crowded situations such as public transport. Presumably because of the resultant difficulty in identifying and charging frotteurs, they rarely come to attention, but it would seem likely that their behavior develops a compulsive quality similar to that of toucheurs, who are charged and referred for treatment. Clinical assessment does not provide evidence of marked psychopathology apart from the deviant behavior.

Masochism and sadism rarely lead to seeking of treatment or criminal charges; therefore, information concerning it is largely obtained by investigating members of "S and M" clubs, of whom 20% to 30% were found to be female. Women were more likely to be bisexual, and most of the men were predominantly heterosexual (Breslow, Evans, & Langley, 1985; Moser & Levitt, 1987). More than 50% of the men and 21% of the women were aware of sadomasochistic interest by age 14. Beating, bondage, and fetishistic practices were common, and more extreme and dangerous practices rare. Members of sadomasochistic clubs were of above-average intelligence and social status and most wished to continue sadomasochistic activities. The rare reports of practicing sadomasochists who seek medical treatment indicate few suffer significant physical damage. When such damage is reported it is usually the result of "fisting," the insertion of the hand and arm into the rectum or the vagina, or of self-insertion of implements. Lee (1979) did not find any nonaccidental instances where sadomasochistic activities escalated to a dangerous level in a 1979 search of the medical and psychiatric literature. The statement in *DSM-IV* that severity of the sadistic acts usually increases over time appears to require support. However, the majority of subjects who identify as sadomasochists by joining a club would not be classified as having the paraphilia in *DSM-IV*, as they are not distressed by their behavior.

Fetishists are almost invariably male. In childhood, they commonly experience a strong interest in particular objects, most frequently clothing, or footwear. At puberty, the interest is associated with sexual arousal disproportionate to that produced by the secondary sexual characteristics of women or men. When the fetish is a body part such as hair, feet or hands, or a deformity or mutilation, the condition is termed *partialism* in the *DSM-IV*. In relation to the use of female clothes to produce sexual arousal accompanying masturbation in adolescent boys, there appears to be a continuum from those who apply them to their body through to those who wear them and, while wearing them, feel they are members of the opposite sex. Those who wear female clothes receive a *DSM-IV* diagnosis of *transvestic fetishism*. The urge to obtain female clothes secretly may lead them to steal from clotheslines or from neighboring houses, leading to criminal charges. An unknown percentage of adolescent boys with transvestic fetishism develop the adult form of transvestism. This is characterized by reduction or, in some cases, reported loss of sexual arousal with cross-dressing as it increasingly produces feelings of relaxation, relief from responsibility, and/or of sensuality, elegance, and beauty (Buhrich, 1977). If, at this stage, the subjects resist the desire to cross-dress, which can arise when they are alone or see women's clothes, they experience increased tension, which appears responsible for the behavior's becoming compulsive. Transvestites are predominantly heterosexual and usually marry. Periodic cross-dressing to enjoy feeling masculine appears not to have been reported in women.

The development of an operation to convert male to female genitalia led to recognition of the separate clinical condition of *transsexualism*. An increasing number of men with the urge to cross-dress, which they usually reported was present from childhood, made strong efforts to obtain the operation and live permanently as women. They and the smaller number of women who, in general, made less strong efforts to obtain some degree of sex-conversion to live permanently as men were termed *transsexuals*. Male transsexuals who had never experienced fetishistic arousal to cross-dressing and sought sex-conversion in early adulthood were, like almost all female transsexuals, typically attracted to members of their biological sex. They were termed *classical transsexuals* to distinguish them from *fetishistic transsexuals*. The latter men gave a history of fetishistic transvestism and were predominantly attracted to women and married (Buhrich & McConaghy, 1978). Compared to nuclear transvestites who had no desire to alter their bodily appearance by taking female hormones or having surgery, fetishistic transsexuals reported having had stronger opposite sex-identity and homosexual feelings since childhood, leading to their seeking sex-conversion later in life, commonly in middle age (McConaghy, 1993). The rare women who sought sex-conversion to live as gay males were considered to be at the end of a continuum of men and women attracted to and/or idealizing homosexual people of the opposite sex, a condition termed *transhomosexuality* by Clare and Tully (1989). Only one of nine female-to-male transsexuals who regarded themselves as homosexual or bisexual in that they were sexually attracted to males reported any fetishism with cross-dressing (Coleman, Bockting, & Gooren, 1993). This is reported by all male-to-female transsexuals who are sexually attracted to women. Transvestites tend to be of higher socioeconomic class than transsexuals and more stable in their relationships and occupation as compared to male but not female transsexuals (McConaghy, 1993).

Presence of marked wishes to be of the opposite sex, accompanied by extreme opposite-sex behavior in childhood—in boys, dressing in female clothes, using cosmetics and jewelry, and walking and posturing like girls and marked tomboy-ism in girls—is termed *gender identity disorder* of childhood. In adulthood, the majority of these boys identify as homosexual (Zuger, 1966, 1984). Less information is available about the outcome of girls with the disorder.

COURSE AND PROGNOSIS

Information concerning the course of most sexual dysfunctions with or without treatment is limited; therefore, only the marked changes in their prevalence with age in both men and women discussed earlier (see Epidemiology section) can be regarded as established. Thirty-six (7%) of a representative sample of middle-aged married women ($N = 497$) reported absence of desire; six years later, half of the 36 had regained desire without treatment, 70%, to a weak extent and 30%, to a moderate extent (Hallstrom & Samuelsson, 1990). Of 50 men mainly over age 50 with erectile dysfunction who took no action following recommendation for treatment, four reported being much better and four were slightly better at two-year follow-up (Tiefer & Melman, 1987). Tiefer and Melman also cited a finding that 30% of men with erectile dysfunction who did not accept or dropped out of behavioral treatment were asymptomatic by 6 to 12 months. De Amicis, Goldberg, LoPiccolo, Friedman, and Davies (1984) were able to follow up 49 of 155 couples (mean age about 35 years) three years after they had a single evaluation at a sexual therapy clinic but were not offered or declined treatment. Women, but not men, reported a significant increase in sexual satisfaction. As to dysfunctions, apart from the 11 with dyspareunia, more women improved than stayed the same or got worse. More men stayed the same or got worse than improved, though 6 of 16 with premature ejaculation and 7 of 16 with erectile dysfunction improved. Half the subjects received treatment elsewhere before follow-up, but this did not appear to modify the outcome. Six of 8 diabetic women and 8 of 14 diabetic men who had sexual dysfunctions at initial assessment when their average age was 35 had recovered six years later (Jensen, 1986). Eight of the 14 women and men who recovered had new partners. Four of the remainder attributed the recovery to improvement in their emotional and social security. Five of the 14 had objective signs of peripheral and autonomic neuropathy at both interviews.

The effect of treatment on the course of sexual dysfunctions has been inadequately evaluated, with the influence of spontaneous improvement often being overlooked. Milan, Kilmann, and Boland (1988) found that women with secondary orgasmic dysfunction randomly allocated to sex therapy or didactic lectures planned to act as a placebo showed equal slight improvement two to six years later. It was decided the lectures were an effective treatment. As discussed earlier, orgasmic ability increases in women with age; therefore, improvement may have occurred without treatment. Munjack et al. (1976) randomly allocated 22 anorgasmic women, most of whom were happily married, either to immediate or delayed treatment with an education, communication, and desensitization program. Following treatment, a third of the treated women were orgasmic on at least 50% of sexual relations, whereas there was no change in the untreated group. Untreated groups are not a satisfactory comparison group. They almost invariably show a markedly poorer response than those treated with placebo psychological therapies, possibly because of low motivation to change while awaiting treatment (McConaghy, 1993). The report of Masters and Johnson (1970) of a low failure rate of about 20% attracted widespread media attention. It was severely criticized by Zilbergeld and Evans (1980). A major objection was that the outcome measure of initiating reversal of the basic symptomatology could mean, not that subjects' dysfunctions were reversed, but rather, that they felt less guilty about sex, became less performance oriented during sex, or enjoyed sex more. In addition, it was not clear if subjects who dropped out were treated as failures. When results comparable to those of Masters and Johnson have been reported by other therapists, they have been open to some of the same criticisms. LoPiccolo and Stock (1986) treated 150 women for orgasmic dysfunction with a behavioral desensitization program that included directed masturbation. Following treatment, 95% were able to reach orgasm with self-masturbation; 85%, with genital stimulation from their partners; and 40%, with penile-vaginal intercourse. No information was provided as to whether any patients dropped out of therapy. Reported dropout rates vary remarkably, ranging from 4% to more than 40% of couples accepting sex therapy (McConaghy, 1993). Forty percent of 140 couples assessed by Hawton et al. (1986) as suitable for treatment did not complete it. In the 86 couples treated completely or incompletely who were still together at follow-up one to six years later, the significant improvement in their general relationship found at termination of therapy was still present. This was despite recurrence or continuing difficulty with the presenting problem in 64 and a new problem in 9. The authors commented that the majority were quite satisfied with their sexual relationship. In some, an effect of therapy was greater acceptance of their difficulties.

In relation to the response of different dysfunctions, 22 of 32 women in the Hawton et al. (1986) study with impaired sexual interest reported its resolution when they ceased treatment. At one- to six-year follow-up, interest had returned in 11 of the 22. The positive outcome in the remainder was comparable to the spontaneous remission after six years in half the women of a community sample who reported absence of sexual desire (Hallstrom & Samuelsson, 1990). De Amicis, Goldberg, LoPiccolo, Friedman, and Davies (1985) found regression to lower than pretherapy levels at three-year follow-up in both men and women treated at a sexual dysfunction clinic for sexual desire disorder, and Kaplan (1977) reported limited success in women with this condition. Schover and Leiblum (1994) found that hypoactive sexual desire disorder had the worst prognosis with therapy. De Amicis et al. found the good immediate response of women with anorgasmia persisted at three-year follow-up in relation to frequency of orgasm with masturbation and genital stimulation. Vaginismus has also been consistently found to respond well to treatment. Success, usually defined as ability to have coitus, was the immediate outcome in 80% of women in 37 studies reviewed by van de Wiel, Jaspers, Schultz, and Gal (1990). Persistence of good outcome was found at one- to six-year follow-up in 18 of 20 female patients (Hawton et al., 1986). The good response at termination of treatment in men with premature ejaculation and with erectile dysfunction was maintained at follow-up only by the latter group (De Amicis et al., 1985; Hawton et al., 1986). Munjack and Kanno (1979) found inadequate but suggestive evidence that retardation and, particularly, absence of ejaculation responded poorly to treatment.

There appear to be marked differences in men who accept psychological as opposed to physical sex therapy. Whereas a quarter of 46 men with erectile dysfunction who self-referred to a sexual dysfunction clinic declined the offer of behavioral sex therapy, more than half of 47 men referred from a urology department did (Segraves, Schoenberg, Zarins, Camic, & Knopf, 1981). Of those who accepted treatment, all the self-referred patients completed six or more sessions; 57% of the urology-referred men dropped out before six sessions. Segraves et al. found urology-referred as compared to self-referred patients much less willing to accept a possible role of psychological factors in their dysfunction. They pointed out that the current models of behavioral sex therapy were developed on a highly sophisticated self-referred population. Catalan, Hawton, and Day (1990) found that couples who dropped out, as compared to those who completed sex therapy, had shown less initial motivation for treatment and more marked relationship and marital problems, and the presenting person had shown greater anxiety. A history of psychiatric disorder, particularly in the female partner, was the major pretreatment predictor of poor outcome at one- to six-year follow-up in the study of Hawton et al. (1986). Couples who rated themselves before treatment as able to communicate anger showed a better response, which the authors considered reflected their general ability to communicate with each other. A hostile relationship with the partner predicted a poor response (Snyder & Berg, 1983b; Takefman & Brender, 1984).

Comparing the format of psychological treatments on the course of sex dysfunctions, Libman, Fichten, and Brender (1985) found equal effectiveness whether administered by therapists to individuals, couple or groups, or as bibliotherapy—that is, by the subject's use of self-help treatment books combined with minimal therapist contact. LoPiccolo and Stock (1986) reported use of a self-treatment book and film for women to become orgasmic, combined with limited therapist contact, as effective as a complete program of therapist-administered sex therapy. Libman et al. (1985) found bibliotherapy alone to be ineffective.

This led G. M. Rosen (1987) to criticize the commercialization of psychotherapy involved in the publication and recommendation for use without therapist supervision of self-help treatment books for sex dysfunctions. Libman et al. (1985) found no empirical support for the frequently expressed beliefs that cotherapists were more effective than single therapists or that the gender of the therapists affected treatment outcome. Review of studies comparing different components of sex therapy revealed that in the treatment of orgasmic dysfunction in women, directed masturbation for primary anorgasmia was more effective than sensate focusing combined with supportive psychotherapy. There were few differences between sensate focusing, systematic desensitization, and communication training (Fichten, Libman, & Brender, 1983). Auerbach and Kilmann (1977) reported group systematic desensitization, combined with relaxation, produced improvement of more than 40% in frequency of successful intercourse in men with secondary erectile dysfunction; relaxation alone produced improvement of 3%. No adequate placebo-controlled studies or studies comparing recommended psychological treatments appear to have been carried out in recent years. Schover and Leiblum (1994) concluded there has been a stagnation of sex therapy.

Consistent with the low correlation between the presence of dysfunctions and sexual satisfaction, the most consistent finding of outcome studies has been that, despite minimal improvement of the specific dysfunction with which they presented, many subjects reported increased sexual interest and enjoyment following psychological treatment (Adkins & Jehu, 1985; De Amicis et al., 1985; Hawton et al., 1986). This finding led LoPiccolo, Heiman, Hogan, and Roberts (1985) to conclude that treatment was more effective in changing the way people think and feel about their sexual life than in totally eliminating the presenting complaint. A good sexual relationship involved more than just an erect penis or an orgasm, and patients should be encouraged to enjoy the sexual process rather than to strive for results. Although this conclusion would seem relevant for subjects who seek and persist in psychological treatment for sexual dysfunctions, it may not be for those who seek physical treatment and if referred for psychological treatment are unlikely to persist with it. It is likely these men are being increasingly catered for following the shift Schover and Leiblum (1994) noted from the belief in the 1970s that almost all sexual problems were psychogenic, to the current belief that they usually have an organic cause. It resulted in what they termed "shopping in the organic market" for chemical means to improve the course of dysfunctions. They pointed out that enhancing erections has become a lucrative industry for urologists, pharmaceutical companies who market the drugs used in intracavernous injection (ICI) therapy, and manufacturers of penile prostheses. Schover and Leiblum believed that urologists often prescribe ICIs or vacuum erection devices for men with psychogenic sexual dysfunction because the patients refuse to see mental health professionals. They suggested that combining sex therapy with ICIs could improve the outcome of erectile dysfunction. They also reported that some urologists used ICIs or vacuum erection devices for premature ejaculation, either believing the treatment will delay orgasm or telling the patient he will be able to go on thrusting after orgasm. Schover and Leiblum said that men invariably told them that such thrusting is a chore. Women partners of men with premature ejaculation treated with ICIs reported their sexual enjoyment was improved (Althof et al., 1992).

Shopping in the organic market would appear to have markedly accelerated with the introduction of sildenafil (Viagra). Manecke and Mulhall (1999) concluded from an extensive review of the literature that based on safety, effectiveness, and ease of use, oral sildenafil citrate was an excellent choice for first-line therapy. They added that based solely on effectiveness, ICI therapy remained the gold standard and should also be offered as an option for the appropriate patient. Tan (2000) noted that sildenafil and the vacuum erection device should be considered first-line strategies for erectile dysfunction, whereas ICI therapy, transurethreal alprostadil (prostaglandid E1) suppositories, and penile prosthesis implants should be reserved for second- or third-line therapy. Boyce and Umland (2001), in their review of recent studies of sildenafil, also noted that it was an effective first-line therapy for erectile dysfunction. They pointed out that its effectiveness had also been demonstrated for the dysfunction when associated with prostatectomy, radiation therapy, diabetes mellitus, some neurological disorders, and drug therapy, such as selective serotonin reuptake inhibitors (SSRIs). It appears generally accepted that most men seeking treatment for erectile dysfunction with sildenafil will receive it from their general practitioners, with some being referred to urologists (Pena & Sweeney, 1999). R. C. Rosen (2000) recommended psychological sex therapy and sildenafil as first-line treatment options, adding that they may be used alone or in combination. It is likely, given the resistance of many men to psychological sex therapy, that form of therapy will be offered only to those interested. Boyce and Umland found sildenafil was less effective in women with sexual dysfunctions, with the exception of those associated with SSRIs. R. C. Rosen and Ashton (1993) had earlier criticized the dearth of studies of the effects of prosexual drugs in women. A number of uncontrolled and a few placebo-controlled studies reported reduction of premature ejaculation with SSRIs. Significantly, greater clinical improvement was reported with paroxetine 20 to 40 mg per day for five weeks than placebo (Waldinger, Hengeveld, & Zwinderman, 1994). Twenty patients with premature ejaculation estimated average time to ejaculation after vaginal penetration increased to 6.1 minutes with clomipramine 25 mg and 8.4 minutes with clomipramine 50 mg, both significantly greater than the estimated time on placebo (Segraves, Saran, Segraves, & Maguire, 1993).

Investigations of the prognosis of untreated sex offenders have reported widely varying rates of reoffending. Marshall and Barbaree (1990) found incest offenders showed the lowest rates, from 4% to 10%. This could be due to reduced opportunities following detection of the offense. Those for rapists were 7% to 35%; for nonfamilial molesters of girls, 10% to 29%; and for nonfamilial molesters of boys, 13% to 40%. Those for exhibitionists were the highest for all sex offenders, 41% to 71%, consistent with the compulsive nature of the paraphilia. Outcome of treated offenders also showed marked variability sufficient to cause Furby, Weinrott, and Blackshaw (1989) to warn that using it for comparison with that of untreated offenders would allow any kind of conclusion. Length of follow-up was a major factor determining outcome. In a long-term follow-up, Hanson, Steffy, and Gauthier (1993) found that, of about 200 child molesters released from prison, 42% were reconvicted for sexual crimes, violent crimes, or both. Ten percent were reconvicted 10 to 31 years after being released. Hanson and Bussiere (1998) carried out a meta-analysis on the findings of 61 recidivism studies to determine the features that characterized sex offenders who recidivated in follow-up periods ranging from 6 months to 23 years, with a mean of 66 months. The studies reviewed followed up approximately 29,000 sex offenders, of whom about 18,000 were child molesters. The variables that significantly predicted recidivism were:

- Demographic variables: young age and single marital status.
- Lifestyle variables: antisocial personality and total number of prior offenses.
- Sexual criminal history: previous criminal convictions, stranger victim (versus acquaintance), extrafamilial victim, offending began at an early age, selected male victim, engaged in diverse sexual crimes.
- Clinical presentation variables: only failure to complete treatment.

None of the other variables, including denial or clinical ratings of low treatment motivation, were related to recidivism. Consistent with their finding that young age had a negative prognosis, adolescent as compared to adult offenders were found to require more intensive treatment independent of the nature of their offense (McConaghy et al., 1989). Marshall and Barbaree (1990) reported that rapists were the least responsive of sex offenders to treatment. This presumably reflected short-term response as few older men are charged with the offense. The failure of denial, as well as low motivation to predict recidivism, in the studies reviewed by Hanson and Bussiere is of particular interest as both factors are commonly believed by clinicians to contribute to recidivism to such an extent that they are targeted in cognitive treatment programs (Barbaree, 1999). That these two factors do not predict recidivism suggests that clinicians who accept these beliefs may have limited ability to predict offenders' likelihood of recurrence. Quinsey, Khanna, and Malcolm (1998) found that sex offenders who were rated by therapists as showing very good gains had sexual rearrest rates of 29%; those who were rated as having very poor gains had rearrest rates of 18%.

Acceptable evidence that treatment alters the prognosis of sex offenders is lacking. Polizzi, MacKenzie, and Hickman (1999) reported an evaluation of 21 studies of programs carried out in the previous 10 years. Only two prison-based programs were assessed as sufficiently rigorous to permit conclusions. In one, treatment resulted in insignificantly more recidivism up to 31 years; in the other, recidivism was significantly less at a follow-up averaging 6 years. Five nonprison-based studies were assessed as sufficiently rigorous. Two showed significantly and one nonsignificantly lower recidivism for sexual offenses in the treated group. One showed lower recidivism for sexual offenses in the untreated group. All the studies compared treated offenders with matched controls. In discussing methodology of evaluation of sex offender treatment, Miner (1997) pointed out the impossibility of matching offenders on all relevant variables. In view of the failure of these studies to employ random allocation of subjects to treatment or no treatment, it was disappointing that Polizzi et al. did not attach greater significance to the study of Marques, Day, Nelson, and West (1994), which did. In concluding that the outcome of that study favored the treatment group, Marques et al. ignored the fact that this was the case only if offenders who had been allocated to treatment but later rejected were excluded. Offenders who do not complete treatment usually have a poorer outcome than those who complete it, commonly because they are more impulsive and exercise less self-control (Marques et al., 1994). To exclude their outcome when it is not possible to exclude from the control group, the outcome of the offenders with equivalent characteristics biases the outcome in favor of treatment. When the outcomes of all offenders randomized to treatment or no treatment were examined, more of those treated had reoffended than those who were not treated (McConaghy, 1999a). Marques (1999) examined post hoc the groups randomly allocated to treatment and no treatment and found that more married offenders had, presumably by chance, been allocated to no treatment. Married subjects who received treatment had a better outcome than the married subjects who were not treated. If this result was not due to chance, the study still showed that the larger number of single offenders had a worse outcome following treatment than those not treated (McConaghy, 1999a). The treatment employed was relapse prevention, a form of cognitive behavioral therapy, which is an integral part of most treatment programs for sex offenders in North America (Marshall, 1996). Polizzi et al. (1999) reported that the evidence was not strong enough to conclude that prison-based programs were effective, but nonprison-based programs that employed cognitive-behavioral techniques were effective.

Failure to base cost-effective assessment and treatment of sex offenders on a critical examination of research findings remains widespread. No attempts have been made to replicate the findings of comparison studies using random allocation, which demonstrated superiority of the nonaversive imaginal desensitization (alternative behavior completion) to electric shock and covert sensitization aversive therapies (McConaghy et al., 1993). The two forms of aversive therapy remain the major methods used to modify sexually offensive behaviors in North America. Quinsey and Earls (1990) found it disturbing that the literature concerning electrical aversive therapy appeared to have dried up. They found no controlled studies since 1983 that investigated its effectiveness in reducing inappropriate sexual arousal and commented that the evidence for the efficacy of covert sensitization was not overwhelming. They noted a variety of techniques had by then been shown to reduce individual men's sexual arousal to deviant stimuli as assessed by penile circumference response (PCR) assessment (the validity of which they accepted), but it was not known which were most efficacious or what procedural details were the most important. Comparison studies would provide valuable information concerning the relative cost effectiveness of the various techniques presently in use. In one such study, 30 sex offenders were randomly allocated—10 to receive alternative behavior completion; 10, low-dosage medroxyprogesterone acetate (MPA) therapy; and 10, the two combined. Twenty-eight ceased deviant behavior at one year following commencement of treatment. Two of the 28 had required the addition of electric shock aversive therapy (McConaghy, Blaszczynski, & Kidson, 1988). Three relapsed in the following two to five years, but responded to the reinstitution of MPA. All subjects who requested treatment were accepted. These results were comparable with those of multimodal programs, which required much longer periods of staff-patient contact and treated selected patients.

The significance of changes in PCR arousal of sex offenders following treatment also needs to be determined. In view of the low validity of this measure and the ability of the men tested to modify it voluntarily (see Psychological and Biological Assessment section), it remains controversial whether treatments result in a change in offenders' sexual preference or their ability to control the preference, which remains unchanged. McConaghy (1999b) noted that the evidence favored the latter position. If it is correct, procedures such as aversive therapy and masturbatory satiation that aim to change preference could be counterproductive. This could account for the evidence of the lack of effectiveness found by Polizzi et al. (1999) of treatments carried out in prison or in high-security hospital settings employed in the Marques et al. study (1994). Offenders are unlikely to learn to control their behaviors when they are not exposed to cues for the behaviors. For rapists, the cue would be the presence of women, and for child molesters, the presence of children.

The *DSM-IV* states that usually the severity of sadistic acts increases over time, and that when severe, and especially when associated with antisocial personality disorder, individuals with sexual sadism may seriously injure or kill their victims. This statement is open to question. As stated earlier (see Epidemiology section), the sadistic acts rarely involved serious physical harm. The *DSM-IV* comment may be meant to apply to the rare sadistic or sexual murderers, whose condition seems different from that of subjects who identify as masochists and sadists by joining clubs (McConaghy, 1993). Fetishism and transvestic fetishism can rarely be eliminated in the subjects who seek this, and the aim of treatment is to give them control over the behaviors so they can be carried out possibly with reduced frequency and in acceptable situations. Treatment of gender identity disorders also aims to minimize any distress because of the condition. The forms of sex-conversion sought by the subject are generally recommended for adults who have shown an ability to live successfully as a member of the opposite sex for an agreed period, commonly two years.

DIAGNOSTIC CONSIDERATIONS

Reliability of *DSM-IV* diagnoses of sexual dysfunctions is likely to be low in view of the number of issues left to the judgment of the individual clinician. *DSM-IV* diagnoses are therefore rarely employed in research studies. No standardized structured interviews have been developed to make such diagnoses for the dysfunctions or the other sexual disorders (Raymond, Coleman, Ohlerking, Christenson, & Miner, 1999). Some researchers have created their own, with individual operationally defined criteria. Kelly, Strassberg, and Kircher (1990) diagnosed the presence of anorgasmia in women who reported that orgasm resulted from 5% or less of all sexual activities with their partners, and its absence, if it resulted from 70% or more of such activities. Strassberg, Mahoney, Schaugaard, and Hale (1990) diagnosed subjects as having premature ejaculation who estimated ejaculation latencies of two minutes or less on at least 50% of intercourse occasions, and who, in addition, perceived lack of control over the onset of orgasm. Such arbitrarily developed criteria may lack validity. Using the criteria of Strassberg et al., none of 110 heterosexual male undergraduates would have received the diagnosis of premature ejaculation, although 4% percent had latencies of less than two minutes and 8% reported no control (Grenier & Byers, 1997). The students' concern with ejaculating faster than desired did not correlate significantly with their estimated latency to ejaculation or with perceived ejaculatory control. Laumann et al. (1994) found in their population sample that 27% of men in the age range of the students reported coming to a climax too quickly. With criteria of seven minutes or less latency to ejaculation, combined with four or less on an eight-point ejaculatory control scale, Grenier and Byers found 24% of the students were classified as rapid ejaculators. Arbitrary criteria for diagnosis of hypoactive or inhibited sexual desire have allowed women and men with evidence of significant sexual interest to receive the diagnosis (McConaghy, 1993). To make the diagnosis in subjects who report acceptable frequencies of sexual activity, it is necessary to establish that they are having intercourse from obligation to their partner rather than from sexual desire, and in subjects who report low frequencies, that they are not avoiding sexual activity because of dissatisfaction with their sexual relationship rather than reduced desire.

Diagnosis of sexual dysfunction often requires that the health professional inquire directly concerning the dysfunction. Studies reporting the results of such inquiry in patients who had previously seen a health professional found that many had sexual dysfunctions that they had not revealed, and the professional had not asked concerning their sexual functioning (McConaghy, 1993). Seidman and Rieder (1994) cited a 1990 report of the Department of Health and Human Services, which charged all health care providers to take a complete sexual and drug use history with all adolescent and adult patients and to give advise and counseling concerning strategies for avoiding infection and unwanted pregnancies. Studies indicated only 11% to 37% of primary care physicians routinely took a sexual history from new patients, and they found that many psychiatrists (and presumably psychologists) were ill at ease with explicit sexual history taking. Seidman and Rieder, in their review of studies of sexual behavior in the United States, reported that most 18- to 24-year-olds had multiple, serial sex partners and did not consistently use condoms. Suarez and Miller (2001) referred to more recent data indicating increased risk behavior in both the United States and abroad, accompanied by increased rates of sexually transmitted diseases and possibility of HIV. They found that "barebacking," the conscious choice to engage in risky sexual behaviors, had gathered an almost cult-like following among men who have sex with men. Seidman and Rieder pointed out that male-to-female transmission of HIV was five times as likely with anal as with vaginal intercourse. Anal intercourse was rarely discussed in the medical literature and was apparently a topic of extreme sensitivity for many individuals, including physicians. Anal intercourse was reported in the last year by 9% of women with opposite sex partners; 1.2% stated it occurred in their last sexual experience (Laumann et al., 1994). In taking a sexual history from adolescents, it is necessary to be aware that most will not reveal sexual activities or feelings that are considered deviant. This awareness was not always shown, even by experienced sexuality researchers. Studies of the effects of exposure to altered levels of sex hormones in utero accepted as valid the reports of 62 child, adolescent, and young adult subjects and 48 controls that only one (a control) reported some degree of homosexual feelings (McConaghy, 1993). Twenty percent of men and women report some homosexual feelings or activity, or both, in answer to anonymous questionnaires (Dunne et al., 2000; McConaghy, 1999b).

The *DSM-IV* diagnosis of paraphilia requires both that the behavior, sexual urges, or fantasies have been present over a period of at least six months, and that they cause clinically significant distress or impairment in social, occupational, or other important areas of functioning. At the same time, it states that many individuals with these disorders assert that the behavior causes them no distress and that their only problem is social dysfunction because of the reaction of others to their behavior. The majority of child molesters have not been detected and so not exposed to the reaction of others. Marshall and Eccles (1991) commented that many rapists, incest offenders, exhibitionists, and a substantial number of nonfamilial child molesters do not display or report deviant sexual preferences, yet they persistently engage in sexually offensive behaviors. Most clinicians, therefore, ignore *DSM* diagnoses. Interviewers should not be misled into regarding sexual arousal in men and women to fantasies of paraphilias or sexual offenses as uncommon or pathological (see Epidemiology section). *DSM-IV* acknowledges the marked prevalence of sexually arousing fantasies commonly regarded as deviant, emphasizing that a paraphilia must be distinguished from the nonpathological use of sexual fantasies, behaviors, or objects as a stimulus for sexual excitement. They are paraphilic only when they lead to clinically significant distress or impairment. Differences in diagnostic criteria produced marked discrepancies in findings concerning adult-child sexual relations, including their prevalence, the sex of the adult, and the relationship of the adult with the child (see Epidemiology section).

The abandonment in the *DSM-IV* of the terms *transvestism* and *transsexualism*, widely accepted by both clinicians and subjects with these conditions, seems likely to confuse rather than clarify the subjects' diagnosis. It has already caused controversy between specialists in the area (McConaghy, 1999b). There is substantial evidence that both conditions exist as clinical entities with fetishistic transsexualism as an intermediate state (McConaghy, 1993). Presumably, most adult transvestites, if distressed about their condition, are meant to receive a *DSM-IV* diagnosis of fetishistic transvestism. When discussing the differential diagnosis from gender identity disorder, *DSM-IV* states that transvestic fetishism occurs in heterosexual or bisexual men for whom the cross-dressing behavior is for the purpose of sexual excitement. Most adult transvestites do not cross-dress for sexual excitement but for periodic enjoyment of the female role. If they still experience sexual excitement with cross-dressing, they dismiss it as insignificant or distracting. Many prefer not to acknowledge any fetishistic aspect to their behavior. A term that emphasizes the fetishistic aspect of the behavior is objectionable to them (McConaghy, 1993). In addition, transvestism has been reported in homosexual men. Buhrich and Beaumont (1981) investigated 216 American and Australian members of transvestite clubs after excluding the 24 who reported they had not experienced fetishism to women's clothes. All were male. Most reported their preference and behavior to be heterosexual. However, when dressed as men, 1.5% reported it to be bisexual, and

3% reported that it was exclusively homosexual. When dressed as women, 8% reported it was bisexual; 3%, predominantly homosexual, and 3.5%, exclusively homosexual. Most transvestites do not conform to criterion B for paraphilias, which requires that they show clinically significant distress. Adding transvestism to the list of sexual behaviors no longer considered disorders, which includes masturbation, oral and anal sex, and homosexuality, would seem a progressive solution. Further additions to the list could be sadism and masochism, as most men and women with these conditions, like transvestites, are not distressed by their condition and do not seek treatment (McConaghy, 1993).

DSM-IV includes the condition of transsexualism in adults and adolescents with cross-gender identification in children as gender identity disorder. It states that gender identity disorder of childhood is not meant to describe a child's nonconformity to stereotypic sex role behavior, as, for example, in "tomboyishness" in girls or "sissyish" behavior in boys. As discussed earlier (see Epidemiology section), the degree to which sissy and tomboyish behaviors are shown in childhood, along with the degree of opposite sex identity both then and in adulthood, correlates with awareness of homosexual feelings and behavior in adulthood. Inquiry concerning the presence of "tomboyish" or "sissyish" behaviors in childhood may be indicated when subjects' balance of homosexual to heterosexual feelings and sex role are relevant.

As to dual diagnosis, those most relevant to sexual disorders are personality disorders, as they influence the likelihood that the men and women with these disorders are willing and able to report their symptoms and behaviors accurately (McConaghy, 1994). van Lankveld and Grothohann (2000) reviewed studies of dual diagnosis involving sexual dysfunctions. All found significant levels of personality and other psychiatric disorders in men and women with sexual dysfunctions, and of sexual dysfunctions in patients with schizophrenia and affective disorders. Medication for schizophrenia and affective disorders contributed to the latter associations. No comparisons were made with levels of the disorders in the normal population. Van Lankveld and Grothohann used the Composite International Diagnostic Interview 1.1 (World Health Organization, 1992) to investigate the presence of *DSM-III-R* Axis I diagnoses in 181 men and 201 women with sexual dysfunctions that met *DSM-IV* criteria. They found a significantly higher prevalence of current anxiety disorder and lifetime affective disorder in both the women and men, compared to their prevalence in the general population. Raymond et al. (1999) found 42 of 45 men who met *DSM-IV* criteria for pedophilia also met the criteria for another Axis I diagnosis: lifetime mood disorder in 67%, anxiety disorder in 64%, psychoactive substance use disorders in 60%, another paraphilia diagnosis in 53%, and sexual function disorder in 24%. Axis II personality disorders were also common. The authors noted that 77.5% did not meet criteria for antisocial personality disorder and 80% did not meet criteria for narcissistic personality disorder. Obsessive-compulsive personality disorder was slightly more prevalent, being present in 25%. No controls were investigated. Diagnoses were made using the Structured Clinical Interview for *DSM-IV* Axis I Disorders, Patient Edition. The reliability of such interviews is more established than their validity (McConaghy, 1993). The frequent presence of antisocial or psychopathic personality in sexual offenders based on their behavioral history was discussed earlier (see Clinical Picture and Course and Prognosis sections).

PSYCHOLOGICAL AND BIOLOGICAL ASSESSMENT

The unstructured interview remains the most common method of psychological assessment of subjects with sexual disorders. It enables the clinician to determine the nature of the disorder while assessing the subject's personality and commencing to establish the appropriate therapeutic relationship, which maximizes the likelihood of cooperation with the chosen therapy (McConaghy, 1998). Use of structured interviews by clinicians would add considerably to the time taken to adequately assess subjects. Their use would result in more reliable diagnoses, that is, diagnoses that agree better with those of other clinicians who use the same interview. This is of no advantage in the treatment of individual patients unless it can be shown that it leads to selection of more appropriate treatment. Currently, there is no evidence that this is the case. Morganstern (1988) pointed out that often the highest treatment priority needed to be given to a different problem from that of which the client initially complained. The therapist is likely to realize this only in the course of an unstructured interview. As to data about which subjects have privacy concerns, Catania, Gibson, Chitwood, and Coates (1990) concluded that current evidence suggested self-administered questionnaires reduced measurement error compared to face-to-face interviews. Anonymous questionnaires may reduce error further. The figure of 20% of homosexual feelings, or behavior, or both, reported by men and women in a number of studies was markedly higher than the percentage found in studies using a mixture of face-to-face interviews and questionnaires (McConaghy, 1999b). Clark and Tifft (1966) asked 45 male sociology students to complete questionnaires before and following their undergoing a polygraph examination, which the subjects believed would detect falsehoods. In the initial questionnaire as compared to the second, percentages of overreporting and underreporting were nearly equal (15% and 17.5%) for vaginal intercourse; 15% underreported and 5% overreported homosexual contacts; and 30% underreported masturbation, 95% admitting it in the second responses. Use of self-reporting of sexual behavior by diary led to increased dropout in comparison to interview (Reading, 1983). The frequency of urges for sexual contact with children reported by pedophiles using the daily diary card did not differ in those receiving the male sex hormone-reducing chemical, medroxyprogesterone, from those receiving placebo (Wincze, Bansal, & Malamud, 1986). This indicated the diary card assessment lacked validity. Medroxyprogesterone has been shown to reduce such urges both clinically (McConaghy, 1993) and in research. Percentage reduction in sex offenders' testosterone levels produced by medroxyprogesterone correlated highly with their global assessment of the degree of reduction of their deviant urges, as reported by questionnaire. Neither the offenders nor the questionnaire administrator knew the degree of reduction (McConaghy et al., 1988). Patients' self-report of behaviors in inventories can of themselves produce changes in behaviors (LoPiccolo & Steger, 1974). Wincze and Carey (1991) pointed out that behavioral inventories have not been widely used in clinical sexuality assessments. They cited Conte's (1983) suggestion that one reason was that many inventories were developed for specific research purposes and had limited clinical utility. They also pointed out that their use could be time consuming and inconvenient in a busy practice. Nevertheless, they used a number of self-report questionnaires in assessing patients with sexual dysfunctions and suggested Conte's review and the compendium of Davis, Yarber, and Davis (1988, now updated to

Davis, Yarber, Bauserman, Schreer, & Davis, 1998) as sources for other measures that could be useful. A further source is the *Dictionary of Behavioral Assessment Techniques* (Hersen & Bellack, 1988). Jacobson et al. (1984) pointed out that differences in the scores of marital satisfaction of subjects who received active and placebo marital therapy could be highly statistically significant when the changes were clinically trivial. They recommended comparing treated subjects' individual scores with the norms of functionally well subjects on the same scales. With this procedure, the mean improvement rate with behavioral marital therapy was about 35%, considerably less than was generally believed.

Sexual or gender identity was first identified in relation to transsexualism (McConaghy, 1993). Because transsexuals claimed to identify totally as members of the biologically opposite sex, the possibility that, in nontranssexuals, sexual identity could be dimensional was not initially considered. The first attempt to assess it dimensionally asked men and women to rate three items on five-point scales—the amount of time from never to all the time they:

1. Felt uncertain of their identity as a member of their sex.
2. Felt like a member of their sex.
3. Felt like a member of the opposite sex.

In a series of studies by McConaghy and colleagues using anonymous questionnaires, the degree of homosexual to heterosexual feelings reported by women and men correlated with their feelings of opposite sex identity assessed by these scales (see Epidemiology section). These replicated findings indicated the three items were validly measuring some concept related to gender identity. Examining the responses of male medical students separately, responses to the three items correlated at most about .5 (McConaghy & Armstrong, 1983), suggesting the concept may not be unified. The correlations were stronger in subjects who reported some awareness of homosexual feelings. These subjects also reported a greater degree of opposite sex identity than exclusively heterosexual subjects. It was suggested that awareness of belonging to a minority produced a stronger and more consistent sense of identity, which, in the case of men with homosexual feelings, was with the opposite sex. Dunne et al. (2000), also using anonymous questionnaires, found a similar relationship in male and female twins between opposite gender identity assessed on a seven-point continuous gender identity scale and homosexual feelings and behaviors. Spence and Buckner (1995) believed that such scales measured men's and women's awareness that they failed to correspond to socially dictated gender expectations, not gender identity, which was essentially dimorphic. They stated that apart from subjects with gender identity disorder, the large majority of males and females maintain an unambiguous and stable sense of their own gender identity. It is not clear if they would exclude men with transvestism from this large majority with a stable gender identity. Some male transvestites felt they had male identity when dressed as men and female identity when dressed as women (Buhrich & McConaghy, 1977). As Spence and Buckner believed people's existential sense of gender identity could not be measured, it would seem impossible to support or refute scientifically their belief that the sense is dichotomously, rather than dimensionally, distributed.

Physiological assessment of men's sexual arousal by measuring their penile volume responses (PVRs) to pictures of male and female nudes of 13-second duration was introduced and validated by Freund (1963). He demonstrated that it classified correctly as individuals the majority of men who reported relatively exclusive heterosexual or homosexual feelings or behaviors. McConaghy (1967) replicated this finding using a simpler apparatus for measuring PVRs to a brief standardized presentation of moving pictures of nude men and nude women of 10-second duration. Subsequently, a strain gauge measuring penile circumference responses (PCRs) introduced to assess penile tumescence during sleep was also used to measure sexual arousal. It was assumed that PCRs and PVRs were identical. PCR assessment was adopted by researchers apart from Freund and McConaghy before studies were published demonstrating PCRs to pictures of nude men, and women did not discriminate heterosexual from homosexual men as individuals (McConaghy, 1993). It was not until 1985 that Sakheim, Barlow, Beck, and Abrahamson demonstrated that, to make this discrimination, it was necessary to use men's PCRs to the more powerful erotic stimuli of moving films of prolonged duration of men and women involved in homosexual (but not heterosexual) activity. Comparison of PCRs and PVRs of individual men to the standardized presentation of films of nudes of 10-second duration revealed that, although in some men the two responses were reasonably equivalent, in others, they were largely reversed to be mirror images (McConaghy, 1974). It was suggested the mirror image responses occurred in men whose initial penile tumescence was associated with a rapid elongation of the penis. The increase in blood flow necessary to maintain the elongation was not sufficient to also maintain an increase in circumference (the response measured by the PCR). While the circumference temporarily diminished, the volume (measured by PVRs) increased. PVRs, therefore, measure the initial stage of penile tumescence more accurately than PCRs, which in some men can only accurately measure the later stage after two minutes or more (McConaghy, 1982). This could account for the greater sensitivity of PVRs in assessing sexual orientation of individual men. The initial stage may more accurately reflect sexual arousal, with the later stage of tumescence possibly being more influenced by haemodynamic factors determining erection. Kuban, Barbaree, and Blanchard (1999) found the mean PCRs and PVRs to one-minute erotic stimuli were almost identical for 32 students whose responses were high. In the 16 whose two responses were low, their mean PCRs were less valid than their PVRs. Kuban et al. suggested this could be because some PCRs are inverse or mirror responses of the valid PVRs.

PCRs to pictures of single male and female nudes were first reported to be unable to correctly differentiate as individuals men who identified as homosexual or heterosexual in 1975. By that time, they had been adopted for use in single-case studies as the major outcome measure of change in individual subjects' heterosexual and homosexual feelings (McConaghy, 1977). The findings of these single-case studies remain the only evidence that widely used techniques such as masturbatory satiation and aversive procedures modify deviant sexual arousal. They continue to be cited in this respect (Laws & Marshall, 1991). Tollison, Adams, and Tollison (1979) reported the PCRs to movies of sexual activity failed to distinguish bisexual from homosexual men. Rather than question the validity of the assessment, they questioned the existence of bisexuality, claiming there was to that date no physiological evidence for bisexual arousal except where this was a by-product of sexual reorientation therapy. In fact, PVR assessments had provided such evidence (McConaghy, 1993). Early studies reported that, as groups, pedophiles and rapists could be distinguished from control subjects by their PCRs to audiotaped or videotaped descriptions of sexual activities or pictures of male and female nudes of various ages. This encouraged the widespread use of these responses in diagnosis and assessment of response to treatment of pedophiles and rapists as individuals. Subsequent studies showed inconsistent results (McConaghy, 1993), possibly due to:

- Lower sensitivity of PCRs compared to PVRs as measures of arousal.
- Ability of subjects to learn to modify their PCRs with the prolonged time these responses require for assessment as compared with PVRs.
- Significant percentage of normal controls who show evidence of arousal to stimuli of children or acts of sexual aggression (McConaghy, 1998).

Lalumiere and Quinsey (1994), using meta-analysis of studies investigating the PCRs of rapists, demonstrated that the assessment did discriminate rapists from nonrapists, as groups. The fact that it was necessary to combine the results of several studies by meta-analysis to obtain convincing statistical evidence that PCR assessment discriminated the two groups would seem evidence that the assessment should be used only to investigate groups, not individuals. Nevertheless, the authors concluded that the result supported its use to identify individual offenders' treatment needs and risk of recidivism.

In the meta-analysis of Hanson and Bussiere (1998), phallometric assessment of sexual interest in children was the strongest predictor of recidivism; that of sexual interest in rape was unrelated. No distinction was made by the authors between PCR and PVR assessments. PCR assessment is as yet unstandardized and the method used may be chosen from several after initial results are examined, increasing the likelihood of false positive errors. In addition, men's ability to modify their PCRs during the prolonged period in which they are exposed to the evoking stimuli is influenced by their intelligence (McConaghy, 1999b). Marshall (1996) suggested the wisest course of action may be to withdraw clinical use of PCR assessment until more adequate data are available. Presumably, because of the small number of women sex offenders, their genital physiological responses do not appear to have been investigated. Changes in sexually functional and dysfunctional women's vaginal, clitoral, or labial blood flow with exposure to erotic stimuli were measured by either the associated temperature changes using a thermistor, or vaginal color changes using a photoplethysmograph. Clitoral responses have also been assessed using a strain gauge. R. C. Rosen and Beck (1988) concluded that photoplethysmograph assessment of vaginal pulse amplitude (VPA) was the most widely used and most sensitive measure of arousal in distinguishing the responses of groups of women to erotic, as compared to nonerotic, stimuli. However, its correlation with subjectively assessed arousal was insignificant in the majority of women studied. This was also reported by Laan, Everaerd, van Bellen, and Hanewald (1994).

Men with hypoactive sexual desire and those whose erectile disorder is not situational (and hence not obviously psychogenically determined) require biological assessment. Situational erectile disorder is that occurring with some but not other partners, or with all partners but not in private masturbation where no pressure to produce an erection is experienced. Physical examination is indicated to exclude conditions such as Peyronie's disease and hypogonadism, and blood and urine screening to exclude diabetes, hyperprolactinaemia (raised levels of the pituitary hormone prolactin HPRL), and thyroid dysfunction. Presumably reflecting differences in patient samples, the percentage of impotent men reported to show hormone abnormalities vary markedly between studies, as do conclusions as to what hormones should be investigated. Some studies recommended that in initial evaluation only men's testosterone levels be measured and prolactin estimations be carried out only if their testosterone levels were low. Although the level of testosterone necessary to maintain erectile function is markedly below that necessary to maintain sexual interest (McConaghy, 1993), testosterone levels are usually routinely investigated in men with nonsituational erectile disorder whether they show physical signs of hypogonadism or not. The widespread prescription of sildenafil by medical practitioners and urologists for erectile dysfunction suggests it is commonly commenced at least by medical practitioners without assessments apart from physical examination, exclusion of diabetes, and possibly testosterone level estimation. Nocturnal penile tumescence (NPT) assessment, with the aim of differentiating erectile dysfunction of psychogenic and organic origin, may be employed by therapists specializing in the treatment of the dysfunction to whom men failing to respond to sildenafil and possibly intracavernous injection therapy are referred. Meisler and Carey (1990) indicated a conservative appraisal was that NPT misdiagnosed as many as 20% of the men investigated. It is advisable for medicolegal purposes in assessment of patients complaining of erectile disorder secondary to compensable accidents or injuries. Impairment of penile blood flow as a cause of erectile dysfunction can be assessed by determination of the penile-brachial index (PBI), the ratio of the blood pressure in the penile arteries, commonly measured by Doppler ultrasound probe, and conventionally measured blood pressure in the brachial artery in the arm. Before the introduction of sildenafil, pharmacological erection tests by intracavernous injection of vasodilating chemicals were increasingly used to assess penile vascular supply in erectile dysfunction. They are likely to be part of the initial assessment carried out by clinicians specializing in its management. When the pharmacological erection test indicates the presence of vascular pathology, further physical investigations are carried out if it is necessary to determine its cause. Assessment of neurogenic factors producing impotence is indicated if the patient has a history of diabetes, pelvic pathology, or radical prostatectomy, or if physical examination reveals the absence of the cremasteric or bulbocavernosal reflex or reduced lower limb reflexes (McConaghy, 1998).

Physical and laboratory examination are more rarely carried out on women with sexual dysfunctions. Although, as in men, it is necessary to exclude illness, medications, or substances as responsible for reduced sexual interest or ability to reach orgasm, the effects of neurological and vascular disease and of medications and drugs of abuse on the sexuality of women are much more poorly documented. Physical examination is necessary to investigate dyspareunia, but hormone studies are not routine in the investigation of sexually dysfunctional women in the absence of evidence of hormonal imbalance such as excessive hirsutism. The significant hormonal fluctuations that occur throughout the menstrual cycle have not been demonstrated to be accompanied by consistent fluctuations in sexual behaviors (McConaghy, 1993).

Determination of serum testosterone levels is of value in monitoring the response of sex offending and paraphilic men to low-dose androgen-reducing chemical therapy. Reduction of their pretreatment level produced therapeutically adequate reduction in deviant arousal without impairing their erectile responses in acceptable sexual activities (McConaghy et al., 1988). A number of studies have reported differences in hypothalamic nuclei in men and women, in homosexual compared to heterosexual subjects, and in male-to-female transsexuals compared to control males (Swaab, Zhou, & Hofman, 1995).

ETIOLOGICAL CONSIDERATIONS

FAMILIAL AND GENETIC CONSIDERATIONS

Women's relationships with their parents and their parents' attitudes to sex or nudity did not distinguish sexually dysfunctional from functional women (McConaghy, 1993). Prentky et al. (1989) found that caregiver inconstancy, sexual deviation within the family, and sexual abuse of the subject were related to severity of sexual aggression in 82 incarcerated sex offenders. Childhood and juvenile institutional history and physical abuse and neglect were associated with severity of nonsexual aggression. Early exposure to family violence, along with childhood sexual abuse and early age of sexual initiation, predicted later sexually aggressive behaviors in the national sample of 2,972 male students investigated by Koss and Dinero (1988). As these behaviors are associated with psychopathy, which is in part inherited (Schulsinger, 1972), genetic factors, as well as modeling of the disturbed childhood relationships, may have contributed to the later aggression of offenders. Of 5,000 treated sex offenders, 27% reported having first-degree relatives with a history of sexual offenses and 44% first-degree relatives with a history of alcoholism (Maletzky, 1991). Alcoholism has also been shown to be, in part, genetically determined.

LEARNING AND MODELING

The increase in women from age 15 to middle age of the ability to reach orgasm in sexual relationships suggests learning, possibly to relinquish control, is involved (McConaghy, 1993). Wolpe's (1958) concept that sexual dysfunctions are due to anxiety concerning sexual activity has been generally accepted by clinicians. Wolpe found that anxiety could be conditioned by faulty cognitions, including expectations about performance, and by experiences occurring at any stage of life, not merely the first five years, as advanced in psychoanalytic theory. This anxiety could partially or totally inhibit the subject's sexual responsiveness. Hale and Strassberg (1990) demonstrated that anxiety about sexual performance was a factor in erectile dysfunctions in men and pointed out that earlier studies that had demonstrated that anxiety did not consistently impair sexual arousal had not investigated anxiety concerning sexual activity.

LIFE EVENTS

Apart from family experiences and illness, childhood sexual abuse (CSA) and sexual assault in adulthood are the life events considered most likely to result in sexual disorders. CSA has been found to be associated with increased sexually inappropriate behaviors in the victims' childhood, and frigidity, sexual orientation confusion, promiscuity, problems of sexual adjustment, and sexual dissatisfaction when they are adult (Beitchman, Zucker, Hood, DaCosta, & Akman, 1991; Beitchman et al., 1992). Studies reporting the problems in adults did not compare their prevalence with that in the general population; therefore, the amount that could be attributed to CSA was unknown. The majority of studies were of subjects from child protection or psychiatric facilities and could overestimate the prevalence and severity of symptomatology associated with CSA in the general population. Rind, Tromovitch, and Bauserman (1998) carried out a meta-analysis of 59 studies of the effect of CSA on college students. Concerning 17 behaviors, including sexual adjustment, the students were slightly less well adjusted than controls. The poorer adjustment could not be attributed to CSA because family environment (FE) was consistently confounded with CSA. FE explained much more adjustment variance than did CSA. CSA-adjustment relationships generally became insignificant when studies controlled for FE. Psychosexual dysfunctions were commonly reported to follow sexual assault in clinical studies. The victims' satisfaction with sexual behaviors with their partners was significantly reduced, particularly behaviors forced on them during the assault, though not all studies reported that the frequency of the behaviors was reduced (McConaghy, 1993). Dysfunctions reported included vaginismus, dyspareunia, and difficulties with arousal and orgasm, which could persist for years following the assault. Psychosexual disorders were also reported to follow the sexual assault of men by women (Sarrel & Masters, 1982) and by men (King, 1992b). Use of alcohol plays a significant role in sexual assault. Police and victims confirmed alcohol intoxication in 70% of rapists (Marshall & Barbaree, 1990). In Ageton's (1983) study, half the adolescent males who reported carrying out sexual assaults reported they had been drinking or taking drugs before the event. Victims considered the offender's being drunk a major factor precipitating the assault. The hypothesis that subjects sexually abused in their childhood become sex offenders through "identification with the aggressor" has been questioned on the basis that sex offenders, particularly child molesters, could report being victimized in childhood to obtain the sympathy of the interviewer or more lenient legal treatment. In addition, they could unconsciously exaggerate remembered events to reduce feelings of guilt (Freund, Watson, & Dickey, 1990). Diseases associated with pain, or which result in debility, anxiety, or depression, may impair sexual desire, arousal, and orgasm, as may a wide range of medications and drugs of abuse. These include antihypertensive agents, diuretics, vasodilators, and psychiatric and anticonvulsant drugs (Schiavi & Segraves, 1995). The effects of neurological and vascular disease on the sexual activity of men is well documented; their effects on that of women, much less so.

GENDER AND RACIAL-ETHNIC

Gender issues are, of course, of major importance in every area of sexuality. There are evident biases in the degree of attention given them. Biological factors determining women's as compared to men's normal and dysfunctional sexual activities are poorly researched, consistent with the suggestion that women's sexuality is more determined by social factors (McConaghy, 1993). Evidence cited to support this suggestion included the failure of numerous studies to find consistent relationships between women's sexual interest or behavior and the wide fluctuations in level of the sex hormones—estrodial, progesterone, and testosterone—which occur throughout the menstrual cycle. In contrast, men's sexual interest is strongly dependent on maintenance of their normal level of testosterone. Marked diminution or loss of such interest is a major side effect of the treatment for prostatic cancer when the level is reduced by castration or androgen-blocking medication. Such medication is also employed to reduce the sexual interest of men with paraphilias. Reduction of sex hormone levels has, in the author's experience, been ineffective in reducing sexual interest in women who complain of their interest being distressingly high and causing socially inappropriate behaviors. The consistent finding that women choose their sexual partners based on loving feelings and the partner's prospective suitability as a husband, whereas men are motivated by sexual desire, has been considered due to evolutionarily determined biological differences.

Laumann et al. (1994), in their representative U.S. study, found women to be somewhat less physically and emotionally satisfied with their sexual relationship than men. The difference became marked in the age range of 55 to 59, when more than 50% of men but less than 30% of women reported extreme satisfaction. The authors suggested it may have been because as men age, they are more likely than women to acquire new partners. Women were more likely to be reporting concerning relationships of long duration when sexual activity may be subsiding. As pointed out earlier (in the Epidemiology section), in women, all dysfunctions as defined by Laumann et al. decreased with age except lack of interest in sex, and reduced ability to the need for lubricate. In men, only problems with achieving or maintaining erection showed a clear relationship with age. Most dysfunctions were much more common in women than in men.

Another major difference in the sexual behavior of men and women is the virtual absence of many paraphilic behaviors in women, including exhibitionism, voyeurism, fetishism, frotteurism, transvestism, and telephone scatologia. Most studies of sexual aggression investigated men only as perpetrators and women only as victims. This was the case with the commonly used Sexual Experiences Survey (Koss & Oros, 1982) developed to investigate the concept that rape represented an extreme behavior on a continuum with normal male sexual behavior. McConaghy & Zamir (1995) modified the questionnaire to allow men and women to report coercive behaviors as both perpetrators and victims. The most common coercive behavior was constant physical attempts to have sexual activity with another person. Twenty percent of men, but also 15% of women, reported having carried out this behavior. The reported perpetration of sexual coercion correlated with masculine sex-role behavior in both men and women. The fact that women rarely seek treatment for, or are diagnosed or charged with, sexual assault or pedophilia, as discussed earlier, appears to be due to the tendency of male children not to regard experiences with older women negatively. Most male children touched sexually by an older person reported that female, unlike male perpetrators, were only a few years older (Laumann et al., 1994). The definition that pedophilic activity was abusive, whether the children considered their reactions neutral or positive, was initially applied only to sexual activity of postpubertal subjects with girl children.

Eklund, Gooren, and Bezemer (1988) found that almost all female-to-male transsexuals presented before the age of 50, whereas a number of male-to-female transsexuals presented after that age. Despite the marked increase in reported prevalence of transsexualism since it was first recognized, Eklund et al. pointed out the ratio of male-to-female as compared to female-to-male transsexuals has tended to remain consistent at about 3:1.

Ethnic differences were found in the prevalence of sexual dysfunctions by Laumann et al. (1994). Black men and women were more likely to report a higher prevalence of most dysfunctions than Whites and Hispanics. Concerning arrests for forcible rape, as with most arrests, Blacks are overrepresented. In 1986, when a little more than 12% of the U.S. population was estimated to be Black, 47% of men arrested for rape were Black. A consistent finding concerning male rape in institutional settings was the disproportionate number of Black aggressors and White victims, both in prisons and juvenile corrective-training schools (King, 1992a). King suggested that coerced sexual assault in all-male institutions may be part of a personalized ethnic power struggle, reflecting a deep-seated resentment of lower-class Blacks against middle-class Whites. It was pointed out that the findings might be influenced by racial prejudice of researchers. They could also reflect differences in the readiness of Black and White victims to report assaults. Fewer Hispanics, compared to non-Hispanic White men and women in the Los Angeles ECA project, reported having been sexually assaulted (Sorenson et al., 1987). The project found women to be perpetrators of 25% of assaults.

Ethnic differences contribute to differences in the reported prevalence of transsexualism between and within countries. Tsoi (1990) suggested in relation to the markedly higher prevalence of transsexualism in men and women born in Singapore, as compared with those born in most Western countries, that the greater availability of sex-conversion surgery may have drawn out the Singapore transsexuals earlier. In addition, Singaporese may have had a stronger need for sex conversion because homosexuality was not accepted by society there. He reported that 200 male transsexuals in Singapore could not be differentiated from male homosexuals from their earlier sexual behavior until they started to cross-dress and sought sex conversion. None had ever married or experienced heterosexual intercourse. The absence among his subjects of fetishistic transsexuals who, in the English-speaking world and Europe, are usually predominantly heterosexual and have married requires explanation. Ninety percent of the transsexual prostitutes investigated by MacFarlane (1984) in Wellington, New Zealand, were half- or quarter-caste Maoris, who made up only 9% of the population. Lothstein and Roback (1984) reported that Black women were grossly underrepresented among applicants for sex conversion to their clinic in Cleveland, Ohio. The few who did apply were all diagnosed by consensus of the entire gender identity team as borderline or frankly schizophrenic, and hence not suitable for sex conversion.

BIOLOGICAL AND PHYSIOLOGICAL

Of biological variables, age appears the most important determinant of the frequency of sexual activity throughout life, as well as of the dysfunctions of inhibited female orgasm and male erectile disorders. In the representative British study of Johnson et al. (1994), more than half of all 45- to 59-year-olds agreed that it was natural for people to want sex less often as they aged. There would appear to be a weaker biological basis for female than male orgasm throughout the mammalian species (Kinsey et al., 1953). Investigators of women's sexual behaviors have commonly concluded that women differ biologically in their ability to learn to reach orgasm (Mead, 1950) and that some women seem unable to do so (Kaplan, 1974). Martin (1981) found the relative frequencies of sexual activity of individual men tended to be constant through their postpubertal lives. He noted that biological rather than social factors must determine the frequency because experiential factors would have varied markedly over the men's lives. If so, the biological factors were also involved in determining the prevalence of sexual dysfunctions in men, independent of aging. Elderly men who had higher levels of sexual activity through their lives were less likely to be partially or totally impotent or to have experienced a long-term problem with premature ejaculation. In opposition to the belief of the 1970s that most cases of erectile disorder were entirely psychogenically determined (LoPiccolo, 1982), it is now generally accepted that organic factors, usually impairment in penile blood flow, commonly contribute to their etiology (Meuleman et al., 1992). Clinical studies of nonincarcerated sex offenders seeking treatment have reported that subjects with evidence of congenital or acquired brain damage are overrepresented (Berlin & Meinecke, 1981; McConaghy et al., 1988). A biological model was advanced to explain reports that men who have repeatedly carried out paraphilic or sexually offensive behaviors experience a compulsion to carry out the behaviors to relieve aversive levels of tension produced by increased autonomic arousal, rather than sexual arousal. It was suggested that, with repetition of a behavior, a neurophysiological behavior completion mechanism is set up in the brain. It produces increase in autonomic arousal if the subject attempts not to carry out the behavior in the presence of cues to do so. The effectiveness of alternative behavior completion therapy based on the model was considered to support it (McConaghy, 1993).

SUMMARY

The most common sexual dysfunctions appear to be erectile dysfunction in men and impairment of sexual interest in women, which both increase with age, and inhibited female orgasm, which decreases with age, at least until middle age. Relationship difficulties are more common and more related to sexual satisfaction than dysfunctions.

Sexual assault and child sexual abuse of women and girls by men are the most studied, but coercive behavior of men by women and sexual activity of prepubertal boys with postpubertal girls are not uncommon. It is calculated that 5% of men and 0.5% of women molest girls and 0.5% of men molest boys. Men who molest boys commonly have many victims. Half the male population is likely to have carried out a sexual offense in adolescence; and they have sexual fantasies currently considered deviant, just as does half of the female population.

Opposite gender identity and sex-linked behaviors in childhood and adulthood are related dimensionally to homosexual feelings in men and women, suggesting gender identity may not be categorical. The replacement in *DSM-IV* of the terms *transvestism* and *transsexualism* by *transvestic fetishism with or without gender dysphoria* and *gender identity disorder* in adolescents or adults is criticized.

Presence of sexually active partners appears of importance in developing and maintaining subjects' sexual functioning. In earlier studies, traditional measures of personality and psychopathology yielded inconsistent findings in men and women with sexual dysfunctions and in sex offenders. Subsequent use of structured interviews, which find high levels of pathology in the normal population, find even higher levels in these two groups.

A significant percentage of sexually assaultive men show delinquent or antisocial personality features. Most commit their offenses while under the influence of alcohol.

Psychological treatment of dysfunctions may frequently increase patient satisfaction by reducing sexual difficulties while the dysfunctions persist. Reduction of difficulties would seem to involve improving couples' communication and the quality of their relationships. Availability of sildenafil has encouraged men with erectile dysfunction who would not accept psychological sex therapy to seek treatment.

Evidence of the effectiveness of treatment of sex offenders is urgently needed, as it is possible that cognitive behavioral therapy administered in prison or high-security environments is counterproductive. No randomized placebo-controlled trials of treatments of offenders have been carried out though imaginal desensitization based on an alternative behavior completion model demonstrated to be superior to aversive electric shock and covert sensitization aversive therapy in random allocation controlled studies. Based on this model, a much lower dose of medroxyprogesterone than that generally used was introduced and was shown to be effective in allowing subjects to control deviant sexual urges. Prediction of recidivism should be based on demographic, lifestyle variables, and criminal history of offenders. Clinicians' judgment of offenders' likelihood of reoffending based on their response to cognitive behavior therapy has proved markedly inaccurate. Use of penile circumference assessment of individual sex offenders should be ceased until a standardized form has proved to be valid in replicated studies.

Etiological contribution to sexual and gender identity disorders of familial and genetic factors, learning and modeling, life events, and gender, racial-ethnic, biological, and physiological variables were discussed.

REFERENCES

Abel, G. G., Becker, J. V., Cunningham-Rathner, J., Mittelman, M., & Rouleau J.-L. (1988). Multiple paraphilic diagnoses among sex offenders. *Bulletin of the American Academy of Psychiatry and Law, 16,* 153–168.

Adkins, E., & Jehu, D. (1985). Analysis of a treatment program for primary orgastic dysfunction. *Behavior Research and Therapy, 23,* 1219–1226.

Ageton, S. S. (1983). *Sexual assault among adolescents.* Lexington, MA: Lexington Books.

Althof, S. E., Turner, L. A., Levine, S. B., Bodner, D., Kursh, E. D., & Resnick, M. I. (1992). Through the eyes of women: The sexual and psychological responses of women to their partner's treatment with self-injection or external vacuum therapy. *Journal of Urology, 147,* 1024–1027.

American Psychiatric Association. (1987). *Diagnostic and statistical manual of mental disorders* (3rd ed., rev.). Washington, DC: Author.

American Psychiatric Association. (1994). *Diagnostic and statistical manual of mental disorders* (4th ed.). Washington, DC: Author.

Auerbach, R., & Kilmann, P. R. (1977). The effects of group systematic desensitization on secondary erectile failure. *Behavior Therapy, 8,* 330–339.

Aytac, I. A., McKinley, J. B., & Krane, R. J. (1999). The likely worldwide increase in erectile dysfunction between 1995 and 2025 and some possible policy consequences. *BJU International, 84,* 50–56.

Barbaree, H. E. (1999). Denial and minimization among sex offenders: Assessment and treatment outcome. *Sex Offender Programming, 3,* 1–7.

Bard, L. A., Carter, D. L., Cerce, D. D., Knight, R. A., Rosenberg, R., & Schneider, B. (1987). A descriptive study of rapists and child molesters: Developmental, clinical, and criminal characteristics. *Behavioral Sciences and the Law, 5,* 203–220.

Beitchman, J. H., Zucker, K. J., Hood, J. E., DaCosta, G. A., & Akman, D. (1991). A review of the short-term effects of child sexual abuse. *Child Abuse and Neglect, 15,* 537–556.

Beitchman, J. H., Zucker, K. J., Hood, J. E., DaCosta, G. A., Akman, D., & Cassavia, E. (1992). A review of the long-term effects of child sexual abuse. *Child Abuse and Neglect, 16*, 101–118.

Berlin, F. S., & Meinecke, C. F. (1981). Treatment of sex offenders with antiandrogenic medication: Conceptualization, review of treatment modalities, and preliminary findings. *American Journal of Psychiatry, 138*, 601–607.

Bowie, S. I., Silverman, D. C., Kalick, S. M., & Edbril, S. D. (1990). Blitz rape and confidence rape: Implications for clinical intervention. *American Journal of Psychotherapy, 44*, 180–188.

Boyce, E. G., & Umland, E. M. (2001). Sildenafil citrate: A therapeutic update. *Clinical Therapeutics, 23*, 2–23.

Breslow, N., Evans, L., & Langley, J. (1985). On the prevalence and roles of females in the sadomasochistic subculture: Report of an empirical study. *Archives of Sexual Behavior, 14*, 303–319.

Bridges, C. F., Critelli, J. W., & Loos, V. E. (1985). Hypnotic susceptibility, inhibitory control, and orgasmic consistency. *Archives of Sexual Behavior, 14*, 373–376.

Buhrich, N. (1977). *Clinical study of heterosexual male transvestism.* Unpublished doctoral dissertation. Sydney, Australia: University of New South Wales.

Buhrich, N., & Beaumont, T. (1981). Comparison of transvestism in Australia and America. *Archives of Sexual Behavior, 10*, 269–279.

Buhrich, N., & McConaghy, N. (1977). The clinical syndromes of femmiphilic transvestism. *Archives of Sexual Behavior, 6*, 397–412.

Buhrich, N., & McConaghy, N. (1978). Two clinically discrete syndromes of transsexualism. *British Journal of Psychiatry, 133*, 73–76.

Burgess, A. W., & Holmstrom, L. L. (1980). Rape typology and the coping behavior of rape victims. In S. L. McCombie (Ed.), *Rape crisis intervention handbook* (pp. 27–42). New York: Plenum Press.

Catania, J. A., Gibson, D. R., Chitwood, D. D., & Coates, T. J. (1990). Methodological problems in AIDS behavioral research: Influences on measurement error and participation bias in studies of sexual behavior. *Psychological Bulletin, 108*, 339–362.

Catalan, J. A., Hawton, K., & Day, A. (1990). Couples referred to a sexual dysfunction clinic psychological and physical morbidity. *British Journal of Psychiatry, 156*, 61–67.

Clare, E., & Tully, B. (1989). Transhomosexuality, or the dissociation of sexual orientation and sex object choice. *Archives of Sexual Behavior, 18*, 531–536.

Clark, J. P., & Tifft, L. L. (1966). Polygraph and interview validation of self-reported deviant behavior. *American Sociological Review, 31*, 516–523.

Coleman, E., Bockting, W. O., & Gooren, L. (1993). Homosexual and bisexual identity in sex-reassigned female-to-male transsexuals. *Archives of Sexual Behavior, 22*, 37–50.

Conte, H. R. (1983). Development and use of self-report techniques for assessing sexual functioning: A review and critique. *Archives of Sexual Behavior, 12*, 555–576.

Crepault, C., & Couture, M. (1980). Men's erotic fantasies. *Archives of Sexual Behavior, 9*, 565–581.

Davis, C. M., Yarber, W. L., Bauserman, R., Schreer, G., & Davis, S. L. (1998). *Handbook of sexuality-related measures.* Thousand Oaks, CA: Sage.

Day, K. (1994). Male mentally handicapped sex offenders. *British Journal of Psychiatry, 165*, 630–639.

De Amicis, L. A., Goldberg, D. C., LoPiccolo, J., Friedman, J., & Davies, L. (1984). Three-year follow-up of couples evaluated for sexual dysfunction. *Journal of Sex and Marital Therapy, 10*, 215–228.

De Amicis, L. A., Goldberg, D. C., LoPiccolo, J., Friedman, J., & Davies, L. (1985). Clinical follow-up of couples treated for sexual dysfunction. *Archives of Sexual Behavior, 14,* 467–489.

DiVasto, P. V., Kaufman, L. R., Jackson, R., Christy, J., Pearson, S., & Burgett, T. (1984). The prevalence of sexually stressful events among females in the general population. *Archives of Sexual Behavior, 13,* 59–67.

Dunne, M. P., Bailey, J. M., Kirk, K. M., & Martin, N. G. (2000). The subtlety of sex-atypicality. *Archives of Sexual Behavior, 29,* 549–565.

Eklund, P. L. E., Gooren, L. J. G., & Bezemer, P. D. (1988). Prevalence of transsexualism in the Netherlands. *British Journal of Psychiatry, 152,* 638–640.

Fedora, O., Reddon, J. R., Morrison, J. W., Fedora, S. K., Pascoe, H., & Yeudall, L. T. (1992). Sadism and other paraphilias in normal controls and aggressive and nonaggressive sex offenders. *Archives of Sexual Behavior, 21,* 1–15.

Fichten, C. S., Libman, E., & Brender, W. (1983). Methodological issues in the study of sex therapy: Effective components in the treatment of secondary orgasmic dysfunction. *Journal of Sex and Marital Therapy, 9,* 191–202.

Finkelhor, D. (1998). Improving research, policy, and practice to understand child sexual abuse. *Journal of the American Medical Association, 280,* 1864–1865.

Finkelhor, D., Hotaling, G., Lewis, I. A., & Smith, C. (1990). Sexual abuse in a national survey of adult men and women: Prevalence, characteristics, and risk factors. *Child Abuse and Neglect, 14,* 19–28.

Frank, E., Anderson, B., & Rubinstein, D. (1978). Frequency of sexual dysfunction in "normal" couples. *New England Journal of Medicine, 299,* 111–115.

Freund, K. (1963). A laboratory method of diagnosing predominance of homo- or hetero-erotic interest in the male. *Behavior Research and Therapy, 12,* 355–359.

Freund, K. (1990). Courtship disorder. In W. L. Marshall, D. R. Laws, & H. E. Barbaree (Eds.), *Handbook of sexual assault* (pp. 195–207). New York: Plenum Press.

Freund, K., & Watson, R. J. (1992). The proportions of heterosexual and homosexual pae-dophiles among sex offenders against children: An exploratory study. *Journal of Sex and Marital Therapy, 18,* 34–43.

Freund, K., Watson, R. J., & Dickey R. (1990). Does sexual abuse in childhood cause pe-dophilia: An exploratory study. *Archives of Sexual Behavior, 19,* 557–568.

Furby, L., Weinrott, M. R., & Blackshaw, L. (1989). Sex offender recidivism: A review. *Psychological Bulletin, 105,* 3–30.

Grenier, G., & Byers, E. S. (1997). The relationships among ejaculatory control, ejaculatory latency, and attempts to prolong heterosexual intercourse. *Archives of Sexual Behavior, 26,* 27–47.

Hale, V. E., & Strassberg, D. S. (1990). The role of anxiety on sexual arousal. *Archives of Sexual Behavior, 19,* 569–581.

Hallstrom, T., & Samuelsson, S. (1990). Changes in women's sexual desire in middle life: The longitudinal study of women in Gothenburg. *Archives of Sexual Behavior, 19,* 259–268.

Hanson, R. K., & Bussiere, M. T. (1998). Predicting relapse: A meta-analysis of sexual of-fender recidivism studies. *Journal of Consulting and Clinical Psychology, 66,* 348–362.

Hanson, R. K., Steffy, R. A., & Gauthier, R. (1993). Long-term recidivism of child moles-ters. *Journal of Consulting and Clinical Psychology, 61,* 646–652.

Hariton, E. B., & Singer, J. L. (1974). Women's fantasies during sexual intercourse. *Journal of Consulting and Clinical Psychology, 42,* 313–322.

Hawton, K., Catalan, J., Martin, P., & Fagg, J. (1986). Long-term outcome of sex therapy. *Behavior Research and Therapy, 24,* 665–675.

Heiman, J. R., Gladue, B. A., Roberts, C. W., & LoPiccolo, J. (1986). Historical and current factors discriminating sexually functional from sexually dysfunctional married couples. *Journal of Marital and Family Therapy, 121,* 163–174.

Helmius, G. (1998). The 1996 Swedish sex survey: An introduction and remarks on changes in early sexual experiences. *Scandinavian Journal of Sexology, 1,* 63–70.

Herman, J. L. (1990). Sex offenders: A feminist perspective. In W. L. Marshall, D. R. Laws, & H. E. Barbaree (Eds.), *Handbook of sexual assault* (pp. 177–193). New York: Plenum Press.

Hersen, M., & Bellack, A. S. (1988). *Dictionary of behavioral assessment techniques.* New York: Pergamon Press.

Hunt, M. (1974). *Sexual behavior in the 1970s.* New York: Dell.

Jacobson, N. S., Follette, W. C., Revenstorf, D., Baucom, D. H., Hahlweg, K., & Margolin, G. (1984). Variability in outcome and clinical significance of behavioral marital therapy: A reanalysis of outcome data. *Journal of Consulting and Clinical Psychology, 53,* 497–504.

Jensen, S. B. (1986). Sexual dysfunction in insulin-treated diabetics: A six-year follow-up study of 101 patients. *Archives of Sexual Behavior, 15,* 271–283.

Johnson, A. M., Wadsworth, J., Wellings, K., Field, J., & Bradshaw, S. (1994). *Sexual attitudes and lifestyles.* Oxford, England: Blackwell.

Kaplan, H. S. (1974). *The new sex therapy.* New York: Brunner/Mazel.

Kaplan, H. S. (1977). Hypoactive sexual desire. *Journal of Sex and Marital Therapy, 3,* 3–9.

Kelly, M. P., Strassberg, D. S., & Kircher, J. R. (1990). Attitudinal and experiential correlates of anorgasmia. *Archives of Sexual Behavior, 19,* 165–177.

Kilpatrick, A. C. (1992). *Long-range effects of child and adolescent sexual experiences.* Hillsdale, NJ: Erlbaum.

King, M. B. (1992a). Male rape in institutional settings. In G. C. Mezey & M. B. King (Eds.), *Male victims of sexual assault* (pp. 67–74). Oxford, England: Oxford University Press.

King, M. B. (1992b). Male sexual assault in the community. In G. C. Mezey & M. B. King (Eds.), *Male victims of sexual assault* (pp. 1–12). Oxford, England: Oxford University Press.

Kinsey, A. C., Pomeroy, W. B., & Martin, C. E. (1948). *Sexual behavior in the human male.* Philadelphia: Saunders.

Kinsey, A. C., Pomeroy, W. B., Martin, C. E., & Gebhardt, P. H. (1953). *Sexual behavior in the human female.* Philadelphia: Saunders.

Knight, R. A., & Prentky, R. A. (1990). Classifying sexual offenders. In W. L. Marshall, D. R. Laws, & H. E. Barbaree (Eds.), *Handbook of sexual assault* (pp. 23–52). New York: Plenum Press.

Knight, R. A., Prentky, R. A., & Cerce, D. D. (1994). The development, reliability, and validity of an inventory for the multidimensional assessment of sex and aggression. *Criminal Justice and Behavior, 21,* 72–94.

Knight, R. A., Rosenberg, R., & Schneider, B. A. (1985). Classification of sexual offenders: Perspectives, methods, and validation. In A. W. Burgess (Ed.), *Rape and sexual assault* (pp. 222–293). New York: Garland Press.

Koss, M. P., & Dinero, T. E. (1988). Predictors of sexual aggression among a national sample of male college students. *Annals of the New York Academy of Sciences, 528,* 133–147.

Koss, M. P., & Oros, C. J. (1982). Sexual experiences survey: A research instrument investigating sexual aggression and victimization. *Journal of Consulting and Clinical Psychology, 50,* 455–457.

Kuban, M., Barbaree, H. E., & Blanchard, R. (1999). A comparison of volume and circumference phallometry: Response magnitude and method agreement. *Archives of Sexual Behavior, 28,* 345–359.

Laan, E., Everaerd, W., van Bellen, G., & Hanewald, G. (1994). Women's sexual and emotional responses to male- and female-produced erotica. *Archives of Sexual Behavior, 23,* 153–169.

Lalumiere, M. L., & Quinsey, V. L. (1994). The discriminability of rapists from nonsex offenders using phallometric measures: A meta-analysis. *Criminal Justice and Behavior, 21,* 150–175.

Langevin, R., & Lang, R. A. (1987). The courtship disorders. In G. D. Wilson (Ed.), *Variant sexuality: Research and theory* (pp. 202–228). London: Croom Helm.

Laumann, E. O., Gagnon, J. H., Michael, R. T., & Michaels, S. (1994). *The social organization of sexuality.* Chicago: University of Chicago Press.

Laws, D. R., & Marshall, W. L. (1991). Masturbatory reconditioning with sexual deviates: An evaluative review. *Advances in Behavior Research and Therapy, 13,* 13–25.

Lee, J. (1979). The social organization of sexual risk. *Alternative Lifestyles, 2,* 69–100.

Libman, E., Fichten, C. S., & Brender, W. (1985). The role of therapeutic format in the treatment of sexual dysfunction: A review. *Clinical Psychology Review, 5,* 103–117.

LoPiccolo, J. (1982). Book review. *Archives of Sexual Behavior, 11,* 277–279.

LoPiccolo, J., Heiman, J. R., Hogan, D. R., & Roberts, C. W. (1985). Effectiveness of single therapists versus cotherapy teams in sex therapy. *Journal of Consulting and Clinical Psychology, 53,* 287–294.

LoPiccolo, J., & Steger, J. C. (1974). The sexual interaction inventory: A new instrument for assessment of sexual dysfunction. *Archives of Sexual Behavior, 3,* 585–595.

LoPiccolo, J., & Stock, W. E. (1986). Treatment of sexual dysfunction. *Journal of Consulting and Clinical Psychology, 54,* 158–167.

Lothstein, L. M., & Roback, H. (1984). Black female transsexuals and schizophrenia: A serendipitous finding. *Archives of Sexual Behavior, 13,* 371–390.

MacFarlane, D. F. (1984). Transsexual prostitution in New Zealand: Predominance of people of Maori extraction. *Archives of Sexual Behavior, 13,* 301–309.

Malamuth, N. M. (1989). The attraction to sexual aggression scale: Part two. *Journal of Sex Research, 26,* 324–354.

Malamuth, N. M., & Check, J. V. P. (1983). Sexual arousal to rape depictions: Individual differences. *Journal of Abnormal Psychology, 92,* 55–67.

Maletzky, B. M. (1991). *Treating the sexual offender.* Newbury Park, CA: Sage.

Manecke, R. G., & Mulhall, J. P. (1999). Medical treatment of erectile dysfunction. *Annals of Medicine, 31,* 388–398.

Marques, J. (1999). How to answer the question "Does sexual offender treatment work?" *Journal of Interpersonal Violence, 14,* 437–451.

Marquis, J., Day, D., Nelson, C., & West, M. (1994). Effects of cognitive-behavioral treatment on sex offender recidivism. *Criminal Justice and Behavior, 21,* 28-34.

Marshall, W. L. (1996). Assessment, treatment, and theorizing about sex offenders. *Criminal Justice and Behavior, 23,* 162–199.

Marshall, W. L., & Barbaree, H. E. (1990). Outcome of comprehensive cognitive-behavioral treatment programs. In W. L. Marshall, D. R. Laws, & H. E. Barbaree (Eds.), *Handbook of sexual assault* (pp. 363–385). New York: Plenum Press.

Marshall, W. L., & Eccles, A. (1991). Issues in clinical practice with sex offenders. *Journal of Interpersonal Violence, 6,* 68–93.

Martin, C. E. (1981). Factors affecting sexual functioning in 60–79-year-old married males. *Archives of Sexual Behavior, 10,* 399–420.

Masters, W. H., & Johnson, V. E. (1970). *Human sexual inadequacy.* Boston: Little, Brown.

McConaghy, N. (1967). Penile volume change to moving pictures of male and female nudes in heterosexual and homosexual males. *Behavior Research and Therapy, 5,* 43–48.

McConaghy, N. (1974). Measurements of change in penile dimensions. *Archives of Sexual Behavior, 3,* 381–388.

McConaghy, N. (1977). Behavioral treatment in homosexuality. In M. Hersen, R. M. Eisler, & P. M. Miller (Eds.), *Progress in behavior modification* (Vol. 5, pp. 309–380). New York: Academic Press.

McConaghy, N. (1982). Sexual deviation. In A. S. Bellack, M. Hersen, & A. E. Kazdin (Eds.), *International handbook of behavior therapy and modification* (pp. 683–716). New York: Plenum Press.

McConaghy, N. (1987). Heterosexuality/homosexuality: Dichotomy or continuum. *Archives of Sexual Behavior, 16,* 411–424.

McConaghy, N. (1993). *Sexual behavior: Problems and management.* New York: Plenum Press.

McConaghy, N. (1994). Sexual dysfunctions and deviations: Paraphilias and gender identity disorders. In M. Hersen & S. M. Turner (Eds.), *Diagnostic interviewing* (2nd ed., pp. 211–239). New York: Plenum Press.

McConaghy, N. (1998). Assessment of sexual dysfunction and deviation. In A. S. Bellack & M. Hersen (Eds.), *Behavioral assessment: A practical handbook* (4th ed., pp. 315–341). New York: Pergamon Press.

McConaghy, N. (1999a). Methodological issues concerning evaluation of treatment for sexual offenders: Randomization, treatment dropouts, no-treatment controls, and within-treatment studies. *Sexual Abuse: A Journal of Research and Treatment, 11,* 183–193.

McConaghy, N. (1999b). Unresolved issues in scientific sexology. *Archives of Sexual Behavior, 28,* 285–318.

McConaghy, N., & Armstrong, M. S. (1983). Sexual orientation and consistency of sexual identity. *Archives of Sexual Behavior, 12,* 317–327.

McConaghy, N., Blaszczynski, A., Armstrong, M. S., & Kidson, W. (1989). Resistance to treatment of adolescent sexual offenders. *Archives of Sexual Behavior, 18,* 97–107.

McConaghy, N., Blaszczynski, A., & Kidson, W. (1988). Treatment of sex offenders with imaginal desensitization and/or medroxyprogesterone. *Acta Psychiatrica Scandinavica, 77,* 199–206.

McConaghy, N., Buhrich, N., & Silove, D. (1994). Opposite sex-linked behaviors and homosexual feelings in the predominantly heterosexual male majority. *Archives of Sexual Behavior, 23,* 565–577.

McConaghy, N., & Silove, D. (1991). Opposite sex behaviors correlate with degree of homosexual feelings in the predominantly heterosexual. *Australian and New Zealand Journal of Psychiatry, 25,* 77–83.

McConaghy, N., & Zamir, R. (1995). Heterosexual and homosexual coercion, sexual orientation, and sexual roles in medical students. *Archives of Sexual Behavior, 24,* 489–502.

McConaghy, N., Zamir, R., & Manicavasagar, V. (1993). Nonsexist sexual experiences survey and scale of attraction to sexual aggression. *Australian and New Zealand Journal of Psychiatry, 27,* 686–693.

Mead, M. (1950). *Male and female.* London: Gollancz.

Meisler, A. W., & Carey, M. P. (1990). A critical reevaluation of nocturnal penile tumescence monitoring in the diagnosis of erectile disorder. *Journal of Nervous and Mental Disease, 178,* 78–89.

Meuleman, E. J. H., Bemelmans, B. L. H., Doesburg, W. H., van Asten, W. N. J., Skotnicki, S. H., & Debruyne, F. M. J. (1992). Penile pharmacological duplex ultrasonography: A dose-effect study comparing papaverine, papaverine/phentolamine, and prostaglandin E1. *Journal of Urology, 148,* 63–66.

Milan, R. J., Kilmann, P. R., & Boland, J. P. (1988). Treatment outcome of secondary orgasmic dysfunction: A two- to six-year follow-up. *Archives of Sexual Behavior, 17,* 463–480.

Miner, M. H. (1997). How can we conduct treatment outcome research? *Sexual Abuse: A Journal of Research and Treatment, 9,* 95–110.

Morganstern, K. P. (1988). Behavioral interviewing. In M. Hersen & A. S. Bellack (Eds.), *Behavioral assessment: a practical handbook* (3rd ed., pp. 86–118). New York: Pergamon Press.

Moser, C., & Levitt, E. E. (1987). An exploratory-descriptive study of a sadomasochistically oriented sample. *Journal of Sex Research, 23,* 322–337.

Mulhall, J. P. (2000). Current concepts in erectile dysfunction. *American Journal of Managed Care, 6*(Suppl. 12), S625–S631.

Munjack, D., Cristol, A., Goldstein, A., Phillips, D., Goldberg, A., Whipple, K., et al. (1976). Behavioral treatment of orgasmic dysfunction: A controlled study. *British Journal of Psychiatry, 129,* 497–502.

Munjack, D. J., & Kanno, P. H. (1979). Retarded ejaculation: A review. *Archives of Sexual Behavior, 8,* 139–150.

Nathan, S. (1986). The epidemiology of the *DSM-III* psychosexual dysfunctions. *Journal of Sex and Marital Therapy, 12,* 267–281.

O'Connor, A. A. (1987). Female sex offenders. *British Journal of Psychiatry, 150,* 615–620.

Pena, B. M., & Sweeney, M. (1999). Erectile dysfunction: Estimating prevalence and modeling future practice patterns. *Asian Journal of Surgery, 22,* 257–262.

Person, E. S., Terestman, N., Myers, W. A., Goldberg, E. L., & Salvadori, C. (1989). Gender differences in sexual behaviors and fantasies in a college population. *Journal of Sex and Marital Therapy, 15,* 187–198.

Pfaus, J. G., Myronuk, L. D. S., & Jacobs, W. J. (1986). Soundtrack contents and depicted sexual violence. *Archives of Sexual Behavior, 15,* 231–237.

Phillips, G., & Over, R. (1995). Differences between heterosexual, bisexual, and lesbian women in recalled childhood experiences. *Archives of Sexual Behavior, 24,* 1–20.

Polizzi, D. M., MacKenzie, D. L., & Hickman, L. J. (1999). What works in adult sex offender treatment? A review of prison- and nonprison-based treatment programs. *International Journal of Offender Therapy and Comparative Criminology, 43,* 357–374.

Prentky, R. A., Knight, R. A., Sims-Knight, J. E., Straus, H., Rokous, F., & Cerce, D. (1989). Developmental antecedents of sexual aggression. *Development and Psychopathology, 1,* 153–169.

Quinsey, V. L., & Earls, C. M. (1990). The modification of sexual preferences. In W. L. Marshall, D. R. Laws, & H. E. Barbaree (Eds.), *Handbook of sexual assault* (pp. 279–295). New York: Plenum Press.

Quinsey, V. L., Khanna, A., & Malcolm, P. B. (1998). A retrospective evaluation of the regional treatment center sex offender treatment program. *Journal of Interpersonal Violence, 13,* 621–644.

Raymond, N. C., Coleman, E., Ohlerking, F., Christenson, G. A., & Miner, M. (1999). Psychiatric comorbidity in pedophile sex offenders. *American Journal of Psychiatry, 156,* 786–788.

Reading, A. E. (1983). A comparison of the accuracy and reactivity of methods of monitoring male sexual behavior. *Journal of Behavioral Assessment, 5,* 11–23.

Rind, B., Tromovitch, P., & Bauserman, R. (1998). A meta-analytic examination of assumed properties of child sexual abuse using college samples. *Psychological Bulletin, 124,* 22–53.

Rosen, G. M. (1987). Self-help treatment books and the commercialization of psychotherapy. *American Psychologist, 42,* 46–51.

Rosen, R. C. (2000). Medical and psychological interventions for erectile dysfunction: Toward a combined treatment approach. In S. R. Leiblum & R. C. Rosen (Eds.), *Principles and practice of sex therapy* (3rd ed., pp. 276–304). New York: Guilford Press.

Rosen, R. C., & Ashton, A. K. (1993). Prosexual drugs: Empirical status of the "new aphrodisiacs." *Archives of Sexual Behavior, 22*, 521–543.

Rosen, R. C., & Beck, J. G. (1988). *Patterns of sexual arousal.* New York: Guilford Press.

Russell, D. E. H. (1983). The incidence and prevalence of intrafamilial and extrafamilial sexual abuse of female children. *Child Abuse and Neglect, 7*, 133–146.

Russell, D. E. H. (1986). *The secret trauma: Incest in the lives of girls and women.* New York: Basic Books.

Sakheim, D. K., Barlow, D. H., Beck, J. G., & Abrahamson, D. J. (1985). A comparison of male heterosexual and male homosexual patterns of sexual arousal. *Journal of Sex Research, 21*, 183–198.

Sarrel, P., & Masters, W. (1982). Sexual molestation of men by women. *Archives of Sexual Behavior, 11*, 117–133.

Schiavi, R. C., Schreiner-Engel, P., Mandeli, J., Schanzer, H., & Cohen, E. (1990). Healthy aging and male sexual function. *American Journal of Psychiatry, 147*, 766–771.

Schiavi, R. C., & Segraves, R. T. (1995). The biology of sexual function. *Psychiatric Clinics of North America, 18*, 7–23.

Schott, R. L. (1995). The childhood and family dynamics of transvestites. *Archives of Sexual Behavior, 24*, 309–327.

Schover, L. R., & Leiblum, S. R. (1994). Commentary: The stagnation of sex therapy. *Journal of Psychology and Human Sexuality, 6*, 5–30.

Schulsinger, F. (1972). Psychopathy heredity and environment. *International Journal of Mental Health, 1*, 190–206.

Segraves, R. T., Saran, A., Segraves, K., & Maguire, E. (1993). Clomipramine versus placebo in the treatment of premature ejaculation: A pilot study. *Journal of Sex and Marital Therapy, 19*, 198–200.

Segraves, R. T., Schoenberg, H. W., Zarins, C. K., Camic, P., & Knopf, J. (1981). Characteristics of erectile dysfunction as a function of medical care system entry point. *Psychosomatic Medicine, 43*, 227–234.

Seidman, S. N., & Rieder, R. O. (1994). A review of sexual behavior in the United States. *American Journal of Psychiatry, 151*, 330–341.

Smukler, A. J., & Schiebel, D. (1975). Personality characteristics of exhibitionists. *Diseases of the Nervous System, 36*, 600–603.

Snyder, D. K., & Berg, P. (1983a). Determinants of sexual dissatisfaction in sexually distressed couples. *Archives of Sexual Behavior, 12*, 237–246.

Snyder, D. K., & Berg, P. (1983b). Predicting couples' response to brief directive sex therapy. *Journal of Sex and Marital Therapy, 9*, 114–120.

Sorensen, R. C. (1973). *Adolescent sexuality in contemporary America.* New York: World Publishing.

Sorenson, S. B., Stein, J. A., Siegel, J. M., Golding, J. M., & Burnam, M. A. (1987). The prevalence of adult sexual assault. *American Journal of Epidemiology, 126*, 1154–1164.

Speckens, A. E. M., Hengeveld, M. W., Lycklama a Nijeholt, G., van Hemert, A. M., & Hawton, K. E. (1995). Psychosexual functioning of partners of men with presumed nonorganic erectile dysfunction: Cause or consequence of the disorder? *Archives of Sexual Behavior, 24*, 157–172.

Spector, I. P., & Carey, M. P. (1990). Incidence and prevalence of the sexual dysfunctions: A critical review of the empirical literature. *Archives of Sexual Behavior, 19*, 389–408.

Spence, J. T., & Buckner, C. (1995). Masculinity and femininity: Defining the indefinable. In P. J. Kalbfleish & M. J. Cody (Eds.), *Gender, power, and communication in human relationships* (pp. 105–138). Hillsdale, NJ: Erlbaum.

Steiner, A. E. (1981). Pretending orgasm by men and women: An aspect of communication in relationships. *Dissertation Abstracts International, 42,* 2553-B. (UMI No. 8126396)

Stermac, L. E., Segal, Z. V., & Gillis, R. (1990). Social and cultural factors in sexual assault. In W. L. Marshall, D. R. Laws, & H. E. Barbaree (Eds.), *Handbook of sexual assault* (pp. 143–159). New York: Plenum Press.

Strassberg, D. S., Mahoney, J. M., Schaugaard, M., & Hale, V. E. (1990). The role of anxiety in premature ejaculation: A psychophysiological model. *Archives of Sexual Behavior, 19,* 251–257.

Stuart, F. M., Hammond, D. C., & Pett, M. A. (1987). Inhibited sexual desire in women. *Archives of Sexual Behavior, 16,* 91–106.

Suarez, T., & Miller, J. (2001). Negotiating risks in context: A perspective on unprotected anal intercourse and barebacking among men who have sex with men—Where do we go from here? *Archives of Sexual Behavior, 30,* 287–300.

Swaab, D. F., Zhou, J. N., & Hofman, M. A. (1995, May 25–27). *Sexual differentiation of the human hypothalamus.* Paper presented at the International Behavioral Development Symposium, Minot State University, Minot, ND.

Takefman, J., & Brender, W. (1984). An analysis of the effectiveness of two components in the treatment of erectile dysfunction. *Archives of Sexual Behavior, 13,* 321–340.

Tan, H. L. (2000). Economic cost of male erectile dysfunction using a decision analytic model: For a hypothetical managed-care plan of 100,000 members. *Pharmacoeconomics, 17,* 77–107.

Templeman, T. L., & Stinnett, R. D. (1991). Patterns of sexual arousal and history in a "normal" sample of young men. *Archives of Sexual Behavior, 20,* 137–150.

Tiefer, L., & Melman, A. (1987). Adherence to recommendations and improvement over time in men with erectile dysfunction. *Archives of Sexual Behavior, 16,* 301–309.

Tollison, C. D., Adams, H. E., & Tollison, J. W. (1979). Cognitive and physiological indices of sexual arousal in homosexual, bisexual, and heterosexual males. *Journal of Behavioral Assessment, 1,* 305–314.

Tsoi, W. F. (1990). Developmental profile of 200 male and 100 female transsexuals in Singapore. *Archives of Sexual Behavior, 19,* 595–605.

van Kesteren, P. J., Gooren, L. J., & Megens, J. A. (1996). An epidemiological and demographic study of transsexuals in the Netherlands. *Archives of Sexual Behavior, 25,* 589–600.

van Lankveld, J. J. D., & Grothohann, Y. (2000). Psychiatric comorbidity in heterosexual couples with sexual dysfunction assessed with the composite international diagnostic interview. *Archives of Sexual Behavior, 29,* 479–498.

Waldinger, M. D., Hengeveld, M. W., & Zwinderman, A. H. (1994). Paroxetine treatment of premature ejaculation: A double-blind, randomized, placebo-controlled study. *American Journal of Psychiatry, 151,* 1377–1379.

Weizman, R., & Hart, J. (1987). Sexual behavior in healthy married elderly men. *Archives of Sexual Behavior, 16,* 39–44.

Wincze, J. P., Bansal, S., & Malamud, M. (1986). Effects of medroxyprogesterone acetate on subjective arousal, arousal to erotic stimulation, and nocturnal penile tumescence in male sex offenders. *Archives of Sexual Behavior, 15,* 293–305.

Wincze, J. P., & Carey, M. P. (1991). *Sexual dysfunction.* New York: Guilford Press.

Wolpe, J. (1958). *Psychotherapy by reciprocal inhibition.* Stanford, CA: Stanford University Press.

World Health Organization. (1992). *Composite international diagnostic interview* (Version 1.1). Geneva, Switzerland: Author, Division of Mental Health.

Zilbergeld, B., & Evans, M. (1980). The inadequacy of Masters and Johnson. *Psychology Today, 14,* 29–43.

Zuger, B. (1966). Effeminate behavior present in boys from early childhood. I: The clinical syndrome and follow-up studies. *Journal of Pediatrics, 69,* 1098–1107.

Zuger, B. (1984). Early effeminate behavior in boys: Outcome and significance for homosexuality. *Journal of Nervous and Mental Diseases, 172,* 90–97.

Zuger, B., & Taylor, P. (1969). Effeminate behavior present in boys from early childhood. II: Comparison with similar symptoms in noneffeminate boys. *Pediatrics, 44,* 375–380.

CHAPTER 15

Eating Disorders

J. KEVIN THOMPSON and BILL N. KINDER

EATING DISORDERS ARE some of the most common and debilitative psychological disorders, especially for young girls and women (Striegel-Moore & Smolak, 2001; Thompson & Smolak, 2001a). The medical and psychological complications of eating dysfunction are numerous and lead it to have the highest mortality rate of any psychiatric disorder (Fairburn, Cooper, Doll, Norman, & O'Connor, 2000). Research efforts focused on understanding eating disorders have increased dramatically in recent years. In this chapter, we report on the latest diagnostic, assessment, and etiological developments.

DESCRIPTION OF EATING DISORDERS

There are four categories of eating disorders currently listed in the *Diagnostic and Statistical Manual of Mental Disorders* (*DSM-IV*; American Psychiatric Association [APA], 1994): anorexia nervosa, bulimia nervosa, eating disorder not otherwise specified, and binge-eating disorder (see Table 15.1). Binge-eating disorder is actually included in an appendix of "criteria sets and axes provided for further study"; however, it is reviewed in this chapter for two reasons: It will likely be included as a bona fide eating disorder category in the next revision of the *DSM*, and the disorder has been the subject of intense empirical study in recent years.

ANOREXIA NERVOSA

Any description of anorexia nervosa should begin with the most obvious and critical feature of the disorder, which is the weight status of the individual. The *DSM-IV* quantifies this criterion as a body weight of "85% of that expected" (APA, 1994, p. 544). Reference to average weight charts for adults or expected weight gain during growth periods (pediatric charts) are often used to assist in this assessment. Typically, individuals who present with the clinical picture of anorexia nervosa have a much lower body weight to height than 85% of that expected. A clinical picture of emaciation or cachexia is often easily observable, and such malnourishment in the absence of any medical or physiological disturbance directs

Table 15.1
Diagnostic and Research Criteria for Eating Disorders

Diagnostic Criteria for Anorexia Nervosa

A. Refusal to maintain body weight at or above a minimally normal weight for age and height (e.g., weight loss leading to maintenance of body weight less than 85% of that expected; or failure to make expected weight gain during period of growth, leading to body weight less than 85% of that expected).

B. Intense fear of gaining weight or becoming fat, even though underweight.

C. Disturbance in the way in which one's body weight or shape is experienced, undue influence of body weight or shape on self-evaluation, or denial of the seriousness of the current low body weight.

D. In postmenarcheal females, amenorrhea, i.e., the absence of at least three consecutive menstrual cycles. (A woman is considered to have amenorrhea if her periods occur only following hormone, e.g., estrogen, administration.)

Specify Type:

Restricting Type: During the current episode of anorexia nervosa, the person has not regularly engaged in binge-eating or purging behavior (i.e., self-induced vomiting or the misuse of laxatives, diuretics, or enemas).

Binge-Eating/Purging Type: During the current episode of anorexia nervosa, the person has regularly engaged in binge-eating or purging behavior (i.e., self-induced vomiting or the misuse of laxatives, diuretics, or enemas).

Diagnostic Criteria for Bulimia Nervosa

A. Recurrent episodes of binge eating. An episode of binge eating is characterized by both of the following:

   1. Eating, in a discrete period of time (e.g., within any 2-hour period), an amount of food that is definitely larger than most people would eat during a similar period of time and under similar circumstances.

   2. A sense of lack of control over eating during the episode (e.g., a feeling that one cannot stop eating or control what or how much one is eating).

B. Recurrent inappropriate compensatory behavior in order to prevent weight gain, such as self-induced vomiting; misuse of laxatives, diuretics, enemas, or other medications; fasting; or excessive exercise.

C. The binge eating and inappropriate compensatory behaviors both occur, on average, at least twice a week for 3 months.

D. Self-evaluation is unduly influenced by body shape and weight.

E. The disturbance does not occur exclusively during episodes of Anorexia Nervosa.

Specify Type:

Purging Type: During the current episode of bulimia nervosa, the person has regularly engaged in self-induced vomiting or the misuse of laxatives, diuretics, or enemas.

Nonpurging Type: During the current episode of bulimia nervosa, the person has used other inappropriate compensatory behaviors, such as fasting or excessive exercise, but has not regularly engaged in self-induced vomiting or the misuse of laxatives, diuretics, or enemas.

Table 15.1   *(Continued)*

Research Criteria for Binge-Eating Disorder

A. Recurrent episodes of binge eating. An episode of binge eating is characterized by both of the following:
   1. Eating, in a discrete period of time (e.g., within any 2-hour period), an amount of food that is definitely larger than most people would eat in a similar period of time under similar circumstances.
   2. A sense of lack of control over eating during the episode (e.g., a feeling that one cannot stop eating or control what or how much one is eating).

B. The binge-eating episodes are associated with three (or more) of the following:
   1. Eating much more rapidly than normal.
   2. Eating until feeling uncomfortably full.
   3. Eating large amounts of food when not feeling physically hungry.
   4. Eating alone because of being embarrassed by how much one is eating.
   5. Feeling disgusted with oneself, depressed, or very guilty after overeating.

C. Marked distress regarding binge eating is present.

D. The binge eating occurs, on average, at least 2 days a week for 6 months.

   Note: The method of determining frequency differs from that used for bulimia nervosa; future research should address whether the preferred method of setting a frequency threshold is counting the number of days on which binges occur or counting the number of episodes of binge eating.

E. The binge eating is not associated with the regular use of inappropriate compensatory behaviors (e.g., purging, fasting, excessive exercise) and does not occur exclusively during the course of anorexia nervosa or bulimia nervosa.

Eating Disorder Not Otherwise Specified

The Eating Disorder Not Otherwise Specified category is for disorders of eating that do not meet the criteria for any specific Eating Disorder. Examples include:

   1. For females, all of the criteria for anorexia nervosa are met except that the individual has regular menses.
   2. All of the criteria for anorexia nervosa are met except that, despite significant weight loss, the individual's current weight is in the normal range.
   3. All of the criteria for bulimia nervosa are met except that the binge eating and inappropriate compensatory mechanisms occur at a frequency of less than twice a week or for a duration of less than 3 months.
   4. The regular use of inappropriate compensatory behavior by an individual of normal body weight after eating small amounts of food (e.g., self-induced vomiting after the consumption of two cookies).
   5. Repeatedly chewing and spitting out, but not swallowing, large amounts of food.
   6. Binge-eating disorder: recurrent episodes of binge eating in the absence of the regular use of inappropriate compensatory behaviors characteristic of bulimia nervosa.

Source: From American Psychiatric Association, 1994, *Diagnostic and Statistical Manual of Mental Disorders* (4th ed.), Washington, DC: Author.

the clinician to a consideration of a diagnosis of anorexia nervosa. Walsh and Garner (1997) also emphasize that a rigid adherence to the weight criterion may not be advisable if the patient meets all other criteria for diagnosis, yet misses the weight cutoff (i.e., weighing 90% of that expected).

Individuals with this disorder also usually report an extreme dissatisfaction or disparagement of their appearance, insisting that they are not underweight and expressing a desire to maintain their current weight status or even lose more weight. Such a disturbance of the "body image" may manifest in subjective dissatisfaction, behavioral avoidance (for instance, of evaluating oneself in a mirror or attending social functions), disturbed cognitions ("Everyone notices my fat stomach"), and, possibly, perceptual overestimation of body size (Thompson, Heinberg, Altabe, & Tantleff-Dunn, 1999). An intense fear of gaining weight, often referred to as a pursuit of thinness, is also very characteristic, and may be indicated by symptoms such as avoidance of highly caloric foods, excessive exercise, and presence of purgative activities (laxative use, diuretics, self-induced vomiting). Purgative activities are often thought of as confined to the diagnosis of bulimia nervosa; however, the *DSM-IV* notes that such behaviors may occur during the time period when an individual meets the weight criteria of anorexia nervosa. Such individuals should receive the subtype specification of *binge-eating/purging type* (APA, 1994, p. 545; see also Table 15.1). Individuals who maintain their low weight status without reliance on purgative methods are classified as *restricting* subtype.

Because of the intense biological disruption engendered by excessive weight loss and caloric restriction, many individuals experience a severe disruption of normal menstrual cycle functioning. The *DSM-IV* requires the absence of three consecutive menstrual periods for a diagnosis of anorexia nervosa, however, this criterion is perhaps the most problematic and controversial of the four criteria. Often menstrual functioning is disrupted and irregular, but amenorrhea does not eventuate. In addition, the criterion is not appropriate or applicable to men. However, the International Classification of Diseases (ICD-10; World Health Organization [WHO], 1992) criteria include evidence of testosterone function alterations in men by indications of loss of sexual potency or interest. For these reasons, many researchers do not require that patients meet this criterion for inclusion in research studies, and its relevance for clinical psychotherapy and/or pharmacological management is debatable.

BULIMIA NERVOSA

This disorder is most easily contrasted with anorexia nervosa in terms of the amount of food consumed. Whereas individuals with anorexia nervosa greatly restrict intake and, even in the case of the binge-purge subtype, typically do not consume excessively large quantities of food, individuals with bulimia nervosa may intake vast quantities of food. The food is normally eaten in a short period of time with psychological concomitants of a sense of distress and a feeling of lack of control over the binging behavior. There is often a sense that once eating begins, it is impossible to stop until finished. Most often, such binges are followed by severe self-disparagement and a sense that something must be done to undo the potential damage of ingesting such a large level of calories. Therefore, commonly, a variety of purgative methods are employed, including self-induced vomiting, laxatives, diuretics, enemas, purgative-inducing medications, fasting, and excessive exercise.

As with anorexia nervosa, there are two subtypes; in the case of bulimia nervosa, the two categories are *purging* type and *nonpurging* type. The distinction is in the type of compensatory procedure that the individual uses to "handle" the excessive food intake so that excessive calories are not stored as fat and enhance weight gain. In the purging type, the individual either self-induces vomiting, uses diuretics or laxatives, or performs enemas. In the nonpurging type, other types of compensatory, yet nonpurging, behaviors are used, such as fasting or excessive exercise.

BINGE-EATING DISORDER

This disorder was recently added to the *DSM,* yet was assigned to a section for disorders in need of further study. It has features in common with bulimia nervosa—the description of the criterion for recurrent binge eating is identical to that for bulimia nervosa (see Table 15.1). However, the frequency requirement is different—for a diagnosis of bulimia nervosa, the binge eating occurs at least twice a week for three months, but for binge-eating disorder, the criterion is two days a week for six months. Of greater importance is the essential defining feature that distinguishes between the two eating disorders; to be diagnosed with binge-eating disorder, the individual does not use any compensatory behaviors (purging or nonpurging types) as a consequence of binging. In addition, there is no body image disturbance criterion for binge-eating disorder, whereas there is for bulimia nervosa. A fourth difference between the two disorders is the chance to rate the occurrence of five different binge-associated features for binge-eating disorder, with three of the options required for diagnosis (see Table 15.1).

EATING DISORDERS NOT OTHERWISE SPECIFIED (EDNOS)

The EDNOS category is used typically for cases in which one or more of the required criteria are not met, yet there is evidence that the individual's level of eating disturbance meets a degree of severity that warrants clinical attention. Other examples might be someone who engages in compensatory behaviors, yet the "binge" consists of small amounts of food that would not meet the *DSM-IV* definition of "an amount of food that is definitely larger than most people would eat during a similar period of time and under similar circumstances" (APA, 1994, p. 549). Another example might be an individual who chews and spits out, but does not swallow, large amounts of food.

Case Study

Case Identification and Presenting Complaints

Ms. T. was a 17-year-old White college freshman who was referred to therapy by her father. At the time of initial assessment, she weighed 85 pounds, distributed on a 5 ft. 5 in. frame. She reported no problem with binge eating or self-induced vomiting; however, she used laxatives occasionally (once a week) to relieve a "feeling of constipation." She exercised approximately one hour each day, reported a fear of obesity, and weighed herself several times a day. Her meals consisted primarily of vegetables, fruits, and cottage cheese.

(Continued)

History

She reported that her problem began approximately four years before when her sister left home to get married. At this time, Ms. T. began to lose weight and was hospitalized. Treatment with a behavior modification program followed, and she gained to within a normal weight range for her age. However, shortly after discharge, she gradually began to lose weight again. Shortly thereafter, she saw a psychiatrist, who prescribed Tagamet for stomach problems, a medication she continued to take. She had most recently been seen by her school counselor. Her weight had fluctuated from 80 to 100 pounds during the four years from onset of dieting to the current assessment.

She reported that her mother was quiet, dependent, prone to stomach problems, and currently seeing a psychiatrist. She described a poor relationship with her father, noting a disdain for his drinking and relating an inability to talk with him. She reported a history of family conflicts about her weight. When she was 10, her father stated that she was "too fat" and required her mother to seek medical assistance for Ms. T.'s problems. She reported that family arguments often took place at the dinner table, causing her to lose her appetite. Recently, her father almost denied her permission to enter college because of her weight status. She stated that her desire to maintain weight following her earlier treatment was challenged by her father, who insisted that she gain weight. She maintained that this attitude contributed to her continued weight loss. She reported considerable difficulty expressing feelings to others and noted that she felt totally dependent on her parents.

She also noted considerable stress at school, despite having no difficulty with academics. At her parents' urging, she had joined a sorority but now had reservations about the decision. She said that sorority-mates constantly commented on her weight, which disturbed her, but she failed to reply, not knowing how to handle the situation. She also reported dissatisfaction with the sorority's focus on appearance and social demands. She reported that a commonality between home and school life was a lack of independence, stating "someone is always telling me what to do." In addition, she reported that her new friends, in repeating an old theme of focusing on her weight, were trying to change her in a manner similar to that of her father. She indicated increasing feelings of confusion, withdrawal, depression, and "being out of control" (case excerpted from Thompson & Williams, 1987, pp. 246–247).

Case Assessment

Assessment included a focus on initial interview and additional measures to document presence of *DSM* criteria and associated features of eating disturbance. The Minnesota Multiphasic Personality Inventory (MMPI), Eating Attitudes Test, Eating Disorder Inventory, and Zung Depression Inventory were administered. Additionally, the patient self-monitored eating behaviors and thoughts/emotions associated with such behaviors. She easily met the weight criteria for anorexia nervosa and also met the other required symptoms for diagnosis. She scored in the moderately depressed range on the Zung, but in the subclinical range on all scales of the MMPI. Her body dissatisfaction scores on a subscale of the Eating Disorder Inventory indicated moderate levels of body dissatisfaction with weight-relevant body sites (waist, hips, thighs). Self-monitoring corroborated self-report in that interpersonal situations and mealtimes were associated with considerable emotional distress and disturbed food-related cognitions.

This case illustrates several of the formative experiences and related features often present in individuals with an eating disorder. Her focus on appearance apparently began at an early age, most likely fostered by her father's feeling that she needed to lose weight. Dependency and lack of control may have been fostered by the decision to take her to a variety of physicians because of her inability to control her weight. She felt an early lack of acceptance by family because of her overweight status. Eating, or not eating (which occurred later) became the central focus of her family interactions and a defining feature of her personality. Mealtimes were associated with stress and family discord, leading to emotional upset and stomach problems, producing a conditioned aversion to meals and food. At an early age, she learned to evaluate herself in terms of body size and appearance. Interpersonal interactions, with family and peers, often centered around food and appearance, rather than a broader array of social and interpersonal topics. After losing a substantial amount of weight, in fact, reaching an anorexic weight status, it became increasingly difficult to eat reasonable amounts of food because of a feeling of fullness and constipation. Such feelings led to greater food avoidance and excessive exercise.

EPIDEMIOLOGY

Considerable effort has gone into analysis of issues related to epidemiology of eating disorders. There is not only some debate concerning the actual prevalence of the well-established eating disorders of anorexia nervosa and bulimia nervosa, but also minimal data on prevalence of binge-eating disorder. Researchers have begun to address, yet not fully determine, if eating disorders are increasing in prevalence. In addition, research on the prevalence with younger ages, that is, childhood and adolescence, offers unique challenges.

The *DSM-IV* puts the prevalence rate for anorexia nervosa at approximately 1% and between 1% to 3% for bulimia nervosa (APA, 1994). These numbers have generally been supported by research studies and other reviews of prevalence and incidence statistics (Lucas, Beard, O'Fallon, & Kurland, 1988; Nielson, 2001; Walters & Kendler, 1995; Williamson, Zucker, Martin, & Smeets, 2001). However, there is some variability across studies and age groups. Walters and Kendler found an overall prevalence rate of 0.51%. Pawluck and Gorey found that the rate for females ages 13 to 19 was five times greater than that for other age groups. Although the data for binge-eating disorder are far less conclusive, it appears that the incidence may be between 1% and 3% (Striegel-Moore et al., 2000; Varnado et al., 1997).

Gender differences are usually prominent, especially for adults. Generally, women outnumber men by a 10 to 1 ratio; however, this ratio may be significantly less for anorexia nervosa and bulimia nervosa at the younger ages and for all ages with reference to binge-eating disorder (Nielson, 2001). Statistics for children and adolescents indicate that the rate for anorexia nervosa and bulimia nervosa may be a bit lower than that found for adults (Thompson & Smolak, 2001b), and the rate of binge-eating disorder is much lower, perhaps around 1% (Rosenvinge, Sundgot-Borgen, & Borresen, 1999). Interestingly, many prevalence rate studies do not include the category of *eating disorder not otherwise specified,* which may add perhaps 50% more cases of possible clinically relevant treatment cases (Nicholls, Chater, & Lask, 2000). These cases, which may also be referred to as *partial syndrome* or *subthreshold* eating disorders, may increase the numbers of individuals considered "eating disturbed" dramatically. For instance, Shisslak, Crago, and Estes (1995), in a review of adolescent studies, found a prevalence rate of partial syndrome that ranged from 1.78% to 13.3%.

One of the most comprehensive examinations of prevalence was recently reported by Lewinsohn (2001). Adolescent females were followed for more than 10 years and assessed periodically for the presence of eating disturbances. By age 24, 1.4% had anorexia nervosa and 2.8% had bulimia nervosa. Additionally, 4.4% met criteria for a partial syndrome.

CLINICAL PICTURE

The clinical presentation of someone with an eating disorder may manifest in many different ways, especially given the recent addition of binge-eating disorder to the research and clinical arena. The classic case of the restricting anorexic who is resistant to treatment and has little insight into her "distorted" body image is one vignette often sensationalized by media, yet this might be a good place to begin, for it offers a distinct clinical picture that allows for a quite clear differentiation with bulimia nervosa and binge-eating disorder. Such individuals typically have an early onset, possibly in the late adolescent years, and have never had a normal menstrual cycle or may even have primary amenorrhea (never having experienced a menstrual period). The restriction is quite severe, and these individuals may consume significantly less than 1,000 calories a day, for an extended period of time. Weight is significantly below average, perhaps at a level of 60% to 70% of expected. Treatment is met with much resistance and even subterfuge, such as hiding ankle weights or other heavy objects under clothing to increase observed weight during weighings. The denial of illness that has often been used to characterize the lack of insight may involve a perceptual inability and/or psychological denial of the emaciated body. Perfectionistic and obsessive-compulsive features are paramount, and may consist of excessive and obligatory exercise patterns, rigid adherence to daily routines, and food hoarding. In fact, a preoccupation with food may include activities such as preparing food for others and conversations that center on food. This seemingly paradoxical behavior (for someone who doesn't eat and is afraid of weight gain) might be explained by the central control issue that food is for the eating-disordered patient: What better way to illustrate to yourself and others a control of eating than by preparing food for others and organizing your life around food, yet not eating it?

This classic picture of the restrictor subtype can now be contrasted with a similar, perhaps stereotypical, view of the individual with bulimia nervosa. Such an individual is usually of normal or average weight, or only slightly overweight, yet is extremely distressed by her weight status. Restriction may have been attempted and, in fact, may have been successful at some point, but now the individual is in a cyclic pattern of overeating and compensating, either via purging or nonpurging means. Overeating, following the *DSM-IV*-required definition, is definitely a binge: Some individuals with bulimia nervosa may consume 30 times the caloric value that is recommended or normal for a single meal (Beumont, 1995). The binging creates a physical sensation of discomfort, along with a psychological state of extreme anxiety and depression. Getting rid of the food is essential to restore some level of equilibrium. Unfortunately, this strategy is generally followed by temporary relief, the return of hunger (due to the lack of satiety), and another attempt at restriction to reduce body weight. Hunger and perhaps unrealistic restriction of food intake set the stage for an eventual failure, that is, eating a forbidden food or too much of some food, leading to another binge. Interpreting any variation from planned restriction a failure, many patients consider even small intakes of forbidden foods a violation of their planned abstinence and feel the relief that they can now eat all they want, having already decided that compensatory activities will be necessary (additionally, overeating along with significant water intake, makes self-induced vomiting easier to achieve).

The typical individual with bulimia nervosa does not evidence the resistance to treatment, denial, and lack of insight into her problem that is often found with the restricting anorexic. Such individuals are very disturbed by the food intake patterns that they have developed, and depression is a common comorbid feature. In addition, there exists a great deal of shame and guilt associated with the depression. In contrast to anorexics' subjective sense that they are in "control" and would prefer to be left alone, bulimics prototypically feel "out of control" and in desperate need of someone to help them handle their problem.

These general vignettes are oversimplifications of the full range of manifestations of individuals with eating disorders. Perhaps 30% to 40% of the individuals who meet the diagnosis of anorexia nervosa also binge and purge, necessitating an assignment to the binge-eating/purging type. These patients may be at an anorexic weight, but the distress, depression, and feeling out of control magnitude is more like that of the bulimic case described than the restrictor anorexic. In fact, except for the weight criterion, the individual would receive assignment to the *DSM* category for bulimia nervosa. Additionally, body image disturbance is a required criterion for both anorexia and bulimia, and this core characteristic has been found empirically to exist in both disorders.

The clinical picture of the individual with binge-eating disorder is very similar to that of the individual with bulimia nervosa. As noted earlier, the diagnostic criteria are quite similar between the two conditions. There is a difference in the frequency-duration criterion concerning binge eating; however, this does not affect the clinical presentation of binging. An additional list of binge-related features is required for binge-eating disorder (i.e., feeling embarrassed, disgusted, or depressed about the binge); however, these features are also present in individuals with bulimia nervosa. The primary *DSM*-related difference is in the requirement that binge-eating-disordered individuals may not engage in any compensatory behaviors. Therefore, the presence of purging and nonpurging compensation (i.e., vomiting, excessive exercise, laxatives, and so on) indicates the bulimia nervosa diagnosis. There is also no weight criterion for distinguishing bulimia nervosa from binge-eating disorder, so these individuals may present similarly in this regard. Evidence suggests that individuals with binge-eating disorder may, on average, be heavier than people with bulimia nervosa (Johnson & Torgrud, 1996). Perhaps this is a consequence of not engaging in compensatory methods.

COURSE AND PROGNOSIS

Eating disorders have the highest mortality rate of any psychiatric disorder (Fairburn et al., 2000) and also have one of the highest rates of hospitalization and suicidality (Newman, Moffitt, Caspi, Magdol, Silva, & Stanton, 1996). Mortality rates vary, but appear to be much higher for individuals with anorexia nervosa. Estimates for anorexia nervosa cluster around 5% to 6% (Agras, 2001; Herzog et al., 2000; Sullivan, 1995), with about half the deaths attributable to suicide and the rest related to physical complications of the disorder. The rate for bulimia nervosa may be closer to 0.5% to 1% or a bit higher (e.g., Agras, 2001; Nielson, 2001). On the positive side, however, Steinhausen (1995) reviewed the treatment outcome literature from the 1950s to the 1980s and found that about one-third of cases of anorexia nervosa improved, one-fifth had a chronic course, and two-fifths recovered. Ten-year follow-up studies also indicate that approximately three-fifths of individuals with bulimia nervosa are in full or partial remission (Herzog et al., 1999).

Much less is known about the course of binge-eating disorder. Fairburn et al. (2000) followed two cohorts of individuals with either bulimia nervosa or binge-eating disorder prospectively for a period of five years. At follow-up, only 9% of the original binge-eating disorder sample still had the disorder; 15% of the original bulimia nervosa group continued to meet criteria for bulimia nervosa. However, some of the individuals in the initial groups developed a different eating disorder at follow-up. For instance, 7% of the original bulimia nervosa sample met criteria for binge-eating disorder and 32% met criteria for EDNOS. For the binge-eating sample, at five-year follow-up, 12% met EDNOS criteria and 3% had bulimia nervosa.

Another interesting aspect of the course of eating disorders is the finding that perhaps 25% to 30% of individuals who seek treatment for bulimia nervosa report a previous history of anorexia nervosa (Klump, Kaye, & Strober, 2001). Herzog and colleagues, in a 7.5-year prospective study, found that 16% of women with restricting anorexia nervosa developed bulimia nervosa and 7% of women with bulimia nervosa developed anorexia nervosa (Herzog et al., 1999). Such findings question the temporal stability of the diagnostic categories, as well as whether a categorical or dimensional model best characterizes eating disturbance (Anderson & Williamson, 2002; Herzog & Delinsky, 2001).

It is important to further evaluate the course for individuals with eating disorder in future studies. Many individuals with binge-eating disorder are also obese; therefore, morbidity and mortality rates might be expected to be higher than in the general population. Excessive weight is associated with a multitude of physical complications (Pomeroy, 1996); such issues, plus the disordered-eating patterns, indicate that individuals with binge-eating disorder may need to be followed carefully from a clinical perspective.

DIAGNOSTIC CONSIDERATIONS

As with many *DSM* categories, there is continuing debate as to utility and accuracy of the current system. Frequency and duration criteria for the binge eating in bulimia nervosa ("twice a week for 3 months") and binge-eating disorder ("2 days a week for 6 months") are often criticized as somewhat arbitrary. Striegel-Moore, Wilson, Wilfley, Elder, and Brownell (1998) found that individuals with binge-eating disorder who met all criteria except these were similar psychologically and behaviorally to individuals who met all criteria. Individuals with bulimia nervosa who binge only once a week do not seem to differ substantially from those who meet the binge criterion (Sullivan, Bulik, & Kendler, 1998; Walsh et al., 1997). Defining what constitutes a *binge* is also a problem that has produced some concern among researchers. The *DSM* criteria require an "objective" binge, yet many individuals define even small amounts of food as a subjective binge, leading them to engage in compensatory methods. Some researchers suggest that the loss of control or dysphoria associated with the binge should be used in defining it (Beglin & Fairburn, 1992; Telch & Agras, 1996).

The amenorrhea criterion for anorexia nervosa is also problematic, given that it is a physical sequelae of starvation and lower body fat/weight, and not generally seen as a cause of either the psychology or physiology of the disorder. In addition, some women, even at low weights, do not experience menstrual flow disruption (Cachelin & Maher, 1998).

The body image criterion, required for the diagnosis of anorexia nervosa and bulimia nervosa, but not binge-eating disorder, is also a topic of dissension among researchers. Research suggests that shape concerns are present in binge-eating disorder, yet there is no criterion related to body image in the *DSM-IV* criteria (Thompson, 1996). Also, the wording of the criteria for anorexia nervosa is more extensive than that for bulimia nervosa, despite little evidence distinguishing the types of body image disturbance between the two eating disorders (Thompson, 1996).

The continuing problem of many cases not meeting the specific criteria of anorexia nervosa, bulimia nervosa, or binge-eating disorder, thus necessitating confinement to the EDNOS category, led Andersen, Bowers, and Watson (2001) to propose an alternative system (see Table 15.2). Their classification scheme allows for a much broader labeling of symptoms for anorexia nervosa and bulimia nervosa and also, controversially, does not include a binge-eating disorder category.

Bulik, Sullivan, and Kendler (2000) also addressed the current classification system problems. They criticized the development of the current *DSM* eating disorder category because of the reliance on clinical samples for data evaluation, noting that only a subset of women seek treatment and that referral bias may be a factor. They sought to evaluate a nonbiased sample by using an epidemiological methodology, assessing via interview 2,163 female twins from a population-based registry. Using latent class analysis, they developed an empirically based categorization of eating disorders. Interestingly, they found that a six-class solution fit the data best, with three of the classes resembling the extant categories (anorexia nervosa, bulimia nervosa, binge-eating disorder). However, they also found potential separate classifications—one based on "distorted eating attitudes without low body weight" and two classes with "low weight without the psychological features of eating disorders" (Bulik et al., 2000, p. 886).

DUAL DIAGNOSIS

Another important issue with respect to diagnostic considerations is the possible co-occurrence of other Axis I disorders or Axis II personality disorders. A

Table 15.2

Proposed Diagnostic Criteria for Anorexia Nervosa, Bulimia Nervosa, and Eating Disorders Not Otherwise Specified

Anorexia Nervosa (AN)

1. Substantial self-induced weight loss (or lack of normal weight gain), leading to significant physiologic, psychologic, and social signs of starvation, including, but not limited to, bradycardia, hypothermia, reproductive hormone abnormally (decreased frequency or intensity of menses in women; decreased sexual drive and lowered testosterone in males), diminished mental concentration, social isolation, and depressive affect. Although the final weight will often be less than 85% of normal population weight, this is not an absolute requirement if weight loss is substantial, usually greater than 20% of initial weight.

2. The presence of a morbid fear of fatness, a relentless drive for thinness that overrides personal awareness of weight loss consequences or both, or the admonitions of a clinician, parent, significant other, or responsible other person, such a teacher or coach, to restore weight.

3. The presence of the weight loss and physiologic, social, or psychologic consequences or a combination of these consequences is present for at least 3 months.

4. Self-esteem and mood are excessively dependent on attaining or sustaining significant weight loss despite medical, social, or psychologic consequences and admonitions of responsible and knowledgeable persons.

5. No clear medical causation is present. In general, most of the physiologic signs and symptoms of AN are secondary to the weight loss and not causative.

   Commonly found, but not essential to diagnosis, are (a) denial of thinness, (b) distorted body image, (c) denial of sexuality, (d) low mood.

   Subtypes:

   A. Pure food restricting AN (ANR), characterized by limitation of food intake, with or without overexercising, but excluding the presence of binge episodes, or purging by vomiting, laxative abuse, or diuretics.

   B. Binge-purge subtype AN (AN/BP) meeting above diagnostic criteria and including binge episodes, purging by any method or both, with or without overexercising.

Bulimia Nervosa (BN)

1. Presence of binge episodes characterized typically by larger than normal amounts of food, usually eaten more quickly than normal, often consisting of increased sweets and fats, consumed to the point of medical discomfort or psychologic distress, especially guilt, remorse, or regret.

2. Presence of a morbid fear of fatness and a pursuit of thinness.

3. Binge episodes present on the average twice a week for 3 months.

4. Excessive dependence of self-esteem or mood on body size and shape.

5. No clear primary medical cause.

   Subtypes:

   A. BN, purging subtype, includes the presence of binge episodes with purging by self-induced vomiting, laxative, diuretics, or other methods.

   B. BN, compensation by nonpurging means, presence of binge episodes, followed by nonpurging compensation including severe food restriction and overexercising.

   C. BN, no compensation, also called BED, includes binge episodes leading to psychologic or medical distress, without consistent compensation.

   D. Night-eating syndrome: includes binge eating occurring only, or primarily, at night.

Table 15.2 *(Continued)*

Eating Disorders Not Otherwise Specified

1. The presence of abnormal attitudes and behaviors toward food and weight, primarily dissatisfaction with body weight or shape, with resulting functional impairment in eating behavior, medical symptomatology, social or psychologic functioning, not meeting criteria for AN or BN.

2. Exclusion of clear primary medical causation.

   Subtypes:

   A. Significant and continued psychologic distress concerning body weight and shape, without significant weight loss.
   B. Abnormal eating behavior not meeting current criteria for AN or BN, for example, chewing and spitting out food when associated with fear of fatness/drive for thinness/distress concerning body size or shape.
   C. Self-induced weight loss, meeting criteria for AN, but without comorbid psychopathology requisite for diagnosis of AN.
   D. Binge or purge episodes without identifiable psychopathology required for BN.

Source: From "A Slimming Program for Eating Disorders Not Otherwise Specified: Reconceptualizing a Confusing, Residual Diagnostic Category," by A. E. Andersen, W. A. Bowers, and T. Watson, 2001, *The Psychiatric Clinics of North America, 24,* pp. 271–281. Reprinted with permission of the author.

variety of disorders are comorbid with anorexia nervosa. Depression meeting *DSM* criteria may be present in one-third of cases and lifetime diagnosis of major depression may reach 60% (Agras, 2001). Symptoms of depression contemporaneous with a diagnosis of anorexia nervosa may be present in an even higher percentage of cases (Williamson et al., 2001). Anxiety disorders, particularly obsessive-compulsive disorder and social phobia, also commonly occur in individuals with anorexia nervosa, with lifetime prevalence data ranging from 20% to 65% (Wonderlich & Mitchell, 1997; Williamson et al., 2000). A secondary diagnosis of personality disorder may approach 50% (Agras, 2001), with disorders such as obsessive-compulsive and avoidant personality common.

Depression is also commonly a feature of bulimia nervosa. Agras (2001) noted that about 20% may have current major depression and one-half may develop major depression at some point concurrent with the eating disorder. Half of patients with bulimia nervosa may experience current anxiety disorders and perhaps two-thirds develop such disorders during the course of their eating disorder (Williamson et al., 2001). Estimates of the comorbidity of personality disorders vary widely from study to study; however, Dennis and Sansone (1997) found an average prevalence rate of 34%. In particular, borderline personality has been found to coexist with bulimia nervosa, with rates ranging from 2% to 47% (Wonderlich, 1995). Substance abuse may be evident in 25% of cases (Agras, 2001).

Binge-eating disorder is also associated with a current diagnosis of major depression in approximately 40% to 50% of cases (Williamson et al., 2001). Personality disorders, including histrionic, borderline, and avoidant may affect one-third or more of cases (Yanovski, Nelson, Dubbert, & Spitzer, 1993). Alcohol abuse may affect one-third of individuals with binge-eating disorder (Eldredge & Agras, 1996).

Methodological issues are of concern when considering comorbidity. The drastic weight loss and compromised biological status of the individual with anorexia nervosa may contribute to the symptomatology of depression. Obsessive-compulsive characteristics may follow, rather than precede, many of the characteristic symptoms of anorexia nervosa (food preoccupation, hoarding, etc.). Axis II diagnoses for individuals with bulimia nervosa are also problematic—borderline is often diagnosed; however, the criterion of impulsivity for borderline notes eating disturbance as one possible facet. Some conceptual overlap may exist between the two disorders, resulting in potential criterion contamination. Coprevalence of disorders certainly has clinical significance; however, it may tell us little about specific mechanisms or the directionality of causality. Future research should address such issues (Westen & Harnden-Fischer, 2001).

PSYCHOLOGICAL AND BIOLOGICAL ASSESSMENT

Any comprehensive assessment of eating disorders includes a broad array of strategies to determine the biological, physiological, behavioral, cognitive, and affective components of the presenting picture. We begin with some of the basic physical assessment methods that should be undertaken, usually by a physician, to understand the biological and physiological aspects of the eating disorder (see also Hill & Pomeroy, 2001; Pomeroy, 1996).

BIOLOGICAL ASSESSMENT

An initial physical exam may reveal abnormalities in various body systems, such as the cardiovascular, hematologic, gastrointestinal, renal, endocrine, and skeletal systems, as well as indicating avenues for laboratory testing. Such an exam might give information concerning the current state of inanition and hydration, and might also include a dental, dermatological, and gynecological evaluation. A history should accompany the exam; it might focus on issues such as weight/dieting, menstrual history, chemical abuse and dependency, and any purgative activity (vomiting, diuretics, laxatives, etc.).

Specific medical complications may be associated with dysfunction of different systems. In terms of the potential cardiovascular problems, tachycardia, hypotension, ventricular arrhythmias, and cardiac failure are possibilities. Arrhythmias may develop, often due to electrolyte problems, and these may be fatal. In the case of bulimic patients who use ipecac to induce vomiting, irreversible myocardial damage may eventuate.

Dermatological assessment may reveal carotenodermia (yellowing skin due to excessive carotene intake) and lanugo hair (emergence of soft, light-colored hair in nontraditional places such as the face and back). Russell's sign, which is a distinct change in the skin over the dorsum of the hand caused by trauma during self-induced vomiting, may be present in some cases. Dental assessment may reveal decalcification of the surfaces of the teeth, as well as possible gum problems.

Gastrointestinal evaluation often finds esophageal complications, such as dismotility. Decreased stomach motility may also present, giving substance to patient complaints of increased fullness and abdominal pain, even on consuming small amounts of food. Transit time in the small intestine may be delayed. Rectal impaction is a potential sequelae of these problems; it is exacerbated by a low volume of liquid intake. Pancreatic problems may also emerge, often as a consequence of refeeding. Parotid gland enlargement may occur, possibly related to a high level of binge eating and purging, high carbohydrate intake, malnutrition, and/or alkalosis. Such enlargement is easily visible because the parotid glands are located bilaterally next to the ear.

A variety of laboratory tests may also reveal problems in these and other bodily systems. Decrease in bone density is a characteristic dysfunction of the skeletal system. Endocrine problems are multifold. Disruption of the primary hypothalamic pituitary gonadotropin axis leads to problems with gonadal growth and function, hypothalamic pituitary adrenal axis overstimulation leads to heightened cortisol activity, and thyroid function may be severely depressed. Renal function may be altered drastically given the vomiting, diuretic, and laxative abuses that can often occur in eating-disordered individuals.

PSYCHOLOGICAL ASSESSMENT

Psychological assessment should be multifaceted, including a focus on discrete eating behaviors, along with a broader evaluation of symptoms necessary for a diagnosis (see Netemeyer & Williamson, 2001; Williamson, 1990; Williamson, Anderson, & Gleaves, 1996). A variety of questionnaire measures and structured interviews have been developed specifically for the assessment of eating disorders.

The Eating Disorder Examination (EDE) is perhaps the most widely used structured interview. It focuses on the evaluation of the symptoms of anorexia nervosa and bulimia nervosa and has been revised 12 times (Fairburn & Cooper, 1993). It yields scores on four subscales: restraint, eating concern, shape concern, and weight concern. The EDE was also found to be appropriate for the assessment of binge eating disorder (Grilo, Masheb, & Williamson, 2001). The Structured Interview for Anorexia and Bulimic Disorders assesses a range of symptoms related to eating disorders and has six factors: body image; general psychopathology; measures to counteract weight gain, fasting, and substance abuse; sexuality and social integration; bulimic symptoms; and atypical binges (Fichter, Herpertz, Quadflieg, & Herpertz-Dahlmann, 1998). The Interview for Diagnosis of Eating Disorders IV was designed to address the specific diagnosis of anorexia nervosa, bulimia nervosa, and binge-eating disorder, along the lines of the *DSM-IV* criteria (Kutlesic, Williamson, Gleaves, Barbin, & Murphy-Eberenz, 1998; Williamson, 1990).

In addition, a host of questionnaire measures can be used for assessing either the full clinical picture of one or more eating disorders, or for evaluating a more specific component of the disorder (see Anderson & Williamson, 2002; Netemeyer & Williamson, 2001; Williamson et al., 1996, for a more detailed discussion). The Eating Disorder Inventory-2 is probably the most widely used self-report index; it has 11 scales: drive for thinness, bulimia, body dissatisfaction, ineffectiveness, perfectionism, interpersonal distrust, interoceptive awareness, maturity fears, asceticism, impulse regulation, and social insecurity (Garner, 1991). Other questionnaire measures that have received considerable use in research and clinical settings include Eating Attitudes Test, Dutch Eating Behavior Questionnaire, Children's Eating Attitudes Test, Kid's Eating Disorder Survey, Bulimia Test-Revised, Dietary Intent Scale, Dieting and Body Image Questionnaire, Children's Eating Behavior Inventory, Mize's Cognitive Distortions Questionnaire, and the Bulimic Cognitive Distortions Scale (see Netemeyer & Williamson, 2001; Williamson, 1990; Williamson et al., 1996, for a detailed examination of these and other measures).

There are also some innovative approaches that should be considered for the measurement of self-report levels of eating symptoms. For instance, Anderson, Williamson, Duchmann, Gleaves, and Barbin (1999) developed the Multiaxial Assessment of Eating Disorders as a brief self-report measure, ideally suited for measuring treatment outcome. It has six subscales: binge eating, purgative behavior, avoidance of forbidden foods, restrictive eating, fear of fatness, and depression. It has excellent psychometric characteristics, including criterion validity (Martin, Williamson, & Thaw, 2000). Stice, Rizvi, and Telch (2000) also describe a very brief (22-item) self-report measure, the Eating Disorder Diagnostic Scale (EDDS), which has excellent psychometric characteristics. In particular, Stice et al. found excellent agreement between the diagnoses of eating disorders from structured interviews and those from the EDDS (99% for anorexia nervosa; 96% for bulimia nervosa; 93% for binge-eating disorder).

Self-monitoring of eating-disordered behaviors and associated cognitive and affective components is also an important aspect of assessment (Williamson et al., 2001). Forms might include sections for the recording of amounts and types of food, purgative activity, environmental circumstances, associated cognitions and feelings, and pre- and posteating behaviors (see Williamson et al., 1996). Test meals have also been advocated for the determination of binge eating level. For instance, Anderson, Williamson, Johnson, and Grieve (2001) evaluated individuals with binge-eating disorder, obese nonbinge-eaters, and controls in a laboratory setting designed to increase the potential of binge eating. Individuals with binge-eating disorder ate more and felt more psychologically out of control of their eating behaviors.

Measurement of body image disturbance, a central feature of all eating disorders, should also be a core aspect of assessment plans. Some of the more widely used measures include Multidimensional Body Self-Relations Questionnaire, Body Dysmorphic Disorder Examination, Body Shape Questionnaire, Body Image Avoidance Questionnaire, and several others developed by Cash and colleagues (www.body-images.com; see Thompson et al., 1999; Thompson & Gardner, 2002; Thompson & van den Berg, 2002, for an extensive selection and discussion of body image measures). Assessment of general psychopathology associated with eating disorders is also very important. A variety of measures might be indicated, including structured interviews and questionnaire methods (MMPI, Beck Depression Inventory, etc.; Crowther & Sherwood, 1997).

ETIOLOGICAL CONSIDERATIONS

In recent years, a tremendous amount of research activity has addressed unidimensional and multifactorial models of the development of eating disorders. There are multiple pathways and precursors to the eventual development of an eating disturbance and often several influences may be apparent for individual cases (see previous case study description). In this section, we first review unitary approaches, followed by a discussion of studies that have examined multiple factors and authors who have posed multicomponent theoretical conceptualizations.

FAMILIAL AND GENETIC

Familial approaches typically indict the parents and, possibly, siblings as agents in the onset and perpetuation of eating disorders. From the early days of eating disorders work, it was noted that families play a central role in understanding eating disorders; families were sometimes kept apart from patients during assessment and treatment (Gull, 1874/1964). Family therapy was one of the earliest and most used methods of intervention (Minuchin, Rosman, & Baker, 1978). As noted by Steinberg and Phares (2001), a variety of different avenues of family effect have been noted, including:

- Level of family functioning.
- Communication patterns with the family.
- Parental modeling of eating patterns.
- Psychological functioning of the parents.
- Specific feedback (i.e., weight-related criticism or teasing) to the child concerning some aspect of appearance.

Several studies have addressed family functioning. Humphrey (1994) found greater rigidity and dependency for families with a restricting anorexic child when compared to families that had either a child with bulimia nervosa or a child of anorexic weight, who also had bulimic characteristics. Horesh et al. (1996), in a sample of adolescent girls with binge-eating disorder, found significant relations between disturbed eating patterns and parental overprotection and pressures. In a direct comparison of individuals with bulimia nervosa and obese binge eaters, Friedman, Wilfley, Welch, and Kunce (1997) found that troubled family functioning was higher for the bulimia nervosa group. In terms of parental functioning, there is little evidence that parents of eating-disordered patients, when compared to control groups of parents with either no eating-disordered offspring or an obese child, have elevated levels of psychopathology (see Steinberg & Phares, 2001).

However, mothers with eating disorders may have a negative effect on their offspring. Strober, Lampert, Morrell, Burroughs, and Jacobs (1990) found that daughters with anorexic mothers were five times more likely to develop eating disorders than daughters without mothers who suffered from eating disorders. Stein, Woolley, Cooper, and Fairburn (1994) found that mothers with eating disorders were also more negative toward infants during feeding time periods than control mothers.

The role of parental attitudes, modeling, and direct feedback in the development of eating disorders has received a great deal of support (Steinberg & Phares, 2001). Such influences may begin early in life, possibly by the time girls are 5 years old. In a series of studies by Birch and colleagues (see Fisher & Birch, 2001), 5-year-old girls' attitudes toward dieting and their own weight concerns were related to mothers' weight concerns and dieting behaviors.

Direct communications may take the form of comments, teasing, or criticism about a child's appearance or eating behaviors. Rieves and Cash (1996), in a study of the sources of teasing, identified high levels for mothers (30%), fathers (24%), and siblings (sister, 36%; brother, 79%). Schwartz, Phares, Tantleff-Dunn, and Thompson (1999) had college students recall teasing experiences from mothers and fathers, and related the levels to current body image dissatisfaction. For women, but not men, levels of teasing were associated with dissatisfaction.

A great deal of work has begun to focus on genetic factors in eating disorders. Bulik, Sullivan, Wade, and Kendler (2000) offer a concise guide to the methodology and findings for the extremely complicated issue of genetic versus environmental contributions to eating disorders. They note that limitations of the existing research, primarily insufficient sample sizes, make it difficult to draw conclusions about the contribution of genetic and environmental factors to anorexia nervosa. However, there is a reasonable database for bulimia nervosa, suggesting that additive genetic effects and unique environmental factors play a role in liability. In their review of twin studies, Klump et al. (2001) concluded that 58% to 76% of the variance in anorexia nervosa was due to genetic factors, with 54% to 83% due to these factors in the case of bulimia nervosa. They also found that eating-disturbed symptoms were heritable: 32% to 72% of factors such as body dissatisfaction, eating and weight concerns, and weight preoccupation were heritable, as were 46% to 72% of dietary restraint, binge eating, and vomiting. One of the most exciting and ambitious enterprises in this area is an international multisite collaborative project designed to map the genetic loci involved in anorexia nervosa (Kaye et al., 2000). This is a much-needed development in the field, given that more than 200 genes that contribute to appetite, hunger, satiety, and other aspects of energy balance have been identified (Yager, 2000).

LEARNING AND MODELING

Relevant to learning and modeling are the data reviewed previously that indicate a role of parents as etiological agents. However, research has demonstrated that media and peer influences may also be powerful modeling and didactic agents that contribute to level of eating disturbance (Thompson et al., 1999). Weight concern, the acceptability of dieting, the normative nature of being dissatisfied with looks, and the details of weight control strategies are just a few of the areas wherein media, parents, and peers exert an influence. The media have often been spotlighted because of the omnipresent nature of a seemingly inexhaustible array of impossibly thin and beautiful models and celebrities. Countless studies have documented the presence of thinness in these images and the associated endless parade of magazine articles that focus on dieting and appearance management (Thompson & Heinberg, 1999). Recently, work in the area of internalization of media images has indicated that women who incorporate or "buy into" the images and messages to the point of desiring thinness or modifying behavior to achieve the perfect "look" are at much greater risk to develop eating disturbances (Thompson & Stice, 2001).

Peers and parents may also model behaviors that connote an imperative to the friend or child that appearance and/or thinness is highly desirable (Smolak & Levine, 2001). For instance, teasing or negative appearance-related comments have received remarkably consistent support as a factor in level or eating disturbance (Thompson, Coovert, Richards, Johnson, & Cattarin, 1995; Wertheim, Koerner, & Paxton, 2001). Comments may also manifest not in teasing or disparagement, but simple encouragement to modify weight. Significant relationships have been found between level of parental comments and level of a daughter's desire to lose weight or body esteem scores (Thelen & Cormier, 1995; Smolak, Levine, & Schermer, 1999). Parents may also express concern about their own weight that may serve to model such attitudes to offspring. Smolak et al. found that a mother's complaints about her weight and weight loss attempts were related to the daughter's body esteem scores. Concerning peers, Vander Wal and Thelen (2000) found that peer modeling of weight and shape concerns and daughters' perception of parental influence to lose or control weight were significant predictors of body image disturbance. A variety of other studies have found that direct (e.g., teasing) and indirect (e.g., modeling, investment in appearance) peer and parental influences are important contributors to body dissatisfaction and eating concerns (Field et al., 2001; Smolak & Levine, 2001; Vander Wal & Thelen, 2000).

LIFE EVENTS

Life events, a relatively heterogeneous category of influences, have the power to radically affect an individual's psychological and, possibly, physical status, leading to body image and eating problems. Common experiences such as a family move to a different city or state, loss of a loved one, and a physical illness can serve as the beginning of a change in eating patterns that may evolve into a full-blown eating disorder. Negative comments in the form of criticism or teasing about appearance or weight, as noted earlier, have also been associated with the onset of eating and shape-related problems. However, perhaps the most studied life event involves the traumatic experiences related to sexual abuse.

Connors (2001) offers an excellent review of the confusing and controversial area of sexual abuse, concluding that it "constitutes a significant risk factor for the development of body image and eating problems" (p. 160). Her review encompasses a wide range of studies, from childhood through early adulthood. She concludes that a variety of factors affect the connection between abuse and level of its effect on eating symptomatology, including familiarity of the perpetrator, level of physical contact, and level of negative reaction at the time of the abuse (the most consistent finding may be that level of negative reaction predicts level of eating pathology). Family factors may also serve as moderators of the effect of abuse on eating, including family variables such as unreliability of parents, reduced expressiveness and warmth, and family chaos (see Connors, 2001).

One of the many relevant methodological issues in this area is the definition of *abuse,* which varies drastically across studies. For instance, some studies require sexual penetration or forced sexual activities as essential for defining sexual abuse, while others use a general definition related to "touching" in a place that was not welcome or doing something "sexual" that should not have been done. Weiner and Thompson (1997) identified two types of sexual abuse via factor analysis: overt and covert. Overt sexual abuse consisted of explicit sexual violations of an individual's body, while covert was defined as a variety of more subtle, yet offensive in nature, activities (such as sexually related staring, verbal harassment about sexual development, inappropriate parental sharing of sexually related information). In regression analyses, covert sexual abuse was found to explain variance in eating problems and body dissatisfaction beyond that accounted for by overt sexual abuse.

GENDER AND RACIAL-ETHNIC

Gender and racial-ethnic factors have been found to play a very large role, historically, in helping researchers and clinicians understand dispositional factors in eating disorders (Thompson, 1996). *Gender* has typically been used synonymously with biological sex (male, female); however, gender is also a term that has been used to connote socialization and social roles (i.e., masculine and feminine). Racial-ethnic etiological factors, additionally, need to consider within- and between-country ethnic comparisons, as well as the identification of respondents with racial-ethnic background or culture.

Feminist theorists and other researchers often focus on the nature of the gender role adopted by the individual and/or promoted by society (Gilbert & Thompson, 1996; Smolak & Murnen, 2001). One such component is the traditional feminine gender role, consisting of the traits of passivity, need for approval, dependence, and a focus on interpersonal relationships. Research is not conclusive at this time on whether the adoption of such a gender role is central to the development of an eating disorder; however, Murnen and Smolak (1998), using meta-analysis, found that high femininity was associated with increased risk for eating problems and high masculinity was related to a decreased risk. They noted, however, that the effect sizes, indicating the degree of association, were quite small. Smolak and Murnen (2001) detail several components of women's "lived experiences" that they think contribute to eating disorders: a culture of thinness, sexual harassment and abuse, and societal limitations on achievement, which function to "focus girls on a good body as the key to success and . . . limit girls' voices" (p. 96).

Men present with the eating disorders of anorexia nervosa and bulimia nervosa much less frequently than women—only about 10% of cases are men. However, the sex ratio is roughly equivalent for binge-eating disorder. The societal ideal of thinness for women is paralleled by a relatively intense pressure on men to achieve a muscular ideal (Andersen, 1995; Thompson et al., 1999). However, men in certain avocations may be at an elevated risk to develop an eating disorder. For instance, athletes who are wrestlers, bodybuilders, jockeys, or gymnasts have size and/or weight imperatives that may induce extreme forms of weight maintenance or loss. Homosexuality appears to be associated with an elevated risk also, with perhaps 20% or more of male cases stating this sexual orientation (Andersen, 1995). However, research on a randomly selected sample of heterosexual and gay males found few differences in eating disturbance or body image, even when groups were further categorized by exercise status (bodybuilders vs. sedentary controls; Boroughs & Thompson, 2002).

Considerable recent work has evaluated the ethnic differences that exist in eating disorders and related disturbances, such as body dissatisfaction. Although the data are still sketchy and no large-scale epidemiological study has been conducted, it is now clear that "no ethnic group is completely immune to developing an eating disorder" (Smolak & Striegel-Moore, 2001, p. 114). Much of the available research is limited, however, because researchers have typically looked at individual symptoms, such as dieting level or body dissatisfaction, rather than a comprehensive assessment and diagnosis of eating disorders. Yet, the data indicate that eating disturbance crosses ethnic boundaries. For example, French et al. (1997), in a study of various ethnic groups, found the following percentages for frequent dieting: Latina, 23.6%; White, 21.5%; American Indian, 20.6%; Asian, 17.4%; and Black, 13.6%. A large-scale study of 34,447 adults revealed similar percentages of individuals across ethnicity who were trying to lose weight (White, 38.4%; Black, 38.6%; Hispanic, 37.7%; Serdula, Collins, Williamson, Anda, Pamuk, & Byers, 1993).

BIOLOGICAL AND PHYSIOLOGICAL

As noted earlier in the section on physical assessment, a variety of metabolic, endocrine, and other physiological changes accompany the severe weight loss of anorexia nervosa. The challenge for any type of biological or physiological theory of eating disorders is to illustrate that physical changes predict or precede the onset of eating-disordered symptoms. Kaye (1995) and colleagues have noted that serotonin may play a role in the pathology of eating disorders. For instance, evidence suggests that serotonin inhibits appetite. High levels of CSF 5-HIAA (a metabolite of serotonin) are found in weight-restored anorexics; these individuals often have traits such as perfectionism and constraint that persist even after weight gain. Kaye notes that such traits are opposite those of impulsivity and aggression, which appear in individuals with low levels of CSF 5-HIAA. Serotonin has also been implicated in bulimia nervosa (Pirke, 1995). Enhancing serotonin activity via agonists leads to a reduction in food intake; use of antagonists leads to an increase in consumption. More recently, Kaye and colleagues found that brain serotonin was altered in recovered bulimic patients (Kaye, Frank, Meltzer, Price, McConaha, & Klump, 2001).

Smolak and Murnen (2001) note a variety of methodological issues that should be considered concerning biological factors. First, prospective studies are lacking—studies have compared clinical versus nonclinical cases in which the eating disorder has already developed. Often, the assumption is that any current biological finding preexisted the eating pathology, which is debatable. Second, comparisons between recovered patients and nonclinical controls are also suspect. Any biochemical differences may not reflect causes of eating disorders, but perhaps the long-term effects of eating pathology on biochemistry (even in recovered cases). Third, it is crucial to equate comparison groups on other psychiatric disorders, such as depression, substance abuse, and personality disorders, which may have unique biochemical associates. Finally, the behavior of dieting, alone, may produce a variety of biochemical changes (e.g., serotonin; Walsh, Oldman, Franklin, Fairburn, & Cowen, 1995) that may be mistaken for precursors to restricting behavior.

Integrative Approaches

Multivariate approaches perhaps offer the most comprehensive and accurate strategy for evaluating etiology and maintenance of eating disorders (Stice, 2001). For instance, Levine and Smolak (1996) developed a cumulative stressor model that proposes that three developmental processes (weight gain from puberty, dating, and academic demands) interact with the societal imperative for a thin ideal to produce dieting and eating disturbance. Stice and colleagues have done considerable work with their dual pathway model, which emphasizes that sociocultural pressures lead an individual to internalize the thin ideal, which leads to body dissatisfaction (Stice, 2001). Body dissatisfaction leads to dieting and negative affect, which leads to bulimic symptoms.

Vohs, Bardone, Joiner, Abramson, and Heatherton (1999) believe that perfectionism and body dissatisfaction lead to effective weight control for those with high self-esteem, but possibly lead to bulimic behavior for those with low self-esteem. Heatherton and Polivy (1992) outline a spiral model of disordered eating. Body dissatisfaction and low self-esteem may produce dieting behavior and, because many diets fail, some individuals develop higher levels of body dissatisfaction and lower self-esteem, possibly spiraling downward into greater and greater distress and negative affect. Compensatory bulimic strategies may then be adopted to help gain control of weight. Thompson et al. (1999) proposed a tripartite influence model that enlists three formative factors (peers, parents, media) in the development of body dissatisfaction and eating disturbances. Such factors may have a direct effect, but may also function via mediational factors such as internalization of societal messages of appearance and elevated appearance comparison tendencies.

SUMMARY

Great advances have been made in the investigation of many facets of eating disorders over the past few years. A wide variety of measures are now available for the assessment of multiple characteristics of anorexia nervosa, bulimia nervosa, and binge-eating disorder. Research continues to address the accuracy and utility of the current diagnostic systems. Exploration of the complex etiological factors involved has given rise to an explosion of interest in putative risk factors. To date, we have made tremendous progress in capturing the clinical picture of the various eating disorders, constructing classification systems, evaluating course and prognosis, and developing multifactorial theoretical models. Perhaps the greatest challenge for future researchers is not the ability to detect relative genetic and environmental causation, but to use this information to inform diagnostic, measurement, treatment, and prevention strategies.

REFERENCES

Agras, W. S. (2001). The consequences and costs of the eating disorders. *Psychiatric Clinics of North America, 24*, 371–379.

American Psychiatric Association. (1994). *Diagnostic and statistical manual of mental disorders* (4th ed.). Washington, DC: Author.

Andersen, A. E. (1995). Eating disorders in males. In K. D. Brownell & C. G. Fairburn (Eds.), *Eating disorders and obesity: A comprehensive handbook* (pp. 177–182). New York: Guilford Press.

Andersen, A. E., Bowers, W. A., & Watson, T. (2001). A slimming program for eating disorders not otherwise specified: Reconceptualizing a confusing, residual diagnostic category. *Psychiatric Clinics of North America, 24*, 271–281.

Anderson, D. A., & Williamson, D. A. (2002). Outcome measurement in eating disorders. In W. W. Ishack, T. Burt, & L. Sedeser (Eds.), *Outcome measurement in clinical psychiatry: A critical review* (pp. 284–301). Washington, DC: American Psychiatric Press.

Anderson, D. A., Williamson, D. A., Duchmann, E. G., Gleaves, D. H., & Barbin, J. M. (1999). Development and validation of a multifactorial treatment outcome measure for eating disorders. *Assessment, 6*, 7–20.

Anderson, D. A., Williamson, D. A., Johnson, W. G., & Grieve, C. O. (2001). Validity of test meals for determining binge eating. *Eating Behaviors, 2*, 105–112.

Beglin, S. J., & Fairburn, C. G. (1992). What is meant by the term "binge"? *American Journal of Psychiatry, 149*, 123–124.

Beumont, P. J. V. (1995). The clinical presentation of anorexia and bulimia nervosa. In K. D. Brownell & C. G. Fairburn (Eds.), *Eating disorders and obesity: A comprehensive handbook* (pp. 151–158). New York: Guilford Press.

Boroughs, M., & Thompson, J. K. (2002). Body image and eating disturbances in men: The moderating effects of exercise status and sexual orientation. *International Journal of Eating Disorders, 31*, 307–311.

Bulik, C. M., Sullivan, P. F., & Kendler, K. S. (2000). An empirical study of the classification of eating disorders. *American Journal of Psychiatry, 157,* 886–895.

Bulik, C. M., Sullivan, P. F., Wade, T. D., & Kendler, K. S. (2000). Twin studies of eating disorders: A review. *International Journal of Eating Disorders, 27,* 1–20.

Cachelin, F. M., & Maher, B. A. (1998). Is amenorrhea a critical criterion for anorexia nervosa? *Journal of Psychosomatic Research, 44,* 435–440.

Connors, M. E. (2001). Relationship of sexual abuse to body image and eating problems. In J. K. Thompson & L. Smolak (Eds.), *Body image, eating disorders, and obesity in youth: Assessment, prevention, and treatment* (pp. 149–167). Washington, DC: American Psychological Association.

Crowther, J. H., & Sherwood, N. E. (1997). Assessment. In D. M. Garner & P. E. Garfinkel (Eds.), *Handbook of treatment for eating disorders* (2nd ed., pp. 34–49). New York: Guilford Press.

Dennis, A. B., & Sansone, R. A. (1997). Treatment of patients' personality disorders. In D. M. Garner & P. E. Garfinkel (Eds.), *Handbook of treatment for eating disorders* (2nd ed., pp. 437–439). New York: Guilford Press.

Eldredge, K. L., & Agras, W. S. (1996). Weight and shape overconcern and emotional eating in binge eating disorder. *International Journal of Eating Disorders, 19,* 73–82.

Fairburn, C. G., & Cooper, Z. (1993). The Eating Disorder examination (12th ed.). In C. G. Fairburn & G. T. Wilson (Eds.), *Binge eating: Nature, assessment and treatment* (pp. 317–360). New York: Guilford Press.

Fairburn, C. G., Cooper, Z., Doll, H. A., Norman, P., & O'Connor, M. (2000). The natural course of bulimia nervosa and binge eating disorder in young women. *Archives of General Psychiatry, 57,* 659–665.

Fichter, M. M., Herpertz, S., Quadflieg, N., & Herpertz-Dahlmann, B. (1998). Structured interview for anorexic and bulimic disorders for *DSM-IV* and ICD-10: Updated (third) revision. *International Journal of Eating Disorders, 24,* 227–249.

Field, A. E., Camargo, C. A., Taylor, C. B., Berkey, C. S., Roberts, S. B., & Colditz, G. A. (2001). Peer, parent, and media influences on the development of weight concerns and frequent dieting among preadolescent and adolescent girls and boys. *Pediatrics, 107,* 54–60.

Fisher, J. O., & Birch, L. L. (2001). Early experience with food and eating: Implications for the development of eating disorders. In J. K. Thompson & L. Smolak (Eds.), *Body image, eating disorders, and obesity in youth: Assessment, prevention and treatment* (pp. 23–39). Washington, DC: American Psychological Association.

French, S. A., Story, M., Neumark-Stzainer, D., Downes, B., Resnick, M. D., & Blum, R. (1997). Ethnic differences in psychosocial and health behavior correlates of dieting and binge eating in a population-based sample of adolescence females. *International Journal of Eating Disorders, 22,* 315–322.

Friedman, M. A., Wilfley, D. E., Welch, R. R., & Kunce, J. T. (1997). Self-directed hostility and family functioning in normal-weight bulimics and overweight binge eaters. *International Journal of Eating Disorders, 22,* 367–375.

Garner, D. M. (1991). *Manual for the Eating Disorder Inventory-2.* Odessa, FL: Psychological Assessment Resources.

Gilbert, S., & Thompson, J. K. (1996). Feminist explanations of the development of eating disorders: Common themes, research findings, and methodological issues. *Clinical Psychology: Science and Practice, 3,* 183–202.

Grilo, C. M., Masheb, R. M., & Wilson, G. T. (2001). A comparison of different methods for assessing the features of eating disorders in patients with binge eating disorder. *Journal of Consulting and Clinical Psychology, 69,* 317–322.

Gull, W. W. (1964). Anorexia nervosa. In R. M. Kaufman & M. Heiman (Eds.), *Evolution of psychosomatic concepts anorexia nervosa: A paradigm*. New York: International Universities Press. (Original work published 1874)

Heatherton, T. F., & Polivy, J. (1992). Chronic dieting and eating disorders: A spiral model. In J. H. Crowther, D. L. Tennenbaum, S. E. Hobfold, & M. A. Parris-Stephens (Eds.), *The etiology of bulimia nervosa: The individual and familial context* (pp. 133–155). Washington, DC: Hemisphere.

Herzog, D. B., & Delinsky, S. S. (2001). Classification of eating disorders. In R. Striegel-Moore & L. Smolak (Eds.), *Eating disorders: Innovative directions in research and practice* (pp. 31–50). Washington, DC: American Psychological Association.

Herzog, D. B., Dorer, D. J., Keel, P. K., Selwyn, S. E., Ekeblad, E. R., Flores, A. T., et al. (1999). Recovery and relapse in anorexia and bulimia nervosa: A 7.5-year follow-up study. *Journal of the American Academy of Child and Adolescent Psychiatry, 38,* 829–837.

Herzog, D. B., Greenwood, D. N., Dorer, D. J., Flores, A. T., Ekeblad, E. R., Richards, A., et al. (2000). Mortality in eating disorders: A descriptive study. *International Journal of Eating Disorders, 28,* 20–26.

Hill, K., & Pomeroy, C. (2001). Assessment of physical status of children and adolescents with eating disorders and obesity. In J. K. Thompson & L. Smolak (Eds.), *Body image, eating disorders, and obesity in youth: Assessment, prevention and treatment* (pp. 171–191). Washington, DC: American Psychological Association.

Horesh, N., Apter, A., Ishai, J., Danziger, Y., Miculincer, M., Stein, D., et al. (1996). Abnormal psychosocial situations and eating disorders in adolescence. *Journal of the American Academy of Child and Adolescent Psychiatry, 35,* 921–927.

Humphrey, L. L. (1994). Family relationships. In K. A. Halmi (Ed.), *Psychobiology and treatment of anorexia nervosa and bulimia nervosa* (pp. 263–282). Washington, DC: American Psychiatric Press.

Johnson, W. G., & Torgrud, L. J. (1996). Assessment and treatment of binge eating disorder. In J. K. Thompson (Ed.), *Body image, eating disorders and obesity: An integrative guide for assessment and treatment* (pp. 321–343). Washington, DC: American Psychological Association.

Kaye, W. H. (1995). Neurotransmitters and anorexia nervosa. In K. D. Brownell & C. G. Fairburn (Eds.), *Eating disorders and obesity: A comprehensive handbook* (pp. 255–260). New York: Guilford Press.

Kaye, W. H., Frank, G. K., Meltzer, C. C., Price, J. C., McConaha, C., & Klump, K. L. (2001). Altered serotonin 2A receptor activity in women who have recovered from bulimia nervosa. *America Journal of Psychiatry, 158,* 1152–1155.

Kaye, W. H., Lilenfield, L. R., Berretini, W. H., Strober, M., Devlin, B., Klump, K., et al. (2000). A genome-wide search for susceptibility loci for anorexia nervosa: Methods and sample description. *Biological Psychiatry, 47,* 794–803.

Klump, K. L., Kaye, W. H., & Strober, M. (2001). The evolving genetic foundations of eating disorders. *Psychiatric Clinics of North America, 24,* 215–225.

Kutlesic, V., Williamson, D. A., Gleaves, D. H., Barbin, J. M., & Murphy-Eberenz, K. P. (1998). The Interview for the Diagnosis of Eating Disorders IV: Application to *DSM-IV* diagnostic criteria. *Psychological Assessment, 10,* 41–48.

Levine, M. P., & Smolak, L. (1996). Media as a context for the development of disordered eating. In L. Smolak, M. P. Levine, & R. Striegel-Moore (Eds.), *The developmental psychopathology of eating disorders* (pp. 235–237). Mahwah, NJ: Erlbaum.

Lewinsohn, P. M. (2001, December). *The role of epidemiology in prevention science.* Paper presented at the Eating Disorders' Research Society, Albuquerque, NM.

Lucas, A. R., Beard, C. M., O'Fallon, W. M., & Kurland, L. T. (1988). Anorexia nervosa in Rochester, Minnesota: A 45-year study. *Mayo Clinic Proceedings, 63,* 433–442.

Martin, C. K., Williamson, D. A., & Thaw, J. M. (2000). Criterion validity of the multiaxial assessment of eating disorders symptoms. *International Journal of Eating Disorders, 28,* 303–310.

Minuchin, S., Rosman, B. L., & Baker, L. (1978). *Psychosomatic families: Anorexia nervosa in context.* Cambridge, MA: Harvard University Press.

Murnen, S., & Smolak, L. (1998). Femininity, masculinity, and disordered eating: A meta-analytic approach. *International Journal of Eating Disorders, 22,* 231–242.

Netemeyer, S. B., & Williamson, D. A. (2001). Assessment of eating disturbance in children and adolescents with eating disorders and obesity. In J. K. Thompson & L. Smolak (Eds.), *Body image, eating disorders, and obesity in youth: Assessment, prevention and treatment* (pp. 215–233). Washington, DC: American Psychological Association.

Newman, D. L., Moffitt, T. E., Caspi, A., Magdol, L., Silva, P. A., & Stanton, W. R. (1996). Psychiatric disorder in a birth cohort of young adults: Prevalence, comorbidity, clinical significance, and new case incidence from ages 11 to 21. *Journal of Consulting and Clinical Psychology, 64,* 552–562.

Nicholls, D., Chater, R., & Lask, B. (2000). Children into *DSM* don't go: A comparison of classification systems for eating disorders in childhood and early adolescence. *International Journal of Eating Disorders, 28,* 317–324.

Nielson, S. (2001). Epidemiology and mortality of eating disorders. *Psychiatric Clinics of North America, 24,* 201–214.

Pirke, K. M. (1995). Physiology of bulimia nervosa. In K. D. Brownell & C. G. Fairburn (Eds.), *Eating disorders and obesity: A comprehensive handbook* (pp. 261–265). New York: Guilford Press.

Pomeroy, C. (1996). Anorexia nervosa, bulimia nervosa, and binge eating disorder: Assessment of physical status. In J. K. Thompson (Ed.), *Body image, eating disorders and obesity: An integrative guide for assessment and treatment* (pp. 177–203). Washington, DC: American Psychological Association.

Rieves, L., & Cash, T. F. (1996). Social developmental factors and women's body-image attitudes. *Journal of Social Behavior and Personality, 11,* 63–78.

Rosenvinge, J. H., Sundgot-Borgen, S., & Borresen, R. (1999). The prevalence of psychological correlates of anorexia nervosa, bulimia nervosa, and binge eating among 15-year-old students: A controlled epidemiological study. *European Eating Disorders Review, 7,* 382–391.

Schwartz, D. J., Phares, V., Tantleff-Dunn, S., & Thompson, J. K. (1999). Body image, psychological functioning, and parental feedback regarding physical appearance. *International Journal of Eating Disorders, 25,* 339–343.

Serdula, M. K., Collins, M. E., Williamson, D. F., Anda, R. F., Pamuk, E., & Byers, T. E. (1993). Weight control practices of U.S. adolescents and adults. *Annals of Internal Medicine, 119,* 667–671.

Shisslak, C. M., Crago, M., & Estes, L. S. (1995). The spectrum of eating disturbances. *International Journal of Eating Disorders, 18,* 1209–1219.

Smolak, L., & Levine, M. P. (2001). Body image in children. In J. K. Thompson & L. Smolak (Eds.), *Body image, eating disorders, and obesity in youth: Assessment, prevention and treatment* (pp. 41–66). Washington, DC: American Psychological Association.

Smolak, L., Levine, M. P., & Schermer, F. (1999). Parental input and weight concerns among elementary school children. *International Journal of Eating Disorders, 25,* 263–272.

Smolak, L., & Murnen, S. K. (2001). Gender and eating problems. In R. H. Striegel-Moore & L. Smolak (Eds.), *Eating disorders: Innovative directions in research and practice* (pp. 91–110). Washington, DC: American Psychological Association.

Smolak, L., & Striegel-Moore, R. (2001). Challenging the myth of the golden girl: Ethnicity and eating disorders. In R. H. Striegel-Moore & L. Smolak (Eds.), *Eating disorders: Innovative directions in research and practice* (pp. 111–132). Washington, DC: American Psychological Association.

Stein, A., Woolley, H., Cooper, S. D., & Fairburn, C. G. (1994). An observational study of mothers with eating disorders and their infants. *Journal of Child Psychology and Psychiatry, 35,* 733–748.

Steinberg, A. B., & Phares, V. (2001). Family functioning, body image, and eating disturbances. In J. K. Thompson & L. Smolak (Eds.), *Body image, eating disorders, and obesity in youth: Assessment, prevention and treatment* (pp. 127–147). Washington, DC: American Psychological Association.

Steinhausen, H. C. (1995). The course and outcome of anorexia nervosa. In K. D. Brownell & C. G. Fairburn (Eds.), *Eating disorders and obesity: A comprehensive handbook* (pp. 234–237). New York: Guilford Press.

Stice, E. (2001). Risk factors for eating pathology: Recent advances and future directions. In R. H. Striegel-Moore & L. Smolak (Eds.), *Eating disorders: Innovative directions in research and practice* (pp. 51–73). Washington, DC: American Psychological Association.

Stice, E., Rizvi, S. L., & Telch, C. F. (2000). Development and validation of the Eating Disorder Diagnostic Scale: A brief self-report measure of anorexia, bulimia, and binge-eating disorder. *Psychological Assessment, 22,* 123–131.

Striegel-Moore, R. H., Dohm, F. A., Solomon, E. E., Fairburn, C. G., Pike, K. M., & Wilfley, D. E. (2000). Subthreshold binge eating disorder. *International Journal of Eating Disorders, 27,* 270–278.

Striegel-Moore, R. H., & Smolak, L. (Eds.). (2001). *Eating disorders: Innovative directions in research and practice.* Washington, DC: American Psychological Association.

Striegel-Moore, R. H., Wilson, G. T., Wilfley, D. E., Elder, K. A., & Brownell, K. D. (1998). Binge eating in an obese community sample. *International Journal of Eating Disorders, 23,* 27–37.

Strober, M., Lampert, C., Morrell, W., Burroughs, J., & Jacobs, C. (1990). A controlled family study of anorexia nervosa: Evidence of familial aggregation and lack of shared transmission with affective disorders. *International Journal of Eating Disorders, 9,* 239–253.

Sullivan, P. F. (1995). Mortality in anorexia nervosa. *American Journal of Psychiatry, 152,* 1073–1074.

Sullivan, P. F., Bulik, C. M., & Kendler, K. S. (1998). The epidemiology of bulimia nervosa: Symptoms, syndromes and diagnostic thresholds. *Psychological Medicine, 28,* 599–610.

Telch, C. F., & Agras, W. S. (1996). Do emotional states influence binge eating in the obese? *International Journal of Eating Disorders, 20,* 271–280.

Thelen, M., & Cormier, J. (1995). Desire to be thinner and weight control among children and their parents. *Behavior Therapy, 26,* 85–99.

Thompson, J. K. (Ed.). (1996). *Body image, eating disorders, and obesity: An integrative guide for assessment and treatment.* Washington, DC: American Psychological Association.

Thompson, J. K., Coovert, M. D., Richards, K. J., Johnson, S., & Cattarin, J. (1995). Development of body image, eating disturbance, and general psychological functioning in female adolescents: Covariance structure modeling and longitudinal investigations. *International Journal of Eating Disorders, 18,* 221–236.

Thompson, J. K., & Gardner, R. M. (2002). Assessment of perceptual body image in adolescents and adults. In T. F. Cash & T. Pruzinsky (Eds.), *Body images: A handbook* (pp. 135–141). New York: Guilford Press.

Thompson, J. K., & Heinberg, L. J. (1999). The media's influence on body image disturbance and eating disorders: We've reviled them, now can we rehabilitate them? *Journal of Social Issues, 55,* 339–353.

Thompson, J. K., Heinberg, L. J., Altabe, M. N., & Tantleff-Dunn, S. (1999). *Exacting beauty: Theory, assessment and treatment of body image disturbance.* Washington, DC: American Psychological Association.

Thompson, J. K., & Smolak, L. (Eds.). (2001a). *Body image, eating disorders, and obesity in youth: Assessment, prevention and treatment.* Washington, DC: American Psychological Association.

Thompson, J. K., & Smolak, L. (2001b). Body image, eating disorders and obesity in youth: The future is now. In J. K. Thompson & L. Smolak (Eds.), *Body image, eating disorders and obesity in youth: Assessment, prevention and treatment* (pp. 1–18). Washington, DC: American Psychological Association.

Thompson, J. K., & Stice, E. (2001). Internalization of the thin-ideal: Mounting evidence for a new risk factor for body image disturbance and eating pathology. *Current Directions in Psychological Science, 11,* 181–183.

Thompson, J. K., & van den Berg, P. (2002). Assessment of body image attitudes in adolescents and adults. In T. F. Cash & T. Pruzinsky (Eds.), *Body images: A handbook* (pp. 142–154). New York: Guilford Press.

Thompson, J. K., & Williams, D. E. (1987). An interpersonally based cognitive-behavioral psychotherapy. In M. Hersen, R. M. Eisler, & P. M. Miller (Eds.), *Progress in behavior modification* (Vol. 21, pp. 230–258). Newbury Park, CA: Sage.

Vander Wal, J. S., & Thelen, M. H. (2000). Predictors of body image dissatisfaction in elementary-age school girls. *Eating Behaviors, 1,* 105–122.

Varnado, P. J., Williamson, D. A., Bentz, G. G., Ryan, D. H., Rhodes, S. K., O'Neil, P. M., et al. (1997). Prevalence of binge eating disorder in obese adults seeking weight loss treatment. *Eating and Weight Related Disorders, 2,* 117–124.

Vohs, K. D., Bardone, A. M., Joiner, T. E., Abramson, L. Y., & Heatherton, T. F. (1999). Perfectionism perceived weight status, and self-esteem interact to predict bulimic symptoms: A model of bulimic symptom development. *Journal of Abnormal Psychology, 108,* 695–700.

Walsh, B. T., & Garner, D. M. (1997). Diagnostic issues. In D. M. Garner & P. E. Garfinkel (Eds.), *Handbook of treatment for eating disorders* (pp. 25–33). New York: Guilford Press.

Walsh, B. T., Oldman, A., Franklin, M., Fairburn, C. G., & Cowen, P. (1995). Dieting decreases plasma tryptophan and increases prolactin response to d-fenfluramine in women but not in men. *Journal of Affective Disorders, 33,* 89–97.

Walsh, B. T., Wilson, G. T., Loeb, K. L., Devlin, M. J., Pike, K. M., Roose, S. P., et al. (1997). *American Journal of Psychiatry, 154,* 523–531.

Walters, E. E., & Kendler, K. S. (1995). Anorexia nervosa and anorexia-like syndromes in a population-based female twin sample. *American Journal of Psychiatry, 152,* 64–71.

Weiner, K., & Thompson, J. K. (1997). Overt and covert sexual abuse: Relationship to body image and eating disturbance. *International Journal of Eating Disorders, 22,* 273–284.

Wertheim, E. H., Koerner, J., & Paxton, S. J. (2001). Longitudinal predictors of restrictive eating and bulimic tendencies in three different age groups of adolescent girls. *Journal of Youth and Adolescence, 30,* 69–81.

Westen, D., & Harnden-Fischer, J. (2001). Personality profiles in eating disorders: Rethinking the distinction between Axis I and Axis II. *American Journal of Psychiatry, 158,* 547–562.

Williamson, D. A. (1990). *Assessment of eating disorders: Obesity, anorexia, and bulimia nervosa.* New York: Pergamon Press.

Williamson, D. A., Anderson, D. A., & Gleaves, D. H. (1996). Anorexia nervosa and bulimia nervosa: Structured interview methodologies and psychological assessment. In J. K. Thompson (Ed.), *Body image, eating disorders and obesity: An integrative guide for assessment and treatment* (pp. 205–233). Washington, DC: American Psychological Association.

Williamson, D. A., Zucker, N. L., Martin, C. K., & Smeets, M. A. M. (2001). Etiology and management of eating disorders. In P. B. Sutker & H. E. Adams (Eds.), *Comprehensive handbook of psychopathology* (3rd ed., pp. 641–670). New York: Kluwer Academic/Plenum Press.

Wonderlich, S. A. (1995). Personality and eating disorders. In K. D. Brownell & C. G. Fairburn (Eds.), *Eating disorders and obesity: A comprehensive handbook* (pp. 171–176). New York: Guilford Press.

Wonderlich, S. A., & Mitchell, J. E. (1997). Eating disorders and comorbidity: Empirical, conceptual, and clinical implications. *Psychopharmacology Bulletin, 33,* 381–390.

World Health Organization. (1992). *The ICD-10 classification of mental and behavioral disorders: Clinical descriptions and diagnostic guidelines.* Geneva, Switzerland: Author.

Yager, J. (2000). Weight perspectives: Contemporary challenges in obesity and eating disorders. *American Journal of Psychiatry, 157,* 851–853.

Yanovski, S. Z., Nelson, J. E., Dubbert, B. K., & Spitzer, R. L. (1993). Association of binge eating disorder and psychiatric comorbidity in obese subjects. *American Journal of Psychiatry, 150,* 1472–1479.

CHAPTER 16

Sleep Disorders: Evaluation and Diagnosis

CHARLES M. MORIN and JACK D. EDINGER

S LEEP DISORDERS ARE common and debilitating conditions that contribute to emotional distress, social and occupational dysfunction, increased risks for injury, and, in some instances, serious medical illnesses. Despite their prevalence and clinical significance, sleep disorders have traditionally received little attention in health provider training programs. This chapter discusses sleep disorders most likely to be encountered in health provider practices. Specifically, this chapter reviews the diagnostic classification, clinical characteristics, course, and prognosis of various sleep disorders and explores the epidemiology of sleep pathology in modern society. In addition, etiological factors involved in the development of sleep disorders are considered, and methods for assessing patients' sleep complaints are described.

CLASSIFICATION

Whereas various nosologies are available for sleep disorder classification, the *International Classification of Sleep Disorders-Revised: Diagnostic and Coding Manual* (ICSD-R; American Sleep Disorders Association [ASDA], 1997) and the Sleep Disorders section of the *Diagnostic and Statistical Manual of Mental Disorders* (*DSM-IV-TR*; American Psychiatric Association [APA], 2000) are currently most widely used. The ICSD-R delineates clinical features and diagnostic criteria for more than 80 highly specific sleep disorders. As such, this system is best suited for sleep specialists. In contrast, the *DSM-IV-TR* describes a smaller number of global diagnostic subtypes, many of which subsume several ICSD-R diagnoses. Although there is considerable overlap between these two diagnostic systems, psychologists and other mental health practitioners are generally more familiar with the *DSM-IV-TR*. Thus, only this system for sleep disorders classification is considered at length herein.

As illustrated in Table 16.1, the *DSM-IV-TR* delineates a variety of discrete diagnostic sleep disorders that are grouped into four broad categories on the basis

Table 16.1

DSM-IV-TR Sleep Disorders Classification

I. Primary Sleep Disorders
   A. Dyssomnias
      1. Primary Insomnia
      2. Narcolepsy
      3. Breathing-Related Sleep Disorders
      4. Primary Hypersomnia
      5. Circadian Rhythm Sleep Disorders
      6. Dyssomnia Not Otherwise Specified
   B. Parasomnias
      1. Nightmare Disorder
      2. Sleep Terror Disorder
      3. Sleepwalking Disorder
      4. Other Parasomnias
II. Sleep Disorders Related to Another Mental Disorder
   A. Insomnia Related to Another Mental Disorder
   B. Hypersomnia Related to Another Mental Disorder
III. Sleep Disorder Related to a General Medical Condition
   A. Insomnia Type
   B. Hypersomnia Type
   C. Parasomnia Type
   D. Mixed Type
IV. Substance-Induced Sleep Disorder*
   A. Insomnia Type
   B. Hypersomnia Type
   C. Parasomnia Type
   D. Mixed Type

---

*The additional specifier "With Onset During Intoxication" should be used with Substance Induced Sleep Disorders if sleep-related symptoms develop during intoxification with the substance; the specifier "With Onset During Withdrawal" should be used when the sleep symptoms develop during or shortly after withdrawal from the substance.
Source: From *Diagnostic and Statistical Manual of Mental Disorders, Text Revision (DSM-IV-TR)*; American Psychiatric Association, 2000.

of their presumed etiologies. *Primary sleep disorders* include various sleep-wake disturbances arising from abnormalities in the biological sleep-wake system and complicated by factors such as conditioned arousal at bedtime, poor sleep hygiene practices, and development of secondary medical illnesses. Included in this broad category are several *dyssomnias* arising from abnormalities in the timing, amount, or quality of sleep, and *parasomnias,* characterized by abnormal events (nightmares) or unusual behaviors (e.g., sleepwalking) during sleep. In contrast, *sleep disorders related to another mental disorder* involve a prominent sleep complaint attributable to a coexisting mental disorder such as a mood or anxiety disorder. Similarly, *sleep disorders due to a general medical condition* include disturbances arising directly from the effects (pain, seizures, etc.) of an active medical illness. Finally, *substance-induced sleep disorders* are presumed to arise from inappropriate use of, or withdrawal from, medications, illicit drugs, stimulants, or alcohol.

Of the various sleep disorders listed in Table 16.1, only those classified as primary sleep disorders may occur in the absence of a coexisting psychiatric, medical, or substance use problem. Moreover, even when a psychiatric, medical, or substance abuse disorder is also present, primary sleep disorders are viewed as having etiologies independent of such comorbid conditions. In contrast, the remaining diagnoses are assigned as codiagnoses only among individuals who present a prominent sleep-wake complaint that warrants separate clinical attention. For example, a patient who presents a clinically prominent complaint of insomnia that is determined to arise from a recurrent *major depressive disorder* would be assigned both a diagnosis of *major depressive disorder-recurrent* and a diagnosis of *insomnia related to another mental disorder*. The ensuing discussion provides descriptions of the various diagnostic subgroups listed in Table 16.1. Inasmuch as the reader is likely to have less knowledge of the primary sleep disorder subtypes, more extensive descriptions of these disorders are provided.

PRIMARY SLEEP DISORDERS: DYSSOMNIAS

Primary Insomnia Primary insomnia, characterized by difficulty initiating or maintaining sleep or persistent poor-quality sleep, is a relatively common form of sleep disturbance that cannot be attributed to an underlying psychiatric, medical, or substance abuse problem. However, the diagnosis of primary insomnia does not imply total absence of psychiatric or medical disorders, but rather a sleep disturbance that is viewed as independent of any coexisting conditions. Indeed, individuals suffering from primary insomnia often complain of mild anxiety, mood disturbances, concentration or memory dysfunction, somatic concerns, and general malaise, but such clinical findings are viewed as common symptoms rather than as causes of their sleep disturbances.

Development and persistence of this condition have been ascribed to myriad psychological, behavioral, and physiological anomalies. As suggested by some writers (Hauri, 2000; Hauri & Fisher, 1986; Spielman, 1986; Stepanski, 2000), primary insomnia, like many other forms of sleep disturbance, arises from a special confluence of endogenous *predisposing characteristics*, sleep-disruptive *precipitating events*, and *perpetuating behaviors or circumstances*. Vulnerabilities, such as proneness to worry, repression of disturbing emotion, physiological hyperarousal, innate propensity toward light, or fragmented sleep—or all of these—may predispose certain individuals to a primary sleep disturbance. Among such individuals, insomnia may develop given sufficient stress or disruption from a precipitating event (e.g., loss of a loved one, undergoing a painful medical procedure, frequent disruption of sleep-wake schedule). Subsequently, primary insomnia persists when conditioned environmental cues and maladaptive habits serve to perpetuate sleep disturbance long after the initial precipitating circumstances are resolved.

Many primary insomnia sufferers report intense preoccupation with sleep and heightened arousal as bedtime approaches (Hauri, 2000). This pattern is demonstrated by the following case study.

Patients such as Ms. P. usually describe bedtime as the worst time of day. A vicious cycle often emerges for such patients in which repetitive unsuccessful sleep attempts reinforce their sleep-related anxiety, which, in turn, contributes to continued sleep difficulty. Through repetitive association with unsuccessful sleep efforts, the bedroom environment and presleep rituals often become cues or stimuli for poor sleep. Moreover, in some cases, formerly benign habits, such as watching television, eating, or reading in bed, may also reduce the stimulus value

---

Case Study 1

Ms. P. was a 71-year-old married woman who presented to a sleep disorders clinic after referral by her primary physician. On presentation, she reported a six-month history of insomnia. She noted her sleep difficulty had begun during a time when she was worried about her husband's medical status. Although her husband's medical condition eventually was resolved, her insomnia persisted and actually had worsened over time. At the time of her initial sleep clinic visit, she reported that she had developed a marked aversion to thoughts of her daily bedtime. Indeed, she noted that her anxiety level typically rose each day as her usual bedtime approached. Reportedly, she typically had great difficulty initiating sleep and, as a result, had resorted to frequent use of prescription sleeping pills to remedy her problem. However, on many occasions, she continued to have increased anxiety about sleep and a less than desirable night's sleep despite the use of prescribed sleep aids. A full work-up, including medical exam by her primary physician and psychological screening assessment by a sleep clinician, revealed no medical or psychiatric cause of her sleep difficulty. As part of the assessment, the patient also completed self-report measures of anxiety and depression and kept a daily sleep diary for a period of two weeks before initiating treatment. Although the patient appeared to have developed some psychological dependence on her sleep medication, such dependence appeared secondary to what was viewed as her primary insomnia problem.

---

of the bed and bedroom for sleep and may further enhance the sleep problem. As a result, it is not unusual for primary insomnia sufferers to report improved sleep in novel settings where conditioned environmental cues are absent and usual presleep rituals are obviated.

Narcolepsy   Narcolepsy is a relatively rare sleep disorder arising from environmental influences acting on specific hereditary factors. Characteristically, this condition results in moderate-to-severe daytime dysfunction. Classic narcolepsy is defined by a tetrad of symptoms including:

1. *Excessive daytime sleepiness* and unintended sleep episodes occurring during situations (e.g., driving, at work, during conversations) when those without sleep disorders typically are able to remain awake.
2. *Cataplexy,* which consists of an abrupt and reversible decrease or loss of muscle tone (without loss of consciousness) precipitated by emotions such as laughter, anger, surprise, or exhilaration.
3. *Sleep paralysis,* which involves awakening from nocturnal sleep with an inability to move.
4. *Hypnagogic hallucinations* consisting of vivid images and dreams, usually just as sleep develops, but sometimes intruding into wakefulness (Guilleminault & Anagnos, 2000; Karacan & Howell, 1988).

Individuals with narcolepsy complain of frequent overwhelming episodes throughout the day during which they feel compelled to sleep despite having obtained a seemingly adequate amount of sleep during the previous night. Although daytime naps are often viewed as momentarily restorative, excessive sleepiness may return shortly thereafter. As the syndrome progresses, naps may lose their restorative value, and even nocturnal sleep may become disturbed (Parks, 1985).

Breathing-Related Sleep Disorders   A variety of breathing-related sleep disorders (BRSDs) may produce significant nocturnal sleep disruption and result in sleep-wake complaints. Patients suffering form *obstructive sleep apnea* experience repetitive partial (hypopneas) or complete (apneas) obstructions of their upper airways during sleep despite continued diaphragmatic effort to breathe. Other patients who suffer from *upper airway resistance syndrome* may show repeated arousals in association with far more subtle periods of reduced patency in the upper airway. In contrast, patients suffering from *central sleep apnea* experience sleep disruption as a result of repeated events during which both airflow and respiratory efforts cease. Finally, patients with *central alveolar hypoventilation syndrome* experience sleep-related worsening of their daytime proneness to hypoventilate. Whatever their exact form, such BRSDs lead to repeated arousals from sleep (to restart normal breathing) and consequent diminution in sleep quality and restorative value.

Although some patients with BRSDs complain of insomnia, most report excessive daytime sleepiness and unintentional sleep episodes occurring while watching television, reading, or driving their motor vehicles. Additional symptoms may include loud snoring, gasping for breath during sleep, frequent dull headaches on awakening, and *automatic behaviors* (i.e., carrying out activities without, at the moment, being aware of their actions). BRSDs may result in psychological consequences such as dysphoria, irritability, concentration difficulties, and memory dysfunction. In addition, they may produce serious medical consequences, including hypertension, cardiac arrhythmias and arrest, cerebral vascular infarction (stroke), sexual dysfunction, and nocturnal enuresis (Guilleminault, 1989; Partinen & Palomaki, 1985). The pathological daytime sleepiness of patients with BRSDs places them at dramatically increased risk for serious daytime mishaps such as traffic accidents (Findley, Unverzadt, & Suratt, 1988; Teran-Santos, Jimenez-Gomez, & Cordero-Guevara, 1999).

Primary Hypersomnia   Primary hypersomnia is a sleep-wake disorder characterized by excessive daytime sleepiness that cannot be attributed to a BRSD, presence of narcolepsy, or a medical, psychiatric, or substance abuse problem. Individuals with this condition present complaints of severe daytime drowsiness that interferes with work performance, social functioning, and general quality of life. Daytime somnolence leads to frequent naps that are not refreshing. Nocturnal sleep is long, undisturbed, and without respiratory impairment. Moreover, there is no evidence of sleep paralysis or cataplexy. Awakening in the morning is often difficult and accompanied by excessive grogginess or *sleep drunkenness* (Billard & Besset, 1998). Like patients with BRSDs or narcolepsy, patients suffering from primary hypersomnia usually require referral to sleep specialists for proper diagnosis and management.

Circadian Rhythm Sleep Disorders   Individuals with circadian rhythm sleep disorders (CRSDs) experience persistent or recurrent sleep-wake difficulties because of a mismatch between their endogenous, circadian sleep-wake rhythms and the sleep-wake schedules imposed on them by their educational pursuits, work settings, or social demands. Alterations of the usual sleep-wake pattern because of jet lag, rotating shift work, or social and recreational pursuits may lead to CRSDs. In some individuals, CRSDs are intermittent or recurrent as a function of frequently changing work or travel schedules. For others, aberrant bedtimes may, over a period, lead to a persistent shift (either advance or delay) in the underlying circadian mechanisms that regulate the timing of when sleep occurs.

These individuals typically complain that their sleep is disrupted or does not occur at a time that is consistent with their desired sleep-wake schedule. In addition, they often report insomnia during their preferred sleep periods and excessive sleepiness during the times they choose to be awake. Among individuals engaged in rotating shift work, alterations in chosen sleep-wake schedules between workdays and days off may perpetuate the sleep-wake complaints. In other cases, the person appears to obtain a normal amount of sleep if it is allowed to occur ad lib and not at the time chosen in response to actual or perceived external demands (Baker & Zee, 2000; Weitzman et al., 1981). Whatever the cause, such individuals usually require interventions designed to resynchronize their endogenous and exogenous sleep-wake rhythms.

PRIMARY SLEEP DISORDERS: PARASOMNIAS

Nightmare Disorder   Nightmare disorder is characterized by repeated awakenings from nocturnal sleep or daytime naps precipitated by disturbing dreams. Typically, such dreams involve threats to the individual's physical, psychological, or emotional well-being. On awakening, the individual appears fully alert, oriented, and cognizant of the arousing dream's content. Whereas anxiety and depressed mood may develop as secondary features of the nightmares, such emotional symptoms do not meet criteria for a psychiatric disorder. Moreover, inasmuch as nightmares are common to children, college students, and many noncomplaining normal adults (Nielsen & Zadra, 2000), nightmare disorder is diagnosed only when recurrent disturbing dreams cause impairment of emotional, social, or occupational functioning (APA, 2000).

Individuals with nightmare disorder complain of repeated disturbing dreams that arouse them from their sleep. Because nightmares arise during rapid eye movement (REM) sleep, individuals with nightmare disorder typically report nightmare-induced awakenings during the latter half of the night, when REM episodes typically become longer and more vivid. Careful interview also usually reveals dream content that reflects a recurrent theme reflective of underlying conflicts, characteristic fears, or more general personality characteristics (A. Kales, Soldatos, Caldwell, Charney, et al., 1980). For example, individuals with obsessive-compulsive traits often report recurrent nightmares during which they find themselves repeatedly unable to finish an important assignment despite their persistent efforts to do so. In addition, individuals with nightmare disorder usually complain of anxiety and sleep disturbance caused by the nightmares as well as resultant disruption of their normal day-to-day functioning. The following case study exemplifies the nature of this condition.

Sleepwalking and Sleep Terror Disorders   In approximately 15% of all patients presenting to sleep centers, aberrant nocturnal behaviors disrupt normal sleep

Case Study 2

Ms. R. was a 45-year–old, successful, upwardly mobile businesswoman who presented to the sleep center with a complaint of frequent disturbing dreams. In particular, she reported being bothered by a recurrent dream that often awakened her and left her feeling anxious. The theme of this dream centered on her trying to arrive on time for a very important job interview. The dream typically began with her leaving her home with the intent to arrive for her interview on time. However, she noted that she typically would be running late and, hence, felt uncertain as to whether she would actually arrive for her interview on schedule. As the dream typically progressed, she arrived at a building where the interview was to take place, at which time she encountered a male doorkeeper standing beside the building entry, which looked very much like a garage door. She would request entry to the building, and the doorkeeper would set into motion an apparatus that looked like a mechanical mouse. This "mouse" would then travel very slowly up the wall beside the door until it reached the unlocking mechanism. At that point, the "mouse" inserted itself into this mechanism and the door opened. The patient reported that she then would typically enter the building and walk down a hallway until she encountered a very similar locked door and another male doorkeeper, who again had to engage the maddeningly slow mechanical mouse to unlock the door. Once this second door opened, she entered another hallway, only to eventually encounter yet another door that had to be opened in similar fashion by an attendant. This process typically repeated several times during the dream, and with each new door she encountered, she noted increased anxiety and fear that she would be late for her interview. Typically, the dream would culminate with her going through a final door and finding herself back outside the building right back where she started. At this point in the dream, she would awaken feeling anxious and frustrated. In addition to assessment of her sleep complaint, the evaluation revealed no significant symptomatology of either anxiety or depression. The patient was asked to keep a daily diary of her nightmares, noting the frequency, intensity, and content of those disturbing dreams. This material was subsequently used for an exposure-based intervention.

(Coleman et al., 1982). Among the more common of these are sleepwalking and sleep terrors. Both phenomena occur early in the sleep period and appear to represent incomplete arousals from the deepest stages of sleep, known as slow-wave sleep. Individuals with *sleepwalking disorder* arise from bed in a stuporous state and amble about their homes but may also walk outdoors (A. Kales, Soldatos, Caldwell, Kales, et al., 1980). Typically, such sleepwalking episodes involve behaviors that are relatively routine, such as using the bathroom, eating, talking, or walking aimlessly about the home. In contrast, individuals with *sleep terror disorder* display episodes during which they suddenly emit a shrill scream, usually after sitting up in bed. Because neither of these conditions is associated with REM sleep, the affected individual usually does not report dream content in association with the event. Moreover, the patient is usually difficult to arouse from the episode and may have no recall of the event the next morning. Because more slow-wave sleep occurs in younger age groups, these events are observed most commonly in children, although they also may develop in adults. At a minimum, such events cause individual embarrassment and may contribute to avoidance of certain situations (e.g., going on trips, overnight visits to friends' homes). However, both sleepwalking and sleep terror episodes may result in injury to the affected individual or to a bed partner. In some cases, acts of violence such as striking out at others may occur during these events, and rare instances of homicide during sleepwalking episodes have been observed (Broughton et al., 1994). Referral to a specialty sleep disorders clinic is indicated whenever historical information suggests such parasomnias pose risks to the affected individual or others.

SLEEP DISORDERS RELATED TO ANOTHER MENTAL DISORDER

Sleep-wake complaints are extremely common among a range of psychiatric disorders (Nofzinger, Buysse, Reynolds, & Kupfer, 1993). However, a small subset of individuals with psychiatric disorders either minimizes the importance of other symptoms or reports disturbances of sleep and wakefulness as the most salient concerns. In such cases, the diagnosis of sleep disorder related to another mental condition is assigned in addition to the diagnosis for the contributing psychiatric condition.

Several clinical case series (Buysse et al., 1994; Coleman et al., 1982; Edinger et al., 1989; Tan, Kales, Kales, Soldatos, & Bixler, 1984) have shown that mood disorders are more prevalent than other psychiatric conditions among patient groups who present to sleep disorders centers. Among such groups, those suffering from depression typically complain of insomnia characterized by sleep-onset difficulty, early morning awakenings, and nonrefreshing, fragmented sleep. Nocturnal sleep recordings generally corroborate these difficulties. In addition, they show a reduced latency to the onset of the first REM period, an increase in the number of eye movements during REM episodes (particularly early in the night), a reduction in deep or slow-wave sleep, and an increase in both lighter sleep stages and arousals (Reynolds & Kupfer, 1987). However, many of these sleep aberrations may be observed in other psychiatric disorders as well (Benca, Obermeyer, Thisted, & Gillin, 1992). Conversely, patients with bipolar disorder show a cyclic pattern of insomnia and hypersomnia corresponding to their manic-depressive swings, but such individuals most often complain of hypersomnia and fatigue during their depressive periods. Finally, individuals with atypical mood disorders (e.g., seasonal depression) complain of hypersomnia, which is manifested by extended nocturnal sleep periods, frequent napping, and feelings of fatigue and lethargy (Walsh, Moss, & Sugerman, 1994).

Anxiety disorders also frequently contribute to sleep disturbances, but proportionately account for a lower percentage of sleep disorder diagnoses than do the mood disorders among those who present to sleep centers (Buysse et al., 1994; Tan et al., 1984). Nonetheless, general population surveys suggest that insomnias associated with anxiety disorders may be slightly more prevalent than insomnias associated with depressive conditions (Ohayon, Caulet, & Lemoine, 1998). Most commonly, those with anxiety disorders report complaints of difficulty initiating or maintaining sleep and less commonly report early morning awakening or complain solely that their sleep is not restorative (Ohayon et al., 1998). Among individuals with phobic or obsessive-compulsive disorders, sleep disturbance may emerge in response to troublesome stimuli or situations, whereas those with generalized anxiety disorders and posttraumatic stress disorders may experience a more pervasive and unrelenting insomnia problem (Walsh et al., 1994). Alternatively, some patients with panic disorder complain of sleep disturbances caused by nocturnal panic attacks occurring during non-REM sleep (Hauri, Friedman, & Ravaris, 1989).

In addition to mood and anxiety disorders, a number of other psychiatric conditions may give rise to a sleep-wake complaint. Insomnia is not uncommon among individuals with somatoform disorders, likely because of their tendencies to somatize emotional or psychological conflicts (Walsh et al., 1994). In contrast, insomnia arises among some Axis II personality disorders because of their chaotic lifestyles and irregular sleep schedules. Insomnia and *night wandering* commonly accompany dementia, as a result of associated anomalies in the biological sleep-wake system (Bliwise, 1993). Finally, marked sleep disturbance is common to schizophrenia and other psychoses, but individuals with such disorders rarely report sleep difficulties as their primary or sole complaint.

Sleep Disorder Due to a General Medical Condition

Sleep-wake disturbances arise in the context of medical disorders that are too numerous to consider here. However, most such medical conditions do not warrant a separate sleep disorder diagnosis, inasmuch as sleep complaints do not dominate their clinical presentation. Nevertheless, a subset of patients with medical conditions complains of sleep difficulties to such a degree that such complaints warrant separate clinical attention. A diagnosis of sleep disorder due to a general medical condition is made in such cases.

Individuals with sleep disorders due to a general medical condition may suffer from an insomnia type, hypersomnia type, parasomnia type, or a mixture (mixed type) of these forms of sleep-wake disturbances. Insomnia may arise from a variety of medical conditions including vascular headaches, cerebrovascular disease, hyperthyroidism, chronic bronchitis, degenerative neurological conditions, and pain accompanying rheumatoid arthritis. In contrast, conditions such as hypothyroidism, viral encephalitis, and chronic fatigue syndrome may result in hypersomnia complaints (Wooten, 1994). Among patients with medically based parasomnias, those with sleep-related epileptic seizures constitute the largest subgroup. Regardless of their presenting sleep difficulties, individuals with a medically based sleep disorder usually require intervention for their contributing medical conditions to realize sleep-wake improvements.

Substance-Induced Sleep Disorder

A variety of medications, illicit drugs, and other substances in common use may contribute to sleep-wake disturbances. Many of these substances produce insomnia, hypersomnia, parasomnias, or a mixture of these symptoms, either while in use or during periods of withdrawal and abstinence. When such sleep-wake disturbances are presented as a predominant clinical complaint, a diagnosis of substance-induced sleep disorder is warranted as a codiagnosis in addition to the *DSM-IV-TR* diagnosis descriptive of the substance abuse problem. Most commonly, such a diagnosis would be associated with excessive use of alcohol, sedating hypnotic medications, and stimulants.

Approximately 10% of men and 3% to 5% of women develop significant alcohol dependence/abuse problems (Schuckit & Irwin, 1988). Various factors may contribute to alcohol dependence, but chronic sleep difficulties may lead many to rely on alcohol as a hypnotic aid. Survey data suggests that 2% to 5% of those between 18 and 45 years of age routinely use alcohol by itself or in combination with other sleep aids to combat insomnia (E. O. Johnson, Roehrs, Roth, & Breslau, 1998). Alcohol ingestion may facilitate sleep onset but usually leads to sleep maintenance difficulties because of sleep fragmentation caused by metabolic withdrawal effects occurring amid the sleep period. In addition, heavy alcohol consumption may result in a variety of parasomnias, such as bedwetting, sleep terrors, and sleepwalking. Moreover, given alcohol's pronounced suppressant effects on REM sleep, vivid, disturbing dreams may emerge during alcohol withdrawal due to a *REM rebound effect* (Gillin & Drummond, 2000). Among chronic alcohol abusers, insomnia may persist through even extended periods of abstinence and serve as the primary catalyst for relapse (Brower, Aldrich, & Hall, 1998).

Like alcohol, sedating prescription medications and sedative-hypnotics in particular may contribute to a substance-induced sleep disorder. Although most sedating medications used as sleep aids are effective for transient sleep disturbances, most such medications lose their effectiveness with continued use. Individuals who frequently use sedating medications for sleep often experience a return of their insomnia as they become tolerant to such drugs. In turn, hypersomnia complaints may emerge among those who increase medication dosages to reestablish drug efficacy. In addition, abrupt withdrawal of some sedating medications with short *half-lives* may lead to a period of *rebound insomnia* during which sleep disturbances worsen (Gillin & Drummond, 2000). Clinical observations suggest that such withdrawal effects often contribute to loss of self-efficacy concerning sleep and encourage many individuals to continue use of hypnotics long after such drugs lose their effectiveness.

In contrast, stimulants such as amphetamines, cocaine, caffeine, and nicotine increase daytime alertness and may disrupt nighttime sleep. As a result, insomnia complaints may arise during periods of use. Conversely, complaints of hypersomnia may emerge during periods of withdrawal and abstinence. However, paradoxical symptoms, such as insomnia during nicotine withdrawal and hypersomnia during periods of heavy caffeine use, have also been observed (Gillin & Drummond, 2000; Regestein, 1989). Whatever their exact characteristics, stimulant-related sleep disorders often may persist for prolonged periods given the addictive properties of many of the substances that perpetuate them.

EPIDEMIOLOGY

Prevalence

Various surveys have suggested high prevalence of intermittent and chronic sleep-wake complaints in industrialized societies. For example, insomnia is reported as an intermittent problem for approximately one-third of the adult population in industrialized countries whereas 10% to 15% of those surveyed report chronic, unrelenting sleep difficulties (Gallup Organization, 1995; Lugaresi, Zucconi, & Bixler, 1987; Mellinger, Balter, & Uhlenhuth, 1985; Weissman, Greenwald, Nino-Murcia, & Dement, 1997). Women are twice as likely to present insomnia complaints than men, and middle-aged and older adults are more prone to this form of sleep difficulty than are younger age groups. Both general population (e.g., Ohayon et al., 1998) and sleep clinic-based (e.g., Buysse et al., 1994) studies suggest that insomnia associated with psychiatric disorders is more prevalent than primary insomnia, and both of these forms of insomnia appear more common than circadian rhythm sleep disorders and substance-induced insomnia problems.

Somewhat less prevalent but still relatively common are hypersomnia complaints, which are presented by 3% to 5% of the adult populations in Western nations (Ford & Kamerow, 1989; Lugaresi et al., 1987). Sleep apnea sufferers likely account for the largest subgroup of these individuals as most population studies suggest between 1% and 4% of adults suffer from this disorder (Partinen & Hublin, 2000). Narcolepsy is a much less prevalent disorder that occurs in 50 of 100,000 individuals, a rate similar to the occurrence of Parkinson's disease. However, genetic factors seemingly cause variation in population prevalence rates. For instance, the Japanese appear to have the highest vulnerability for this disease, with prevalence estimates ranging between 160 and 590 per 100,000 individuals (Honda, 1979; Partinen & Hublin, 2000). The population prevalence of primary hypersomnia remains unknown in part because this diagnosis is derived by exclusion of many other medical, psychiatric, and sleep disorder diagnoses that are difficult to assess by common epidemiological survey methodology.

Less is known about prevalence of parasomnias, but limited data suggest prevalence of 3% to 9% for frequent nightmares and 0.1% to 1.0% for sleepwalking among adults. Among children, 2% to 11% are bothered by frequent nightmares, whereas sleepwalking occurs in 1% to 3% on a regular basis. Finally, sleep terrors hit a peak prevalence in children between the ages of 5 and 7 years old but occur at a rate of less than 1% in the adult population (Lugaresi et al., 1987; Partinen & Hublin, 2000).

PSYCHOLOGICAL, BEHAVIORAL, AND MEDICAL CONSEQUENCES

Sleep disorders may impart significant psychological, behavioral, and medical morbidity to those who suffer from such conditions. Studies suggest that presence of insomnia, in the absence of significant psychiatric and medical disease, dramatically increases the risk for the subsequent onset of major depressive illness and other psychiatric disorders even many years after the insomnia is first identified (Chang, Ford, Mead, Cooper-Patrick, & Klag, 1997; Weissman et al., 1997). Other studies have suggested that those who suffer from insomnia report a reduced quality of life, a greater propensity for work-related accidents, and higher alcohol consumption than do those without sleep complaints (E. O. Johnson et al., 1998; L. C. Johnson & Spinweber, 1983; Zammit, Weiner, Damato, Sillup, & McMillan, 1999). Moreover, both primary insomnia and insomnia complicated by comorbid conditions enhance use of the health care system and absenteeism from work settings (Simon & VonKorff, 1997; Weissman et al., 1997).

Like insomnia, hypersomnia complaints, in the absence of other psychiatric symptoms, increase the risk for subsequent depressive disorders (Ford & Kamerow, 1989; Lugaresi et al., 1987). In addition, several studies have implicated BRSDs in the development of serious medical conditions such as hypertension, cardiac arrhythmias, myocardial infarction, stroke, and some forms of dementia, all of which increase risk of mortality (Partinen & Hublin, 2000). Traffic fatalities also are more common among those who suffer from chronic hypersomnia, but the exact rate of sleep disordered-related accidents is difficult to ascertain because excessive sleepiness as a causal factor is often difficult, if not impossible, to ascertain after the accident occurs. However, one study found that drivers' falling asleep behind the wheel caused 27% of all traffic accidents, and such occurrences accounted for 83% of all observed fatalities (Parson, 1986).

Circadian rhythm disorders, like many other sleep disorders, may impart considerable morbidity to affected individuals. Circadian disturbances caused by frequent exposure to jet lag or shift work often lead to gastrointestinal or cardiac disorders. Furthermore, various psychiatric disturbances may arise from chronic sleep disruption due to shift work and other causes of circadian disorders (National Commission on Sleep Disorders Research, 1993). Along with their potential contribution to driver errors, improper sleep scheduling and resultant sleep loss have been implicated in serious railroad and maritime accidents as well as in accidents in the workplace (Mitler et al., 1988). Hence, the sleep disorders discussed herein may contribute to significant psychological, behavioral, and medical disorders that result in serious consequences for the affected individuals.

COURSE AND PROGNOSIS

Insomnia can begin at any time during the course of the life span, but onset of the first episode is more common in young adulthood (A. Kales & Kales, 1984; Morin, 1993). It is often triggered by stressful life events, with the most common precipitants involving separation or divorce, death of a loved one, occupational stress, and interpersonal conflicts (Healy et al., 1981; Vollrath, Wicki, & Angst, 1989). In a small subset of cases, insomnia begins in childhood, in the absence of psychological or medical problems, and persists throughout adulthood (Hauri & Olmstead, 1980). Insomnia is a frequent problem among women during menopause and often persists even after other symptoms (e.g., hot flashes) have resolved. The first episode of insomnia can also occur in late life, although it must be distinguished from normal age-related changes in sleep patterns and from sleep disturbances due to medical problems or prescribed medications (Lichstein & Morin, 2000).

For the large majority of insomnia sufferers, sleep difficulties are transient in nature, lasting a few days, and resolving themselves once the initial precipitating event has subsided. Its course may also be intermittent, with repeated brief episodes of sleep difficulties following a close association with the occurrence of stressful events (Vollrath et al., 1989). Even when insomnia has developed a chronic course, typically there is extensive night-to-night variability in sleep patterns, with an occasional restful night's sleep intertwined with several nights of poor sleep. The subtype of insomnia (i.e., sleep onset, maintenance, or mixed insomnia) may also change over time (Hohagen et al., 1994).

There are several hypothetical risk factors for insomnia (e.g., female gender, advancing age, emotional factors), and a history of insomnia itself increases the risk for future episodes of sleep difficulties (Klink, Quan, Kaltenborn, & Lebowitz, 1992). This pattern of recurrence is present in both primary insomniacs and in patients whose sleep difficulties are associated with affective or anxiety disorders (Vollrath et al., 1989). The prognosis for insomnia varies extensively across individuals and is probably mediated by psychological factors. It can also be complicated by prolonged usage of hypnotic drugs.

In narcolepsy, primary symptoms of excessive daytime sleepiness and irresistible sleep attacks usually develop during late adolescence. While onset of the syndrome may occur at any time between childhood and the fifth decade of life, accurate diagnosis is often made when an individual has already experienced symptomatology for many years. Cataplexy, sleep paralysis, and hypnagogic hallucinations almost always follow rather than precede onset of daytime sleepiness, and some features may not develop at all. Although drug therapy can provide some relief for sleep attacks and cataplexy, narcolepsy is a lifelong disorder. Excessive daytime sleepiness may worsen over time, and nighttime sleep can become impaired as a result of stimulant medications used to stay awake during the day. Other symptoms may decrease or fluctuate in intensity over the life span (Billard, Dauvilliers, & Carlander, 1998).

The most common form of BRSDs, obstructive sleep apnea, can occur at any age. It is, however, much more prevalent among middle-aged obese males (Guilleminault, 1989). When left untreated, its course is usually progressive and, in most severe cases, it can lead to significant daytime impairments (sleepiness, memory and concentration difficulties) and severe medical complications (e.g., hypertension, heart failures). Onset of primary hypersomnia usually occurs between ages 15 and 30, and symptoms develop gradually over several weeks or months.

CRSDs due to jet lag and shift work have a recurrent course that is directly linked to the frequency of traveling or schedule change. Following a transmeridian flight, it takes approximately one day for each time zone crossed for the circadian rhythm to become resynchronized with local time. Likewise, after a week of work on the night shift, it takes up to 10 days to become fully reacclimated to working in the daytime and sleeping at night. Adjustment to frequent changes in sleep schedules is more difficult with advancing age. Shift workers tend to consume more stimulants to stay awake and more hypnotics to sleep than those working regular day shifts. Working on shifts for several years may increase risk of sleep difficulties when returning to a regular daytime shift.

Most parasomnias occur first in childhood. Sleep terror and sleepwalking have a typical onset between ages 5 and 12 and tend to resolve spontaneously by mid-adolescence, suggesting a developmental course to these conditions. Their persistence, and especially onset, in adulthood has been associated with greater likelihood of concomitant psychopathology (J. D. Kales, Kales, et al., 1980; A. Kales, Soldatos, Caldwell, Kales, et al., 1980). Sleepwalking is more common than sleep terrors, but their co-occurrence is also frequent. In some individuals, both conditions may develop at the same time, whereas in others, they may develop at different times. Following sleep deprivation, there is an increase in the amount of deep sleep during the recovery period. As such, sleep deprivation can increase incidence of sleep terror and sleepwalking, which originates from deep sleep (stages 3 to 4). Fever and sleeping in an unfamiliar environment have also been associated with higher risks for these parasomnias. Nightmares can occur at any age, but their first occurrence is usually between 3 and 5 years of age. Frequency and course of nightmares are highly variable. Emotional stress can trigger nightmares in both children and adults, although they can also be isolated phenomena, independent of anxiety (Wood & Bootzin, 1990).

Sleep pathologies due to mental, medical, or substance abuse disorder tend to closely parallel the temporal course of the underlying disorder. Conditioning factors may contribute to or perpetuate a sleep problem, especially insomnia, even after the underlying condition has resolved. For example, sleep disturbances associated with major depression may persist long after the depression has lifted (Rush et al., 1986). Likewise, sleep difficulties associated with chronic use of benzodiazepines or with alcohol abuse may continue even after complete withdrawal from the substance (Morin et al., 2001).

CLINICAL PICTURE AND DIAGNOSTIC CONSIDERATIONS

This section outlines the most important issues to consider in making a differential diagnosis. After outlining the clinical picture of the four broad categories of sleep-wake complaints, we review the distinguishing features leading to specific sleep disorder diagnoses.

INSOMNIA

The clinical features of insomnia involve a subjective complaint of difficulty initiating or maintaining sleep, or nonrestorative sleep that causes significant distress or impairments in social or occupational functioning. *DSM-IV-TR* does not provide specific operational criteria to define insomnia severity. In clinical research, however, insomnia is generally defined as a sleep-onset latency or wake after sleep onset (or both) greater than 30 minutes per night for more than three nights per week (Lacks & Morin, 1992), with a corresponding sleep efficiency (ratio of time asleep to time spent in bed) of less than 85%. Sleep duration alone is not always useful to diagnose insomnia because of individual differences in sleep needs. Some people may function well with as little as 5 to 6 hours of sleep and would not necessarily complain of insomnia; conversely, others needing 9 to 10 hours may still complain of inadequate sleep when they sleep for only 7 or 8 hours. Thus, the patient's subjective complaint is crucial in establishing a diagnosis of primary or secondary insomnia. Associated features of insomnia often include complaints of daytime fatigue, cognitive impairments (attention, memory, concentration), social discomfort, and mood disturbances.

Although numerous factors can produce a subjective complaint of insomnia (e.g., emotional, medical, environmental), the main differential diagnosis is usually between primary insomnia and insomnia related to another mental disorder. This distinction is not always easily made. There is a high rate of comorbidity between sleep and psychiatric disorders in general and, more specifically, between insomnia, depression, and anxiety conditions (Morin & Ware, 1996; Ohayon et al., 1998). A difficult issue is that sleep disturbance is a common feature of several psychiatric disorders. Problems falling asleep are often linked to anxiety conditions, and early morning awakenings are linked to major depression. Nonetheless, many individuals may present insomnia with concurrent features of anxiety, depression, or both, that do not meet criteria for a psychiatric disorder. In the presence of coexisting insomnia and anxiety or depression, it is essential to clarify relative onset and course of each disorder to determine which condition is primary and which is secondary in nature. The diagnosis of primary insomnia is made when its onset and course are independent of a mental disorder. Conversely, a diagnosis of insomnia associated with psychopathology is indicated when onset of the sleep problem coincided with, and its subsequent course occurred exclusively in association with, psychopathology. Data from clinical case series suggest that between 35% and 44% of patients presenting to a sleep clinic with a primary complaint of insomnia receive a diagnosis of insomnia related to another mental disorder (Buysse et al., 1994; Coleman et al., 1982).

Insomnia can also result from another sleep disorder. *Restless legs syndrome,* a condition characterized by an unpleasant and creeping sensation in the calves of the legs, can produce severe sleep-onset insomnia. *Periodic limb movements* is a related condition characterized by stereotyped and repetitive leg twitches that can produce sleep maintenance difficulties. Some breathing-related sleep disorders, especially central sleep apnea, can also produce difficulties maintaining sleep. Obstructive sleep apnea more typically leads to a complaint of excessive daytime sleepiness. The clinical history, combined with daily monitoring of sleep-wake schedules, is usually sufficient to determine whether insomnia is related to an underlying circadian rhythm disorder. Some parasomnias, especially nightmares, can cause awakenings, but the main diagnostic focus is the nightmare. Insomnia might also arise from various medical conditions (e.g., hyperthyroidism, pain, congestive heart failure, pulmonary disease) or from use or withdrawal of prescribed medications (e.g., steroids, bronchodilators), sedative-hypnotics, alcohol, or illicit stimulants (e.g., cocaine). In those instances, the primary diagnosis would be, respectively, a sleep disorder associated with a medical condition or a substance-induced sleep disorder.

HYPERSOMNIA

The main sleep disorders with a predominant complaint of excessive daytime sleepiness are narcolepsy, breathing-related sleep disorders, and primary hypersomnia. The differential diagnosis among those conditions is based on history, clinical features, nocturnal sleep recordings, and measurement of daytime sleepiness. The first diagnostic consideration with a complaint of excessive daytime sleepiness is whether a person is allowing enough time for sleep. This possibility is suggested when a person reports fewer than six or seven hours of sleep per night and by evidence of adequate daytime alertness when sleep duration is extended to eight or nine hours. Such presentation is more likely among chronically sleep-deprived individuals with highly demanding occupational and family schedules. When time is available to catch up on sleep, such as on weekends, daytime alertness is much improved. Conversely, individuals with narcolepsy, breathing-related sleep disorders, and primary hypersomnia experience daytime sleepiness regardless of the amount of nocturnal sleep they obtain. Several additional symptoms help to distinguish among those conditions (see Table 16.2).

The most prominent symptoms in breathing-related sleep disorders, especially obstructive sleep apnea, include loud snoring and pauses in breathing. These symptoms are typically witnessed by a bed partner. In narcolepsy, the main clinical features are repeated and irresistible sleep attacks throughout the day with or without accompanying symptoms of cataplexy, hypnagogic hallucinations, and sleep paralysis. A short latency to REM sleep is a diagnostic feature of narcolepsy. In both apnea and narcolepsy, sleep continuity is impaired and the proportion of time spent in stages 3 to 4 sleep is significantly reduced. Conversely, nocturnal sleep is usually long, deep, and undisrupted in primary hypersomnia. This latter diagnosis is often made by default, in the absence of other classic symptoms.

Table 16.2

Symptoms Associated with Sleep Apnea, Narcolepsy, and Primary Hypersomnia

Symptom	Apnea	Narcolepsy	Primary Hypersomnia
Snoring	+	–	–
Breathing lapses	+	–	–
Sleep attacks	–	+	–
Cataplexy	–	+	–
Hypnagogic hallucinations	–	+	–
Sleep paralysis	–	+	–
Restless sleep	+	+	–
Excessive daytime sleepiness	+	+	+
Sleep drunkenness	+	–	+
Automatic behaviors	+	+	+

Daytime napping is refreshing in narcoleptics but not in patients with apnea or primary hypersomnia. Sleep drunkenness, which is characterized by difficult arousal and disorientation, is more often associated with primary hypersomnia and apnea than with narcolepsy. Automatic behaviors may be present in all disorders associated with hypersomnia. Onset of the disorder can provide additional clues for the differential diagnosis; narcolepsy typically occurs early in life (i.e., late adolescence), whereas sleep apnea is much more prevalent among middle-aged obese males. Patients suspected of sleep apnea, narcolepsy, or primary hypersomnia should always be referred to a sleep disorders center for nocturnal polysomnography and a daytime multiple sleep-latency test, two assessment procedures essential to confirm these diagnoses.

Several additional factors should be considered in the differential diagnosis of hypersomnia. In shift workers, a complaint of excessive sleepiness is typically due to the underlying desynchronization of circadian rhythms. Hypersomnia may also occur in the context of another mental disorder. This is more common in major affective disorder, especially in bipolar patients. Hypersomnia is usually part of the depressive phase, whereas insomnia is predominant during the manic phase. Several medical conditions (e.g., hypothyroidism and chronic fatigue syndrome) and prescribed drugs (e.g., antihypertensives) may cause hypersomnia. Use or withdrawal from substances (e.g., alcohol and sedative-hypnotics) can also impair daytime wakefulness. Individuals with primary insomnia often report fatigue and tiredness, but they are not necessarily sleepy during the day. When there is evidence of daytime sleepiness, insomnia is more likely to be associated with another medical problem (pain) or sleep disorder (apnea).

Circadian Rhythm Sleep Disorders

Most circadian rhythm sleep disorders (CRSDs) can produce insomnia, hypersomnia, or a combination of both. The main feature distinguishing CRSDs from other sleep disorders is a poor timing of sleep and wake episodes with reference to the desired schedule. In shift work and jet lag, sleep and wakefulness are compromised by frequently changing schedules or traveling across several time zones. Insomnia due to a delayed sleep phase is characterized by intractable difficulty falling asleep until early in the morning (e.g., 3:00 A.M.). There is usually no difficulty staying asleep once sleep has been achieved. More common in younger people, particularly college students, this condition is presumed to arise from an endogenous delay in the biological clock (Weitzman et al., 1981), but it may also be exacerbated by irregular sleep schedules and a natural tendency to stay up late. The main differential diagnosis is with primary sleep-onset insomnia, which is more strongly associated with sleep-anticipatory anxiety and concomitant psychological symptomatology. In the phase advance syndrome, the presenting complaint involves a compelling difficulty in staying awake during the evening (e.g., after 8:00 or 9:00 P.M.), followed by early morning awakening (e.g., 4:00 A.M.). Total sleep duration is not shortened. More frequent in older adults, this condition must be distinguished from early morning awakening, which is also a common form of sleep maintenance insomnia in both depression and late life. Duration of the previous sleep episode must be considered instead of relying exclusively on the actual clock time of the final awakening. In true early morning awakening, the final awakening is premature regardless of bedtime on the previous night.

PARASOMNIAS

The main differential diagnosis among parasomnias involves sleep terrors and nightmares. The former is characterized by a piercing scream, confusion, excessive autonomic arousal, and partial awakening. There is no recollection of disturbing dreams or of the incident on awakening in the morning. In contrast, nightmares trigger a full awakening, followed by a quick return to consciousness and vivid recall of a disturbing dream. The timing of the abnormal or distressful event is critical to make an accurate diagnosis. Sleep terrors originate from stage 3 to 4 sleep, which occurs almost exclusively in the first third of the night, whereas nightmares arise from REM sleep, which is more predominant and more intense in the last third of the night. The distinction between sleepwalking and sleep terrors is more difficult. These conditions often occur together and are considered by some as manifestations of the same arousal disorder with varying intensity. Parasomnias do not always lead to a complaint of insomnia or hypersomnia, although in the most severe forms, either of these difficulties may be present.

Because parasomnias may accompany other primary sleep disorders such as narcolepsy and breathing-related sleep disorders, those conditions should be excluded before a diagnosis of parasomnia is made. Nightmare is also a common symptom of posttraumatic stress disorder (Ross, Ball, Sullivan, & Caroff, 1989) and major depressive episodes; therefore, it is important to exclude such psychiatric conditions from consideration as well. Nocturnal panic attack may present features similar to sleep terrors and nightmares. Unlike sleep terror, nocturnal panic attack leads to a full awakening, and unlike nightmares, there is no recollection of disturbing dreams. A seizure disorder is the most common medical condition producing symptoms similar to those of parasomnias. Finally, the introduction (L-dopa compounds and certain antihypertensive drugs) and withdrawal (antidepressants and benzodiazepines) of certain medications may lead to transient increases in nightmare activity, but such occurrences are not indicative of a nightmare disorder.

PSYCHOLOGICAL AND BIOLOGICAL ASSESSMENT

Accurate diagnosis of sleep disorders rests on thorough evaluation. This principle applies to all psychiatric disorders but is even more relevant to sleep disorders because sleep is affected by a host of psychological, medical, pharmacological, and circadian factors. The differential diagnosis of sleep disorders requires a multifaceted evaluation involving a clinical interview, psychological and physical examinations, daily sleep monitoring, and, for some disorders, more specialized diagnostic procedures.

CLINICAL HISTORY

A detailed clinical history is the most important diagnostic tool for evaluation of sleep disorders. The clinical history should elicit type of complaint (insomnia, hypersomnia, unusual behaviors during sleep), chronology, course, exacerbating and alleviating factors, and responses to previous treatments. In particular, it is important to inquire about life events, psychological disorders, substance use, and medical illnesses at the time of onset of the sleep problem to help establish its etiology. At least three interviews are available to gather this information in a structured format. The *Structured Interview for Sleep Disorders* (Schramm et al., 1993), designed according to *DSM-III-R* criteria, is helpful to establish a preliminary differential diagnosis among the different sleep disorders. The *Structured Interview for Insomnia* (Morin, 1993) is more specifically geared for patients with a suspected diagnosis of primary or secondary insomnia. More recently, Spielman and Anderson (1999) have developed the *CCNY Interview for Insomnia*, which enables the interviewer to rate symptomatology in relation to the different ICSD diagnoses, while considering psychological, social, and physiological etiology of sleep disturbances. Finally, Espie (2000) has outlined a plan for conducting a sleep history assessment specifically with older adults.

Determining whether the course of the symptomatology has been chronic or intermittent is crucial in the diagnosis of some disorders. For instance, patients with narcolepsy have persistent daytime sleepiness, whereas patients with hypersomnia related to depression have more intermittent symptoms. Duration and course of insomnia can be transient, intermittent, or chronic; these distinctions can have important implications for diagnosis and treatment planning. For example, transient insomnia may require an intervention that focuses directly on precipitating conditions, whereas chronic insomnia almost always requires an intervention that also targets perpetuating factors (e.g., maladaptive sleep habits and dysfunctional cognitions). In light of the high comorbidity between sleep disturbances and psychiatric disorders, the history should identify relative onset and course of each condition to establish whether the sleep disorder is primary or secondary in nature.

Careful functional analysis of exacerbating and alleviating factors also can be quite useful diagnostically. For insomnia patients, detailed analysis of the following factors is crucial: sleeping environment; activities leading up to bedtime; patient's cognitions at bedtime or in the middle of the night; perceived impact of sleep disruptions on mood, performance, and relationships; coping strategies; and secondary gains. Interviewing the bed partner can yield most valuable diagnostic information about a patient suspected of sleep apnea or some forms of parasomnia.

Patients may be unaware of their own snoring or breathing pauses in their sleep, and they may deny or underestimate their degree of daytime sleepiness. Patients suffering from sleepwalking or sleep terrors typically have no recollection of such events, and the bed partner (or parents) represents a most important source of clinical information.

DAILY SELF-MONITORING

Prospective daily sleep diary monitoring is extremely useful for establishing a diagnosis of some sleep disorders, especially insomnia. A typical sleep diary includes entries for bedtime, arising time, sleep latency, number and duration of awakenings, sleep duration, naps, use of sleep aids, and various indices of sleep quality and daytime functioning (Morin, 1993). These data provide information about a patient's sleep habits and schedules, the nature of the sleep problem, and its frequency and intensity, all of which may vary considerably from the patient's global and retrospective report during a clinical interview. Despite some discrepancies between subjective and objective measurements of sleep parameters, daily morning estimates of specific sleep parameters represent a useful index of insomnia (Coates et al., 1982). The sleep diary is a practical and economical assessment tool for prospectively tracking sleep patterns over long periods of time in the home environment. Self-monitoring is also helpful to establish a baseline before initiating treatment and to monitor progress as the intervention unfolds. Because of the extensive night-to-night variability in sleep patterns of insomnia sufferers, it is recommended that baseline data for at least one or two weeks be obtained (Lacks & Morin, 1992). Self-monitoring can be helpful not only for elucidating insomnia complaints, but also for diagnosing circadian rhythm sleep disorders or even for distinguishing daytime sleepiness due to insufficient sleep from that due to other sleep pathologies. Recording the timing of unusual events in sleep can also assist the clinician in differentiating between a sleep terror or a nightmare.

PSYCHOLOGICAL ASSESSMENT

Clinical indications for psychological assessment vary according to the specific sleep disorders. Although any sleep disorder can be associated with comorbid psychopathology, and chronic sleep disturbances of any kind can produce psychological symptoms, such findings are less probable when the presenting complaint is hypersomnia or the suspected diagnosis is circadian rhythm sleep disorders. Psychopathology is also rare among children with parasomnias, whereas its incidence is more variable among adults. Psychological assessment should be an integral component in the evaluation of insomnia. At the very least, a screening assessment is indicated because insomnia is frequently associated with psychopathology, and even when formal criteria for specific psychiatric disorders are not met, clinical features of anxiety and depression are extremely common among patients with insomnia complaints (Sateia, Doghramji, Hauri, & Morin, 2000).

Although the Minnesota Multiphasic Personality Inventory (MMPI) has been extensively used to document rate of psychopathology and predict outcome among insomnia patients (Edinger, Stout, & Hoelscher, 1988), a more cost-effective approach is to use brief screening instruments that target specific psychological features (e.g., emotional distress, anxiety, and depression) most commonly associated with insomnia complaints. Instruments such as the Brief Symptom Inventory, the Beck Depression Inventory, and the State-Trait Anxiety Inventory can yield valuable screening data. As for all self-report measures, these instruments are subject to bias resulting from denial or exaggeration of symptoms and should never be used in isolation to make a diagnosis. Psychometric screening should always be complemented by a more in-depth clinical interview.

Numerous other self-report measures tapping various dimensions of insomnia can also yield useful information (see Table 16.3). Some instruments are used as global measures of quality (Pittsburgh Sleep Quality Index; Buysse, Reynolds, Monk, Berman, & Kupfer, 1989), satisfaction (Coyle & Watts, 1991), or impairment of sleep (Morin, 1993). Other scales are designed to evaluate mediating factors of insomnia, such as state (Pre-Sleep Arousal Scale; Nicassio, Mendlowitz, Fussell, & Petras, 1985) and trait arousal (Arousal Predisposition Scale; Coren, 1988), dysfunctional sleep cognitions (Beliefs and Attitudes about Sleep Scale; Morin, 1994), sleep-incompatible activities (Sleep-Behavior Self-Rating Scale; Kazarian, Howe, & Csapo, 1979), and sleep hygiene principles (Sleep Hygiene Awareness and Practice Scale; Lacks & Rotert, 1986). Measures of fatigue, daytime performance, and quality of life can also be quite useful to evaluate the impact of insomnia. All these measures are particularly useful for designing individually tailored insomnia interventions and assessing their outcome.

Three self-report measures can provide useful screening data on daytime sleepiness: the Epworth Sleepiness Scale (Johns, 1991), a global and retrospective measure assessing the likelihood (on a four-point scale) of falling asleep in several situations (e.g., watching TV, or riding in a car); the Stanford Sleepiness Scale (Hoddes, Zarcone, Smythe, Phillips, & Dement, 1973), a seven-point Likert-type scale measuring subjective sleepiness at a specific moment in time; and the Karolinska Sleepiness Scale (Akerstedt & Gillberg, 1990), also a Likert-type (nine-point) rating scale. As for any self-report measure, the score from these sleepiness scales cannot be taken in isolation as evidence of a sleep disorder; however, when the clinical history is positive for other symptoms, a high score should be confirmed with more objective measures.

Table 16.3
Self-Report Measures of Insomnia and Associated Features

Measures/Authors
Pittsburg Sleep Quality Index (Buysse et al., 1989)
Insomnia Severity Index (Morin, 1993)
Sleep Satisfaction Questionnaire (Coyle & Watts, 1991)
Pre-Sleep Arousal Scale (Nicassio et al., 1985)
Arousal Predisposition Scale (Coren, 1988)
Dysfunctional Beliefs and Attitudes about Sleep Scale (Morin, 1993)
Sleep-Behavior Self-Rating Scale (Kazarian et al., 1979)
Sleep Hygiene Awareness and Practice Scale (Lacks & Rotert, 1986)
The Stanford Sleepiness Scale (Hoddes et al., 1973)
The Epworth Sleepiness Scale (Johns, 1991)
The Karolinska Sleepiness Scale (Akersdedt & Gillberg, 1990)

BEHAVIORAL ASSESSMENT DEVICE

Of several behavioral assessment devices available to monitor sleep, wrist actigraphy is increasingly being used for ambulatory data collection. This activity-based monitoring system uses a microprocessor to record and store wrist activity, along with actual clock time. Data are processed through microcomputer software, and an algorithm is used to estimate sleep and wake based on wrist activity. Despite some limitations in assessing specific sleep parameters (e.g., sleep latency), wrist actigraphy is a useful method for confirming the diagnosis of insomnia and some circadian rhythm sleep disorders; it can also be used for monitoring compliance with some behavioral treatment procedures (e.g., restriction of time spent in bed) and for evaluating treatment outcome (Sadeh, Hauri, Kripke, & Lavie, 1995).

POLYSOMNOGRAPHIC EVALUATION

Polysomnography   Nocturnal polysomnography (PSG) involves monitoring of electroencephalogram (EEG), electro-oculogram (EOG), and electromyogram (EMG) readings. These three parameters are sufficient to distinguish sleep from wake and to quantify the proportion of time spent in various stages of sleep. Several additional variables such as respiration, EKG, oxygen saturation, and leg movements are usually monitored to detect other sleep-related abnormalities (e.g., breathing pauses and leg twitches) not recognized by the sleeping person. A PSG evaluation is essential for the diagnosis of sleep apnea, narcolepsy, and periodic limb movements. It can also yield useful data to document the severity of insomnia, especially in light of discrepancies between subjective complaints and objective findings. However, its clinical utility in the assessment and differential diagnosis of insomnia is more controversial. Some authors (Kales & Kales, 1984) claim that clinical evaluation is sufficient and reliable to diagnose insomnia, whereas others (Edinger et al., 1989; Jacobs, Reynolds, Kupfer, Lovin, & Ehrenpreis, 1988) argue that laboratory findings can significantly alter initial diagnostic impressions. Whether information gained from one night of PSG evaluation is of sufficient clinical value to improve treatment recommendations and outcome is still a matter of debate. The high cost of PSG remains a major deterrent to its routine use. Most insurance companies do not cover the cost of a sleep study for a suspected diagnosis of insomnia, whereas they reimburse for sleep apnea or narcolepsy. Although it is standard practice to conduct a PSG evaluation in the sleep laboratory when the suspected diagnosis is sleep apnea, there are several advantages to conducting ambulatory sleep assessment in the patient's home, a method that yields more naturalistic sleep data, particularly for those with insomnia complaints.

Multiple Sleep Latency Test (MSLT)   Assessment of daytime sleepiness should be an integral component of the evaluation process when daytime alertness is compromised by a sleep disorder. The MSLT is a daytime assessment procedure in which a person is offered five or six 20-minute nap opportunities at two-hour intervals throughout the day. Latency to sleep onset provides an objective measure of physiological sleepiness. Individuals who are well rested and without sleep disorders take 10 minutes or more to fall asleep or do not fall asleep at all. A mean sleep latency of less than 5 minutes is considered pathological and is associated with increased risks of falling asleep at inappropriate times or places, such as while driving. The MSLT is also a diagnostic test for narcolepsy in that patients with this condition enter REM sleep in two or more of the scheduled naps, whereas normal sleepers rarely get into REM sleep during daytime naps. The MSLT is performed almost exclusively on patients with a presenting complaint of excessive daytime sleepiness. Although insomnia patients may complain about daytime tiredness, typically, they do not display pathological sleepiness on the MSLT.

Combining nocturnal PSG and daytime MSLT provides the most comprehensive assessment of sleep disorder inasmuch as these procedures are recognized by many as the "gold standards" in assessing sleep and its disorders. These evaluation procedures are clinically indicated when the presenting complaint is excessive daytime sleepiness and when symptoms suggestive of breathing-related disorders, narcolepsy, and periodic limb movements are present (Reite, Buysse, Reynolds, & Mendelson, 1995). The diagnosis of insomnia, particularly sleep-onset insomnia in younger patients, can be established fairly reliably through careful clinical evaluation complemented by daily sleep diaries. A clinician can always initiate treatment, and if the patient is unresponsive, a PSG evaluation can still be conducted to screen for another disorder that was missed during the clinical evaluation. A sleep study may have a higher yield of diagnostically useful information in older patients, especially those with a subjective complaint of sleep maintenance insomnia, because this segment of the population is at increased risk for several sleep pathologies (Edinger et al., 1989; Lichstein & Morin, 2000). Patients with circadian rhythm sleep disorders usually do not require PSG evaluation. These disorders can be reliably established by clinical history, sleep diary monitoring, and, possibly, with ambulatory monitoring of rest-activity cycles using a wrist-actigraphy device. PSG is usually not indicated for patients with most parasomnias such as sleepwalking, sleep terrors, or nightmares. Because these conditions rarely occur on a nightly basis, a single night of sleep monitoring is unlikely to capture the disorder. However, PSG may be warranted if other disorders (e.g., seizures) are suspected.

ETIOLOGICAL CONSIDERATIONS

FAMILIAL AND GENETIC

Familial and genetic factors may predispose some individuals to development of certain sleep disorders. For instance, individuals suffering from sleep disorders often report positive family history for a similar condition. In addition, twin studies indicate that monozygotic twins have a higher concordance of sleep habits and sleep difficulties than dizygotic twins (Heath, Kendler, Eaves, & Martin, 1990). Although some evidence suggests that the complaint of insomnia runs in families (Bastien & Morin, 2000), it is unclear whether this is strictly due to genetic predisposition, influence of familial and social learning factors, or a combination of both. Narcolepsy is the only sleep disorder for which there is strong evidence of genetic transmission (Guilleminault & Anagnos, 2000). Studies of human leukocyte antigens (HLA) have traced two antigens (DR2 and DQwl) in 90% to 100% of narcoleptic patients. These antigens are also present in up to 35% of nonnarcoleptic individuals as well as in other autoimmune diseases (e.g., lupus and multiple sclerosis). Nonetheless, first-degree relatives of a narcoleptic proband are eight times more likely to have a disorder of excessive daytime sleepiness than are individuals in the general population. A familial predisposition has also been suggested for other sleep disorders such as sleep terrors and sleepwalking (A. Kales,

Soldatos, Bixler, et al., 1980). Risk of sleepwalking increases to 45% when one parent is affected and to 60% when both are affected. Prevalence of these conditions is up to 10 times greater in first-degree relatives of an affected individual than in the general population. The association of nightmares to familial and genetic factors has not been documented.

Except for narcolepsy, relatively few studies have examined the role of familial and genetic factors as predisposing factors to sleep disorders. It may be that hereditary factors predispose some individuals to develop sleep disorders, but the actual manifestation of the disorder may be influenced by psychological and environmental factors as well.

LEARNING AND MODELING

Primary insomnia is the sleep disorder with the strongest learning component. An earlier section of this chapter outlines the role of conditioning factors in both development and maintenance of insomnia. Briefly, insomnia may initially be precipitated by a variety of stressful life events but, rapidly, a negative association is established between sleeplessness and temporal (bedtime) and environmental (bed/bedroom) stimuli previously associated with sleep. This conditioning process may develop more rapidly among those individuals already predisposed to insomnia. Over time, the combination of maladaptive sleep habits (e.g., daytime napping, excessive amounts of time spent in bed) and dysfunctional sleep cognitions (e.g., unrealistic sleep expectations, fear of the consequences of insomnia) contribute to perpetuate sleep disturbances. For instance, primary insomnia sufferers are prone to many sleep-disruptive practices that initially may emerge as a means of combating their sleep disturbances. For example, poor sleep at night may lead to daytime napping or sleeping late on weekends in efforts to catch up on lost sleep. Alternatively, such individuals may lie in bed for protracted periods trying to *force* sleep, only to find themselves becoming increasingly awake. Such practices are particularly common among middle-age and older adults due to an increase in sleep fragmentation and shortening of their natural biological sleep-wake rhythm due to aging (Bliwise, 1993; Edinger, Wohlgemuth, Radtke, Marsh, & Quillian, 2001). In addition, other practices, such as routinely engaging in physically or mentally stimulating activities shortly before bed or failing to adhere to a regular sleep-wake schedule, may emerge as a function of lifestyle choices or perceived social obligations and also contribute to sleep difficulty. Dysfunctional sleep cognitions, such as unrealistic expectations and amplification of the consequences of insomnia, can exacerbate or perpetuate what might otherwise have been a transient sleep problem (Edinger et al., 2000; Morin, 1993).

Although the role of behavioral and cognitive factors is more clearly established in primary insomnia, these factors are most likely involved in all forms of chronic insomnia, whether primary or secondary in nature (Morin, 1993). Likewise, it is plausible that learning factors are also involved in other forms of chronic sleep disturbances such as nightmares.

LIFE EVENTS

The role of life events in the etiology of sleep disorders is more clearly documented for insomnia, a condition with a stronger psychological component, than for any other disorders. One study by Healy and colleagues (1981) found that individuals with insomnia reported more stressful life events in the year preceding onset of their insomnia than in the following year. A longitudinal study (Vollrath et al., 1989) has also confirmed the role of stressful life events in the onset or exacerbation of insomnia. While there is no evidence that sleep disorders such as sleep apnea are associated with life events, one study found that narcolepsy, a disorder with a predominant biological origin, was associated with environmental factors (e.g., stressful life events, change in sleep schedule) in about half of the narcoleptic patients surveyed (Orellana et al., 1994). Among the different forms of parasomnias, nightmares and night terrors are the only conditions that have been associated with major life events such as combat experience, sexual aggression, and natural disasters.

Age, Gender, and Racial-Ethnic

Insomnia complaints are twice as common among women as among men, and such complaints increase across the life span. The nature of insomnia complaints also changes with aging. Sleep-onset insomnia is more common among younger people, whereas difficulties maintaining sleep, such as nocturnal or early morning awakenings, are more prevalent in middle-age and older people. Although women report more sleep difficulties, their sleep patterns are apparently better preserved with aging. Among noncomplaining older adults, men display more sleep pathologies than women (Reynolds et al., 1985). BRSDs also increase with aging, but unlike insomnia, obstructive sleep apnea is much more prevalent in men than in women. After menopause, women may have a higher predisposition to central apnea. Some limited data suggest that in adults, nightmares are more common in females, whereas in children, sleep terrors are more frequent in boys (J. D. Kales, Kales, et al., 1980; Kales, Soldatos, Caldwell, Kales, et al., 1980). There are no data on age, gender, or cultural differences in circadian rhythm sleep disorders. However, older adults may have more difficulties adjusting to schedule changes. Aside from a suspected higher incidence of isolated sleep paralysis in African Americans and a higher predisposition for narcolepsy among Japanese, there is no other evidence of racial or ethnic differences in any of the sleep disorders.

Biological and Physiological

A biological component is probably involved in the etiology of all sleep disorders, even among those with a predominant psychological etiology. For instance, in primary insomnia, there is increased physiological arousal (e.g., heart rate, body temperature, skin conductance) both before sleep onset and during the sleep period, relative to baseline and to normal control sleepers (Bonnet & Arand, 1995). There is also a higher frequency of fast (Beta) brain-wave activity before sleep onset and during sleep among insomniacs, reflecting some cognitive hyperactivity, relative to noncomplaining good sleepers (Merica, Blois, & Gaillard, 1998; Perlis, Smith, Andrews, Orff, & Giles, 2001). Although it is unclear whether hyperarousal is causal, a covariation, or even the consequence of insomnia, it is likely to contribute to sleep disturbances at least in some people complaining of insomnia.

Most sleep disorders associated with a subjective complaint of excessive daytime sleepiness have a predominantly biological origin. Sleep apnea is primarily the result of a physical/anatomical obstruction in the upper-airway area causing breathing impairment during sleep. Although the etiology of narcolepsy is still unknown, it is primarily a neurological disorder involving brain structures controlling the regulation of REM sleep.

All circadian rhythm disorders share a chronobiological component, in which some physiological parameters (body temperature, melatonin secretion) that are normally regulated by a circadian rhythm (e.g., light-darkness) become out of phase with the desired sleep period. For example, in shift work, a person has to stay awake at night when his or her biological clock is ready to go to sleep. In jet lag, a mismatch between the internal circadian sleep propensity and the new required sleep-wake schedule often hampers the sleep of individuals who travel across multiple time zones. While some circadian disorders have an intrinsic chronobiological origin, other forms of sleep disturbances resulting from a rotating or night shift are generally caused by scheduling factors imposed by societal or occupational obligations.

Parasomnias are disorders of arousal involving unusual behaviors during sleep. Most of these disorders are more prevalent in childhood and are manifestations of abnormal or excessive activation of the central nervous system, involving changes in autonomic or skeletal muscle activity (ASDA, 1997). Sleepwalking and night terrors are disorders of arousal occurring mostly during the transition from deep sleep to lighter sleep. These parasomnias, which involve a dissociative state during which there is a lack of awareness of the environment accompanied by automatic behaviors, are predominantly explained by a hyperactivation of electrophysiological activity of the brain during sleep. While infrequent nightmares are considered normal phenomenon, an increase in dopaminergic or noradrenergic activity may increase the frequency of these episodes.

SUMMARY

Sleep disorders are extremely prevalent in the general population and even more so in patients with psychiatric and medical disorders. Consequences of sleep disorders include impairment of daytime functioning, diminishing quality of life, and even significant health and public safety hazards. Increasing evidence suggests that sleep disturbances may increase vulnerability to psychiatric disorders and, perhaps, prevent or delay recovery (see Billard, Partinen, Roth, & Shapiro, 1994; Morin & Ware, 1996). Unless a systematic inquiry about sleep-wake complaints is integrated in a clinical evaluation, many of those disorders can go unrecognized and remain untreated. A detailed sleep history is often sufficient to make a preliminary diagnosis. When a more medically based sleep disorder (e.g., sleep apnea or narcolepsy) is suspected, referral to a sleep disorders center is essential to confirm the diagnosis and initiate appropriate treatment. Mental health practitioners are more likely to encounter patients with a primary sleep disorder such as insomnia or sleep complaints co-occurring with psychopathology. An accurate differential diagnosis has important implications for treatment planning. When sleep disturbance is a core symptom of underlying psychopathology, treatment should focus on the basic psychopathology. If, on the other hand, the sleep disorder is primary in nature, treatment should be primarily sleep focused. At times, sleep and psychological symptomatology coexist without clear evidence of a specific cause-effect relationship. In such a case, multifocused interventions targeting both symptom clusters may be required to optimize treatment outcome.

REFERENCES

Akerstedt, T., & Gillberg, M. (1990). Subjective and objective sleepiness in the active individual. *International Journal of Neuroscience, 52*, 29–37.

American Psychiatric Association. (2000). *Diagnostic and statistical manual of mental disorders* (4th ed., text rev.). Washington, DC: Author.

American Sleep Disorders Association. (1997). *International classification of sleep disorders (ICSD): Diagnostic and coding manual* (Rev. ed.). Rochester, MN: Author.

Baker, S. K., & Zee, P. C. (2000). Circadian disorders of the sleep-wake cycle. In M. H. Kryger, T. Roth, & W. C. Dement (Eds.), *Principles and practice of sleep medicine* (3rd ed., pp. 606–614). Philadelphia: Saunders.

Bastien, C. H., & Morin, C. M. (2000). Familial incidence of insomnia. *Journal of Sleep Research, 9*, 49–54.

Benca, R. M., Obermeyer, W. H., Thisted, R. A., & Gillin, J. C. (1992). Sleep and psychiatric disorders: A meta analysis. *Archives of General Psychiatry, 49*, 651–668.

Billard, M., & Besset, A. (1998). L'hypersomnie idiopathique. In M. Billard (Ed.), *Le sommeil normal et pathologique* [Normal and pathological sleep] (2nd ed., pp. 292–298). Paris: Masson.

Billard, M., Dauvilliers, Y., & Carlander, B. (1998). La narcolepsie. In M. Billard (Ed.), *Le sommeil normal et pathologique* [Normal and pathological sleep] (2nd ed., pp. 278–292). Paris: Masson.

Billard, M., Partinen, M., Roth, T., & Shapiro, C. (1994). Sleep and psychiatric disorders. *Journal of Psychosomatic Research, 38*(Suppl. 1), 1–2.

Bliwise, D. L. (1993). Sleep in normal aging and dementia. *Sleep, 16*, 40–81.

Bonnet, M. H., & Arand, D. L. (1995). 24-Hour metabolic rate in insomniacs and matched normal sleepers. *Sleep, 18*, 581–588.

Broughton, R., Billings, R., Cartwright, R., Doucette, D., Edmeads, J., Edwrdh, M., et al. (1994). Homicidal somnambulism: A case report. *Sleep, 17*, 253–264.

Brower, K. J., Aldrich, M. S., & Hall, J. M. (1998). Polysomnographic and subjective sleep predictors of alcoholic relapse. *Alcohol Clinical and Experimental Research, 22*, 1864–1871.

Buysse, D. J., Reynolds, C. F., Kupfer, D. J., Thorpy, M. J., Bixler, E., Manfredi, R., et al. (1994). Clinical diagnoses in 216 insomnia patients using the International Classification of Sleep Disorders (ICSD), *DSM-IV*, and ICD-10 categories: A report from the APA/NIMH *DSM-IV* field trial. *Sleep, 17*, 630–637.

Buysse, D. J., Reynolds, C. F., Monk, T. H., Berman, S. R., & Kupfer, D. J. (1989). The Pittsburgh Sleep Quality Index: A new instrument for psychiatric practice and research. *Psychiatry Research, 28*, 193–213.

Chang, P. P., Ford, D. E., Mead, L. A., Cooper-Patrick, L., & Klag, M. J. (1997). Insomnia in young men and subsequent depression: The Johns Hopkins Precursors Study. *American Journal of Epidemiology, 146*, 105–114.

Coates, T. J., Killen, J. D., George, J., Marchine, F., Silverman, S., & Thoresen, C. (1982). Estimating sleep parameters: A multitrait multimethod analysis. *Journal of Consulting and Clinical Psychology 50*, 345–352.

Coleman, R. M., Roffwarg, H. P., Kennedy, S. J., Guilleminault, C., Cinque, J., Cohn, M. A., et al. (1982). Sleep-wake disorders based on a polysomnographic diagnosis: A national cooperative study. *Journal of the American Medical Association, 247*, 997–1003.

Coren, S. (1988). Prediction of insomnia from arousability predisposition scores: Scale development and cross-validation. *Behavior Research and Therapy, 26*, 415–420.

Coyle, K., & Watts, F. N. (1991). The factorial structure of sleep dissatisfaction. *Behavior Research and Therapy, 29*, 513–520.

Edinger, J. D., Fins, A. I., Glenn, D. M., Sullivan, R. J., Jr., Bastian, L. A., Marsh, G. R., et al. (2000). Insomnia and the eye of the beholder: Are there clinical markers of objective sleep disturbances among adults with and without insomnia complaints? *Journal of Consulting and Clinical Psychology, 68,* 586–593.

Edinger, J. D., Hoelscher, T. J., Webb, M. D., Marsh, G. R., Radtke, R. A., & Erwin, C. W. (1989). Polysomnographic assessment of DIMS: Empirical evaluation of its diagnostic value. *Sleep, 12,* 315–322.

Edinger, J. D., Stout, A. L., & Hoelscher, T. J. (1988). Cluster analysis of insomniacs' MMPI profiles: Relation of subtypes to sleep history and treatment outcome. *Psychosomatic Medicine, 50,* 77–87.

Edinger, J. D., Wohlgemuth, W. K., Radtke, R. A., Marsh, G. R., & Quillian, R. E. (2001). Efficacy of cognitive-behavioral therapy for treating primary sleep-maintenance insomnia: A randomized controlled trial. *Journal of the American Medical Association, 285,* 1856–1864.

Espie, C. E. (2000). Assessment and differential diagnosis. In K. L. Lichstein & C. M. Morin (Eds.), *Treatment of late-life insomnia* (pp. 81–108). Thousand Oaks, CA: Sage.

Findley, L. J., Unverzadt, M., & Suratt, P. (1988). Automobile accidents in patients with obstructive sleep apnea. *American Review of Respiratory Disease. 138,* 337–340.

Ford, D. E., & Kamerow, D. B. (1989). Epidemiologic study of sleep disturbances and psychiatric disorders: An opportunity for prevention? *Journal of the American Medical Association, 262,* 1479–1484.

Gallup Organization. (1995). *Sleep in America.* Princeton, NJ: Author.

Gillin, J. C., & Drummond, S. P. A. (2000). Medication and substance abuse. In M. H. Kryger, T. Roth, & W. C. Dement (Eds.), *Principles and practice of sleep medicine* (3rd ed., pp. 1176–1195). Philadelphia: Saunders.

Guilleminault, C. (1989). Clinical features and evaluation of obstructive sleep apnea. In M. H. Kryger, T. Roth, & W. C. Dement (Eds.), *Principles and practice of sleep medicine* (pp. 552–558). Philadelphia: Saunders.

Guilleminault, C., & Anagnos, A. (2000). Narcolepsy. In M. H. Kryger, T. Roth, & W. C. Dement (Eds.), *Principles and practice of sleep medicine* (3rd ed., pp. 676–686). Philadelphia: Saunders.

Hauri, P. J. (2000). Primary insomnia. In M. H. Kryger, T. Roth, & W. C. Dement (Eds.), *Principles and practice of sleep medicine* (3rd ed., pp. 633–639). Philadelphia: Saunders.

Hauri, P. J., & Fisher, J. (1986). Persistent psychophysiological (learned) insomnia. *Sleep, 9,* 38–53.

Hauri, P. J., Friedman, M., & Ravaris, C. L. (1989). Sleep in patients with nocturnal panic attacks. *Sleep, 12,* 323–337.

Hauri, P. J., & Olmstead, E. M. (1980). Childhood-onset insomnia. *Sleep, 3,* 59–65.

Healy, E. S., Kales, A., Monroe, L. J., Bixler, E. O., Chamberlin, K., & Soldatos, C. R. (1981). Onset of insomnia: Role of life-stress events. *Psychosomatic Medicine, 43,* 439–451.

Heath, A. C., Kendler, K. S., Eaves, L. J., & Martin, N. G. (1990). Evidence for genetic influences on sleep disturbance and sleep pattern in twins. *Sleep, 13,* 318–335.

Hoddes, E., Zarcone, V., Smythe, H., Phillips, R., & Dement, W. C. (1973). Quantification of sleepiness: A new approach. *Psychophysiology, 10,* 431–436.

Hohagen, F., Kappler, C., Schramm, E., Riemann, D., Weyerer, S., & Berger, M. (1994). Sleep onset insomnia, sleep maintaining insomnia and insomnia with early morning awakening: Temporal stability of subtypes in a longitudinal study on general practice attenders. *Sleep, 17,* 551–554.

Honda, Y. (1979). Census of narcolepsy, cataplexy and sleep life among teenagers in Fujisawa City. *Sleep Research, 2*, 191.

Jacobs, E. A., Reynolds, C. F., Kupfer, D. J., Lovin, P. A., & Ehrenpreis, A. B. (1988). The role of polysomnography in the differential diagnosis of chronic insomnia. *American Journal of Psychiatry, 145*, 346–349.

Johns, M. W. (1991). A new method for measuring daytime sleepiness: The Epworth Sleepiness Scale. *Sleep, 14*, 540–545.

Johnson, E. O., Roehrs, T., Roth, T., & Breslau, N. (1998). Epidemiology of alcohol and medication as aids to sleep in early adulthood. *Sleep, 21*, 178–186.

Johnson, L. C., & Spinweber, C. L. (1983). Quality of sleep and performance in the Navy: A longitudinal study of good and poor sleepers. In C. Guilleminault & E. Lugaresi (Eds.), *Sleep/wake disorders: Natural history, epidemiology, and long-term evolution* (pp. 13–28). New York: Raven Press.

Kales, A., & Kales, J. D. (1984). *Evaluation and treatment of insomnia.* New York: Oxford University Press.

Kales, A., Soldatos, C. R., Bixler, E. O., Ladda, R. L., Charney, D. S., Weber, G., et al. (1980). Hereditary factors in sleepwalking and night terrors. *British Journal of Psychiatry, 137*, 111–118.

Kales, A., Soldatos, C. R., Caldwell, A. B., Charney, D. S., Kales, J. D., Markel, D., et al. (1980). Nightmares: Clinical characteristics and personality patterns. *American Journal of Psychiatry, 137*, 1197–1201.

Kales, A., Soldatos, C. R., Caldwell, A. B., Kales, J. D., Humphrey, F. J., Charney, D. S., et al. (1980). Somnambulism: Clinical characteristics and personality patterns. *Archives of General Psychiatry, 37*, 1406–1410.

Kales, J. D., Kales, A., Soldatos, C. R., Caldwell, A. B., Charney, D. S., & Martin, E. D. (1980). Night terrors: Clinical characteristics and personality patterns. *Archives of General Psychiatry, 37*, 1413–1417.

Karacan, I., & Howell, J. W. (1988). Narcolepsy. In R. L. Williams, I. Karacan, & C. A. Moore (Eds.), *Sleep disorders: Diagnosis and treatment* (pp. 87–108). New York: Wiley.

Kazarian, S. S., Howe, M. G., & Csapo, K. G. (1979). Development of the sleep behavior self-rating scale. *Behavior Therapy, 10*, 412–417.

Klink, M. E., Quan, S. F., Kaltenborn, W. T., & Lebowitz, M. D. (1992). Risk factors associated with complaints of insomnia in a general adult population: Influence of previous complaints of insomnia. *Archives of Internal Medicine, 152*, 1572–1575.

Lacks, P., & Morin, C. M. (1992). Recent advances in the assessment and treatment of insomnia. *Journal of Consulting and Clinical Psychology, 60*, 586–594.

Lacks, P., & Rotert, M. (1986). Knowledge and practice of sleep hygiene techniques in insomniacs and poor sleepers. *Behavior Research and Therapy, 24*, 365–368.

Lichstein, K. L., & Morin, C. M. (Eds.). (2000). *Treatment of late-life insomnia.* Thousand Oaks, CA: Sage.

Lugaresi, E., Zucconi, M., & Bixler, E. O. (1987). Epidemiology of sleep disorders. *Psychiatric Annals, 17*, 446–453.

Mellinger, C. D., Balter, M. B., & Uhlenhuth, E. H. (1985). Insomnia and its treatment. *Archives of General Psychiatry, 42*, 225–232.

Merica, H., Blois, R., & Gaillard, J. M. (1998). Spectral characteristics of sleep EEG in chronic insomnia. *European Journal of Neurosciences, 10*, 1826–1834.

Mitler, M. M., Carskadon, M. A., Czeisler, C. A., Dement, W. C., Dinges, D. F., & Graeber, R. C. (1988). Catastrophes, sleep, and public policy: Consensus report. *Sleep, 11*, 100–109.

Morin, C. M. (1993). *Insomnia: Psychological assessment and management.* New York: Guilford Press.

Morin, C. M. (1994). Dysfunctional beliefs and attitudes about sleep: Preliminary scale development and description. *Behavior Therapist, 17,* 163–164.

Morin, C. M., Bastien, C., Guay, B., Radouco-Thomas, M., Leblanc, J., & Vallières, A. (2001). The role of cognitive-behavior therapy and supervised tapering in the discontinuation of benzodiazepines among chronic insomniacs. Paper presented in A. Harvey (Chair), *Insomnia.* Symposium presented at the meeting of World Congress of Behavioral and Cognitive Therapies, Vancouver, Canada.

Morin, C. M., & Ware, C. (1996). Sleep and psychopathology. *Applied and Preventive Psychology, 5,* 211–224.

National Commission on Sleep Disorders Research. (1993). *Wake up America: A national sleep alert.* Washington, DC: Author.

Nicassio, P. M., Mendlowitz, D. R., Fussell, J. J., & Petras, L. (1985). The phenomenology of the presleep state: The development of the presleep arousal scale. *Behavior Research and Therapy, 23,* 263–271.

Nielsen, T. A., & Zadra, A. (2000). Dream disorders. In M. H. Kryger, T. Roth, & W. C. Dement (Eds.), *Principles and practice of sleep medicine* (3rd ed., pp. 753–772). Philadelphia: Saunders.

Nofzinger, E. A., Buysse, D. J., Reynolds, C. F., & Kupfer, D. J. (1993). Sleep disorders related to another mental disorder (Nonsubstance/Primary): A *DSM-IV* literature review. *Journal of Clinical Psychiatry, 54,* 244–255.

Ohayon, M. M., Caulet, M., & Lemoine, P. (1998). Comorbidity of mental and insomnia disorders in the general population. *Comprehensive Psychiatry, 39,* 185–197.

Orellana, C., Villemin, E., Tafti, M., Carlander, B., Besset, A., & Billard, M. (1994). Life events in the year preceding the onset of narcolepsy. *Sleep, 17,* S50–S53.

Parks, J. D. (1985). *Sleep and its disorders.* London: Saunders.

Partinen, M., & Hublin, C. (2000). Epidemiology of sleep disorders. In M. H. Kryger, T. Roth, & W. C. Dement (Eds.), *Principles and practice of sleep medicine* (3rd ed., pp. 558–579). Philadelphia: Saunders.

Partinen, M., & Palomaki, H. (1985). Snoring and cerebral infarction. *Lancet, 2,* 1325–1326.

Perlis, M. L., Smith, M. T., Andrews, P. J., Orff, H., & Giles, D. E. (2001). Beta/Gamma EEG activity in patients with primary and secondary insomnia and good sleeper controls. *Sleep, 24,* 110–117.

Regestein, Q. R. (1989). Pathologic sleepiness induced by caffeine. *American Journal of Medicine, 87,* 586–588.

Reite, M., Buysse, D., Reynolds, C., & Mendelson, W. (1995). The use of polysomnography in the evaluation of insomnia. *Sleep, 18,* 58–70.

Reynolds, C. F., & Kupfer, D. J. (1987). Sleep research in affective illness: State of the art circa 1987. *Sleep, 10,* 199–215.

Reynolds, C. F., Kupfer, D. J., Taska, L. S., Hoch, C. C., Sewitch, D. W., & Spiker, D. G. (1985). The sleep of healthy seniors: A revisit. *Sleep, 8,* 20–29.

Ross, R. J., Ball, W. A., Sullivan, K. A., & Caroff, S. N. (1989). Sleep disturbance as the hallmark of posttraumatic stress disorder. *American Journal of Psychiatry, 146,* 697–707.

Rush, A. J., Erman, M. K., Giles, D. E., Schlesser, M. A., Carpenter, G., Vasavada, N., et al. (1986). Polysomnographic findings in recently drug-free and clinically remitted depressed patients. *Archives of General Psychiatry, 43,* 878–884.

Sadeh, A., Hauri, P., Kripke, D. F., & Lavie, P. (1995). The role of actigraphy in the evaluation of sleep disorders. *Sleep, 18,* 288–302.

Sateia, M., Doghramji, K., Hauri, P., & Morin, C. M. (2000). Evaluation of chronic insomnia. *Sleep, 23,* 243–308.

Schramm, E., Hohagen, F., Grasshoff, U., Rieman, D., Hujak, G., Weeb, H.-G., et al. (1993). Test-retest reliability and validity of the structured interview for sleep disorders according to *DSM-III-R. American Journal of Psychiatry, 150,* 867–872.

Schuckit, M. A., & Irwin, M. (1988). Diagnosis of alcoholism. *Medical Clinics of North America, 72,* 1133–1153.

Simon, G. E., & VonKorff, M. (1997). Prevalence, burden, and treatment of insomnia in primary care. *American Journal of Psychiatry, 154,* 1417–1423.

Spielman, A. J. (1986). Assessment of insomnia. *Clinical Psychology Review, 6,* 11–25.

Spielman, A. J., & Anderson, M. W. (1999). The clinical interview and treatment planning as a guide to understanding the nature of insomnia: The CCNY Interview for Insomnia. In S. Chokroverty (Ed.), *Sleep disorders medicine: Basic science, technical considerations and clinical aspects* (2nd ed., pp. 385–426). Boston: Butterworth-Heinemann.

Stepanski, E. J. (2000). Behavioral therapy for insomnia. In M. H. Kryger, T. Roth, & W. C. Dement (Eds.), *Principles and practice of sleep medicine* (3rd ed., pp. 647–656). Philadelphia: Saunders.

Tan, T., Kales, J. D., Kales, A., Soldatos, C. R., & Bixler, E. O. (1984). Biopsychobehavioral correlates of insomnia. IV: Diagnoses based on *DSM-III. American Journal of Psychiatry, 141,* 356–362.

Teran-Santos, J., Jimenez-Gomez, A., & Cordero-Guevara, J. (1999). The association between sleep apnea and the risk for traffic accidents. *New England Journal of Medicine, 340,* 847–851.

Vollrath, M., Wicki, W., & Angst, J. (1989). The Zurich study. VIII: Insomnia: Association with depression, anxiety, somatic syndromes, and course of insomnia. *European Archives of Psychiatry and Neurological Sciences, 239,* 113–124.

Walsh, J. K., Moss, K. L., & Sugerman, J. (1994). Insomnia in adult psychiatric disorders. In M. H. Kryger, T. Roth, & W. C. Dement (Eds.), *Principles and practice of sleep medicine* (2nd ed., pp. 500–508). Philadelphia: Saunders.

Weissman, M. M., Greenwald, S., Nino-Murcia, G., & Dement, W. C. (1997). The morbidity of insomnia uncomplicated by psychiatric disorders. *General Hospital Psychiatry, 19,* 245–250.

Weitzman, E. D., Czeisler, C. A., Coleman, R. M., Spielman, A. J., Zimmerman, J. C., Dement, W. C., et al. (1981). Delayed sleep phase syndrome: A chronological disorder with sleep onset insomnia. *Archives of General Psychiatry, 38,* 737–746.

Wood, J. M., & Bootzin, R. R. (1990). The prevalence of nightmares and their independence from anxiety. *Journal of Abnormal Psychology, 99,* 64–68.

Wooten, V. (1994). Medical causes of insomnia. In M. H. Kryger, T. Roth, & W. C. Dement (Eds.), *Principles and practice of sleep medicine* (2nd ed., pp. 509–522). Philadelphia: Saunders.

Zammit, G. R., Weiner, J., Damato, N., Sillup, G. P., & McMillan, C. A. (1999). Quality of life in people with insomnia. *Sleep,* 22(Suppl. 2), S379–S385.

CHAPTER 17

Personality Disorders

RALPH C. SERIN and WILLIAM L. MARSHALL

DESCRIPTION OF THE DISORDER

INDIVIDUALS WITH PERSONALITY disorders are seen to be reasonably normal people who nevertheless have personal styles or personalities that upset others and interfere with their interaction with others. Key features of their personalities are persistently displayed over time and across situations, such that their behavior is not particularly influenced by context. In addition, even when initiating appropriate behavior, they cannot sustain it for long periods of time or when under stress.

The primary criteria identified in the *Diagnostic and Statistical Manual for Mental Disorders* (*DSM-IV*; American Psychiatric Association [APA], 1994) for diagnosing personality disorders include "an enduring pattern of inner experience and behavior that deviates markedly from the expectations of an individual's culture, (that) is pervasive and inflexible, has an onset in adolescence or early adulthood, is stable over time, and leads to distress or impairment" (p. 629). It is important to note, however, that many, if not most, individuals deemed to have a personality disorder are not themselves distressed by the disorder, although their lives may be objectively determined to be impaired. For many of these people, their personality functioning is egosyntonic and this, of course, presents a problem in securing their cooperation in treatment. Research, for example, has revealed that 80% or more of people with personality disorder never seek treatment for their problems (Drake & Vaillant, 1985).

There are reasons for concern about possible cultural and gender biases in diagnostic practices. However, these are simply aspects of the larger problems concerning the reliability and validity of personality disorder diagnoses—problems that have beset these disorders since they were first included in the diagnostic manual.

Obviously, these problems concern researchers and no doubt confuse clinicians. Nevertheless, by far the majority of clinicians agree that some people consistently show maladaptive, inflexible, and restricted ways of behaving and thinking that seem best described as personality disorders. The problem is not so much whether these disorders exist, but rather, how they can be defined in a way that is not prejudicial, is reliable, and leads to effective treatment. Further, diagnostic categories are not mutually exclusive, potentially obfuscating the identification and prioritizing of treatment targets.

It has been suggested (Livesley, Schroeder, Jackson, & Jang, 1994; Widiger & Costa, 1994) that the solution to many of these problems would be to adopt a dimensional rather than categorical system of classification. Proposals for 10 or more dimensions to classify patients with personality disorders have been made (Livesley, Jackson, & Schroeder, 1992; Millon, 1983). This would present practical difficulties for diagnosticians because of the complexity of interpretation compared to the simpler categorical systems. However, other research has suggested that as few as three or, at most, five dimensions are sufficient to identify all the features of the diverse personality disorders (Widiger & Trull, 1992; Wiggins & Pincus, 1989). Although a dimensional system was considered for both *DSM-III-R* and *DSM-IV*, agreement among committee members was not achieved (Widiger, Frances, Spitzer, & Williams, 1988), so the manual retained the categorical approach.

DSM-IV identifies 10 distinct personality disorders (and one nonspecific category), which are grouped into three clusters:

1. *Cluster A.* Odd and eccentric disorders (paranoid, schizoid, and schizotypal).
2. *Cluster B.* Dramatic, emotional, or erratic disorders (antisocial, borderline, histrionic, and narcissistic).
3. *Cluster C.* Anxious and fearful disorders (avoidant, dependent, and obsessive-compulsive).

While two of these clusters (A and C) appear to have sufficient features in common for the clusters to make sense, cluster B is a rather confusing grouping (Widiger & Costa, 1994). In fact, there is little in the way of evidence to support the identity of any of these clusters (Frances, 1985), and there seems to be limited clinical utility to them.

RELIABILITY OF DIAGNOSIS

Before reviewing prevalence rates of personality disorders, it is important to consider diagnostic reliability. Original field trials and subsequent examinations have revealed rather poor reliability for the personality disorders, suggesting that clinicians fail to agree about a particular diagnosis for a given patient (Dahl, 1986; Rogers, Duncan, Lynett, & Sewell, 1994). Specific to the diagnosis of antisocial personality disorder (APD), Rogers, Dion, and Lynett (1992) found only 3 of 13 studies provided evidence for satisfactory reliability. Importantly, strategies to enhance reliability, such as using structured interviews and expanding the breadth of information collected, have been proposed and appear to be effective. However, these suggested diagnostic procedures require a greater time investment by clinicians and few appear willing to spend the extra time. Nonetheless, diagnostic reliability is essential if diagnoses are to be used to identify and prioritize treatment targets and if prevalence rates are to be considered meaningful.

Personality disorders present more diagnostic problems than do most of the Axis I disorders, partly because of the lower reliability of their diagnosis (Rogers et al., 1994) and their poorly understood etiology (Marshall & Barbaree, 1984), as well as weak treatment efficacy (Kelly et al., 1992). With respect to diagnosis, two indexes of reliability are important. Interrater reliability, that is, the agreement between two raters, ranges from 0.86 to 0.97 for the personality disorders (Maffei et al., 1997). Test-retest reliability, that is, agreement in diagnosis over time, is much weaker, ranging from 0.11 to 0.57 (Zimmerman, 1994). Indeed, the defining criteria introduced with *DSM-III* (APA, 1980), and subsequently modified in *DSM-III-R* (APA, 1987) and *DSM-IV* (APA, 1994), were meant to reduce diagnostic unreliability, but there is little evidence to suggest that they have been successful. Neither expanding the breadth of information collected (Zimmerman, Pfohl, Stangl, & Corenthal, 1986) nor using structured interviews (Loranger, Oldham, Russakoff, & Susman, 1987) appears to increase reliability.

PREVALENCE

Studies of the prevalence of personality disorders have examined rates among inpatient samples, outpatients, and in the community at large. Depending on the sample chosen, prevalence rates vary quite considerably. Data in Table 17.1 describe results of a community study conducted in the United States. Similar studies in Europe reveal different rates with the lifetime prevalence for most disorders being somewhat lower than that observed in the United States (Maier, Lichtermann, Klingler, Heun, & Hallmayer, 1992). Comparisons of these and other findings suggest that approximately 6% to 9% of the population will have one or more personality disorders during their lifetime (Merikangas & Weissman, 1986).

Widiger and his colleagues (Widiger & Frances, 1989; Widiger & Rogers, 1989) reviewed prevalence studies and found that, in general, rates were higher among inpatient psychiatric patients than among outpatients. For example, borderline

Table 17.1
Lifetime Prevalence

Disorder	Percent
Cluster A	
Paranoid	0.4
Schizoid	0.7
Schizotypal	3.0
Cluster B	
Antisocial	3.0
Borderline	1.7
Histrionic	3.0
Narcissistic	0.0
Cluster C	
Avoidant	1.3
Dependent	1.7
Obsessive-compulsive	1.7

Source: Data from "Diagnosing Personality Disorder in the Community: A Comparison of Self-Report and Interview Measures," by M. Zimmerman and W. Coryell, 1990, *Archives of General Psychiatry, 47,* p. 527.

personality disorder (BPD), which was the most commonly diagnosed personality disorder among patients in treatment, was reported in 11% of outpatients and 19% of inpatients (Widiger & Frances, 1989). Similarly, outpatient prevalence figures for schizotypal personality disorder range between 10% and 15% (Bornstein, Klein, Mallon, & Slater, 1988), while among inpatients, the rates vary between 20% and 30% (Widiger & Rogers, 1989). Antisocial personality disorder rates differ depending on whether psychiatric patients or prisoners are surveyed. In psychiatric outpatients, the prevalence rates for APD are near 5%; in psychiatric outpatients, the rates are 12% to 37%; while in prison populations, the rates range from 30% to 70% (Widiger & Rogers, 1989). The quite variable latter rates for prisoners reflect differences in the diagnostic criteria used and apparently in the particular population of prisoners that were sampled.

Depending on the sample chosen, prevalence rates vary considerably. In addition, prevalence rates vary as a function of the method used for specific diagnoses. For example, self-report measures are likely to yield underestimates of APD relative to structured interviews because individuals are reluctant to indicate that they have antisocial traits and behaviors. Other disorders, such as those in cluster C, may be overrepresented by self-report questionnaires, because patients may endorse particular items, even though the severity of the associated symptoms may not be sufficient to merit a clinical diagnosis. The issue of multimethod assessment, then, is pertinent to broader diagnostic issues, although this has not been rigorously investigated.

COMORBIDITY AND DIAGNOSTIC OVERLAP

The terms *comorbidity* and *overlap* are often used as synonyms in the literature when, in fact, they refer to two conceptually distinct features of diagnosis. *Comorbidity* should be used to describe the co-occurrence in the same person(s) of two or more diagnostically distinct disorders. *Overlap*, on the other hand, refers to the similarity of symptoms in two or more different disorders (i.e., the disorders overlap for diagnostic criteria). Insofar as the diagnostic criteria for different disorders are distinct, overlap should not occur. However, the criteria for the personality disorders remain sufficiently vague, or require significant inferential skill by the diagnostician, so overlap seems certain to occur.

Comorbidity of personality disorders and Axis I disorders and overlap between the various personality disorders remain issues of concern. Attempts to resolve the problem by encouraging use of multiple diagnoses has advantages for clinical practice, but it causes problems for researchers in identifying homogeneous samples. Further, it has produced debate as to the true nature of the various disorders.

This similarity of symptoms across disorders has encouraged multiple diagnoses to be applied to individuals in recent revisions of the diagnostic manual. This strategy, therefore, eliminates the earlier requirement by the clinician to make a determination of a primary diagnosis and exclude all others. Despite clear practical benefits, researchers generally require a single clear diagnosis to identify distinct groups of subjects in their studies, and they are then faced with difficult decisions that may lead to confusion in the possible interpretations of their findings. Furthermore, a specific diagnosis often implies a course of treatment and differential prognosis, and this is complicated by use of multiple diagnoses. This similarity of symptoms across disorders also results in blurred boundaries between diagnoses, perhaps confusing clinicians. To highlight this concern, Morey (1988) found that eight of the personality disorders diagnosed according to *DSM-III-R* (APA, 1987) overlapped in their diagnostic criteria with other diagnoses by as much as 50%. This represented a marked increase in overlap from *DSM-III*. Currently, as many as two-thirds of patients who receive one diagnosis of a personality disorder also meet the criteria for at least one other personality disorder (Clarkin, Widiger, Frances, Hurt, & Gilmore, 1983). Comorbidity of personality disorders and Axis I disorders, and overlap between the various personality disorders remain concerns (Clarkin et al., 1983; Pfohl, Coryell, Zimmerman, & Stangl, 1986) and influence outcome in correctional samples (Porporino & Motiuk, 1995). In particular, comorbidity in borderlines has been the focus of considerable debate. Patients diagnosed as borderline have commonly been found to possess schizotypal features, and considerable overlap has been observed between borderline diagnoses and other personality disorders (Pfohl et al., 1986). For example, 47% of borderlines met the criteria for APD, and 57% met the criteria for histrionic disorder in one study (Widiger, Frances, & Trull, 1987). These findings were replicated by Morey, who also reported high diagnostic overlap in borderlines with paranoid, histrionic, narcissistic, avoidant, and dependent personality disorder diagnoses. Comorbidity between BPD and affective disorders is common (Andrulonis & Vogel, 1984; Gunderson & Elliott, 1985; McManus, Lerner, Robbins, & Barbour, 1984; Perry, 1985). This has led to suggestions that borderline disorder might be best classified as a subtype of affective disorder (Nakdimen, 1986).

Avoidant disorder patients manifest symptoms (e.g., social inadequacy and hypersensitivity to negative evaluations) remarkably similar to those that identify social phobia (an Axis I disorder). Reich, Noyes, and Troughton (1987), for example, found that phobic patients were far more likely than nonphobics to meet the criteria for a cluster C personality disorder; and Turner, Beidel, Dancu, and Keys (1986) reported that social phobics and avoidant patients displayed the same physiological reactivity, and the content of their cognitions was similar. In fact, both *DSM-III-R* and *DSM-IV* explicitly note the overlap in these two disorders but suggest the solution is to apply both diagnoses. This suggestion will not help researchers, and no differential treatment approaches are described by the authors of the diagnostic manuals.

Millon (1996) presented an overview of the likelihood of specific comorbid diagnoses within the *DSM-IV* personality disorders. For instance, he rank-ordered diagnoses in order of their likelihood of comorbidity with APD. In ascending order, Millon found that sadistic personality, narcissistic personality, and substance abuse were all commonly comorbid with APD. Furthermore, he provided a concise clinical description of the unique features for each potentially overlapping disorder that was meant to assist clinicians to more accurately distinguish among a rather heterogeneous group of patients. For instance, in distinguishing other disorders from antisocial personality, he noted that narcissistic individuals are similarly egocentric, but tend not to be impulsive. Also, relative to antisocial personality patients, the borderlines' manipulative behavior tends not to be aggrandizing nor aimed at gaining power. Millon's descriptions highlight pervasiveness, severity, and motivation, as well as personality style, and indicate that a diagnosis should be much more than a simple compilation of behaviors or symptoms.

GENDER AND CULTURAL ISSUES

The diagnostic manual insists that clinicians determine, in the case of recent immigrants or members of minority groups, that the client's functioning, while differing from the expectations of his or her current or broader society, is not reflective of appropriate response in the client's society of origin or minority group. Recent immigrants or members of minority cultures may be susceptible to misdiagnosis unless the diagnostician makes the effort to determine which attitudes and behaviors are appropriate for a person from a distinct culture. The same is true of gender biases in the diagnosis of personality disorders. For example, clinicians have been shown to be reluctant to diagnose males as having histrionic personality disorder and loathe to consider females as having APD (Widiger & Spitzer, 1991).

Prevalence studies also have found that personality disorders occur more frequently in urban populations than in rural residents, and that they are differentially distributed according to gender (Merikangas & Weissman, 1986). Schizoid and schizotypal disorders are more frequently diagnosed in males, as is APD, whereas histrionic and borderline disorders are identified more commonly in women. All the disorders in cluster C (primarily anxieties and fearful symptoms) are diagnosed most frequently in women. Some authors have suggested that these apparent differential rates for males and females are the product of sex-role stereotype biases reflected in both the diagnostic criteria and their application (Brown, 1992). In the case of histrionic personality disorder, more women receive this diagnosis, but an epidemiological survey of more than 3,000 community adults revealed approximately the same prevalence (2.2%) in males and females (Nestadt et al., 1990). This suggests that either referral to psychiatric clinics for people with histrionic features are gender biased, or the application of the diagnosis among those who are referred is gender biased. These problems of gender bias do not, unfortunately, appear to have disappeared with the current diagnostic manual. These cultural and gender issues are also relevant with respect to treatment (Coatsworth, Szapocznik, Kurtines, & Santisteban, 1997) in that one application of a diagnosis is the development of a course of intervention. If the diagnosis itself is biased, the treatment is clearly compromised.

Sensitivity to cultural norms and differences in the expression of the features of APD is particularly important (Yung & Hammond, 1997). Also, the emphasis on aggressivity in the prerequisite diagnosis of conduct disorder may yield underdiagnosis in females because of gender differences in the prevalence and expression of aggression.

As to diagnosis of psychopathy using the Hare Psychopathy Checklist (PCL-R; Hare, 1991) with male offenders, there appear to be differences between African Americans and Caucasians, with African Americans scoring significantly higher. Whether this reflects true differences between these two groups or whether it, more likely, results from differences in social circumstances and opportunities remains to be seen. Economically disadvantaged African Americans living in inner cities can be expected to learn as children self-interested strategies to survive, and these strategies may, in the eyes of a privileged clinician, appear to reveal a psychopathic character. There is also the suggestion of gender differences on the PCL-R (Vitale & Newman, 2001), with females having lower rates than males. Further, there are cultural differences with respect to norms, although similar factor solutions for the PCL-R have been found when comparing results from different countries (Cooke, 1999).

Together, these studies suggest that, at a minimum, there are cultural and gender differences in the way in which psychopathy is expressed (Hare, 1991) and perhaps in the way certain features may be recorded as evidence for or against psychopathic traits in an examinee.

Henry and Cohen (1983) suggested that clinicians typically overdiagnosed BPD in women. Widiger and Trull (1993) responded to this by pointing to the results of 75 prevalence studies estimating the percentage of women diagnosed as borderline. Comparing studies that used semistructured interviews versus those that used unstructured interviews, prevalence differences derived by the two approaches, even though statistically significant, were not remarkable—an average of 80% of the subjects identified as borderline by structured interviews were women, with a figure of 73% using the unstructured method. While gender bias may not occur in the application of the diagnostic criteria, this may still have led to the identification of diagnostic criteria that are more likely to identify women as disordered.

In an early review of what was then called *hysterical* personality (now identified as *histrionic personality disorder*), Chodoff and Lyons (1958) wrote that, given the history of the concept of *hysteria*, it was inevitable that gender biases in diagnosis would emerge. They suggested that even the traits said to characterize the disorder are no more than features of the traditional female stereotype. Changing the name of the disorder to *histrionic* from *hysterical* in *DSM-III* was meant, at least in part, to diminish these biases, but the impact does not seem to have been profound. Histrionic personality disorder is still diagnosed much more commonly in females than in males (Kass, Spitzer, & Williams, 1983; Reich, 1987). Furthermore, studies that ask subjects to rate the diagnostic criteria indicate that most people view the features of the disorder as decidedly feminine (Sprock, Blashfield, & Smith, 1990).

In an interesting examination of gender bias, Warner (1978) had 175 mental health professionals make a diagnosis after reading a case history. The patient was described as a woman in half the cases and as a male in the other half, but the case description remained the same. Of those clinicians who were given the female case, 76% diagnosed the patient as suffering from a hysterical personality disorder, while only 49% applied that diagnosis when the patient was described as a man. Ford and Widiger (1989) also examined these issues, but looked at gender bias both in the diagnostic criteria and in the application of the overall diagnosis. They found no influence of gender of the patient for the individual criteria, but a noticeable influence of gender in the assignment of the diagnosis. There is no evidence that these problems of gender bias have disappeared with the subsequent revisions of the diagnostic manual.

Reich (1987) used both a structured interview and two self-report measures completed by patients and found that the rates for dependent personality disorder were the same for males and females. Morey and Ochoa (1989) had clinicians indicate both their diagnoses of the patients they were seeing and whether *DSM-III-R* diagnostic criteria were present in these patients. Overdiagnosis occurred when the clinician assigned a diagnosis but the appropriate criteria were not present, and underdiagnosis occurred when the criteria were present but the diagnosis was not applied. Gender of the patient did not predict either the underdiagnosis or overdiagnosis of dependent personality.

Subsequently, Sprock et al. (1990) had undergraduates place *DSM-III-R* diagnostic criteria for personality disorder on a dimension of masculinity-femininity. Criteria for dependent disorder received the highest femininity ratings of any of the personality disorders. These findings tend to support Kaplan's (1983) view that the diagnostic criteria for dependent personality disorder represented no more than the male concept of females as submissive, passive, and inadequate. Apparently, this issue remains unresolved.

ETIOLOGY

Research as to the factors that cause personality disorders is generally unavailable. This is problematic because an improved understanding of the etiology of these disorders is important for preventative purposes and would also inform intervention strategies. In the area of antisocial behavior, certain events during critical developmental periods may influence the trajectory toward psychopathology (Stoff, Breiling, & Maser, 1997). Several authors have suggested that personality disorders have their origin in childhood resulting from failure in the attachment bonds with their parents (see Marshall & Barbaree, 1991, for elaboration of this view). Attachment bonds with parents provide the developing child with a template for later relationships (Bowlby, 1977). If attachments are poor, the child typically develops adult relationship styles that are characterized by ambivalence, fear, or avoidance (Bartholomew, 1990). In addition, poor attachments fail to instill in the child the self-confidence and social skills needed to develop appropriate intimacy (Marshall, 1989; Marshall, Hudson, & Hodkinson, 1993). Levy (2000) has argued that poor attachment bonds are an antecedent to violence and antisocial patterns in children. Such disadvantaged individuals can be expected to adopt various maladaptive ways of dealing with interpersonal relations, and a failure to function effectively in such relationships has been said to characterize the personality disorders (Marshall & Barbaree, 1984; Patrick, Hobson, Castle, & Howard, 1994). Others have shown that if parent-child attachments are poor, the child typically develops adult relationship styles that are characterized by ambivalence, fear, or avoidance (Bartholomew, 1990; Dutton, Saunders, Starzomski, & Bartholomew, 1994). The fact that personality disorders are understood to typically emerge during late adolescence, when the demands for social interaction and interpersonal relationships become preeminent, strengthens these suggestions concerning the origins of personality disorders and the nature of the problems of these patients. Consistent with these claims, R. L. Goldberg, Mann, Wise, and Segall (1985) found that personality-disordered patients typically described their parents as either uncaring or overprotective, or both.

In the literature that distinguishes between APD and psychopathy, there has been some effort to identify processes that underlie psychopaths' maladaptive behavior. Through a series of laboratory and process-based investigations, Newman and his colleagues conclude that psychopaths suffer from a generalized information-processing deficiency involving the automatic directing of attention to stimuli that are peripheral to ongoing directed behavior (Wallace, Vitale, & Newman, 1999). That is, once engaged in reward-based behavior, the psychopath cannot attend to other cues to modulate his or her ongoing response. Given that APD involves schema-based deficits (antisocial schemas and cognitive distortions), they suggest psychopathy and APD are different diagnoses, implying different etiology, intervention, and prognosis.

THE SPECIFIC DISORDERS

Two of the specific personality disorders continue to receive the bulk of research attention over the past several years: APD and BPD. Accordingly, the primary focus of our discussion of the specific disorders is on these two with only brief descriptions of the remaining disorders.

CLUSTER A: ODD AND ECCENTRIC DISORDERS

Paranoid Personality Disorder   Pervasive suspiciousness over the motives of other people and a tendency to interpret what others say and do as personally meaningful in a negative way are the primary features of paranoid patients. They consistently misread the actions of others as threatening or critical, and they expect other people to exploit them. Consequently, paranoid personalities tend to be hypervigilant and take extreme precautions against potential threats from others. They believe that other people intend to hurt them, and they are reluctant to share anything personal for fear it might be used against them. In addition, they typically are humorless and eccentric, and are seen by others as hostile, preoccupied with power and control, and jealous. Not surprisingly, they have considerable problems in relationships, as most people cannot tolerate their need to control and, particularly, their destructive jealousy. Frequently, paranoid patients become socially isolated, and this seems only to add to their persecutory ideas.

These features identified in both the diagnostic criteria and in clinical reports have been confirmed in research. For example, Turkat and his colleagues have found that, compared with normal subjects, paranoid personalities experienced far more paranoid thoughts both currently and during their school days (Turkat & Banks, 1987), had greater difficulty in dealing with ambiguity, were more suspicious (Thompson-Pope & Turkat, 1988), and were more likely to misread social cues as evidence of hostility by others (Turkat, Keane, & Thompson-Pope, 1990).

Kendler, Masterson, and Davis (1985) reported that paranoid personality occurs quite commonly in the relatives of schizophrenics, which suggests the possibility that paranoid personality might be a subtype of schizophrenia or that there is a genetic link between the two disorders. However, paranoid personality disorder overlaps more significantly with avoidant and borderline personality disorders than it does with schizophrenia (Morey, 1988).

In a large-scale study of the prevalence and stability of personality disorder among adolescents in upstate New York communities, Bernstein et al. (1993) identified the presence of moderate or severe forms of the various disorders on two occasions separated by a two-year interval. They found that paranoid disorder was one of the four most persistent types of personality disorder.

Schizoid Personality Disorder   Individuals with this condition seem determined to avoid intimate involvement with others, and they display little in the way of emotional responsiveness. These clients often indicate that they rarely experience intense emotions and may be puzzled by the enthusiasms of others. Schizoid clients are typically loners who are cold and indifferent toward others and display social indifference. In fact, they seem not to enjoy relationships of any type with others, apparently preferring to be alone. They enjoy solitary activities and do not seek or seem to desire sexual relations. There seems little doubt that most do not have the skills necessary for effective social interaction, but they also appear uninterested in acquiring such skills.

One of the main problems with this diagnostic category is that little methodologically sound research has been done on the problem. As a consequence, we know little more about it than we did several years ago, and clinical speculations remain unfettered by data. Studies that do appear in the literature frequently confound schizoid and schizotypal features and do not, therefore, permit any reasonable conclusions.

Schizotypal Personality Disorder   The major presenting feature of these patients is eccentricity of thought and behavior. Many schizotypal patients are extremely superstitious. Their ideation and behavior are peculiar, and these features tend to turn other people away; therefore, schizotypal patients are typically socially isolated. No doubt, such isolation from others increases the likelihood that they will have unusual thoughts and perceptions, as they have little opportunity to check the sense of their cognitions. Their thinking tends to be magical and full of odd beliefs and ideas of reference. They typically believe in paranormal phenomena such as telepathy and clairvoyance.

Although their beliefs, perceptual experiences, speech, and behaviors are quite odd and tend to isolate them from others, they are not considered so eccentric as to meet the criteria for delusional or hallucinatory experiences. There is, however, considerable disagreement on this issue. For example, McGlashan (1987) claimed that transient psychoses characterize these patients, and Kendler (1985) concluded that schizotypal disorder is simply a subtle form of schizophrenia. Research examining biological features has found strong similarities between schizotypal patients and schizophrenics (Baron, Levitt, Gruen, Kane, & Asnis, 1984; Siever, 1985), and many family members of schizophrenics exhibit schizotypal symptoms (Kendler, 1985). Indeed, Widiger and Shea (1991) suggested that schizotypal disorder may be a prodromal or residual stage of schizophrenia. This obviously is an issue that deserves greater attention although diagnostic overlap with BPD is also considerable (Morey, 1988) and also warrants further research. Finally, the long-term prognosis for schizotypal patients is poor.

CLUSTER B: DRAMATIC, EMOTIONAL, OR ERRATIC DISORDERS

As noted earlier, this cluster does not seem to have as much in common as is implied by grouping these four disorders. While histrionic and borderline disorders may be seen as dramatic, it is hard to see what this descriptor has to do with APD. Indeed, except for a limited range of emotional expression, none of the descriptors of cluster B seem to fit the antisocial patients. In fact, it might be better to consider the antisocial patients as belonging to a separate category of personality disorder.

Antisocial Personality Disorder
   DEVELOPMENT OF *DSM-IV* CRITERIA   This section reviews the *DSM-IV* changes in the diagnostic criteria for APD, providing a context for current assessment and treatment issues as to this population. Distinct from other personality disorders, the essential feature of APD is a "pervasive pattern of disregard for and violation of, the rights of others that begins in childhood or early adolescence and continues into adulthood" (APA, 1994, p. 645). It is important to note that alternate diagnostic strategies such as Hare's Psychopathy Checklist-Revised (PCL-R; Hare,

1991) are gaining prominence in the forensic literature (Harris, Skilling, & Rice, 2001). The PCL-R enjoys widespread popularity, and it is increasingly being used in assessments to inform judicial decisions, principally because of its predictive validity as to recidivism (Serin & Brown, 2000). Nonetheless, there is an absence of a cogent body of jurisprudential thought as to psychopathy, and little distinction is made between APD and psychopathy in the law (Lyon & Ogloff, 2000).

The goal of the *DSM-IV* task force was to simplify and shorten the *DSM-III-R* criteria for APD without sacrificing reliability of diagnosis. In reviewing the *DSM-III-R* criteria, the *DSM-IV* task force considered correlation with overall criteria, complexity, prevalence, and interrater reliability. Widiger and Corbitt (1993) summarized arguments by various authors (Hare, Hart, & Harpur, 1991; Millon, 1981) for greater emphasis on personality traits and the need for a briefer, simpler criterion set. They also commented on the generally acceptable degree of inclusiveness and validity of the *DSM-III-R* criteria, although this has been disputed (Rogers et al., 1994).

Reliance on behavioral indexes of the disorder since *DSM-II* has raised concerns as to the relation of the *DSM* criteria to clinical conceptions of a related construct, that of psychopathy (Hare, 1996; Wulach, 1983). The relatively few criteria reflecting affective and interpersonal processes (Millon, 1981) and prototypicality studies (Rogers et al., 1994) comparing *DSM-IV* and other measures of APD (PCL-R; ICD-10, dyssocial personality disorder) underscore this concern.

DSM-IV criteria for diagnosis of APD present seven exemplars reflecting the violation of the rights of others: nonconformity, callousness, deceitfulness, irresponsibility, recklessness, impulsivity, and aggressiveness. Three or more of these must be met. These criteria represent a reduced and simplified version of the *DSM-III-R* criterion set. Three items from the *DSM-III-R* criteria—parental irresponsibility, failure to sustain a monogamous relationship, and inconsistent work—were dropped as they failed to meet acceptable levels of association with APD, prevalence, interrater reliability, or all of these (Rogers et al., 1994; Widiger & Corbitt, 1993). Widiger and Corbitt reached the important conclusion that the *DSM-IV* diagnostic criterion had a 98% concordance with the *DSM-III-R* diagnosis.

The *DSM-IV* (APA, 1994) cautions clinicians to ensure that in the assessment of antisocial traits, the social and economic context should be carefully considered. For instance, the antecedents or motivation for antisocial behavior may be significantly different among individuals. Clinicians must ensure, therefore, that this behavior is not exclusively in response to trauma or part of a broader protective strategy (Herman, 1992).

A final concern expressed (Rogers et al., 1994) is the temporal instability of the diagnosis of APD. Because of the early onset and long course of the disorder, diagnostic inconsistency over time with the *DSM-III* is disconcerting (Helzer, Spitznagel, & McEnvoy, 1987). It remains to be seen whether *DSM-IV* criteria reflect greater temporal stability. Comparisons of prevalence symptoms and correlates of APD in four countries (Taiwan, New Zealand, Canada, and the United States) suggest a similar pattern, although there are differences in continuity across these countries (Zoccolillo, Price, Ji, & Hwu, 1999).

PREVALENCE   The *DSM-IV* reported prevalence rates for APD of approximately 3% in males and 1% in females in community samples. These results are comparable to the National Comorbidity Survey (Kessler et al., 1994), which reported prevalence rates of 5.8% in males and 1.2% in females.

The incidence in forensic and correctional settings are understandably higher, yet contemporary estimates are unavailable for *DSM-IV*. Estimates in Great Britain are that approximately 25% to 33% of patients in special hospitals are psychopathic, which is quite high, presumably because those offenders considered treatable are diverted to these special hospitals while those considered untreatable are simply imprisoned (Chiswick, 1992). Hare (1983, 1985) reported higher estimates using *DSM-III-R,* where approximately 40% of Canadian prisoners were diagnosed with APD. Special hospitals are part of the mental health system in the United Kingdom. They admit offenders who have committed crimes but found mentally ill, but in contrast to other countries, diagnosis of personality disorder is a sufficient criterion for a finding of mental illness. Similar data for a correctional sample were provided by Hart and Hare (1989), reflecting the relative overdiagnosis of *DSM-III* (50% incidence of APD) compared with an early version PCL (12.5% incidence of psychopathy). Rates of psychopathy among prisoners also appear to vary according to security level, with psychopaths being overrepresented in maximum security prisons (Wong, 1984). Further, Cooke (1999) compared prevalence rates for Scottish and North American incarcerated samples and concluded that Scotland has lower rates.

DESCRIPTION OF THE DISORDER   The description of a persistent pattern of antisocial behavior has a long clinical tradition (Pinel, 1809), which is described by Cleckley (1976). Individuals, thus identified, have been referred to as *psychopaths, sociopaths,* or *dyssocial personalities,* with these terms sometimes being used interchangeably (Schlesinger, 1980). In correctional settings, psychopathy and APD have been used interchangeably, albeit incorrectly, given research over the past decade. Some authors (Harding, 1992) suggest that the reluctance to use the term *psychopathic* stems from its pejorative connotation. Further, sensationalism in the media has not been instructive given that all criminal psychopaths are not serial rapists and murderers.

Psychopathy, however, is a resilient term and has enjoyed a relative resurgence in use in correctional and forensic settings, notably in North America, with the emergence of Hare's checklist (Hare, 1991). The PCL-R has been demonstrated to be a reliable and more specific construct than APD (Hare, 1983) and has greater predictive validity (Hare, 1991; Harris, Rice, & Quinsey, 1993). For example, psychopaths, as defined by the PCL-R, have a greater number and variety of criminal offenses than do nonpsychopaths (psychopaths and nonpsychopaths are defined as approximately the top and bottom 15% of the distribution of PCL-R scores; Kosson, Smith, & Newman, 1990). Use of the PCL-R in Britain (Raine, 1985) and Scotland (Cooke, 1999) yielded factor structures similar to North American studies (Hare et al., 1990) but had noticeably lower mean scores.

The APD versus psychopathy debate has led to some confusion, possibly obscuring theoretical advances and improvements in the identification of treatment targets (Lilienfeld, 1994). Central to this issue is whether existing assessment strategies (*DSM-IV*), with fixed indicators of a trait, sufficiently reflect the *personality* domain of the disorder. Employing essentially behavioral criteria may increase diagnostic reliability but also yield a group of antisocial individuals who are markedly heterogeneous in terms of personality traits (Blackburn, 1992; Lilienfeld, 1994; Millon, 1981). At the same time, patients whose personality structure is representative of the disorder, but whose behavior is not specifically antisocial, are excluded (Hare et al., 1991; Lilienfeld, 1994). Further, using process measures rather than self-report or interview-based information suggests that psychopaths and those diagnosed with APD are uniquely different (Wallace, Schmitt, Vitale, & Newman, 2000).

Consistent with factor analytic studies of the PCL-R, it has been proposed that two factors, personality traits and lifestyle instability, should be *necessary* and *sufficient* for a diagnosis of APD (Hare et al., 1991; Rogers et al., 1994). Such an approach may address concerns as to the over- and underinclusiveness of existing criteria (Lilienfeld, 1994) and might eventually yield a more dimensional model of APD (Rogers et al., 1994). Meloy (1995) attempted to address this difficulty by describing psychopathic versus nonpsychopathic APD. This distinction may be helpful for correctional and forensic applications but may confuse rather than illuminate all but the highly informed clinician. This proposal, however, highlights the present conundrum for clinicians in these settings. That is, use an existing diagnostic nosology (APD), which is overinclusive and has limited predictive or prognostic utility, or adopt the highly reliable PCL-R with its wealth of empirical literature in the area of risk assessment (Harris et al., 1993; Hart, Kropp, & Hare, 1988; Serin & Brown, 2000; Skeem & Mulvey, 2001). Specific guidelines for the forensic use of the PCL-R are also now available to inform those who choose to use it clinically (Gacono, 2000; Gacono & Hutton, 1994; Hare, 1991). Further, interview guidelines are now available that address the interpersonal behavior of psychopaths and clinicians' reactions to this group (Kosson, Gacono, & Bodholdt, 2000).

CLINICAL PICTURE   Notwithstanding this debate over the most preferred assessment strategy, there is consensus concerning the clinical picture presented by those broadly diagnosed with APD. APD individuals have been described as:

- Failing to comply with societal norms and repeatedly performing acts that are grounds for arrest.
- Disregarding the wishes, rights, and feelings of others.
- Being frequently deceitful and manipulative to gain personally.
- Displaying a pattern of impulsivity through a failure to plan ahead or acting without due regard to the consequences.
- Acting irritably and aggressively in nondefensive situations.
- Being reckless and irresponsible in various aspects of their lives.
- Displaying little remorse for their behavior.
- Being indifferent and quick to rationalize.

Callousness, contempt for others, and inflated self-appraisals are also indisputable characteristics of this group, but they are not specifically reflected in the *DSM-IV* criteria. Such descriptors, however, are central to, or prototypical of, clinicians' formulations of APD (Rogers et al., 1994) and are represented in ICD-10 criteria for dyssocial personality.

COURSE AND PROGNOSIS   Robins and Regier (1991) reported the average duration of APD (*DSM-III*) to be 19 years, from first to last symptom. Such remittance over time of symptoms has been described as the "burnout" factor, with expectations of symptom alleviation by the fourth decade of life. Harpur and Hare (1994) presented cross-sectional data suggesting that personality style, as reflected by Factor 1 of the PCL-R, does not appreciably diminish with age. Accordingly, a diagnosis of psychopathy may be less age dependent than is APD (Harpur & Hare, 1994). These data are consistent with views that psychopathy is a taxon (Harris,

Rice, & Quinsey, 1994). Further, various case studies exist that refute the burnout hypothesis, at least for persistent offenders.

While onset of antisocial behavior as an adolescent is requisite, much is to be gained from an appreciation of the developmental literature, particularly conduct disorder. This should not be surprising, because some of these youths become APD adults. Moffitt (1993) provided a model for understanding developmental antecedents of adult psychopathology and developmental trajectories of antisocial behavior. The pattern and pervasiveness of antisocial behavior by the individuals she described as "life-course persistent" are important markers for adult difficulties in a broad range of societal and relationship interactions. Kazdin (1987, 1993) presented a *contextual* evaluation of treatment considerations for conduct-disordered youth, with emphasis on problem-solving skills training *and* parent management training. He described impediments to treatment compliance and the need for prescriptive intervention that is broad-based and multifaceted. Failure to attend to this literature greatly limits the utility of assessment and treatment initiatives for adults. Kazdin's (1993) analogy of a chronic care model is important because it provides for the shared responsibility of the disorder and its sequelae. Treatment, then, becomes management and symptom reduction, not cure. This view is consistent with suggestions in the adult literature (Rice & Harris, 1997; Serin & Preston, 2001b).

TREATMENT CONSIDERATIONS   Reviews of the empirical literature on treatment efficacy for APD patients, and for psychopaths in particular, have been unequivocally pessimistic (Suedfeld & Landon, 1978), leading to conclusions of therapeutic impotence (Harding, 1992). Many earlier studies, however, suffered from poor methodology. Further, the programs delivered in previous decades did not reflect contemporary knowledge of effective treatment programs for resistant clients (Gendreau, 1996; Miller & Rollnick, 1991). Unfortunately, however, treatment studies have been no more encouraging. Psychopaths tend to exploit unstructured programs, masking their resistance with verbal skills, and may in fact do more poorly when provided inappropriate intervention (Rice, Harris, & Cormier, 1992). Attrition from treatment programs is also high (Ogloff, Wong, & Greenwood, 1990) and has proved to be of prognostic value (Marques, Day, Nelson, & West, 1994). Last, in substance abuse treatment, APD patients fare more poorly than non-APD patients (Alterman & Cacciola, 1991; Poldrugo & Forti, 1988).

Surprisingly, as Meloy (1995) noted, therapeutic hope has not vanished. Approximately two-thirds of psychiatrists think that psychopaths are sometimes treatable (Tennent, Tennent, Prins, & Bedford, 1993). Despite a poor response to hospitalization, prognosis is improved for APD patients if there is a treatable anxiety or depression (Gabbard & Coyne, 1987) or a demonstration of therapeutic alliance (Gerstley et al., 1989).

Treatment of other groups of resistant clients (Miller & Rollnick, 1991) suggests that the noncompliance of APD patients may be a responsivity factor. That is, treatment must be responsive or matched to a particular patient's needs and interpersonal style. Poor treatment performance may be influenced, in part, by an intervention that is of insufficient intensity (Gendreau, 1996), viewed by patients as irrelevant (Miller & Rollnick, 1991), or involuntary (Gabbard & Coyne, 1987). Newman and Wallace (1993) provide an analogy between psychopathy and learning disability to emphasize how to make intervention more responsive for this group of patients. They extend this point by providing laboratory evidence in support of their hypothesis that psychopaths have specific information-processing deficits that must be considered in the delivery of treatment programs.

Overviews of relevant treatment needs and models for delivering such programs are presently available (Blackburn, 1993a; Rice, Harris, & Quinsey, 1996), but there is little evidence that these are prescriptively applied. Furthermore, programs vary according to the extent that personality and criminality are emphasized, and yet a *problems-based* approach may enhance compliance and efficacy (Nezu & Nezu, 1993; Rice et al., 1996; Rice & Harris, 1997). Cognitive models of intervention predominate (Beck, Freeman, & Associates, 1990; Blackburn, 1993b), but there is still strong interest in alternate psychotherapeutic approaches (Gallwey, 1992), despite rather scant empirical support for their efficacy. An outcome study of a cognitively based treatment program, however, is encouraging (Robinson, 1995). Similar programs for juveniles have yielded good treatment gains, but with limited generalization of effects (Guerra & Slaby, 1990).

While treatment targets for forensic and correctional samples have obscured the distinction between criminality and antisocial personality, they typically include some combination of aggressive and antisocial attitudes and beliefs, impulsivity or poor self-regulation, social skills, anger, assertiveness, substance abuse, empathy, problem solving, and moral reasoning (Rice & Harris, 1997). For many of these targets, there exist structured program materials; however, assessment technology to measure treatment gain remains relatively unsophisticated (Rice & Harris, 1997). Further, overreliance on self-report assessment methods is problematic for a population for whom candor is suspect (Serin & Kuriychuk, 1994).

Another management strategy for antisocial or acting-out behavior, particularly in closed settings, has been pharmacotherapy. Short-term use of psychopharmocologic agents is most often used to manage difficult or threatening behavior (Karper & Krystal, 1997; Rice, Harris, Varney, & Quinsey, 1989). However, problems of side effects of long-term drug use and noncompliance have been noted in forensic patients (Harris, 1989). While short-term use of antipsychotic, antianxiety, and sedative medications is not uncommon (Tupin, 1987), symptom alleviation is rarely sustained, and patients are typically provided no new skills to improve their ability to deal with future situations. For some patients, medication may reduce arousal level sufficiently for them to participate more fully in cognitive-behavioral treatment (Rice & Harris, 1993).

FAMILIAL, BIOLOGICAL, AND GENETIC CONSIDERATIONS   The developmental literature (Moffitt, 1993), at the very least, confirms that familial and genetic risk factors are present in many disordered youth, contributing to present and future difficulties and various diagnoses. How these factors interact to increase the risk of subsequent diagnosis, however, is unclear (Moffitt, 1993). Nonetheless, presence of neuropsychological damage or difficulties (e.g., emotional reactivity, temperament, impulse control, and cognitive abilities) and familial or environmental factors (e.g., criminogenic environments, neglect or physical abuse, and poor parenting skills) are predispositional factors that contribute to increased risk. In combination, these markers appear to make children particularly vulnerable to psychopathology (Rutter, 1997). Improved identification of behavioral or neuropsychological markers (White et al., 1994) and intervention strategies (Kazdin, 1993) is important in promotion of a preventative perspective for adult APD (see Stoff et al., 1997).

Previous reviews by Rutter et al. (1990) dispute genetic influences on juvenile delinquency and, hence, antisocial behavior. Raine (1993), however, noted there is stronger support when self-reported delinquency is considered versus legal definitions (Grove et al., 1990). For instance, he summarizes twin study analyses, citing that 51.5% of MZ = monzygotic twins are concordant for crime compared to 20.6% for DZ = dizygotic twins, yet concedes that adoption studies also highlight the importance of environmental variables and their crucial interaction effect.

Summaries of biochemical influences on crime and antisocial behavior show that antisocials are characterized by reduced central serotonin and norepinephrine, with no effect for dopamine (Schalling, 1993; Virkkunen & Linnoila, 1993). These conclusions are also supported by meta-analyses of 29 studies summarized by Raine (1993). He further noted that norepinephrine was reduced in only those antisocials who also displayed affective stability and alcoholism. Raine concluded that these biochemical findings support a behavioral disinhibition theory of antisocial behavior, yet there remains no singular pharmocologic intervention guided by such research (Bond, 1993).

COMORBIDITY OF DISORDERS Meta-analytic reviews of studies comparing substance abuse disorder and APD have suggested a strong association (Schubert, Wolf, Patterson, Grande, & Pendelton, 1988). However, Gerstley, Alterman, McLellan, and Woody (1990) caution that the lack of independence between substance use disorders and APD may lead to an overdiagnosis of APD in substance-use patients. At issue is whether the antisocial behavior is independent of the need to obtain drugs. The *DSM-IV* criteria for substance dependence and substance abuse are explicit concerning dependency and abuse, but this does not appear to preclude a diagnosis of APD if the criteria are met because of the patients' addictions. The suggestion by Gerstley et al. to use the PCL-R to focus on personality traits is similar to Meloy's (1995) proposal; that is, make certain accommodations for particular settings or comorbid disorders.

When APD and substance use are comorbid in a community sample, the treatment response is poorer (Gerstley et al., 1990). In a related vein, postrelease performance is also poorer in those offenders released to the community with both disorders, using Diagnostic Interview Schedule (DIS) criteria (Porporino & Motiuk, 1995). They found that neither the presence of an Axis I diagnosis nor alcohol abuse alone affected recidivism. Further, alcohol plus APD was only marginally more indicative of recidivism than APD alone.

Millon (1996) presented an overview of the likelihood of specific comorbid diagnoses within the *DSM-IV* personality disorders, although this is a rationally derived model. For instance, he ranked diagnoses in order of likelihood of comorbidity with APD. In ascending order, they are sadistic personality, narcissistic personality, and substance abuse. Furthermore, he provided a concise clinical description of unique features for each potentially overlapping disorder to assist clinicians in more accurately distinguishing among a rather heterogeneous group of patients. For instance, in distinguishing from antisocial personality, he noted narcissistic individuals are egocentric but tend not to be impulsive. Similarly, relative to antisocial patients, the borderlines' manipulative behavior tends not to be aggrandizing or to gain power. These descriptions highlight pervasiveness, severity, motivation, and personality style, emphasizing that a diagnosis should be much more than a simple compilation of behaviors or symptoms.

SUMMARY The goal of the *DSM-IV* task force to develop simplified, yet reliable, criteria for APD appears to have been met. These changes, however, have not served to bridge the conceptual differences between divergent views concerning the preferred assessment. It is important that alternative strategies to *DSM*, such as the PCL-R and ICD-10, yielded the most prototypical items, as reported by experienced clinicians (Rogers et al., 1994). In part, setting and time available to the clinician might dictate the approach taken, as the PCL-R requires more specific training, the use of a semistructured interview and collateral collaborative information, and, perhaps, greater time. Some clinicians in community settings, for whom APD is a less frequent and, therefore, less prognostic diagnosis, may choose *DSM-IV* criteria. Rogers et al. proposed a screening model, with the *DSM-IV* acting as a triage for the more intensive PCL-R strategy. It seems such suggestions, while sensitive to the present reality, fail to address the fundamental issue of whether the nosology sufficiently reflects the assessment technology and theory of the constructs of APD or psychopathy.

In the meantime, treatment initiatives can only partly be guided by theory (Rice & Harris, 1997; Serin & Preston, 2001b). Prognosis, even after treatment, remains relatively poor for APD patients, yet conceptualizing treatment as a management strategy rather than a cure is perhaps a more helpful framework, likely to insulate clinicians from undue optimism (Serin & Preston, 2001a). Furthermore, improved treatment responsivity for APD patients may yield enhanced treatment efficacy, but this remains an empirical question.

Borderline Personality Disorder   Fluctuations in mood, an unstable sense of their own identity, and instability in their relationships characterize borderline patients. This overriding instability in all aspects of their functioning makes borderlines unpredictable and impulsive, and, along with their irritability and argumentative style, these features tend to seriously interfere with their relationships. However, they seem not able to tolerate being alone and, accordingly, display a desperateness concerning relationships, although they typically alternate between idealizing and devaluing their partners.

Millon (1992) and Widiger, Miele, and Tilly (1992) described origins of the present conceptualization of BPD. Perry and Klerman (1978) examined four influential reports on what was variously called *borderline personality organization* (Kernberg, 1967), *the borderline syndrome* (Grinker, Werble, & Drye, 1968), *borderline states* (Knight, 1953), and simply *borderline patients* (Gunderson & Singer, 1975). Perry and Klerman found that of the 104 different criteria identified in these four reports, 55 appeared in only one of the reports. In fact, only one of the criteria (the patient's behavior at interview is adaptive and appropriate) appeared in all four reports. After reviewing the literature, Spitzer, Endicott, and Gibbon (1979) concluded that the label *borderline* had been used up to that time to identify two different constellations of symptoms:

1. Instability and vulnerability.
2. A set of features described by Kety, Rosenthal, Wender, and Schulsinger (1971) as *borderline schizophrenia.*

The former constellation provided the basis for identifying BPD in *DSM-III*, while the latter became schizotypal personality disorder. Perhaps not surprisingly, there have been consistent observations ever since of considerable overlap and even confusion between these two disorders (Jacobsberg, Hymowitz, Barasch, & Frances, 1986; McGlashan, 1983; Rosenberger & Miller, 1989; Serban,

Conte, & Plutchik, 1987). Oddly enough, the *DSM-III* characteristic (intolerance of being alone) that most accurately distinguished borderlines from schizotypals (McGlashan, 1987; Plakun, 1987) has been dropped from the diagnostic criteria in *DSM-III-R* and *DSM-IV*.

Borderline disorder has a lifetime occurrence in approximately 2% of the population and is said to be more common in women than in men (Swartz, Blazer, George, & Landerman, 1986), although claims about gender differences in personality disorders have, as we noted earlier, been seriously challenged (Brown, 1992). Borderline disorder, which typically onsets in adolescence (McGlashan, 1983), has been shown to display reasonable stability over time (Barasch, Frances, Hurt, Clarkin, & Cohen, 1985; Pope, Jonas, Hudson, Cohen, & Gunderson, 1983). However, Stone (1993) reported that of patients diagnosed during early adulthood as borderline, only 25% still met the diagnostic criteria in middle age.

Debate continues concerning the nature of borderline disorders with Millon (1986), Kernberg (1984), and Gunderson and Zanarini (1987), in particular, expressing strong disagreement as to the appropriate diagnostic criteria. Widiger et al. (1992) reviewed the various alternative perspectives on the diagnosis and found considerable inconsistencies in the results of research aimed at evaluating the diagnostic formulations they examined. They attribute these inconsistencies in findings to differences in the research samples across different settings and, most important, to variability in the interpretations of the diagnostic criteria. This latter observation is consistent with the observed low reliability of the diagnosis of borderline using *DSM* criteria (Hurt, Clarkin, Koenigsberg, Frances, & Nurmberg, 1986; Widiger, Hurt, Frances, Clarkin, & Gilmore, 1984). In fact, a field trial of *DSM-III* criteria revealed very poor reliability ($r = .29$) for this diagnosis (Mellsop, Varghese, Joshua, & Hicks, 1982).

These disagreements about the appropriate criteria for borderlines and the unreliability of the application of diagnostic criteria challenge the value of attempting to integrate research findings. It is no surprise that inconsistencies typify the results of research with these patients. Consistent with this, raters have been found to vary in their identification of the presence or absence of each of the diagnostic criteria (Angus & Marziali, 1988; Skodol, Rosnick, Kellman, Oldham, & Hyler, 1988). When researchers report satisfactory interrater reliabilities, it is apparently because of the establishment of clear but local operational definitions that, unfortunately, vary across settings (Widiger et al., 1992). Once again, reliability has been shown to be superior when dimensional ratings rather than categorical distinctions are used (Widiger et al., 1992), and use of various rating scales and structured interviews facilitate this approach (Reich, 1992). Interestingly, in a sample of incarcerated women, a greater degree of affect dysregulation, notably poor anger modulation, was significantly related to APD when controlling for BPD and trauma (Zlotnick, 1999). This suggests that, in distinct samples where BPD is frequently comorbid with other Axis II disorders, treatment planning must be carefully considered.

The etiology of borderline disorder has been debated for many years with the different views emphasizing childhood experiences, biological factors, psychodynamic processes, or social learning. Certainly, the evidence strongly implicates disruptions in the family of origin and childhood abuse and neglect as very significant factors in the development of borderline disorder (Links, 1992; Marziali, 1992). Borderline patients typically recall their parents as either neglectful (R. L. Goldberg et al., 1985; Paris & Frank, 1989) or abusive (Bryer, Nelson, Miller, &

Krol, 1987). However, retrospective studies present problems of interpretation when there is no available check on the accuracy of recall. In fact, problems of distorted recall of parental behaviors may be even more problematic with borderline patients than with other populations. Briere and Zaidi (1989), in the examination of 100 females seen at an emergency service, found that among the sexually abused females, a diagnosis of BPD was five times more likely to be given than to female patients who were not sexually abused. Physical abuse by parents has also been found to be typical of the childhoods of borderlines (Zanarini, Gunderson, Marino, Schwartz, & Frankenburg, 1989).

Despite problems with some of these studies, the findings suggest that attachment problems with parents may be a significant etiological factor in borderline disorder. Borderline patients, as we have seen, have very significant problems with adult relationships, and this may be understood to result from a fear of, or ambivalence about, intimacy. People who have problems with adult intimacy are considered to have developed these difficulties as a result of poor parent-child attachments (Berman & Sperling, 1994), which fail to instill the self-confidence and skills necessary for effective intimacy (Bartholomew, 1989) and fail to provide an adequate template for adult intimate relationships (Bowlby, 1988). The features of borderline disorder may then be seen as attempts to adjust to their distrust of intimacy.

Murray (1979) suggested an association between minimal brain dysfunction (MBD) and development of borderline disorder. He suggested that the distorting effects of MBD on perceptual processes may interfere with effective parent-child relationships and that these effects may continue to disrupt relationships throughout the life span. Confused perceptions, emotional instability, and poor impulse control typical of MBD were said to lead to the development of borderline behavior. Research that has examined this claim has generally supported the idea that a subset of borderlines has soft neurological signs (Marziali, 1992), but the evidence is certainly not convincing.

Available evidence suggests a relatively high incidence of borderline features in the first-degree relatives of borderline patients (Links, 1992), and this has been taken by some to suggest familial transmission of the disorder (Baron, Risch, Levitt, & Gruen, 1985; Loranger, Oldham, & Tulis, 1983). Torgersen (1984) examined the genetic contribution to the development of both borderline disorder and schizotypal disorder using Norwegian twins. Diagnoses were done by a clinician blind to the zygosity of the subjects. Results did not offer support for a genetic etiology because none of the three monozygotic twins were concordant for borderline disorder and only two of the seven dyzygotic twins were. However, this was a limited examination of the issue given that the number of subjects was quite small.

Histrionic Personality Disorder   Attention-seeking behaviors distinguish people with this disorder. They are overly dramatic in their emotional displays, self-centered, and constantly attempt to be the center of attention.

The flamboyant displays characteristic of histrionics are apparently intended to have others focus on them as they seem unable to tolerate being ignored. Associated with this tendency is the overresponsiveness of histrionic patients to what others might consider insignificant events. Their insincerity and shallowness, however, make it difficult for histrionics to hold other people's attention for long and, as a consequence, they typically have few friends. Because of their very strong need for attention, they tend to be very demanding and inconsiderate when they are involved in relationships, and, not surprisingly, their relationships are often short-lived and emotionally tumultuous. Again, as a result of needing to be the center of attention, histrionic patients are often flirtatious, and they seem unable to develop any degree of intimacy in relationships. Their behavior causes considerable distress to themselves and to others with whom they become involved.

Histrionic patients are frequently depressed and often suffer from poor health (Nestadt et al., 1990). The primary problem of overlap with other disorders, however, is with BPD (Pfohl et al., 1986; Pope et al., 1983). Widiger, Trull, et al. (1987), for example, found that 57% of borderline patients also met the criteria for histrionic personality disorder.

Narcissistic Personality Disorder   Narcissistic patients grandiosely consider themselves to have unique and outstanding abilities. They have an exaggerated sense of self-importance, and, indeed, egocentricity is the hallmark of narcissistic patients. They are so preoccupied with their own interests and desires that they typically have difficulty feeling any concern for others, although they are themselves easily hurt. Similarly, their self-esteem is readily shattered by negative feedback from others, presumably because they desire only admiration and approval (Kernberg, 1975). The self-absorption of these patients frequently leads to an obsession with unrealistic fantasies of success. They expect, and demand, to be treated as special, and this, along with their lack of empathy, leads them to exploit others. Like histrionic patients, the typical behaviors of narcissists alienate others, and they are frequently lonely and unhappy individuals.

Ronningstam and Gunderson (1990) claim that research has validated these features as characteristic of narcissistic personality disorder. However, while Morey (1988) has reported a remarkable increase (from 6.2% of patients to 22%) in the application of the diagnosis from *DSM-III* to *DSM-III-R*, Zimmerman and Coryell (1989) could find no cases of narcissistic personality disorder in a sample of 800 community subjects. When narcissistic personality disorder is diagnosed, there is considerable overlap with borderline personality disorder (Morey, 1988).

CLUSTER C: ANXIOUS AND FEARFUL DISORDERS

Although avoidant and dependent disorders appear to share anxieties and fears as primary features, the obsessive-compulsive patient seems to be more characterized by a preoccupation with orderliness and rules. Again, there seems to be little value in clustering these disorders in the same category.

Avoidant Personality Disorder   A pervasive pattern of avoiding interpersonal contacts and an extreme sensitivity to criticism and disapproval characterize the avoidant client. They actively avoid intimacy with others although they clearly desire affection. As a result, they frequently experience emotional loneliness. Social discomfort and a fear of being evaluated negatively are common features of these patients. Avoidant clients are afraid of criticism, and so they restrict the range of their social interactions to those people they trust not to denigrate them; but even with these people, they refrain from getting too close. These fears cause problems for them not only in interpersonal relationships but also in their choice of jobs, academic pursuits, and leisure activities. Their avoidance of intimacy also distresses other people who may wish to form a close relationship with the avoidant person.

People with avoidant styles were identified in the literature for many years before the inclusion of this personality disorder in the diagnostic manual. For instance, Horney (1945) pointed out that there were people who found interpersonal relationships of any kind to be such an intolerable strain that "solitude becomes primarily a means of avoiding it" (p. 73). Millon (1969) was the first to use the term *avoidant personality* to describe people who actively avoided social interactions. He (Millon, 1981) suggested that a child rejected by his or her parents would lack self-confidence and would, as a consequence, avoid others for fear of further rejection. This notion fits with the extensive literature on parent-child attachments and the consequences for adult relationships of parental rejection (Bartholomew, 1989, 1990; Berman & Sperling, 1994). Children who have poor parental bonds typically grow up to be afraid of intimate relationships and carefully avoid any depth in whatever relationships they form. These are just the characteristics that identify avoidant personality clients.

Trull, Widiger, and Frances (1987) found considerable overlap between avoidant personality disorder and dependent disorder, and Morey (1988) reports overlap with borderline disorder. As we noted earlier, there is also a problem concerning the distinction between avoidant disorder and social phobia. In particular, Turner, Beidel, Dancu, and Keys (1991) found considerable overlap between these two disorders, and they appear to differ only in the severity of their symptoms (Holt, Heimberg, & Hope, 1992).

Dependent Personality Disorder   These patients appear to be afraid to rely on themselves to make decisions. They seek advice and direction from others, need constant reassurance, and seek relationships where they can adopt a submissive role to their partner. Dependent patients not only allow other people to assume responsibilities for important aspects of their lives, but they seem to desperately need others to do so. They seem unable to function independently and typically ask their spouses or partners to decide what jobs they should seek or what clothes they should purchase, and indeed, they defer to others for all the decisions in their lives. Dependent personality patients subordinate their needs to those of other people in their lives, even people they hardly know. This style often gets them involved in abusive relationships or destroys relationships with partners who could be beneficial to their lives.

Reich (1990) observed that the relatives of male dependent patients were likely to experience depression, whereas the relatives of female dependents were more likely to have panic disorder. Panic-disordered patients have also been found to have comorbidity with various personality disorders, including the dependent disorder (Johnson, Weissman, & Klerman, 1990).

Obsessive-Compulsive Personality Disorder   Inflexibility and perfection characterize this disorder. It is the centrality of these two features and the absence of obsessional thoughts and compulsive behaviors that distinguish this personality disorder from the Axis I obsessive-compulsive disorder. Preoccupation with rules and order makes these patients rigid and inefficient as a result of focusing too much on the details of a problem. Obsessive-compulsive personality patients also attempt to ignore feelings because they consider emotions unpredictable. They tend to be moralistic and judgmental, and this causes problems in dealing with others.

Turkat and Levin (1984) could find no reports in the literature that they considered at all helpful in understanding obsessive-compulsive personality disorder.

Most of the research they reviewed was concerned with the psychoanalytic notion of the anal retentive character, which was thought to be related to obsessive-compulsive personality. It is not clear, however, if the results of this research are helpful in understanding the personality disorder. Very little research on this disorder has emerged over the years since *DSM-III-R* was published, except that which concerned distinguishing this personality disorder from obsessive-compulsive disorder. Those studies using objective measures have found a clear independence, whereas those using projective techniques or clinical interviews find co-occurrence of the two disorders (Cawley, 1974; Coursey, 1984; Slade, 1974). In fact, Joffe, Swinson, and Regan (1988) found that other personality disorders (e.g., avoidant, dependent, and schizotypal) were more likely to co-occur with obsessive-compulsive disorder than was obsessive-compulsive personality disorder.

TREATMENT

As Gorton and Akhtar (1990) observed, there are two important factors that make it difficult to evaluate treatment with the personality disorders:

1. Many of these patients are not themselves upset by their characteristic personality styles and so do not seek treatment.
2. The dropout rate from treatment among these patients is extremely high (Kelly et al., 1992).

There is no doubt that these patients constitute a serious challenge for the therapist. All of them have considerable difficulties with relationships and this affects the therapeutic alliance. In addition, most have problems maintaining focus between sessions on the therapeutic process. Even when the focus in treatment is on an Axis I disorder, those patients who also have a personality disorder do more poorly than those who are free of such problems (Reich & Green, 1991). In recent years, however, far more efforts have been devoted to developing treatment programs for these patients, although to date outcome data are limited.

TREATMENT RESISTANCE

Before considering specific intervention strategies for individuals diagnosed with personality disorders, some general issues concerning treatment resistance may be instructive. Individuals with Axis II disorders are notable in terms of their poor response to treatment. This response ranges from initial treatment refusal, program dropout, and poorer prognosis following intervention. Preston (2001) identified a host of treatment resistance factors that interfere with successful program completion and posttreatment outcome. These include:

- Disorder variables (e.g., personality disorders, schizophrenia, psychopathy, organic and neurological disorders, intellectual deficits, and substance abuse).
- Personality characteristics (e.g., hostility, defensiveness, rejecting authority, demanding, controlling).
- Behavioral variables (lack of motivation, interpersonal skills deficits, aggressivity, suicidal).

- Client fears (e.g., lack of confidence, hopelessness about change, lack of understanding about purpose of program).
- Self-serving motives (e.g., secondary gains).

For individuals with personality disorders, several of these factors interact to impede involvement and progress in treatment. Increasingly, programs for such treatment-resistant clients include sessions on motivational enhancement and cost-benefit analyses to engage them in treatment (Preston & Murphy, 1997). Motivational interviewing (Miller & Rollnick, 1991) and an understanding of stages of change (Prochaska & DiClemente, 1992) are also important in enhancing client motivation. In addition, broader responsivity factors such as therapist characteristics, setting, gender, culture, age, and client-therapist relationship influence treatment response (Kennedy & Serin, 1999; Serran, Fernandec, & Marshall, 1999). In the case of highly resistant clients, such as those diagnosed with personality disorder, these issues are as relevant to program effectiveness as the actual program content.

A related area is that of comorbidity. Although comorbidity is discussed in the context of assessment and diagnosis, it is also important in terms of treatment. Axis II diagnoses increased prediction of relapse in substance use (Pettinati, Pierce, Belden, & Meyers, 1999). Also, comorbid personality diagnoses have been shown to inform the choice of treatment paradigm and outcome (Mennin & Heimberg, 2000). Further, among substance abusers with comorbid personality disorders, the type of disorder yielded a differential impact on severity and type of relapse (Skodol, Oldham, & Gallaher, 1999). Finally, even in a group of substance abusers diagnosed with APD, presence or absence of depression was related to prognosis (Cecero, Ball, Tennen, Kranzler, & Rounsaville, 1999). An understanding of comorbidity is essential for the effective intervention and management of personality-disordered clients.

Given the characteristics of clients diagnosed as personality disordered and their resistance to treatment, there are significant difficulties in relying on self-reports of treatment gain (Kennedy & Serin, 1999). In addition to considering the influence of social desirability, clinicians are encouraged to consider behavioral measures. Fortunately, efforts are underway to develop such measures specifically for personality-disordered clients (Marziali, Munroe-Blum, & McCleary, 1999). As well, structured assessments concerning treatment gains are beginning to be reported in the literature (Kennedy & Serin, 1999). In general, multimethod assessments are recommended in determining both treatment needs and in evaluating treatment response (Serin & Preston, 2001a).

In terms of formal intervention, essentially three approaches have been developed: object-relations therapy, cognitive-behavioral approaches, and the use of medications. These approaches are discussed in the following sections.

OBJECT-RELATIONS THERAPY

The leading proponents of such an approach have been Kernberg (1975, 1985) and Kohut (1977). In their view, treatment should be aimed at correcting the flaws in the self that have resulted from their unfortunate formative experiences. The transference relationship between patient and therapist serves as a vehicle for confronting, in a supportive way, the patient's defenses and distortions. This process is slow and, if successful, produces gradual changes. Thus, treatment is seen as necessarily long term.

In the only controlled evaluation of this approach available, Stevenson and Meares (1992) treated, then followed up 30 borderline patients for one year. At follow-up, 30% of the patients no longer met *DSM* criteria for BPD. Single case reports of similar treatment programs with narcissistic patients have provided encouraging results (Kinston, 1980), but we await more extensive and rigorous evaluations.

Although Stone (1985) and Walsh (1990) have suggested that a psychotherapeutic approach emphasizing a supportive relationship and aimed at enhancing social skills may be useful with schizotypal patients, as long as the goals are limited, there have not, as yet, been any controlled evaluations of such an approach.

Cognitive-Behavioral Approaches

Beck et al. (1990) has extended his cognitive analyses to the personality disorders and has suggested that treatment must correct the cognitive distortions of these patients to be successful. Beck's treatment is directed at challenging the core schemas and beliefs that are thought to underlie the problems of these patients. Cognitive restructuring techniques provide bases for change, along with skills training and behavioral practices. To date, however, adherents of this promising approach have not produced controlled evaluations. This appears to be at least partly explained by the relatively recent development of this approach and because Beck et al.'s claim that, unlike the application of cognitive therapy to other problems, treatment of personality disorders takes far longer.

Linehan and Heard (1992) developed what they call *dialectical behavior therapy*. To date, this approach has been used only with borderline patients, but there does not seem to be any reason that it cannot be adapted to the problems of other personality disorders. One of the main features of this approach is the acceptance by the therapist of the patient's demanding and manipulative behaviors. In addition, several standard behavioral procedures are used, such as exposure to external and internal cues that evoke distress, skills training approaches, contingency management, and cognitive restructuring. The dialectical process describes "both the coexisting multiple tensions . . . and the thought processes and styles used and targeted in the treatment strategies" (p. 249).

Linehan, Armstrong, Suarez, Allmon, and Heard (1991) compared the treatment outcome of 22 female borderline patients randomly assigned to dialectical behavior therapy with 22 patients randomly assigned to "treatment as usual." At the end of one year of treatment, those assigned to dialectical behavior therapy had made fewer suicidal attempts and had spent less time in hospitals than those allocated to the other treatment program. An important additional observation was that while only 17% of the dialectically treated patients dropped out, almost 60% of the other group withdrew before treatment termination. Although both groups displayed less depression and hopelessness after treatment, there were no group differences on these measures. A second study (Linehan, Heard, & Armstrong, 1993) produced similar positive results.

Behavioral approaches employing social skills training and desensitization have been effective in ameliorating the problems of avoidant personality-disordered patients (Alden, 1989; Renneberg, Goldstein, Phillips, & Chambless, 1990; Stravynski,

Lesage, Marcouiller, & Elie, 1989). However, the benefits of these programs have not been evaluated at long-term follow-up, and Alden (1989) observed that most of these patients remained socially uncomfortable.

Pharmacologic Interventions

Borderline patients have been successfully treated with a variety of pharmacologic agents, including amitriptyline (Soloff et al., 1986), thiothixene (S. C. Goldberg et al., 1986), and carbemazepine (Gardner & Cowdry, 1986). It has been suggested that different subtypes of borderline patients may be differentially responsive to either antipsychotics or antidepressant medications. Goldberg et al., for example, found antipsychotics to be most effective with borderlines displaying psychotic-like features, while Cole, Saloman, Gunderson, Sunderland, and Simmonds (1984) found maximal improvements for antidepressants with those patients who also met the criteria for a major depression. In addition, Waldinger and Frank (1989) indicate that medications may facilitate psychotherapy with borderline patients.

S. C. Goldberg et al. (1986) and Schulz (1986) also found low doses of thiothixene to be beneficial with schizotypal-disordered patients. In addition, schizotypals seem to respond to antidepressants (Markowitz, Calabrese, Schulz, & Meltzer, 1991); however, the benefits of any medications with schizotypal disorder are modest at best (Gitlin, 1993).

SUMMARY

Other than the rather extensive research on borderline and antisocial personality disorders, and, to a lesser extent, on schizotypal patients, the personality disorders remain a neglected domain in the field of psychopathology. There is no doubt that diagnostic problems continue to hamper progress in this field. Whether switching from a categorical classification to a dimensional system is the best solution to this problem is not clear, although research focusing on dimensional analyses seems most likely to enhance our understanding of these disorders. As long as the authors of the diagnostic manual insist on pursuing a categorical system, problems of heterogeneity, comorbidity, and overlap will make research difficult. Issues of gender and culture must also be addressed if the diagnoses of personality disorders are to be meaningful in populations that are increasingly ethnoculturally diverse.

Whatever decision is made on classification, clinicians and researchers must give greater emphasis to developing and properly evaluating treatment programs for the personality disorders. Controlled, long-term outcome studies of large numbers of patients are required to determine the effectiveness of treatment. Of course, for the low-incidence personality disorders, such studies may not be feasible; but this should not deter researchers from making the best effort they can within the restrictions imposed by these low frequencies. Much can be learned from intervention and management strategies for resistant populations and applied to the area of personality disorders. Further, specific characteristics of effective therapists appear related to enhanced program performance and outcome. Last, the meta-analytic literature provides support for the effectiveness of interventions, but little is known concerning the integration of these group-based results for individual cases. Decision guidelines and performance-based measures are required to inform clinicians in such applications.

REFERENCES

Alden, L. (1989). Short-term structured treatment for avoidant personality disorder. *Journal of Consulting and Clinical Psychology, 57,* 756–764.

Alterman, A. I., & Cacciola, J. S. (1991). The antisocial personality disorder diagnosis in substance abusers. *Journal of Nervous and Mental Diseases, 179,* 401–409.

American Psychiatric Association. (1980). *Diagnostic and statistical manual of mental disorders* (3rd ed.). Washington, DC: Author.

American Psychiatric Association. (1987). *Diagnostic and statistical manual of mental disorders* (3rd ed., rev.). Washington, DC: Author.

American Psychiatric Association. (1994). *Diagnostic and statistical manual of mental disorders* (4th ed.). Washington, DC: Author.

Andrulonis, P. R., & Vogel, N. G. (1984). Comparison of borderline personality subcategories to schizophrenic and affective disorders. *British Journal of Psychiatry, 144,* 358–363.

Angus, L. E., & Marziali, E. (1988). A comparison of three measures for the diagnosis of borderline personality disorder. *American Journal of Psychiatry, 145,* 1453–1454.

Barasch, A., Frances, A., Hurt, S., Clarkin, J., & Cohen, S. (1985). Stability and distinctness of borderline personality disorder. *American Journal of Psychiatry, 142,* 1484–1486.

Baron, M., Levitt, M., Gruen, R., Kane, J., & Asnis, L. (1984). Platelet monoamine oxidase activity and genetic vulnerability to schizophrenia. *American Journal of Psychiatry, 141,* 836–842.

Baron, M., Risch, N., Levitt, M., & Gruen, R. (1985). Familial transmission of schizotypal and borderline personality disorders. *American Journal of Psychiatry, 142,* 927–934.

Bartholomew, K. (1989). *Attachment styles in young adults: Implications for self-concept and interpersonal functioning.* Unpublished doctoral dissertation, Stanford University, Stanford, CA.

Bartholomew, K. (1990). Avoidance of intimacy: An attachment perspective. *Journal of Personal and Social Relationships, 7,* 147–178.

Beck, A. T., Freeman, A., & Associates. (1990). *Cognitive therapy of personality disorders.* New York: Guilford Press.

Berman, W. H., & Sperling, M. B. (1994). The structure and function of adult attachment. In M. B. Sperling & W. H. Berman (Eds.), *Attachment in adults: Clinical and developmental perspectives* (pp. 3–28). New York: Guilford Press.

Bernstein, D. P., Cohen, P., Velez, C. N., Schwab-Stone, M., Siever, L. J., & Shinsato, L. (1993). Prevalence and stability of the *DSM-III-R* personality disorders in a community-based survey of adolescents. *American Journal of Psychiatry, 50,* 1237–1243.

Blackburn, R. (1992). Criminal behavior, personality disorder, and mental confusion: The origins of confusion. *Criminal Behavior and Mental Health, 2,* 66–77.

Blackburn, R. (1993a). Clinical programs with psychopaths. In K. Howells & C. Hollins (Eds.), *Clinical approaches to the mentally disordered offender* (pp. 179–208). Chichester, England: Wiley.

Blackburn, R. (1993b). *The psychology of criminal conduct.* Chichester, England: Wiley.

Bond, A. J. (1993). Prospects for antiaggressive drugs. In C. Thompson & P. Cowen (Eds.), *Violence: Basic and clinical services* (pp. 147–170). London: Butterworth-Heinemann.

Bornstein, R. F., Klein, D. N., Mallon, J. C., & Slater, J. F. (1988). Schizotypal personality disorder in an outpatient population: Incidence and clinical characteristics. *Journal of Clinical Psychology, 44,* 322–325.

Bowlby, J. (1977). The making and breaking of affectional bonds. I: Aetiology and psychopathology in the light of attachment theory. *British Journal of Psychiatry, 30,* 301–310.

Bowlby, J. (1988). *A secure base: Parent-child attachment and health human development*. New York: Basic Books.

Briere, J., & Zaidi, L. Y. (1989). Sexual abuse histories and sequelae in female psychiatric emergency room patients. *American Journal of Psychiatry, 146,* 1602–1606.

Brown, L. S. (1992). A feminist critique of the personality disorder. In L. S. Brown & M. Ballou (Eds.), *Personality and psychopathology: Feminist reappraisals* (pp. 176–189). New York: Guilford Press.

Bryer, J. B., Nelson, B. A., Miller, J. B., & Krol, P. K. (1987). Childhood sexual and physical abuse as factors in adult psychiatric illness. *American Journal of Psychiatry, 144,* 1426–1430.

Cawley, R. (1974). Psychotherapy and obsessional disorders. In H. R. Beech (Ed.), *Obsessional states* (pp. 259–290). London: Methuen.

Cecero, J. J., Ball, S. A., Tennen, H., Kranzler, H. R., & Rounsaville, B. J. (1999). Concurrent and predictive validity of antisocial personality disorder subtyping among substance abusers. *Journal of Nervous and Mental Diseases, 187,* 478–486.

Chiswick, D. (1992). Compulsory treatment of patients with psychopathic disorder: An abnormally aggressive or seriously irresponsible exercise. *Criminal Behavior and Mental Health, 2,* 106–113.

Chodoff, P., & Lyons, H. (1958). Hysteria, the hysterical personality and "hysterical" conversion. *American Journal of Psychiatry, 114,* 734–740.

Clarkin, J. F., Widiger, T. A., Frances, A. J., Hurt, S. W., & Gilmore, M. (1983). Prototypic typology and the borderline personality disorder. *Journal of Abnormal Psychology, 92,* 263–275.

Cleckley, H. (1976). *The mask of sanity* (5th ed.). St. Louis, MO: Mosby.

Coatsworth, J. D., Szapocznik, J., Kurtines, W., & Santisteban, D. A. (1997). Culturally competent psychosocial interventions with antisocial problem behavior in Hispanic youths. In D. M. Stoff, J. Breiling, & J. D. Maser (Eds.), *Handbook of antisocial behavior* (pp. 395–404). New York: Wiley.

Cole, J. O., Saloman, M., Gunderson, J., Sunderland, P., & Simmonds, P. (1984). Drug therapy for borderline patients. *Comprehensive Psychiatry, 25,* 249–254.

Cooke, D. J. (1999). Psychopathy across cultures: North America and Scotland compared. *Journal of Abnormal Psychology, 108,* 58–68.

Coursey, D. (1984). The dynamics of obsessive-compulsive disorder. In T. R. Insel (Ed.), *New findings in obsessive-compulsive disorder* (pp. 104–121). Washington, DC: American Psychiatric Press.

Dahl, A. R. (1986). Some aspects of *DSM-III* personality disorder illustrated by a consecutive sample of hospitalized patients. *Acta Psychiatrica Scandinavian, 73,* 61–67.

Drake, R. E., & Vaillant, G. E. (1985). A validity study of Axis II of *DSM-III. American Journal of Psychiatry, 142,* 553–558.

Dutton, D. G., Saunders, K., Starzomski, A., & Bartholomew, K. (1994). Intimacy-anger and insecure attachment as precursors of abuse in intimate relationships. *Journal of Applied Social Psychology, 24,* 1367–1386.

Fernandez, Y., Serran, G., & Marshall, W. L. (1999). *The reliable identification of therapist features in the treatment of sexual offenders*. Paper presented at Association of Treatment of Sexual Abusers annual conference, Orlando, FL.

Ford, M. R., & Widiger, T. A. (1989). Sex bias in the diagnosis of histrionic and antisocial personality disorders. *Journal of Consulting and Clinical Psychology, 57,* 301–305.

Frances, A. J. (1985). Validating schizotypal personality disorders: Problems with the schizophrenic connection. *Schizophrenia Bulletin, 11,* 595–597.

Gabbard, G. O., & Coyne, L. (1987). Predictors of response of antisocial patients to hospital treatment. *Hospital and Community Psychiatry, 38,* 1181–1185.

Gacono, C. (Ed.). (2000). *The clinical and forensic assessment of psychopathy: A practitioner's guide.* Mahwah, NJ: Erlbaum.

Gacono, C. B., & Hutton, H. E. (1994). Suggestions for the clinical and forensic use of the Hare Psychopathy Checklist-Revised (PCL-R). *International Journal of Law and Psychiatry, 17,* 303–317.

Gallwey, P. (1992). The psychotherapy of psychopathic disorder. *Criminal Behavior and Mental Health, 2,* 159–168.

Gardner, D. L., & Cowdry, R. W. (1986). Positive effects of carbamazepine on behavioral dyscontrol in borderline personality disorder. *American Journal of Psychiatry, 143,* 519–522.

Gendreau, P. (1996). The principles of effective intervention with offenders. In A. T. Harland (Ed.), *Choosing correctional options that work: Defining the demand and evaluating the supply* (pp. 117–130). Thousand Oaks, CA: Sage.

Gerstley, L. J., Alterman, A. I., McLellan, A. T., & Woody, G. E. (1990). Antisocial personality disorder in patients with substance abuse disorders: A problematic diagnosis? *American Journal of Psychiatry, 147,* 173–178.

Gerstley, L. J., McLellan, A. T., Alterman, A. I., Woody, G. E., Luborsky, L., & Prout, M. (1989). Ability to form an alliance with the therapist: A possible marker of prognosis for patients with antisocial personality disorder. *American Journal of Psychiatry, 146,* 508–512.

Gitlin, M. J. (1993). Pharmacotherapy of personality disorders: Conceptual framework and clinical strategies. *Journal of Clinical Psychopharmacology, 13,* 343–353.

Goldberg, R. L., Mann, L. S., Wise, T. N., & Segall, E. R. (1985). Parental qualities as perceived by borderline personality disorder. *Hillside Journal of Clinical Psychiatry, 7,* 134–140.

Goldberg, S. C., Schulz, S. C., Schulz, P. M., Resnick, R. J., Hamer, R. M., & Friedel, R. O. (1986). Borderline and schizotypal personality disorder treated with low-dose thiothixene versus placebo. *Archives of General Psychiatry, 43,* 680–686.

Gorton, G., & Akhtar, S. (1990). The literature on personality disorders, 1985–1988: Trends, issues, and controversies. *Hospital and Community Psychiatry, 41,* 39–51.

Grinker, R. R., Werble, B., & Drye, R. C. (1968). *The borderline syndrome.* New York: Basic Books.

Grove, W. M., Eckert, E. D., Heston, L., Bouchard, T. J., Segal, N., & Lykken, D. T. (1990). Heritability of substance abuse and antisocial behavior: A study of monozygotic twins reared apart. *Biological Psychiatry, 27,* 1293–1304.

Guerra, N. G., & Slaby, R. G. (1990). Cognitive mediators of aggression in adolescent offenders. II: Intervention. *Developmental Psychology, 26,* 269–277.

Gunderson, J. G., & Elliott, G. R. (1985). The interface between borderline personality disorder and affective disorder. *American Journal of Psychiatry, 142,* 277–288.

Gunderson, J. G., & Singer, M. T. (1975). Defining borderline patients: An overview. *American Journal of Psychiatry, 132,* 1–10.

Gunderson, J. G., & Zanarini, M. C. (1987). Current overview of borderline diagnosis. *Journal of Clinical Psychiatry, 43,* 5–11.

Harding, T. W. (1992). Psychopathic disorder: Time for a decent burial of a bad legal concept? *Criminal Behavior and Mental Health, 2,* vi–ix.

Hare, R. D. (1983). Diagnosis of antisocial personality disorder in two prison populations. *American Journal of Abnormal Psychiatry, 140,* 887–890.

Hare, R. D. (1985). A comparison of procedures for the assessment of psychopathy. *Journal of Consulting and Clinical Psychology, 53,* 7–16.

Hare, R. D. (1991). *The Hare Psychopathy Checklist-Revised.* Toronto, Ontario, Canada: Multi-Health Systems.

Hare, R. D. (1996). Psychopathy: A clinical construct whose time has come. *Criminal Justice and Behavior, 21,* 25–54.

Hare, R. D., Harpur, T. J., Hakstian, A. R., Forth, A. E., Hart, S. D., & Newman, J. P. (1990). The Revised Psychopathy Checklist: Reliability and factor structure. *Psychological Assessment: A Journal of Consulting and Clinical Psychology, 2,* 338–341.

Hare, R. D., Hart, S. D., & Harpur, T. J. (1991). Psychopathy and *DSM-IV* criteria for antisocial personality disorder. *Journal of Abnormal Psychology, 100,* 391–398.

Harpur, T. J., & Hare, R. D. (1994). The assessment of psychopathy as a function of age. *Journal of Abnormal Psychology, 103,* 604–609.

Harris, G. T. (1989). The relationship between neuroleptic drug dose and the performance of psychiatric patients in a maximum security token economy program. *Journal of Behavior Therapy and Experimental Psychiatry, 20,* 57–67.

Harris, G. T., Rice, M. E., & Quinsey, V. L. (1993). Violent recidivism of mentally disordered offenders: The development of a statistical prediction instrument. *Criminal Justice and Behavior, 20,* 315–335.

Harris, G. T., Rice, M. E., & Quinsey, V. L. (1994). Psychopathy as a taxon: Evidence that psychopaths are a discrete class. *Journal of Consulting and Clinical Psychology, 62,* 387–397.

Harris, G. T., Skilling, T. A., & Rice, M. E. (2001). The construct of psychopathy. In M. Tonry & N. Morris (Eds.), *Crime and justice: An annual review of research* (Vol. 28, pp. 197–264). Chicago: University of Chicago Press.

Hart, S. D., & Hare, R. D. (1989). Discriminant validity of the Psychopathy Checklist in a forensic psychiatric population. *Psychological Assessment: A Journal of Consulting and Clinical Psychology, 1,* 211–218.

Hart, S. D., Kropp, P. R., & Hare, R. D. (1988). Performance of male psychopaths following conditional release from prison. *Journal of Consulting and Clinical Psychology, 56,* 227–232.

Helzer, J. E., Spitznagel, E. L., & McEnvoy, L. (1987). The predictive validity of lay Diagnostic Interview Schedule diagnoses in the general population: A comparison with physician examiners. *Archives of General Psychiatry, 44,* 1069–1077.

Henry, K., & Cohen, C. (1983). The role of labeling in diagnosing borderline personality disorder. *American Journal of Psychiatry, 140,* 1527–1529.

Herman, J. L. (1992). *Trauma and recovery.* New York: Basic Books.

Holt, C. S., Heimberg, R. G., & Hope, D. A. (1992). Avoidant personality disorder and the generalized subtype of social phobia. *Journal of Abnormal Psychology, 101,* 318–325.

Horney, K. (1945). *Our inner conflicts.* New York: Norton.

Hurt, S. W., Clarkin, J. F., Koenigsberg, H. W., Frances, A., & Nurmberg, H. G. (1986). Diagnostic interview for borderlines: Psychometric properties and validity. *Journal of Consulting and Clinical Psychology, 54,* 256–260.

Jacobsberg, L. B., Hymowitz, P., Barasch, A., & Frances, A. J. (1986). Symptoms of schizotypal personality disorder. *American Journal of Psychiatry, 143,* 1222–1227.

Joffe, R. T., Swinson, R. P., & Regan, J. J. (1988). Personality features of obsessive-compulsive disorder. *American Journal of Psychiatry, 145,* 1127–1129.

Johnson, J., Weissman, M. M., & Klerman, G. L. (1990). Panic disorder and suicide attempts. *Archives of General Psychiatry, 47,* 805–808.

Kaplan, M. (1983). A woman's view of *DSM-III. American Psychologist, 38,* 786–792.

Karper, L. P., & Krystal, J. H. (1997). Pharmacotherapy of violent behavior. In D. M. Stoff, J. Breiling, & J. D. Maser (Eds.), *Handbook of antisocial behavior* (pp. 436–444). New York: Wiley.

Kass, F., Spitzer, R., & Williams, J. (1983). An empirical study of the issue of sex bias in the diagnostic criteria of *DSM-III* Axis II personality disorders. *American Psychologist, 38,* 799–801.

Kazdin, A. E. (1987). Treatment of antisocial behavior in children: Current status and future directions. *Psychological Bulletin, 102,* 187–203.

Kazdin, A. E. (1993). Treatment of conduct disorder: Progress and directions in psychotherapy research. *Development and Psychopathology, 5,* 277–310.

Kelly, T., Soloff, P. H., Cornelius, J., George, A., Lis, J. A., & Ulrich, R. (1992). Can we study (treat) borderline patients? Attrition from research and open treatment. *Journal of Personality Disorders, 6,* 417–433.

Kendler, K. S. (1985). Diagnostic approaches to schizotypal personality disorder: A historical perspective. *Schizophrenia Bulletin, 11,* 538–553.

Kendler, K. S., Masterson, C. C., & Davis, K. L. (1985). Psychiatric illness in first degree relatives of patients with paranoid psychosis, schizophrenia and medical controls. *British Journal of Psychiatry, 147,* 524–531.

Kennedy, S., & Serin, R. (1999). Examining offender readiness to change and the impact on treatment outcome. In P. M. Harris (Ed.), *Research to results: Effective community corrections* (pp. 215–230), Lanham, MD: American Correctional Association.

Kernberg, O. F. (1967). Borderline personality organization. *Journal of the American Psychoanalytic Association, 15,* 641–685.

Kernberg, O. F. (1975). *Borderline conditions and pathological narcissism.* New York: Aronson.

Kernberg, O. F. (1985). *Borderline conditions and pathological narcissism.* Northvale, NJ: Aronson.

Kessler, R. C., McGonagle, K. A., Zhao, S., Nelson, L. B., Hughes, M., Eslheman, S., et al. (1994). Lifetime and 12-month prevalence of *DSM-III-R* psychiatric disorders in the United States: Results from the National Comorbidity Study. *Archives of General Psychiatry, 51,* 8–19.

Kety, S. S., Rosenthal, D., Wender, P. H., & Schulsinger, F. (1971). Mental illness in the biological and adoptive families of adopted schizophrenics. *American Journal of Psychiatry, 128,* 302–306.

Kinston, W. (1980). A theoretical and technical approach to narcissistic disturbance. *International Journal of Psychoanalysis, 61,* 383–393.

Knight, R. (1953). Borderline states. *Bulletin of the Menninger Clinic, 17,* 1–12.

Kohut, H. (1977). *The restoration of the self.* New York: International Universities Press.

Kosson, D. S., Gacono, C. B., & Bodholdt, R. H. (2000). Assessing psychopathy: Interpersonal aspects and clinical interviewing. In C. Gacono (Ed.), *The clinical and forensic assessment of psychopathy: A practitioner's guide* (pp. 203–229). Hillsdale, NJ: Erlbaum.

Kosson, D. S., Smith, S. S., & Newman, J. P. (1990). Evaluation of the construct validity of psychopathy in Black and White male inmates: Three preliminary studies. *Journal of Abnormal Psychology, 99,* 250–259.

Levy, T. M. (2000). *Handbook of attachment interventions.* San Diego, CA: Academic Press.

Lilienfeld, S. O. (1994). Conceptual problems in the assessment of psychopathy. *Clinical Psychology Review, 14,* 17–38.

Linehan, M. M., Armstrong, H. E., Suarez, A., Allmon, D., & Heard, H. L. (1991). Behavioral treatment of chronically parasuicidal borderline patients. *Archives of General Psychiatry, 48,* 1060–1064.

Linehan, M. M., & Heard, H. L. (1992). Dialectical behavior therapy for borderline personality disorder. In J. F. Clarkin, E. Marziali, & H. Munroe-Blum (Eds.), *Borderline personality disorder: Clinical and empirical perspectives* (pp. 248–267). New York: Guilford Press.

Linehan, M. M., Heard, H. L., & Armstrong, H. E. (1993). Naturalistic follow-up of a behavioral treatment for chronically parasuicidal borderline patients. *Archives of General Psychiatry, 50,* 971–974.

Links, P. S. (1992). Family environment and family psychopathology in the etiology of borderline personality disorder. In J. F. Clarkin, E. Marziali, & H. Munroe-Blum (Eds.), *Borderline personality disorder: Clinical and empirical perspectives* (pp. 45–66). New York: Guilford Press.

Livesley, W. J., Jackson, D. N., & Schroeder, M. L. (1992). Factorial structure of traits delineating personality disorders in clinical and general population samples. *Journal of Abnormal Psychology, 101,* 432–440.

Livesley, W. J., Schroeder, M. L., Jackson, D. N., & Jang, K. L. (1994). Categorical distinctions in the study of personality disorder: Implications for classification. *Journal of Abnormal Personality, 103,* 6–17.

Loranger, A., Oldham, J., Russakoff, L. M., & Susman, V. (1987). Structured interviews and borderline personality disorder. *Archives of General Psychiatry, 41,* 565–568.

Loranger, A., Oldham, J., & Tulis, E. H. (1983). Familial transmission of *DSM-III* borderline personality disorders. *Archives of General Psychiatry, 40,* 975–979.

Lyon, D. R., & Ogloff, J. R. P. (2000). Legal and ethical issues in psychopathy assessment. In C. Gacono (Ed.), *The clinical and forensic assessment of psychopathy: A practitioner's guide* (pp. 139–173). Hillsdale, NJ: Erlbaum.

Maffei, C., Fossati, A., Agostoni, I., Barraco, A., Bagnato, M., Deborah, D., et al. (1997). Interrater reliability and internal consistency for the Structured Clinical Interview for *DSM-IV* Axis II Personality Disorders (SCID-II), version 2.0. *Journal of Personality Disorders, 11,* 279–284.

Maier, W., Lichtermann, D., Klingler, T., Heun, R., & Hallmayer, J. (1992). Prevalence of personality disorders (*DSM-III-R*) in the community. *Journal of Personality Disorders, 6,* 187–196.

Markowitz, P. J., Calabrese, J. R., Schulz, C. S., & Meltzer, H. Y. (1991). Fluoxetine in the treatment of borderline and schizotypal personality disorders. *American Journal of Psychiatry, 148,* 1067–1076.

Marques, J. K., Day, D. M., Nelson, C., & West, M. A. (1994). Effects of cognitive-behavioral treatment on sex offender recidivism: Preliminary results of a longitudinal study. *Criminal Justice and Behavior, 21,* 28–54.

Marshall, W. L. (1989). Intimacy, loneliness and sexual offenders. *Behavior Research and Therapy, 27,* 491–503.

Marshall, W. L., & Barbaree, H. E. (1984). Disorders of personality, impulse and adjustment. In S. M. Turner & M. Hersen (Eds.), *Adult psychopathology: A behavioral perspective* (pp. 406–449). New York: Wiley.

Marshall, W. L., & Barbaree, H. E. (1991). Personality, impulse control and adjustment disorders. In M. Hersen & S. M. Turner (Eds.), *Adult psychopathology and diagnosis* (2nd ed., pp. 360–391). New York: Wiley.

Marshall, W. L., Hudson, S. M., & Hodkinson, S. (1993). The importance of attachment bonds in the development of juvenile sex offending. In H. E. Barbaree, W. L. Marshall, & S. M. Hudson (Eds.), *The juvenile sex offender* (pp. 164–181). New York: Guilford Press.

Marziali, E. (1992). The etiology of borderline personality disorder: Developmental factors. In J. F. Clarkin, E. Marziali, & H. Munroe-Blum (Eds.), *Borderline personality disorder: Clinical and empirical perspectives* (pp. 27–44). New York: Guilford Press.

Marziali, E., Munroe-Blum, H., & McCleary, L. (1999). The Objective Behavioral Index: A measure for assessing treatment response of patients with severe personality disorders. *Journal of Nervous and Mental Diseases, 187,* 290–295.

McGlashan, T. M. (1983). The borderline syndrome. I: Testing three diagnostic systems. *Archives of General Psychiatry, 40,* 1311–1318.

McGlashan, T. M. (1987). Testing *DSM-III* symptom criteria for schizotypal and borderline personality disorders. *Archives of General Psychiatry, 44,* 143–148.

McManus, M., Lerner, H. D., Robbins, D., & Barbour, C. (1984). Assessment of borderline symptomatology in hospitalized adolescents. *Journal of the American Academy of Child Psychiatry, 23,* 685–694.

Mellsop, G., Varghese, F., Joshua, S., & Hicks, A. (1982). The reliability of Axis II of *DSM-III. American Journal of Psychiatry, 139,* 1360–1361.

Meloy, J. R. (1995). Treatment of antisocial personality disorder. In G. Gabbard (Ed.), *Treatments of psychiatric disorders: The DSM-IV Edition* (pp. 2273–2290). Washington, DC: American Psychiatric Press.

Mennin, D. S., & Heimberg, R. G. (2000). The impact of comorbid mood and personality disorders in the cognitive-behavioral treatment of panic disorder. *Clinical Psychology Review, 20,* 339–357.

Merikangas, K. R., & Weissman, M. M. (1986). Epidemiology of *DSM-III* Axis II personality disorders. In A. J. Frances & R. E. Hales (Eds.), *The American Psychiatric Association annual review* (pp. 49–74). Washington, DC: American Psychiatric Press.

Miller, W. R., & Rollnick, S. (1991). *Motivational interviewing.* New York: Guilford Press.

Millon, T. (1969). *Modern psychopathology: A biosocial approach to maladaptive learning and functioning.* Philadelphia: Saunders.

Millon, T. (1981). *Disorders of personality: DSM-III: Axis II.* New York: Wiley.

Millon, T. (1983). An integrative theory of personality and psychopathology. In T. Millon (Ed.), *Theories of personality and psychopathology* (pp. 3–19). New York: Hold, Rinehart and Winston.

Millon, T. (1986). Personality prototypes and their diagnostic criteria. In T. Millon & G. L. Klerman (Eds.), *Contemporary directions in psychopathology* (pp. 671–712). New York: Guilford Press.

Millon, T. (1992). The borderline construct: Introductory notes on its history, theory, and empirical grounding. In J. F. Clarkin, E. Marziali, & H. Munroe-Blum (Eds.), *Borderline personality disorder: Clinical and empirical perspectives* (pp. 3–23). New York: Guilford Press.

Millon, T. (1996). *Disorders of personality: DSM-IV and beyond* (2nd ed.). New York: Wiley.

Moffitt, T. E. (1993). Adolescence-limited and life-course-persistent antisocial behavior: A developmental taxonomy. *Psychological Review, 100,* 674–701.

Morey, L. C. (1988). Personality disorders in *DSM-III* and *DSM-III-R:* Convergence, coverage, and internal consistency. *American Journal of Psychiatry, 145,* 573–577.

Morey, L. C., & Ochoa, E. (1989). An investigation of adherence to diagnostic criteria: Clinical diagnosis of the *DSM-III* personality disorders. *Journal of Personality Disorders, 3,* 180–192.

Murray, M. E. (1979). Minimal brain dysfunction and borderline personality adjustment. *American Journal of Psychotherapy, 33,* 391–403.

Nakdimen, K. A. (1986). A new formulation for borderline personality disorder? *American Journal of Psychiatry, 143,* 1069.

Nestadt, G., Romanoski, A. J., Chahal, R., Merchant, A., Folstein, J. F., Gruenberg, E. M., et al. (1990). An epidemiological study of histrionic personality disorder. *Psychological Medicine, 20,* 413–422.

Newman, J., & Wallace, J. F. (1993). Psychopathy and cognition. In K. S. Dobson & P. C. Kendall (Eds.), *Psychopathology and cognition* (pp. 293–349). Orlando, FL: Academic Press.

Nezu, A. M., & Nezu, C. M. (1993). Identifying and selecting target problems for clinical interventions: A problem-solving model. *Psychological Assessment, 5,* 254–263.

Ogloff, J. P. R., Wong, S., & Greenwood, A. (1990). Treating criminal psychopaths in a therapeutic community program. *Behavioral Sciences and the Law, 8,* 81–90.

Paris, J., & Frank, H. (1989). Perceptions of parental bonding in borderline patients. *American Journal of Psychiatry, 146,* 1498–1499.

Patrick, M., Hobson, R. P., Castle, D., & Howard, R. (1994). Personality disorder and the mental representation of early social experiences. *Development and Psychopathology, 6,* 375–388.

Perry, J. C. (1985). Depression in borderline personality disorder: Lifetime prevalence at interview and longitudinal course of symptoms. *American Journal of Psychiatry, 142,* 15–21.

Perry, J. C., & Klerman, G. L. (1978). The borderline patient: A comparative analysis of four sets of diagnostic criteria. *Archives of General Psychiatry, 35,* 141–150.

Pettinati, H. M., Pierce, J. D., Jr., Belden, P., & Meyers, K. (1999). The relationship of Axis II personality disorders to other known predictors of addiction treatment outcome. *American Journal on Addictions, 8,* 136–147.

Pfohl, B., Coryell, W., Zimmerman, M., & Stangl, D. (1986). *DSM-III* personality disorders: Diagnostic overlap and internal consistency of individual *DSM-III* criteria. *Comprehensive Psychiatry, 27,* 21–34.

Pinel, P. (1809). *Traite medico-phiosophique sur l'alienation mentale* (2nd ed.). Paris: Chez J. Ant Brosson.

Plakun, E. M. (1987). Distinguishing narcissistic and borderline personality disorders using *DSM-III* criteria. *Comprehensive Psychiatry, 28,* 437–443.

Poldrugo, F., & Forti, B. (1988). Personality disorders and alcoholism treatment outcome. *Drug and Alcohol Dependence, 21,* 171–176.

Pope, H. G., Jonas, J. M., Hudson, J. I., Cohen, B. M., & Gunderson, J. G. (1983). Borderline personality disorder: A phenomenologic, family history, treatment response and long-term follow-up study. *Archives of General Psychiatry, 40,* 23–30.

Porporino, F. J., & Motiuk, L. L. (1995). The prison careers of mentally disordered offenders. *International Journal of Law and Psychiatry, 18,* 29–44.

Preston, D. L. (2001). Addressing treatment resistance in corrections. In L. L. Motiuk & R. C. Serin (Eds.), *Compendium 2000 on effective corrections* (pp. 47–55). Correctional Service Canada, Ministry of Supply and Services.

Preston, D. L., & Murphy, S. (1997). Motivating treatment-resistant clients in therapy. *Forum on Corrections Research, 9*(2), 39–43.

Prochaska, J. O., & DiClemente, C. C. (1992). Stages of change in the modification of problem behaviors. *Progress in Behavior Modification, 28,* 183–218.

Raine, A. (1985). A psychometric assessment of Hare's checklist for psychopathy in an English prison population. *British Journal of Clinical Psychology, 24,* 247–258.

Raine, A. (1993). *The psychopathology of crime: Criminal behavior as a clinical disorder.* San Diego, CA: Academic Press.

Reich, J. (1987). Sex distribution of *DSM-III* personality disorders in psychiatric outpatients. *American Journal of Psychiatry, 144,* 485–488.

Reich, J. (1990). Comparison of males and females with *DSM-III* dependent personality disorder. *Psychiatry Research, 33,* 207–214.

Reich, J. (1992). Measurement of *DSM-III* and *DSM-III-R* borderline personality disorder. In J. F. Clarkin, E. Marziali, & H. Munroe-Blum (Eds.), *Borderline personality disorder: Clinical and empirical perspectives* (pp. 116–148). New York: Guilford Press.

Reich, J., & Green, A. I. (1991). Effect of personality disorders on outcome of treatment. *Journal of Neurons and Mental Disease, 179,* 74–82.

Reich, J., Noyes, R., & Troughton, E. (1987). Dependent personality disorder associated with phobic avoidance in patients with panic disorder. *American Journal of Psychiatry, 144,* 323–326.

Renneberg, B., Goldstein, A. J., Phillips, D., & Chambless, D. L. (1990). Intensive behavioral group treatment of avoidant personality disorder. *Behavior Therapy, 21,* 363–377.

Rice, M. E., & Harris, G. T. (1993). Treatment for prisoners with mental disorder. In J. H. Steadman & J. J. Cocozza (Eds.), *Mental illness in America's prisons* (pp. 91–130). Seattle, WA: National Coalition for the Mentally Ill in the Criminal Justice System.

Rice, M. E., & Harris, G. T. (1997). The treatment of adult offenders. In D. M. Stoff, J. Breiling, & J. D. Maser (Eds.), *Handbook of antisocial behavior* (pp. 425–435). New York: Wiley.

Rice, M. E., Harris, G. T., & Cormier, C. (1992). Evaluation of a maximum security therapeutic community for psychopaths and other mentally disordered offenders. *Law and Human Behavior, 16,* 399–412.

Rice, M. E., Harris, G. T., & Quinsey, V. L. (1996). Treatment of forensic patients. In B. Sales & S. Shah (Eds.), *Mental health and the law: Research, policy, and practice* (pp. 141–190). New York: Carolina Academic Press.

Rice, M. E., Harris, G. T., Varney, G. W., & Quinsey, V. L. (1989). *Violence in institutions: Understanding, prevention, and control.* Toronto, Ontario, Canada: Hans Huber.

Robins, L. N., & Regier, D. A. (1991). *Psychiatric disorders in America.* New York: Free Press.

Robinson, D. (1995). The impact of cognitive skills training on postrelease recidivism among Canadian federal offenders. *Research Report R-34.* Ottawa, Canada: Correctional Service of Canada.

Rogers, R., Dion, K. L., & Lynett, E. (1992). Diagnostic validity of antisocial personality disorder: A prototypical analysis. *Law and Human Behavior, 16,* 677–689.

Rogers, R., Duncan, J. C., Lynett, E., & Sewell, K. E. (1994). Prototypical analysis of antisocial personality disorder: *DSM-IV* and beyond. *Law and Human Behavior, 18,* 471–484.

Ronningstam, E., & Gunderson, J. G. (1990). Identifying criteria for narcissistic personality disorder. *American Journal of Psychiatry, 147,* 918–922.

Rosenberger, P. H., & Miller, G. A. (1989). Comparing borderline definitions: *DSM-III* borderline and schizotypal disorders. *Journal of Abnormal Psychology, 92,* 161–169.

Rutter, M. (1997). Antisocial behavior: Developmental psychopathology perspectives. In D. M. Stoff, J. Breiling, & J. D. Maser (Eds.), *Handbook of antisocial behavior* (pp. 115–124). New York: Wiley.

Rutter, M., Boltin, P., Harrington, R., Le Couteur, A., Macdonald, H., & Simonoff, E. (1990). Genetic factors in child psychiatric disorders. I: A review of research strategies. *Journal of Child Psychology and Psychiatry, 31,* 5–37.

Schalling, D. (1993). Neurochemical correlates of personality, impulsivity, and disinhibitory suicidality. In S. Hodgins (Ed.), *Mental disorder and crime* (pp. 208–226). Newbury Park, CA: Sage.

Schlesinger, L. B. (1980). Distinctions between psychopathic, sociopathic and antisocial personality disorders. *Psychological Reports, 47,* 15–21.

Schubert, D. S., Wolf, A. W., Patterson, M. B., Grande, T. P., & Pendelton, L. (1988). A statistical evaluation of the literature regarding the associations among alcoholism, drug abuse, and antisocial personality disorder. *International Journal of the Addictions, 23,* 797–808.

Schulz, S. C. (1986). The use of low-dose neuroleptics in the treatment of "schizo-obsessive" patients. *American Journal of Psychiatry, 143,* 1318–1319.

Serban, G., Conte, H. R., & Plutchik, R. (1987). Borderline and schizotypal personality disorders: Mutually exclusive or overlapping? *Journal of Personality Assessment, 5,* 15–22.

Serin, R. C., & Brown, S. L. (2000). The clinical use of the Hare Psychopathy Checklist-Revised in contemporary risk assessment. In C. Gacono (Ed.), *The clinical and forensic assessment of psychopathy: A practitioner's guide* (pp. 251–268). Hillsdale, NJ: Erlbaum.

Serin, R. C., & Kuriychuk, M. (1994). Social and cognitive processing deficits in violent offenders: Implications for treatment. *International Journal of Law and Psychiatry, 17,* 431–441.

Serin, R. C., & Preston, D. L. (2001a). Designing, implementing and managing treatment programs for violent offenders. In G. A. Bernfeld, D. P. Farrington, & A. W. Leischied (Eds.), *Offender rehabilitation in practice: Implementing and evaluating effective programs* (pp. 204–221. Chichester, England: Wiley.

Serin, R. C., & Preston, D. L. (2001b). Managing and treating violent offenders. In J. B. Ashford, B. D. Sales, & W. Reid (Eds.), *Treating adult and juvenile offenders with special needs* (pp. 249–272). Washington, DC: American Psychological Association.

Siever, L. J. (1985). Biological markers in schizotypal personality disorders. *Schizophrenia Bulletin, 11,* 564–575.

Skeem, J. L., & Mulvey, E. P. (2001). Psychopathy and community violence among civil psychiatric patients: Results from the MacArthur Violence Risk Assessment study. *Journal of Consulting and Clinical Psychology, 69,* 358–374.

Skodol, A. E., Oldham, J. M., & Gallaher, P. E. (1999). Axis II comorbidity of substance use disorders among patients referred for treatment of personality disorders. *American Journal of Psychiatry, 156,* 733–738.

Skodol, A. E., Rosnick, L., Kellman, D., Oldham, J. M., & Hyler, S. E. (1988, May). *The validity of structured assessments of Axis II.* Paper presented at the 141st annual meeting of the American Psychiatric Association, Montreal, Canada.

Slade, P. D. (1974). Psychometric studies of obsessional illness and obsessional personality. In H. R. Beech (Ed.), *Obsessional states* (pp. 95–112). London: Methuen.

Soloff, P. H., George, A., Nathan, R. S., Schulz, P. M., Ulrich, R. F., & Perel, J. M. (1986). Progress in pharmacotherapy of borderline disorders. *Archives of General Psychiatry, 43,* 691–697.

Spitzer, R. L., Endicott, J., & Gibbon, M. (1979). Crossing the border into borderline personality and borderline schizophrenia. *Archives of General Psychiatry, 36,* 17–24.

Sprock, J., Blashfield, R. K., & Smith, B. (1990). Gender weighting of *DSM-III-R* personality disorder criteria. *American Journal of Psychiatry, 147,* 586–590.

Stevenson, J., & Meares, R. (1992). An outcome study of psychotherapy for patients with borderline personality disorder. *American Journal of Psychiatry, 149,* 358–362.

Stoff, D. M., Breiling, J., & Maser, J. D. (Eds.). (1997). *Handbook of antisocial behavior.* New York: Wiley.

Stone, M. (1985). Schizotypal personality: Psychotherapeutic aspects. *Schizophrenia Bulletin, 11,* 576–589.

Stone, M. (1993). Long-term outcome in personality disorders. *British Journal of Psychiatry, 162,* 299–313.

Stravynski, A., Lesage, A., Marcouiller, M., & Elie, R. (1989). A test of the therapeutic mechanism in social skills training with avoidant personality disorder. *Journal of Neurons and Mental Disease, 177*, 739–744.

Suedfeld, P., & Landon, P. B. (1978). Approaches to treatment. In R. D. Hare & D. Schalling (Eds.), *Psychopathic behavior: Approaches to research* (pp. 347–376). Chichester, England: Wiley.

Swartz, M., Blazer, D., George, L., & Landerman, R. (1986). Somatization disorder in a community population. *American Journal of Psychiatry, 143*, 1403–1408.

Tennent, G., Tennent, D., Prins, H., & Bedford, A. (1993). Is psychopathic disorder a treatable condition? *Medicine, Science, and the Law, 33*, 63–66.

Thompson-Pope, S. K., & Turkat, I. D. (1988). Reactions to ambiguous stimuli among paranoid personalities. *Journal of Psychopathology and Behavioral Assessment, 10*, 21–32.

Torgersen, S. (1984). Genetic and nosological aspects of schizotypal and borderline personality disorders. *Archives of General Psychiatry, 41*, 546–554.

Trull, T. J., Widiger, T. A., & Frances, A. (1987). Covariation of criteria for avoidant, schizoid, and dependent personality disorders. *American Journal of Psychiatry, 144*, 767–771.

Tupin, J. P. (1987). Psychopharmacology and aggression. In L. H. Roth (Ed.), *Clinical treatment of the violent person.* New York: Guilford Press.

Turkat, I. D., & Banks, D. S. (1987). Paranoid personality and its disorder. *Journal of Psychopathology and Behavioral Assessment, 9*, 295–304.

Turkat, I. D., Keane, S. P., & Thompson-Pope, S. K. (1990). Social processing in paranoid personalities. *Journal of Psychopathology and Behavioral Assessment, 12*, 263–269.

Turkat, I. D., & Levin, R. A. (1984). Formulation of personality disorders. In H. E. Adams & P. B. Sutker (Eds.), *Comprehensive handbook of psychotherapy* (pp. 495–522). New York: Plenum Press.

Turner, S. M., Beidel, D. C., Dancu, C. V., & Keys, D. J. (1986). Psychopathology of social phobia and comparison to avoidant personality disorder. *Journal of Abnormal Psychology, 95*, 389–397.

Turner, S. M., Beidel, D. C., Dancu, C. V., & Keys, D. J. (1991). Social phobia: Axis I and II correlates. *Journal of Abnormal Psychology, 100*, 102–106.

Virkkunen, M., & Linnoila, M. (1993). Serotonin in personality disorders with habitual violence and impulsivity. In S. Hodgins (Ed.), *Mental disorder and crime* (pp. 194–207). Newbury Park, CA: Sage.

Vitale, J. E., & Newman, J. P. (2001). Using the Psychopathy Checklist-Revised with female samples: Reliability, validity, and implications for clinical utility. *Clinical Psychology: Science and Practice, 8*(1), 117–132.

Waldinger, R. J., & Frank, A. F. (1989). Transference and the vicissitudes of medication use by borderline patients. *Psychiatry, 52*, 416–427.

Wallace, J. F., Schmitt, W. A., Vitale, J. E., & Newman, J. P. (2000). Experimental investigations of information-processing deficiencies in psychopaths: Implications for diagnosis and treatment. In C. Gacono (Ed.), *The clinical and forensic assessment of psychopathy: A practitioner's guide* (pp. 87–109). Hillsdale, NJ: Erlbaum.

Wallace, J. F., Vitale, J. E., & Newman, J. P. (1999). Response modulation deficits: Implications for the diagnosis and treatment of psychopathy. *Journal of Cognitive Psychotherapy, 13*(1), 55–70.

Walsh, J. (1990). Assessment and treatment of the schizotypal personality disorder. *Journal of Independent Social Work, 4*, 41–59.

Warner, R. (1978). The diagnosis of antisocial and hysterical personality disorders: An example of sex bias. *Journal of Nervous and Mental Diseases, 166,* 839–845.

White, J. L., Moffitt, T. E., Caspi, A., Bartusch, B. J., Needles, D. J., & Stouthamer-Loeber, M. D. (1994). Measuring impulsiveness and examining its relationship to delinquency. *Journal of Abnormal Psychology, 103,* 192–205.

Widiger, T. A., & Corbitt, E. M. (1993). Antisocial personality disorder: Proposals for *DSM-IV. Journal of Personality Disorders, 7,* 63–77.

Widiger, T. A., & Costa, P. T. (1994). Personality and personality disorders. *Journal of Abnormal Psychology, 103,* 78–91.

Widiger, T. A., & Frances, A. J. (1989). Epidemiology, diagnosis, and comorbidity of borderline personality disorder. In A. Tasman, R. E. Hales, & A. J. Frances (Eds.), *Review of psychiatry* (Vol. 8, pp. 8–24). Washington, DC: American Psychiatric Press.

Widiger, T. A., Frances, A. J., Spitzer, R. L., & Williams, J. B. W. (1988). The *DSM-III* personality disorder: An overview. *American Journal of Psychiatry, 145,* 786–795.

Widiger, T. A., Frances, A. J., & Trull, T. J. (1987). A psychometric analysis of the social-interpersonal and cognitive-perceptual items for the schizotypal personality disorder. *Archives of General Psychiatry, 44,* 741–745.

Widiger, T. A., Hurt, S. W., Frances, A. J., Clarkin, J. F., & Gilmore, M. (1984). Diagnostic efficiency and *DSM-III. Archives of General Psychiatry, 41,* 1005–1012.

Widiger, T. A., Miele, G. M., & Tilly, S. M. (1992). Alternative perspectives on the diagnosis of borderline personality disorder. In J. F. Carkin, E. Marziali, & H. Munroe-Blum (Eds.), *Borderline personality disorder: Clinical and empirical perspectives* (pp. 89–115). New York: Guilford Press.

Widiger, T. A., & Rogers, J. H. (1989). Prevalence and comorbidity of personality disorders. *Psychiatric Annals, 19,* 132–136.

Widiger, T. A., & Shea, T. (1991). Differentiation of Axis I and Axis II disorders. *Journal of Abnormal Psychology, 100,* 399–406.

Widiger, T. A., & Spitzer, R. L. (1991). Sex bias in the diagnosis of personality disorders: Conceptual and methodological issues. *Clinical Psychology Review, 11,* 1–22.

Widiger, T. A., & Trull, T. J. (1992). Personality and psychopathology: An application of the five-factor model. *Journal of Personality, 60,* 363–393.

Widiger, T. A., & Trull, T. J. (1993). Borderline and narcissistic personality disorders. In P. B. Sutker & H. E. Adams (Eds.), *Comprehensive handbook of psychopathology* (2nd ed., pp. 371–397). New York: Plenum Press.

Widiger, T. A., Trull, T. J., Hurt, S. W., Clarkin, J. F., & Frances, A. J. (1987). A multidimensional scaling of the *DSM-III* personality disorders. *Archives of General Psychiatry, 44,* 557–563.

Wiggins, J. S., & Pincus, A. L. (1989). Conceptions of personality disorders and dimensions of personality. *Psychological Assessment: A Journal of Consulting and Clinical Psychology, 1,* 305–316.

Wong, S. (1984). *Criminal and institutional behaviors of psychopaths.* (Programs Branch Users Report). Ottawa: Ministry of the Solicitor General of Canada.

Wulach, J. S. (1983). Diagnosing the *DSM-III* antisocial personality disorder. *Professional Psychology: Research and Practice, 14,* 330–340.

Yung, B. R., & Hammond, W. R. (1997). Antisocial behavior in minority groups: Epidemiological and cultural perspectives. In D. M. Stoff & J. Breiling (Eds.), *Handbook of antisocial behavior* (pp. 474–495). New York: Wiley.

Zanarini, M. C., Gunderson, J. G., Marino, M. F., Schwartz, E. O., & Frankenburg, F. R. (1989). Childhood experiences of borderline patients. *Comprehensive Psychiatry, 30,* 18–25.

Zimmerman, M. (1994). Diagnosing personality disorders: A review of issues and research methods. *Archives of General Psychiatry, 51,* 225–245.

Zimmerman, M., & Coryell, W. (1989). *DSM-III* personality disorder diagnoses in a nonpatient sample. *Archives of General Psychiatry, 46,* 682–689.

Zimmerman, M., & Coryell, W. (1990). Diagnosing personality disorder in the community: A comparison of self-report and interview measures. *Archives of General Psychiatry, 47,* 527–531.

Zimmerman, M., Pfohl, B., Stangl, D., & Corenthal, C. (1986). Assessment of *DSM-III* personality disorders: The importance of interviewing an informant. *Journal of Clinical Psychiatry, 47,* 261–263.

Zlotnick, C. (1999). Antisocial personality disorder, affect dysregulation and childhood abuse among incarcerated women. *Journal of Personality Disorders, 13,* 90–95.

Zoccolillo, M., Price, R., Ji, T. H. C., & Hwu, H. (1999). Antisocial personality disorder: Comparison of prevalence, symptoms, and correlates in four countries. In P. Cohen (Ed.), *Historical and geographical influences on psychopathology* (pp. 249–277). Hillsdale, NJ: Erlbaum.

Author Index

651

Greenwood, D. N., 564
Greist, J. H., 84, 85, 374
Grella, C. E., 43, 48
Grenier, G., 532
Grieder, T., 335
Grieve, C. O., 570
Griffen, M. L., 41
Griffith, E. E. H., 268
Griffith, J. L., 455
Griffith, J. M., 45
Griffith, M. E., 455
Griffiths, J., 296
Grills, C., 213
Grilo, C. M., 569
Grimes, K., 255
Grinker, R. R., 488, 629
Grisham, J. R., 10
Grisso, T., 254
Grissom, G., 241
Grisson, T., 45
Grochocinski, V. J., 341
Grof, P., 326
Groome, C. S., 46
Gross, J. J., 5
Gross, S., 482
Grossman, H., 45
Grossman, L. S., 43
Grossman, R. G., 183
Grothaus, L., 296
Groth-Marnat, G., 452
Grothohann, Y., 534
Grove, W. M., 75, 78, 82, 99, 628
Grubb, H. J., 385
Gruber, R., 105, 136
Gruen, R., 621, 631
Gruen, W., 118
Gruenbeg, E. M., 456, 618, 632
Grunebaum, H., 267
Guay, B., 596
Gueldner, S. H., 113
Guerra, N. G., 627
Guido, J. R., 46
Guilford, J. P., 108
Guilford, J. S., 108
Guilleminault, C., 118, 586–590, 595, 597, 604
Gull, W. W., 571
Gully, R., 391

Gunderson, J., 617, 629–632, 637
Gunderson, J. G., 17, 24, 25
Gunnarsdottir, E. D., 298
Gur, R. C., 438
Guralnik, O., 482, 483
Gureje, O., 426, 427
Gurguis, G., 455
Gurland, B., 334
Guroff, J., 318
Guroff, J. J., 55, 438, 492, 494
Gursky, D. M., 369
Gusella, J. F., 184
Guthrie, E., 448
Gutierrez, R., 7
Guze, S. B., 15, 169, 422, 427, 430, 436, 451

Haas, G., 40, 57
Haas, G. L., 255, 265
Haatainen, J., 295
Hackmann, A., 434
Hadzi-Pavlovic, D., 382
Haellstroem, T., 372
Hafner, H., 255
Hagekull, B., 110
Hahlweg, K., 536
Hahn, S. R., 426
Haiman, C., 395
Hakko, H., 341
Hakstian, A. R., 624
Hale, V. E., 532, 540
Hale, W. E., 113
Haley, J., 264
Haley, R., 479, 495
Halford, W. K., 263
Hall, J. A., 16
Hall, J. M., 592
Hall, K., 334, 478, 495
Hall, W., 444
Hallam, R., 423
Halligan, P. W., 435
Hallmayer, J., 615
Hallstrom, T., 513, 525, 526
Halmi, K. A., 140
Halstead, W. C., 157
Halverson, C. F., 109, 110
Hamann, M. S., 394–395

Hamburger, R., 333
Hamburger, S. D., 164
Hamer, R. M., 637
Hamilton, J. A., 6
Hamilton, M., 21, 205
Hamilton, N., 48
Hammen, C., 385
Hammond, D. C., 519, 520
Hammond, W. R., 618
Hamovit, J., 55, 318
Hand, I., 378
Handel, M. H., 267
Handelsman, L., 50
Handrinos, D., 427
Hanewald, G., 538
Hanin, I., 317
Hanna, G. L., 383
Hans, S. L., 255
Hansell, S., 437
Hansom, J., 456
Hanson, L., 372
Hanson, R. K., 529, 538
Hanusa, B. H., 423
Hanwella, T., 435
Happel, R. L., 427
Harakal, T., 137
Harding, C. M., 256
Harding, P. S., 425
Harding, T. W., 624, 626
Hare, R. D., 618, 619, 622–625
Harford, T. C., 39
Hariton, E. B., 518
Harkness, A. R., 442
Harlow, B. L., 428
Harnden-Fischer, M., 568
Harper, D., 129
Harpin, R. E., 382
Harpur, T. J., 623–625
Harrington, R., 627
Harris, E. C., 253
Harris, G. J., 335
Harris, G. T., 623–627, 629
Harris, L., 297
Harris, M., 48, 254, 267
Harris, T. O., 304
Harris, T. R., 211
Harrison, T. C., 243

Subject Index